Web Services

Visit the *Web Services: Principles and Technology* Companion Website at **www.pearsoned.co.uk/papazoglou** to find valuable **student** learning material including:

- Links to useful sites on the web

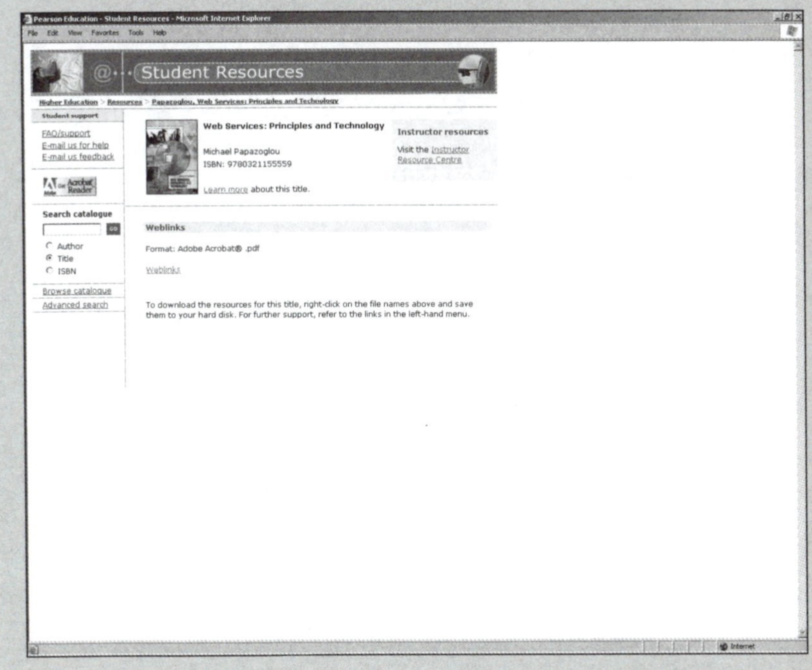

We work with leading authors to develop the strongest educational materials in computing, bringing cutting-edge thinking and best learning practice to a global market

Under a range of well-known imprints, including Prentice Hall, we craft high-quality print and electronic publications which help readers to understand and apply their content, whether studying or at work

To find out more about the complete range of our publishing, please visit us on the World Wide Web at: www.pearsoned.co.uk

Web Services: Principles and Technology

Michael P. Papazoglou

INFOLAB/CRISM, Tilburg University, The Netherlands

Harlow, England • London • New York • Boston • San Francisco • Toronto • Sydney • Singapore • Hong Kong
Tokyo • Seoul • Taipei • New Delhi • Cape Town • Madrid • Mexico City • Amsterdam • Munich • Paris • Milan

Pearson Education Limited
Edinburgh Gate
Harlow
Essex CM20 2JE
England

and Associated Companies throughout the world

Visit us on the World Wide Web at:
www.pearsoned.co.uk

First published 2008

ISBN 978-0-321-15555-9

British Library Cataloguing-in-Publication Data
A catalogue record for this book is available from the British Library

10 9 8 7 6 5 4 3 2 1
11 10 09 08 07

Typeset in 10/12pt Times by 35
Printed and bound in Great Britain by Henry Ling Ltd.,
at the Dorset Press, Dorchester, Dorset

The publisher's policy is to use paper manufactured from sustainable forests.

This book is dedicated to Marion without whose support, continuous encouragement, and infinite patience this book would have been impossible.

Contents

Supporting resources

Visit **www.pearsoned.co.uk/papazoglou** to find valuable online resources

Companion Website for students

- Links to useful sites on the web

For instructors

- Complete, downloadable Solutions Manual
- PowerPoint slides that can be downloaded and used for presentations

For more information please contact your local Pearson Education sales representative or visit **www.pearsoned.co.uk/papazoglou**

Preface

The Internet-based economy is shifting attention from the hype of portals and Website traffic and is gearing towards the world of fully automated, complex electronic transactions. We have embarked on a new paradigm of Web computing: Web services. Web services have emerged as the next generation of Web-based technology for exchanging information over the Internet and, as part of the service-oriented computing paradigm, promise to revolutionize the process of developing and deploying distributed software applications.

Web services hold the promise of moving beyond the simple exchange of information – the dominating mechanism for application integration today – to the concept of accessing, programming, and integrating application services that are encapsulated within old and new applications. An important economic benefit of the Web services computing paradigm is that it enables application developers to dynamically grow application portfolios more quickly than ever before, by creating compound application solutions that use internally existing organizational software assets (possibly based on legacy systems) which they appropriately combine with external components possibly residing in remote networks. This represents a fundamental change to the socio-economic fabric of the software developer community that improves the effectiveness and productivity in software development activities and enables enterprises to bring new products and services to the market more rapidly.

The visionary promise of Web services technologies is a world of cooperating services where application components are assembled with little effort into a network of services that can be loosely coupled to create dynamic business processes and agile applications that span organizations and computing platforms. It is therefore expected that Web services technologies will increasingly help shape modern society as a whole, especially in vital areas such as dynamic business, health, education, and government services.

As Web services technologies mature and as the infrastructure is being put in place it is expected that most companies will begin to focus on a few very strategic business processes, which they will package up as Web services that they will offer on the Web. This will enable in the future most kinds of electronic business applications to be handled by a series of Web services interacting with one another, and handling each other's requests. For example, a service in one application would decide to engage a service fronted by another enterprise.

With every new technology, such as Web services, there is still a lot of groundwork to be put in place. In fact, today, developing complex Web services applications is still an increasingly complex undertaking. However, once the groundwork and infrastructure are in place then things will be dramatically simpler. Applying Web services technologies will then be a matter of simply exposing and reusing core business functionality and combining processes in unanticipated ways to create value-added propositions. This will then lead to reduced complexity and costs, increased flexibility, and improving operational efficiency. For all these reasons, it is expected that the Web services computing paradigm will exhibit a steeper adoption curve, as it solves expensive and intractable business and technology problems, and will infiltrate more of the applications portfolio, than previous application technologies.

One of the ramifications of the growth of Web services is the increase in the number of professions where an understanding of Web services technologies is essential for success. This has led to a proportionate increase to the number of people – who come from a variety of academic and professional backgrounds – wanting to understand the concepts, principles, and technologies underpinning Web services. Therefore, the purpose of this book is to address this phenomenon by providing a comprehensive and systematic coverage and treatment of the concepts, foundations, issues, and technologies in Web services and in particular to pave the way for understanding the directions in which the field is currently developing and is likely to develop in the future.

What is unique about this book?

The subject of Web services is vast and enormously complex, spanning many concepts, protocols, and technologies that find their origins in disciplines such as distributed computing systems, computer networking, computer architectures and middleware, software engineering, programming languages, database systems, security, and knowledge representation, which are woven together in an intricate manner. In addition there is a need to merge technology with an understanding of business processes and organization, a combination of recognizing an enterprise's pain points and the potential solutions that can be applied to correct them.

The material in this book spans an immense and diverse spectrum of the literature, in origin and in character. I had to read a huge body of literature, conduct a lot of research, comprehend and critically distil the material. To make requisite connections between radically diverse sources of subject matter, I adopted and developed a comprehensive approach based on analyzing the material, making new connections, finding links in hitherto neglected spheres of work, and synthesizing the ensuing material in a meaningful and coherent manner. I took pains to make my research conform to the most fastidious criteria and tried diligently to present the results in such a form that it is easily readable and allows the readers to see through the complexity of Web services technologies. Readers will learn about the distinct concepts, technologies, protocols, and standards in one part of the architecture while seeing the big picture of how all parts fit together in the Web services landscape.

Many excellent books about Web services standards and programming have been written over the past few years. It was never my intention to write yet another such book. Unlike all these books, this book is neither about Web services standards nor about Web services programming techniques, it is rather about teaching readers the concepts and principles underlying Web services and the technologies that make Web services happen.

This book is unique in terms of its coverage, approach, and treatment of its subject matter. More specifically, this book aims to:

- present a solid foundation for understanding what Web services are;
- place emphasis on acquiring deep knowledge, insight, and understanding of the concepts, principles, mechanisms, and methodologies underpinning Web services, not on programming or implementation;
- provide sufficient depth for readers to have a basic understanding of each of the technologies that underlie the Web services paradigm and where each fits in the Web services landscape;
- explain how Web services are introduced in organizations, in particular how they are designed, deployed, and used; and
- introduce key standards necessary for Web services development at a level where they are understandable by the lay reader.

Another important characteristic of this book is that it tries to make Web services understandable to readers who do not necessarily have a strong technical background while still providing substance comprehensive enough to challenge experienced readers. The book is written with this mix of readership in mind by concentrating on the theoretical and technical underpinnings of Web services and connecting them to Web standards and novel developments.

To ensure thorough understanding of the material presented in this book, Web services concepts, techniques, and problems are presented in many forms, e.g., through informal descriptions and illustrative examples, abstractly in models, and concretely in XML and related Web services standards. A large number of graphical illustrations and abundant real-world examples are used as a means to gaining greater insight, understanding, and confidence in the material that is presented here. Simple concepts and enabling technologies are introduced first and as the book progresses, new concepts are elaborated on their bases, thereby helping the readers to get a better understanding and grasp of the core concepts Web services rely on. The book reports on material and recent developments that are very scattered in the literature.

Running example

One distinguishing feature of this book is that the technologies and standards that make up the Web services concept are examined in the context of a running example involving a non-trivial order management scenario. The running example is used to enhance readers' understanding and add insight to the theoretical exposure and explanation of the concepts. In this book I adopt a progressive disclosure approach as I follow the running example continuously and add to it the layers of Web services technologies and standards. It is also used in the context of service-oriented architectures and services design and in the development sections of the book.

Content and organization of the book

The book is divided into 10 parts. This has been done to compartmentalize topics and assist readers and instructors. The order of the book is such that when the readers read the book sequentially, the introductory parts and chapters largely precede the more advanced topics that build on them. The book parts and their respective chapters are as follows:

Part I Basics (Chapter 1)

This part includes only Chapter 1 and serves to introduce foundation material and the concept of Web services to the reader.

Chapter 1 introduces the concept of Web services and presents several examples of Web services development and use. It compares Web services applications to traditional Web-based application development and concludes with a discussion about the types and features of Web services.

Part II Enabling infrastructure (Chapters 2 and 3)

This part serves to provide a general overview of Web services computing and introduces support concepts and technologies.

Chapter 2 is an introductory chapter that examines the types of systems and technologies that fall under the umbrella terms "enterprise application integration" and "cross-enterprise computing," which are key enabling technologies that enable the development of distributed applications for Web services.

Chapter 3 deals with XML, which is used as an enabling technology that makes it possible for business document forms and messages to be comprehensible and interoperable. XML is one of the key ingredients that will accelerate the reality of a network economy and new business models for e-business applications.

Part III Core functionality and standards (Chapters 4, 5, and 6)

This part serves to cover core Web services technologies and standards. It provides a comprehensive treatment of the Web services architecture, Web services standards, and technologies for representing, registering, and discovering Web services. This part gives a solid basis for the rest of the book.

Chapter 4 provides a comprehensive introduction to the Simple Object Access Protocol (SOAP). This includes overviews of the SOAP specification and SOAP data structures, and explains by means of examples how SOAP is used to provide a consistent serialization format and general protocol for Web services.

Chapter 5 gives an in-depth coverage of the Web Services Description Language (WSDL) and explains how WSDL is key to making Web services the enabling technology for developing loosely coupled Web applications. It includes an overview of the WSDL specification and data structures as well as WSDL examples.

Chapter 6 provides a comprehensive coverage of the Universal Description, Discovery, and Integration (UDDI) framework. This includes an overview of the UDDI data model and numerous examples for publishing business data on UDDI and discovering UDDI-based information. It also explains in some detail how Web services represented in WSDL can be accommodated in UDDI and can be discovered by Web-services-enabled applications.

Part IV Event notification and service-oriented architectures (Chapters 7 and 8)

This part serves to introduce service-oriented architectures (SOAs) and the concepts of event processing and notification on which these rely.

Chapter 7 introduces the concept of the notification pattern for SOAs whereby an information-providing service sends messages to one or more interested receivers. In this pattern the message frequently carries information about an event that has occurred rather than a request that some specific action should occur.

Chapter 8 introduces the SOAs and explains their general characteristics and functionality. It presents the Enterprise Service Bus, which offers a whole range of functions designed to offer a manageable standards-based IT backbone connecting heterogeneous components and systems.

Part V Service composition and service transactions (Chapters 9 and 10)

This part serves to introduce the concepts of business processes and Web services transactions that rely on them and are used to create assemblies of services that cross organizational boundaries, which may also exhibit advanced transactional properties.

Chapter 9 explains how core workflow technologies can be used to combine and orchestrate Web services in order to develop Web services applications across different enterprises and computing platforms.

Chapter 10 introduces the concept of Web services transactions and discusses its unique features and requirements for supporting cross-enterprise computing applications composed of Web services.

Part VI Service security and policies (Chapters 11 and 12)

This part serves to introduce security mechanisms as well as the use of policies and agreements for Web services applications.

Chapter 11 introduces the concept of security for Web services and explains the different security mechanisms and protocols used for developing Web-services-based applications. This chapter also looks at authentication and authorization protocols that can be used in conjunction with these applications.

Chapter 12 introduces the concept of service policies that is used for communicating such information as security requirements, supported features, preferred ways of invoking the service, and so on, among Web services. It also explains how to create and describe contracts, agreements, and guarantees from offers between a service provider and a service client for Web services applications.

Part VII Service semantics and business protocols (Chapters 13 and 14)

This part serves to introduce the problems of semantic interoperability and how metadata, standard vocabularies, and semantic taxonomies help alleviate these problems.

Chapter 13 discusses the problems of enabling disparate systems to understand the information that is being shared appropriately, which relates to the logical aspect of using and sharing data and business processes based on their intended meaning. The chapter also introduces the Resource Description Framework (RDF), the World Wide Web Consortium's official format for describing metadata, which is used to supplant WSDL constructs to facilitate an understanding of the business domain underlying Web services.

Chapter 14 discusses semantic problems when attempting to integrate business processes that span organizations and presents business protocols, specifications, and concepts for business process integration and interoperability that are especially relevant to Web services.

Part VIII Service design and development (Chapter 15)

This part describes how to design and specify enterprise-scale and cross-enterprise business processes and the business conditions and requirements driving the development of their underlying applications.

Chapter 15 introduces a methodology for designing cross-enterprise computing applications using Web services. This chapter explains that Web services are not just an approach to complex business solving using abstract interfaces and modular pieces of software functionality. It includes several design guidelines such as various forms of coupling and cohesion, organizational guidelines and policies, and specialized modeling techniques.

Part IX Service management (Chapter 16)

This part contains one chapter that explores various Web services management approaches and their underlying architectural concepts.

Chapter 16 describes service management techniques and mechanisms that enable enterprises to monitor and measure service levels for processes that are distributed and federated. Such functionality helps to diagnose and combat problems as they occur so as to ensure that the Web services supporting a given business task are performing in accordance with service-level objectives.

Part X Emerging trends (Chapter 17)

This part contains one chapter that describes emerging trends and developments in the field of Web services.

Chapter 17 describes recent developments such as grid services and mobile services, evaluates their merits, introduces their architectural features, and examines the consanguinity between Web services and mobile technologies and Web services and grid technologies.

Logical organization and suggested paths

There is sufficient material in this book for at least two one-semester courses. An entire term basic course can be built around the first three parts of the book followed by either Part IV or Part V or even elements of both depending on the interests of the instructor

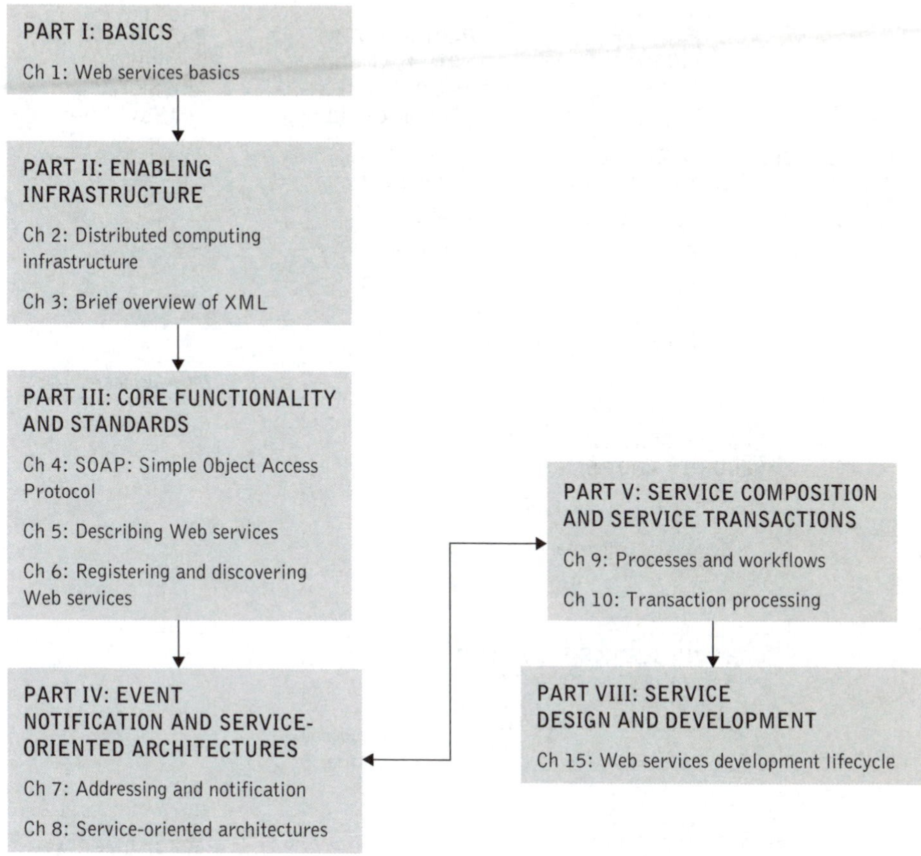

Figure P.1 Suggested paths for an introductory course

and students. I would also strongly advise instructors to use Part VIII as a component of an introductory course to Web services. The logical organization of the book along with suggested paths through it for an introductory course is shown in Figure P.1. A more advanced course (or second-level course on Web services) could skim through Parts I, III, IV, and V, and be followed by Parts VI, VII, VIII, and IX. By organizing the book in this way, I have attempted to provide an instructor with a number of teaching options. The logical organization of the book along with suggested paths through it for an advanced course is shown in Figure P.2.

Intended readership

This book targets a broad audience with a detailed coverage of the major issues, topics, and technologies underlying Web services. The book is intended both as a textbook and a reference book.

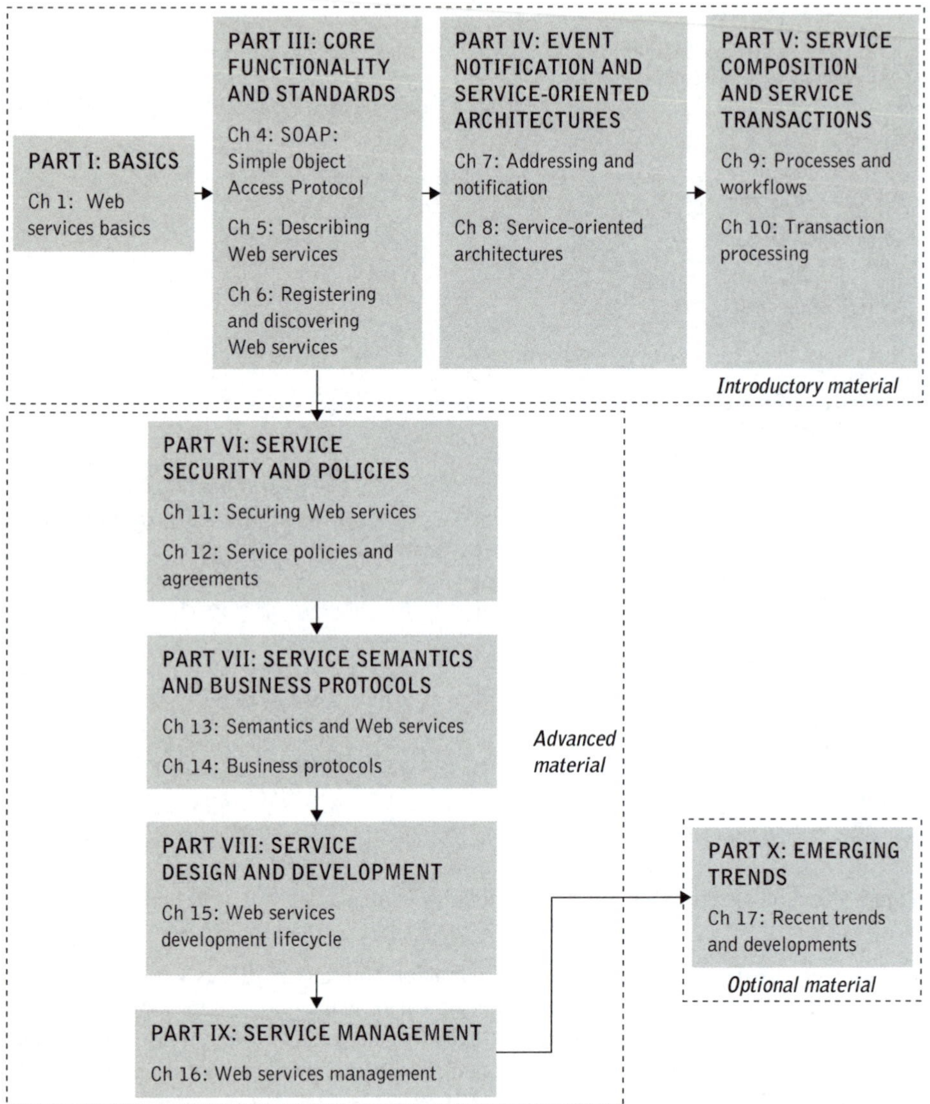

Figure P.2 Suggested paths for an advanced course

The style has been tailored to bring out the key points and reach those who feel intimidated by the jargon, bewildering plethora of standards, and programming techniques in the current Web services literature. More specifically, the book is aimed at advanced undergraduate/postgraduate students, researchers, professionals such as IT planners, architects, software analysts, designers, developers, software engineers, and programmers, and, in general, individuals who wish to develop a deep understanding of the concepts, technologies, scope, and extent of Web services and wish to learn how to apply them to complex applications such as electronic business problems. Equally it is aimed at business strategists, business process engineers, and business architects. More significantly, my hope is for the book to also reach business-minded individuals, especially the new breed of professionals and students that is emerging as the dividing lines between business requirements and IT grow increasingly blurred. Many of the issues and problems raised in this book are directly related to the design of software solutions for business applications.

The reader will learn several aspects of Web services and enterprise computing in depth and will understand how these are applied in the context of business-to-business commerce. For the advanced student I provide a comprehensive and in-depth treatment of the concepts, issues, standards, and technical underpinnings of Web services, thereby enabling them to acquire important skills in understanding how complex distributed systems and applications work and how they can be developed. For the practitioner I show how to use Web services technology effectively to solve real-life problems and offer approaches to reasoning and designing complex distributed systems and applications on the basis of the Web services paradigm. To achieve its stated objectives, the book makes heavy use of illustrations, examples, and realistic business scenarios. The book seldom mentions specific platforms or vendors.

Companion Website to the book

Supplementary material, including overhead slides, solutions to exercises, and additional publications and sources can be found at the book's dedicated website:
www.pearsoned.co.uk/papazoglou.

About the author

Michael P. Papazoglou holds the chair of Computer Science and is director of the INFOLAB/CRISM at the University of Tilburg in the Netherlands. He is also an honorary professor at the University of Trento in Italy. Prior to this (1991–6), he was full professor and head of School of Information Systems at the Queensland University of Technology (QUT) in Brisbane, Australia. He has also held senior academic positions at the Australian National University, the University of Koblenz, Germany, FernUniversität in Hagen, Germany, and was principal research scientist at the National German Research Centre for Computer Science (GMD) in St Augustin from 1983 to 1989.

Professor Papazoglou serves on several international committees and on the editorial board of nine international scientific journals and is co-editor in charge of the MIT book series on information systems. He has chaired numerous well-known international scientific conferences in computer science. These include the International Conference on Data Engineering (ICDE), International Conference on Distributed Computing Systems (ICDCS), International Conference on Digital Libraries (ICDL), International Conference on Cooperative Information Systems (CoopIS), International Conference on Entity/Relationship Modeling, and others. He is the founder of the International Conference on Cooperative Information Systems (CoopIS) and more recently of the International

Conference on Service Oriented Computing (ICSOC). He has authored or edited 15 books and over 150 scientific journal articles and refereed international conference papers. His latest book is on the organizational and technical foundations of e-business, published by John Wiley & Sons in April 2006. His research was/is funded by the European Union, the Australian Research Council, the Japanese Society for the Promotion of Science, and Departments of Science and Technology in Europe and Australia. He is a golden core member and a distinguished visitor of the Institute of Electrical and Electronics Engineers (IEEE), Computer Science Section.

Acknowledgements

Writing this book was quite a challenge in many ways but something that I aspired to for a long time. It was a daunting exercise that took the better part of three years to complete. In the process I did extensive research, used a huge number of sources, and had discussions with numerous individuals and experts in the field who made invaluable suggestions. This has broadened my scientific horizons and knowledge, inspired many ideas found in this book, and led to a more comprehensive treatment of its subject matter.

This book would not have been possible without a great deal of help from a lot of people, and I relish this opportunity to thank them.

Reviewers have played a significant role in the development of this project by making pertinent and constructive comments that helped me improve the quality of this book. I would especially like to acknowledge the following people who gave their time unstintingly to review substantial portions of the final draft, resulting in substantial improvements: Athman Bouguettaya at Virginia Tech, Schahram Dustdar at the Vienna University of Technology, Tiziana Margaria at the University of Potsdam, Monica Martin at Sun Microsystems, Anne Ngu at Texas State University, Robert Steele at the Sydney University of Technology, and Farouk Toumani at Blaise Pascal University.

I am also indebted to the following people for reviewing chapters in the manuscript at various stages and for all of their helpful suggestions and insight: Gregory Antoniou at the University of Crete, who reviewed Chapter 13; Dave Chappell at Sonic Software, who reviewed Chapter 8; Jean Jacques Dubray at Attachmate and editor of OASIS ebXML, who reviewed Chapter 1; George Feuerlicht at Sydney University of Technology, who reviewed Chapter 15; Rania Khalaf at IBM TJ Watson Research Labs, who reviewed Chapter 9; Heather Kreger at IBM TJ Watson Research Labs, who reviewed Chapter 16; Heiko Ludwig at IBM TJ Watson Research Labs, who reviewed Chapter 12; Willem Jan van den Heuvel at Tilburg University, who reviewed Chapters 8 and 15; and Andrea Zisman at City University in London, who reviewed Chapters 5 and 6.

I am also grateful to the following people who provided me with feedback or gave me tips and suggestions on how to improve the manuscript: Marco Aiello at the University of Groningen, Fabio Casati at HP Labs, Paco Curbera at IBM TJ Watson Research Labs, Vincenzo d'Andrea at the University of Trento, Asit Dan at IBM TJ Watson Research Labs, Bernd Krämer at the FernUniversität in Hagen, Frank Leymann at Stuttgart University, Maurizio Marchese at the University of Trento, John Mylopoulos at the University of Toronto, and Paolo Traverso at the IRST Research Center.

My sincere thanks also go to Vassilios Andrikopoulos, Benedikt Kratz, and Bart Orriens at Tilburg University, Stefan Pottinger and Thorsten Scheibler at the University of Stuttgart, Michele Manchioppi and Manuel Zanoni at the University of Trento, who helped by providing tips and solutions for several of the exercises in this book.

Finally, I wish to thank the entire Pearson team, who have done an outstanding job. Particular thanks go to Kate Brewin and Owen Knight, my original editors at Pearson, for their continuous encouragement, perseverance, and especially patience with me. This book took a very long time to complete. My sincere thanks also go to Simon Plumtree and Joe Vella, for guiding me over the last and most painful hurdles of this book and giving me invaluable advice and assistance.

Michael P. Papazoglou

Publisher's acknowledgements

Figures 2.4, 2.7 and 2.17: Papazoglou, M. P. and Ribbers, P. M. A., *e-Business: Organizational and Technical Foundations*. Chichester: John Wiley & Sons Ltd, April 2006; Figure 5.8: Kifer, M., Bernstein, A. and Lewis, P. M., *Database Systems: An Application-Oriented Approach*, Second Edition. Boston: Addison Wesley, 2005, Figure 5.8., p. 165. Copyright © 2005 Pearson Education, Inc. Reproduced by permission of Pearson Education, Inc. All rights reserved; Figures 9.16 and 9.17: Graham, S., Boubez, T., Daniels, G., Davis, D., Nakamura, Y., Neyama, R. and Simeonov, S., *Building Web Services with Java*, Second Edition. Indianapolis, IN: Sams Publishing, 2005. Copyright © 2005 Pearson Education, Inc. Reproduced by permission of Pearson Education, Inc. All rights reserved; Figure 10.12: Little, M., Maron, J., and Pavlik, G., *Java Transaction Processing*, Upper Saddle River, NJ: Prentice Hall, 2004. Copyright © 2004 Pearson Education, Inc. Reproduced by permission of Pearson Education, Inc. All rights reserved; Figures 10.25, 10.27 and 11.26: Bunting, D., *et al.*, *Web Services Composite Application Framework (WS-CAF)*, July 2003, http://developers. sun.com/techtopics/webservices/wscaf/index.html. Reproduced with permission from Sun Microsystems, Inc.; Figures 11.12 and 11.13: Steel, C., Nagappan, R. and Lai, R., *Core Security Patterns: Best Practices and Strategies for J2EE™, Web Services, and Identity Management*, Upper Saddle River, NJ: Prentice Hall 2006. Copyright © 2006 Pearson Education, Inc. Reproduced by permission of Pearson Education, Inc. All rights reserved; Figure 14.6: 'Cluster 3: Order Management Segment A: Quote and Order Entry PIPs 3A4, 3A7, 3A8, 3A9', *RosettaNet Implementation Guide*, April 2004, (www.rosettanet.org/usersguides/); Figure 16.9: Vambenepe, W. (ed), 'Web services distributed management: management using web Services (MUWS 1.0) Part 1', *OASIS Standard*, March 2005 (http://docs. oasis-open.org/wsdm/2004/12/wsdm-muws-part1-1.0.pdf). Copyright © OASIS Open 2003–2006. All rights reserved; Figure 16.10: Sedukhin, I., 'Web services distributed management: management of web services (WSDM-MOWS) 1.0', OASIS Standard, March 2005, http://docs.oasis-open.org/wsdm/2004/12/wsdm-mows-1.0.pdf. Copyright © OASIS Open 2003–2006. All rights reserved.

PART I

Basics

CHAPTER 1

Web services basics

Learning objectives

Web services are an emerging technology that enables disparate applications running on different machines to exchange data and integrate with one another without requiring additional, proprietary third-party software or hardware. Applications that rely on the Web services paradigm can exchange data regardless of the language, platform, or internal protocols they use. Web services are self-describing and self-contained network-available modules that perform concrete business functions and are deployed easily because they are based on common industry standards and existing technology, such as XML and HTTP. They reduce application interface costs, and provide a universal mechanism for integrating business processes within an enterprise and, ultimately, among multiple organizations.

After completing this chapter readers will understand the following key concepts:

- The nature, broad characteristics, and types of Web services.
- The difference between Web services and the application service provider model and Web-based applications.
- The concepts of tight and loose coupling.
- The concepts of stateful and stateless services.
- The notion of the service-oriented architecture and its main building blocks.
- The Web services technology stack and how Web services standards help develop distributed applications.
- Functional versus non-functional services characteristics and the notion of quality of service.

1.1 Introduction

Service-oriented computing is an emerging computing paradigm that utilizes services as the constructs to support the development of rapid, low-cost composition of distributed applications. Services are self-contained modules – deployed over standard middleware platforms – that can be described, published, located, orchestrated, and programmed using XML-based technologies over a network. Any piece of code and any application component deployed on a system can be transformed into a network-available service. Services reflect a "service-oriented" approach to programming, based on the idea of describing available computational resources, e.g., application programs and information system components, as services that can be delivered through a standard and well-defined interface. Services perform functions that can range from answering simple requests to executing business processes requiring peer-to-peer relationships between service consumers and providers. Services are most often built in a way that is independent of the context in which they are used. This means that the service provider and the consumers are loosely coupled. Service-based applications can be developed by discovering, invoking, and composing network-available services rather than building new applications.

Service-oriented computing represents the fusion of several technologies including distributed systems, software engineering, information systems, computer languages, Web-based computing, and XML technologies rather than being a new technology. This technology is expected to have an impact on all aspect of software construction at least as wide as that of object-oriented programming.

The premise of the foundation of service-oriented computing is that an application can no longer be thought of as a single process running within a single organization. The value of an application is actually no longer measured by its functional capabilities but rather by its ability to integrate with its surrounding environment [Papazoglou 2003]. For instance, services can help integrate applications that were not written with the intent to be integrated with other applications and define architectures and techniques to build new functionality leveraging existing application functionality. A new breed of applications can be developed solely on the basis of collections of interacting services offering well-defined interfaces to their potential users. These applications are often referred as *composite applications*. Service orientation enables loosely coupled relationships between applications of transacting partners. At the middleware level, the concept of loose coupling requires that the "service-oriented" approach be independent of specific technologies or operating systems. The service-oriented model does not even mandate any kind of predetermined agreements before the use of an offered service is allowed.

The service-oriented model allows for a clear distinction to be made between *service providers* (organizations that provide the service implementations, supply their service descriptions, and provide related technical and business support); *service clients* (end-user organizations that use some service); and *service aggregators* (organizations that consolidate multiple services into a new, single orchestrated service offering what is commonly known as a business process).

Since services may be offered by different enterprises and communicate over the Internet, they provide a distributed computing infrastructure for both intra- and cross-enterprise application integration and collaboration. Clients of services can be other solutions or applications within an enterprise or clients outside the enterprise, whether these are external applications, processes, or customers/users. This distinction between service providers and consumers is independent of the relationship between consumer and provider, which can be either client/server or peer to peer. For the service-oriented computing paradigm to exist, we must find ways for the services to be technology neutral, loosely coupled, and support location transparency.

To be *technology neutral* services must be invoked through standardized lowest common denominator technologies that are available to almost all IT environments. This implies that the invocation mechanisms (protocols, descriptions, and discovery mechanisms) should comply with widely accepted standards. To be *loosely coupled* services must not require knowledge or any internal structures or conventions (context) at the client or service side. Finally, to *support location transparency* services should have their definitions and location information stored in a public repository such as the Universal Description and Discovery and Integration Repository (see Chapter 6) and be accessible by a variety of clients that can locate and invoke them irrespective of their location.

One of the major advantages of services is that they may be implemented on a single machine or on a large number and variety of devices and be distributed on a local area network or more widely across several wide area networks (including mobile and ad hoc networks).

A particularly interesting case is when the services use the Internet (as the communication medium) and open Internet-based standards. This results in the concept of Web services, which share the characteristics of more general services, but they require special consideration as a result of using a public, insecure, low-fidelity mechanism, such as the Internet, for distributed service interactions.

1.1.1 What are Web services?

A *Web service* is a self-describing, self-contained software module available via a network, such as the Internet, which completes tasks, solves problems, or conducts transactions on behalf of a user or application. Web services constitute a distributed computer infrastructure made up of many different interacting application modules trying to communicate over private or public networks (including the Internet and Web) to virtually form a single logical system.

A Web service can be: (i) a self-contained business task, such as a funds withdrawal or funds deposit service; (ii) a full-fledged business process, such as the automated purchasing of office supplies; (iii) an application, such as a life insurance application or demand forecasts and stock replenishment; or (iv) a service-enabled resource, such as access to a particular back-end database containing patient medical records. Web services can vary in function from simple requests (e.g., credit checking and authorization, pricing enquiries, inventory status checking, or a weather report) to complete business applications that access and combine information from multiple sources, such as an insurance brokering system, an insurance liability computation, an automated travel planner, or a package tracking system.

Web services address the problems of rigid implementations of predefined relationships and isolated services scattered across the Internet. The long-term goal of Web services technology is to enable distributed applications that can be dynamically assembled according to changing business needs, and customized based on device (such as personal computers, workstations, laptops, WAP-enabled cellular phones, personal digital assistants), network (such as cable, UMTS, XDSL, Bluetooth, etc.) and user access while enabling wide utilization of any given piece of business logic wherever it is needed. Once a Web service is deployed, other applications and Web services can discover and invoke it.

A more complete definition of Web services is given in section 1.3 after readers have familiarized themselves with the concept of software-as-a-service and understood the differences between Web services and Web-based applications.

1.1.2 Typical Web services scenarios

Web services efforts focus on reusing existing applications (including legacy code) for lightweight integration with other applications, often motivated by the desire for new forms of sharing of services across lines of business, or between business partners.

To better understand the mission of Web services, consider, as an example, an insurance company that decides to offer an on-line quoting Web service to its customers. Rather than developing the entire application from scratch, this enterprise looks to supplement its home-grown applications with modules that perform industry standard functions. Therefore, it may seamlessly link up with the Web service of another enterprise that specializes in insurance liability computations. The insurance liability Web service may present a quote form to the customer to collect customer information based on the type of the desired insurance. Subsequently, the Web service would present the customer with a quote including a premium estimate. If the customer selected to buy that particular insurance policy, the system would take the customer's payment information and run it through a payment Web service offered by yet another company (service provider). This payment Web service will ultimately return billing information to the customer and to the originating company.

Enterprise applications, such as the insurance quoting Web service, are among the most likely candidate applications that can benefit from the use of Web services technologies. Enterprise applications cover a wide spectrum of Web services scenarios including interactions between the departments within an organization as well as interactions between business partners. Enterprises can typically use a single Web service to accomplish a specific business task, such as billing or inventory control, or they may compose several Web services together to create a distributed enterprise application such as customized ordering, customer support, procurement, and logistical support. These enterprise application scenarios require both the reuse and integration of existing back-end systems within an enterprise, which are the target of enterprise application integration or EAI, see section 2.9. More sophisticated enterprise applications may focus on e-business, or cross-enterprise interactions involving transacting business partners over the Internet (also covered in section 2.9), which is typical of the way in which large companies procure, manufacture, sell, and distribute products [Papazoglou 2006].

Case study: Order management process

In the following we introduce an order management process that is crafted in such a way as to interweave Web services principles and concepts that will be covered in later chapters in this book. The case study is built around a simple order management scenario that manages a purchase order submitted by a customer to a specific supplier. An order management solution supports an end-to-end order fulfillment process that can be represented by means of a complex set of interacting Web services requiring a lot of synchronization and coordination. Such Web services may configure and order customized products; provide customers with accurate, real-time information on global product availability; provide interactive pricing options; offer real-time status enquiry; perform inventory and warehouse management; and so forth.

In the simple purchase order scenario examined in this book the customer or buying organization initially creates a purchase order and sends the request to fulfill that order to a supplier. The supplier offers a purchase order Web service that receives the purchase order and responds with either acceptance or rejection based on a number of criteria, including availability of the goods and the credit of the customer. Figure 1.1 shows how such a purchase order process can be developed at the supplier's side in terms of interacting Web services that involve purchase orders, credit checks, automated billing, stock updates, and shipping originating from various

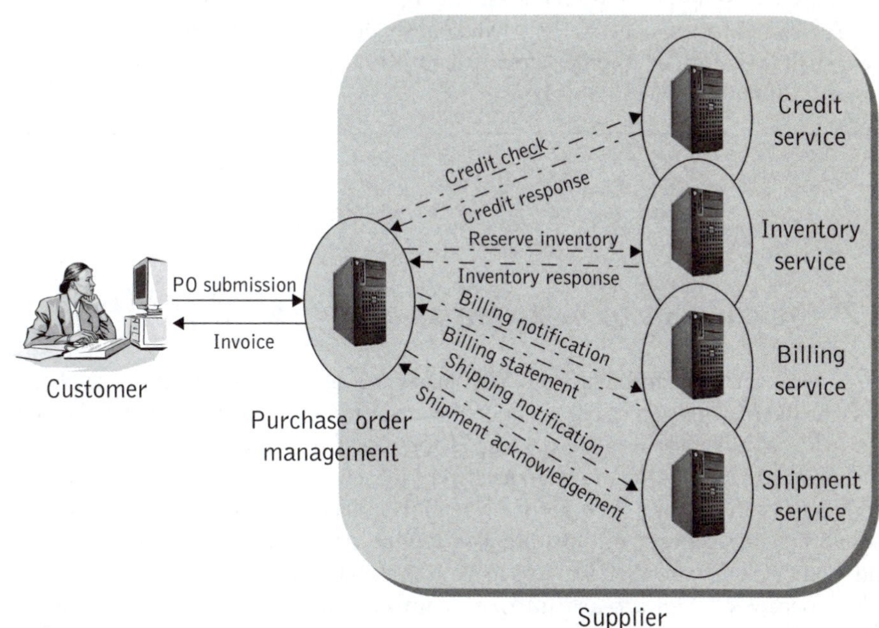

Figure 1.1 A purchase order application involving interacting Web services

service providers whose offerings are packaged to create turnkey products. On receiving the purchase order from a customer, the purchase order process may initiate several tasks concurrently: checking the creditworthiness of the user, determining whether or not an ordered part is available in the product inventory, calculating the final price for the order and billing the customer, selecting a shipper, and scheduling the production and shipment for the order. While some of the processing can proceed concurrently, there are synchronization dependencies between these tasks. For instance, the customer's creditworthiness must be ascertained first before accepting the order, the shipping price is required to finalize the price calculation, and the shipping date is required for the complete fulfillment schedule. When these tasks are completed successfully, invoice processing can proceed and the invoice will be sent to the customer.

A purchase order Web service, like the one we described earlier, can also handle more elaborate tasks. For instance, it could provide tracking and adjusting facilities that track and adjust purchase orders due to unexpected events such as the customer initiating a purchase order change or cancellation. These tasks involve a lot of coordination work and call for the use of reactive Web services. If a single event in the purchase order needs to change or is cancelled, the entire purchase order process can unravel instantly. Employing a collection of Web services that work together to adjust purchase orders for such situations creates an automated solution to this problem. In the case of a purchase order cancellation the purchase order Web service can automatically reserve a suitable replacement product and notify the billing and inventory services of the changes. When all of these Web services interactions have been completed and the new adjusted schedule is available, the purchase order Web service notifies the customer, sending the customer an updated invoice.

The order management example will help set the stage for the following chapters. We shall revisit it and appropriately extend it to explicate the key aspects of Web services introduced later in this book.

1.2 The concept of software as a service

Web services are very different from Web pages that also provide access to applications across the Internet and across organizational boundaries. Web pages are targeted at human users, whereas Web services are developed for access by humans as well as automated applications. As terminology is often used very loosely, it is easy to confuse someone by describing a "service" as a Web service when it is in fact not. Consequently, it is useful to examine first the concept of software-as-a-service on which Web services technology builds and then compare Web services to Web server-based functionality.

The concept of *software-as-a-service* is revolutionary and appeared first with the applications service provider software model. *Application service providers* (ASPs) are companies that package software and infrastructure elements together with business and professional services to create a complete solution that they present to the end customer as a service on a subscription basis. An ASP is a third-party (service organization) that deploys, hosts, and manages access to packaged applications at a centrally managed facility for multiple customers across a network, offering application availability and security. Applications are delivered over networks on a subscription or rental basis, and end users access these applications remotely using Internet or leased lines. In essence, ASPs were a way for companies to outsource some or even all aspects of their IT needs.

The basic idea behind an ASP is to "rent" applications to subscribers. The whole application is developed in terms of the user interface, workflow, business, and data components that are all bound together to provide a working solution. An ASP hosts the entire application and the customer has little opportunity to customize it beyond setting up tables, or perhaps the final appearance of the user interface (such as adding company logos). Access to the application for the customer is provided simply via browsing and manually initiated purchases and transactions occur by downloading reports. This activity can take place by means of a browser. This is not a very flexible solution, but offers considerable benefits in terms of deployment providing the customer is willing to accept it "as is".

By providing a centrally hosted Internet application, the ASP takes primary responsibility for managing the software application on its infrastructure, using the Internet as the conduit between each customer and the primary software application. What this means for an enterprise is that the ASP maintains the application, the associated infrastructure, and the customer's data, and ensures that the systems and data are available whenever needed.

An alternative of this is where the ASP is providing a software module that is downloaded to the customer's site on demand – this is for situations where the software does not work in a client/server fashion, or can be operated remotely via a browser. This software module might be deleted at the end of the session, or may remain on the customer's machine until replaced by a new version, or the contract for using it expires.

Although the ASP model introduced the concept of software-as-a-service first, it suffered from several inherent limitations such as the inability to develop highly interactive applications, inability to provide complete customizable applications, and inability to integrate applications. This resulted in monolithic architectures, highly fragile, customer-specific, non-reusable integration of applications based on tight coupling principles.

Today we are in the midst of another significant development in the evolution of software-as-a-service. The new architecture allows for loosely coupled asynchronous interactions on the basis of eXtensible Markup Language (XML) standards with the intention of making access to, and communications between, applications over the Internet easier.

The Web services paradigm allows the software-as-a-service concept to expand to include the delivery of complex business processes and transactions as a service.

Perceiving the relative benefits of Web services technology, many ASPs are modifying their technical infrastructures and business models to be more akin to those of Web services providers. The use of Web services provides a more flexible solution for ASPs. The core of the application – the business and data components – remains on the ASP's machines, but is now accessed programmatically via Web services interfaces. The customers can now build their own custom business processes and user interfaces, and are also free to select from a wide variety of Web services that are available over the network and satisfy their needs.

When comparing Web services to Web-based applications we may distinguish four key differences [Aldrich 2002]:

- Web services act as resources to other applications that can request and initiate those Web services, with or without human intervention. This means that Web services can call on other Web services to outsource parts of a complex transaction to those other Web services. This provides a high degree of flexibility and adaptability not available in today's Web-based applications.
- Web services are modular, self-aware, and self-describing applications; a Web service knows what functions it can perform and what inputs it requires to produce its outputs, and can describe this to potential users and to other Web services. A Web service can also describe its *non-functional properties*: for instance, the cost of invoking the service, the geographical areas the Web service covers, security measures involved in using the Web service, performance characteristics, contact information, and more (see section 1.8).
- Web services are more visible and manageable than Web-based applications; the state of a Web service can be monitored and managed at any time by using external application management and workflow systems. Despite the fact that a Web service may not run on an in-house (local) system or may be written in an unfamiliar programming language, it still can be used by local applications, which may detect its state (active or available) and manage the status of its outcome.
- Web services may be brokered or auctioned. If several Web services perform the same task, then several applications may place bids for the opportunity to use the requested service. A broker can base its choice on the attributes of the "competing" Web services (cost, speed, degree of security).

1.3 A more complete definition of Web services

In the previous sections we have provided the reader with enough information to understand the origin of Web services and their main differences from Web-based applications. In this section we shall provide a more in-depth description of the key functional characteristics of Web services.

Web services form the building blocks for creating distributed applications in that they can be published to and accessed over the Internet and corporate intranets. They rely on a set of open Internet standards that allow developers to implement distributed applications – using different tools provided by many different vendors – to create corporate applications that join together possible existing software modules from systems in diverse organizational departments or from different enterprises. For example, an application that tracks the inventory level of parts within an enterprise can provide a useful service that answers queries about the inventory level. But more importantly, Web services can also be combined and/or configured by these distributed applications, behind the scenes to perform virtually any kind of (business-related) task or transaction.

Web services can discover and communicate with other Web services and trigger them to fulfill or outsource part of a higher-level transaction by using a common vocabulary (business terminology) and a published directory of their capabilities according to a reference architecture called the service-oriented architecture (see section 1.6).

The modularity and flexibility of Web services make them ideal for e-business application integration [Papazoglou 2006]. For example, the inventory Web service can be accessed together with other related Web services by a business partner's warehouse management application or can be part of a new distributed application that is developed from scratch and implements an extended value chain supply planning solution.

At this stage a more complete definition of a Web service can be given. A Web service is a platform-independent, loosely coupled, self-contained, programmable Web-enabled application that can be described, published, discovered, coordinated, and configured using XML artifacts (open standards) for the purpose of developing distributed interoperable applications. Web services possess the ability to engage other services in a common computation in order to: complete a concrete task, conduct a business transaction, or solve a complex problem. In addition, Web services expose their features programmatically over the Internet (or intranet) using standard Internet languages (based on XML) and standard protocols, and can be implemented via a self-describing interface based on open Internet standards.

In the following we shall examine the above definition more closely and deconstruct its meaning:

> *Web services are loosely coupled software modules:* Web services are distinctly different from predecessor distributed computing architectures because of one key point: Web services protocols, interfaces, and registry services enable applications to work cooperatively together using the principle of loose coupling. To achieve this requirement, the service interface is defined in a neutral manner that is independent of the underlying platform, the operating system, and the programming language the service is implemented in. This allows services, built on a variety of such systems, to interact with each other in a uniform and universal manner. This feature of having a neutral interface definition, which is not strongly tied to a particular implementation, is known as loose coupling between services. Because loose coupling is a concept of paramount importance to understanding how Web services function, we shall revisit it in section 1.4.4 where we discuss the characteristics of Web services.
>
> *Web services semantically encapsulate discrete functionality:* A Web service is a self-contained software module that performs a single task. The module describes its own interface characteristics, i.e., the operations available, the parameters, data typing, and the access protocols, in such a way that other software modules can determine what it does, how to invoke its functionality, and what result to expect in

return. In this regard, Web services are contracted software modules as they provide publicly available descriptions of the interface characteristics used to access the service so that potential clients can bind to it. The service client uses a Web service's interface description to bind to a service provider and invoke its services.

Web services can be accessed programmatically: A Web service provides programmable access – this allows embedding Web services into remotely located applications. This enables information to be queried and updated, thus improving efficiency, responsiveness, and accuracy – ultimately leading to high added value to the Web services clients. Unlike Websites, Web services are not targeted at human users. Rather, Web services operate at the code level; they are called by and exchange data with other software modules and applications. However, Web services can certainly be incorporated into software applications designed for human interaction.

Web services can be dynamically found and included in applications: Unlike existing interface mechanisms, Web services can be assembled to serve a particular function, solve a specific problem, or deliver a particular solution to a customer.

Web services are described in terms of a standard description language: the Web Services Description Language or WSDL describes both functional as well as non-functional service characteristics. Functional characteristics include operational characteristics that define the overall behavior of the service while non-functional characteristics mainly describe characteristics of the hosting environment (refer to sections 1.4.2 and 1.8).

Web services are distributed over the Internet: Web services make use of existing, ubiquitous transport Internet protocols like HTTP. By relying on the same, well-understood transport mechanism as Web content, Web services leverage existing infrastructure and can comply with current corporate firewall policies.

1.4 Characteristics of Web services

This section introduces the most important characteristics of Web services such as simple and complex Web services, stateful and stateless services, services granularity, loose coupling, synchronous and asynchronous services, and so on.

1.4.1 Types of Web services

Topologically, Web services can come in two flavors, see Figure 1.2. Informational, or type I, Web services, which support only simple request/response operations and always wait for a request; they process it and respond. Complex, or type II Web services implement some form of coordination between inbound and outbound operations. Each of these two models exhibits several important characteristics and is in turn subdivided in more specialized subcategories.

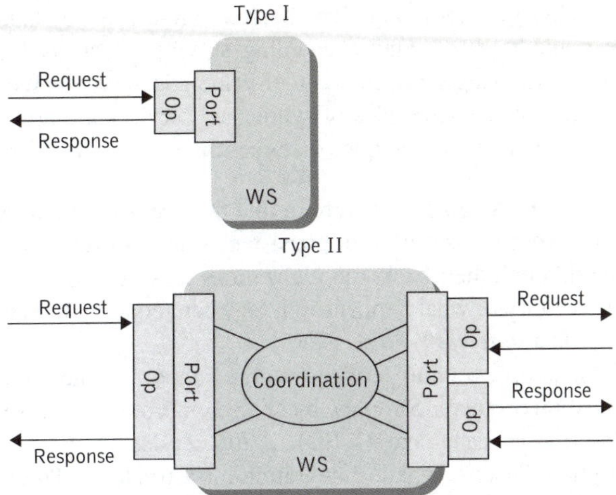

Figure 1.2 High-level view of informational and complex services

1.4.1.1 Simple or informational services

Informational services are services of relatively simple nature. They either provide access to content interacting with an end user by means of simple request/response sequences, or alternatively may expose back-end business applications to other applications. Web services that typically expose the business functionality of the applications and components that underlie them are known as *programmatic services*. For instance, they may expose function calls, typically written in programming languages such as Java/EJB, Visual Basic, or C++. The exposed programmatic simple services perform a request/response type of business task and can be viewed as "atomic" (or singular) operations. Applications access these function calls by executing a Web service through a standard programmatic interface specified in the Web Services Description Language or WSDL (see Chapter 5).

Informational services can be subdivided into three subcategories according to the business problems they solve:

1. Pure *content services*, which give programmatic access to content such as weather report information, simple financial information, stock quote information, design information, news items, and so on.
2. *Simple trading services*, which are more complicated forms of informational services that can provide a seamless aggregation of information across disparate systems and information sources, including back-end systems, giving programmatic access to a business information system so that the requestor can make informed decisions. Such service requests may have complicated realizations. Consider, for example, "pure" business services, such as logistic services, where automated services are the actual front-ends to fairly complex physical organizational information systems.
3. *Information syndication services*, which are value-added information Web services that purport to "plug into" commerce sites of various types, such as e-marketplaces,

or sell-sites. Generally speaking, these services are offered by a third party and run the whole range from commerce-enabling services, such as logistics, payment, fulfillment, and tracking services, to other value-added commerce services, such as rating services. Typical examples of syndicated services might include reservation services on a travel site or rate quote services on an insurance site.

Informational services are singular in nature in that they perform a complete unit of work that leaves its underlying datastores in a consistent state. However, they are not transactional in nature (although their back-end realizations may be). An informational service does not keep any memory of what happens to it between requests. In that respect this type of service is known as a *stateless Web service*.

Informational and simple trading services require support by the three evolving standards: (i) communication protocol (Simple Object Access Protocol), (ii) service description Web Service Description Language (WSDL), (iii) service publication and discovery (Universal Description, Discovery, and Integration infrastructure). These are described in Chapters 4, 5, and 6 of this book.

1.4.1.2 Complex services or business processes

Enterprises can use a singular (discrete) service to accomplish a specific business task, such as billing or inventory control. However, for enterprises to obtain the full benefit of Web services, business process and transactional-like Web services functionality is required that is well beyond that found in informational Web services. When enterprises need to compose several services together to create a business process such as customized ordering, customer support, procurement, and logistical support, they need to use complex Web services. Complex (or *composite*) services typically involve the assembly and invocation of many pre-existing services possibly found in diverse enterprises to complete a multi-step business interaction. Consider for instance a supply-chain application involving order taking, stocking orders, sourcing, inventory control, financials, and logistics. Numerous document exchanges will occur in this process including requests for quotes, returned quotes, purchase order requests, purchase order confirmations, delivery information, and so on. Long-running transactions and asynchronous messaging will also occur, and business "conversation" and even negotiations may occur before the final agreements are reached. This functionality is a typical characteristic of business processes (or complex services).

Complex Web services can in turn be categorized according to the way that they compose simple services. Some complex Web services compose simple services that exhibit programmatic behavior whereas others compose services that exhibit mainly interactive behavior where input has to be supplied by the user. This makes it natural to distinguish between the following two types of complex Web services:

1. *Complex services that compose programmatic Web services:* The clients of these Web services can assemble them to build complex services. An example typical of a simple service exhibiting programmatic behavior could be an inventory checking service that comprises part of an inventory management process.

2. *Complex services that compose interactive Web services:* These services expose the functionality of a Web application's presentation (browser) layer. They frequently expose a multi-step Web application behavior that combines a Web server, an

application server, and underlying database systems and typically deliver the application directly to a browser and eventually to a human user for interaction. Clients of these Web services can incorporate interactive business processes into their Web applications, presenting integrated (aggregated) applications from external service providers. Obviously interactive services can be combined with programmatic services thus delivering business processes that combine typical business logic functionality with Web browser interactivity.

Complex services exhibit *coarse-grained* functionality and are stateful. A *stateful Web service* maintains some state between different operation invocations issued by the same or different Web service clients (see section 1.4.3).

The complex Web services standards are still evolving and are converging on the communication protocol (Simple Object Access Protocol), WSDL, Universal Description, Discovery, and Integration infrastructure, WS-MetaDataExchange (which allows service endpoints to provide metadata information to requestors and support the bootstrapping of Web service interactions) and the Web services Business Process Execution Language or BPEL.

1.4.2 Functional and non-functional properties

Services are described in terms of a description language. A service description has two major interrelated components: its functional and non-functional characteristics. The *functional description* details the operational characteristics that define the overall behavior of the service, i.e., defines details of how the service is invoked, the location where it is invoked, and so on. This description focuses on details regarding the syntax of messages and how to configure the network protocols to deliver messages. The *non-functional description* concentrates on service quality attributes, such as service metering and cost, performance metrics, e.g., response time or accuracy, security attributes, authorization, authentication, (transactional) integrity, reliability, scalability, and availability. Non-functional descriptions force the service requestor's run-time environment to include, for instance, SOAP headers that specify non-functional requirements that may influence which service provider a service requestor may choose. An example of this may be a security policy statement (refer to Chapter 12 for details regarding service security policies).

Functional properties of services are examined in Chapter 5, while non-functional ones are examined in section 1.8 of this chapter.

1.4.3 State properties

Services could be stateless or stateful. If services can be invoked repeatedly without having to maintain context or state they are called stateless, while services that may require their context to be preserved from one invocation to the next are called stateful. The services access protocol is always connectionless. A *connectionless protocol* means that the protocol has no concept of a job or a session and does not make any assumptions about eventual delivery (see section 2.1.1.2).

A Web service in its simplest form, e.g., an informational weather report service, does not keep any "memory" of what happens to it between requests. Such Web services are known as *stateless* Web services. The concept of statelessness means that each time a consumer interacts with a Web service, an action is performed. After the results of the service invocation have been returned, the action is finished. There is no assumption that subsequent invocations are associated with prior ones. Consequently, all the information required to perform the service is either passed with the request message or can be retrieved from a data repository based on some information provided with the request.

In contrast to a stateless Web service, a *stateful* Web service maintains some state between different operation invocations issued by the same or different Web service clients. If a particular "session" or "conversation" involves composite Web services then transient data between operation invocations is stateful. A message sent to a Web service stateful instance would be interpreted in relation to that instance-specific state. Typically, business processes specify stateful interactions involving the exchange of messages between partners, where the state of a business process includes the messages that are exchanged as well as intermediate data used in business logic and in composing messages sent to partners. Consider, for instance, an order management application, where a seller's business process might offer a service that begins an interaction by accepting a purchase order through an input message, and then returns an acknowledgement to the customer if the order can be fulfilled. The application might later send further messages to the customer, such as shipping notices and invoices. The seller's business process must "remember" the state of each such purchase order interaction separately from other similar interactions. This is necessary when a customer has many purchase processes with the same seller that are executed simultaneously.

1.4.4 Loose coupling

Web services interact with one another dynamically and use Internet standard technologies, making it possible to build bridges between systems that otherwise would require extensive development efforts. The term *coupling* indicates the degree of dependency any two systems have on each other.

In a *tightly coupled* exchange, applications need to know how their partner applications behave. They also need to know intimate details of how their partner requires to be communicated with – the number of methods it exposes and the details of the parameters that each method accepts, and the type of results it returns. In addition, tightly coupled applications need to know the location of the applications with which they work (and this implies a certain "security" guarantee). Traditional application design depends upon a tight coupling of all subsidiary elements, often running in the same process. Consequently, a key design pattern in tightly coupled environments is synchronous interactions. Tight coupling requires that the interfaces between the different components of an application are tightly interrelated in function and form, thus making them brittle when any form of change or replacement is required to parts or the whole application. It is often quite difficult and cumbersome to build tightly coupled applications because when the number of applications and services increases, the number of interfaces that need to be created and maintained quickly becomes unwieldy. This requires that a lot of time needs to be spent in defining the connections and relationships between any two cooperating applications.

As opposed to tight coupling principles that require agreement and shared context between communicating systems as well as sensitivity to change, loose coupling allows systems to connect and interact more freely (possibly across the Internet). In a loosely

Table 1.1 Tight versus loose coupling

	Tight coupling	*Loose coupling*
Interaction pattern	Synchronous	Asynchronous
Messaging style	RPC style	Document style
Message path	Hard coded	Routed
Underlying platform	Homogeneous	Heterogeneous
Binding protocol	Static	Dynamic – late binding
Objective	Reuse	Flexibility, broad applicability

coupled exchange, applications need not know how their partner applications behave or are implemented. The benefit of a loosely coupled system lies in its agility and the ability to survive evolutionary changes in the structure and implementation of the internals of each service, which make up the whole application. Systems that are loosely coupled in time have an asynchronous or event-driven model rather than a synchronous model of interaction (see section 2.4). Loose coupling of applications provides a level of flexibility and interoperability that cannot be matched using traditional approaches to building highly integrated, cross-platform, program-to-program communications environments.

With the Web services approach, the binding from a service requestor to a service provider is loosely coupled. This means that the service requestor has no knowledge of the technical details of the provider's implementation, such as the programming language, deployment platform, and so forth. The service requestor typically invokes operations by way of messages – a request message and the response – rather than through the use of application programming interfaces or file formats.

Table 1.1 summarizes the differences between loose and tight coupling.

1.4.5 Service granularity

Web services may vary in function from simple requests to complex systems that access and combine information from multiple sources. Even simple service requests may have complicated realizations. Simple services are discrete in nature, exhibit normally a request/reply mode of operation, and are of fine granularity, i.e., they are atomic in nature. In contrast, complex services are coarse grained, for instance the `SubmitPurchaseOrder` process, and involve interactions with other services and possibly end users in a single or multiple sessions. Coarse-grained communication implies larger and richer data structures, i.e., those supported by XML schema, and enables looser coupling, which in turn enables asynchronous communication where the information exchange is the minimal required to complete the task.

1.4.6 Synchronicity

We may distinguish between two programming styles for services: synchronous or remote procedure call (RPC) style versus asynchronous or message (document) style, see sections 2.4 and 2.5:

Synchronous services: Clients of synchronous services express their request as a method call with a set of arguments, which returns a response containing a return value. This implies that when a client sends a request message, it expects a response message before continuing with its computation. This makes the whole invocation an all-or-nothing proposition. If one operation is unable to complete for any reason, all other dependent operations will fail. Because of this type of bilateral communication between the client and service, RPC-style services require a tightly coupled model of communication between the client and service provider. RPC-style Web services are normally used when an application exhibits the following characteristics:

- The client invoking the service requires an immediate response.
- The client and service work in a back-and-forth conversational way.

Examples of typical simple synchronous services with an RPC-style include returning the current price for a given stock; providing the current weather conditions in a particular location; or checking the credit rating of a potential trading partner prior to the completion of a business transaction.

Asynchronous services: Asynchronous services are document-style or message-driven services. When a client invokes a message-style service, the client typically sends it an entire document, such as a purchase order, rather than a discrete set of parameters. The service accepts the entire document, it processes it and may or may not return a result message. A client that invokes an asynchronous service does not need to wait for a response before it continues with the remainder of its application. The response from the service, if any, can appear hours or even days later.

Asynchronous interactions (messaging) are a key design pattern in loosely coupled environments. Messaging enables a loosely coupled environment in which an application does not need to know the intimate details of how to reach and interface with other applications. This allows a communication operation between any two processes to be a self-contained, standalone unit of work. Document-style Web services are normally used when an application exhibits the following characteristics:

- The client does not require (or expect) an immediate response.
- The service is document oriented (the client typically sends an entire document, e.g., a purchase order, rather discrete parameters).

Examples of document-style Web services include processing a purchase order; responding to a request for quote order from a customer; or responding to an order placement by a particular customer. In all these cases, the client sends an entire document, such as a purchase order, to the Web service and assumes that the Web service is processing it in some way, but the client does not require an immediate answer.

1.4.7 Well-definedness

The service interaction must be well defined. WSDL allows applications to describe to other applications the rules for interfacing and interacting. WSDL provides a uniform mechanism for describing abstract service interfaces and specific protocol bindings that support the service. As such it is a widely supported way of describing the details required by a service requestor for binding to a service provider. The service descriptions focus on how operations interact with a service; how messages invoke operations; details of constructing such messages; and details of where to send messages for processing, i.e., determining service access points.

WSDL does not include any technology details of the implementation of a Web service. The service requestor neither knows nor cares whether the service is implemented in a programming language such as Java, C#, C, and so on. As long as the Web service can handle SOAP messages, it does not matter which platform the service is developed and implemented on.

These issues are described further in section 1.5 where we distinguish between the service interface and service implementation sections of a service definition.

1.4.8 Service usage context

In addition to the types and characteristics of Web services mentioned above it also useful to divide information services into different categories based on the Web service requestor's perspective. Here, we may distinguish between replaceable and mission-critical services.

A *replaceable Web service* is a service provided by several providers and replacing one provider with another does not affect application functionality as long as the service interfaces are identical. The productivity is not impacted severely if the service is unavailable for a short period of time as another provider may be chosen. A discrete (enumerated) discovery process involving several alternative possibilities may be pursued here. An example of this kind of service is a car rental service. Here we may pursue different car rental agencies, e.g., Avis, Hertz, Budget, and choose the first service response that arrives and satisfies our needs. This type of service is usually well integrated with the consumer processes (e.g., rent-a-car activity) and does not exchange any critical business data.

A *mission-critical Web service* is a service possibly provided by a single specific provider, which if replaced compromises severely the functionality of an entire application. If the service is unavailable for a period of time it would drastically reduce the productivity of the application. This type of service would typically hold some critical business data and be integrated at the process level.

1.5 Service interface and implementation

One important aspect of services is that they make a sharp distinction between an interface and implementation part [Alonso 2004].

The *service interface* part defines service functionality visible to the external world and provides the means to access this functionality. The service describes its own interface characteristics, i.e., the operations available, the parameters, data typing, and the access protocols, in such a way that other software modules can determine what it does, how to invoke its functionality, and what result to expect in return. In this regard, services are contractible software modules as they provide publicly available descriptions of the interface characteristics used to access the service so that potential clients can bind to it. The service client uses the service's interface description to bind to the service provider and invoke its functionality.

The *service implementation* part realizes a specific service interface whose implementation details are hidden from the users of the service. Different service providers using any programming language of their choice may implement the same interface. One service implementation might provide the functionality itself directly, while another service implementation might use a combination of other services to provide the same functionality.

It is important to distinguish between service interfaces and service implementations because in many cases the organizations that provide service interfaces are not the same as the organizations that implement the services. A service is a business concept that should be specified with an application or the user of the service in mind, while the service realization, i.e., the *service content*, may be provided by a software package, e.g., an enterprise resource planning (ERP) package, a special-purpose built component, a commercial off-the-shelf application, or a legacy application that represents a consistent chunk of business logic.

To better understand how to design and develop services, it is important to understand the relationship between services, interfaces, and components. When designing an application developers produce a logical model of what an enterprise does in terms of business objects (such as product, customer, order, bill, etc.) and the services the business requires from these business objects (what the stock level is, what the delivery schedule is, and so on). The developer may implement these concepts as a blend of interface specifications in terms of services and component implementations (the business objects). Component technology is normally used to implement (realize) the service functionality. A *component* is an independent, encapsulated part of a system, which is simple enough to implement a well-defined set of responsibilities and has well-defined limits to its functionality. In summary, we are dealing with two largely complementary elements: the service interface and its corresponding implementation component that realizes the Web service implementation.

The only way a singular service can interact with another is via its interface. A service is usually a business function implemented in software, wrapped with a formal documented interface that is well known and locatable not only by agents who designed the service but also by agents who do not know about how the service has been designed and yet want to access and use it. This type of black-box encapsulation inherits its features from the principles of modularity in software engineering. Services are different from all of these forms of modularity in that they represent complete business functions; they are intended to be reused and combined in unanticipated ways in new transactions not at the level of an individual program or even application but at the level of the enterprise or even across enterprises.

To a service client it is irrelevant whether the services are provided by a fine-grained suite of components, or a single monolithic system such as ERP. However, it is important that the developer who implements the service still thinks about granularity so that they can optimize its performance possibly by changing parts of the implementation with the minimum amount of disruption to other components, applications, and services (see Chapter 15 which deals with service design and development concerns).

To cater for service assemblage into business processes we need to introduce the concept of *service orchestration interface* in addition to the concept of an interface. The service orchestration interface must explicitly describe all the interfaces that a client of an aggregate (composite) service expects as well as the service interfaces that must be provided by the environment into which the service is assembled/composed. The service orchestration interface serves as a means to define how a composite service interface can be specified by means of imported (possibly singular) service interfaces. In this sense the service orchestration interface has a mission identical to a composition meta-model that provides a description of how the Web service interfaces interact with each other and how to define a new Web service interface (or `<PortType>`, see section 5.2.1) as a collection (assembly) of existing ones (imported `<PortType>`s).

The concept of a service orchestration interface is shown in Figure 1.3, where it defines the encapsulation boundary of a service. This is the only way to design services reliably using imported services without knowledge of their implementations. As service

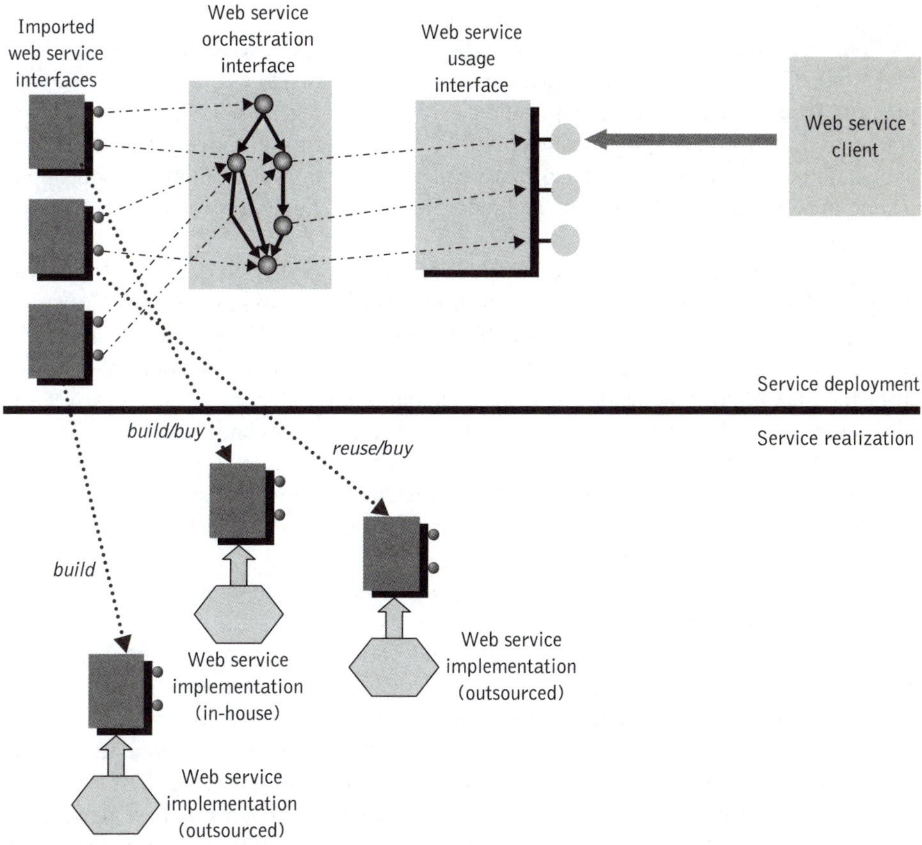

Figure 1.3 Services, interfaces, and service realizations

development requires that we deal with multiple imported service interfaces it is useful to introduce at this stage the concept of *service usage interface*. A service usage interface is simply the interface that the service chooses to expose to its clients whom it shields from the details of the internal service orchestration interface (if present). The service usage interface is the only interface viewed by a client application.

Figure 1.3 distinguishes between two broad aspects of services: service deployment, which we have examined already, and service realization. The service realization strategy involves choosing from an increasing diversity of different options for services, which may be mixed in various combinations including: in-house service design and implementation, purchasing/leasing/paying for services, outsourcing service design and implementation, and using wrappers and/or adapters (see section 2.7.1) for converting the legacy functionality, encapsulating it inside components, and combining it with modern applications. The service realization options are described in Chapter 15 where we introduce aspects of service design and development.

1.6 The service-oriented architecture

Web services hold the promise of moving beyond the simple exchange of information – the dominating mechanism for application integration today – to the concept of accessing, programming, and integrating application services that encapsulate existing and new applications. This means organizations will be able not only to move information from application to application, but also to create complex customizable composite applications, leveraging any number of back-end and older (legacy) technology systems found in local or remote applications.

Key to this concept is the service-oriented architecture (SOA). SOA is a logical way of designing a software system to provide services to either end-user applications or to other services distributed in a network, via published and discoverable interfaces. To achieve this, SOA reorganizes a portfolio of previously siloed software applications and support infrastructure in an organization into an interconnected collection of services, each of which is discoverable and accessible through standard interfaces and messaging protocols. Once all the elements of an SOA are in place, existing and future applications can access the SOA-based services as necessary. This architectural approach is particularly applicable when multiple applications running on varied technologies and platforms need to communicate with each other.

The essential goal of an SOA is to enable general-purpose interoperability among existing technologies and extensibility to future purposes and architectures. SOA lowers interoperability hurdles by converting monolithic and static systems into modular and flexible components, which it represents as services that can be requested through an industry-standard protocol. Much of SOA's power and flexibility derives from its ability to leverage standards-based functional services, calling them when needed on an individual basis, or aggregating them to create composite applications or multi-stage business processes. The building-block services might employ pre-existing components that are reused, and can also be updated or replaced without affecting the functionality or integrity of other independent services. In this latter regard, the services model offers numerous advantages over large monolithic applications, in which modifications to some portions of the code can have unintended and unpredictable effects on the rest of the code to which it is tightly bundled. Simply put, an SOA is an architectural style, inspired by the service-oriented approach to computing, for enabling extensible interoperability.

SOA as a design philosophy is independent of any specific technology, e.g., Web services or J2EE. Although the concept of SOA is often discussed in conjunction with Web services, these two are not synonymous. In fact SOA can be implemented without the use of Web services, e.g., using Java, C#, or J2EE. However, Web services should be seen as a primary example of a message delivery model that makes it much easier to deploy an SOA. Web services standards are key to enabling interoperability as well as key issues including quality of service (QoS), system semantics, security, management, and reliable messaging.

1.6.1 Roles of interaction in the SOA

The main building blocks of an SOA are three-fold and they are determined on the basis of three primary roles that can be undertaken by these architectural modules. These are the service provider, the service registry, and the service requestor (client). Providers are software agents that provide the service. Providers are responsible for publishing a description of the service(s) they provide on a services registry. Clients are software agents that request the execution of a service. Agents can be simultaneously both service clients and providers. Clients must be able to find the description(s) of the services they require and must be able to bind to them. To achieve this functionality SOA builds on today's Web services baseline specifications of SOAP, WSDL, UDDI, and the Business Process Execution Language for Web services that are going to be examined in Chapters 4, 5, 6, and 9.

1.6.1.1 Web services provider

The first important role that can be discerned in the Web service architecture is that of the Web services provider. From a business perspective the Web services provider is the organization that owns the Web service and implements the business logic that underlies the service. From an architectural perspective this is the platform that hosts and controls access to the service.

The Web services provider is responsible for publishing the Web services it provides in a service registry hosted by a service discovery agency. This involves describing the business, service, and technical information of the Web service, and registering that information with the Web services registry in the format prescribed by the discovery agency.

1.6.1.2 Web services requestor

The next major role in the Web services architecture is that of the Web services requestor (or client). From a business perspective this is the enterprise that requires certain functions to be satisfied. From an architectural perspective, this is the application that is looking for, and subsequently invoking, the service.

The Web services requestor searches the service registry for the desired Web services. This effectively means discovering the Web services description in a registry provided by a discovery agency and using the information in the description to bind to the service. Two different kinds of Web services requestors exist. The requestor role can be played either by a browser driven by an end user or by another Web service as part of an application without a user interface.

1.6.1.3 Web services registry

The last important role that can be distinguished in the Web services architecture is that of the Web services registry, which is a searchable directory where service descriptions can be published and searched. Service requestors find service descriptions in the registry and obtain binding information for services. This information is sufficient for the service requestor to contact, or bind to, the service provider and thus make use of the services it provides.

The Web services discovery agency is responsible for providing the infrastructure required to enable the three operations in the Web services architecture as described in the previous section: publishing the Web services by the Web services provider, searching for Web services by Web services requestors, and invoking the Web services.

1.6.2 Operations in the SOA

For an application to take advantage of the Web services interactions between the three roles in the SOA three primary operations must take place. These are publication of the service descriptions, finding the service descriptions, and binding or invocation of services based on their service description. These three basic operations can occur singly or iteratively.

A logical view of the SOA is given in Figure 1.4. This figure illustrates the relationship between the SOA roles and operations. First, the Web services provider publishes its Web service(s) with the discovery agency. Next, the Web services client searches for desired Web services using the registry of the discovery agency. Finally, the Web services client, using the information obtained from the discovery agency, invokes (binds to) the Web services provided by the Web services provider.

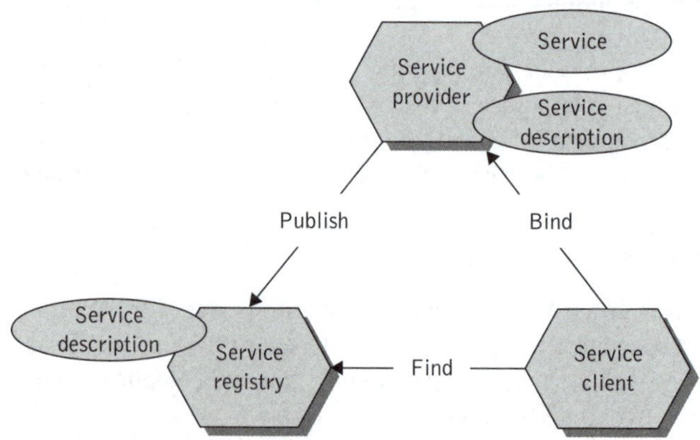

Figure 1.4 Web service roles and operations

1.6.2.1 The publish operation

Publishing a Web service so that other users or applications can find it actually consists of two equally important operations. The first operation is *describing* the Web service itself; the other is the actual *registration* of the Web service.

The first requirement for publishing Web services with the service registry is for a service provider to properly describe them in WSDL. Three basic categories of information necessary for proper description of a Web service can be discerned:

- business information: information regarding the Web service provider or the implementer of the service;
- service information: information about the nature of the Web service;
- technical information: information about implementation details and the invocation methods for the Web service.

The next step in publishing a Web service is registration. Registration deals with storing the three basic categories of descriptive information about a service in the Web services registry. For Web services requestors to be able to find a Web service this service description information needs to be published with at least one discovery agency.

1.6.2.2 The find operation

In a similar fashion to publishing, finding Web services is also a two-fold operation. Finding the desired Web services consists of first discovering the services in the registry of the discovery agency and then selecting the desired Web service(s) from the search results.

Discovering Web services involves querying the registry of the discovery agency for Web services matching the needs of a Web services requestor. A query consists of search criteria such as type of service, preferred price range, what products are associated with this service, with which categories in company and product taxonomies this Web service is associated as well as other technical service characteristics (see Chapter 6). A query is executed against the Web service information in the registry entered by the Web services provider. The find operation can be involved in two different instances by the requestor. The find operation can be specified statically at design time to retrieve a service's interface description for program development or dynamically (at run-time) to retrieve a service's binding and location description for invocation.

Selection deals with deciding about which Web service to invoke from the set of Web services the discovery process returned. Two possible methods of selection exist: *manual* and *automatic* selection. Manual selection implies that the Web services requestor selects the desired Web service directly from the returned set of Web services after manual inspection. The other possibility is automatic selection of the best candidate between potentially matching Web services. A special client application program provided by the Web services registry can achieve this. In this case the Web services requestor has to specify preferences to enable the application to infer which Web service the Web services requestor is most likely to wish to invoke.

1.6.2.3 The bind operation

The final operation in the Web services architecture and perhaps the most important one is the actual invocation of the Web services. During the binding operation the service requestor invokes or initiates an interaction at run-time using the binding details in the service description to locate and contract to the service. The technical information entered in the registry by the Web services provider is used here. Two different possibilities exist for this invocation. The first possibility is direct invocation of the Web service by the Web services requestor using the technical information included in the description of the service. The second possibility is mediation by the discovery agency when invoking the Web service. In this case all communication between the Web services requestor and the Web services provider goes through the Web services registry of the discovery agency.

1.6.3 SOA: an example involving complex services

As already explained in the previous section, an SOA introduces a new philosophy for building distributed applications where elementary services can be published, discovered, and bound together to create more complex valued-added services. To exemplify this, let us consider the example of a business process that implements the processing of a purchase order submitted by a manufacturing company. Here, we assume that a large manufacturer has built a business based on providing "specialty" and custom-fabricated plastics components on a spot and contract basis. Its role in the middle of the supply chain – between commodity suppliers like refiners and the plants of manufacturers like consumer packaged goods – requires that the company manages relationships with multiple business partners and even acts as an intermediary between its suppliers and customers.

The purchase order process can be developed in terms of interacting Web services involving purchase orders, credit checks, automated billing, stock updates, and shipping originating from various service providers who can gradually package their offerings to create turnkey products. To simplify things we assume that the purchase order process employs a relatively simple composite service that is provided by a commodity supplier that composes two separate singular services, namely an inventory and a distribution service. The SOA representation of this type of aggregate service is illustrated in Figure 1.5. This figure shows a usage relationship, which is critical for understanding dependency management as well as for visualizing the overall picture.

To address the requirements of composite Web services, Figure 1.5 involves a hierarchical service provision scheme whereby a requestor (client) sends a request to an aggregator, a system that offers a composite Web service for an application such as order management (step 1). The aggregator (parts supplier) which is just another service provider receives the initial request and decomposes it into two parts, one involving an inventory check service and a distribution service request. The aggregator thus acts as a Web services requestor and forwards the order request to the inventory (step 2) service provider. This service provider determines whether or not the ordered parts are available in the product inventory and sends its response to the aggregator (step 3). If all is well, the aggregator selects a distributor which schedules the shipment for the order (steps 4 and 5).

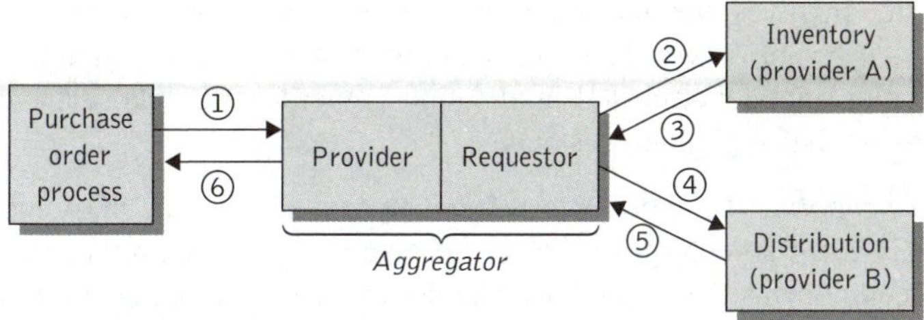

Figure 1.5 SOA: composite service example

Finally, the aggregator reverts to its role as service provider and calculates the final price for the order, bills the customer, and relays its final response to the client process (step 6).

1.6.4 Layers in an SOA

SOA introduces a flexible architectural style that provides an integration framework through which software architects can build applications using a collection of reusable functional units (services) with well-defined interfaces, which it combines in a logical flow. Applications are integrated at the interface (contract) and not at the implementation level. This allows greater flexibility since applications are built to work with any implementation of a contract, not to take advantage of a feature or idiosyncrasy of a particular system or implementation. For example, different service providers (of the same interface) can be dynamically chosen based on policies, such as price, performance, or other QoS guarantees, current transaction volume, and so on.

Another important characteristic of an SOA is that it allows many-to many integration, i.e., a variety of consumers across an enterprise can use and reuse applications in a variety of ways. This ability can dramatically reduce the cost/complexity of integrating incompatible applications and increase the ability of developers to quickly create, reconfigure, and repurpose applications as business needs arise. Benefits include reduced IT administration costs, ease of business process integration across organizational departments and with trading partners, and increased business adaptability.

Organizations that use SOAs may distinguish between three distinct SOA entry points on the basis of their business requirements and priorities: implementing enterprise service orchestrations, service enabling the entire enterprise, and implementing end-to-end collaborative business processes:

> *Implementing enterprise service orchestrations:* This basic SOA entry point focuses on a typical implementation within a department or between a small number of departments and enterprise assets and comprises two steps. First, transforming enterprise assets and applications into an SOA implementation. This can start by service enabling existing individual applications or creating new applications using Web services technology. This can begin by specifying a Web service interface into an individual application or application element (including legacy systems). The next step after this basic Web service implementation is implementing service orchestrations out of the service-enabled assets or newly created service applications.

This step involves integrating multiple services into a process that accomplishes a particular business task. This step supports a range of integration types, including integrating interdepartmental applications, interdepartmental data, business processes, and heterogeneous systems.

Service enabling the entire enterprise: The next stage in the SOA entry point hierarchy is when an enterprise seeks to provide a set of common services based on SOA components that can be used across the entire organization. Enterprise-wide service integration is achieved on the basis of commonly accepted standards. This results in achieving service consistency across departmental boundaries and is a precursor to integrating an organization with its partners and suppliers. Consistency is an important factor for this configuration as it provides both a uniform view to the enterprise and its customers as well as ensuring compliance with statutory or business policy requirements.

Implementing end-to-end collaborative business processes: The term *end-to-end business process* signifies that a succession of automated business processes and information systems in different enterprises (which are typically involved in inter-company business transactions) are successfully integrated. The aim is to provide seamless interoperation and interactive links between all the relevant members in an extended enterprise – ranging from product designers, suppliers, trading partners and logistics providers to end customers. At this stage an organization moves into the highest strategic level of SOA implementation. Deployment of services becomes ubiquitous, and federated services collaborate across enterprise boundaries to create complex products and services. Individual services in this extended enterprise may originate from many providers, irrespective of company-specific systems or applications.

One problem when implementing an SOA at the enterprise level or implementing a cross-enterprise collaborative SOA is how to manage the SOA model, how to categorize the elements in this model, and how to organize them in such a way that the different stakeholders reviewing the model can understand it. It is often convenient to think of the SOA as comprising a number of distinct layers of abstraction that emphasize service interfaces, service realizations, and compositions of services into higher-level business processes [Arsanjani 2004].

The layered approach to SOA development is shown in Figure 1.6. In this figure an SOA is shown to comprise six distinct layers: domains, business processes, business services, infrastructure services, service realizations, and operational systems. Each of these describes a logical separation of concerns by defining a set of common enterprise elements. In Figure 1.6 each layer uses the functionality of the layer below it, adding new functionality, to accomplish its objective.

The logical flow employed in the layered SOA development model may focus on a top-down development approach, which emphasizes how business processes are decomposed into a collection of business services and how these services are implemented in terms of pre-existing enterprise assets. Other variations include a bottom-up (where emphasis is placed on enterprise information systems) and the more common meet-in-the-middle approach. The bottom-up approach emphasizes how existing enterprise assets

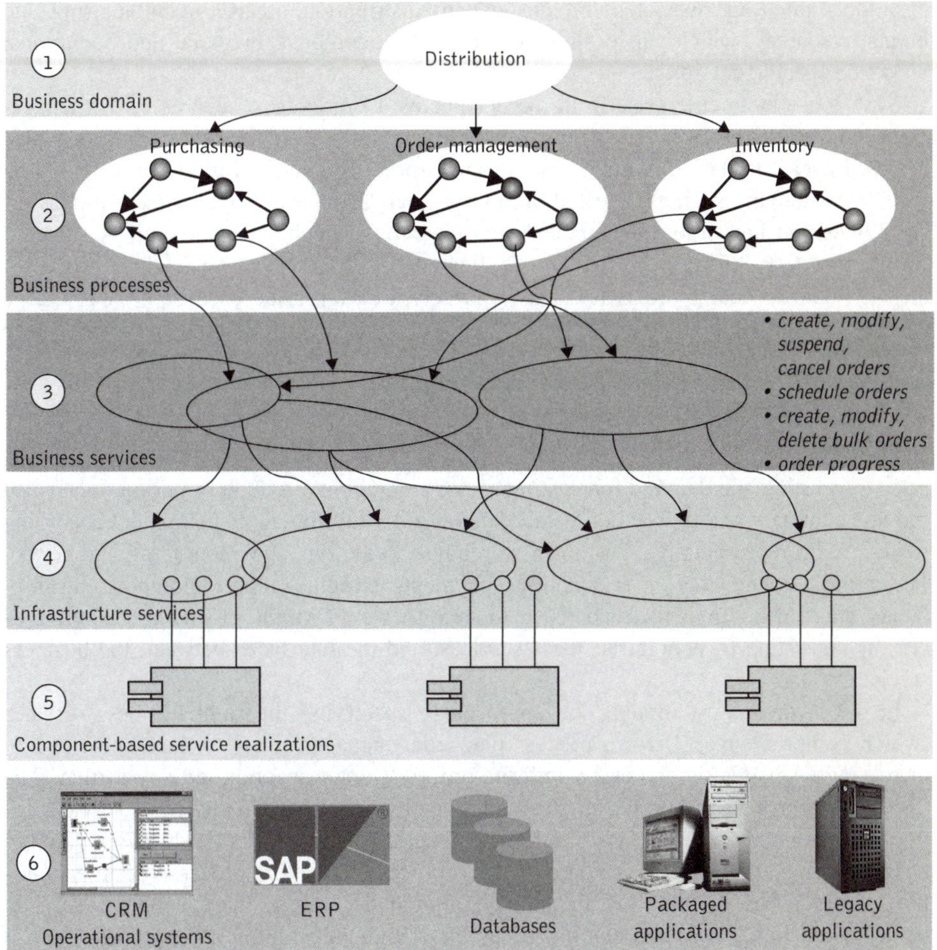

Figure 1.6 Layers in an SOA

are transformed into business services and how business services are in turn composed into business processes. All these Web services development options are part of the Web services design and development methodology that we introduce in Chapter 15. In the following we shall analyze the layered SOA development model starting with a downwards flow from the top.

The topmost layer (layer 1) is formed on the basis of the observation that all business process constellations in an enterprise target a particular business domain. A *business domain* is a functional domain comprising a set of current and future business processes that share common capabilities and functionality and can collaborate with each other to accomplish a higher-level business objective, such as loans, insurance, banking, finance, manufacturing, marketing, human resources, etc. In this way, an enterprise can be partitioned into a set of disjoint domains. In our case study, we assume that a business is partitioned into four associated domains, namely distribution, finance, manufacturing, and human resources, which can be linked to provide a complete financial and operational view of a specific enterprise.

SOA looks at an enterprise from the perspective of processes, such as order management, and perceives an enterprise as a complete set of well-defined, core business processes. Layer 2 in the SOA model, the business process layer, is formed by subdividing a business domain, such as distribution, into a small number of core business processes, such as purchasing, order management, and inventory, which are made entirely standard for use throughout the enterprise. This is illustrated in Figure 1.6. These three processes are well-defined coarse processes. This is largely a design issue because having a large number of fine-grained processes leads to tremendous overhead and inefficiency (see section 15.8.1, which describes process design criteria). Clearly, having a small collection of coarser-grained processes that are usable in multiple scenarios is a better option.

Now let us concentrate on the order management process and deconstruct its meaning and functionality. This process typically performs order volume analysis, margin analysis, sales forecasting and demand forecasting across any region, product, or period. It can also provide summary and transaction detail data on order fulfillment and shipment according to item, sales representative, customer, warehouse, order type, payment term, and period. Furthermore, it can track order quantities, payments, margins on past and upcoming shipments, and cancellations for each order. In an SOA we may think of such a business process as consisting of people, business services, and the interfaces between the business services.

In the layered SOA model, one approach to specifying the right business services (which comprise layer 3) for a process like order management is to decompose it into increasingly smaller subprocesses until the process cannot decomposed any further. The resulting subprocesses then become candidate indivisible (singular) business services for implementation. *Business services* automate generic business tasks that provide value to an enterprise and are part of standard business process. The more processes that an enterprise decomposes in this way the more commonality across these subprocesses can be achieved. In this way, an enterprise has the chance of building an appropriate set of reusable business services.

This layer relies on the orchestration interface of a collection of business-aligned services to realize reconfigurable end-to-end business processes (see Figure 1.3). Individual services or collections of services that exhibit various levels of granularity are combined and orchestrated to produce "new" composite services that not only introduce new levels of reuse but also allow the reconfiguration of business processes.

The order management process in Figure 1.6 is shown to comprise generic business activities for creating, modifying, suspending, cancelling, querying orders, and scheduling order activities, which exemplify (singular) business services. Business services in this process are used to create and track orders for a product, a service, or a resource, and capture customer-selected service details. They can also create, modify, and delete bulk orders and order activities, and inform customers of the progress of an order and its order activities. Such business services exhibit a fine granularity and simply automate specific business tasks that are part of the order management process. Information that is captured as part of a purchase order may include customer account information, product offering scheduling information, and so forth. A common data vocabulary is used to describe this kind of information so that various business services (that may belong to different organizations) can interpret messages unambiguously, communicate with each other, and be easily orchestrated and used together under the order management process (for further details on surmounting semantic ambiguities in service messages refer to Chapter 13, which presents mechanisms for the semantic enrichment of Web services descriptions).

The interfaces get exported as service descriptions in this layer using a service description language, such as WSDL (see Chapter 5). The service description can be implemented by a number of service providers, each offering various choices of qualities of service based on technical requirements in the areas of availability, performance, scalability, and security.

During the exercise of defining business services it also important to take existing utility logic, ingrained in code, and expose it as services which themselves become candidate services that specify not the overall business process, but rather the mechanism for implementing the process. This exercise should thus yield two categories of services: business functionality services that are reusable across multiple processes, and a collection of fine-grained *utility* (or *commodity*) *services* (not shown in Figure 1.6), which provide value to and are shared by business services across the organization. Examples of utility services include services implementing calculations, algorithms, directory management services, and so on.

An SOA requires the provision of infrastructure services, which are not specific to a single line of business but are reusable across multiple lines of business. Infrastructure services[1] are subdivided into technical utility services, access services, management and monitoring services, and interaction services. *Technical services* in layer 4 are coarse-grained services that provide the technical infrastructure enabling the development, delivery, maintenance, and provisioning of singular business services (in layer 3) and their integration into processes (in layer 2) as well as capabilities that maintain QoS such as security, performance, and availability. To achieve their mission technical services rely on a reliable set of capabilities, such as intelligent routing, protocol mediation, transaction management, identity management, event handling, and so on. They also include mechanisms that seamlessly interlink services that span enterprises. This can, for example, include the policies, constraints, and specific industry messages and interchange standards (such as the need to conform to specific industry message and interchange standards like EDIFACT, SWIFT, xCBL, ebXML BPSS, or RosettaNet) that an enterprise, say within a particular vertical marketplace, must conform to in order to work with other similar processes. *Access services* are dedicated to transforming data and integrating legacy applications and functions into the SOA environment. This includes the wrapping and service enablement of legacy functions. In the distributed computing systems literature access services are commonly known as adapters (see section 2.7.1). In the layered SOA model, access services are distinctly responsible for rendering these adapters as services so that they can help transform elements of legacy assets and enterprise application systems into singular business services and business processes. Infrastructure services also provide *management and monitoring services*. Management services manage resources both

[1] We shall henceforth not differentiate between business and infrastructure services and use the generic term Web services to refer to either term, unless it is necessary for a distinction to be made.

within and across system boundaries, gather information about managed systems and managed resource status and performance, and offer specific management tasks such as root cause failure analysis, Service-Level Agreement monitoring and reporting, and capacity planning. Monitoring services monitor the health of SOA applications, giving insights into the health of systems and networks, and into the status and behavior patterns of applications, thus making them more suitable for mission-critical computing environments. Management and monitoring services rely on emerging standards such as WS-Management, which are covered in Chapter 16. *Interaction services* support the interaction between applications and end users. Interactions with the external world are not limited to just interactions with humans. In some cases, interaction logic needs to orchestrate the interface to vehicles, sensors, radio frequency identification (RFID) technology devices, environmental control systems, process control equipment, and so on. All types of infrastructure services are considered as integral parts of the Enterprise Service Bus, which is the technical infrastructure that enables standards-based integration in an SOA environment (see Chapter 8).

Layer 5 in Figure 1.6 is the component realization layer that is used for implementing services out of pre-existing applications and systems found in the operational systems layer (layer 6). This layer uses components to implement (realize) the required service functionality. Component realizations are then used by the technical services in layer 4 to define the content of and construct business services, e.g., using transformation facilities and orchestrating business services with other related business services to create business processes. Component technology is the preferred technology for service implementations (see section 1.10 for a comparison between Web services and component technologies). Components comprise autonomous units of software that may provide a useful service or a set of functionality to a client (business service), and have meaning in isolation from other components with which they interoperate. Because components are autonomous units of functionality they provide natural demarcation of implementation work. The implementation of a business service will often consist of an entire assembly of application and middleware functionality potentially integrated across different application origins. Such functionality is provided by operational systems in layer 6.

Finally, the operational systems in layer 6 are used by components to implement business services and processes. Layer 6 is shown to contain existing enterprise systems or applications, including customer relationship management (CRM) and ERP systems and applications, legacy applications, database systems and applications, other packaged applications, and so on. These systems are usually known as enterprise information systems (see section 2.9). This explains how an SOA can leverage existing systems and integrate them using a service-oriented style of integration.

1.7 The Web services technology stack

The goal of Web services technology is to allow applications to work together over standard Internet protocols, without direct human intervention. By doing so, we can automate many business operations, creating new functional efficiencies and new, more effective ways of doing business. The minimum infrastructure required by the Web services

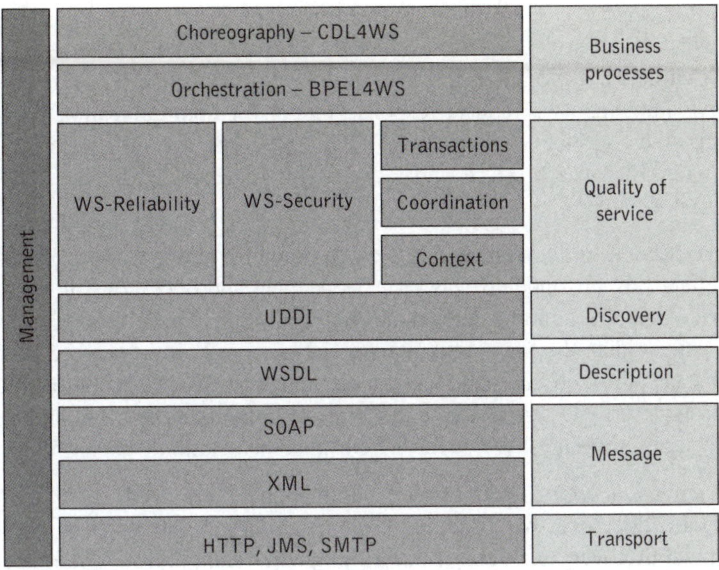

Figure 1.7 The Web services technology stack

paradigm is purposefully low to help ensure that Web services can be implemented on and accessed from any platform using any technology and programming language.

By intent, Web services are not implemented in a monolithic manner, but rather represent a collection of several related technologies. The more generally accepted definition for Web services leans on a stack of specific, complementary standards, which are illustrated in Figure 1.7. The development of open and accepted standards is a key strength of the coalitions that have been developing the Web services infrastructure. At the same time, as can be seen in Figure 1.7, these efforts have resulted in the proliferation of a dizzying number of emerging standards and acronyms. In order to simply things we provide a classification scheme for the most important standards in the Web services technology stack, which we introduce briefly below.

Enabling technology standards. Although not specifically tied to any specific transport protocol, Web services build on ubiquitous Internet connectivity and infrastructure to ensure nearly universal reach and support. For instance, at the transport level Web services take advantage of HTTP, the same connection protocol used by Web servers and browsers. Another enabling technology is the *Extensible Markup Language (XML)*. XML is a widely accepted format for all exchanging data and its corresponding semantics. Web services use XML as the fundamental building block for nearly every other layer in the Web services stack. We cover XML briefly in Chapter 3.

Core services standards. The core Web services standards comprise the baseline standards SOAP, WSDL, and UDDI:

Simple Object Access Protocol: SOAP is a simple XML-based messaging protocol on which Web services rely to exchange information among themselves. It is based on XML and uses common Internet transport protocols like HTTP to carry its data. SOAP implements a request/response model for communication between interacting Web services, and uses HTTP to penetrate firewalls, which are usually configured to accept HTTP and FTP service requests. We cover SOAP in some detail in Chapter 4.

Service description: Web services can be used effectively when a Web service and its client rely on standard ways to specify data and operations, to represent Web service contracts, and to understand the capabilities that a Web service provides. To achieve this, the functional characteristics of a Web service are first described by means of a Web Services Description Language. WSDL defines the XML grammar for describing services as collections of communicating endpoints capable of exchanging messages. We cover WSDL in some detail in Chapter 5.

Service publication: Web service publication is achieved by UDDI, which is a public directory that provides publication of on-line services and facilitates eventual discovery of Web services. Companies can publish WSDL specifications for services they provide and other enterprises can access those services using the description in WSDL. In this way, independent applications can advertise the presence of business processes or tasks that can be utilized by other remote applications and systems. Links to WSDL specifications are usually offered in an enterprise's profile in the UDDI registry. We cover UDDI in some detail in Chapter 6.

Service composition and collaboration standards. These include the following standards:

Service composition: Describes the execution logic of Web-services-based applications by defining their control flows (such as conditional, sequential, parallel, and exceptional execution) and prescribing the rules for consistently managing their unobservable business data. In this way enterprises can describe complex processes that span multiple organizations – such as order processing, lead management, and claims handling – and execute the same business processes in systems from other vendors. The Business Process Execution Language (BPEL), which we cover in Chapter 9, can achieve service composition for Web services [Andrews 2003].

Service collaboration: Describes cross-enterprise collaborations of Web service participants by defining their common observable behavior, where synchronized information exchanges occur through their shared contact points, when commonly defined ordering rules are satisfied. Service collaboration is materialized by the Web Services Choreography Description Language (WS-CDL) [Kavantzas 2004], which specifies the common observable behavior of all participants engaged in business collaboration. Each participant could be implemented not only by BPEL but also by other executable business process languages.

Coordination/transaction standards: Solving the problems associated with service discovery and service description retrieval is the key to success of Web services. Currently there are attempts underway towards defining transactional interaction among Web services. The WS-Coordination and WS-Transaction initiatives complement BPEL to provide mechanisms for defining specific standard protocols for use by transaction processing systems, workflow systems, or other applications that wish to coordinate multiple Web services. These three specifications work in tandem to address the business workflow issues implicated in connecting and executing a number of Web services that may run on disparate platforms across organizations involved in e-business scenarios. We cover WS-Coordination and WS-Transaction in some detail in Chapter 10.

Value-added standards: Additional elements that support complex business interactions must still be implemented before Web services can automate truly critical business processes. Value-added services standards include mechanisms for security and authentication, authorization, trust, privacy, secure conversations, contract management, and so on. We cover value-added services standards such as WS-Security, WS-Policy, and WS-Management in Chapters 11, 12, and 16.

Today there are several vendors including companies such as IBM, Microsoft, BEA, and Sun Microsystems which supply products and services across the realm of Web services functionality and implement Web services technology stack. These vendors are considered as platform providers and provide both infrastructure, e.g., WebSphere, .NET framework, WebLogic, for building and deploying Web services in the form of application servers, as well as tools for orchestration and/or composite application development for utilizing Web services within business operations.

1.8 Quality of service (QoS)

A significant requirement for an SOA-based application is to operate in such a way that it functions reliably and delivers a consistent service at a variety of levels. This requires not only focusing on the functional properties of services but also concentrating on describing the environment hosting the Web service, i.e., describing the non-functional capabilities of services. Each service hosting environment may offer various choices of QoS based on technical requirements regarding demands for around-the-clock levels of service availability, performance and scalability, security and privacy policies, and so on, all of which must be described. It is thus obvious that the QoS offered by a Web service is becoming the highest priority for service providers and their customers.

QoS refers to the ability of the Web service to respond to expected invocations and to perform them at the level commensurate with the mutual expectations of both its provider and its customers. Several quality factors that reflect customer expectations, such as constant service availability, connectivity, and high responsiveness, become key to keeping a business competitive and viable as they can have a serious impact upon service provision. QoS thus becomes an important criterion that determines the service usability and utility, both of which influence the popularity of a particular Web service, and an important selling and differentiating point between Web services providers.

Delivering QoS on the Internet is a critical and significant challenge because of its dynamic and unpredictable nature. Applications with very different characteristics and requirements compete for all kinds of network resources. Changes in traffic patterns, securing mission-critical business transactions, and the effects of infrastructure failures, low performance of Web protocols, and reliability issues over the Web create a need for Internet QoS standards. Often, unresolved QoS issues cause critical transactional applications to suffer from unacceptable levels of performance degradation.

Traditionally, QoS is measured by the degree to which applications, systems, networks, and all other elements of the IT infrastructure support availability of services at a required level of performance under all access and load conditions. While traditional QoS metrics apply, the characteristics of Web services environments bring both greater availability of applications and increased complexity in terms of accessing and managing services and thus impose specific and intense demands on organizations, which QoS must address. In the Web services' context, QoS can be viewed as providing assurance on a set of quantitative characteristics. These can be defined on the basis of important functional and non-functional service quality properties that include implementation and deployment issues as well as other important service characteristics such as service metering and cost, performance metrics (e.g., response time), security requirements, (transactional) integrity, reliability, scalability, and availability. These characteristics are necessary requirements to understand the overall behavior of a service so that other applications and services can bind to it and execute it as part of a business process.

The key elements for supporting QoS in a Web services environment are summarized in what follows and were inspired by [Mani 2002]:

1. *Availability:* Availability is the absence of service downtimes. Availability represents the probability that a service is available. Larger values mean that the service is always ready to use while smaller values indicate unpredictability over whether the service will be available at a particular time. Also associated with availability is time-to-repair (TTR). TTR represents the time it takes to repair a service that has failed. Ideally smaller values of TTR are desirable.

2. *Accessibility:* Accessibility represents the degree with which a Web service request is served. It may be expressed as a probability measure denoting the success rate or chance of a successful service instantiation at a point in time. A high degree of accessibility means that a service is available for a large number of clients and that clients can use the service relatively easily.

3. *Conformance to standards:* Describes the compliance of a Web service with standards. Strict adherence to correct versions of standards (e.g., WSDL version 2.0) by service providers is necessary for proper invocation of Web services by service requestors. In addition, service providers must stick to the standards outlined in Service-Level Agreements between service requestors and providers.

4. *Integrity:* Describes the degree with which a Web service performs its tasks according to its WSDL description as well as conformance with Service-Level Agreement (SLA). A higher degree of integrity means that the functionality of a service is closer to its WSDL description or SLA.

5. *Performance:* Performance is measured in terms of two factors: throughput and latency. *Throughput* represents the number of Web service requests served at a

given time period. *Latency* represents the length of time between sending a request and receiving the response. Higher throughput and lower latency values represent good performance of a Web service. When measuring the transaction/request volumes handled by a Web service it is important to consider whether these come in a steady flow or burst around particular events like the open or close of the business day or seasonal rushes.

6. *Reliability:* Reliability represents the ability of a service to function correctly and consistently and provide the same service quality despite system or network failures. The reliability of a Web service is usually expressed in terms of number of transactional failures per month or year.
7. *Scalability:* Scalability refers to the ability to consistently serve the requests despite variations in the volume of requests. High accessibility of Web services can be achieved by building highly scalable systems.
8. *Security:* Security involves aspects such as authentication, authorization, message integrity, and confidentiality (see Chapter 11). Security has added importance because Web service invocation occurs over the Internet. The amount of security that a particular Web service requires is described in its accompanying SLA, and service providers must maintain this level of security.
9. *Transactionality:* There are several cases where Web services require transactional behavior and context propagation. The fact that a particular Web service requires transactional behavior is described in its accompanying SLA, and service providers must maintain this property.

As organizations depend on business units, partners, and external service providers to furnish them with services, they rely on the use of SLAs to ensure that the chosen service provider delivers a guaranteed level of service quality. An SLA is a formal agreement (contract) between a provider and client, formalizing the details of a Web service (contents, price, delivery process, acceptance and quality criteria, penalties, and so on, usually in measurable terms) in a way that meets the mutual understandings and expectations of both the service provider and the service requestor.

An SLA is basically a QoS guarantee typically backed up by charge-back and other mechanisms designed to compensate users of services and to influence organizations to fulfill SLA commitments. Understanding business requirements, expected usage patterns, and system capabilities can go a long way towards ensuring successful deployments. An SLA is an important and widely used instrument in the maintenance of service provision relationships as both service providers and clients alike utilize it.

An SLA may contain the following parts [Jin 2002]:

- *Purpose:* This field describes the reasons behind the creation of the SLA.
- *Parties:* This field describes the parties involved in the SLA and their respective roles, e.g., service provider and service consumer (client).
- *Validity period:* This field defines the period of time that the SLA will cover. This is delimited by start time and end time of the agreement term.

- *Scope:* This field defines the services covered in the agreement.
- *Restrictions:* This field defines the necessary steps to be taken in order for the requested service levels to be provided.
- *Service-level objectives:* This field defines the levels of service that both the service customers and the service providers agree on, and usually includes a set of service level indicators, like availability, performance, and reliability. Each of these aspects of the service level will have a target level to achieve.
- *Penalties:* This field defines what sanctions should apply in case the service provider underperforms and is unable to meet the objectives specified in the SLA.
- *Optional services:* This field specifies any services that are not normally required by the user, but might be required in case of an exception.
- *Exclusion terms:* These specify what is not covered in the SLA.
- *Administration:* This field describes the processes and the measurable objectives in an SLA and defines the organizational authority for overseeing them.

SLAs can be either static or dynamic in nature. A *static SLA* is an SLA that generally remains unchanged for multiple service time intervals. Service time intervals may be calendar months for a business process that is subject to an SLA, or may be a transaction or any other measurable and relevant period of time for other processes. They are used for assessment of the QoS and are agreed between a service provider and service client. A *dynamic* SLA is an SLA that generally changes from service period to service period, to accommodate changes in provision of service.

To enter into a Web services SLA, specific QoS metrics that are evaluated over a time interval to a set of defined objectives should be employed. Measurement of QoS levels in an SLA will ultimately involve tracing Web services through multi-domain (geographical, technological, application, and supplier) infrastructures. In a typical scenario, each Web service may interact with multiple Web services, switching between the roles of being a service provider in some interactions to being a consumer in other interactions. Each of these interactions could potentially be governed by an SLA. The metrics imposed by SLAs should correlate with the overall objectives of the services being provided. Thus an important function that an SLA accomplishes is addressing QoS at the source. This refers to the level of service that a particular service provides [Mani 2002].

To achieve measurement of an SLA in an organized manner, it is convenient to group the Web services QoS elements we introduced earlier under the following three broad categories.

1. *Performance and capacity:* This category considers such issues as transaction volumes, throughput rates, system sizing, utilization levels, whether underlying systems have been designed and tested to meet these peak load requirements, and, finally, how important are request/response times.
2. *Availability:* This category considers such issues as mean time between failure for all or parts of the system, disaster recovery mechanisms, mean time to recovery, whether the business can tolerate Web services downtime and how much, whether

there is adequate redundancy built in so that services can be offered in the event of a system or network failure, and so on.

3. *Security/privacy:* This category considers such issues as response to systematic attempts to break into a system, privacy concerns, authentication/authorization mechanisms provided, and so on.

To address QoS concerns, the evolving Web services suite of standards supports a standard policy framework that makes it possible for developers to express the policies of services and for Web services to understand policies and enforce them at run-time. The Web Services Framework (WS-Policy) [Bajaj 2006a] assists this undertaking by providing building blocks that may be used in conjunction with other Web service and application-specific protocols to assist in expressing, exchanging, and processing the policies governing the interactions between Web services endpoints (see Chapter 12).

1.9 Web services interoperability

Details of Web services specifications, implementations, and best practices are gradually becoming established. Given the potential to have many necessary interrelated specifications at various versions and schedules of development, it becomes a very difficult task to determine which products support which levels of the Web services specifications. In many situations, there are versions of products that implement the specifications in ways that are different enough to prevent their implementations from being fully interoperable. This requires that individual enterprises provide individual interpretations of how their specifications are to be used. This has resulted in many Web services applications that were isolated and could serve only a limited community and certainly defies the purpose of Web services interoperability. Web services interoperability needs among other things to address the problem of ambiguity among the interpretation of standards that have been agreed upon and insufficient understanding of the interaction among the various specifications (see **www.ws-i.org**).

Web services interoperability concerns are addressed by the Web Services Interoperability Organization (WS-I). WS-I is an open, industry consortium chartered to promote Web services interoperability across platforms, operating systems, and programming languages. This organization works across the industry and standards organizations to respond to developer needs by providing guidance, best practices, and resources for developing Web services solutions that are interoperable.

WS-I brands versions of Web services specification as interoperable profiles. Interoperable profiles identify target Web services technologies and provide clarifications on their usage both individually and in conjunction. WS-I *profiles* contain a list of named and versioned Web services specifications together with a set of implementation and interoperability guidelines recommending how the specifications should be used to develop interoperable Web services. WS-I is developing a core collection of profiles that support interoperability for general-purpose Web services functionality. Profiles make it easier to discuss Web services interoperability at a level of granularity that makes sense for developers, users, and executives making investment decisions about Web services and Web services products.

Basic Profile 1.0 includes implementation guidelines on using core Web services specifications together to develop interoperable Web services and concentrates on conventions around messaging, description, and discovery. Those specifications include SOAP 1.1, WSDL 1.1, UDDI 2.0, XML 1.0, and XML Schema. The availability of Basic Profile 1.0 sets the stage for unified Web services support in technologies such as the next major version of the enterprise Java specification, J2EE 1.4, and the IBM WebSphere Studio development environment. Version 1.0 of the profile is intended to provide a common framework for implementing interoperable solutions while giving customers a common reference point for purchasing decisions. Meanwhile WS-I has also developed Basic Profile 1.1, which extends version 1.0, and is currently busy establishing a new working group, the Reliable Secure Profile Working Group, which will deliver guidance to Web services architects and developers concerning reliable messaging with security.

Among the key deliverables of WS-I are testing tools, which developers can use to test conformance of their Web services with the test assertions that represent the interoperability guidelines of established WS-I profiles. The process used to develop these profiles, interoperability guidelines, test assertions, and testing tools generates other related resources useful to developers. The tools developed monitor the interactions with a Web service, record those interactions, and analyze them to detect implementation errors.

1.10 Web services versus components

Web services are primarily developed to provide a standard framework for distributed applications to communicate with each other in a way that promotes understanding, reuse, development, and integration of independently developed applications. As distributed components share the same concerns at first, it may seem that Web services and components are simply different flavors of the same type of distributed computing. However, when compared to distributed component software, which is traditionally used to develop tightly coupled solutions, Web services are not an attempt to define a new component model but rather a functional distributed service specification that can be layered over any existing component model, language, or execution environment.

The primary requirement for an integration solution as advocated by both Web services and components is to support neutrality along various dimensions by establishing an abstraction layer (implemented either as Web services or as components) that hides the specifics of the endpoint implementations. The integration solution should be neutral to platforms, languages, application component models, transaction models, security models, transport protocols, invocation mechanisms, data formats, endpoint availability models, and so on. The challenges for achieving this endeavor can be naturally grouped under five dimensions: communication patterns, types of coupling between the endpoints, types of interfaces, types of invocation, and finally, type of brokering. We shall use these to serve as the set of criteria for a brief comparison between Web services and distributed components:

Type of communication: The distributed component style of interaction for components is based on the RPC paradigm and typically involves passing a small number of individual data items in multiple requests, and synchronously getting a small number of reply data items in return. Communication at the component method level results in fine-grained communication at the object level over a network. This is often unreliable and expensive.

As opposed to components that use synchronous communication, services employ both synchronous and asynchronous communication to perform computations. While simple services can be developed using a request/response RPC-style synchronous behavior with fine-grained object interactions, complex Web services require a more loosely coupled asynchronous mode, which is typical of message-based systems.

Type of coupling between endpoints: Distributed components rely on tightly coupled interactions that typically involve invocation of multiple fine-grained APIs (Application Programming Interfaces). Such tightly coupled interactions largely depend upon a general acceptance of the component model on which the application is designed. This forces the use of a homogeneous infrastructure on both the client and service machines and thus distributed component platforms cannot interoperate easily. For example, CORBA requires all applications to conform to IDL (Interface Description Language) and use of an Object Request Broker and Java Remote Method Invocation requires the communicating entities to be written using Java. While implementations that are tightly coupled to specific component technologies are perfectly acceptable in a controlled environment, they become impractical and do not scale on the Web. As the set of participants in an integrated business process changes, and as technology changes over time, it becomes increasingly difficult to guarantee a single, unified infrastructure among all participants.

On the other hand, Web services do not bind to each other using application-specific interfaces. Instead, they make use of abstract message definitions to mediate their binding with respect to each other, focusing on the message definitions instead of method signatures. This supports general-purpose message definitions such that the application code can independently handle the complexity of processing specific message instances, which makes the interfaces reusable. By focusing solely on messages, Web services are completely language, platform, and object model agnostic. Applications that consume the service can also be implemented on any platform in any programming language.

Type of interface: Components expose fine-grained object-level interfaces to applications. With the distributed component approach, the sender makes many assumptions about the recipient regarding how the application will be activated, the kinds of interfaces that are called, and their signatures. In contrast, whereas services expose application-level interfaces, messaging systems as used by Web services, on the other hand, form the contract at the wire format level. The only assumption the requestor makes is that the recipient will be able to understand the message being sent. The requestor makes no assumptions about what will happen once the message is received, nor does it make any assumptions about what might occur between the sender and the receiver.

With the Web services approach, application-level interfaces are coarse-grained interfaces that describe services that are useful at the business level. For instance, with a Web services approach an inventory service would expose the inventory replenishment service and associated parameters. Unlike a component-based approach it would not expose the inventory object and all its interfaces, the replenishment object and its interfaces, which are of no interest to a business application.

Type of invocation: Components focus on locating services by name – for instance, CORBA uses naming contexts. In contrast to this, Web services introduce the concept of service capability. Service capability describes the classification, functionality, and conditions under which a particular service can be published, discovered, and invoked. For example, we may be able to find the categories of services that a number of businesses may offer, e.g., manufacturing or logistics services, and choose the most appropriate one on the basis of pricing and QoS – including technical parameters such as response times, load balancing, and so on.

Type of request brokering: Traditional approaches to distributed computing, e.g., component frameworks, rely on predefined interfaces to invoke remote objects: the code that uses the service understands the message formats of the target service. Services rely on a quite different service binding paradigm: static binding where the application knows the details of the collaborating service as this has been determined during the design time, and dynamic binding where the application knows how to ask a service broker for the precise collaborating service.

Other important differences include the wide use of open standards by Web services, which components lack, and advanced functionality provided only by Web services technologies. Such advanced functionality includes run-time negotiable QoS (by choosing between various service providers according to QoS criteria), reactive services and processes (where services can respond to environmental demands without compromising on operational efficiencies), and, finally, advanced workflow, coordination, and transactional features for service-based applications.

In conclusion, component systems are best suited to building systems with well-defined architectural considerations that are very much oriented towards the intranet and the enterprise integration architectures of a single organization. For instance, distributed component technologies, such as CORBA, are better suited for building distributed applications in controlled environments, where it is possible to share a common object model among all distributed entities, where there are no restrictions on the granularity or volume of the communications between the distributed entities, and where the deployment is more or less permanent such that the system may find a benefit in mapping the network addresses directly to object references. While distributed component technologies provide excellent support in integrating disparate endpoints, they do not inherently (or at least not easily) support building business process management solutions. It is difficult to create the technical agreement and coordination needed to build a distributed object system that spans enterprises.

Because Web services provide a semantically rich integration environment, they can build intra- and cross-enterprise business process management solutions. Web services are best suited for implementing shared business tasks between enterprises; they could, however, also be used for enterprise application integration purposes, see section 2.9.

1.11 Impact and shortcomings of Web services

In this chapter we have explained the nature and characteristics of Web services and have focused on the positive aspects of their use. However, despite the great promise that Web services hold for improving efficiency and broadening application portfolios, there is still a lot of work that needs to be done to augment the Web services paradigm in order to enable Web services applications to be run in production, mission-critical computing environments using formal standards.

This section first describes the impact of Web services for business applications and then goes on to identify the primary concerns of making Web services a robust, reliable, secure, and manageable technology capable of being used in the challenging, mission-critical, industrial-strength environments of the future.

The true potential for Web services technologies lies in supporting businesses functions by addressing recurring business problems and changing market demands. Coupled with a well-designed service-oriented architecture, Web services technology enables enterprises to effectively achieve reuse of business functionality and reduce time to market of new applications. Consequently, Web services are widely viewed by enterprises as a means to extend existing investments in information repositories, applications, and business processes both within organizations and across extended value chains.

The most appealing characteristic of Web services is that they are evolving to embrace the convergence of e-business, EAI, traditional middleware, and the Web. Web services are not a replacement for traditional middleware, but when used in combination with middleware and EAI techniques, Web services provide a simplified and standards-based approach to integration. To this effect Web services offer:

- A standard way to expose legacy application functionality as a set of reusable self-contained, self-describing services that can interoperate with other services in a well-behaved, manageable way.
- A standard, easy, and flexible way to help overcome application integration issues that leads to rapid application assembly out of tested, trusted, interoperable modules that implement application functionality.
- A standard way to develop and/or assemble Internet-native applications for both the internal and the extended enterprise by using internally or externally created services as building blocks that can be assembled in whole sections into full applications.
- A common facade for cross-enterprise specific systems, making it easier to create the SLAs needed for business-to-business integration.

As the business requirements that drive Web services become ever more complex, Web services technologies require additional capabilities to handle demanding situations that severely test the most obvious current shortcomings of Web services. These include performance issues, lack of appropriate support for sophisticated transaction management, lack of expressing business semantics, and, especially, achieving widespread agreement and harmonization on a wide range of existing and emerging standards. Going without these capabilities can expose a company to risks and degrade the value of its Web services. We shall examine these Web services shortcomings in turn in what follows.

A much maligned problem with Web services lies in sharing and employing data between different flavors of Web services software. This includes simple tasks such as sending a video clip from a handheld computer to a desktop and major jobs such as exchanging large documents among several collaborators, which can severely impact performance. A major part of the problem is that Web services applications are based on XML, which takes a lot of bandwidth and significantly slows down applications when binary data – such as a picture – is encoded in XML format and transferred across the network.

Recently, Web services standards organizations have been making strides to improve the performance, effectiveness, and enterprise readiness of Web services. In January 2005 the World Wide Web Consortium (W3C) published three new standards to help vendors improve Web services performance for customers. These new standards are XML-binary Optimized Packaging, SOAP Message Transmission Optimization Mechanism, and Resource Representation SOAP Header Block to help developers package and send binary data in a SOAP 1.2 message.

The first specification, XOP (XML-binary Optimized Packaging), represents a standard way to include binary data with an XML document in a package. As a result, applications need less space to store the data and less bandwidth to transmit it. The second specification, MTOM (Message Transformation Optimization Mechanism), employs XOP to address SOAP messages and optimize transmission of the messages. The third recommendation is known as the RRSHB (Resource Representation SOAP Header Block), which enables SOAP message receivers to access cached versions of the content in the message. In instances where bandwidth or size restrictions might come into play, RRSHB gives users the choice of accessing the original file or a cached copy.

XOP aims to allow XML to support large binary media types and is an indication of the prevalence of XML use for new applications that are outside the bounds originally conceived for the language. MTOM and RRSHB, on the other hand, aim to boost efficiency by trimming the traffic that SOAP messages can create.

Today, Web services transactional standards, e.g., WS-Transaction and the Web Services Composite Application Framework, which we shall examine in Chapter 10, are still evolving and rather immature. Therefore, Web services that provide transactional services should be carefully considered, designed, and implemented. When building service-based transactional solutions, it is important to keep a sharp eye on maintaining interoperability, reducing complexity of client integration, and utilizing the "right" type of standards – those that are accepted industry-wide. Designing reliable and secure business transactions and advanced applications by creating and deploying proprietary extensions is quite possible. However, developing such ad hoc solutions is time consuming and expensive and enterprises must resolve these solutions separately with each partner or customer. This approach obviously encroaches upon a central value area of Web services – cross-organizational interoperability. Thus there is a clear need to provide advanced transactional capabilities required by more sophisticated Web services on a broader basis to unleash the full power and promise of Web services development.

In contrast to business transactions, progress has been achieved in the area of security where WS-Security describes how to use the existing W3C security specifications, XML Signature and XML Encryption, to ensure the integrity and confidentiality of SOAP messages. Together, these specifications form the bottom layer of comprehensive modular security architecture for XML Web services. Future security specifications will build on these basic capabilities to provide mechanisms for credential exchange, trust management, revocation, and other higher-level capabilities.

With SOAs in place, applications can be built quickly to provide a collection of applications and processes that function as a unified and clearly understandable unit. However, alignment is not possible when business processes using diverse business terminologies try to communicate with each other across organizational boundaries, and, more importantly, when there is lack of commonly accepted and understood processes and commonly accepted business protocols that drive the business process exchanges and interactions. In an SOA it becomes imperative for the service requestors and providers to communicate meaningfully with each other, notwithstanding the heterogeneous nature of the underlying information structures, business processes, and artifacts. This requirement is known as semantic interoperability and will be examined in Chapters 13 and 14.

The good news is that a prime formalism in the Semantic Web, the Resource Description Format, which is a formal specification for describing and exchanging metadata, has successfully penetrated various business domains with highly practical applications in knowledge management, knowledge engineering, production support, and large-scale database applications. As we shall see in Chapter 13, RDF is the basis for interoperability among diverse metadata, and is considered the cornerstone of Semantic Web efforts.

One of the most serious pitfalls that hinder wide acceptance of Web services is the existence of many different standards out there that are either overlapping or conflicting. There are no fewer than four organizations – Liberty Alliance, Oasis, W3C, and WS-I – that are vying to preside over the process, each with different goals, each with differing degrees of power and influence. It is these standards bodies that make Web services function. But in addition to that there are also vendor coalitions that also define specifications. A vendor coalition actually develop a lot of the Web services specifications initially. They work on it for some period of time until they feel that it is reasonably mature and then they generally submit it to a standards body for standardization. Currently, two opposing camps of vendors have emerged: an uneasy alliance of IBM and Microsoft versus companies such as Sun, Oracle, SAP, and a few other vendors. Both camps are proposing Web services specifications – some proprietary, some not – with unclear patent and licensing implications for companies.

Today there are an overwhelming number of existing and emerging standards. Trying to understand how the different standards, some of which are still in flux, must interact to fulfill the Web services vision is in itself a daunting task. Unless these standards mature enough to the degree that they are harmonized and can act together, the long-term viability of Web services applications being used in mission-critical, production computing environments will be severely tested.

Despite all these problems there were several signs of collaboration and goodwill between opposing standards camps. For example, in August 2004, IBM, Microsoft, BEA, SAP, and Sun Microsystems submitted the WS-Addressing specification to W3C. Originally, IBM, Microsoft, BEA, and SAP developed WS-Addressing, and Sun was not involved. It is expected that such activities will continue in the future.

1.12 Summary

The service-oriented computing paradigm allows the software-as-a-service concept to expand to include the delivery of complex business processes as a service, while permitting applications to be constructed on-the-fly and services to be reused everywhere and by anybody. Services are self-describing, platform-agnostic computational elements that support rapid, low-cost, and easy composition of loosely coupled distributed applications.

Web services are a distinct family of automated services that use the Internet (as the communication medium) and open Internet-based standards. A Web service is a service available via a network such as the Internet that completes tasks, solves problems, or conducts transactions on behalf of a user or application. Web services are used for composing applications by discovering and invoking network-available services rather than building new applications or by invoking available applications to accomplish some task.

The Web services approach is based on loose coupling between a service requestor and a service provider. This means that the service requestor has no knowledge of the technical details of the provider's implementation, such as the programming language, deployment platform, and so forth. The service requestor typically invokes operations by way of messages – a request message and the response – rather than through the use of APIs or file formats. This is possible because Web services distinguish the service interface part, which is defined in a neutral manner, that is independent from the implementation part of a Web service.

Key to the concept of Web services is the service-oriented architecture. SOA is a logical way of designing a software system to provide services to either end-user applications or to other services distributed in a network, via published and discoverable interfaces. The basic SOA defines an interaction between software agents as an exchange of messages between service requestors (clients) and service providers. Clients are software agents that request the execution of a service, while providers are software agents that provide the service. Agents can be simultaneously both service clients and providers.

Coupled with a well-designed SOA, Web services technology enables enterprises to effectively achieve reuse of business functionality and reduce time to market of new applications. However, Web services currently present several limitations that include: performance issues, lack of advanced transaction management facilities, lack of appropriate support for business semantics, and, finally, the proliferation of a wide range of existing and emerging standards that partially overlap or even conflict. The lack of these capabilities can expose a company to risks and degrade the value of its Web services.

Review questions

- What are Web services?
- How do Web services differ from application service providers and Web-based applications?
- Name and briefly describe each of the types of Web services.

- What are stateful and stateless services? Give examples.
- What is service granularity? Give examples of typical fine-grained and coarse-grained services.
- How do synchronous services differ from asynchronous services?
- What is loose coupling and how does it compare to tight coupling? Give examples of technologies that use tight and loose coupling.
- Define and describe the significance of a service-oriented architecture.
- List and describe the roles and operations in an SOA.
- List some benefits of an SOA.
- What are the main layers in an SOA and what is their purpose?
- What is the Web services technology stack?
- What is quality of service and why is it important for Web services? What is the role of a Service-Level Agreement?
- List some of the benefits and some of pitfalls of Web services.

Exercises

1.1 Mention a few typical examples that make use of Web services to solve complex business applications. Explain how these differ from conventional business solutions that use paper, fax, and e-mail exchanges.

1.2 Develop an application that comprises a number of singular Web services that are composed to create complex services (business processes). Explain whether the business processes that you designed are stateless or stateful. Justify your answer. Compare the granularity level of simple and complex services. What do you observe?

1.3 Consider a consumer electronics company that manufactures customizable personal computers and devices. This company delivers to its customers new versions of products on a very frequent basis, say every six months. For example, the personal computer that a customer may buy today is a different product version to that the same customer might have bought six months ago. Typically there is constant reconfiguration of components delivering new or specialized functionality using existing interfaces on the motherboard. Develop an SOA solution so that customers of this company may make frequent changes to very limited areas of their computer configuration to upgrade its functionality in a highly manageable and controllable fashion. Explain your design choices and describe the services that your are going to introduce to the SOA solution.

1.4 The purchasing process in the distribution domain in Figure 1.6 provides purchase order details (quantity, unit price, and extended price) according to purchase order, vendor, buyer, authorizer, inventory item, any chart of accounts combination, and non-invoiced receipts. In this way purchasing departments are able to research purchases made through blanket orders, planned orders, and standard purchase orders and can also analyze vendor performance, lead time based on the promised-by date and the need-by date. The process can also help analyze goods received and invoice received, and shipped-item costs for distribution to charged accounts. Decompose this standard business process into a number of appropriate services and indicate how these services interact with each other.

1.5 The distribution inventory process in the distribution domain in Figure 1.6 helps track the amount of inventory on hand and expected arrival of items, and monitors the movement of physical inventory. It also helps analyze inventory transactions through various accounts, warehouses, and subinventories as well as tracking inventory on-hand, by warehouse, across the organization at any time. Inventory items can be monitored by arrival date, per geographic location, ensuring correct inventory levels are met. In this way slow-moving inventory and obsolete inventories can be quickly identified, allowing the department managers to reduce the cost of the inventory. Decompose this standard business process into a number of appropriate services and indicate how these services interact with each other.

1.6 Explain which of the services in the inventory business process are synchronous and which are asynchronous.

PART II

Enabling infrastructure

CHAPTER 2

Distributed computing infrastructure

Learning objectives

Distributed computing has evolved significantly over the past decades introducing new techniques and developments for interprocess communication and remote methods invocation, distributed naming, security mechanisms, data replication, distributed transaction mechanisms, and so on. New developments in distributed computing technologies in conjunction with the advent of XML technologies eventually led to the current dominant paradigm of Web services.

This chapter acts as a launching pad to discuss a number of key technologies that are pertinent to Web services. In particular, this chapter introduces the material that is necessary to understand more advanced concepts that use the services technical infrastructure. After completing this chapter the reader will understand the following key enabling technologies that facilitate the development of distributed applications for Web services:

- Internet protocols.
- Synchronous and asynchronous forms of communication.
- Publish/subscribe messaging and event processing mechanisms.
- Message-oriented middleware and integration brokers.
- Transaction monitors.
- Enterprise application and e-business integration technologies and architectures.

2.1 Distributed computing and Internet protocols

A distributed system is characterized as a collection of (probably heterogeneous) networked computers, which communicate and coordinate their actions by passing messages. Distribution is transparent to the user so that the system appears as a single integrated facility. This is in contrast to a network infrastructure, where the user is aware that there are several machines, is also aware of their location, storage replication, and load balancing, and functionality is not transparent.

A distributed system has numerous operational components (computational elements, such as servers and other processors, or applications) which are distributed over various interconnected computer systems. Components are autonomous as they posses full control over their parts at all times. In addition, there is no central control in the sense that a single component assumes control over all the other components in a distributed system. Distributed systems usually use some kind of client–server organization. A computer system that hosts some component of a distributed system is referred to as a *host*. Distributed components are typically heterogeneous in that they are written in different programming languages and may operate under different operating systems and diverse hardware platforms. The sharing of resources is the main motivation for constructing distributed systems. As a consequence of component autonomy, distributed systems execute applications concurrently. Consequently, there are potentially as many processes in a distributed system as there are components. Furthermore, applications are often multi-threaded. They may create a new thread whenever they start to perform a service for a user or another application. In this way the application is not blocked while it is executing a service and is available to respond to further service requests.

One important characteristic of a distributed system is that processes are not executed on a single processor but rather span a number of processors. This requires that interprocess communication mechanisms are introduced to manage interaction between processes executing on different machines. Another important characteristic of a distributed system is that it can fail in many ways [Coulouris 2001]. For example, faults in the network result in isolation of the computers that are connected to it, but this does not mean that these computers should stop running. In fact the programs running on them may not be able to detect whether the network has failed. Similarly, the failure of a computer, or an unexpected application crash, is not immediately detected by other components with which the failed computer communicates. Each component in a distributed system can fail independently, leaving others still running.

Distributed computing has evolved significantly over the past decades in self-contained and distinct stages. For example, interprocess communication and remote invocation techniques, distributed naming, security mechanisms, distributed filing systems, data replication, distributed transaction mechanisms, and so forth were introduced over the past two decades. Each stage introduced new architectural modes and new sets of protocols.

2.1.1 Internet protocols

To enable data to be transmitted across the Internet typical distributed platforms, such as J2EE, rely on the support of Internet protocols. Internet protocols are essentially methods of data transport across the Internet. They define, in general, the standards by which the different components in a distributed system communicate with each other and with remote components. Internet protocols, just like other conventional protocols, define the format and the order of messages exchanged between two or more communication entities, as well as the actions taken on the transmission and/or receipt of a message or event [Kurose 2003].

The most prominent of the Internet protocols is the Transport Control Protocol over Internet Protocol (or TCP/IP). The Internet Protocol (IP), the basic protocol of the Internet, enables the unreliable delivery of individual packets from one host to another. IP makes no guarantees as to whether the packet will be delivered, how long it will take, or if multiple packets will arrive in the order they were sent. The Transport Control Protocol (TCP) adds the notions of connection and reliability. These two protocols provide for the reliable delivery of streams of data from one host to another across communication networks, and the Internet in particular.

To be able to identify a host within an interconnected network, each host is assigned an address, called an IP address. Internet protocol addresses, or IP addresses, uniquely identify every network or host on the Internet. The IP address consists of two parts: a network identifier and a host identifier. The *network identifier* part of the IP address identifies the network within the Internet and is assigned by a central authority and is unique throughout the Internet. The authority for assigning the *host identifier* part of the IP address resides with the organization that controls the network identified by the network number. The dividing line between the network identifier and the host identifier is not constant. Instead, IP addresses are split into three classes which allow for a small number of very large networks, a medium number of medium-sized networks, and a large number of small networks.

Before we examine the TCP/IP model closer we shall first summarize the layers of the ISO Open Systems Interconnection (OSI) model. Knowing the OSI layer at which the TCP/IP model operates is one of the keys to understanding the different layers of the TCP/IP model.

2.1.1.1 The Open Systems Interconnection reference model

The Open Systems Interconnection (OSI) reference model is an abstract description of the digital communications between application processes running in distinct systems distributed over a network. A *reference model* is a conceptual blueprint of how communications should take place. It addresses all the processes required for effective communication and divides these processes into logical groupings called layers. When a communication system is designed in this manner, it is known as *layered architecture*.

The OSI model employs a hierarchical structure of seven layers, see Figure 2.1. Each layer performs value-added service at the request of the adjacent higher layer and, in turn, requests more basic services from the adjacent lower layer. The OSI layers are as follows:

> *Physical layer* (or Layer 1): This is the lowest of seven hierarchical layers in the ISO/OSI reference model and specifies the electrical, mechanical, procedural, and functional requirements for activating, maintaining, and deactivating a physical link between end systems.

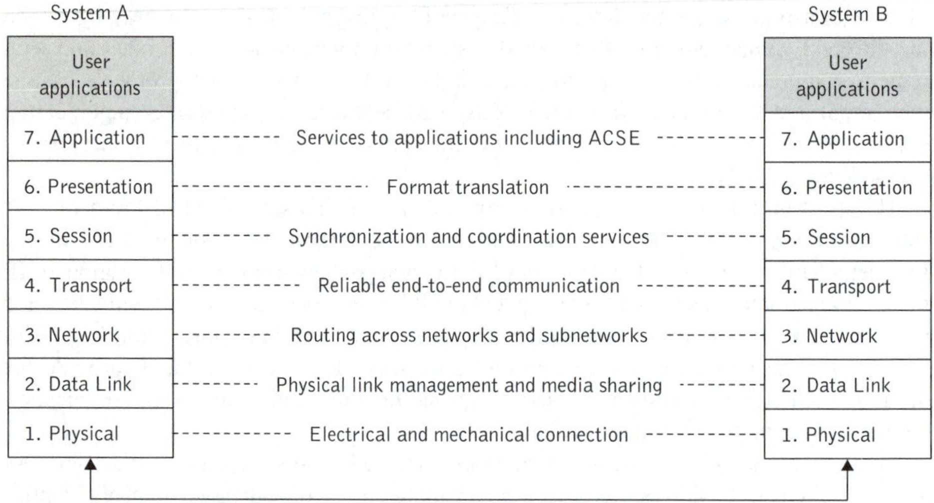

Figure 2.1 The ISO/OSI reference model

Data Link layer (or Layer 2): This layer provides the means to transfer data between network entities and to detect and possibly correct errors that may occur in the physical layer. The data link layer provides the physical transmission of the data and handles error notification, network topology, and flow control. The data link layer formats the messages into pieces, called a *data frame*, and adds a customized header containing the hardware destination and source address.

Network layer (or Layer 3): This layer responds to service requests from the transport layer (its immediate higher-level layer) and issues service requests to the data link layer. The network layer provides the functional and procedural means of transferring variable length data sequences from a source to a destination via one or more networks. This layer performs network routing, flow control, segmentation/de-segmentation, and error control functions.

Transport layer (or Layer 4): This layer responds to service requests from the session layer (its immediate higher-level layer) and issues service requests to the network layer. The purpose of the transport layer is to provide transparent transfer of data between end users, thus relieving the upper layers from any concern with providing reliable and cost-effective data transfer. Data integrity is ensured at the transport layer by maintaining flow control and by allowing users to request reliable data transport between systems.

Session layer (or Layer 5): This layer provides the mechanism for managing the dialogue between end-user application processes. The session layer is responsible for setting up, managing, and then tearing down sessions between presentation layer entities. This layer coordinates communication between systems, and serves to organize their communication by offering three different modes: simplex, half duplex, and full duplex. It also establishes check-pointing, termination, and restart procedures.

Presentation layer (or Layer 6): This layer presents data to the application layer and is responsible for data translation and code formatting. Tasks like data compression, decompression, encryption, and decryption are associated with this layer.

Application layer (or Layer 7): This is the highest layer in the ISO/OSI reference model that gives an application program access to the OSI network. This layer interfaces directly to and performs common application services required by the application programs and also issues requests to the presentation layer. The common application services provide syntactic conversion between associated application processes.

Layers 1 through 4 deal with the communication, flow control, routing, and error handling needed to transport data end to end across the network. Below the transport layer, there can be many different types of physical networks – for example, an X.25 packet-switched data network (PSDN) or a local area network (LAN). Layers 5 through 7 deal with the coordination of applications across the network and the way that information is presented to the applications. A wide range of application programs providing various types of end-user services can be supported by a common transport layer implementation.

2.1.1.2 The TCP/IP network protocol

The TCP/IP is a layered protocol [Moss 1997]. Each layer builds upon the layer below it, adding new functionality. This layered representation leads to the term *protocol stack* that refers to the stack of layers in the protocol suite through the use of which TCP/IP operates. The protocol stack is a hierarchical arrangement of all predefined protocols necessary to complete a single transfer of data between two computing systems.

The TCP/IP stack is shown in Figure 2.2 in association with the various layers of the ISO/OSI model. This figure shows that each level of the TCP/IP stack builds on the

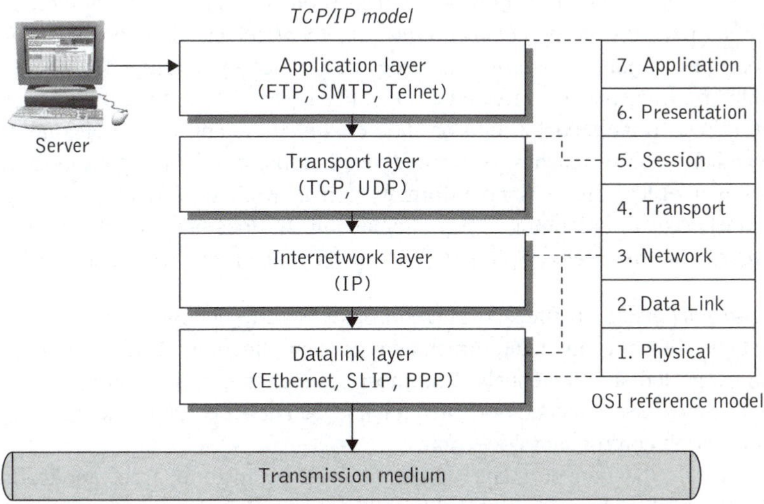

Figure 2.2 The TCP/IP stack and its relation to the ISO reference model

services provided by the layer below it. Layers communicate with those above and below via concise interfaces. Intercommunication requirements are handled at the lowest level within the stack. The lowest-level protocol is concerned purely with sending and receiving data using specific network hardware. At the top are protocols designed specifically for tasks like transferring files or delivering e-mail. In between are protocol levels concerned mainly with routing and reliability.

Note that there is no standard TCP/IP model, and some sources include an additional physical layer at the bottom of the stack. Figure 2.2, however, illustrates that TCP/IP is a four-layer protocol [Moss 1997], [Rodriguez 2001], where the physical connection standards are included as part of the data link layer. The TCP/IP stack comprises the following layers:

Data link layer: The data link layer, or simply link layer, is the lowermost layer and provides the interface to the actual network hardware. This interface may or may not provide reliable delivery, and may be packet or stream oriented. In fact, TCP/IP does not specify any protocol at this level but can use almost any network interface available, which illustrates the flexibility of the IP layer.

Internetwork layer: The internetwork layer, also called the Internet layer or the network layer, is the next layer up from the data link layer. This layer is responsible for routing *datagrams* – a term which basically means "blocks of data" – from one host to another. The internetwork layer provides the "virtual network" image of an Internet (this layer shields the higher levels from the physical network architecture below it). IP is the most important protocol in this layer; IP is the bedrock protocol of TCP/IP. Every message and every piece of data sent over any TCP/IP network is sent as an IP packet. IP provides a routing function that attempts to deliver transmitted messages to their destination.

IP uses the link layer protocol to enable data to be transmitted across and between networks. IP is a connectionless protocol that does not assume reliability from lower layers. A *connectionless protocol* means that the protocol has no concept of a job or a session and does not make any assumptions about eventual delivery. Each packet is treated as an entity in itself. IP simply routes packets, one at a time, to the next location on the delivery route and is also unconcerned with whether a packet reaches its eventual destination, or whether packets arrive in the original order. There is no information in a packet to identify it as part of a sequence or as belonging to a particular job. IP does not provide reliability, flow control, or error recovery. These functions must be provided at a higher level.

Transport layer: The transport layer provides end-to-end data transfer by delivering data between the client and server sides of an application. Multiple applications can be supported simultaneously. The most used transport layer protocol is the TCP, which provides connection-oriented reliable data delivery, duplicate data suppression, congestion control, and flow control.

TCP is the transport layer protocol used by most Internet applications, like Telnet, the File Transfer Protocol (FTP), and HTTP. It is a *connection-oriented protocol*. The connection-oriented reliable service guarantees that the data transmitted from a sender to a receiver will eventually be delivered to the receiver in order and in its entirety. This means that two hosts – one a client, the other a server – must establish a connection before any data can be transferred between them. Once a connection has been made, data can be sent. TCP is a *sliding window protocol*, so there is no need to wait for one segment to be acknowledged before another can be sent. Acknowledgements are sent only if required immediately, or after a certain interval has elapsed. This makes TCP an efficient protocol for bulk data transfers. TCP provides reliability. An application that uses TCP knows that the data it sends is received at the other end, and that it is received correctly.

Application layer: The application layer is responsible for supporting network applications. The application layer is provided by the program that uses TCP/IP for communication. An application is a user process cooperating with another process usually on a different host (there is also a benefit to application communication within a single host). Examples of applications include Telnet, FTP, and the Simple Mail Transfer Protocol (SMTP). The interface between the application and transport layers is defined by port numbers and sockets.

TCP/IP programs are usually initiated over the Internet and most of them are client–server oriented. When each connection request is received, the server program communicates with the requesting client machine. To facilitate this process, each application (FTP or Telnet, for example) is assigned a unique address, called a *port*. The application in question is bound to that particular port and when any connection request is made to this port, the corresponding application is launched. Table 2.1 shows some of the most common ports and the applications that are typically bound to them.

2.1.2 Middleware

Middleware is connectivity software that is designed to help manage the complexity and heterogeneity inherent in distributed systems by building a bridge between different systems thereby enabling communication and transfer of data. *Middleware* could be defined as a layer of enabling software services that allow application elements to interoperate across network links, despite differences in underlying communications protocols, system architectures, operating systems, databases, and other application services. The role of middleware is to ease the task of designing, programming, and managing distributed

Table 2.1 Common ports and their corresponding applications

Application	*Port*
File Transfer Protocol (FTP)	21
Telnet	23
Simple Mail Transfer Protocol (SMTP)	25
HyperText Transfer Protocol (HTTP)	80
Network News Transfer Protocol (NNTP)	119

applications by providing a simple, consistent, and integrated distributed programming environment. Essentially, middleware is a distributed software layer, or "platform," that lives above the operating system and abstracts over the complexity and heterogeneity of the underlying distributed environment with its multitude of network technologies, machine architectures, operating systems, and programming languages.

Middleware services provide a more functional set of *Application Programming Interfaces* (APIs) than the operating system and network services to allow an application to:

- locate applications transparently across the network, thereby providing interaction with another or service;
- shield software developers from low-level, tedious, and error-prone platform details, such as socket-level network programming;
- provide a consistent set of higher-level network-oriented abstractions that are much closer to application requirements in order to simplify the development of distributed systems;
- leverage previous developments and reuse them rather than rebuild them for each usage;
- provide a wide array of services such as reliability, availability, authentication, and security that are necessary for applications to operate effectively in a distributed environment;
- scale up in capacity without losing function.

Modern middleware products mask heterogeneity of networks and hardware, operating systems, and programming languages. They also permit heterogeneity at the application level by allowing the various elements of the distributed application to be written in any suitable language. Finally, programming support offered by the middleware platform can provide transparency with respect to distribution in one or more of the following dimensions: location, concurrency, replication, and failure. This means that applications can interoperate irrespective of whether they are located in diverse geographical locations, whether operations execute concurrently, and whether data is replicated in multiple locations.

Figure 2.3 shows that the middleware layers are interposed between applications and internet transport protocols. The figure shows that the middleware abstraction comprises two layers. The bottom layer is concerned with the characteristics of protocols for communicating between processes in a distributed system and how the data objects, e.g., a sales order, and data structures used in application programs can be translated into a suitable form for sending messages over a communications network, taking into account that different computers may rely on heterogeneous representations for simple data items. The layer above is concerned with interprocess communication mechanisms, while the layer above that is concerned with non-message- and message-based forms of middleware. *Non-message-based* forms of *middleware* provide synchronous communication mechanisms designed to support client–server communication. *Message-based* forms of *middleware* provide asynchronous messaging and event notification mechanisms to exchange messages or react to events over electronic networks.

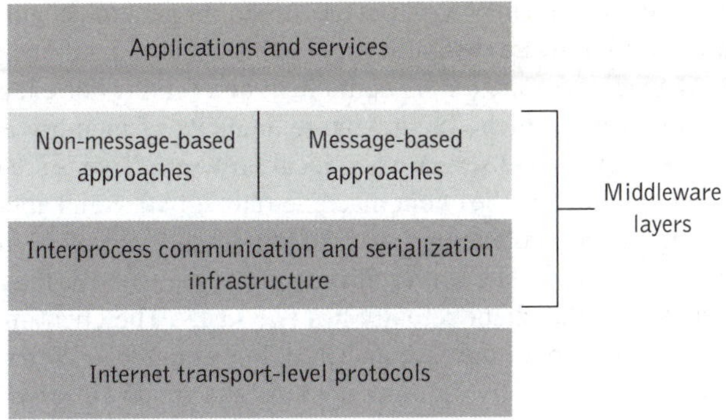

Figure 2.3 Middleware layers

Before concentrating on the middleware layers depicted in Figure 2.3, we shall describe the characteristics of client–server architectures as these are the most prevalent structure for Internet applications and central to the material that follows.

2.2 The client–server model

A widely applied form of distributed processing is client–server computing. The client–server architecture is one of the common solutions to the conundrum of how to handle the need for both centralized data control and widespread data accessibility. In short, a client–server architecture (Figure 2.4) is a computational architecture in which processing and storage tasks are divided between two classes of network members, clients and servers. Client–server involves client processes (service consumers) requesting service from server processes (service providers). Servers may in turn be clients of other servers. For instance, a Web server is often a client of a local file server (or database server) that manages the

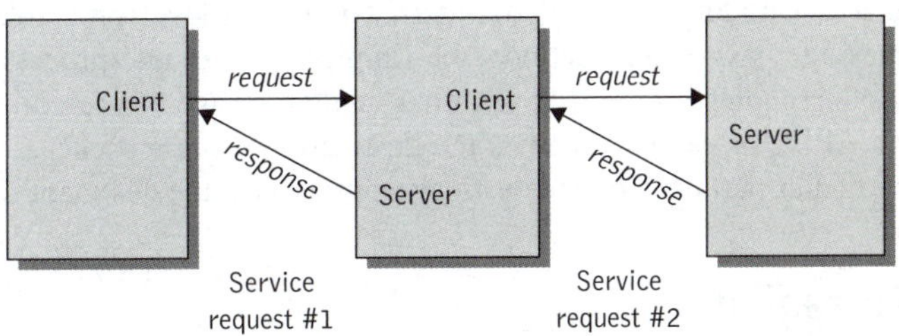

Figure 2.4 Client–server architecture
Source: From M. P. Papazoglou and P. M. A. Ribbers, *e-Business: Organizational and Technical Foundations*, J. Wiley & Sons, 2006. Reproduced with permission.

files (storage structures) in which Web pages are stored. In general, client–server computing does not emphasize hardware distinctions; it rather focuses on the applications themselves. The same device may function as both client and server. For example, there is no reason why a Web server – which contains large amounts of memory and disk space – cannot function as both client and server when local browser sessions are run there.

In a client–server architecture the client machine runs software and applications that are stored locally. Some of the applications may be stored and executed on the server, but most of them are on the client. The server also provides the data for the application. In a client–server architecture, the client actually has two tasks. The client makes requests to servers and is also responsible for the user interface. For example, a Web browser software (which is a client process) not only requests documents from Web servers, but must also display those documents for the user to make requests by typing a URL or by clicking on links. The Web server must store all of the documents and must be able to respond to requests from clients.

The client–server model is the most prevalent structure for Internet applications. The Web, e-mail, file transfer, Telnet applications, newsgroups, and many other popular Internet-based applications adopt the client–server model. Since a client program typically runs on one computer and the server program runs on another computer, client–server Internet applications are, by definition, distributed applications. The client program and the server program interact with each other by sending each other messages over the Internet.

The term *thin client* is used to differentiate the client used in Web-based applications from the client in traditional client–server architectures, which stores large parts of the application locally. This architecture has the characteristic that it does not download the code of applications into the client's computer; instead it executes them on a powerful computer server. In Web-based applications the server provides execution code as well as data to the client as needed. The browser is the client's interface. Consequently, the only software that the client needs, in this case, is operating system software, browser software, and software to convert downloaded code.

2.3 Characteristics of interprocess communication

Processes on two different end systems (with potentially different operating systems) communicate with each other by exchanging messages across a computer network. Figure 2.3 indicates that the middleware API to Internet transport-level protocols, such as UDP, provide a message-passing abstraction – the simplest form of interprocess communication. This enables the sending process to transmit a single message to a receiving process. In the case of Java APIs, the sender specifies the destination using a socket – an indirect reference to a particular port used by the destination process at the destination computer.

2.3.1 Messaging

Distributed systems and applications communicate by exchanging messages. *Messaging* is a technology that enables high-speed, asynchronous, program-to-program communication with reliable delivery. Programs communicate by sending packets of data called *messages* to each other. The concept of a message is a well-defined, data-driven text format – containing the business message and a network routing header – that can be sent between two or more applications. A message typically comprises three basic elements: a *header*, its *properties*, and a *message payload* or *body*. The message header is used by both the messaging system and the application developer to provide information about characteristics such as the destination of a message, the message type, the message expiration time, and so forth. The properties of a message contain a set of application-defined name/value pairs. These properties are essentially parts of the message body that get promoted to a special section of the message so that filtering can be applied to the message by clients or specialized routers [Chappell 2004]. The message body carries the actual "payload" of the message. The format of the message payload can vary across messaging implementations. Most common formats are plain text, a raw stream of bytes for holding any type of binary data, or a special XML message type that allows the message payload to be accessed using any number of common XML parsing technologies.

The message can be interpreted simply as data, as the description of a command to be invoked on the receiver, or as the description of an event that occurred in the sender. The business data usually contains information about a business transaction, such as a sales order, payment processing, or shipping and tracking. The simplest form of messaging is a request/reply message, whereby the sender sends a message and may pick a reply from the message recipient (if there is one) at a later time.

Message passing between a pair of processes is supported by two message communication operations: *send* and *receive*, defined in terms of destinations and messages [Coulouris 2001]. In order for one process to communicate with another, one process sends a message to a destination and another process at the destination receives the message. This activity involves the communication of data from the sending process to the receiving process and may involve the synchronization of the two processes. A receiving process receives the messages and may respond by sending messages back. Distributed applications have application layer protocols that define the format and orders of the messages exchanged between processes, as well as the actions taken on the transmission or receipt of a message.

The data stored in application programs in distributed systems is normally represented as data structures, for instance, a series of interlinked objects in Java, whereas the messages exchanged between interacting processes consist of byte sequences. Irrespective of the form of communication used, the data structures must be flattened (converted to a sequence of bytes) before transmission and rebuilt on arrival. To enable two or more heterogeneous computers to exchange data values, the principle of marshalling is used.

Marshalling is the process of taking an object or any other form of structured data items and breaking it up so that it can be transmitted as a stream of bytes over a communications network in such a way that the original object or data structure can be reconstructed easily on the receiving end. *Unmarshalling* is the process of converting the assembled stream of bytes on arrival to produce an equivalent object or form of structured data at the destination point. Therefore, marshalling comprises the transformation of structured data items and primitive values into an agreed standard form of representation for transmission across the network. Similarly, unmarshalling comprises the generation of primitive values from their external data representation and the reconstruction of the same (equivalent) data structures at the receiving end. Java and XML use the terms *serialization* and *deserialization* to denote the process of marshalling and unsmarshalling, respectively. In this book we shall use the terms serialization and marshalling interchangeably.

2.3.2 Message destinations and sockets

In section 2.1.1 we explained that in the case of Internet protocols, messages are sent to ports. For interprocess communication processes may use multiple ports from which to receive messages. Servers usually publicize their port numbers for use by clients and processes use multiple ports from which to receive messages. Any process that knows the identifier of a port can send a message to it.

During interprocess communication messages are sent to (Internet address, local port) pairs. A local port is a message destination within a computer, specified as an identifier. There is a serious drawback with this approach in a case where the client uses a fixed address to a service: then that service must always run on the same computer for its address to remain valid. This can be avoided either if client applications refer to services by name and use a name server to translate names into server locations at run-time, or by having the operating system provide location-independent identifiers for messages allowing service relocation [Coulouris 2001].

Many applications involve two processes in different hosts communicating with each other over a network. These two processes communicate with each other by exchanging (sending and receiving) messages. A process sends messages into, and receives messages from, the network through its *socket*. A process's socket could be thought of as the entry point to the process. Interprocess communication consists of transmitting a message between a client and a socket in another process, as illustrated in Figure 2.5. Once the message arrives at its destination, it passes through the receiving process's socket and the receiving process then acts on the message. Figure 2.5 illustrates that for a particular

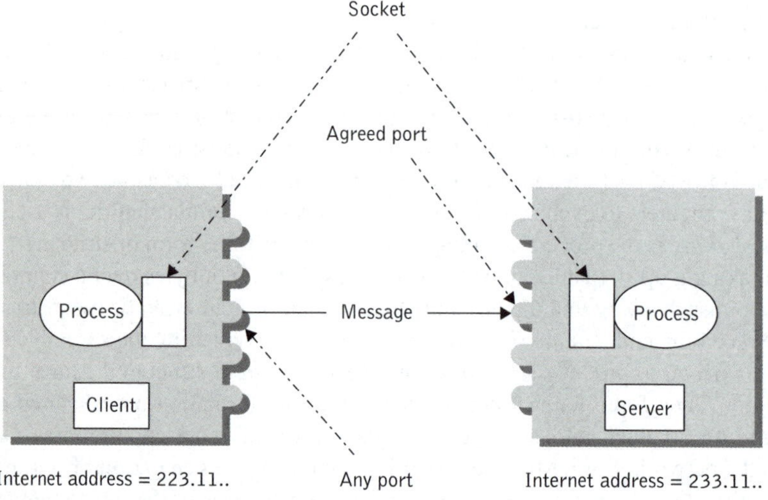

Figure 2.5 Ports and sockets

process to receive messages, its socket must be bound to a local port and must refer to the Internet address of the computer on which it is hosted.

2.3.3 Synchronous and asynchronous forms of message communication

Whilst there are different types of messaging middleware, they all can support one, or sometimes two, basic modes of message communication. These modes are: *synchronous* or time dependent and *asynchronous* or time independent.

The defining characteristic of a synchronous form of execution is that message communication is synchronized between two communicating application systems, which must both be up and running, and that execution flow at the client's side is interrupted to execute the call. Both the sending and the receiving application must be ready to communicate with each other at all times. A sending application initiates a request (sends a message) to a receiving application. The sending application then blocks its processing until it receives a response from the receiving application. The receiving application continues its processing after it receives the response. Figure 2.6 shows this form of synchronous request/response mode of communication. Synchronous communication is exemplified by remote procedure calls (discussed in section 2.4).

When using asynchronous messaging, the caller employs a *send and forget* approach that allows it to continue to execute after it sends the message. With asynchronous communication, an application sends (requestor or sender) a request to another while it continues its own processing activities. The sending application does not have to wait for the receiving application to complete and for its reply to come back. Instead it can continue processing other requests. Unlike the synchronous mode, both application systems (sender and receiver) do not have to be active at the same time for processing to occur.

Asynchronous messaging is usually implemented by some queuing mechanism. Two types of message queues exist: these are *store and forward* and *publish/subscribe* and are described in section 2.5.

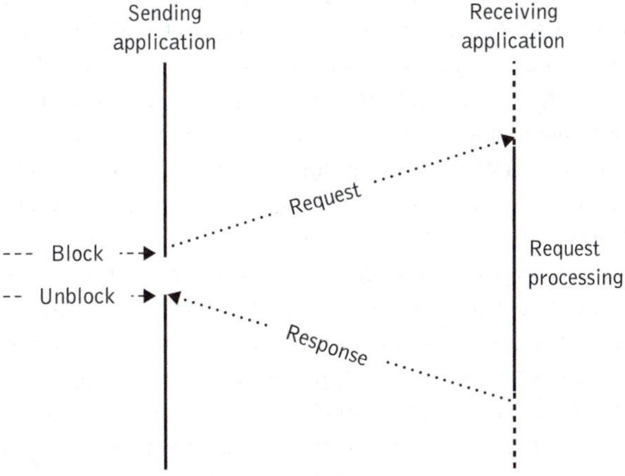

Figure 2.6 Synchronous messaging

In choosing a type of communication infrastructure, it is important to consider the tradeoffs between loosely and tightly coupled interfaces, and asynchronous versus synchronous modes of interaction. We shall examine these modes of communication in some detail in the following two sections.

2.4 Synchronous forms of middleware

Programming models for synchronous forms of middleware are composed of cooperating programs running in several interacting distributed processes. Such programs need to be able to invoke operations synchronously in other processes, which frequently run in different computing systems.

The most familiar approaches to non-message-based forms of middleware are typified by the remote procedure call (RPC) and the remote method invocation (RMI). We shall concern ourselves with examining these two approaches in this section.

2.4.1 Remote procedure calls

RPC is a basic mechanism for interprogram communication. In effect, RPC is the middleware mechanism used to invoke a procedure that is located on a remote system, and the results are returned. With this type of middleware the application elements communicate with each other synchronously, meaning that they use a request/wait-for-reply model of communication. By design, the RPC programming style mimics the serial thread of execution that a "normal" non-distributed application would use, where each statement is executed in sequence. The RPC mechanism is the simplest way to implement client–server applications because it keeps the details of network communications out of the application code.

Figure 2.7 shows the relationship between application code and the RPC mechanism during an RPC. In RPC-style programming, an object and its methods are "remoted" such that the invocation of the method can happen across a network separation. In client application code, an RPC looks like a local procedure call, because it is actually a call to a local proxy known as a *client stub* (a surrogate code that supports RPCs). The client stub mimics the interface of the remote object and its methods. It essentially behaves like a local procedure to the client, but instead of executing the call, it marshals the procedure identifier and the arguments into a request message, which it sends via its communication module to the server. The client stub communicates with a *server stub* using the RPC runtime library, which is set of procedures that support all RPC applications. A server stub is like a *skeleton* method in that it unmarshals the arguments in the request message, calls the corresponding service procedure, and marshals the return results for the reply message. The server stub communicates its output to the client stub, again by using the RPC runtime library. Finally, the client stub returns to the client application code.

RPCs work well for smaller, simple applications where communication is primarily point to point (rather than one system to many). RPCs do not scale well to large, mission-critical applications, as they leave many crucial details to the programmer, including handling network and system failures, handling multiple connections, and synchronization between processes. This can be understood by the fact that when performing a

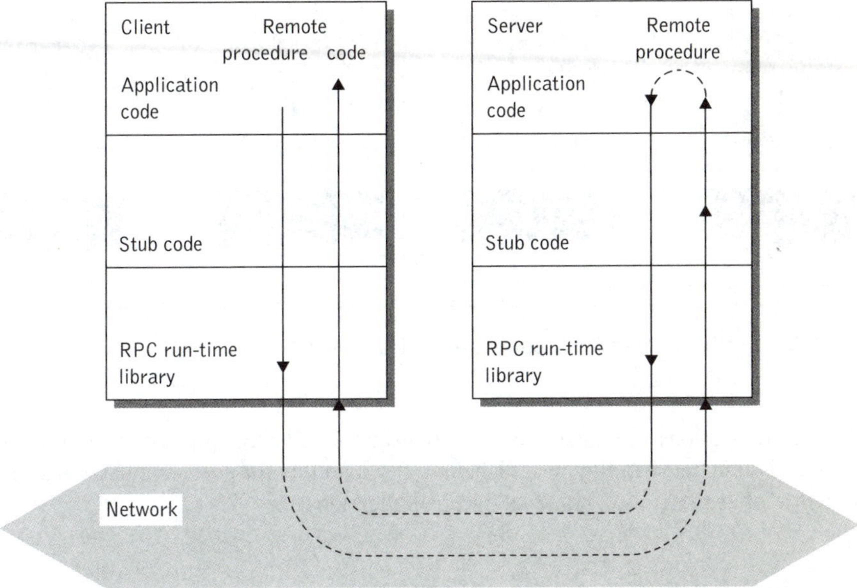

Figure 2.7 RPC communication
Source: From M. P. Papazoglou and P. M. A. Ribbers, *e-Business: Organizational and Technical Foundations*, J. Wiley & Sons, 2006. Reproduced with permission.

synchronous operation across multiple processes, the success of one RPC call depends on the success of all downstream RPC-style calls that are part of the same synchronous request/response cycle. This makes the invocation a whole-or-nothing proposition [Chappell 2004]. If one operation is unable to complete for any reason, all other dependent operations will fail with it. This is shown in Figure 2.8.

Figure 2.8 illustrates that RPC-style programming leads to *tight coupling* of interfaces and applications. In an RPC environment each application needs to know the intimate details of the interface of every other application – the number of methods it exposes and the details of each method signature it exposes. This figure clearly shows that the synchronized nature of RPC tightly couples the client to the server. The client cannot proceed – it is blocked – until the server responds and the client fails if the server fails or is unable to complete.

RPC-style programming has had reasonable adoption in the industry for a number of years. Technologies that predominantly use RPC-style communication include the Common Object Request Broker Architecture (CORBA), the Java Remote Method Invocation (RMI), DCOM, Active X, Sun-RPC, Java API for XML-RPC (JAX-RPC), and the Simple Object Access Protocol (SOAP) v1.0 and v1.1. Component-based architectures such as Enterprise Java Beans are also built on top of this model. However, due to their synchronous nature, RPCs are not a good choice to use as the building blocks for enterprise-wide applications where high performance and high reliability are needed. The synchronous tightly coupled nature of RPCs is a severe hindrance in system-to-system processing where applications need to be integrated together. Under synchronous

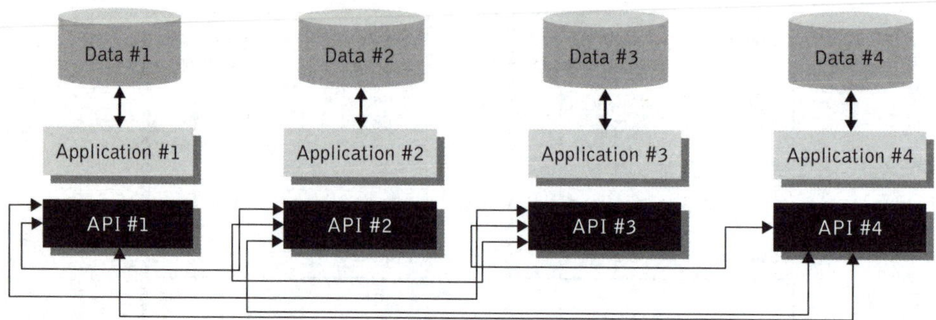

Figure 2.8 Tightly coupled RPC point-to-point integrations

solutions, applications are integrated by connecting APIs together on a point-to-point basis. This is illustrated in Figure 2.11 below. If we do this for every application scenario it implies a lot of integration points between applications.

2.4.2 Remote method invocation

Traditional RPC systems are language neutral, and therefore cannot provide functionality that is not available on all possible target platforms. The Java RMI provides a simple and direct model for distributed computation with Java objects on the basis of the RPC mechanism.

The Java RMI establishes interobject communication. If the particular method happens to be on a remote machine, Java provides the capability to make the RMI appear to the programmer to be the same as if the method is on the local machine. Thus, Java makes RMI transparent to the user. RMI applications comprise two separate programs: a server and a client. RMI provides the mechanism by which the server and the client communicate and pass information back and forth.

There are two different kinds of classes that can be used in RMI: *remote* and *serializable* classes. A remote object is an instance of a remote class. When a remote object is used in the same address space, it can be treated just like an ordinary object. But if it is used externally to the address space, the object must be referenced by an object handle. Correspondingly, a serializable object is an instance of a serializable class. A serializable object can be copied from one address space to another. This means that a serializable object can be a parameter or a return value. Note that if a remote object is returned, it is the object handle being returned.

2.5 Asynchronous forms of middleware

As we already explained in section 2.3.3, in an environment where multiple applications and Web services need to interact with each other, it is not practical to expect that each application knows the signature characteristics of every other application's methods.

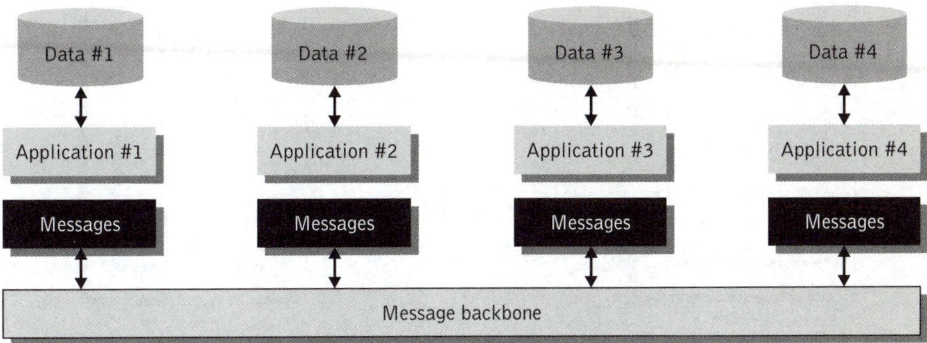

Figure 2.9 Loose coupling of asynchronous interfaces

Instead, the intricacies of the service interface should not necessarily be known to all interacting applications. Asynchronous communication promotes a loosely coupled environment in which an application does not need to know the intimate details of how to reach and interface with other applications. Each participant in a multi-step business process flow need only be concerned with ensuring that it can send a message to the messaging system. This is illustrated in Figure 2.9.

Asynchronous communication is exemplified by the two approaches to messaging store and forward and publish/subscribe. As the publish/subscribe approach employs the concept of event notification, which is very appealing to the world of Web services, we shall introduce this topic in this section. Finally, we shall also examine another interesting approach to messaging: point-to-point queuing.

2.5.1 Store and forward messaging

With the store and forward queuing mechanism, messages are placed on a virtual channel called a *message queue* by a sending application and are retrieved by the receiving application as needed. Messages are exchanged through a queue, which is the destination to which senders send messages and a source from which receivers receive messages. The queue is a container that can keep hold of a message until the recipient collects it. The message queue is independent of both the sender and receiver applications and acts as a buffer between the communicating applications. In this form of communication, two applications can be senders and receivers relative to the message queue, see Figure 2.10.

This figure shows an example of a common messaging scenario from the application's point of view. Messages are placed on a message queue by an application and reviewed by another application (application system #2 in Figure 2.10). The implication in this diagram is that the physical location of the queue is not known to either application. Similarly, the physical details of the host platform are not known either. All that is required is that an application is in some way registered or connected to the message queue subsystem. This provides a useful form of abstraction that enables physical implementations to be changed on either platform, without affecting the rest of the implementation. Asynchronous

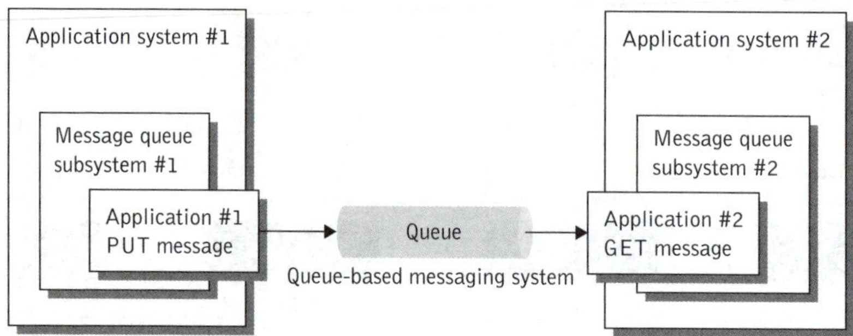

Figure 2.10 Store and forward messaging

communication with the store and forward queuing mechanism allows work to be performed whenever applications are ready.

The message delivery semantics include several delivery options which range from *exactly-once delivery* to *at-least-once delivery* and to *at-most-once delivery*. It is critical for many applications to ensure guaranteed delivery of a message to its final destination and elimination of duplicates. This level of message service delivery is referred to as exactly-once message delivery. The at-least-once message delivery mode guarantees that messages will be delivered to their final destination at least once. The at-most-once delivery mode guarantees that messages will be delivered to their final destination at most once. This latter mode of delivery is a less stringent QoS setting on a message as it implies that the messaging system is permitted to occasionally lose a message in the event of hardware, software, or network breakdown. The exactly-once guarantee of message delivery is a characteristic of message reliability, which we shall examine as part of the Web services standards in section 8.4.2, and is accomplished in part by the store and forward queuing mechanism.

The store and forward queuing mechanism is typical of a many-to-one messaging paradigm where multiple applications can send messages to a single application. The same application can be sender, receiver, or both sender and receiver. Message queuing provides a highly reliable, although not always timely, means of ensuring that application operations are completed.

In many applications there is an additional requirement that the concept of store and forward is capable of being repeated across multiple message servers that are chained together. This leads to the configuration illustrated in Figure 2.11. In this configuration, each message server uses the principle of store and forward and message acknowledgements to get the message to the next server in the chain of interconnected message servers. A *message acknowledgement* is a mechanism that allows the messaging system to monitor the progress of a message so that it knows when the message was successfully produced and consumed. With this kind of knowledge, message-oriented middleware systems can manage the distribution of messages to their destinations and guarantee their delivery.

In Figure 2.11 each server-to-server handoff procedure maintains the reliability and quality of service requirements that were specified by the sender of the message. This is accomplished in a manner that is transparent to both the server and receiver.

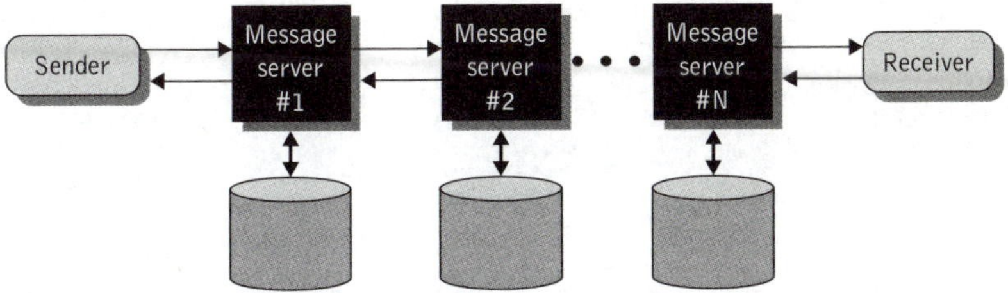

Figure 2.11 Store and forward involving multiple chained message servers

2.5.2 Publish/subscribe messaging

Another form of reliable messaging is publish/subscribe messaging. This mode of messaging is a slightly more scalable form of messaging when compared to the store and forward mechanism. With this type of asynchronous communication the application that produces information publishes it and all other applications that need this type of information subscribe to it. Messages containing the new information are placed in a queue for each subscriber by the publishing application. Each application in this scheme may have a dual role: it may act as a publisher or subscriber of different types of information.

The publish/subscribe messaging works as follows. Suppose that a publisher application publishes messages on a specific topic, such as sending out new product prices or new product descriptions to retailers. Multiple subscribing applications can subscribe to this topic and receive the messages published by the publishing application. Figure 2.12 shows message publishers publishing messages by sending them to topics and all the message subscribers who had registered to the topic for messages receiving them as soon as the publisher makes them available. This figure describes how the publish/subscribe semantics work:

1. Publishers publish messages to specific topics.
2. A message server keeps track of all the messages, and all its currently active and durable subscribers (subscribers who specifically expressed a durable interest in the topic). The message server provides a secure environment for the messaging system by handling authorization and authentication.
3. As soon as messages are published on a specific topic, they are distributed to all of its subscribers. Durable subscribers, who were not connected at the time of message delivery, can retrieve the messages if they come up within a specified time.

The message server takes the responsibility of delivering the published messages to the subscribing applications based on the subscribed topic. Every message has an expiration time that specifies the maximum amount of time that it can live from the time of its publication in a topic. The message server first delivers messages to its associated active subscribers, and then checks to make sure if there are any non-active durable subscribers

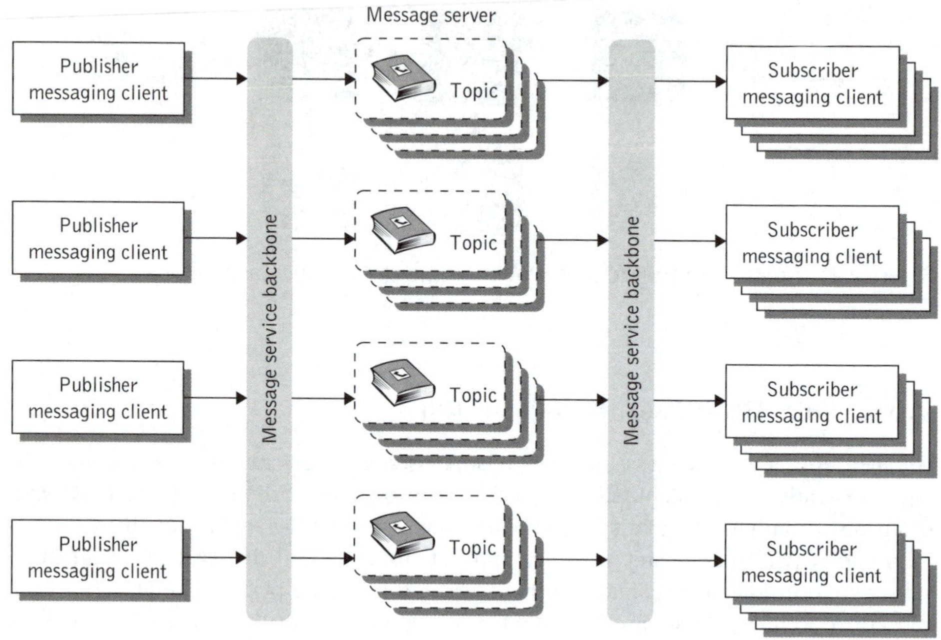

Figure 2.12 Publish/subscribe messaging

subscribed to the published topic. If, after the initial delivery, any of the durable subscribers did not acknowledge receipt of the message, the message is retained in the message server for the period of the expiration time, in the hope that the durable subscribers, if any, will connect to the message server and accept delivery of the message.

All subscribers have a message event listener that takes delivery of the message from the topic and delivers it to the messaging client application for further processing. Subscribers can also filter the messages that they receive by qualifying their subscriptions with a message selector. Message selectors evaluate a message's headers and properties (not their bodies) with the provided filter expression strings.

The subscription list can be easily modified, on-the-fly, providing a highly flexible communications system that can run on different systems and networks. The publish/subscribe messaging mode usually includes the ability to transform messages, acting as an interpreter, which enables applications that were not designed to work together to do so.

In summary, asynchronous communication enables a loosely coupled environment in which an application does not need to know the intimate details of how to reach and interface with other applications. In general, asynchronous communication is often the preferred solution for EAI and cross-enterprise computing, especially when applications want to transfer data between internal enterprise information systems, e.g., databases and ERP packages, or between their systems and those of their partners. In these cases the reply from clients may not be important, or, if it is, its contents are not. For example, when sending a group of new product prices out to the enterprise information systems of retail partners, the publisher of those messages is not expecting an answer. It simply wants to make sure that the partners have received the information.

2.5.3 Event-driven processing mechanisms

The familiar one-to-one request/reply interaction pattern that is commonly used in client–server systems is inadequate for systems that must react to events representing changes in the environment, information of interest, or process status, which are particularly well suited for distributed environments without central control. Applications such as process support systems and workflow management systems are best constructed using event middleware, realizing the control flow and intertask dependencies by event-driven task managers.

Traditional addressing and routing mechanisms in networks, both unicast and multicast, are based on the use of explicit and specialized addressing and routing information attached to, or otherwise associated with, messages. The actual data, e.g., attributes of business events, contained within messages, referred to as *content* (or sometimes message body or payload), are typically invisible to the transport mechanism and, therefore, are not considered when performing addressing or routing operations. In traditional network addressing and routing mechanisms, the flow of information between a message producer and a message consumer can be seen as the result of producers directing messages to selected consumers, given their use of explicit destination specifications and explicit identity attributes. A rather different approach is to expose the content to the network transport mechanism so that it can influence the addressing and routing of messages. In the extreme, no information other than the content is used; a network that takes this approach is said to use a *content-based* addressing and routing scheme [Carzaniga 2000]. Unlike the flow of information in traditional network addressing and routing mechanisms, the content-based addressing and routing mechanism implicitly emerges from the circumstantial interplay between expressions of interest and any messages that are generated. The content-based scheme is usually based on the processing of incoming events. Under this approach, message producers will generate messages, but with no particular destinations intended. The destinations are determined by clients expressing interest in the delivery of messages satisfying some arbitrary predicates on the content, independent of the producers of the messages.

The asynchrony, heterogeneity, and inherent loose coupling that characterize modern applications in a wide area network promote event interaction as a natural design abstraction for a growing class of software systems. Such systems are based on a technical infrastructure known as an *event notification service* [Rosenblum 1997].

An event notification service complements other general-purpose middleware services, such as point-to-point and multicast communication mechanisms, by offering a many-to-many communication and integration facility. Clients in an event notification scheme are of two kinds: *objects of interest*, which are the producers of notifications, and *interested parties*, which are the consumers of notifications. It is noteworthy that a client can act as both an object of interest and an interested party. An event notification service typically realizes the publish/subscribe asynchronous messaging scheme that we described earlier in this section. In a publish/subscribe system, clients publish event (or notification) messages with highly structured content, and other clients make available a filter (a kind of pattern) specifying the subscription: the content of events to be received at that client. Event message distribution is handled by an underlying content-based routing network, which is a set of server nodes interconnected as a peer-to-peer network. The content-based router is responsible for sending copies of event messages to all clients whose filters match that message.

Clients use the access points of their local servers to advertise the information about notifications that they generate and to publish the advertised notifications. Clients also use the access points to subscribe for individual notifications or compound patterns of notifications of interest. In its most generic form, a notification can be viewed as a set of attributes, where each attribute can have a name, a type, and a value. Some clients publish notifications about events that have occurred, and other (but possibly the same) clients subscribe for notifications of interest. A notification is addressed to all subscribers whose subscriptions match the content of the notification. The selection service is responsible for selecting the notifications whose contents are of interest to clients and delivering those notifications to the clients via the access points. Because there may be multiple such subscribers, the event notification service is thus a multicast service. However, the use of content-based addressing and routing makes the event notification service fundamentally different from traditional multicast services.

The event notification service performs a *selection* process to determine which of the published notifications are of interest to which of its clients, routing and delivering notifications only to those clients that are interested. In addition to serving clients' interests, the selection process also can be used by the event notification service to optimize communication within the network. The information that drives the selection process originates with clients. More specifically, the event notification service may be directed to apply a *filter* to the contents of event notifications on behalf of a client such that it will deliver only notifications that contain certain specified data values. The selection process may also be asked to look for *patterns* of multiple events, such that it will deliver only sets of notifications associated with that pattern of event occurrences (where each individual event occurrence is matched by a filter) [Carzaniga 2001].

A filter selects event notifications by specifying a set of attributes and constraints on the values of those attributes. For example, an inventory service might be interested in receiving notifications about significant stock drops for a particular product, and so issues a subscription that includes a filter specifying the product name and a stock differential. While a filter is matched against a single notification based on the notification's attribute data, a pattern is matched against two or more notifications based on both their attribute data and the combination they form. At its most generic, a pattern might correlate events according to any compound relation. For example, a customer might be interested in receiving price change notifications for a certain product if a change in the price of this product is introduced simultaneously by specific suppliers of the product.

In order to achieve scalability in a wide area network, the event notification service by necessity must be implemented as a distributed network of servers. It is the responsibility of the event notification service to route each notification through the network of servers to all subscribers that registered matching subscriptions, and to keep track of the identity of the subscriber that registered each subscription. From this informal description of event notification, we can identify a number of important properties.

The event notification scheme is particularly appealing for developing service-based applications, see section 7.4. The fact that notifications are delivered based on their content rather than on an explicit destination address adds a level of indirection that provides a great deal of flexibility and expressive power to clients of the service. However, this may complicate the final implementation of the service. Furthermore, the behavior of subscribers is dynamic, since they add and remove subscriptions. Yet this dynamism is transparent to publishers of notifications, since they simply generate content irrespective of its eventual recipients.

2.5.4 Point-to-point queuing

Many large systems are divided into several separate units. The point-to-point messaging model allows clients to send and receive messages both synchronously and asynchronously via queues. The point-to-point messaging model provides reliable communication for multi-staged applications. This model has traditionally been a *pull-based* or *polling-based model*, where messages are requested from a queue instead of being pushed to the client automatically as is the case with publish/subscribe model. The publish/subscribe approach is based on a *push-based model*, which means that messages are delivered to consumers without having to request them.

In the point-to-point messaging model the producer is called a *sender* and the consumer is called a *receiver* [Monson-Haefel 2001]. Messages are exchanged through a queue. A given queue may be used by multiple receivers, but only a single receiver may consume each message delivered to the queue. Each message is consumed only once by the next available receiver in a group. For instance, in an order management application under the point-to-point messaging model, the Web front-end sends a message including new order information and a single warehouse receives the message and processes the order. The messaging system guarantees that multiple warehouses do not fulfill the same order. This is illustrated in Figure 2.13.

As in the publish/subscribe messaging model, point-to-point messaging is based on the concept of sending a message to a named destination. One important difference between the publish/subscribe messaging and the point-to-point messaging is that point-to-point messages are always delivered, regardless of the current connection status of a receiver. Once a message is delivered to a queue it stays there even if there is no consumer currently connected to it [Monson-Haefel 2001]. The point-to-point messaging model also offers reliability guarantees regarding dispatched messages. This feature is in contrast to the

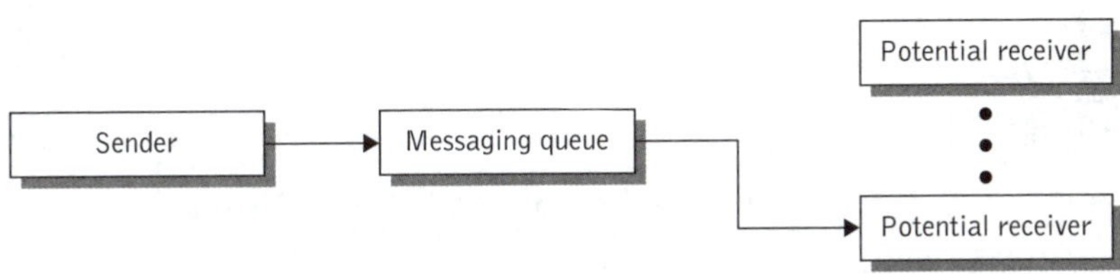

Figure 2.13 Point-to-point queuing

publish/subscribe model where a message may be directed to multiple receivers. In the point-to-point messaging model, how a message delivered to a queue is distributed to the queue's receivers depends on the policies of the sender.

2.6 Request/reply messaging

Most of the asynchronous messaging mechanisms that we have examined so far follow the *"fire-and-forget" messaging* principle. This means that the sending application can conduct its work as usual once a message was asynchronously sent. As already explained, the sending application assumes that the message will arrive safely at its destination at some point in time. This mode of asynchronous messaging does not necessarily preclude the necessity to perform request/reply operations.

On many occasions applications require that request/reply messaging operations be performed. Here, we can distinguish between two types of request/reply messaging operations: synchronous request/reply messaging and asynchronous request/reply messaging operations. Synchronous request/reply messaging is often necessary when trying to integrate with a Web service client that blocks and waits for a synchronous response to return to it [Chappell 2004]. In the asynchronous version of request/reply messaging, the requestor (sender) expects the reply to arrive at a later time and continue its work unaffected.

Figure 2.14 illustrates a simple request/reply asynchronous messaging configuration. Observe that in this figure message delivery channels are not bidirectional. To perform a request/reply operation the sender must use two channels: one for the request and one for the reply. The request message needs to contain reference to the receiver's endpoint, along with a correlation identifier that is needed to correlate the request with the response message. The requestor needs to poll a reply channel for the reply message.

Both request/reply messaging modes can be layered on top of message-oriented middleware. Some message-oriented middleware systems can further automate this process by managing the contents of the request/reply message.

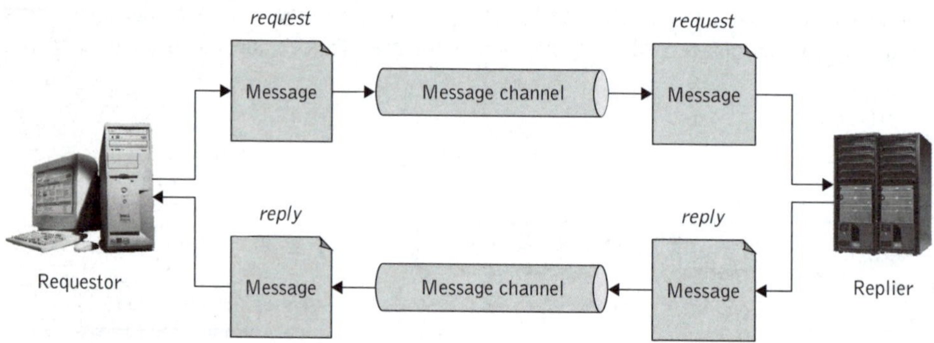

Figure 2.14 Asynchronous request/reply messaging

Request/reply messaging is a useful mechanism for Web services and we shall be referring to it later in this book (section 8.4.2) in the context of reliable messaging and associated Web services standards.

2.7 Message-oriented middleware

Message-oriented middleware (MOM) is an infrastructure that involves the passing of data between applications using a common communication channel that carries self-contained messages. In an MOM-based communication environment, messages are usually sent and received asynchronously. Using message-based communications, applications are abstractly decoupled as senders and receivers are not aware of each other. Instead they send and receive messages from the messaging system and it is the responsibility of the messaging system, namely the MOM, to forward the messages to their intended destination.

MOM is interposed between the client and the server part of client–server architecture and handles asynchronous calls between clients and servers, see Figure 2.15. To support this asynchronous model, MOM products typically use message queues to store calls temporarily and allow clients and servers to run at different times. Messages in the queue can consist of formatted data, requests for action, or both.

The messaging system is responsible for managing the connection points between messaging clients, and for managing multiple channels of communication between the connection points. The messaging system is usually implemented by a software module known as the *message* (or *integration*) *broker*, see Figure 2.15 and section 2.7.1. Integration brokers are usually capable of being grouped together to form clusters that provide advanced capabilities such as load balancing, fault tolerance, and various routing mechanisms using managed security domains [Chappell 2004].

When an event occurs, the client application hands off to the messaging middleware application the responsibility of notifying a server that some action needs to be taken. Messages containing requests for action can trigger other messages to be fired. Normally

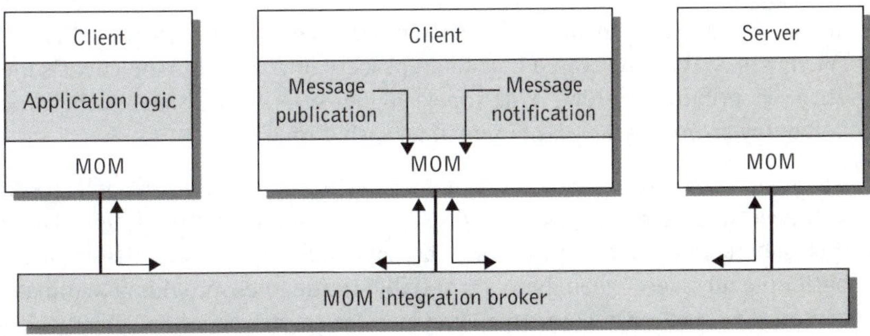

Figure 2.15 Message-oriented middleware (MOM)
Source: From M. P. Papazoglou and P. M. A. Ribbers, *e-Business: Organizational and Technical Foundations*, J. Wiley & Sons, 2006. Reproduced with permission.

when an event occurs, a notification is required. The natural form of communication here is to publish events to which various listeners (clients) subscribe.

MOM products, in general, cover more than just passing information; they usually include services for translating data, security, broadcasting data to multiple programs, error recovery, locating resources on the network, cost routing, prioritization of messages and requests, and extensive debugging facilities. MOM messaging systems also help divide long-running tasks into multiple transactions for greater efficiency. As opposed to RPC and ORB (Object Request Broker) products, MOM does not assume that a reliable transport layer exists. MOM tries to handle all problems that may surface when the transport layer is unreliable.

Modern MOM technologies typically possess features that can be used as a springboard for developing Web services technologies, including:

- Message multicast supporting event-driven processing, i.e., the publish/subscribe model.
- Reliability and serialization of messages thus guaranteeing message delivery in the appropriate order.
- Subject-based (textual) names and attributes to abstract from the physical names and addresses that are interpreted and implemented by the network.
- Support for multiple communications protocols such as store and forward, request/reply, and publish/subscribe.
- Support for transactional boundaries.

In summary, there are several features that make the MOM particularly appealing when integrating applications. These include – but are not limited to – the following:

- *Transparent cooperation of heterogeneous systems:* The integration broker provides transformation software to transform application data running under diverse programming environments, operating systems, and hardware platforms.
- *Prioritization of requests:* In many cases some services need higher priority than others. All messages in an MOM environment may have priority attached to them. When a message is delivered to a client process, it is added to the client's message queue in prioritized order. This forces higher-priority messages to be processed before lower-priority messages sent at an earlier time.
- *Automatic message buffering and flow control:* A distributed application often will need to read messages from diverse applications and programs. To support this undertaking each application can have message queues that transparently buffer the messages when there are variable traffic rates, providing automatic flow control. This method of communication increases performance and greatly simplifies development.
- *Persistent messaging:* This brings reliability and ensures that messages are guaranteed to be delivered at most once to their subscribers.

- *Flexibility and reliability:* Flexibility with MOM is achieved because an application does not need an immediate answer; it can send its messages whenever it decides, independently of the recipient's availability. Senders and recipients are independent and thus unattached. Reliability is achieved because a persistent message is never lost.
- *Load balancing:* The asynchronous nature of MOM provides flexibility for load balancing. Load balancing is achieved as messages can be forwarded from a relatively busy application system to a less busy one. For example, if an application system is busy then messages could be forwarded to a parallel process in an alternate location – if one exists. Dynamic load balancing can be designed into an MOM environment using selected algorithms including "least busy" and "round robin." This results in a cost-effective use of network facilities. In addition, the load balancing facility generates highly available message queues and enables an effective peak-hours network management. With this configuration, a low-bandwidth system may still attain acceptable performance, whereas it would have collapsed in a synchronous messaging environment.
- *Scalability and optimal use of resources:* When process volumes increase MOM brokers employ *dynamic routing* and *multiplexing* techniques. Dynamic routing allows clients and servers that are not preprogrammed to communicate as the MOM automatically connects the requestor to the necessary service, without developer intervention. In addition, in case of a server breakdown, the MOM platform can dispatch a message to another backup server. Multiplexing is a function offered by MOM brokers that enables several applications to share a message queue. Processing volumes of several hundreds of messages per second on a local network are quite typical.

MOM has demonstrated an ability to deliver the benefits of asynchronous messaging for applications and process-to-process interoperability, distributed transaction processing (such as banking, brokerage, airline reservations), distributed enterprise workflow (such as process manufacturing, insurance claims processing), real-time automation (such as utility and process control), and systems management (such as distributed backup, software distribution), among others.

One of the disadvantages of message queues used in MOM is that they can suffer from overloading because of temporary storage leading to an overworked network. It is very possible for a client application to keep transferring data messages to a server that is not able to consume them in a timely way. A nice feature of many MOM implementations, however, is that they can switch between synchronous and asynchronous communication mode. Although MOM is in principle an asynchronous peer-to-peer protocol, some implementations can handle synchronous message passing too.

2.7.1 Integration brokers

Before leaving the subject of MOM, it would be useful to complement it with a short description of integration brokers.

Integration brokers perform necessary content and format transformation to translate incoming messages into a scheme that the destination system(s) can understand and utilize. Integration brokers are usually built on top of some MOM implementations and so the general principles of MOM also apply to them. Initially integration brokers were called message brokers but this name often led to a mischaracterization and confusion between message brokers and message-oriented middleware. More recently, message brokers have been renamed integration brokers, which is a more descriptive name for the features they provide.

An *integration broker* is an application-to-application middleware service that is capable of one-to-many, many-to-one, and many-to-many message distribution. An integration broker is a software hub that records and manages the contracts between publishers and subscribers of messages. When a business event takes place, the application will publish the message(s) corresponding to that event. The broker reviews its lists of subscriptions and activates delivery to each subscriber for this type of message so that subscribers receive only the data to which they subscribe. An integration broker is a high-performance communication module and supports large volumes of messages. Several hundreds of messages per second are quite typical of integration brokers.

An integration broker is usually built on a queue manager and routes messages to applications. The integration broker allows multiple applications to implement a published service with the broker providing application integration. In addition to these functions, integration brokers account for any differences at the structural level of applications. Integration brokers take care of structural mismatches by keeping track of message schemas and by changing accordingly the content of messages to the semantics of a specific application. These unique capabilities of integration brokers enable them to broker not only between applications but also between types of middleware.

Integration brokers consist of components that provide the following functions: message transformation, business rules processing, routing services, naming services, adapter services, repository services, and events and alerts. We examine these components in turn.

The integration broker transforms application-specific messages into commonly understood messages, e.g., between different XML schemas using eXtensible Stylesheet Language Transformations, see section 3.5.2. To achieve transformation the integration broker uses transformation rules defined by an application developer by means of a graphical mapping tool. The message transformation functionality "understands" the format of all messages transmitted among applications. This is possible since the integration broker holds a repository of schemas of interchanged messages. Using this knowledge, the broker can translate between schemas by restructuring the data of these messages. In this way, receiving applications can make sense of received messages.

A *business rule* is a precise statement that describes, constrains, and controls the structure, operations, and strategies of an enterprise [BRCommunity 2005]. Business rules can express pricing and billing policies, quality of service, process flow – where they describe routing decisions, actor assignment policies, etc. – regulations, and so on. The business rules processing functionality is usually implemented as a rules processing engine within the broker. Often, there is a need for a message created in one system to be used in more than one other application, and the broker can follow business rules to decide where the message should be sent. The integration broker allows the application of business rules to messages, so that new application logic can reside within the integration broker.

The routing functionality takes care of the flow control of messages. It identifies the origin of the message and routes it to the appropriate target application. It also uses the message transformation functionality since messages usually have to be translated for a receiving application to understand its content. The business rules engine may also be involved to determine under which conditions the message can be sent to the recipient.

The directory services functionality is needed since integration brokers function in a distributed environment and need a way to locate and use network resources. Applications using the integration broker are able to find other applications or hardware on the network.

The integration broker deploys communications middleware and associated protocols of various types as applicable to the particular application target. Many integration brokers use *adapters* as layers between the broker and large enterprise's back-end information systems to convert the data formats and application semantics from the source application to the target application. Adapters provide the integration broker with both data and process access to disparate applications within an enterprise.

Adapters map the differences between two distinct interfaces: the integration broker interface and the native interface of the source or target application. Adapters hide the complexities of that interface from the end user or even the developer using the integration broker. For instance, an integration broker vendor may have adapters for several different source and target applications (such as packaged ERP applications), or adapters for certain types of databases (such as Oracle, Sybase, or DB2), or even adapters for specific brands of middleware. The adapters may reside in the integration broker or in the target application environment and link an application in one environment with one in another taking advantage of the application's API.

The widespread adoption of standards, such as J2EE and XML, has laid the foundation for a standardized approach to the development of adapters. Perhaps the most significant of these standards for application integration is the J2EE Connector Architecture (CA) [Sharma 2001]. The J2EE CA defines a standardized approach for the development of adapters connecting the J2EE platform to heterogeneous enterprise information systems (see section 2.9). The adoption of standards such as J2EE CA enables organizations to develop adapters that work on any J2EE-compliant application server (see section 8.5.4.2 for a description of application servers). This ability to transform messages as they are distributed provides relief for applications by isolating them from the message formats that every other connected application uses.

Repository services are implemented by using a repository holding extensive information on target and source applications. The repository keeps track of input/output to the applications, its data elements, interrelationships between applications, and all the metadata from the other subsystems of the broker like the rules processing component. In short, the repository houses information on rules, logic, objects, and metadata. Metadata is one of the key elements of any integration solution as it is used to describe the structure of information held in the disparate systems and processes. This may range from the structure of a relational database schema to the description of a process that sets up a new customer account. When repositories are used in conjunction with adapters they enable the integration broker to understand the source and target applications and interact with them by relying on metadata about the source and target applications.

Messages passing through the integration broker may trigger events or alerts based on specified conditions. Such conditions may be used for tracking business processes that move outside given parameters, and create a new message, run a special-purpose application, or send an alert, in response.

2.7.2 The Java Message Service (JMS)

Until recently, MOM products required use of their own proprietary programmatic interfaces. This meant that all applications needed to be recorded to adapt to a middleware package. Thus, in-house applications that were designed for use with one middleware product could not be used with another middleware product. Several times during the last decade, middleware vendors attempted to standardize programming interfaces to MOM packages, but with little success. This changed in 1999 when Java launched the Java Message Service (JMS), a framework that specified a set of programming interfaces by which Java programs could access MOM software.

JMS is a vendor-agnostic API for enterprise messaging that can be used with many different MOM vendors. JMS acts as a wrapper around different messaging products, allowing developers to focus on actual application development and integration, rather on the particulars of each other's APIs. Application developers use the same API to access many different systems. JMS is not a messaging system itself. It is an abstraction of the interfaces and classes needed by messaging clients when communicating with different messaging systems. JMS not only provides a Java API for connectivity to MOM systems, but also supports messaging as a first-class Java distributed computing paradigm on an equal footing with RPC [Monson-Haefel 2001].

JMS-based communication is a potential solution in any distributed computing scenario that needs to pass data either synchronously or asynchronously between application elements. A common application for JMS involves interfacing Enterprise Java Beans (EJBs) with legacy applications and sending legacy-related data between the two. JMS provides the two principal models of MOM messaging: point-to-point queuing and publish/subscribe.

The JMS messaging point-to-point model allows JMS clients to send and receive messages both asynchronously and synchronously via queues. A given queue may have multiple receivers, but only one receiver may consume each message. This guarantees that, for example, if a packaging order is sent to multiple warehouses a single warehouse receives the message and processes the order.

In the JMS publish/subscribe messaging model, publishers send messages to a named topic, and subscribers receive all messages sent to this topic. There may be multiple message listeners subscribed to each topic and an application can be both sender and receiver.

JMS supports different message-sending configurations, including: *one-to-one messages*, *one-to-many messages*, and *many-to-many messages*. One-to-one messages allow one message to be sent from one publisher (sender) to one subscriber (receiver). This concept is, as we already explained earlier in this chapter, known as point-to-point messaging. One-to-many messages allow one message to be sent from one publisher to numerous subscribers. Many-to-many messages allow many messages to be sent from many publishers to numerous subscribers.

JMS supports two types of message delivery: *reliable message delivery* and *guaranteed message delivery*. With reliable message delivery, the messaging server will deliver a message to its subscribing client as long as there are no application or network failures. Delivery would fail if some disruption were to occur. This characteristic is known as "at-most-once delivery." With guaranteed message delivery, the message server will deliver a message even if there are application or network failures. The messaging server will store the message in its persistent store and then forward the message to its subscribing clients. After the client processes the message, it sends an acknowledgement to the messaging server and verifies the receipt of the message.

In addition to this basic messaging functionality, JMS works with other Java technologies, such as the Java Transactions API, to provide features like distributed transaction support. There exist some typical middleware issues that are not specified in the JMS standard including: administration and monitoring, load balancing, fault tolerance, error and advisory notification, routing methodologies, wire protocols, and security.

2.8 Transaction-oriented middleware

Transaction-oriented middleware encompasses transaction processing monitors, which coordinate information movement and method sharing between many different resources. Although transaction management for Web services is covered in depth in Chapter 10, we shall briefly examine transaction monitors as part of middleware for reasons of completeness.

Transaction processing (TP) monitor technology provides the distributed client–server environment with the capacity to efficiently and reliably develop, execute, and manage transaction applications. TP monitors enable building on-line TP by coordinating and monitoring the efforts of separate applications. TP monitors reside between front-end applications and back-end applications and databases to manage operations on transactional data. They manage processes and orchestrate applications by breaking complex applications into a set of transactions. The transaction is the mechanism that binds the client to one or more servers and is the fundamental unit of recovery, consistency, and concurrency in a client–server system. From the perspective of application integration, transactions are more than just business events. They have become an application's design philosophy that guarantees consistency and robustness in distributed systems.

A TP monitor is needed for transactions requiring guaranteed completion of multiple discrete functions on multiple application systems. Under the control of a TP monitor, a transaction can be managed from its point of origin – typically on a client – across one or more servers and back to the originating client. When a transaction ends, all parties involved agree that it either succeeded or failed. Transaction models define when a transaction starts, when it ends, and what the appropriate units of recovery are in case of failure.

TP monitors were invented to run applications that serve large numbers of clients. By interjecting themselves between clients and servers, TP monitors can manage transactions, route them across systems, load balance their execution, and restart them after failures. The router subsystem of a TP monitor brokers the client request to one or more server processes. Each server in turn executes the request and responds. Typically, the server manages a file system, database, or other mission-critical resources, shared among several clients. A TP monitor can manage transactional resources on a single server or across multiple servers, and it can cooperate with other TP monitors in federated arrangements.

TP can adversely affect application performance because the processing of a transaction is synchronous, from the point of view of the transaction's requestor. The requestor must wait until all the processing of the transaction has completed before it can proceed with further computations. Moreover, during the processing of a transaction all the resources used by it are locked until the transaction completes. No other application can use these resources during the execution of a transaction. Another problem is that TP monitors are much more intrusive than MOM. This means that they demand more modification of the applications themselves in order take advantage of the TP monitor's specific services.

2.9 Enterprise application and e-business integration

Until a few years ago, traditional enterprise architectures grouped the classical bureaucratic organization model into functional compartments, like sales, manufacturing, and procurement. The results of this architectural approach were multi-functional businesses that were effectively being run in silos where mission-critical data was "locked" within disparate information systems. These systems were primarily designed to support functional departments and were completely isolated from each other and as a result did not require any degree of cross-functional coordination. Application systems within such enterprises essentially ran as autonomous independent automated stovepipes exchanging data through batch file transfer, if they exchanged data at all.

For many years, the solution to the siloed enterprise architecture was to integrate disparate systems by building point-to-point bridges between them. *Point-to-point integration* is an architectural approach where applications are linked through hand-coded, custom-built connectivity systems and data is interchanged directly between any two systems. The approach is generally to "build an interface" for each and every connection between information systems. This tactical approach has enormous limitations as with each new connection point-to-point solutions become unyielding, unmanageable, and unproductive.

One of the key enabling technologies that has emerged to help organizations eliminate islands of data and automation and to integrate diverse custom and package applications (including legacy) is enterprise application integration. The objective of enterprise application integration (EAI) is to transform an organization's internal applications into a cohesive corporate framework. To achieve this, EAI enables applications throughout the enterprise to communicate and integrate seamlessly in the form of business processes.

The internal applications in an enterprise that EAI attempts to integrate are called enterprise information systems (EISs). An EIS encompasses the business processes and IT assets used within enterprises and delivers the information infrastructure internal to an enterprise [Sharma 2001]. An EIS exposes a set of services to its users at differing levels of abstraction – including data level, function level, business object, or process level. Many different applications and systems qualify collectively as EISs:

- Custom applications that have been developed by an enterprise to meet specific business needs and are developed using different programming languages, such as C, C++, or Java.
- Legacy systems and database applications that manage mission-critical data to the business processes within an enterprise. Database and legacy systems may support

core business tasks such as taking and processing orders, initiating production and delivery, generating invoices, crediting payments, distribution, inventory management, and related revenue-generating, cost-saving, and accounting tasks. Legacy systems are the subject of section 8.5.6.

- ERP systems: These are management information systems that provide a unified, organization-wide view of business processes and associated information by integrating and automating many of the business practices associated with the operations or production aspects of a company. They typically include manufacturing, logistics, distribution, inventory, shipping, invoicing, and accounting. ERP systems are often called "back-office" systems, indicating that customers and the general public are not directly involved.
- CRM systems: These provide functionality that supports the process of creating relationships with customers through the introduction of reliable service automated processes, personal information gathering and processing, and self-service throughout the supplying company in order to create value for the customer. CRM systems achieve their functionality by accessing and analyzing data from disparate databases within the enterprise, drawing heavily on data already available in ERP systems. CRM systems are known as "front-office" systems that help the enterprise deal directly with its customers.
- TP systems and applications, which coordinate data movement between various data repositories.

EAI solutions combine a fast, robust communications backbone with integration broker technology, business process workflow, business process management (BPM) facilities and tools that provide for explicit management of cross-functional business processes (see section 8.5.4.3), and application-specific adapters – along with complete end-to-end application control and management – to create an environment that enables new business processes for competitive advantage [Papazoglou 2006]. Figure 2.16 shows a typical EAI solution integrating various EISs.

Integration brokers in the EAI architecture focus on the message and process flow and are responsible for brokering messages exchanged between two or more applications, providing the ability to transform, store, and route messages and also to apply business rules and respond to events. Integration brokers use messaging systems to move information between systems and as such they may include process and workflow management, which introduce the capability to manage state and long-running transactions. Most integration brokers support some sort of asynchronous transport layer, either proprietary or open. Some integration brokers offer the ability to select any number of messaging systems, even to mix and match messaging systems to meet the requirements of the problem domain. Integration brokers may utilize several abstraction layers around the types of applications to be integrated. For example, there may be an abstraction for common middleware services (such as distributed objects, MOM, and transactional middleware).

EAI solutions normally use *application servers* to connect an enterprise with the outside world. An application server is a natural point for application integration as it provides a platform for development, deployment, and management of Web-based, transactional,

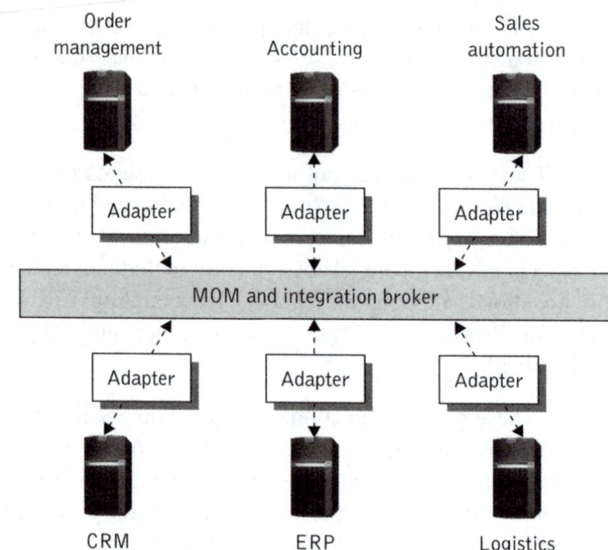

Figure 2.16 Typical EAI solution

secure, distributed, and scalable enterprise applications (see also section 8.5.4.2). Application servers can be used in tandem with integration brokers through a cooperative interface. In this mode the integration broker functions as a service provider to the application server by providing data access, transformations, and content-based routing.

E-business (or business-to-business) integration solutions grow on the back of successful internal EAI solutions and provide the capability to link together disparate processes between trading partners. E-business integration makes systems internal to an enterprise able to interact with those of customers, suppliers, and partners. For instance, e-business integration solutions focus on supply-chain integration by providing seamless interoperability between multiple systems, e.g., manufacturing, inventory management and warehousing, logistics, and billing, across the integrated supply chain. A supply chain essentially has three main parts: the supply, manufacturing, and distribution. The supply side concentrates on how, from where, and when raw materials are procured and supplied to manufacturing. Manufacturing converts these raw materials to finished products and distribution ensures that these finished products reach the final customers through a network of distributors, warehouses, and retailers. By integrating information and processes across their supply chain network, manufacturers expect to reduce procurement costs while increasing inventory turns. Interoperability in a supply chain is necessary to gather useful business information such as consumption forecasts and trends to improve visibility into these systems, thereby seamlessly integrating and coordinating cross-functional and cross-firm business processes in the supply chain.

Sharing business logic between applications is an important factor when attempting to integrate applications that originate from different enterprises. Application servers provide a flexible platform for integrating business applications, not only because they provide a platform for development, deployment, and management of Web-based business

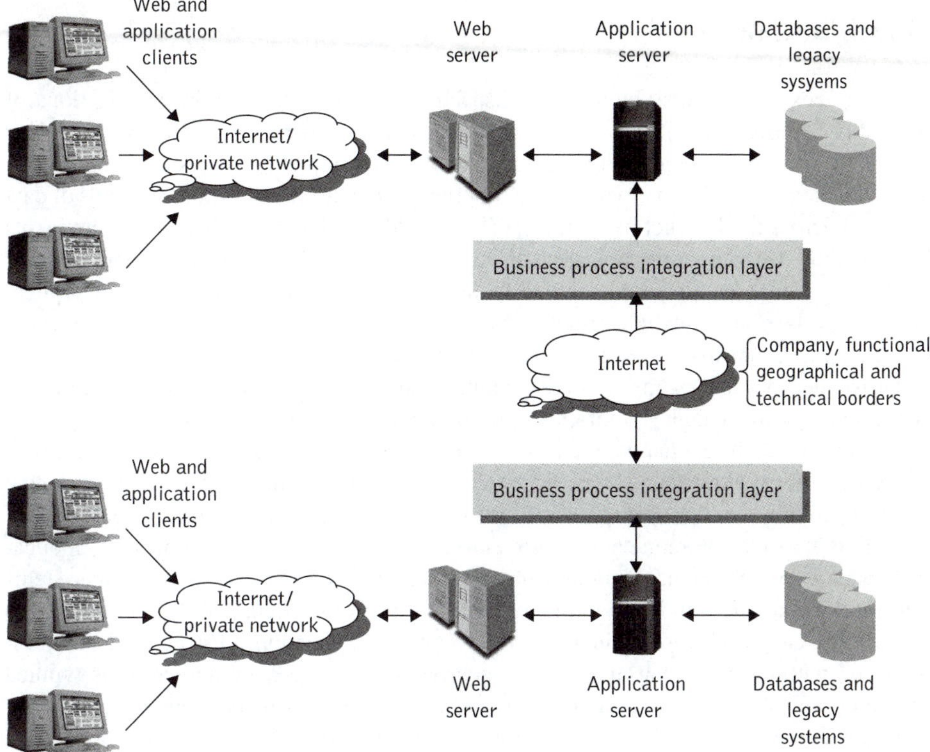

Figure 2.17 Typical e-business integration solution
Source: From M. P. Papazoglou and P. M. A. Ribbers, *e-Business: Organizational and Technical Foundations*, J. Wiley & Sons, 2006. Reproduced with permission.

applications, but also because they can be interconnected using either synchronous or asynchronous communication methods. The ability to interconnect application servers is a key requirement for integrating e-business applications. Application servers coordinate the sequence of complex integration steps with support for checkpoints and transaction boundaries.

Figure 2.17 illustrates how application servers interlink business applications across partners by accommodating business and integration logic. Figure 2.17 also illustrates that business process integration introduces an additional independent coordination layer that provides a non-invasive fit into the existing application server architectures. Rather than being primarily focused on integrating physical entities such as data or business components, the business process integration layer involves the integration of logical entities represented as business process elements. The application server thus encapsulates the process logic of application integration in its business process integration layer. This moves integration logic out of the applications codifying the logic, including the sequencing of events and data flow, and ensuring transaction integrity for transactions that span multiple organizations.

2.10 Summary

Web services technologies build upon distributed systems that comprise collections of (probably heterogeneous) networked computers that communicate and coordinate their actions by passing messages. Web services also rely on Internet protocols to enable data to be transmitted across the Internet. Typical Internet protocols are essentially methods of data transport across the Internet by defining the standards by which the different components in a distributed system communicate with each other and with remote components.

Other key enabling technologies that facilitate the development of distributed applications for Web services include remote procedure calls, message-based middleware, event processing mechanisms, message-oriented middleware, and integration brokers.

Distributed systems and applications communicate by exchanging messages. Messaging is a technology that enables program-to-program communication by allowing programs to communicate via the exchange of packets of data called messages. Whilst there are different types of messaging middleware, they all can support synchronous or time-dependent and asynchronous or time-independent forms of messaging. With a synchronous form of execution message communication is synchronized between two communicating application systems. Synchronous communication requires that any two communicating systems must both be up and running, and that execution flow at the client's side is interrupted to execute the call. Both the sending and the receiving application must be ready to communicate with each other at all times. Synchronous message communication is typified by the concepts of remote procedure call and remote method invocation. Asynchronous communication is exemplified by store and forward and publish/subscribe approaches. The publish/subscribe approach is based on the concept of event notification, which is very appealing to the world of Web services.

Message-oriented middleware is an infrastructure that involves the passing of data between applications using a common communication channel that carries self-contained messages. The asynchronous nature of MOM makes it most appropriate for event-driven Web services applications. A particular type of MOM with appealing properties for Web services applications is an integration broker. An integration broker is an application-to-application middleware service that is capable of one-to-many, many-to-one, and many-to-many message distribution. In the Web services world integration brokers can be used as the software hub that records and manages the contracts between publishers and subscribers of messages.

Review questions

- What are Internet protocols?
- Describe the two types of message communication. What are their main differences?
- What are remote procedure calls and what is remote method invocation?
- What are the most popular forms of asynchronous messaging?

- List and describe the characteristics of publish/subscribe messaging and event-driven processing. How are they related to each other?
- What is point-to-point queuing and how does it differ from publish/subscribe messaging?
- List and describe the role and features of message-oriented middleware.
- List some benefits of message-oriented middleware.
- What is an integration broker and how is it used in MOM solutions?
- Define and describe the concept of enterprise application integration.
- Define and describe the concept of e-business integration.
- What are enterprise information systems and what problems do they cause if they are not appropriately integrated?

Exercises

2.1 Write a Java program that:

(a) Takes a host address and checks whether a connection is available on port 80. If the connection is available the application sends an HTTP request echoing on the reply.

(b) Acts as a server listening on port 8888 and echoes any request it receives.

2.2 Implement a simple store and forward queuing system such as the one shown in Figure 2.10, where a J2EE application client sends several messages to a queue. The messages that are sent to the queue are asynchronously received by a server, which processes them.

2.3 Implement a distributed application that distributes computations among many clients. The clients are located on different machines and they connect themselves to a single server in a network using sockets. A single task is to be divided into many jobs, which may be assigned to different clients at different times.

2.4 Write a Java Web application to implement a simple e-commerce application that represents a shopping cart in an on-line bookstore. Clients may add a book to the cart, remove a book, or retrieve the cart's contents. For information on how to develop such Web applications on the J2EE platform readers are referred to **https://blueprints.dev.java.net/petstore/**.

2.5 Develop a simple publish/subscribe messaging stock ticker application. A stock ticker works by continuously presenting all the trades that occur in a stock exchange, providing the name of the company, the number of shares traded, and the price of the trade. A stock ticker application can be seen as one that sends an event to a topic for every trade that occurs in a stock exchange to many traders.

Traders receive only the desired events from selected companies' trades by subscribing to the appropriate topic and specifying the desired companies. In this case, the message selector is the company name or symbol. Every participant (trader) in a stock trading session uses this stock trading program to join a specific stock (topic), and deliver and receive messages to and from the producer of this topic.

2.6 Topic-based bulletin board systems consist of a set of newsgroups, which are classified according to subject (e.g., wine, cooking, holiday resorts, clothing, etc.). Users can send messages to these newsgroups or read messages from them. Bulletin board systems usually have one or more central servers, which store messages, and many clients, which make requests to servers for reading or sending messages. Implement a distributed architecture for a bulletin board system which does not rely on a central server. Your implementation should rely on a peer-to-peer architecture where peers can send to or read messages from other peers. It is recommended that you use JXTA technology (**http://www.jxta.org/**) to solve this problem. JXTA is a set of open protocols that allow connected devices on the network ranging from cell phones and wireless PDAs to PCs and servers to communicate and collaborate in a peer-to-peer manner. JXTA peers create a virtual network where any peer can interact with other peers and resources directly even when peers and resources are on different network transports.

CHAPTER 3

Brief overview of XML

Learning objectives

In Chapter 2 we covered the distributed and Web-based computing roots of Web services. In this chapter we explain how XML structures, describes, and exchanges information. One of the appealing features of XML is that it enables diverse applications to flexibly exchange information and therefore is used as the building block of Web services. All Web services technologies are based on XML and the XML Schema Definition Language that make possible precise machine interpretation of data and fine tuning the entire process of information exchange between trading enterprises and heterogeneous computing infrastructures.

It is important that readers have a good understanding of XML, XML namespaces, and the W3C Schema Language so that they are in a position to understand fundamental Web services technologies such as SOAP, WSDL, UDDI, and BPEL. Therefore, this chapter provides a brief overview of XML to help readers understand the material that follows in this book. It specifically covers the following topics:

- XML document structure.
- XML namespaces.
- Defining schemas.
- Reusing schemas by deriving complex type extensions and polymorphic types.
- Reusing schemas by importing and including schemas.
- Document navigation and the XML Path Language.
- Document transformation and the eXtensible Stylesheet Language Transform.

For more details about XML and XML schemas, in particular, we refer interested readers to the following books: [Walmsley 2002], [Skonnard 2002], [Valentine 2002].

3.1 XML document structure

XML is an extensible markup language used for the description and delivery of marked-up electronic text over the Web. Two important characteristics of XML distinguish it from other markup languages: its document type concept and its portability.

An important aspect of XML is its notion of a *document type*. XML documents are regarded as having types. XML's constituent parts and their structure formally define the type of a document.

Another basic design feature of XML is to ensure that documents are portable between different computing environments. All XML documents, whatever language or writing system they employ, use the same underlying character encoding scheme. This encoding is defined by the international standard Unicode, which is a standard encoding system that supports characters of diverse natural languages.

An XML document is composed of named containers and their contained data values. Typically, these containers are represented as declarations, elements, and attributes. A *declaration* declares the version of XML used to define the document. The technical term used in XML for a textual unit, viewed as a structural component, is *element*. Element containers may be defined to hold data, other elements, both data and other elements, or nothing at all.

An XML document is also known as an *instance* or *XML document instance*. This signifies the fact that an XML document instance represents one possible set of data for a particular markup language. The example in Listing 3.1 typifies an XML document instance. This example shows billing information associated with a purchase order issued by plastics manufacturer. We assume that this company has built a business based on providing "specialty" and custom-fabricated plastics components on a spot and contract basis.

```
<?xml version="1.0" encoding="UTF-8"?>
<BillingInformation>
    <Name> Right Plastic Products </Name>
    <BillingDate> 2002-09-15 </BillingDate>
    <Address>
      <Street> 158 Edward st. </Street>
      <City> Brisbane </City>
      <State> QLD </State>
      <PostalCode> 4000 </PostalCode>
    </Address>
</BillingInformation>
```

Listing 3.1 Example of an XML document instance

3.1.1 XML declaration

The first few characters of an XML document must make up an XML declaration. The XML processing software uses the declaration to determine how to deal with the

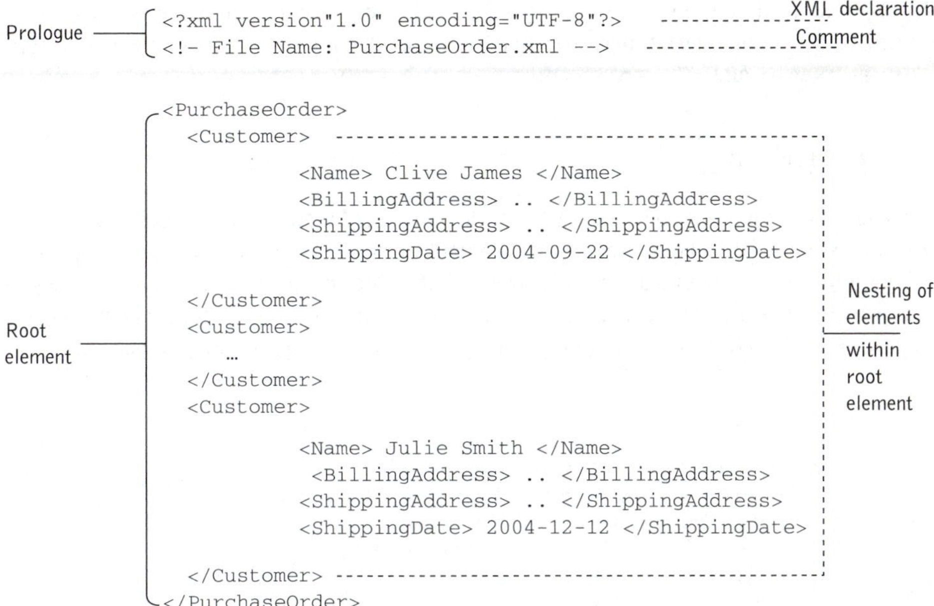

Figure 3.1 Layout of typical XML document

subsequent XML content. A typical XML declaration begins with a *prologue* that typically contains a declaration of conformity to version 1.0 of the XML standard and to the UTF-8 encoding standard: `<?xml version="1.0" encoding="UTF-8"?>`. This is shown in Figure 3.1.

3.1.2 Elements

The internal structure of an XML document is roughly analogous to a hierarchical directory or file structure. The topmost element of the XML document is a single element known as the *root element*. The content of an element can be character data, other nested elements, or a combination of both. Elements contained in other elements are referred to as *nested elements*. The containing element is the *parent* element and the nested element is called the *child* element. This is illustrated in Figure 3.1, where a `Purchase Order` element is shown to contain a `Customer` element, which in turn contains `Name` and `BillingAddress` and `ShippingAddress` elements.

The data values contained within a document are known as the *content* of the document. When descriptive names have been applied to the elements and attributes that contain the data values, the content of the document becomes intuitive and self-explanatory to a person. This signifies the "self-describing" property of XML [Bean 2003].

Different types of elements are given different names, but XML provides no way of expressing the meaning of a particular type of element, other than its relationship to other element types. For instance, all one can say about an element such as `<Address>` in

Listing 3.2 is that instances of it may (or may not) occur within elements of type `<Customer>`, and that it may (or may not) be decomposed into elements of type `<StreetName>` and `<StreetNumber>`.

3.1.3 Attributes

Another way of putting data into an XML document is by adding *attributes* to start tags. Attributes are used to better specify the content of an element on which they appear by adding information about a defined element. An attribute specification is a name–value pair that is associated with an element. Listing 3.2 is an example of an element declaration using an attribute (shaded) to specify the type of a particular customer as being a manufacturer.

```
<?xml version="1.0" encoding="UTF-8"?>
<BillingInformation customer-type="manufacturer">
    <Name> Right Plastic Products </Name>
    <BillingDate> 2002-09-15 </BillingDate>
    <Address>
      <Street> 158 Edward st. </Street>
      <City> Brisbane </City>
      <State> QLD </State>
      <PostalCode> 4000 </PostalCode>
    </Address>
</BillingInformation>
```

Listing 3.2 Example of attribute use for Listing 3.1

Each attribute is a name–value pair where the value must be in either single or double quotes. Unlike elements, attributes cannot be nested. They must also always be declared in the start tag of an element.

3.2 URIs and XML namespaces

The Web is a universe of resources. A resource is defined to be anything that has identity. Examples include documents, files, menu items, machines, and services, as well as people, organizations, and concepts [Berners-Lee 1998]. A Web architecture starts with a uniform syntax for resource identifiers, so that one can refer to resources, access them, describe them, and share them. The Uniform Resource Identifier (URI) is the basis for identifying resources in WWW. A URI consists of a string of characters that uniquely identifies a resource. The URI provides the capability for an element name to be unique, such that it does not conflict with any other element names.

The W3C uses the newer and broader term URI to describe network resources rather than the familiar but narrower term Uniform Resource Locator (URL). URI is all-inclusive, referring to Internet resource addressing strings that use any of the present or future addressing schemes [Berners-Lee 1998]. URIs include URLs, which use traditional addressing schemes such as HTTP and FTP, and Uniform Resource Names (URNs). URNs are another form of URI that provide *persistence* as well as *location independence*. URNs address Internet resources in a location-independent manner and unlike URLs they are stable over time.

XML allows designers to choose the names of their own tags and as a consequence it is possible that name clashes (i.e., situations where the same tag name is used in different contexts) occur when two or more document designers choose the same tag names for their elements. XML *namespaces* provide a way to distinguish between elements that use the same local name but are in fact different, thus avoiding name clashes. For instance, a namespace can identify whether an address is a postal address, an e-mail address, or an IP address. Tag names within a namespace must be unique.

To understand the need for namespaces consider the example in Listing 3.3. This listing illustrates an example of an XML document containing address information without an associated namespace.

```
<?xml version="1.0" encoding="UTF-8"?>
    <Address>
      <Street> 158 Edward st. </Street>
      <City> Brisbane </City>
      <State> QLD </State>
      <PostalCode> 4000 </PostalCode>
    </Address>
```

Listing 3.3 XML example with no associated namespace

Now, if we compare the instance of the `Address` markup in Listing 3.3 against the `BillingInformation` markup in Listing 3.2, we observe that both markups contain references to `Address` elements. In fact, the `Address` markup has its own schema in XML Schema Definition Language. It is desirable that every time that address information is used in an XML document that the `Address` declaration is reused and is thus validated against the `Address` markup schema. This means that the `Address` element in Listing 3.2 should conform to the `Address` markup while the rest of the elements in this listing conform to the `BillingInformation` markup. We achieve this in XML by means of namespaces.

Namespaces in XML provide a facility for associating the elements and/or attributes in all or part of a document with a particular schema. All namespace declarations have a scope, i.e., all the elements to which they apply. A namespace declaration is in scope for the element on which it is declared and of that element's children. The namespace name and the local name of the element together form a globally unique name known as a *qualified name* [Skonnard 2002]. A qualified name is often referred to as *QName* and consists of a prefix and the local name separated by a colon.

A namespace declaration is indicated by a URI denoting the namespace name. The URI may be mapped to a prefix that may then be used in front of tag and attribute names, separated by a colon. In order to reference a namespace, an application developer needs to first declare one by creating a *namespace declaration* using the form

```
xmlns:<Namespace Prefix> = <someURI>
```

When the prefix is attached to local names of elements and attributes, the elements and attributes then become associated with the correct namespace. An illustrative example can be found in Listing 3.4. As the most common URI is a URL, we use URLs as namespace names in our example (always assuming that they are unique identifiers). The two URLs used in this example serve as namespaces for the `BillingInformation` and `Address` elements, respectively. These URLs are simply used for identification and scoping purposes and it is, of course, not necessary that they point to any actual resources or documents.

```
<?xml version="1.0" encoding="UTF-8"?>
<BillingInformation customer-type="manufacturer"
   xmlns="http://www.plastics_supply.com/BillInfo">
  <Name> Right Plastic Products </Name>
  <Address xmlns="http://www.plastics_supply.com/Addr">
    <Street> 158 Edward st. </Street>
    <City> Brisbane </City>
    <State> QLD </State>
     <PostalCode> 4000 </PostalCode>
   </Address>
   <BillingDate> 2002-09-15 </BillingDate>
</BillingInformation>
```

Listing 3.4 An XML example using namespaces

The `xmlns` declarations in Listing 3.4 are the *default namespaces* for their associated element and all of its declarations. The scope of a default element applies only to the element itself and all of its descendants. This means that the declaration `xmlns="http://www.plastics_supply.com/Addr"` applies only to elements nested within `Address`. The declaration `xmlns="http://www.plastics_supply.com/BillInfo"` applies to all elements declared within `BillingInformation` but not to `Address` elements as they define their own default namespace.

Using default namespaces can get messy when elements are interleaved or when different markup languages are used in the same document. To avoid this problem, XML defines a shorthand notation for associating elements and attributes with namespaces. Listing 3.5 illustrates.

```
<?xml version="1.0" encoding="UTF-8"?>
<bi:BillingInformation customer-type="manufacturer"
     xmlns:bi="http://www.plastics_supply.com/BillInfo"
     xmlns:addr="http://www.plastics_supply.com/Addr">

    <bi:Name> Right Plastic Products </bi:Name>
    <addr:Address>
      <addr:Street> 158 Edward st. </addr:Street>
      <addr:City> Brisbane </addr:City>
      <addr:State> QLD </addr:State>
      <addr:PostalCode> 4000 </addr:PostalCode>
    </addr:Address>
    <bi:BillingDate> 2002-09-15 </bi:BillingDate>
</bi:BillingInformation>
```

Listing 3.5 Using qualified names in XML

The example in Listing 3.5 illustrates the use of QNames to disambiguate and scope XML documents. As already explained earlier, QNames comprise two parts: the XML namespace and the local name. For instance, the QName of an element like `City` is composed of the `"http://www.plastics_supply.com/Addr"` namespace and the local name `City`.

The use of valid documents can greatly improve the quality of document processes. Valid XML documents allow users to take advantage of content management, e-business transactions, enterprise integration, and all other kinds of business processes that require the exchange of meaningful and constrained XML documents.

3.3 Defining structure in XML documents

A way to define XML tags and structure is with schemas. Schemas provide much needed capabilities for expressing XML documents. They provide support for metadata characteristics such as structural relationships, cardinality, valid values, and data types. Each type of schema acts as a method of describing data characteristics and applying rules and constraints to a referencing XML document [Bean 2003]. The term *schema* is commonly used in the area of databases to refer to the logical structure of a database. When the term is used in the XML community, it refers to a document that defines the content of and structure of a class of XML documents.

3.3.1 The XML Schema Definition Language

The XML Schema Definition Language (XSD) as proposed by W3C provides a type system for XML processing environments. XSD provides a granular method for describing the content of an XML document and provides extensive capabilities in the areas of data types, customization, and reuse [Bean 2003]. XSD provides a very powerful and flexible way in which to validate XML documents. It includes facilities for declaring elements and attributes, reusing elements from other schemas, defining complex element definitions, and for defining restrictions for even the simplest of data types. This gives the XML schema developer explicit control over specifying a valid construction for an XML document. For instance, a document definition can specify the data type of the contents of an element, the range of values for elements, the minimum as well as maximum number of times an element may occur, annotations to schemas, and much more.

An XML schema is made up of *schema components*. These are building blocks that make up the abstract data model of the schema. Element and attribute declarations, complex and simple type definitions, and notifications are all examples of schema components. Schema components can be used to assess the validity of well-formed element and attribute information items and furthermore may specify augmentations to those items and their descendants.

XML schema components include the following [Valentine 2002]: data types which embrace both simple and complex/composite and extensible data types; element type and attribute declarations; constraints; relationships which express associations between elements; and namespaces and import/include options to support modularity as they make it possible to include reusable structures, containers, and custom data types through externally managed XML schemas.

3.3.2 The XML schema document

Schemas are more powerful when validating an XML document because of their ability to clarify data types stored within the XML document. Because schemas can more clearly define the types of data that are to be contained in an XML document, they allow for a closer check on the accuracy of XML documents. Listing 3.6 illustrates an XML schema for a sample purchase order.

```
<?xml version="1.0" encoding="UTF-8"?>
<xsd:schema
  xmlns:xsd="http://www.w3.org/2001/XMLSchema"
  xmlns:PO="http://www.plastics_supply.com/PurchaseOrder"
  targetNamespace="http://www.plastics_supply.com/PurchaseOrder">

  <!-- Purchase Order schema -->
  <xsd:element name="PurchaseOrder" type="PO:PurchaseOrderType"/>

  <xsd:complexType name="PurchaseOrderType">
    <xsd:all>
      <xsd:element name="ShippingInformation" type="PO:Customer"
           minOccurs="1" maxOccurs="1"/>

      <xsd:element name="BillingInformation" type="PO:Customer"
           minOccurs="1" maxOccurs="1"/>
      <xsd:element name="Order" type="PO:OrderType" minOccurs="1"
           maxOccurs="1"/>
    </xsd:all>
  </xsd:complexType>
```

```
<xsd:complexType name="Customer">
  <xsd:sequence>
    <xsd:element name="Name" minOccurs="1" maxOccurs="1">
      <xsd:simpleType>
        <xsd:restriction base="xsd:string"/>
      </xsd:simpleType>
    </xsd:element>
    <xsd:element name="Address" type="PO:AddressType"
       minOccurs= "1" maxOccurs="1"/>
      <xsd:choice>
      <xsd:element name="BillingDate"  type="xsd:date"/>
      <xsd:element name="ShippingDate" type="xsd:date"/>
    </xsd:choice>
  </xsd:sequence>
</xsd:complexType>

<xsd:complexType name="AddressType">
  <xsd:sequence>
    <xsd:element name="Street"          type="xsd:string"/>
    <xsd:element name="City"            type="xsd:string"/>
    <xsd:element name="State"           type="xsd:string"/>
    <xsd:element name="PostalCode"      type="xsd:decimal"/>
  <xsd:sequence>
</xsd:complexType>

<xsd:complexType name="OrderType">
  <xsd:sequence>
    <xsd:element name="Product" type="PO:ProductType"
                 minOccurs= "1" maxOccurs="unbounded"/>
  </xsd:sequence>
  <xsd:attribute name="Total">
    <xsd:simpleType>
      <xsd:restriction base="xsd:decimal">
        <xsd:fractionDigits value="2"/>
      </xsd:restriction>
    </xsd:simpleType>
  </xsd:attribute>
  <xsd:attribute name="ItemsSold" type="xsd:positiveInteger"/>
</xsd:complexType>

<xsd:complexType name="ProductType">
  <xsd:attribute name="Name" type="xsd:string"/>
  <xsd:attribute name="Price">
    <xsd:simpleType>
      <xsd:restriction base="xsd:decimal">
        <xsd:fractionDigits value="2"/>
      </xsd:restriction>
    </xsd:simpleType>
  </xsd:attribute>
  <xsd:attribute name="Quantity" type="xsd:positiveInteger"/>
</xsd:complexType>
</xsd:schema>
```

Listing 3.6 A sample purchase order schema

Listing 3.6 depicts a purchase order for various items. This document allows a customer to receive the shipment of the goods at the customer's manufacturing plant and billing information to be sent to the customer's headquarters. This document also contains specific information about the products ordered, such as how much each product cost, how many were ordered, and so on. The root element of an XML schema document, such as the purchase order schema, is always the `schema` element. Nested within the `schema` element are element and type declarations. For instance, the purchase order schema consists of a schema element and a variety of sub-elements, most notably element `complexType` and `simpleType` that determine the appearance of elements and their content in instance documents. These components are explained in the following sections.

The `schema` element assigns the XML schema namespace `("http://www.w3.org/2001/XMLSchema")` as the default namespace. This schema is the standard schema namespace defined by the XML schema specification and all XML schema elements must belong to this namespace. The `schema` element also defines the `targetNamespace` attribute, which declares the XML namespace of all new types explicitly created within this schema. The `schema` element is shown to assign the prefix `PO` to the `targetNamespace` attribute. By assigning a target namespace for a schema, we indicate that an XML document whose elements are declared as belonging to the schema's namespace should be validated against the XML schema. Therefore, the `PO` `targetNamespace` can be used within document instances so that they can conform to the purchase order schema.

As the purpose of a schema is to define a class of XML documents, the term *instance document* is often used to describe an XML document that conforms to a particular schema. Listing 3.7 illustrates an instance document conforming to the schema in Listing 3.6.

The remainder of this section is devoted to understanding the XML schema for the XML document shown in Listing 3.6.

3.3.3 Type definitions, element, and attribute declarations

The XSD differentiates between *complex types*, which define their content in terms of elements that may consist of further elements and attributes, and *simple types*, which define their content in terms of elements and attributes that can contain only data. The XSD also introduces a sharp distinction between *definitions* that create new types (both simple and complex) and *declarations* that enable elements and attributes with specific names and types (both simple and complex) to appear in document instances. To *declare* an element or attribute in a schema means to allow an element or attribute with a specified name, type, and other features to appear in a particular context within a conforming XML document.

3.3.3.1 Element declarations

Elements are the primary ingredients of an XML schema and can be declared using the `<xsd:element>` element from the XSD. The element declaration defines the element name, content model, and allowable attributes and data types for each element type. W3C XML schemas provide extensive data type support, including numerous built-in and

```
<?xml version="1.0" encoding="UTF-8"?>

<PO:PurchaseOrder
 xmlns:PO="http://www.plastics_supply.com/PurchaseOrder"
 xmlns:xsi="http://www.w3.org/2001/XMLSchema-instance"
 xsi:schemaLocation="http://www.plastics_supply.com/PurchaseOrder
     purchaseOrder.xsd">

  <ShippingInformation>
    <Name> Right Plastic Products Co. </Name>
    <Address>
      <Street> 459 Wickham st. </Street>
      <City> Fortitude Valley </City>
      <State> QLD </State>
      <PostalCode> 4006 </PostalCode>
   </Address>
    <ShippingDate> 2002-09-22 </ShippingDate>
  </ShippingInformation>

  <BillingInformation>
    <Name> Right Plastic Products Inc. </Name>
    <Address>
      <Street> 158 Edward st. </Street>
      <City> Brisbane </City>
      <State> QLD </State>
      <PostalCode> 4000 </PostalCode>
    </Address>
    <BillingDate> 2002-09-15 </BillingDate>
  </BillingInformation>

  <Order Total="253000.00" ItemsSold="2">
    <Product Name="Injection Molder" Price="250000.00"
     Quantity="1"/>
    <Product Name="Adjustable Worktable" Price="3000.00"
     Quantity="1"/>
  </Order>
</PO:PurchaseOrder>
```

Listing 3.7 An XML instance document conforming to the schema in Listing 3.6

derived data types that can be applied as constraints to any elements or attribute. The `<xsd:element>` element either denotes an element declaration, defining a named element and associating that element with a type, or is a reference to such a declaration [Skonnard 2002].

The topmost element container in an XML document is known as the *root element* (of which there is only one per XML document). Within the root element, there may be many occurrences of other elements and groups of elements. The containing of elements by other elements presents the concept of nesting. Each layer of nesting results in another hierarchical level. Elements may also contain attributes. Some elements may also be defined intentionally to remain empty.

The location at which an element is defined determines its availability within the schema. The element declarations that appear as immediate descendants of the `<xsd:schema>` element are known as *global element declarations* and can be referenced from anywhere within the schema document or from other schemas. For example, the `PurchaseOrderType` in Listing 3.6 is defined globally and in fact constitutes the root element in this schema. Global element declarations describe elements that are always part of the target namespace of the schema. Element declarations that appear as part of complex type definitions either directly or indirectly – through a group reference – are known as *local element declarations*. In Listing 3.6 local element declarations include elements such as `Customer` and `ProductType`.

An element that declares an element content may use *compositors* to aggregate existing types into a structure, define, and constrain the behavior of child elements. A compositor specifies the sequence and selective occurrence of the containers defined within a complex type or group. There are three types of compositors that can be used within XML schemas. These are `sequence`, `choice`, and `all`. The `sequence` construct requires that the sequence of individual elements defined within a complex type or group must be followed by the corresponding XML document (content model). The construct `choice` requires that the document designer make a choice between a number of defined options in a complex type or group. Finally, the construct `all` requires that all the elements contained in a complex type or group may appear once or not at all, and may appear in any order.

3.3.3.2 Attribute declarations

Attributes in an XML document are contained by elements. XML attributes cannot be nested and do not exhibit cardinality or multiplicity. To indicate that a complex element has an attribute, we use the `<attribute>` element of the XSD. For instance, from Listing 3.6 we observe that, when declaring an attribute (such as `Total`), we must specify its type. This type must be one of the simple types: `boolean`, `byte`, `date`, `dateTime`, `decimal`, `double`, `duration`, `float`, `integer`, `language`, `long`, `short`, `string`, `time`, `token`, etc. This example shows that an attribute may be defined based on `simpleType` elements.

3.3.4 Simple types

Most programming languages only allow developers to arrange the various built-in types into a structured type of some sort, but do not allow developers to define new simple types that have user-defined value spaces. XML Schema is different in this regard because it allows users to define their own custom simple types, whose value spaces are subsets of the predefined built-in types. In XML custom data types can be defined by creating a `simpleType` with one of the supported data types as a base and adding constraining facets to it.

Listing 3.6 indicates that the values of the simple element `Name` in `Customer` are restricted to only string values. Moreover, this listing specifies that each of the simple attributes Name, BillingDate, and ShippingDate must appear exactly once as a child of the Customer element. This is indicated by the presence of the occurrence constraint attributes minOccurs and maxOccurs, which specify that the minimum and maximum number of times these elements may appear is set to one. By the same token Listing 3.6 indicates that simple attribute types like Total and Price are restricted to decimal values only with two digits allowed to the right of the decimal point.

3.3.5 Complex types

The complexType element is used to define structured types. An element is considered to be a complex type if it contains child elements and/or attributes. Complex type definitions appear as children of an xsd:schema element and can be referenced from elsewhere in the schema and from other schemas. Complex types typically contain a set of element declarations, element references, and attribute declarations.

An example of a complex type in Listing 3.6 is PurchaseOrderType. This particular element contains three child elements – ShippingInformation, BillingInformation, and Order – as well as the attribute Total. The use of the maxOccurs and minOccurs attributes on the element declarations, with a value of one for these attributes, indicates that the element declarations specify that they must occur only once within the PurchaseOrderType element.

An element declared with a content model can contain one or more child elements of the specified type or types, as well as attributes. To declare an element with element content, a schema developer must define the type of the element using the xsd:complexType element and include within a content model that describes all permissible child elements the arrangement of these elements, and rules for their occurrences. In the XSD the following elements, all, choice, sequence, or a combination of them, can be used for this purpose. As an example, notice the use of the xsd:sequence and xsd:choice composition elements in Listing 3.6 that defines Customer as a complex type element. The xsd:sequence element is used to indicate when a group of elements or attributes is declared within an xsd:sequence schema element; they must appear in the exact order listed. This is the case with the Name and Address elements in the complex type Customer. The <xsd:choice> element is used to indicate when a group of elements or attributes is declared within an <xsd:choice> schema element; any one, but not all, of the child elements may appear in the context of the parent element. This is the case with the BillingDate and ShippingDate attributes in the complex type Customer.

3.4 XML schemas reuse

In enterprise-level solutions, one of the most challenging problems facing XML designers is how to design structures that can be reused. There are many benefits to designing XML schemas using reusable components. These benefits lead directly to shorter development cycles, reducing application development costs, simpler maintenance of code, as well as promoting the use of enterprise data standards.

3.4.1 Deriving complex types

XML Schema allows the derivation of a complex type from an already existing simple or complex type. Complex types are derived from other types either *by extension or by restriction* [Walmsley 2002]. Extension allows for adding additional descendants and/or attributes to an existing (base) type. Restriction restricts the value contents of a type. The values of the new type are a subset of those for the base type.

3.4.1.1 Complex type extensions

Complex types may be extended by adding attributes and adding to the content model but one cannot modify or remove existing attributes. When defining a complex content extension the XML processor handles the extensions by appending the new content model after the base type's content model, as if they were together in a `sequence` compositor construct.

```
<?xml version="1.0" encoding="UTF-8"?>

<xsd:schema
  xmlns:xsd="http://www.w3.org/2001/XMLSchema"
  xmlns:PO="http://www.plastics_supply.com/PurchaseOrder"
  targetNamespace="http://www.plastics_supply.com/PurchaseOrder">

      <xsd:complexType name="Address">
         <xsd:sequence>
             <xsd:element name="Number" type="xsd:decimal"/>
             <xsd:element name="Street" type="xsd:string"/>
             <xsd:element name="City" type="xsd:string"
               minOccurs="0"/>
         </xsd:sequence>
      </xsd:complexType>

      <xsd:complexType name="AustralianAddress">
          <xsd:complexContent>
              <xsd:extension base="PO:Address">
                      <xsd:sequence>
                             <xsd:element name="State"
                              type="xsd:string"/>
                             <xsd:element name="PostalCode"
                              type="xsd:decimal"/>
                             <xsd:element name="Country"
                              type="xsd:string"/>
                      </xsd:sequence>
              </xsd:extension>
          </xsd:complexContent>
      </xsd:complexType>
</xsd:schema>
```

Listing 3.8 Extending XML complex types

Listing 3.8 illustrates how to extend a complex type such as Address (which includes number, street, and city). The City element in the listing is optional and this is indicated by the value of zero for the attribute minOccurs. The base type Address in Listing 3.8 can be used to create other derived types, such as EuropeanAddress or USAddress as well.

3.4.1.2 Complex type restrictions

Complex types may be restricted by eliminating or restricting attributes, and subsetting content models. When restriction is used, instances of the derived type will always be valid for the base type as well.

For instance, a developer can create an additional type, named AustralianPostalAddress, from the AustralianAddress type that omits the City element, as shown in Listing 3.9. If the state and postal code are included in an Australian address it is not necessary to include the city as well.

```
<!-- Uses the data type declarations from Listing 3.8 -->
<xsd:complexType name="AustralianPostalAddress">
   <xsd:complexContent>
      <xsd:restriction base="PO:AustralianAddress">
         <xsd:sequence>
            <xsd:element name="Number" type="xsd:decimal"/>
            <xsd:element name="Street" type="xsd:string"/>
            <xsd:element name="City" type="xsd:string"
             minOccurs="0" maxOccurs="0"/>
            <xsd:element name="State" type="xsd:string"/>
            <xsd:element name="PostalCode" type="xsd:decimal"/>
            <xsd:element name="Country" type="xsd:string"/>
         </xsd:sequence>
      </xsd:restriction>
   </xsd:complexContent>
</xsd:complexType>
```

Listing 3.9 Defining complex types by restriction

The purpose of the complex content restrictions is to allow designers to restrict the content model and/or attributes of a complex type. Listing 3.9 shows how the restriction element achieves this purpose. In this example, the derived type AustralianPostalAddress contains the Number, Street, State, PostalCode, and Country elements but omits the City element. It is omitted as the value of both attributes minOccurs and maxOccurs is set to zero.

3.4.1.3 Polymorphism

One of the attractive features of XML Schema is that derived types can be used polymorphically with elements of the base type. This means that a designer can use a derived type in an instance document in place of a base type specified in the schema.

Listing 3.10 defines a variant of the PurchaseOrder type introduced in Listing 3.6 to use the base type Address for its billingAddress and shippingAddress elements.

```
<!-- Uses the data type declarations from Listing 3.8 -->

  <xsd:complexType name="PurchaseOrder">
    <xsd:sequence>
      <xsd:element name="Name" minOccurs="1" maxOccurs="1">
        <xsd:simpleType>
          <xsd:restriction base="xsd:string"/>
        </xsd:simpleType>
      </xsd:element>
      <xsd:element name="shippingAddress" type="PO:Address"
                                  minOccurs= "1" maxOccurs="1"/>
      <xsd:element name="billingAddress" type="PO:Address"
                                  minOccurs= "1" maxOccurs="1"/>
        <xsd:choice minOccurs="1" maxOccurs="1">
            <xsd:element name="BillingDate" type="xsd:date"/>
            <xsd:element name="ShippingDate" type="xsd:date"/>
        </xsd:choice>
    </xsd:sequence>
</xsd:complexType>
```

Listing 3.10 Defining types polymorphically

Since XML Schema supports polymorphism, an instance document can now use any type derived from base type Address for its billingAddress and shippingAddress elements. Listing 3.11 illustrates that the PurchaseOrder type uses the derived AustralianAddress type as its billingAddress and the derived Australian-PostalAddress type as its shippingAddress elements.

3.4.2 Importing and including schemas

W3C XML schemas provide extensive capabilities in the area of cross-domain reuse. Leveraging W3C XML schemas for cross-domain reuse implies that a schema (or sub-schema) can represent a repeatable pattern, and it can be used in different contexts and by different applications. The method of implementation is to define modular W3C XML schemas as external subschemas. When combined these modules provide the complete framework for the document module. This approach allows developers to reuse schema components and each other's schemas and thus reduces the complexity of developing schemas, while easing development, testing, and maintainability.

```
<!-- Uses type declarations from Listing 3.10 -->

<?xml version="1.0" encoding="UTF-8"?>
<PO:PurchaseOrder xmlns:
               PO="http://www.plastics_supply.com/PurchaseOrder">

    <Name> Plastic Products </Name>
    <shippingAddress xsi:type="PO:AustralianAddress">
      <Number> 459 </Number>
      <Street> Wickham st. </Street>
      <City> Fortitude Valley </City>
      <State> QLD </State>
      <PostalCode> 4006 </PostalCode>
      <Country> Australia </country>
    </shippingAddress>

    <billingAddress xsi:type="PO:AustralianAddress">
      <Number> 158 </Number>
      <Street> Edward st. </Street>
      <State> QLD </State>
      <PostalCode> 4000 </PostalCode>
      <Country> Australia </Country>
    </billingAddress>
      <BillingDate> 2002-09-15 </BillingDate>
</PO:PurchaseOrder>
```

Listing 3.11 Using polymorphism in an XML schema instance

Combining schemas can be achieved by using the `include` and `import` elements in the XSD. Through the use of these two elements, we can effectively "inherit" attributes and elements from referenced schemas.

3.4.2.1 Including schemas

The `include` element allows for modularization of schema documents by including other schema documents in a schema document that has the same target namespace. The `include` syntax targets a specific context using a namespace to provide uniqueness. This option is useful when a schema becomes large and difficult to manage. In this case it is desirable to partition the schema into separate subschemas (modules), which we can eventually combine by using the `include` element.

The declaration in Listing 3.12 illustrates that the `Customer` type has been placed in its own schema document, which has the same target namespace as the purchase order schema depicted in Listing 3.6. We also assume that the same applies for the `ProductType` type which has been placed in its own schema document and has the same target namespace as the purchase order schema (shaded in the listing).

```
<?xml version="1.0" encoding="UTF-8"?>
<xsd:schema
  xmlns:xsd="http://www.w3.org/2001/XMLSchema"
  xmlns:PO="http://www.plastics_supply.com/PurchaseOrder"
  targetNamespace="http://www.plastics_supply.com/PurchaseOrder">

  <xsd:complexType name="Customer">
      <xsd:sequence>
        <xsd:element name="Name" minOccurs="1" maxOccurs="1">
          <xsd:simpleType>
            <xsd:restriction base="xsd:string"/>
          </xsd:simpleType>
        </xsd:element>
        <xsd:element name="Address" type="PO:AddressType"
                                   minOccurs= "1" maxOccurs="1"/>
          <xsd:choice minOccurs="1" maxOccurs="1">
          <xsd:element name="BillingDate"  type="xsd:date"/>
          <xsd:element name="ShippingDate" type="xsd:date"/>
        </xsd:choice>
      </xsd:sequence>
  </xsd:complexType>
</xsd:schema>
```

Listing 3.12 Sample customer subschema

Now these two subschemas can be combined in the context of the purchase order schema using the `include` element. This is illustrated in Listing 3.13, where the two `include` statements are shaded.

Notice that in Listing 3.13 we do not need to specify the namespaces for the two included schemas, as these are expected to match the `namespace` of the purchase order schema.

3.4.2.2 Importing schemas

The `import` element is used when we wish to use schema modules that belong to different namespaces. An `import` element is used to instruct the XML parser that it should refer to components from other namespaces. The `import` element differs from the `include` element in two important ways [Walmsley 2002]. First, the `include` element can only be used within the same namespace, while the `import` element is used across namespaces. The second, subtler distinction, is their general purpose. The purpose of the `include` element is specifically to introduce other schema documents, while the purpose of the `import` element is to record dependency on another namespace, not necessarily another schema document. The `import` mechanism enables designers to combine schemas to create a larger, more complex schema. It is very useful in cases where some parts of a schema, such as address types, are reusable and need their namespace and schema.

```
<?xml version="1.0" encoding="UTF-8"?>
<xsd:schema xmlns:xsd="http://www.w3.org/2001/XMLSchema"
 xmlns:PO="http://www.plastics_supply.com/PurchaseOrder"
 targetNamespace="http://www.plastics_supply.com/PurchaseOrder">

  <xsd:include
    schemaLocation="http://www.plastics_supply.com/customerType.
    xsd"/>

  <xsd:include
    schemaLocation="http://www.plastics_supply.com/productType.
    xsd"/>

  <xsd:element name="PurchaseOrder" type="PO:PurchaseOrderType"/>

  <xsd:complexType name="PurchaseOrderType">
    <xsd:all>
      <xsd:element name="ShippingInformation" type="PO:Customer"
                               minOccurs="1" maxOccurs="1"/>
      <xsd:element name="BillingInformation" type="PO:Customer"
                               minOccurs="1" maxOccurs="1"/>
      <xsd:element name="Order" type="PO:OrderType" minOccurs="1"
                               maxOccurs="1"/>
    </xsd:all>
  </xsd:complexType>

  <xsd:complexType name="AddressType">
    <xsd:sequence>
      <xsd:element name="Street"        type="xsd:string"/>
      <xsd:element name="City"          type="xsd:string"/>
      <xsd:element name="State"         type="xsd:string"/>
      <xsd:element name="PostalCode "   type="xsd:decimal"/>
    <xsd:sequence>
  </xsd:complexType>

  <xsd:complexType name="OrderType">
    <xsd:sequence>
      <xsd:element name="Product" type="PO:ProductType"
                   minOccurs= "1" maxOccurs="unbounded"/>
    </xsd:sequence>
    <xsd:attribute name="Total">
      <xsd:simpleType>
        <xsd:restriction base="xsd:decimal">
          <xsd:fractionDigits value="2"/>
        </xsd:restriction>
      </xsd:simpleType>
    </xsd:attribute>
    <xsd:attribute name="ItemsSold" type="xsd:positiveInteger"/>
  </xsd:complexType>
</xsd:schema>
```

Listing 3.13 Using the `include` element in the purchase order schema

```
<?xml version="1.0" encoding="UTF-8"?>

<xsd:schema xmlns:xsd="http://www.w3.org/2001/XMLSchema"
 xmlns:addr=http://www.plastics_supply.com/NewAddress
 targetNamespace="http://www.plastics_supply.com/NewAddress">
 <xsd:import namespace="http://www.plastics_supply.com/Address"
             schemaLocation="addressType.xsd"/>


  <xsd:complexType name="AddressType" abstract="true">
    <xsd:sequence>
      <xsd:element name="Number" type="xsd:decimal"/>
      <xsd:element name="Street" type="xsd:string"/>
      <xsd:element name="City"   type="xsd:string" minOccurs="0"/>
    <xsd:sequence>
  </xsd:complexType>

  <xsd:complexType name="AustralianAddress">
    <xsd:complexContent>
      <xsd:extension base="addr:AddressType">
        <xsd:sequence>
           <xsd:element name="State"        type="xsd:string"/>
           <xsd:element name="PostalCode "  type="xsd:decimal"/>
           <xsd:element name="Country"      type="xsd:string"/>
        <xsd:sequence>
      </xsd:extension>
   </xsd:complexContent>
  </xsd:complextype>

  <xsd:complexType name="AustralianPostalAddress">
    < xsd:complexContent>
      <xsd:restriction base="addr:Austtralian Address">
        <xsd:sequence>
           <xsd:element name="Number"       type="xsd:decimal"/>
           <xsd:element name="Street"       type="xsd:string"/>
           <xsd:element name="State"        type="xsd:string"/>
           <xsd:element name="PostalCode "  type="xsd:decimal">
           <xsd:element name="Country"      type="xsd:string"/>
        </xsd:sequence>
      </xsd:restriction>
   </xsd:complexContent>
  </xsd:complextype>
</xsd:schema>
```

Listing 3.14 The address markup schema

Listing 3.14 defines a separate schema and namespace for all types related to addresses in the purchase order example. This schema defines a complete address markup language for purchase orders that contains all address-related elements such as the `AddressType`, `AustralianAddress`, `EuropeanAddress`, `USAddress`, `AustralianPostalAddress`, `EuropeanPostalAddress`, and so on. The namespace attribute for the address markup schema is "http://www.plastics_supply.com/Address", which is a distinct and separate namespace from that of the purchase order elements.

As the purchase order example depends on the AddressType type, we shall need to import the address markup schema into the purchase order schema as illustrated in Listing 3.15.

Listing 3.15 shows the use of both the import and the include elements. These appear together at the top level of the purchase order schema definition document. In particular, it illustrates that the import statement references the namespace and location of the schema document that contains the address markup language for purchase orders. The imported namespace needs to be assigned a prefix before we can use it. In this case it is assigned the prefix addr. In this way, the declaration of the Address element in the complex type Customer is able to reference the AddressType type by using this prefix. For reasons of brevity we included the definition of the complex type Customer as part of the purchase order schema, instead of defining it in a separate subschema document as we did with Listing 3.12.

3.5 Document navigation and transformation

In contrast to languages such as HTML, XML is primarily used to describe and contain data. Although the most obvious and effective use of XML is to describe data, other technologies such as the eXtensible Stylesheet Language Transform (XSLT) can also be used to format or transform XML content for presentation to users. XML transactions that are targeted for direct viewing by individuals will generally require an applied stylesheet transformation (by means of XSLT). The XSLT process transforms an XML structure into presentation technology such as HTML or into any other required forms and structures.

XSLT intensively uses the XML Path Language or XPath (defined as a separate specification at the W3C) to address and locate sections of XML documents [Gardner 2002]. XPath is a standard for creating expressions that can be used to find specific pieces of information within an XML document.

3.5.1 The XML Path Language

The XPath data model views a document as a tree of nodes. Nodes correspond to document components, such as elements and attributes. It is very common to think of XML documents as trees comprising roots, branches, and leaves. This is quite natural as trees are hierarchical in nature, just as XML documents are.

XPath uses genealogical taxonomy to describe the hierarchical makeup of an XML document, referring to children, descendants, parents, and ancestors [Goldfarb 2001]. The parent is the element that contains the element under discussion, while an element's list of ancestors includes its parent as the entire set of nodes preceding its parent in a directed path leading from this element up to the root. A list of descendants includes the children of an element in a direct path from this element all the way down to leaf nodes. The topmost node in XPath is known as the *root* or *document root*. The root is not an element. It is

```
<?xml version="1.0" encoding="UTF-8"?>
<xsd:schema xmlns:xsd="http://www.w3.org/2001/XMLSchema">
 targetNamespace=http://www.plastics_supply.com/PurchaseOrder
 xmlns:PO="http://www.plastics_supply.com/PurchaseOrder"
 xmlns:addr="http://www.plastics_supply.com/Address">

  <xsd:include
    schemaLocation="http://www.plastics_supply.com/
    productType.xsd"/>

  <xsd:import namespace="http://www.plastics_supply.com/Address"
    schemaLocation="http://www.plastics_supply.com/
    addressType.xsd"/>

  <xsd:element name="PurchaseOrder" type="PO:PurchaseOrderType"/>

  <xsd:complexType name="PurchaseOrderType">
    <xsd:all>
      <xsd:element name="ShippingInformation" type="PO:Customer"
                               minOccurs="1" maxOccurs="1"/>
      <xsd:element name="BillingInformation" type="PO:Customer"
                               minOccurs="1" maxOccurs="1"/>
      <xsd:element name="Order" type="OrderType" minOccurs= "1"
                               maxOccurs="1"/>
    </xsd:all>
  </xsd:complexType>

  <xsd:complexType name="Customer">
    <xsd:sequence>
      <xsd:element name="Name" minOccurs="1" maxOccurs="1">
        <xsd:simpleType>
          <xsd:restriction base="xsd:string"/>
        </xsd:simpleType>
      </xsd:element>
      <xsd:element name="Address" type="addr:AddressType"
                             minOccurs= "1" maxOccurs="1"/>
      <xsd:choice minOccurs="1" maxOccurs="1">
          <xsd:element name="BillingDate"  type="xsd:date"/>
          <xsd:element name="ShippingDate" type="xsd:date"/>
      </xsd:choice>
    </xsd:sequence>
  </xsd:complexType>

  <xsd:complexType name="OrderType">
    <xsd:sequence>
      <xsd:element name="Product" type="PO:ProductType"
                             maxOccurs="unbounded"/>
    </xsd:sequence>
    <xsd:attribute name="Total">
      <xsd:simpleType>
        <xsd:restriction base="xsd:decimal">
            <xsd:fractionDigits value="2"/>
        </xsd:restriction>
      </xsd:simpleType>
    </xsd:attribute>
    <xsd:attribute name="ItemsSold" type="xsd:positiveInteger"/>
  </xsd:complexType>
</xsd:schema>
```

Listing 3.15 A purchase order schema using `import` and `include` statements together rather a logical construct that holds the entire XML document. The *root element* is the single element from which all other elements in the XML document instance are children or descendants. The root element is itself the child of the root. The root element is also known as the *document element*, because it is the first element in a document and it contains all other elements in the document.

Figure 3.2 exemplifies the previous points as it shows an abridged version of the logical (XPath tree) structure for the instance document defined in Listing 3.7. Note that the root element in this figure is `Purchase Order`. Attributes and namespaces are associated directly with nodes (see dashed lines) and are not represented as children of an element. The document order of nodes is based on the tree hierarchy of the XML instance. Element nodes are ordered prior to their children (to which they are connected via solid lines), so the first element node would be the document element, followed by its descendants. Children nodes of a given element (as in conventional tree structures) are processed prior to sibling nodes. Finally, attributes and namespace attachments of a given element are ordered prior to the children of the element.

The code in Listing 3.7 provides a good baseline sample XML structure that we can use for defining XPath examples. Listing 3.16 illustrates a sample XPath expression and the resulting node set.

```
XPath Query#1: /PurchaseOrder/Order[2]/child::*

Resulting Node Set#1:
=====================
    <Product Name="Adjustable Worktable" Price="3000.00"
     Quantity="1"/>
```

Listing 3.16 Sample XPath query and resulting node set

The XPath query in Listing 3.16 consists of three location steps, the first one being `PurchaseOrder`. The second location step is `Order[2]`, which specifies the second `Order` element within the `PurchaseOrder`. Finally, the third location step is `child::*`, which selects all child elements of the second `Order` element. It is important to understand that each location step has a different context node. For the first location step (`PurchaseOrder`), the current context node is the root of the XML document. The context for the second location step (`Order[2]`) is the node `PurchaseOrder`, while the context for the third location step is the second `Order` node (not shown in Figure 3.2).

More information on XPath and as well as sample XPath queries can be found in books such as [Gardner 2002], [Schmelzer 2002].

3.5.2 Using XSLT to transform documents

To perform document transformation, a document developer usually needs to supply a style sheet, which is written in XSLT. The *style sheet* specifies how the XML data will be

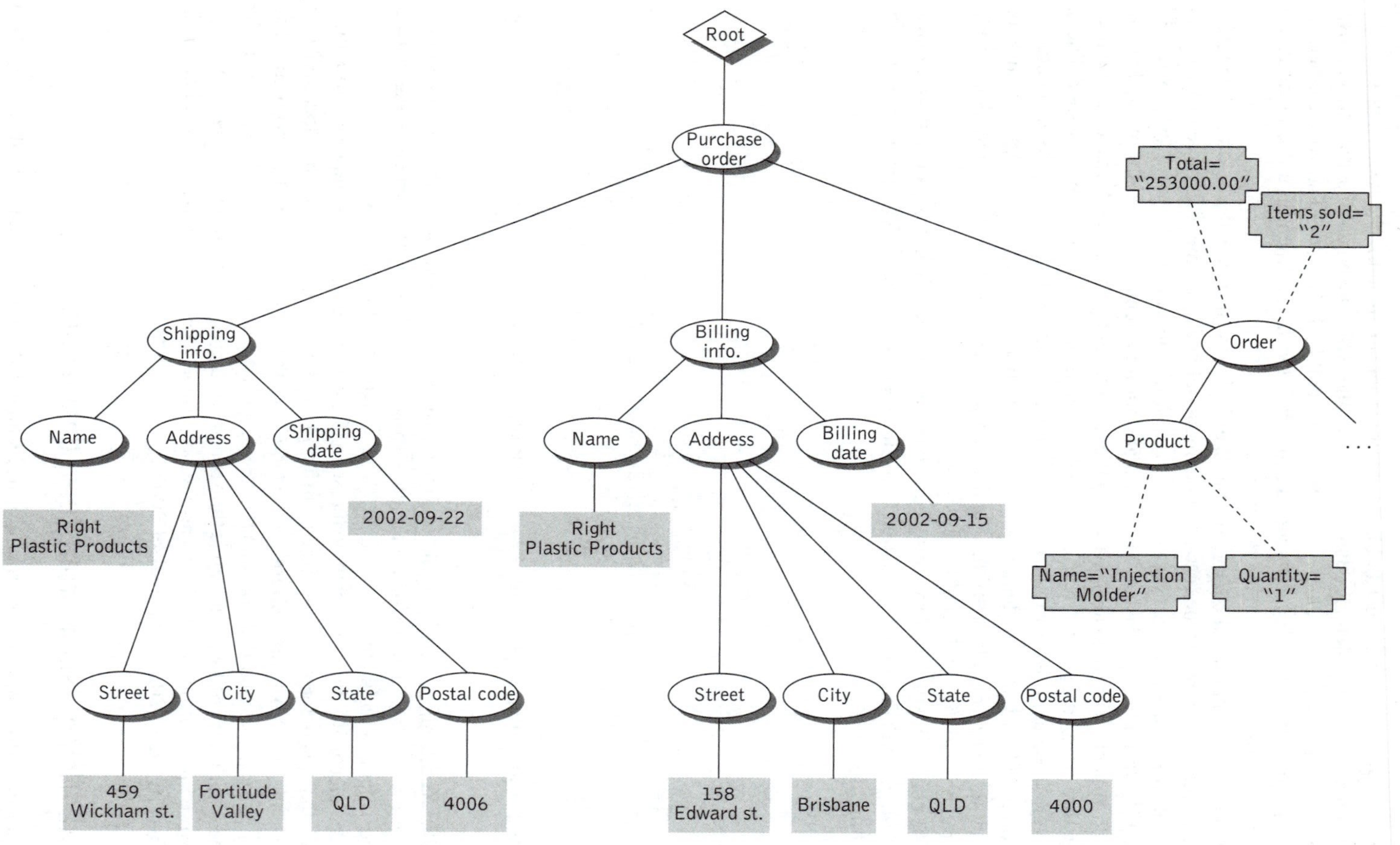

Figure 3.2 XPath tree model for instance document in Listing 3.7

displayed. XSLT uses the formatting instructions in the style sheet to perform the transformation. The converted document can be another XML document or a document in another format, such as HTML, that can be displayed on a browser. Formatting languages, such as XSLT, can access only the elements of a document that are defined by the document structure, e.g., XML schema.

An XSLT style sheet or script contains instructions that inform the transformation processor of how to process a source document to produce a target document. This makes XSLT transformations very useful for business applications. Consider, for example, XML documents generated and used internally by an enterprise that may need to be transformed into an equivalent format that customers or service providers of this enterprise are more familiar with. This can help to easily transfer information to and from an enterprise's partners.

Figure 3.3 shows an example of such a transformation. This figure shows an XML fragment which represents the billing element of a purchase order message. As shown in this message the source XML application uses separate elements to represent street numbers, street addresses, states, postal codes, and countries. The target application is shown to use a slightly different format to represent postal codes as it uses seven characters to represent postal codes by combining state information with conventional four-digit postal codes.

More information on XSLT and transformations as well as examples can be found in books such as [Gardner 2002], [Tennison 2001].

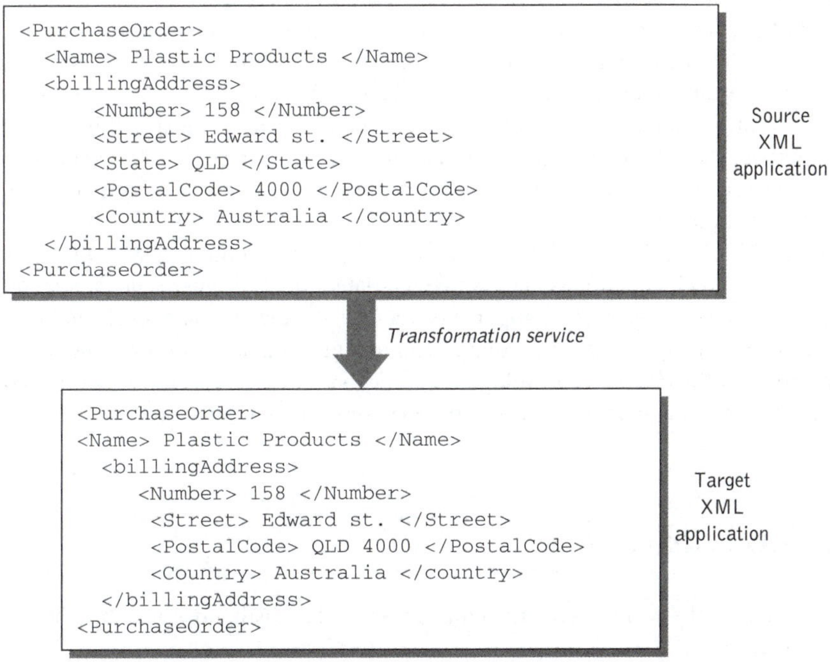

```
<PurchaseOrder>
  <Name> Plastic Products </Name>
  <billingAddress>
      <Number> 158 </Number>
      <Street> Edward st. </Street>
      <State> QLD </State>
      <PostalCode> 4000 </PostalCode>
      <Country> Australia </country>
  </billingAddress>
<PurchaseOrder>
```

Source XML application

Transformation service

```
<PurchaseOrder>
<Name> Plastic Products </Name>
  <billingAddress>
     <Number> 158 </Number>
      <Street> Edward st. </Street>
      <PostalCode> QLD 4000 </PostalCode>
      <Country> Australia </country>
  </billingAddress>
<PurchaseOrder>
```

Target XML application

Figure 3.3 Using XSLT to transform business-related information

3.6 Summary

XML is an extensible markup language used for the description and delivery of marked-up electronic text over the Web. Important characteristics of XML are its emphasis on descriptive rather than prescriptive (or procedural) markup, its document type concept, its extensibility, and its portability. In XML, the instructions needed to process a document for some specific purpose, e.g., to format it, are sharply distinguished from the descriptive markup, which occurs within the actual XML document. With descriptive instead of procedural markup the same document can readily be processed in many different ways, using only those parts of it that are considered relevant.

An important aspect of XML is its notion of a document type. XML documents are regarded as having types. Its constituent parts and their structure formally define the type of a document. XML Schema describes the elements and attributes that may be contained in a schema-conforming document and the ways that the elements may be arranged within a document structure. Schemas are more powerful when validating an XML document because of their ability to clarify data types stored within the XML document.

XML can be perceived as a dynamic trading language that enables diverse applications to exchange information flexibly and cost-effectively. XML allows the inclusion of tags pertinent to the contextual meaning of data. These tags make possible precise machine interpretation of data, fine tuning the entire process of information exchange between trading enterprises. In addition the ability of the XML schemas to reuse and refine the data model of other schema architectures enables reuse and extension of components, reduces the development cycle, and promotes interoperability.

As XML can be used to encode complex business information it is ideally suited to support open standards, which are essential to allow rapid establishment of business information exchange and interoperability. For example, XML is well suited to transactional processing in a heterogeneous, asynchronous, open, and distributed architecture that is built upon open standard technologies, such as parsers and interfaces. This applies equally well to enterprise application integration as well as to the e-business style of integration with trading partners.

The ability of XML to model complex data structures combined with the additional ability of XML Schema to reuse and refine the data model of other schema architectures enables reuse and extension of components, reduces the development cycle and promotes interoperability. It is precisely the suite of technologies that are grouped under XML that had profound influence on the development of Web services technologies and provide the fundamental building blocks for Web services and service-oriented architectures.

Review questions

- What are the two important features of XML that distinguish it from other markup languages?
- What are XML elements and what are XML attributes? Give examples of both.

- Describe URIs and XML namespaces using examples.
- What is the purpose of the XML Schema Definition Language?
- List and describe the main XML schema components.
- What are simple and what are complex XML types?
- How do you achieve reusability in XML?
- Give an example of a derived complex type.
- Define and describe the concept of polymorphism in XML.
- What is the purpose of the `include` and `import` elements in the XML Schema Definition Language? How do they differ?
- What is the purpose of the XPath data model? Describe how it views an XML document.
- How can XSLT help with document transformation?

Exercises

3.1 Define a simple purchase order schema for a hypothetical on-line grocery. Each purchase order should contain various items. The schema should allow one customer to receive the shipment of the goods and an entirely different individual, e.g., spouse, to pay for the purchase. This document should include a method of payment that allows customers to pay by credit card, direct debit, check, etc., and should also contain specific information about the products ordered, such as how much each product cost, how many items were ordered, and so on.

3.2 Extend the purchase order schema in the previous exercise to describe the case of an on-line grocery that sells products to its customers by accepting only credit cards as a payment medium. This simple order processing transaction should contain basic customer, order, and product type information as well as different methods of delivery, and a single method of payment, which includes fields for credit card number, expiration date, and payment amount. Show how this purchase order schema can import schema elements that you developed for Exercise 3.1.

3.3 Define a schema for a simple clearinghouse application that deals with credit card processing and (PIN-based) debit card processing for its customers who are electronic merchants. In order to process a credit card a merchant will need to have a valid merchant account with the clearinghouse. A merchant account is a commercial bank account established by contractual agreement between a merchant and the clearinghouse and enables a merchant that provides shopping facilities to accept credit card payments from its customers. A merchant account is required to authorize transactions. A typical response for a credit card is authorized, declined, or cancelled. When the clearinghouse processes credit card sales it returns a transaction identifier (TransID) only when a credit card sale is authorized. If the merchant needs to credit or void a transaction the TransID of the original credit card sale will be required. For simplicity assume that one credit is allowed per sale and that a credit amount cannot exceed the original sale amount. The application should be able to process a number of payments in a single transmission as a batch transaction.

3.4 Define a schema for a flight availability request application that requests flight availability for a city pair on a specific date for a specific number and type of passengers. Optional request information can include: time or time window, connecting cities, client preferences, e.g., airlines, flight types, etc. The request can be narrowed to request availability for a specific airline, specific flight, or specific booking class on a specific flight.

3.5 Define a schema for handling simple requests for the reservation of rental vehicles. The schema should assume that the customer has already decided to use a specific rental branch. It should then define all the information that is needed when requesting information about a vehicle rental. The schema should include information such as rate codes, rate type, promotional descriptions, and so on, as well as rate information that had been supplied in a previous availability response, along with any discount number or promotional codes that may affect the rate. For instance, the customer may have a frequent renter number that should be associated with the reservation. Typically rates are offered as either leisure rates or corporate rates. The schema should also define the rental period, as well as information on a distance associated with a particular rate, e.g., limited or unlimited miles per rental period, and customer preferences regarding the type of vehicle and special equipment that can be included with the reservation of a rental vehicle.

3.6 Define a simple hotel availability request schema that provides the ability to search for hotel products available for booking by specific criteria that may include: dates, date ranges, price range, room types, regular and qualifying rates, and/or services and amenities. A request can also be made for a non-room product, such as banquets and meeting rooms. An availability request should be made with the intent to ultimately book a reservation for an event or for a room stay. The schema should allow a request for "static" property data published by the hotel that includes information about the hotel facilities, amenities, services, etc., as well as "dynamic" (e.g., rate-oriented) data. For example, a hotel may have an AAA rate, a corporate rate (which it does not offer all the time), or may specify a negotiated code as a result of a negotiated rate, which affects the availability and price of the rate.

PART III

Core functionality and standards

CHAPTER 4

SOAP: Simple Object Access Protocol

Learning objectives

Conventional distributed object communication protocols, such as CORBA, DCOM, Java/RMI, and other application-to-application communication protocols for server-to-server communications, present severe weaknesses for client-to-server communications. These weaknesses are especially notable when the client machines are scattered across the Internet. Conventional distributed communications protocols have a *symmetrical* requirement: both ends of the communication link would need to be implemented under the same distributed object model and would require the deployment of libraries developed in common. To address such limitations the Simple Object Access Protocol (SOAP) was developed. SOAP facilitates interoperability among a wide range of programs and platforms, making existing applications accessible to a broader range of users.

This chapter introduces SOAP, describes its main characteristics and the structure of SOAP messages, and concentrates on the following topics:

- The use of SOAP as a messaging protocol.
- How SOAP promotes interoperability.
- The structure of SOAP messages.
- RPC and document style messages.
- Error handling in SOAP.
- The use of HTTP as transport protocol with SOAP.
- Advantages and limitations of SOAP.

4.1 Inter-application communication and wire protocols

In the emerging world of Web services, it is possible for enterprises to leverage mainstream application development tools and Internet application servers to bring about inter-application communication. This enables enterprises to conduct business electronically by making a broader range of services available faster and cheaper. This undertaking can only take place successfully if proprietary systems running on heterogeneous infrastructures are overcome. It is interesting to note that the tools and common conventions required to interconnect these systems were lacking until recently.

To address the problem of overcoming proprietary systems running on heterogeneous infrastructures, Web services rely on SOAP, an XML-based communication protocol for exchanging messages between computers regardless of their operating systems, programming environment, or object model framework. SOAP was originally an acronym for Simple Object Access Protocol (now it is just a name). SOAP is the *de facto* standard messaging protocol used by Web services. SOAP's primary application is inter-application communication. SOAP codifies the use of XML as an encoding scheme for request and response parameters using HTTP as a means for transport. In particular, a SOAP method is simply an HTTP request and response that complies with the SOAP encoding rules. A SOAP endpoint is simply an HTTP-based URL that identifies a target for method invocation.

Even though SOAP was originally an "object" access protocol, it does not mandate any object-oriented approach like CORBA does. SOAP rather defines a model for using simple request and response messages written in XML as the basic protocol for electronic communication.

SOAP provides a wire protocol in that it specifies how service-related messages are structured when exchanged across the Internet. SOAP can be defined as a lightweight wire protocol for exchanging structured and typed information back and forth between disparate systems in a distributed environment, such as the Internet or even a LAN (Local Area Network), enabling remote method invocation [Cauldwell 2001]. The term *lightweight wire protocol* means that SOAP possesses only two fundamental properties. It can send and receive HTTP (or other) transport protocol packets, and process XML messages [Scribner 2000]. This can be contrasted with distributed object architecture protocols, such as the Internet Inter-ORB Protocol (IIOP), which is the wire protocol for CORBA, where the proper run-time environments must be installed and the users have to configure their systems to accommodate the distributed infrastructure and administer these systems, in addition to managing an application's particular needs [Scribner 2000].

One distinction that many people find confusing is the difference between the wire protocol (format) and the transport protocol. Whereas the wire protocol specifies the form or shape of the data to be exchanged between disparate applications, and eventually systems, the transport protocol is the method by which that data is transferred from system to system. The transport protocol is responsible for taking its payload from its point of origin to its destination.

4.1.1 SOAP as a wire representation

SOAP makes use of *openly available* technologies that, when combined, specify a wire protocol. SOAP commonly uses HTTP to transport XML-encoded serialized method argument data from system to system. This serialized argument data is used on the remote end to execute a client's method call on that system, rather than on a local system. If HTTP is used as a SOAP transport protocol, then SOAP processing is very much aligned with the Internet, which specifies a stateless programming model. The combination of the open XML encoding style and the pervasive HTTP makes SOAP possibly the most interoperable wire protocol invented [Scribner 2000].

Wire protocols, such as SOAP, are designed to meet specific design criteria, including [Scribner 2002] compactness, protocol efficiency, coupling, scalability, and interoperability:

> *Compactness* refers to how terse a network package becomes while conveying the same information. Small degree of compactness is usually best.
>
> *Protocol efficiency* is directly related to compactness. Efficiency is rated by examining the overhead required to send the payload. The more overhead required, the less efficient the protocol is.
>
> *Coupling* is the rate at which the client application needs to adapt to changes. Loosely coupled protocols are quite flexible and can easily adapt to changes, while tightly coupled protocols require significant modifications to both the server and existing clients.
>
> *Scalability* addresses the ability of a protocol to work with a large number of potential recipients. Some protocols are limited to a few hundreds of clients, while others can easily handle millions.
>
> *Interoperability* refers to the ability of the protocol to work with a variety of computing platforms. For instance, general-purpose protocols enable clients to send information to a variety of systems.

Protocols, including XML and SOAP, generally lie on a continuum of these characteristics. No single protocol achieves all properties. For instance, XML and SOAP are both loosely coupled and interoperable. This adversely affects compactness and efficiency. Both XML and SOAP as document-based protocols are rather verbose and this makes them rather inefficient. The SOAP commonly uses HTTP and is therefore very scalable in its native form. It is far more scalable than distributed object architecture protocols.

4.2 SOAP as a messaging protocol

The goal of SOAP is to diffuse the barriers of heterogeneity that separate distributed computing platforms. SOAP achieves this by following the same recipe as other successful Web protocols: simplicity, flexibility, firewall friendliness, platform neutrality, and XML messaging-based (text-based). SOAP is simply an attempt to codify the usage of existing Internet technologies to standardize distributed communications over the Web, rather than being a new technological advancement.

A SOAP XML document instance is called a SOAP *message* (or SOAP envelope) and is usually carried as the payload of some other network protocol. As already explained, the

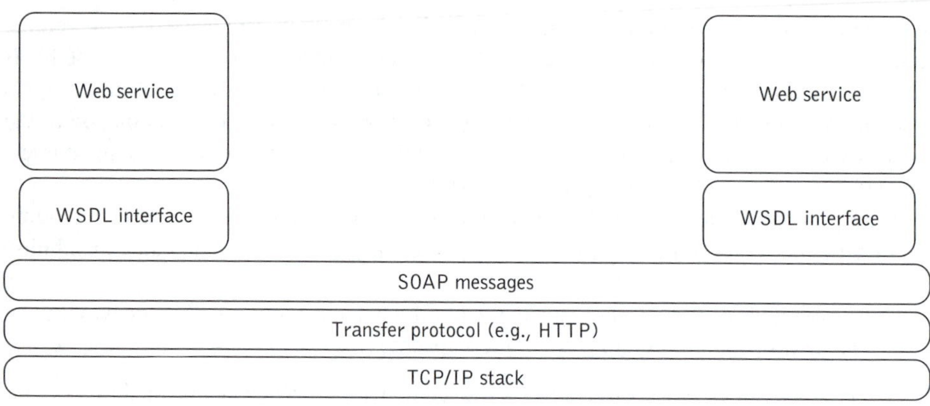

Figure 4.1 The Web services communication and messaging network

most common way to exchange SOAP messages is via HTTP, used by Web browsers to access HTML Web pages. HTTP is simply a convenient way of sending and receiving SOAP messages.

SOAP has a clear purpose: exchanging data over networks. Specifically, it concerns itself with encapsulating and encoding XML data and defining the rules for transmitting and receiving that data [Monson-Haefel 2004]. In short, SOAP is a network application protocol that is used to transfer messages between service instances described by WSDL interfaces. Figure 4.1 illustrates this situation and also shows that SOAP messages use different protocols such as HTTP to transport messages and locate the remote systems associated with interacting Web services. SOAP describes how a message is formatted but it does not specify how it is delivered. The message must be embedded in a transport-level protocol to achieve this purpose. HTTP is the most commonly used transport protocol but also other protocols, such as SMTP, FTP, or RMI, may be used.

The SOAP message, shown in Figure 4.1, becomes the body of an HTTP message and is sent to its destination. At the next layer in the protocol hierarchy illustrated in Figure 4.1, the HTTP message becomes data in a TCP stream sent over a connection. At the other end (destination) an HTTP listener passes the body of the HTTP message on to a SOAP processor that understands the syntax of SOAP messages and is capable of processing the message it receives. We shall elaborate further on this below.

SOAP is fundamentally a stateless, one-way message exchange paradigm, but applications can create more complex interaction patterns (e.g., request/response, request/multiple responses, etc.) by combining such one-way exchanges with features provided by an underlying protocol and/or application-specific information. SOAP does not itself define any application semantics such as a programming model or implementation specific semantics; rather it defines a simple mechanism that provides a modular packaging model and encoding mechanisms for encoding data within modules. This allows SOAP to be used in a large variety of systems ranging from messaging systems to RPC. It also does not concern itself with such issues as the routing of SOAP messages, reliable data transfer, firewall traversal, and so on. However, SOAP provides the framework by which application-specific information may be conveyed in an extensible manner. Also, SOAP provides a full description of the required actions taken by a SOAP node on receiving a SOAP message.

The basic requirement for an Internet node to play the role of requestor or provider in XML messaging-based distributed computing is the ability to construct and parse a SOAP message and the ability to communicate over the network by sending and receiving messages. Any SOAP run-time system executing in a Web application server performs these functions. Although SOAP may use different protocols such as HTTP, FTP, or RMI to transport messages and locate the remote system and initiate communications, its natural transport protocol is HTTP. Layering SOAP over HTTP means that a SOAP message is sent as part of an HTTP request or response, which makes it easy to communicate over any network that permits HTTP traffic (see section 4.6). SOAP uses HTTP to transport XML-encoded serialized method argument data from system to system. SOAP's serialization mechanism converts method calls to a form suitable for transportation over the network, using special XML tags and semantics. The serialized argument data is used on the remote end to execute the client's method call on that system's, rather than on the client's, local system. Because SOAP can reside on HTTP, its request/response method operates in a very similar way to HTTP. When a client makes an HTTP request, the server attempts to service the request and can respond in one of two ways. Either it can respond that communication was successful by returning the requested information. Alternatively, it can respond with a fault message notifying the client of the particular reason why the request could not be serviced.

SOAP plays the role of a *binding* mechanism between two conversing endpoints. A SOAP endpoint is simply an HTTP-based URL that identifies a target for a method invocation. It is the goal of SOAP to allow for flexible binding. For example, a particular Web service might provide two bindings. A client may submit a SOAP request using either HTTP or as an e-mail using SMTP. It is important to realize that the type of the binding used does not affect the design of the SOAP message format.

For simple Web services SOAP specifies a structure for a single message exchange. However, in many cases where business processes or complex Web services are involved there is a need to exchange multiple messages. Usually, this may be achieved using a conversational mode that has no fixed pattern. The decision as to who sends a message or when to send the next message may be determined by examining the body SOAP messages exchanged. This is due to the fact that the SOAP body carries the XML documents exchanged between interacting Web services. In other cases, there might be a predetermined pattern such as a request/response pattern, which is the simplest and most natural pattern for procedure-like invocations. This pattern is commonly known as RPC-style SOAP. We shall discuss the SOAP communication modes in section 4.4 after we examine the structure of a SOAP message.

In its most recent version (SOAP version 1.2 [Mitra 2003]), SOAP adds clear rules for supporting new transport protocols like SMTP or FTP, making it a global exchange protocol. In addition SOAP introduces the concept of intermediaries (stops between a SOAP call and the endpoint that do not affect the contents of the message, useful for information routing). This notion of endpoint means a SOAP message can send a piece of information all the way along a chain of intermediaries to a final recipient. The information concerning the various intermediaries and the data dedicated to them is found in the header of the

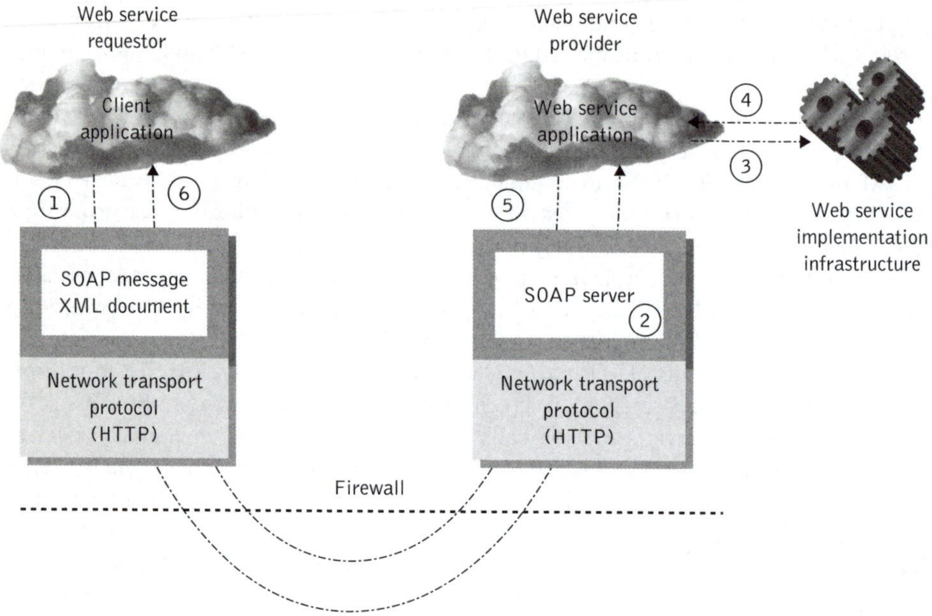

Figure 4.2 Distributed messaging using SOAP

SOAP message. The information in the body of the SOAP message is destined for the message end user.

Distributed application processing with SOAP can be achieved in terms of the basic steps illustrated in Figure 4.2 and outlined below.

A service requestor's application creates a SOAP message as a result of a request to invoke a desired Web service operation hosted by a remote service provider (1). The request is formed by the SOAP client, which is a program that creates an XML document containing the information needed to remotely invoke a method in a distributed system. The XML code in the body of the SOAP request is the location where the method request and its arguments are placed. The service requestor forwards the SOAP message together with the provider's URI (typically over HTTP) to the network infrastructure.

The network infrastructure delivers the message to the message provider's SOAP run-time system (e.g., a SOAP server) (2). The SOAP server is simply special code that listens for SOAP messages and acts as a distributor and interpreter of SOAP documents. The SOAP server routes the request message to the service provider's Web service implementation code (3). The SOAP server ensures that documents received over an HTTP SOAP connection are converted from XML to programming-language-specific objects required by the application implementing the Web services at the provider's site. This conversion is governed by the encoding scheme found within the SOAP message envelope. In doing so the SOAP server also ensures that the parameters included in the SOAP document are passed to the appropriate methods in the Web service implementation infrastructure.

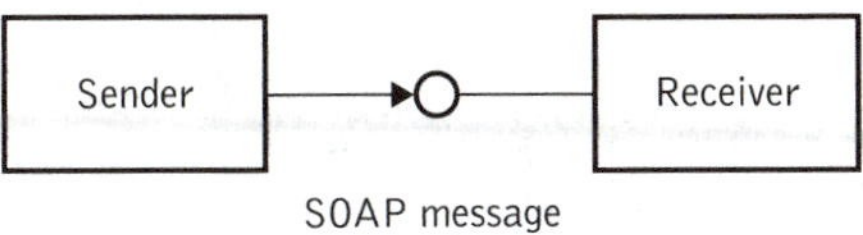

Figure 4.3 One-way messaging

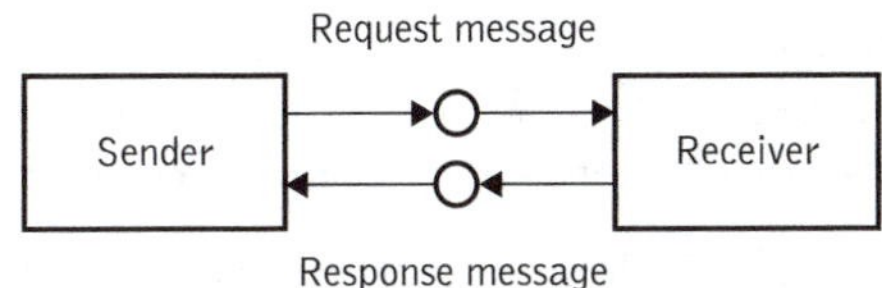

Figure 4.4 Request/response messaging exchange pattern

The Web service is responsible for processing the request and formulating a response as a SOAP message. The response SOAP message is presented to the SOAP run-time system at the provider's site with the service requestor's URI as its destination (4). The SOAP server forwards the SOAP message response to the service requestor over the network (5).

The response message is received by the network infrastructure on the service requestor's node. The message is routed through the SOAP infrastructure, potentially converting the XML response into objects understood by the source (service requestor's) application (6).

Web services can use *one-way messaging* or *request/response messaging*. In the former, SOAP messages travel in only one direction, from a sender to a receiver. In the latter, a SOAP message travels from the sender to the receiver, which is expected to send a reply back to the sender. SOAP allows for any number of message exchange patterns, of which request/response is just one. Other examples include solicit/response (the reverse of request/response), notifications, and long-running peer-to-peer conversations. Figure 4.3 illustrates a simple one-way message where the sender does not receive a response. The receiver could, however, send a response back to the sender as illustrated in Figure 4.4.

4.3 Structure of a SOAP message

The current SOAP specification v1.2 describes how the data types defined in associated XML schemas are serialized over HTTP or other transport protocols [Gudgin 2003]. Both the provider and requestor of SOAP messages must have access to the same XML schemas in order to exchange information correctly. The schemas are normally posted on the Internet, and may be downloaded by any party in an exchange of messages. A SOAP message contains a payload and every SOAP message is essentially an XML document.

A SOAP message consists of an `<Envelope>` element containing an optional `<Header>` and a mandatory `<Body>` element [Gudgin 2003]. The contents of these

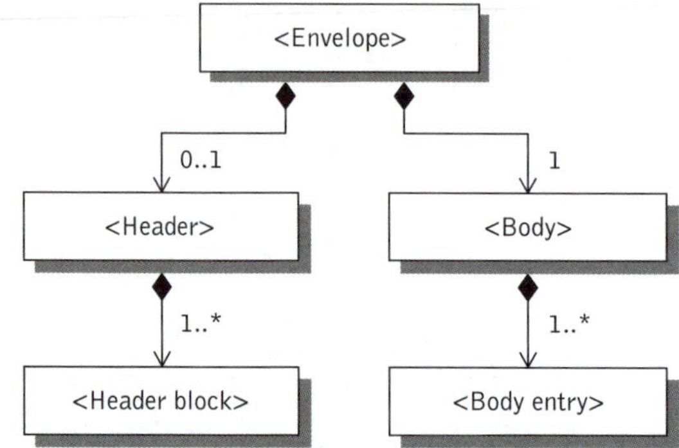

Figure 4.5 The SOAP message containment structure described in UML

elements are application defined and not a part of the SOAP specifications, although the latter do have something to say about how such elements must be handled. A SOAP `<Header>` element contains blocks of information relevant to how the message is to be processed. This provides a way to pass information in SOAP messages that is not part of the application payload. Such "control" information includes, for example, passing directives or contextual information related to the processing of the message, e.g., routing and delivery settings, authentication or authorization assertions, and transaction contexts. This allows a SOAP message to be extended in an application-specific manner. The immediate child elements of the `<Header>` element are called header blocks, and represent a logical grouping of data, which can individually be targeted at SOAP nodes that might be encountered in the path of a message from a sender to an ultimate receiver. The SOAP `<Body>` element is the mandatory element within the SOAP `<Envelope>`, which implies that this is where the main end-to-end information conveyed in a SOAP message must be carried. A pictorial representation of the SOAP message structure is shown in Figure 4.5.

4.3.1 SOAP envelope

The purpose of SOAP is to provide a uniform way to transport messages between two endpoints. The SOAP envelope serves to wrap any XML document interchange and provide a mechanism to augment the payload with additional information that is required to route it to its ultimate destination. The SOAP envelope is the single root of every SOAP message and must be present for the message to be SOAP compliant. The `<Envelope>` element defines a framework for describing what is in a message and how to process it.

Listing 4.1 shows the structure of a SOAP message. This listing shows that in SOAP the `<Envelope>` element is the root element, which may contain an optional `<Header>` section and a mandatory `<Body>` section. If a `<Header>` element is used, it must be the immediate child of the `<Envelope>` element, and precede the `<Body>` element. The `<Body>` element is shown to delimit the application-specific data. A SOAP message may have an XML declaration, which states the version of XML used and the encoding format, as shown in the snippet in Listing 4.1.

```
<?xml version="1.0" encoding="UTF-8"?>
<env:Envelope
   xmlns:env="http://www.w3.org/2003/05/soap-envelope">

   <env:Header> <!-- optional -->
    <!-- header blocks go here . . . -->
   </env:Header>

   <env:Body>
    <!-- payload or Fault element goes here . . . -->
   </env:Body>
</env:Envelope>
```

Listing 4.1 Structure of SOAP message

All elements of the SOAP envelope are defined using W3C XML Schema. Notice that the SOAP message takes full advantage of namespaces. Recall from Chapter 3 that namespaces differentiate elements and attributes with similar names, so that they can both occupy the same XML document without confusion. More importantly, namespaces allow SOAP messages to be extensible: by referencing different namespaces a SOAP message can extend its semantic scope and the receiver of the message can interpret the new message by referencing the same namespace [Schmelzer 2002].

In SOAP namespaces are declared as usual with the `xmlns` keyword. To actually identify the envelope tag as to belong to the SOAP namespace, it must contain the reference to the SOAP envelope namespace URI. The URI where the envelope schema is located for the SOAP v1.2 specification (used throughout this chapter) is `"http://www.w3.org/2003/05/soap-envelope"`. The expression `env` is used as the namespace qualifier referring to this URI. The expression `env` namespace qualifier in Listing 4.1 is shown to include not only the `<Envelope>` element but also the `<Header>` and `<Body>` sections. If a SOAP application receives a message that is based on some other namespace, it will generate a fault. This rule ensures that all conforming messages are using exactly the same namespace and XML schema, and therefore the same processing rules.

A SOAP envelope can specify a set of encoding rules serializing the application-defined XML data over the network. Both the provider and requestor must agree on the encoding rules (typically by downloading the same XML schema that defines them). To allow two or more communicating parties that agree on a specific encoding style for XML messages to express that agreement in the SOAP messages, they can use the global `encodingStyle` attribute. This attribute mandates a certain encoding style (typically defined by the schema) for the element on which it appears and all child elements thereof. Encoding style is simply a set of rules that describes how data can be expressed (serialized to XML) by the parties to enable interoperability between their systems. The attribute is "global," because it may appear at any level and on any tag of the SOAP message, including custom headers and body entries. In order to allow for added flexibility SOAP allows applications to define their own encoding style. For example, if two applications use an array as argument in a SOAP message one application may serialize the array as a sequence of rows using one set of tags while another may serialize the array as a sequence of columns using a different set of tags. The set of rules that is used must be identified using the `encodingStyle` attribute. In most cases the standard SOAP encoding rules are indicated. For more information the `encodingStyle` attribute refer to section 4.4.

SOAP defines a data model that can be used to represent arbitrary data structures, e.g., integers, arrays, records, and then it specifies the rules for transforming the instances of this model into serialized ASCII strings that are contained in SOAP messages. It is up to the client and service provider to map an instance of a data type specified in the client's or provider's representation language into an instance of the model. The term *client* in this context is associated with the initial sender of a request message. Given that the encoding rules specify the serialization of each model instance, each client's and service provider's type instance is, as a result, mapped to a serialized string. Both client and service provider must then provide serialization and deserialization mechanisms that realize that mapping. Many vendors provide programs that implement the SOAP encoding rules for simple and structured data types defined in SOAP for programming languages such as Java or C#.

```
<env:Envelope
    xmlns:env="http://www.w3.org/2003/05/soap-envelope"
    env:encodingStyle="http://schemas.xmlsoap.org/soap/
                                             encoding/">
    ...
</env:Envelope>
```

Listing 4.2 Example of a SOAP envelope

The SOAP specification allows the envelope tag to contain any number of additional, custom attributes. However, each of these custom attributes must be namespace qualified. This means that a custom prefix must be associated with the custom attribute's namespace URI through an `xmlns` declaration and that prefix must be used for the custom attribute. This is illustrated in Listing 4.2, which is a brief example of the SOAP `<Envelope>` element syntax.

4.3.2 SOAP header

SOAP divides any message into two parts contained in a SOAP `<Envelope>`: `<Header>` and `<Body>`. The `<Envelope>` may contain at most one `<Header>` child element, which contains all processing hints that are relevant for the endpoints or intermediate transport points. The `<Header>` may contain information about where the document shall be sent, where it originated, and may even carry digital signatures. This type of information must be separated from the SOAP `<Body>` which is mandatory and contains the SOAP payload (the XML document).

The purpose of the <Header> is to encapsulate extensions to the message format without having to couple them to the payload or to modify the fundamental structure of SOAP. This allows specification of additional features and functionality such as security, transactions, object references, billing, QoS attributes, and many others, which can be added over time to SOAP messages without breaking the specification. Moreover, SOAP can be used with a variety of messaging systems (asynchronous, synchronous, RPC, one way, and others), which can be combined in non-traditional ways. This allows for Web service clients to place extra data in the header of the message so that every single method call on that service does not have to accept that data as an argument. For example, the header information can be used to supply authentication credentials to a Web service. Rather than requiring every single method call on the Web service to ask for user name and password, this information can be included in the SOAP <Header>.

The SOAP <Header> provides a mechanism for providing further detailed information describing the payload being carried by the SOAP <Body>. When a <Header> is included in a SOAP message it must be the first child element of the SOAP <Envelope> element. The schema for the optional SOAP header element allows for an unlimited number of child elements to be placed within the header. The immediate child elements of the <Header> element are called *header blocks*, and represent a logical grouping of data that can individually be targeted at SOAP nodes that might be encountered in the path of a message from a sender to an ultimate receiver. Each header block in the <Header> element should have its own namespace. This is a particularly important issue since namespaces help SOAP applications identify header blocks and process them separately. A variety of standard header blocks that deal with topics such as security, transactions, and other service characteristics are in development by organizations such as W3C and OASIS. Each of the proposed standards defines its own namespaces and XML schemas, as well as processing requirements.

```
<env:Envelope
    xmlns:env="http://www.w3.org/2003/05/soap-envelope" >
     ...
    <env:Header>
       <tx:transaction-id
           xmlns:tx="http://www.transaction.com/transaction"
             env:mustUnderstand="true">
                512
       </tx:transaction-id>
       <notary:token xmlns:notary="http://www.notarization-
                                            services.com/token"
              env:mustUnderstand="true">
                 GRAAL-5YF3
       </notary:token>
    </env:Header>
     ...
</env:Envelope>
```

Listing 4.3 Example of a SOAP header

Listing 4.3 shows an example of a <Header> element involving two header blocks. The first block presumably deals with the transactional integrity rules associated with the payment of orders. The second header block includes a notarization service to associate a token with a particular purchase order, as a third-party guarantee that the purchase order was dispatched and contained the particular items that were ordered. In this way each header block provides different extensibility options by encapsulating extensions to the SOAP message format.

As already explained in the previous section, SOAP leverages the capabilities of XML namespaces and defines protocol versions, such as SOAP 1.1 versus SOAP 1.2, to be associated with the URI of the SOAP <Envelope> element. Namespaces enable a SOAP receiver to handle different versions of a SOAP message, without impairing backward compatibility or requiring different Web service endpoints for each version of a particular SOAP message. Differences in a particular version of a header block, for example, can affect how a receiver processes messages, so identifying the header-block version by its namespace enables a receiver to switch processing models, or to reject messages if it does not support the specified version. This modularity enables different parts of a SOAP message to be processed independently of other parts and to evolve separately. For instance, the version of the SOAP <Envelope> or <Header> blocks may change over time, while the structure of the application-specific contents in the <Body> element remains the same. Similarly, the application-specific contents may change while the version of the SOAP message and the header blocks do not.

The modularity of SOAP messaging permits the code that processes the SOAP messages to be also modular [Monson-Haefel 2004]. The code that processes the <Envelope> element is independent of the code that processes the <Header> blocks, which in turn is independent of the code that processes application-specific data in the SOAP <Body> element. Modularity enables developers to use different code libraries to process different parts of a SOAP message as shown in Figure 4.6, which is based on [Monson-Haefel 2004]. This figure shows the structure of a SOAP message and the code modules that are used to process each of its parts. The code modules in gray boxes are associated with namespaces used in the current SOAP message, while the code modules in white boxes represent alternatives. These alternatives are associated with different namespaces, used to process alternative versions of the SOAP message.

The SOAP <Header> element also provides for extensibility. SOAP *extensibility* refers to the fact that additional information required for a particular service, such as security requirements that the requestor be authenticated before a method is invoked or that a method must have transactional properties, can be added to SOAP without changing the body of the message that contains the information meant to be for the intended receiver of the message, e.g., the invocation information. To this end a <Header> element can contain any number of child elements, as we already explained in a previous section. This is also illustrated in Figure 4.6 where a <Header> element can contain a header block specifying a digital signature extension.

4.3.2.1 SOAP intermediaries

SOAP headers have been designed in anticipation of various uses for SOAP, many of which will involve the participation of other SOAP processing nodes – called SOAP

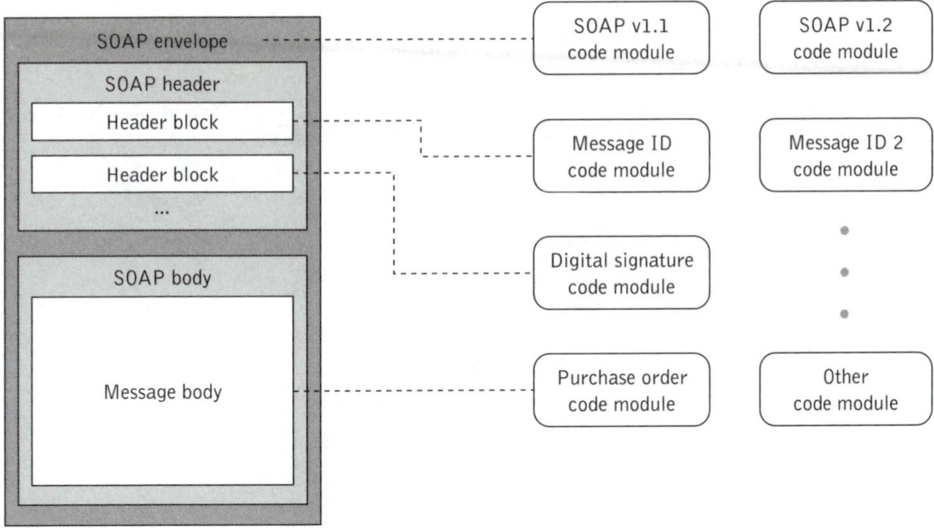

Figure 4.6 Using different code libraries to process parts of a SOAP message

intermediaries – along a message's path from an initial SOAP sender (point of origin) to an ultimate SOAP receiver (final destination). The route taken by an SOAP message, including all intermediaries it passes through, is called the SOAP *message path*.

A SOAP message travels along the message path from a sender to a receiver. All SOAP messages start with the initial sender, which creates the SOAP message, and end with the ultimate receiver. Figure 4.7 illustrates the message path for validating a purchase order SOAP message that is generated by a customer. In this figure the purchasing service node validates that the purchase order was indeed send to it by a particular customer. This intermediary service verifies that the customer's digital signature header block embedded in the SOAP message is actually valid. The SOAP message is automatically routed to the intermediary node (signature verification service), which extracts the digital signature from the SOAP message, validates it, and adds a new hear block telling the purchasing service whether the digital signature is valid.

Intermediaries can both accept and forward SOAP messages. They receive a SOAP message, process one or more of the header blocks, and send it on to another SOAP application. As a SOAP message travels along the message path, its header blocks may be intercepted and processed by any number of SOAP intermediaries along the way. Headers may be inspected, inserted, deleted, or forwarded by SOAP nodes encountered along a SOAP message path. The applications along the message path (the initial sender, intermediaries, and ultimate receiver) are commonly referred to as SOAP *nodes*. Three key use cases define the need for SOAP intermediaries: crossing trust domains, ensuring scalability, and providing value-added services along the message path.

To illustrate how nodes in a message path process a header we use Listing 4.4. In Listing 4.4, the `<Header>` element contains two header blocks, each of which is defined in its own XML namespace and which represents some aspect pertaining to the overall processing of the body of the SOAP message. For this order processing application, such

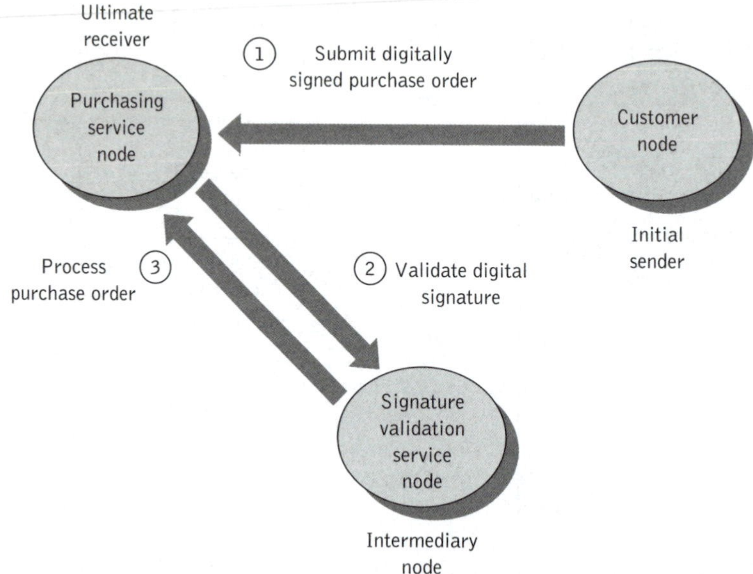

Figure 4.7 The SOAP message path for validating a purchase order

"meta" information pertaining to the overall request is an order header block, which provides an order number and time stamp for this order instance, and the customer's identity in the customer block.

In Listing 4.4 the header block's order and customer must be processed by the next SOAP intermediary encountered in the message path. The fact that the header block's purchase order and customer are targeted by the next SOAP node encountered en route is indicated by the presence of the attribute `env:role` with the value `"http://www.w3.org/2003/05/soap-envelope/role/next"`, which is a role that all SOAP nodes must be willing to play. This indicates the fact that while processing a message, a SOAP node may be willing to assume one or more *roles* to influence how SOAP header blocks and the `<Body>` are processed. Roles are given unique names (in the form of URIs) so they can be identified during processing. When a SOAP node receives a message for processing, it must first determine what roles it will assume. It may inspect the SOAP message to help make this determination. SOAP defines the (optional) `env:role` attribute that may be present in a header block, which identifies the role played by the intended target of that header block. A SOAP node is required to process a header block if it assumes the role identified by the value of the URI. How a SOAP node assumes a particular role is not a part of the SOAP specifications. The `env:role` attribute in Listing 4.4 is used in combination with the XML namespaces to determine which code module will process a particular header block.

After a SOAP node has correctly identified the header blocks (and possibly the body) targeted at itself using the `env:role` attribute, the additional attribute, `env:mustUnderstand`, in the header elements determines further processing actions that have to be taken. In order to ensure that SOAP nodes do not ignore header blocks, which

```
<?xml version="1.0" encoding="UTF-8"?>
<env:Envelope
   xmlns:env="http://www.w3.org/2003/05/soap-envelope">
 <env:Header>
  <m:order
     xmlns:m="http://www.plastics_supply.com/purchase-order"
      env:role="http://www.w3.org/2003/05/soap-envelope/role/next"
           env:mustUnderstand="true">
    <m:order-no >uuid:0411a2daa</m:order-no>
    <m:date>2004-11-8</m:date>
  </m:order>
  <n:customer xmlns:n="http://www.supply.com/customers"
     env:role="http://www.w3.org/2003/05/soap-envelope/role/next"
           env:mustUnderstand="true">
     <n:name> Marvin Sanders </n:name>
  </n:customer >
 </env:Header>
 <env:Body>
     <-- Payload element goes here -->
 </env:Body>
</env:Envelope>
```

Listing 4.4 Example of a header block with message routing

are important to the overall purpose of the application, SOAP header blocks also provide for the additional optional attribute, `mustUnderstand`. The presence of an `env:mustUnderstand` attribute with value "true" indicates that the node(s) processing the header must absolutely process these header blocks in a manner consistent with their specifications, or else not process the message at all and report a fault. For instance in Listing 4.3, the header indicates that a message is part of an ongoing (hypothetical) transaction, which uses the `mustUnderstand` attribute to require the provider to support transactions if the client wants to use them. If the provider (the recipient of the message) does not support transactions, the receipt of this message will raise an error. The special attribute called `mustUnderstand` is meant for `<Header>` child elements.

The choice of what data is placed in a header block and what goes in the SOAP body are decisions taken at the time of application design. The main point to observe is that header blocks may be targeted at various nodes that might be encountered along a message's path from a sender to the ultimate recipient. Such intermediate SOAP nodes may provide value-added services based on data in such headers.

4.3.3 SOAP body

The SOAP body is the area of the SOAP message where the application-specific XML data (payload) being exchanged in the message is placed. The `<Body>` element must be present and must be an immediate child of the envelope. It may contain an arbitrary number of child elements, called body entries, but it may also be empty. All body entries that are immediate children of the <Body> element must be namespace qualified. By default, the body content may be an arbitrary XML and is not subject to any special encoding rules. The body must be contained within the envelope, and must follow any headers that might be defined for the message.

The <Body> element contains either the application-specific data or a fault message. Application-specific data is the information that is exchanged with a Web service. It can be arbitrary XML data or parameters to a method call. The SOAP <Body> is where the method call information and its related arguments are encoded. It is where the response to a method call is placed, and where error information can be stored. The <Body> element has one distinguished root element, which is either the request or the response object. A fault message is used only when an error occurs. The receiving node that discovers a problem, such as a processing error or a message that is improperly structured, sends it back to the sender just before it in the message path. A SOAP message may carry either application-specific data or a fault, but not both. Examples involving the <Body> element are given in the following section.

4.4 The SOAP communication model

The Web services communication model describes how to invoke Web services and relies on SOAP. The SOAP communication model is defined by its communication style and its encoding style. SOAP supports two possible communication styles: RPC and document (or message). The SOAP encoding style conveys information about how the contents of a particular element in the header blocks or the <Body> element of a SOAP message are encoded. We shall first describe the SOAP encoding style and then the two SOAP communication styles in some detail.

SOAP defines encoding rules (commonly known as *encoding styles*) for serialization of a graph of typed objects. Encoding styles are about how applications on different platforms share and exchange data, even though they may not have common data types or representations. The encoding rules help in two areas. First, given a schema in any notation consistent with the type system described, a schema for an XML grammar may be constructed. Second, given a type-system schema and a particular graph of values conforming to that schema, an XML instance may be constructed, using this schema and elements in the SOAP <Body>. In reverse, given an XML instance produced in accordance with these rules, and given also the original schema, a copy of the original value graph may be constructed. The SOAP encoding rules are identified by the URI `"http://www.w3.org/2003/05/soap-encoding"`. SOAP messages using this particular serialization should indicate that fact by using the SOAP `encodingStyle` attribute. The encoding style of a particular set of SOAP elements is defined through the use of the `encodingStyle` attribute, which can be placed anywhere in the document and applies to all subordinate children of the element on which it is located.

The SOAP communication styles come in four flavors: RPC/Literal, Document/Literal, RPC/Encoded, and Document/Encoded. The WS-I Basic Profile 1.0 permits the use of RPC/Literal or Document/Literal only (which we describe in the following two sections). The RPC/Encoded and Document/Encoded modes are explicitly prohibited.

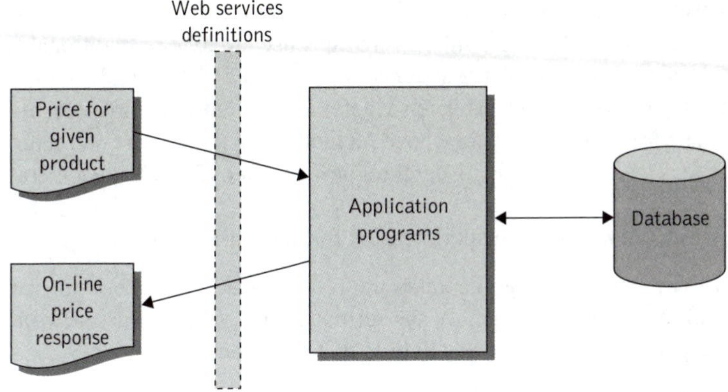

Figure 4.8 RPC-style Web service for calculating the price of a given product

4.4.1 RPC-style Web services

An RPC-style Web service appears as a remote object to a client application. The interaction between a client and an RPC-style Web service centers around a service-specific interface. Clients express their request as a method call with a set of arguments, which returns a response containing a return value. These are represented as sets of XML elements embedded within a SOAP message as shown in Figure 4.8.

RPC style supports automatic serialization/deserialization of messages, permitting developers to express a request as a method call with a set of parameters, which returns a response containing a return value. Because of this type of bilateral communication between the client and Web service, RPC-style Web services require a tightly coupled (synchronous) model of communication between the client and service provider.

```
<env:Envelope
 xmlns:SOAP="http://www.w3.org/2003/05/soap-envelope"
 xmlns:m="http://www.plastics_supply.com/product-prices">
    <env:Header>
       <tx:Transaction-id
           xmlns:t="http://www.transaction.com/transactions"
           env:mustUnderstand='1'>
               512
       </tx:Transaction-id>
    </env:Header>
    <env:Body>
       <m:GetProductPrice>
          <product-id> 450R6OP </product-id >
       </m:GetProductPrice >
    </env:Body>
</env:Envelope>
```

Listing 4.5 Example of an RPC-style SOAP body

The RPC/Literal messaging enables SOAP messages to issue method calls with parameters and return values. RPC/Literal messaging is used to expose traditional components as Web services, such as a servlet, a stateless session bean, a Java RMI object, a CORBA object, or a DCOM component [Monson-Haefel 2004]. These components do not explicitly exchange XML data; rather, they have methods with parameters and return values.

The rules for packaging an RPC/Literal request in a SOAP envelope are quite simple:

- A URI identifying the transport address for the call is required.
- An RPC request message contains the method name and the input parameters of the call. The method call is always formatted as a single structure with each in or in–out parameter modeled as a field in that structure.
- The names and the physical order of the parameters must correspond to the names and physical order of the parameters in the method being invoked.
- An RPC response message contains the return value and any output parameters (or a fault). Method responses are similar to method calls in that the structure of the response is modeled as a single structure with a field for each parameter in the method signature.

Listing 4.5 is an example of a SOAP `<Body>` specification. It illustrates a price quote service that requests the product price be associated with a specified plastic product. As shown from this listing, the SOAP `<Body>` element contains the actual method call (as its first child element). Notice the existence of the message namespace qualifier (`m:`), which is part of the information needed for the method call to be successful. The namespace identifies the URI of the target object. In addition, the method call requires the method name (`GetProductPrice`) and the parameters (`product-id`).

Once a SOAP message containing a call body (a method element and arguments in the `<Body>` element) has been sent, it is reasonable to expect that a response message will ensue. The response message will contain a `<Body>` element that includes the results of the remote method call. The response message corresponding to the price quote request made in Listing 4.5 could look like the response in Listing 4.6.

```
<env:Envelope
 xmlns:SOAP="http://www.w3.org/2003/05/soap-envelope"
 xmlns:m="http://www.plastics_supply.com/product-prices">
    <env:Header>
       <--! - Optional context information -->
    </env:Header>
    <env:Body>
       <m:GetProductPriceResponse>
          <product-price> 134.32 </product-price>
       </m:GetProductPriceResponse>
    </env:Body>
</env:Envelope>
```

Listing 4.6 Example of a SOAP RPC response message

A useful feature of the HTTP binding when RPC-style messages are transmitted is that it provides a way to automatically associate the request with the corresponding response. This feature is important for applications where a client communicates with multiple providers. In this case an application may have several outstanding requests and it is necessary to correlate an arriving response with its corresponding request.

4.4.2 Document (message)-style Web services

SOAP can also be used for exchanging documents containing any kind of XML data. This enables complete reuse of code, from systems of any type, both within an enterprise and between business partners by fostering transparent integration to heterogeneous systems and infrastructures. Unlike some other routed messaging and distributed access protocols, e.g., Java/RMI or CORBA's protocol, SOAP provides no means for encoding source and destination information into the envelope. Rather, it is up to the individual client of SOAP to decide where and how the information is to be transmitted. For instance, in the case of Web service applications, the Web services infrastructure determines how and where to send the SOAP messages. Typically, sending non-coded XML content in the body is known as document-style SOAP, since it focuses on the message as an XML document rather than an abstract data model that happens to be encoded into XML. With document-style SOAP applications, there are no restrictions on the contents of the SOAP `<Body>` element.

Document-style Web services are message driven. When a client invokes a message-style Web service, the client typically sends it an entire document, such as a purchase order, rather than a discrete set of parameters, see Figure 4.9. The Web service is sent an entire document, which it processes; however, it may or may not return a response message. This style is thus asynchronous in that the client invoking the Web service can continue with its computation without waiting for a response. A client that invokes a Web service does not need to wait for a response before it continues with the remainder of its application. The response from the Web service, if any, may appear at any time later. Unlike the RPC style, the document style does not support automatic serialization/

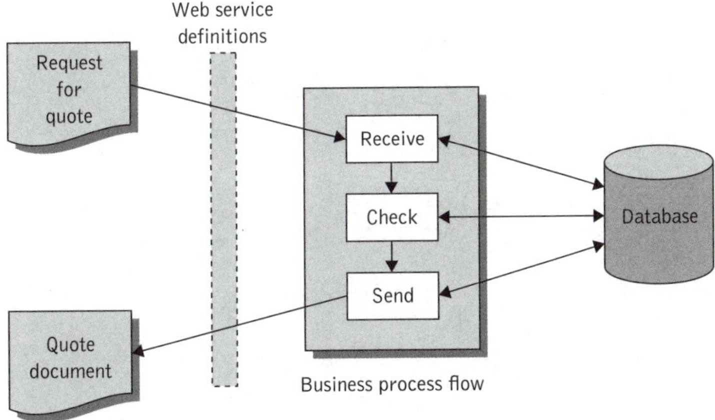

Figure 4.9 Processing a request for a price quote

deserialization of messages. Rather it assumes that the contents of the SOAP message are well-formed XML documents. For instance, a set of XML elements that describes a purchase order, embedded within a SOAP message, is considered an XML document fragment. In fact, the purchase order SOAP message, which is used as an example throughout this chapter, is a Document/Literal message.

In the Document/Literal mode of messaging, a SOAP `<Body>` element contains an XML document fragment, a well-formed XML element that contains arbitrary application data that belongs to an XML schema and namespace separate from that of the SOAP message. The `<Body>` element reflects no explicit XML structure. The SOAP run-time environment accepts the SOAP `<Body>` element as it stands and hands it over to the application it is destined for unchanged. There may or may not be a response associated with this message.

Listing 4.7 shows a purchase order SOAP message, which contains a purchase order XML document fragment ordering two injection molders of a certain type on behalf of a plastics manufacturing company. This application data upload scenario is not very well suited for an RPC-like request, such as the one shown in Listing 4.6. Instead, the application aims to transfer the application data in one piece to a service provider for further processing. Under

```
<env:Envelope
 xmlns:SOAP="http://www.w3.org/2003/05/soap-envelope">

    <env:Header>
      <tx:Transaction-id
          xmlns:t="http://www.transaction.com/transactions"
          env:mustUnderstand='1'>
              512
    </env:Header>
    <env:Body>
      <po:PurchaseOrder orderDate="2004-12-02"
          xmlns:m="http://www.plastics_supply.com/POs">
          <po:from>
            <po:accountName> RightPlastics </po:accountName>
            <po:accountNumber> PSC-0343-02 </po:accountNumber>
          </po:from>
          <po:to>
            <po:supplierName> Plastic Supplies Inc.
                                                  </po:supplierName>
            <po:supplierAddress> Yara Valley Melbourne
                                              </po:supplierAddress>
          </po:to>
          <po:product>
            <po:product-name> injection molder </po:product-name>
            <po:product-model> G-100T </po:product-model>
            <po:quantity> 2 </po:quantity>
          </po:product>
      </ po:PurchaseOrder >
    </env:Body>
</env:Envelope>
```

Listing 4.7 Example of a document-style SOAP body

this scenario a document-style SOAP message carrying the entire application data as part of one concise, self-contained XML document (called purchase order) is the preffered option.

4.4.3 Communication modes and messaging exchange patterns

Some people often confuse Document/Literal and RPC/Literal modes of messaging with the one-way and request/response message exchange patterns, although the concepts are quite distinct. When the SOAP communication mode is either Document/Literal or RPC/Literal, we usually describe the payload of the SOAP message: an XML document fragment or an XML representation of the parameters and return values associated with an RPC. In contrast, the one-way and request/response message exchange patterns refer to the flow of messages, not their contents. One-way messaging is unidirectional, while request/response is bidirectional. The Document/Literal mode of communication can be used with either one-way or request/response messaging. The RPC/Literal mode of messaging can also be used with either one-way or request/response messaging, although it is usually used with request/response messaging.

4.5 Error handling in SOAP

SOAP provides a model for handling situations when faults arise in the processing of a message. SOAP distinguishes between the conditions that result in a fault and the ability to signal that fault to the originator of the faulty message or another node. The SOAP `<Body>` element has another distinguishing role in that it is the place where fault information is placed.

The SOAP fault model requires that all SOAP-specific and application-specific faults be reported using a special-purpose element called `env:Fault`. The `env:Fault` element is a reserved element predefined by the SOAP specification whose purpose is to provide an extensible mechanism for transporting structured and unstructured information about problems that have arisen during the processing of a SOAP message.

Listing 4.8 shows a SOAP message returned in response to the RPC request in Listing 4.5 that indicates a failure to process the RPC. The `env:Fault` element in this figure is shown to be carried within the `<Body>` element. The `env:Fault` element contains two mandatory sub-elements, `env:Code` and `env:Reason`, and (optionally) application-specific information in the `env:Detail` sub-element. In Listing 4.8, the immediate sub-element of the `env:Fault` is shown to be an `env:Code` element. This element contains two sub-elements, a mandatory element called `env:Value` and an optional one called `env:Subcode`. The `env:Value` element contains a number of standardized fault codes (values) in the form of XML qualified names (QNames) each of which identifies the kind of error that occurred. The value `env:Sender` indicates that the sender of the message incorrectly formed the message (syntax error) or the message was lacking information (missing parameters or authentication information). In addition, the `env:Subcode` element indicates that an `InvalidPurchaseOrder` error defined by the namespace `"http://www.plastics_supply.com/product-prices"` is the cause of the failure to process the request. The `env:Reason` sub-element contains a human-readable description that gives an account of the fault situation. Finally, the `env:Detail` element, when present, is a place where application-specific error information can be placed. This error

```
<env:Envelope
 xmlns:SOAP="http://www.w3.org/2003/05/soap-envelope"
 xmlns:m="http://www.plastics_supply.com/product-prices">
    <env:Header>
       <tx:Transaction-id
           xmlns:t="http://www.transaction.com/transactions"
           env:mustUnderstand='1'>
               512
       </tx:Transaction-id>
    </env:Header>
    <env:Body>
       <env:Fault>
          <env:Code>
             <env:Value>env:Sender</env:Value>
             <env:Subcode>
                <env:Value> m:InvalidPurchaseOrder </env:Value>
             </env:Subcode>
          </env:Code>
          <env:Reason>
             <env:Text xml:lang="en-UK"> Specified product
              did not exist </env:Text>
          </env:Reason>
          <env:Detail>
            <err:myFaultDetails
              xmlns:err="http://www.plastics_supply.com/
              faults">
              <err:message> Product number contains invalid
              characters
              </err:message>
              <err:errorcode> 129 </err:errorcode>
            </err:myFaultDetails>
          </env:Detail>
       </env:Fault>
    </env:Body>
</env:Envelope>
```

Listing 4.8 Example of a fault SOAP message

information is not likely to be generally understood by all SOAP nodes, only nodes aware of the specific application that generated the error information.

4.6 SOAP over HTTP

SOAP codifies the use of XML as an encoding scheme for request and response parameters typically using HTTP as a transport protocol to reach any destination in the Internet without needing any additional wrapping or encoding. In particular, a SOAP method is simply an HTTP request and response that complies with the SOAP encoding rules, while a SOAP endpoint is simply an HTTP-based URL that identifies a target for method invocation. SOAP does not require that a specific object be tied to a given endpoint. Rather, it is up to the implementer to decide how to map the object endpoint identifier onto a provider-side object.

In the following we examine briefly the concept of HTTP binding with the SOAP request/response message exchange pattern using the HTTP POST method. Note that the use of this message exchange pattern in the SOAP HTTP binding is available to all applications, whether or not they involve the exchange of general XML data or RPCs encapsulated in SOAP messages. SOAP requests are transported in the body of an HTTP POST method, which transmits the request content in the body of the HTTP request message. With POST, the SOAP envelope becomes the data part of an HTTP request message. The SOAP response is returned in the HTTP response (see Figure 4.10).

The code snippet in Listing 4.9 illustrates the use of the purchase order SOAP RPC request message depicted in Listing 4.5 within an HTTP POST operation, which means the message is being posted to some service provider. When RPC-style SOAP is used to format the SOAP message, for instance the message in Listing 4.9, a procedure is being invoked and results are generated which are returned in a SOAP response message. The SOAP response (see Listing 4.10) is carried in the data part of the HTTP response.

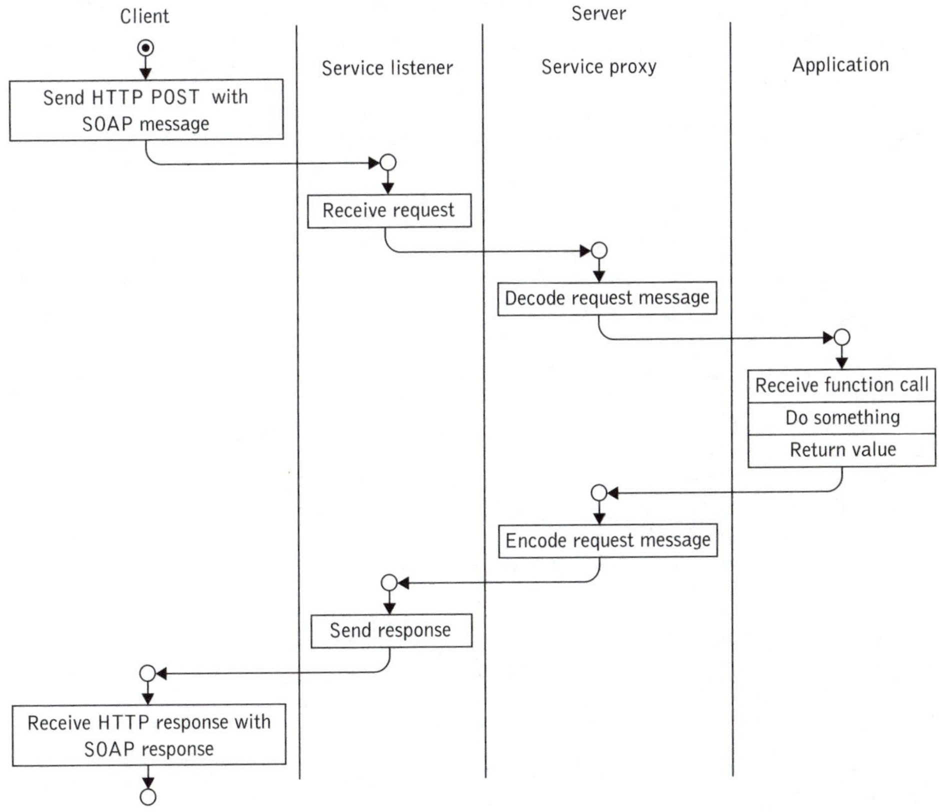

Figure 4.10 Usage of the SOAP HTTP POST method

```
POST /Purchase Order HTTP/1.1
Host: http://www.plastics_supply.com  <! - Service provider -- >
Content-Type:application/soap+xml;
charset = "utf-8"
Content-Length: nnnn

<?xml version="1.0" ?>
<env:Envelope
 xmlns:SOAP="http://www.w3.org/2003/05/soap-envelope"
 xmlns:m="http://www.plastics_supply.com/product-prices">
    <env:Header>
       <tx:Transaction-id
           xmlns:t="http://www.transaction.com/transactions"
           env:mustUnderstand='1'>
               512
       </tx:Transaction-id>
    </env:Header>
    <env:Body>
       <m:GetProductPrice>
          <product-id>  450R6OP  </product-id >
       </m:GetProductPrice >
    </env:Body>
</env:Envelope>
```

Listing 4.9 Sample HTTP/SOAP enveloped request

```
HTTP/1.1 200 OK
Content-Type:application/soap+xml;
charset = "utf-8"
Content-Length: nnnn

<?xml version="1.0" ?>
<env:Envelope
 xmlns:SOAP="http://www.w3.org/2003/05/soap-envelope"
 xmlns:m="http://www.plastics_supply.com/product-prices">
    <env:Header>
       <--! - Optional context information -->
    </env:Header>
    <env:Body>
       <m:GetProductPriceResponse>
          <product-price> 134.32 </product-price>
       </m:GetProductPriceResponse>
    </env:Body>
</env:Envelope>
```

Listing 4.10 RPC return sent by the purchase order service application

Listing 4.10 shows the RPC return sent by the purchase order service application in the corresponding HTTP response to the request from Listing 4.6. SOAP, using HTTP transport, follows the semantics of the HTTP status codes for communicating status information in HTTP. For example, the 200 series of HTTP status codes indicate that the client's request was successfully received, understood, and accepted.

While it is important to understand the SOAP foundation for services, most Web service developers will not have to deal with this infrastructure directly. Most Web services use optimized SOAP bindings generated from WSDL. In this way, SOAP implementations can self-configure exchanges between Web services while masking most of the technical details.

4.7 Advantages and disadvantages of SOAP

As with any other protocol, several aspects of using SOAP can be seen as advantages, whereas other aspects can be seen as limitations. The primary advantages of SOAP are summarized as follows:

- Simplicity: SOAP is simple as it based on XML, which is highly structured and easy to parse.
- Portability: SOAP is portable without any dependencies on the underlying platform like byte-ordering issues or machine-word widths. Today, XML parsers exist for virtually any platform from mainframes to write-watch-size devices.
- Firewall-friendly: Posting data over HTTP means not only that the delivery mechanism is widely available but also that SOAP is able to get past firewalls that pose problems for other methods.
- Use of open standards: SOAP uses the open standard of XML to format the data, which makes it easily extendable and well supported.
- Interoperability: SOAP is built on open, rather than vendor-specific, technologies and facilitates true distributed interoperability and loosely coupled applications. Because SOAP is a wire protocol based on XML and HTTP, it is possibly the most widely interoperable protocol to date and can be used to describe message exchanges between autonomous technical environments and highly diverse enterprise applications.
- Universal acceptance: SOAP is the most widely accepted standard in the message communication domain.
- Resilience to changes: Changes to the SOAP infrastructure will likely not affect applications using the protocol, unless significant serialization changes are made to the SOAP specification.

There are, however, several aspects of SOAP that can be considered as disadvantageous. These include [Scribner 2000] the following:

- SOAP was initially tied to HTTP and this mandated a request/response architecture that was not appropriate for all situations. HTTP is a relatively slow protocol and of course the performance of SOAP suffered. The latest version of the SOAP specification loosens this requirement.
- SOAP is stateless. The stateless nature of SOAP requires that the requesting application must reintroduce itself to other applications when more connections are required as if it had never been connected before. Maintaining the state of a connection is desirable when multiple Web services interact in the context of business processes and transactions.
- SOAP serializes by value and does not support serialization by reference. Serialization by value requires that multiple copies of an object will, over time, contain state information that is not synchronized with other dislocated copies of the same object. This means that currently it is not possible for SOAP to refer or point to some external data source (in the form of an object reference).

4.8 Summary

SOAP is a lightweight protocol for exchange of information in a decentralized, distributed environment. SOAP defines a simple and extensible XML messaging framework that can be used over multiple protocols with a variety of different programming models. SOAP messages are effectively service requests sent to some endpoint on a network. That endpoint may be implemented in any number of ways – Remote Procedure Call server, Component Object Model (COM) object, Java servlet, Perl script – and may be running on any platform. Thus, SOAP specifies a wire protocol for facilitating highly distributed applications and is all about interoperability between applications running on potentially disparate platforms using various implementation technologies in various programming languages.

SOAP is fundamentally a stateless, one-way message exchange paradigm, but applications can create more complex interaction patterns (e.g., request/response, request/multiple responses, etc.) by combining such one-way exchanges with features provided by an underlying protocol and/or application-specific information. SOAP is silent on the semantics of any application-specific data it conveys as it is on issues such as the routing of SOAP messages, reliable data transfer, firewall traversal, etc. However, SOAP provides the framework by which application-specific information may be conveyed in an extensible manner. Also, SOAP provides a full description of the required actions taken by a SOAP node on receiving a SOAP message.

SOAP defines a complete processing model that outlines how messages are processed as they travel through a path. Overall, SOAP provides a rich and flexible framework for defining higher-level application protocols that offer increased interoperability in distributed, heterogeneous environments.

SOAP consists of three parts. An envelope provides a mechanism to augment the payload with additional information that is required to route it to its ultimate destination. The `<Header>` element contains all processing hints that are relevant for the endpoints or intermediate transport points and provides an extension hook that allows SOAP to be extended in arbitrary ways to specify security, transactional, and other conventions. Finally, the `<Body>` element carries the application-specific XML data being exchanged.

Review questions

- What are wire protocols and what is the purpose of SOAP?
- What does a stateless one-way exchange protocol do?
- Describe how SOAP processes distributed applications.
- Describe how SOAP works with WSDL.
- What are the two most popular forms of messaging used with SOAP?
- List and describe the elements in a SOAP message.
- How is modularity achieved with SOAP?
- Give an example of a SOAP intermediary and explain how it functions.
- Describe the two SOAP communication models.
- How is HTTP used with SOAP?
- How does SOAP achieve interoperability?
- Describe how SOAP achieves serialization.

Exercises

4.1 Write a simple SOAP program that returns information about commercial flights from the XML Schema of Exercise 3.4.

4.2 Write a simple SOAP program that charges the credit card of a traveler that made a reservation for a particular trip.

4.3 Write a simple SOAP program that returns the value of a particular stock ticker symbol.

4.4 Assume that you have written a simple Java method that checks the status of an order you have placed with the following signature `checkOrderStatus(String OrderNumber, String companyID)` that can be invoked with the following arguments: `("ZRA56782C", "Mega Electronics Ltd.")`. Write a simple method embedded within a SOAP message that achieves the same result.

4.5 Write a SOAP message that declines charging the credit card of a client in Exercise 4.2 due to an invalid card number.

4.6 Write a simple SOAP program that:

(a) Uses an RPC-style message to check the inventory for a particular product. The message should accept two arguments: the product identifier and the number of products to be shipped.

(b) Converts the SOAP RPC-style message into an equivalent SOAP document-style message.

CHAPTER 5

Describing Web services

Learning objectives

In the previous chapter we have explained how SOAP can be used to encapsulate XML data exchanged between any two Web services. SOAP does not, however, describe the functional characteristics of Web services and how data may be exchanged between interacting services. Thus, a SOAP service requires some documentation detailing the service operations exposed along with their parameters. A service description language addresses this problem. A service description language is an XML-based language that describes the mechanics of interacting with a particular Web service. It essentially specifies a "contract" that governs the interaction between requestor and provider parties – and not information that is relevant only to one party or the other, such as internal implementation details.

This chapter concentrates on describing the Web Services Description Language, an XML dialect for describing Web services. In this chapter we focus on WSDL version 1.1, which is being standardized by W3C and has found wide acceptance and support from many vendors. Another reason for this decision is that the Business Process Execution Language, BPEL, which we discuss in Chapter 9, is based on WSDL version 1.1.

After completing this chapter readers will understand the following key concepts:

- Why a Web services description language is needed.
- The Web Services Description Language.
- The difference between a Web services interface definition and a Web services implementation.
- Defining Web services interfaces and implementations in WSDL.
- The WSDL message exchange conventions.
- How WSDL accommodates non-functional service characteristics.

5.1 Why is a service description needed?

To develop service-based applications and business processes, which comprise service assemblies, Web services need to be described in a consistent manner. In this way Web services can be published by service providers, discovered by service clients and developers, and assembled in a manageable hierarchy of composite services that are orchestrated to deliver value-added service solutions and composite application assemblies. However, in order to accomplish this, consumers must determine the precise XML interface of a Web service along with other miscellaneous message details a priori. In the Web services world, XML Schema can partially fill this need as it allows developers to describe the structure of XML messages understood by Web services. However, XML Schema alone cannot describe important additional details involved in communicating with a Web service such as service functional and non-functional characteristics (see section 1.8) or service policies.

Service description is a key to making the SOA loosely coupled and reducing the amount of required common understanding, custom programming, and integration between the service provider and the service requestor's applications. Service description is a machine-understandable specification describing the structure, operational characteristics, and non-functional properties of a Web service. It also specifies the wire format and transport protocol that the Web service uses to expose this functionality. It can also describe the payload data using a type system. The service description combined with the underlying SOAP infrastructure sufficiently isolates all technical details, e.g., machine- and implementation-language-specific elements, from the service requestor's application and the service provider's Web service. In particular, it does not mandate any specific implementation on the service requestor side provided that the contract specified in a standard service description language is abided by. Later in the book we shall discover that service description may also include metadata, behavioral properties, and descriptions of policies (see Chapters 13 and 15).

5.2 WSDL: Web Services Description Language

To use SOAP with a particular Web service would require some documentation explaining the structure of SOAP messages, which protocol will be employed (HTTP or SMTP, for instance), operations exposed along with their parameters in a machine-understandable standard format, and the Internet address of the Web service in question. WSDL makes it easy to reap the benefits of SOAP by providing a way for Web services providers and users of such services to work together easily. WSDL is the service representation language used to describe the details of the complete interfaces exposed by Web services and thus is the means to accessing a Web service. It is through this service description that the service provider can communicate all the specifications for invoking a particular Web service to the service requestor. For instance, neither the service requestor nor the provider should be aware of each other's technical infrastructure, programming language, or distributed object framework (if any). Although WSDL has been designed such that it can express bindings to protocols other than SOAP, our main concern in this chapter is WSDL as it relates to SOAP over HTTP.

WSDL is an XML-based specification schema for describing the public interface of a Web service. This public interface can include operational information relating to a Web service such as all publicly available operations, the XML message protocols supported by the Web service, data type information for messages, binding information about the specific transport protocol to be used, and address information for locating the Web service. WSDL allows the specification of services in terms of XML documents for transmission under SOAP. Although a Web service description in WSDL is written exclusively from the point of view of the Web service (or the service provider that publishes that service), it is inherently intended to constrain both the service provider and the service requestor that make use of that service. This implies that WSDL represents a "contract" between the service requestor and the service provider, in much the same way that an interface in an object-oriented programming language, e.g., Java, represents a contract between client code and the actual object itself. The prime difference is that WSDL is platform and language independent and is used primarily (but not exclusively) to describe SOAP-enabled services. This situation is illustrated in Figure 5.1. The Web service description is therefore concerned only with information that both parties must agree upon – not information that is relevant only to one party or the other, such as internal implementation details. Essentially, WSDL is used to describe precisely *what* a service does, i.e., the operations the service provides, *where* it resides, i.e., details of the protocol-specific address, e.g., a URL, and *how* to invoke it, i.e., details of the data formats and protocols necessary to access the service's operations.

WSDL provides a mechanism by which service providers can describe the basic format of Web requests over different protocols (e.g., SOAP) or encoding (e.g., Multipurpose Internet Messaging Extensions or MIME). It also allows most of the WSDL elements to

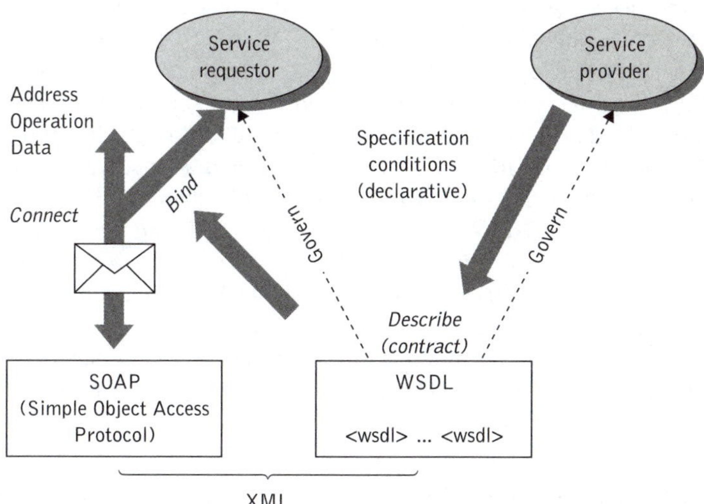

Figure 5.1 WSDL service description governing interaction between a service requestor and a service provider

be extended with elements from other namespaces. The language specification further defines standard extensions for SOAP, HTTP GET/POST operations, as well as MIME attachments. Extensibility is a useful feature as extensibility elements can be commonly used to specify some technology-specific binding. They allow innovation in the area of network and message protocols without having to revise the base WSDL specification.

WSDL is used simply to describe operations. In doing so it does not indicate the order of execution of these operations. This is the responsibility of BPEL, which we shall examine in Chapter 9.

WSDL has unique capabilities that make it a useful and flexible language. Because it is based on XML, instance documents can be validated against a schema as well as leverage the flexibility of namespaces. WSDL documents can be separated into distinct sections that isolate the argument types, the operational interface, the message encoding and transport format, and the service location. In fact, the WSDL specification can be conveniently divided into two parts: the service interface definition (abstract interface) and the service implementation (concrete endpoint). This enables each part to be defined separately and independently, and reused by other parts:

- The *service interface definition* describes the general Web service interface structure. This contains all the operations supported by the service, the operation parameters, and abstract data types.
- The *service implementation part* binds the abstract interface to a concrete network address, to a specific protocol, and to concrete data structures. A Web service client may bind to such an implementation and invoke the service in question.

The service interface definition together with the service implementation definition make up a complete WSDL specification of the service. The combination of these two parts contains sufficient information to describe to the service requestor how to invoke and interact with the Web service at a provider's site. Using WSDL, a requestor can locate a Web service and invoke any of the publicly available operations. With WSDL-aware tools, this process can be entirely automated, enabling applications to easily integrate new services with little or no manual coding. If a service requestor's environment supports automated discovery of Web services, the service requestor's application can then point to the service provider's WSDL definitions and generate proxies for the discovered Web service definitions automatically. This simplifies the invocation of Web services by the service requestor's applications as it eliminates the need for constructing complex calls and thus saves many hours of coding.

There are several design decisions that lie behind the development of WSDL; platform and language independence, which we examined earlier, is one of the most important ones. Others include: support for multiple protocols and encoding schemes, extensibility, uniform support for messages and RPC constructs, and no ordering of operations. We shall examine these briefly in turn.

5.2.1 WSDL interface definition

Service clients interact with a Web service by means of invoking its operations. Related operations are grouped into the interfaces of the Web service. Clients must know not only the interfaces of a Web service and the operations it contains, but also what communication protocol to use for sending messages to the service, along with the specific mechanics involved in using the given protocol, such as the use of commands, headers, and error codes. A binding specifies the concrete details of what is transferred on the wire by outlining how to map abstract messages onto a particular network-level communication protocol. A binding also influences the way abstract messages are encoded on the wire by specifying the style of service (WSDL serves as a unifying substrate to support both messaging and synchronous RPC-like conventions to process requests) and the encoding mechanism (literal versus encoded). A service can support multiple bindings for a given interface, but each binding should be accessible at a unique address identified by a URI, also commonly referred to as a *service endpoint*.

WSDL specifies a grammar and syntax that describes Web services as a collection of communicating endpoints (see also section 7.2.1 that describes an addressing scheme for Web service resources). WSDL is layered on top of the XML schema and provides the means to group messages into operations and operations into interfaces. The data being exchanged between the endpoints is specified as part of *messages* and every kind of processing activity allowed at an endpoint is considered as an *operation*. Collections of permissible operations at an endpoint are grouped together into *port types*. WSDL also provides a way to define bindings for each interface and protocol combination along with the endpoint address for each one. This situation is illustrated in Figure 5.2. A complete WSDL definition contains all of the information necessary to invoke a Web service.

The Web service interface definition describes messages, operations, and port types in a platform- and language-independent manner. The Web service interface definition

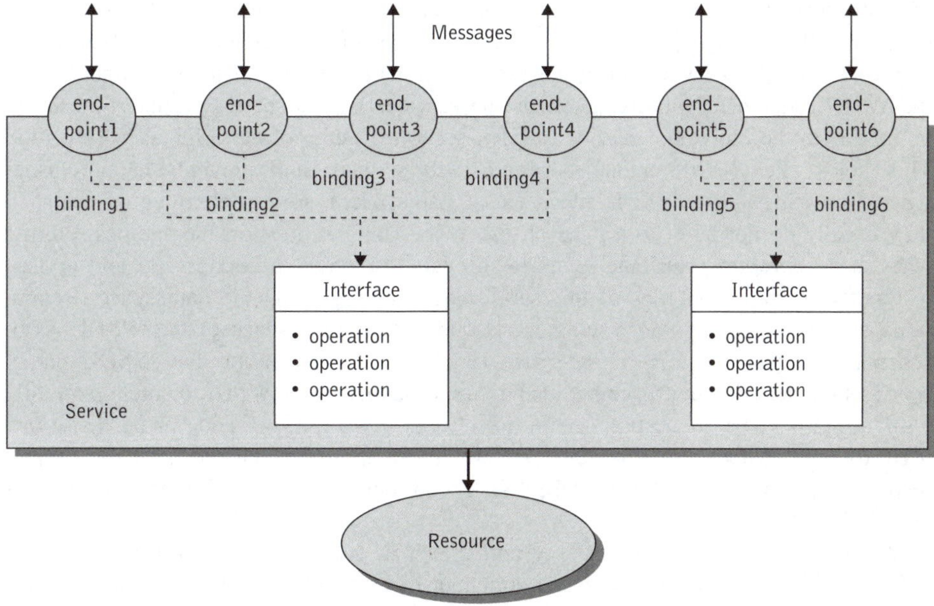

Figure 5.2 Web service endpoints

is considered as an *abstract definition* of a Web service in that it does not carry any deployment-specific details and is used to describe a specific type of interface provided by the service. It describes exactly what types of messages need to be sent and how the various Internet standard messaging protocols and encoding schemes can be employed in order to format the message in a manner compatible with the service provider's specifications. A service interface definition is an abstract service description that can be instantiated and referenced by multiple concrete service implementations. This allows common industry-standard service types to be defined and implemented by multiple service implementers.

In a WSDL document the `<types>`, `<message>`, `<part>`, `<portType>`, and `<operation>` elements describe the abstract interface of a Web service. The `<portType>` element is essentially an abstract interface (analogous to a Java interface definition) that combines `<operation>` and `<message>` definitions. Each `<message>` definition describes the payloads of outgoing and incoming messages, i.e., messages that are sent or received by a Web service. Messages consist of `<part>` elements, each of which represents an instance of a particular type (typed parameter). Each `<operation>` element is declared by a `<portType>` element and contains a number of `<message>` definitions describing its input and output parameters as well as any faults. The abstract interface of a Web service is described in the following and is also shown in Figure 5.3, which describes the relationship between the WSDL interface definition data structures in UML.

Listing 5.1 shows an excerpt of a WSDL interface definition describing a purchase order service. This service takes a purchase order number, a date, and customer details as input and returns an associated invoice document. The root element in Listing 5.1 (and every WSDL specification) is the `<definitions>` element, which encapsulates the entire WSDL document and provides it with its name. The `<definitions>` element as a root element in WSDL usually contains several XML namespace definitions. The first attribute in the `<definitions>` element is `name`, which is used to name the entire WSDL document. The `<definitions>` element also declares an attribute called `targetNamespace`, which identifies the logical namespace for elements defined within the WSDL document and characterizes the service. This element is usually chosen to be unique to the individual service (a URL set to the name of the original WSDL file). This helps clients differentiate between Web services and prevents name clashes when importing other WSDL files. These namespaces are simply unique strings – they usually do not point to a page on the Web. The `xmlns:tns` (sometimes referred to as *this namespace*) attribute is set to the value of `targetNamespace` and is used to qualify (scope) properties of this service definition. Among the namespace declarations of the `<definitions>` element is one for the namespace of the WSDL XML schema `"http://schemas.xmlsoap.org/wsdl/"`. Declaring the WSDL namespace as the default namespace avoids having to qualify every WSDL element explicitly with a prefix. The namespace definitions `xmlns:soapbind` and `xmlns:xsd` are used for specifying SOAP-binding specific information as well as XSD data types, respectively. The `wsdl:types` definition encapsulates schema definitions of all types using XML XSD.

WSDL adopts as its basic type system the W3C XML Schema built-in types. The WSDL `<types>` element serves as a container that contains all abstract data types that define a Web service interface. The WSDL `<types>` element is used to contain XML schemas or external references to XML schemas that describe the data type definitions

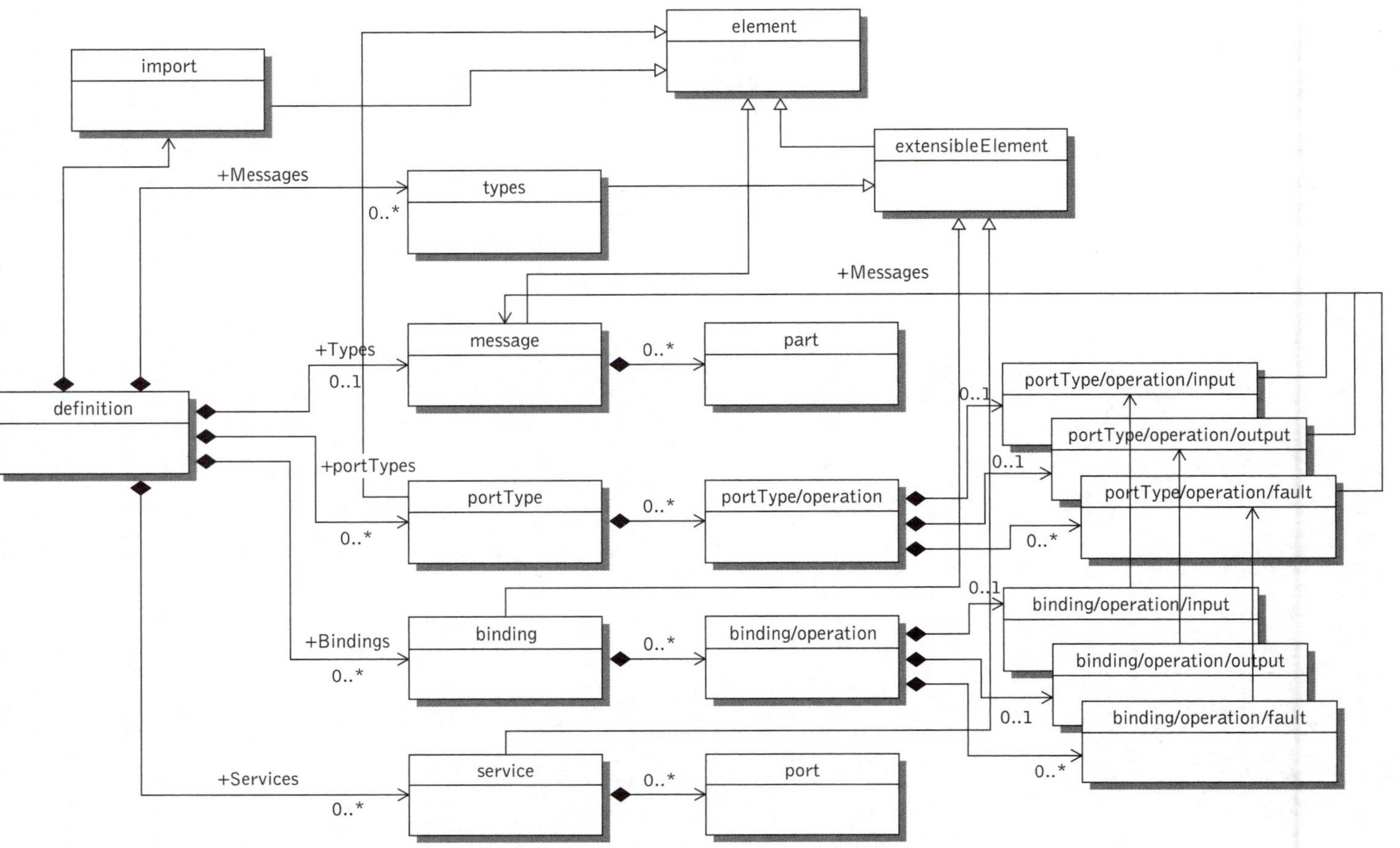

Figure 5.3 WSDL interface definition meta-model expressed in UML

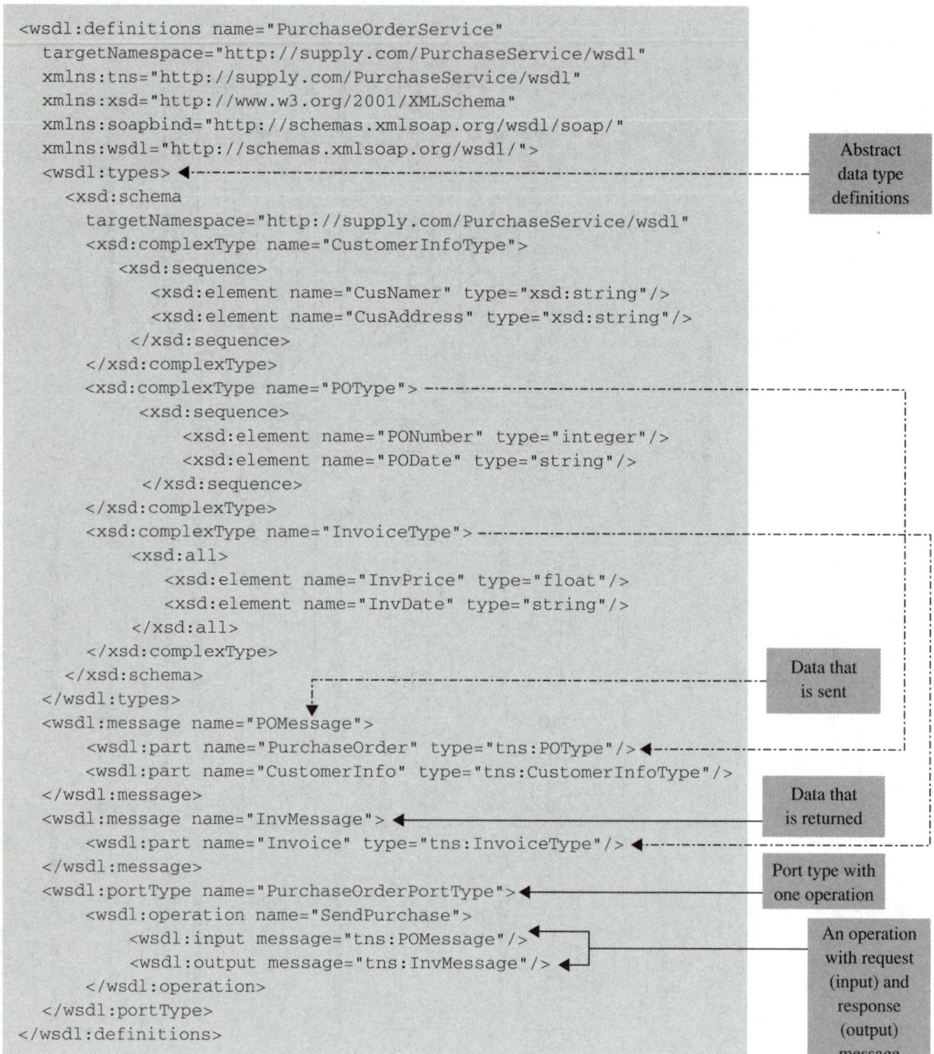

```
<wsdl:definitions name="PurchaseOrderService"
   targetNamespace="http://supply.com/PurchaseService/wsdl"
   xmlns:tns="http://supply.com/PurchaseService/wsdl"
   xmlns:xsd="http://www.w3.org/2001/XMLSchema"
   xmlns:soapbind="http://schemas.xmlsoap.org/wsdl/soap/"
   xmlns:wsdl="http://schemas.xmlsoap.org/wsdl/">
   <wsdl:types>
      <xsd:schema
        targetNamespace="http://supply.com/PurchaseService/wsdl"
        <xsd:complexType name="CustomerInfoType">
           <xsd:sequence>
              <xsd:element name="CusNamer" type="xsd:string"/>
              <xsd:element name="CusAddress" type="xsd:string"/>
            </xsd:sequence>
        </xsd:complexType>
        <xsd:complexType name="POType">
             <xsd:sequence>
                <xsd:element name="PONumber" type="integer"/>
                <xsd:element name="PODate" type="string"/>
             </xsd:sequence>
        </xsd:complexType>
        <xsd:complexType name="InvoiceType">
            <xsd:all>
               <xsd:element name="InvPrice" type="float"/>
               <xsd:element name="InvDate" type="string"/>
            </xsd:all>
        </xsd:complexType>
      </xsd:schema>
   </wsdl:types>
   <wsdl:message name="POMessage">
        <wsdl:part name="PurchaseOrder" type="tns:POType"/>
        <wsdl:part name="CustomerInfo" type="tns:CustomerInfoType"/>
   </wsdl:message>
   <wsdl:message name="InvMessage">
        <wsdl:part name="Invoice" type="tns:InvoiceType"/>
   </wsdl:message>
   <wsdl:portType name="PurchaseOrderPortType">
        <wsdl:operation name="SendPurchase">
            <wsdl:input message="tns:POMessage"/>
            <wsdl:output message="tns:InvMessage"/>
        </wsdl:operation>
   </wsdl:portType>
</wsdl:definitions>
```


Listing 5.1 Simple WSDL interface definition

used within the WSDL document. This element helps define all data types that are described by the built-in primitive data types that XML Schema Definition defines, such as `int`, `float`, `long`, `short`, `string`, `boolean`, and so on, and allows developers to either use them directly or build complex data types based on those primitive ones before using them in messages. This is why developers need to define their own namespace when referring to complex data types.

Listing 5.1 illustrates two complex types that have been defined in its `<types>` section: `POType` and `InvoiceType`. These two complex types are assigned the `xmlns:tns` namespace by the `targetNamespace` attribute. The elements

<sequence> and <all> are standard XSD elements. The construct <sequence> requires that the content model follows the element sequence defined, while the construct <all> denotes that all the elements that are declared in the <complexType> statement must appear in an instance document. The WSDL document must be aware of all namespaces used in the document.

Messages in WSDL are abstract collections of typed information cast upon one or more logical units, used to communicate information between systems. A <message> element describes the payload of outgoing and incoming messages. The <message> element corresponds to a single piece of information moving between the invoker and a Web service. Consequently, a regular round-trip method call is modeled as two messages, one for the request and one for the response.

While a message represents the overall data type formation of an operation, <part> elements may further structure this formation. A message can consist of one or more <part> elements with each part representing an instance of a particular type (typed parameter). When WSDL describes a software module, each <part> element maps to an argument of a method call. The <part>s of a message (message payload) use XML Schema built-in types, complex types or elements that are defined in the WSD document's <types> element or defined in external WSDL elements linked to by the <import> element. In addition, the message element can describe contents of SOAP header blocks and fault detail elements [Monson-Haefel 2004].

The following code snippet in Listing 5.1 illustrates that the message called POMessage (when associated with the <portType> element PurchaseOrderPortType) describes the input parameters of the service while the message InvMessage represents the return (output) parameters:

```
<!-- message elements that describe input and output parameters
    for the PurchaseOrderService -->
<!--input message -->
<wsdl:message name="POMessage">
      <wsdl:part name="PurchaseOrder" type="tns:POType"/>
      <wsdl:part name="CustomerInfo" type="tns:CustomerInfoType"/>
</wsdl:message>
<! -- output message -->
<wsdl:message name="InvMessage">
      <wsdl:part name="Invoice" type="tns:InvoiceType"/>
</wsdl:message>
```

The input message POMessage in this code snippet is shown to contain two <part> elements, PurchaseOrder and CustomerInfo, that refer to the complex types POType and CustomerInfoType (defined in Listing 5.1), respectively. POType consists of PONumber and PODate elements. The dashed arrow at the right hand side of the WSDL definition in Listing 5.1 links the POType definition to the input message. The same applies to the output message InvMessage and the InvoiceType definition. A message is defined depending on which mode of messaging is used, i.e., RPC-style or document-style messaging. When RPC-style messaging is used, <message> elements describe the payloads of the SOAP request and reply messages. If RPC-style messaging is used, messages commonly have more than one part. This is, for example, shown in the code snippet above where the input message POMessage contains the two <part> elements PurchaseOrder and CustomerInfo.

The following code snippet defines a document-style message where the <message> element definition refers to a top-level element in the <types> definition section. The code snippet shows that the PurchaseOrder service now defines one document-style <message> element using a PurchaseOrder <types> element.

```
<!-- message element that describes input and output parameters -->
<wsdl:message name="POMessage">
      <wsdl:part name="PurchaseOrder" element="tns:PurchaseOrder"/>
</wsdl:message>
```

In document-style messaging a message part may declare an <element> instead of a <type> attribute. WSDL allows a message part to declare either an <element> or a <type> attribute, but not both. A document-style <message> element commonly uses one-way messaging where there is no reply message. Document-style messaging exchanges XML document fragments and refers to their top-level (global) elements. In document-style messaging the <input> is the XML document fragment sent to the Web service, and the <output> is the XML document fragment sent back to the client.

The central element externalizing a service interface description in WSDL is the <portType> element. A <portType> element defines an abstract type and its operations but not an implementation. A WSDL <portType> and its <operation> elements are analogous to a Java interface and its method declarations. The rest of the elements in a WSDL description are essentially details that the <portType> element depends upon. A <portType> element is simply a logical grouping of operations, which describe the interface of a Web service and define its methods. A <portType> element describes the kinds of operations that a Web service supports – the messaging mode and payloads – without specifying the Internet protocol or physical address used. A <portType> element is used to bind the collection of logical operations to an actual transport protocol such as SOAP, thus providing the linkage between the abstract and concrete portions of a WSDL document. In WSDL the <portType> element is implemented by the <binding> and <service> elements, which dictate the Internet protocols, encoding schemas, and an Internet address used by the Web service implementation.

A WSDL definition can contain zero or more <portType> definitions. Typically, most WSDL documents contain a single <portType>. This convention separates out different Web service interface definitions into different documents. This granularity allows each business process to have separate binding definitions, providing for reuse, significant implementation flexibility for different security, reliability, transport mechanism, and so on [Cauldwell 2001].

A WSDL <portType> element may have one or more <operation> elements, each of which defines an RPC-style or document-style Web service method. Each <operation> element is composed of at most one <input> or one <output> element and any number of <fault> elements. Operations in WSDL are the equivalent of method signatures in programming languages. They represent the various methods being exposed by the service. An operation defines a method on a Web service, including the name of the method and the input and output parameters. A typical operation defines the input and output parameters or exceptions (faults) of an operation.

The WSDL example in Listing 5.1 defines a Web service that contains a single <portType> named PurchaseOrderPortType that supports a single <operation>, which is called SendPurchase. The example in Listing 5.1 assumes that the service is deployed using SOAP v1.1 as its encoding style, and is bound to HTTP.

An operation holds all messages potentially exchanged between a Web service consumer and a Web service provider. If fault messages had been defined, these would also be part of the <operation> element.

In Listing 5.1, the <portType> PurchaseOrderPortType <operation> element is an RPC-style operation that declares the message POMessage as its <input> and the message Inv(oice)Message as its <output> message. The <input> message represents the payload sent to the Web service, and the <output> message represents the payload sent to the client. In Listing 5.1, the <operation> element SendPurchase will be called using the message POMessage and will return its results using the message Inv(oice)Message. The input and output message elements of an operation link the services method, SendPurchase, in the case of Listing 5.1, to SOAP messages that will provide the transport for input parameters and output results. Operations can be used in a Web service in four fundamental patterns: request/response, solicit/response, one-way, and notification. The operation SendPurchase is a typical example of a request/response style of operation as it contains an input and an output message. The WSDL operation patterns are described in section 5.2.3.

5.2.2 WSDL implementation

In the previous section WSDL operations and messages have been defined in an abstract manner without worrying about the details of implementation. In fact, the purpose of WSDL is to specify a Web service abstractly and then to define how the WSDL developer will reach the implementation of these services. The *concrete* or *implementation level* of a service specifies how the abstract definition of a service is implemented. The service implementation part of WSDL contains the elements <binding> (although sometimes this element is considered as part of the service definition), <port>, and <service> and describes how a particular service interface is implemented by a given service provider. The service implementation describes where the service is located, or more precisely, to which network address the message must be sent in order to invoke the Web service. A service implementation document can contain references to more than one service interface document by means of <import> elements. The Web service implementation elements are shown in Figure 5.3 and summarized below.

The WSDL example in Listing 5.2 is an implementation description for the abstract service interface (<portType> element) shown in Listing 5.1. The central element of the implementation description is the <binding> element. The <binding> element specifies how the client and Web service should exchange messages. The client uses this information to access the Web service. This element binds the port type, i.e., the service interface description, to an existing service implementation and provides information about the protocol and the concrete data formats expected by a service offered from a distinct network address [Zimmermann 2003]. In WSDL a <binding> element contains information of how the elements in an abstract service interface (<portType> and <operation> elements) are mapped to a concrete representation in a particular combination of concrete protocols (e.g., SOAP or HTTP), messaging styles (e.g., RPC or documents styles), and formatting (encoding) styles (e.g., literal or SOAP encoding) to be associated with the <portType> element. For example, if a message is to be sent using SOAP over HTTP, the binding describes how the message parts are mapped to elements in the SOAP <Body> and <Header> and what the values of the corresponding attributes are. Each type of protocol, e.g., MIME, SOAP, or HTTP GET or POST, has its own set of protocol-specific elements and its own namespace. Figure 5.4 shows how WSDL elements can be used to implement endpoints. This figure also illustrates how the elements of the WSDL interface and implementation are related to each other.

The structure of the <wsdl:binding> element (henceforth referred to as <binding> element) resembles that of the <portType> element. This is no coincidence, as the binding must map an abstract port type description to a concrete implementation. The <type> attribute identifies which <portType> element this binding describes. The <binding> element declared in Listing 5.2 is actually composed of two different namespaces. On the one hand, there are elements that are members of the WSDL 1.1 namespace "http://schemas.xmlsoap.org/wsdl/", which is declared in

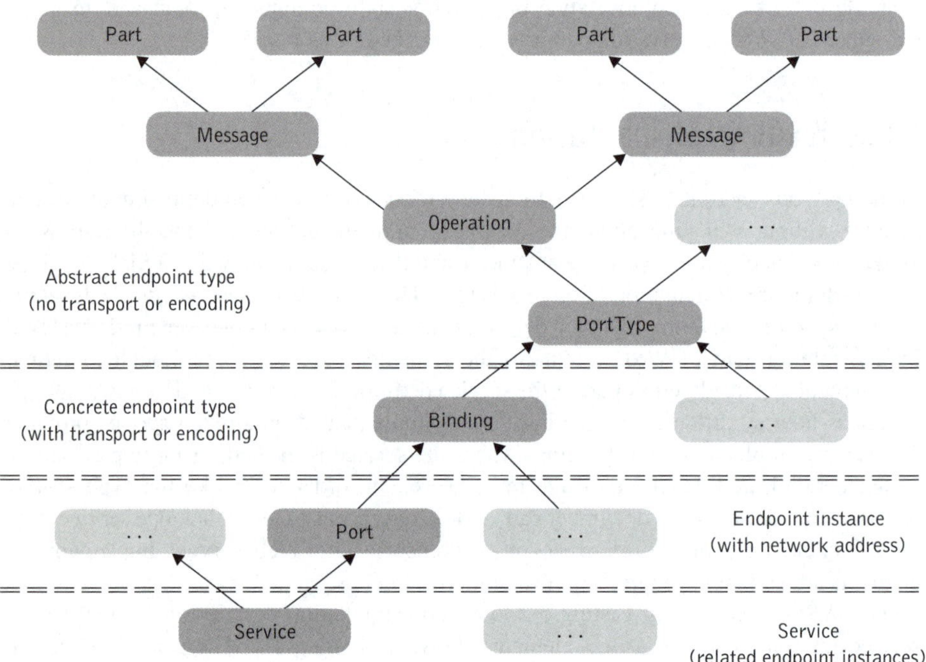

Figure 5.4 Using WSDL elements to define endpoints

Listing 5.1 and is the default namespace of the WSDL document. On the other hand, the soapbind:binding, soapbind:operation, and soapbind:body elements are SOAP-specific elements that are members of the namespace for the SOAP–WSDL binding "http://schemas.xmlsoap.org/wsdl/soap/" that is also declared in Listing 5.1. The soapbind:binding (not to be confused with the WSDL <binding> element) and soapbind:body elements are to express the SOAP-specific details of the Web service. More specifically, in Listing 5.2 the purpose of the SOAP binding element <soapbind:binding> is to signify that the messaging style is RPC (via the soapbind:operation construct and the style attribute which defines the type of default operations within this binding), the lower-level transport service that this binding will use is HTTP (specified via the transport attribute), and the SOAP format is going to be used as a binding and transport service. This declaration applies to the entire binding. It signifies that all operations of the PurchaseOrderPortType are defined in this binding as SOAP messages. It then becomes the responsibility of SOAP to take the client from the abstract WSDL specification to its implementation. Since SOAP is used for this purpose, SOAP's namespace must also be used. The <soapbind:body> element enables applications to specify the details of the input and output messages and enable the mapping from the abstract WSDL description to the concrete protocol description. In particular, the <soapbind:body> element specifies the SOAP encoding style and the namespace associated with the specific service (PurchaseOrderService in our case). In Listing 5.2 the <soapbind:body> construct specifies that both the input and output messages are literally encoded, while the term literal indicates that the XML document fragment can be validated against its XML schema. The sub-elements of the <binding> element (<operation>, <input>, and <output>) map directly to the corresponding children of the <portType> element. In Listing 5.2 the <soapbind:operation> element is used to indicate the binding of a specific operation, e.g., SendPurchase, together with the mapping of its input and output messages from the abstract service interface description (see Listing 5.1) to a specific SOAP implementation. The data types of these messages that are abstractly described by means of XSD in the service interface description should be SOAP encoded for the transfer.

Several bindings may represent various implementations of the same <portType> element. If a service supports more than one protocol, then the WSDL <portType> element should include a <binding> for each protocol it supports. For a given <portType> element, a <binding> element can describe how to invoke operations using a single messaging/transport protocol, e.g., SOAP over HTTP, SOAP over SMTP, or a simple HTTP POST operation, or any other valid combination of networking and messaging protocol standards. Currently, the most popular binding technique is to use SOAP over HTTP. It must be noted that a binding does not contain any programming language or service-implementation-specific details. How a service is implemented is an issue completely external to WSDL.

As already explained, the binding in Listing 5.2 is shown to contain a single operation SendPurchase, which maps each of the input, output, and fault elements of operation SendPurchase from the PurchaseOrderPortType (see Listing 5.1) to its SOAP on-the-wire format. In this way, the PurchaseOrderService Web service can be accessed. The soapbind:operation in Listing 5.2 specifies the messaging style (RPC or document) for a specific operation and the value of the SOAPAction header field. In

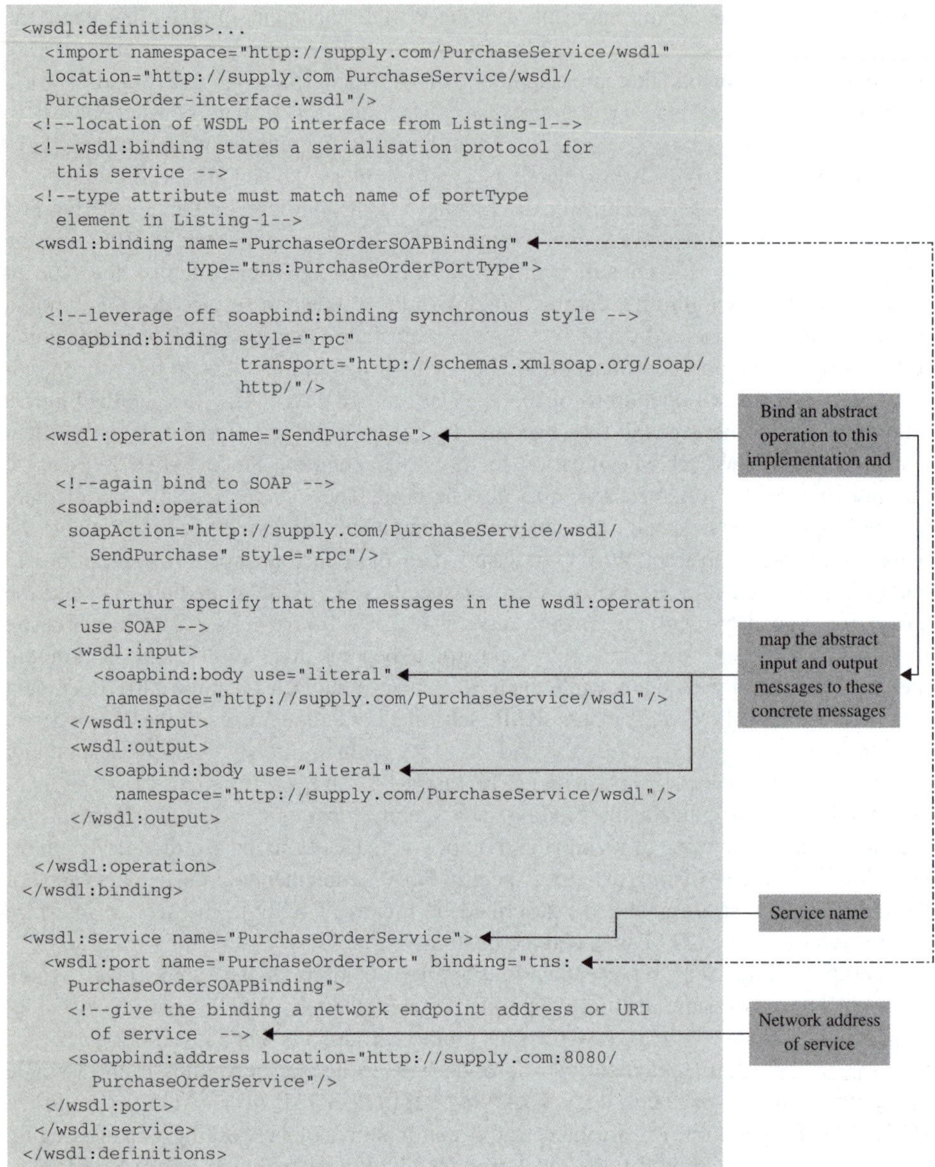

```
<wsdl:definitions>...
  <import namespace="http://supply.com/PurchaseService/wsdl"
  location="http://supply.com PurchaseService/wsdl/
  PurchaseOrder-interface.wsdl"/>
 <!--location of WSDL PO interface from Listing-1-->
 <!--wsdl:binding states a serialisation protocol for
   this service -->
 <!--type attribute must match name of portType
   element in Listing-1-->
 <wsdl:binding name="PurchaseOrderSOAPBinding"
               type="tns:PurchaseOrderPortType">

  <!--leverage off soapbind:binding synchronous style -->
  <soapbind:binding style="rpc"
                    transport="http://schemas.xmlsoap.org/soap/
                    http/"/>

  <wsdl:operation name="SendPurchase">

   <!--again bind to SOAP -->
   <soapbind:operation
    soapAction="http://supply.com/PurchaseService/wsdl/
      SendPurchase" style="rpc"/>

   <!--furthur specify that the messages in the wsdl:operation
     use SOAP -->
    <wsdl:input>
      <soapbind:body use="literal"
       namespace="http://supply.com/PurchaseService/wsdl"/>
    </wsdl:input>
    <wsdl:output>
      <soapbind:body use="literal"
        namespace="http://supply.com/PurchaseService/wsdl"/>
    </wsdl:output>

 </wsdl:operation>
</wsdl:binding>

<wsdl:service name="PurchaseOrderService">
  <wsdl:port name="PurchaseOrderPort" binding="tns:
    PurchaseOrderSOAPBinding">
    <!--give the binding a network endpoint address or URI
      of service  -->
    <soapbind:address location="http://supply.com:8080/
      PurchaseOrderService"/>
  </wsdl:port>
 </wsdl:service>
</wsdl:definitions>
```


Listing 5.2 WSDL implementation description

WSDL the style attribute is optional. It can be used to override the default messaging style declared by the <soapbind:binding> element. The SOAPAction attribute in the <soap:operation> element is an attribute that a SOAP client will use to make a SOAP request. The SOAPAction attribute of the <soapbind:operation> is used to specify the HTTP SOAPAction header, which in turn can be used by SOAP servers as an indication of the action that should be taken by the receipt of a message at run-time. This usually captures the name of a method to invoke in a service implementation. The `SOAPAction` attribute is a server-specific URI used to indicate the intent of request. It can contain a message routing parameter or value that helps the SOAP run-time system dispatch the message to the appropriate service. The purpose of this is to achieve interoperability between client and service provider applications. The SOAP client will read the SOAP structure from the WSDL file and coordinate with a SOAP server on the other end.

The style of messaging has a direct impact on how the body of the SOAP message is constructed, thus declaring the correct `style`, "rpc" or "document," is important. When RPC-style messaging is used then the `<Body>` of the SOAP message will contain an element that represents the operation that needs to be performed. This element receives its name from the `<operation>` defined in the `<portType>` element, i.e., `SendPurchase`. Figure 5.5 illustrates how the `<operation>` defined in the `<portType>` element and its message parts (e.g., purchase order) are mapped to an RPC-style SOAP message.

```
<wsdl:message name="POMessage">
    <wsdl:part name="PurchaseOrder" type="tns:POType"/>
    < wsdl:part name="CustomerInfo"type="tns:CustomerInfoType"/>
</wsdl:message>
    <wsdl:message name="InvMessage">
<wsdl:part name="Invoice" type="tns:InvoiceType"/>
</wsdl:message>

<wsdl:portType name="PurchaseOrderPortType">
    <wsdl:operation name="SendPurchase">
        <wsdl:input message="tns:POMessage"/>
        <wsdl:output message="tns:InvMessage"/>
    </wsdl:operation>
</wsdl:portType>

<wsdl:binding name="POMessageSOAPBinding"
             type="tns:PurchaseOrderPortType">

 <soapbind:binding style="rpc"
      transport="http://schemas.xmlsoap.
      org/soap/http/"/>
 <wsdl:operation name="SendPurchase">

 <soapbind:operation style="rpc"
           soapAction="http://supply.com/
           PurchaseService/wsdl/SendPurchase"/>

  <wsdl:input>
    <soapbind:body  use="literal"
     namespace="http://supply.com/PurchaseOrderService/wsdl"/>
  </wsdl:input>
  <wsdl:output>
    <soapbind:body  use="literal"
     namespace="http://supply.com/PurchaseOrderService/wsdl"/>
  </wsdl:output>
 </wsdl:operation>
</wsdl:binding>
```

```
<?xml version= "1.0"encoding=
 "UTF-8"?>
<soap:Envelope
xmlns:soapbind="http://schemas.
xmlsoap.org/soap/envelope"
  xmlns:tns="http://supply.com/
  PurchaseService/wsdl">
    <soap:Body>
      <tns:SendPurchase>
        <POtype>
          <PONumber>223451
            </PONumber>
          <PODate>10/28/2004
            </PODate>
        </POtype>
        ...
      <tns:SendPurchase>
    </soap:Body>
</soap:Envelope>
```

Figure 5.5 Mapping `SendPurchase` and its message parts to an RPC-style SOAP message

```
<wsdl:input>
    <soapbind:body use="literal"
     namespace="http://supply.com/PurchaseOrderService/wsdl"/>
</wsdl:input>

<wsdl:output>
     <soapbind:body use="literal"
      namespace="http://supply.com/PurchaseOrderService/wsdl"/>
</wsdl:output>
```

The code snippet above comes from Listing 5.2 and illustrates how the input and output messages of the <operation> SendPurchase appear in the parts of the SOAP message. The <input> and <output> elements for the <operation> SendPurchase specify exactly how the input and output messages of this operation should appear in the SOAP message. Both input and output contain a <soapbind:body> element with the value of its namespace corresponding to the name of the service that is deployed on the SOAP server. In RPC-style messages, the namespace attribute must be specified with a valid URI. This URI can be the same as the targetNamespace attribute of the WSDL document. In contrast, document-style messages must not specify the targetNamespace attribute in the <soapbind:body> element. The namespace of the XML document fragment is then derived from its XML schema.

Consider the <input> element for the SendPurchase operation. The entire POMessage message from the <portType> declaration for the SendPurchase operation is declared to be abstract. This is indicated by the use="literal" attribute. This means that the XML defining the input message and its parts is in fact abstract, and the real, concrete representation of the data is to be derived. The purpose of the use attribute within the <soapbind:body> element enables applications to specify how the parts of the message are defined. The "literal" encoding indicates that the resulting SOAP message contains data formatted exactly as specified in the abstract WSDL definitions. It essentially means that the parameter element in a SOAP message body is an ASCII string that is a literal instance of the <part>'s type as specified in the message declaration. Consequently, the data type that the message part references will be serialized according to its exact representation in the type definition section, i.e., according to the XML schema. This means that the schema would be used to validate an instance of each individual message part. If we had used the encoded instead of the literal form of encoding, the additional encodingStyle attribute would have to be used to denote the specific way that the message is serialized. This implies that the message should appear as part of the <soapbind:body> element and that the SOAP run-time system on the service provider's network should deserialize the data from XML to another format, e.g., Java data types, according to the encoding rules defined in the SOAP specification.

The <service> element finally binds the Web service to a specific network-addressable location. It takes the bindings that were declared previously and ties them to one or more <port> elements, each of which represents a Web service. A <service> is modeled as a collection of related WSDL <port> elements – where a <port> element is a single

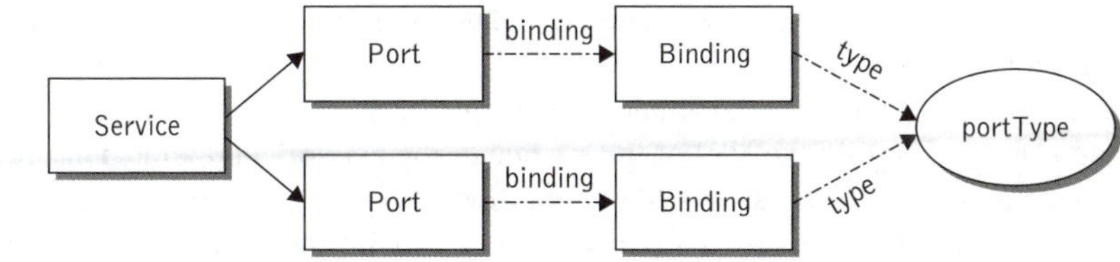

Figure 5.6 Connecting the service interface with the service implementation

endpoint defined as a combination of a binding and a network address – at which a service is made available. Each `<service>` element is named, and each name must be unique among all services in a WSDL document. Taken together the `<port>`s of a `<service>` element host a set of related operations that are offered to clients.

In WSDL a `<port>` element defines the location at which the operations of a specific `<portType>` using a particular transport protocol, can be invoked. A `<port>` associates an endpoint, for instance, a network address location, or URL – with a specific WSDL `<binding>` element – to denote the physical endpoint that service requestors must use to connect to the service. Since the `<binding>` specifies a `<portType>`, the `<port>` element effectively ties the `<portType>` to an address.

Figure 5.6 illustrates the fact that a single service contains multiple ports that all use the same `<portType>`. This implies that there could be multiple service implementations for the same service interface provided by different service providers. These all have different bindings and/or addresses. For instance, a standard `<portType>` for order management may be provided by a particular vertical industry. Different manufacturers may then provide different order management services that implement the same `<portType>`. All these implementations should provided the semantically equivalent behavior. Alternatively, a service implemented by a particular provider may contain several `<port>`s for the same `<portType>`, each of which is provided by a different `<binding>`. This allows a service requestor to choose the most convenient way to communicate with the service provider which implements the service.

In Listing 5.2 the `<binding>` element named `POMessageSOAPBinding` links the `<portType>` element named `PurchaseOrderPortType` (refer to Listing 5.1) to the `<port>` element named `PurchaseOrderPort`. This is effected through the binding `name POMessageSOAPBinding` as can be seen from the dashed arrow in Listing 5.2. This listing contains only one Web service, namely the `PurchaseOrderService`, thus only the `<port>` element named `PurchaseOrderPort` is used to reveal the service location. However, as already explained, the service `PurchaseOrderService` could, for instance, contain three ports, all of which use the `PurchaseOrderPortType` but are bound to SOAP over HTTP, SOAP over SMTP, and HTTP GET/POST, respectively. A client that wishes to interact with the service can then choose which protocol it wants to use to communicate with the service (possibly programmatically by using the namespaces in the bindings), or which address is closest [Cauldwell 2001]. By employing different bindings, the service is more readily accessible on a wider range of platforms. For instance, a PC desktop application may use SOAP over HTTP, while a WAP application designed to run on a cellular phone may use HTTP GET/POST, since an XML parser is typically not available in a WAP application. All three services are semantically equivalent in that they all take a purchase order number, a date, and customer details as input and return an associated invoice.

The `<soapbind:address>` attribute in Listing 5.2 is another SOAP extension to WSDL and is used to signify the URI of the service or the network endpoint. This element simply assigns an Internet address to a SOAP binding via its `location` attribute. A Web service client is expected to bind to a port and interact with the service provided that it understands and respects the concrete message expected by the service.

Figure 5.7 summarizes several of the constructs introduced in the previous discussion by illustrating the various WSDL elements involved in a client–service interaction. This figure shows one client invoking a Web service by means of SOAP over HTTP and another client invoking the same service by means of HTTP. Figure 5.7 depicts a single service that contains multiple ports. This figure shows that a service may contain more than one port, which are bound to binding elements, which are associated with a `<portType>`. Service providers all have different bindings and/or addresses. Port addresses are specified by the `<soapbind:address>` element of `<port>`, as already explained.

Finally, Figure 5.8 represents an overview of how the concrete and abstract levels of WSDL are connected. The indented items in this figure denote information represented by child elements. In Figure 5.8 attributes are italicized to distinguish them from elements.

5.2.3 WSDL message exchange patterns

WSDL interfaces support four types of operations. These operations represent the most common interaction patterns for Web services. Since each operation defined by WSDL can have an input and/or an output, the four WSDL interaction patterns represent possible combinations of input and output messages [Cauldwell 2001]. The WSDL operations correspond to the incoming and outgoing versions of two basic operation types: an incoming single message passing operation and its outgoing counterpart ("one-way" and "notification" operations), and the incoming and outgoing versions of a synchronous two-way message exchange ("request/response" and "solicit/response"). These message exchange patterns are shown in Figure 5.9 and summarized below. For reasons of brevity we only provide sample code listings of the two most popular message exchange patterns: one-way and request/response.

One-way operation. A one-way operation is an operation in which the service endpoint receives a message, but does not send a response. An example of a one-way operation might be an operation representing the submission of an order to a purchasing system. Once the order is sent, no immediate response is expected. This message exchange pattern is typically thought of as asynchronous messaging. A one-way message defines only an input message. It requires no output message and no fault.

If an `<operation>` element is declared with a single `<input>` element but no `<output>` element, it defines a one-way operation. By listing only an `<input>` message, the `<operation>` element indicates that clients will send messages to the Web service without expecting any responses. The following snippet illustrates the `SubmitPurchaseOrder` `<portType>` that defines a one-way operation and has been adapted from [Monson-Haefel 2004]:

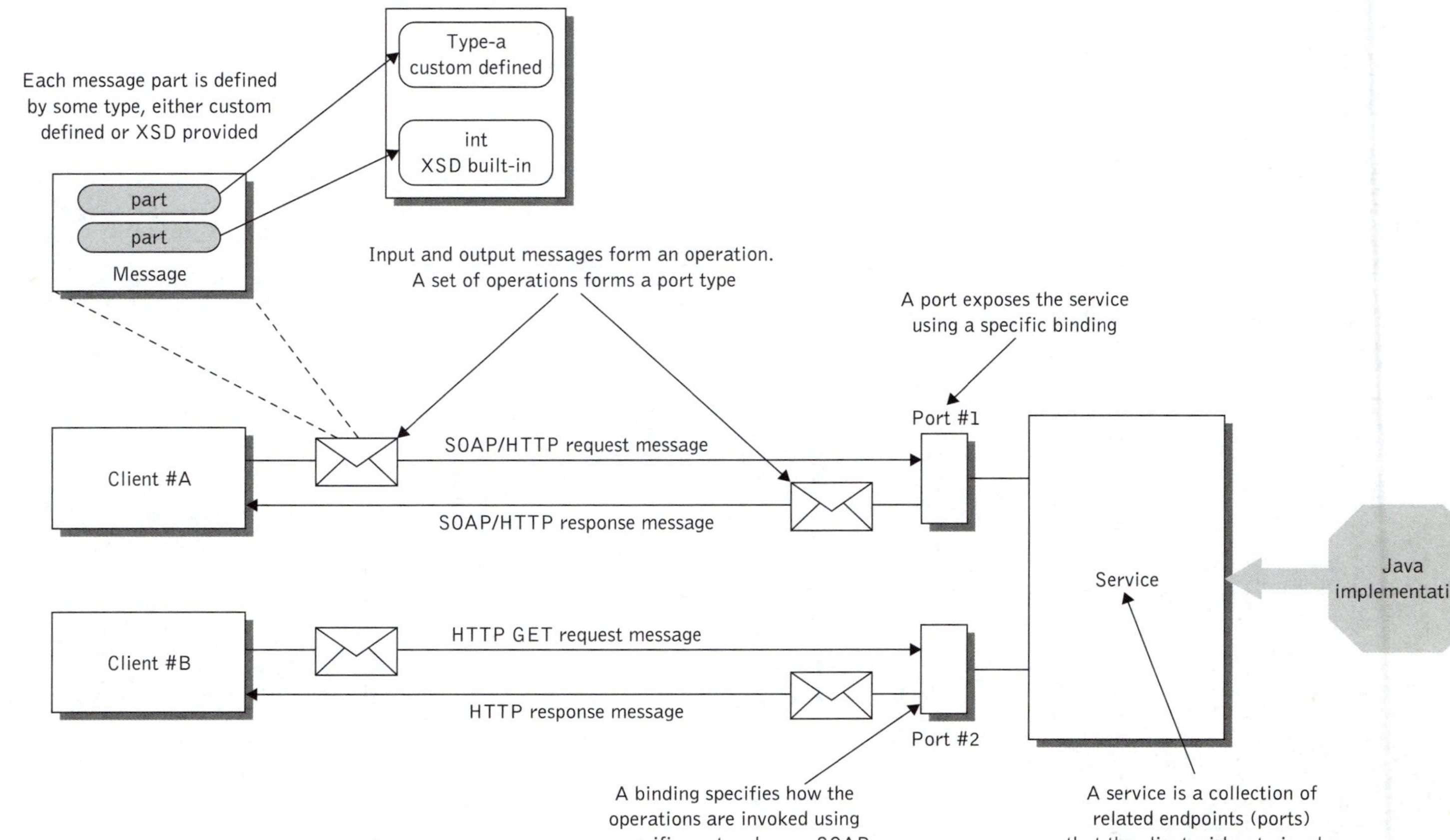

Figure 5.7 Elements of the WSDL as part of requestor–service interaction

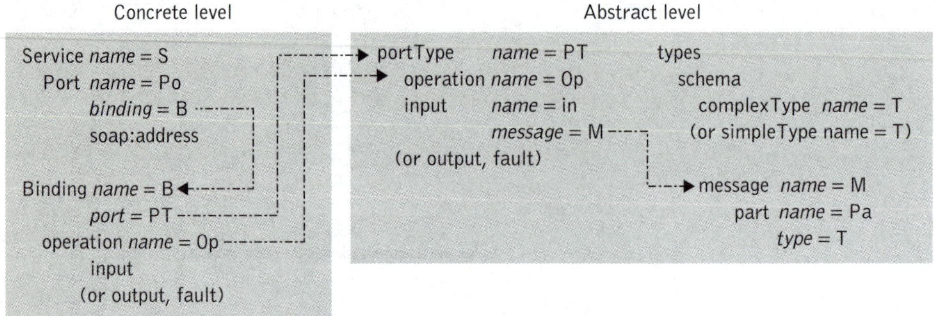

Figure 5.8 Connecting the abstract and concrete levels of a Web service
Source: M. Kifer, A. Bernstein and P. M. Lewis, *Database Systems: An Application-Oriented Approach*, Second Edition, Addison Wesley, 2005. Reproduced with permission.

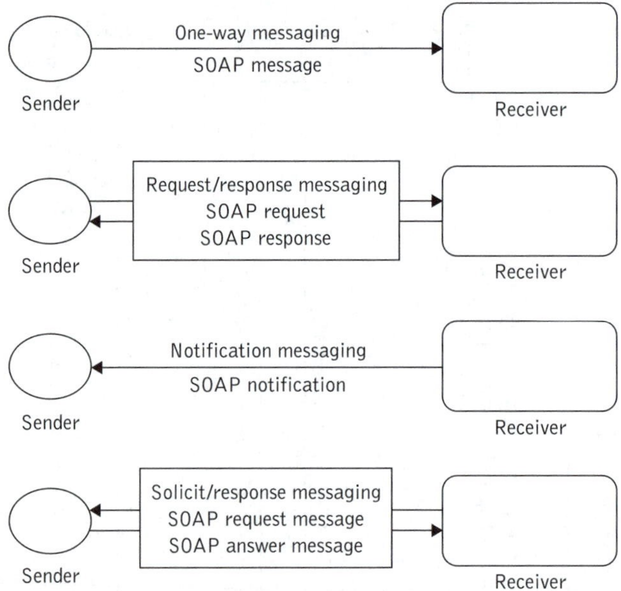

Figure 5.9 WSDL messaging patterns

```
<!-- portType element describes the abstract interface of a Web
 service -->
<wsdl:portType name="SubmitPurchaseOrder_PortType">
     <wsdl:operation name="SubmitPurchaseOrder">
           <wsdl:input name="order"
            message="tns:SubmitPurchaseOrder_Message"/>
     </wsdl:operation>
</wsdl:portType>
```

Request/response operation. A request/response operation is an operation in which the service endpoint receives a message and returns a message in response. In the request/response message pattern a client requests that some action is taken by the service provider. If an <operation> element is declared with a single <input> element followed by a single <output> element, it defines a request/response operation. By listing the <input> tag first, the <operation> indicates that the Web service receives a message that is sent by the client. Listing the <output> tag second indicates that the Web service should respond to the message. An example of this is the following code snippet taken from Listing 5.1, which illustrates the SendPurchase operation as an example of the request/response messaging pattern. The SendPurchase operation receives as input a message containing a purchase order (order number and date) and customer details and responds with a message containing an invoice. In an RPC environment, this is equivalent to a procedure call, which takes a list of input arguments and returns a value.

```
<!-- portType element describes the abstract interface of a Web
 service -->
<wsdl:portType name="PurchaseOrder_PortType">
     <wsdl:operation name="SendPurchase">
           <wsdl:input message="tns:POMessage"/>
           <wsdl:output message="tns:InvMessage"/>
     </wsdl:operation>
</wsdl:portType>
```

Notification operation. A notification operation is an operation in which the service endpoint sends a message to a client, but it does not expect to receive a response. This type of messaging is used by services that need to notify clients of events. A Web service that uses the notification messaging pattern follows the *push model* of distributed computing. The assumption is that the client (subscriber) has registered with the Web service to receive messages (notifications) about an event. Notification is when a <portType> element contains an <output> tag but no <input> message definitions. An example of this could be a service model in which events are reported to the service and where the endpoint periodically reports its status. No response is required in this case, as most likely the status data is assembled and logged and not acted upon immediately.

Solicit/response operation. A solicit/response operation is an operation in which the service endpoint sends a message and expects to receive an answering message in response. This is the opposite of the request/response operation since the service endpoint is initiating the operation (soliciting the client), rather than responding to a request. Solicit/response is similar to notification messaging, except that the client is expected to respond to the Web service. As with notification messaging, clients of the solicit/response Web services must subscribe to the service in order to receive messages. With this type of messaging the <portType> element first declares an <output> tag and then an <input> message definition – exactly the reverse of a request/response operation. An example of this operation might be a service that sends out order status to a client and receives back a receipt.

Table 5.1 Summary of WSDL message exchange patterns

Type	*Definition*
One-way	The operation can receive a message but will not return a response
Request/response	The operation can receive a request and will return a response
Notification	The operation can send a message but will not wait for a response
Solicit/response	The operation can send a request and will wait for a response

Table 5.1 summarizes and compares the four WSDL messaging patterns described in the previous section.

It should be noted that any combination of incoming and outgoing operations can be included in a single WSDL interface. As a result, the four types of operations presented above provide support for both push and pull interaction models at the interface level. The inclusion of outgoing operations in WSDL is motivated by the need to support loosely coupled peer-to-peer interactions between services.

5.3 Using WSDL to generate client stubs

In this chapter we have introduced several elements of WSDL to help readers understand the WSDL foundation for Web services. Understanding this technology is fundamental to comprehending the Web services model. However, most Web services developers will not have to deal with this infrastructure directly. There are a number of Web services development toolkits to assist with this undertaking. There are currently many tools, which automate the process of mapping WSDL to programming languages, such as Java, for both the service requestor and the service provider. One of the most popular tools for achieving this is WSDL2Java provided by Axis. Axis is an open source toolkit that is developed as part of Apache (**xml.apache.org**). Axis allows developers to write Java code and deploy that code as a Web service. In the following, we shall concentrate on how code generation tools allow automatic generation of WSDL definitions and creation of Web services.

Developers can implement Web services logic within their applications by incorporating available Web services and certainly without having to build new applications from scratch. The mechanism that makes this possible is the proxy class. Proxy classes enable developers to reference remote Web services and use their functionality within a local application, as if the data the services return was generated locally. The application developer communicates with any remote objects by sending messages to these local objects, which are commonly known as proxy objects. The proxy classes (or stub classes) are client-side images of the remote (provider) object classes that implement the Web services. The server-side counterparts are commonly known as skeletons in the distributed computing systems parlance, see section 2.4.1. Proxies implement the same interfaces as the remote class counterparts and forward the invoked methods on their local instances to corresponding remote instances (skeletons). The proxy object is simply a local object with methods that are merely a pass-through to the Web service it is representing. There exists

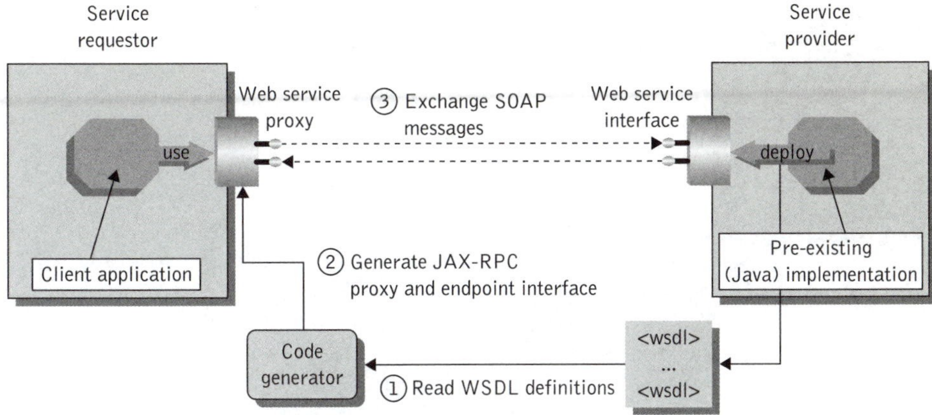

Figure 5.10 Generating proxies from WSDL code generators

exactly one proxy for each remote object for which a local object (application) holds a remote object reference. A proxy implements the methods in the remote interface of the service provider object it represents. This ensures that method invocations are suitable for the remote object in question. The role of the proxy class is to act as the local representative for the remote object and basically is, to the client, the remote reference. However, instead of executing an invocation, the proxy forwards it in a message to a remote object. The proxy hides the details of the remote object reference, the marshaling of arguments to the remote object methods using object serialization, and sends the marshaled invocation across the wire to the service provider's site. It also handles the unmarshaling of results that are received from the remote object implementing the service.

WSDL is well suited for code generators that can read WSDL definitions and generate a programming interface for accessing a Web service. For instance, a JAX-RPC provider may use WSDL 1.1 to generate Java RMI interfaces and network stubs, which can be used to exchange messages with a Web service interface. Figure 5.10 shows how a WSDL toolkit, such as JAX-RPC [Monson-Haefel 2004], can generate a Java RMI (an endpoint) interface and networking proxy that implements that interface. From the WSDL definition of a Web service, such as `PurchaseOrderService`, the Web service development tool generates a (Java) client proxy, which uses service requests from a local application (also shown to be coded in Java in Figure 5.10) to interact with a remote Web service implementing the WSDL interface.

WSDL code generator tools allow automatic creation of Web services, automatic generation of WSDL files, and invocation of Web services. These toolkits speed the creation of Web services by generating the service implementation template code from the WSDL specifications, leaving only the application-specific implementation details to the developer. They also simplify the development of client applications by generating service proxy code from the WSDL specification. Several code generators can generate interfaces and network stubs from WSDL documents.

Once the proxy class is built, the client simply calls the Web method from it, and the proxy, in turn, performs the actual request of the Web service. This request may, obviously, have its endpoint anywhere in the network. When we reference the Web service in

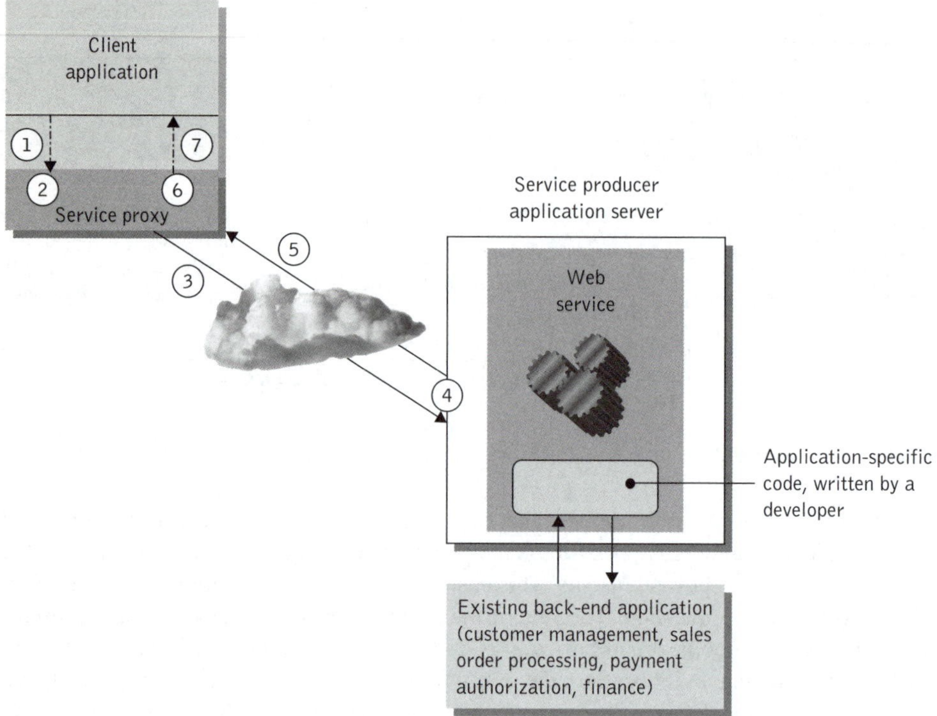

Figure 5.11 Communicating between proxy classes and Web services

the client application, it appears to be part of the consumer application itself, just like a normal internal function call. Figure 5.11 illustrates the process of communicating between a proxy and a Web service. This is shown to include the following steps:

1. The client-side application performs a call in the proxy class, passing any appropriate arguments to it, unaware that the proxy is actually invoking a remote Web service.
2. The proxy receives the call and formulates the request to the service, using the parameters the client application provides.
3. The call is transported from the proxy to the Web service across the network.
4. The Web service uses the parameters provided by the proxy to execute its Web service callable operations and expresses the result in XML.
5. The resulting data from the Web service is returned to the proxy at the client.
6. The proxy parses the XML returned from the Web service to retrieve the individual data values that are generated. These values may be simple or complex data types as already explained in this section.
7. The application receives the expected values in a normalized form from the proxy operation, completely unaware that they resulted from a Web service call.

5.4 Non-functional descriptions in WSDL

From what we have seen so far, one can understand that WSDL specifies the syntactic signature for a service but does not specify any non-functional service aspects. However, in section 1.8, we argued that non-functional characteristics are an integral part of any Web service. The Web services platform should be capable of supporting a multitude of different types of applications with different QoS requirements. In fact, programmers and applications need to be able to understand the QoS characteristics of Web services to be able to develop applications that invoke Web services and interact with them. Thus, the non-functional characteristics of a Web service should be described too.

QoS-enabled Web services require a separate language to describe non-functional characteristics of Web services. Currently, the most widely used approach to describing non-functional Web services characteristics is the combination of two specifications, which we shall examine in Chapter 12. These are WS-Policy and WS-PolicyAttachment. The Web services policy framework provides an additional description layer for services and offers a declarative policy language for expressing and programming policies. By employing this policy language, characteristics of the hosting environment can be described including security characteristics (including authentication and authorization) at the provider's endpoint, transactional behavior, the levels of QoS and quality of protection offered by the provider, privacy policies observed by the provider, and application-specific service options, or capabilities and constraints specific to a particular service domain.

When considering QoS-aware Web services, the service interface specifications need to be extended with statements on QoS that can be associated to the whole interface or to individual operations and attributes. It would be helpful if these non-functional service descriptions were to be added to WSDL in a standard manner. WS-PolicyAttachment accomplishes this objective (see section 12.4.3). It offers a flexible way of associating policy expressions with existing and future Web services artifacts. For instance, WS-PolicyAttachment addresses the requirements for associating Web services policy with a policy subject such as a WSDL `<portType>` or `<message>` and can even attach policies to UDDI entities.

5.5 Summary

A service description language is an XML-based language that describes the mechanics of interacting with a particular Web service and is inherently intended to constrain both the service provider and all requestors who make use of that service.

The Web Services Description Language is an XML-based specification schema providing a standard service representation language used to describe the details of the public interface exposed by a Web service. This public interface can include operational information relating to a Web service such as all publicly available operations, the XML message protocols supported by the Web service, data type information for messages, binding information about the specific transport protocol to be used, and address information for locating the Web service. WSDL allows the specification of services in terms of XML documents for transmission under SOAP.

The service implementation part of WSDL describes how a particular service interface is implemented by a given service provider. The service implementation describes where the service is located, or more precisely, to which network address the message must be sent in order to invoke the Web service.

WSDL specifies the syntactic signature for a service but does not specify any non-functional service aspects. The most widely used approach to describing non-functional Web services characteristics is by means of the Web services policy framework which provides an additional description layer for services and offers a declarative policy language for expressing and programming policies. This framework adds non-functional service descriptions to WSDL in a standard manner. In this way QoS characteristics such as performance, security (including authentication and authorization) at the provider's endpoint, transactional behavior, the levels of quality of protection offered by the provider, privacy policies observed by the provider, and so on, can be attached to the Web services description.

Currently, the World Wide Web Consortium is busy standardizing WSDL. Although WSDL 1.1, which we use throughout this book, is the *de facto* standard, WSDL 2.0 is the version of WSDL that the W3C is currently standardizing. WSDL 2.0 is a simpler and more usable language than WSDL 1.1. It provides several improvements over WSDL 1.1, including language clarifications and simplifications, support for interoperation, and making it easier for developers to understand and describe services. The recent WSDL 1.2 definition has introduced some changes, among which `<portType>` elements are renamed to `<interface>` elements [Weerawarana 2005]. The WSDL 1.2 definition also supports a useful new feature in the form of the `<extends>` attribute, which allows multiple `<interface>` declarations to be aggregated together and further extended to produce a completely new `<interface>` element. It is expected that the adoption of WSL 2.0 will take quite some time given the wide support that WSDL 1.1 enjoys in terms of tooling and run-time support environments [Weerawarana 2005].

Review questions

- Why is a service description necessary for representing Web services?
- What is the purpose of the Web Services Description Language? How does WSDL achieve its objective?
- Define and describe the Web services interface.
- Define and describe the Web services implementation.
- How do the Web services interface and implementation relate to each other?
- Describe the parts of the Web services `<portType>` element.
- Describe the parts of the Web services `<wsdl:binding>` element.
- How can you define RPC and document-style Web services in WSDL?

- Can a single service contain multiple ports? What is the implication?
- How does a one-way operation differ from a request/response operation?
- How does a notification operation differ from a solicit/response operation?
- How can you use WSDL to create client stubs?

Exercises

5.1 Define a simple stock trading Web service in WSDL that requests the stock price associated with a specified stock ticker symbol. This exercise is similar to Exercise 4.3.

5.2 Define a simple insurance claim Web service in WSDL using both RPC/literal and document bindings.

5.3 Define a simple Web service in WSDL that returns flight information regarding flights of a particular flight operator, see Exercise 3.4.

5.4 Define a simple Web service in WSDL that uses the car rental reservation schema in Exercise 3.5 to reserve vehicles on the basis of a customer request.

5.5 Define a WSDL interface on the basis of the card processing schema that you defined in Exercise 3.3. Typical operations should be "CreditCardSale" for credit card debit authorization, "DebitCardSale" for debit card debit authorization, "CancelCreditCardSale" for cancelling a credit card sale, "CheckCardDebitStatus" for determining the current status of a credit card sale, "CreditCardUserDetails" for getting the details of a credit card user, and so on.

5.6 Develop a simple inventory checking service. The inventory service should check the availability of an item. Based on this check, the inventory service should respond either that the purchase order could be fulfilled or by issuing a fault stating that the order cannot be completed.

CHAPTER 6

Registering and discovering Web services

Learning objectives

Service registration and discovery are two core functions of the service-oriented architecture (SOA) approach. In Web services applications a service registry is necessary to keep track of what services an organization has to offer and the characteristics of those services. To address the challenges of service registration and discovery, the Universal Description, Discovery, and Integration specification was created. UDDI is a cross-industry initiative to create a registry standard for Web service description and discovery together with a registry facility that supports the publishing and discovery processes.

In this chapter we describe the role of service registries and the service discovery process for Web services. After completing this chapter readers will understand the following key concepts:

- The use of UDDI as a standard registry.
- The UDDI data structures and their relationship to WSDL documents.
- The UDDI to WSDL mapping model.
- The UDDI APIs.
- How the UDI APIs are used to publish Web services in UDDI and enquire about Web services contained in the UDDI.
- Different UDDI usage models and variants.

6.1 Service registries

To exploit the full potential of e-business, organizations must be able to discover each other, make their needs and capabilities known, and compose Web services from diverse organizations into new services and business processes. The solution is to enable businesses to discover and reach each other, to learn what kinds of capabilities their potential trading partners have, and to continuously discover new potential trading partners, understand what their capabilities are, and seamlessly conduct e-business with them. This solution requires the creation of a service registry architecture that enables enterprises to introduce a global, platform-independent, open framework for businesses to (i) discover each other, (ii) define how they interact over the Internet, and (iii) share information in a global registry that will more rapidly accelerate the global adoption of e-business.

As we have already explained in section 1.6.2.1, publishing a Web service in a service registry so that other applications can find it entails two equally important operations: describing and registering the Web service. Publication of a service requires proper description of a Web service in terms of business, service, and technical information. Registration deals with persistently storing the Web service descriptions in the Web services registry.

Service registries are all about visibility and control. At the simplest level, a service registry keeps track of what services an organization has and characteristics of those services. In general, two types of e-business registries can be discerned: the *document*-based and the *metadata*-based service registry. These registries differ from one another in the way that they handle descriptive service information.

A document-based service registry enables its clients to publish information by storing XML-based service documents, such as business profiles or technical specifications (including WSDL descriptions of the service), in the registry. When these descriptive documents are submitted to the registry, service providers must also provide descriptive information about each document in the form of service metadata. Metadata is one of the key elements of any integration solution because it is used to describe the structure of information held in the disparate systems and processes, see section 13.2. This may range from the structure of XML schemas, interface definitions, or endpoints in locations across the network to the detailed description of an entire process (e.g., a process that sets up a new customer account or processes a customer-initiated order). Metadata is stored in the service registry and is used by the registry to provide meaningful attachments to its descriptive documents, which are made persistent in the storage facility of the service registry. The registry is completely oblivious to the content of the service documents themselves.

In the metadata-based service registry a different approach is used to deal with service-related information. Service providers simply submit documents that contain service information. However, these documents are not stored as such. Instead, the registry reads the information contained in the service documents and creates metadata, which captures the essence of the submitted document. The metadata is stored in the service registry in an internal format. In this case, the service registry is not oblivious to the published information. It is possible that the metadata contains references to content, to which the registry is oblivious. However, the registry does not manage these documents in this situation. Rather, the registry provides links to the documents.

In summary, an advanced registry offers several appealing characteristics including the following:

- Maximizes Web services reuse and encourages broad usage by all potential users in an SOA solution.
- Creates a management and governance structure to grow and sustain a successful SOA implementation.
- Contains all the metadata about Web services and their associated objects. It also contains information about service providers, consumers, and their relationships.
- Provides general- and special-purpose interfaces that address the needs of providers, consumers, administrators, and operators.
- Ensures that the evolving SOA can handle the growing number of services and service consumers and quickly adapt to changing business requirements.

6.2 Service discovery

Service discovery is an important element of an SOA. *Service discovery* is the process of locating Web service providers, and retrieving Web service descriptions that have been previously published. Web service discovery entails locating and interrogating Web service definitions, which is a preliminary step for accessing a Web service. It is through this discovery process that Web services clients learn that a particular Web service exists, what its capabilities are, and how to properly interact with it. Interrogating services involves querying the service registry for Web services matching the needs of a service requestor. A query consists of search criteria such as the type of the desired service, preferred price, and maximum number of returned results and is executed against service information published by the service provider. After the discovery process is complete, the service developer or client application should know the exact location of a Web service (a URI for the selected service), its capabilities, and how to interface with it. *Service selection* involves deciding on what Web service to invoke from the set of Web services the discovery process returned.

There are two basic types of service discovery: *static* and *dynamic* [Graham 2004a]. Static service discovery generally occurs at design time, whereas dynamic discovery occurs at run-time.

With static discovery, the service implementation details such as the network location and network protocol to use are bound at design time and service retrieval is performed on a service registry. A human designer usually examines the results of the retrieval operation and the service description returned by the retrieval operation is incorporated into the application logic.

With dynamic discovery, the service implementation details such as the network location and network protocol to use are left unbound at design time so that they can be determined at run-time. In this case, the Web service requestor has to specify preferences to enable the application to infer which Web service(s) the requestor is most likely to want to invoke. The application issues a retrieval operation at run-time against the service registry to locate one or more service implementation definitions that match the service interface definition used by the application. Based on application logic, QoS considerations such as best price, performance, security certificates, and so on, the application chooses the most appropriate service, binds to it, and invokes it.

6.3 UDDI: Universal Description, Discovery, and Integration

To address the challenges of service registration and discovery, the Universal Description, Discovery, and Integration specification was created. UDDI is a cross-industry initiative to create a registry standard for Web service description and discovery together with a registry facility that supports the publishing and discovery processes. The UDDI specifications take advantage of World Wide Web Consortium (W3C) and Internet Engineering Task Force (IETF) standards such as XML, HTTP, and Domain Name System (DNS) protocols. UDDI is designed for use by developer tools and applications that use Web services standards such as SOAP/XML and WSDL. UDDI provides a global, platform-independent, open framework making it easier to publish an enterprise's preferred means of conducting business, find trading partners, and interoperate with these trading partners over the Internet. By automating the registration and interrogation processes, UDDI enables service providers to describe their services and business processes in a global, open environment on the Internet, thus extending their reach. It also enables service clients to discover information about enterprises offering Web services; find descriptions of the Web services these enterprises provide; and, finally, find technical information about Web service interfaces and definitions of how the enterprises may interact over the Internet.

UDDI is a registry that contains relatively lightweight data. As a registry its prime purpose is to provide network addresses to the resources it describes, e.g., schemas, interface definitions, or endpoints, in locations across the network. The core concept of the UDDI initiative is the UDDI business registration, an XML document used to describe a business entity and its Web services. Conceptually, the information provided in a UDDI business registration consists of three interrelated components: "white pages", including address, contact, and other key points of contact; "yellow pages" , the classification of information according to industrial classifications based on standard industry taxonomies; and "green pages", the technical capabilities and information about services that are exposed by the business including references to specifications for Web services and pointers to various file- and URL-based discovery mechanisms. Using a UDDI registry, enterprises can discover the existence of potential trading partners and basic information about them (through white pages), find companies in specific industry classifications (through yellow pages), and uncover the kind of Web services offered to interact with the enterprises (through green pages). The information that is stored in the UDDI registry allows applications and developers to determine *who* the business entity represents, *what* they do, *where* the services they provide can be found, and *how* they can be accessed.

UDDI has been designed in a highly normalized fashion, not bound to any technology. In other words, an entry in the UDDI registry can contain any type of resource, independently of whether the resource is XML based or not. For instance, the UDDI registry could contain information about an enterprise's electronic document interchange (EDI) system, DCOM or CORBA interface, or even a service that uses the fax machine as its primary communication channel. The point is that, while UDDI itself uses XML to represent the data it stores, it allows for other kinds of technology to be registered. As UDDI uses SOAP as its transport layer, enterprises can interact with UDDI both at design time and at run-time through SOAP-based XML API calls in order to discover technical data about an enterprise's services. In this way enterprises can link up with service providers and invoke and use their services.

One key difference between a UDDI registry and other registries and directories is that UDDI provides a mechanism to categorize businesses and services using taxonomies. For example, service providers can use a taxonomy to indicate that a service implements a specific domain standard, or that it provides services to a specific geographic area [Manes 2004]. UDDI uses standard taxonomies so that information can be discovered on the basis of categorization. Such taxonomies make it easier for consumers to find services that match their specific requirements. Once a Web service has been developed and deployed it is important that it is published in a registry, such as UDDI, so that potential clients and service developers can discover it.

A business may set up multiple *private* UDDI registries in-house to support intranet and e-business operations by connecting departments in an organization. In addition, a business may use UDDI registries set up by its customers and business partners. Once a Web service has been developed and deployed it is important that it is published in a *public* UDDI registry so that potential clients and service developers can discover it. The Universal Business Registry (UBR) is a free, public registry operated by IBM, Microsoft, SAP, and NTT. The UBR provides a global directory about accessing publicly available Web services. UBR has a role analogous to the role that DNS (Domain Name Service) has in the Internet infrastructure. It enables users to locate businesses, services, and service specifications.

The companies that host the UDDI global registry are called the UDDI *operator nodes*. These operators manage and maintain the directory information, cater for replication of business information, and other directory-related functions. These sites provide a Web interface to the UDDI registry for browsing, publishing, and un-publishing business information. The UDDI operators allow businesses to publish their information and services they offer over the Web and they follow a well-defined replication scheme.

The UDDI usage model involves standard bodies and industry consortia publishing the descriptions of available services. The basic UDDI usage model is illustrated in Figure 6.1. Once the descriptions of available services have been published, service providers implement and deploy Web services conforming to these type definitions. Prospective clients can then query the UDDI registry based on various criteria such as the name of the business, product classification categories, or even services that implement a given service type definition. These clients can then get the details of the service type definition from the location specified. Finally, the clients can invoke the Web service because they have the service endpoint, and also the details on how to exchange messages with it.

6.3.1 UDDI data structures

For Web services to be meaningful there is a need to provide information about them beyond the technical specifications of the service itself. Central to UDDI's purpose is the representation of data and metadata about Web services. Through UDDI, enterprises can publish and discover information about other businesses and the services they provide. This information can be classified using standard taxonomies so that information can be discovered on the basis of categorization. UDDI also contains information about the technical interfaces of an enterprise's services.

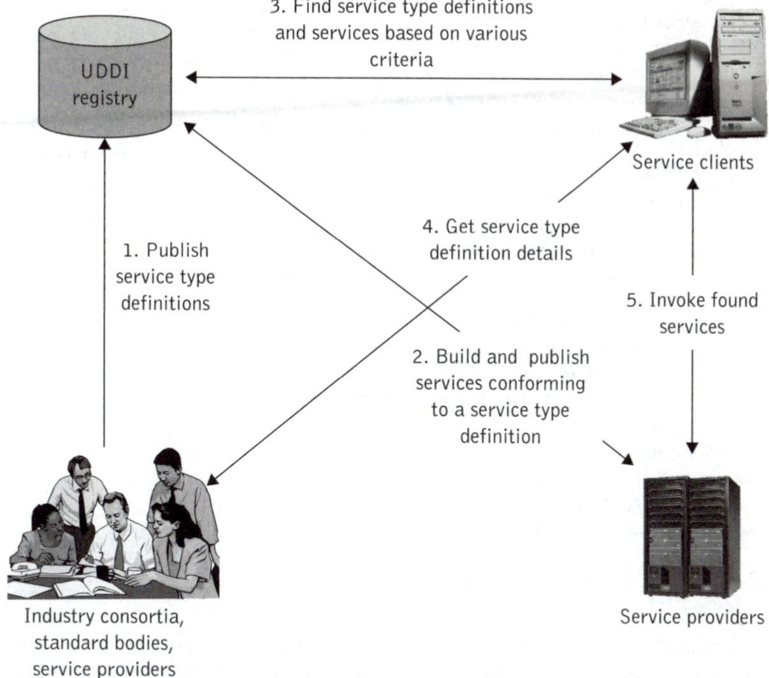

Figure 6.1 The UDDI usage model

A UDDI registry, either for use in the public domain or behind the firewall, offers a standard mechanism to classify, catalogue, and manage Web services, so that they can be discovered and consumed. Whether for the purpose of e-business or alternate purposes, businesses and providers can use UDDI to represent information about Web services in a standard way such that queries can then be issued to a UDDI registry – at design time or run-time. Queries address the following scenarios [Bellwood 2003]:

- Find Web services implementations that are based on a common abstract interface definition.
- Find Web service providers that are classified according to a known classification scheme or identifier system.
- Issue a search for services based on a general keyword.
- Determine the security and transport protocols supported by a given Web service.
- Cache the technical information about a Web service and then update that information at run-time.

UDDI defines a data structure standard for representing company and service description information. The data model used by the UDDI registries is defined in an XML schema. XML was chosen because it offers a platform-neutral view of data and because it allows

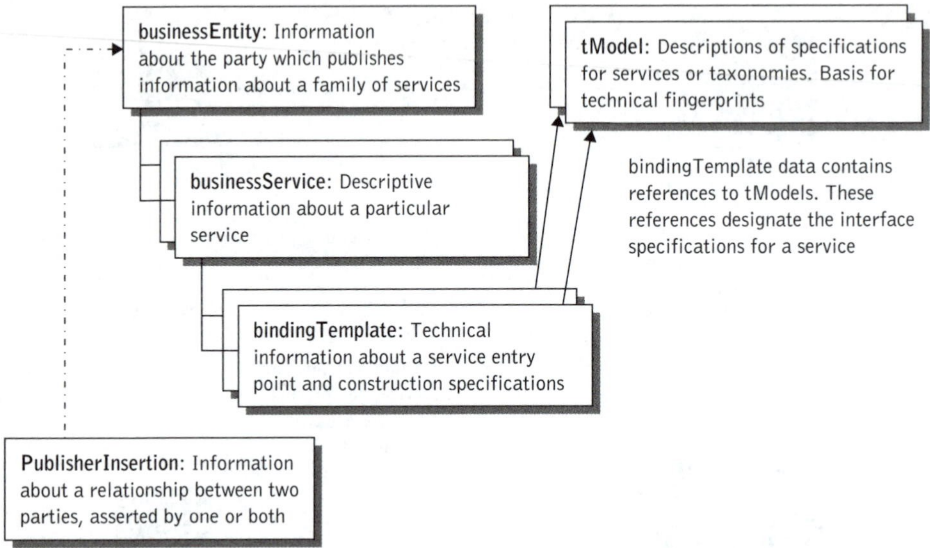

Figure 6.2 Overview of UDDI data structures

hierarchical relationships to be described in a natural way. The UDDI XML schema defines four core types of information that provide the white/yellow/green page functions. These are: business entities, business services, binding templates; and information about specifications for services (technical or `tModels`) [OASIS 2004].

Figure 6.2 provides a high-level view of the UDDI data structures, while the relationship between the UDDI data structures expressed in UML is shown in Figure 6.3. The diagram in Figure 6.2 shows the relationships between the various UDDI structures, their substructures, and attributes. The UDDI XML schema specifies information about the business entity, e.g., a company, that offers the service (`<businessEntity>`), describes the services exposed by the business (`<businessService>`), and captures the binding information (`<bindingTemplate>`) required to use the service. The `<bindingTemplate>` captures the service endpoint address, and associates the service with the `<tModel>`s that represent its technical specifications. A service implementation registration represents a service offered by a specific service provider. Each `<businessService>` can be accessed in one or more ways. For example, a retailer might expose an order entry service accessible as a SOAP-based Web service, a regular Web form, or even a fax number. To convey all the ways a service is exposed each service is bound to one or more `<tModel>`s via a binding template. Each of these four core UDDI structures has for identification purposes a unique key called a universal unique identifier (UUID).

Figure 6.3 also shows that there is a hierarchical relationship among the UDDI data structures. A business publishes a business entity containing, among other things, one or more business services. A business service has descriptive information about a service that a business provides, and can have one or more binding templates. The binding template has information on how to access a service entry point. It also has references to `<tModel>`s (using `<tModel>` keys) that point to the specification or interface definitions

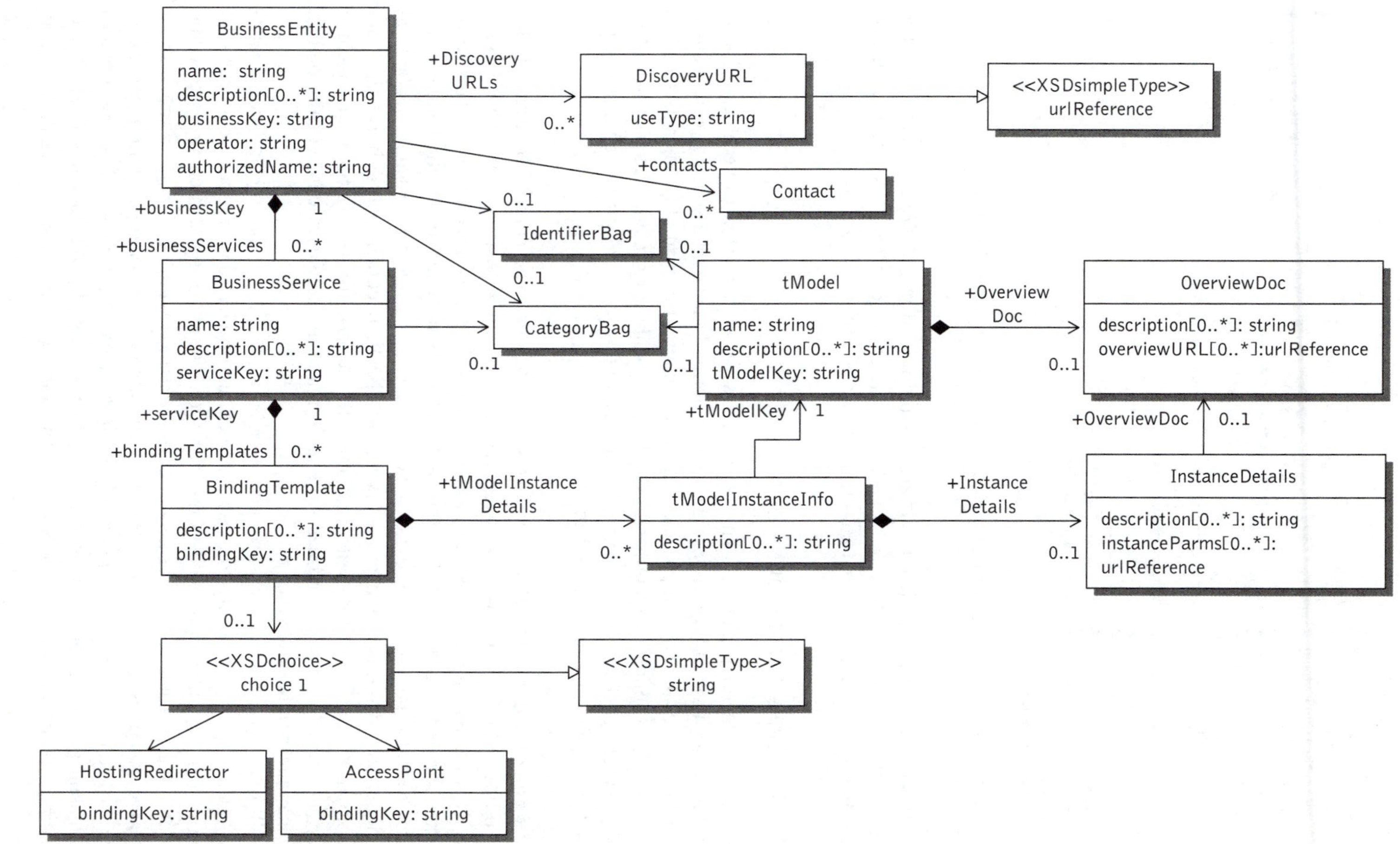

Figure 6.3 Relationships between the UDDI structures expressed in UML

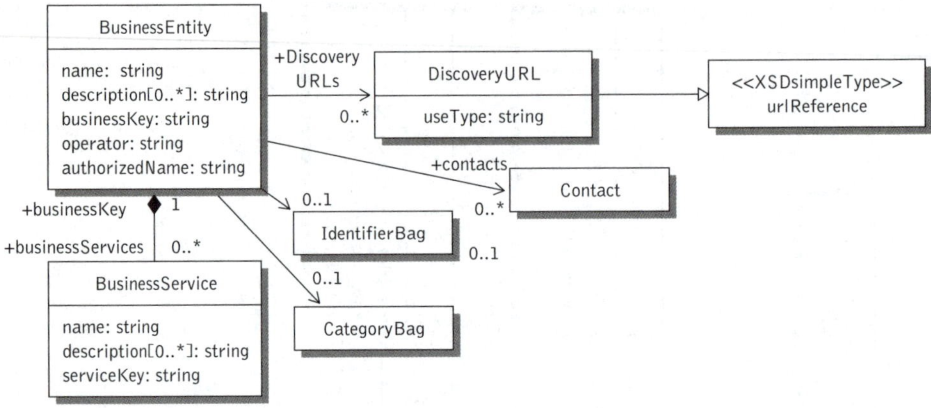

Figure 6.4 The `<businessEntity>` data structure expressed in UML

for a service. The interface definitions are usually in the form of WSDL definitions. The relationship between `<tModel>`s and `<bindingTemplate>`s is many-to-many. Accordingly, `<tModel>`s are not unique to `<bindingTemplate>`s.

6.3.1.1 Service provider information

Partners and potential clients of an enterprise's services that need to be able to locate information about the services provided would normally have as a starting point a small set of facts about the service provider. They will know, for example, either its business name or perhaps some key identifiers, as well as optional categorization and contact information (white pages). Service provider information is recorded by the data structures depicted in Figure 6.4 and outlined below.

The business entity element and business key attribute. The core XML elements for supporting publishing and discovering information about a business – the UDDI Business Registration – are contained in an element named `<businessEntity>`. This XML element serves as the top-level structure and contains white page information about a particular business unit (service provider). The `<businessEntity>` structure can be used to model any businesses and providers within UDDI. It contains descriptive information about the business or provider and about the services it offers. This would include information such as names and descriptions in multiple languages, contact information, and classification information.

All other non-business or provider elements related to the organization that a `<businessEntity>` entity represents, such as service descriptions and technical information, are either contained in this entity or referred to by elements nested within it. For instance, each `<businessService>` contained within a `<businessEntity>` structure describes a logical service offered by the business or organization. Similarly, each `<bindingTemplate>` contained within a given `<businessEntity>` provides the technical description of a Web service that belongs to the logical service that is described by the `<businessService>`. An example of a `<businessEntity>` data structure is given in Listing 6.1. This listing illustrates the attributes and elements in a <businessEntity>, while Figure 6.4 illustrates the <businessEntity> data structure and its contents expressed in UML.

```
<businessEntity businessKey="d2300-3aff-.."
                xmlns = "urn:uddi-org:api_v2">
<name xml: lang="en"> Automotive Equipment Manufacturing Inc.
</name>
<description xml: lang="en">
   Automotive Equipment, Accessories and Supplies for European firms
</description>
<contacts>
   <contact useType="Sales Contact">
      <description xml: lang="en"> Sales Representative
       </ description>
      <personName> Reginald Murphy </personName>
      <email useType="primary"> joe.murphy@automeq.com </email>
      <address useType="http">
         <addressLine> http://www.medeq.com/sales/ </addressLine>
      </address>
   </contact>
</contacts>
<businessServices>
   <!-- Business service information goes here -->
</businessServices>
<identifierBag>
   <!-- DUNS Number identifier System -->
   <keyedReference keyName="DUNS Number" keyValue="…"
    tModelKey="…"/>
</identifierBag>
<categoryBag>
   <!--North American Industry Classification System (NAICS) -->
   <keyedReference
            keyName="Automotive parts distribution" keyValue="…"
            tModelKey="…"/>
   ……
</categoryBag>
</businessEntity>
```

Listing 6.1 Example of a <businessEntity> structure

The <businessEntity> in Listing 6.1 is shown to contain a <businessKey> element, which is a unique business identifier for that <businessEntity>. The value of this attribute is a UUID, which the UDDI registry generates automatically and assigns to the <businessEntity> when it is first created. Entities like <businessService>, <bindingTemplate>, and <tModel> also contain UUID keys. A prospective partner (client) can search the UDDI on the basis of one or more of the <businessEntity> attributes in Listing 6.1 and locate matching enterprises.

The discovery URLs element. This is an optional element and contains the URLs that point to alternate Web addressable (via HTTP GET) discovery documents.

An example of a <discoveryURL>, generated by a UDDI node that is accessible at **www.medeq.com** and rendered by the publisher of the <businessEntity> that is identified by the hypothetical <businessKey> attribute uddi:medeq.com:registry:sales:55, is

```
<discoveryURL useType="businessEntity">
   http://www.
   medeq.com?businessKey=uddi:example.com:registry:sales:55
</discoveryURL>
```

The name element. The name element contains the common name of the organization that a business entity represents. A <businessEntity> may contain more than one name. Multiple names are useful; for example, in order to specify both the legal name and a known abbreviation of a <businessEntity>. In Listing 6.1 the attribute xml:lang="en" signifies that the company's name is specified in English.

The description element. This element is a short narrative description for the business. A <businessEntity> can contain several descriptions, e.g., in different languages.

The contacts element. This element is an optional list of contact information for the organization, see Listing 6.1. The contact structure records contact information for a person or a job role within the <businessEntity> so that someone who finds the information can make human contact for any purpose.

The business services element. This is an optional list containing information describing logical families of the business services that this business entity provides. This simple container holds one or more <businessService> entities, each of which represents a Web service implementation. The <businessService> data structure is covered in some detail in the following section.

The identifier bag element. In addition to the descriptive information the UDDI registry provides information about enterprises and their services; it also provides formal identifiers for business entities. The UDDI specification requires that UDDI products support several identifier systems, including two industry standards, the Dunn and Bradstreet's Data Universal System Number Identification System (DUNS) and the Thomas Register Supplier Identifier Code system. These systems are useful for looking up companies in the UDDI registry and provide unique supplier identification digits.

The <identifierBag> is an optional list of name–value pairs that can act as alternative identifiers for the company: for example, the US tax code, business identifiers such as DUNS. A company may have multiple identifiers in this field. An <identifierBag> structure is modeled as a list of "tModelKey/keyName/keyValue". Each such triplet is called a *keyed reference*. An <identifierBag> is a list of one or more <keyedReference> structures, each representing a single identification.

A <tModel> (see section 6.3.1.3) is a data structure that identifies the specifications for a specific taxonomy or classification system [Monson-Haefel 2004]. Each <tModel> has a unique <tModelKey> element that can be used to look up the <tModel> in a UDDI registry.

The <keyedReference> contains three attributes: <tModelKey>, <keyName>, and <keyValue>. The required <tModelKey> refers to the <tModel> element that represents the identifier system, and the required <keyValue> contains the actual identifier within this system. For instance, identifying SAP AG by its DUNS number, using the corresponding <tModelKey> element within the UBR, is accomplished as follows:

```
<identifierBag>
   <keyedReference
      tModelKey="uddi:uddi.org:ubr:identifier:dnb.com:d-u-n-s"
      keyName="SAP AG"
      keyValue="31-626-8655" />
</identifierBag>
```

The category bag element. A <categoryBag> element is similar to the <identifierBag>. This element is a list of one or more <keyedReference> structures that tag the business entity with specific classification information, e.g., industry, product, or geographic codes. This could be in the form of industry taxonomy classifiers, e.g., the Universal Standard Products and Services Classification (UNSPC), which is an open, global coding system for classifying products and services, or geographic classifiers, or the North American Industry Classification System (NAICS), which likewise defines codes for business and product categories.

6.3.1.2 Web service description information

The top-level entity <businessEntity> declares an element called a <businessServices> entity. This entity in turn contains one or more <businessService> data structures, with each <businessService> construct being the logical descendant of a single <businessEntity>. Each <businessService> data structure represents a logical service classification about a family of Web services offered by a company and contains descriptive information in business terms. At the Web service information level, there is still no technical information provided about Web services; rather, the <businessService> structure provides the ability to assemble a set of services under a common rubric.

The <businessService> structure is a descriptive container that is used to group a series of Web services related to either a business process or category of services. It is used to reveal service-related information such as the name of a Web service aggregate, a description of the Web service, or categorization details. Examples of business processes that would include related Web service information include purchasing services, shipping services, and other high-level business processes. Such <businessService> information sets as these can each be further categorized, allowing Web service

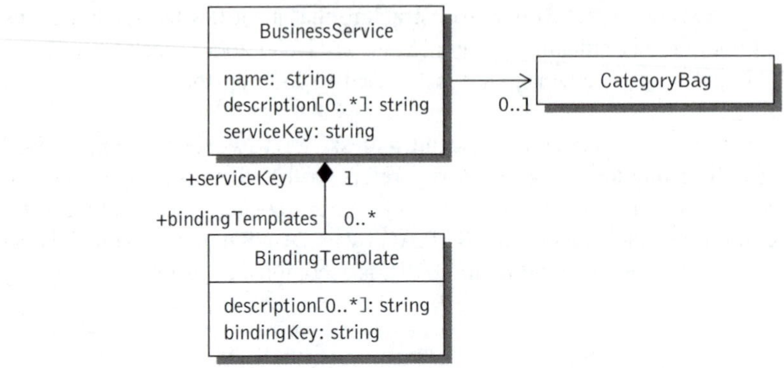

Figure 6.5 The <businessService> data structure expressed in UML

descriptions to be segmented along combinations of industry, product, and service or geographic category boundaries. Each <businessService> outlines the purpose of the individual Web services found within it. For example, a <businessService> structure could contain a set of purchase order Web services (submission, confirmation, and notification) that are provided by a business. Figure 6.5 illustrates the <businessService> data structure expressed in UML.

A <businessService> contains one or more <bindingTemplate> entities. The relationship between a <businessService> and <bindingTemplate> entity is similar to the relationship between a WSDL <service> and the WSDL <port> elements. A <bindingTemplate> describes a Web service endpoint and represents the "technical fingerprint" of a Web service [Monson-Haefel 2004]. This means that it lists all <tModel> types that describe a Web service, which uniquely identify the technical specifications of a Web service.

The kind of information contained in a <businessService> element maps to the "yellow pages" information about a company. Just like any other data structure in UDDI, the <businessService> structure is described by an XML schema complex type. The example in Listing 6.2 shows a sample <businessService> instance in the UDDI registry corresponding to the company modeled in Listing 6.1. This information was not shown in Listing 6.1. As can be seen in the listing, <businessService> contains the service name, description, and classification information (<categoryBag> element).

A prospective partner can search the UDDI to locate businesses which service a particular industry or product category, or which are located within a specific geographic region.

A given <businessService> entity is uniquely identified by its service key. The <businessKey> attribute uniquely identifies the <businessEntity> which is the provider of the <businessService>. The service key is assigned by the operator node when the service is registered. Every <businessService> element is contained in exactly one <businessEntity>, see Figure 6.3. Simple textual information about the <businessService>, potentially in multiple languages, is given by its name and short service description. The name of a <businessService> entity is adorned with a unique

```
<businessServices>
   <businessService serviceKey=" ">
      <name> Search the Automotive Equipment Manufacturing parts
                                                   Registry </name>
         <description lang="en">
            Get to the Automotive Equipment Manufacturing parts
            Registry
         </description>
         <bindingTemplates>
            <bindingTemplate bindingKey="..">
               <description lang="en">
                  Use your Web Browser to search the parts
                  registry
               </description>
               <accessPoint URLType="http">
                  http://www.automeq.com/b2b/actions/search.jsp
               </accessPoint>
               <tModelInstanceDetails>
                  <tModelInstanceInfo
                      tModelKey="uddi:.."/>
               <tModelInstanceDetails>
            </bindingTemplate>
         </bindingTemplates>
   </businessService>
</businessServices>
```

Listing 6.2 Example of a `<businessService>` structure

`xml:lang` value to signify the language it is expressed in. The `<categoryBag>` element contained in a `<businessService>` data structure is the same type that is used in the `<businessEntity>` structure. The `<categoryBag>` contains a list of business categories where each describes a specific business aspect of the `<businessService>` (e.g., industry, product category, or geographic region). A given `<businessService>` contains a `<bindingTemplates>` element, which is a list of technical descriptions for the Web services provided. More information on binding templates is given below.

6.3.1.3 Web service access and technical information

Each `<businessService>` may potentially contain multiple `<bindingTemplate>` structures, each of which describes a Web service (see Figure 6.6). More precisely, each `<bindingTemplate>` represents a different Web service `<port>` or `<binding>`. All access information required to invoke a service is described in the information element named `<bindingTemplate>`. In contrast with the `<businessEntity>` and `<businessService>` structures, which are oriented towards auxiliary information about providers and services, a `<bindingTemplate>` element provides the technical information needed by applications to bind (map the name of a service to its WSDL

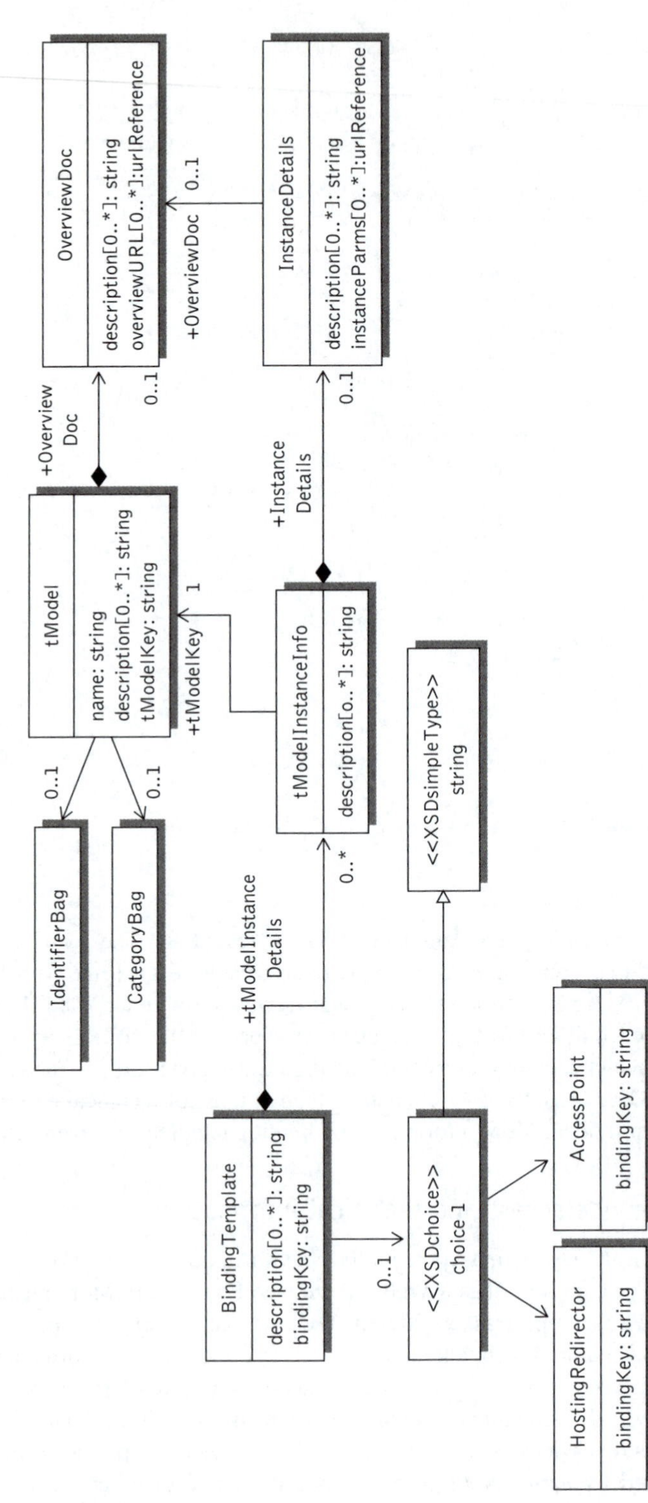

Figure 6.6 The `<bindingTemplate>` and `<tModel>` data structures expressed in UML

description) and interact with the Web service being described. It must contain either the access point for a given service or an indirection mechanism that will lead one to the access point. Technical descriptions of Web services – the "green pages" data – reside within the <bindingTemplate> elements listed in the <bindingTemplate> element of a <businessService>. These structures provide support for determining a technical endpoint or optionally support remotely hosted services, as well as a lightweight facility for describing unique technical characteristics of a given implementation. Support for technology- and application-specific parameters and settings is also provided. This information is relevant for application programs and clients that need to connect to and then communicate and invoke a remote Web service.

Listing 6.3 shows the <bindingTemplate> structure that corresponds to the <businessService> structure in Listing 6.2. The <bindingTemplate> in this listing provides references to details about data formats and requirements of the trading partners.

```
<bindingTemplate bindingKey="..">
   <description lang="en">
      Use your Web Browser to search the parts registry
   </description>
   <accessPoint URLType="http">
      http://www.automeq.com/b2b/actions/search.jsp
   </accessPoint>
   <tModelInstanceDetails>
       <tModelInstanceInfo
          tModelKey="uddi:.."/>
   <tModelInstanceDetails>
</bindingTemplate>
```

Listing 6.3 An example of a <bindingTemplate> structure

When a <bindingTemplate> structure is defined, the designer declares either an <accessPoint> or a <hostingRidirector> element (but not both). The <accessPoint> element is an attribute-qualified pointer to a service entry point. In other words, it provides the exact electronic address of a Web service. Valid access point values can include the URL, e-mail, or even a phone number. The <accessPoint> has a <URLType> attribute to facilitate searching for entry points associated with a particular type of service. An example could be a purchase order service that provides three types of entry points: one for HTTP, one for SMTP, and one for fax ordering. A <bindingTemplate> may have only a single <accessPoint> element. If a Web service is accessible via more than one URL, then a different <bindingTemplate> structure must be defined for each URL. The <hostingRidirector> element indicates that the actual <bindingTemplate> element points to another <bindingTemplate> that ultimately provides the required binding information. Redirection is useful if multiple service descriptions may profit from a given <bindingTemplate>, or if the service is hosted remotely.

It is not always enough simply to know where to contact a particular Web service. For instance, if we know that a service provider provides a Web service that accepts purchase orders, knowing the URL for that service is not enough. There is a clear requirement to understand the technical details regarding a service, such as what format the purchase order should be sent in, which protocols are appropriate, what security is required, and what form of response will result after sending the purchase order. This objective is met by using the UDDI <tModel> (short for "Technology Model"). A <tModel> provides green page information describing the technical details of a service. In particular a <tModel> contains (within the <overviewDoc> element) a pointer to a file that could contain the WSDL description of the service. These technical details are supplied in the specification of the service, which we described in section 5.2. A common use of the technical fingerprint is referring to a Web service WSDL in the <bindingTemplate>. To understand the relationship between a binding template and a technology model we need to realize that a <businessService> structure can support several business protocols or specifications (XML vocabularies, EDI standards, RosettaNet Partner Interface Processes, and so on) each having a separate <bindingTemplate>. The <bindingTemplate> can reference each such protocol or specification with a specific <tModel>.

When describing how a Web service is to interact with its clients, the primary role that a <tModel> plays is to provide a technical specification. For instance, in the case of a purchase order, the Web service that accepts a purchase order exhibits a set of well-defined behaviors if the proper document format is sent to the proper address in the right way. A UDDI registration for this service would consist of an entry for the business partner <businessEntity>, a logical service entry that describes the purchasing service <businessService>, and a <bindingTemplate> entry that describes the purchase order service by listing its URL and a reference to a <tModel> that is used to provide information about the service's interface and its technical specification. In the purchase order example, the <tModel> reference (<tModelKey>) found in its <bindingTemplate> is a pointer to information about the specifics of this purchase order Web service that contain such information as software settings that the service provider's system needs in order to connect and exchange data. The designers of the purchase order specifications can thus establish a unique technical identity within a UDDI registry by registering information about the specification in a <tModel>. In this way the <tModel> becomes a technical fingerprint that is unique to a given specification. This refers to any technical specifications such as service types, bindings, and wire protocols or prearranged agreements on how to conduct business. Once registered in this way, other parties can express the availability of Web services that are compliant with a specification by simply including a reference to the <tModel> identifier (called a <tModelKey>) in their technical service descriptions <bindingTemplate> data. The reference itself is a pledge by the enterprise that exposes the Web service that it has implemented a service that is compatible with the <tModel> referenced. In this way, many companies can provide Web services that are compatible with the same specifications. This approach facilitates searching for registered Web services that are compatible with a particular specification and promotes interoperability between disparate software systems.

It is important that taxonomies are used when publishing data in a UDDI registry. To facilitate the discovery of businesses, services, bindings, or service types, UDDI registration data could be marked with a set of categories that can universally be searched on. To achieve this, the <tModel> defines an abstract namespace reference that is used to identify or classify business entities, business services, and even <tModel>s. A namespace <tModel> represents a scoping domain. For example, the Universal Standard Products and Services Classification (UNSPSC), a set of categorization codes representing product and service categories, could be used to specify a product and service offering of a particular business in a more formalized way. Irrespective of whether identification systems, e.g., the DUNS number system which identifies companies globally, are used to uniquely identify information, standard codes (such as the UNSPSC) are used to classify businesses, or a new taxonomy is created and distributed, it is imperative that UDDI data – `businessEntity`, `businessService`, `bindingTemplate`, and `tModel` elements alike – are attributed with metadata.

The <tModel> data structure expressed in UML is illustrated in Figure 6.6. A given <tModel> structure is uniquely identified by its <tModelKey> attribute. These too are assigned by the operator node in a manner similar to the business, service, and binding keys. The name element is the name of this <tModel>. The <description> element is a short narrative description for this technical model, which may appear multiple times for different languages. The <overviewDoc> element is a reference to remote instructions or descriptions related to the <tModel> and an <overviewURL> element. The <overviewURL> element can be any valid URL, but the convention is to use a URL that points to a file, e.g., a WSDL definition of a service, which can be obtained with a standard HTTP GET operation, or downloaded using a common Web browser. The <identifierBag> element is an optional list of name–value pairs that are used to record identification numbers for this <tModel>. The <categoryBag> element is an optional list of name–value pairs that are used to record specific taxonomy information, e.g., industry, product or geographic codes, for this <tModel>. These elements were described in section 6.3.1.1.

Listing 6.4 shows a sample <tModel> entry in the UDDI registry for a RosettaNet Partner Interface Process (PIP) for enabling trading partners to request and provide quotes. RosettaNet defines a set of standards for IT, an electronic component, and a semiconductor manufacturing supply chain (see section 14.3). RosettaNet PIPs define business processes between trading partners. Listing 6.4 refers to the PIP 3A1 "Request Quote" which enables a buyer to request a product quote from a provider, and a provider to respond with either a quote or a referral. As can be seen from Listing 6.4, the specification is not stored in the UDDI registry; instead the <tModel> has a URL <overviewDoc> element that points to where it can be found.

Published "best practices" for using a UDDI registry to store information about WSDL services recommend that a <bindingTemplate> contains two different <tModelKey> attributes that point to two different <tModel>s for a specific Web service [Kifer 2005]. One <tModel> entry points to a file containing the WSDL description of the <portType> of the service while the other points to a file containing the WSDL description of its <binding>. One reason for this recommendation for having two different <tModel>s for a specific Web service is that the <portType> of the service might be shared by many businesses providing the same service. For instance, there might be a

```
<tModel tModelKey="…" >

 <name> RosettaNet-Org </name>
 <description xml:lang="en">
      Supports a process for trading partners to request and
        provides quotes
 </description >

 <overviewDoc>
    <description xml:lang="en">
         This compressed file contains the specification in a word
         document, the html guidelines document, and the XML schemas.
    </ description>
    <overviewURL>
          http://www.rosettanet.org/rosettanet/Doc/0/
          K96RPDQA97A1311M0304UQ4J39/3A1_RequestQuote.zip
    </overviewURL>
  </overviewDoc>

  <categoryBag>
      <keyedReference  keyName="Trading quote request and
                                                 provision"
                       keyValue="80101704" tModelKey=" ….."/>
  </categoryBag>
</tModel>
```

Listing 6.4 Example of a sample <tModel> entry

standard order management service having a generic <portType> available to the entire electronics manufacturing sector. Many individual enterprises within this sector may provide the same service, each with their own binding. The <bindingTemplate>s of each of these enterprises would then point to the same <tModel> <portType> and to different <tModel>s for their individual <binding>s. This means that all manufacturing enterprise order management services are semantically equivalent but are implemented differently. Another reason for having two different <tModel>s for a specific Web service is that a single provider may wish to provide the same <portType> with different <binding>s for a particular service.

UDDI, just like WSDL, draws a sharp distinction between abstraction and implementation. In fact, as we have already seen, a <tModel> fulfills the role of providing technical fingerprints, abstract types of metadata, and interfaces. An example might be a specification that outlines wire protocols and interchange formats. These can, for instance, be found in the RosettaNet PIPs, the Open Applications Group Integration Specification, and various EDI efforts, and so on.

6.3.1.4 The publisher assertion structure

Many enterprises are not effectively represented by a single <businessEntity>, since their description and, hence, their discovery are likely to be diverse. For instance, large multinational organizations have many divisions and departments that may need to create their own UDDI entries for Web services they offer, but still want to be recognized as part of a larger organization. As a consequence, several <businessEntity> structures can be published representing individual divisions or subsidiaries of an organization. This objective can be achieved using a <publisherAssertion> structure.

A <publisherAssertion> structure defines relationships between pairs of <businessEntity> structures. Two (or more) related enterprises may use the <publisherAssertion> structure to publish assertions of business relationships, which are mutually acceptable to both parties.

```
<publisherAssertion>
    <fromKey> FE565 … <\fromKey>
    <toKey> A237B   … <\toKey>
    <keyedReference tModelKey="uuid:807A .. " />
                    keyName="subsidiary"
                    keyValue="parent-child">
    </ keyedReference >
</publisherAssertion>
```

Listing 6.5 Example of a sample <publisherAssertion> entry

Listing 6.5 shows a <publisherAssertion> structure expressing the relationship between a fictitious corporation and one of its divisions. In this listing, the <fromKey> and <toKey> constructs contain the business keys of two related companies. The <tModelKey> attribute in the <keyedReference> element refers to the type of relationship, e.g., business partners, holding company, or franchise, which represents the relationship between these organizations. UDDI has defined a canonical <tModel> for such business relationship types. This allows for three valid <keyeValue>s in this canonical tModel: parent–child (for organizational hierarchies such as holding company/subsidiary), peer-to-peer (for companies on an equal footing such as business partners or departments in a company), and identity (for indicating that the two business entities represent the same company).

6.3.2 WSDL to UDDI mapping model

Due to the fact that both UDDI and WSDL schema have been architected to delineate clearly between interface and implementation, these two constructs will quite complementarily work together naturally. By decoupling a WSDL specification and registering it in UDDI, we can populate UDDI with standard interfaces that have multiple implementations, providing a landscape of business applications that share interfaces.

The WSDL to UDDI *mapping model* is designed to help users find services that implement standard definitions. The mapping model describes how WSDL <portType> and

`<binding>` element specifications can become `<tModel>`s; how the `<port>`s of WSDL become UDDI `<bindingTemplate>`s; and how each WSDL service is registered as a `<businessService>`.

As already explained, UDDI provides a method for publishing and finding service descriptions. The service information defined in WSDL documents is complementary to the information found in UDDI business and service entries. Since UDDI strives to accommodate many types of service descriptions it has no direct support for WSDL. However, since UDDI and WSDL distinguish clearly between interface and implementation, these two constructs work together quite naturally. The primary focus in this section is on how to map WSDL service description into a UDDI registry, which is required by existing Web service tools and run-time environments.

In this section we use the term *WSDL interface file* to denote a WSDL document that contains the `<types>`, `<message>`, `<portType>` elements, and the term *WSDL binding file* to denote a WSDL document that contains the `<binding>` element. The term *WSDL implementation file* denotes a WSDL document that contains the `<service>` and `<port>` elements. The WSDL implementation file imports the interface and binding file, while the binding file imports the interface file.

A complete WSDL service description is a combination of a service interface, service binding, and a service implementation document. Since the service interface and service binding represent a reusable definition of a service, they are published in a UDDI registry as a `<tModel>`. The service implementation describes instances of a service. Each instance is defined using a WSDL `<service>` element. Each `<service>` element in a service implementation document is used to publish a UDDI `<businessService>` and the service `<port>`s of WSDL become UDDI binding templates. When publishing a WSDL service description, a service interface must be published as a `<tModel>` before a service implementation is published as a `<businessService>`. By decoupling a WSDL specification and registering it in UDDI, we can populate UDDI with standard interfaces that have multiple implementations. An overview of this mapping is given in Figure 6.7. We summarize this process in two major steps: publication of service interfaces and service implementations.

6.3.2.1 Publishing service interfaces and service bindings

When trying to publish a service, the first step is to create the service interface definition, which includes service interfaces and protocol bindings, both publicly available. Any Web service registered with UDDI must be associated with a `<tModel>`. This `<tModel>` describes the abstract interface, i.e., a set of operations, exposed by a specific Web service. As WSDL allows a `<portType>` and a `<binding>` to have the same name, a `<keyedReference>` is used to differentiate two `<tModel>`s, one of which relates to a `<portType>` and the other to a `<binding>` [Colgrave 2004], [Colgrave 2003a].

A WSDL `<portType>` is represented by a UDDI `<tModel>`. This `<tModel>` is categorized as a WSDL `<portType tModel>` to distinguish it from any other type of `<portType>`. In this `<tModel>` only metadata is stored about a `<portType>`. As the detailed information in the `<portType>` relating to messages, operations, and so on is not duplicated in UDDI the `<portType tModel>` must refer to the WSDL document in which the `<portType>` is defined. In this way application development tools that wish to

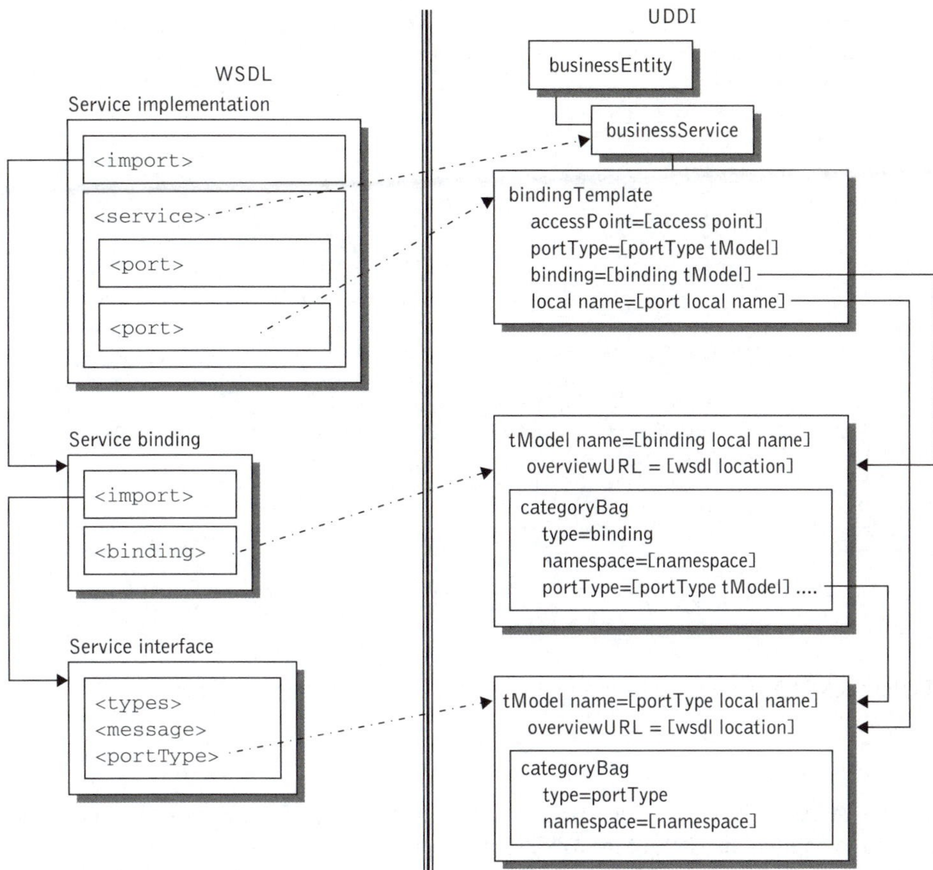

Figure 6.7 Mapping WSDL to UDDI schemas

generate a programming language interface from the <portType>, or sophisticated systems that wish to validate requests against the definition of the <portType>, can retrieve the WSDL document.

Listing 6.6 contains the UDDI <portType tModel> corresponding to the Web service interface definition illustrated in Listing 5.1.

The WSDL `binding` entity maps to a <tModel>. The <tModel> name is the same as the WSDL binding local name. The <tModel> contains a <categoryBag> that specifies the WSDL namespace, it indicates that the <tModel> is of type "binding" to differentiate a <binding tModel> from a <portType tModel>, it supplies a pointer to the <portType tModel>, and it indicates what protocols are supported by the binding. The name of the binding <tModel> is the name of the binding. The namespace of the <binding> element is represented by a <keyedReference> in the <categoryBag> of the <binding tModel>.

As the detailed information in the binding is not duplicated in UDDI, the <binding tModel> refers to the WSDL document in which the binding is defined. In this way application development tools that need this information can retrieve it from the WSDL

```
<tModel tModelKey="uuid:e8cf1163…" >
   <name>
      PurchaseOrderPortType
   </name>
   <overviewDoc>
      <!-- WSDL service interface definition -->
      <overviewURL>
         http://supply.com:8080/PurchaseOrderService.wsdl
      <overviewURL>
   <overviewDoc>
   <categoryBag>
      <keyedReference
         tModelKey="uuid:d01987d1…"
         keyName="portType namespace"
         keyValue="http://supply.com/PurchaseService/wsdl" />
      <keyedReference
         tModelKey="uuid:6e090afa…"
         keyName="WSDL type"
         keyValue="portType" />
   </categoryBag>
</tModel>
```

Listing 6.6 UDDI <tModel> created from WSDL <portType> element

document. As in the case of the <portType tModel>, the <overviewURL> construct is used to point to the URL of the WSDL document.

Listing 6.7 contains the UDDI <binding tModel> corresponding to the Web service interface definition illustrated in Listing 5.2.

Registering a Web service as a <tModel> provides flexible design patterns for applications using Web services. For example, there might be a standard interface for Web services that provide purchase orders. Assuming that many providers may create Web services that implement this standard interface, clients can search the UDDI registry for a list of these companies and select the most suitable one based on such criteria as cost or response time. Furthermore, if a client uses the purchase order service from a preferred service provider and finds out that for some reason the service is unavailable, then the client's application can dynamically query the UDDI for another company that implements the same interface, i.e., that has the same <tModel>, and use that service instead.

6.3.2.2 Publishing service implementations

A WSDL service is represented by a UDDI <businessService> element and the WSDL port entity maps to a <bindingTemplate>. If the WSDL service represents a Web service interface for an existing service, there may be an existing UDDI <businessService> element that is relevant. In this case, the WSDL information can be added to that existing service. If there is no suitable existing service then a new UDDI

```
<tModel tModelKey="uuid:49662926-f4a…">
<name>
     PurchaseOrderSOAPBinding
  </name>
  <overviewDoc>
     <overviewURL>
        http://supply.com:8080/PurchaseOrderService.wsdl
     <overviewURL>
  <overviewDoc>
  <categoryBag>
     <keyedReference
        tModelKey="uuid:d01987…."
        keyName="binding namespace"
        keyValue="http://supply.com/PurchaseService/wsdl" />
     <keyedReference
        tModelKey="uuid:6e090af…"
        keyName="WSDL type"
        keyValue="binding" />
     <keyedReference
        tModelKey="uuid:082b0851… "
        keyName="portType reference"
        keyValue="uuid:e8cf1…" />
     <keyedReference
        tModelKey="uuid:4dc741…"
        keyName="SOAP protocol"
        keyValue= "uuid:aa254…" />
     <keyedReference
        tModelKey="uuid:e5c439…"
        keyName="HTTP transport"
        keyValue="uuid:68DE9…" />
     <keyedReference
        tModelKey="uuid:c1acf…"
        keyName="uddi-org:types"
        keyValue="wsdlSpec" />
  </categoryBag>
</tModel>
```

Listing 6.7 UDDI <tModel> created from WSDL <binding > element

<businessService> can be created. This new service must be deployed and registered in the UDDI repository. This can be accomplished either manually or, using WSDL- and UDDI-aware tooling, a UDDI <businessService> data structure is created, and then registered. The information contained in the new <businessService> references the industry-implemented standards and provides additional deployment details such as:

- The <businessService> name is generated from the service name in the WSDL service implementation document.

- A <bindingTemplate> is created for each service access endpoint. The network address of the <soap:address> extension element in the service implementation is encoded in the <accessPoint> element.
- One <tModelInstanceInfo> is created in the <bindingTemplate> for each <tModel> that is relevant to the service endpoint being described.

A WSDL <port> is represented by a UDDI <bindingTemplate>. The containment relationship between a WSDL service and its ports is exactly mirrored by the containment relationship between a UDDI <businessService> and its <bindingTemplate>s.

The <businessService> structure for the service implementation found in Listing 5.2 is given below (see Listing 6.8).

The service registered in Listing 6.8 shows its compliance by referring to the <portType> <tModelKey> of the purchase order service in Listing 6.6 (as in uuid:e8cf1163...) and to the <binding> <tModelKey> of the purchase order service in Listing 6.7 (as in uuid:49662926-f4a...) in the <tModelInstanceInfo> structure. It also includes the <accessPoint> element, which refers to the endpoint of the service, or the location where it can be accessed. This corresponds to the network address of the service specified in the WSDL <service> element, and in particular the <location> attribute value of the SOAP <address> extensibility in Listing 5.2.

Figure 6.8 gives an overview of the mapping from the WSDL service interface and service implementation definitions to the appropriate UDDI entries and gives a high-level view of how the listing in the service interface (Listing 5.1) and service implementation (Listing 5.2) are associated with UDDI schema entries such as the <tModel>s in Listings 6.6 and 6.7 and <businessService> and <bindingTemplate> in Listing 6.8.

6.3.2.3 Summary of WSDL to UDDI mapping model

This section summarizes the WSDL to UDDI mapping model. In particular, Tables 6.1 to 6.4 summarize the mapping of WSDL artifacts to the UDDI data structures <tModel>, <businessService>, and <bindingTemplate> according to the UDDI Technical Note [Colgrave 2004].

Table 6.1 shows that a wsdl:portType must be mapped to uddi:tModel categorized as a <portType>. The minimum information that must be captured about a wsdl:portType is its entity type, its local name, its namespace, and the location of the WSDL document that defines the <portType> [Colgrave 2004]. Capturing the entity

Table 6.1 Summary of mapping of wsdl:portType to uddi:tModel

WSDL	*UDDI*
portType	tModel (categorized as portType)
Local name of portType	tModel name
Namespace of portType	keyedReference in categoryBag
Location of WSDL document	overviewURL

```
<businessService
      serviceKey="102b114a…"
      businessKey="1e65ea29…">
   <name> Purchase Order Service </name>
   <bindingTemplates>
      <bindingTemplate
            bindingKey="f793c521…"
            serviceKey="102b114a…">
         <accessPoint URLType="http">
            http://supply.com:8080/PurchaseOrderService
         </accessPoint>
         <tModelInstanceDetails>
            <tModelInstanceInfo
               tModelKey="uuid:49662926-f4a…">
               <description xml:lang="en">
                  The wsdl:binding that this wsdl:port implements.
                  The instanceParms specifies the port local name.
               </description>
               <instanceDetails>
                  <instanceParms> PurchaseOrderPort </instanceParms>
               </instanceDetails>
            </tModelInstanceInfo>
            <tModelInstanceInfo
               tModelKey="uuid:e8cf1163…">
               <description xml:lang="en">
                  The wsdl:portType that this wsdl:port implements.
              </description>
            </tModelInstanceInfo>
         </tModelInstanceDetails>
      </bindingTemplate>
   </bindingTemplates>
   <categoryBag>
      <keyedReference
         tModelKey="uuid:6e090afa…"
         keyName="WSDL type"
         keyValue="service" />
      <keyedReference
         tModelKey="uuid:d01987d1…"
         keyName="service namespace"
         keyValue=""http://supply.com/PurchaseService/wsdl" />
      <keyedReference
         tModelKey="uuid:2ec65201… "
         keyName="service local name"
         keyValue="PurchaseOrderService" />
   </categoryBag>
</businessService>
```

Listing 6.8 UDDI <businessService> created from WSDL service implementation

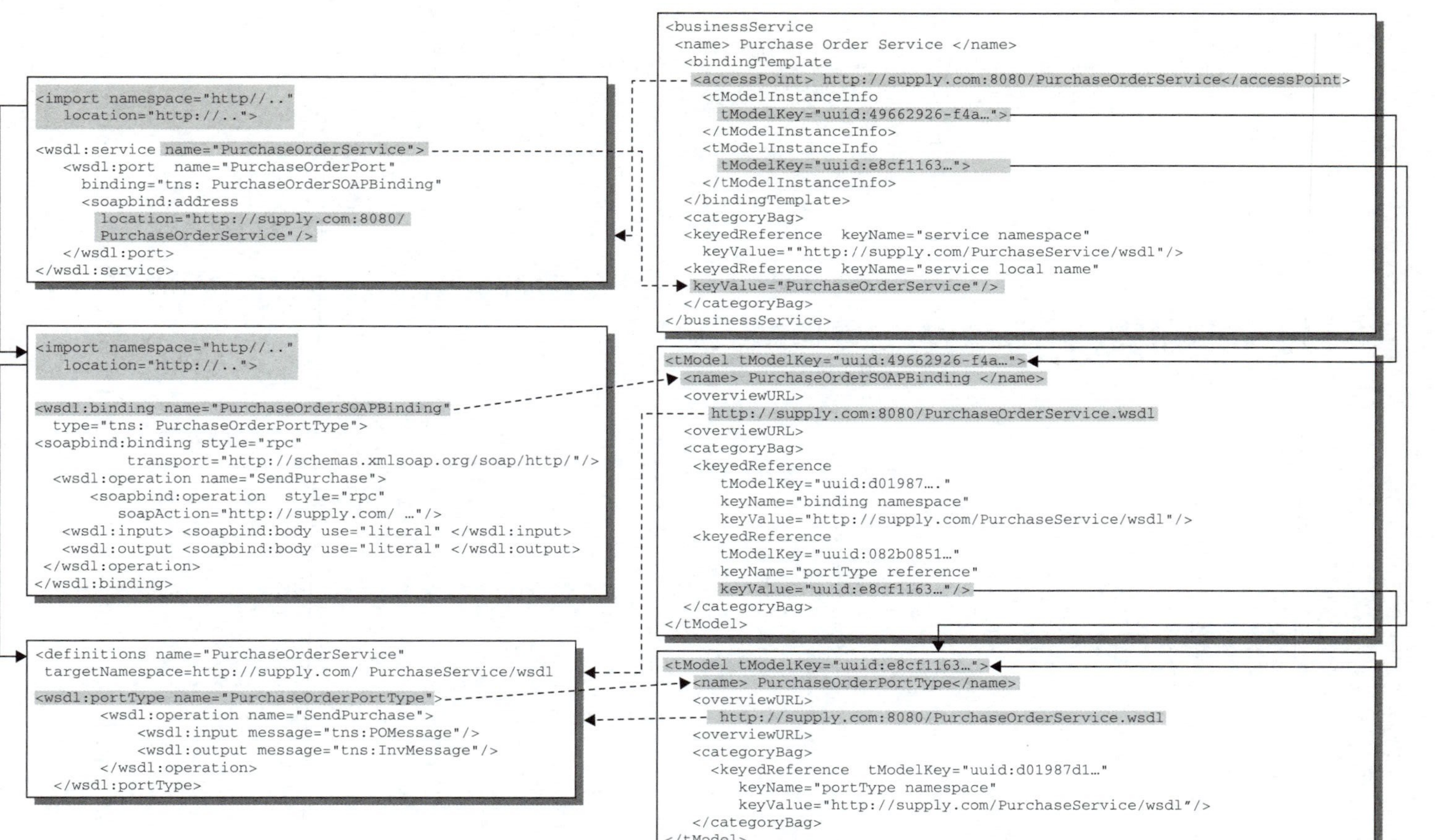

Figure 6.8 Overview of WSDL to UDDI mapping

Table 6.2 Summary of mapping of wsdl:binding to uddi:tModel

WSDL	*UDDI*
Binding	tModel (categorized as binding and wsdlSpec)
Local name of binding	tModel name
Namespace of binding	keyedReference in categoryBag
Location of WSDL document	overviewURL
portType binding relates to	keyedReference in categoryBag
Protocol from binding extension	keyedReference in categoryBag
Transport from binding extension (if there is one)	keyedReference in categoryBag

type enables users to search for <tModel>s that represent <portType> artifacts. Capturing the local name, namespace, and WSDL location enables users to locate the definition of the specified portType artifact.

Table 6.2 shows that a wsdl:binding must be modeled as a uddi:tModel categorized as a <binding>. The minimum information that must be captured about a binding is its entity type, its local name, its namespace, the location of the WSDL document that defines the binding, the <portType> that it implements, its protocol, and, optionally, the transport information [Colgrave 2004]. Capturing the entity type enables users to search for <tModel>s that represent binding artifacts. Capturing the local name, namespace, and WSDL location enables users to locate the definition of the specified binding artifact. The link to the <portType> enables users to search for bindings that implement a particular <portType>.

Table 6.3 shows that a wsdl:service must be modeled as a uddi:businessService. An existing <businessService> may be used or a new <businessService> created. Only one wsdl:service can be modeled by an individual uddi:businessService.

The minimum information that must be captured about a wsdl:service is its entity type, its local name, its namespace, and the list of ports that it supports [Colgrave 2004]. Capturing the entity type enables users to search for services that are described by a WSDL definition. The list of ports provides access to the technical information required to consume the service.

Table 6.3 Summary of mapping of wsdl:service to uddi:businessService

WSDL	*UDDI*
service	businessService (categorized as service)
Namespace of service	keyedReference in categoryBag
Local name of service	keyedReference in categoryBag; optionally also the name of the service

Table 6.4 Summary of mapping of wsdl:port to uddi:bindingTemplate

WSDL	*UDDI*
port	bindingtemplate
Namespace	Captured in keyedReference of the containing businessService
Local name of port	InstanceParms of the tModelInstanceInfo relating to the tModel for the binding
Binding implemented by port	tModelInstanceInfo with tModelKey of the tModel corresponding to the binding
portType implemented by port	tModelInstanceInfo with tModelKey of the tModel corresponding to the portType

The <bindingTemplate>s element of the <businessService> must include <bindingTemplate> elements that model the ports of the <wsdl:service>, as shown in Table 6.4. A <wsdl:port> must be modeled as a <uddi:bindingTemplate>. The minimum information that must be captured about a port is the binding that it implements, the <portType> that it implements, and its local name. By capturing the binding, users can search for services that implement a specific binding. By capturing the <portType>, users can search for services that implement a particular <portType> without necessarily knowing the specific binding implemented by the service.

6.3.3 The UDDI API

A UDDI registry offers a standard mechanism to classify, catalogue, and manage Web services, so that they can be discovered and consumed. Businesses and providers can use UDDI to represent information about Web services in a standard way such that queries can then be issued against a UDDI registry – at design time or run-time. UDDI uses SOAP as its transport layer; thus enterprises can interact with UDDI registries through SOAP-based XML API calls in order to discover technical data about an enterprise's services.

The UDDI API is an interface that accepts XML messages wrapped in SOAP envelopes [McKee 2001]. All UDDI interactions use a request/response model, in which each message requesting a service from a UDDI registry generates some kind of response. The UDDI specifications allow two types of exchanges with UDDI-registered sites: enquiries and publishing. The enquiry API is used to search and read data in a UDDI registry, while the publishing API is used to add, update, and delete data in a UDDI registry.

6.3.3.1 Enquiry API

Requestors can obtain information from a UDDI registry using its enquiry interface. Enquiries enable trading organizations to find businesses, services, or bindings (technical characteristics) meeting certain criteria. The corresponding <businessEntity>,

`<businessService>`, or `<bindingTemplate>` information matching the search criteria is then returned. The UDDI enquiry API has two usage patterns: *browse* and *drill down*. A developer would, for instance, use a browse pattern (find API calls) to get a list of all entries satisfying broad criteria to find the entries, services, or technical characteristics and then use the drill-down pattern (get API calls) to get the more specific features. For example, a `find_business` call could be first issued to locate all businesses in a specific category area, and then a `get_BusinessDetail` call could be used to get additional information about a specific business.

The browse pattern allows for searching the UDDI registry for data structures that match some criteria. It uses the following five operations: `find_business`, `find_relatedBusinesses`, `find_service`, `find_binding`, and `find_tModel`.

The operation `find_business` helps locate one or more `<businessEntity>` entries that match the search criteria. The search criteria are expressed in terms of categories, identifiers, `<tModel>`s, or `<discoveryURL>`s. The search can be performed on the partial name of the business, the business identifiers, the category/classification identifiers, or the technical fingerprints of the services. The operation returns a lightweight list of `<businessEntity>` listings, including their keys, names, descriptions, and `<businessService>` names and keys.

The operation `find_relatedBusinesses` is used to locate information about `<businessEntity>` registrations that are related to a business entity. This operation returns a lightweight list of all the businesses that have visible `<publisherAsertion>` relationships with a specified organization. The search can be modified to list a subset of all related businesses, according to `<keyedReference>` elements. The operation `find_service` returns a lightweight list of business service entries that match the search criteria, which are expressed in terms of given categories, `<tModel>` keys, or both. The operation `find_binding` is used to locate specific bindings within a registered business service and returns the `<bindingTemplate>` entries whose `<tModel>`s match the search criteria. The binding templates have information on invoking services. The operation `find_tModel` returns a list of `<tModel>`s that match the names, identifiers, or categories listed in the request message. This operation returns a lightweight list of `<tModel>` keys.

The drill-down UDDI usage pattern allows specific data structures to be requested by their unique identifiers. A drill-down or get operation can return one or many of the same types of data structure, depending on how many unique identifiers are supplied in the request message.

The drill-down pattern uses the following five methods: `get_BusinessDetail`, `get_BusinessDetailExt`, `get_serviceDetail`, `get_bindingDetail`, and `get_tModelDetail`. The method `get_BusinessDetail` requests one or more `<businessEntity>` data structures by their unique business keys. This operation returns the complete `<businessEntity>` object for one or more business entities. The operation `get_BusinessDetailExt` is identical to the method `get_BusinessDetail`, but returns extra attributes in case the source registry is not an operator node. The operation `get_serviceDetail` requests one or more `<businessService>` data structures by their unique service keys. This operation returns the complete `<businessService>` object for a given business service. The operation `get_bindingDetail` requests one or more `<bindingTemplate>` data structures by their unique binding keys. This operation returns the run-time binding information (`<bindingTemplate>` structure) used for invoking methods against a business service. Finally, the operation get_tModelDetail requests one or more <tModel> data structures by their unique <tModel> keys. It returns <tModel> details.

6.3.3.2 Publishing API

The publishing interface can be used by enterprises to store and update information contained in a UDDI registry. UDDI sites use publishing functions to manage the information provided to requestors. The publishing API essentially allows applications to save and delete the five UDDI data structures <businessEntity>, <businessService>, <bindingTemplate>, <tModel>, and <publisherAssertion> described earlier in this chapter. These calls are used by service providers and enterprises to publish and un-publish information about themselves in the UDDI registry. These API calls require authenticated access to the registry, unlike the enquiry API [Cauldwell 2001].

The publishing API supports four kinds of operations: authorization, save, delete, and get operations. The authorization operations allow a client to authenticate itself, obtain an authorization token, and terminate a session and its authentication token. The save operations allow a client to add or update the primary UDDI data structures. The delete operations allow a client to delete the primary UDDI data structures. The get operations allow a client to view <publisherAssertion>s.

There are two authorization operations: get_authtoken that logs a client into the registry and discard_authtoken that terminates a session and logs a client out of a registry. To start a publishing session with a UDDI operator, a client must first establish an HTTPS connection with a UDDI operator and then send it a get_authtoken message containing its login credentials. When a client finishes accessing the UDDI publishing endpoint, it terminates its session by sending a discard_authtoken operation that instructs the registry to invalidate the authentication token. Further accesses with this token will fail. If the discard_authtoken is not sent, the session will simply time out, effectively invalidating the authentication token.

The save operations allow a client to add or update information in the UDDI. Each of the primary UDDI data structures has a corresponding save operation except for <publisherAssertion>, which has special add and set operations that add and update one or more <publisherAssertion> entries.

The delete operations allow a client to remove information from the UDDI. Each of the primary UDDI data structures has a corresponding delete operation. The get operations allow for obtaining summary data about data structures published by a client.

As taxonomies and identifiers play an important role within UDDI, UDDI facilitates the registration of new business identifiers and taxonomies. The UDDI version 2 specifications add the ability to accommodate validated classification and identification taxonomies. This capability allows any company to extend the support that all UDDI operators use to manage validated taxonomies. In UDDI version 2, two types of taxonomies are supported to encourage registrants to categorize their businesses, services, and service descriptions. These are unchecked and checked categorization and identification taxonomies [McKee 2001]. A provider of a taxonomy or identifier system that wishes to publish its taxonomy or business identifier in UDDI can allow unrestricted references to it or may choose to validate references. Taxonomy and identifier systems that allow for unrestricted references are called *unchecked*. Unchecked taxonomies are registered by simply registering a new <tModel> with a UDDI operator, and classifying that <tModel> as either an identifier or as a categorization taxonomy. Conversely, a taxonomy or identifier system that requires references to be validated is called *checked*. Checked taxonomies are used when the publisher of a taxonomy wishes to make sure that the categorization code values or identifiers registered represent accurate and validated information. NAICS, UNSPC, and ISO 3166 are all checked classifications, which means that the UDDI registry must validate the values submitted by a client as correct. UDDI version 2 supports third parties that wish to create new checked taxonomies of identifiers and categorizations. Registering a checked taxonomy is an involved process between two parties: the organization providing the taxonomy or identifier system and the UDDI registry operator with which the <tModel> of the taxonomy is to be published [McKee 2001].

6.3.4 Querying the UDDI model

The sample queries described in this section are based on the enquiry API and can be issued at design/build time or at run-time, depending on the type of application being developed. The main scenario is that at design/build time, a <portType> is chosen and, if necessary, a particular binding occurs, from which a stub or similar programming artifact is generated. At run-time, implementations of this <portType> and, optionally, <binding> are searched for.

The queries in this section are based on sample queries found in [Colgrave 2003b], [Colgrave 2004] and are issued against the listings found in section 6.3.1. The criteria used in find operations are based on <tModel> values (both WSDL and taxonomy <tModel>s), data fields, and modifiers of the default searching rules used by UDDI.

```
<find_business generic="2.0" xmlns="urn:uddi-org:api_v2">
   <name xml: lang="en"> Automotive Equipment Manufacturing Inc.
                                                         </name>
   <name xml: lang="en"> Manufacturing Goods Co. </name>
</find_business>
```

Query 6.1 Finding business entities by name

Query 6.1 performs an OR search (default case) for businesses matching the names specified in the query predicate. Query 6.1 returns the business entity with name Automotive Equipment Manufacturing Inc. and businesKey="d2300-3aff..." found in Listing 6.1.

Query 6.2 returns a list of businesses with matching <keyedReference> values. Only those <businessEntity> entries that declare the <keyedReference> values involved in the <categoryBag> in the query will yield a match. Query 6.2 returns the business entity with businesKey="d2300-3aff..." found in Listing 6.1.

```
<find_business generic="2.0" xmlns="urn:uddi-org:api_v2">

<categoryBag>
   <!--North American Industry Classification System (NAICS) -->
   <keyedReference
            keyName="Automotive parts distribution"
            keyValue="…"
            tModelKey="…"/>
    …
</categoryBag>
</find_business>
```

Query 6.2 Finding <businessEntity> entries by category

In the remainder of this section we shall concentrate mainly on issuing queries involving <tModel>s to retrieve technical information regarding services that are the point of interest. Recall from the previous section that all WSDL service interfaces are published in a UDDI registry as a <tModel> (see Figure 6.5). Each of these <tModel>s is categorized to identify it as a WSDL service description. WSDL service interface descriptions can be found using the UDDI enquiry API. The UDDI `find_tModel` message is used to retrieve <tModel>s that have been categorized. This message will return a list of <tModel> keys. Using the drill-down `get_tModelDetail` message, applications and developers can then retrieve a specific service interface description. This message could, for instance, return a <tModel> such as the one given in Listings 6.6 and 6.7. Additional <keyedReference>s can be added to the <categoryBag> to limit the set of <tModel>s that are returned in response to the `find_tModel` message. After a <tModel> has been retrieved, the overview URL can be used to retrieve the contents of a WSDL service interface document [Brittenham 2001].

```
<find_tModel generic="2.0" xmlns="urn:uddi-org:api_v2">
   <name> PurchaseOrderPortType </name>
   <categoryBag>
      <keyedReference
         tModelKey="uuid:d01987d1…"
         keyName="portType namespace"
         keyValue="http://supply.com/PurchaseService/wsdl" />
      <keyedReference
         tModelKey="uuid:6e090afa…"
         keyName="WSDL type"
         keyValue="portType" />
   </categoryBag>
</tModel>
```

Query 6.3 Finding the <tModel> for <portType> name

Query 6.3 is a simple query that finds the `<portType tModel>` for `Purchase-OrderPortType` in the namespace `"http://supply.com/PurchaseService/wsdl"`. This query should return the `tModelKey="uuid:e8cf1163…"` found in Listing 6.6.

```
<find_tModel generic="2.0" xmlns="urn:uddi-org:api_v2">
   <categoryBag>
      <keyedReference
         tModelKey="uuid:6e090afa…"
         keyName="WSDL type"
         keyValue="binding" />
      <keyedReference
         tModelKey="uuid:082b0851… "
         keyName="portType reference"
         keyValue="uuid:e8cf1…" />
   </categoryBag>
</tModel>
```

Query 6.4 Find all `<binding tModel>` for `PurchaseOrderPortType`

Query 6.4 finds all `<binding tModel>` for a `PurchaseOrderPortType` that has a corresponding `<portType tModel>` with a key of `tModelKey="uuid:082b0851…"`, regardless of the protocol and/or transport specified in the binding. This query returns the `tModelKey="uuid:49662926-f4a…"` found in Listing 6.7. If a particular protocol and/or transport is required, then extra `<keyedReference>`s involving a messaging protocol, such as SOAP, and/or transfer protocol, such as HTTP, can be added to the predicate of the previous query as necessary.

More information about the WSDL to UDDI mapping as well as the UDDI APIs can be found in references such as [Brittenham 2001], [Colgrave 2003b], [Colgrave 2004].

6.3.5 UDDI usage model and deployment variants

In section 6.3, we explained that UDDI comes basically in two flavors: public and private UDDI registries. In fact, the UDDI usage model envisages different business information provider roles such as:

1. *Registry operators:* These refer to the organizations (referred to earlier as operator nodes) that host and operate the UBR. The operator nodes manage and maintain the directory information, and cater for replication of business information and other directory-related functions. These operators provide a Web interface to the UDDI registry for browsing, publishing, and un-publishing business information. An enterprise does not need to register with each of these operators separately; it can register at any one of the operator companies. The registry works on a "register once, published everywhere" principle. This means that a client searching for a

business or service can do so at any of the registry operators – they should get the same information. This happens since the operator nodes registries replicate their data with each other on a regular basis.

2. *Standards bodies and industry consortia:* These publish descriptions in the form of service type definitions (<tModel>s). These <tModel>s do not contain the actual service definitions, instead they have a URL that points to the location where the service descriptions are stored (definitions can be in any form; however, UDDI, recommends using WSDL).
3. *Service providers:* Commonly implement Web services conforming to service type definitions supported by UDDI. They publish information about their business and services in the UDDI. The published data also contains the endpoint of the Web services offered by these enterprises.

The structure of the UDDI allows the possibility of a variety of private UDDI nodes. Currently, we may distinguish the following UDDI deployment possibilities [Graham 2004a]:

1. *The e-marketplace UDDI:* e-marketplaces are local communities of service providers and requestors organized in vertical markets and gathering around portals. An e-marketplace, a standards body, or a consortium of organizations that participate and compete in the industry can host this private UDDI node. The entries in this private UDDI relate to a particular industry or narrow range of related industries. This gives rise to the idea of a Web services discovery agency (or service broker) that is the organization (acting as a third trusted party) whose primary activities focus on hosting the registry, publishing, and promoting Web services. The service discovery agency can further improve the searching functionality for Web service requestors by adding advertising capabilities to this infrastructure and by supporting facilities for Web service matchmaking between providers and requestors. The e-marketplace node can then provide value-added services such as QoS monitoring and validation of content published by companies, ensure that participants in the UDDI registry have been vetted by a rigorous selection procedure, and also ensure that all entries pertain to the market segment of interest. In such an environment, publish and find operations provided by an API could be restricted to the legitimate businesses registered with the marketplace.
2. *The business partner UDDI registry:* This variant of the above scheme is a private UDDI node hosted behind one of the business partner's firewalls and only trusted or vetted partners can access the registry. It also contains Web service description metadata published by trusted business parties (i.e., those organizations with which the hosting organization has formal agreements/relationships).
3. *The portal UDDI:* This type of deployment is on an enterprise's firewall and is a private UDDI node that contains only metadata related to the enterprise's Web services. External users of the portal would be allowed to invoke find operations on the registry; however, a publish operation would be restricted to services internal to the portal. The portal UDDI gives a company ultimate control over how the

metadata describing its Web services is used. For example, an enterprise can restrict access. It can also monitor and manage the number of lookups being made against its data and potentially get information about who the interested parties are.

4. *The internal UDDI:* This allows applications in different departments of the organization to publish and find services, and is useful for large organizations. The major distinction of this UDDI variant is the potential for a common administrative domain that can dictate standards (e.g., a fixed set of `tModels` can be used).

The closed registries covered above offer some advantages over the global UBR. This registry does not restrict how the service is described; hence an enterprise could describe its services by a variety of means. It could use a URL pointing to a text description of the service, a description in WSDL, or whatever means the company chooses to use. While this allows for flexibility, it severely restricts the ability of applications to interoperate, as an application can not really do anything meaningful with the results of a find operation. Instead, if the description (metadata) were modeled using WSDL (this is recommended as best practice), an application could use dynamic find and bind operations on the service [Wahli 2004].

6.4 Summary

To address the challenges of service registration and discovery, the Universal Description, Discovery and Integration specification was created. UDDI is a cross-industry initiative to create a registry standard for Web service description and discovery together with a registry facility that facilitates the publishing and discovery processes. The UDDI specification provides a platform-independent way of describing services, discovering businesses, and integrating business services using the Internet.

The core concept of the UDDI initiative is the UDDI Business Registration, an XML document used to describe a business entity and its Web services. Conceptually, the information provided in a UBR consists of three interrelated components: "white pages," including address, contact, and other key points of contact; "yellow pages," a classification information according to industrial classifications based on standard industry taxonomies; and "green pages," the technical capabilities and information about services that are exposed by the business including references to specifications for Web services and pointers to various file- and URL-based discovery mechanisms. The UDDI data structures provide a framework for the description of basic business and service information, and architects an extensible mechanism to provide detailed service access information using any standard service description mechanism. UDDI also contains information about the technical interfaces of an enterprise's services.

The chief architectural change in version 3 of the UDDI specification is the concept of "registry interaction." This implies that UDDI should support a variety of infrastructural permutations. For UDDI, this business requirement dictates an increased emphasis on providing a means to define the relationships among a variety of UDDI registries, not simply access to one public registry of business services, namely the UBR. Registry interaction refers to using UDDI to support a variety of network/infrastructure topologies. The possibilities have expanded from a standalone, single-registry approach to include hierarchical, peer-based, delegated, and other approaches. In short, the structure of a UDDI registry (or registries) can now reflect the realities and relationships of the underlying business processes that it supports.

Review questions

- What are service registries and what is service discovery?
- What is the UDDI and what are its major characteristics?
- What are operator nodes?
- Describe the UDDI data structures and their interrelationships in UML.
- What is a `<businessEntity>` and what are its major sub-elements?
- Which data structure in UDDI is used to describe Web service access information?
- What is a `<tModel>` and how does it describe technical service information?
- How does UDDI differentiate between service interface and service implementation?
- What is the purpose of a WSDL to UDDI mapping model?
- Define and describe the concept of a UDDI API.
- Describe how the UDDI model can be queried.
- Explain why it is useful to have various UDDI deployment variants. Briefly describe two important private UDDI variants.

Exercises

6.1 Give an example of a `<businessEntity>` and a `<tModel>`.

6.2 Give an example of a `<businessService>` associated with the `<businessEntity>` you specified in Exercise 6.1. Additionally, give an example of a `<bindingTemplate>` associated with this `<businessService>`.

6.3 Write a query that finds all the implementations of the `PurchaseOrderPortType` in Listing 6.6. This query should use the APIs `find_service` and `find_binding`.

6.4 If we wish to query `<businessService>`s in their own right, as opposed to querying them as part of querying `<bindingTemplate>`s, then it is possible to use any combination of the service's WSDL-related information (the service name, its namespace, and the fact that the `<businessService>` corresponds to a WSDL service) and generic UDDI information, primarily categorizations of the service. Write a query that finds the `<businessService>` for `PurchaseOrderService` in the namespace `"http://supply.com/PurchaseService/wsdl"` in Listing 6.6.

6.5 Consider Listings 5.1 and 5.2, which describe a purchase order service. Show how these WSDL documents can be decomposed into two `<tModel>`s (one for the `portType` and one for the binding) and one `<businessService>` with one `<bindingTemplate>`.

6.6 Write queries to find the `portType` `<tModel>` and all bindings for the `PurchaseOrderPortType`.

PART IV

Event notification and service-oriented architectures

CHAPTER 7

Addressing and notification

Learning objectives

Real-life SOA implementations need to rely on event processing and notification. This form of processing introduces a notification pattern for SOAs whereby an information-providing service sends messages to one or more interested parties. In this pattern the message frequently carries information about an event that has occurred rather than a request that some specific action should occur. This pattern unifies the principles and concepts of SOA with those of event-based programming.

In this chapter we start by describing critical components of the notification infrastructure such as mechanisms for handling stateful resources as well as transport-neutral mechanisms for addressing Web services and messages. Subsequently, we concentrate on a standard Web services approach to notification using topic-based publish/subscribe mechanisms. After completing this chapter readers will understand the following key concepts:

- Representing stateful resources in a Web services environment.
- The concept of an endpoint reference.
- Mechanisms for routing messages and addressing Web services.
- Event processing and notification mechanisms for Web services.
- The WS-Notification family of specifications.
- Peer-to-peer notifications and topic-based notification patterns.

The material presented in this chapter is used to lay the groundwork for more advanced material that relates to event-driven SOAs and the Enterprises Service Bus (see Chapter 8).

7.1 Web services and stateful resources

Generally speaking, the effect of a computation on volatile storage could be described as taking a series of snapshots, called states (see also section 1.4.3). A program's state refers to its ability to "remember" information between successive computations. Usually, procedure (method) invocations cause these computations and change the state of a program (or of an object). As explained in Chapter 1, an interaction spans two modes: stateful and stateless. A stateful interaction keeps track of client state between method invocations, whereas a stateless interaction does not.

Like programs, Web services must also often provide their users with the ability to access and manipulate state. State concerns data values that persist across, and evolve as a result of, Web service interactions. Web services are typically implemented by stateless components such as Java servlets or Enterprise Java Bean stateless session beans. While Web services implementation is typically stateless, Web services interfaces must frequently allow for the manipulation of state [Foster 2004]. For example, an on-line order fulfillment process must maintain state concerning purchase order status, purchases or orders made by specific customers, and the system itself: its current location, load, and performance. Web service interfaces that allow requestors to query purchase order status, make or cancel orders, change order status, and manage the order processing system must necessarily provide access to this state.

In the Web services world, state is any piece of information, outside the contents of a Web services request message, which a Web service needs in order to properly process the request. While Web services successfully implement applications that manage state, it is also desirable to define Web services conventions to enable the discovery of, introspection on, and interaction with stateful resources in standard and interoperable ways [Foster 2004]. The information that forms the state is often bundled together in what is known as a *stateful resource*. A stateful resource exhibits three major properties [Foster 2004]: it is a specific set of state data expressible as an XML document that defines the type of the resource; it has a well-defined identity and lifecycle; and it is known to, and acted upon, by one or more Web services.

Stateful resources are elements that can be modeled and range from physical entities (such as servers) to logical constructs (such as business agreements and contracts). Access to these stateful resources enables customers to realize business efficiencies including just-in-time procurement with multiple suppliers, systems outage detection and recovery, and workload balancing. A stateful resource can also be a collection or group of other stateful resources.

The previous definition concerns itself with how a stateful resource is modeled but not with how it is implemented. The state of a specific resource may be implemented as an actual XML document that is stored in memory, in the file system, in a database, or in some XML repository. Alternatively, the same resource may be implemented as a logical projection over data constructed or composed dynamically from programming language objects (such as an EJB entity bean) or from data returned by executing a command on a private communications channel to a traditional procedural application or data system.

Several aspects of stateful resources are of interest to Web services applications that need to reason about state. These include [Graham 2004a]:

- How a stateful resource is used as the data context for the execution of Web service message exchanges.
- How stateful resources can be created, assigned an identity, and destroyed.
- How the elements of a stateful resource can be modified.
- How the type definition of a stateful resource can be associated with the interface description of a Web service to enable well-formed queries against the resource via its Web service interface, and the state of the stateful resource can be queried and modified via Web service message exchanges.
- How a stateful resource is identified and referenced by other components in the system.

All these aspects are addressed by elements of the WS-Resource Framework (WS-RF), which is concerned primarily with the creation, addressing, inspection, and lifetime management of stateful resources. The relationship between Web services and stateful resources sits at the core of WS-RF.

There are many motivations behind the WS-RF specifications [Foster 2004]. The most notable contribution is the intersection of grid computing and Web services standards and their alignment with SOA principles. In particular, WS-RF helps define how Web services can maintain stateful information, aiming to unify grid and Web services. Through this alignment with the Web services stack, grid services can use existing Web services standards, such as WS-Notification, WS-Addressing, and WS-Security, and build extensions for extended capabilities such as service state data, lifetime, grouping, and reference management. As we shall see in Chapter 17, grid services are particular types of services that are used to represent stateful resources in the context of grid computing. In WS-RF, these stateful resources are called WS-Resources. A grid service has an identity, service data, and lifetime management mechanisms, while a WS-Resource has a name, resource properties, and lifetime management mechanisms.

7.2 Introduction to the WS-Resource Framework

WS-RF is a collection of specifications that provide the ability to model stateful resources (resources whose behavior is defined with respect to their underlying state) using Web services. The framework provides the means to express state as stateful resources and relates to well-known Web services standards such as XML, WSDL, WS-Addressing [Bosworth 2004], WS-Security [Nadalin 2004], and WS-Notification [Graham 2004b].

WS-RF relates to a set of six Web services specifications that define what is termed the WS-Resource approach to representing and managing state. These specifications are listed in Table 7.1. The first five specifications in Table 7.1 are named collectively the WS-Resource Framework [Czajkowski 2004], while the WS-Notification family of specifications addresses notification (event) subscription and delivery. Figure 7.1 shows WS-RF in relation with other Web services standards.

Table 7.1 Summary of WS-RF specifications

Name	*Description*
WS-ResourceProperties	Describes associating stateful resources and Web services to produce WS-Resources, and how elements of publicly visible properties of a WS-Resource are retrieved, changed, and deleted
WS-ResourceLifetime	Allows a requestor to destroy a WS-Resource either immediately or at a scheduled future point in time
WS-RenewableReferences	Annotates a WS-Addressing endpoint reference with information needed to retrieve a new endpoint reference when the current reference becomes invalid
WS-ServiceGroup	Creates and uses heterogeneous by-reference collections of Web services
WS-BaseFault	Describes a base fault type used for reporting errors
WS-Notification family of specifications	Standard approaches to notification using a topic-based publish and subscribe pattern

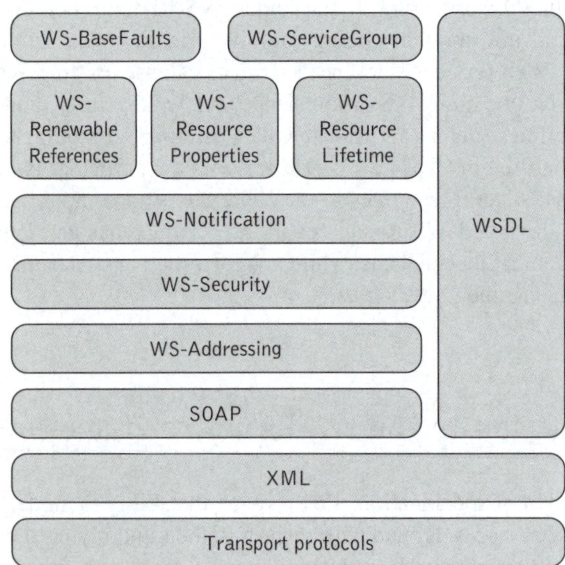

Figure 7.1 Relationship between WS-RF and other Web services standards

WS-RF provides the means to express state as stateful resources and codifies the relationship between Web services and stateful resources in terms of what is known as an implied resource pattern. An *implied resource pattern* is a set of conventions on Web services technologies, particularly XML, WSDL, and WS-Addressing, which as we shall see in section 7.2.1 helps route Web services messages and deliver them to their true

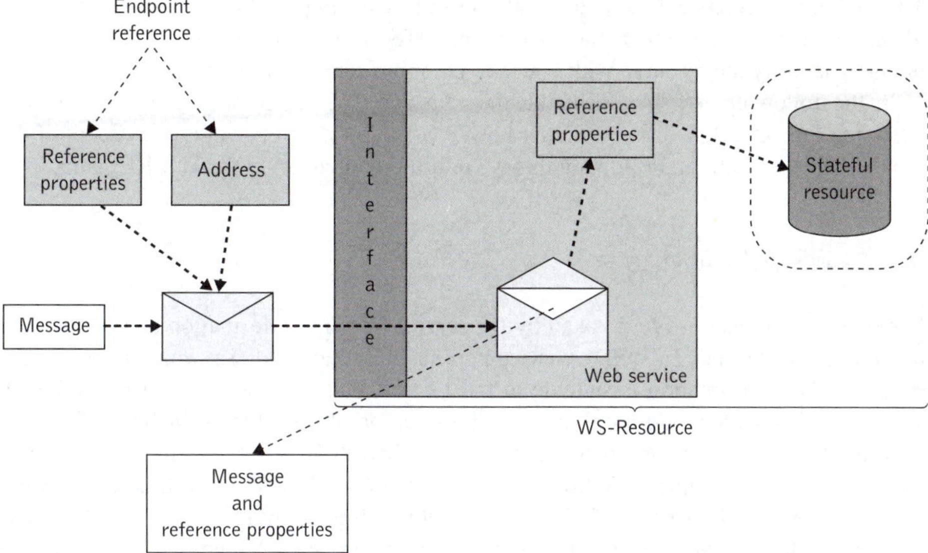

Figure 7.2 Implied resource pattern

destination. In particular, the term implied resource pattern describes the way WS-Addressing is used to associate a stateful resource with the execution of message exchanges implemented by a Web service. An implied resource pattern defines how a particular stateful resource is associated with the mechanisms for processing a Web services message [Czajkowski 2004]. This is illustrated in Figure 7.2 where it is shown how an implied resource pattern helps establish a specific kind of relationship between a Web service and one or more stateful resources.

The term *implied* is used because the identity of the stateful resource associated with a given message exchange is not part of the request message itself. Instead, the stateful resource is implicitly associated with the execution of the message exchange. This can occur either statically or dynamically [Foster 2004]. Finally, the term *pattern* is used to indicate that the relationship between Web services and stateful resources is codified by a set of conventions on existing Web services technologies, in particular XML, WSDL, and WS-Addressing. A stateful resource that is taking part in this implied resource pattern is called WS-Resource, see section 7.2.2. The WS-RF describes the WS-Resource definition and also how to make the properties of a WS-Resource accessible through a Web service interface, and to manage and reason about a WS-Resource's lifetime.

A stateful resource is associated with the Web service statically in the situation where the association is made when a Web service is deployed. Alternatively, when the association is made during execution of message exchanges the stateful resource is dynamically associated with the Web service. When the association is performed dynamically then the stateful resource identifier used to designate that the implied stateful resource may be encapsulated in the WS-Addressing endpoint reference is used to address the target Web service at its endpoint. A Web service *endpoint reference* (described in some detail in the following section) is the equivalent of an XML representation of a Web service pointer.

The endpoint reference is a pattern of message exchange with the implicit resource identifier in the context of a message (using WS-Addressing reference properties) to uniquely identify the resource with which to communicate, see Figure 7.2.

In the following we shall describe the role that WS-Addressing plays in the WS-Resource Framework, and in particular how WS-Addressing relates to the concept of the implied resource pattern. Following this we return our attention to the WS-RF again.

7.2.1 WS-Addressing

Normally, Web services are invoked by the service endpoint information that is provided by WSDL. For instance, a WSDL service port has a location address, which identifies the endpoint. This information is suitable in most cases, with the exception of stateful Web services and cases that add more dynamic information to the address, including instance information, policy, complex binding, and so on [Joseph 2004]. This requires a client or run-time system to uniquely identify a service at run-time, based on run-time information like this. This binding-specific information could include a unique identifier. Currently, there is no standard way by which this information can be exchanged and then mapped to the run-time engine while the service is accessed. The WS-Addressing specification tackles this problem by providing a lightweight mechanism for identifying and describing the endpoint information and mapping that information into the SOAP message headers.

WS-Addressing provides transport-neutral mechanisms to address Web services and messages. WS-Addressing was introduced in order to standardize the notion of a pointer to a Web service [Graham 2004a]. The main purpose of WS-Addressing is to incorporate message addressing information into Web services messages. SOAP itself does not provide any feature to identify endpoints. Normal endpoints like message destination, fault destination, and message intermediary were delegated up to the transport layer. Combining WS-Addressing with SOAP makes it a real message-oriented specification. WS-Addressing provides a uniform addressing method for SOAP messages traveling over synchronous and/or asynchronous transports. Additionally, it provides addressing features to help Web services developers build applications around a variety of messaging patterns beyond the typical exchange of requests and responses.

WS-Addressing defines how message headers direct messages to a service, provides an XML format for exchanging endpoint references, and defines mechanisms to direct replies or faults to a specific location. It also enables messaging systems to support message transmission through networks that include processing nodes such as endpoint managers, firewalls, and gateways in a transport-neutral manner.

The WS-Addressing standard designates that addressing and action information normally embedded in communication transport headers should be placed within the SOAP envelope. WS-Addressing defines two constructs that convey information that is typically provided by transport protocols and messaging systems in an interoperable manner. These constructs normalize this kind of information into a uniform format that can be processed independently of transport or application. The two constructs are endpoint references and message information headers [Bosworth 2004].

The WS-Addressing standard defines a schema for a portable address construct known as an endpoint reference. An endpoint reference provides an address, not an identity, of its target and is defined as an XML type. The address construct is a URI that is used to provide the logical address of an endpoint, and appears in the header block of every SOAP message targeted at that endpoint.

A service endpoint in WS-Addressing follows the implied resource pattern by providing three critical pieces of information required at run-time for interaction with an endpoint: a base address, sets of reference properties, and reference parameters. Reference properties and reference parameters are collections of arbitrary XML elements used to complement the base address construct by providing additional routing or processing information for messages. Reference properties help address collections of WSDL entities that share a common URL and scope. Endpoint references must contain the address along with metadata descriptions, such as service name, port name, port type, and WS-Policy statements that describe the requirements, capabilities, and preferences of the service. Such properties allow discovery of contract details and policies.

To enable interacting with endpoints, WS-Addressing defines a set of headers in SOAP messages that are sent to relevant Web services endpoints. More specifically, it defines a set of four headers (`ReplyTo`, `FaultTo`, `RelatesTo`, `MessageID`) used to dynamically define the message flow between different endpoints. This kind of support not only enables further independence of a SOAP message from its communication protocol, but also defines a means by which Web services may pass references to themselves and other services. The WS-Addressing headers are explained below in conjunction with Listing 7.1.

The sample code in Listing 7.1 illustrates the use of these WS-Addressing mechanisms in a SOAP message being sent from the site `http://myclient.com/business/someClient` to the site `http://www.plastics_supply.com/purchasing`.

```
<Soap:Envelope xmlns:Soap="http://www.w3.org/2003/05/soap-envelope"
               xmlns:wsa="http://www.w3.org/2004/12/addressing">
    <Soap:Header>
        <wsa:MessageID>
            uuid:SomeUniqueMessageIdString
        </wsa:MessageID>
        <wsa:ReplyTo>
            <!-- Endpoint reference for intended receiver of
             message reply -->
            <wsa:Address> http://myclient.com/business/someClient
            </wsa:Address>
        </wsa:ReplyTo>
        <!-- Endpoint reference for ultimate receiver of message -->
        <wsa:To> http://www.plastics_supply.com/purchasing
        </wsa:To>
        <wsa:Action> http://www.plastics_supply.com/SubmitPO
        </wsa:Action>
    </Soap:Header>
    <Soap:Body>
        <!-- The message body of the SOAP request appears here -->
        <SubmitPO> … </SubmitPO>
    </Soap:Body>
</Soap:Envelope>
```

Listing 7.1 A typical SOAP message using WS-Addressing

In Listing 7.1, the lines included in the SOAP header first specify the identifier for this message and the endpoint to which replies to this message should be sent as an endpoint reference. The construct <wsa:MessageID> specifies a URI that uniquely identifies a message, the construct <wsa:From> specifies the endpoint where the message originated from, while the construct <wsa:To> specifies the address of the intended receiver of this message. The construct <wsa:ReplyTo> specifies an endpoint reference that identifies the intended receiver for replies to this message. If a reply is expected, a message must contain a <wsa:ReplyTo> header. The sender must use the contents of the <wsa:ReplyTo> header to formulate the reply message. If the <wsa:ReplyTo> header is absent, the contents of the <wsa:From> header may be used to formulate a message to the source. This property may be absent if the message has no meaningful reply. The last two statements in the SOAP header specify the address URI of the ultimate receiver of this message and a <wsa:Action> element, which is an identifier that uniquely (and opaquely) identifies the action semantics implied by this message, e.g., the submission of a purchase order.

The example in Listing 7.2 shows a sample WS-Addressing endpoint reference. The service's URI is specified in the <Address> element and is shown to the purchase order service specified in Chapter 5 (Listings 5.1 and 5.2). The <Address> element contains the transport-specific address of the Web service. In this case it is an HTTP URL.

The WS-Addressing <EndpointReference> includes a <ReferenceProperties> child element that identifies the resource to be associated with the execution of all message exchanges performed using this <EndpointReference>, see also Figure 7.2. A reference property in this figure is used to identify the endpoint at which a service is deployed.

```
<wsa:EndpointReference
   xmlns:wsa="http://schemas.xmlsoap.org/ws/2003/03/addressing"
   xmlns:wsp="http://schemas.xmlsoap.org/ws/2004/09/policy"
   xmlns:tns="http://supply.com/PurchaseService/wsdl"
>
   <wsa:Address> http://supply.com/PurchaseService/wsdl
   </wsa:Address>
   <wsa:PortType> tns:PurchaseOrderPortType </wsa:PortType>
   <wsa:ServiceName PortName="tns:PurchaseOrderPort">
        tns:PurchaseOrderService
   </wsa:ServiceName>
   <wsa:ReferenceProperties>
       <tns:CustomerServiceLevel> Premium
       </tns:CustomerServiceLevel>
   </wsa:ReferenceProperties>
   <wsp:Policy>
       <!-- policy statement omitted for brevity -->
   </wsp:Policy>
</wsa:EndpointReference>
```

Listing 7.2 Specifying an endpoint reference

The WS-Addressing `<ReferenceProperty>` element indicates that a reference may contain a number of individual properties that are required to identify the entity or resource being conveyed. For instance, the reference property in Listing 7.2 indicates that the purchase order is from a version of the service that provides purchase services with discount prices available for premium customers.

Two endpoint references that share the same URI but specify different reference property values represent two different services. Reference properties are used to dispatch a request to the appropriate service. For example, an application might deploy two different versions of a service and have requests specify a target version in their reference parameters. One service version may target basic service-level customers while the other could target premium service-level customers.

Finally, policies may be included in an endpoint to facilitate easier processing by the consuming application. This is achieved by using the `<Policy>` element in Listing 7.2, which describes the behavior, requirements, and non-functional capabilities of the endpoint according to the WS-Policy specification, see Chapter 12.

WS-Addressing is independent of the other Web services specifications but can be used in conjunction with them. More specifically, WS-Addressing extends and incorporates some concepts from WSDL to identify a full description of the service endpoint. This relationship is shown in Figure 7.3, which depicts the connection among the data structures in the endpoint reference, the WSDL constructs, and the WS-Addressing headers that appear in a SOAP message. As shown in this figure, WS-Addressing makes use of `<Service>` and `<PortType>` constructs. These are very similar to their WSDL counterparts. As in WSDL, the `<Service>` and `<PortType>` name are QNames (qualified names) in WS-Addressing. The `<Service>` and `<PortType>` name in a WS-Addressing endpoint reference are meant to provide compatibility with WSDL rather than to replace it entirely. The `<PortType>` element in Listing 7.2 gives the name of the `<PortType>` implemented by the Web service located at the location `"http://supply.com/PurchaseService/wsdl"`, i.e., the `PurchaseOrderPortType`. Finally, Figure 7.3 indicates that WS-Addressing works in conjunction with WS-Policy to identify various non-functional characteristics that are associated with a specific Web service. This is also illustrated in Listing 7.2. WS-Addressing can also be used with other Web services standards. For example, an application might use WS-Addressing to identify a message's source and destination and also use WS-Security to authenticate the source to the destination.

7.2.2 WS-Resource

A WS-Resource is defined as the combination of a Web service and a stateful resource [Czajkowski 2004]. This combination is expressed as an association of an XML document with defined type with a Web services `<PortType>` element, and addressed and accessed according to the implied resource pattern.

With the WS-Resources construct the relationship between Web services and stateful resources is encoded in such a way that the properties of a WS-Resource are accessible through a Web service interface. This is shown in Figure 7.4. A WS-Resource has a network-wide endpoint reference to identify the Web service and a set of reference properties to uniquely identify the specific resource through the WS-Addressing reference properties.

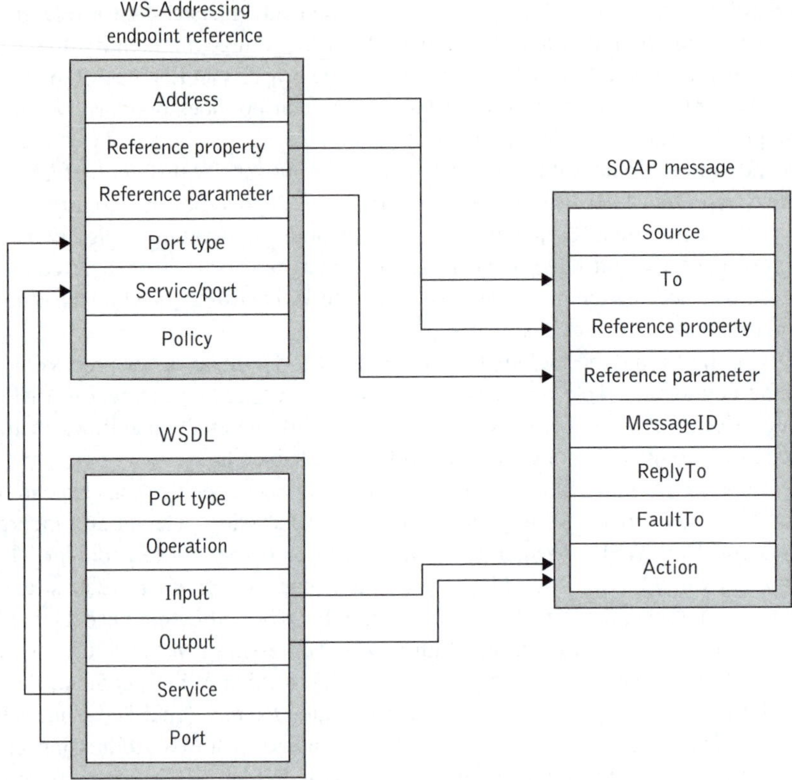

Figure 7.3 WS-Addressing message headers embedded in a SOAP message

For example, Figure 7.4 shows three stateful resources associated with a single Web service. The stateful resource component of a WS-Resource is identified through the use of a stateful resource identifier carried in the reference properties component in WS-Addressing.

Each WS-Resource has at least one form of identity that identifies that unique WS-Resource within the context of the Web service that provides access to that WS-Resource [Foster 2004]. This identity is not the same as the identity of the Web service, but the Web service can construct an address for an associated WS-Resource by including the local identity information of a WS-Resource into the reference properties portion of a WS-Addressing endpoint reference. Such an endpoint reference is then said to be WS-Resource-qualified. A WS-Resource-qualified endpoint reference can be made available to other entities in a distributed system, which can subsequently use it to direct requests to the WS-Resource.

Using the WS-Resource construct, it is possible to completely separate a Web service from its state, which results in a stateless Web service. Such a stateless service acts upon stateful resources, provides access, and manipulates a set of logical stateful resources based on messages it sends and receives.

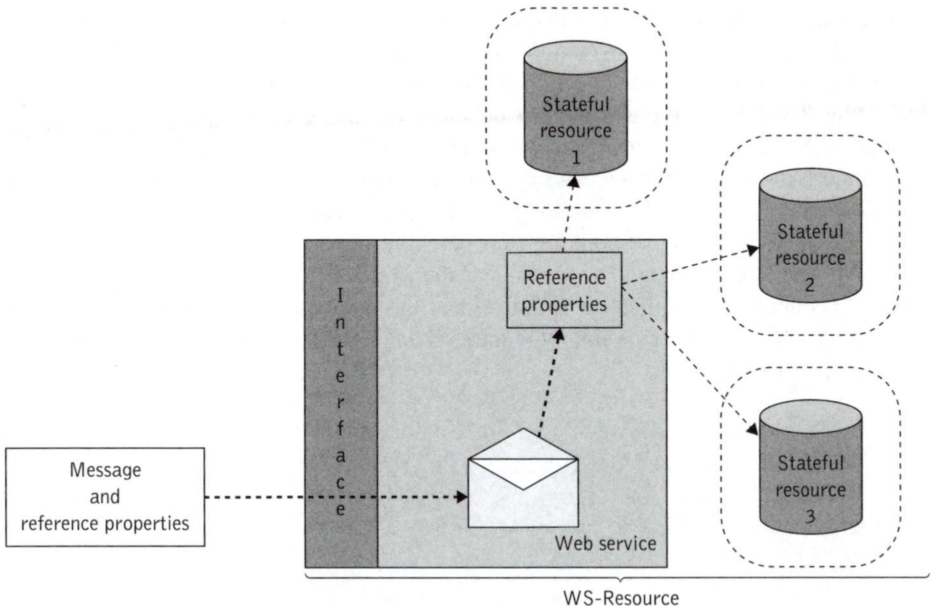

Figure 7.4 Web service and associated WS-Resources

To exemplify the use of WS-Resource consider the purchase order service that we introduced in Chapter 5 and appears in Listing 7.3, which illustrates the `PurchaseOrderPortType`. Here, we assume that purchase orders need to be stateful entities that need to be modeled as WS-Resources that maintain the state associated with the processing of each purchase order request.

```
<wsdl:message name="POMessage">
      <wsdl:part name="PurchaseOrder" type="tns:POType"/>
      <wsdl:part name="CustomerInfo" type="tns:CustomerInfoType"/>
</wsdl:message>

<wsdl:message name="InvMessage">
      <wsdl:part name="Invoice" type="tns:InvoiceType"/>
</wsdl:message>

<wsdl:portType name="PurchaseOrderPortType">
      <wsdl:operation name="SendPurchase">
           <wsdl:input message="tns:POMessage"/>
               <wsdl:output message="tns:InvMessage"/>
      </wsdl:operation>
</wsdl:portType>
```

Listing 7.3 The `PurchaseOrderPortType` from Chapter 5

According to the WS-Resource definition given earlier in this section, a WS-Resource can be defined as the composition of the purchase order Web service and a stateful resource accessed according to the implied resource pattern. The operation `SendPurchase` in Listing 7.3 then becomes a factory operation to create a new purchase order WS-Resource. As we shall see in section 7.2.4, the WS-RF defines simply the factory pattern that supports an operation that creates and returns endpoint references for one or more new WS-Resources. The response is no longer an invoice as can be seen from Listing 7.3, but rather an endpoint reference pointing to a purchase order WS-Resource. This purchase order WS-Resource is created as a result of the `SendPurchase` operation issued by a client. This allows an application to implement the purchase order service by using the implied resource pattern. This simply requires changing the output (response) message in Listing 7.3 as follows:

```
<wsdl:message name="InvMessage">
     <wsdl:part name="POEndPointReference"
      element="tns:POReference"/>
</wsdl:message>
```

The `POReference` element can be defined in the type elements section of the WSDL interface definition file as follows:

```
<xsd: element name="POReference"
      type="wsa: EndPointReferenceType"/>
</xsd:message>
```

The `<PortType>` element responsible for purchase order WS-resources provides operations to allow a client to query the contents of a purchase order that the client submitted, query the status of a submitted purchase order, cancel a purchase order, and so on. This `<PortType>` element will be examined in the following section.

The final item that we need to consider in this section is how to handle responses to a `SendPurchase` operation issued by a client. The content of the response message to a `SendPurchase` operation contains a WS-Resource qualified endpoint reference to a purchase order WS-Resource. This is shown in Figure 7.5. This figure identifies three important constructs of the endpoint reference to the purchase order WS-Resource. These are:

1. The `<Address>` element in WS-Addressing that identifies a URL to a Web service that can perform operations on the purchase order WS-Resource.
2. The reference properties element that uniquely identifies the specific resource specified by the `<Address>` element. More specifically, the reference properties element contains the identifier of the purchase order stateful resource created after performing the `SendPurchase` operation.

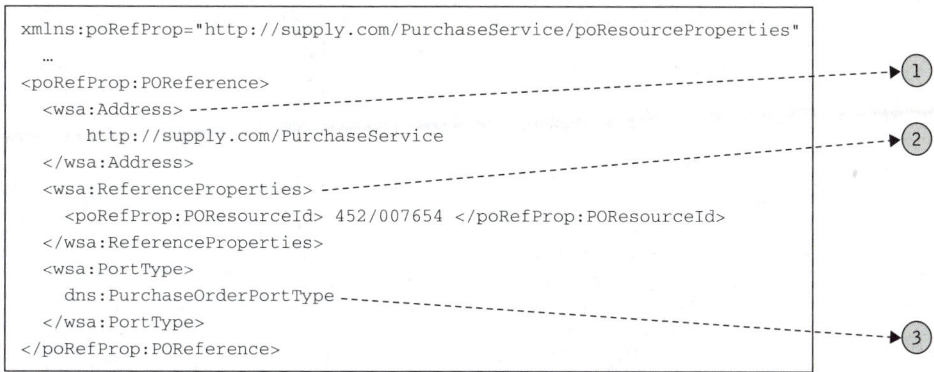

Figure 7.5 Constructs of the endpoint reference to a purchase order created after the `SendPurchase` operation

3. The interface of the Web service, which is identified by the `<Address>` element. The Web service interface is described by the annotated `PurchaseOrderPortType` that we shall examine later in Listing 7.5.

7.2.3 Resource properties

As can be established from the previous discussion an important requirement for stateful resources concerns mechanisms for defining the message exchanges that can be used to access the state of a stateful entity. More specifically, we require the ability to determine the type of the state and the specific message exchanges that may be supported, and issue read update requests and queries against state components [Czajkowski 2004]. To address these requirements the WS-RF specification uses standard XML Schema global element declarations to define resource property elements, which may be declared as part of the Web services interface.

A WS-Resource represents state in a Web services context by means of a set of components called resource property elements. A *resource property element* represents an atomic element of state that can be read or updated. A set of resource property elements is gathered together into a *resource property document*, which is an XML document that can be queried by client applications using XPath or other query language expressions.

The WS-RF WS-ResourceProperties document essentially represents a projection of the resource properties of the WS-Resource, e.g., projecting the utilization of a certain processor, essentially exposing the stateful resource component within a WS-Resource. The WS-Resource properties document defines a basis for access to the resource properties through the Web services interface [Graham 2004c]. A WS-Resource properties document collects resource property elements and is associated with a Web services interface by using an XML attribute on the WSDL 1.1 `<portType>`. In this way the existence and type of a resource properties document is captured, as well as its association with a particular `<portType>`. The annotated `<portType>` defines the overall type of the WS-Resource.

```
<xsd:schema xmlns:xsd="http://www.w3.org/2001/XMLSchema"
  targetNamespace="http://supply.com/PurchaseService/
                                poResourceProperties"
  xmlns:poRefProp="http://supply.com/PurchaseService/
                                poResourceProperties"
  xmlns:po="http://supply.com/PurchaseService/PurchaseOrder"
  ... ... >
  ... ...
<wsdl:types>
    <xsd:element name="dateReceived" type="xsd:dateTime" />
    <!-- Resource properties document declaration -->
      <xsd:element name="execution-status">
         <xsd:simpleType>
            <xsd:restriction base="xsd:string">
               <xsd:element value="received" />
               <xsd:element value="paid" />
               <xsd:element value="pending" />
               <xsd:element value="invoiced" />
               <xsd:element value="terminated" />
            </xsd:restriction>
         </xsd:simpleType>
      </xsd:element>
       …
      <xsd:element name="statusDate" type="xsd:dateTime" />
      <xsd:element name="terminationDate" type="xsd:dateTime" />
      <xsd:element name="handlingPerson" type="xsd:string" />
      <xsd:element name="handlingDepartment" type="xsd:string" />

      <xsd:element name="poResourceProperties">
         <xsd:complexType>
            <xsd:sequence>
               ... ...
               ... ...
            <!-- Resource property element declarations specific
                                          to Purchase Order -->
               <xsd:element ref="po:po" minOccurs="1"
                                               maxOccurs="1" />
               <xsd:element ref="poRefProp:dateReceived"
                                    minOccurs="1" maxOccurs="1" />

               <xsd:element ref="poRefProp:execution-status"
                                    minOccurs="1" maxOccurs="1" />
               <xsd:element ref="poRefProp:statusDate"
                                    minOccurs="1" maxOccurs="1" />
               <xsd:element ref="poRefProp:handlingPerson"
                                    minOccurs="1" maxOccurs="1" />

               <xsd:element ref="poRefProp:handling-Department"
                                    minOccurs="1" maxOccurs="1" />

            </xsd:sequence>
         </xsd:complexType>
      </xsd:element>
  </xsd:schema>
</wsdl:types>
```

Listing 7.4 Sample WS-ResourceProperties document

The WS-Resource properties specification does not dictate the means by which a service implements a resource properties document [Graham 2004c]. Some service implementations may choose to realize implementation of the resource properties document as an actual XML instance document, stored in memory, in the file system, in a database, or in some XML repository. Other service implementations may dynamically construct the resource property elements and their values from data held in programming language objects (such as a J2EE EJB Entity Bean) or by executing a command on a private communications channel to a physical resource.

The WS-Resource properties specification defines an XML attribute named `<ResourceProperties>`, which developers include with WSDL 1.1 `<PortType>` elements to specify the XML definition of the state of a WS-Resource. This XML attribute also indicates that the application developed adheres to the WS-ResourceProperties standard. Using this approach we can specify that the format of a purchase order resource properties document is an XML element of type `POResourceProperties`. This is illustrated in the code snippet in Listing 7.4. The code in this example is based on [Graham 2004a] and has been adapted to suit the purchase order example as defined in Chapter 5.

The actual definition of the `POResourceProperties` element in Listing 7.4 appears at the bottom of the listing. There also appears the original purchase order submitted by the customer, the date that the original purchase order was submitted by the customer, the current processing status of the purchase order, the name of the person handling the order, the department where this person works, and so on.

WS-ResourceProperties defines a collection of message exchanges (operations) that standardize the means by which a requestor can retrieve values of resource properties, update values of resource properties, and issue queries against resource properties [Graham 2004c].

Listing 7.5 shows the new purchase order WSDL definitions, which encompass WS-ResourceProperty concepts and operations. As expected, this listing also includes a new annotated `PurchaseOrderPortType` element.

The following code snippet represents the request message used to retrieve two resource property elements – the execution status of the purchase order and the person handling it – from the WS-Resource that implements the `PurchaseOrderPortType` element.

```
<wsrp:GetMultipleResourceProperties
  xmlns:tns="http://supply.com/PurchaseService/wsdl" … >
      <wsrp:ResourceProperty> tns:executionStatus
       </wsrp:ResourceProperty>
      <wsrp:ResourceProperty> tns:handlingPerson
       </wsrp:ResourceProperty>
</wsrp:GetMultipleResourceProperties>
```

```
<wsdl:definitions name="PurchaseOrder"
 xmlns:tns="http://supply.com/PurchaseService/wsdl"
 ... >

<!– Type definitions -->
<wsdl:types>
   <xsd:schema
        targetNamespace="http://supply.com/PurchaseService/
        poResource.wsdl">
           ... ...
        <xsd:element name="ErrorMessage" type="xsd:string" />
        <xsd:element name="poResourceID"
         type="xsd:positiveInteger" />
   </xsd:schema?
</wsdl:types>
<!-- Message definitions -->
<wsdl:message name="ErrorMessage">
   <wsdl:part name="ErrorMessage" element="poRefProp:ErrorMessage" />
</wsdl:message>
<wsdl:message name="GetInvoiceRequest">
  ... ...
</wsdl:message>
<wsdl:message name="GetInvoiceResponse">
   <wsdl:part name="GetInvoiceRequest" element="inv:invoice" />
</wsdl:message>

<!-- Association of resource properties document to a portType -->
<wsdl:portType name="PurchaseOrderPortType"
        wsrp:ResourceProperties="poRefProp:poResourceProperties">

   <!–Operations supported by the PO PortType -->
   <wsdl:operation name="getInvoice">
         <wsdl:input name="GetInvoiceRequest"
                     message="poRefProp:GetInvoiceRequest" />
         <wsdl:output name="GetInvoiceResponse"
                      message="poRefProp:GetInvoiceResponse" />
         <wsdl:fault name="FaultyInvoice"
                     message="poRefProp:ErrorMessage" />
    </wsdl:operation>
    <wsdl:operation name="dispatch-order"> ... </wsdl:operation>
    <wsdl:operation name="cancel-order"> ... </wsdl:operation>

    <!-- WS-RF operations supported by this portType -->
    <wsdl:operation name="GetResourceProperty"> ...
                                             </wsdl:operation>
    <wsdl:operation name="GetMultipleResourceProperties"> ...
                                             </wsdl:operation>
    <wsdl:operation name="QueryResourceProperties"> ...
                                             </wsdl:operation>
    <wsdl:operation name="SetResourceProperties"> ...
                                             </wsdl:operation>

     :
 </wsdl:portType>
</wsdl:definitions>
```

Listing 7.5 Resource property operations for purchase order

The following is a sample response to the previous simple request:

```
<wsrp:GetMultipleResourcePropertiesResponse
   xmlns:ns1= xmlns:tns="http://supply.com/PurchaseService/wsdl" … >
   <ns1:executionStatus> paid </ns1:executionStatus>
   <ns1: handlingPerson> Charles Simpson </ns1: handlingPerson>
</wsrp:GetMultipleResourcePropertiesResponse>
```

Detailed definitions of WS-ResourceProperties constructs and operations can be found in [Graham 2004c]. Additional listings and examples of how to use the WS-ResourceProperties standard can be found in [Graham 2004a].

7.2.4 Resource lifecycle

The lifecycle of a WS-Resource (stateful entity) is defined to be the period between its creation and its destruction and can be either static or dynamic [Shaikh 2004]. Resources with a static lifecycle are those that are created on or deployed to the system and remain there in a permanent or semi-permanent fashion. By contrast, dynamic lifecycle resources are created and destroyed more frequently. WS-RF addresses three aspects of the entity lifecycle: creation, identity assignment, and destruction.

WS-RF addresses the concept of service creation via by some out-of-bound mechanism or by applying the *factory pattern*, a term used to denote a Web service that supports an operation that creates, and returns endpoint references for, one or more new WS-Resources. A WS-Resource factory is any Web service capable of bringing a WS-Resource into existence and assigning the new WS-Resource an identity. The creation of a new WS-Resource results in the creation of one new WS-Resource-qualified endpoint reference containing a WS-Resource context that refers to the new WS-Resource. The endpoint reference may be returned to the service creator or saved somewhere, e.g., into a registry, for later retrieval.

The WS-ResourceLifetime [Srinivasan 2004] part of WS-RF (see Table 7.1) standardizes the means by which a WS-Resource can be destroyed. The specification also defines the means by which the lifetime of a WS-Resource can be monitored. Normally, a service requestor's interest in a WS-Resource is for some foreseeable period of time. In many scenarios, it is appropriate for clients of a WS-Resource to cause its immediate destruction. In such cases, the WS-Resource might support a message exchange pattern that allows a service requestor to request that resource's destruction. This is the *immediate destruction* mechanism identified in the WS-ResourceLifetime specification. The immediate destruction of a WS-Resource may be accomplished using the message exchanges defined in the WS-ResourceLifetime specification. To destroy a WS-Resource immediately a service requestor must use the appropriate WS-Resource-qualified endpoint reference for the destroy message.

The WS-ResourceLifetime specification also provides a time-based mechanism for managing the destruction of a WS-Resource. This type of distraction mechanism is known as *scheduled destruction*. WS-ResourceLifetime defines a standard message exchange by which a service requestor can establish and renew a scheduled termination time for the WS-Resource, and defines the circumstances under which a service requestor can determine that this termination time has elapsed [Srinivasan 2004]. Using a WS-Resource-qualified endpoint reference, a service requestor may establish and later also renew a scheduled termination time of the WS-Resource.

7.2.5 Service groups

The term *service group* refers to a standard mechanism for creating a heterogeneous by-reference collection of Web services [Maguire 2005]. Service groups can form a wide variety of collections of services, including building registries of services and associated WS-Resources. Members of a ServiceGroup are represented using components called entries. A *service group entry* is a WS-Resource.

The WS-ServiceGroup specification [Maguire 2005] defines a means by which Web services and WS-Resources can be aggregated or grouped together for a domain-specific purpose. In order for requestors to form meaningful queries against the contents of the ServiceGroup, membership in the group must be constrained in some fashion. The constraints for membership are expressed by intension using a classification mechanism. Further, the members of each intension must share a common set of information over which queries can be expressed. The Web service associated with a ServiceGroup entry can be composed from a variety of Web services standards including WS-ResourceProperties [Graham 2004c], WS-ResourceLifetime [Srinivasan 2004], and WS-BaseNotification [Graham 2004d] (which we examine in the following section).

In the WS-ServiceGroup specification (Figure 7.6), the ServiceGroup membership rules, membership constraints, and classifications are expressed using the resource property model. Groups are defined as a collection of members that meet the constraints of the group as expressed through resource properties. A ServiceGroup maintains information about a collection of Web services. Each of the Web services represented in the collection

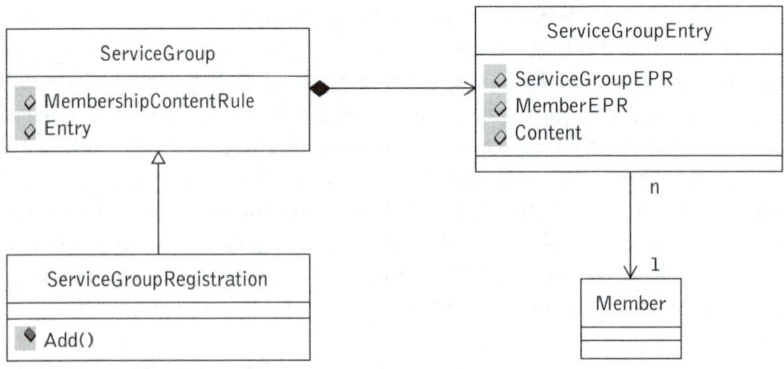

Figure 7.6 ServiceGroup interfaces

may be a component of a WS-Resource. These Web services may be members of a ServiceGroup for a specific reason, such as being part of a federated service, or they may have no specific relationship, such as the Web services contained in an index or registry operated for Web service discovery purposes.

A detailed description of the WS-ServiceGroup specification as well as examples of its use can be found in [Maguire 2005].

7.3 Web Services Notification

As we have already seen in Chapter 2, publish-and-subscribe processing is at the heart of the functionality embodied in event-driven architectures and message-oriented middleware. Event-driven processing and notification is especially important for the event-driven SOA model (see Chapter 8) where Web services interact with each other through the exchange of asynchronous messages.

Event-driven processing and notification introduces a pattern known as the *notification pattern* for SOA implementations. In the notification pattern (sometimes also referred to as the event pattern), an information-providing service sends one-way messages to one or more interested receivers. It is possible that more than one consuming service is registered to consume the same information. In addition, the information-providing (distributing) service may send any number of messages to each registered consuming service as the application may require. In this pattern the message frequently carries information about an event that has occurred rather than a request that some specific action should occur. Another requirement is that message receivers are registered prior to receiving the notifications. Service registration may be initiated either by the consuming services themselves, or by a third party. Registration may be preconfigured or may happen dynamically.

The OASIS Web Services Notification is a family of related specifications that define a standard Web services approach to notification using a topic-based publish/subscribe pattern. The WS-Notification specification defines standard message exchanges to be implemented by service providers that wish to participate in notifications and standard message exchanges – allowing publication of messages from entities that are not themselves service providers. The basic approach taken is to define mechanisms and interfaces that allow clients to subscribe to topics of interest, such as resource property value changes for a WS-Resource. From the perspective of WS-Notification, WS-RF thus provides useful building blocks for representing and structuring notifications. From the perspective of WS-RF, the WS-Notification family of specifications extends the utility of WS-Resources by allowing requestors to ask to be asynchronously notified of changes to resource property values. In addition to WS-RF, WS-Notification is also intended to work together with WS-Policy and WS-ReliableMessaging.

The WS-Notification family of standards provides support for both brokered as well as peer-to-peer publish/subscribe notification and proposes three normative specifications: WS-BaseNotification, WS-Topics, and WS-BrokeredNotification, which are examined in succession in what follows.

7.3.1 Peer-to-peer notification

The WS-BaseNotification specification defines the standard interfaces of notification consumers and producers. This specification includes standard message exchanges to be implemented by service providers that wish to act in these two roles, along with operational requirements expected of them. With this specification notification producers have to expose a `subscribe` operation that notification consumers can use to request a subscription. Consumers, in turn, have to expose a `notify` operation that producers can use to deliver the notification. The configuration where a NotificationConsumer is subscribed directly to the NotificationProducer is referred to as the peer-to-peer, direct, or point-to-point notification pattern. There are other variations of the notification pattern, where the NotificationConsumer is subscribed to an intermediary NotificationBroker service. These are covered by the WS-Brokered Notification specification, see section 7.3.3.

The WS-BaseNotification is the base specification on which the other WS-Notification specification documents depend. The WS-BaseNotification describes three basic roles that are required to allow a subscriber to register interest in receiving notification messages from a notification producer [Graham 2004d]. These roles are: notification producer, notification consumer, and a subscriber. It includes standard message exchanges to be implemented by service providers that wish to act in these roles, along with operational requirements expected of them. The three basic roles in WS-BaseNotification and their message interaction patterns are depicted in Figure 7.7 and are examined below.

A *notification producer* is a Web service that is responsible for managing the actual process of notification. The notification producer is responsible for maintaining a list of interested receivers and arranging for notification messages to be delivered to those receivers. This may involve a matching step, which compares each notification message against the interests expressed by the individual receivers (notification consumers).

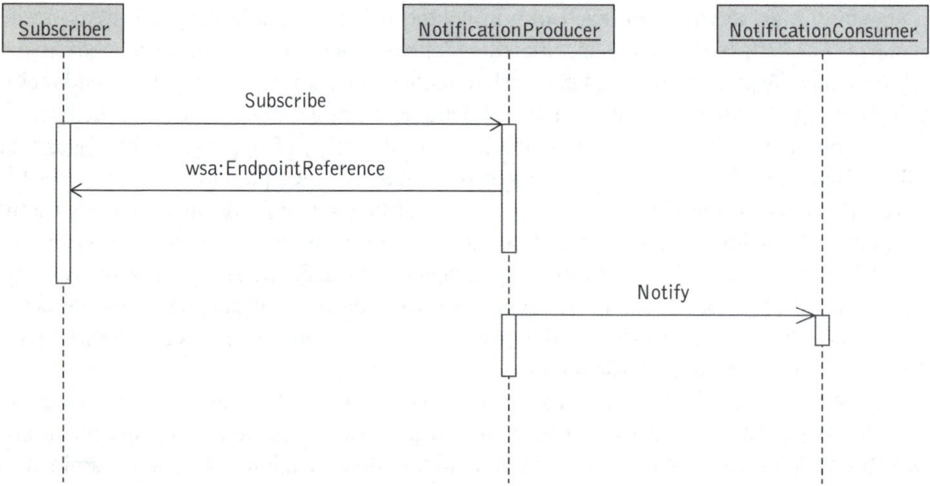

Figure 7.7 Base message exchange pattern

A notification producer performs two functions: it produces notifications and handles notification subscriptions.

As shown in Figure 7.7, a notification producer accepts incoming `subscribe` requests where each `subscribe` request identifies one or more topics of interest and a reference to a notification consumer. If the notification producer is willing to accept this request, it creates a new subscription and adds it to its list of active subscriptions. The notification producer is then in a position where it can start delivering notification messages to the relevant notification consumer.

A *notification consumer* is a Web service that is the counterpart of a notification producer and receives notification messages from a notification producer. A notification can concern anything: a change in the value of a resource property, e.g., a change of status of a purchase order, a time-based event, such as payment expiry, some other internal change in the state of the notification producer, or some other "situation" within the environment.

A *publisher*, which could be a notification producer that acts under this role, is an entity that creates notification messages, based upon situation(s) that it is capable of detecting and translating into notification message artifacts. The publisher selects the appropriate type of notification message and constructs a notification message instance containing information relevant to a particular situation. If the notification producer does not act as publisher, it is referred to as a *notification broker* and does not actually create notification messages, but instead manages the notification process on behalf of one or more publishers, see section 7.3.3.

A *situation* identifies an object of interest reacting to an event. Situations in WS-Notification relate to changes of state, e.g., the purchase order changing status from pending to invoiced; time-based events, e.g., expiry of a timer; or system-resource-related events, e.g., server breakdown. For instance, the purchase order WS-Resource that we examined earlier in this chapter is an object that can detect situations related to a purchase order and generate related notification messages. What is important to the notification pattern is that information relating to a particular situation can be communicated to interested services.

WS-Notification uses the term *notification* to refer to the one-way message that conveys information about a particular situation to other services. The sender of a notification message could choose to format this information in whatever way it sees fit and use a different representation for each occurrence of each situation. Notification messages include the topic associated with the message, the dialect used to specify the topic, and an optional endpoint reference to the producer. Notification messages serve as a general notification–delivery approach because they can contain any type of application-specific notification message.

A single `notify` message can contain multiple notification messages, which are essential to bundle up raw messages with notification-specific information [Vinovski 2004], thus supporting a form of efficient batch-notification delivery. The `notify` message allows the notification producer to supply additional WS-Notification-defined information (such as the topic) in addition to the application-specific notification message content. The notification producer maintains a list of subscriptions. A *topic* is the concept used to categorize notifications and their related notification message schemas. Topics are used as part of the matching process that determines which (if any) subscribing notification consumers should receive a notification message. When the notification producer has a notification to distribute, it matches the notification against the interest registered in each subscription known to it. If it identifies a match it issues the notification to the notification consumer associated with that subscription.

A *subscription* is an entity that represents the relationship between a notification consumer and a notification producer. It records the fact that the notification producer is interested in some or even all of the notifications that a notification producer can provide, and can contain filter expressions, policies, and context information. Each notification producer holds a list of active subscriptions, and when it has a notification to perform it matches this notification against the interest registered in each subscription in its list. If it identifies a match it performs the notification to the notification consumer associated with that subscription.

WS-Notification models a subscription as a WS-Resource, following the implied resource pattern as defined in section 7.2. A subscription is a stateful resource that is created by a `subscribe` request and uses operations defined by the WS-ResourceLifetime (see section 7.2.4) to manage the lifetime of a subscription. In essence, a subscription represents the relationship between a notification consumer, a notification producer, a topic, and various other optional filter expressions, policies, and context information.

Finally, a *subscriber* is an entity (often a Web service) that acts as a service requestor, sending the `subscribe` request message to a notification producer, see Figure 7.7. This results in creating a subscription resource. Note that a subscriber may be a different entity than the notification consumer that actually receives the notification messages. For example, the Web service that places a purchase order request (by invoking a `SendPurchase` operation on the `PurchaseOrderPortType`) might subscribe for changes in the status of the purchase order. Alternatively, it may indicate that a separate inventory management system is the notification consumer.

To create a subscription, a subscriber must send specific information to a notification producer. This information includes a consumer endpoint reference to which the producer can send notification messages; a topic expression, which identifies the topics the consumer is interested in; and a dialect for that expression [Vinovski 2004]. The response to a subscription request is an endpoint reference that includes an identifier for the newly created subscription, as well as an address for a subscription manager service, which can manage the subscription (when contacted).

Figure 7.8 illustrates the WS-BaseNotification entities that we described above. The figure shows a subscriber making a `subscribe` request to a notification producer on behalf of a notification consumer (shown via the dashed lines). As a result of this request, the notification producer adds a subscription to its list of subscriptions and sends a response to the subscriber. Each subscription entry records the identity of the notification consumer along with other properties of the subscription such as the termination time of the subscription and any filter expressions associated with it. As soon as the publisher detects a situation (e.g., expiry date of an invoice has been exceeded), then the notification producer sends a notification to the notification consumer.

7.3.1.1 WS-BaseNotification interfaces

The WS-BaseNotification document's main contribution is two-fold: defining the notification producer interface (supported by applications that accept notification subscriptions

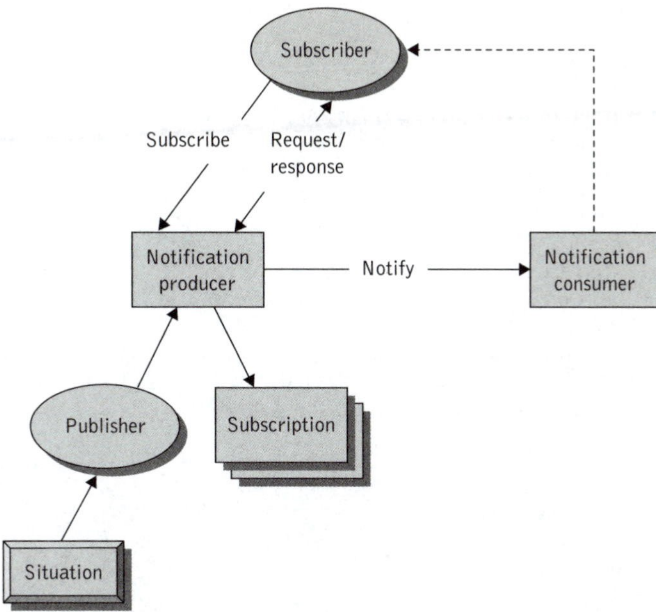

Figure 7.8 WS-BaseNotification entities

and send notification messages) and the notification consumer interface (supported by applications that subscribe to notification messages). These are briefly summarized in the following.

The notification consumer interface. WS-Notification allows a notification producer to send a notification message to a notification consumer in either one of two ways. The notification producer may simply send the raw notification message, i.e., the application-specific content, to the notification consumer. Alternatively, the notification producer may send the notification message data using the `notify` operation. This operation implies that the notification consumer can receive a wide range of notification messages without having to explicitly provide support for each one in its WSDL.

Listing 7.6 is an example of a `notify` message using SOAP. Note the use of the `wsa:ReferenceProperties` elements in the message. These are examples of WS-Resource-qualified endpoint references, following the implied resource pattern as outlined in Section 7.2.

The notification producer interface. A subscriber registers interest in receiving notification messages on one or more topics by issuing a `subscribe` message (operation). The subscriber sends a message to a notification producer in order to register the interest of a notification consumer for notification messages related to one or more topics. As part of the processing of a `subscribe` request message, the notification producer must create a subscription resource representing the subscription. In response, the

```
<Soap:Envelope
   xmlns:Soap="http://www.w3.org/2003/05/soap-envelope"
   xmlns:wsa="http://schemas.xmlsoap.org/ws/2003/03/addressing"
   xmlns:wsnt="http://www.ibm.com/xmlns/stdwip/Web-services/
     WS-BaseNotification"
   xmlns:ncex="http://www.consumer.org/RefProp"
   xmlns:npex="http://www.producer.org/RefProp">
  <Soap:Header>
    <wsa:Action>
        http://www.ibm.com/xmlns/stdwip/Web-services/
        WS-BaseNotification/Notify
    </wsa:Action>
    <wsa:To s12:mustUnderstand="1">
        http://www.consumer.org/ConsumerEndpoint
    </wsa:To>
    <ncex:NCResourceId>
       uuid: … …
    </ncex:NCResourceId>
  </Soap:Header>
  <Soap:Body>
    <wsnt:Notify>
      <wsnt:NotificationMessage>
        <wsnt:Topic dialect="http://www.ibm.com/xmlns/stdwip/
         Webservices/WSTopics/
         TopicExpression/simple">
             npex:SomeTopic
        </wsnt:Topic>
        <wsnt:ProducerReference
             xmlns:npex="http://www.producer.org/RefProp">
          <wsa:Address>
              http://www.producer.org/ProducerEndpoint
          </wsa:Address>
          <wsa:ReferenceProperties>
             <npex:NPResourceId>
                 uuid: … … …
             </npex:NPResourceId>
          </wsa:ReferenceProperties>
        </wsnt:ProducerReference>
        <wsnt:Message>
            <npex:NotifyContent>exampleNotifyContent
                                </npex:NotifyContent>
        </wsnt:Message>
      <wsnt:NotificationMessage>
    </wsnt:Notify>
  </Soap:Body>
</Soap:Envelope>
```

Listing 7.6 Use of the notify message in conjunction with SOAP subscriber receives from the notification producer a WS-Resource-qualified endpoint reference to a "subscription" WS-Resource. This endpoint reference includes the address of a subscription manager service and a reference property containing the identity of the subscription resource. The subscription WS-Resource models this relationship between the subscriber and the notification producer, and uses WS-ResourceProperties and WSR-esourceLifetime to help manage this relationship.

The notification producer interface supports message exchanges that allow the notification producer to advertise its support for one or more topics, and allow a subscriber to create subscriptions or to control the delivery of notification messages by the notification producer.

To allow a newly subscribed notification consumer to get the last notification message that other notification consumers have received, a `GetCurrentMessage` message can be sent to the notification producer. In response to a `GetCurrentMessage` message, the notification producer may return the last notification message published to a given topic.

Listing 7.7 illustrates how notification producer interface messages can be attached to the `PurchaseOrderPortType` defined in Listing 7.5.

The subscription manager interface. When a notification producer accepts a subscription request, it returns an endpoint reference in its response to this request as a reference to the subscription. The Web service whose address is carried in the endpoint reference is in fact a subscription manager, which is a service that allows a service requestor to query, delete, or renew subscriptions [Niblett 2005]. The subscription manager provides this query capability by supporting a number of resource properties that return, for example, the subscription's filter expressions, the consumer endpoint reference, and the scheduled termination time. The subscription manager is another example of a stateful Web service [Niblett 2005].

The subscription manager interface defines message exchanges to manipulate subscription resources [Graham 2004d]. The subscription manager supports the required message exchanges associated with the WS-ResourceProperties specification. In addition to supporting WS-ResourceProperties operations, the subscription manager must also support the message exchanges defined for both forms of resource lifetime (immediate and scheduled destruction) by WS-ResourceLifetime. These message exchanges define the means by which subscription resources can be explicitly destroyed, or destroyed using a scheduled (time-based) mechanism.

The subscription manager defines a `PauseSubscription` and a `Resume-Subscription` operation. These operations work to stop and restart the process of sending notification messages to the notification consumer based on a given subscription.

7.3.1.2 Subscription filtering

Filter expressions serve to indicate the kind of notification that the consumer is interested in by restricting the messages to be sent to a subscriber on a subscription. Filtering occurs on a per subscription basis. This means that a given notification producer may have several active subscriptions, each with different filter expressions. Moreover, a notification consumer can be the target of multiple subscriptions, each involving different filter expressions.

```
<wsdl:definitions name="PurchaseOrder"
 xmlns:tns="http://supply.com/PurchaseService/wsdl"
 ... >

  <!-- Type definitions -->
      ... ...
  <!-- Message definitions -->
      ... ...
  <!-- portType defnitions -->
  <wsdl:portType name="PurchaseOrderPortType"
                 wsrp:ResourceProperties="
                 poRefProp:poResourceProperties">

     <!--Operations supported by the PO PortType -->
     <wsdl:operation name="getInvoice"> ... </wsdl:operation>
     <wsdl:operation name="dispatch-order"> ... </wsdl:operation>
     <wsdl:operation name="cancel-order"> ... </wsdl:operation>

     <!-- WS-RF operations supported by this portType -->
     <wsdl:operation name="GetResourceProperty"> ...
                                             </wsdl:operation>
     <wsdl:operation name="GetMultipleResourceProperties"> ...
                                             </wsdl:operation>
     <wsdl:operation name="QueryResourceProperties"> ...
                                             </wsdl:operation>
     <wsdl:operation name="SetResourceProperties"> ...
                                             </wsdl:operation>

     <!-- WS-Notication operations supported by this portType -->
     <wsdl:operation name="Subscribe"> ... </wsdl:operation>
     <wsdl:operation name="GetCurrentMessage"> ...
                                             </wsdl:operation>
          :
  </wsdl:portType>
</wsdl:definitions>
```

Listing 7.7 Including notification operators in `PurchaseOrderPortType`

WS-Base Notification defines three basic kinds of filter expression. However, developers are free to augment this set with filter expressions defined outside the standard. The three kinds of filter expression defined by WS-Base Notification are [Graham 2004b]:

1. *Message filters:* A message filter is a Boolean expression evaluated over the content of a notification message. A message filter excludes all messages which do not evaluate to true. An example of a message filter is when an inventory service requires automatic replenishment for products that fall below a certain threshold.

2. *Topic filters:* As we shall see in the next section, topics provide a convenient way of categorizing kinds of notification. A topic filter excludes all notifications which do not correspond to the specified topic or list of topics.
3. *Notification producer state filters:* These filters involve expressions on the basis of some state of the notification producer itself, which is not carried in message exchanges, and which the subscriber needs to know about.

7.3.2 Notification topics

Applications that use notifications typically declare their interest in receiving notification messages that fulfill certain criteria, e.g., having particular content, and it is this expression of interest that is used to route messages through the network to notification consumers.

WS-Notification supports specific topics that help consumers receive only those notification messages of specific interest. The WS-Topics specification defines the features required to allow applications to work with topic-oriented notification systems. In particular, it defines a mechanism to organize and categorize items of interest for subscription known as "topics." These are used in conjunction with the notification mechanisms defined in WS-Base Notification.

A topic is a category of notification message (see section 7.3.1 for a proper definition of the term *topic*). When a subscriber creates a subscription, it associates the subscription with one or more topics to indicate which kinds of notification it is interested in. A subscriber does this by supplying a topic filter, rather than a filter specified in terms of the message body. This allows more flexibility, as topic filters are not tied to notification messages. The topic name does not have to appear in the message itself and more than one message type can be associated with a given topic.

When a subscriber creates a subscription, it associates this subscription with one or more topics. In addition to detecting situations and creating notification messages, the notification producer is responsible for matching notifications against the list of subscriptions and for sending the notification messages to each appropriately subscribed consumer. To achieve this task, the notification producer uses topic lists as part of the matching process [Graham 2004a]. When the notification producer has a notification to perform, it matches this notification against subscriber interest registered in topics in its topic list. When the producer identifies a match it performs the notification to the notification consumer who subscribed with that topic [Vambenepe 2004]. This organization allows the notification producer to declare the types of situations for which it produces notification messages. In this way, it allows a requestor to understand what topics and information it can subscribe for.

A collection of related topics is used to organize and categorize a set of notification messages. It provides a convenient means by which subscribers can reason about notifications of interest. As part of the publication of a notification message, the publishing application (publisher) associates it with one or more topics.

Topics are organized hierarchically into a *topic tree*, where each topic may have zero or more child topics and a child topic can itself contain further child topics [Vambenepe 2004]. Each topic tree contains a *root topic*. This hierarchical topic structure allows subscribers to subscribe against multiple topics. For example, a subscriber can subscribe against an entire topic tree or a subset of the topics in a topic tree. This reduces the number of subscription requests that a subscriber needs to issue if it is interested in a large subtree. It also means that a subscriber can receive notification messages related to descendant topics without having to be specifically aware of their existence.

Topics are arranged within *topic spaces*, which use XML namespaces to avoid topic–definition clashes. A topic space is a collection (forest) of topic trees. The topic space contains additional metadata describing how its member topics can be modeled as an XML document. All root topics must have unique names within their topic space. A topic space associates topic trees with a namespace in such a way that each topic tree can be uniquely identified by the name of the root of its topic tree. Child topics can only be referred to relative to their ancestor root topic using a path-based topic expression dialect.

A topic space is not tied to a particular notification producer. It contains an abstract set of topic definitions, which can be used by many different notification producers. It is also possible for a given notification producer to support topics from several different topic spaces. A notification producer can support an entire topic tree, or just a subset of the topics in that topic tree. The list of topics supported by the notification producer may change over time by supporting additional topics from a topic space not previously supported or by supporting extension topics to a (new or already supported) topic space.

The WS-Notification topic-based approach allows message filtering within the notification producer, the consumer, or a combination of both, which is important for scalability. Filtering occurs in the notification producer on the basis of the topics specified for a consumer's subscription, along with any selector expressions and precondition expressions associated with that subscription. Notification consumers can then apply further criteria to filter messages that arrive from a producer.

As an example of a sample topic space containing two hierarchically organized topic trees consider the diagram depicted in Figure 7.9. This figure describes a topic space named `"http://supply.com/topicsSpace/order-mgt-example/"`. This topic space uses WS-Notification to specify two root topics, one describing payment methods

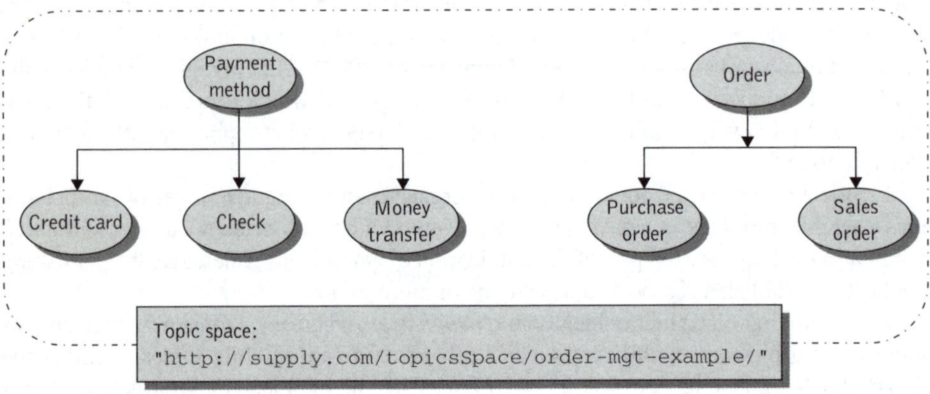

Figure 7.9 Sample topic space

while the other represents company orders. As part of a payment application, one can model a payment method that is the root topic of all topics related to payment. There might be several subcategories of the payment method, including paying by credit card, by check, or direct transfer order. These subtopics are organized as descendants of the payment method root topic in Figure 7.9.

The code snippet in Listing 7.8 illustrates how a topic space can be specified using the WS-Topics XML model for topics. This listing illustrates that an optional name can be assigned to each topic space element for documentation purposes. Each topic may contain a `messageTypes` attribute that defines the types of notification message that may be used in conjunction with the topic. The purpose of this attribute is to scope the contents of

```
<?xml version="1.0" encoding="UTF-8"?>
<wstop:topicSpace name="TopicSpaceOrderMgt-Example"
   targetNamespace="supply.com/topicsSpace/orderMgt-example"
   xmlns:tns="http://supply.com/topicsSpace/orderMgt-example"
   xmlns:wsrp="http://www.ibm.com/xmlns/stdwip/Web-services/WS-
                                              ResourceProperties"
   xmlns:wstop="http://www.ibm.com/xmlns/stdwip/Web-services/
                                                       WS-Topics">
   <wstop:topic name="PaymentMethod">
      <wstop:topic name="CreditCard"
             messageTypes="tns:CreditCardPaymentNotification"/>
      <wstop:topic name="Check"
             messageTypes="tns:CheckPaymentNotification"/>
      <wstop:topic name="MoneyTransfer"
             messageTypes="tns:MoneyTransferNotification"
             final="false">
           <wstop:documentation>
               All money transfers, including urgent money
               transfers appear under this topic.
           </wstop:documentation>
           <wstop:topic name="UrgentMoneyTransfer"
              <wsrp:QueryExpression
                  dialect="http://www.w3.org/TR/2003/
                  WD-xpath20-20031112" >
                  Boolean(/*/order/@orderStatus="urgent")
              </wsrp:QueryExpression>
           </wstop:topic>
   </wstop:topic>
   <wstop:topic name="Order">
      <wstop:topic name="PurchaseOrder"
             messageTypes="tns:m1" … />
      <wstop:topic name="SalesOrder"
             messageTypes="tns:m2" … />
         … … …
   </wstop:topic>
</wstop:topicSpace>
```

Listing 7.8 Sample WS-Topic topic space definition

notification messages associated with the topic [Vambenepe 2004]. For example, in the case of a money transfer payment, the listing indicates that all notification messages associated with the money transfer topic are `tns:MoneyTransferNotification`-conformant messages. The `messageTypes` attribute thus contains information helpful to design the appropriate selector expressions to filter messages on a `subscribe` request. Each topic may also contain an optional attribute, called `final`, whose default value is "false." If the value is "true" it indicates that the notification producer cannot dynamically add any further child topics to this topic.

The child topic `UrgentMoneyTransfer` in Listing 7.8 demonstrates the use of the message pattern feature of the XML model of topics in WS-Notification. The `wsrp:QueryExpression` operation is used here to describe a *message pattern* or specify further constraints on the type of a message associated with a given topic such as money transfer. Listing 7.8 illustrates that a message to the `UrgentMoneyTransfer` topic is not only `tns:MoneyTransferNotification` compliant but can also indicate to a potential subscriber that it deals with money transfer payments which are related with orders that have an urgent order status. The message pattern is expressed in terms of a `wsrp:QueryExpression` operation, which is a WS-ResourceProperties operation designed to allow applications to issue query expressions, such as XPath, against the resource properties document of a WS-Resource.

The WS-Topics specification supports several *topic expressions*, which are used to specify topics in `subscribe` and `notify` messages, as well as to indicate the topics that notification producers support. The WS-Topics standard specifies several topic expressions, ranging from a simple approach that refers only to root topics within a given topic space to an approach that uses XPath-like expressions to refer to topics. The three topic expression dialects that can be used as subscription expressions in WS-Topic are as follows:

Simple topic expressions: These are defined in terms of a simple topic expression language for use by resources that are constrained entities in the WS-Notification system that deal only with simple topic spaces.

Concrete topic path expressions: These are used to identify exactly one topic within a topic space by employing a path notation. Concrete path expressions employ a simple path language that is similar to file paths in hierarchical directory structures.

Full topic path expressions: The full topic expression dialect builds on the concrete topic dialect by adding wildcard characters and logical operations. Full topic path expressions are made up of XPath expressions, which are evaluated over a document whose nodes are made up of the topics in the topic space and where topics include their child topics as contained XML elements.

Additional examples of WS-Topic expressions can be found in [Vambenepe 2004] and [Graham 2004a].

7.3.3 Brokered notification

The kind of direct connection approach adopted by the peer-to-peer notification (or direct) pattern is useful in closed systems in which producer and consumer applications know each other and are unaffected by the coupling introduced by direct connections between notification producers and consumers. However, most event-based systems (see, for instance, the event-driven Enterprise Service Bus in section 8.5) seek to completely decouple notification producers and consumers. To achieve this, the WS-BrokeredNotification specification was created [Chappell 2004]. This specification introduces an additional role, called a notification broker, as an intermediary, which allows the publisher/subscribers to be decoupled and thus provides greater scalability.

A notification broker is an intermediary Web service that is designed to provide scalable notification handling that decouples notification consumers from publishers. Notification brokers operate as intermediaries between producer and consumer applications, such that producers and consumers each know about the broker but do not know about each other. A notification broker takes on the role of both notification producer and notification consumer (as defined in WS-Base Notification), and its interactions with other notification producers and notification consumers are largely defined by the WS-Base Notification specification.

Because applications that produce or consume notifications are not normally designed to also fulfill large-scale notification requirements, brokers can improve system scalability by offloading the difficult aspects of notification handling (such as dealing with subscriptions, filtering, efficient delivery to multiple consumers, and message persistence) [Vinovski 2004]. By doing so, brokers help keep infrastructure concerns separate from application concerns.

The notification broker as defined by WS-BrokeredNotification is an extension of the capabilities offered by a basic notification producer. These extensions include [Graham 2004b]:

- Relieving a publisher from having to implement message exchanges associated with notification producer. The notification broker takes on the duties of a subscription manager (managing subscriptions) and notification producer (distributing notification messages) on behalf of the publisher.
- Reducing the number of interservice connections and references, in cases where there exist many publishers and many notification consumers.
- Acting as a finder service to facilitate potential publishers and subscribers to effectively find each other.
- Providing anonymous notification, so that publishers and notification consumers need not be aware of each other's identity.

The notification broker on the incoming side fulfills the notification consumer interface, while on the outgoing side, it fulfills the notification producer interface. To a notification producer, the broker appears as a consumer, but to a consumer, it appears as a producer.

An implementation of a notification broker may provide additional added-value function that is beyond the scope of the WS-BrokeredNotification specification. For example, WS-Notification features and composable features of related standards, which provide facilities such as logging notification messages for auditing purposes, or using facilities such as authentication, message persistence, message integrity, message encryption, delivery

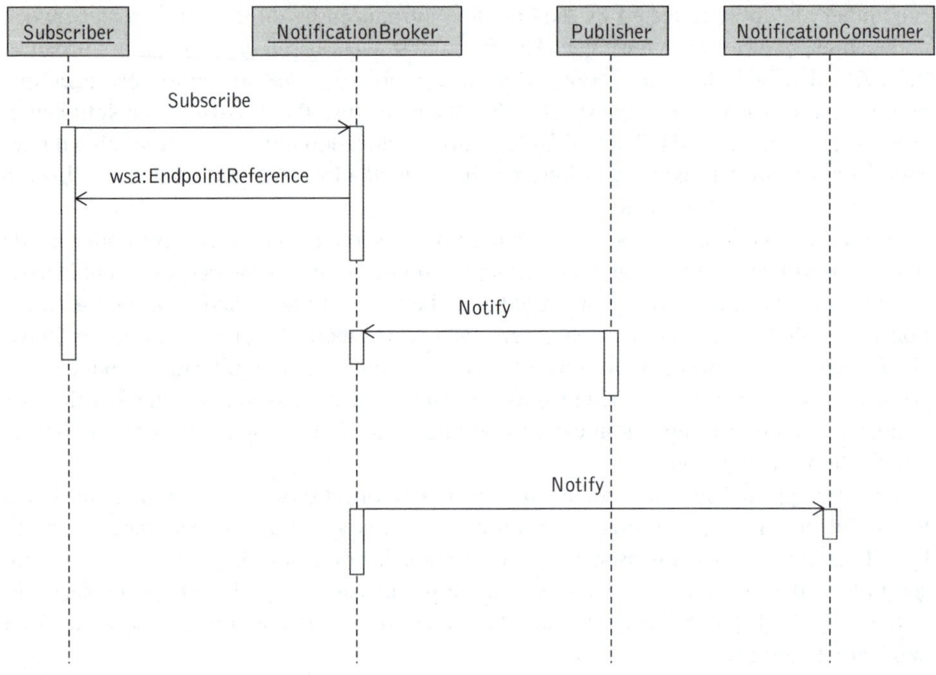

Figure 7.10 Brokered message exchange patterns

guarantees, and so on, are offloaded to a broker. This brokered implementation has one additional benefit, namely that publishers need never know anything about any of the subscribers. The complete decoupling of subscribers from publishers along with the centralized subscription and topic management provides enterprises with more control and allows more accurate measures of performance against SLAs.

The diagram depicted in Figure 7.10 illustrates a possible sequence of brokered message exchanges. In the brokered case, the sequence of message exchanges between a subscriber and the notification broker is the same as the sequence of message exchanges between a subscriber and notification producer in the non-brokered case [Graham 2004b], see Figure 7.7. Instead of interacting directly with the ultimate notification consumers, publishers interact with the notification broker using a sequence of message exchanges supported by the notification broker. The publisher publishes a notification message to the notification broker, using the `notify` message. Subsequently, the notification broker delivers the notification messages to any notification consumer identified by subscriptions that match the publication. Because the publish function is implemented by sending the `notify` message, a notification broker appears to the publisher as any other notification consumer. This allows notification brokers to be inserted into the message flow (for instance, for auditing purposes) without the publisher needing to change the way it sends its notification messages.

The `notify` message exchange in Figure 7.10 can be used for two purposes [Graham 2004b]. First, it can be used to issue a notification message to the notification broker. It can also be used to deliver a notification message to a notification consumer. This allows chaining of notification brokers and anonymous intermediation of notification brokers between notification producers (publishers) and notification consumers.

As a final remark, the WS-Notification family of standards currently outlines only the push delivery mode for notifications, which is based on a full-fledged publish/subscribe model. The push model is one in which notifications are pushed to the consumer. An advantage of the push model is that notifications are routed to the consumer as soon as they are available. WS-Notification also incorporates support for delegated delivery of notifications, where an intermediary, the broker, can push notifications to the consumer.

7.4 Web Services Eventing

Recently, a specification called Web Services Eventing (WS-Eventing) that also addresses event-driven processing for Web services was published by companies such as BEA Systems, Microsoft, Sun Microsystems, and Tibco Software. This specification is intended to define a baseline set of operations that allow Web services to provide simple asynchronous notifications of events between Web services to interested parties. WS-Eventing is a set of protocols, message formats, and interfaces that allow a Web service to subscribe or accept subscriptions for event notifications. For example, an event notification could pertain to shipping of an order or could pertain to making a request to process a particular transaction and when the process is complete, the sender receives a message assuring the transaction has been processed.

The WS-Eventing specification defines a protocol for one Web service (called a *subscriber*) to register interest (called a *subscription*) with another Web service (called an *event source*) in receiving messages about events (called *notifications* or *event messages*). An event source is a Web service that sends notifications and accepts requests to create subscriptions. A notification in WS-Eventing is a one-way message sent to indicate that an event has occurred. The Web service that receives notifications is called an *event sink*. A *subscriber* is a Web service that sends requests to create, renew, and/or delete subscriptions. The subscriber may manage the subscription by interacting with a special-purpose Web service (called the *subscription manager*) designated by the event source. The subscription manager accepts requests to manage, get the status of, renew, and/or delete subscriptions on behalf of an event source.

Figure 7.11 depicts the main components and message exchanges in WS-Eventing. This figure shows that when an event sink `subscribes` with an event source, the source includes information regarding the subscription manager in its response. Subsequent operations, such as getting the status of a subscription, renewing a subscription and unsubscribing – relating to previously registered subscriptions – are all directed to the subscription manager. In case an event source needs to terminate a subscription it sends a `subscriptionEnd` message signifying the end of the registered subscription to the sink. To update the expiration for a subscription, a subscription manager supports requests to `renew` subscriptions. An event source may support filtering to limit notifications that are delivered to the event sink. If it does, and a subscribe request contains a filter, the event

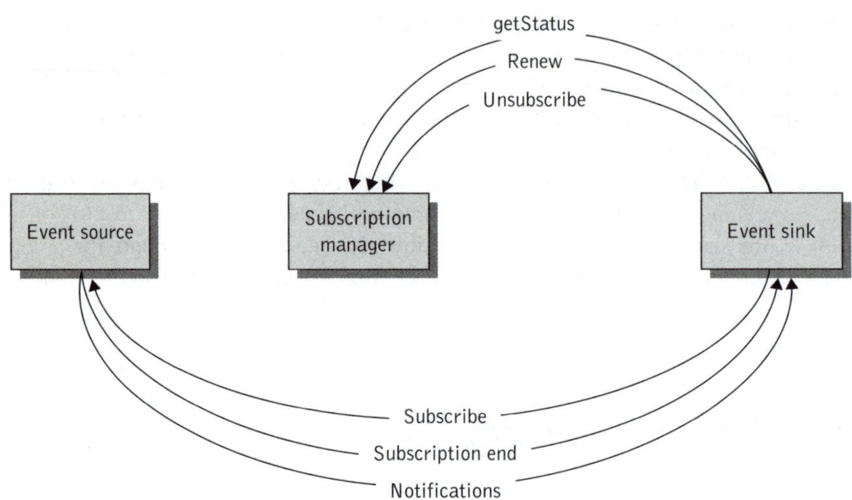

Figure 7.11 WS-Eventing message exchanges

source sends only notifications that match the requested filter. The event source sends notifications until one of the following happens: the subscription manager accepts an unsubscribe request for the subscription; the subscription expires without being renewed; or the event source cancels the subscription prematurely.

The latest version of WS-Eventing includes improvements such as the use of endpoint references (that rely on WS-Addressing, WS-ReferenceProperties, and reference parameters) in place of subscription identifiers to enhance interoperability, new delivery modes that allow events to be pushed asynchronously, and addition of extensibility points to allow the possibility of adding other modes in the future.

From what we have presented so far, it is easy to understand that the WS-Eventing specification provides similar functionality to that of WS-Base Notification. Both WS-Eventing and WS-Notification are intended to work together with other Web services standards such as WS-Security and assorted specifications, WS-Policy, and WS-ReliableMessaging. The major difference between the two specifications (WS-Eventing and WS-Notification) is that the model of WS-Eventing requires tight coupling between the "event filter" declaration and the format of the streaming content, which use XPath expressions, while WS-Notification uses a more loosely coupled topic-based subscription method. Another difference is that WS-Notification supports intermediary brokering technologies for publish-and-subscribe Web services paradigms while WS-Eventing currently does not. A detailed analysis and comparison of these two notification-related specifications for Web services can be found in [Pallickara 2004].

Recently, the OASIS WS-Notification Technical Committee recognized that WS-Eventing and WS-Base Notification address a very similar problem area and are architecturally similarly structured. While it noted that there were differences, it recognized that the overlapping subset is significant enough to warrant further investigation and has invited the authors of WS-Eventing and WS-Base Notification to jointly work on a unified infrastructure, meeting the requirements of both specifications.

7.5 Summary

Web services must provide their users with the ability to access and manipulate state, i.e., data values that persist across, and evolve as a result of, Web service interactions. The information that forms the state is often bundled together in what is known as a stateful resource. A stateful resource is associated with the Web service statically in the situation where the association is made when a Web service is deployed. Alternatively, when the association is made during execution of message exchanges, the stateful resource is dynamically associated with the Web service. The WS-Resource Framework is concerned primarily with the creation, addressing, inspection, and lifetime management of stateful resources.

Stateful Web services add more dynamic information to the Web services addressing scheme by including instance information, policy, complex binding, and so on. This requires a client to be in a position to uniquely identify a service at run-time, based on run-time information like the previous. This problem is tackled by WS-Addressing, which enables the description of complex message paths in SOAP message headers. This message addressing mechanism enables intermediate message handling, message forwarding, and multiple message transports in a single message path.

WS-Notification is a family of related specifications that define a standard Web services approach to notification using a topic-based publish/subscribe pattern. The WS-Notification specification defines standard message exchanges to be implemented by service providers that wish to participate in notifications and standard message exchanges – allowing publication of messages from entities that are not themselves service providers. WS-Topics, which is related to WS-Notification, defines three topic expression dialects that can be used as subscription expressions in subscribe request messages and other parts of the WS-Notification system. It further specifies an XML model for describing metadata associated with topics.

Review questions

- What is a stateful resource and why do Web services need to deal with stateful resources?
- What is the purpose of the WS-Resource Framework?
- Which specifications does the WS-Resource Framework provide?
- What is meant by the term "implied resource pattern"?
- Describe the problem of addressing with stateful Web services.
- What is Web services addressing and what is a Web service endpoint reference?
- How does Web services addressing apply the implied resource pattern?
- What is the purpose of WS-Resource?
- What is the purpose of WS-Base Notification and what kind of notifications does it support?

- What are notification topics?
- Describe the three topic expression dialects that can be used with the WS-Topic standard.
- What is WS-BrokeredNotication and how does it differ from WS-Base Notification?

Exercises

7.1 Assume that when an insurance claim is submitted from an insurance agent to an insurance company, message routing and delivery information, such as endpoint addresses, must be provided. Use WS-Addressing headers in SOAP messages with reference properties and parameters to achieve this purpose.

7.2 Extend Exercise 5.2 by assuming that insurance claims need to be stateful entities, which need to be modeled as WS-Resources that maintain the state associated with the processing of each insurance claim. The WS-Resource implementation should include WSDL definitions as well as WS-ResourceProperty statements.

7.3 In a domestic application, autonomous devices may interact asynchronously using WS-Notification publish/subscribe mechanisms. The events could be, for instance, topic-based representing critical factors such as fire, gas presence, and the health status of an inhabitant. Write a program to manage a simple WS-Notification topic namespace like the one illustrated in the example below. The program must be able to parse the XML file, recognize its tree structure, and show it to the user in a meaningful way. Moreover, the program should allow the user to modify the tree (adding, renaming, or removing nodes as required). All the events the publisher can generate are specified in the topic namespace below.

```
<?xml version="1.0" encoding="UTF-8"?>

<wstop:topicSpace name="Event"
targetNamespace="http://publisher.domotic.com/topicnamespace.xml"
xmlns:wstop="http://www.ibm.com/xmlns/stdwip/web-services/
                                                        WS-Topics" >
  <wstop:topic name="Alarm events" >
        <wstop:topic name="Fire presence" />
        <wstop:topic name="Gas presence" />
  </wstop:topic>
  <wstop:topic name="Health events" >
        <wstop:topic name="Arm dislocation" />
        <wstop:topic name="Irregular heartbeat" />
  </wstop:topic>
</wstop:topicSpace>
```

7.4 Extend Exercise 7.3 by adding the possibility to read and store incoming WS-Notification subscription messages to specific topics. You can store the subscription in an XML file similar to the topic namespace that will look like the following code snippet:

```
<?xml version="1.0" encoding="UTF-8"?>

<wstop:topicSpace name="Event"
targetNamespace="http://publisher.domotic.com/topicnamespace.xml"
xmlns:domPub="http://publisher.domotic.com/xmlnamespace.xml"
xmlns:wstop="http://www.ibm.com/xmlns/stdwip/web-services/
                                                WS-Topics" >
  <wstop:topic name="Alarm events" >
        <wstop:topic name="Fire presence" />
        <wstop:topic name="Gas presence" />
  </wstop:topic>
  <wstop:topic name="Health events" >
        <wstop:topic name="Arm dislocation" />
        <wstop:topic name="Irregular heartbeat" />
        <domPub:Address name="simpleSubscriber:1234" />
  </wstop:topic>
</wstop:topicSpace>
```

To do that you also need a simple WS-Notification subscriber able to send SOAP message as follows:

```
<s12:Envelope xmlns:s12="http://www.w3.org/2003/05/soap-envelope"
xmlns:wsa="http://schemas.xmlsoap.org/ws/2003/03/addressing"
xmlns:wsnt="http://www.ibm.com/xmlns/stdwip/web-services/WS-
BaseNotification"
xmlns:domPub="http://publisher.domotic.com/xmlnamespace.xml">
  <s12:Header/>
  <s12:Body>
        <wsnt:Subscribe>
            <wsnt:ConsumerReference>
                  <wsa:Address>
                       simpleSubscriber:1234
                  </wsa:Address>
            </wsnt:ConsumerReference>
            <wsnt:UseNotify>
               true
            </wsnt:UseNotify>
            <wsnt:TopicExpression
                      dialect=http://publisher.domotic.com/
                          topicdialect.ebnf>
                          domPub:Event/Health events
            </wsnt:TopicExpression>
        </wsnt:Subscribe>
  </s12:Body>
</s12:Envelope>
```

7.5 Extend Exercises 7.3 and 7.4 to implement a simple WS-Notification event broker, able to receive notification messages and forward them to registered subscribers. To do that you also need a simple WS-Notification publisher able to send SOAP messages such as follows:

```
<s12:Envelope xmlns:s12="http://www.w3.org/2003/05/soap-envelope"
xmlns:wsa="http://schemas.xmlsoap.org/ws/2003/03/addressing"
xmlns:wsnt="http://www.ibm.com/xmlns/stdwip/web-services/WS-
BaseNotification"
xmlns:domBro="http://broker.domotic.com/xmlnamespace.xml">
  <s12:Header/>
  <s12:Body>
        <wsnt:Notify>
             <wsnt:NotificationMessage>
                  <wsnt:Topic dialect="+dialect+">
                       domBro:Event/Health events/Arm Dislocation
                  </wsnt:Topic>
                  <wsnt:Message>
                      Arm dislocation detected!
                  </wsnt:Message>
             </wsnt:NotificationMessage>
        </wsnt:Notify>
  </s12:Body>
</s12:Envelope>
```

7.6 Figure 7.12 shows an insurance claims topic tree. Descendant topics of the root topic insurance claim include property, health, and casualty claims. Use the WS-Topics notation to represent the insurances claim topic tree in Figure 7.12.

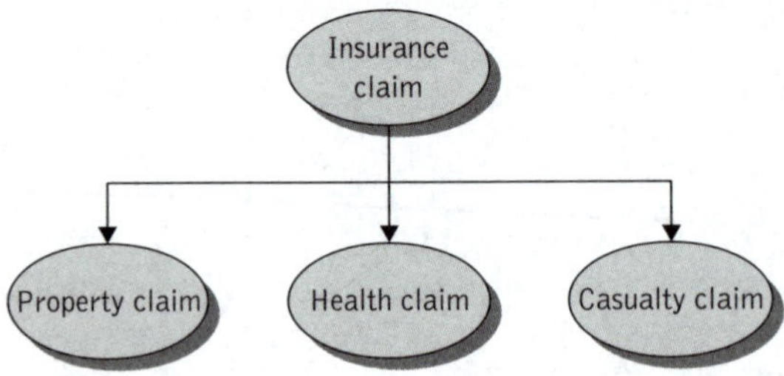

Figure 7.12 Sample insurance claims topic tree

CHAPTER 8

Service-oriented architectures

Learning objectives

The challenges in automated business integration have fueled new approaches and architectures to address the requirements of loosely coupled, standards-based, and protocol-independent distributed computing applications culminating in the introduction of the service-oriented architecture. Much of SOA's power derives from its ability to leverage standards-based functional services, calling them when needed on an individual basis, or aggregating them to create composite applications or multi-stage business processes. The building-block services can be stored and reused and can also be updated or replaced without affecting the functionality or integrity of other independent services. Typically, business operations running in an SOA comprise a number of invocations of these different services, often in an event-driven or asynchronous fashion that reflects the underlying business process needs.

In this chapter we describe technologies and approaches that unify the principles and concepts of SOA with those of event-based programming. After completing this chapter readers will understand the following key concepts:

- The concept of software architecture.
- The purpose of reliable messaging.
- The structure of WS-ReliableMessaging.
- The meaning of event-driven computing for SOA applications.
- The Event Service Bus integration infrastructure for SOA applications.
- Connectivity, integration and scalability issues in the Event Service Bus.

8.1 What is a software architecture?

Building distributed software systems involves fitting together resources and systems from diverse organizations as well as developing implementation code. For example, when automating business processes crossing enterprise boundaries, these will traverse diverse systems in various organizations, leveraging shared resources such as Web servers, business logic components, security systems, and back-end enterprise information systems, e.g., databases or ERP systems. In this environment, partners must not only agree on a core set of interfaces and standards, but also agree on how to use those interfaces and standards. Central to such considerations is the concept of software architecture.

Software architecture of a computing system involves the description of the structures from which systems are built (software components), the externally visible properties of those components, their interrelationships as well as principles and guidelines governing their design and evolution over time [Shaw 1996], [Bass 2003]. Externally visible properties are assumptions other components can make of a specific component, such as its provided interfaces and services, performance characteristics, fault handling, shared resource usage, and so on.

More precisely, software architecture is the high-level structure of a software system – including distributed and service-oriented systems – that is commonly specified in terms of functional components and interactions/interconnections among those components. Components are identified and assigned responsibilities that client components interact with through "contracted" interfaces [Soni 1995]. Component interconnections specify communication and control mechanisms, and support all component interactions needed to accomplish system behavior.

Software architecture forms the backbone for building successful software-intensive systems; it represents a capitalized investment in the form of an abstract reusable model that can be transferred from one system to the next. Important properties of software architecture include [Bass 2003]:

- It is at a high-enough level of abstraction that the system can be viewed as a whole and yet it must provide enough information to form a basis for analysis, decision making, and hence risk reduction.
- The structure must support the functionality required of the system. Thus, the dynamic behavior of the system must be taken into account when designing the architecture.
- It must conform to the *system qualities* (captured in SLAs or non-functional requirements). These likely include performance, security, interoperability, and reliability requirements associated with current functionality, as well as flexibility or extensibility requirements associated with accommodating future functionality at a reasonable cost of change. As system qualities may conflict, tradeoffs are an essential part of designing architecture. These tradeoffs need to be made among alternative solutions and must take into account the relative priorities of the system qualities.
- At the architectural level, all implementation details are hidden.

Two essential elements of a software architecture are its functional requirements and its system qualities. Functional requirements capture the intended behavior of the system – or what the system will do. This behavior may be expressed in terms of services, tasks, or functions that the system is required to perform.

In this chapter we briefly re-examine the nature and implications of system quality requirements, which we first introduced in section 1.8, to improve reader understandability. Service development techniques that concentrate on functional requirements of SOAs are presented in Chapter 15.

8.1.1 System quality attributes

While the design of software systems concentrates on satisfying the functional requirements for a system, the design of the software architecture for systems concentrates on the non-functional or quality requirements of systems. Quality requirements of systems are described in terms of quality attributes, which are those system properties over and above the functionality of the system that determine the technical qualities of the system. System quality attributes describe how well behavioral or structural aspects of a system are accomplished. System qualities are judged by some externally observable/measurable property of the system behavior and not its internal implementation. These may be judged by the user in terms of some characteristic that the user values or is concerned about.

There are two types of quality attributes: run-time qualities and development-time quality attributes [Bass 2003]. *Run-time qualities* provide value to the user and have more to do with short-term competitive differentiation. *Development-time qualities*, for the most part, provide business value (as opposed to direct value to the end user) and have to do with the long-term competitiveness of the business.

Run-time quality attributes include: usability (ease of use, learnability, memorability, efficiency, etc.); configurability and supportability; correctness, reliability, availability; technical system requirements such as performance (throughput, response time, transit delay, latency, etc.); safety properties such as security and fault tolerance; and operational scalability including support for increased user involvement, additional system nodes, and higher transaction volumes.

In addition to developing systems that satisfy user requirements, the properties of the artifacts (architecture, design, code, etc.) of the development process play an important role for software architecture. These influence the effort and cost associated with software development as well as support for future changes or uses (maintenance, enhancement, or reuse). Examples of development-time quality requirements include: maintainability; extensibility – ability to add (unspecified) future functionality; evolvability – support for new capabilities or ability to exploit new technologies; composability – ability to compose systems from plug-and-play components; and reusability – ability to (re)use in future systems.

To understand the impact of development-time qualities consider the client–server architectural pattern. This pattern describes collaboration between the providers and users of a set of services by separating one collection of responsibilities (the client's) from another (the server's). The consequence of this separation is enhanced modifiability and upgradeability. Modifying the implementation of the services or modifying the number of servers providing services is invisible to the clients. Moreover, the addition of new clients has no effect on the server. On the downside is the fact that, although this separation of computations might improve reliability, increased network traffic might increase the vulnerability to certain types of security attacks. Therefore, special attention needs to be paid to security considerations.

To specify quality attribute requirements, quality attribute scenarios are used very much in the same way that use cases are essential in determining functional requirements. A collection of quality attribute general (system-independent) scenarios for five important quality attributes (modifiability, performance, availability, security, and usability) can be found in [Bass 2001].

8.1.2 Common architectural concerns

A distinctive characteristic of architectural decisions is that they need to be made from a broad-scoped or technical system perspective. This is due to the fact that architectural decisions impact, if not the entire system, at least different parts of the system. A broad-scoped perspective is required to take this impact into account, and to make the necessary tradeoffs across the system. Key concerns that need to be addressed by (distributed) software architectures, include but are not limited to [Bass 2003], [Malan 2002]:

- *Meta-architecture:* This is a set of architectural vision, style, principles, key communication and control mechanisms, and concepts that results in high-level decisions that will strongly influence the integrity and structure of the system. The meta-architecture, through style, patterns of composition or interaction, principles, and philosophy, rules certain structural choices out and guides selection decisions and tradeoffs among others.
- *Architectural patterns:* Over time, software developers distinguish patterns in the way that systems are structured, and as these patterns become widespread they become dominant designs. Patterns allow the architect to start with a problem and a vision for the solution, and then find a pattern that fits that vision. Subsequently, the architect can further define the additional functional pieces that the application will need to succeed. For instance, well-tested patterns such as client–server, three-tier, and multi-tier (layered) architectures have become prevalent within the IT industry. Architectural patterns are gradually emerging also in an SOA to address system decomposition concerns and how to achieve system properties [Chappell 2004], [Endrei 2004].
- *Architectural views:* Software architectures are best envisioned in terms of a number of complementary views or models. In particular, structural views help document and communicate the architecture in terms of the components and their relationships, and are useful in assessing architectural qualities like extensibility. Behavioral views are useful in thinking through how the components interact to accomplish their assigned responsibilities and evaluating the impact of what-if scenarios on the architecture. Behavioral models are especially useful in assessing run-time qualities such as performance and security. Execution views help in evaluating physical distribution options and documenting and communicating decisions.

- *System decomposition principles and good interface design:* These identify the high-level components of the system and the relationships among them. Their purpose is to direct attention at an appropriate decomposition of the system without delving into unnecessary details. Subsequently, externally visible properties of the components are made precise and unambiguous through well-defined interfaces and component specifications and key architectural mechanisms are detailed. Concerns such as whether the components fit together and whether the congruence of structural pieces achieves the necessary degree of system integrity and consistency are important decisions and need to be factored into architectural decisions.
- *Key architectural design principles:* These include abstraction, separation of concerns, postponing decisions, and simplicity, and related techniques such as interface hiding and encapsulation.

Such architectural concerns play a fundamental role in the success of SOA-based applications. The first concern relates mainly to system functional and quality requirements and is addressed in this chapter while the remaining concerns deal with design principles and characteristics of SOAs and are addressed in Chapter 15.

8.2 The SOA revisited

As we have learned from section 1.6, SOA is a meta-architectural style that supports loosely coupled services to enable business flexibility in an interoperable, technology-agnostic manner. In an SOA, coarse-grained software resources and functions are made accessible via the network and access to them is provided by business-aligned services, which are realized using interface-based service descriptions. Business-aligned services are well-defined, self-contained (elementary) business process steps, such as "create invoice," "customer lookup," or "bill customer," and are independent of the state or context of other services. In SOA, business-aligned services are used as the basis for constructing flexible and dynamically reconfigurable end-to-end business processes. Another important characteristic of an SOA is that business-aligned services are implemented with standard ways to invoke them and are "loosely coupled" in that they can be invoked without the caller needing to understand anything about the technology choice or location of the service provider. In this way a service such as "bill customer" can be invoked from any other business application that requires customer information.

SOA is focused on creating a design style, technology, and process framework that will allow enterprises to develop, interconnect, and maintain enterprise applications and services efficiently and cost-effectively. While this objective is not new, SOA seeks to eclipse previous efforts such as modular programming, code reuse, and object-oriented software development techniques. SOA represents a significant advance in the "abstracted development" of software applications. An SOA provides a set of guidelines, principles, and techniques by which business processes, information, and enterprise assets can be effectively (re)organized and (re)deployed to support and enable strategic plans and productivity levels that are required by competitive business environments. This ability enables enterprises to satisfy new and changing business requirements with existing assets in a timely manner. An SOA is based on the combination of and interaction between services, associated with messages, and governed by policies (see Chapter 12). In this way, new business processes and alliances can be routinely mapped to services that can be used, modified, built, or orchestrated.

SOA is designed to allow developers to overcome many complex implementation challenges such as distributed software, application integration, multiple platforms and protocols, and numerous access devices, while leveraging the potential of the Internet. The driving goal of SOA is to eliminate these barriers so that applications integrate and run seamlessly. It is widely believed that SOA, by providing this kind of flexibility and by leveraging new and existing applications and abstracting them as modular, coarse-grained services that map to discrete business functions, represents the future enterprise technology solution that can deliver the flexibility and agility that business users require. A well-constructed SOA can empower a business environment with a flexible infrastructure and processing environment by provisioning independent, reusable, automated business processes (which it deploys as services), and providing a robust architectural backbone for leveraging these services.

A service in SOA is an exposed piece of functionality with three essential properties. An SOA-based service is a self-contained (i.e., the service maintains its own state) and platform-independent (i.e., the interface contract to the service is platform independent) service that can be dynamically located and invoked. The primary value of SOA is that it enables the reuse of existing services, either as standalone or as part of composite applications that perform more complex functions by orchestrating numerous services and pieces of information. A simple service is reused in different ways and combined with other services to perform a specific business function.

Services in an SOA exhibit the following characteristics [Channabasavaiah 2003]:

1. All functions in an SOA are defined as services. This includes purely business functions, business transactions composed of lower-level functions, and system service functions as well. Services used in composite applications in an SOA may be brand-new service implementations, they may be fragments of old applications that were adapted and wrapped, or they may be combinations of the above.

2. All services are independent of each other. Service operation is perceived as opaque by external services. Service opaqueness guarantees that external components neither know nor care how services perform their function; they merely anticipate that they return the expected result. The technology and location of the application providing the desired functionality are hidden behind the service interface.

3. Service interfaces are invokable. This means that at the architectural level, it is irrelevant whether services are local (within a specific system) or remote (external to the immediate system), what interconnect scheme or protocol is used to effect the invocation, or what infrastructure components are required to make the connection. The service may be within the same application or in a different address space on an entirely different system.

SOA's loose-coupling principles – especially the clean separation of service interfaces from internal implementations – to guide planning, development, integration, and

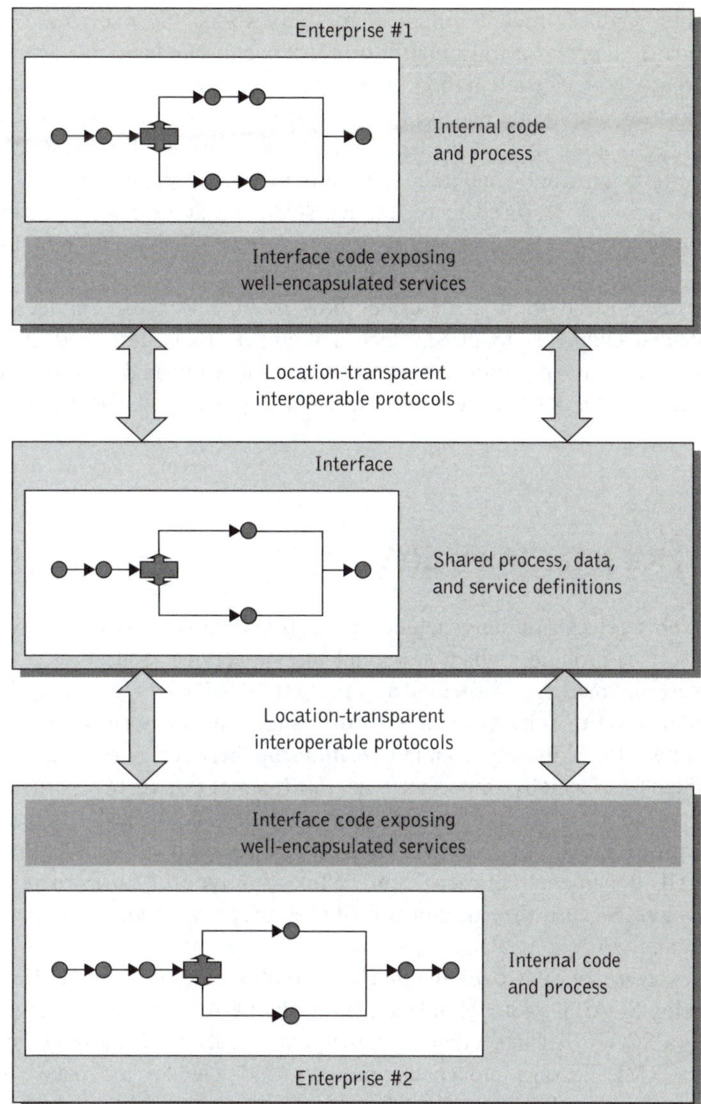

Figure 8.1 Intercommunicating services in an SOA
Source: [Channabasavaiah 2003]

management of their network application platforms make them indispensable for enterprise-wide and cross-enterprise applications. Figure 8.1 illustrates the use of well-defined interfaces to define and encapsulate a reusable business function (termed internal process in Figure 8.1) while hiding its implementation details.

Although SOAs can be implemented using different technologies, such as established middleware technologies like J2EE, CORBA, and JMS, Web services are the preferred environment for realizing the SOA promise of maximum service sharing, reuse, and interoperability. Unlike previous middleware frameworks, the evolving Web services suite of standards supports a truly platform-independent, language-independent, loosely coupled approach to service integration. A Web services SOA realization reduces application complexity by employing encapsulation principles and minimizes the requirements for shared understanding by a clear definition of interfaces. Additionally, Web services enable just-in-time integration and interoperability of legacy applications.

When Web services are used to realize an SOA, the description of the interface is expressed in the Web Service Description Language (see Chapter 5). WSDL supports a complete description of the operations available and the parameters required to use those business services. In addition, it describes how to bind to those services, specifying the protocols and endpoints required. Once a Web service is described, its description can be published in a repository that conforms to the Universal Description and Discovery Interface standard. Clients can then query the repository to discover an appropriate service.

8.3 Service roles in an SOA

SOAs and Web services solutions include two well-known key roles: a service requestor (client) and service provider, which communicate via service requests (see section 1.6). Service requests are messages formatted according to SOAP (see Figure 8.2). In Chapter 4 we explained that SOAP is by nature a platform-neutral and vendor-neutral standard. This capability allows for a loosely coupled relationship between a service requestor and provider, which is especially important over the Internet where two parties may be in different organizations or enterprises. However, SOA does not necessarily require the use of SOAP. Prior to SOAP, for example, some companies used IBM's WebSphere MQ to exchange XML documents between them. While this type of infrastructure is clearly not Web services because they do not use SOAP, they are another example of service invocation in an SOA.

SOAP messages are sent over the Internet employing HTTP or HTTPS (although strictly speaking SOAP is protocol independent). The SOAP request is received by a run-time service (a SOAP "listener") that accepts it, extracts its XML message body portion, transforms the XML message into a native protocol, and delegates the request to the actual business process within the enterprise. These run-time capabilities may be hosted within a Web services container, which provides facilities such as location, routing, service

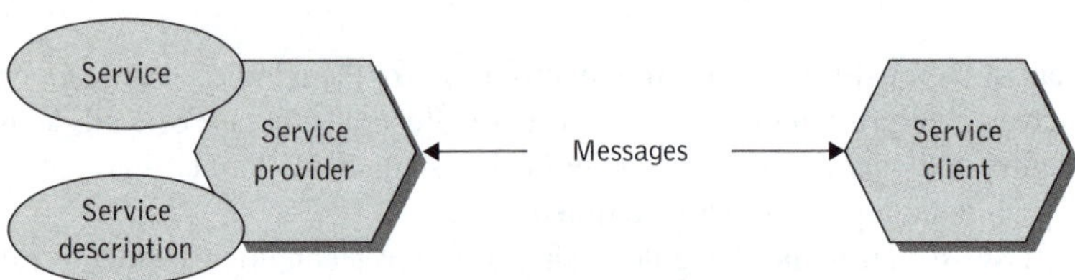

Figure 8.2 Service client and service provider roles

invocation, and management. Finally, the response that the provider sends back to the client takes again the form of an SOAP envelope carrying an XML message.

A *service container* provides deployment and a run-time support environment that makes a Web service highly distributed. In particular, a service container is the physical manifestation of the abstract service endpoint, and provides the implementation of the service interface. It allows applications to monitor and manage supported components as well as the service(s) that monitor and manage the components. It also provides facilities for lifecycle management such as startup, shutdown, and resource cleanup. A Web services container is similar to a J2EE container [Anagol-Subbaro 2005] and serves as an interface between business services and low-level infrastructure services, thus providing a variety of facilities that a service implementation may have at its disposal. A service container can host multiple services, even if they are not part of the same distributed process. Thread pooling allows multiple instances of a service to be attached to multiple listeners within a single container [Chappell 2004].

While SOA services are visible to the service client, their underlying component implementations are transparent. The service consumer does not have to be concerned with the implementation or realization of the service, as long as it supports the required functionality and QoS. This represents the *client view* of SOA. For the service provider, the design of components, their service exposure, and management reflect key architecture and design decisions that enable services in SOA. The *provider view* offers a perspective on how to design the realization of the component that offers the services its architectural decisions and designs.

The process of a service requestor having to directly communicate with a service provider exposes service requestors to the potential complexity of negotiating and reserving services between different service providers. An alternative approach is for an organization to provide this combined functionality direct to the service requestor. This service role could be described as a *service aggregator*. The service aggregator (see also section 1.6.3) performs a dual role. First, it acts as an application service provider as it constructs a complete "service" solution, by creating composite, higher-level services, which it provides to the service client. Service aggregators can accomplish this composition using specialized choreography languages like BPEL (which we describe in section 9.7). Second, it acts as a service requestor as it may need to request and reserve services from other service providers. This process is shown in Figure 8.3.

While service aggregation may offer direct benefits to the requestor, it is a form of service brokering that offers a convenience function – all the required services are grouped "under one roof." However, an important question that needs to be addressed is how does a service requestor determine which one out of a number of several application service providers should be selected for its service offerings? The service requestor could retain the right to select an application service provider based on those that can be discovered from a registry service, such as UDDI. SOA technologies such as UDDI, and security and privacy standards such as SAML and WS-Trust, introduce a third role called a *service broker* [Colan 2004].

Service brokers (also known as certification authorities, see section 11.3) are trusted parties that force service providers to adhere to information practices that comply with privacy laws and regulations, or, in the absence of such laws, industry best practices. In this way broker-sanctioned service providers are guaranteed to offer services that are in

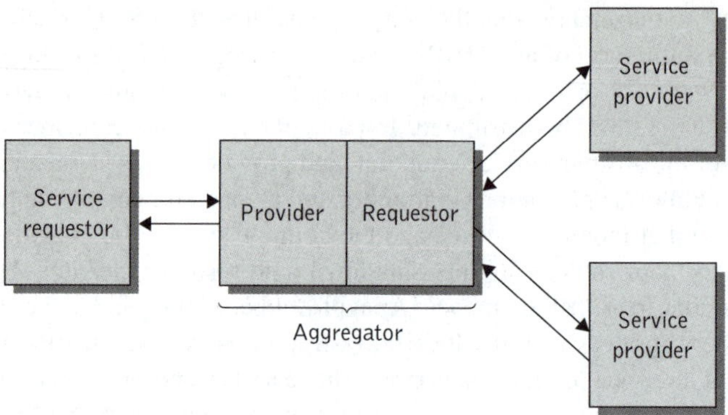

Figure 8.3 The role of service aggregator

compliance with local regulations and create a more trusted relationship with customers and partners. A service broker maintains an index of available service providers. The service broker is able to "add value" to its registry of application service providers by providing additional information about its services. This may include differences about the reliability, trustworthiness, quality of the service, SLAs, and possible compensation routes, to name but a few.

Figure 8.4 shows an SOA where a service broker serves as an intermediary that is interposed between service requestors and service providers. The classical Web services SOA that we illustrated in Figure 1.4 falls under this category with the service registry (UDDI operator) being a specialized instance of a service broker. Under this configuration the

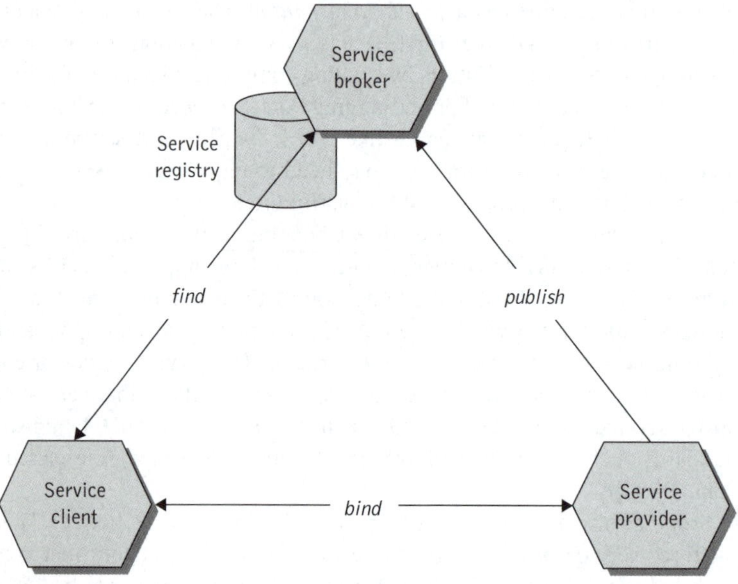

Figure 8.4 Service brokering

UDDI registry serves as a broker where the service providers publish the definitions of the services they offer using WSDL and where the service requestors find information about the services available.

SOA implementations are based around messages exchanged between services, where SOAP messages were chosen as the recommended intercommunication mechanism, and services are defined as network-addressable entities that send and receive messages. When multiple Web services interact to complete a common task involving service orchestration, they cannot rely on proprietary protocols for message exchanges. They require the use of a common protocol that guarantees end-to-end reliable interoperable messaging. Consequently, before we concentrate on the infrastructure layer that facilitates SOA implementations on the basis of event processing and notification, we shall introduce the concept of reliable messaging which is a critical technology standard for event-driven SOA implementations. Reliable messaging is also a critical technology for coordination and transactional behavior of Web services, which we shall examine in Chapter 10.

8.4 Reliable messaging

The main objective of SOAP is to package the data needed by a message recipient and a binding to a transport action. One of the main characteristics of SOAP is that it helps exchange messages between endpoints over unreliable communication channels, such as the Internet, employing unreliable data transfer protocols, e.g., HTTP, TCP, SMTP, and FTP. These protocols are considered unreliable as they do not offer the reliable messaging services such as guaranteed delivery needed by Web services applications. Furthermore, these protocols perceive the message path only as a pair of interlinked endpoints. Given the fact that certain Web services implementations may require a SOAP message to be modified en route or be delegated for processing to other services before reaching its final destination, it is clear that SOAP messages need a more holistic view of which destination they are intended for and how they can reach it. There might even be a need during the message routing for a SOAP message to be transformed from one transport protocol to another, e.g., from HTTP to TCP. Unfortunately, the core SOAP specification does not provide reliability mechanisms addressing such complex message routing requirements. Therefore, there is a clear need for more robust SOAP-based messaging specifications to guarantee that messages are being received by their intended recipients and that message addressing remains consistent despite the fact that messages might be routed to Web services implemented on different platforms, e.g., .NET or J2EE, using heterogeneous messaging transport protocols.

8.4.1 Definition and scope of reliable messaging

Reliability at the level of messages is often referred to as *reliable messaging*. Reliable messaging for Web services is the execution of a transport-agnostic, SOAP-based protocol providing QoS in the reliable delivery of messages. When specifying reliable messaging features there are three aspects that must be addressed equally. First, we need to make certain that both the sender and recipient of a message know whether or not a message was actually sent and received, and that the message received is the same as the one sent. Second, we need to make sure that the message was sent once and only once to the intended recipient. And, third, we need to guarantee that the received messages are in the same order as they were sent. Reliable messaging becomes one of the first problems that need to be addressed for Web services to become truly enterprise-capable technologies.

Reliable messaging is a problem that has overwhelmed Internet application development since its inception. The Internet is, by its very nature, unreliable. In particular, the protocols used to connect senders and receivers were not designed to support reliable messaging constructs, such as message identifiers and acknowledgements (see section 2.6). Recipients of messages must be able to acknowledge the fact that they actually did in fact receive the message. Senders of messages must be able to cache those messages in the event that an acknowledgement is not received and the message needs to be sent again. The fundamental technology that drives the Internet of today does not support such mechanisms. As a consequence, developers are forced to implement proprietary protocols and technology implementations that address these needs.

As Web services messaging is replacing traditional message-oriented middleware, they are expected to offer reliability as a core QoS capability at the infrastructural level, implemented using interoperable and widely deployed standards. Reliability guarantees an agreed-upon quality of delivery in spite of network, software, and hardware failures. It allows message senders and receivers to overcome the unreliability of the Internet/intranet environment, and otherwise guarantees some awareness of failure conditions.

The ability to ensure the delivery of a message is a critical component of Web services. Until recently the mechanisms for ensuring message reliability have traditionally been designed into the application operating at each end of message exchange and transaction systems. This situation is changing with the introduction of standard mechanisms for exchanging secure, reliable messages in a Web services environment. Organizations are therefore no longer faced with the need to develop costly, ad hoc solutions, which are unable to interoperate across platforms to address reliability.

A standard reliable messaging protocol simplifies the code that developers have to write to transfer messages under varying transport assurances. The underlying infrastructure verifies that messages have been properly transferred between the endpoints, retransmitting messages when necessary. Applications do not need any additional logic to handle the message retransmissions, or duplicate message elimination or message acknowledgement that may be required to provide the delivery assurances. Currently, reliable messaging in the world of Web services comes in two flavors, WS-Reliability (published by Sun Microsystems, Oracle, and others as an OASIS standard) and WS-ReliableMessaging (published by IBM, Microsoft, BEA, and TIBCO). These are examples of specifications for an acknowledgement infrastructure that leverages the SOAP extensibility model. Both these specifications define protocols that are independent of the underlying transport layer.

The two nascent reliability specifications largely overlap and it is expected that they will eventually merge. A key difference between these two competing specifications is that WS-ReliableMessaging includes usage of other critical Web services specifications, such as WS-Security and WS-Addressing. In practice, this means that WS-ReliableMessaging uses specific expressions from other standards for supplying reliability features, whereas WS-Reliability supports the reliable messaging features but does not yet rely on expressions provided by other Web services standards. In the following, we shall concentrate on describing WS-ReliableMessaging as it naturally meshes with other Web services standards that we shall examine in this chapter, such as WS-Addressing and WS-Notification. Details of the WS-Reliability specification as well as examples of its usage can be found in [Iwasa 2004].

8.4.2 WS-ReliableMessaging

WS-ReliableMessaging provides a protocol for ensuring that unreceived and duplicate SOAP messages can be detected and received messages can be processed in the order in which they were sent. Messages can also be exchanged with varying levels of delivery assurances. The WS-ReliableMessaging protocol depends upon other Web services specifications for the identification of service endpoint addresses and policies. When WS-ReliableMessaging is used in conjunction with WS-Addressing see (section 7.2.1) it enables transport-neutral, bidirectional, synchronous, asynchronous, and stateful service interactions across networks that include the likes of endpoint managers, firewalls, and gateways. Each specification defines a SOAP binding for interoperability across platforms.

The WS-ReliableMessaging standard has been developed to provide a framework for interoperability between different reliable transport infrastructures [Bilorusets 2005]. More specifically, the WS-ReliableMessaging protocol determines invariants maintained by the reliable messaging endpoints and the directives used to track and manage the delivery of a sequence of messages. WS-ReliableMessaging provides an interoperable protocol that a *reliable messaging source* and *reliable messaging destination* use to provide the application source and the application destination with a guarantee that a message that is sent will be delivered. The WS-ReliableMessaging model is illustrated in Figure 8.5. Implementation of the WS-ReliableMessaging model is distributed across the initial sender and ultimate receiver (service), as shown in the figure. This figure also illustrates that there might be multiple receivers interposed between the initial message sender and the ultimate receiver. The message is transmitted using the reliable messaging protocol. First, both interacting endpoints establish preconditions for message exchange. Subsequently, the sender formats the message to the transport protocol "agreed." The messaging handler of the receiver then forwards the message to the appropriate recipient. Finally, the messaging handler in the receiver transforms the message into a form that is suitable for use for the receiver application. While reliable messaging actions, e.g., retransmission of a message due to transport loss, are handled transparently by the messaging infrastructure, other end-to-end characteristics, such as in-order delivery, require that both the messaging infrastructure and the receiver application collaborate [Cabrera 2005d].

WS-ReliableMessaging distinguishes two important traits:

1. The reliability protocol between message handlers, which they implement using the same notions of sequence of messages within which each message is identified by a sequence number, and using a resending mechanism combined with a notion of acknowledgement.

2. The reliability QoS contract, which provides a delivery assurance and a QoS to the communicating parties.

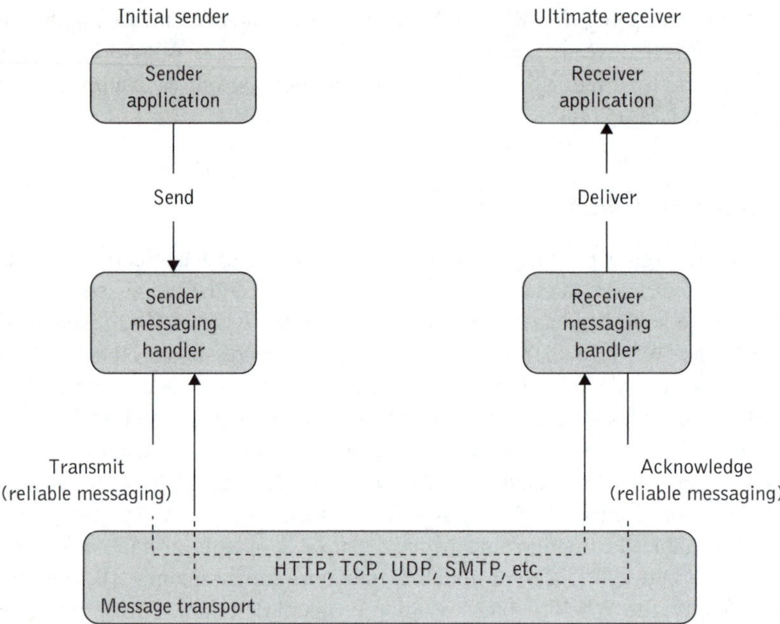

Figure 8.5 Reliable messaging model

In WS-ReliableMessaging the guarantee for delivery is specified as a delivery assurance. Endpoints that implement the WS-ReliableMessaging protocol provide delivery assurances for the delivery of messages sent from the initial sender to the ultimate receiver. It is the responsibility of the reliable messaging source and reliable messaging destination to fulfill the delivery assurances, or raise an error. There are four basic delivery assurances that endpoints provide and are supported by WS-ReliableMessaging. These are [Bilorusets 2005]:

- *AtLeastOnce Delivery:* This feature guarantees that every message sent will be delivered or an error will be raised on at least one endpoint. Some messages may be delivered more than once.
- *AtMostOnce Delivery:* This feature guarantees that every message will be delivered at most once without duplication or an error will be raised on at least one endpoint. It is possible that some messages in a sequence may not be delivered.
- *ExactlyOnce Delivery:* This feature guarantees that every message sent will be delivered without duplication or an error will be raised on at least one endpoint. This delivery assurance is the logical AND of the two prior delivery assurances.
- *InOrder Delivery:* This feature enforces the delivery of a sequence of messages at the destination, in the same order as the submission order by the sending application. This delivery assurance says nothing about duplications or omissions.

Due to the transport-independent nature of the Web services architecture, all delivery assurances are guaranteed irrespective of the communication transport or combination of transports used. Using WS-ReliableMessaging simplifies system development due to the smaller number of potential delivery failure modes that a developer must anticipate.

WS-ReliableMessaging takes advantage of the algorithms used in reliable messaging and transaction protocols. More specifically, WS-ReliableMessaging provides a flexible acknowledgement scheme in which receivers can efficiently convey the range of messages that have (and have not) been received. WS-ReliableMessaging also provides an efficient ordering mechanism to ensure that receivers can process messages in the same order in which they were sent, even in the face of reordering due to retransmissions or multi-path routing.

WS-ReliableMessaging was designed to comply with the existing Web service infrastructure. In particular, WS-ReliableMessaging is meant to be layered on top of existing application protocols and interfaces described in WSDL and XML Schema [Box 2003]. This means that in an application that involves two interacting parties, such as a distributor and a supplier, the two parties do not need to redesign their application-level message schemas or exchange patterns. If the implementations of the distributor and supplier applications use the WSDL and XML Schema elements that define the business interfaces of the services, then these implementations can be extended with the necessary reliable messaging functions.

The correct implementation of the WS-ReliableMessaging protocol requires that a number of constraints are met prior to the processing of an initial message sent from a source to a destination [Bilorusets 2005]. The reliable messaging source must have an endpoint reference that uniquely identifies the reliable messaging destination endpoint. In addition, the reliable messaging source must also have knowledge of the destination's policies, if any, and must also be capable of formulating messages that adhere to this policy. Policy assertions can be expressed using the mechanisms defined in WS-Policy (see section 12.4.1). If a secure exchange of messages is required, then the reliable messaging source and the reliable messaging destination must have established a security context. The WS-ReliableMessaging standard assumes that communications can be secured using WS-Security and associated standards.

To guarantee correct behavior during the lifetime of the protocol, two invariants are introduced [Bilorusets 2005]. First, a reliable messaging source must assign each reliable message a sequence number. Second, every acknowledgement issued by a reliable messaging destination must include within an acknowledgement range the sequence number of every message successfully received by the reliable messaging destination, while excluding sequence numbers of any messages not yet received.

8.4.2.1 Structure of WS-ReliableMessaging

WS-ReliableMessaging is developed around three core elements.

- *Sequences:* The WS-ReliableMessaging specification models a message exchange between two endpoints always as a sequence irrespective of whether only one or an entire sequence of messages transmitted as a group are exchanged. The protocol uses the `<Sequence>` element to identify and track a group of messages, which are given a globally unique sequence identifier (an absolute URI) that is common to all messages in the sequence.

- *Message numbers:* Individual messages in a sequence are identified by an ascending sequence number. This numbering scheme makes it simple to detect missing or duplicate messages, and simplifies acknowledgement generation and processing.
- *Acknowledgements:* An acknowledgement is an indication that a message was successfully transferred to its destination.

8.4.2.2 WS-ReliableMessaging examples

Listing 8.1 is an example of a message containing the `<Sequence>` element. The message in the example is the third in sequence and is identified by some URI. As the listing illustrates, in addition to mandatory `<Identifier>` and `<MessageNumber>` elements, the `<Sequence>` header may include a `<LastMessage>` element to indicate that a particular message is the last in the exchange. The `<LastMessage>` element has no content.

```
<Soap:Envelope
  xmlns:Soap="http://www.w3.org/2003/05/soap-envelope"
  xmlns:wsrm="http://schemas.xmlsoap.org/ws/2005/02/rm"
  xmlns:wsa="http://www.w3.org/2004/12/addressing">
  <Soap:Header>
       ...
    <wsrm:Sequence>
        <wsrm:Identifier> xs:anyURI </wsrm:Identifier>
            ...
        <wsrm:MessageNumber> 3 </wsrm:MessageNumber>
        <wsrm:LastMessage/>
            ...
    </wsrm:Sequence>

  </Soap:Header>
  <Soap:Body>
     <GetOrder xmlns="http://supply.com/orderservice"
          ...
     </GetOrder>
  </Soap:Body>
</Soap:Envelope>
```

Listing 8.1 Sample sequence element in WS-ReliableMessaging

WS-ReliableMessaging proposes the use of a `<SequenceAcknowledgement>` header element, which is used to return a receipt acknowledgement for one or more messages in a given sequence, either in an arbitrary response message or in a response created exclusively to return the acknowledgement.

Listing 8.2 is an example of a message containing the <SequenceAcknowledgement> element. As shown in this listing, an acknowledgement uses a number of <AcknowledgementRange> elements to indicate that the range of messages in the sequence being acknowledged is not contiguous. The example in the listing specifies that while messages number 1, 2, and 4 have been received, message number 3 in the sequence has not been received by the reliable messaging destination.

```
<Soap:Envelope
 xmlns:Soap="http://www.w3.org/2003/05/soap-envelope"
 xmlns:wsrm="http://schemas.xmlsoap.org/ws/2005/02/rm"
 xmlns:wsa="http://www.w3.org/2004/12/addressing">
 <Soap:Header>
      ...
  <wsrm:SequenceAcknowledgement>
      <wsrm:Identifier> http://supply.com/abc </wsrm:Identifier>
      <wsrm:AcknowledgementRange Upper="2" Lower="1"/>
      <wsrm:AcknowledgementRange Upper="4" Lower="4"/>
      <wsrm:Nack> 3 </wsrm:Nack>
  </wsrm:SequenceAcknowledgement>
  <Soap:Body>
      ...
  </Soap:Body>
</Soap:Envelope>
```

Listing 8.2 Sample acknowledgement element in WS-ReliableMessaging

Reliable message delivery does not require an explicit coordinator. When using WS-ReliableMessaging, the participants must recognize the protocol based on the information sent in SOAP message headers. A message sequence can be established either by the initiator/sender or the Web service, and often by both when establishing a duplex association. When the initiator attempts to establish a sequence, the service is informed of this request by the inclusion of a WS-ReliableMessaging <Sequence> header block in the request. If the ultimate receiver agrees to collaborate in this behavior, this is indicated by including the <SequenceAcknowledgement> header block in the response message. A rejection means that the sequence is not established. Alternately, the service may establish a message sequence when asked. This typically happens during the initial message exchange and is often used for duplex communications.

WS-ReliableMessaging leverages the ability of WS-Addressing to allow messages to be sent asynchronously in either direction in several ways [Box 2003]. Rather than send an acknowledgement message for every message received, WS-ReliableMessaging allows the destination to cumulatively acknowledge every message it has received in a single, compact control element. This control element can be sent in its own message or included with a subsequent application message that is sent back to the source (e.g., a response message in a request/reply conversation). In addition, the fault definitions defined in WS-ReliableMessaging reference fault abstract properties that are defined in the WS-Addressing specification.

8.5 The Enterprise Service Bus

To surmount problems of system heterogeneity and information model mismatches in an SOA implementation an EAI middleware supporting hub-and-spoke integration patterns could be used (see section 2.9). The hub-and-spoke approach introduces an integration layer between the client and server modules that must support interoperability among and co-exist with deployed infrastructure and applications, and not attempt to replace them. However, this approach has its own drawbacks as a hub can be a central point of failure and can quickly become a bottleneck.

A scalable distributed architecture such as an SOA needs to employ a constellation of hubs (see section 8.5.4). The requirements to provide an appropriately capable and manageable integration infrastructure for Web services and SOA are coalescing into the concept of the Enterprise Service Bus (ESB), which will be the subject of this section. The two key ideas behind this approach are to loosely couple the systems taking part in the integration and break up the integration logic into distinct, easily manageable pieces [Graham 2005].

The *Enterprise Service Bus* is an open standards-based message backbone designed to enable the implementation, deployment, and management of SOA-based solutions with a focus on assembling, deploying, and managing distributed service-oriented architectures. An ESB is a set of infrastructure capabilities implemented by middleware technology that enable an SOA and alleviate disparity problems between applications running on heterogeneous platforms and using diverse data formats. The ESB supports service invocations, message, and event-based interactions with appropriate service levels and manageability. The ESB is designed to provide interoperability between larger-grained applications and other components via standards-based adapters and interfaces. The bus functions as both transport and transformation facilitator to allow distribution of these services over disparate systems and computing environments.

An ESB provides an implementation backbone for an SOA that treats applications as services. The ESB is about configuring applications rather than coding and hardwiring applications together. It is a lightweight infrastructure that provides plug and play enterprise functionality. It is ultimately responsible for the proper control, flow, and even translations of all messages between services, using any number of possible messaging protocols. An ESB pulls together applications and discrete integration components to create assemblies of services to form composite business processes, which in turn automate business functions in an enterprise. It establishes proper control of messaging as well as applying the needs of security, policy, reliability, and accounting, in an SOA architecture. With an ESB SOA implementation, previously isolated ERP, CRM, supply-chain management, financial, and other legacy systems can become SOA enabled and integrated more effectively than when relying on custom, point-to-point coding or proprietary EAI technology. The end result is that with an ESB it is then easier to create new composite applications that use pieces of application logic and/or data that reside in existing systems.

The ESB distributed processing infrastructure is aware of applications and services and uses content-based routing facilities to make informed decisions about how to communicate with them. In essence the ESB provides "docking stations" for hosting services that can be assembled and orchestrated and are available for use to any other service on the

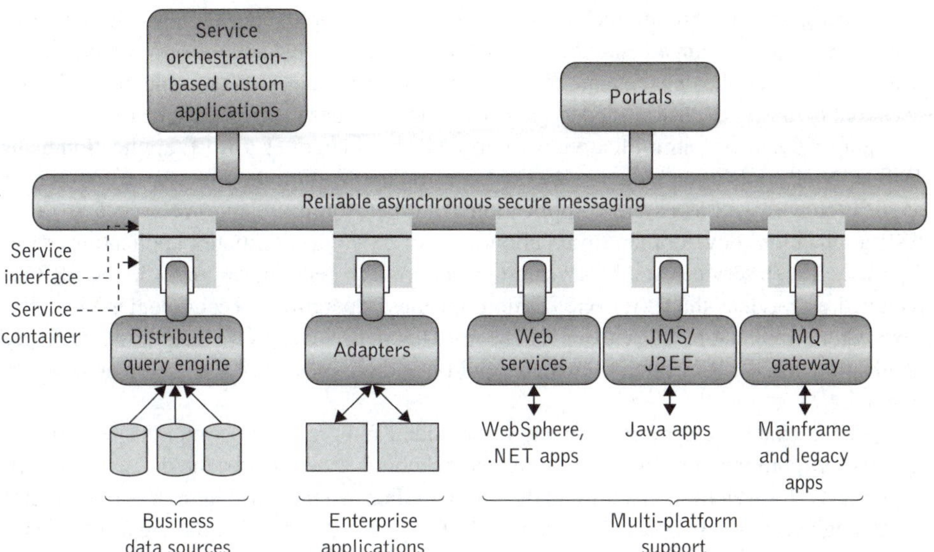

Figure 8.6 ESB connecting diverse applications and technologies

bus. Once a service is deployed into a service container it becomes an integral part of the ESB and can be used by any application or service connected to it. The service container hosts, manages, dynamically deploys services, and binds them to external resources, e.g., data sources, enterprise and multi-platform applications, such as shown in Figure 8.6.

Conceptually, the ESB has evolved from the store and forward mechanism found in middleware products and now is a combination of EAI, Web services, XSLT, and orchestration technologies, such as BPEL. To achieve its operational objectives the ESB draws from traditional EAI broker functionality in that it provides integration services such as connectivity and routing of messages based on business rules, data transformation, and adapters to applications [Chappell 2005a]. These capabilities are themselves SOA based in that they are spread out across the bus in a highly distributed fashion and hosted in separately deployable service containers. This is a crucial difference from traditional integration brokers, which as we shall see in section 8.5.4.1 are usually heavyweight, highly centralized, and monolithic in nature [Papazoglou 2006]. The ESB approach allows for the selective deployment of integration broker functionality exactly where it is needed with no additional over-bloating where it is not required.

One of the primary use cases for ESB is to act as the intermediary layer between a portal server and the back-end data and processing sources that the portal server needs to interact with. This is also shown in Figure 8.6. A portal is a user-facing visual aggregation point of a variety of resources represented as services, e.g., retail, divisional, corporate employee, and business partner portals. A portal enables unified and secure access to multiple applications, self-service publishing, on-line collaboration, and process automation. The portal draws content from a variety of different systems and presents this content and associated functionality on a browser as a single screen. For example, a sales portal at a business may contain sales information, calendars of special events, e.g., sales discounts, sales forecasting, and so on. Each of these separate areas on the portal may originate from a different system within an enterprise. Some of the content may come from external organizations. Web services provide an effective means for reducing the complexity and overhead that comes with custom-coded interfaces and manages changes efficiently.

Figure 8.6 shows a simplified view of an ESB that integrates a J2EE application using JMS, a .NET application using a C# client, an MQ application that interfaces with legacy applications, as well as external applications and data sources using Web services. In an ESB application, development tools allow new or existing distributed applications to be exposed as Web services and be accessed via a portal. In general, resources in the ESB are modeled as services that offer one or more business operations. Technologies like J2EE Connector Architecture (JCA) may also be used to create services by integrating packaged applications (like ERP systems), which would then be exposed as Web services (see section 8.5.4.2).

An ESB enables the more efficient value-added integration of a number of different application components, by positioning them behind a service-oriented facade and by applying Web services technology to the problem. For instance, in Figure 8.6 a distributed query engine, which is normally based on XQuery or SQL, enables the creation of business data services, e.g., sales order data or available product sets, by providing uniform access to a variety of disparate business data sources or organization repositories.

Endpoints in the ESB depicted in Figure 8.6 provide abstraction of physical destination and connection information (like TCP/IP host name and port number). In addition, they facilitate asynchronous and highly reliable communication between service containers using reliable messaging conventions (see section 8.4). Endpoints allow services to communicate using logical connection names, which an ESB will map to actual physical network destinations at run-time. This destination independence gives the services that are part of the ESB the ability to be upgraded, moved, or replaced without having to modify code and disrupt existing ESB applications. For instance, an existing ESB invoicing service could be easily upgraded or replaced with a new service without disrupting other applications. Additionally, duplicate processes can be set up to handle fail-over if a service is not available. The endpoints can be configured to use several levels of QoS, which guarantee communication despite network failures and outages [Chappell 2004].

The distributed nature of the ESB container model allows individual event-driven services to be plugged into the ESB backbone on an as-needed basis. It allows them to be highly decentralized and work together in a highly distributed fashion, while they are scaled independently from one another. This is illustrated in Figure 8.6 where applications running on different platforms are abstractly decoupled from each other, and can be connected together through the bus as logical endpoints that are exposed as event-driven services. The WS-Notification family of specifications, which we examined in Chapter 7, will bring the publish/subscribe functionality to ESB-focused current incarnations of Web services standards.

To successfully build and deploy a distributed SOA, there are five design/deployment and management aspects that need to be addressed first:

1. *Service analysis and design:* A service development methodology should be used to enable service-oriented development and the reuse of existing applications and resources.

2. *Service enablement:* The service development methodology should determine which discrete application elements need to be exposed as services.

3. *Service orchestration:* Distributed services need to be configured and orchestrated in a unified and clearly defined distributed process.

4. *Service deployment:* Emphasis should also be placed on the production environment that addresses security, reliability, and scalability concerns.

5. *Service management:* Services must be audited, maintained, and reconfigured and corresponding changes in processes must be made without rewriting the services or underlying application.

The above issues will be addressed in Chapter 15, which examines service design and development methodologies, and in Chapter 16, which focuses on service management technology and mechanisms. In this chapter we assume that services in an ESB are well designed according to the principles of a services development methodology and can be managed appropriately by a services management framework.

8.5.1 The event-driven nature of SOA

An SOA requires an additional fundamental technology beyond the services aspect to realize its full potential: event-driven computing. Ultimately, the primary objective of most SOA implementations is to automate as much processing as necessary and to provide critical and actionable information to human users when they are required to interact with a business process. This requires the ESB infrastructure itself to recognize meaningful events and respond to them appropriately. The response could be either by automatically initiating new services and business processes or by notifying users of business events of interest, putting the events into topical context and, often, suggesting the best courses of action. In the enterprise context business events, such as a customer order, the arrival of a shipment at a loading dock, or the payment of a bill, and so forth, affect the normal course of a business process and can occur in any order at any point in time. Consequently, applications that use orchestrated processes that exchange messages need to communicate with each other using a broad capability known as an event-driven SOA.

An *event-driven SOA* is an architectural approach to distributed computing where events trigger asynchronous messages that are then sent between independent software components that need not have any information about each other by abstracting away from the details of underlying service connectivity and protocols. An event-driven SOA provides a more lightweight, straightforward set of technologies to build and maintain the service abstraction for client applications [Bloomberg 2004].

In an ESB-enabled event-driven SOA, applications and services are treated as abstract service endpoints, which can readily respond to asynchronous events [Chappell 2005a]. Applications and event-driven services are tied together in an ESB-enabled event-driven SOA in a loosely coupled fashion, which allows them to operate independently from each other while still providing value to a broader business function. An event source typically sends messages through the ESB that publishes the messages to the objects that have subscribed to the events. The event itself encapsulates an activity, and is a complete description of a specific action. To achieve its functionality, the ESB must support both the established Web services technologies such as SOAP, WSDL, and BPEL, as well as emerging standards like WS-ReliableMessaging and WS-Notification (see Chapter 7).

To achieve a more lightweight arrangement an event-driven SOA requires that two participants in an event (server and client) be decoupled. With fully decoupled exchanges the two participants in an event need not have any knowledge about each other before engaging in a business transaction. This means that there is no need for a service contract in WSDL that explicates the behavior of a server to the client. The only relationship is indirect, through the ESB, to which clients and servers are subscribed as subscribers and publishers of events. Despite the notion of decoupling in event-driven SOA, recipients of events require metadata about those events. In such situations recipients of events still have some information about those events. For instance, the publishers of the events often organize them on the basis of some (topical) taxonomy or, alternatively, provide details about the event, including its size, format, etc., which is a form of metadata. In contrast to service interfaces, however, metadata that is associated to events is generated on an ad hoc basis as metadata tends to come along with the event rather than being contained in a separate service contract. In particular, *ad hoc metadata* describes published events that consumers can subscribe to, the interfaces that service clients and providers exhibit as well as the messages they exchange, and even the agreed format and context of this metadata, without falling into the formal service contracts themselves.

To effectively orchestrate the behavior of services in a distributed process, the ESB infrastructure includes a distributed processing framework and XML-based Web services. To exemplify these features, the simplified distributed procurement business process shown in Figure 8.7 will be later configured and deployed using an ESB. Figure 8.7 shows a simplified distributed procurement business process where an automated inventory system initiates a replenishment signal and thereby triggers an automated procurement process flow. During this procurement process flow a series of logical steps need to be performed. First, the sourcing service queries the enterprise's supplier reference database

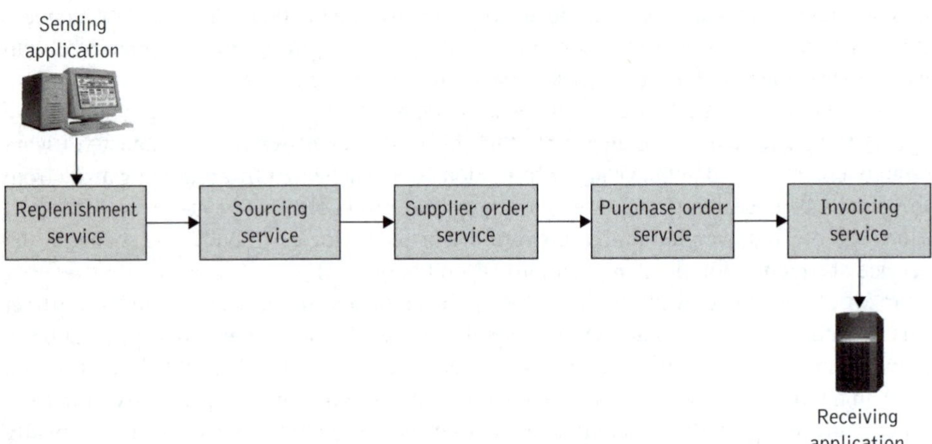

Figure 8.7 Simplified distributed procurement process

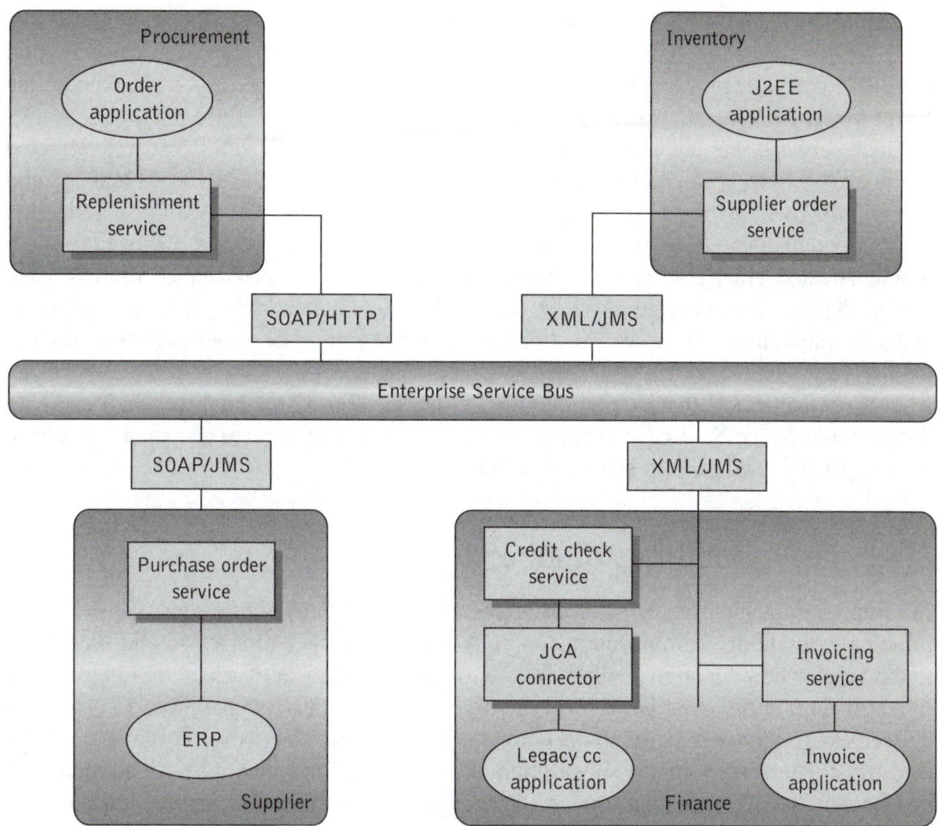

Figure 8.8 ESB connecting remote services

to determine the list of possible suppliers, which could be prioritized on the basis of existing contracts and supplier metrics. A supplier is then chosen based on some criterion and the purchase order is automatically generated in an ERP purchasing module and is sent to the vendor of choice. Finally, this vendor uses an invoicing service to bill the customer.

The services that are part of the simplified distributed procurement business process depicted in Figure 8.7 can be seen in use in Figure 8.8. The service implementation of the procurement business process reuses and service enables any standard processes found in back-end systems such as ERP, supply-chain management, or any other enterprise applications. These processes are then orchestrated to create a fragment of the functionality required by the procurement business process. In the example of Figure 8.7 we assume that the inventory is out of stock and the replenishment message is routed to a supplier order service. Although this figure shows only a single supplier order service as part of the inventory, in reality a plethora of supplier services may exist. The supplier order service, which executes a remote Web service at a chosen supplier to fulfill the order, is assumed to generate its output in an XML message format that is not understood by the purchase order service. To avoid heterogeneity problems, the message from the supplier order service leverages the ESB's transformation service to convert the XML into a format that is acceptable by the purchase order service. This figure also shows that JCA is used within the ESB to allow legacy applications, such as a credit check service, to be placed onto the ESB through JCA resource adapters.

Once services that are part of the distributed procurement business process depicted in Figure 8.8 have been chained together, it is necessary to provide a way to manage and reconfigure them to react to changes in business processes. The ESB is a federated environment that can be managed from any point. Ideally, this could be achieved through a sophisticated graphical business process management tool that can be used to configure, deploy, and manage services and endpoints. This allows the free movement and reconfiguration of services without requiring rewriting or modifying the services themselves.

In the remainder of this chapter and throughout the rest of this book we shall make no distinction between SOAs and event-driven SOAs (unless necessary) and shall henceforth use the generic term SOA to stand for both terms.

8.5.2 Key capabilities of an ESB

In order to implement an SOA, both applications and infrastructure must support SOA principles. Enabling an application for SOA involves the creation of service interfaces to existing or new functions, either directly or through the use of adapters. Enabling the infrastructure, at the most basic level, involves provision of the capabilities to route and deliver secure service requests to the correct service provider. However, it is also vital that the infrastructure supports the substitution of one service implementation by another with no effect on the clients of that service. This requires not only that the service interfaces be specified according to SOA principles, but also that the infrastructure allows client code to invoke services irrespective of the service location and the communication protocol involved. Such service routing and substitution are among the many capabilities of the ESB. Additional capabilities can be found in the following list that describes detailed functional requirements of an ESB. Some of the ESB functional requirements described in the list below have also been discussed by other authors such as [Robinson 2004], [Candadai 2004], [Channabasavaiah 2003], [Chappell 2004]. It should be noted that not all of the capabilities described below are offered by current commercial ESB systems.

Dynamic connectivity capabilities: Dynamic connectivity is the ability to connect to Web services dynamically without using a separate static API or proxy for each service. Most enterprise applications today operate on a static connectivity mode, requiring some static piece of code for each service. Dynamic service connectivity is a key capability for a successful ESB implementation. The dynamic connectivity API is the same regardless of the service implementation protocol (Web services, JMS, EJB/RMI, etc.).

Reliable messaging capabilities: Reliable messaging can be primarily used to ensure guaranteed delivery of these messages to their destination and for handling events. This capability is crucial for responding to clients in an asynchronous manner and for a successful ESB implementation.

Topic- and content-based routing capabilities: The ESB should be equipped with routing mechanisms to facilitate not only topic-based routing, but also more sophisticated content-based routing. *Topic-based routing* assumes that messages can be grouped into fixed, topical classes, so that subscribers can explicate interest in a topic and as a consequence receive messages associated to that topic. *Content-based routing*, on the other hand, allows subscriptions on constraints of actual properties (attributes) of business events (see section 2.5.3). Content-based routing forwards messages to their destination based on the context or content of the service. Content-based routing is usually implemented using techniques that can examine the content of a message and apply a set of rules to its content to determine which endpoints in the ESB infrastructure it may need to be routed to next. Content-based routing logic (rules) is usually expressed in XPath or a scripting language, such as JavaScript. For example, if a manufacturer provides a wide variety of products to its customers, only some of which are made in-house, depending on the product ordered it might be necessary to route the message directly to an external supplier, or route it internally to be processed by a warehouse fulfillment service. Content-based ESB capabilities could be supported by emerging standard efforts such as WS-Notification, see section 7.3.

Transformation capabilities: A critical ability of the ESB is the ability to route service interactions through a variety of transport protocols, and to transform from one protocol to another where necessary. Another important aspect of an ESB implementation is the ability to support service messaging models and data formats consistent with the SOA interfaces. A major source of value in an ESB is that it shields any individual component from any knowledge of the implementation details of any other component. The ESB transformation services make it possible to ensure that messages and data received by any component are in the format it expects, thereby removing the need to make changes. The ESB plays a major role in transforming between differing data formats and messaging models, whether between basic XML formats and Web services messages, or between different XML formats (e.g., transforming an industry-standard XML message to a proprietary or custom XML format). The ESB connectivity and translation infrastructure is discussed in section 8.5.5.

Service enablement capabilities: Service enablement includes the ability to access already existing resources such as legacy systems – technically obsolete mission-critical elements of an organization's infrastructure – and include them in an SOA implementation. Tactically legacy assets must be leveraged, service enabled, and integrated with modern service technologies and applications. This important issue is the subject of section 8.5.6.

Endpoint discovery with multiple QoS capabilities: The ESB should support the basic SOA need to discover, locate, and bind to services. As many network endpoints can implement the same service contract, the ESB should make it possible for the client to select the best endpoint at run-time, rather than hard-coding endpoints at build time. The ESB should therefore be capable of supporting various QoSs and allow clients to discover the best service instance with which to interact based on QoS properties. Such capabilities should be controlled by declarative policies associated with the services involved using a policy standard such as the WS-PolicyFramework.

Long-running process and transaction capabilities: Service orientation, as opposed to distributed object architectures such as .NET or J2EE, more closely reflects real-world processes and relationships. Hence, SOA represents a much more natural way to model and build software that solves real-world business processing needs. Accordingly, the ESB should provide the ability to support business processes and long-running services – services that tend to run for long duration, exchanging message (conversation) as they progress. Typical examples are an on-line reservation system, which interacts with the user as well as various service providers (airline ticketing, insurance claims, mortgage and credit product applications, etc.). In addition, in order to be successful in business environments it is extremely important that the ESB provides certain transactional guarantees. More specifically, the ESB needs to be able to ensure that complex transactions are handled in a highly reliable manner and if failure should occur, transactions should be capable of rolling back processing to the original, pre-request state. Long-duration transactional conversations could be made possible if implemented on the basis of messaging patterns using asynchrony, store and forward, and itinerary-based routing techniques. It should be noted that the base definition of an ESB as currently used by the ESB analyst and vendor community does not mandate a long-duration transaction manager [Chappell 2005b]. Chapters 9 and 10 discuss business processes, long-running services, and transactions.

Security capabilities: Generically handling and enforcing security is a key success factor for ESB implementations. The ESB needs both to provide a security model to service consumers and to integrate with the (potentially varied) security models of service providers. Both point-to-point (e.g., SSL encryption) and end-to-end security capabilities will be required. These end-to-end security capabilities include federated authentication, which intercepts service requests and adds the appropriate user name and credentials; validation of each service request and authorization to make sure that the sender has the appropriate privilege to access the service; and, lastly, encryption/decryption of XML content at the element level for both message requests and responses. To address these intricate security requirements the ESB must rely on WS-Security and other security-related standards for Web services that have been developed recently, see sections 11.4 and 11.5.

Integration capabilities: To support SOA in a heterogeneous environment, the ESB needs to integrate with a variety of systems that do not directly support service-style interactions. These may include legacy systems, packaged applications, or other EAI technologies. When assessing the integration requirements for ESB, several types or "styles" of integration must be considered, e.g., process versus data integration.

Management and monitoring capabilities: In an SOA environment, applications cross system (and even organizational) boundaries, they overlap, and they can change over time. Managing these applications is a serious challenge. Examples include dynamic load balancing, fail-over when primary systems go down, and achieving topological or geographic affinity between the client and the service instance, and so on. Effective systems and application management in an ESB requires a management framework that is consistent across an increasingly heterogeneous set of participating component systems, while supporting complex aggregate (cross-component) management use cases, like dynamic resource provisioning and demand-based routing, and SLA enforcement in conjunction with policy-based behavior (e.g., the ability to select service providers dynamically based on the quality of service they offer compared to the business value of individual transactions). An additional requirement for a successful ESB implementation is the ability to monitor the health, capacity, and performance of services. Monitoring is the ability to track service activities that take place via the bus and provide visibility into various metrics and statistics. Of particular significance is the ability to spot problems and exceptions in the business processes and move towards resolving them as soon as they occur. Chapter 16 examines the management and monitoring of distributed Web services platforms and applications.

Scalability capabilities: With a widely distributed SOA, there will be the need to scale some of the services or the entire infrastructure to meet integration demands. For example, transformation services are typically very resource intensive and may require multiple instances across two or more computing nodes. At the same time, it is necessary to create an infrastructure that can support the large nodes present in a global service network. The loose-coupled nature of an SOA requires that the ESB uses a decentralized model to provide a cost-effective solution that promotes flexibility in scaling any aspect of the integration network. A decentralized architecture enables independent scalability of individual services as well as the communications infrastructure itself. Scalability is discussed further in section 8.5.7.

Finally, Table 8.1 summarizes the most typical ESB functional capabilities along with their related standards. As ESB integration capabilities in the above list are central in understanding the material that follows and a key element of the ESB when performing service-oriented integration, we shall consider them next in some detail in the following section. The discussion is partly based on points raised in [Channabasavaiah 2003].

8.5.3 ESB integration styles

ESBs employ a service-oriented integration solution that leverages among other things open standards, loose coupling, and the dynamic description and discovery capabilities of Web services to reduce the complexity, cost, and risk of integration. Other salient characteristics of the ESB architectural integration style are that it is technology agnostic (it encompasses more than one particular set of technologies) and can reuse functionality in existing applications to support new application development. There is a series of important technical requirements that need to be addressed by a service-oriented integration solution in the context of an ESB. These are briefly described in the following.

Integration at the presentation tier. Integration at the presentation tier is concerned with how the complete set of applications and services a given user accesses are fabricating a

Table 8.1 ESB functional areas and related standards

Functional area	*Capabilities*	*Relevant standards*
Connectivity	Transport Guaranteed delivery Routing	SOAP WS-ReliableMessaging WS-Addressing
Content-based routing and event notification	Content-based routing Topic-based routing Business event notification	XPath WS-Topic WS-Notification
Transformation	Protocol transformation Message transformation Data transformation	XSLT WS-Addressing WS-ReourceFramework
Service enablement	Wrapping Transformation Access to legacy resources	WSDL BPEL
Service orchestration	Process description Process execution Long-running processes	BPEL
Transaction management	Transactional services Coordination	WS-Transaction WS-Coordination
Security	Authentication Authorization Access rights Encryption	WS-Security WS-SecurePolicy
Discovery with multiple QoS	Run-time service discovery using multiple QoS capabilities and policies	WS-PolicyFramework
Management and monitoring	Monitoring QoSs Enforcing SLAs Controlling tasks Managing resource lifecycles	WS-DistributedManagement WS-Policy

highly distributed yet unified portal framework that provides a usable, efficient, uniform, and consistent presentation tier. In this way the ESB can provide one face to the users resulting in consistent user experience, with unified information delivery while allowing underlying applications to remain distributed. Two complementary industry standards that are emerging in the portal space and can assist with these efforts [Rana 2004] are:

- JSR 168: This is an industry standard that defines a standard way to develop portlets. It allows portlets to be interoperable across portal vendors. For example, portlets developed for BEA WebLogic Portal can be interoperable with IBM Portal. This allows organizations to have a lower dependency on the portal product vendor.

- WSRP (Web Service for Remote Portals): This is an industry standard that allows remote portlets to be developed and consumed in a standard manner and facilitates federated portals. WSRP combines the power of Web services and portal technologies and is fast becoming the major enabling technology for distributed portals in an enterprise.

JSR 168 complements WSRP by dealing with local rather than distributed portlets. A portal page may have certain local portlets, which are JSR 168 compliant, and some remote, distributed portlets that are executed in a remote container. A portlet may be an ESB service, which allows the portlet developer to view the entire universe of back-end systems in a normalized fashion through the ESB, see Figure 8.6. With JSR 168 and WSRP maturing, the possibility of a true EJB federated portal can become a reality.

Application connectivity. Application connectivity is an integration style concerned with all types of connectivity that the ESB integration layer must support. At one level, this means things such as synchronous and asynchronous communications, routing, transformation, high-speed distribution of data, and gateways and protocol converters. On another level, application connectivity also relates to the virtualization of input and output, or sources and sinks. It requires that inputs are received and passed to applications in the ESB in a source-neutral way. Special-purpose front-end device and protocol handlers should make that possible. For connectivity, an ESB can utilize J2EE components such as the Java Message Service for MOM connectivity, and JCA for connecting to application adapters. An ESB can also integrate easily with applications built with .NET, COM, C#, C++, and C. In addition, an ESB can integrate easily with any application that supports SOAP and Web services.

An ESB allows these different kinds of application to connect together by supporting notification features such as those embodied in WS-Notification (which we examined in section 7.4). For example, a notification message might be published by a JMS application and received by a notification consumer as defined by WS-Notification.

The ESB can also mediate between request/response SOA and event-oriented SOA services by managing a set of topic spaces in its registry and by providing an implementation of one or more distributed notification brokers as defined by WS-Notification. Traditional MOM applications are unaware of the WS-Notification aspect of these brokers – they simply publish or subscribe to topics on the broker of their choice. The ESB administrator can configure one or more WS-Notification-style notification brokers to be used by WS-Notification publishers or subscribers. Moreover, the ESB administrator can arrange that these be federated together with each other, and/or with the traditional publish/subscribe applications.

Application connectivity has to deal with the following types of integration:

Application integration: Application integration is concerned with building and evolving an integration backbone capability that enables fast assembly and disassembly of various platform and component technologies. Application integration is an integral part of the assembly process that facilitates combining legacy applications, acquired packages, external application subscriptions, and newly built components. The ESB should focus on a service-based application integration style that enables better-structured integration solutions that deliver applications comprised of interchangeable parts that are designed to be adaptable to business and technology change.

Business process integration: Process integration is concerned with the development of automated processes that map to and provide solutions for business processes, integration of existing applications into processes, and integrating processes with other processes. Process-level integration at the level of an ESB may include the integration of business processes and applications within the enterprise (i.e., EAI solutions). It also may involve the integration of whole processes, not just individual services, from external sources, such as supply-chain management or financial services that span multiple institutions. For such application and process integration needs, technologies such as BPEL can be used, see section 9.7.

Business data integration: Data integration is the process of providing consistent access to business data in the enterprise, by all the applications that require it, in whatever form they need it, without being restricted by the format, source, or location of the data. This requirement, when implemented, might involve adapters and transformation facilities, aggregation services to merge and reconcile disparate data, e.g., merging two customer profiles, and validation to ensure data consistency, e.g., minimum income should be equal to or exceed a certain threshold. Business data should be transformed irrespective of the formats under which it exists, the operating system that manages it, and the location where it is stored. Access to distributed business data is provided by a distributed query engine such as the one shown in Figure 8.6.

Integration design and development methodology: One of the requirements for the application development environment must be that it takes into account all the styles and levels of integration that could be implemented within the enterprise, and provides for their development and deployment. To be truly robust, the development environment must rely on a methodology that clearly prescribes how ESB services and components are designed and built in order to facilitate reuse, eliminate redundancy, and simplify integration, testing, deployment, and maintenance.

All of the styles of integration listed above will have some form of incarnation within any enterprise, even though in some cases they might be simplified or not clearly defined. It is important to note that all integration styles must be considered when embarking on an ESB implementation.

8.5.4 Elements of an ESB solution

There are alternative ways to implement an ESB. The ESB itself can be a single centralized service or even a distributed system consisting of peer and subpeer ESBs – in the form of an ESB federation – all working in tandem to keep the SOA system operational.

In small-scale implementations of integration solutions, the physical ESB infrastructure is likely to be a centralized ESB topology. A *centralized ESB topology* is concentrated on a single cluster, or hub, of servers. This solution is reminiscent of hub-and-spoke middleware topologies, which use a central node that manages all interactions between applications and prevents an application having to integrate multiple times with several other applications [Linthicum 2003], [Papazoglou 2006]. The hub-and-spoke approach simply carries out one integration process on the central node, which is a central point of control responsible for integration/translation activities, maintaining routing information, service naming, and so forth. The most popular hub-and-spoke EAI solution for the interenterprise arena is integration brokering (see section 2.7.1 and section 8.5.4.1).

Even though a hub-and-spoke solution is capable of being stretched out across organizational boundaries, it still does not allow the local autonomy that individual business units require to operate semi-independently of each other. This is usually caused by the integration broker's inability to easily span firewalls and network domains. However, as explained earlier in this chapter, the most serious drawback of this approach is that hub-and-spoke solutions can quickly become a point of contention for large-scale implementations. In an environment of loosely coupled units it does not make sense for business processes flow between localized applications or security domains to be managed by a single centralized authority like an integration broker.

In circumstances where the organizational or geographically dispersed units need to act independently from one another, the infrastructure may become more physically distributed while retaining at least logically the central control over configuration. This calls for a federated hub solution. This is shown in Figure 8.9, which shows a *federated ESB* allowing different enterprises such as manufacturers, suppliers, and customers to plug together their integration domains into a larger federated integration network. This topology allows for local message traffic, integration components, and adapters to be locally installed, configured, secured, and managed, while allowing for a single integrated transaction and security model. In this figure a federated ESB solution is used to form a virtual network of trading partners across industries and services able to take advantage of the wider range of options and partnering models.

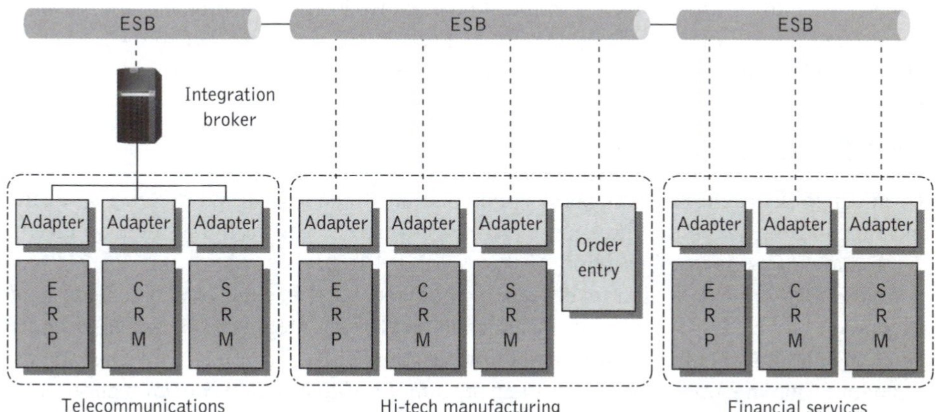

Figure 8.9 Distributed ESB allowing geographically dispersed organizations to cooperate (ERP = Enterprise Resource Planning, CRM = Customer Relationship Management, SRM = Supplier Relationship Management)

The physical deployment of the ESB depends on candidate ESB technologies such as specialized MOM, integration brokers, application servers, etc. The use and combination of different candidate ESB technologies results in a variety of ESB patterns, each having its own requirements and constraints in connection with its physical deployment. Some ESB configurations might be suited to very widespread distribution to support integration over large geographical areas, while others might be more suited to deployment in localized clusters to support high availability and scalability. Matching the requirements for physical distribution to the capabilities of candidate technologies is an important aspect of ESB design. Also important is the ability to incrementally extend the initial deployment to reflect evolving requirements, to integrate additional systems, or to extend the geographical reach of the ESB infrastructure [Robinson 2004].

Irrespective of its implementation topology, the main aim of the ESB is to provide virtualization of the enterprise resources, allowing the business logic of the enterprise to be developed and managed independently of the infrastructure, network, and provision of those business services. Implementing an ESB requires an integrated set of middleware facilities that support the following interrelated architectural styles [Endrei 2004]:

- Service-oriented architectures, where distributed applications are composed of granular reusable services with well-defined, published, and standards-compliant interfaces.
- Message-driven architectures, where applications send messages through the ESB to receiving applications.
- Event-driven architectures, where applications generate and consume messages independently of one another.

The ESB supports the above architectural styles and service interaction capabilities, and provides the integrated communication, messaging, and event infrastructure to enable them, as explained in the previous section. To achieve its stated objectives the ESB amalgamates functional capabilities of application servers, integration brokers, and business process management technologies and product sets into a single integrated infrastructure. These middleware solutions are discussed in turn in the following sections.

8.5.4.1 Integration brokers

To integrate disparate business applications one must concentrate on the characteristics and functions of integration brokers, which we covered as part of the introduction to the distributing infrastructure in section 2.7.1.

Figure 8.10 presents a high-level view of the typical architecture for implementing an integration broker. In particular, it illustrates the use of an integration broker to integrate functions and information from a variety of back-end EISs. To effectively illustrate the behavior of the integration broker, we use the simplified distributed procurement process as shown in Figure 8.7. Figure 8.10 shows that when an automated inventory system triggers a replenishment signal, an automated procurement process flow is triggered and first the enterprise's supplier reference database is queried to determine the list of possible suppliers, which could be prioritized on the basis of existing contracts and supplier

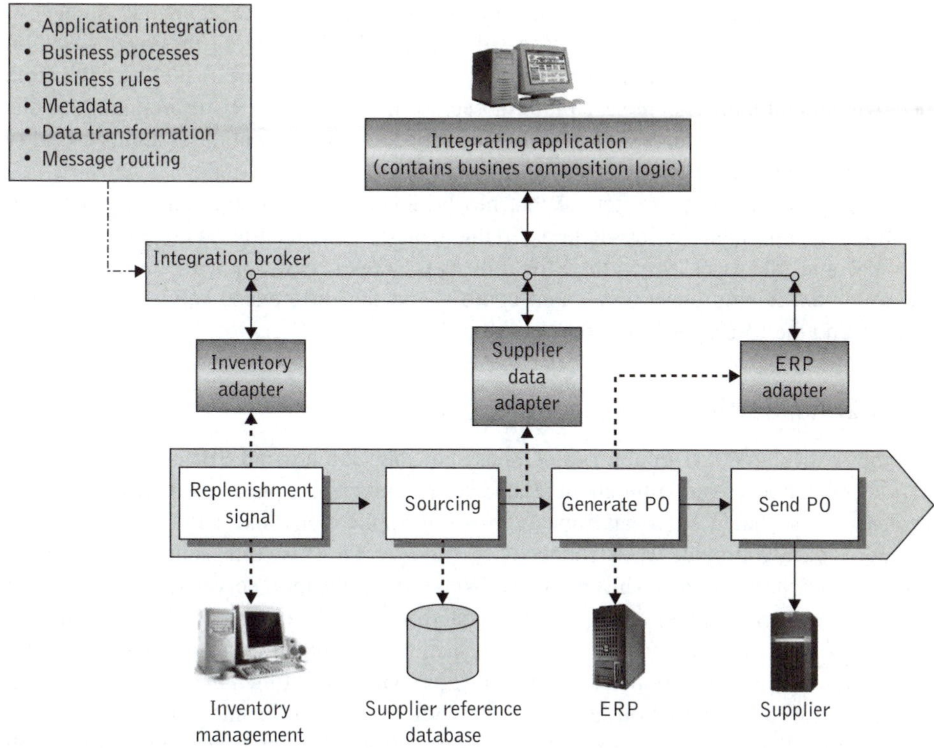

Figure 8.10 Integration broker integrating disparate back-end systems (PO = Purchase Order)

metrics. A supplier is then chosen and the purchase order is automatically generated in the ERP purchasing module and is sent to the vendor of choice.

The figure illustrates that the integration broker is the system centerpiece. The integration broker facilitates information movement between two or more resources (source and target applications), shown by means of solid lines in Figure 8.10, and accounts for differences in application semantics and heterogeneous platforms. The various existing (or component) EISs, such as CRM, ERP systems, transaction processing monitors, legacy systems, and so on, in this configuration are connected to the integration broker by means of resource adapters. This is illustrated by the presence of dashed lines in Figure 8.10. A resource adapter in this figure is used to provide access to a specific EIS and enable non-invasive application integration in a loosely coupled configuration.

The integration broker architecture presents several advantages given that integration brokers try to reduce the application integration effort by providing pre-built functionality common to many integration scenarios. The value proposition rests on reuse (in terms of middleware infrastructure and the application integration logic) across multiple applications and initiatives. Modern integration brokers incorporate integration functionality such as transformation facilities, process integration, business process management and trading partner management functionality, packaged adapters, and user-driven applications through front-end capabilities such as Java Server Pages (JSP).

In an ESB, the functionality of an integration broker, such as messaging and connectivity, application adapters, a data transformation engine, and routing of messages based on business rules, is spread out across a highly distributed architecture that allows selective deployment and independent scalability of each of those pieces. This is an important difference from the classic integration broker model where these capabilities are localized to a central monolithic server.

In many situations it is essential that newly developed ESB solutions be bridged to existing integration broker installations. In this scenario, the integration broker installation now becomes the asset, which the ESB utilizes to support new application development. To better understand these issues and comprehend the differences between integration brokers and the ESB approach refer to section 8.5.7.

8.5.4.2 Application servers

Another critical middleware infrastructure used in connection with ESBs is application servers. Application servers offer an integrated development environment for developing and deploying distributed Web- and non-Web-based applications and services. Application servers typically provide Web connectivity for extending existing solutions and bring transaction processing mechanisms to the Web. An application server is a natural point for application integration as it provides a platform for development, deployment, and management of Web-based, transactional, secure, distributed, and scalable enterprise applications. The application server middleware enables the functions of handling business processes and transactions as well as extending back-end business data and applications to the Web to which it exposes them through a single interface, typically a Web browser. This makes application servers ideal for portal-based ESB development. Unlike integration brokers, application servers do not integrate back-end systems directly but rather act as an integrated development and support framework for integrating business processes between enterprises. An application server expects the integration broker to function as a service provider providing data access, transformations, and content-based routing.

Figure 8.11 illustrates the use of an application server for a wholesale application that brings together ERP capabilities with sophisticated customer interfaces to open up new models of sales and distribution. In Figure 8.11 the adapter/component wrapper modules are responsible for providing a layer of abstraction between the application server and the component EIS. This layer allows for EIS component communications, as if the component EIS were executed within the application server environment itself. Execution in this type of architecture occurs among component wrappers within the application server. The component wrappers in this figure facilitate point integration of component systems by wrapping legacy systems and applications and other back-end resources such as databases, ERP, CRM, and SRM, so that they can express data and messages in the standard internal format expected by the application server. The application server is oblivious to the fact that these components are only the external facade of existing EISs that do the real processing activities [Lubinsky 2001].

In the previous section we explained the need to employ wrappers to encapsulate legacy and/or package functionality. The functions of wrappers are, in general, not very well understood outside the EAI community. Moreover, as in the Web services literature

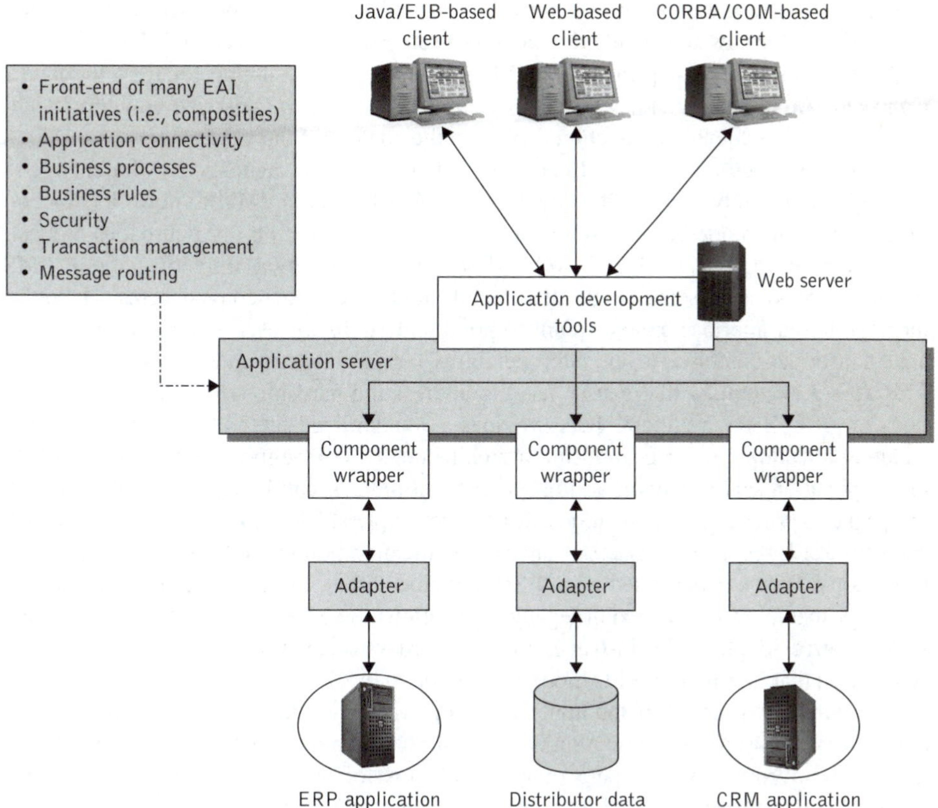

Figure 8.11 Application server providing access to back-end systems

there seems to be a lot of confusion regarding the concept of wrappers and adapters, it is useful to clarify their meaning and intended purpose.

A (component) wrapper is nothing but an abstract component that provides a service implemented by legacy software that can be used to hide existing system dependencies. In a nutshell, a wrapper performs specific business functions, has a clearly defined API, and can appear as "standard" components for clients and be accessed by using modern industry protocols. Wrappers are normally deployed in modern, distributed environments, such as J2EE or .NET. A wrapper can provide a standard interface on one side, while on the other it interfaces with existing application code in a way that is particular to the existing application code. The wrapper combines the existing application functionality that it wraps with other necessary service functionality and represents it in the form of a virtual component that is accessed via a standard service interface by any other service in an ESB.

When a legacy business process is wrapped, its realization comprises code to access an adapter that invokes the legacy system, see Figure 8.11. An adapter, unlike a wrapper, does not contain presentation or business logic functions. It is rather a software module interposed between two software systems in order to convert between their different technical and programmatic representations and perceptions of their interfaces. Resource adapters translate the applications' messages to and from a common set of standards – standard data formats and standard communication protocols, see section 2.7.1.

Application servers are principally J2EE based and include support for JMS, the Java 2 Connector Architecture, and Web services. In what follows, we describe how these technologies help implement application servers in the context of the ESB.

Recall from section 2.7 that JMS is a transport-level vendor-agnostic API for enterprise messaging that can be used with many different MOM vendors. JMS frameworks function in asynchronous mode but also offer the capability of simulating a synchronous request/response mode [Monson-Haefel 2001]. For application server implementations, JMS provides access to business logic distributed among heterogeneous systems. Having a message-based interface enables point-to-point and publish/subscribe mechanisms, guaranteed information delivery, and interoperability between heterogeneous platforms.

JCA is a technology that can be used to address the hardships of integrating applications in an ESB environment. JCA provides a standardized method for integrating disparate applications in J2EE application architectures. JCA defines a set of functionality that application server vendors can use to connect to back-end EISs, such as ERP, CRM, and legacy systems and applications. It provides support for resource adaptation, which maps the J2EE security, transaction, and communication pooling to the corresponding EIS technology. When JCA is used in an ESB implementation, the ESB could provide a JCA container that allows packaged or legacy applications to be plugged into the ESB through JCA resource adapters. For instance, a process order service uses JCA to talk to a J2EE application that internally fulfills incoming orders.

The centralized nature of the application-server-centric model of integrating applications, just like the case of integration broker solutions, can quickly become a point of contention and introduce severe performance problems for large-scale integration projects. The application server model of integrating applications is generally based on developing integration code. The crucial difference between this model and the ESB integration model is that an ESB solution is more about configuration than coding. However, application servers have an important place in an enterprise architecture, and are best when used for what they were originally intended for – to provide a component model for hosting business logic in the form of EJB, and to serve up Web pages in an enterprise portal environment. Application servers can plug into an ESB using established conventions such as JMS and MessageDrivenBeans.

8.5.4.3 Business process management

Today enterprises are striving to become electronically connected to their customers, suppliers, and partners. To achieve this, they are integrating a wide range of discrete business processes across application boundaries of all kinds. Application boundaries may range from simple enquiries about a customer's order involving two applications to complex, long-lived transactions for processing an insurance claim involving many applications and human interactions, and to parallel business events for advanced planning, production, and shipping of goods along the supply chain involving many applications, human interactions, and business to business interactions. When integrating on such a scale, enterprises need a greater latitude of functionality to overcome multiple challenges arising from the existence of proprietary interfaces, diverse standards, and approaches targeting the technical, data, automated business process, process analysis, and visualization levels. Such challenges are addressed by business process management (BPM) technology. In this section we shall only provide a short overview of BPM functionality in the context of ESB implementations.

BPM is the term used to describe the new technology that provides end-to-end visibility and control over all parts of a long-lived, multi-step information request or transaction/process that spans multiple applications and human actors in one or more enterprises. BPM also provides the ability to monitor both the state of any single process instance and all process instances in an aggregate, using real-time metrics that translate actual process activity into key performance indicators.

BPM is driven primarily by the common desire to integrate supply chains, as well as internal enterprise functions, without the need for even more custom software development. This means that the tools must be suitable for business analysts, requiring less (or no) software development. They reduce maintenance requirements because internally and externally integrated environments routinely require additions and changes to business processes. For more details about this technology, readers can refer to section 9.3.

Specialized capabilities such as BPM software solutions provide workflow-related business processes, process analysis, and visualization techniques in an ESB setting. In particular, BPM allows the separation of business processes from the underlying integration code. When sophisticated process definitions are called for in an ESB, a process orchestration engine – that supports BPEL or some other process definition language such as ebXML Business Process Specification Schema (BPSS) – may be layered onto the ESB. The process orchestration may support long-running stateful processes. It may also support parallel execution paths, with branching, and merging of message flow execution paths based on join conditions or transition conditions being met. Sophisticated process orchestration can be combined with stateless itinerary-based routing to create an SOA that solves complex integration problems. An ESB uses the concept of *itinerary-based routing* to provide a message with a list of routing instructions. In an ESB, routing instructions, which represent a business process definition, are carried with the message as it travels through the bus across service invocations. The remote ESB service containers determine where to send the message next.

8.5.4.4 ESB transport-level choices

Finally, before we close this section, it is important to understand the transport-level protocol choices that can be used in conjunction with an ESB. Web services in the ESB can communicate using SOAP messages over a variety of protocols. Each protocol effectively provides a service bus connecting multiple endpoints. Currently, the most common service bus transport layer implementations include SOAP/HTTP(S) and SOAP/JMS [Keen 2004].

The SOAP over HTTP service bus is the most familiar way to send requests and responses between service requestors and providers. As already explained in section 2.1.1, HTTP is a client–server model in which an HTTP client opens a connection and sends a request message to an HTTP server. The client request message is to invoke a Web service. The HTTP server dispatches a response message containing the invocation and closes the connection. Use of an ESB enables the service requestor to communicate using HTTP and permits the service provider to receive the request using a different transport mechanism. Many ESB implementation providers have an HTTP service bus in addition to at least one other protocol. Any of these protocols can be used for ESB interactions and often are chosen based on service-level requirements.

JMS, part of the J2EE standard, provides a conventional way to create, send, and receive enterprise messages. While it does not quite provide the level of interoperability based on the wide adoption that the HTTP ESB can boast, the SOAP/JMS ESB brings advantages in terms of QOS. A SOAP/JMS ESB can provide asynchronous and reliable messaging to a Web service invocation. This means that the requestor can receive acknowledgement of assured delivery and communicate with enterprises that may not be available. A SOAP/JMS Web service is a Web service that implements a JMS queue-based transport. As in the case of the SOAP/HTTP, the SOA/JMS service bus enables service requestors and providers to communicate using different protocols.

8.5.5 Connectivity and translation infrastructure

For the most part, business applications in an enterprise are not designed to communicate with other applications. There is often an impedance mismatch between the technologies used within internal systems and with external trading partner systems. In order to seamlessly integrate these disparate applications, there must be a way in which a request for information in one format can easily be transformed into a format expected by the called service. For instance, in Figure 8.6 the functionality of a J2EE application needs to be exposed to non-J2EE clients such as .NET applications and other clients. In doing so, a Web service may have to integrate with other instances of EISs in an organization, or the J2EE application itself may have to integrate with other EISs. In such scenarios, how the application exchanges information with the ESB depends on the application accessibility options. There are three alternative ways an application can exchange information with the ESB include [Keen 2004]:

1. *Application-provided Web services interface:* Some applications and legacy application servers have adopted the open standards philosophy and have included a Web services interface. WSDL defines the interface to communicate directly with the application business logic. Where possible, taking a direct approach is always preferred.
2. *Non-Web services interface:* The application does not expose business logic via Web services. An application-specific adapter can be supplied to provide a basic intermediary between the application API and the ESB.
3. *Service wrapper as interface to adapter:* In some cases the adapter may not supply the correct protocol (JMS, for example) that the ESB expects. In this case, the adapter would be Web services enabled.

As complementary technologies in an ESB implementation, (resource) adapters and Web services can work together to implement complex integration scenarios, see Figure 8.12. Data synchronization (in addition to translation services) is one of the primary objectives of resource adapters. Adapters can thus take on the role of data synchronization and translation services, whereas Web services will enable application functions to interact

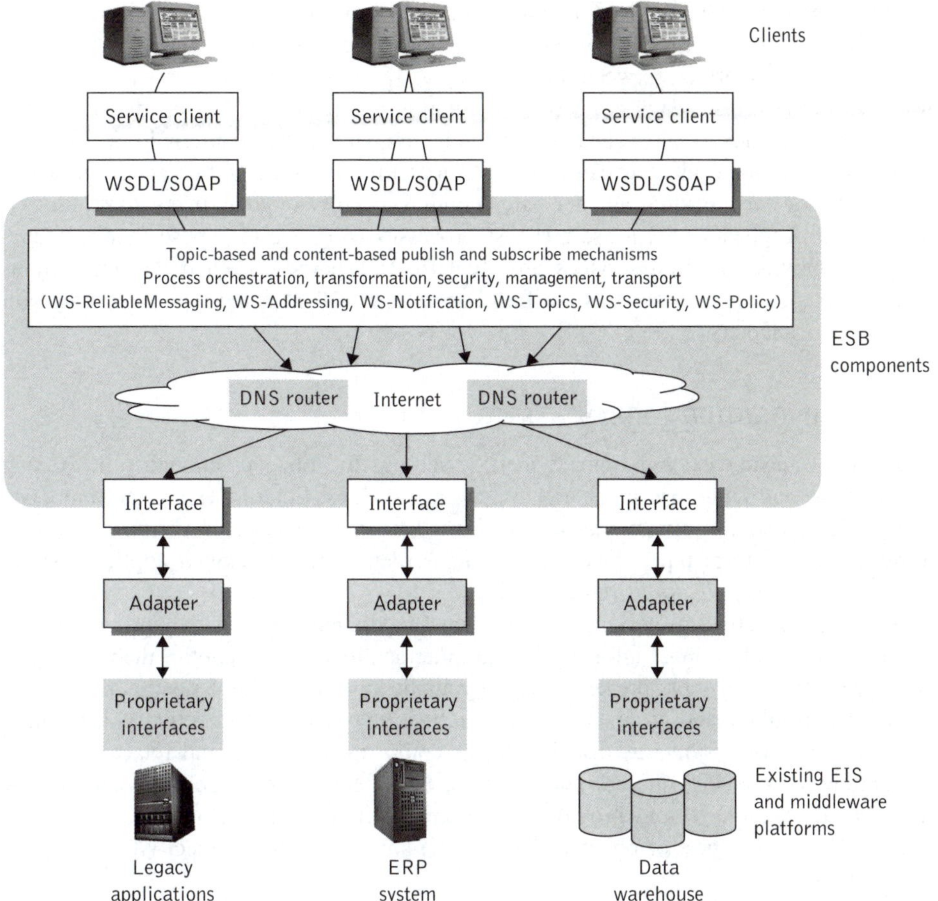

Figure 8.12 Combining Web services with resource adapters

with each other. Web services are an ideal mechanism for implementing a universally accessible application function (service) that may need to integrate with other applications to fulfill its service contract. The drivers of data synchronization and Web services are also different. Web services will generally be initiated by a user request/event, whereas data synchronization is generally initiated by state changes in data objects (e.g., customer, item, order, and so on). The following points explicate.

An event to which a Web service reacts could be a user-initiated request such as a purchase order or an on-line bill payment, for example. User events can naturally be generated by applications such as an order management application requiring a customer status check from an accounting system. On the other hand, a state change in a data object can be an activity like the addition of a new customer record in the customer service application or an update to the customer's billing address. These state changes trigger an adapter to add the new customer record or update the customer record in all other applications that keep their own copies of customer data.

Reverting to the J2EE to .NET application connectivity scenario, a connectivity service in the form of a resource adapter is required. In this implementation strategy, Web services can become the interface between the company and its customers, partners, and suppliers, whereas the resource adapters become integration components tying up different EISs inside the company. This is just one potential implementation pattern in which Web services and resource adapters can co-exist. Another potential integration pattern in which Web services and resource adapters are required to collaborate is in business process integration. Applications that use business processes will have to expose required functionality. Obviously, Web services are ideal for this purpose. When the applications need to integrate with other EISs to fulfill their part in the business process, they will use resource adapters.

8.5.6 Leveraging legacy assets

There is a fundamental requirement in ESB settings to utilize functionality in existing applications and repurpose it for use in new applications. Enterprises are still burdened with older-generation operational applications that were constructed to run on various obsolescent hardware types, programmed in obsolete languages. Such applications are known as *legacy applications* [Ulrich 2002].

Legacy applications are critical assets of any modern enterprise as they provide access to mission-critical business information and functionality and thus control the majority of an organization's business processes. Legacy applications could implement core business tasks such as taking and processing orders, initiating production and delivery, generating invoices, crediting payments, distribution, inventory management, and related revenue-generating, cost-saving, and accounting tasks. Being able to leverage this value in new ESB-based solutions would provide an extremely attractive return on existing investments. Therefore a best-of-breed ESB characteristic is to offer connectivity for legacy applications.

It is not possible to properly integrate legacy systems into Web services solutions without extensive, intrusive modifications to these systems. Modifications are needed to reshape legacy systems to provide a natural fit with the Web services architectural requirements and carefully retrofit business logic so that it can be used with new applications. Therefore, legacy applications need to be re-engineered in order to reuse the core business processes entrenched in legacy applications. The legacy system re-engineering process involves the disciplined evolution of an existing legacy system to a new "improved" environment by reusing as much of it (implementation, design, specification, requirements) as possible and by adding new capabilities. Through re-engineering business processes become more modular and granular exposing submodules that can be reused and are represented as services.

The primary focus of legacy re-engineering and transformation is enterprises, business processes, the EAI, and how a legacy system can contribute to implementing the architecture without propagating the weaknesses of past designs and development methods. In its most fundamental form the process of re-engineering includes three basic tenets. These are:

- understanding of an existing application, resulting in one or more logical descriptions of the application;

- restructuring or transformation of those logical descriptions into new, improved logical descriptions;
- development of the new application based on these improved logical descriptions.

These three broad phases comprise a series of six steps briefly described in the following. The re-engineering and transformation steps below have been considerably simplified. The purpose of these steps is to facilitate the process of legacy application modernization by modularizing legacy processes and business logic separately from presentation logic and data management activities and representing them as components. These components can then be used to create interfaces for new services, thereby service enabling legacy applications.

1. *Understanding existing applications:* Before beginning the modernization process, the first task is to understand the structure and architecture of the existing application's architecture. This task includes gathering statistics about size, complexity, the amount of dead or unused code, and the amount of bad programming for each application [Comella-Dorda 2000], [Seacord 2001]. In addition, in selecting which programs to improve together, selecting the ones that affect common data is a critical step when planning to move through all of the modernization stages, including re-engineering for reuse and/or migration.

2. *Rationalizing business logic:* A typical legacy system is composed of a large number of independent programs. These programs work together in a hardwired net of business process flows. Once an application's program code is clean, any programming anomalies have been removed, and non-business logic has been filtered, it is possible to apply pattern-matching techniques across all of the application's programs to identify and segregate candidate common business logic.

3. *Identifying business rules:* When candidate reusable business logic has been rationalized to a subset of distinct, single occurrences of each service, it is then possible to determine whether each should become part of a process or express a business rule. For a definition and examples of use of business rules refer to section 9.2. To achieve this, sophisticated algorithms are used to extract business rules from monolithic legacy systems within which business rules exist in many different guises. The extraction of business rules from legacy code is generally termed *business rule recovery*. The accuracy with which this task is performed is key to legacy application modernization.

4. *Extracting components:* Extracted business rules can be grouped together based on their contribution to achieve the intended business functionality. A group of rules is normally processing some common set of data to achieve intended business functions. Candidate business rules and associated business data are then extracted and appropriately represented as a cohesive legacy component. The number of rules that need to be grouped together is a matter of choice, depending on the desired granularity of the legacy component. A callable interface needs to be provided for these components.

5. *Wrapping component implementations:* Legacy systems were, for the most part, not implemented in a fashion that lends itself to componentization. Presentation logic is often intertwined with business logic, which is intertwined with systems and data access logic. During this step system-level and presentation-level legacy components are identified and separated from business-level legacy components. In this way candidate components are identified for wrapping. Wrapping provides legacy functionality for new service-based solutions in much shorter time than it would take to build a replacement from scratch and recreate those dependencies. Wrapping requires that the appropriate level of abstraction for components be determined. When it comes to wrapping and legacy componentization one should concentrate on identifying coarse-grained components. Reusing a larger component saves more effort, and thus larger components have greater value. Smaller components are more likely to be frequently used, but their use saves less effort. This implies that fine-grained components are less cost effective.

6. *Creating service interfaces:* Component wrappers result in well-defined boundaries of functionality and data. However, the modernized legacy system as a whole is still tightly coupled with components hardwired to each other via program-to-program calls. The SOA approach to large-scale system coupling requires removing from the individual component wrappers any direct knowledge of any other such components. This can be accomplished by breaking up program-to-program connectivity and replacing it with service-enabled APIs that can be used in conjunction with event-driven and business-process orchestration mechanisms.

For a more detailed description of the re-engineering and transformation steps, interested readers are referred to [Comella-Dorda 2000], [Seacord 2001], [Ulrich 2002], [Papazoglou 2006].

8.5.7 Scalability issues in an ESB

Scalability is a particularly important issue for any automated business integration solution. Scalability concerns in the case of ESB translate to how well the particular ESB implementation has been designed. For example, parallel execution of business operations and itinerary-based routing significantly contribute to the highly distributed nature of the ESB, as there is no centralized rules engine to refer back to for each step in the process. The use of asynchronous communications, message itineraries, message and process definitions allow different parts of the ESB to operate independently of one another. This results in a decentralized model providing complete flexibility in scaling any aspect of the integration network. Such a decentralized architecture enables independent scalability of individual services as well as the communications infrastructure itself.

The ESB approach comes in stark contrast to the approach followed by typical integration broker technologies that handle scalability using a centralized hub-and-spoke model, i.e. they handle changes in load and configuration by increasing broker capacity or by adding brokers in a centralized location. A centralized rules engine for the routing of messages, such as those offered by the typical hub-and-spoke EAI broker approach, can quickly become a bottleneck, and also a single point of failure. Figure 8.13 shows a common strategy used by the integration broker approach when integrating services from multiple enterprises.

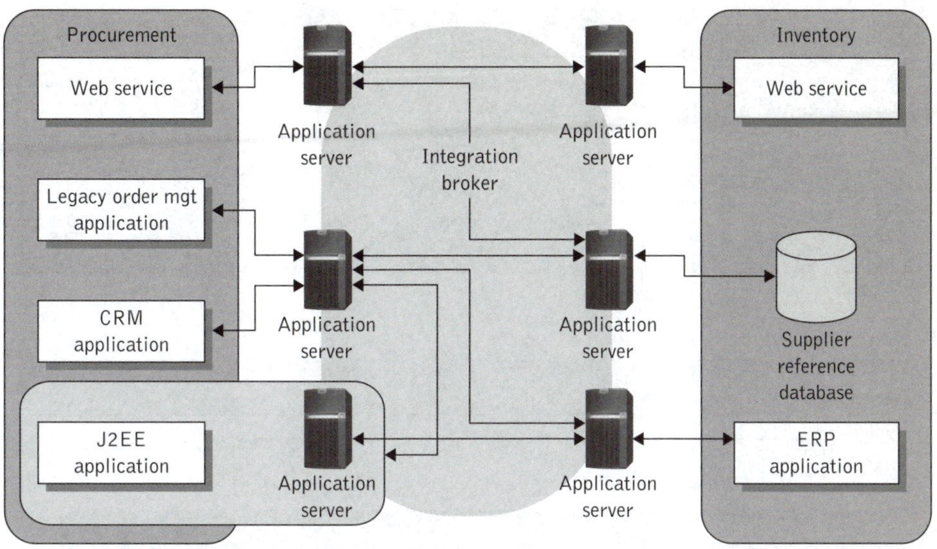

Figure 8.13 The integration broker approach to ESB
Source: adapted from [Chappell 2004]

This figure illustrates that integration brokers, including those built on top of an application server stack, require that the entire integration broker/application server stack be installed everywhere the integration broker functionality is required. This means installing an application server at a remote server at a remote location simply so it can host a JCA container/adapter pair, which acts as a channel to an ERP system [Chappell 2004].

To understand how scalability is treated in the context of an ESB, consider the distributed procurement process connecting procurement, outside suppliers, and warehouse systems. To meet demand by outside customers, additional supplier order services may be easily added to the inventory system in Figure 8.8. These additional services, running on additional computing systems, support scalability requirements without the need for replicating complete integration broker instances. In another example, the procurement system may increase throughput of the already existing replenishment service by increasing the number of threads that this service can handle. Both previous approaches allow capacity to be added where it is most needed – at the service itself. This differs from typical EAI integration broker models, which add capacity solely through the use of additional integration brokers [Chappell 2004].

In some circumstances, it may be desirable to increase overall scalability by expanding the throughput capacity of the enterprise-class backbone. Figure 8.14 illustrates the integration broker functionality that is incorporated in the ESB. When the capacity of a single broker is reached, brokers can be combined into clusters. These may act as a single virtual broker to handle increased demand from users and applications. The ESB's use of integration brokers and broker clusters increases scalability by allowing brokers to communicate and dynamically distribute load on the bus. For example, in the event that an increase in the use of the inventory services has overloaded the capacity of their host machine(s), new machines and new brokers can be added to handle the load without the need to change any of the services themselves and without requiring any additional development or

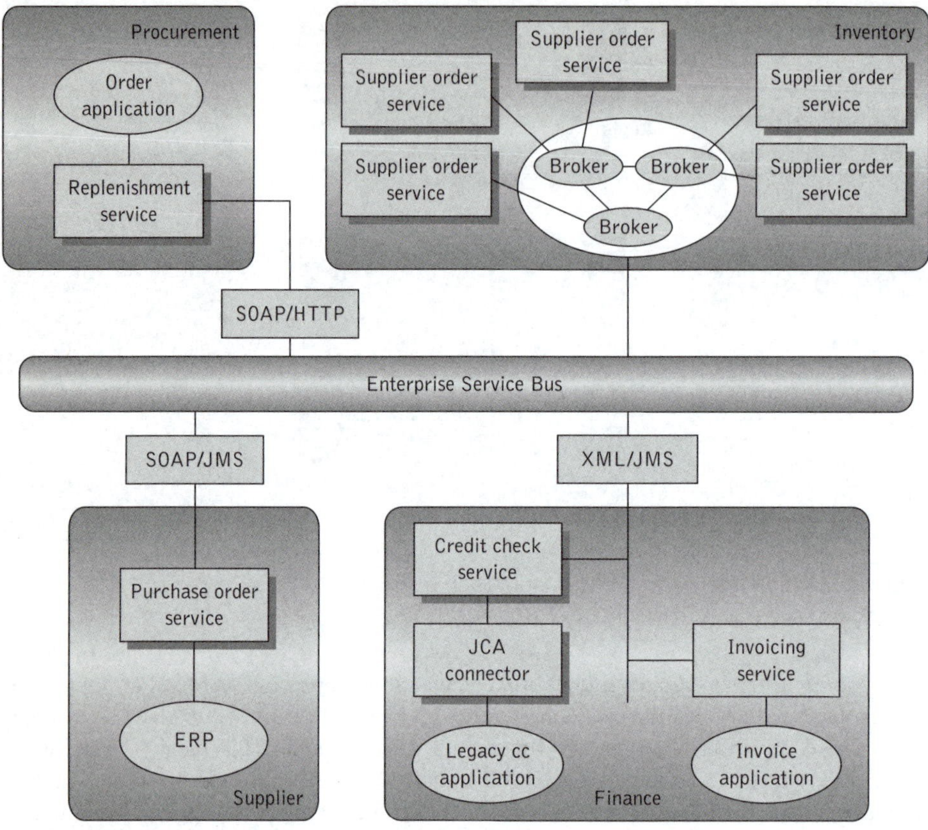

Figure 8.14 Scaling services in the ESB
Source: adapted from [Chappell 2004]

administration changes to the messaging system. The notion of a separately deployable, separately scalable messaging topology combined with a separately deployable, separately scalable ESB service container model is what uniquely distinguishes this architectural configuration. The distributed functional pieces are able to work together as one logical piece with a single, globally accessible namespace for locating and invoking services.

The scalability options that we described in the previous section allow distributed SOAs to be deployed in geographically diverse environments that are seamlessly integrated. To manage this complex network, the ESB relies on a set of graphical BPM (namely, BPM-like) tools that provide the ability to monitor communications on the ESB, look for scalability issues, and reconfigure any portion of the ESB to balance loads without bringing systems down [Chappell 2004].

8.5.8 Integration patterns using an ESB

Choosing the appropriate tools and technologies is an important factor; however, it is not sufficient on its own to achieve SOA success. The use of appropriate message exchange and integration patterns is equally important. These enabling patterns allow organizations to deliver and utilize services in a repeatable manner to ensure consistency and adherence to the best practices necessary to scale SOA across the organization.

One way to increase the flexibility and integration of services in an SOA and to benefit from Web services technologies is to move applications to an ESB. This requires that applications that are hooked into an ESB are service enabled and loosely coupled. Figure 8.14 shows one possible way to implement a simple integration pattern using an ESB. To understand this simple integration scenario, which we call a standalone integration pattern, assume that a new supplier needs to be added to the procurement system and the enterprise's supplier reference database. The processing logic to add one or more new supplier(s) could be implemented as a number of listeners, which are waiting for a message from the ESB. These listeners could be part of different enterprise systems (or standalone applications associated with them) that need to be aware of all possible suppliers in the procurement system. A message containing the supplier information is then placed on the ESB. This message targets an event queue that only the ESB will read. Based on a schedule, e.g., every fixed time interval, the ESB will access the message in the queue, note its source and destination, and forward it to the appropriate event listeners for further processing.

The benefits of this type of integration pattern are that it breaks a fairly complex process into multiple smaller, manageable pieces. Unfortunately, this integration pattern is clearly not scalable as it creates an unmanageable number of small, segregated standalone pieces of integration logic that implement simple business rules.

A better way to approach integration is by means of a business orchestration service. An orchestration service is a special processing engine that can be plugged into the ESB to compose and coordinate services that "live" on the ESB. An orchestration engine, in addition to supporting process description languages such as BPEL, offers additional BPM capabilities that provide visibility into the state of business activities, as well as integrated data access and transformation services.

An integration service can manage stateful information about a business process that spans a considerable length of time. For example, a step in the business process may require human interaction, such as approval of a purchase order or of a new supplier. Changes in the state of one service, e.g., the addition of a new supplier or placement of a new purchase order, will be automatically propagated to all affected services that are part of the business process. Itinerary-based routing requires that itineraries can carry state, and recover from failures if the messages carrying the itineraries are transported over reliable messaging. Alternatively, if all messages reach their destination and there are no failures then the business process can terminate successfully and deliver its results; see Chapters 9 and 10 for more information on this topic.

A business process integration pattern is the preferred solution for most ESB applications because it offers many advantages. Its single drawback is dealing with sometimes excess process complexity.

ESBs are already being put to use in a variety of industries, including financial services, insurance, manufacturing, retail, telecommunications, food, and so on. An excellent source regarding ESB features and functionality as well as implementation case studies is [Chappell 2004]. Integration patterns are also gradually finding their way into ESB settings. Details regarding several proven integration patterns that can be used to increase the speed of developing and deploying e-business applications and to start implementing SOAs using an ESB can be found in [Keen 2004].

8.6 The extended SOA

When we look at the capabilities of the ESB we realize that it offers a wide range of service functionality at various levels. At the lower level it offers a functionality typical of service containers including communication and connectivity capabilities, routing, run-time support, discovery, transformation, security, and so on. At a higher (middle) level it offers long-running processes, unconventional transaction support, and service orchestration capabilities. At the topmost level it provides service management and monitoring capabilities that transcend both the middle and lower levels. Therefore, it becomes obvious that there is a clear necessity to be able to streamline and group together related service functionality and stratify it in such a way that it can tackle efficiently the functional requirements of complex applications that make use of the ESB. Such overarching concerns are addressed by the extended SOA (xSOA).

The xSOA [Papazoglou 2003], [Papazoglou 2005a] is an attempt to provide a layered service-based architecture that appropriately extends conventional SOAs. The architectural layers in the xSOA, which are depicted in Figure 8.15, describe a logical separation

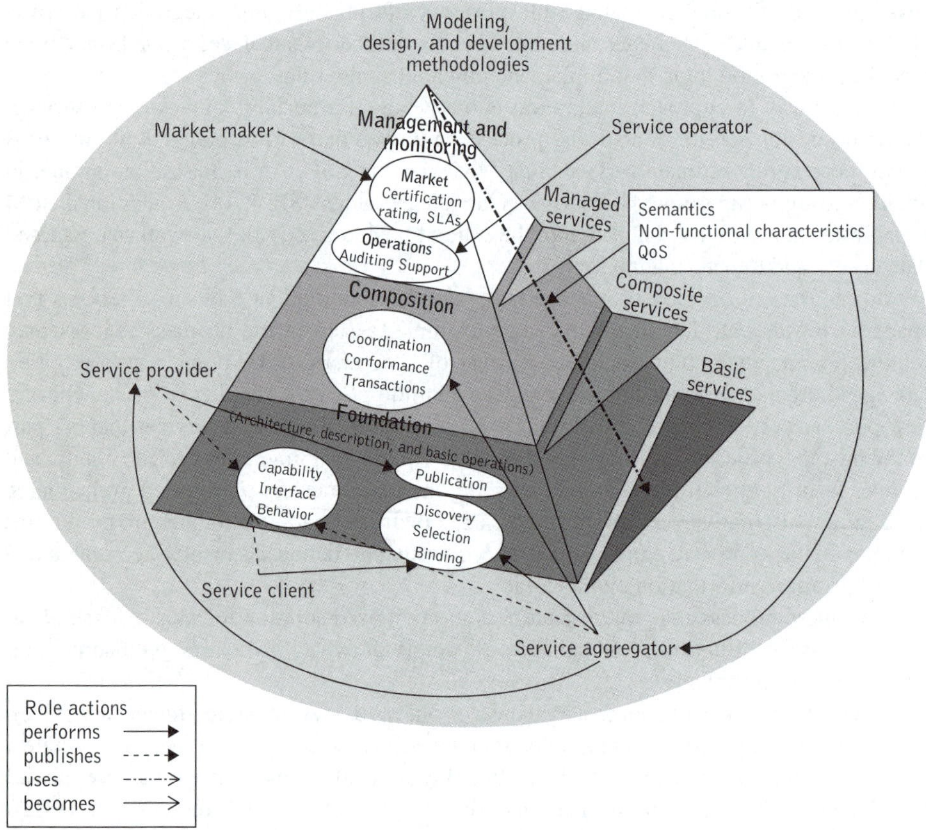

Figure 8.15 The xSOA

of functionality in such a way that each layer defines a set of constructs, roles, and responsibilities and leans on constructs of its preceding layer to accomplish its mission. The logical separation of functionality is based on the need to separate basic service capabilities provided by the conventional SOA (e.g., building relatively simple service-based applications) from more advanced service functionality needed for composing services and the need to distinguish between the functionality for composing services from that for the management of services. The overall objective of these functional layers is to provide facilities for ensuring consistency across the organization, high availability of services, security of non-public services and information, orchestration of multiple services as part of mission-critical composite applications – all essential requirements for business-quality services.

As illustrated in Figure 8.15, xSOA offers three planes: the foundation, the composition, and the management and monitoring. The lowermost plane in the xSOA is the foundation plane, which supports Web services communication primitives and utilizes the basic service middleware and architectural constructs and functionality for describing, publishing, discovering, and executing services, which are widely accepted and implemented quite uniformly. Higher-level planes are layered on top of the foundation plane and define business processes and the management and monitoring of Web service processes and applications. The perpendicular axis in Figure 8.15 designates service characteristics that cut across all three planes. These include semantics, non-functional service properties, and QoS. The xSOA is shown to support a variety of roles. In addition to the classical roles of service client and provider it also supports the roles of service aggregator, service operator, and market maker. In the following we shall focus briefly on the characteristics of the individual xSOA planes.

The service foundations plane provides a service-oriented middleware backbone that realizes the run-time SOA infrastructure that connects heterogeneous components and systems, provides a variety of communication protocols, as well as supports multiple-channel access to services, e.g., via mobile devices, palmtops, handheld devices, over a variety of networks including the Internet, cable, UMTS, XDSL, Bluetooth, and so on. This run-time infrastructure allows definition of the classical SOA functions involving communication and the description, publishing, finding, and binding of services. Five sets of standards implement the service foundations plane. These are SOAP, WSDL, UDDI, WS-Notification (see section 7.4), and WS-MetaDataExchange (see Chapter 13).

The service foundations plane supports the roles of service provider and service client. A service may exhibit characteristics of one, the other or even both. In Figure 8.15 we assume that service clients, providers, and aggregators could act as service brokers or service discovery agencies and publish the services they deploy.

The full potential of Web services as a means of developing dynamic e-business solutions can only be realized when applications and business processes are able to integrate their complex interactions into composite added-value services. Services technologies offer a viable solution to this problem since they support coordination and offer an asynchronous and message-oriented way to communicate and interact with application logic. However, it is important to differentiate between the baseline specifications of SOAP, UDDI, and WSDL that provide the infrastructure that supports publishing, finding, and binding operations in the service-oriented architecture and higher-level specifications, which are required for syndicating Web services. These higher-level specifications provide functionality that supports and leverages services and enables specifications for integrating automated business processes, and resides in the service composition plane.

The service composition plane encompasses roles and functionality that are necessary for the aggregation of multiple (possibly singular) services into a single composite service. Resulting composite services may be used as discrete services in further service compositions or may be offered as complete applications/solutions to service clients. Service aggregators accomplish this task. The role actions in Figure 8.15 indicate that service aggregators can become service providers by publishing the service descriptions of the composite service they create. Service aggregators develop specifications and/or code that permit the composite service to perform functions that are based on features such as metadata descriptions, standard terminology, and reference models (see Chapters 13 and 14); service conformance; service coordination to control the execution of the composite services (i.e., processes), Web services transactions, and manage data flow as well as control flow between composite services (see Chapter 10); and policy enforcement (see Chapter 12).

Currently, standards such as BPEL and WS-CDL operate at the level service composition plane in xSOA and enable the creation of large service collaborations that go far beyond allowing two companies to conduct business in an automated fashion. We also expect to see much larger service collaborations spanning entire industry groups and other complex business relationships. These developments necessitate the use of tools and utilities that provide insights into the health of systems that implement Web services and into the status and behavior patterns of loosely coupled applications. Therefore, managing loosely coupled applications in an SOA is an absolute requirement.

In an SOA application performance depends on the combined performance of cooperating services and their interactions. Failure or change of a single application component can bring down numerous interdependent enterprise applications. Similarly, the addition of new applications or components can overload existing components, causing unexpected degradation or failure of seemingly unrelated systems. To counter such situations, enterprises need to constantly monitor the health of their applications. The performance should be in tune at all times and under all load conditions.

A consistent management and monitoring infrastructure is essential for production-quality Web services and applications and is provided by the management and monitoring plane in xSOA. This requires that a critical characteristic be realized: that services be managed and monitored. Service management encompasses the control and monitoring of SOA-based applications throughout their lifecycle. Service management spans a large number of activities that range from installation and configuration to collecting metrics and tuning to ensure responsive service execution and to efficiently managing service operations. Service management and monitoring includes many interrelated functions such as SLA management, auditing, monitoring, and troubleshooting, service lifecycle/state management, performance management, services and resources provisioning, scalability, availability and extensibility, and others. In addition, it includes managing service operations by providing global visibility of running processes, comparable to that provided by BPM tools. Because of its importance service management is treated in a dedicated chapter (Chapter 16).

A trend that has emerged with the introduction of SOA and Web services is the rise in service-mediated interaction with customers, suppliers, regulators, financial institutions, and literally every outside party involved in an enterprise's operations. This trend is expected to trigger *open service markets* (or *service-based trading communities*) whose purpose is to create opportunities for buyers and sellers to meet and conduct business electronically, or aggregate service supply/demand by offering added-value business services and grouping buying power. The scope of such a service marketplace would be limited only by the ability of enterprises to make their offerings visible to other enterprises and establish industry-specific protocols by which to conduct business. Service markets typically support integrated value networks by providing to their members a unified view of products and services, standard business terminology and naming conventions, standard business data formats, services, and processes, as well as standard definitions of process orchestrations for enterprises connected over the Internet. In addition, service markets must offer a comprehensive range of services supporting industry–trade, including services that provide business transaction negotiation and facilitation, financial settlement, service certification and quality assurance, rating services, service metrics such as number of current service requestors, average turnaround time, and manage the negotiation and enforcement of SLAs. This kind of functionality introduces the role of a market maker, which is the entity that supports and maintains an open service market.

Finally, a quintessential requirement for developing advanced applications is that they are stratified according to the xSOA planes is the use of an SOA lifecycle methodology. A service development methodology starts with analyzing and modeling the business environment including key performance indicators of business goals and objectives, translating that model into service design, deploying that service system, and managing that deployment. These and related topics are the focus of Chapter 15.

8.7 Summary

Unless the message exchanges of Web services are made reliable, organizations will not be able to trust them for deployment in industrial-strength business applications and for mission-critical operations such as complex business-to-business transactions or real-time enterprise integrations. In this chapter we described a messaging protocol and associated standards, which allow messages to be delivered reliably between distributed applications despite software, hardware, or network failures. The protocol is described in a transport-independent manner allowing it to be implemented using different network technologies.

Reliable messaging protocols are at the heart of service-oriented computing architectural approaches that serve as the enabling facilitator for addressing the requirements of loosely coupled, standards-based, and protocol-independent distributed computing. We have explained how service-oriented architectures and technologies offer the means to achieve the desired levels of business integration effectively, mapping IT implementations more closely to the overall business process flow. In particular, we focused on technologies and approaches that unify the principles and concepts of service-oriented architecture with those of event-based programming. These architectural approaches serve as the enabling springboard for business integration projects and deliver a flexible and adaptable environment that enables Web services integration to be put in place productively, effectively, and in a staged manner. Of particular interest is the Enterprise Service Bus, which provides a whole range of functions designed to offer a manageable, standards-based IT backbone that extends messaging-oriented middleware functionality throughout the entire business value chain, connecting heterogeneous components and systems.

Combining Web services standards with an ESB infrastructure can potentially deliver the broadest connectivity between systems. An ESB supports Web services with more established application-integration techniques, enabling the power of the new to be combined with the reach of the old.

As a final remark it is important to understand that ESBs are not yet ready for widespread EAI replacement. While ESBs can be flexible, low-cost integration alternatives, they are not yet suitable for widespread replacement of EAI solutions due to their limitations in key functional areas, such as complex data transformations, support for application adapters, and business process modeling. These features are commonly found in EAI products. However, this situation is expected to change in the near future.

Review questions

- What are system quality attributes and how do they relate to software architectures?
- Briefly describe the common architectural constraints and explain how they relate to the SOA.
- What is reliable messaging and why is it important for SOA-based applications?
- Briefly describe the WS-ReliableMessaging model.
- What is the Enterprise Service Bus and how does it relate to SOA?
- What is the purpose of an event-driven SOA?
- How is the event-driven SOA realized by an Enterprise Service Bus?
- Briefly describe the key capabilities of an Enterprise Service Bus.
- Which are the most common Web services standards used by an Enterprise Service Bus solution?
- Briefly describe the integration styles employed in an ESB solution.
- How are integration brokers and application servers used in an ESB solution?
- How is scalability achieved in an ESB solution?

Exercises

8.1 Assume that the purchase order service allows its clients to make bulk order submissions under the condition that bulk orders are submitted as part of the same sequence and that WS-ReliableMessaging is used to perform the submissions.

Encode an SOAP header using WS-ReliableMessaging to address this problem. Use the code snippet in Listing 8.1 to help you develop your solution.

8.2 An organization that produces goods and relies on the services of carriers to distribute them to its customers wishes to develop an SOA solution that enables it to integrate its systems with those of carriers, suppliers, and customers. As the organization tends to do business with a variety of carriers, it requires that a single interface be provided to those carriers. Moreover, the organization requires that the integration solution should offer functionality that would help it to manage visibility of orders as they move outbound in its distribution chain to its customers. The use of open standards is preferred as the organization has no direct control over the technologies used by its partners. Develop an SOA-compliant architecture based on a Web services broker required to provide secure, manageable access from external parties to those applications.

8.3 The solution for the previous exercise should be modified so that the service interactions between the transacting enterprises should combine at some level to form business processes and workflow solutions. These processes should be explicitly modeled and executed using an appropriate business process execution language in compliance with appropriate open standards.

8.4 Broadly speaking, business process integration may result in several business integration patterns whose aim is to manage and support business automation and integration across distributed enterprises [Papazoglou 2006]. The business process integration patterns include: the integrated enterprise, the brokered enterprise, and the federated enterprise integration patterns. Selecting the most appropriate business process pattern for an organization depends on the business needs, structure, and business priorities of an enterprise.

The integrated business pattern is about ensuring that end-to-end business processes are managed and monitored in a complete fashion across and within all business units. Business processes are viewed across the entire enterprise, where activities span organizational units and are carried out by separate business sections that have a responsibility for them. This business integration pattern assumes that workflow and integration process may cross organizational units and are managed by a group within the enterprise. This group is also responsible for setting policies on toolset selection and on message standards. The integrated enterprise business pattern is most suitable for small enterprises or larger enterprises where a common standard integration toolset is imposed.

Design an ESB solution for a large enterprise employing the integrated enterprise business pattern. In this enterprise, end-to-end business process flows occur between departmental units and the activities carried out in the various departments can be treated as organizational activities within business units (which may contain one or more departments). The role of the various business units is simply to identify the responsibility to carry out activities and as such business unit boundaries have no impact on the business process flow. In the ESB solution an external partner is responsible for carrying out the logistics and distribution processes such as warehousing, distribution, and management inventory. The logistical workflow should be seamlessly integrated into the end-to-end business processes of the enterprise and is dependent on the exchange and processing of consignment notes, goods advice, invoices, and other business documents.

8.5 The brokered enterprise business pattern is about ensuring that processes are managed and monitored across all business units by means of a broker business unit. This is a distributed business enterprise scheme, where business units are fairly autonomous but use the business broker to manage communication and interoperation. The individual business units still own the processes provided, but must maintain standards for both messages and interbusiness unit processing and must register the services they provide and the processes supporting them with the broker unit registry. With this scheme all requests are handled by the broker unit, so a service client is not aware of which organizational unit provides the business process handling the service. The brokered enterprise pattern is applicable to organizations where the individual organization units want to maintain their autonomy but benefit from the advantages of a hub-style service management and a common messaging infrastructure.

Design an ESB solution for a large enterprise employing the brokered enterprise business pattern.

8.6 The federated enterprise business pattern is driven by the expectation that individual business units in a large enterprise, or an integrated value chain, are completely autonomous and are expected to cooperate when there is a need for it. As there is no overall business management and monitoring, business processes are not viewed end to end and each unit is responsible for providing and maintaining standard interfaces so that it can cooperate with other such units. Common standards for messaging and for describing the services provided are introduced with each business unit managing its own service repository. The federated enterprise pattern is applicable to organizations where the individual organization units want to maintain their autonomy but benefit from the advantages of cooperating with other business units in the organization and the use of a common messaging infrastructure and cooperation standards.

Design an ESB solution for a large enterprise employing the federated enterprise business pattern.

PART V

Service composition and service transactions

CHAPTER 9

Processes and workflows

Learning objectives

To create business processes Web services need to be composed. Service composition refers to the aggregation of Web services. Various Web services composition languages and technologies have emerged to provide the mechanisms for describing how individual Web services can be composed to create reliable and dependable business-process-based solutions with the appropriate level of complexity.

In this chapter we introduce workflow and business process technologies and explain how they can support linking together applications comprising Web services. After reading this chapter readers will understand the following key concepts:

- Business processes and workflow systems.
- How business processes can be integrated and managed.
- The main ingredients of a business process solution, such as flow modeling, and composition of Web services.
- The concepts of process orchestration and process choreography.
- The main constructs of the Business Process Execution Language for Web services.
- A high-level view of the Web services Choreography Description Language.

9.1 Business processes and their management

A *process* is an ordering of activities with a beginning and an end; it has inputs (in terms of resources, materials, and information) and a specified output (the results it produces). We may thus define a process as any sequence of steps that is initiated by an event, transforms information, materials, or commitments, and produces an output [Harmon 2003a]. A *business process* is a set of logically related tasks performed to achieve a well-defined business outcome. A (business) process view implies a horizontal view of a business organization and looks at processes as sets of interdependent activities designed and structured to produce a specific output for a customer or a market. A business process defines the results to be achieved, the context of the activities, the relationships between the activities, and the interactions with other processes and resources. A business process may receive events that alter the state of the process and the sequence of activities. A business process may produce events for input to other applications or processes. It may also invoke applications to perform computational functions, and it may post assignments to human worklists to request actions by human actors. Business processes can be measured, and different performance measures apply, like cost, quality, time, and customer satisfaction.

Each enterprise has unique characteristics that are embedded in its business processes. Most enterprises perform a similar set of repeatable routine activities that may include the development of manufacturing products and services, bringing these products and services to market, and satisfying the customers who purchase them. *Automated business processes* can perform such activities. We may view an automated business process as a precisely choreographed sequence of activities systematically directed towards performing a certain business task and bringing it to completion. Examples of typical processes in manufacturing firms include among other things new product development (which cuts across research and development, marketing, and manufacturing), customer order fulfillment (which combines sales, manufacturing, warehousing, transportation, and billing), and financial asset management. The possibility to design, structure, measure processes, and determine their contribution to customer value makes them an important starting point for business improvement and innovation initiatives.

The largest possible process in an organization is the *value chain*. The value chain is decomposed into a set of core business processes and support processes necessary to produce a product or product line. These core business processes are subdivided into activities. An *activity* is an element that performs a specific function within a process. Activities can be as simple as sending or receiving a message, or as complex as coordinating the execution of other processes and activities. A business process may encompass complex activities some of which run on back-end systems, such as a credit check, automated billing, a purchase order, stock updates and shipping, or even such frivolous activities as sending a document, and filling a form. A business process activity may invoke another business process in the same or a different business system domain. Activities will inevitably vary greatly from one company to another and from one business analysis effort to another.

At run-time, a business process definition may have multiple *instantiations*, each operating independently of the other, and each instantiation may have multiple activities that are concurrently active. A process instance is a defined thread of activity that is being *enacted* (managed) by a workflow engine. In general, instances of a process, its current state, and the history of its actions will be visible at run-time and expressed in terms of the business process definition so that users can determine the status of business activities and business specialists can monitor the activity and identify potential improvements to the business process definition.

9.1.1 Characteristics of business processes

A business process is typically associated with operational objectives and business relationships, e.g., an insurance claims process, or an engineering development process. A process may be wholly contained within a single organizational unit or may span different organizations, such as in a customer–supplier relationship. Typical examples of processes that cross organizational boundaries are purchasing and sales processes jointly set up by buying and selling organizations, supported by EDI and value-added networks. The Internet is now a trigger for the design of new business processes and the redesign of existing ones. For instance, new expectations have arisen with setting up Web services, which aim at the design of standardized business-process-based solutions.

Every process has a customer and is initiated by a customer order. The customer may be external, like the final customer for whom a service or product is produced, or internal, like another process for which the output of the process under consideration forms an input. Not every process is directly triggered by a customer order. It is possible that a process is triggered by a standard procedure (event). For example, salary payments are triggered by a date in the month.

Every business process implies processing: a series of activities (processing steps) leading to some form of transformation of data or products for which the process exists. Transformations may be executed manually or in an automated way. A transformation will encompass multiple processing steps. For example, the process "authorizing invoices" will encompass the steps "checking whether the invoice has not yet been paid," "checking the agreed purchasing conditions," "checking the receiving report," "checking calculations," and "checking name, address, and bank account of the creditor." If and only if all the checkpoints are correct, the invoice will be registered in the accounts payable administration.

Typically, a workflow application is associated with business processes and their activities. This is irrespective of whether the issue is the management of a logistics chain, supply-chain planning, or simply the exchange of documents between trading partners, or any other kind of business-process-centered application.

Processes have *decision points*. Decisions have to be made with regard to routing and allocation of processing capacity. In a highly predictable and standardized environment, the trajectory in the process of a customer order will be established in advance in a standard way. Only if the process is complex and if the conditions of the process are not predictable will routing decisions have to be made on the spot. In general the customer orders will be split into a category that is highly proceduralized (and thus automated) and a category that is complex and uncertain. Here human experts will be needed and manual processing is a key element of the process.

Finally, every process delivers a product, like a mortgage or an authorized invoice. The extent to which the end product of a process can be specified in advance and can be standardized impacts the way that processes and their workflows can be structured and automated.

To summarize this discussion, a real business process may characterized by the following behavior:

- It may contain defined conditions triggering its initiation in each new instance (e.g., the arrival of a claim) and defined outputs at its completion.
- It may involve formal or relatively informal interactions between participants.
- It has a duration that may vary widely.

- It may contain a series of automated activities and/or manual activities. Activities may be large and complex, involving the flow of materials, information, and business commitments.
- It exhibits a very dynamic nature, so it can respond to demands from customers and to changing market conditions.
- It is widely distributed and customized across boundaries within and between organizations, often spanning multiple applications with very different technology platforms.
- It is usually long running – a single instance of a process such as order to cash may run for months or even years.

9.2 Workflows

Closely related to business processes are workflows. A workflow system automates a business process, in whole or in part, during which documents, information, or tasks are passed from one participant to another for action, according to a set of procedural rules [WfMC 1999]. Workflows are based on document lifecycles and forms-based information processing, so generally they support well-defined, static, "clerical" processes. They provide transparency, since business processes are clearly articulated in the software, and they are agile because they produce definitions that are fast to deploy and change.

We may define a *workflow* as the sequence of processing steps (execution of business operations, tasks, and transactions), during which information and physical objects are passed from one processing step to another. Workflow is a concept that links together technologies and tools able to automatically route events and tasks with programs or users.

Process-oriented workflows are used to automate processes whose structure is well defined and stable over time, which often coordinate subprocesses executed by machines and which only require minor user involvement (often only in specific cases). An order management process or a loan request is an example of a well-defined process. Certain process-oriented workflows may have transactional properties.

The process-oriented workflow is made up of tasks that follow routes, with checkpoints represented by business rules, e.g., "pause for a credit approval." Such business process rules govern the overall processing of activities, including the routing of requests, the assignment or distribution of requests to designated roles, the passing of workflow data from activity to activity, and the dependencies and relationships between business process activities.

A workflow involves activities, decision points, routes, rules, and roles. These are briefly described below.

Just like a process, a workflow normally comprises a number of logical steps, each of which is known as an *activity*. An activity is a set of actions which are guided by the workflow. As Figure 9.1 illustrates, an activity may involve manual interaction with a user or workflow participant or might be executed using diverse resources such as application programs or databases. A *work item* or data set is created, and is processed and changed in

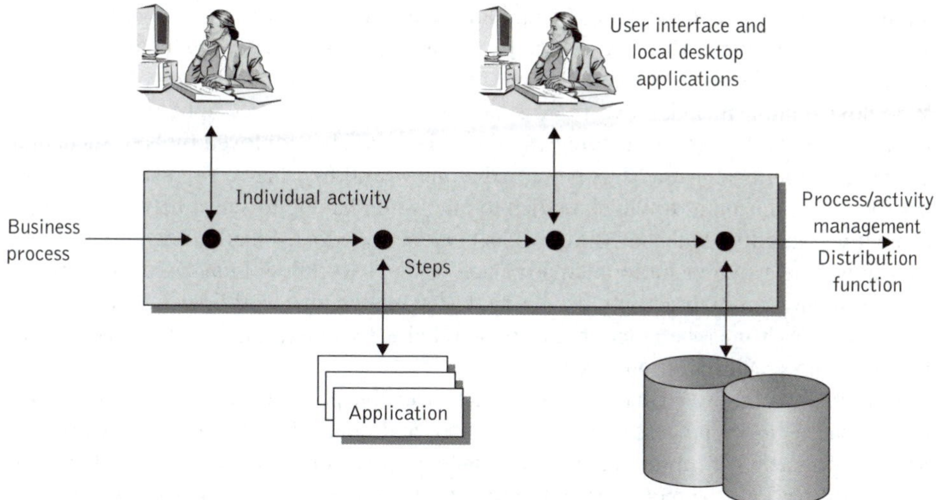

Figure 9.1 The workflow management coalition diagram of process flow across applications

stages at a number of processing or decision points (steps in Figure 9.1) to meet specific business goals. Most workflow engines can handle very complex series of processes.

A workflow can depict various aspects of a business process including automated and manual activities, decision points and business rules, parallel and sequential work routes, and how to manage exceptions to the normal business process.

A workflow can have logical *decision points* that determine which branch of the flow a work item may take in the event of alternative paths. Every alternate path within the flow is identified and controlled through a bounded set of logical decision points. An instantiation of a workflow to support a work item includes all possible paths from beginning to end.

Workflow technology enables developers to describe full intra- or inter-organizational business processes with dependencies, sequencing selections, and iteration. It effectively enables the developers to describe the complex rules for processing in a business process, such as merging, selection based on field content, time-based delivery of messages, and so on. To achieve these objectives workflows are predicated upon the notion of prespecified routing paths. These define the path taken by the set of objects making up the workflow. The routes of a workflow may be sequential, circular, or parallel work routes. Routing paths can be sequential, parallel, or cyclic. A segment of a process instance under enactment by a workflow management system, in which several activities are executed in sequence under a single thread of execution, is called *sequential routing*. A segment of a process instance under enactment by a workflow management system, where two or more activity instances are executing in parallel within the workflow, giving rise to multiple threads of control, is called *parallel routing*. Parallel routing normally commences with an AND-Split (or split) and concludes with an AND-Join (or join or rendezvous) point. A *split point* is a synchronization point within the workflow where a single thread of control splits into two or more threads that are executed in parallel within the workflow, allowing multiple activities to be executed simultaneously. A *join point* in the workflow is a synchronization point where two or more parallel executing activities converge into a single common thread of control. No split or join points occur during sequential routing. Workflow routing includes two more synchronization points: OR-Split (or conditional routing) and OR-Join (or asynchronous join), which can be employed by both sequential and parallel routing constructs. A point within the workflow where a single thread of control makes a decision as to which branch to take when having to select between multiple alternative workflow branches is known as *condition routing*. Finally, a point within the workflow where two or more alternative activity(ies) workflow branches reconverge to form a single common activity as the next step within the workflow is known *asynchronous join*. It must be noted that as no parallel activity execution has occurred at the join point, no synchronization is required.

Within a workflow, business rules in each decision point determine how workflow-related data is to be processed, routed, tracked, and controlled. *Business rules* are core business policies that capture the nature of an enterprise's business model and define the conditions that must be met in order to move to the next stage of the workflow. Business rules are represented as compact statements about an aspect of the business that can be expressed within an application and as such they determine the route to be followed [vonHalle 2002]. For instance, for a healthcare application, business rules may include policies on how new claim validation, referral requirements, or special procedure approvals are implemented. Business rules can represent among other things typical business situations such as escalation ("send this document to a supervisor for approval"), managing exceptions ("this loan is more than $500,000, send it to the CFO"), or progression assurance ("make sure that we deal with this within 30 min or as specified in the customer's service-level agreement").

Roles in a workflow define the function of the people or programs involved in the workflow. A *role* is a mechanism within a workflow that associates participants to a collection of workflow activity(ies). The role defines the context in which the user participates in a particular process or activity. The role often embraces organizational concepts such as structure and relationships, responsibility or authority, but may also refer to other attributes such as skill, location, value data, time or date, etc.

The definition, creation, and management of the execution of workflows is achieved by a *workflow management system* running on one or more workflow engines. A workflow management system (WMS) is capable of interpreting the process and activity definitions, interacting with workflow participants, and, where required, invoking the use of software-enabled tools and applications, see Figure 9.1. Most WMSs integrate with other systems used by an enterprise, such as document management systems, databases, e-mail systems, office automation products, geographic information systems, production applications, and so on. This integration provides structure to a process that employs a number of otherwise independent systems. It can also provide methods, e.g., a project folder, for organizing documents and data from diverse sources.

Modern workflow products extend their functionality into the domain of both enterprise and e-business integration by automating business processes whose structure is well-defined and stable over time. They achieve this by integrating middleware, process sequencing, and orchestration mechanisms as well as transaction processing capabilities. A business activity, such as a submission of an order, invoicing, triggering a business transaction, and so on, forms part of a business process with which a workflow is associated.

In the following we concentrate on a variant of the order management scenario that we introduced in earlier chapters of this book and consider it as a basis for illustrating the steps involved in a fairly complex process-oriented workflow. Activities in the order management process include receiving the sales order, allocating inventory, shipping products, billing, and making sure that the payment is received. Some of these processes may execute for long periods of time, while others may execute in milliseconds. Several activities are executed at the supplier's site, such as checking the creditworthiness of the customer, determining whether or not an ordered part is available in the product inventory, calculating the final price for the order and billing the customer, selecting a shipper, and scheduling the production and shipment for the order.

A simplified version of this business process is depicted in Figure 9.2. All steps in this figure involve a process-to-process coordination and conversation, with customized alerts set up across the network to track exceptions and provide manual intervention if necessary.

In the previous example, the business order management process describes how a product is sent from a supplier to a client. An instance of this process is actually dispatching a product(s) to a specific client. The instance of a process comprises activity instances that include the actual work items that are passed to a workflow participant – the client, supplier, shipper roles – within this activity for action, or to another process for action. For instance, in the order management process a specific shipping company may receive all shipment-related documents for a specific product and may be asked to come up with a specific shipment date and shipping price for the proposed shipment.

Workflow technology tends to relegate integration functions, such as synchronizing data between disparate packaged and legacy applications, to custom code within its activities – and thus outside the scope of the process model [Silver 2003]. Moreover, it uses a tightly coupled integration style that employs low-level APIs and that has confined workflow to local, homogeneous system environments, such as within a department or division. Therefore, traditional workflow implementations are closely tied to the enterprise in which they are deployed, and cannot be reliably extended outside organizational borders to customers, suppliers, and other partners. As a consequence, one of the major limitations of WMSs is integration: they are not good at connecting cross-enterprise systems together. Modern workflow technology tries to address this deficiency by extending this functionality to cross-enterprise process integration by employing business process management functionality. This issue is discussed in some length in section 9.3.

9.3 Business process integration and management

Business processes are the defining elements of a particular organization in that they control and describe precisely how business is conducted both internally and externally. This can relate to how customers are placing an order, goods requisition from partners and suppliers, or employees updating internal systems. Thus it is not surprising that enterprises have come to realize that they need to create end-to-end business processes for internal and cross-enterprise integration in order to bring ultimate value to their customers. It is indeed the entire value chain, not a single enterprise, that delivers the products or services and makes enterprises competitive and successful. Value chain management is now clearly recognized as the next frontier for gaining new productivity and competitive advantage

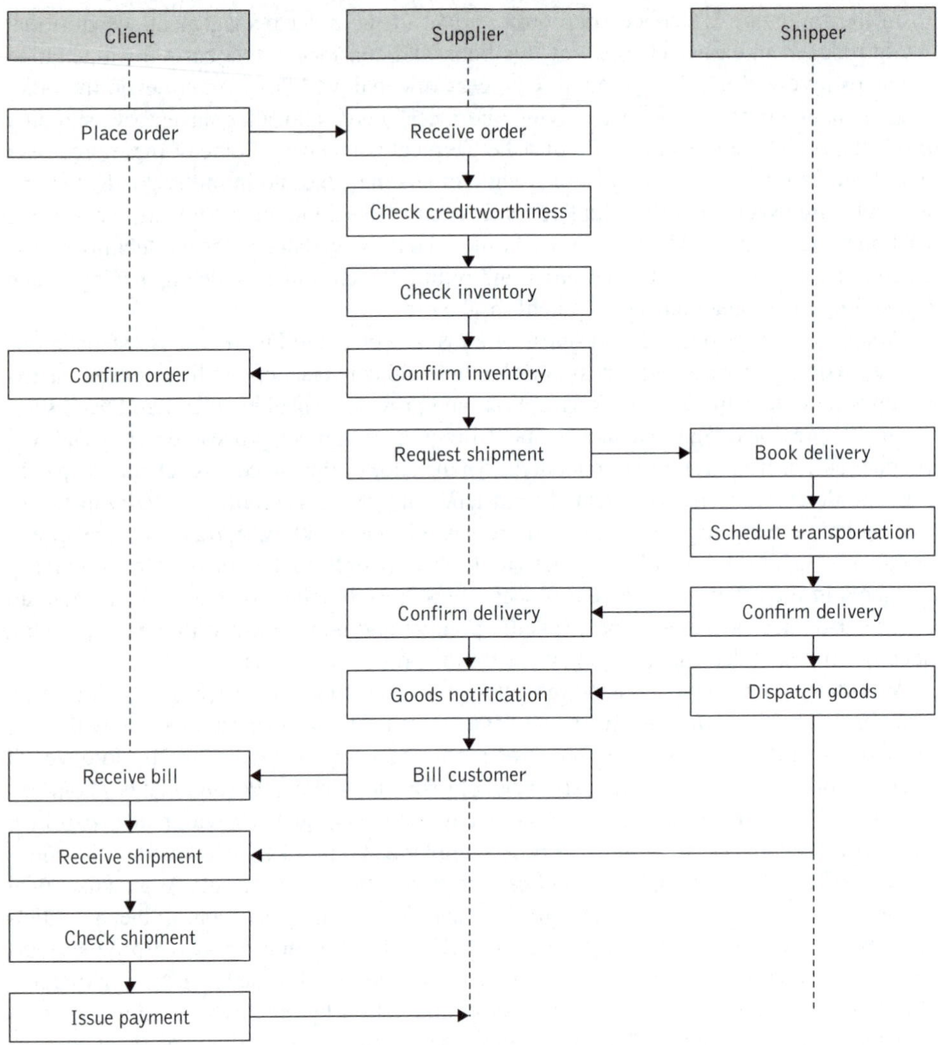

Figure 9.2 Order management process flow diagram

[Papazoglou 2006]. Consequently, internal and cross-enterprise integration initiatives must be managed and deployed in a systematic and coherent fashion.

Business process integration (BPI) can be described as the ability to define a commonly accepted business process model that specifies the sequence, hierarchy, events, execution logic, and information movement between systems residing in the same enterprise (namely, EAI) and systems residing in multiple interconnected enterprises. BPI is an integration solution that provides enterprises with end-to-end visibility and control over the contributing parts of a multi-step information request or transaction, which include people, customers, partners, applications, and databases. For instance, this might include all the steps in an order management, inventory management, or fulfillment process.

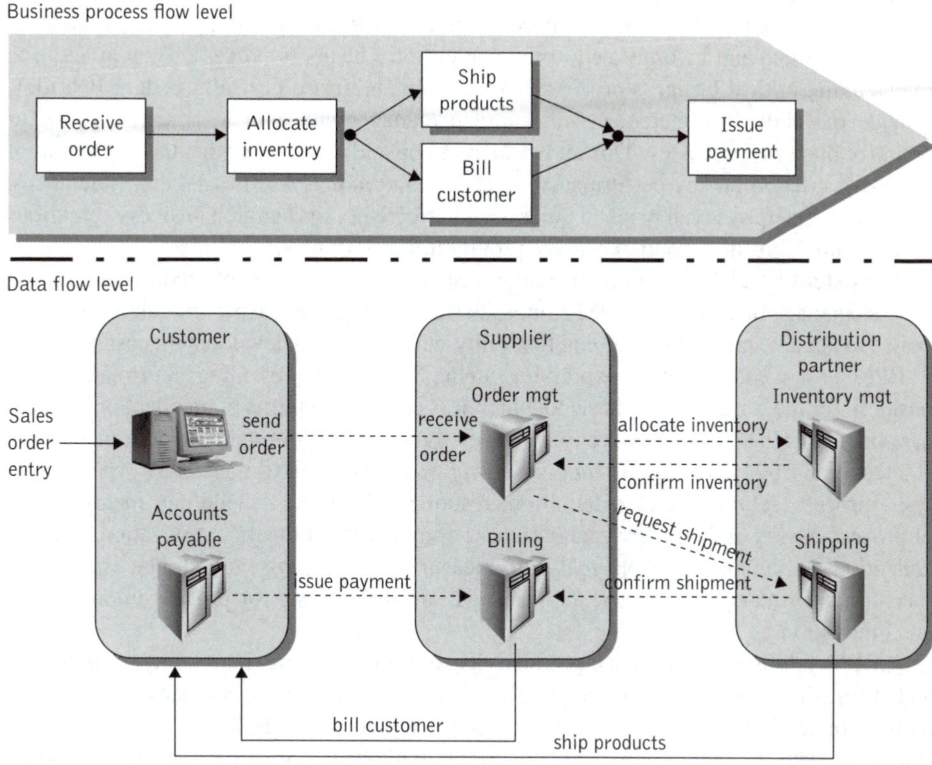

Figure 9.3 Example of BPI workflow

The primary problem with BPI lies not in the translation of data formats and routing, but rather that the business process embedded in one application is being bridged into the process of another. The business processes linked together are not defined as information but rather in terms of activities or workflows.

BPI solutions allow enterprises to take advantage of systems that are already in place by automating and managing the business processes that span these systems. With BPI, enterprises can preserve major investments in legacy systems thereby avoiding the expense of having to write additional code to replicate existing functionality.

Figure 9.3 illustrates a typical application of a process integration workflow involving an order management process that ranges across organizational borders. This typical business process is shown to span multiple functional areas within an enterprise and even between enterprises. The figure shows how processes specified at the business flow level map to corresponding EISs at the information flow level. The figure also shows a split point involving the activities `ship products` and `bill customer` that are executed in parallel and a join point where these activities converge to trigger the activity issue payment. At the information flow level these two activities are shown using solid lines to distinguish them from other activities (messages) represented as dashed lines.

Business processes can range from being straightforward and fully automated to complex and intricate processes that require human input and intervention. This is where workflow technology needs to be embedded into the integration solution. The rules that govern how, when, and which users need to interact with the business process, need to be clearly identified and incorporated in the context of a business process. Thus in addition to extending critical business processes outside the enterprise firewall, modern BPI tools provide the ability to intercede at the human management level to adjust or refine or optimize business processes. This allows alerts to business processes that have gone out of boundaries, based on key performance indicators and indices used to set their tolerances. In this way enterprises can respond quickly and effectively to changing business conditions without time-consuming and expensive programming activities.

The extension of BPI with management aspects is commonly referred to as business process management (BPM). BPM emphasizes the management aspect of automating processes to achieve maximum ongoing flexibility with minimum development cost and time.

BPM is a commitment to expressing, understanding, representing, and managing a business (or the portion of business to which it is applied) in terms of a collection of business processes that are responsive to a business environment of internal or external events [McGoveran 2004]. The term *management of business processes* includes process analysis, process definition and redefinition, resource allocation, scheduling, measurement of process quality and efficiency, and process optimization. Process optimization includes collection and analysis of both real-time measures (monitoring) and strategic measures (performance management), and their correlation as the basis for process improvement and innovation.

A BPM solution is a graphical productivity tool for modeling, integrating, monitoring, and optimizing process flows of all sizes, crossing any application, company boundary, or human interaction. BPM is driven primarily by the common desire to integrate supply chains, as well as internal enterprise functions, without the need for even more custom software development. BPM codifies value-driven processes and institutionalizes their execution within the enterprise [Roch 2002]. This implies that BPM tools can help analyze, define, and enforce process standardization. BPM provides a modeling tool to visually construct, analyze, and execute cross-functional business processes.

BPM is more than process automation, or traditional workflow. It adds conceptual innovations and technology from EAI and e-business integration and reimplements it on an e-business infrastructure based on Web and XML standards. BPM software thus really means the combination of workflow, EAI, and e-business components in an integrated modeling and execution environment based on Web technology standards. BPM within the context of EAI and e-business integration provides the flexibility necessary to automate cross-functional processes. To understand this issue, consider a typical e-business scenario involving the linking of purchasing and sales applications such as the one depicted in Figure 9.2. While such applications may provide traditional workflow features, these features work well only within their local environment. Integrated process management is then required for processes spanning organizations. Automating cross-functional activities, such as checking or confirming inventory between an enterprise and its distribution partners, enables corporations to manage processes by exception based on real-time events driven from the integrated environment [Roch 2002]. Process execution then becomes automated, requiring human intervention only in situations where exceptions occur, e.g., inventory level has fallen below a critical threshold, or manual tasks and approvals are required.

Modern workflow systems incorporate several of the advanced features of BPM technology and target the same problem space, i.e., integration of applications across organizational boundaries. Therefore, on the surface modern workflow and BPM technologies seem to be the same. However, they have subtle differences. Their differentiation lies deep in their architecture and applicability.

The distinction between BPM and workflow is mainly based on the management aspect of BPM systems. Although BPM technology covers the same space as workflow, its focus is on the business user, and provides more sophisticated management and analysis capabilities. BPM tools place considerable emphasis on management and business functions. This fact accentuates the business applicability of BPM, instead of a technological solution, which is the case with workflow systems. With a BPM tool the business user is able to manage all the process of a certain type, e.g., claim processes, and should be able to study them from historical or current data; produce costs, or other business measurements; and produce on the basis of these measurements business charts or reports. In addition, the business user should also be able to analyze and compare the data or business measurements based on the different types of claims. This type of functionality is typically not provided by modern workflow systems.

9.4 Cross-enterprise business processes

Web services provide standard and interoperable means of integrating loosely coupled Web-based components that expose well-defined interfaces, while abstracting the implementation- and platform-specific details. Core Web services standards such as SOAP, WSDL, and UDDI provide a solid foundation to accomplish this. However, these specifications primarily enable development of simple Web services applications that can conduct simple interactions. However, the ultimate goal of Web services is to facilitate and automate business process collaborations both inside and outside enterprise boundaries. Useful business applications of Web services in EAI and business–business environments require the ability to compose complex and distributed Web services integrations and the ability to describe the relationships between the constituent low-level services. In this way, collaborative business processes can be realized as Web services integrations.

In the world of Web services, a business process specifies the potential execution order of operations originating from a logically interrelated collection of Web services, each of which performs a well-defined activity within the process. A business process also specifies the shared data passed between these services, the trading partners' roles with respect to the process, joint exception handling conditions for the collection of Web services, and other factors that may influence how Web services or organizations participate in a process [Leymann 2002]. This allows, in particular, specifying long-running transactions between Web services in order to increase the consistency and reliability of business processes that are composed out of Web services (see Chapter 10).

The platform-neutral nature of services creates the opportunity for building composite services by combining existing elementary or complex services (the *component* services) from different enterprises and in turn offering them as high-level services or processes. We use the term *composability* to describe independent service specifications that can be combined to provide capabilities that are more powerful. Composite services (and processes) integrate multiple services – and put together new business functions – by combining new and existing application assets in a logical flow. Service composition combines services following a certain composition pattern to achieve a business goal, solve a problem, or provide new service functions. The definition of composite services requires coordinating the flow of control and information between the component services. Business logic can be seen as the ingredient that sequences, coordinates, and manages interactions among Web services. To program a complex cross-enterprise workflow task or business transaction, for example, it is possible to logically chain discrete Web services activities into cross-enterprise business processes. Techniques for Web services composability draw heavily on business process modeling and workflow processing languages.

A service composition infrastructure relies on lightweight workflow-like and process integration technologies and enables an organization to seamlessly integrate or compose internal business processes and dynamically integrate them with those of its partners. Composed services can then be offered as value-added services. Service composition provides a mechanism for Web services internal to an enterprise to be seamlessly combined in order to describe a business process to support all kinds of EAI scenarios [Papazoglou 2006]. In addition, Web services from multiple enterprises can be coordinated in order to describe partner interactions. This typically supports e-business integration scenarios. For example, an order management process can be developed by combining elementary services such as checking the creditworthiness of the customer; determining whether an ordered part is available in the inventory; calculating the final price and billing the customer; selecting a shipper; and scheduling the production and shipment for the order.

With EAI and e-business applications, business processes can drive their collaboration to achieve a shared business task by enabling highly fluid networks of collaborating Web services. Accordingly, in a Web services environment the business process workflow is made up of activities that are implemented as a set of scoped operations that may span multiple Web services. These Web-services-centric activities follow routes with checkpoints represented by business conditions and rules.

With e-business applications trading partners must run their own, private business processes (workflows), which need to be orchestrated and coordinated to ensure that the outcome of the collaborative business process is reliable and does not fail or hang waiting for another processes or system to respond to a request. This requires that processes be able to communicate asynchronously when appropriate and is opposed to BPI schemes based on synchronous technologies such as CORBA or DCOM.

Enterprise workflow systems today support the definition, execution, and monitoring of long-running processes that coordinate the activities of multiple business applications. However, because these systems are activity-oriented and not communication (message)-oriented, they do not separate internal implementation from external protocol description [Leymann 2000]. When processes span business boundaries, loose coupling based on precise external protocols is required because the parties involved do not share application and workflow implementation technologies, and will not allow external control over the use of their back-end applications. Such business interaction protocols are by necessity message-centric; they specify the flow of messages representing business actions among trading partners, without requiring any specific implementation mechanism. With such applications the loosely coupled, distributed nature of the Web prevents a central workflow authority (or a centralized implementation of middleware technology) from exhaustively and fully coordinating and monitoring the activities of the enterprise applications that expose the Web services participating in message exchanges [Arkin 2001]. The reasons for this are summarized in the following:

- Traditional workflow models rely on message-based computing methods that are tightly coupled to protocols for e-business or application integration. These protocols assume a tightly linked and controllable environment, which is not the nature of the Web.
- Traditional workflow models do not separate internal implementation from external protocol description.
- Participants in traditional workflow are, normally, known in advance. When moving to the Web environment, it is highly probable that Web services will be dynamically chosen to fulfill certain roles.

A trio of standards tackles the problem of choreographing Web services. These specifications are: the Business Process Execution Language for Web Services (BPEL4WS or BPEL for short) [Andrews 2003], WS-Coordination (WS-C), and WS-Transaction (WS-T) [Cabrera 2005a], [Cabrera 2005b], [Cabrera 2005c]. These three specifications work together to form the bedrock for reliably choreographing Web-services-based applications, providing BPM, transactional integrity, and generic coordination facilities. BPEL is a workflow-like definition language that describes sophisticated business processes that can orchestrate Web services. WS-Coordination and WS-Transaction complement BPEL to provide mechanisms for defining specific standard protocols for use by transaction processing systems, workflow systems, or other applications that wish to coordinate multiple Web services. We shall examine BPEL in a subsequent section of this chapter, while we shall concentrate on the transactional aspects of Web services and cover WS-Coordination and WS-Transaction (among other coordination and transaction protocols) in Chapter 10.

9.5 Service composition meta-model

This section describes the ingredients of a service composition meta-model, which enables linking applications together and overlaying those applications on a workflow (BPM) system. The meta-model represents the concepts, constructs, semantics, and relationships that are inherent in Web services composition. It is language independent and uses generic constructs based on workflow definitions that are employed by Web services choreography and orchestration languages. The purpose of this meta-model is to make it easier for readers to understand the concepts and constructs that are introduced later in this chapter.

9.5.1 Flow modeling concepts

Flow models are used for the specification of complex service interactions. A *flow model* describes a usage pattern of a collection of available services, so that the composition of those services provides the functionality needed to achieve a certain business objective [Leymann 2000]. The flow model describes how activities (implemented as Web services

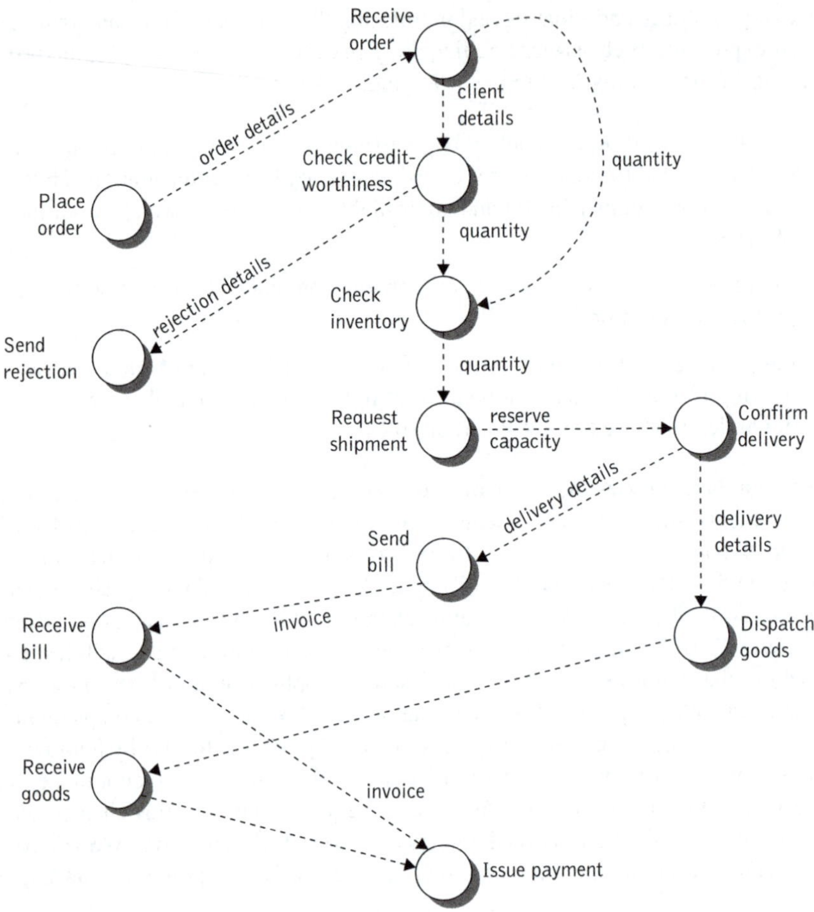

Figure 9.4 Order management process sample flow

operations) are combined, specifies the order in which these steps are executed, the decision points where steps may or may not have to be performed, and the passing of data items between the steps involved.

Figure 9.4 shows a simplified example of a flow model for the order management process depicted in Figure 9.2. This figure consists of a series of activities that are executed in a certain order. An activity is an element that performs a specific function as single step within a process. Activities are normally implemented as operations of Web services. Activities are represented as nodes in a directed acyclic graph (DAG) describing process flows. This means that loops are not allowed within the control structure of a flow. The figure also shows how data items are passed between activities. These comprise the edges in the graph. For instance, client details are passed to the activity that checks customer creditworthiness. As can be discerned from this figure, the key ingredients for the description of a flow model are activities; the specification of the control flow describing the sequencing of these activities and decision points; and the specification of the associated data flow describing the passing of data between them. These three concepts are represented in the service composition meta-model by activities, control links, and data links, respectively. We shall examine these three concepts in subsequent sections of this chapter.

In the example introduced in Figure 9.4, the activity that checks customer creditworthiness could be defined as follows:

```
<activity name="CheckCreditWorthiness">
        <input name="ClientDetails" message="tns:Client"/>
        <output name="Result" message="tns:CreditWorthiness"/>
        <implement> … </implement>
</activity>
```

The fragment specifies that the `CheckCreditWorthiness` activity expects a WSDL message of type `Client` and produces a WSDL message of type `CreditWorthiness` as a result.

The syntax in the above code snippet was inspired by the Web Services Flow Language (WSFL) [Leymann 2001] that preceded BPEL. It is interesting to note that the above code snippet differentiates between an activity specification and its implementation. The specification of an activity defines how this activity is embedded into the process flow. The implementation of an activity describes the actual operation that is invoked when the activity is reached during execution of the flow. The implementing operation of an activity could be defined either internally or externally (by a service provider). The implementation in this case could be provided by a check method in Java or EJB.

Activities in Figure 9.4 are interconnected by means of control links. A *control link* is a directed edge that prescribes the order in which activities will have to be performed. This signifies the potential flow of control between the activities comprising a business process. The need for executing two activities in a certain order follows from logical dependencies between them. If no such dependencies exist, then the activities can be executed simultaneously, thus speeding up the execution of the flow.

A control link is a sequencing relationship between two activities A_1 and A_2 that prescribes the order of their execution, e.g., A_1 must precede A_2. The endpoints of the set of all control links that leave a given activity A represent the possible successor activities A_1, $A_2, \ldots, A_n$ of the activity A.

A control link points from its source activity to its target activity; that is, from an activity to its (or one of its) potential successor activities. Next, such an edge is "guarded" by a transition condition that determines the actual flow of control. Transition conditions determine which of the activities $A_1, A_2, \ldots, A_n$ need to be performed in a business process. A *transition condition* is a predicate expression that is associated with a control link [Leymann 2000]. The formal parameters of this expression can refer to messages that have been produced by some of the activities that preceded the source of the control link in the flow. When an activity A completes, it is succeeded by those control links that originate from this activity whose transition conditions evaluate to true. This set of activities is referred to as "actual successor activities" of A in contrast to the full set $\{A_1, A_2, \ldots, A_n\}$ of "potential successor activities" of the activity A. For instance, in the case of the activity

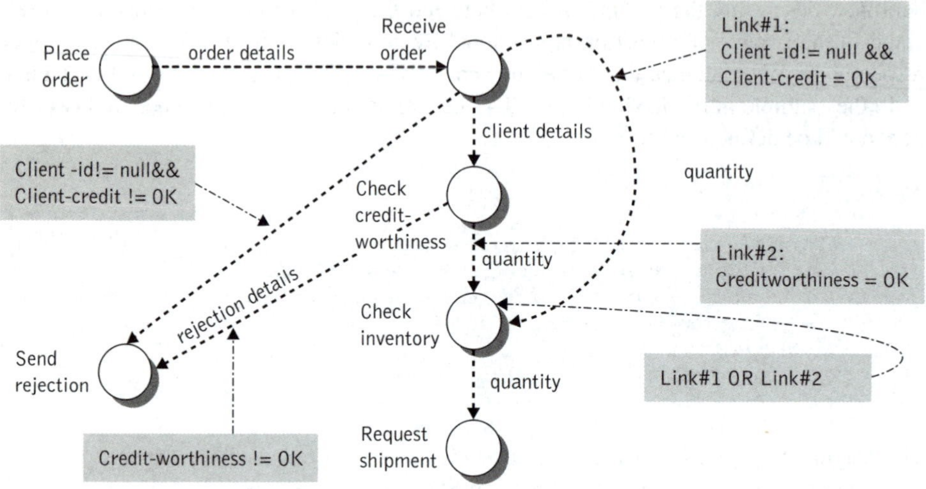

Figure 9.5 Transition conditions and control links for flow model in Figure 9.4

CheckCreditWorthiness either activity SendRejection or CheckInventory are chosen. The chosen activity is the actual successor activity to CheckCreditWorthiness whereas both these activities are in its potential successor activity set. At most one control link between two different activities is allowed and the resulting directed graph must be acyclic as pointed out earlier in this section.

Figure 9.5 shows control details for a fragment of the example flow model in Figure 9.4. This figure shows that there exist transition conditions, i.e., decision points such as determining the credit history of an existing customer, which are evaluated at run-time. Depending on the evaluation, control moves from activity such as CheckCredit-Worthiness to either activity SendRejection or to activity CheckInventory.

The following code fragment specifies that the activity RequestShipment will be reached only after all of its incoming control links have been traversed and only if one of them (link1 or link2) evaluates to true:

```
<activity name="RequestShipment">
       <input name="QuantityOrdered" message="tns:Client"/>
       <output name="ReserveCapacity" message="tns:Shipment"/>
       <implement> … </implement>
  <join condition = "link1" OR "link2"/>
</activity>
<controlLink name="link1"
       source="ReceiveOrder" target="CheckInventory"
       transitionCondition="client_id!= null && client_credit=OK" />

<controlLink name="link2"
       source="CheckCreditWorthiness" target="CheckInventory"
       transitionCondition="credit_worthiness=OK" />
```

The flow model's data flow part specifies how the result message of a given activity is consumed by one (or more) of its successor activities. A *data link* in the service composition meta-model specifies that its source activity passes some data item(s) to its target activity(ies). A data link can be specified only if the target of the data link is reachable from the source of the data link through a path of (directed) control links. Generally speaking, the data flow has to be superimposed on the control flow. This makes certain that error-prone situations are avoided. For example, when trying to consume data that has not yet been produced, it is possible that an activity receives data items from multiple other activities (a data join).

The following code fragment indicates a data flow between the activities `ReceiveOrder` and `CheckCreditWorthiness` in Figure 9.5:

```
<dataLink source="ReceiveOrder" target="CheckCreditWorthiness">
        <map sourceMessage="tns:clientdetails"
         targetMessage="tns:CreditWorthiness"
         sourcePart="data" targetPart="record"
/dataLink>
```

9.5.2 Composing Web services

In the previous section we introduced the basic ingredients of a service composition meta-model without concentrating on the actual realizations of flow activities. In this section we shall concentrate on the composition of flows that perform the coordination of Web services, which implement the individual activities in a process flow. The material in this section provides a high-level description of Web services compositions and is partly based on the Web Services Flow Language [Leymann 2000]. Its aim is to provide readers with enough intuition regarding the characteristics of service compositions so that they can understand much easier the material in section 9.7.

Service providers are the units that participate in service compositions in the service flow model. Service providers represent the functionality that a flow model requires from business partners in a business process. A service provider presents a public interface in the form of a set of WSDL `portTypes` that gives a formal representation of the service or services that each service provider must offer in order to participate in the flow model. This defines essentially the ways in which this service provider can interact with other providers. A composition consists of a set of interconnected service providers, which in turn may be used as a new service provider (aggregator) in other compositions. Compatibility of operations is required between interacting service providers for the service composition to be successful. For instance, a solicit/response operation defined by one service provider requires a matching request/response operation to be provided by another service provider.

One goal of service composition is to enable discrete Web services as implementations of activities of business processes. For this purpose, an activity may refer to an operation of the service provider type's port type that defines the external interface of the flow model to specify which kind of service is required at run-time to perform the business task represented by an activity. For example, Figure 9.6 shows a flow in which an activity called *A* is

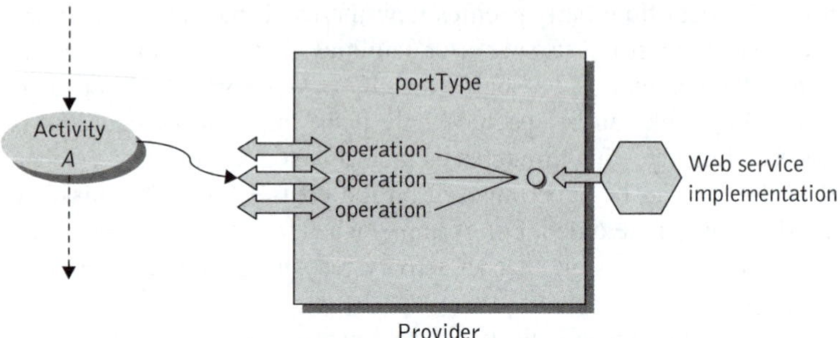

Figure 9.6 Service providers and port types

implemented by a service that realizes operation $operation_1$ of a port type *pt*. At run-time, when navigation encounters *A*, a concrete port is chosen that provides an implementation of port type *pt* and operation $operation_1$. A corresponding binding is used to actually invoke this implementation.

Flow models specify the usage of a service instance of a given type, rather than the service itself. Several flows can use a single Web service simultaneously, whereas a single flow model can use more than one service provider for service of a given type. Figure 9.7 shows an updated version of the flow model illustrated in Figure 9.4, where two activities have been outsourced to a business partner (service provider).

The following code fragment shows how a service provider which plays the role of a logistics provider in Figure 9.7 performs activities by invoking Web services for the order management flow. A service provider type in the meta-model indicates the external interface a business partner makes available. This interface may comprise multiple port types and multiple operations. In the following example the `LogisticsProvider` is shown to offer two operations from two port types.

```
<flowModel name="OrderManagement">
<serviceProvider name="myShipper" type="LogisticsProvider"/>
...
</flowModel>

<serviceProviderType name="LogisticsProvider">
   <portType name="ConfirmDeliveryHandler">
      <operation name="confirmation"/>
   </portType>
   <portType name="DispatchGoodsHandler">
      <operation name="delivery"/>
   </portType>
</serviceProviderType>
```

Binding service providers to actual business partners, which offer the required services, can happen either statically or dynamically. When the binding is static we simply locate the actual business partner which acts as a specific service provider by means of a direct reference to a WSDL service that provides the required operations. The specific WSDL

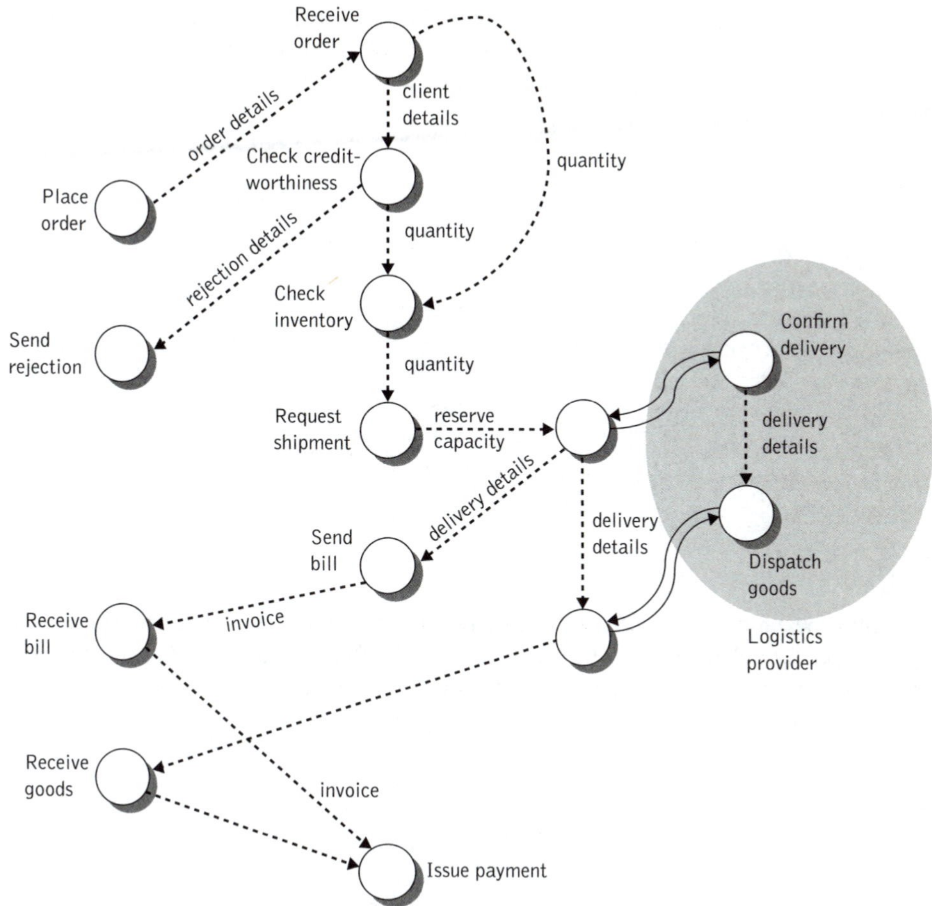

Figure 9.7 Flow model using Web services

service to which we bind statically implements the interface defined by the service provider of the required type. This is illustrated in the following code snippet:

```
<flowModel name="OrderManagement">
<serviceProvider name="myShipper" type="LogisticsProvider">
  <location type = "static" service="abc:LogisticsServices"/>
</serviceProvider>
...
</flowModel>
```

Alternatively, one can bind to a service provider dynamically by looking up the UDDI directory according to some specified criteria, e.g., performance, price, etc., to find a suitable service provider of the required type. Subsequently, the most suitable service is chosen (according to some QoS criterion) and bound. The following example shows how to locate a logistics provider dynamically. The flow engine executes the specified UDDI query, which returns a set of potential logistics providers. These are filtered using a user-defined method (`selectionPolicy`) to return the cheapest logistics provider.

```
<flowModel name="OrderManagement">
<serviceProvider name="myShipper" type="LogisticsProvider">
  <location type = "UDDI"
     selectionPolicy="user-defined" invoke="leastcost.wsdl"/>
   <uddi-api:find-service businessKey= "..." >
     ...
   </ uddi-api>
  </location>
</serviceProvider>
...
</flowModel>
```

The implementation of an outsourced activity needs to reference the operations provided by a service provider, e.g., logistics provider, which offers this activity. For this to occur the service providers that the service composition meta-model uses must be specified first. This situation is shown in the following code snippet:

```
<activity name="ConfirmDelivery">
  ...
  <performedBy serviceProvider="LogisticsProvider"/>
   <implement>
     <internal>
        <target portType="ConfirmDeliveryHandler" operation
          name="confirmation"/>
     </internal>
   </implement>
</activity >
```

The above example assumes that the implementation of the operation can be provided "internally," thus requiring no access to an "external" service provider. The operation `confirmation` shown in the above example is part of `ConfirmDeliveryHandler portType` and implements the flow model's `ConfirmDelivery` operation.

Once the flow model of a certain process such as order management has been implemented in terms of Web services it can be made available to applications so that they can use it. Figure 9.8 shows how the order management process flow can be externalized as

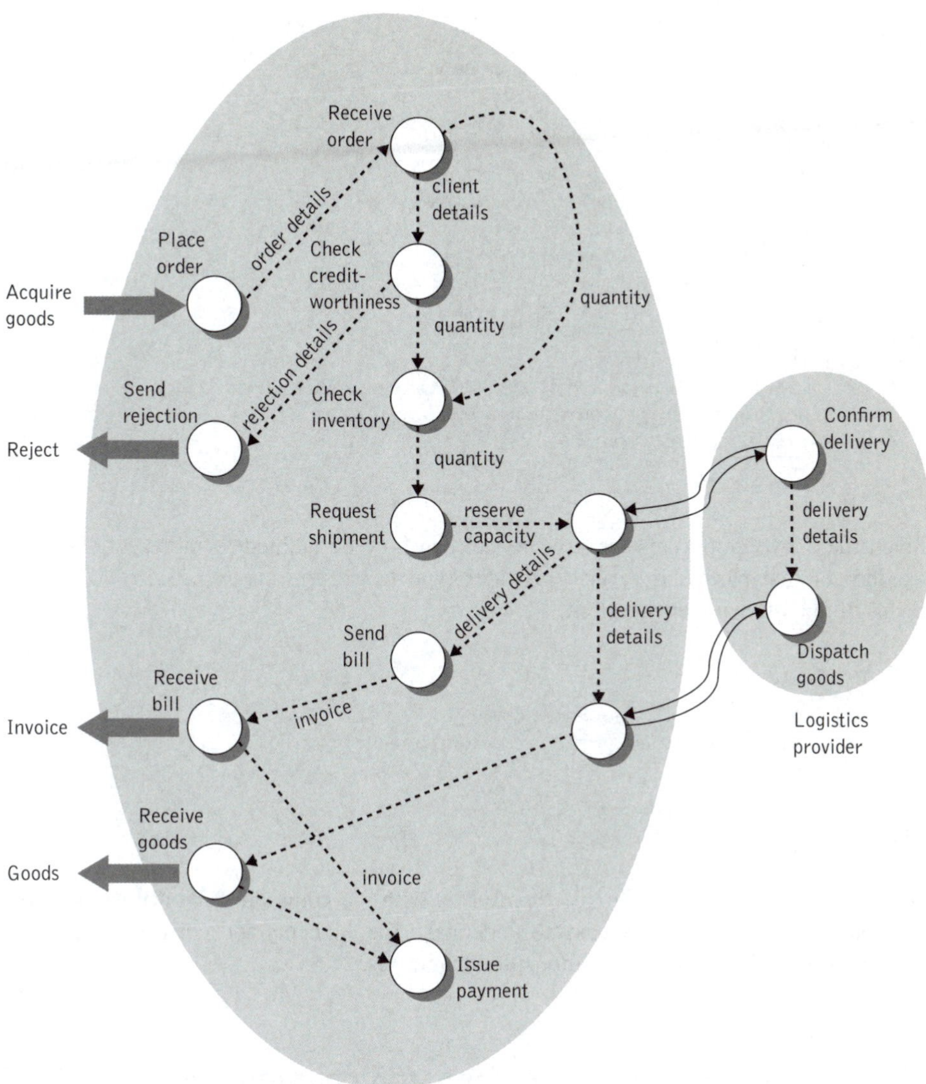

Figure 9.8 Externalizing a process flow as a Web service

a Web service so that client interfaces can connect to it. The flow model's interface is shown to comprise four operations depicted as thick arrows. Three of these operations are outbound whereas one of them is inbound. Initially, the client that uses this Web service interface sends a request for ordering manufacturing parts (goods in the figure), upon which it receives either a rejection or an invoice followed by the actual delivery of goods. The following code fragment illustrates this situation:

```
<portType name="OrderManagementHandler">
   <operation name="acquireGoods">
     <input name="theOrder" message="tns:Order"/>
   </operation>
   <operation name="reject">
     <output name="theRejection" message="tns:RejectionNotice"/>
   </operation>
   <operation name="invoice">
     <output name="theInvoice" message="tns:Invoice"/>
   </operation>
  ...
</portType>
<serviceProviderType name="OrderManagementProvider">
   <portType name="OrderManagementHandler">
</serviceProviderType>
```

Given the above definitions the flow model can now be defined to represent a service provider of that particular service provider type (`OrderManagementProvider`) by means of the following declaration:

```
<flowModel name="OrderManagement">
    serviceProviderType=" OrderManagementProvider"/>
  ...
</flowModel>
```

Now that readers have familiarized themselves with the commonest workflow concepts and constructs, it is relatively easy to understand the concepts and constructs found in Web services orchestration and composition languages.

9.6 Web services orchestration and choreography

The full potential of Web services as a means of developing e-business solutions will only be realized when applications and business processes are able to integrate their complex interactions. Web services technologies offer a viable solution to this problem since they support coordination and offer an asynchronous and message-oriented way to communicate and interact with application logic. Models for e-business interactions typically require specifying sequences of peer-to-peer message exchanges between a collection of Web services, both synchronous and asynchronous, within stateful, long-running interactions involving two or more parties. Such interactions require that business processes are described in terms of a business protocol (or abstract business model) that precisely specifies the mutually visible (public) message exchange behavior of each of the parties involved in the protocol, without revealing their internal (private) implementation. It also

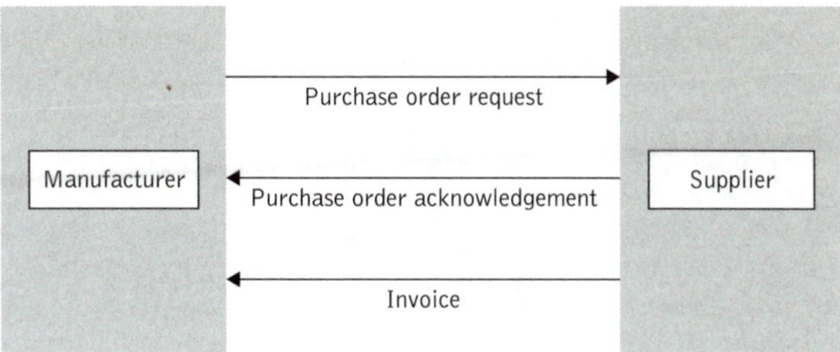

Figure 9.9 A simplified business process

requires modeling the actual behavior of participants involved in a business interaction. To define such business processes and protocols, a formal description of the message exchange protocols used by business processes in their interactions is needed [Bloch 2003].

9.6.1 Orchestration versus choreography

In the previous section, we used terms such as "Web services composition" and "Web services flow" interchangeably to describe the composition of Web services in a process flow. More recently, the terms *orchestration* and *choreography* have been used to describe this phenomenon. There is an important distinction between Web services orchestration and choreography [Pelz 2003], as explained below:

> *Orchestration* describes how Web services can interact with each other at the message level, including the business logic and execution order of the interactions from the perspective and under control of a single endpoint. This is for instance the case of the process flow described in Figure 9.9 where the business process flow is seen from the vantage point of a single supplier. Orchestration refers to an executable business process that may result in a long-lived, transactional, multi-step process model. With orchestration, the business process interactions are always controlled from the (private) perspective of one of the business parties involved in the process.
>
> *Choreography* is typically associated with the public (globally visible) message exchanges, rules of interaction, and agreements that occur between multiple business process endpoints, rather than a specific business process that is executed by a single party. Choreography tracks the sequence of messages that may involve multiple parties and multiple sources, including customers, suppliers, and partners, where each party involved in the process describes the part it plays in the interaction and no party "owns" the conversation. Choreography is more collaborative in nature than orchestration. It is described from the perspectives of all parties (common view), and, in essence, defines the shared state of the interactions between business entities. This common view can be used to determine specific deployment implementations for each individual entity. Choreography offers a means by which the rules of participation for collaboration can be clearly defined and agreed to, jointly. Each entity may then implement its portion of the choreography as determined by their common view.

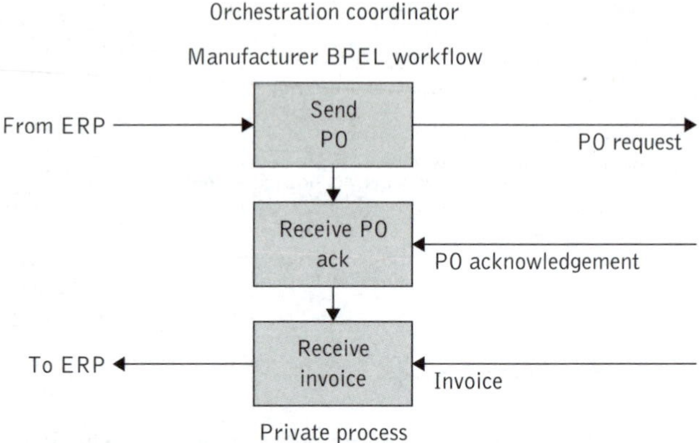

Figure 9.10 PO from an orchestration perspective

We use Figure 9.9 to exemplify the concept of orchestration and choreography in terms of a simplified order management process. This figure shows a typical business process comprising a purchase order. A manufacturer may start a correlated message exchange with a supplier by sending a purchase order (PO) and using a PO number in the PO document. The supplier can use this PO number in the PO acknowledgement. The manufacturer may later send an invoice containing an invoice document that carries both the PO number, to correlate it with the original PO, and an invoice number.

Figure 9.10 shows the PO process from an orchestration perspective. This process is shown from the perspective of a back-end application, such as an Enterprise Resource Planning (ERP) application, which can be employed to check inventory, place orders, and organize the manufacturer's resources. The private manufacturer process can be specified using a typical business process execution language such as BPEL (introduced in the following section).

Figure 9.11 shows the PO from a choreography perspective involving an observable public exchange of messages surrounded by dashed lines. This choreography can be

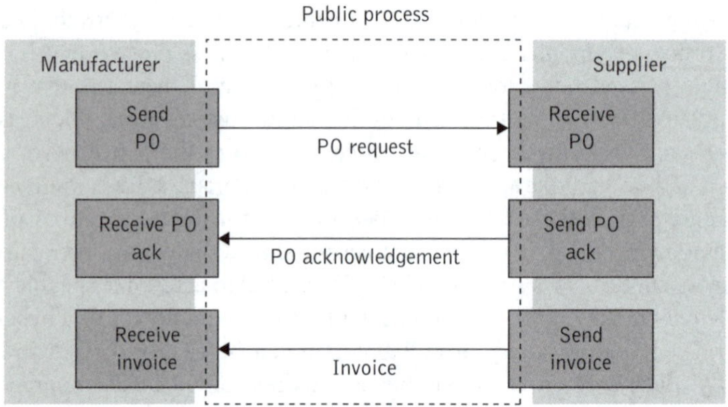

Figure 9.11 PO from a choreography perspective

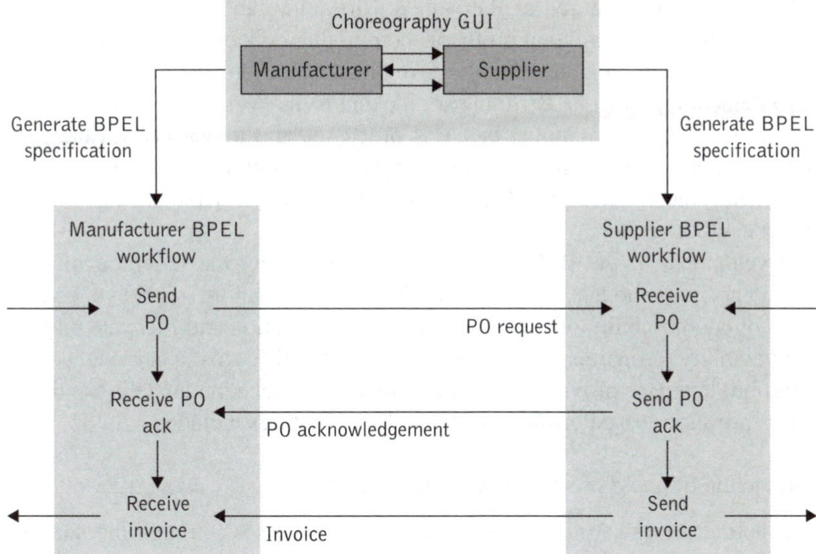

Figure 9.12 Combining choreography and orchestration

specified using a service choreography specification language such as WS-CDL (see section 9.8).

Finally, in Figure 9.12, the manufacturer and supplier are shown to integrate their business processes. This figure assumes that the respective business analysts at both companies have agreed upon the rules and processes involved for the process collaboration. Using a GUI and a tool that can serve as a basis for the collaboration, the manufacturer and supplier agree upon their interactions and generate a WS-CDL representation. The WS-CDL representation can then be used to generate a BPEL workflow template for both the manufacturer and supplier. The two BPEL workflow templates reflect the business agreement.

In the following section we shall first concentrate on the Business Process Execution Language for Web Services (BPEL for short), which is the standard industry specification that is designed specifically for Web-services-based orchestration, and subsequently shall summarize important elements of WS-CDL.

9.7 The Business Process Execution Language (BPEL)

Web services orchestration specifications pick up things from where WSDL ends. WSDL essentially permits definition of the static interface of a Web service. The interaction model of a WSDL `portType` is stateless and static without any correlation of interactions at the level of the interface defined. Additionally, WSDL describes interfaces from the perspective of a service (provider) and hence it is geared towards a client–server model of interaction. Collaborative process models typically involve both client–server and peer-to-peer types of interactions with long-running and stateful conversations involving two or more parties, which WSDL is not equipped to deliver. Hence, the Web services orchestration specifications use WSDL as a basis and extend its functionality.

BPEL has recently emerged as the standard to define and manage business process activities and business interaction protocols comprising collaborating Web services. This is an XML-based flow language for the formal specification of business processes and business interaction protocols. By doing so, it extends the Web services interaction model and enables it to support complex business processes and transactions. Enterprises can describe complex processes that include multiple organizations – such as order processing, lead management, and claims handling – and execute the same business processes in systems from other vendors.

The development of the BPEL language was guided by the requirement to support service composition models that provide flexible integration, recursive composition, separation of composability of concerns, stateful conversation and lifecycle management, and recoverability properties [Weerawarana 2005]. BPEL as a service composition (orchestration) language provides several features to facilitate the modeling and execution of business processes based on Web services. These features include:

- modeling business process collaboration (through `<partnerLink>`s);
- modeling the execution control of business processes (through the use of a self-contained block and transition structured language that support representation of directed graphs);
- separation of abstract definition from concrete binding (static and dynamic selection of partner services via endpoint references);
- representation of participants' roles and role relationships (through `<partnerLinkType>`s);
- compensation support (through fault handlers and compensation);
- service composability (structured activities can be nested and combined arbitrarily);
- context support (through the `<scope>` mechanism);
- spawning off and synchronizing processes (through `<pick>` and `<receive>` activities); and
- event handling (through the use of event handlers).

BPEL can also be extended to provide other important composition language properties such as support for Web services policies and security and reliable messaging requirements.

In this section we summarize the most salient BPEL features and constructs. Our intention is to provide a sound understanding of BPEL concepts and features and not to present a detailed tutorial of BPEL and its constructs. More information about this language can be found in [Andrews 2003].

9.7.1 BPEL structure

A BPEL process is a flow-chart-like expression specifying process steps and entry points into the process that is layered on top of WSDL, with WSDL defining the specific operations allowed and BPEL defining how the operations can be sequenced [Curbera 2003].

The role of BPEL is to define a new Web service by composing a set of existing services through a process-integration-type mechanism with control language constructs. The entry points correspond to external WSDL clients invoking either input-only (request) or input/output (request/response) operations on the interface of the composite BPEL service. Figure 1.7 illustrates how BPEL is related to other Web services standards.

At the core of the BPEL process model lies the notion of peer-to-peer interaction between services described in WSDL. Both the process and its Web service partners are modeled in WSDL. BPEL uses WSDL to specify activities that should take place in a business process and describes the Web services provided by the business process. A BPEL document leverages WSDL in the following three ways [Pelz 2003]:

1. Every BPEL process is exposed as a Web service using WSDL. WSDL describes the public entry and exit points for the process.
2. WSDL data types are used within a BPEL process to describe the information that passes between requests.
3. WSDL might be used to reference external services required by a business process.

BPEL provides a mechanism for creating implementation- and platform-independent compositions of services woven strictly from the abstract interfaces provided in the WSDL definitions. The definition of a BPEL business process also follows the WSDL convention of strict separation between the abstract service interface and service implementation. In particular, a BPEL process represents parties and interactions between these parties in terms of abstract WSDL interfaces (by means of `<portType>`s and `<operation>`s), while no references are made to the actual services (binding and address information) used by a process instance. Both the interacting process as well as its counterparts are modeled in the form of WSDL services. Actual implementations of the services themselves may be dynamically bound to the partners of a BPEL composition, without affecting the composition's definition. Business processes specified in BPEL are fully executable portable scripts that can be interpreted by business process engines in BPEL-conformant environments.

BPEL distinguishes five main sections: the *message flow*, the *control flow*, the *data flow*, the *process orchestration*, and the *fault and exception handling* sections. These sections are shown in Listing 9.1, while Figure 9.13 illustrates how the BPEL data structures are connected to each other by means of a UML meta-model.

The message flow section of BPEL is handled by basic activities that include invoking an operation on some Web service, waiting for a process operation to be invoked by some external client, and generating the response of an input/output operation. The control flow section of BPEL is a hybrid model principally based on block structured definitions with the ability to define selective state transition control flow definitions for synchronization purposes. The data flow section of BPEL comprises variables that provide the means for holding messages that constitute the state of a business process. The messages held are often those that have been received from partners or are to be sent to partners. Variables can also hold data that are needed for holding state related to the process and never exchanged with partners. Variables are scoped and the name of a variable should be unique within its own scope. The process orchestration section of BPEL uses partner links

```
<process name="PurchaseOrderProcess" ... >
  <!– Roles played by actual process participants at endpoints of
   an interaction -->
  <partnerLinks> ... </partnerLinks >

  <!- Data used by the process -->
  <variables> ... </variables >

  <!- Supports asynchronous interactions -->
  <correlationSets> ... </correlationSets>

  <!- Activities that the process performs -->
   (activities)*

  <!-Exception handling: Alternate execution path to deal with
     faulty situations -->
  <faultHandlers> ... </faultHandlers>

  <!-Code that is executed when an action is "undone" -->
  <compensationHandlers> ... </compensationHandlers>

  <!-Handling of concurrent events -->
  <eventHandlers> ... </eventHandlers>
</process>
```

Listing 9.1 Structure of BPEL process

to establish peer-to-peer partner relationships. Finally, the fault and exception handling section of BPEL deals with errors that might occur when services are being invoked with handling compensations of units of work and dealing with exceptions during the course of a BPEL computation.

We shall summarize each of the five BPEL sections giving examples in BPEL 1.1 (which is based on version 1.1 of WDSL) where appropriate in subsequent sections after we define the concepts of abstract and executable processes in BPEL.

9.7.1.1 Abstract and executable processes

BPEL distinguishes between two levels of process description: abstract and executable business processes. An abstract process specifies the external message exchange between Web services and does not contain any internal details of the business process. This type of process is typically used to model the public message interaction (business protocol) between two Web services without exposing the internal business logic of these services and therefore is not executable. In contrast, an *executable process* defines both the external message exchange and the complete internal details of the business logic and is executable. It contains all the actual detailed interactions and behavior of participants in the overall

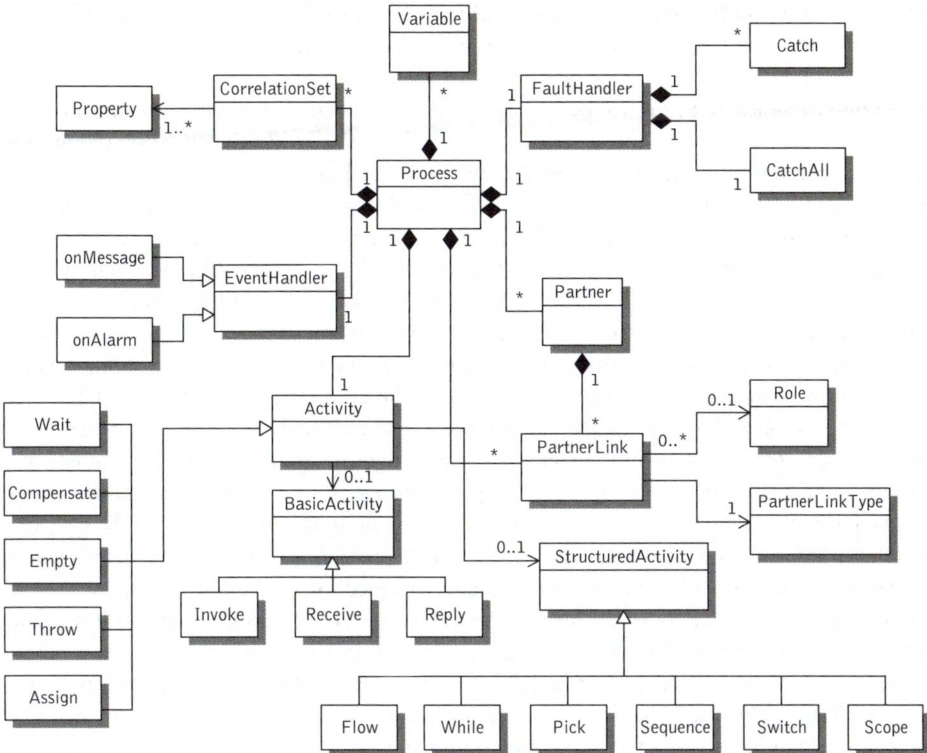

Figure 9.13 BPEL 1.1 UML meta-model

business process flow, essentially modeling a *private* workflow. An executable process contains all the details of the process, including a full description of the process state and how it is processed. We can think of an abstract business process as the projection of an executable process. BPEL provides the same language constructs to define both abstract and executable processes.

There are two main differences between abstract and executable processes. First, abstract processes are modeled as business protocols in BPEL. A business protocol specifies the public interaction of business partners via messages and their potential sequence, i.e., the order in which messages between partners are exchanged in order to achieve a concrete business objective. The details of what else happens internally to realize these protocols are not important and are thus ignored. Unlike executable business processes, business protocols are not executable and do not reveal the internal (private) details of a process flow. Abstract processes (unlike executable processes) are useful for specifying expected protocols and the publicly visible message exchanges of each of the parties leveraging the protocol without too much detail. For instance, the types of products that are ordered by an order management process are not protocol relevant. However, the protocol might be sensitive to the method of payment as the sequence of messages exchanged may depend on the mode of payment. Abstract business processes link Web service interface definitions with behavioral specifications that can be used to control the business roles and define the behavior that each party is expected to perform within the overall business process.

Another important difference between abstract and executable processes is that abstract processes approach data handling in a way that reflects the level of abstraction required to identify protocol-relevant data embedded in messages [Bloch 2003]. Abstract processes view properties as *transparent data* relevant to public aspects as opposed to *opaque data* that internal/private functions use [Bloch 2003]. Opaque data is usually related to back-end systems. Opaque data affects the business protocol only by creating non-determinism because the manner in which it affects decisions is opaque. In contrast, transparent data affects the public business protocol in a direct way. Abstract processes ignore the details of a computation that appears in a corresponding executable process by executing opaque assignments to hide private aspects of behavior. The computation in the executable process is thus replaced by an opaque assignment in the corresponding abstract process. An *opaque (variable) assignment* is a statement that assigns a variable a non-deterministically chosen value. The value is usually a result produced by an internal implementation involving a particular computation or algorithmic implementation. For instance, in the case of a purchase order business protocol the supplier may provide a service that receives a purchase order and responds with either acceptance or rejection of the transaction based on a number of criteria, such as availability of the goods, the creditworthiness of the buyer, etc. The decision process is opaque; however, the result of the decision is reflected as behavior alternatives exhibited by the external business protocol. In other words, the protocol acts as a "switch" within the behavior of the seller's service, while the selection of the decision branch taken in the process flow is non-deterministic.

Figure 9.14 illustrates an abstract process corresponding to the order management process flow diagram in Figure 9.2. In this figure the manufacturer (client) and the supplier have two distinct roles, each with its own port types and operations. The structure of their relationship at the interface level is typically modeled as a publicly visible exchange of messages.

9.7.1.2 Message flow

The message flow section of BPEL deals with the sending and the receiving of messages so that a process (Web service) instance can communicate with other Web services. The message flow section of BPEL is handled by basic activities that include invoking an operation on some Web service (`<invoke>`), waiting for an input-only process operation to be invoked by some external client (`<receive>`), and generating the response of an input/output operation (`<reply>`). As a language for composing Web services, BPEL processes interact by making invocations to other services and receiving invocations from clients. The former is done using the `<invoke>` activity, and the latter using the `<receive>` and `<reply>` activities. A business process provides services to its partners and communicates with them by means of the `<receive>` and `<reply>` activities. These three constructs are briefly described below.

BPEL calls other service partners. A *partner* is a Web service that a process invokes and/or any client that invokes a process. It is essentially a mapping to a WSDL `portType` description of a physical partner's Web service [Chatterjee 2004]. A BPEL process

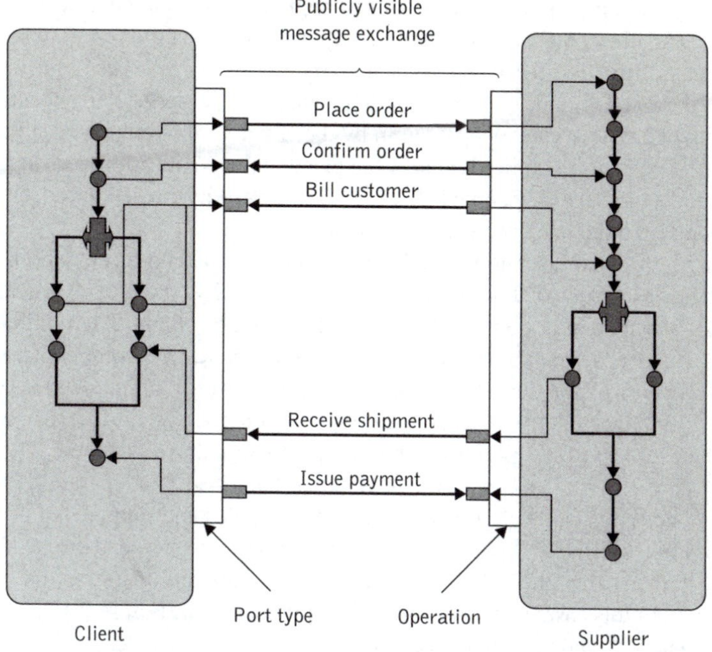

Figure 9.14 Abstract process corresponding to process flow diagram in Figure 9.2

interacts with each partner using a <partnerLink> construct. A *partner link* is an instance of typed connector that a particular process offers to or requires from its partner at the other end of the link [Weerawarana 2005]. A <partnerLink> element reflects the fact that such a link is a conversational interface rather than reflective of a business relationship. In other words, a <partnerLink> can be perceived as a channel that establishes a peer-to-peer conversation with a partner. This is illustrated in Figure 9.14. Each of the <invoke>, <receive>, and <reply> activities in the message flow section of BPEL specifies the <partnerLink> – <portType> operation and the variables that it relates to [Weerawarana 2005]. For more details on <partnerLink>s refer to section 9.7.1.5, which describes the concept of process orchestration in BPEL.

To invoke a Web service a process uses the <invoke> construct. This construct allows the business process to invoke either a synchronous (request/response) or an asynchronous (one-way) operation on a <portType> offered by a partner Web service. The Web service is identified by the <partnerLink> and its respective WSDL <portType> and operation. In addition to the <portType>, partner, and operation, the <invoke> element specifies input and output variables, for the input and output of the operation being invoked. A synchronous Web service requires both input and output variables to be passed in. In the case of asynchronous operation invocations, only an input variable is required.

Whereas an <invoke> activity allows a process to call an operation of a partner's Web service, the <receive> activity specifies a Web service operation implemented by the process for use by Web service partners. In this way a partner triggers the execution of a process by calling its services. In BPEL a process usually starts with a <receive> or

<pick> activity, implying that a process must begin by being called as a service of a particular type. Therefore, the <receive> activity is a process activity onto which a WSDL operation maps. Just like the <invoke> activity, <receive> uses <partnerLink>, WSDL <portType>, and <operation> to identify the service it expects a specific partner to invoke. The arguments passed in by the caller are bound to a specified variable. In this way, <receive> explicitly marks the place in the business process logic where an inbound request message is accepted. A <receive> activity is used to receive a message that has been sent either synchronously or asynchronously.

The <reply> construct allows the business process to send a message in reply to a message that was received through a <receive> activity. A <reply> activity is the place where a response is conveyed to the Web services client. The combination of a <receive> and a <reply> forms a synchronous request/response operation on the WSDL <portType> for the process. The effect is that of a single Web service call in which the <receive> activity accepts the input and the <reply> passes back the output, while the process may perform arbitrary computations in between. The <reply> activity must match the <partnerLink>, <portType>, and operation attributes of <receive> activity, while its variable attribute specifies the output. An asynchronous process does not use the <reply> activity. If such an activity needs to send a reply to the client, it then uses the <invoke> activity to call an operation on the client's <portType>. In this case an output variable is not necessary. Figure 9.15 shows the synchronous (request/response) and asynchronous (one-way) modes of communication, which involve the <receive>, <reply>, and <invoke> activities. This figure indicates that the provider's asynchronous response (if it is forthcoming) in the asynchronous mode of communication is referred to as *callback*.

Multiple <reply> activities may be defined in the process to answer a partner's call. However, only one matching <reply> may become active at any one time. Matching of the appropriate <reply> activity is done at run-time, when the process looks for such an activity that is ready to run and has the same <portType>, <operation>, and <partner> as the <receive>.

9.7.1.3 Control flow

A fundamental part of a BPEL specification is the definition of the activities and the sequence of steps required to make up a given process. This is where basic and structured activities are employed.

BPEL comprises basic and structured activities. *Basic activities* are the simplest form of interaction with a service. They are not sequenced and comprise individual steps to interact with a service, manipulate the exchange data, or handle exceptions encountered during execution. For example, basic activities would handle receiving or replying to message requests as well as invoking external services. The typical scenario is that there is a message received into the BPEL process. The process may then invoke a series of external services to gather additional data, and then respond to the requestor in some fashion. BPEL activities such as <receive>, <reply>, and <invoke> all represent basic activities that allow a business process to exchange messages with the services it composes. Other basic activities include exception handling mechanisms and state management activities. In addition to basic activities, BPEL uses *structured activities* (BPEL messages

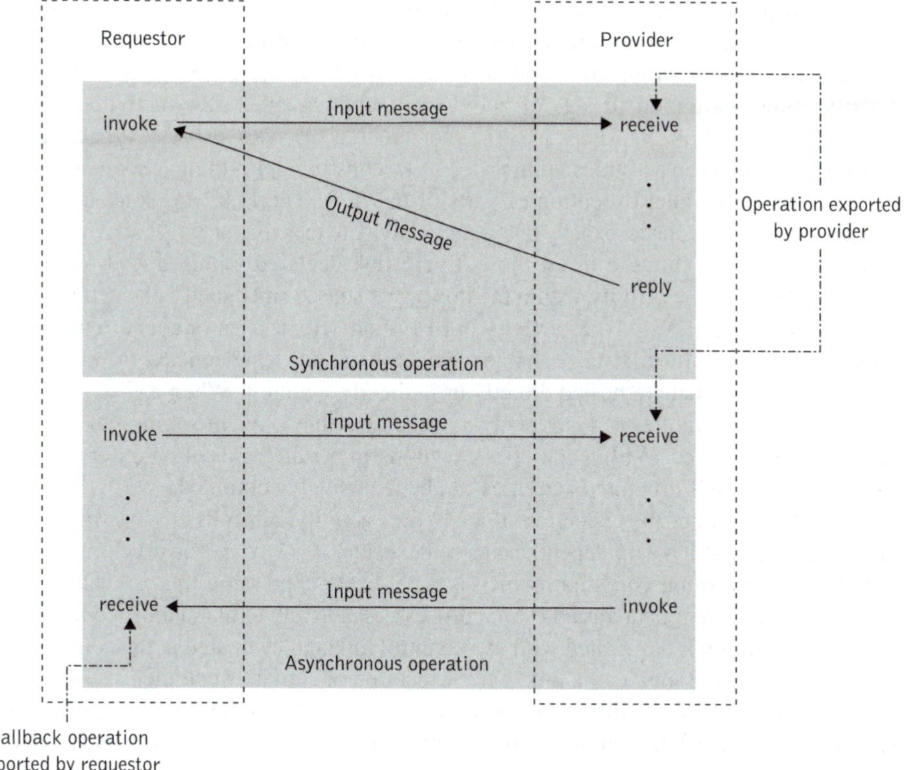

Figure 9.15 Synchronous and asynchronous modes of communication in BPEL

including `<sequence>`, `<switch>`, `<while>`, `<pick>`, and `<flow>`) to manage the overall process control flow, specifying the order in which activities execute.

Structured activities specify which activities should run sequentially (via the <sequence> activity) or in parallel (via the <flow> activity). These describe how a business process is created by composing the basic activities it performs into structures that express control patterns, data flow, fault handling, external event handling, and coordination of message exchanges between process instances. One may think of structured activities as the underlying programming logic for BPEL. Structured activities describe how a business process can be created by composing the basic activities it performs into structures.

The control flow section of BPEL has the ability to define selective state transition control flow definitions for synchronization purposes. The control flow part of BPEL includes the ability to define an ordered sequence of activities (<sequence>), to have activities run in parallel (<flow>), have branching activities (<switch>), to define iterations (<while>), and to execute one of several alternative paths (non-deterministic choice) based on external events (<pick>).

The <sequence> activity contains one or more activities that are executed absolutely sequentially. The activities are executed in the order in which they appear within the <sequence> element. When the final activity in the <sequence> has completed, the <sequence> activity itself is complete.

Parallelizing activities that have no dependencies can be accomplished by enclosing the activities that are to run in parallel within a <flow> construct. This construct provides concurrency and synchronization and also the ability to define guarded links. A <flow> activity allows definition of sets of activities (including other flow activities) that are connected via <links>. The <links> construct is used to express synchronization dependencies between activities within a <flow> construct, providing among other things the potential for parallel execution of parts of the flow. The links are defined inside the flow and are used to connect exactly one source activity to exactly one target activity that must both be the logical children of the flow. Every link declared within a <flow> activity must have exactly one activity within the flow as its source and exactly one activity within the flow as its target. A <flow> activity in BPEL may create a set of concurrent activities directly nested within it. It also enables synchronization dependencies to be expressed between activities that are nested directly or indirectly within it. When a <flow> activity is started, all the activities in it are ready to run unless they have incoming links that have not yet been evaluated. Within activities executing in parallel, execution order constraints can be specified. All structured activities can be recursively combined.

At the beginning of the execution of a <flow> activity, all links are inactive and only those activities that have no dependencies can execute. A <link> construct may be associated with a transition condition, which is a predicate expression that is evaluated over values in the different data variables in a process. As already explained in section 9.5.1, a transition condition is associated with each control link and evaluated at the completion of an activity that is the source of a link. Once execution of activities completes, each activity evaluates its transition condition to determine the status of its outgoing links, which were inactive prior to the completion of this activity. Once all incoming links to an activity are active (they have been assigned a true or false state as a result of the evaluation of their respective transition conditions, see Figure 9.5), the activity's join condition is evaluated. A *join condition* is a Boolean expression associated with each activity that is a target of a link. A join condition decides whether the activity should execute based on the value of the transition conditions of the links (paths) that point at it. This condition evaluates every one of the incoming links (there can be more than one and each one must have a Boolean value in order to continue), and decides whether or not the activity will be executed. For instance, a join condition may specify that a process may expect that either all of its incoming paths have completed successfully or just a single path needs to be successful before proceeding with the execution of a specific activity in the flow.

The <switch> activity functions much like the switch construct that occurs in many traditional programming languages, e.g., C or Java. There is an ordered list of one or more conditional branches, defined by <case> elements, followed by an optional <otherwise> element. Each <case> branch specifies a Boolean XPath expression, and the expressions are evaluated in the order in which they appear. The <switch> activity allows branches in a workflow to be navigated. Navigation is conducted on the basis of conditions defined in <case> elements. In case these conditions are not satisfied, a specific branch can be specified. The switch activity finishes when the activity of the selected branch completes.

Activities are iterated by nesting them within a <while> activity. The <while> activity in BPEL evaluates a condition defined in an XPath expression and if that condition evaluates to true, another iteration of the enclosed activities is executed.

The <pick> activity is akin to an asynchronous event-driven <switch> activity and contains a set of event handlers [Duftler 2002], [Chatterjee 2004]. A <pick> activity is a set of branches of the form event/activity, and exactly one of the branches will be selected based on the occurrence of the event associated with it before any others. After the <pick> activity has accepted an event for handling, all other events are ignored. Possible events include the arrival of some message in the form of the invocation of an inbound one-way or request/response operation, or an "alarm" based on a timer. The event handlers include alarm handlers, which specify an event duration (time relative from now) or deadline (fixed future time), and message handlers (onMessage) which wait for messages from a particular partner, portType, and operation triplet. A <pick> activity completes when one of the branches is triggered by the occurrence of its associated event and the corresponding activity completes.

Each <pick> activity may contain at least one message handler (onMessage event). The onMessage events dictate when an activity becomes active, i.e., when a matching message is received. Only the first event handler to receive its event will run, and the <pick> activity will complete once that handler's activity completes. The message handlers are able to create a process instance in the same way as a <receive> activity. In this way a <pick> activity can provide the entry point into a process and acts very much like a <receive> activity. The key difference is that a <pick> activity can initiate a process based on a number of messages rather than the single message that the <receive> activity supports [Chatterjee 2004].

9.7.1.4 Data flow

Business processes in BPEL specify stateful interactions involving the exchange of messages between partners. The state of a business process includes the content of the messages that are exchanged as well as intermediate data used in business logic and in composing messages sent to partners. To maintain the state of a business process, state variables, which are called <variable>s, are used in BPEL. The data flow section of BPEL requires that information is visible data. In addition, state data can be extracted and combined by means of data expressions to control the behavior of processes. Finally, state update requires a notion of assignment. BPEL provides these features for XML data types and WSDL message types.

In BPEL data <variable>s specify the business context of a particular process. These are collections of WSDL messages, which represent data that is important for the correct execution of the business process, e.g., for routing decisions to be made or for constructing messages that need to be sent to partners. Data <variable>s are used to manage the persistence of data across Web service requests. These provide the means for holding message content that constitute altogether the state of a business process. The messages held are often those that have been received from partners or are to be sent to partners; <variable>s can also hold data that are needed for holding state related to the process and never exchanged with partners [Bloch 2003]. Variables may exchange specific data elements via the use of <assign> statements.

The <assign> statement is used to copy data messages (messages, parts of messages, and service references) between variables. A BPEL variable is a typed data structure that stores messages associated with a workflow instance in order to facilitate stateful interactions among Web services [Chatterjee 2004]. In a workflow the state of the application is simply a function of the messages that have been exchanged and these can be stored in variables. Variables begin their lives initialized and are populated over time by the arrival of messages or computations that are being executed. An `<assign>` activity follows one of several paths depending on what is being assigned. In all assignment activity forms type compatibility between the source and the destination of the assignment must be maintained. Therefore valid assignments can only occur where both the `<from>` (source) and `<to>` (destination) reference variables hold the same message types, or where both endpoints of an assignment are the same. The `<assign>` statement allows not only data manipulation, but also dynamic binding to different service implementations.

9.7.1.5 Process orchestration

In BPEL, business processes from one enterprise must be able to interact through Web service interfaces with the processes of other enterprises. This requires the ability to model a partner process. WSDL already describes the functionality of a service provided by a partner, at both the abstract and concrete levels. The relationship of a business process to a partner is typically peer to peer, requiring a two-way dependency at the service level [Andrews 2003]. In other words, a partner represents both a consumer of a service provided by the business process and a provider of a service to the business process. This is especially the case when the interactions are based on asynchronous messaging rather than on remote procedure calls. BPEL provides also a mechanism for capturing the roles undertaken by business partners in a Web-services-based workflow through *partner linking*, and *endpoint references*.

The process composition (orchestration) section of BPEL uses `<partnerLink>`s to establish peer-to-peer partner relationships by specifying the roles of each party and the (abstract) interface that each provides. `<partnerLink>`s are the most abstract form of relation supported in BPEL and specify the shape of a relationship with a partner by defining the message and port types used in the interactions in both directions between any two partners, i.e., the operations provided or invoked by a business process. The actual partner service may be dynamically determined within the process. Another BPEL element, the `<partnerLinkType>`, is used to describe the communication relationship between two partners by defining the type of role that each partner plays when two processes interact and the port types used in the interactions in both directions. Finally, BPEL defines the notion of endpoint reference to represent the static or dynamic data required to address a message. Endpoint references are defined as given in WS-Addressing. We shall start the description of the BPEL process orchestration section by first describing `<partnerLinkType>` elements.

The services with which a business process interacts are modeled as partners in BPEL. The process orchestration section of BPEL uses a type-based approach as it composes services at the `<portType>` level rather than at the port/instance level [Weerawarana 2005]. Partners are connected to a process in a bilateral manner using a `<partnerLinkType>` element, and `<partnerLinkType>`s represent the interaction between a BPEL process and the involved parties, which include the Web services that the BPEL process invokes and the client that invokes the BPEL process. More than one partner can be characterized by the same <partnerLinkType>. For example, a certain procurement process might use more than one vendor for its transactions, but might use the same <partnerLinkType> for all vendors. A <partnerLinkType> is a declaration of a relationship between two or more services, which is exposed as a set of roles with each role indicating a list of <portType>s. A BPEL partner is then defined to play a role from a given <partnerLinkType>. The service relationship defines a link between any two services, qualified by the targetNamespace of the WSDL document. Thus, the role element of the <partnerLinkType> points to a WSDL <portType>, where one partner provides a one-way or request/response operation that is consumed by the other partner.

It is important to understand that <partnerLinkType>s are actually not part of the BPEL process specification document. This is due to the fact that <partnerLinkType>s belong to the service and not the process specification. They can therefore be placed in the WSDL document that describes the partner Web service of a BPEL process using the WSDL extensibility mechanisms. Alternatively, we can place all the <partnerLinks> specifications in the WSDL document that describes the BPEL process. However, this practice is not recommended as it violates the principle of encapsulation [Juric 2006].

For synchronous operations, there is a single role for each <partnerLinkType> because the operation is only invoked in a single direction. In this case, the BPEL process has to wait for completion of the operation and gets a response only after the operation is completed. If a <partnerLinkType> specifies only one role, one service in the relationship must implement a WSDL <portType>. In the following code snippet a creditCheck process defines a <partnerLinkType> with a single role creditChecker. The role creditChecker refers to an initiate-credit-check WSDL operation through a <portType> called creditCheckPT.

```
<partnerLinkType name="creditCheckPLT">
    <role name="creditChecker"
                portType="tns:creditCheckPT">
    </role>
</partnerLinkType>
```

The initiate-credit-check operation defines an input to be sent to a service provider, and expects either a reply or a fault. Here, the service that implements the creditChecker role must also implement creditCheckPT.

For asynchronous callback operations, two roles need to be specified. The first role describes the invocation of the operation by the client. The second role describes the invocation of a callback operation. If a <partnerLinkType> element specifies two roles, each of the two services that participate in the relationship must implement one role. In the following code snippet a creditCheck process defines the two roles creditRequestor and creditChecker:

```
<partnerLinkType name="creditChecPLT">
   <role name="creditRequestor"
               portType="tns:creditCheck-CallbackPT">
   </role>
   <role name="creditChecker"
               portType="tns:creditCheckPT">
   </role>
</partnerLinkType>
```

Here, the service that implements the `creditRequestor` role must also implement `creditCheckCallbackPT`, while the service that implements the `creditChecker` role must implement `creditCheckPT`.

A `<partnerLinkType>` in BPEL describes a requirement on the port types supported by two processes that interact, but it does not identify the processes themselves. Many pairs of processes might satisfy the requirements described in a `<partnerLinkType>` specification. To achieve this objective, the services with which a business process interacts are modeled as `<partnerLink>`s in BPEL. The `<partnerLink>`s define different parties that interact with the BPEL process. Each `<partnerLink>` element is characterized by a `<partnerLinkType>`, the role of that business process, and the role of its partner (the process at the other end of the link).

The `<partnerLink>` can specify a single role, which is usually the case with synchronous request/response operations. A synchronous BPEL process is one that returns the results of processing back to the client immediately. The client is blocked until the results are returned. The WSDL interface for this process will have a request/response-type endpoint, see Figure 9.15. The synchronous type of process typically follows the following logic and syntax pattern:

```
<process>
    <receive partnerLink="CreditChecking"
     portType="CreditCheckPT"
     operation="initiate-credit-check" variable="creditCheckVar">

    ... perform processing ...

   <reply partnerLink="CreditChecking" portType="CreditCheckPT"
    operation="initiate-credit-check"
    variable="creditCheckResponseVar">
</process>
```

Asynchronous BPEL processes can be used in a scenario where it takes a long time to compute the results. When using an asynchronous BPEL process, the client need not block the call. Instead, the client implements a callback interface, and once the results are available, the BPEL process simply makes a callback invocation on the client. One scenario where an asynchronous BPEL process can be used is if the underlying Web services to be orchestrated are asynchronous. The asynchronous type of process typically follows the following logic and syntax pattern:

```
<process>
    <receive partnerLink="CreditChecking" portType="CreditCheckPT"
     operation="initiate-credit-check" variable="creditCheckVar">

     ...Perform time-consuming processing ...

    <!--Perform an invocation on the client to return the results-->
    <invoke partnerLink="CreditChecking" portType="
     CreditCheck-CallBackPT"
     operation="credit-check-response"
     inputVariable="creditCheckResponseVar">
</process>
```

For asynchronous operations it specifies two roles. For each partner service involved in a process, a <partnerLinkType> element identifies the WSDL <portType> elements referenced by <partnerLink> elements within the process definition.

Figure 9.16 exemplifies the preceding asynchronous BPEL mode of communication. More specifically, this figure shows the relationship between partner links, partner link types, and associated port types for a purchase order and associated credit-check process. As usual, partner links are used for operations provided or invoked by a business process.

BPEL allows business processes to become adaptive and portable by decoupling business logic from available service endpoints. Before operations on a partner's service can be invoked via a <partnerLink>, the binding and communication data for the partner service must be available [Andrews 2003]. When a process needs to execute, each <partnerLink> must be bound to a concrete endpoint. Four binding schemes are possible [Weerawarana 2005]. A process might be bound *statically at design time* to known endpoints. A process can also be bound *statically at deployment time* by specifying a set of endpoints into which the process is deployed. This scheme is useful if instances of a particular process deployment must use the same endpoints. Because in BPEL partners are likely to be stateful, the service endpoint information needs to be extended with instance-specific information. This requires that actual partner services be selected and assigned *dynamically*. In BPEL the endpoint references implicitly present in <partnerLink>s can be selected, extracted, and assigned dynamically in one of two ways. First, by using *lookups* by evaluating criteria attached to a <partnerLink> that might include QoS policies, transactional capabilities, or functional requirements. Second, by means of using *passed-in endpoints* that are copied from variables previously assigned not by the process itself but by either a response to an invocation (as a result of an <invoke> activity) or a request from a partner (as an input to a <receive> activity).

Figure 9.17 illustrates the binding of the two roles of a <partnerLink> as depicted in Figure 9.16 to Web service endpoints. This binding is shown from the point of view of the purchase order process. For the credit requestor role, the WSDL port contains the address where the operations of the process are provided. For the credit checker role, the WSDL

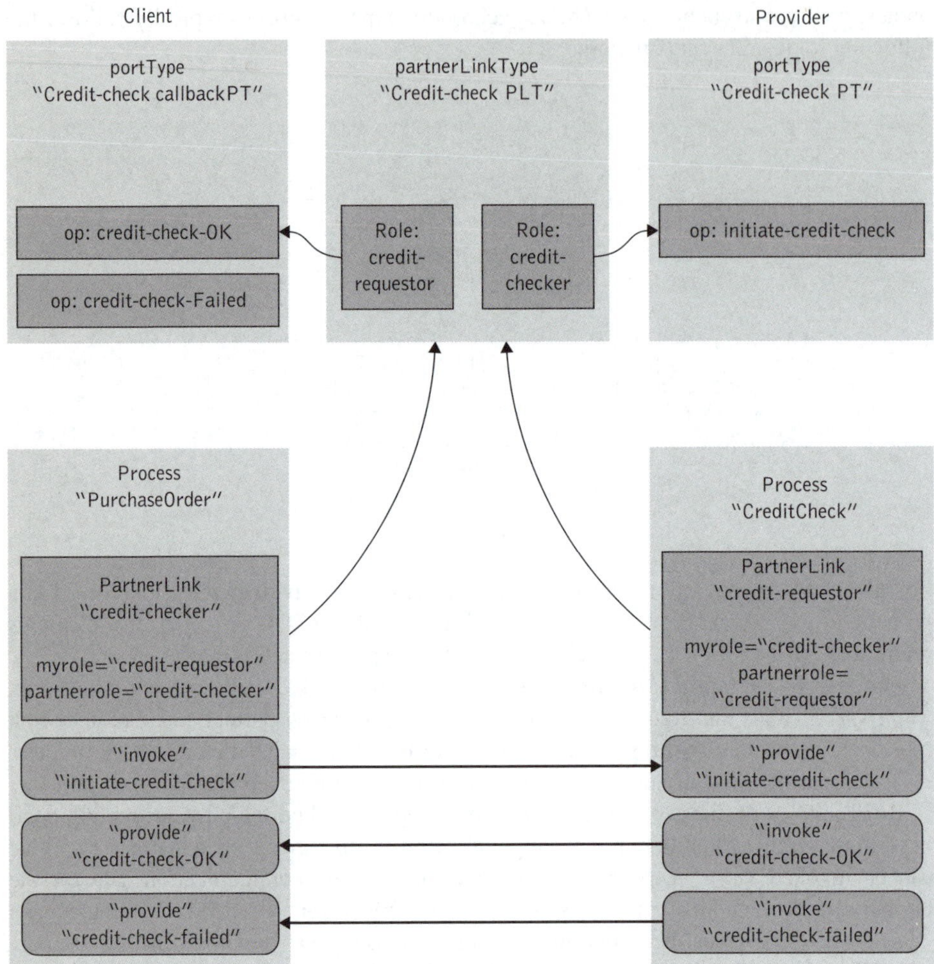

Figure 9.16 Partner links and associated link types
Source: S. Graham, T. Boubez, G. Daniels, D. Davis, Y. Nakamura, R. Neyama, S. Simeonov, *Building Web Services with Java*, Second Edition, SAMS Publishing, 2005. Reproduced with permission.

port contains the address of the Web service provided by the business partner of the purchase order process.

9.7.1.6 Message correlation

Message correlation is the BPEL mechanism that allows multiple processes to participate in stateful conversations. As there can be many instances of the same process running simultaneously, there must be some mechanism for deciding which process instance a particular message is meant for. When a message arrives for a Web service, which has been implemented using BPEL, that message must be delivered somewhere – either to a new or an existing instance of the process. Message correlation determines to which particular conversation a message belongs, i.e., in BPEL's case this is the task of locating/instantiating

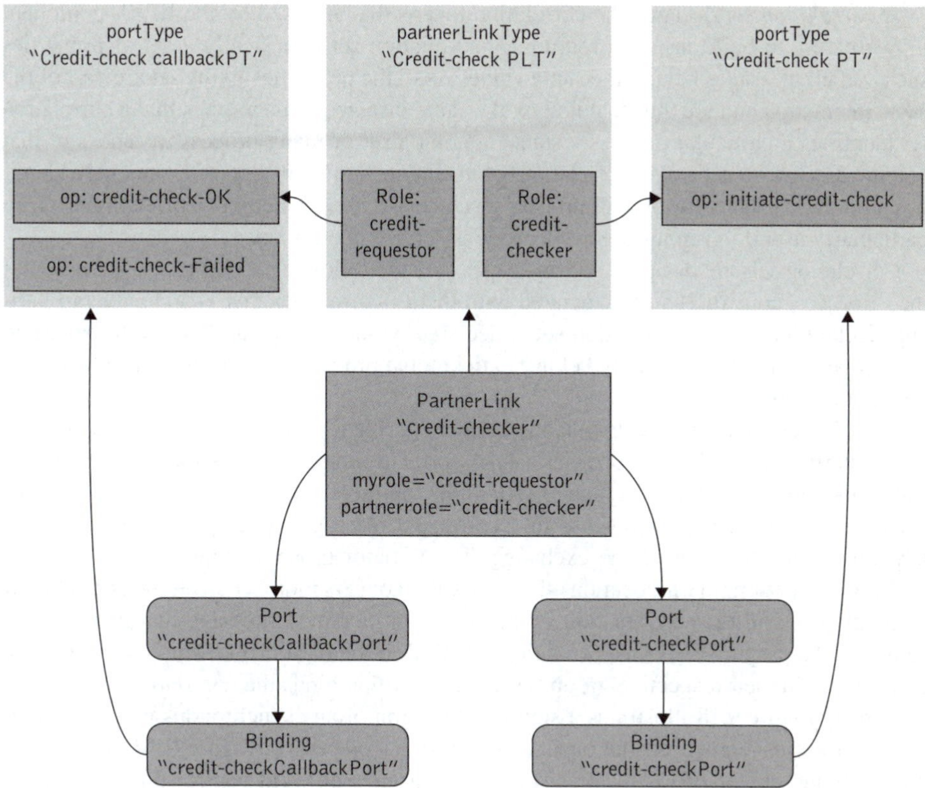

Figure 9.17 Binding a `partnerLink` to Web service endpoints
Source: S. Graham, T. Boubez, G. Daniels, D. Davis, Y. Nakamura, R. Neyama, S. Simeonov, *Building Web Services with Java*, Second Edition, SAMS Publishing, 2005. Reproduced with permission.

a process instance. Correlation can be used, for instance, to match returning or known customers to long-running multi-party business processes that may be running concurrently. A correlation set can be used with all types of activities that deal with sent or received messages. As `<receive>` and `<pick>` activities provide the entry points into a process, correlation sets often appear on them to enable message-to-instance routing.

Message correlation is the concept tying messages together. Usually it occurs when one service calls another service asynchronously and passes *correlation tokens*. For example, a supplier identification number might be used as a correlation token to identify an individual supplier in a long-running multi-party business process relating to a purchase order. In a correlation, the property name, e.g., supplier-id, purchase-order-id, invoice-number, vendor-id, and so on, must have global significance to be of any use. The notation of *property* is used to represent data elements within a message exchanged. A set of correlation tokens is defined as a set of properties shared by all messages in the correlated group. Such a set of properties is called a correlation set. Using correlators, BPEL enables a business process engine to create new instances of a process for handling inbound requests or to route inbound requests to existing process instances based on the values of message properties within the requests.

A *correlation set* declares the correlation tokens that are used by the BPEL-compliant infrastructure to build instance routing. A correlation set is basically a set of properties such that all messages having the same values of all the properties in the set are part of the same interaction and are thus handled by the same instance. This implies that a correlation set identifies a particular process instance among a set of many process instances of that specific process. In general, a correlation set in conjunction with a <port> uniquely identifies a process instance among all process instances at a host machine. Correlation sets are particularly useful in supporting asynchronous service operations.

Correlation sets are declared within scopes (see the following section for a definition of the <scope> construct) and associated with them in a manner that is analogous to variable declarations. Each correlation set is declared within a scope and is said to belong to that scope. Correlation sets may belong to the global process scope or may also belong to other, non-global scopes.

In multi-party business protocols, the partner starting a message exchange and creating the property values of the properties in the correlation set that tags the conversation is called the *initiator* of the exchange. All other partners are *followers* of the message exchange. Each participant process in a correlated message exchange acts either as the initiator or as a follower of the exchange. The initiator process sends the first message (as part of an operation invocation) that starts the conversation. The followers bind their correlation sets in the conversation by receiving an incoming message that provides the values of the properties in the correlation set. Both initiator and followers must mark the first activity in their respective groups as the activity that binds the correlation set.

Finally Figure 9.18 illustrates a simplified version of an asynchronous purchase order (PO) process developed on the basis of the abstract process in Figure 9.14. This figure illustrates the use of BPEL mechanisms including message and control flow constructs, <partnerLinkType>s, endpoint references – defined in WS-Addressing – as well as message correlation by means of identifiers.

9.7.1.7 Fault handling

The BPEL <faultHandlers> section contains structures defining the activities that must be performed in response to faults resulting from the invocation of services. In BPEL, all faults, whether internal or resulting from a service invocation, are identified by a qualified name. In particular, each WSDL fault is identified in BPEL by a qualified name formed by the target namespace of the WSDL document in which the relevant <portType> and fault are defined, and the name of the fault [Bloch 2003]. Certain operations can return faults, as defined in their WSDL definitions.

Fault handling in a business process can be thought of as a mode switch from the normal processing in a scope. The <scope> activity provides fault and compensation handling capabilities to the activities nested within it. A <scope> activity is a means of explicitly packaging activities (or sets of activities gathered under a common structured activity, such as <sequence> or <flow>) together and providing an activity context such that the activities packaged within a scope can share common error handling and compensation methods. A <scope> activity consists of a set of optional fault handlers, a single optional compensation handler, and the primary activity of the scope that defines its behavior. In addition to fault handlers, scopes provide a way to declare variables that are visible within the scope.

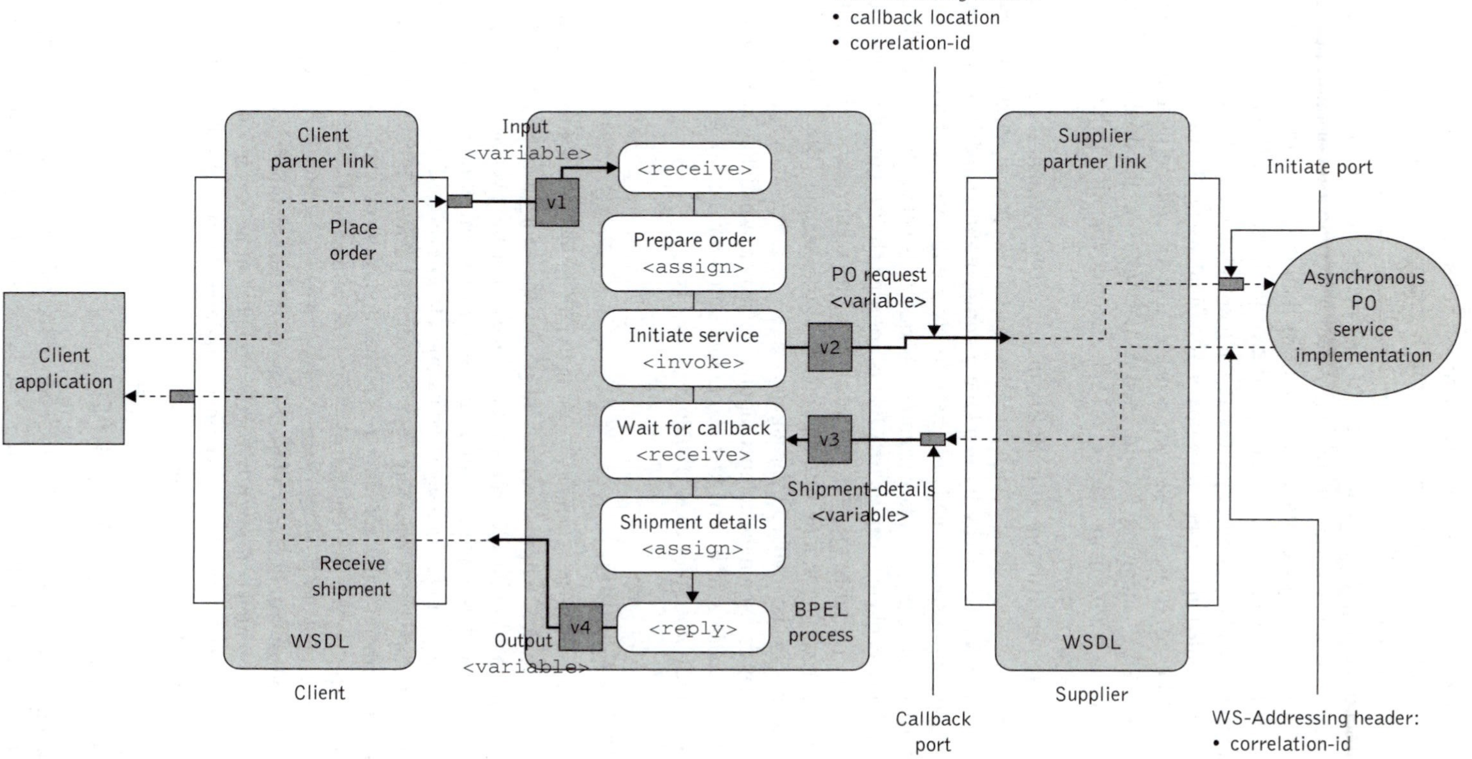

Figure 9.18 Asynchronous BPEL process corresponding to the abstract process in Figure 9.14

A fault handler can be defined on any scope and is bound either to a particular kind of fault (defined by the fault's qualified name, or its message type) or to any faults not caught by a more specific handler. The optional fault handlers attached to a scope provide a way to define a set of custom fault handling activities, syntactically defined as `<catch>` activities. Each `<catch>` activity is defined to intercept a specific kind of fault. For example, the `<catch>` activity might contain a reply activity that notifies a partner that an error has occurred. The first thing a `<scope>` activity does once it receives a fault is to stop all its nested activities. Handlers allow any scope to intercept a fault and take appropriate action. Once a fault is handled in a scope, the scope ends normally with the values of its outgoing links being evaluated as usual. The core concepts and executable pattern extensions of BPEL define several standard faults with their names and data. In addition to these, there might also be other platform-specific faults such as communication failures that can occur in a business process instance.

To set up a transactional context in BPEL, the `<scope>` element is used. This element groups related activities together. Each fault handler of a scope can initiate the reversal of the results of a previous activity by invoking a compensation handler. Compensation is used when application-specific activities need to reverse the effects of a previous activity that was carried out as part of a larger unit of work that is being abandoned when a two-phase commit protocol (see section 10.3.1.1) is not used. BPEL provides a compensation protocol that has the ability to define fault handling and compensation in an application-specific manner, resulting in long-running (business) transactions [Bloch 2003]. The compensation handler can be invoked by using the `<compensate>` activity, which names the `<scope>` element for which the compensation is to be performed; that is, the scope whose compensation handler is to be invoked. A compensation handler for a scope is available for invocation only when the scope completes normally.

9.7.1.8 Event handling

In addition to the `<receive>` and `<pick>` activities in its control structure, BPEL provides the means to deal with the concurrent processing of asynchronous events through *event handlers*. An event handler enables the scope to react to events, or the expiration of timers, at any point during the execution of a scope. `<eventHandlers>` can deal with two kinds of events, namely message events and alarm events. A *message event* implements a request/response or one-way operation that a business process implements. An *alarm event* implements temporal semantics in that it may occur whenever a specified time is reached or expires. The `<eventHandlers>` are similar to a `<pick>` activity insofar as they contain a number of `<onMessage>` or `<onAlarm>` activities. However, unlike a `<pick>` activity that specifies that a business process must wait for events to occur, event handlers can be executed concurrently with the process if the corresponding events occur. This allows concurrent processing within a single scope where previously concurrent "threads" of control were not permitted.

9.7.2 A simple example in BPEL

In this section we shall use a simplified version of the purchase order application shown in Figure 9.4 to explain the BPEL constructs we introduced in the previous section. In this

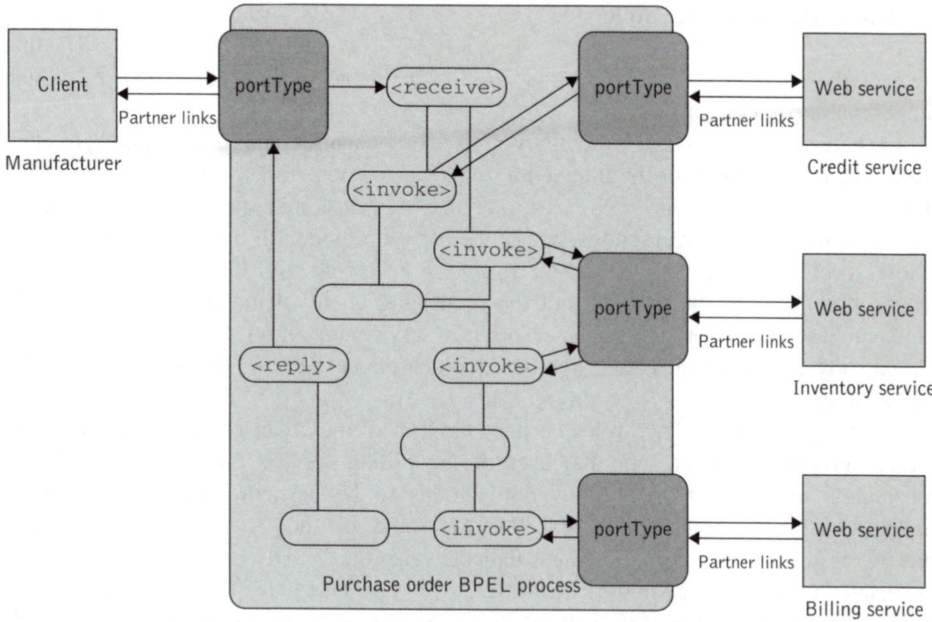

Figure 9.19 Sample BPEL purchase order process

example, we show a manufacturer placing a purchase order and a supplier who tries to fulfill the manufacturer's request. The supplier communicates with credit service, billing service, and inventory service providers to fulfill the client's wishes. Once an invoice is generated, it is then sent back to the client. A high-level view of this process is given in Figure 9.19.

We shall begin developing this example by concentrating on the process orchestration section of BPEL. In this section several BPEL details are skipped in the interest of brevity.

9.7.2.1 Process orchestration

When defining a business process in BPEL we are effectively creating a new Web service that combines existing elementary Web services. The WSDL specification for this new composite Web service defines the relationships between this and other Web services (also defined in WSDL). The WSDL specification for the process specifies the port types it exposes to its clients as well as operations, messages, partner link types, and properties of interest to the process. Relationships between the process and partner Web services (e.g., credit, check, inventory, billing, etc.) are achieved by means of the `<partnerLinkType>` construct. As already explained in section 9.7.1.5, a `<partnerLinkType>` element specifies the relationship between two services by defining the role that each service implements. Each role specifies exactly one WSDL `<portType>` that must be implemented by the service that implements that role. In this example, we define the following <partnerLinkType> elements: "Purchase-OrderPLT", "CreditCheckPLT", "InventoryPLT", and "BillingPLT". The first two of these <partnerLinkType>s are shown in the portion of Listing 9.2 which appears at the bottom of this page.

Each <partnerLinkType> defines up to two role names, and lists the port types that each role must support for the interaction to be carried out successfully. In this example, the <partnerLinkType> "PurchaseOrderPLT" lists a single role because, in the corresponding service interactions, one of the parties provides all the invoked operations. More specifically, the "PurchaseOrderPLT" <partnerLinkType> represents the connection between the process and the requesting client (manufacturer), where only the purchase order service needs to offer a service operation ("sendPurchase"). As already explained, this fact signifies a synchronous mode of communication. The three other <partnerLinkType>s, "CreditCheckPLT", "InventoryPLT", and "BillingPLT", define two roles because the user of the credit check service, the user of the inventory service, and the user of the billing service must provide callback operations to enable asynchronous notifications to be asynchronously sent to their invoker. This is shown in Listing 9.2 for some of the <partnerLinkType>s. Each <partnerLinkType> element indicates also the WSDL <portType>s that are associated with each role via the <partnerLinkType> element. The <partnerLink-Type> element defines the dependencies between the services and the WSDL <portType>s used. For instance, in Listing 9.2 it is shown that the WSDL <portType> "PurchaseOrderPortType" is associated with a request initiated with the client. The PurchaseOrder process will also have a reference to the "CreditCheck" provider for requesting a credit service for the client and receiving a credit check response. This communication occurs by means of the two port types "CreditCheck-CallBackPT" and "CreditCheck-CallBackPT" (mentioned in section 9.7.1.5 but not shown in Listing 9.2).

```
<partnerLinks>
    <partnerLink name="Purchasing"
      partnerLinkType="PurchaseOrderPLT"
      myRole="PurchaseService"/>
    <partnerLink name="CreditChecker"
      partnerLinkType="CreditCheckPLT"
      myRole="CreditRequestor"
      partnerRole="CreditChecker"/>
    <partnerLink name="InventoryChecker"
      partnerLinkType="InventoryCheckPLT"
      myRole="InventoryRequestor"
      partnerRole="InventoryService"/>
    <partnerLink name=" BillingService"
      partnerLinkType="BillingPLT"
      myRole="BillRequestor"
      partnerRole="Biller"/>
</partnerLinks>
```

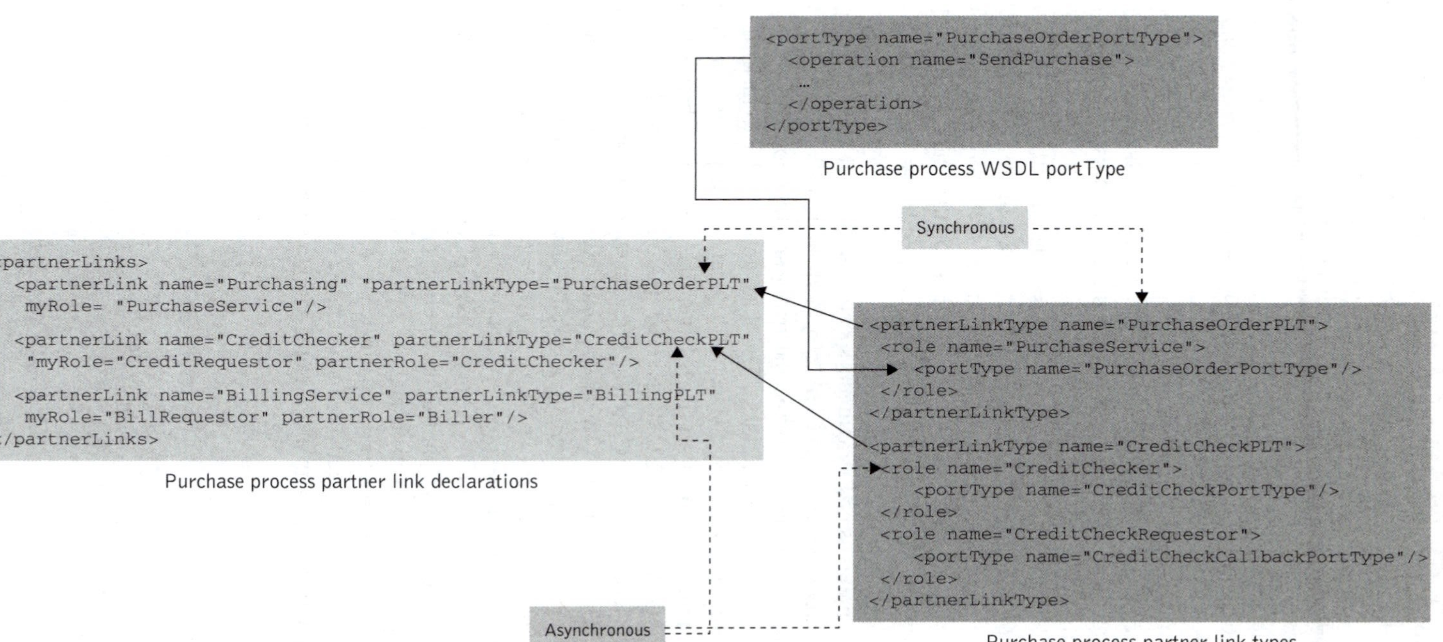

Listing 9.2 Definition of roles in the preceding BPEL snippet

Now we can focus our attention on the main element for specifying partner declarations within a BPEL workflow, which is the <partnerLinks> element. The <partnerLinks> section defines the different parties that interact with the business process in the course of processing an order and contains several <partnerLink> elements. Each of the latter is an individual partner declaration, which specifies the role of an enterprise and its partners on the basis of <partnerLinkType> elements. This information identifies the functionality that must be provided by the business process and by the partner service for the relationship to succeed; that is, the port types that the purchase order process and the partner need to implement. The four <partnerLink> definitions shown in the preceding code snippet correspond to the sender of the order (client or manufacturer), as well as the credit check, inventory, and billing providers. Some of these are also shown in Listing 9.2.

In Listing 9.2 the "PurchaseOrder" process is defined from the perspective of the purchase order supplier (the BPEL process itself). When the manufacturer (client) interacts with the purchase order supplier, the manufacturer is the requestor while the supplier is the credit requestor and bill requestor (on behalf of the manufacturer). Conversely, the roles are reversed when the supplier interacts with the "CreditChecker" or "BillingService" providers.

At this point the previous code fragments specify the types of services an application is interacting with (through <partnerLinkType> element declarations) and the roles of the enterprises that are going to provide the necessary functionality for achieving this (through <partnerLink> declarations). The final step in order to make business interrelationships concrete is to specify the network locations of partners such that we can discover and consume their Web services. Given the distinction between abstract and concrete interfaces in WSDL, BPEL needs to be in a position to bridge the gap between abstract partner declarations, and to exchange messages over the network with real services at run-time. This is addressed by an endpoint reference element, which is part of a workflow that acts as a typed reference to a specific service [Andrews 2003]. The fundamental use of endpoint references in BPEL is to serve as the mechanism for dynamic communication of port-specific data for services. An endpoint reference makes it possible to dynamically select a provider for a particular type of service and to invoke their operations. For instance, many clients can use the "initiate-credit-check" operation of a credit check service. These partners need to identify themselves in order to enable the credit check service to respond to the correct partner. An endpoint reference element allows consuming services to bind abstractly defined partners to physical network endpoints, and expose those endpoints (along with other useful data) to workflow activities.

```
<wsa:EndpointReference xmlns:wsa="...">
    <wsa:Address>http://www.someendpoint.com</wsa:Address>
        <wsa:PortType>PurchaseOrderPortType</wsa:PortType>
</wsa:EndpointReference>
```

Listing 9.3 Endpoint reference declaration

BPEL uses the notion of endpoint reference defined in WS-Addressing (see section 7.3.1). Every partner role in a `<partnerLink>` in a BPEL process instance is assigned a unique endpoint reference statically or dynamically by an activity within the process. Listing 9.3 shows a simplified example of an endpoint reference for two parties involved in a purchase order. More details can be found in Listing 7.3, which specifies the endpoint where the purchase order message originated from and the address of the intended receiver of this message.

The final part now is the definition of the process itself (`"PurchaseOrder"`). This is accomplished by means of the `<process>` element at the process root level (see Listing 9.1). The `<process>` element provides a name for the process and supplies references to the XML namespaces used. In this way the process places WSDL-specific references in a BPEL process definition.

9.7.2.2 Data handling

BPEL processes manage the flow of data between partners represented by their service interfaces. The `<variables>` section of BPEL defines the data variables used by the process, providing their definitions in terms of WSDL message types and XML Schema elements. Variables provide the means for holding messages that constitute a part of the state of a business process. The messages held are often those that have been received from partners or are to be sent to partners. Variables can also hold data that is needed for holding state related to the process and never exchanged with partners.

The `messageType`, `type`, or `element` attributes are used to specify the type of a variable. Attribute `messageType` refers to a WSDL message type definition. Attribute `type` refers to an XML Schema simple or complex type. Attribute `element` refers to an XML Schema element. For example, a purchase order business process may store a `POMessage` in a `PO` variable, see Listing 9.4.

Using `<assign>` and `<copy>`, data can be copied and manipulated between variables. The `<assign>` element is used to copy data (messages, parts of messages, and service references) between variables, while `<copy>` supports XPath queries to sub-select data expressions. A typical example of an assignment is where (parts of) the contents of one message are copied to another. This is shown in Listing 9.4 where the `PurchaseOrder` part of `POMessage` is assigned to the `PurchaseOrder` part of a `creditRequestor`. This message is stored in the `creditRequest` variable once received. The process (purchase order) then may pass on the `creditRequest` variable to the credit service provider. This message uses the part-purchase-order `PO` variable, which is used by the credit service provider to process the request. Each variable shown in Listing 9.4 is followed by a reference to a specific WSDL message type and through it is associated with a corresponding WSDL `<message>` element.

9.7.2.3 Control flow

A key part of a BPEL application is the definition of the basic sequence of steps required to handle the request. This is where basic and structured activities come into play. The process flow in Listing 9.5 is shown to comprise an initial request from a manufacturer (client) asking for a purchase order, followed by an invocation of credit check service and

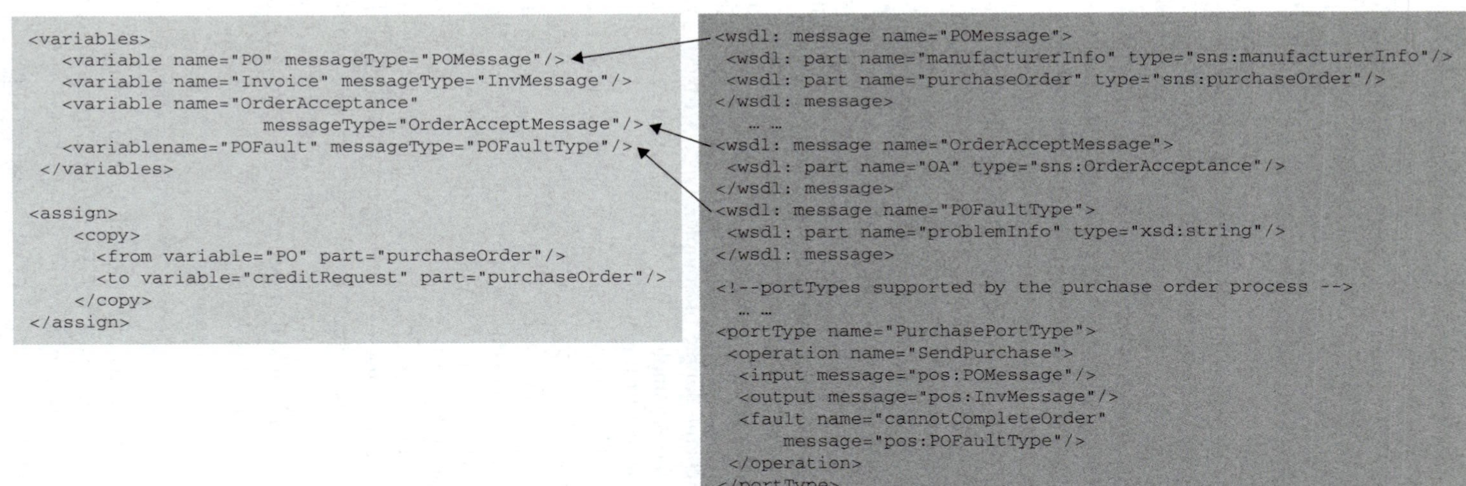

```
<variables>
   <variable name="PO" messageType="POMessage"/>
   <variable name="Invoice" messageType="InvMessage"/>
   <variable name="OrderAcceptance"
                      messageType="OrderAcceptMessage"/>
   <variablename="POFault" messageType="POFaultType"/>
 </variables>

<assign>
    <copy>
      <from variable="PO" part="purchaseOrder"/>
      <to variable="creditRequest" part="purchaseOrder"/>
    </copy>
</assign>
```

```
<wsdl: message name="POMessage">
 <wsdl: part name="manufacturerInfo" type="sns:manufacturerInfo"/>
 <wsdl: part name="purchaseOrder" type="sns:purchaseOrder"/>
</wsdl: message>
  … …
<wsdl: message name="OrderAcceptMessage">
 <wsdl: part name="OA" type="sns:OrderAcceptance"/>
</wsdl: message>
<wsdl: message name="POFaultType">
 <wsdl: part name="problemInfo" type="xsd:string"/>
</wsdl: message>

<!--portTypes supported by the purchase order process -->
  … …
<portType name="PurchasePortType">
 <operation name="SendPurchase">
  <input message="pos:POMessage"/>
  <output message="pos:InvMessage"/>
  <fault name="cannotCompleteOrder"
      message="pos:POFaultType"/>
 </operation>
</portType>
```

Purchase order process WSDL definitions

Listing 9.4 BPEL data variables for the purchase order process

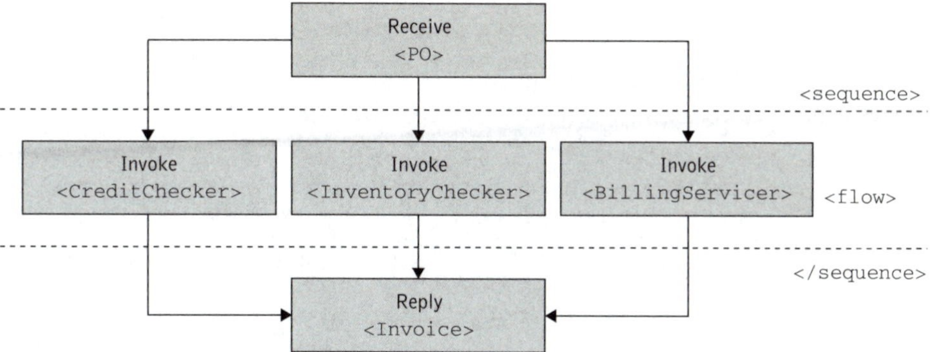

Figure 9.20 Sequencing and flow activities for the purchase order process

inventory check service and billing service providers in parallel; a billing service that bills the customer once credit and inventory checks have succeeded; and ultimately a response to the manufacturer from the supplier sending an invoice. This situation is represented pictorially in Figure 9.20.

In Listing 9.5 the structure of the main processing section is defined by the outer `<sequence>` element, which states that the activities contained inside it are performed in order. The manufacturer request is received (`<receive>` element), then processed (inside a `<flow>` section that enables concurrent asynchronous behavior by issuing multiple `<invoke>` activities), and a `reply` message with the final approval status of the request is sent back to the customer (`<reply>`). The `<invoke>` activity is used to call Web services offered by service providers via `<partnerLink>`s. All the activities that are contained within a `<flow>` element exhibit potentially concurrent behavior that is executed according to the dependencies expressed by `<link>` elements. The first step in the process flow is the initial manufacturer request. Once the request is received, there is a set of parallel activities that are executed using the `<flow>` element. Here, an inventory service is contacted in order to check the inventory, and a credit service is contacted in order to receive a credit check for the customer. Finally, a billing service is contacted to bill the customer. Each references a specific WSDL operation (e.g., `SendPurchase` or `CheckCredit`), and uses the available variables for input and output. Upon receiving the responses back from the credit, inventory, and billing services, the supplier would construct a message back to the customer. This could involve use of the XPath language to take the variables received from the service providers and build a final proposal to the buyer. Note that the `<receive>` and `<reply>` elements are matched respectively to the `<input>` and `<output>` messages of the `Purchase` operation invoked by the customer (see also Listing 9.4). The activities performed by the process between the `<receive>` and `<reply>` elements represent the actions taken in response to the customer request, from the time the request is received to the time the response is sent back (`reply`). The above example assumes that the customer request can be processed in a reasonable amount of time, justifying the requirement that the invoker must wait for a synchronous response (because this service is offered as a request/response operation).

The synchronization dependencies between activities contained within a `<flow>` in Listing 9.5 are expressed by using `<links>` to connect them. The `<links>` are defined

```
<sequence>
  <receive partnerLink="Purchasing"
                portType="lns:PurchaseOrderPortType"
                operation="SendPurchase" variable="PO"
                createInstance="yes" >
  </receive>
  <flow>
      <links>
            <link name="inventory-check"/>
            <link name="credit-check"/>
      </links>
      <!-- Check inventory -->
      <invoke partnerLink="inventoryChecker"
                 portType="lns:InventoryPortType"
                 operation="checkInventory"
                 inputVariable="inventoryRequest"
                 outputVariable="inventoryResponse">
                <source linkName="inventory-check"/>
                …
      </invoke>
      <!-- Check credit -->
      <invoke partnerLink="creditChecker"
                 portType="lns:CreditCheckPortType"
                 operation="checkCredit"
                 inputVariable="creditRequest"
                 outputVariable="creditResponse">
                <source linkName="credit-check"/>
                …
      </invoke>
      <!-- Issue bill once inventory and credit checks are
                                                  successful -->
      <invoke partnerLink="BillingService"
                 portType="lns:BillingPortType"
                                         operation="billClient"
                 inputVariable="billRequest"
                                       outputVariable="Invoice"
                 joinCondition="getLinkStatus
                                        ("inventory-check") AND
                             getLinkStatus("credit-check")">
                 <target linkName="inventory-check"/>
                 <target linkName="credit-check"/>
                 …
      </invoke>
  </flow>
    ...
  <reply partnerLink="Purchasing" portType="lns:purchaseOrderPT"
   operation="Purchase" variable="Invoice"/>
</sequence>
```

Listing 9.5 BPEL process flow for the purchase order process inside the <flow> and are used to connect a source activity to a target activity. Note that each activity declares itself as the source or target of a <link> by using the <source> and <target> elements. Note that the transition conditions attached to the <source> elements of the links determine which links get activated. In the absence of links, all activities nested directly inside a flow proceed concurrently. In the purchase order example, however, the presence of two links introduces control dependencies between the activities performed inside each sequence. The links `inventory-check` and `credit-check`, which are the <source> elements of the `invoke` activities `inventoryChecker` and `creditChecker`, are <target> elements for the `invoke` activity `billingService`. The `joinCondition` attribute in the `invoke` activity `billingService` performs a logical AND operation on the status of each incoming link and will, therefore, only allow this service to execute once all of its preceding activities (i.e., `inventoryChecker` and `creditChecker` invocations) have indicated that there are no problems with checks they performed. This is not indicated in Listing 9.5 (due to reasons of brevity and simplicity) but could be implemented as a `transitionCondition` on the `inventoryChecker` and `creditChecker` activity invocations.

9.7.2.4 Correlations

Figure 9.21 shows a graphical representation of a correlation, while Listing 9.6 shows a BPEL specification corresponding to this graphical representation. In particular, this figure shows that there exists a unique purchase order identifier for each purchase order forwarded by a manufacturer and received by a supplier and a unique number for each corresponding invoice created by the supplier. A manufacturer may start a correlated exchange with a supplier by sending a purchase order (PO) and using a PO id in the PO document as the correlation token. The supplier uses this PO id in the PO acknowledgement. The supplier may later send an invoice document that carries both the PO id, to correlate it with the original PO, and an invoice number. In this way future payment-related messages may carry only the invoice number as the correlation token. The invoice message thus carries two separate correlation tokens and participates in two overlapping correlated exchanges. The scope of correlation is not, in general, the entire interaction specified by a service, but may span a part of the service behavior.

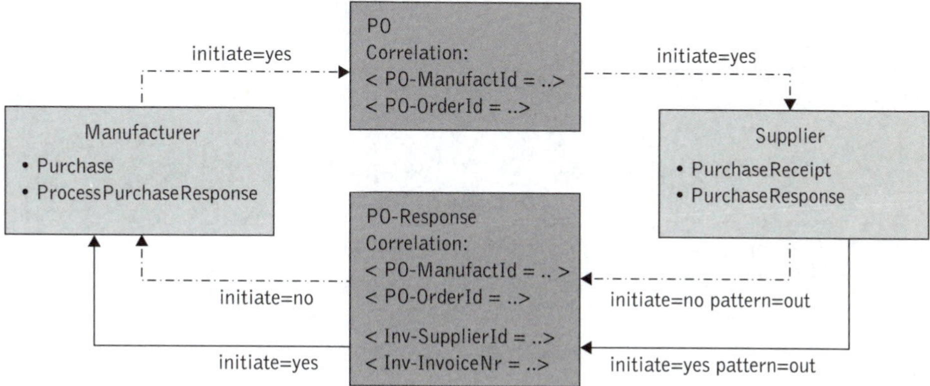

Figure 9.21 Correlation properties and sets for the purchase order (PO) process

```
<!-- define correlation properties -->
    <bpws:property name="manufactID" type="xsd:string"/>
    <bpws:property name="orderNumber" type="xsd:int"/>
    <bpws:property name="supplierID" type="xsd:string"/>
    <bpws:property name="invoiceNumber" type="xsd:int"/> …
 <!—define schema types and messages for PO and invoice
   information -->
 <types>
        <xsd:complexType name="PurchaseOrder">
            <xsd:element name="CID" type="xsd:string"/>
            <xsd:element name="order" type="xsd:int"/>
            ...
         </xsd:complexType>
         <xsd:complexType name="PurchaseOrderResponse">
            <xsd:element name="CID" type="xsd:string"/>
            <xsd:element name="order" type="xsd:int"/>
            ...
         </xsd:complexType>
 </types>
  <message name="POMessage">
        <part name="PO" type="tns:PurchaseOrder"/>
  </message>
  <message name="POResponse">
        <part name="RSP" type="tns:PurchaseOrderResponse"/>
  </message>
            …
 <correlationSets>
    <correlationSet name="POCorr" properties="cor:manufactId
     cor:orderId"/>
    <correlationSet name="InvoiceCorr" properties="cor:supplierId
     cor:invoiceNumber"/>

 </correlationSets> ...

 <receive partnerLink="Manufacturer"
                                   portType="POSubmissionPortType"
      operation="SubmitPurchase" variable="PO">
   <correlations>
      <correlation set="POCorr" initiate="yes">
   </correlations>
 </receive> …

 <invoke partnerLink="Manufacturer"
                                  portType="orderCallbackPortType"
     operation="PurchaseResponse" inputVariable="POResponse">
 <correlations>
    <correlation set="POCorr" initiate="no" pattern="out">
    <correlation set="InvoiceCorr" initiate="yes" pattern="out">
 </correlations>
</invoke> …
```

Listing 9.6 Code fragment representing constructs in Figure 9.21

Correlation set names are shown in this listing to be used in invoke and receive activities. These sets are used to indicate which correlation sets occur in the messages being sent and received. The example in Listing 9.6 shows an interaction in which a PO is received in a one-way inbound request and a confirmation including an invoice is sent in the asynchronous response. The PO `correlationSet` is used in both activities so that the asynchronous response can be correlated to the request. The `<receive>` activity initiates the PO `correlationSet`. As previously explained, in BPEL the partner starting a message exchange and creating the property values is called the initiator. The other partners are followers of the message exchange. The manufacturer is therefore the initiator and the receiving business process (supplier) is a follower for the PO `correlationSet`. The `<invoke>` activity sending the asynchronous response also initiates a new `correlationSet` invoice. The `<invoke>` activity specifies the WSDL `<portType>` and operation to be invoked from the partner (manufacturer) and also that the PO `correlationSet` has been initialized prior to this activity. The business process is in this case the initiator of this correlated exchange and the manufacturer is a follower. The response message in the listing is thus a part of two separate conversations which it links up.

9.7.2.5 Fault handling and compensations

Listing 9.7 illustrates the case where there is an error when a manufacturer submits a purchase order. In this situation the supplier may use a fault handler (`"OrderNotComplete"`) employing a `<reply>` element to return a fault to the manufacturer.

```
<faultHandlers>
 <catch faultName="OrderNotComplete"
        faultVariable="POFault">
  <reply partnerLink="Manufacturer"
         portType="PurchasePortType"
         operation="Purchase"
         variable="POFault"
         faultName="OrderNotComplete"/>
 </catch>
</faultHandlers>
```

Listing 9.7 A simple fault handler for the PO process

To exemplify the concept of compensation handling consider the case where a purchase is made and this purchase needs to be canceled. This situation is shown in Listing 9.8. In this example, the original `invoke` activity makes a purchase and in case that purchase needs to be compensated, the `compensationHandler` invokes a cancellation operation at the same port of the same WSDL `partner`, using the response to the purchase order as its input.

```
<invoke partnerLink="Seller" portType="SP:Purchasing"
        operation="SyncPurchase"
        inputVariable="sendPO"
        outputVariable="getResponse">
   <correlations>
       <correlation set="PurchaseOrder" initiate="yes"
        pattern="out"/>
   </correlations>
   <compensationHandler>
     <invoke partnerLink="Seller" portType="SP:Purchasing"
          operation="CancelPurchase"
          inputVariable="getResponse"
          outputVariable="getConfirmation">
        <correlations>
           <correlation set="PurchaseOrder" pattern="out"/>
        </correlations>
      </invoke>
  </compensationHandler>
</invoke>
```

Listing 9.8 Possible compensation activity

The BPEL specification suggests WS-Transaction (see Chapter 10) as the protocol of choice for coordinating distributed transactions across workflow instances. Thus, when a scope containing invocations on a partner's Web services is compensated, the underlying BPEL engine should ensure that the appropriate WS-Transaction messages are sent to the transaction coordinator so that any partner's systems can be informed of the need to compensate the invoked activities.

9.8 Choreography

Business applications that involve multiple organizations or independent processes are engaged in a collaborative fashion to achieve a common business goal such as order management. For the collaboration to work successfully, long-lived, peer-to-peer message interchanges between the participating services, i.e. choreographies, within or across the trusted domains of an organization must be performed. The primary goals of a choreography definition are: to verify at run-time that all message interchanges are proceeding according to plan, and to guarantee that changes in the implementations of services are still in compliance with the message interchange definition.

9.8.1 Uses of choreography description

A choreography description is a multi-party contract that describes from a global viewpoint the external observable behavior across multiple clients (which are generally Web services) in which external observable behavior is defined as the presence or absence of messages that are exchanged between a Web service and its clients. As such choreography is not an executable business process description language or an implementation language, such as Java or C#, it is rather monitored and validated (or invalidated). Its role is to specify truly interoperable peer-to-peer collaborations between any type of party regardless of the supporting platform or programming model used by the implementation of the hosting environment.

Figure 9.12 illustrates how a business choreography language relates to the business process languages layer. A choreography description language (CDL) is the means by which multi-party collaborations are described. Figure 9.12 illustrates that a GUI and a toolset are used to specify interactions between a manufacturer and supplier and generate a WS-CDL representation (see next section). This WS-CDL representation can then be used to generate a BPEL workflow template for both the manufacturer and supplier reflecting the nature of their business agreement.

The main use of a choreography description is to precisely define the sequence of interactions between a set of cooperating Web services in order to promote a common understanding between participants and to make it possible to validate conformance, ensure interoperability, and to generate code skeletons [Austin 2004]. A choreography description can be used to generate the necessary code skeletons that implement the required external observable behavior for those Web services. For example, a choreography description that is used to describe the multi-party contract between a manufacturing company, a number of potential suppliers, and a number of distributors might be used by any potential participant to generate a code skeleton for a Web service that can be guaranteed to be interoperable with that particular manufacturing company.

9.8.2 Web Services Choreography Description Language

The Web Services Choreography Description Language is an XML specification suitable for composing interoperable, long-running, peer-to-peer collaboration between any type of party regardless of the supporting platform or programming model used by the implementation of the hosting environment. WS-CDL describes the global view of observable behavior of message exchange of all Web services participants that are involved in the business collaboration. Using the WS-CDL specification a contract containing a "global" definition of the common ordering conditions and constraints under which messages are exchanged is produced that describes from a global viewpoint the common and complementary observable behavior of all the parties involved. Each party can then use the global definition to build and test solutions that conform to it. WS-CDL is purely for specifying "abstract business processes," independent of platform and programming languages that are used to implement the Web services participation.

In the WS-CDL specification, the message interchanges take place in a jointly agreed set of ordering and constraint rules. Choreography definitions can involve two (binary) or more (multi-party) participants. WS-CDL describes a global view of the message interchange without taking any participants' point of view, unlike the BPEL abstract process that takes the point of view of one participant. This approach is a lot more scalable when the number of participants increases. However, and like BPEL, WS-CDL is an infrastructure specification which does not contain any business semantics (e.g., resources, commitments, agreements, and so on).

A choreography definition in WS-CDL is always defined abstractly between *roles* which are later bound to *participants*. Roles are related to each other via *relationships*. A relationship is always between exactly two roles. A participant may implement any number of non-opposite roles in the choreography. A distributor may implement the buyer-to-manufacturer and seller-to-customer roles, which is yet different from the seller-to-distributor role. Roles in WS-CDL are somewhat similar to `<partnerLink>`s in BPEL.

Choreographies are composed of activities. The main activity is called an *interaction* and is the basic building block of a choreography, which results in the exchange of messages between participants and possible synchronization of their states and the actual values of the exchanged information. Interactions specify the unit of message exchange between roles. An interaction corresponds to the invocation of a Web service operation on a role. Consequently, an interaction is defined as a request with zero or more responses. Interactions can involve ordering activities (*sequence, parallel, choice*) or can compose another choreography in the parent choreography. Choreography definitions may be data driven, i.e. the data contained in the messages impacts the ordering of interactions. Data is modeled as *variables*, which may be associated to message content, a *channel*, or the *state* of roles involved in the choreography. *Tokens* are aliases that may represent parts of a variable. Tokens in WS-CDL relate to the concept of properties in a BPEL correlation set.

A WS-CDL document is simply a set of definitions. The WS-CDL definitions are named constructs that can be referenced. There is a *package* element at the root, and individual choreography definitions inside it. A WS-CDL package contains a set of one or more choreographies and a set of one or more collaboration type definitions. The WS-CDL package construct allows aggregation of a set of choreography definitions.

The example in Listing 9.9 shows a sample choreography specified in WS-CDL. The `<package>` element is shown to contain exactly one top-level `<choreography>`, which is explicitly marked as the root `<choreography>`. This root choreography can be

```
<package name="ManufacturerSupplierChoreography" version="1.0"
    <informationType name="purchaseOrderType"
                     type="pons:PurchaseOrderMsg"/>
    <informationType name="purchaseOrderAckType"
                     type="pons:PurchaseOrderAckMsg"/>
    <token name="purchaseOrderID" informationType="tns:intType"/>
    <token name="supplierRef" informationType="tns:uriType"/> ......
    <role name="Manufacturer">
         <behavior name="manufacturerForSupplier"
                   interface="cns:ManufacturerSupplierPT"/>
         <behavior name="manufacturerForWarehouse"
                   interface="cns:SupplierWarehousePT"/>
    </role>
    <role name="Supplier">
         <behavior name="supplierForManufacturer"
                   interface="rns:ManufacturerSupplierPT"/>
    </role>
```

```
        <relationship name="ManufacturerSupplierRelationship">
              <role type="tns:Manufacturer" behavior=
                                              "manufacturerForSupplier"/>
              <role type="tns:Supplier"
                                    behavior="supplierForManufacturer"/>
        </relationship>
        <channelType name="ManufacturerChannel">
              <role type="tns:Manufacturer"/>
              <reference>
                  <token type="tns:manufacturerRef"/>
              </reference>
               <identity>
                   <token type="tns:purchaseOrderID"/>
               </identity>
        </channelType> ......
        <choreography name="ManufacturerSupplierChoreo" root="true">
           <relationship type="tns:ManufacturerSupplierRelationship"/>
           <variableDefinitions>
           <variable name="purchaseOrder"
                     informationType="tns:purchaseOrderType"/> ......
           <variable name="supplier-channel"
                                     channelType="tns:supplierChannel"/>
                  ...
           <interaction channelVariable="tns:supplier-channel"
                        operation="handlePurchaseOrder"
                        align="true"initiateChoreography="true">
              <participate
                relationship="tns:ManufacturerSupplierRelationship"
                fromRole="tns:Manufacturer" toRole="tns:Supplier "/>
              <exchange messageContentType="tns:purchaseOrderType"
                        action="request"/>
                  <use variable="cdl:getVariable(tns:purchaseOrder,
                       tns:Manufacturer)"/>
                 <populate variable="cdl:getVariable
                            (tns:purchaseOrder,tns:Supplier)"/>
              </exchange>
              <exchange messageContentType="purchaseOrderAckType"
                        action="respond">
                  <use variable="cdl:getVariable
                       (tns:purchaseOrderAck,tns:Supplier)"/>
                  <populate variable="cdl:getVariable
                             (tns:purchaseOrderAck,tns:Manufacturer)"/>
              </exchange>
             <record role="tns: Supplier "action="request">
                 <source variable="cdl:getVariable(tns:purchaseOrder,
                         PO/Manufacturer Ref, tns: Supplier)"/>
                 <target variable="cdl:getVariable
                         (tns:manufacturer-channel,tns:Supplier)"/>
             </record>
          </interaction>
      </choreography>
    </package>
```

Listing 9.9 A sample choreography in WS-CDL

initiated and is shown to involve one interaction. The interaction happens from role manufacturer to role supplier on the channel "supplier-channel" as a request/response message exchange. In this listing the message purchaseOrder is sent from a manufacturer to a supplier as a request message while the message purchaseOrderAck is sent from a supplier to a manufacturer as a response message.

The <variable> consumer-channel is populated at a supplier at the end of the request using the <record> element. The element <record> is used to create/change one or more states at both the roles at the ends of the <interaction>. For example, the PurchaseOrder message contains the channel of the <role> "manufacturer" when sent to the <role> "supplier". This can be copied into the appropriate state variable of the "supplier" within the <record> element. When align is set to "true" for the <interaction>, it also means that the manufacturer knows that the supplier now has the address of the manufacturer. Another use case of the <record> element is that it can be used to record the states at each <role>. The manufacturer sets the state "OrderSent" to "true" and the retailer sets the state "OrderReceived" to "true" at the end of the request part of the <interaction>. Similarly, the customer sets "OrderAcknowledged" "true" at the end of the <interaction>. The <source> and the <target> elements within the <record> element represent the <variable> names related to the <role> element that is specified in the role attribute of the <record> element.

In Listing 9.9 the <interaction> activity happens on the supplier channel which has a <token> purchaseOrderID used as an identity of the channel. This identity element is used to identify the business process of the supplier. The request message purchaseOrder contains the identity of the supplier business process, while the response message purchaseOrderAck contains the identity of the manufacturer business process.

WS-CDL represents an important new layer of the Web services stack that complements BPEL. AS WS-CDL is still in its early phase in the W3C specification process, it is difficult to picture exactly what the final recommendation will be and whether or not the OASIS BPEL and W3C WS-CDL Working Group will come to an agreement on how the two standards would work together.

9.9 Other initiatives and languages

Several XML-based process definition languages besides BPEL and WS-CDL have been proposed over the past few years. Each of these provides a model for expressing executable processes, which addresses all aspects of enterprise business processes, and is based on differing paradigms. In the following we shall examine briefly two such initiatives: XML Process Definition Language (XPDL) and Business Process Modeling Language (BPML).

XPDL (**http://www.wfmc.org/standards/XPDL.htm**) was proposed by the Workflow Management Coalition (WfMC) as the mechanism for process definition interchange between different workflow products. XPDL forms a common interchange standard that enables products to continue to support arbitrary internal representations of process definitions with an import/export function to map to/from the standard at the product boundary. A variety of different mechanisms may be used to transfer process definition data between systems according to the characteristics of the various business scenarios. The process definition is expressed in a consistent form, which is derived from the common set of objects, relationships, and attributes expressing its underlying concepts. The XPDL process definition can be generated by workflow modeling and simulation tools, or can be manually coded, or can be exported from another XPDL-compliant workflow engine.

BPML (**http://www.bpmi.org/BPML.htm**) is an XML-based meta-language developed by the Business Process Management Initiative (BPMI) as a means of modeling business processes. BPML (already outdated) defines a formal model for expressing abstract and executable processes that address all aspects of enterprise business processes, including activities of varying complexity, transactions and their compensation, data management, concurrency, exception handling, and operational semantics. The BPML specification provides an abstract model and XML syntax for expressing business processes and supporting entities. BPML itself does not define any application semantics such as particular processes or application of processes in a specific domain; rather it defines an abstract model and grammar for expressing generic processes.

A useful comparison of XPDL, BPML, and BPEL can be found in [Shapiro 2002].

9.10 Summary

A business process specifies the shared data passed between services, the trading partners' roles with respect to the process, joint exception handling conditions for the collection of Web services, and other factors that may influence how Web services or organizations that participate in a process. Process-oriented workflows are used to automate business processes whose structure is well defined and stable over time. The business process workflow is made up of activities that are implemented as a set of scoped operations that may span multiple Web services. These Web-services-centric activities follow routes with checkpoints represented by business conditions and rules.

To specify how individual Web services can be composed to create reliable and dependable business process-based solutions with the appropriate level of complexity, various Web services composition languages have emerged. Service composition languages span service orchestration and service choreography. Service orchestration describes how Web services can interact with each other at the message level from the perspective and under control of a single endpoint. In contrast to orchestration, choreography is typically associated with peer-to-peer collaborations of Web services participants by defining from a global viewpoint their common and complementary observable behavior, where information exchanges occur, when jointly agreed ordering rules are satisfied.

The Business Process Execution Language for Web Services has recently emerged as the standard to define and manage business process activities and business interaction protocols comprising collaborating Web services from an orchestration point of view.

The Web Services Choreography Description Language is an XML specification targeted at describing the global view of observable behavior of message exchange of all Web services participants that are involved in the business collaboration.

Review questions

- Briefly describe the major characteristics of automated business processes.
- List and describe the main components of a workflow system.
- Give an example of a workflow application using UML.
- What is business process integration and how does it differ from business process management?
- Describe the purpose of cross-enterprise business processes and their relationship to workflow systems.
- What is the purpose of a service composition meta-model?
- What is a flow model and what are control links and transition conditions?
- How are Web services composed?
- What are Web services orchestration and choreography languages? How do they differ from each other?
- List and describe the main components of BPEL.
- How does BPEL orchestrate Web services?
- What is the purpose of WS-CDL and how can it work with BPEL?

Exercises

9.1 Further develop the sample BPEL process in section 9.7.2 to include credit check and billing service providers.

9.2 Develop an abstract BPEL process for a simplified shipping service. This service handles the shipment of orders, which are composed of a number of items. The shipping service should offer two options, one for shipments where the items are shipped all together, and one for partial shipments where the items are shipped in groups until the order is fulfilled.

9.3 Extend the BPEL process in Exercise 9.1 to offer an inventory check service, consumed by the BPEL process that provisions the purchase order service. When the purchase order service provider receives the client request, the following events should occur:

(a) The purchase order service provider assigns the price and the current date of the request, and

(b) invokes the inventory service to check inventory status.

(c) The inventory service checks the availability of an item and reports to the purchase order service provider.

(d) Based on the result from the inventory service, the purchase order service provider responds either by fulfilling the purchase order or by issuing a fault stating that the order cannot be completed.

Develop your solution by assuming the service client and inventory check service provider use exclusively synchronous operations.

9.4 In your solution for the previous exercise replace all synchronous operations with asynchronous operations that achieve the same results.

9.5 Develop a simple BPEL process for travel booking. This process should be partially based on Exercises 5.3, 5.4, and 5.5 and involve interactions with partners such as flight, hotel, and car reservation services as well as a simple credit checking service.

9.6 Use BPEL to develop a simple application involving a credit card holder and an electronic merchant. The card holder sends a message containing the order instructions and payment details to the merchant. The merchant then initiates a payment authorization request at its bank to determine whether or not the purchase request contains valid information about the buyer's account and financial status. If authorization of payment is successful then the merchant receives a payment approval response and dispatches the ordered goods to the purchaser.

CHAPTER 10

Transaction processing

Learning objectives

In situations where business processes need to drive their collaboration to achieve a shared business task by enabling highly fluid networks of collaborating Web services, transactional support may be needed. This kind of support is required in order to orchestrate loosely coupled services into cohesive units of work and guarantee consistent and reliable execution. However, classical atomic transactions and extended transaction models based on them are far too constraining – by virtue of being short running and synchronous – for loosely coupled applications as these rely on long-lived activities and services that are disjoint in both time and location.

In this chapter we focus on the features, requirements of, and architectural support for transactional Web services. After completing this chapter readers will understand the following key concepts:

- Transaction support for both centralized and distributed systems.
- Distributed transaction architectures.
- Concurrency control and coordination mechanisms for distributed transactions.
- Closed and open nested transactions.
- Transactional workflows.
- Properties and models of transactional Web services.
- Transactional Web services standards and frameworks that work with other Web services standards, such as BPEL, WS-Policy, and WS-Security.

10.1 What is a transaction?

Transaction processing systems are widely used by enterprises to support mission-critical applications. These applications need to store and update data reliably, provide concurrent access to data by large numbers of users, and maintain data integrity despite failures of individual system components. Given the complexity of contemporary business requirements, transaction processing occupies one of the most complex and important segments of business-level distributed applications to build, deploy, and maintain.

A transaction is a series of operations performed as a single unit of work that either completely succeeds, or fails with all partially completed work being undone. By tying a set of related operations together in a transaction, one can ensure the consistency and reliability of the system despite any errors that occur. All operations in a transaction must complete successfully in order to make the transaction successful.

A transaction has a beginning and an end that specify its boundary within which it can span processes and machines. Application programs must be able to start and end transactions, and be able to indicate whether data changes are to be made permanent or discarded. Indicating transaction boundaries for an application program is called *transaction demarcation*.

An *atomic transaction* is a computation consisting of a collection of operations that take place indivisibly in the presence of both failures and concurrent computations. That is, either all of the operations prevail or none of them prevails, and other programs executing concurrently cannot modify or observe intermediate states of the computation. A transaction ends when one of two things happens: either the transaction is committed by the application; or the transaction is rolled back by application or system failure, or when a commit operation fails (e.g., due to inadequate resources or data consistency violations). If the transaction successfully commits, changes associated with that specific transaction will be written to persistent storage and made visible to new transactions. If the transaction is rolled back, all changes made by it will be discarded; it will be as if the transaction never happened at all.

In the pseudo-code shown in Figure 10.1, the `begin transaction` statement begins a new transaction. A transaction can end either by committing changes to the database using the `commit transaction` statement or by undoing all the changes if any error occurs using the `rollback transaction` statement. Operations are of two types: operations that read from the database and operations that update (write) some data items in the database.

Figure 10.2 illustrates a state transition diagram for a transaction. In this diagram a transaction is shown to have the following states:

- *Active:* This state indicates that the transaction is performing some work (operations). A transaction enters this state immediately after it starts execution.
- *Partially committed:* A transaction that has executed its final (`end transaction`) statement. At this stage, recovery protocols need to be tested to ensure that a system failure will not result in an inability to record the changes of the transaction permanently. In case this check is successful, any updates can be safely recorded and the transaction can move to the `committed` state. If any of these checks fail then the transaction transits to the `failed` state.

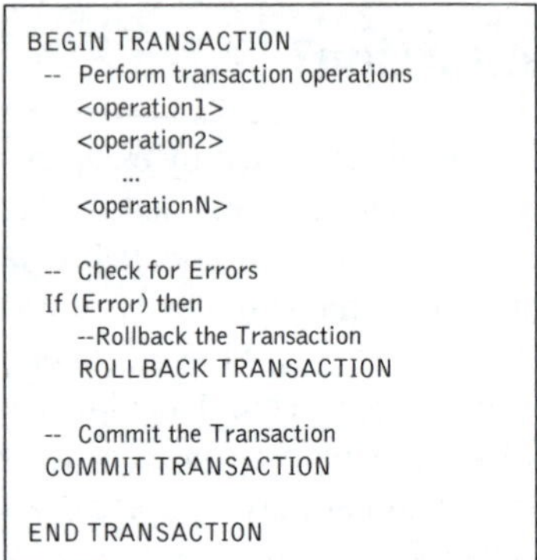

```
BEGIN TRANSACTION
  -- Perform transaction operations
     <operation1>
     <operation2>
        ...
     <operationN>

  -- Check for Errors
  If (Error) then
     --Rollback the Transaction
     ROLLBACK TRANSACTION

  -- Commit the Transaction
  COMMIT TRANSACTION

END TRANSACTION
```

Figure 10.1 Transaction structure

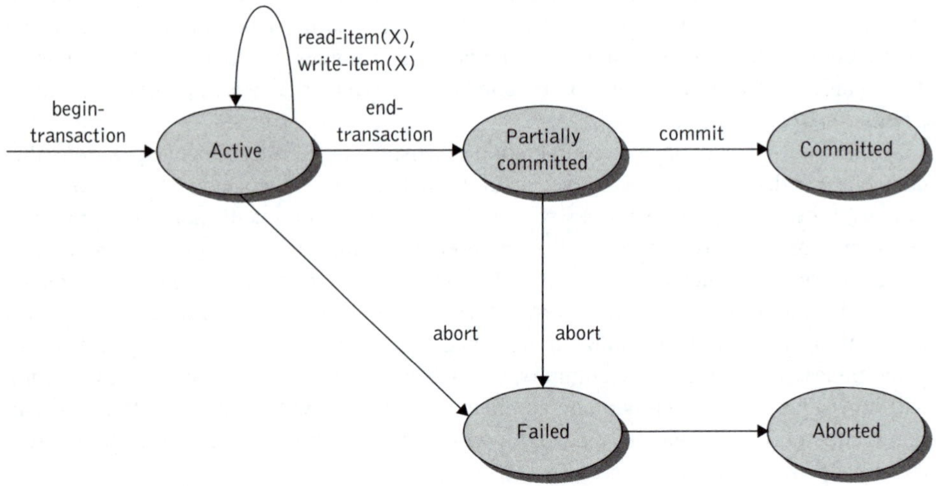

Figure 10.2 State transition diagram for a transaction

- *Committed:* A transaction that has performed all of its work successfully and terminated is said to have committed by making its changes permanent in persistent storage.
- *Failed:* A transaction that was initially in active state but cannot be committed.
- *Aborted:* A transaction that does not execute successfully and rolls back all of the work it has performed. This can happen either due to a recovery check failure or if the transaction is aborted during its active state.

10.1.1 Properties of transactions

To maintain consistency across resources within a transaction boundary, a transaction must exhibit ACID properties, namely Atomicity, Consistency, Isolation, and Durability.

Atomicity means that a transaction is an indivisible unit of work: either all of the operations of a transaction are applied to the application state, or none of them is applied. If the transaction cannot complete successfully, it will roll back to the state before the beginning of the transaction.

Consistency means that the transaction must correctly transition data from one consistent state to another, preserving the data semantics and referential integrity. This means that any integrity constraints implicit in the application are not violated by the transaction. In practice, the notion of consistency is application specific. For example, in an accounting application, consistency would include the integrity constraint that the sum of all asset accounts equals the sum of all liability accounts.

When multiple transactions execute concurrently, one transaction may want to read or write the same data another transaction has changed but not committed. Until the latter transaction commits, the changes it has made should be treated as transient state, because it could roll back these changes. *Isolation* requires that several concurrent transactions must produce the same results in the data as those same transactions executed sequentially, in some (unspecified) order. Isolation guarantees that the execution of concurrent transactions is controlled and coordinated since they are accessing a shared database and may potentially interfere with one another. Concurrent transactions are executed in a manner that gives the illusion that each transaction is executing in isolation while in reality it may work concurrently with other transactions on the same database items. Isolation is generally implemented using a locking mechanism.

Durability means that committed updates are made permanent. Failures that occur after a commit cause no loss of data. Durability also implies that data for all committed transactions can be recovered after a system or media failure.

Atomic transactions are useful for activities that manipulate data, transform data from one or more sources to one or more targets, or coordinate multiple transaction participants (for more detail, see section 10.2.2). The all-or-nothing (atomicity) guarantee ensures that all data changes and messages exchanged in the context of the transaction retain their consistency, regardless of how many steps are required in order to complete the transaction.

10.1.2 Concurrency control mechanisms

When transactions execute concurrently, for instance in financial or commercial applications where there is a need for multiple applications to access the same database at the same time, they may interfere with each other and cause the database to become inconsistent. This may happen despite the fact that the transactions preserve individually the consistency of the database.

When two or more transactions are executing concurrently, their database operations *interleave*. This means that operations from one transaction may execute in between operations from another transaction and thus interfere with them. This interleaving can cause serious problems by corrupting the consistency of data, thereby leading the database to an inconsistent state. The objective of concurrency control is to combat this interference and thereby avoid any potential errors.

Concurrency control is a method for the management of contention for data resources. This mechanism is used to ensure that database transactions are executed in a safe manner (i.e., without loss of data). Concurrency control is especially applicable to relational databases and database management systems, which must ensure that transactions are executed safely and that they follow the ACID rules. The database management system must be able to ensure that only serializable, recoverable schedules are allowed, and that no actions of committed transactions are lost while undoing aborted transactions.

A *serializable schedule* is a schedule, *S*, of some set of concurrently executing transactions that is the equivalent (or has the same effects) of some (serial) schedule, S_{ser}, that executes the transactions of that set sequentially. Informally speaking, what is required is that in both schedules the values returned by the corresponding read operations are the same and updates to each data item occur in the same order.

This means that if the read operations return the same values in *S* and S_{ser} the computations of the transactions will be identical in both schedules and consequently the transactions will write the same values back to the database. Given that the write operations occur in the same order in both schedules, *S* will have the same effect as (and therefore is equivalent to) S_{ser}.

Serial equivalence, when applied to a transaction, means that when a number of transactions are applied concurrently the effect of these transactions will be the same as if they were applied sequentially (or one after the other). This, in effect, provides a hard requirement for the transaction server that ensures that effects of such inconsistent updates do not occur. Typical problems here include the dirty read, the lost update problem, the inconsistent update, and the cascading abort problems [Ullman 1988].

Traditionally concurrency mechanisms for database systems can be managed by means of locking. When a concurrency control mechanism uses locks, transactions must request and release locks in addition to reading and writing data items. At the most fundamental level, locks can be classified into (in an increasingly restrictive order) shared, update, and exclusive locks. A *shared* (or read) lock signifies that another transaction can take an update or another shared lock on the same piece of data. Shared locks are used when data is read. If a transaction locks a piece of data with an *exclusive* (write) lock, it signifies its intention to write this data item and no other transaction may take a lock on the same item. Some database systems provide an *update* lock, which can be used by transactions that initially want to read a data item but later may want to update it. An update lock allows a transaction to read but not write a data item and indicates that the lock is likely to be upgraded later to a write lock. An update lock ensures that another transaction can take only a shared lock on the same data item. To achieve transaction consistency the following two general rules must apply [Garcia-Molina 2002]:

1. A transaction can only read or write a data item if it previously requested a lock on that item and has not yet released that lock.
2. If a transaction locks a data item it must later unlock that data item.

Most concurrency control mechanisms in commercial systems implement serializability using a *strict two-phase locking protocol* [Eswaran 1976]. This protocol uses locks associated with items in the database and requires that a transaction acquires the appropriate lock (read or write) before it accesses a specific data item in the database for either reading or writing. Once a transaction needs to read (or write) a data item, it must be granted a read (or write) lock (as the case may be) on this data item before it can perform this operation. The locks on a transaction can be released only after the transaction has committed/aborted. This version has the disadvantage that some locks may be maintained longer than they are needed; however, it eliminates all kinds of anomalies. Proofs of the fact that a concurrency control mechanism that uses a strict two-phase locking protocol produces only serializable schedules can be found in [Ullman 1988].

Transaction isolation levels are achieved by taking locks on the data items that they access until the transaction completes. There are two general mechanisms for managing concurrency control by taking locks: pessimistic and optimistic. These two modes are necessitated by the fact that when a transaction accesses data, its intention to change (or not change) the data may not be readily apparent. A concurrency control scheme is considered *pessimistic* when it locks a given data resource early in the data access transaction – to prevent more than one application from updating the database simultaneously – and does not release it until the transaction is closed (see section 10.3.1.2). A concurrency control scheme is considered *optimistic* when it is based on the assumption that database transactions mostly do not conflict with other transactions, and that allows this scheme to be as permissive as possible in allowing transactions to execute. Under optimistic concurrency, control locks are not obtained, thus allowing for maximum concurrency in reading and a read is performed immediately before a write to ensure that the data item in question has not changed in the interim. There are three phases in the optimistic concurrency control scheme: a read phase, a validation phase, and a write phase. In the read phase the required data items are read from the database and write operations are performed on local copies of these items. During the validation phase a check for serializability is performed. When a transaction commits, the database checks if the transaction could have possibly conflicted with any other concurrent transaction. If there is a possibility of conflict, the transaction aborts, and is restarted. Otherwise, the transaction commits and the data items modified by the transaction are written into the database (write phase). If there are few conflicts, validation can be done efficiently, and leads to better performance than other concurrency control methods. Unfortunately, if there are many conflicts, the cost of repeatedly restarting transactions impacts performance significantly. The objective of optimistic concurrency is to minimize the time over which a given resource would be unavailable for use by other transactions. This is especially important with long-running transactions (for more detail, see section 10.4.3.2), which under a pessimistic scheme would lock up a resource for unacceptably long periods of time.

10.2 Distributed transactions

In today's complex distributed environments, transactions are fundamental to many distributed operations. Consider, for example, the guaranteed delivery and ordering of a series of messages exchanged between two distributed application components. In this scenario, the message exchange should take place within an atomic execution sequence.

Atomic transactions greatly simplify the coding of distributed applications. Atomic transactions are mechanisms for building reliable distributed systems in the presence of failures. As we already explained, they provide two important properties: recoverability and serializability. Recoverability implies that actions in a transaction exhibit an "all-or-nothing" behavior: an action either executes to completion, in which case it commits, or has no effect on the persistent state of a database, in which case it aborts. Serializability implies that the actual effect of executing transactions concurrently is equivalent to the effect of executing these actions in some serial order. Recoverability thus protects from failures, while serializability allows reasoning about concurrency by considering the effect of each action separately.

Typically, transaction semantics are provided by some underlying system infrastructure (usually in the form of products such as Transaction Processing Monitors [Gray 1993]). This infrastructure deals with failures, and performs the necessary recovery actions to guarantee the property of atomicity. Applications programming is therefore greatly simplified since the programmer does not have to deal with a multitude of possible failure scenarios.

Distributed transaction processing provides the necessary mechanism to combine multiple software components into a cooperating unit that can maintain shared data, potentially spanning multiple physical processors or locations, or both. This enables construction of applications that manipulate data consistently using multiple products that can easily be scaled by adding additional hardware and software components.

A *distributed transaction* bundles multiple operations in which at least two network hosts are involved. Distributed transactions can span heterogeneous transaction-aware data resources and may include a wide range of activities such as retrieving data from an SQL Server database, reading messages from a message queue server, and writing to other databases. A distributed transaction is simply a transaction that accesses and updates data on two or more networked resources, and therefore must be coordinated among those resources. Programming of distributed transactions is simplified by software, such as TP Monitors, that coordinates commit and abort behavior and recovery across several data resources.

10.2.1 Distributed transaction architectures

The components involved in the distributed transaction processing model that are relevant to our discussion are (Figure 10.3): the application program, the application server, the resource manager, the resource adapter, and the transaction manager.

The simplest form of distributed transaction processing involves only the application program, a resource manager, and an application server. The application program implements the desired function of the end-user enterprise, e.g., an order processing application. Each application program specifies a sequence of operations that involves shared resources such as databases. An application program defines the start and end of transactions, accesses to resources within transaction boundaries, and normally makes the decision whether to commit or roll back each transaction.

A resource manager provides and manages access to shared resources. These may be accessed using services that the resource manager provides. Examples for the resource manager are database management systems, a file access method such as X/Open ISAM, and a print server. To simplify the discussion, we concentrate in this section only on examples involving relational databases systems. The resource manager could thus be a relational database management system (RDBMS), such as Oracle or SQL Server. All of the actual database management is handled by this component.

A resource adapter (see section 2.7.1) is a software component that allows application components to access and interact with the underlying resource manager of a specific resource, e.g., a relational database. Because a resource adapter is specific to its resource

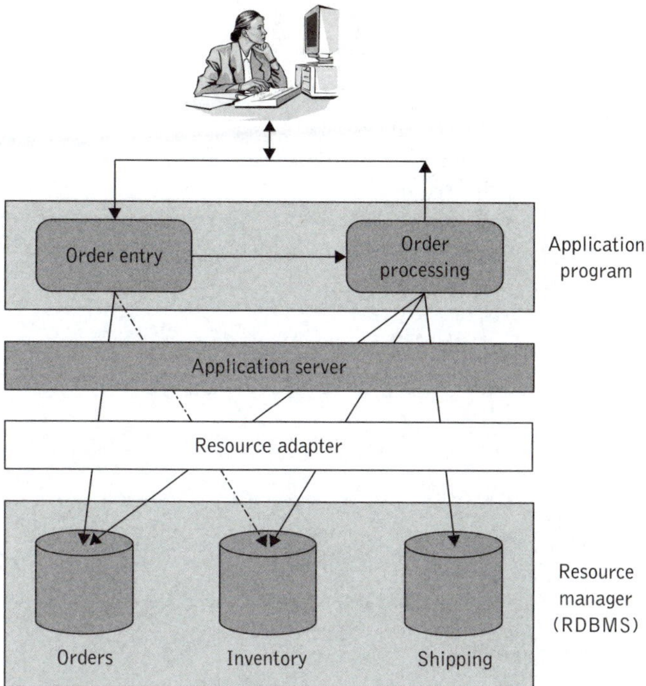

Figure 10.3 Transaction architecture involving only local transactions

manager, typically there is a different resource adapter for each type of database or enterprise information system, such as an enterprise resource planning or legacy system (managing transactions, external functionality, and data). The resource adapter is the component that is the communications channel, or request translator, between the "outside world," in this case a transactional application, and the resource manager.

Transactions that are managed internal to a resource manager are called *local transactions*. If a single resource manager participates in a transaction the application server usually lets the resource manager coordinate the transaction internally. The application program (client) sends a request for data to the resource adapter via an application server. Application servers handle the bulk of application operations and initiate transactions on behalf of clients. The application server handles "house-keeping" activities such as the network connections, protocol negotiation, and other advanced functionality such as transaction management, security, database connection pooling, and so on. The resource adapter then translates the request and sends it across the network to the RDBMS. The RDBMS returns the data to the resource adapter, which then translates the result to the application. This situation is illustrated in Figure 10.4, where an application issues transactional requests (such as `order entry` and `order processing`) against three relational databases (`orders`, `inventory`, and `shipping`) that are housed on a single server and are managed within the confines of a single resource manager. Solid arrows indicate activities that both read and write from the database while dashed arrows denote a read operation.

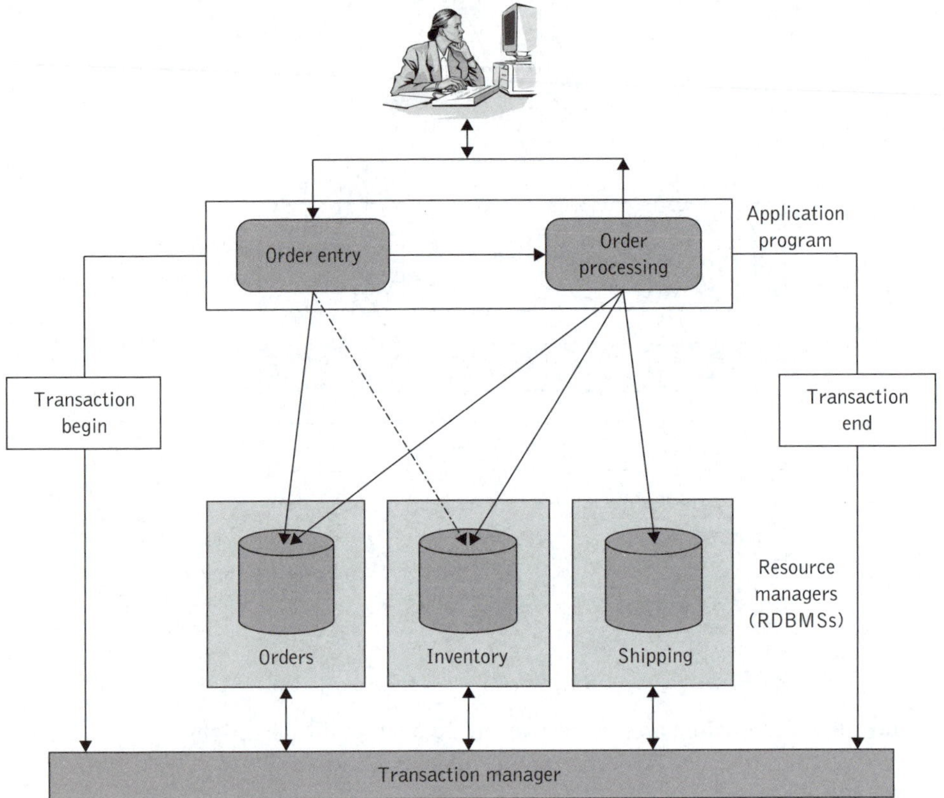

Figure 10.4 Distributed transaction architecture

The above example illustrates a single, local transaction and describes four components involved in a distributed transaction model. An additional fifth component, the transaction manager, comes into consideration only when transactions are to be distributed. The transaction manager is the intermediary between the clients and/or application server and the distributed transaction functionality.

In enterprise computing, it is often the case that several network resources (hosts) are involved, each hosting different servers, e.g., Web servers, several different RDBMSs, EJB servers, or Java Message Service (JMS) servers. A distributed transaction involves coordination among the various resource managers, which is the function of the transaction manager. Transaction demarcation enables work done by distributed application components to be bound by a distributed transaction.

A transaction manager works with applications and application servers to provide services to control the scope and duration of distributed transactions. A transaction manager also helps coordinate the completion of distributed transactions across multiple transactional resource managers (e.g., DBMSs), provides support for transaction synchronization and recovery, and coordinates the decision to start distributed transactions and commit them or roll them back. This ensures atomic transaction completion. A transaction

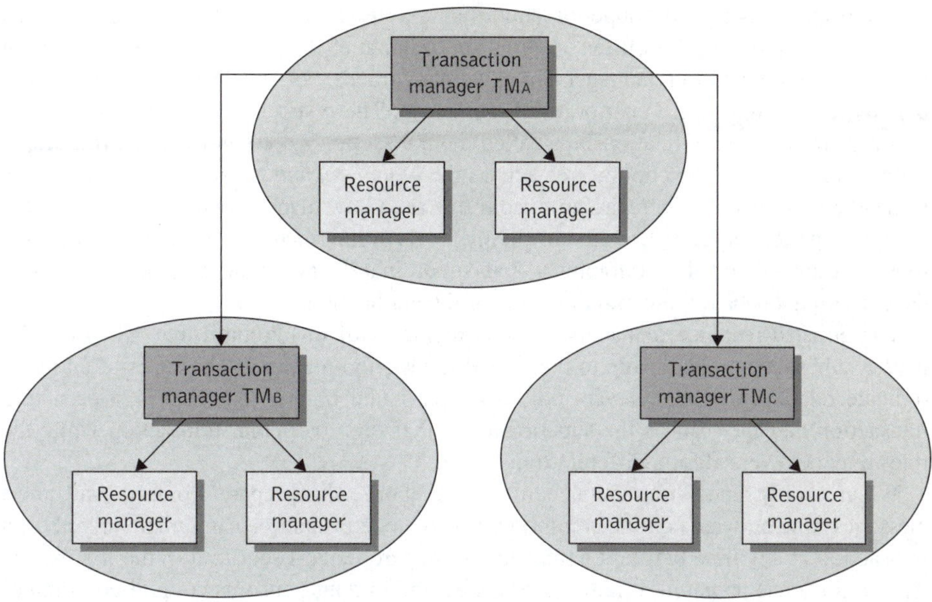

Figure 10.5 Collaborating transaction managers

manager may provide the ability to communicate with other transaction manager instances. In order to satisfy a client's dependence on a guarantee for an atomic sequence of operations, a transaction manager is responsible for creating and managing a distributed transaction that encompasses all operations against the implied resources. The transaction manager accesses each resource, e.g., a relational database system, through the respective resource manager. This situation is illustrated in Figure 10.5.

In this environment resource managers provide two sets of interfaces: one set for the application components to get connections and perform operations on the data, and the other set for the transaction manager to participate in the two-phase commit and recovery protocol. In addition, the resource manager may, directly or indirectly, register resources with the transaction manager so that the transaction manager can keep track of all the resources participating in a transaction. This process is known as *resource enlistment*. The transaction manager uses this information to coordinate transactional work performed by the resource managers and to drive the two-phase commit and recovery protocol.

When two or more transaction managers cooperate within a distributed transaction, the transaction manager that works on behalf of the application program making the request is designated the superior transaction manager and is referred to as the *root transaction coordinator* or simply *root coordinator*. Any transaction manager that is subsequently enlisted or created for an existing transaction (e.g., as the result of interposition, see section 10.4.4) becomes a subordinate in the process. Such a coordinator is referred to as a subordinate transaction coordinator or simply *subordinate coordinator*, and by registering a resource becomes a *transaction participant*. Recoverable servers are always transaction participants.

The principle behind the superior–subordinate transaction manager relationship is that the superior system drives all the systems subordinate to it using the two-phase commit protocol. Each transaction manager can have many transaction managers subordinate to it but can have at most one superior, see Figure 10.5. These superior and subordinate relationships form a tree of relationships called the transaction's commit tree. The root transaction coordinator of the commit tree acts as the *global commit coordinator* for the entire distributed transaction. There are no fixed limits as to how many subordinate coordinators a single superior can have, or as to how many levels of intermediates there are between the root coordinator and the bottommost leaf subordinate. The actual creation of the tree depends on the behavior and requirements of the application.

The enlisted resource managers are also members of this commit tree. They usually have a subordinate relationship to their local transaction manager. The superior and subordinate relationships are relevant only for a particular transaction. That is, a particular transaction manager can be the superior to another on a particular transaction while the roles may be reversed for a different transaction.

When a distributed transaction commits or aborts, the prepare, commit, and abort messages flow outwards on the commit tree. Any node of the tree can unilaterally abort a transaction at any time before it agrees to the prepare request sent to it in the first phase. After a node has prepared, it remains prepared and in doubt until its commit coordinator instructs it to commit or abort the transaction. The global commit coordinator makes the decision to either commit or abort the entire transaction and is never in doubt.

System or communication failures can leave transactions in doubt for extended periods of time. While a transaction is in doubt, the resources modified by the transaction remain locked and unavailable to others. These situations require manual intervention and normally rely on the use of an administrative tool to resolve transactions that remain in doubt.

A typical transactional application begins a transaction by the client application issuing a request to a transaction manager to initiate a transaction. In response, the transaction manager starts a transaction and associates it with the calling transaction branch. A transaction branch is associated with a request to each resource manager involved in the distributed transaction. Although the final commit/rollback decision treats the distributed transaction as a single logical unit, there can be many transaction branches (threads) involved. For instance, transactional requests to different RDBMSs result in an equal number of transaction branches. Since multiple application components and resources participate in a transaction, it is necessary for the transaction manager to establish and maintain the state of the transaction as it occurs. This is usually done in the form of the transaction context. The *transaction context* covers all the operations performed on transactional resources during a transaction, associates the transactional operations with resources, and provides information about the components invoking these operations. Conceptually, a transaction context is a data structure that contains a unique transaction identifier, a timeout value, and the reference to the transaction manager that controls the transaction scope. A transaction manager associates a transaction context with the currently executing thread. Therefore, during the course of a transaction, all the threads participating in the transaction share the transaction context and are associated with the same transaction context dividing a transaction's work into parallel tasks, if possible. The context also has to be passed from one transaction manager to another if a transaction spans multiple transaction managers.

10.2.2 Two-phase commit protocol

In order to respect transaction atomicity, each transaction branch in distributed transaction topology must be committed or rolled back by its local resource manager. The transaction manager controls the boundaries of the transaction and is responsible for the final decision as to whether or not the total transaction should commit or roll back. This decision is made in two phases and the protocol that governs them is widely known as the *two-phase commit protocol* (2PC).

The 2PC is a method of coordinating a single transaction across two or more resource managers. It guarantees data integrity by ensuring that transactional updates are committed in all of the participating databases, or are fully rolled back out of all the databases, reverting to the state prior to the start of the transaction. In other words, either all the participating databases are updated, or none of them is updated. In the 2PC we assume that the transaction coordinator of one site, called the *coordinator*, plays a special role in deciding whether the entire distributed transaction can commit. The coordinator is normally associated with the site at which the distributed transaction originates.

10.2.2.1 Phase I: preparation

In the first phase:

1. As an initial step of the 2PC, the coordinator for distributed transaction *T* decides when to attempt to commit this transaction. In order to achieve this it first polls all of the resource managers (RDBMSs) involved in the distributed transaction *T* by issuing a prepare message `<prepare T>` to see if each resource manager is ready to commit. The prepare message notifies each resource manager to prepare for the commitment of the transaction. The resource manager of each site receiving the message `<prepare T>` decides whether to commit its component of *T* or veto the transaction commit operation. If a resource manager cannot commit, it responds negatively and aborts its particular part of the transaction so that data is not altered. A site can delay if its transactional component has not completed its activity but must eventually respond to the `<prepare T>` message.
2. If a site decides to commit its component it enters a state called the *pre-committed state*. During this state the resource manager performs all actions necessary to ascertain that this portion of *T* will not have to abort, even in the presence of a system failure. The resource manager of this site then forwards the message `<ready T>` to the coordinator. If the resource manager of this site decides to abort its portion of *T* it then forwards the message `<donot commit T>` to the coordinator. It must be noted that once a site is in the pre-committed state, it cannot abort its portion of *T* without an explicit directive by the coordinator.

10.2.2.2 Phase II: commitment/abortion

In the second phase (commitment/abortion), the coordinator determines the fate of the transaction. If all resource managers have voted to commit their portion of transaction *T* (by sending `<ready T>`) the coordinator commits the whole transaction by sending a

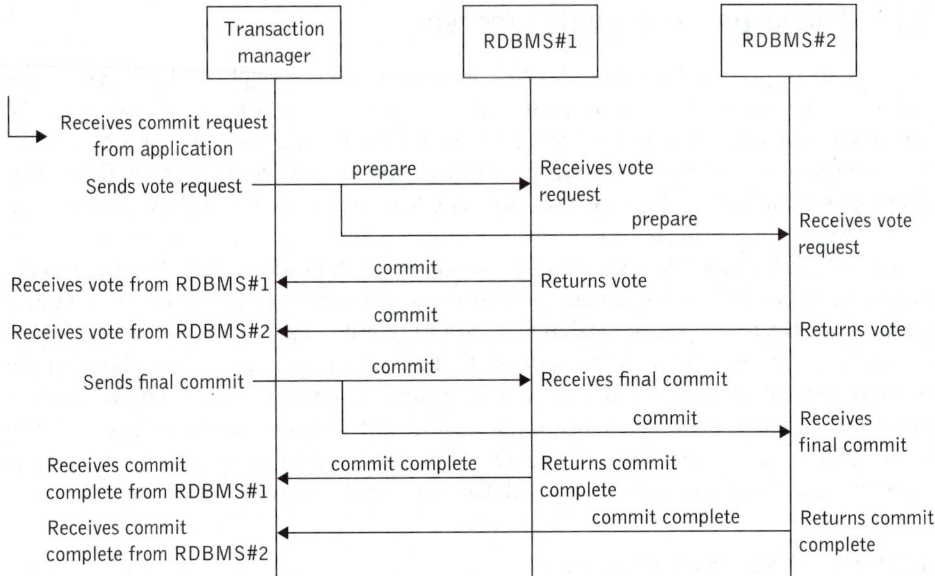

Figure 10.6 The 2PC for distributed transactions

`<commit T>` message to all resource coordinators involved in the transaction. Subsequently, the coordinator returns the results to the application program. If any of the resource managers have responded negatively by sending the message `<donot commit T>` then the coordinator sends an `<abort T>` message to all resource managers involved in the transaction. This effectively rolls back the entire transaction. In case a resource manager in the transaction has not responded with either a `<commit T>` or `<donot commit T>` message, the coordinator will assume that this site has responded with a `<donot commit T>` message after a suitable timeout period.

The 2PC is illustrated in Figure 10.6. This figure shows the sequence of events during a two-phase commit operation involving two RDBMSs. The process begins with a call by the application to commit the transaction. Once the application issues the commit request, the transaction manager prepares all the resources (in this case RDBMS 1 and RDBMS 2) for a commit operation (by conducting a voting). The resource managers respond (in this case they both voted to commit). Subsequently, the resource manager analyzes the votes it has received and, based on whether all resources are ready for a commit or not, issues a commit or rollback request to all the resources. In Figure 10.6 a commit operation is issued to both resource managers.

10.3 Nested transactions

Distributed transactions have evolved from the need to integrate transactions from different servers into a single transaction unit. This is due to the fact that over the years enterprises have developed a number of dedicated applications and transaction processing

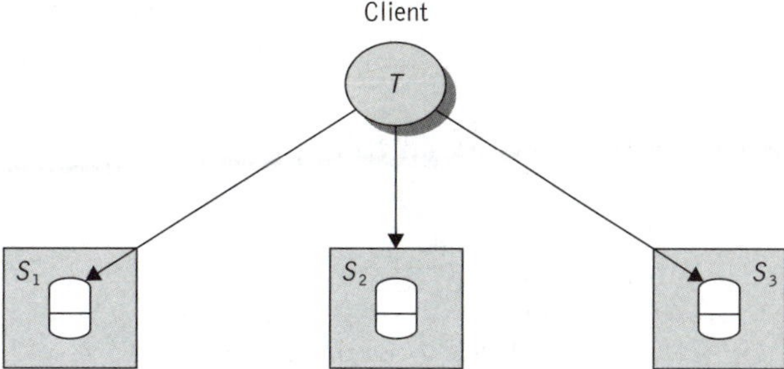

Figure 10.7 Example of a flat transaction

systems to automate business functions, such as billing, inventory control, payroll, and so on. These systems were developed in many cases independently under different hardware platforms and DBMSs.

Transaction managers can provide transactional support for applications using different implementation models. The most common is the transaction model that we described in section 10.1, which is the classical transaction model that involves a database on a single server and has no internal structure and is commonly referred to as a *flat transaction*. A transaction manager that follows the flat transaction model does not allow transactions to be nested within other transactions. Figure 10.7 illustrates a flat transaction accessing data items (through their respective resource managers) in three different servers S_1, S_2, and S_3. In a flat transaction model, the only way to correctly control the scope of transactions that span multiple transaction services is to reach an agreement beforehand on how these services will be combined for a business activity and to apply appropriate transaction policies for the services by agreement.

As the requirements for automation increase, enterprises face the necessity to construct new transaction applications by composing already existing transactional systems. Hence the need for developing distributed transactions as modules, which may be composed freely from existing transactions exported from several servers. With distributed transactions the transaction server controls the function of each exported (local) transaction. Any commit/abort decisions are controlled by the local transactions separately. This rules out transaction designers from explicitly controlling the structure of distributed transactions. As a result of this type of bottom-up approach, transactions may not reflect a clean functional decomposition of the application [Kifer 2005].

Nested transactions evolved from the requirement to allow transaction designers to design complex functionally decomposable transactions from the top down. A nested transaction model allows transaction services to be built independently and later combined into applications. Each service can determine the scope of its transaction boundaries. The application or service that orchestrates the combination of services controls the scope of the top-level transaction. A *sub-transaction* in this model is a transaction that is started within another transaction. It occurs when a new transaction is started on a session that is already inside the scope of an existing transaction. This new sub-transaction is said to be *nested* within (or below the level of) the existing (parent) transaction. *Nested transactions* allow an application to create a transaction that is embedded in an existing transaction. The existing transaction is called the *parent* of the sub-transaction; the sub-transaction is

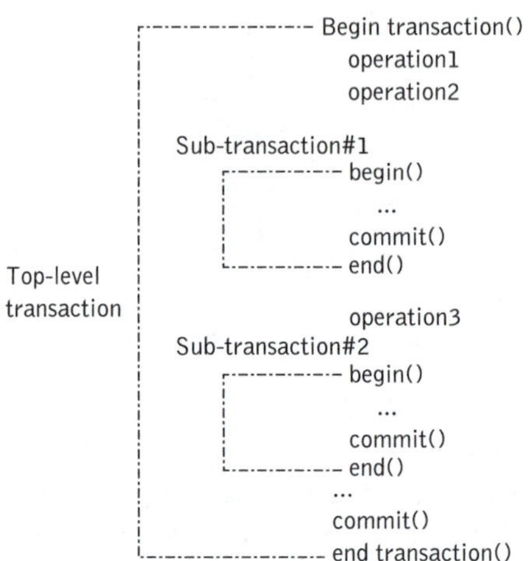

Figure 10.8 Nested transaction structure

called a *child* of the parent transaction. Multiple sub-transactions can be embedded in the same parent transaction. The children of one parent are called *siblings*.

The ancestors of a transaction are the parents of the sub-transaction and (recursively) the parents of its ancestors. The descendants of a transaction are the children of the transaction and (recursively) the children of its descendants. A top-level transaction is one with no parent, see Figure 10.8. A top-level transaction and all of its descendants are called a *transaction family*. A sub-transaction is similar to a top-level transaction in that the changes made on behalf of a sub-transaction are either committed in their entirety or rolled back. However, when a sub-transaction is committed, the changes remain contingent upon commitment of all of the transaction's ancestors. Nesting can occur to an arbitrary depth; the resulting structure can be described using a transaction tree.

Like distributed transactions, sub-transactions have recoverability and serializability properties and control their commit/abort decision; however, the handling of this decision is quite different. Instead of the all-or-nothing approach of the distributed transaction model, individual sub-transactions in a transaction tree can fail independently from their parents without aborting the entire transaction. Changes made within the sub-transaction are invisible to its parent transaction until the sub-transaction is committed. This provides a kind of *checkpointing* mechanism: the work accomplished by a parent transaction prior to starting a child will not be lost if the child aborts. In Figure 10.8 the complete operation will be committed into the database only when the outermost `commit()` is called. The inner `commit()` methods do not control operation completion.

A number of models have been proposed for nested transactions. These fall under two broad categories: closed versus open transaction models.

10.3.1 Closed nested transactions

The closed nested model due to Moss [Moss 1985] views a top-level transaction and all of its sub-transactions as a transaction tree, see Figure 10.9. The nodes of the tree represent

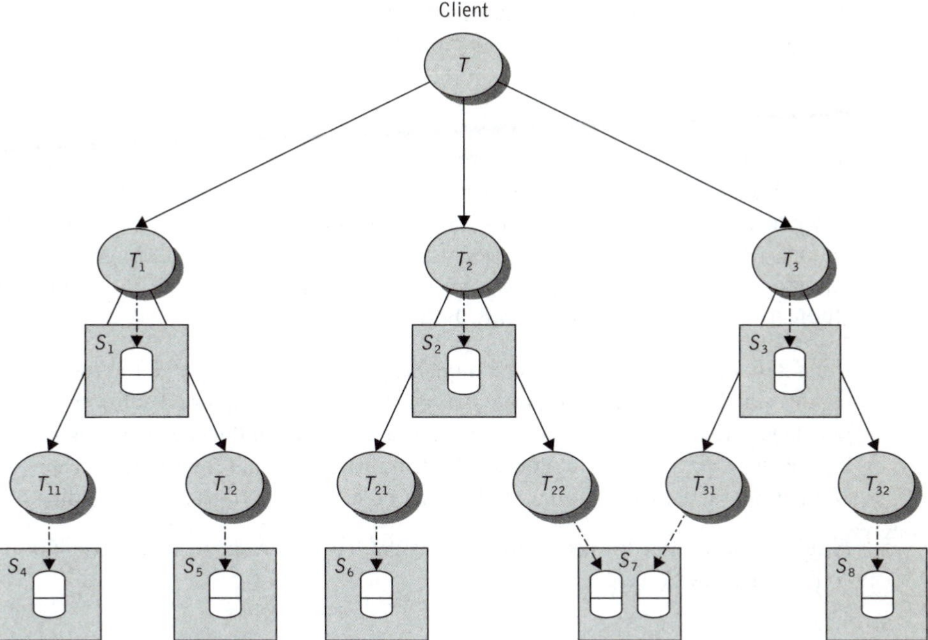

Figure 10.9 Example of a nested transaction

transactions, and the edges illustrate the parent/child relationships between the related transactions. The terms parent, child, ancestor, descendant, and siblings have their usual meanings. In this nested transaction model, the top-level transaction can spawn sub-transactions down to any depth of nesting. Figure 10.9 shows a client top-level transaction T that spawns three sub-transactions T_1, T_2, and T_3. Sub-transactions T_1, T_2, and T_3 access data objects at servers S_1, S_2, and S_3, respectively. Sub-transactions at the same level such as T_1, T_2, and T_3 can run concurrently on different servers. Sub-transactions such as T_{11}, T_{12}, T_{21}, T_{22}, etc., that have no children are called *leaves*. Not all leaves need be at the same level. The six sub-transactions at the leaf level in Figure 10.9 can also run concurrently.

The semantics of the nested transaction model can be summarized as follows [Kifer 2005]:

1. A parent can create children sequentially so that one child finishes before the next one starts. Alternatively, the parent can specify that some of its children can run concurrently. The transaction tree structure in Figure 10.9 does not distinguish between children that run concurrently or sequentially. A parent node does not execute concurrently with its children. It waits until all children in the same level are complete and then resumes execution. It may then decide to spawn additional children.

2. A sub-transaction and all of its descendants appear to execute as a single isolated unit with respect to its concurrent siblings. For instance if T_1 and T_2 run concurrently, T_2 views the sub-tree T_1, T_{11}, T_{12} as a single isolated transaction and does not

observe its internal structure or interfere with its execution. The same applies for T_1 and the sub-tree T_2, T_{21}, T_{22}. Siblings are thus serializable and the effect of their concurrent execution is the same as if they had executed sequentially in some serial order.

3. Sub-transactions are atomic. Each sub-transaction can commit or abort independently. The commitment and the durability of the effects of sub-transactions are dependent on the commitment of its parent. A sub-transaction commits and is made durable when all of its ancestors (including the top-level transaction) commit. At this point the entire nested transaction is said to have committed. If an ancestor aborts then all of its descendants are aborted.

4. If a sub-transaction aborts, its operations have no effect. Control is returned to its parent, which may take appropriate action. In this way, an aborted sub-transaction may have an impact on the state of the database as it may influence its parent to alter its execution path. This situation can be contrasted with flat transactions where an aborted transaction cannot alter the transaction path of the transaction coordinator.

5. A sub-transaction is not necessarily consistent. However, the nested transaction is consistent as a whole.

10.3.1.1 The two-phase commit protocol for nested transactions

The operation of the two-phase commit protocol (2PC) for nested transactions is similar to that of distributed transactions. The only difference is that a server involved in a sub-transaction makes either a decision to abort or a provisional decision to commit a transaction. A provisional commit is not the same as being prepared. It is simply a local decision to perform a *shadow write* (a write that updates a temporary copy of the actual data).

In the 2PC for nested transactions, a client starts a set of nested transactions by opening a top-level transaction (using an `openTransaction()` operation). This operation returns a transaction identifier for the top-level transaction. The client starts a sub-transaction by invoking an `openSub-transaction()` operation, whose argument specifies its parent transaction via its transaction identifier. The new sub-transaction automatically joins the parent transaction, and a transaction identifier by the sub-transaction is returned [Coulouris 2001]. The identifier of a sub-transaction is constructed in such a way that the transaction identifier of its parent can always be recognized from the sub-transaction identifier. Sub-transaction identifiers are globally unique. The transaction manager (coordinator) of a transaction provides an operation to open a sub-transaction, together with an operation enabling the coordinator of a sub-transaction, to enquire about the status of its parent, i.e., whether it has yet committed or aborted.

The client makes a set of nested transactions come to completion by invoking the `closeTransaction()` or `abortTransaction()` on the coordinator of the top-level transaction. Meanwhile, each of the sub-transactions carries out its operations. When they are finished, the server managing a sub-transaction records information as to whether the sub-transaction committed provisionally or aborted. Note that, as already explained, if a parent of a sub-transaction aborts then the sub-transaction will be forced to abort. A real commit operation occurs only when all descendants of a transaction have had their status examined. The sub-transactions will wait until the entire transaction that contains them is committed. Because sub-transactions adhere to the semantics of transactions they can be aborted without causing the parent transaction to abort. The parent transaction may contain code that handles the abortion of any of its sub-transactions. For instance, the parent transaction of an aborted transaction may decide to forward a new sub-transaction to a server holding replicated data.

When a top-level transaction completes, its coordinator carries out a 2PC. The only reason for a participant sub-transaction being unable to complete is if it has crashed since it completed its provisional commit. A coordinator of each parent transaction has a list of all of its descendant sub-transactions. When a sub-transaction commits provisionally it reports its status and the status of its descendants to its parent. The top-level transaction eventually receives a list of all the sub-transactions in the tree together with the status of each of them. Descendants of aborted sub-transactions are omitted from this list.

The top-level transaction plays the role of *coordinator* in the 2PC. The *participants* list consists of the coordinators (transaction mangers) of all sub-transactions in the tree that have provisionally committed but have no aborted ancestors. At this stage, the business logic in the application program determines whether the top-level transaction can commit whatever is left in the tree in spite of aborted sub-transactions. The coordinator will then ask the participants to vote on the outcome of the transaction. If they vote to commit, then they must prepare their transactions by saving their transaction context in permanent storage. This context is recorded as belonging to the top-level transaction of which it will eventually form a part.

The second phase of the 2PC is the same as that for the non-nested case. The coordinator collects the votes and then informs the participants as to the outcome. When it is complete, coordinator and participants will have committed or aborted their respective transactions.

Figure 10.10 clarifies the 2PC for nested transactions. This figure shows a top-level transaction that contains three further sub-transactions that correspond to the sub-transactions T_1, T_2, and T_3 in Figure 10.9. Sub-transactions T_1, T_2, and T_3 access data objects at servers S_1, S_2, and S_3, respectively. This figure shows the status of each sub-transaction at a point in time with each transaction being labeled with either provisional commit or abort. In Figure 10.10 the decision as to whether transaction T can commit is based on whether T_1, T_3 can commit by virtue of transaction T_2 having aborted. Each sub-transaction of these transactions has also either provisionally committed or aborted. For example, T_{11} has aborted while T_{12} has provisionally committed. The fate of T_{12} depends on that of its parent T_1 and eventually on the recommendation of the top-level transaction. T_2 has aborted; thus the whole sub-tree T_2, T_{21}, T_{22} must abort despite the fact that T_{21} has provisionally committed. The sub-tree T_3, T_{31}, T_{32} could also commit depending on the top-level transaction. Assume that T decides to commit in spite of the fact that T_2 has aborted.

The information held by each coordinator in the example shown in Figure 10.10 is given in Table 10.1. Note that sub-transactions T_{22} and T_{31} share a coordinator as they both run at server S_7. Sub-transactions T_{21} and T_{22} are called orphans as their parent T_2 has aborted. When aborting a transaction does not pass any information about its descendants to its parent. Thus T_2 has not passed any information about T_{21} and T_{22} to the top-level transaction T. A provisionally committed sub-transaction of an aborted transaction must abort irrespective of whether the top transaction decides to commit or not. In Figure 10.9,

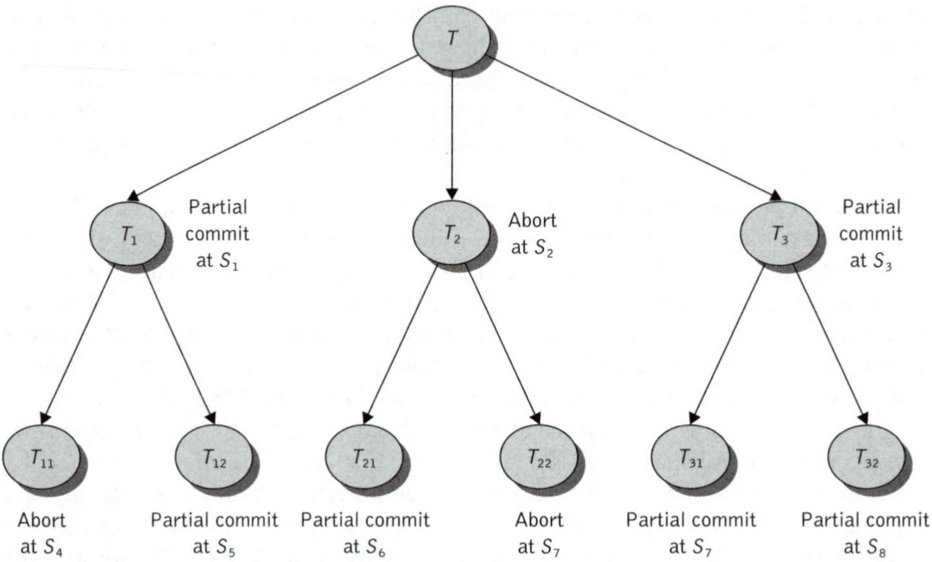

Figure 10.10 Example of the two-phase commit tree for the example in Figure 10.9

Table 10.1 Information held by coordinators of nested transactions

Coordinator of transaction	*Child transactions*	*Participant*	*Provisional commit list*	*Abort list*
T	T_1, T_2, T_3	Yes	T_1, T_{12}, T_3, T_{31}, T_{32}	T_{11}, T_2
T_1	T_{11}, T_{12}	Yes	T_1, T_{12}	T_{11}
T_2	T_{21}, T_{22}	No (aborted)		T_2, T_{22}
T_3	T_{31}, T_{32}	Yes	T_{31}, T_{32}	
T_{11}		No (aborted)		T_{11}
T_{12}		Yes	T_{12}	
T_{21}		No (parent aborted)	T_{21}	
T_{22}, T_{31}		T_{31} but not T_{22}	T_{31}	T_{22}
T_{32}		T_{32}	T_{32}	

the coordinators of T, T_1, T_{12}, T_3, T_{31}, and T_{32} are participants and will eventually be asked to vote on the outcome during the 2PC.

10.3.1.2 Concurrency control

In the closed nested paradigm locks are acquired as in two-phase locking, but additional policies are needed to determine the behavior of sub-transactions with respect to each other. More precisely, several sub-transactions of a top-level transaction may execute concurrently and request conflicting database applications. This requires that additional rules be enforced regarding how sub-transactions of a single (nested) transaction are granted locks.

The closed nested transaction is governed by the following rules [Kifer 2005]:

1. Each transaction must be in its entirety isolated and thus serializable with respect to other nested transactions.
2. A parent sub-transaction never executes concurrently with its children.
3. Each child sub-transaction (including all its descendants) must be isolated and hence serializable with respect to each sibling (together with all of its descendants).

The rules for locking for a nested transaction implement the previous steps and are as follows [Gray 1993]:

1. If a sub-transaction T_i of a nested transaction T requires a read lock on a shared data item then the lock is granted provided that no other nested transaction holds a write lock on that item and any sub-transactions of T that are holders of a write lock on the same data item are all ancestors of T_i (and thus not executing).
2. If a sub-transaction T_i of a nested transaction T requires a write lock on a shared data item then the lock is granted provided that no other nested transaction holds a read or write lock on that item and any sub-transactions of T that are holders of a read or write lock on the same data item are all ancestors of T_i (and thus not executing).
3. All locks obtained by a sub-transaction are held until this sub-transaction aborts or commits. As soon as a sub-transaction finishes any locks that it obtained and which its parent does not hold are passed on to it. Only then can a sibling inherit these locks whenever it needs access to the same data. Without this feature, children of the same parent could potentially block each other. When a sub-transaction aborts, any locks that it obtained and which are not held by its parent are released.

To summarize the previous discussion regarding the nested transaction model, ACID properties apply only to top-level transactions. Sub-transactions appear atomic to other transactions and may commit and abort independently. Aborting a sub-transaction does not affect the outcome of the transactions not belonging to the sub-transaction's hierarchy, and hence sub-transactions act as firewalls, shielding the outside world from internal failures. The concurrency control scheme introduced by the closed nested transaction model guarantees isolated execution for sub-transactions and that the schedules of concurrent nested transactions are serializable.

10.3.2 Open nested transactions

Business processes are found across a broad spectrum of industries and may involve transactional services like finance, logistics, and transportation. Typically, such processes perform transactions upon goods, instruments, and services, such as product delivery, trade settlement, and service provisioning. Typical workflow-based business applications rely on collaborative activities that result in complex interactions between business processes that often create critical interdependencies. In addition, they often require the ability to define complex processes by nesting simpler ones within each other. This in turn requires the support of nested transactions for the transactional execution of such nested processes. Such applications must coordinate their update operations to create a consistent outcome across collaborating/transacting parties. However, classical (ACID) transactions and even nested transaction models based on the ACID transactions are too constraining for the applications that include activities/services that are disjoint in both time and location. The traditional transaction model, which provides ACID guarantees for each transaction, is ideal for applications that are synchronous and involve small numbers of parties: a customer debiting a bank account, a customer ordering goods, a traveler reserving a plane seat, or a stock trader completing a buy transaction. These applications are typically simple in nature and have a relatively short duration.

The closed nested transaction model is incapable of handling process-based applications because it adheres strictly to the classical serializability paradigm to control network-wide transaction management and provide full isolation at the global level. Business processes usually involve *long-running transactions* that cannot be implemented with the traditional 2PC. Because this protocol requires the locking of transactional resources over the lifespan of any transaction. The 2PC is not appropriate for transactions that could take hours, days, weeks, and even years to complete. The failure atomicity requirement of the closed nested transaction model dictates that all work must be rolled back in the event of failures. This requirement is unsuitable for long-lived transactions due to the fact that much work might have been done and will be lost in the event of a failure. In addition, long-lived transactions typically access many data items during the course of their execution. Due to the isolation requirement of the traditional transaction model, these data items cannot be released until the transaction commits. As long-lived transactions run for extended periods of time they can cause short transactions to wait excessively long (as they remain locked) to access data items accessed by long-lived transactions. This increases the possibility of denial-of-service attacks and results in non-functional systems. It is a clear requirement that the isolation property (which controls locking) be relaxed in such applications.

Several extensions to the conventional closed nested transaction model – collectively referred to as *open nesting* – have been proposed to increase transaction concurrency and throughput, by relaxing the atomicity and isolation properties of the traditional transaction model [Elmagarmid 1992]. Open nested models usually involve a mix of coordinated transactions that can be automatically rolled back with the 2PC and extended transactions that require the explicit definition of compensated transactions that are invoked when the extended transaction cannot be committed due to a system failure.

Most open nested transactions are based on a variation of the *saga* model [Garcia-Molina 1987]. Sagas is a transaction model introduced to adequately serve the requirements of long-lived transactions. A saga consists of a set of independent sub-transactions $T_1, T_2, \ldots, T_n$ (called *component transactions*). Each sub-transaction is a conventional (short-duration) transaction that maintains the ACID properties and can interleave with any other transaction. Sub-transactions use conventional concurrency control mechanisms, such as locking. The sub-transactions $T_1, T_2, \ldots, T_n$ execute serially in a predefined order and may interleave arbitrarily with sub-transactions of other sagas.

Sagas are organized in a graph [Garcia-Molina 2002] that comprises nodes that are either sub-transactions or the special `abort` and `complete` nodes. Arcs in the graph link pairs of nodes. The special `abort` and `complete` nodes are *terminal* nodes, with no arcs leaving them. The node at which a saga starts is called the `start` node. Those paths that lead to the `abort` node represent sequences of sub-transactions that cause the overall transaction to be rolled back. These sequences of sub-transactions should leave the state of the database unchanged. Paths to the `complete` node represent successful sequences of sub-transactions. The effects of such sub-transactions become permanent.

Each sub-transaction T_i in a saga has an associated compensating transaction CT_i. Compensating transactions semantically undo the effects of their respective sub-transaction. Compensation is the logic for reversing the effects of a failed transaction. Compensation is the act of making amends when something has gone wrong or when plans are changed. If a sub-transaction aborts, then the entire saga aborts by executing the compensating transactions in reverse order to the order of the commitment of the relevant sub-transactions.

Since the component transactions of a saga may arbitrarily interleave with the component transactions of other sagas, consistency is compromised. Furthermore, once a component transaction completes execution, it is allowed to commit and release its partial results to other transactions thereby relaxing the isolation property. Despite all this, sagas preserve both the atomicity and durability properties.

Figure 10.11 illustrates a simplified transactional workflow version of the order processing example used earlier in this book, whereby products can be scheduled for production if there are insufficient quantities in a warehouse to fulfill an order. The transactional workflow indicates that once the customer has been billed and shipment has been made, the order is fulfilled and the workflow can complete. The workflow in Figure 10.11 comprises a set of interrelated activities. An activity is a unit of (distributed) work that may or may not be transactional. During its lifetime an activity may have transactional and non-transactional periods. An activity is created, made to execute, and then completed. The result of a completed activity is its outcome, which can be used to determine subsequent flow of control to other activities. Activities can run over long periods of time and can thus be suspended and then resumed later.

The paths in the graph of Figure 10.11 that lead to the `abort` node comprise the activities a_1, a_2 and a_1, a_2, a_3, a_5. The path in the graph of Figure 10.11 that leads to the `complete` node comprises the activities a_1, a_2, a_3, a_4, a_5, a_6, a_7, a_8, a_9. To understand how a compensating transaction works consider the activities a_7 (schedule shipment) and a_9 (order fulfillment). Activity a_9 (order fulfillment) assumes that if an order was shipped it was also successfully sent. However, in case the transportation has not arrived, due to a breakdown, strike, etc., then a_7 (schedule shipment) needs to be cancelled (by issuing a compensating activity to undo the effects of the activity schedule shipment). In this case the business logic in the application may automatically reissue a new schedule shipment activity so that the goods can arrive at their destination safely. In fact this is the assumption with the workflow scenario depicted in Figure 10.11.

10.3.2.1 Transactional workflows

Several variants of sagas have been proposed. One variant requires serial execution of sub-transactions while other variants allow concurrent execution of sub-transactions. Other variants adopt a forward recovery policy where the remaining sub-transactions are executed in the event of a sub-transaction aborting, while other variants adopt a backward recovery policy of executing the compensating transactions of all the already committed transactions (see the following section). One interesting variant of open nested transactions is a transactional workflow.

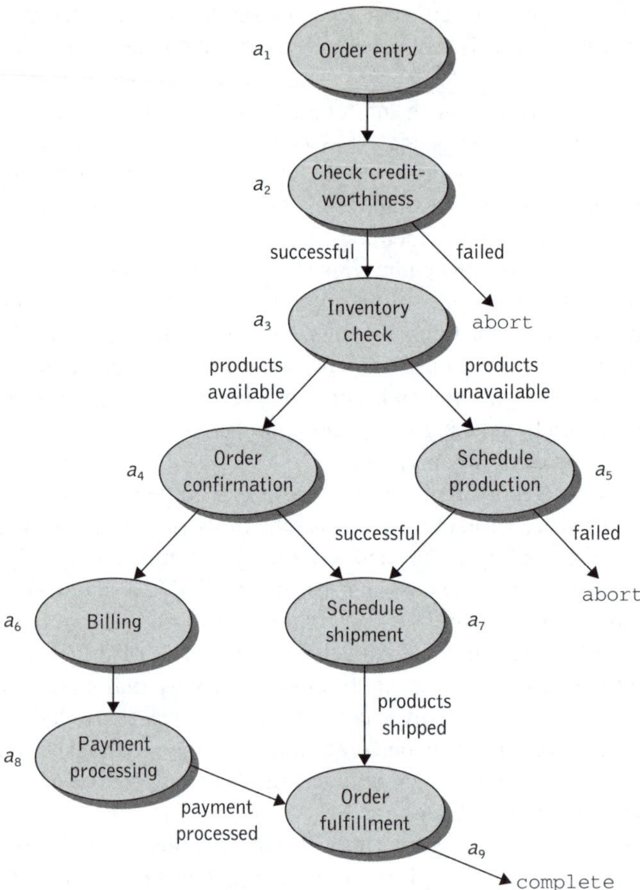

Figure 10.11 Simplified transactional workflow graph for order processing application

The term *transactional workflow* is used to emphasize the relevance of transactional properties for collaborative workflows. Collaborative workflows implement public (visible) processes that transcend functional units within an enterprise or cross-enterprise boundaries. Strictly speaking, a collaborative workflow is a public workflow only if the workflow has not been customized to execute private processes. For the sake of simplicity, the terms *collaborative workflow* and *transactional workflow* are considered interchangeable in this book.

Transactional workflow systems provide scripting facilities for expressing the composition of an activity (or a business process) and offer a flexible way of building application-specific open nested transactions. A transactional workflow manages processes – such as order fulfillment, new product introduction, and cross-enterprise supply-chain management – that span separate functional units in an enterprise and that integrate their activities with those of other organizations. A transactional workflow involves coordinated execution of activities (or processes) which can have logical decision points that determine which branch of the flow a work item may take at run-time in the event of alternate paths. Every alternate path within the flow is identified and controlled through a bounded set of logical decision points. Business rules in each decision point determine how workflow-related data is to be processed, routed, tracked, and controlled. The same workflow definition yields different instantiated multiple times and may be traversed in different ways if the flow contains decision points.

The coordination requirements are expressed by control flow dependencies that specify an invariant controlling the execution of each activity. These invariants in an activity are based on the execution states of other activities within the transactional workflow, i.e., whether they are active committed or aborted; response parameters of other activities; and on external variables, such as time properties.

For instance, assume that the invariant (business rule) that governs the execution of activity a_3 (inventory check) in Figure 10.11 is a workflow variable (Boolean) – response parameter of activity a_2 (check creditworthiness) – that states that a particular customer is creditworthy. A workflow variable is typically used to store application-specific information required by the workflow at run-time. Variables are created and assigned values largely to control the logical path through a workflow instance. Likewise, the invariant for execution of activity a_7 (schedule shipment) is that either of the activities a_4 (order confirmation) or a_5 (schedule production) has completed successfully.

Processes in transactional workflows must be adapted to specific circumstances, such as inventory outages or negative responses to new products. For instance, sagas do not support executing processes to abort an order after the order has been delivered to the customer. In addition, sagas assume that there is always a semantically equivalent compensation transaction that undoes the effects of a sub-transaction. This may not always be true. In some cases compensating transactions may not be able to guarantee complete backward recovery. Consider a cancelled order entry workflow transaction (see Figure 10.11), which may issue a compensating activity (performing backward recovery) by returning goods to the supplier. This activity will still incur shipping and restocking costs, for the supplier may decide to charge the customer a cancellation fee. For such transactional requirements, existing open nested transaction models, e.g., sagas, often do not provide adequate support. A transactional workflow may require varying isolation levels within its internal structure. This means that the isolation requirements between some activities in a transactional workflow may differ from others.

Not all activities in a transactional workflow need to occur for the transactional workflow to commit. Some activities may be optional while other activities may have alternatives defined. Also, not all activities need to be compensated for a transactional workflow to abort. In addition, the same activity if used in different workflows may have different compensation transactions. Finally, the aborting of a transactional workflow may require the execution of complex business processes. Compensating transactions are so fundamental to automating business processes that BPEL includes an explicit declarative mechanism to embed them for failed Web services activities, see section 9.7.1.7.

10.3.2.2 Recovery mechanisms

The open nested transaction model relaxes the classical isolation requirement of ACID transactions. There are two possible modes of recovery for open nested transactions: backward recovery and forward recovery.

Backward recovery is used in case the transaction aborts to guarantee that the encompassing transaction will return to the consistent state that existed before execution of the aborted transaction. This includes the contexts of its children, if any. To achieve this outcome the transaction initiates some compensating activity that will cancel the effects of the failed transaction. An open nested transaction may not be able to guarantee complete backward recovery in all cases because it may include activities with non-reversible side effects. For this reason, the transactional workflow must define the appropriate business logic to perform backward recovery as already explained. Note that not all activities of transactional workflows are transactional. Obviously, non-transactional activities do not require atomic properties and hence compensating transactions. For instance, there is no need to compensate activities such as sending quotes to a customer, calculating quotes, or receiving a purchase order from a customer.

Forward recovery is a guarantee that in the event of system failure, the transaction state can be restored to a consistent state and its execution can resume and continue reliably past the point of failure. Forward recovery assumes that the resource manager of each sub-transaction durably maintains the state and results produced by it. With forward recovery a sub-transaction is allowed to continue its execution taking into account that the transaction failed. Compensating activities are used wherever the execution of an activity cannot be rolled back (such as when an order is shipped).

Compensation is the logic for implementing recovery and reversing the effects of a completed activity or transaction. Compensation activities, which may perform forward or backward recovery, are typically application specific.

The relation between recovery and compensation is as follows [Arkin 2002]:

- Forward recovery happens before the transaction completes in order for it to proceed towards completion.
- Backward recovery happens while the transaction aborts in order to cancel the effects of the transaction.
- Compensation occurs after the transaction completes in order to reverse the effects of the completed transaction.
- During backward recovery, a parent transaction will compensate for any descendant sub-transactions that it performed by using the compensate activity.
- A (sub-)transaction can specify its compensation logic as part of its definition, if that logic depends on the activities that the transaction performs. The logic is invoked when applicable using the compensate activity for that particular transaction. The logic that compensates for the transaction after its completion is defined separately from the logic that performs backward recovery in order to abort the transaction.

The separation between the compensation logic of a transaction and the activities that invoke the compensation as part of a larger context allows for different activities, performed in different contexts or flows, to compensate the same transaction using the same logic.

10.4 Transactional Web services

The Web services vision is often understood as being about building integration bridges that span independent enterprises and their systems by linking the elements of business together into a cohesive whole. Cross-enterprise service applications are distributed applications that appropriately fuse together business functionality and business logic from disparate client applications to provide a range of automated processes such as procurement and order management; collaborative planning, forecasting, and replenishment; demand and capacity planning; production scheduling; marketing information management; shipping/integrated logistics; and so on. This approach aggregates several back-end technology components into high-level, business-oriented services and allows easier migration from legacy applications to new solutions. One key requirement in making cross-enterprise business process automation happen is the ability to describe the collaboration aspects of the business processes, such as commitments and exchange of monetary resources, in a standard form that can be consumed by tools for business process implementation and monitoring. Business collaboration requires transactional support in order to guarantee consistent and reliable execution. Collaborating business processes span everything from short-lived real-time transactional systems to long-lived extended collaborations. This creates demanding requirements for transactional integrity, resilience, and scalability in the extended enterprise.

The push towards sophisticated business applications makes reliable, consistent, and recoverable composition of back-end services more important, as inconsistencies and failures become quickly visible to the entire value chain. A Web services solution must thus be able to support the advanced transaction management solutions that we described in the preceding sections.

Traditional transactions depend upon tightly coupled (synchronous) protocols, and thus are often not well suited to more loosely coupled Web-services-based applications, although they are likely to be used in some of the constituent technologies. As we already explained in this chapter, strict ACIDity and isolation, in particular, is not appropriate to a loosely coupled world of autonomous trading partners, where security and inventory control issues prevent hard locking of local resources that is impractical in the business world. A Web services environment requires more relaxed forms of transactions – those that do not strictly have to abide by the ACID properties – such as collaborations, workflow, real-time processing, and so on. In the loosely coupled environment represented by Web services, long-running applications will require support for coordination, recovery, and compensation, because processors may fail, processes may be cancelled, and services may be moved or withdrawn. Another important requirement is that Web services transactions must span multiple transaction models and protocols native to the underlying infrastructure onto which the Web services are mapped. Finally, there is a need to group Web services into applications that require some form of correlation, but do not necessarily require transactional behavior.

Associated with both business processes and Web-services-based applications will be business rules that express deeper business semantics, conditional logic, calculations, priorities, and failure. Business rules govern the duration and character of participation in a transaction. They determine the set of viable outcomes, which may involve non-critical partial failures, or selection among contending service offerings, rather than the strict all-or-nothing assumption of conventional ACID transactions.

In this section we shall look at how the concepts of traditional and open nested transactions are coalescing with those of Web services and examine the general characteristics and behavior of Web services transactions. Subsequently, we shall concentrate on three standard specifications designed to support Web services transactions. These are WS-Coordination, WS-Transaction, and the Web Service Composite Application Framework.

10.4.1 Definitions and general characteristics of Web services transactions

Web services transactions[1] are a new "generation" of transaction management that builds out from core transactional technology, particularly from distributed coordinated transactions, open nested transactions, transactional workflows, and different forms of recovery. A Web services transaction is a consistent change in the state of the business that is driven by a well-defined business function. At the end of a Web services transaction the state of transacting parties must be aligned, i.e., they must have the same understanding of the outcome of the message interchange throughout the duration of the Web services transaction. A Web services transaction in its simplest form could represent an order of some goods from some company. The completion of an order results in a consistent change in the state of the affected business: the back-end order database is updated and a document copy of the purchase order is filed. More complex Web services transactions may involve activities such as payment processing, shipping and tracking, coordinating and managing marketing strategies, determining new product offerings, granting/extending credit, managing market risk, product engineering, and so on. Such complex Web services transactions are usually driven by interdependent transactional workflows, which must interlock at points to achieve a mutually desired outcome. This synchronization is one part of a wider business coordination protocol (such as WS-Coordination which we shall examine later in this chapter) that defines the public, agreed interactions between interacting business parties.

One question that remains to be answered is at which level of the Web services technology stack should Web services transactions be introduced? While SOAP might seem to be a natural candidate on top of which Web services transactions are developed, HTTP, which is currently the most commonly used transport mechanism for SOAP messages, is simply not a viable option for implementing transactions.

HTTP is a connectionless one-way request/response protocol and therefore makes it difficult for the transaction participants to enter into a bidirectional conversation about the outcome of the transaction. Moreover, the transaction participants that must be coordinated are not merely the application-level endpoints, but also any additional participating resource managers like, for instance, DBMSs. Currently, database transaction coordination interfaces are not reachable via SOAP, simply because there is no SOAP mapping for such coordination protocols. This shows that implementing Web services requiring joint two-phase commit transactions routed exclusively via SOAP/HTTP is not a viable solution.

[1] Web services transactions are also frequently referred to as business transactions or business process transactions.

Considering a SOAP solution for building larger-scale, federated applications out of transactional Web services is also not a viable solution. The chaining of Web services to form an interoperable application sometimes has special requirements because the result of one SOAP request/response pair may affect the operation of some other SOAP message. In such cases, the application developer must identify each SOAP message to coordinate the outcome of one request/response pair with the operation of other messages. This requires maintaining a logical coordination across different SOAP request/response pairs, which is obviously not a practical solution.

An important requirement for Web services transactions is that they provide a mechanism for maintaining transactional behavior and a transactional coordination context at a higher/level of abstraction (on top of SOAP messages) capable of expressing the real nature and imperfect determinism of business processes (which are designed to cope with innumerable variations and with incremental and partial successes). This is shown in Figure 10.12, which depicts a high-level view of a Web services transaction architecture.

The Web services transaction architecture depicted in Figure 10.12 is based on the notion of a transaction coordinator, transaction participants, and transaction contexts [Little 2004]. As this figure illustrates, the application client interacts with a Web services transaction coordinator in a similar manner to conventional distributed transaction systems. Specific details of how a client and a transaction coordinator interact depend on the transaction protocol used, e.g., WS-Transaction or WS-TXM. Context information in this

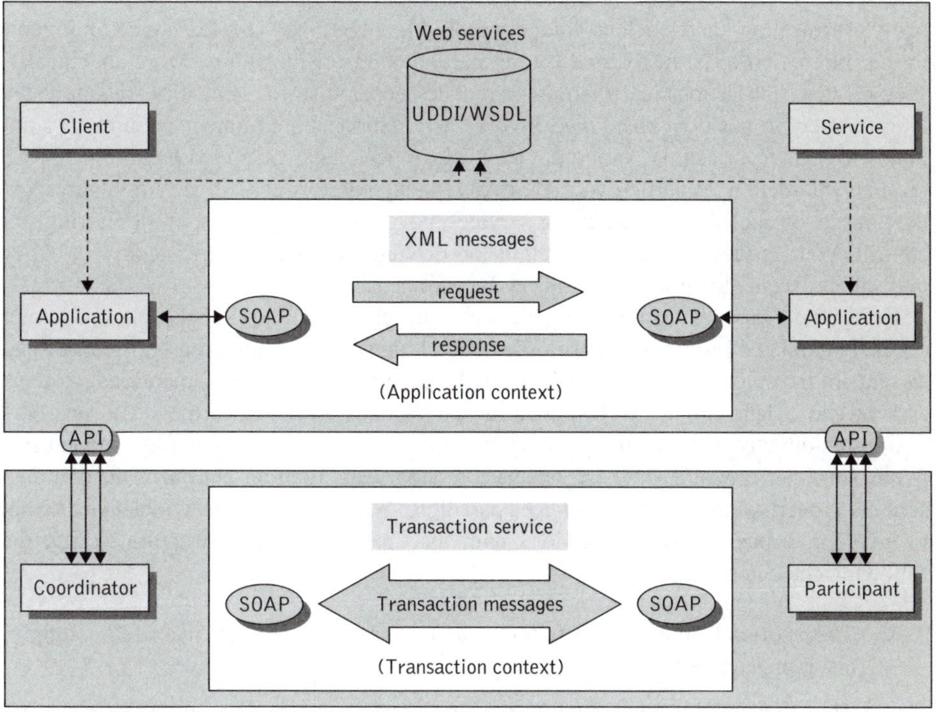

Figure 10.12 Web services transaction architecture
Source: M. Little, J. Maron, G. Pavlik, *Java Transaction Processing*, Prentice Hall, 2004. Reproduced with permission.

architecture is as usual propagated between clients and services to provide a flow of application context information between interacting distributed systems. This may happen using SOAP header information as the figure indicates.

Whenever transactional services are required the Web services transactional infrastructure (bottom part in figure) is responsible for propagating the context to the requested service. When a service that has transactional properties receives an application invocation that also carries a transaction context with it, it registers a participant with the transaction referenced in the context. The transactional service, e.g., an inventory control system, must ultimately (through its container) handle concurrent accesses by different clients and guarantee transactional consistency and the integrity of critical data, e.g., ordered product quantities.

Once a participant is registered then its work is controlled by the transaction coordinator in Figure 10.12. Web services transaction participants are also similar to participants in conventional distributed database systems. All interactions between a transaction coordinator and participant take place according to the specifics of the transactional protocol under which the service is invoked.

10.4.2 Operational characteristics of Web services transactions

In a Web services environment transactions are complex, involve multiple parties, span many organizations, and can have long duration. Moreover, they also require commitments to the transaction to be negotiated by the participating organizations. More specifically, Web services transactions that attempt to emulate deeper business semantics are automated long-running propositions that could involve negotiations, commitments, contracts, shipping and logistics, tracking, varied payment instruments, and exception handling. A Web services transaction, in particular, may involve many enterprises with varying interests in the transaction such as the products or services, payment arrangements, or monitoring and control. Web services transactions retain the driving ambition of consistency, i.e., they may either execute to completion (succeed) or fail as a unit.

Every Web services transaction generates multiple business processes such as credit checks, automated billing, purchase orders, stock updates, and shipping on the back-end systems of the enterprises involved. The challenge is how to integrate operational systems and enterprise data with the Web applications, to enable customers, partners, and suppliers to transact directly with an enterprise's corporate systems such as inventory, accounting, purchasing. Performance of these business-related tasks requires the infusion of transactional properties onto the Web services paradigm. Web services transactions that attempt to incorporate business-level decisions with the transactional infrastructure exhibit the following characteristics:

- They normally represent a function that is critical to the business, e.g., supply-chain management.
- They can involve more than two parties (organizations) and multiple resources operated independently by each party, such as business applications, databases, and ERP systems.

- They define communications protocol bindings that target the domain of Web services, while preserving the ability to carry Web services transaction messages also over other communication protocols. Protocol message structure and content constraints are schematized in XML, and message content is encoded in XML instances.

- They should be based on a formal trading partner agreement, expressed in terms of business protocols such as RosettaNet, PIPs, or ebXML Collaboration Protocol Agreements, see Chapter 14.

When a business function is invoked through a Web service as part of a larger business process, the overall transactional behavior associated with that business process depends on the transactional capabilities of the Web service. Rather than having to compose ever more complex end-to-end offerings, application developers choose those elements that are most appropriate, combining the transactional and non-transactional Web service fragments into a cohesive service.

10.4.3 Web services transaction types

Web services transactions are structured around activities. An activity is a general-purpose computation carried out as a set of scoped operations on a collection of Web services that require a mutually agreed outcome. Cooperating Web services are called *participants* in a transactional unit of work. Participants are Web services that share a common transaction context. As already mentioned in section 10.2.1, transaction context is a data structure containing information pertinent to the shared purpose of the participants, such as the identification of a shared resource, collection of results, common security information, or pointer to the last-known stable state of a business process. Web services transactions comprise two different types of transactional activities: atomic actions (or short-lived transactions) and long-duration activities.

10.4.3.1 Atomic actions

Atomic actions are small-scale interactions made up of services that all agree to enforce a common outcome (commit or abort) of the entire transaction. The atomic action guarantees that all participants will see the same consistent outcome in which all participants complete, otherwise they will be reversed into their original state. In case of a success, all services make the results of their operation durable (i.e., they commit). In case of a failure all services undo (compensate or roll back) operations that they invoked during the course of the transaction. The atomic action does not necessarily follow the ACID properties. It may in fact relax isolation and durability depending on the coordination protocol applied, e.g., volatile or durable 2PC. The atomic action could be nested (closed nesting model) and gives an all-or-nothing guarantee to the group of atomic activities that are executed as part of the transaction. In summary, an atomic action is considered as an independent, coordinated, transactional short-duration unit of work (atomic unit of work) performed by a participant of a Web services transaction.

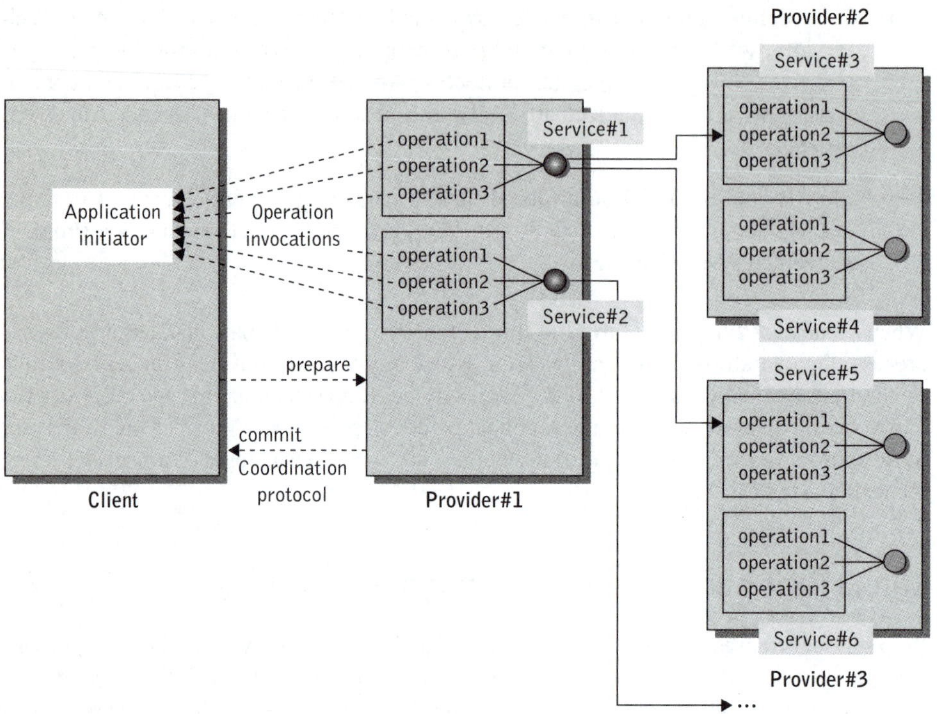

Figure 10.13 Web services transactions and applications

To understand the nature of atomic actions we revert to our running example again. Assume that a client application (application initiator in Figure 10.13) decides to invoke one or more operations from a particular service such as `order confirmation`, or `inventory check`. It is highly likely for the client application to expect these operations to succeed or fail as a unit. We can thus view the set of operations used by the client in each Web service as constituting an atomic unit of work (namely, atomic action). An atomic transaction is the simplest unit of work and behaves like existing X/Open XA-compliant, two-phase commit transactions. An atomic action must either fully commit or fully roll back. Within an atomic action, the operations exposed by a single transactional Web service and the internal processes of the service, e.g., support processes, would usually make up a single atomic action. Atomic actions frequently appear when the business model represents one of the core business processes, e.g., order entry of an enterprise. Non-atomic Web services activities usually support the service atoms and are frequently found within ancillary processes, e.g., travel expense accounts.

Atomic actions use a 2PC (with presumed abort) whereby a coordinating process is required to manage the coordination protocol messages, e.g., prepare, commit, cancel, that are sent to the participating services within a given atomic transaction (see Figure 10.13). This coordinating process might be implemented within the application itself, or, more likely, it will be a specialized Web service [Webber 2001]. Once the actual work involving the consumed Web services in an atomic action has finished, the client application (service client) can begin the two-phase commit coordination of those Web services. The client (transaction initiator) is expected to control all aspects of the 2PC, i.e., prepare phase and confirm phase. The rationale behind allowing the client to govern when prepare and confirm calls are made on the atomic transaction is to permit maximum flexibility within the protocol. Allowing the client to decide upon timings implicitly permits reservation-style business processes to be carried out with ease. For instance, this can apply to an order reservation system, where the prepare phase of the 2PC reserves a number of products, and the confirm phase actually buys the reserved products.

10.4.3.2 Long-duration transactions

Recall that business processes are long running, e.g., a single instance of a process such as order to cash may run for months, and very dynamic, thus responding to demands from customers and to changing market conditions. Accordingly, business processes are usually large and complex, involving the flow of materials, information, and business commitments. *Long-duration (business) activities* are aggregations of several atomic actions and may exhibit the characteristics and behavior of open nested transactions and transactional workflows. A long-duration activity aggregates atomic actions with conventional business logic functions into a cohesive Web services transaction. The initiator of a Web service transaction (typically a client application) can manipulate the embedded atomic actions in a long-duration transaction. Long-duration activities are non-atomic in the sense that they allow the selective confirm (commit) or cancel (rollback) of participants (even if they are capable of committing). Atomic activities can be part of a long-duration activity. The actions of the embedded short-lived transactions are committed and made visible before the long-running business activity completes. In the event of the long-running business activity failing, the effects of such short-lived (atomic) transactions need to be compensated for. The atomic actions forming a particular long-duration business activity do not necessarily need to have a common outcome. Under application control (business logic), some of these may be performed (confirmed), while others may fail or raise exceptions such as timeouts or failure.

Figure 10.14 illustrates the concept of transactional nesting for both long-duration as well as atomic activities. Because long-duration activities can be nested, there exists a

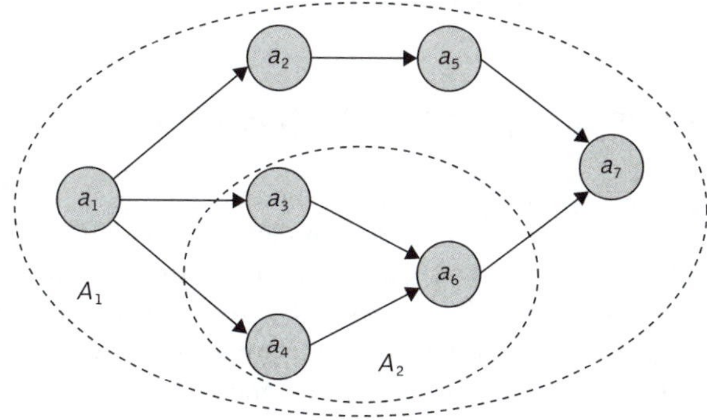

Figure 10.14 Atomic activities, long-duration activities, and nesting

certain parent–child relationship not only between long-duration activities (in Figure 10.14 activity A_2 is nested within activity A_1) but also between long-duration activities and atomic actions (in the same figure atomic actions a_3, a_4, and a_6 are nested within activity A_2 and atomic actions a_1, a_2, a_5, and a_7 are nested within activity A_1). A client application can dictate whether an atomic activity within the long-duration activity succeeds or fails, even if the service is capable of succeeding.

To exemplify a long-duration business activity consider a slight variation of the order processing scenario where a manufacturer asks one of its suppliers to provide it with valuable and fragile piece of equipment. Now consider that one atomic action arranges for the purchase of this product, while a second arranges for its insurance, and a third one for its transportation. If the client application is not risk averse (due to excessive costs), then even if the insurance operation (atomic action) votes to cancel, the client might still confirm the Web services transaction and get the item shipped uninsured. Most likely, however, the client application would probably retry to obtain insurance for the item. In this case the Web services infrastructure comes into play, and the client would opt for another insurer via, for instance, the UDDI service infrastructure. Once the client discovers a new insurer, it can try again to complete the long-duration business activity with all the necessary atomic actions voting to confirm on the basis of the particular coordination protocol used.

Splitting a long-duration activity into atomic actions introduces flexibility because not all individual atomic actions need to lock resources at the same time. In addition, in case a failure occurs at one atomic action level, the overall long-duration activity can still continue using an alternate path either to compensate already done tasks or to do other tasks (e.g., trying out a different insurer or using a safer transportation medium in case the preferred insurer is too expensive).

One of the major problems with Web services is that their underlying implementations are located remotely and hosted by third parties (service providers in Figure 10.13), thus, there is an increased risk of failure during their application. To cater for this threat a long-duration activity may decide to selectively cancel atomic transactions and create new ones during its lifetime. Thus, the membership of long-duration activity is established dynamically by the business logic part of a client application. For instance, a transaction composition service (invoked by the client application) may take interim "polls" to discover whether atomic activities are ready or have been cancelled or it may decide to withdraw its participants because of a timeout.

10.4.4 Consensus groups and interposition

In a Web services transaction consensus about the outcome of specific tasks among the participants is of high importance. This is true in particular because of the often involved monetary value of the transaction. To share consensus, participants are grouped into *consensus groups* in which participants are structured so that they see the same outcome (i.e., consensus of opinion). Another term for consensus groups is *transaction scope*. A scope is a business task consisting of a general-purpose computation carried out as a bounded set of operations on a collection of Web services that require a mutually agreed outcome. Different participants of a Web services transaction can be part of different consensus groups, so that participants in one group can observe a different outcome than participants in other groups. Every consensus group can have a particular level of atomicity. These characteristics distinguish Web services transactions from traditional transactions. Another distinction from traditional transactions is the fact that a participant of a consensus group can also leave the consensus group before the transaction is terminated.

Related to the consensus groups is the notion of nesting. Consensus groups containing tasks or lower-level activities (children) that are required to perform a higher-level activity (parent) can be regarded as child scopes. Child scopes can complete independently of a parent. The parent may, however, have some ultimate control of the child scopes. Child scopes may terminate bottom up, but the parent scope may have ultimate control over them. So, for example, a nested scope (child scope) may think it has terminated, when in fact the parent scope will eventually complete and tell the child what to do.

Next to the flexible consensus groups and nesting, another important notion for Web services transactions is the concept of interposition of subordinate coordinators. Recall from section 10.2.1 that the first coordinator created for a specific top-level transaction (root coordinator) is responsible for driving the 2PC. Any coordinator that is subsequently created for an existing transaction (e.g., as the result of interposition) becomes a subordinate in the process. The root coordinator initiates the 2PC and participants respond to the operations that implement the protocol. A coordinator in Web services transactions can take the responsibility for notifying the participants of the outcome, making the outcomes of the participants persistent, and managing the transaction context. A coordinator becomes a participant when it registers itself with another coordinator for the purpose of representing a set of other, typically local participants. When a coordinator represents a set of local participants, this is known as *interposition*. This technique allows a proxy to handle the functions of a coordinator in the importing domain (server) and is generally used to increase performance (when the number of participants increases beyond a certain threshold) and security in a Web services transaction. Interposed coordinators act as subordinate coordinators. An interposed coordinator registers as a participant in the transaction.

The relationships between coordinators in the transaction form a tree as shown in Figure 10.15. The root coordinator is responsible for completing the Web services transaction (top-level transaction). A coordinator is not concerned with what the participant implementation is. One participant may interact with a database to commit a transaction (e.g., participants of enterprises 1 and 5 in Figure 10.15), another may just as readily be responsible for forwarding the (root) coordinators' messages to a number of back-end systems essentially acting as a coordinator itself as shown (participant at enterprise 4). In this case, the participant is acting like a proxy for the coordinator (the root coordinator). In the example of Figure 10.15 the proxy coordinator (participant at enterprise 4) is responsible for interacting with two participants (enterprises 2 and 3) when it receives an invocation from the root coordinator and collates their responses (along with its own) for the root coordinator. As far as the root coordinator is concerned, the interposed (child) coordinator is a participant that obeys the parent's transaction protocol (typically two-phase). However, each child coordinator will be tailored to the domain in which it operates and the protocol(s) that domain uses.

An interposed participant (i.e., a subordinate coordinator) forwards information from its own participants to the next higher-level (superior) coordinator and receives decisions

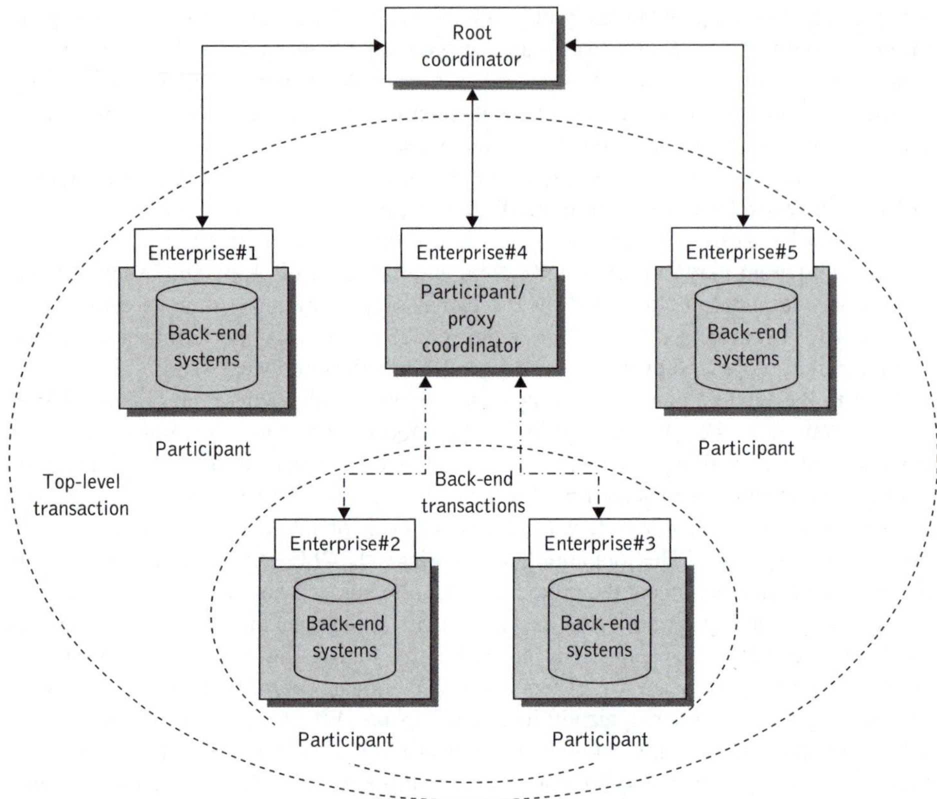

Figure 10.15 Transaction interposition

from a higher-level coordinator and forwards these to its participants. It cannot make decisions on its own. Such an interposed actor does not manage but just coordinates transactions, e.g., across processes or machines. In interposition participants of a subordinate coordinator cannot complete autonomously, but must be instructed by their coordinator. If a participant exits, the subordinate coordinator cannot do anything about that and cannot make other decisions based on this fact.

This last point is a crucial difference between the principles of interposition and nesting (parent–child scopes). With nesting, applications have the control to properly manage scopes because of the parent–child relationship. If a parent completes its work and sees what the child has done, it can react to that by compensating, accepting its descendant's work, terminating the child, or start invoking other services (e.g., if the child exited). This means that there is full control by the parent.

Interposition of subordinate coordinators assists in achieving interoperability because the interposed coordinator can also translate a neutral-outcome protocol into a platform-specific protocol. This is illustrated in Figure 10.15 where the proxy coordinator shields the internal business process infrastructure in enterprises 2 and 3 from the root coordinator. Not only does the interposed domain (enterprises 2 and 3) require the use of a different context when communicating with services within the domain, but also each domain may use different protocols to those outside of the domain. The subordinate coordinator may then act as a translator from protocols outside the domain to protocols used within the domain. The main benefit of adding transaction-based protocols is that the participants and the coordinator negotiate a set of agreed actions or behaviors based on the outcome, such as rollback, compensation, three-phase commit, etc.

10.4.5 States of Web services transactions

Each Web services transaction instance transitions through a number of states in a similar fashion to transition states for conventional transactions (see Figure 10.2). These are depicted in Figure 10.15 and described in what follows [Arkin 2002]:

- *Active:* The transaction is active and performs the activities stated in its transaction context.
- *Preparing to complete:* The transaction has performed all the activities in its activity set and is now preparing to complete. This may involve additional work such as making data changes persistent, performing two-phase commit, and coordinating nested Web services transaction completion (i.e., context completion).
- *Completed:* The transaction has performed all the work required in order to complete successfully.
- *Preparing to abort:* The transaction has failed to complete successfully and is now preparing to abort. This may involve additional work such as reversing data by running compensating transactions, communicating the outcome to transaction participants (for atomic transactions only), and coordinating nested Web services transaction abortion.
- *Aborted:* The transaction has failed to complete successfully and has performed all the work required to abort.
- *Preparing to compensate:* The transaction is now executing activities within its own compensation activity set.
- *Compensated:* The transaction has performed successfully all the work within its own compensation activity set.

A transaction instance always starts in the active state and transitions to the preparing to complete and completion state if all its work is performed successfully (see Figure 10.16). A transaction will transition to the preparing to abort and aborted if an exception is raised, e.g., timeout, or fault occurs, or one of its parents raises an exception, or the transaction cannot complete successfully. The transaction then performs all the work required, in particular the activities that were related to the exception and need completion.

It is possible to compensate for a transaction once it is in the complete state (see Figure 10.16). The initial attempt to compensate a Web services transaction will transition

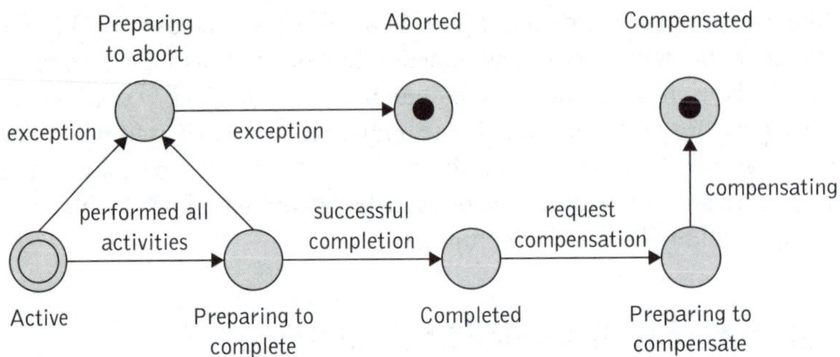

Figure 10.16 Transition diagram for Web services transaction instance states

it to the compensating state. The transaction will then perform all of the activities in its compensation activity set before moving to the compensated state. Note that in Figure 10.16 only the aborted and compensated states are terminal states.

10.4.6 Web services transaction frameworks

When a business function is invoked through a Web service as part of a larger business process, the overall transactional behavior associated with that business process depends on the transactional capabilities of the Web service. Moreover, a business process may involve one or more business functions (invoked through one or more Web services). To support the desired transactional behavior, coordination across all or some of these participants may be required. Coordination must respect the loose coupling and the autonomy of Web services and must be imposed by a business coordination protocol. Without a failure-resilient coordination protocol business interactions become cluttered with multiple out-of-band messages for error recovery, which throws responsibility onto the internal business processes in respect of durable recording of the state of progress. The motivation is to create a Web services transaction framework (WSTF) that orchestrates loosely coupled Web services into a single Web services transaction.

The WSTF builds on a Web services orchestration/choreography infrastructure that offers the ability to create complex processes by defining different activities that invoke Web services operations that are part of dynamic service compositions, manipulate and coordinate data flows, use exception and error handling mechanisms, and so on. Such advanced functionality is typically offered by the BPEL and WS-CDL standards that we covered in Chapter 9. In addition to the services orchestration/choreography facilities, the WSTF should provide the following three interrelated components that offer incremental layers of transactional functionality:

1. A *Web services transaction type* for expressing long-lived workflow transactions, conventional short-duration transactions, exception handling mechanisms, and compensating activities. The WSTF should offer transactional support in terms of coordinating distributed autonomous business functionality and should guarantee coordinated, predictable outcomes for the trading partners participating in a shared business process.

2. *Coordination framework:*[2] The WSTF should include a coordination framework that leverages Web services transactional models for coordinating transactional and non-transactional operations of Web services across distributed applications. The framework should enable an application to create the context needed to propagate an activity to other services and to register for diverse coordination protocols. The WSTF should also enable existing workflow and transaction processing systems of organizations engaging in Web services transactions to coordinate their activities and interoperate by hiding their proprietary protocols and heterogeneity.

3. Support for *business protocols:* At a higher (semantic) level, the WSTF should be able to capture the information and exchange requirements between trading partners, identifying the timing, sequence, and purpose of each business collaboration and information exchange. This functionality is typical of business protocols that we shall examine in Chapter 14. A business protocol defines the ordering in which a particular partner sends messages to and expects messages from its partners based on an actual business context and captures all behavioral aspects that have cross-enterprise business significance. If there is a standard protocol available, each participant can then understand it and plan for conformance to it without engaging in the process of human agreement that adds so much to the difficulty of establishing cross-enterprise automated business processes. Developers can use such ready-made solutions for rapid Web-services-based application development. In addition, adherence to industry-standard protocols for transactional Web services helps in achieving better interoperability.

The Web Services Composite Application Framework that we shall examine in section 10.6 is an example of a WSTF that supports various transaction models, coordination protocols, and architectures in a single interoperable framework.

At this point readers have enough information to help them understand the current breed of transactional Web services standards that are used in advanced business applications. We shall first concentrate on examples of coordination protocols and a transaction model as provided by the WS-Co-ordination and WS-Transaction specifications. Subsequently we shall examine the Web Services Composite Application Framework. We shall revisit business protocols in Chapter 14 where we explain several standard protocols that are able to express transactional behavior at a high abstraction level.

10.5 WS-Coordination and WS-Transaction

WS-Coordination and WS-Transaction are specifications being jointly prepared by BEA, IBM, and Microsoft [Cabrera 2005a], [Cabrera 2005b], [Cabrera 2005c]. The purpose of these specifications is to define a mechanism for transactional Web services. These

[2] Note that the WS-Coordination framework that we examine in section 10.5.1 names its transaction types as coordination types.

transaction specifications encompass Web services transaction types and coordination protocols and support different transactional application requirements.

The WS-Coordination and WS-Transaction initiatives complement BPEL to provide mechanisms for defining specific standard protocols for use by transaction processing systems, workflow systems, or other applications that wish to coordinate multiple Web services. WS-Coordination provides a framework for coordinating the actions of distributed applications via context sharing. WS-Coordination leverages a separate protocol aimed solely at outcome determination and processing. This protocol is WS-Transaction, which provides standards for atomic transactions as well as long-running transactions and associated coordination protocols.

10.5.1 WS-Coordination

A business process may involve a number of Web services working together to provide a common solution. Each service needs to be able to coordinate its activities with those of the other services for the process to succeed. Such applications often take some time to complete due to business latencies, network latencies, and waiting for users to interact with the application. Coordination refers to the act of organizing a number of independent entities to achieve a specific goal. Coordination is necessary to ensure correct behavior when more than one transactional resource is involved in a Web services transaction. This is because transaction managers in the individual resources need to be coordinated to correctly perform a commit or rollback. Typically, coordination is the act of one entity (known as the coordinator) disseminating information to a number of participants for some domain-specific reason, e.g., reaching consensus on a decision like a distributed transaction protocol, or simply to guarantee that all participants obtain a specific message, as occurs in a reliable multicast environment [Webber 2003a]. When parties are being coordinated, information known as the coordination context is propagated to tie together operations that are logically part of the same activity.

The WS-Coordination specification [Cabrera 2005a] can be viewed as the facility to organize a number of independent applications into a coordinated activity and as such it describes an extensible framework for supporting a variety of protocols that coordinate the actions of distributed applications. The fundamental idea underpinning WS-Coordination is that there is a generic need for a coordination infrastructure in a Web services environment as a lot of issues related to Web services, like security, transaction management, replication, workflow, authentication, and so on, require coordination. WS-Coordination coordinates operations in a process that spans interoperable Web services and enables participants to reach consistent agreement on the outcome of distributed activities. Coordination (transaction) types and protocols are used to support a number of applications, including those that need to reach consistent agreement on the outcome of distributed transactions. The set of coordination types is open ended. New types can be defined by an implementation, as long as each service participating in the joint work has common understanding of the required behavior.

The specification provides for extensibility along two dimensions. It allows for the publication of new coordination protocols and the selection of a specific protocol from a coordination type and the definition of extension elements that can be added to protocols and message flows.

The WS-Coordination specification describes a framework for a coordination service (or coordinator) that aggregates three component services:

- An activation service with an operation that enables an application to create a coordination instance and its associated context.
- A registration service with an operation that enables an application to register for coordination protocols that coordinate the execution of distributed operations in a Web services environment.
- A protocol service that implements the coordination type and specific set of coordination protocols that are used to carry out a coordination activity. The protocol service may typically support the two coordination types atomic transaction and business activity, which are defined as part of WS-Transaction as we shall explain later in this chapter (see section 10.5.2). Each of these types defines a set of its own coordination protocols which represent a set of coordination rules that are imposed on activities under the control of the specific coordination type, e.g., durable or volatile 2PC for atomic activities.

Another important element for the coordination of activities is the entity that drives the coordination protocol through to its completion. This entity is usually a client (application) that controls the application as a whole and that is not defined in the coordination framework. The three WS-Coordination component services and their interrelationships are illustrated in Figure 10.17.

To initiate a joint piece of work, an application first contacts the target activation service to create an activity, which is identified by a coordination context. The coordination context is a SOAP header block that uniquely identifies the joint piece of work that needs to be undertaken by means of an activity identifier. When a request is received at one of the endpoints, unless the request is for creating a new activity, in which case a new coordinator is created, it is simply passed on to the coordinator responsible for the activity concerned. The respective coordinator then handles the requested operations. A coordinator is an entity that is responsible for keeping track of transactions and the various Web services involved in each one. For instance, if a purchase order service needs to make several Web services calls to some of its suppliers to order products, the coordinator is then responsible for keeping track of which suppliers were called and the overall status of a transaction. A coordinator normally exposes transaction-related operations.

The coordination service maintains a central repository of all active coordinators. When a new request arrives at any of the endpoints, the activity identifier is used to look up the coordinator coordinating the particular activity to dispatch the request. To facilitate this process, the coordination service uses activity identifier as a reference property (see section 7.2.1 on WS-Addressing) at all of its endpoints.

Web services that participate in the same activity receive application messages with the coordination context attached. Web services then use the context to identify the registration service and register as participants to the original activity. Registration is a key operation in the coordination framework as it allows the tying up of all the different Web services that desire to coordinate to perform a joint unit of work.

The registration service is responsible for the registration of new participants (i.e., the registration of Web services) with the coordinator and the selection of the coordination

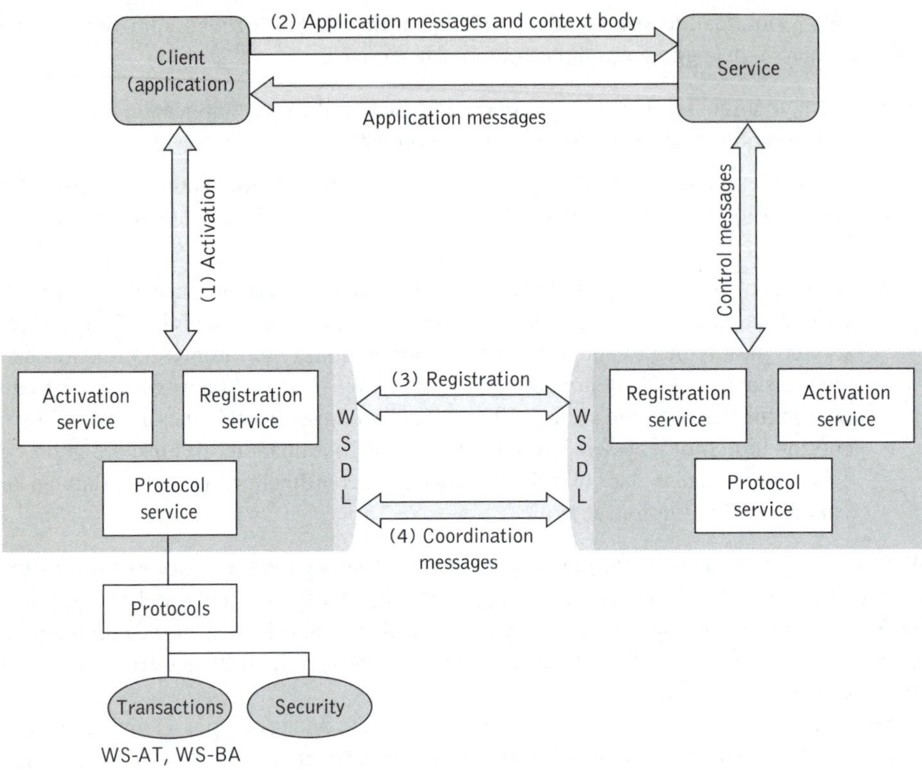

Figure 10.17 Overview of WS-Coordination architecture

protocol. This enables the participants to receive the context and protocol messages of the coordinator during the application's lifetime. This last responsibility is provided by the coordination service. This service ensures that the registered Web services are driven through to completion by using the selected protocol. The protocol defines the behavior and the operations that are required for the completion of an activity. When creating the coordinator, one of the supported protocol types is chosen by the instantiating application. Later, when the coordination context is propagated to other applications, the other applications choose the coordination protocol supported by that coordination type to participate in the transaction.

The activation and registration endpoints are defined by the WS-Coordination specification. All other endpoints are defined by coordination type specific specification such as WS-AtomicTransaction and WS-BusinessActivity. The purpose of all other endpoints is to facilitate communication between participants and the coordination service based on specific coordination protocols. Hence these are known as *protocol services*.

The role of a transaction terminator is generally played by the client application. The client application will at an appropriate point ask the coordinator to perform its particular coordination function with any registered participants in order to drive the protocol

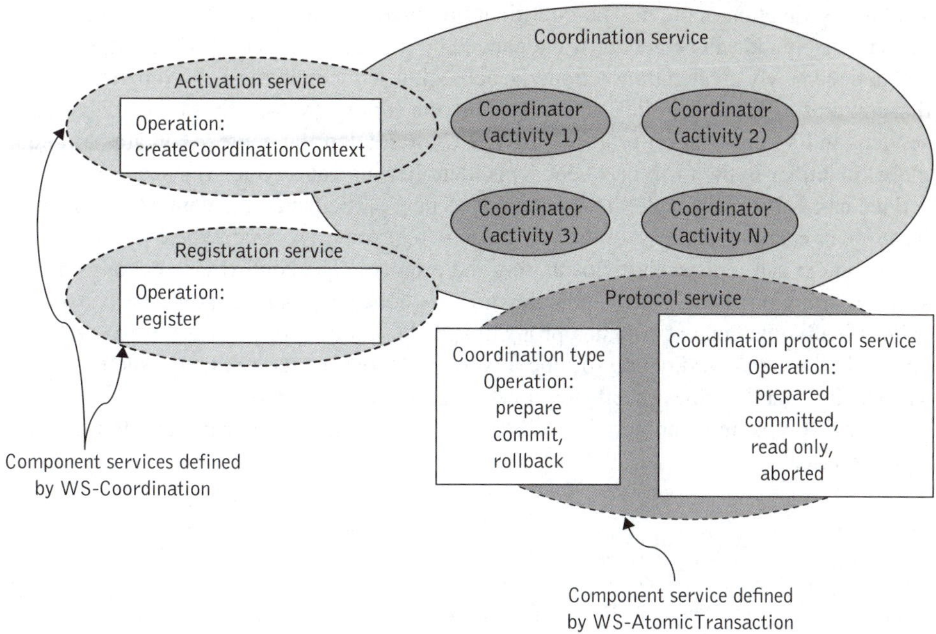

Figure 10.18 Coordination service and its constituent component services

through to its completion [Webber 2003a]. Upon completion, the client application may be informed of an outcome for an activity. This may vary from simple succeeded/failed notification through to complex structured data detailing the activity's status.

Figure 10.18 illustrates the coordination service and its constituent components as well as the relationship between WS-Coordination and WS-Transaction. The figure indicates that the coordination type used is WS-AtomicTransaction (which defines operations such as prepare, commit, and rollback) and the coordination protocol used is durable 2PC (which defines operations such as prepared, aborted, committed, and read-only). In addition, the figure shows that at any given time the number of active coordinators resident in the coordination service is equal to the number of activities coordinated by the service. This is due to the fact that as new activities are created and existing activities are terminated, as a result coordinators also get created and destroyed.

10.5.1.1 Coordination context

`CoordinationContext` is a distinct context type that is defined to pass coordination information to the participants involved in a Web services transaction. In WS-Coordination context information is critical to coordination since it contains the information necessary for services to participate in the coordination protocol. The coordination context provides the mechanism to share processing information between interacting Web services and to bind all of constituent Web services of an application together into a single coordinated application. To propagate an activity to another Web service, the initiating client must send a coordination context. The coordination context is sent as part of the application message itself and can be generally exchanged by using the header in SOAP messages.

For each newly created transaction, the activation service returns a coordination context that contains a global identifier, an expiry field, the address (WS-Address) of a registration service, and a coordination protocol. In WS-Coordination the context contains a unique global identifier in the form of a URI. This identifier indicates which transaction the Web service call is for. To enable the enrollment of new participants, the context contains the location, or endpoint address, of the coordinator (registration service) where parties receiving a context can register participants into the protocol. The context also contains a time stamp (expiration) field, which indicates for how long the context should be considered valid. Finally, the context contains protocol-specific information (`CoordinationType`) about the actual coordination protocol supported by the coordinator, such as WS-Transaction that describes specific completion processing behavior.

Listing 10.1 is an example of `CoordinationContext` supporting an atomic transaction service.

```
<?xml version="1.0" encoding="utf-8"?>
<soap:Envelope xmlns:soap="http://www.w3.org/2001/12/
  soap-envelope"
    <soap:Header>
        . . .
        <wscoor:CoordinationContext
            xmlns:wsu="http://schemas.xmlsoap.org/ws/2002/07/
                                                    utility"
            xmlns:wsa="http://schemas.xmlsoap.org/ws/
                                        2004/08/addressing"
            xmlns:wscoor="http://schemas.xmlsoap.org/ws/2004/10/
                                                    wscoor">
            <wscoor:Expires> 2012 </wscoor:Expires>
            <wscoor:Identifier>
                http://supply.com/trans345
            </wscoor:Identifier>
            <wscoor:CoordinationType>
              http://schemas.xmlsoap.org/ws/2004/10/wsat
            </wscoor:CoordinationType>
            <wscoor:RegistrationService>
                <wsa:Address>
                  http://example.com/mycoordinationservice/
                  registration
                </wsa:Address>
                . . .
            </wscoor:RegistrationService>
            . . .
        </wscoor:CoordinationContext>
        . . .
    </soap:Header>
```

Listing 10.1 Sample coordination context

10.5.1.2 Activation service

When an application wants to start a new transaction, it asks the coordinator to create a new context. It does so by invoking the `CreateCoordinationContext` operation of the coordinator activation service, passing the coordination type, its own port type reference (for the coordinator to send back the response), the port type reference of activation service, and other information. The coordinator in return calls the `CreateCoordinationContextResponse` operation of the requestor, passing back the requestor endpoint reference, the coordination context created in response to the `CreateCoordinationContext` operation call, and other information.

Listing 10.2 is an example of a simple `CreateCoordinationContext` request message. This operation has only one actual parameter, which defines the type of transaction in use.

```
<?xml version="1.0" encoding="utf-8"?>
<soap:Envelope xmlns:soap="http://www.w3.org/2001/12/soap-
  envelope"
    <soap:Header>
        . . .
    </soap:Header>
      <soap:Body>
        <wscoor:CreateCoordinationContext
            xmlns:wsa="http://schemas.xmlsoap.org/ws/2004/08/
                                                 addressing"
            xmlns:wscoor="http://schemas.xmlsoap.org/ws/2004/10/
                                                     wscoor">
          <wscoor:Expires> 2012 </wscoor:Expires>
          <wscoor:CoordinationType>
              http://schemas.xmlsoap.org/ws/2004/10/wsat
          </wscoor:CoordinationType>
        </wscoor:CoordinationContext>
        . . .
    </soap:Body>
</soap:envelope>
```

Listing 10.2 Activation service definition

Listing 10.3 is an example of a response to the above request message. The requesting application (purchase order service in our case) has asked the coordinator to create a new coordination context, which is subsequently returned to the requestor (purchase order service). As part of the newly created coordination context, the registration service endpoint reference of the coordinator is also returned.

The response in Listing 10.3 contains a context with a unique identifier, an expiry time, and the transaction that was passed to the request. The remaining element `RegistrationService` contains a reference pointer to the coordinator's registration

```
<?xml version="1.0" encoding="utf-8"?>
<soap:Envelope xmlns:soap="http://www.w3.org/2001/12/soap-
 envelope"
    <soap:Header>
        . . .
    </soap:Header>
      <soap:Body>
        <wscoor:CreateCoordinationContextResponse>
         <wscoor:CoordinationContext>
              <wscoor:Identifier>
                 http://supply.com/trans345
              </wscoor:Identifier>
              <wscoor:Expires> 2012 </wscoor:Expires>
              <wscoor:CoordinationType>
               http://schemas.xmlsoap.org/ws/2004/10/wsat
              </wscoor:CoordinationType>
              <wscoor:RegistrationService>
                <wsa:Address>
                  http://coordinator.com/registration
                </wsa:Address>
                 . . .
              </wscoor:RegistrationService>
            . . .
         </wscoor:CoordinationContext>
      </wscoor:CreateCoordinationContextResponse>
    </soap:Body>
</soap:envelope>
```

Listing 10.3 Response message

service. This is an endpoint reference as defined by the WS-Addressing specification. This service is the one that each participant in the transaction would invoke to notify the coordinator that it is in the scope of the transaction (see following section). For example, a purchase order service may contact several supplier services; those services will use the above address to register with the coordinator. In this way, the coordinator knows which suppliers to contact if they need to take some action on behalf of the transaction, e.g., prepare, commit, or rollback.

10.5.1.3 Registration service

Once a coordinator has been instantiated and a corresponding context created by the activation service, a registration service is then created and exposed. This service allows participants to register to receive protocol messages associated with a particular coordinator. Like the activation service, the registration service requires port type references on both the coordinator side for the request and the requestor side for the response. This allows the coordinator and requestor to exchange messages.

```
<?xml version="1.0" encoding="utf-8"?>
<soap:Envelope>
 <soap:Header>
  <wscoor:CoordinationContext soap:mustUnderstand="1">
          <wscoor:Identifier>
             http://supply.com/trans345
          </wscoor:Identifier>
          <wscoor:Expires> 2012 </wscoor:Expires>
          <wscoor:CoordinationType>
            http://schemas.xmlsoap.org/ws/2004/10/wsat
          </wscoor:CoordinationType>
          <wscoor:RegistrationService>
            <wsa:Address>
               http://coordinator.com/registration
            </wsa:Address>
                 . . .
          </wscoor:RegistrationService>
            . . .
   </wscoor:CoordinationContext>
 </soap:Header>
 <soap:body>
  <wscoor:Register>
   <wscoor:ProtocolIdentifier>
      http://schemas.xmlsoap.org/ws/2004/10/wsat#Durable2PC
   </wscoor:ProtocolIdentifier>
   <wscoor:ParticipantProtocolService>
       <wsa:Address>
          http://supplier.com/DurableParticipant
       </wsa:Address>
      . . .
   </wscoor:ParticipantProtocolService>
  </wscoor:Register>
 </soap:body>
</soap:Envelope>
```

Listing 10.4 Defining a registration service

If the purchase order service wishes to invoke an operation such as `checkInventory()` on one of its suppliers then the entire coordination context is passed as a SOAP header to denote to the coordinator which transaction the supplier service is likely to register for. When the supplier service receives the message, it then examines the information in the context to decide whether it can participate in the transaction under the coordination type specified there.

For a requestor, e.g., supplier service, to register itself to the coordinator, the requestor uses the registration service reference returned by the coordinator in response to the creation of a context. The requestor then calls the `Register` operation of the coordinator registration service, passing the coordinator registration service endpoint reference, endpoint reference of itself (PartcipantProtocolService) to allow the coordinator to invoke transactional operations on this participant and send back transaction status information, URI of the coordination protocol selected for registration (ProtocolIdentifier), and other information. In this example the coordination protocol selected is Atomic and follows the two-phase commit protocol (wsat#Durable2PC). All this is shown in Listing 10.4.

```
<?xml version="1.0" encoding="utf-8"?>
<soap:Envelope>
 <soap:Header>
  <wscoor:CoordinationContext soap:mustUnderstand="1">
          <wscoor:Identifier>
             http://supply.com/trans345
          </wscoor:Identifier>
          <wscoor:Expires> 2012 </wscoor:Expires>
          <wscoor:CoordinationType>
            http://schemas.xmlsoap.org/ws/2004/10/wsat
          </wscoor:CoordinationType>
          <wscoor:RegistrationService>
            <wsa:Address>
               http://coordinator.com/registration
            </wsa:Address>
                 . . .
          </wscoor:RegistrationService>
            . . .
    </wscoor:CoordinationContext>
 </soap:Header>
 <soap:body>
  <wscoor:RegisterResponse>
   <wscoor:CoordinatorProtocolService>
       <wsa:Address>
          http://coordinator.com/coordinator-service
       </wsa:Address>
   </wscoor:CoordinatorProtocolService>
  </wscoor:RegisterResponse>
 </soap:body>
</soap:Envelope>
```

Listing 10.5 Coordinator response to a registration operation

The coordinator in return calls the RegisterResponse operation on the requestor. This operation returns the address the coordinator wants the registered participant to use for the coordination protocol (CoordinatorProtocolService), see Listing 10.5. At this stage both the coordinator and the requestor have each other's endpoint reference and can exchange protocol messages. When a participant is registered with a coordinator through the registration service, it receives messages that the coordinator sends. These could be, for instance, prepare to complete and complete messages if a two-phase protocol is used as in the case of Listing 10.5. Alternatively, if a participant (supplier service) that has registered with the coordinator wishes to invoke a message such as `abort` on the coordinator it will use the `PartcipantProtocolService` address.

Although WS-Coordination defines only two core operations (`CreateCoordinationContext` and `Register`), the coordination service can be extended with additional transaction-specific operations. WS-Coordination also supports the concept of interposition. Registered participants at a coordinator can also be a coordinator, enabling interposition and creating a tree of sub-coordinators. WS-Coordination does this by making it an integral part of the protocol. The context messages therefore (can) also contain information about other participants and about recovery information.

10.5.1.4 Typical message exchange between two applications

In this section we present an example showing a typical message exchange between two Web services employing WS-Coordination. The example is taken from [Cabrera 2005a] and assumes that the two Web services (applications 1 and 2) will create their own coordinators (coordinators A and B) to interact with each other.

Figure 10.19 illustrates how two application services (Application 1 and Application 2) with their own coordinators (Coordinator A and Coordinator B) interact as the activity propagates between them. The sequence of message exchanges in this example is explained in what follows.

1. Application 1 calls the `CreateCoordinationContext` operation on Coordinator A to begin a new transaction and specifies the coordination type, say CT, that governs this transaction. The application receives the coordination context (CC_a) that contains the activity identifier A_1, the coordination type CT, and an endpoint reference to Coordinator A's registration service RS_a.

2. Application 1 sends an application message containing the coordination context CC_a as a SOAP header to Application 2. This acts as an invitation to Application 2 to participate in the activity using one of the coordination protocols for the coordination type in CC_a. The service that receives this invitation can either register to participate or not.

3. Application 2 creates its own coordinator instead of using the coordinator sent by Application 1. Application 2 calls the `CreateCoordinationContext` operation on Coordinator B with the coordination context CC_a that it received from Application 1. Coordinator B creates its own coordinator context CC_b. This new coordinator context CC_b contains the same activity identifier and coordination type as CC_a but has its own registration service RS_b.

4. Application 2 determines the coordination protocol supported by the coordination type CT and registers for a coordination protocol CP at Coordinator B, thereby exchanging endpoint references for Application 2 and the protocol instance CP_b. All messages on protocol CP can now be exchanged between Application 2 and Coordinator B.

5. The registration of Application 2 with Coordinator B triggers another registration. It causes Coordinator B to forward the registration on to Coordinator A's registration

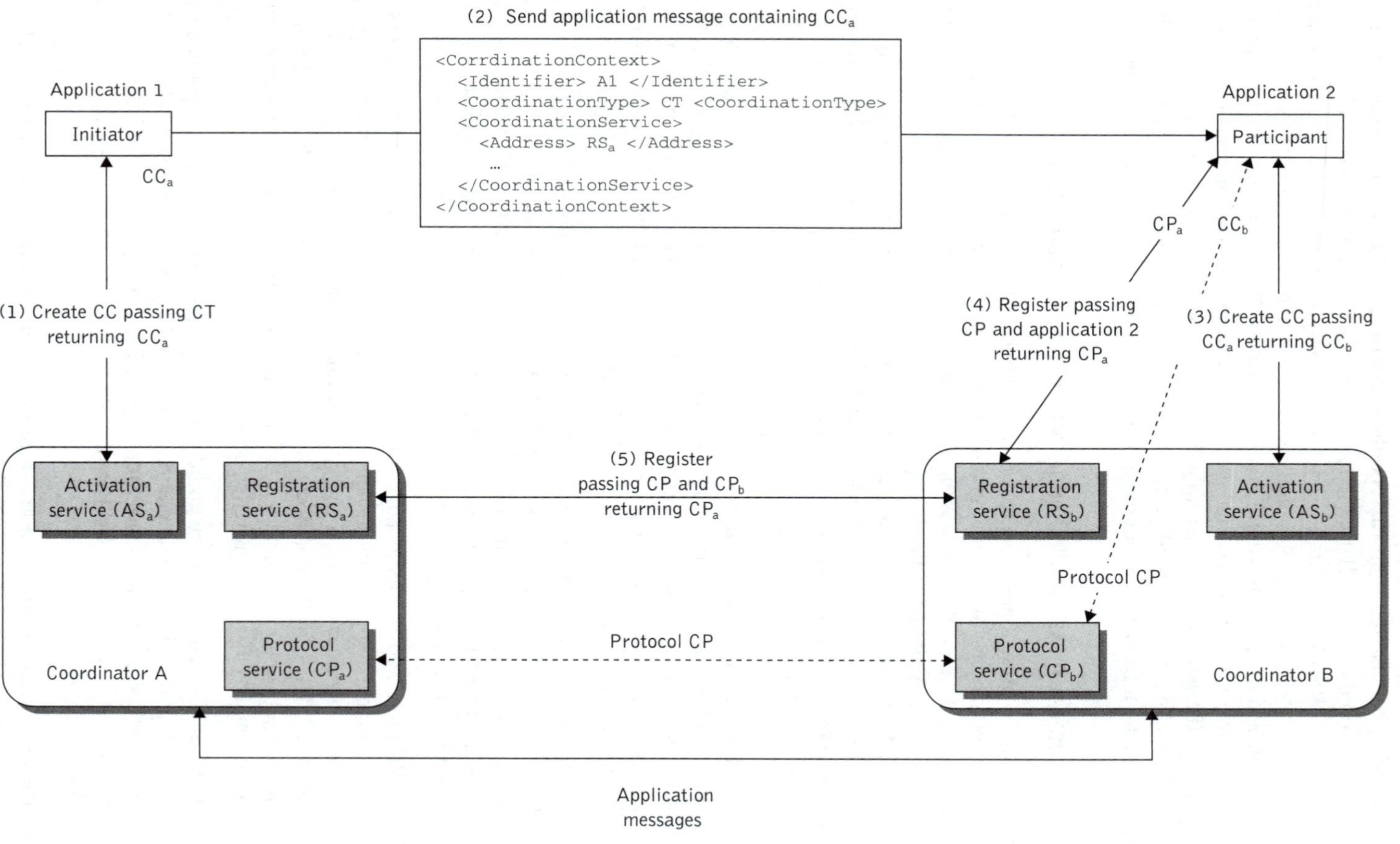

Figure 10.19 Two interacting applications using WS-Coordination with their own coordinator

service RS_a, exchanging port references for the protocol instances CP_b and CP_a. Enrollment and protocols selection allow the Web services involved in the two applications to establish the traditional roles of transaction coordinator and participants. Following this, all messages on protocol CP can be exchanged between the coordinator and participant and hence between the two applications.

10.5.2 WS-Transaction

The WS-Coordination specification does not define a protocol for terminating a coordination protocol instance. WS-Transaction is used for defining the transaction types that are used with WS-Coordination. An important aspect of WS-Transaction that differentiates it from traditional transaction protocols is that it does not assume a synchronous request/ response model. This derives from the fact that WS-Transaction is layered upon the WS-Coordination protocol whose own communication patterns are asynchronous. The WS-Transaction specification leverages WS-Coordination by extending it to define specific protocols for transaction processing. The WS-Transaction specification monitors the success of specific, coordinated activities in a business process. WS-Transaction uses the structure that WS-Coordination provides to make sure the participating Web services end the business process with a shared understanding of its outcome.

WS-Transaction leverages the context management framework provided by WS-Coordination in two ways [Little 2003a]. First, it extends the WS-Coordination context to create a transaction context. Second, it augments the activation and registration services to support transaction models with a number of associated transaction coordination protocols.

The two transaction (coordination protocol) types that can be executed within the WS-Coordination framework are: *atomic transaction* and *business activity*. WS-Transaction supports these two transaction types by supplying the WS-AtomicTransaction [Cabrera 2005b] (for specifying atomic transactions) and WS-BusinessActivity [Cabrera 2005c] (for specifying long-duration transactions.) Atomic transactions are suggested for transactions that are short-lived atomic units of work within a trust domain, while business activities are suggested for transactions that are long-lived units of work comprising activities of potentially different trust domains. Each transaction type may employ a number of transaction coordination protocols, e.g., two phase commit (durable and volatile), participant completion, coordination completion. Various participants may choose to register for one or more of these protocols. Based on the transaction coordination protocol that a participant registers for, a well-defined number and type of message becomes available to the participant for exchanging with the coordinator.

10.5.2.1 Atomic transaction

Atomic transactions compare to the traditional distributed database transaction model (short-lived atomic transactions). They also provide simple agreement coordination protocols for closely coupled systems that desire all-or-nothing outcomes.

WS-AtomicTransaction [Cabrera 2005b] is usually confined to individual organizations where a client needs to consolidate operations across various internal applications. As explained earlier in this chapter, coupling several transaction resources of different companies together using traditional ACID semantics is not a wise choice.

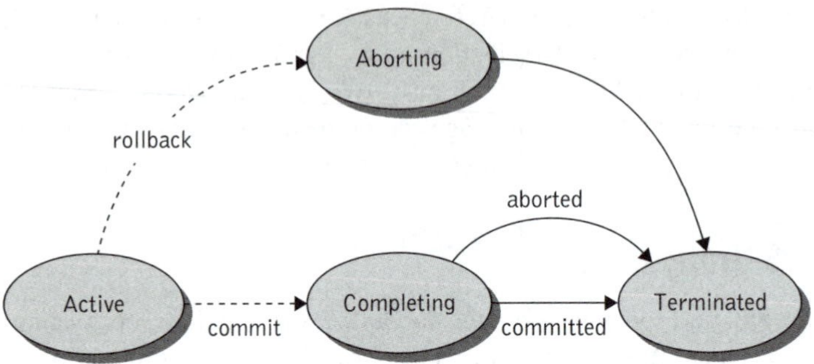

Figure 10.20 Completion state transitions
Source: [Cabrera 2005b]

The WS-AtomicTransaction maps to existing ACID transaction standards and offers three kinds of transaction coordination protocols for atomic transactions. Different participants in the same activity can register for different transaction coordination protocols such as the ones outlined below.

Completion protocol. This protocol is used by the application that controls the atomic transaction. When an application starts an atomic transaction, it establishes a coordinator that supports the WS-AtomicTransaction protocol. The application registers for this protocol and instructs the coordinator to commit or to abort the transaction after all the necessary application work has been done. The sequence of actions during this protocol is illustrated in Figure 10.20 where solid arcs signify coordinator-generated actions and dashed arcs signify participant-generated actions. The state transition diagram assumes that a coordinator will receive either a `commit` or `rollback` message from a participant. In this way, the application can detect whether the desired outcome is successful or not.

Durable 2PC. This protocol is the same as the traditional 2PC used to ensure atomicity between participants. This protocol is based on the classic two-phase commit with presumed abort technique, where the default behavior in the absence of a successful outcome is to roll back all actions in an activity. The durable 2PC is used to coordinate a group of participants that all need to reach the same decision, either a commit or an abort. After receiving a `commit` notification in the completion protocol, the root coordinator begins the `prepare` phase (phase 1) for durable 2PC participants. All participants registered for this protocol must respond with `prepared` or `aborted` notification. During the second (commit) phase, in case the coordinator has received a `prepared` response from the participants, it indicates a successful outcome by sending a `commit` notification to all registered participants. All participants then return a `committed` acknowledgement. Alternatively, if the coordinator has received an `aborted` response from one or more of the participants, it indicates a failed outcome by sending a `rollback` notification to all remaining participants. The participants then return `aborted` to acknowledge the result.

Figure 10.21 illustrates the state transitions of a WS-Transaction atomic transaction with a durable phase commit protocol and the message exchanges between coordinator

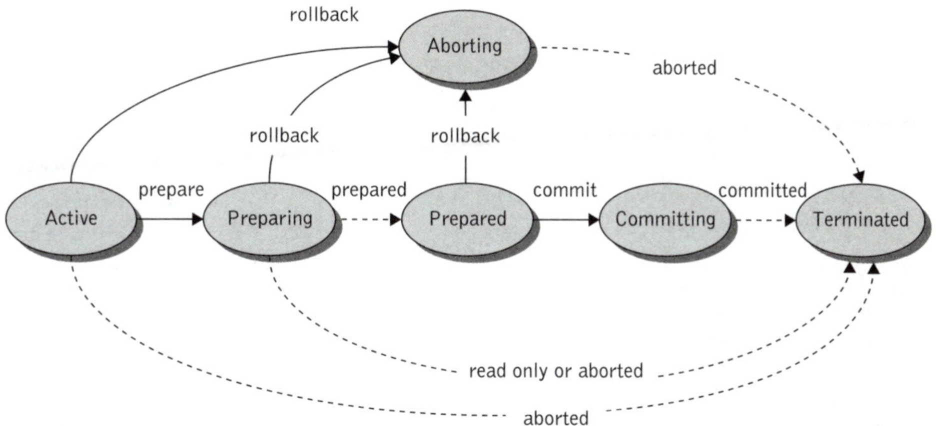

Figure 10.21 Durable two-phase commit state transitions
Source: [Cabrera 2005b]

and participant. The coordinator-generated messages are indicated by solid lines, whereas the participant messages are indicated by dashed lines.

Volatile 2PC. Accessing durable data storage for the duration of a transaction, as already explained, leads to hard locking of local resources and performance bottlenecks. Alternatively, operating on cached copies of data can significantly improve performance. However, volatile data on which a transaction has worked will eventually have to be written back to back-end enterprise information systems such as databases, or ERP systems – where the state being managed by the applications ultimately resides – prior to this transaction committing. Supporting this requires additional coordination infrastructure. For example, to enable flushing of their updated cached state to the back-end servers, participants need to be notified before 2PC begins. In the WS-AtomicTransaction specification, this is achieved by volatile 2PC. This protocol is identical to durable 2PC with only some subtle exceptions. During phase 1, the coordinator sends a `prepare` message to those participants which have registered for volatile 2PC first, before sending this message to those participants registered for durable 2PC. Only when all volatile 2PC participants have voted `prepared` are `prepare` messages sent to participants registered for durable 2PC. During phase 2, the coordinator indicates the successful outcome, sending a `commit` notification to both volatile and durable participants.

Figure 10.22 illustrates the sequencing of the messages at commit for the scenario of a successful commit where three participants are involved, one for each of the above coordination protocols (completion, volatile 2PC, durable 2PC):

1. When all of the work has completed, the completion participant (i.e., the application) initiates the commit process by trying to commit. To achieve this it sends a `commit` message to the coordinator (step 1). The coordinator initiates the prepare phase on the volatile 2PC participant by sending it a `prepare` message (step 2). Each volatile 2PC participant signals that it has successfully finished preparing by sending a `prepared` message.

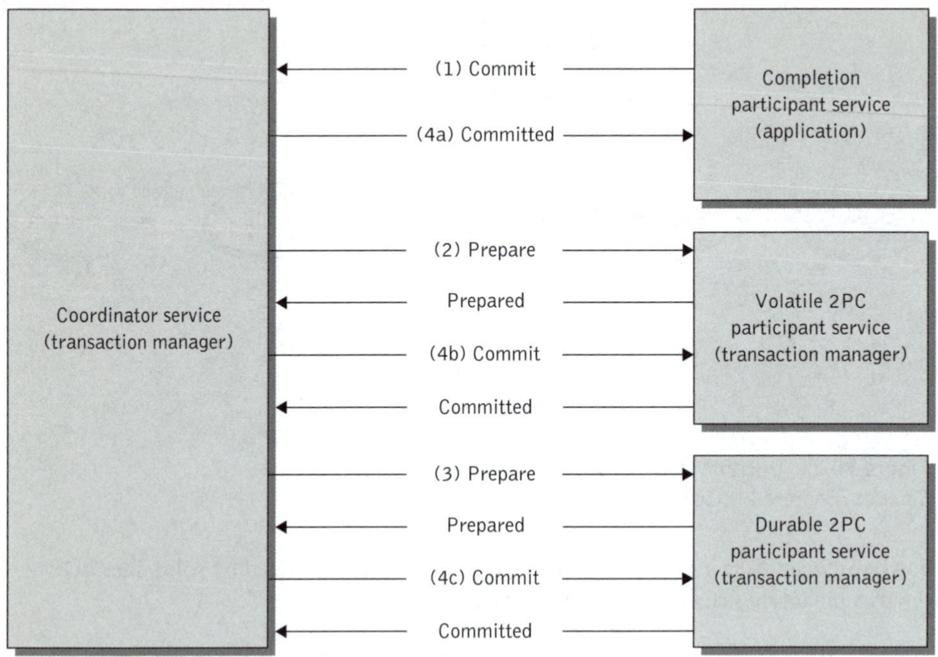

Figure 10.22 WS-AtomicTransaction successful commit scenario
Source: [Cabrera 2005b]

2. The coordinator initiates the prepare phase on the volatile 2PC participant by sending a `prepare` message. Each volatile 2PC participant signals that it has successfully finished preparing by sending a `prepared` message.

3. When all `prepared` messages have been received from volatile 2PC participants, the root coordinator initiates the prepare phase on the durable 2PC participant by sending a `prepare` message (step 3). Each durable 2PC participant signals that it has successfully finished preparing by sending a `prepared` message.

4. When all `prepared` messages have been received from durable 2PC participants, the root coordinator decides to commit, sends the `committed` message to the completion participant (step 4a), and also sends the `commit` message to both the volatile 2PC and durable 2PC participants (steps 4b and 4c). It must be noted that there are no ordering constraints among messages 4a, 4b, and 4c.

WS-AtomicTransaction is superior to existing coordination protocols for traditional atomic transactions. It promotes interoperability as it is SOAP based, thus enabling its use by participants that have been developed on different platforms. It can also work together with other standards such as WS-Security, WS-Policy, and WS-Trust to express policy assertions and provide secure end-to-end operations in arbitrary network topologies.

10.5.2.2 Business activity

The WS-BusinessActivity coordination type [Cabrera 2005c] supports transactional coordination of potentially long-duration activities. These differ from atomic transactions in that they take much longer to complete and do not require resources to be held for long periods of time. This allows many clients to reserve the same product for a specific period of time while eventually only one may obtain it (if it is the final item in the inventory). It also avoids denials of service that occur when resources are locked indefinitely. To minimize the latency of access by other potential users of the resources used by a business activity, the results of interim operations need to be realized prior to completing the overall activity. They also require that business logic be applied to handle exceptions. Participants are viewed as business tasks (scopes) that are children of the business activity for which they register. Participants may decide to leave a business activity (e.g., to delegate processing to other services), or a participant may declare its outcome before being solicited to do so.

Business activity does not maintain the full ACID transaction properties for maximum flexibility. This allows business activities to query multiple participants in order to finally select the most appropriate one and cancel the other ones. It also allows that results of completed tasks (e.g., transactions) within a business activity can be seen prior to the completion of the business activity, thereby relaxing isolation. These tasks are in fact tentative and in case there is need for them to be compensated, business logic is required to make that possible.

As an example of a business activity involving multiple services, consider a manufacturer (client) service that sends a purchase order to multiple supplier services. The manufacturer service picks one of the quotes according to its standard selection criteria and instructs the other suppliers to cancel. In this case, the WS-BusinessActivity coordination protocol adds a standard structure to the application, but at the same time allows arbitrary application logic to handle the coordination. In another example, a manufacturer may issue a purchase order process, which may contain various activities that have to complete successfully but may run simultaneously (at least to some extent), such as credit checks, inventory controls, billing, and shipment. The combination of WS-Transaction and WS-Coordination makes sure that these tasks succeed or fail as a unit.

Business activity can be partitioned in scopes with a scope being defined as a collection of operations that need to be executed to finish a task. The operations executed may be on different participants who participate to finish the task. A hierarchy of scopes can be created to finish a business activity. Nesting of scopes allows for various options. For instance, the parent can select which of its children to include in the outcome protocol thus making non-atomic results possible. The WS-BusinessActivity protocol defines a consensus group that allows the relaxation of atomicity based on business-level decisions [Weerawarana 2005]. Additionally, parents can catch exceptions thrown by their children's scope, apply an exception handler, and continue doing processing. The state of the business activity is durably saved between steps in order to reach a desired goal, even if exceptions occur.

The participants of a business activity can be coordinated in an all-or-nothing fashion by the coordinator. The coordinator in a business activity is not as restricted as the coordinator in an atomic transaction. What the behavior of the coordinator will be is determined by the application driving the activity. A participant after registering in the business activity is allowed to leave the activity at any point in time during the transaction. This is opposite to how an atomic transaction handles its participants. Any participant once registered in an atomic transaction coordination type must confirm with the other participants, but if it chooses to cancel, it forces other participants also to cancel the task.

As with atomic transactions, WS-BusinessActivity defines two coordination protocols: Business Agreement with Participant Completion and Business Agreement with Coordinator Completion. However, unlike the WS-AtomicTransaction protocol that is driven from the coordinator down to participants, this protocol is driven much more from the participants upwards [Little 2003b].

Business Agreement with Participant Completion. With this protocol, a participant (child) activity is initially created in the `active` state. If the participant task finishes and wishes to be involved in the business activity further, then it must be in a position to compensate for the work it has performed. In this case it sends a `completed` message to the coordinator and waits to receive the final outcome of the business activity from the coordinator. This outcome will be either a `close` message, meaning the business activity has completed successfully, or a `compensate` message indicating that the coordinator activity requires that the participant reverses the effects of its work. Alternatively, if a participant activity finishes the work it was created to do and decides it no longer needs to participate within the scope of the WS-BusinessActivity, then the participant can unilaterally send an `exited` message to the coordinator, which is equivalent to the participant resigning from the Web services transaction.

Figure 10.23 illustrates the state transitions of a WS-BusinessActivity with Participant Completion protocol and the message exchanges between coordinator and participant. As usual the coordinator-generated messages are indicated by solid lines, whereas the participant messages are indicated by dashed lines.

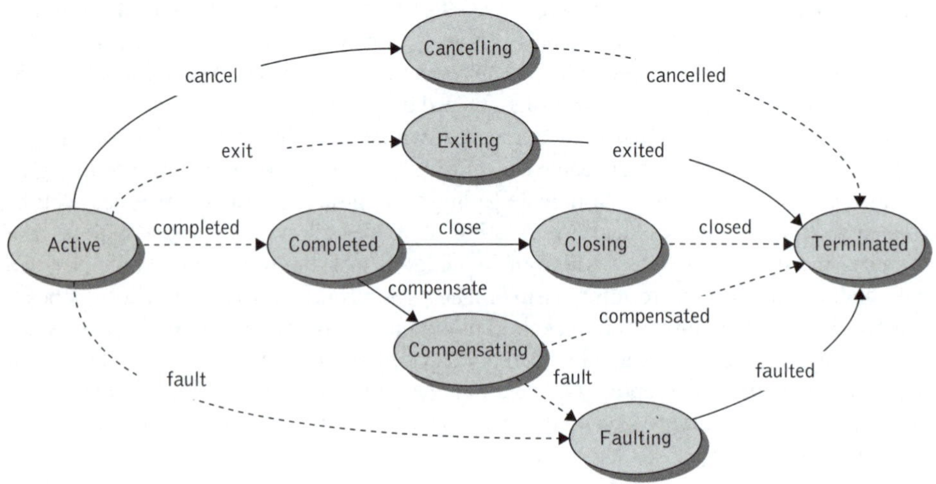

Figure 10.23 Business agreement with participant completion state transitions
Source: [Cabrera 2005c]

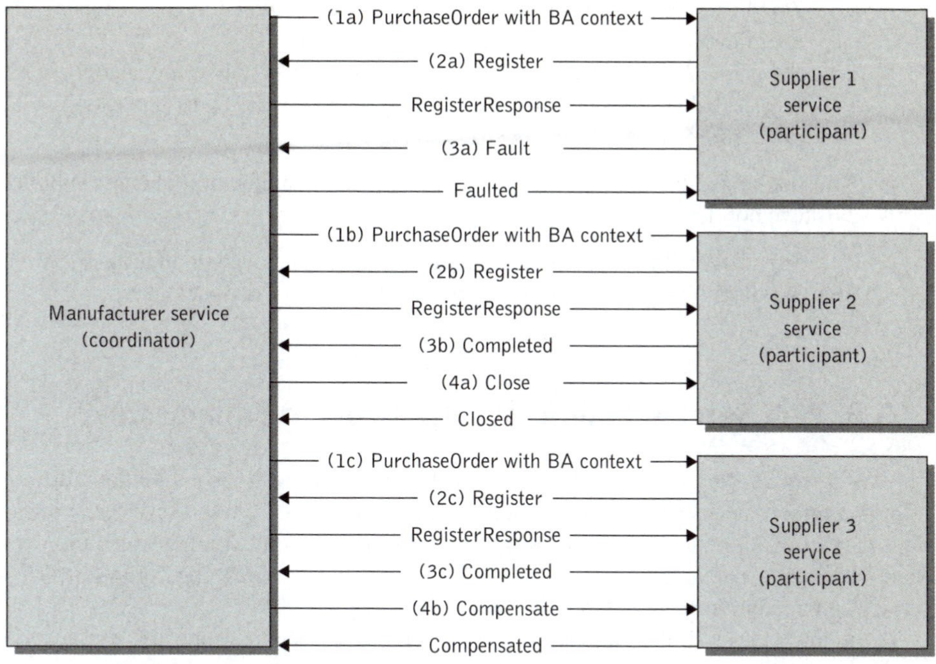

Figure 10.24 Business-activity-based order processing example
Source: [Cabrera 2005c]

Business Agreement with Coordinator Completion. This protocol is identical to the Business Agreement with Participant Completion protocol with the exception that the participant cannot unilaterally decide to end its participation in the business activity, even if it can be compensated. Rather the participant task relies on the coordinator to inform it when it has received all requests for it to perform work. To accomplish this, the coordinator sends the `complete` message to the participant. The participant then acts in a similar fashion as it does in the Business Agreement with Participant Completion protocol.

Figure 10.24 clarifies some of the points raised above. This figure illustrates an order processing application (adapted from [Cabrera 2005c]) in which a manufacturer service asks for quotes from three supplier services under the Business Agreement with Participant Completion protocol and chooses the best deal. The steps in this protocol interaction are as follows:

1. The manufacturer service (coordinator) sends each seller a `PurchaseOrder` message with a `CoordinationContext` header for this business activity. These messages can all be sent simultaneously.
2. All three suppliers (participants) register for the Business Agreement with Participant Completion protocol.
3. From this point onwards, each of the three suppliers has different flows, such as:

(a) Supplier 1 cannot make a quote. It notifies the manufacturer service using the coordination protocol `Fault` message.
(b) Suppliers 2 and 3 can make a quote. They each notify the manufacturer service using the coordination protocol `completed` message along with price information.

4. After looking at the quotes from both suppliers, the manufacturer chooses supplier 2. It then notifies:

(a) Supplier 2 with the coordination protocol `close` message (to indicate success).
(b) Supplier 3 with the coordination protocol `compensate` message.

10.6 Web Service Composite Application Framework

The Web service transaction models that we described in the previous sections do not offer a common means for managing shared context in composite Web services applications as part of long-duration business process executions. Context allows operations to share a common outcome and is important for applications comprising composite Web services grouped in transactions.

To address these shortcomings the OASIS Web Services Composite Application Framework (WS-CAF) defines a context management service to manage and coordinate the use of shared context data across composite Web services applications. The WS-CAF set of specifications addresses these two major unresolved areas of Web services transaction standardization as follows:

1. It solves the problem of managing the information context shared across multiple Web services that are composed into a larger unit of work, e.g., processing a purchase order and executing a series of Web services within a transaction, by providing a flexible, standard mechanism to manage Web Service Context that improves interoperability, and eliminates potential duplication of effort.
2. It is specifically designed as an open "pluggable" framework to support a variety of Web services transaction protocols, including WS-Transaction, and interoperability across them. WS-CAF can act as a bridge between diverse transaction models such as MQ Series and J2EE transactions.

WS-CAF presents a well-abstracted view of the architecture needed to support long-running interactions between Web services. It is divided into three broad parts, which define incremental layers of functionality. These are [Bunting 2003a]: Web Service Context (WS-CTX), a lightweight framework for context management; Web Service Coordination Framework (WS-CF) a sharable mechanism to manage context augmentation and lifecycle; and Web Services Transaction Management (WS-TXM), which builds on WS-CF to provide transactional coordination.

The individual parts of WS-CAF are designed to complement Web services orchestration and choreography technologies such as BPEL and WS-Choreography, and work with existing Web services specifications such as WS-Security and WS-Reliability. WS-CAF confines itself to the management of information required by the various supporting distributed computing infrastructures while other standards such as BPEL are used to create such interdependencies. The BPEL context management system defines how messages are correlated within the flow execution engine, but does not address how to share context across the Web services executions in the flow. These are the responsibility of WS-CAF.

10.6.1 Web Service Context

Web services share a common context when they perform related activities such as multiple interactions with a data management resource, interactive display, or automated business process. Through the use of shared context Web services from different sources can effectively become part of the same application because they share common system information. Typical applications that rely on shared context include common security domains where multiple Web services execute within the scope of a single authorized session; common outcome negotiation where each party within the activity needs to know whether each of the other participants successfully completed their work; establishing continuous connections to back-end systems; and so on [Webber 2003b], [Newcomer 2005].

WS-CTX defines the context, the scope of context sharing, and basic rules for context management. WS-CTX describes how to define an *activity* in which multiple Web services are related through shared context. An activity is essentially a way of *scoping application-specific work* [Bunting 2003b]. WS-CTX represents a Web services interaction of a number of activities related to an overall application. WS-CTX defines demarcation points that specify the start and endpoints of an activity, registers Web services so that they that can become participants in the lifecycle of an activity and manage and augment the context associated with that activity, and propagates context information across the network [Bunting 2003b].

WS-CTX is not aimed specifically at a single service type or application domain: it is a more low-level and fundamental service concerned purely with the management of abstract activity entities through shared context. The main components of WS-CTX are [Bunting 2003b]:

> *Context service:* This defines the scope of an activity and how information about it (the context) can be referenced and propagated in a distributed environment. To manage activities the context service maintains a repository of shared contexts associated with execution environments. Whenever messages are exchanged within the scope of an activity, the context service can supply the associated context, which may then be propagated with those messages [Webber 2003b]. The context service also manages hierarchies of contexts to support nesting and concurrency.
>
> *Context:* This provides a way to correlate a set of messages into an activity by sharing common information. For this purpose it contains information necessary for multiple Web services to be associated with the same activity, which may be dynamically updated by services as the application or process makes progress.

In WS-CTX the services that are involved within an activity span two categories, namely application services and activity lifecycle services.

In addition to the context service, each Web service participating in an activity may register an *activity lifecycle service* (ALS) with the context service. The ALS participates in the lifecycle of an activity (is informed when it starts, ends, etc.). During execution, when a context is required for the activity associated with the current execution environment, the context service calls each registered ALS and obtains additional content for the basic context from it. From this it eventually assembles the entire context document that can be propagated to participants. For example, a context service may have a transaction ALS and security ALS registered with it. These may define the scope of an activity to be the scope of a security and transaction domain.

Application services are the services that an application uses to obtain the functional aspects of the task. For example, a purchase order application may have several activities which involve checking customer creditworthiness, checking product inventory, calculating the final price for the order and billing the customer, selecting a shipper, and so forth. For both application services and ALS the definition of the activity is directly related to the need for a group of Web services to share common information, such as a purchase order. An activity is itself implemented as a Web service, and a Web service may be enrolled with an activity in order to define it.

The relationships between ALS and context service, application services, and applications are shown in Figure 10.25.

10.6.2 Web Service Coordination Framework

The Web Service Coordination Framework (WS-CF) allows the management and coordination in a Web services interaction of a number of activities related to an overall application. It builds on the WS-CTX specification and provides a coordination service that plugs into WS-CTX. WS-CF allows applications and services to tie into it and customize it on a per

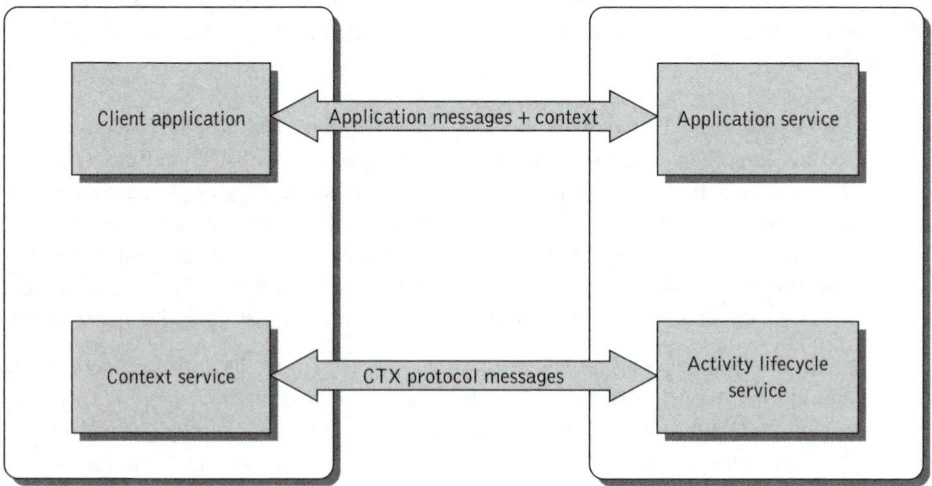

Figure 10.25 Linking ALS, context service, application services, and applications
Source: [Bunting 2003a]

service or application basis. This addresses the need for Web services to be designed to be transaction protocol independent and map to multiple underlying technologies.

WS-CF defines demarcation points, which specify the start and endpoints of coordinated activities. It also defines demarcation points where coordination of participants occurs, i.e., the points at which the appropriate SOAP messages are sent to participants. It registers participants for the activities that are associated with the application. And, finally, it propagates coordination-specific information across the network by enhancing the default context structure provided by WS-CTX.

WS-CF comprises the following main building blocks [Bunting 2003c]:

Coordinator: This component provides an interface for the registration of participants (such as activities) triggered at coordination points. The coordinator is responsible for communicating the outcome of the activity to the list of registered activities.

Participant: This component provides operations that are performed as part of coordination sequence processing.

Coordination Service: This defines the behavior for a specific or customizable coordination model. The coordination service provides a processing pattern that is used for outcome processing. For example, a possible implementation of a coordination service is an ACID transaction service that provides a two-phase protocol, extended transaction patterns such as collaborations, open, and closed nested transactions, and non-transactional patterns such as cohesions and correlations. Coordination services can also be used to group related non-transactional activities.

Figure 10.26 illustrates how individual Web services and composite applications can register as participants with a coordinator. The coordinator takes over responsibility for context management and notifying participants of the outcome of a series of related Web services executions. As this figure shows, a coordinator can register itself with another coordinator and become a participant, thereby improving interoperability.

While WS-CF is seemingly similar to WS-Coordination, the main differentiator is that WS-CF defines more of the coordinator's architecture than WS-Coordination (which leaves most things up to the services that use it) [Webber 2003b]. In many respects, WS-CF can be considered a superset of the WS-Coordination.

10.6.3 Web Services Transaction Management

Web Services Transaction Management (WS-TXM) defines a set of pluggable transaction protocols (two-phase commit, long-running actions, and business process flows) that can be used with a coordinator to negotiate a set of actions for all participants to execute based on the outcome of a series of related Web services executions. The executions are related through the use of shared context (scopes) that can be both nested (parent–child relationships) and concurrent.

To achieve its stated objective WS-TXM builds on the WS-CF and WS-CTX specifications. It does this by defining specific coordinator and participant services and augmenting the distribution context. Figure 10.27 illustrates the layering of WS-TXM protocols.

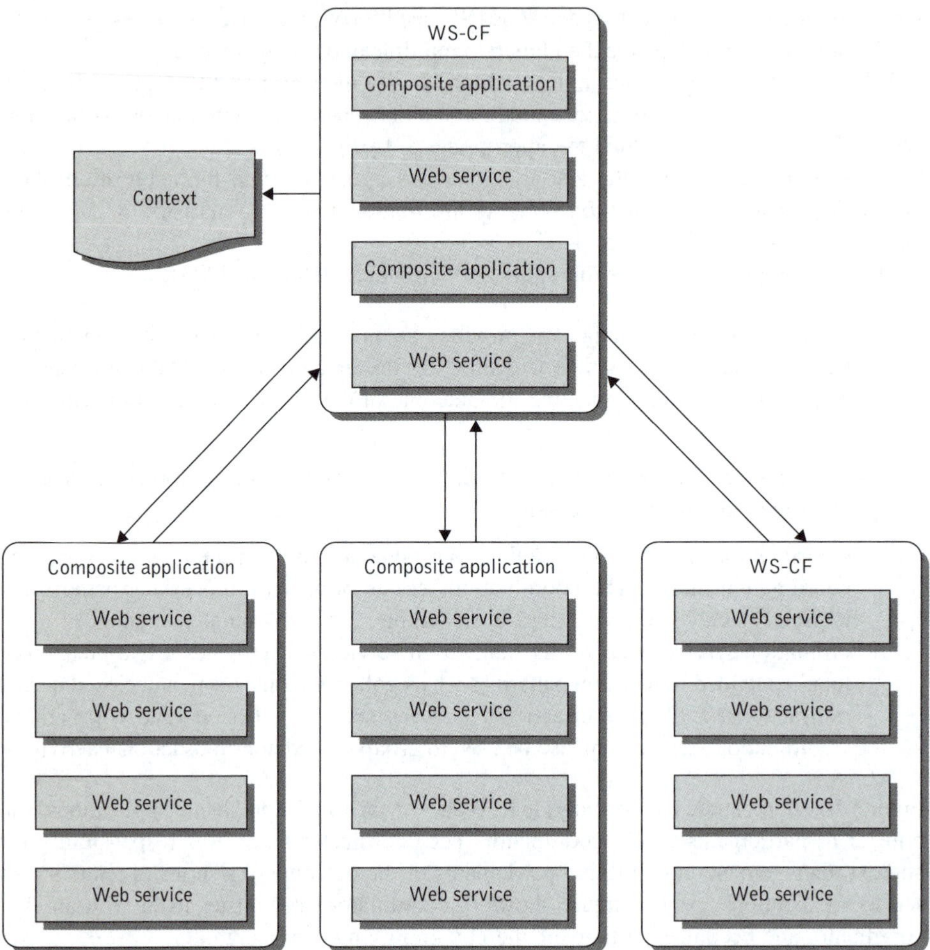

Figure 10.26 Relationship of coordinator to Web services and composite applications
Source: [Bunting 2003a]

Currently, there are three transaction protocols defined by WS-TXM [Bunting 2003d]. These are: ACID transaction, long-running action, and business process transaction.

ACID transaction is a traditional database-like transaction designed for interoperability across existing transaction infrastructures via Web services. In the ACID model, each activity is bound to the scope of a transaction, so that the end of an activity automatically triggers the termination (commit or rollback) of the associated transaction.

A long-running action (LRA) is an activity, or group of activities, which does not necessarily possess the guaranteed ACID properties. Participants within an LRA may use forward (compensation) or backward error recovery to ensure atomicity. The LRA model simply defines the triggers for compensation actions and the conditions under which those triggers are executed. Isolation is also considered a back-end implementation responsibility.

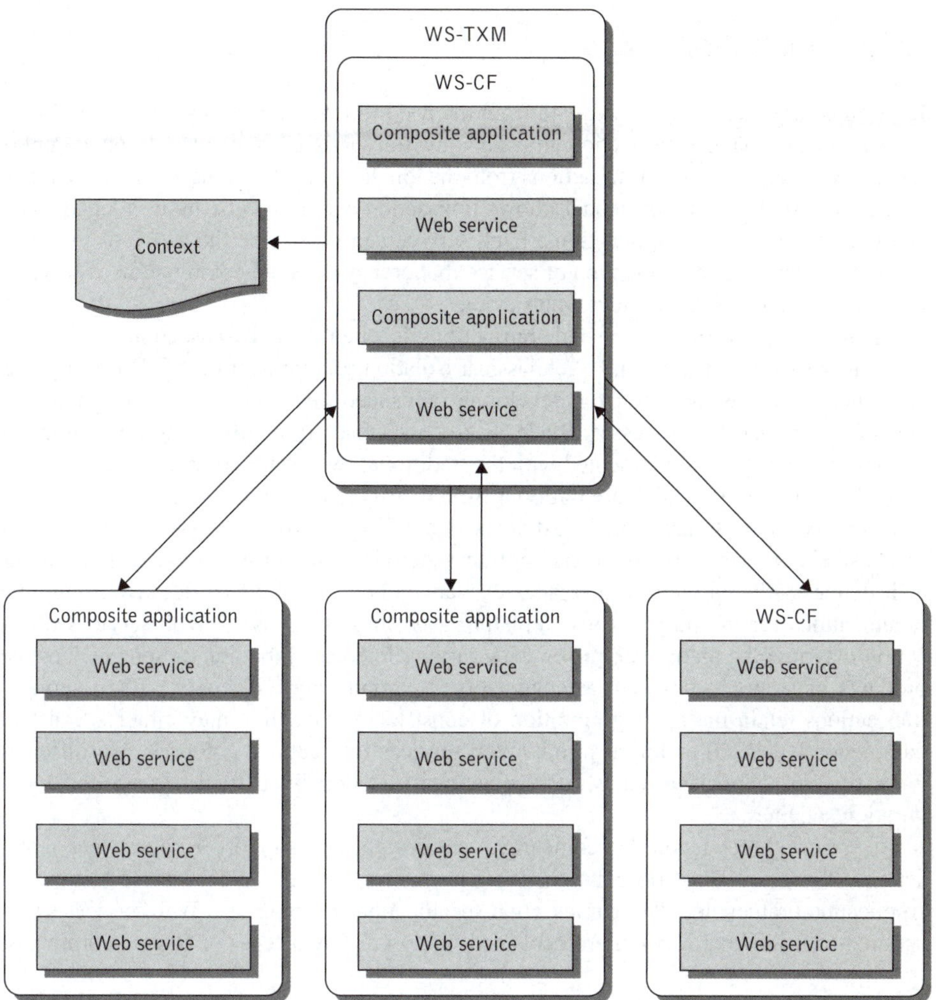

Figure 10.27 Relationships of transactions to coordination framework
Source: [Bunting 2003d]

Finally, business process transaction is an activity, or group of activities, that is responsible for performing some application-specific work. A business process may be structured as a collection of atomic transactions or LRAs depending upon the application requirements. The business process protocol is significantly different from any of the other transaction models such as WS-Transaction. This model mainly targets e-business applications and is specifically aimed at tying heterogeneous transaction domains together into a single business-to-business transaction. For example, with the business process transaction model it is possible to have a long-running Web services transaction spanning messaging, workflow, and traditional ACID transactions, allowing enterprises to leverage their existing enterprise assets [Webber 2003b].

10.7 Summary

Distributed transactions have evolved from the need to integrate transactions from different servers into a single transaction unit. To allow transaction designers to design complex functionally decomposable transactions from the top down, nested transactions were introduced. A nested transaction model allows transaction services to be built independently and later combined into applications. Each service can determine the scope of its transaction boundaries. The application or service that orchestrates the combination of services controls the scope of the top-level transaction.

An interesting variant of nested transactions is open nested transactions and transactional workflows. These relax the classical isolation requirement of ACID transactions and can be used as the basis for developing advanced business applications involving collaborating business processes. Business processes usually involve long-running transactions that cannot be implemented with the traditional two-phase commit protocol.

Web services transactions are built out from distributed coordinated transactions, open nested transactions, transactional workflows, and different forms of recovery. The concept of a business transaction (or Web services transaction) is central to Web services applications as it defines a shared view of messages exchanged between Web services from multiple organizations for the purpose of completing a business process. A Web services transaction may involve many enterprises with varying interest in the transaction, such as the products or services, payment arrangements, or monitoring and control. Web services transactions retain the driving ambition of consistency, i.e., they may either execute to completion (succeed) or fail as a unit. Web services transactions comprise two different types of transactional activities: atomic actions (or short-lived transactions) and long-duration activities.

At present three standard specifications are designed to support Web services transactions. These are WS-Coordination, WS-Transaction, and the Web Service Composite Application Framework. These transaction specifications encompass a Web services transaction model and coordination protocols and support different types of business protocols.

Review questions

- What is a transaction and what are its major properties? What are distributed transactions and how do they differ from centralized transactions?
- Describe the main building blocks of a distributed transaction architecture involving local and global transactions.
- What is a coordinator and what are subordinate coordinators and (transaction) participants?
- Briefly describe the two-phase commit protocol. What is its purpose?
- Briefly describe the concept of closed nested transactions and the two-phase commit protocol for nested transactions.

- What are open nested transactions and what are long-running activities?
- Compare closed nested with open nested transactions.
- Why are long-running activities important for Web services transactions? Describe the two types of Web services transactions and discuss their relative merits.
- What is interposition and why is it important for Web services?
- What are the main component services of WS-Coordination and how does it relate to WS-Transaction?
- Describe the two types of Web services transactions supported by WS-Transaction and their most important coordination protocols.
- What is the Web Service Composite Application Framework and how does it differ from WS-Coordination and WS-Transaction?

Exercises

10.1 Develop a simple sequence diagram illustrating the WS-Coordination flow for an application involving a purchase order service that forwards orders for products and needs to make several Web services calls to some of its suppliers to order products, and a coordinator service that acts as both activation and registration service on behalf of WS-Coordination. Assume that the purchase order service invokes an operation called `checkInventory()` to accomplish its task.

10.2 Develop a simple sequence diagram illustrating the WS-Coordination flow for an application involving a sales service that receives orders for products and wishes to query an inventory service that provides inventory information from a warehouse about the availability of products, a shipping service that schedules shipments, and a coordinator service that acts as both activation and registration service on behalf of WS-Coordination.

10.3 Modify the solution to Exercise 10.2 to include durable 2PC. If all the products are available the activity should commit, otherwise the entire activity should roll back. Again draw a sequence diagram and use message exchanges defined in specifications such as WS-Coordination and WS-Transaction to show how messages are exchanged (excluding faults) between the initiator and participant.

10.4 Replace the WS-AtomicActivity protocol by a WS-BusinessActivity protocol. The solution should include a purchase order service (acting on behalf of a customer), a coordination service associated with the purchase order service and, finally, a sales service (acting on behalf of a supplier). Assume that the buyer wants to buy three specific products and wants to know if the supplier can provide all these three products. If the supplier has no problem supplying all three products, the distributor will confirm the order. If there are problems with delivery of any of the three products, the buyer would like to reconsider the entire purchase activity. For example, the buyer may want to contact some other supplier to ask about the availability of the three items and may eventually buy only one product from the supplier in question. To solve this exercise you should take into account that the WS-BusinessActivity is nested. This means that the overall purchase activity can be considered as a parent activity, while there can be a number of child activities for this activity, where each child represents the purchase of a single product. Notice that each child activity may further consist of one or more WS-AtomicTransactions. Demonstrate the actual exchange of messages that accomplishes this activity using WS-Coordination and WS-Transaction.

10.5 Extend the solution to Exercise 10.1 by assuming that the application uses durable 2PC and involves one initiator (purchase order) and a single participant (supplier). Again draw a sequence diagram and use message exchanges defined in specifications such as WS-Coordination and WS-Transaction to show how messages are exchanged (excluding faults) between the initiator and participant.

10.6 Extend the solution to Exercise 10.3 assuming that there is a rollback initiated by the participant (supplier service).

PART VI

Service security and policies

CHAPTER 11

Securing Web services

Learning objectives

With Web services applications security becomes a major concern. Web services use the insecure Internet for mission-critical transactions with the possibility of establishing dynamic, short-term relationships. Part of the flexibility and benefits of Web services creates potential security gaps. This calls for securing them against a wide range of security attacks. Ensuring the integrity, confidentiality, and security of Web services through the application of a comprehensive security model is critical, for both organizations and their customers.

In this chapter we describe a comprehensive security model for Web services. This security model relies on the integration of currently available technologies with the evolving security requirements of future Web services applications, which require a unifying technological (secure messaging) and business (policy, risk, trust) approach. After completing this chapter readers will understand the following key concepts:

- Common security threats for Web services and countermeasures.
- Network- and application-level security mechanisms.
- Architectural approaches to security.
- XML security services and standards such as XML Encryption, XML Signature, and SAML.
- Use cases for Web services security.
- Use of WS-Security to develop SOA-based solutions.
- The family of WS-Security standards.

11.1 Web services security considerations

A major characteristic of services in SOA is that they are designed to be combined with each other in unanticipated ways. The current deployment of Web services technology is a promising early initiative in this direction. However, before SOAs can support mission-critical, long-lived Web services transactions, serious security requirements must be addressed. Enterprises that undertake Web services integration initiatives must place additional reliance on electronic means for protecting and safeguarding business-critical information, transactions, and communications.

In the physical world enterprises rely on conventional security measures to protect and safeguard confidential corporate information. Traditional enterprise security has focused almost entirely on keeping intruders out by using tools such as firewalls and content filters. Firewalls act as a secure interface between a private, trusted enterprise network and external untrusted networks. A firewall can be used to control access to and from the enterprise network and uses content filters to permit/deny packet flow on the basis of the origin and destination of the packet's addresses and ports. This includes access to resources such as application services and specific hosts. When properly configured to implement a judicious security policy, firewalls can protect an enterprise network from intrusion and compromise.

Traditional distributed computing security was modeled by islands of security, which describe systems and users on isolated networks or subnetworks. The network acted as an island, with its own perimeter security, but users within the network were considered to be trusted, whereas users outside the network were considered as untrusted. As a result of this, until recently, enterprises have controlled and managed access to resources by building authorization and authentication into every application that transcended enterprise boundaries. This piecemeal approach is not only time consuming but also error-prone, and expensive to build and maintain. Eventually, this technique becomes unsustainable as an enterprise's e-business portfolio grows, and as on-line interactions between enterprises become more complex. The "trusted" versus "untrusted" dichotomy breaks down in a service-oriented model, because applications can access "spontaneously" services located on systems across one or more enterprises. In an interface-driven environment, application functionality is much more exposed compared to traditional, stove-piped applications. The concept of trusted groups no longer has meaning; instead, enterprises must institute policies that apply to their entire enterprise network (including participants invited from outside), and administer that security in a tiered or hierarchical fashion [Bloomberg 2004]. What we require is a comprehensive Web services security solution that is easily managed and satisfies a demanding set of application and developer security requirements and provides capabilities such as performance, speed of deployment, and scalability, as well as the flexibility to accommodate evolving technologies such as wireless services.

Web services integration initiatives are forcing enterprises to move away from private communication networks to open public networks such as the Internet where they need to open their private network applications and information assets to customers, suppliers, and business partners. This means letting customers and business partners into the private enterprise network, essentially through the firewall, but in a selective and controlled manner, so that they access only applications permitted to them. As a result, existing network infrastructures, e.g., routers, firewalls, and load balancers, that operate at the network layer rather than at the application layer, are entirely unable to provide the application layer security that Web services require. This means a careful migration from network-level to application-level security is required to be able to protect business-critical information, transactions, and communication with a large number of trading partners, customers, and suppliers, exchanged over insecure networks such as the Internet. Web services security involves the complex interaction of multiple computer environments, communication protocols, policies, and procedures. These must all be considered when implementing a coherent, consistent approach to Web services security.

Web services security marks a departure from traditional security as it poses new security requirements in connection with access (authentication, authorization), confidentiality, non-repudiation, and integrity of information. These are the issues that will be of concern to us throughout this chapter. However, before we introduce and explain these topics it is important to understand what kind of security threats Web services face.

11.1.1 Security threats for Web services

The objective of Web services is to expose standardized interfaces to new and existing applications to allow the construction of applications and business processes that span organizational networks. Service aggregation makes it easy to create new value-added services, e.g., an application that enables resellers to check the availability and pricing of a manufacturer's products, place orders, and track order status on-line. Unfortunately, it also introduces a new set of security risks – as no previous technology has created this level of exposure to critical business applications. One major concern is that Web services are designed to penetrate firewalls, evading their usefulness at the application layer. Web services are designed to go through network firewalls, e.g., through port 80, and provide only rudimentary content inspection. Application-level security is required to protect against XML and Web-services-related security threats. While network firewalls continue to be absolutely essential to provide IP-based access control and network-level protection, a service (or XML) firewall is required to protect Web services. To achieve this, service firewalls must understand who the requestors are, what information is being requested, and what specific services are being requested. In addition, they must be able to intercept incoming XML traffic and take policy-based actions based on the content of that traffic. This type of functionality is a prerequisite to providing the necessary security to protect Web services and SOA environments.

An additional security concern is that Web services are standardized and self-describing. Given that Web services interfaces are standardized, they can be attacked in consistent ways. Intruders can more easily gain access to a standardized interface than a proprietary interface since more is known about the standardized interface. Further, SOAP messages provide information and structure for each message. A packaged application, for instance, may have a large number of critical operations exposed, all accessible through port 80. In addition, attackers have more information available to them. Since WSDL specifications and UDDI entries are self-describing, they can provide detailed information that enables an intruder to gain entry to mission-critical applications. WSDL documents provide significant information about each Web service, including where the service is located, how to access it, what kind of information to send to it, and what type of information a developer should expect to receive. This provides significant information to a potential intruder to inappropriately access the service. Again this points to a migration from network-level security to application-level security.

The fact that Web services applications must operate at the application layer of the OSI stack poses a challenge, because all data-specific network traffic appears to be the same to lower-level devices. Current network and transport security layer solutions use conventional mechanisms such as firewalls, routers, proxies, load balancing, restricting access to known IP addresses, and use of Secure Socket Layer to secure Web transactions independent of the programming of Web services applications. However, such solutions are inadequate as they are simply network aware. Instead, they must be able to be XML aware. Application layer security plays a pivotal role in Web services applications and involves inspecting the content of the network traffic, making authentication and authorization decisions for that content as well as verifying the individual parts of XML transactions and performing activities as security policies dictate. Application layer security also addresses confidentiality and privacy – using encryption to protect messages, guarantee message integrity, and provide audit functionality.

Web services security presents many similarities to application security with distributed technologies and is based on an understanding of:

- the resources being managed and protected by an application;
- the vulnerabilities relevant to the application's base technology;
- the vulnerabilities relevant to the application's specific logic; and
- the techniques that can be used to mitigate these risks.

To address Web services security concerns the WS-I Basic Security Profile [Davis 2004] has identified several security threats and challenges for Web services as well as countermeasures (technologies and protocols) used to mitigate each threat. Below we group the threats identified by the WS-I Basic Security Profile into four broad categories to illustrate some of the most frequent security concerns that come up with Web services:

1. *Unauthorized access:* Information within the message is viewable by unintended and unauthorized participants, e.g., an authorized party obtains a credit card number.
2. *Unauthorized alteration of messages:* These threats affect message integrity, whereby an attacker may modify parts (or the whole) message. Message information is altered by inserting, removing, or otherwise modifying information created by the originator of the information and mistaken by the receiver as being the originator's intention. For example, an attacker may delete part of a message, or modify part of a message, or insert extra information into a message. This broad category may include: attachment alteration, replay attacks (signed messages are intercepted and sent back to a targeted site), session hijacking, forged claims, and falsified messages.
3. *Man in the middle:* In this kind of assault it is possible for an attacker to compromise a SOAP intermediary and then intercept messages between the Web service

requestor and the ultimate receiver. The original parties will think that they are communicating with each other. The attacker may just have access to the messages or may modify them. Threats known as *routing detours* comprise also a form of a "man-in-the-middle" attack which compromises routing information. Routing information (whether in the HTTP headers or in WS-Routing headers) can be modified en route to direct sensitive messages to an outside location. Traces of the routing can be removed from the message so that the receiving application does not realize that a routing detour has occurred. Mutual authentication techniques can be used to alleviate the threats of this attack.

4. *Denial-of-service attacks:* Here the objective is to render target systems inaccessible by legitimate users. A flood of plain messages or messages with large numbers of encrypted elements or signed elements may cause system resources to be tied up and service levels to be affected. This can cause severe disruption to a system.

All the above issues point out that securing open, loosely coupled systems requires a sophisticated security approach to support distributed clients (applications) and systems that may have different policies and possibly different security mechanisms. At the same time, because Web services have a high degree of interaction with varied clients, it is important to keep security measures from being overly intrusive and thus maintain the ease of use of a service. A service needs to promote its interoperability features and make its security requirements and policies known to its clients. As a result, to ensure the appropriate security to the network of Web services a fundamental requirement is to be able to operate on the security context of applications that invoke services. *Security context* is a set of information regarding the use of services on behalf of an application (or user), including the rules and policies that apply to the application, as well as information about the business process or transaction that the application is currently participating in. When the application is separated from the service, that context is lost.

11.1.2 Countermeasures

Although not all Web services threats can be eliminated, there are many circumstances where exposure can be reduced to an acceptable level through the use of *application security*. Application security applies to networked (distributed) applications and platforms, such as J2EE, and contains six basic requirements, expressed in terms of the messages exchanged between parties [Pilz 2003]. Such messages include any kind of communication between the sender (the party who wishes to access a network accessible application) and the recipient (the application itself). The six requirements for application-level security include authentication, authorization, message integrity, confidentiality, operational defense, and non-repudiation. These countermeasures are addressed in section 11.3, where we discuss application-level solutions for networked applications and distributed platforms, and in section 11.6 where we describe application-level solutions for Web-services-enabled applications.

In the next section we take a closer look at a variety of technology-based solutions that address network-level security concerns.

11.2 Network-level security mechanisms

Network-level security refers to the protection of the process by which data items are communicated from a network to an end system [Ford 1997]. In particular, this topic excludes any coverage of what happens within the end system – both client and server systems. Network-level security incorporates embedded encryption functionality within network devices or operating systems utilizing Internet Protocol Security (IPSec). Network-level solutions are usually designed to terminate the secure connections at the corporate firewall. Enterprises employing network-level security solutions usually rely on two main technologies to protect their networks: firewalls and vulnerability assessment.

11.2.1 Firewalls

A firewall is a network security infrastructure placed between networks to logically separate and protect the privacy and integrity of business communications across these networks, and to safeguard against malicious use. Firewalls are built between an organization's internal network and the Internet backbone and help define the network perimeter where an enterprise meets the Internet.

Firewalls examine message traffic coming into and leaving an organization and block all access to local networks except authorized messages. They identify incoming traffic by name, IP address, application, and so on. This information is checked against the access rules that have been programmed into the firewall system. Because firewalls determine what traffic is allowed to pass into an enterprise from the Internet, they are the essential first line of defense against intruders. A firewall that is a perfect brick wall admits no outside traffic and ensures perfect security for an enterprise. This is, however, hardly practical for Web applications because it isolates the company from its customers and partners. Instead, firewalls can be used to block unwanted protocols by blocking the TCP ports that they use while leaving Web ports, i.e., ports 80 and 443 for SSL, open for Web browsing purposes. This has the effect of bypassing firewalls without compromising security as firewalls continue to guard against lower layers of communication. Thus only authorized traffic, as defined by the local security policy, will be allowed to pass a firewall while any unauthorized communication between the internal and the external network is prevented.

Functions typically provided by a firewall include [Ford 1997]:

- Limiting the set of applications for which traffic can enter the internal network from the Internet, and limiting the internal addresses to which traffic for different applications can go.
- Authenticating the sources of incoming traffic.
- Limiting the ability of internal enterprise networks and systems to establish connections to the external Internet, on the basis of the application used and other relevant information.
- Acting as a security gateway and encrypting and/or integrity checking all traffic over the Internet backbone to or from some other security gateway. Such a continuation

is known as a virtual private network (VPN). VPNs allow organizations to use their corporate networks and the Internet as a wide area network to achieve secure connectivity with their branches, suppliers, customers, and remote users.

11.2.1.1 Firewall architectures

The level of protection that any firewall is able to provide in securing a private network when connected to the Internet is directly related to the architecture(s) chosen for the firewall. Firewall architectures rely on information generated by protocols that function at various layers of the OSI model, see section 2.1.1.1. The higher up in the OSI layer at which a firewall architecture examines IP packets, the greater the level of protection the architecture provides as more information is available upon which to base security-related decisions.

There are three general classes of firewall architectures: packet filtering, circuit and application proxies, and stateful inspection. We shall examine these in turn.

IP packet filtering. Packet filtering firewalls are the oldest firewall architectures. A filtering firewall works at the network level (see Figure 11.1). This type of firewall employs a filtering process by examining individual IP packets. As packets arrive they are filtered by their type, source address, destination address, and port information (contained in each IP packet).

There are two types of packet filtering firewalls: static and stateful. A *static packet filter* firewall examines data in the IP header and the TCP header and compares this information against prespecified packet filtering (access) rules that dictate whether the firewall should deny or permit packets to pass the firewall. IP header information allows specifying packet filtering rules that deny or permit packets to and from a specific IP address or range of IP addresses, see Figure 11.1. TCP header information allows the specification of service specific rules, i.e., allow or deny packets to or from ports related to specific services. For example, with a static packet filter the network administrator may write rules that allow certain services such as HTTP from any IP address to view the Web pages on a protected Web server, while blocking other IP addresses from using the HTTP service and viewing the Web pages. The *stateful packet filter* firewall is the next step in the evolution of the static packet filter. This type of firewall inspects packets in isolation (as its static counterpart does) as it maintains state information on connections, and tracks open, valid connections without reprocessing the access rule set and can implement complex policies. The typical stateful packet filter is aware of the difference between a new and an established connection. As checked for new versus established connections are performed at the kernel level, substantial performance increase over a static packet filter is observed.

IP filtering is performed usually by a process within the operating system kernel of a router for performance purposes. If multiple firewalls are used, the first may mark certain packets for more exhaustive examination by a later firewall, allowing only "clean" packets to proceed. For example, a network administrator could configure a packet filter firewall to disallow FTP traffic between two networks while allowing HTTP and SMTP traffic between the two, further refining the granularity of control on protected traffic between sites.

The main advantages of packet filter firewalls are that they are fairly easy to implement and they are transparent to the end users, unlike some of the other firewall methods. However, even though packet filters can be easy to implement, they can prove difficult to

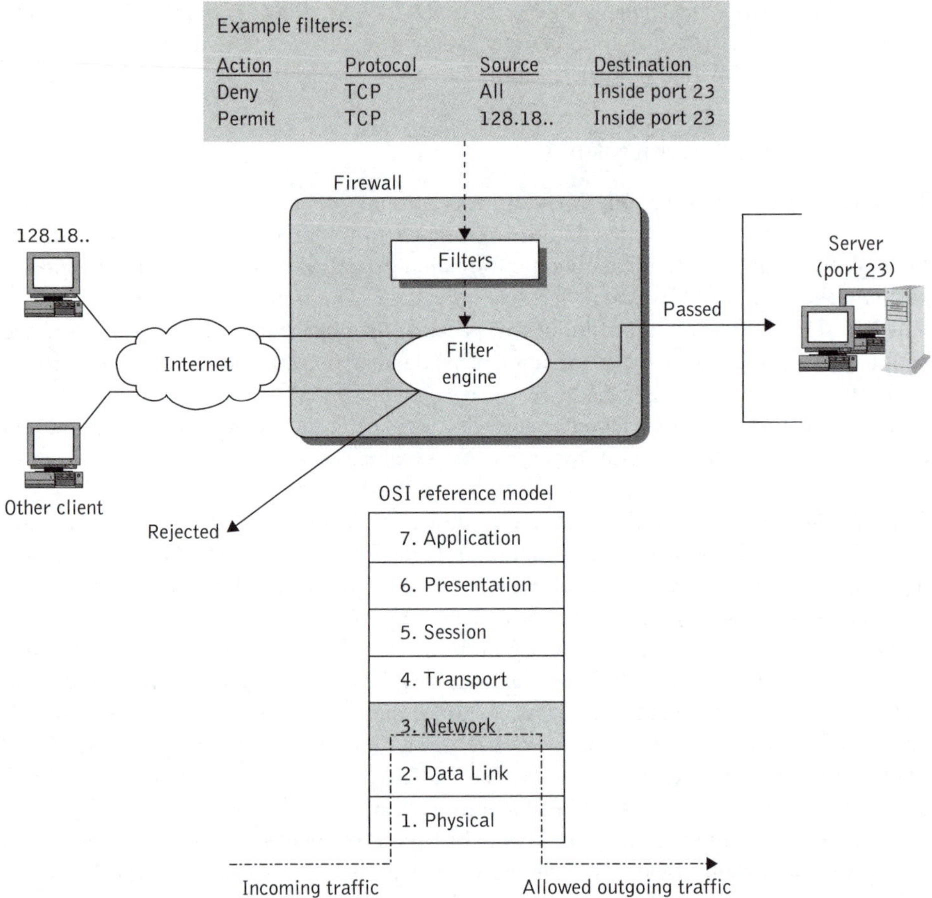

Figure 11.1 Packet filtering firewall

configure properly, particularly if a large number of rules have to be generated to handle a wide variety of application traffic and users. One of the main deficiencies is that packet filters are based on IP addresses, not authenticated user identification. Packet filtering also provides little defense against man-in-the-middle attacks and no defense against forged IP addresses. Additional limitations include lack of packet payload awareness, lack of state awareness, and susceptibility to application layer attacks.

Circuit-level gateway. The circuit-level gateway (circuit proxy) is an extension of a packet filter that performs basic packet filter operations and then adds verification of proper handshaking and verification of the legitimacy of the sequence numbers used in establishing the connection. This firewall enables users to utilize a proxy to communicate with secure systems, hiding valuable data and servers from potential attackers.

The proxy accepts a connection from the other side and, if the connection is permitted, makes a second connection to the destination host on the other side. The client attempting the connection is never directly connected to the destination. Because proxies can act on

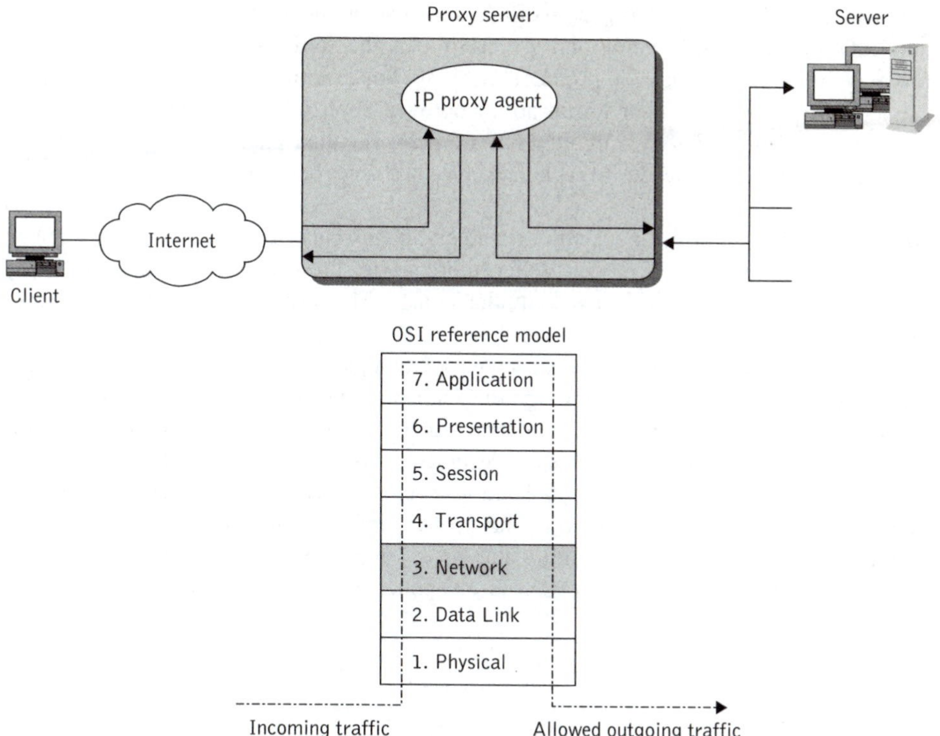

Figure 11.2 Circuit-level gateway

different types of traffic or packets from different applications, a *proxy firewall* (or *proxy server*, as it is often called) is usually designed to use proxy agents, in which an agent is programmed to handle one specific type of transfer, e.g., TCP traffic or FTP traffic. The more types of traffic that need to pass through the proxy, the more proxy agents need to be loaded and running on the proxy server.

Circuit-level gateways focus on the TCP/IP layers, using the network IP connection as a proxy. The circuit-level gateway operates at the session layer (OSI Layer 5), see Figure 11.2. The circuit-level gateway applies security mechanisms when a TCP or UDP connection is established. In particular, it examines and validates TCP and User Datagram Protocol (UDP) sessions before opening a connection, or circuit, through the firewall. Outbound connections are passed based on policy, and inbound connections are blocked. Management control is based primarily on port addresses. A circuit proxy is typically installed between an enterprise's network router and the Internet, communicating with the Internet on behalf of the enterprise network. Real network addresses can be hidden because only the address of the proxy is transmitted on the Internet.

Once a circuit-level gateway establishes a connection, any application can run across that connection because a circuit-level gateway filters packets only at the session and network layers of the OSI model. A circuit-level gateway cannot examine the application data content of the packets it relays between a trusted network and an untrusted network.

This can make the circuit proxy more efficient than an application proxy, which examines application data, but may compromise security. Another serious drawback of the circuit proxy is the lack of application protocol checking. For example, if two cooperating users use an approved port number to run an unapproved application, a circuit relay will not detect the violation. Finally, circuit proxies are slower than packet filters because they must reconstruct the IP header to each packet to its correct destination.

Application-level gateway. Packet filters and circuit gateways look exclusively at some of the lower layers of the OSI model. Better, more secure firewalls can be designed if they examine all layers of the OSI model simultaneously. This principle led to the creation of application-level gateways.

Application-specific proxies check each packet that passes through the gateway, verifying the contents of the packet up through the application layer (Layer 7) of the OSI model. These proxies can filter on particular information or specific individual commands in the application protocols that the proxies are designed to copy, forward, and filter.

Like a circuit-level gateway, an application-level gateway intercepts incoming and outgoing packets, runs proxies that copy and forward information across the gateway, and functions as a proxy server, preventing any direct connection between a trusted server or client and an untrusted host. The proxies that an application-level gateway runs (Figure 11.3)

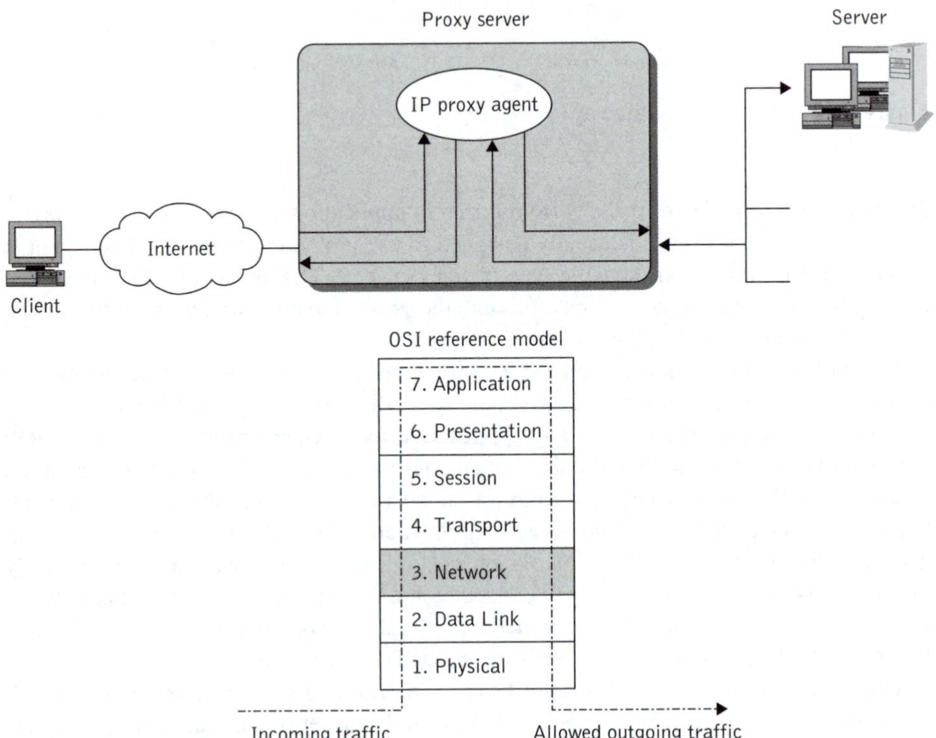

Figure 11.3 Application-level proxy server

often differ in two important ways from the circuit-level gateway: the proxies are application specific and examine the entire packet and can filter packets at the application layer of the OSI model.

The application-level gateway runs proxies that examine and filter individual packets, rather than simply copying them and recklessly forwarding them across the gateway. Unlike the circuit gateway, the application-level gateway accepts only packets generated by services that they are designed to copy, forward, and filter. For example, only an HTTP proxy can copy, forward, and filter HTTP traffic. If a network relies only on an application-level gateway, incoming and outgoing packets cannot access services for which there exists no proxy. All other services would be blocked.

Because application proxies operate as one-to-one proxies for a specific application, a proxy agent needs to be installed for every IP Service (HTTP/HTML, FTP, SMTP, and so on) to which an enterprise wants to control access. This leads to two of the disadvantages of application proxies: a lag usually exists between the introduction of new IP services and the availability of appropriate proxy agents; and the application proxy requires more processing of the packets, leading to lower performance.

One important differentiating feature of application proxies is their capability to identify users and applications. This identification can enable more secure user authentication, because digital certificates or other secure token-based methods can be used for identifying and authenticating use.

11.2.2 Intrusion detection systems and vulnerability assessment

One possible technology for network protection is intrusion detection systems (abbreviated as IDSs). An IDS is a defense system which detects and responds to hostile activities targeted at computing and networking resources. IDS tools are capable of distinguishing between insider attacks originating from inside the organization (coming from its own employees or customers) and external ones (attacks and the thread posed by hackers). One key feature of IDSs is their ability to provide a view of unusual activity and issue alerts notifying administrators and/or block a suspected connection. With an IDS, an organization discovers hacking attempts or actual break-ins by analyzing its networks or hosts for inappropriate data or other anomalous activity.

IDS solutions raise alerts that an attack may be taking place. However, this is inadequate for business-to-business applications. What is needed is a more proactive approach that determines susceptibility to attacks before networks are compromised. This is provided by vulnerability assessment.

Vulnerability assessment is a methodical approach to identifying and prioritizing vulnerabilities, enabling enterprises to non-intrusively test their networks from the "hacker's perspective." Vulnerability assessment automatically identifies vulnerabilities and network misconfigurations; identifies rogue devices, including wireless and VPN access points; detects and prioritizes vulnerability exposures; validates firewall and IDS configurations; and provides remedies for known vulnerabilities. The process of vulnerability assessment identifies potential vulnerabilities before they can be exploited, and the IDS notifies the company when anomalous activity has occurred. Vulnerability assessment works hand in hand with firewalls and IDS. It enables an enterprise to identify and close obvious holes so that the IDS produces a manageable volume of alerts. Vulnerability assessment also works in conjunction with firewalls to continuously and seamlessly monitor for vulnerabilities that may have inadvertently been introduced by firewall policy changes.

11.2.3 Securing network communications

Automated business processes and transactions using Web applications must flow over the public Internet. They, therefore, involve a large number of routers and servers through which the transaction packets flow. This situation is very different from a private network where dedicated communication lines are established between communicating parties. On unsecured networks, such as TCP/IP, there is a concern for both the sender and the receiver about the security of messages exchanged over the network. A number of technologies are available to protect the security of Internet communications, the most basic of which is message encryption.

Cryptography enables the user to encrypt and decrypt messages, allowing only authorized persons to read them. Both processes require a key, to transform the original text (called *plain text*) into a coded message (called *cipher text*) and back. *Encryption* is a process where the plain text is placed into a codified algorithm and an encryption key to transform the plain text into cipher text. The encryption key is used in the algorithmic formula to scramble the information in question in such a way that it could not easily be descrambled without knowledge of the secret encryption key. *Decryption*, on the other hand, is the reverse of encryption with the cipher text as input and the plain text as output. The function involves both an algorithm and a decryption key.

The security functions enabled by cryptography address four dimensions of the application-level security requirements: authentication, confidentiality, message integrity, and non-repudiation. There are currently three main cryptographic techniques that are used to protect the security of Internet communications and which we examine in this section. These are symmetric encryption or secret-key cryptography, or asymmetric encryption of public-key cryptography, digital certificates, and signatures.

11.2.3.1 Symmetric encryption

Symmetric-key encryption, also called *shared-key encryption* or *secret-key cryptography*, uses a single key that both the sender and recipient possess, see Figure 11.4. The term *symmetric* refers to the fact that the same key is used for both encryption and decryption. This key is called a secret key (also referred to as a symmetric or shared key). Symmetric-key encryption is an efficient method for encrypting large amounts of data. Many algorithms exist for symmetric-key encryption, but all have the same purpose – the reversible transformation of plain text into cipher text. Cipher text is scrambled using an encryption key and is meaningless to anyone who does not have the decryption key. Deciphering is accomplished by retracing the key's algorithms in reverse order. Because symmetric key cryptography uses the same key for both encryption and decryption, the security of this process depends on no unauthorized person obtaining the symmetric key.

The advantage of symmetric encryption is that it is easily and quickly implemented. If the key is to be used only a few times, it works very effectively because there are only a

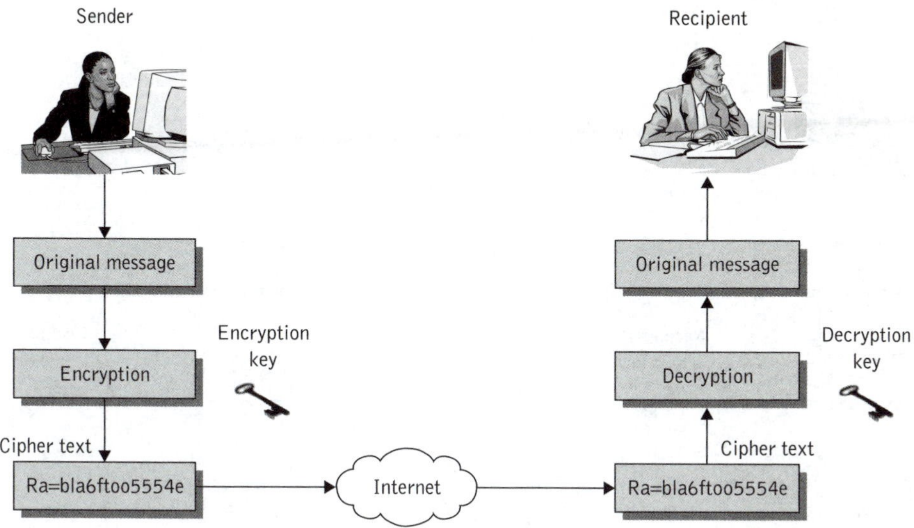

Figure 11.4 Symmetric-key cryptography

limited number of previous messages with which to compare a new cipher text. The disadvantage is that every pair or group of users needs its own key – otherwise everyone can read along – which results in a large number of keys. And if one key is lost or made public, all other keys must be replaced as well. Of the security requirements, symmetric encryption ensures confidentiality only: nobody but the sender and the receiver can read the message.

11.2.3.2 Asymmetric encryption

In order to overcome the disadvantages of symmetric encryption, a different cryptographic system, which involves the use of different keys for encryption and decryption, has been devised. This type of encryption is called *asymmetric encryption* or *public-key cryptography*. The most widely used public-key algorithm, especially for data sent over the Internet, is the Rivest–Shamir–Adleman (RSA) cryptographic algorithm.

In contrast to symmetric encryption, the primary characteristic of asymmetric encryption (public-key cryptography) is the fact that instead of one key, both the sender and the receiver need two keys, one of which is public and the other private. These two keys share a specific property in that when one of these keys (public key) is used to perform encryption, only the other key (private) is able to decrypt the data. These two keys are created during the same process and are known as a *key pair*. All keys are mathematically related to one another, so that data encrypted with one key can be decrypted using the other. This allows applications that are not possible with symmetric-key encryption.

Figure 11.5 illustrates a message encrypted with a public key. Once a message is encrypted using the public key, it is sent over the Internet and can be decrypted only with its matching private key. The private key is a secret key that only the recipient keeps. Both keys are different, and the key used for encrypting messages cannot be used for decrypting

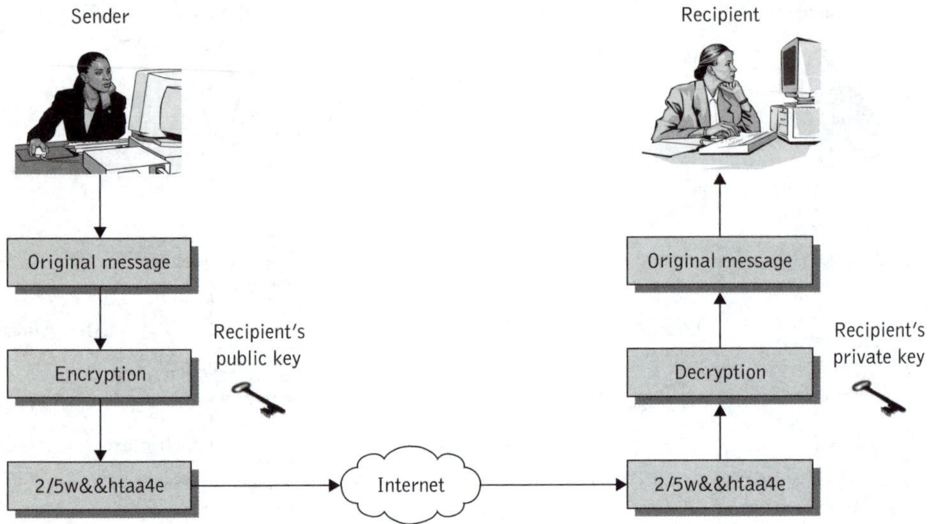

Figure 11.5 Asymmetric-key cryptography

the same message. The public key can be passed openly between the parties or published in a public repository, but the related private key remains private. Thus with the asymmetric encryption scheme both confidentiality and the receiver's authenticity are guaranteed. However, this scheme does not achieve accountability or non-repudiation and does not guarantee the sender's authenticity, since anybody can use the receiver's public key.

To overcome the issue of accountability, digital signing can be used in conjunction with the public-key encryption scheme to provide confidentiality, integrity, and non-repudiation. Figure 11.6 illustrates how digital signing and encryption work together. This figure illustrates that the sender creates a "secret" message that encrypts (signs) using the sender's own private key. The sender further encrypts (signs) the message using the recipient's public key and the message is sent to the recipient over the Internet. On the other side, the recipient first decrypts the message using the recipient's own private key and then decrypts it further using the sender's public key. Finally, the recipient receives the original message sent by the sender.

The asymmetric cryptography suffers from performance. The digital signature algorithm (DSA) [Kaufman 1995] is a technique used to address such concerns. The DSA is a public-key cryptosystem used only to calculate digital signatures (and not for data encryption). The DSA is optimized for speed of generating a signature, anticipating its use on low-power microprocessors such as those on smart cards.

11.2.3.3 Digital certificates and signatures

Public-key encryption gives rise to another kind of encryption that is absolutely necessary for business-to-business interactions: digital certificates and signatures.

A *digital certificate* is a document that uniquely identifies a party (person or organization) that owns the certificate, the time period for which the certificate is valid, the organization

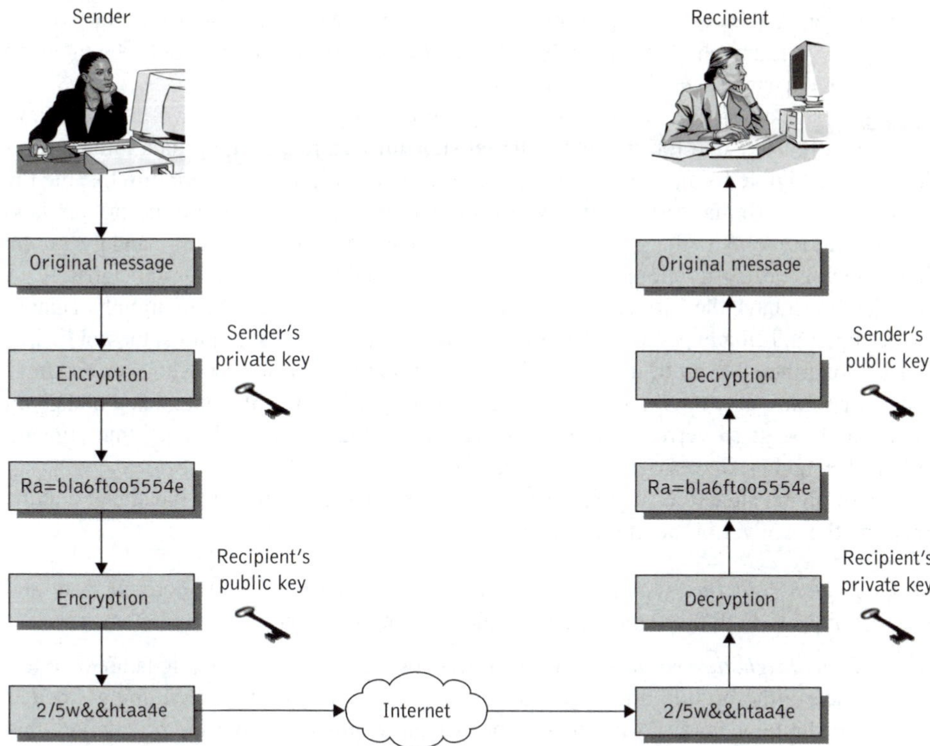

Figure 11.6 Asymmetric-key cryptography using digital signing and public-key encryption

that issued the certificate, and a digital signature that verifies the issuing organization's identity. Digital certificates are exchanged during the set up of communication links to verify that the trading partner on the other end of the wire is the intended recipient of a message transmission and to prove the sender's identity. A digital certificate is issued by a *certification authority* and binds an entity's identification to its public key. This intermediary guarantees that the key belongs to the party identified, and announces this by signing and publishing the file containing the key owner's personal specifics and public key. This digital certificate is then sent along with the encrypted message. The certification authority's signature ensures the authenticity, integrity, and incontrovertibility of the certificate as well as the accuracy of the public key. In order to prevent a massive spread of certificates, the Internet Engineering Task Force (IETF) is developing standards for them.

Digital certificates are interlinked with digital signatures, which can solve the problem of authenticating a public key. *Digital signatures* guarantee that the enterprise or person represented in the digital certificate sent the message. A digital signature is a block of data created by applying a cryptographic signing algorithm to some data using the signer's private key. Digital signatures may be used to authenticate the source of a message and to assure message recipients that no one has tampered with a message since the time it was sent by the signer. These are attached to the message body to identify the sender. The receiver verifies the digital signature by decrypting it with the sender's public key to retrieve the message. In this way authentication mechanisms ensure that only the intended parties can exchange sensitive information.

Digital signatures use asymmetric encryption techniques whereby two different keys are generally used, one for creating a digital signature or transforming data into a seemingly unintelligible form, and another key for verifying a digital signature or returning the message to its original form. The keys for digital signatures are termed the private key, which is known only to the signer and is used to create the digital signature, and the public key, which is ordinarily more widely known and is used to verify the digital signature. A recipient must have the corresponding public key in order to verify that a digital signature is the signer's. If many people need to verify the signer's digital signatures, the public key must be distributed to all of them, e.g., by publication in an on-line repository or directory where they can easily obtain it. Although many people will know the public key of a given signer and use it to verify that signer's signatures, they cannot discover that signer's private key and use it to forge digital signatures.

Use of digital signatures comprises two processes, one performed by the signer and the other by the receiver of the digital signature:

1. *Digital signature creation* is the process of computing a code derived from and unique to both the signed message and a given private key.
2. *Digital signature verification* is the process of checking the digital signature by reference to the original message and a public key, and thereby determining whether the digital signature was created for that same message using the private key that corresponds to the referenced public key.

A *hashing algorithm* is used in both creating and verifying a digital signature [Steel 2006]. Hashing algorithms enable the software for creating digital signatures to operate on smaller and predictable amounts of data, while still providing a strong evidentiary correlation to the original message content. A *digest* (hashing) *algorithm* creates a *message digest* of the message, which is a code usually much smaller than the original message but nevertheless unique to it. Digest algorithms consume (digest) data to calculate a hash value, called a message digest. The message digest depends upon the data as well as the digest algorithm. If the message changes, the hash result of the message will invariably be different. The digest value can be used to verify the integrity of a message; that is, to ensure that the data has not been altered while on its way from the sender to the receiver. The sender sends the message digest value with the message. On receipt of the message, the recipient repeats the digest calculation. If the message has been altered, the digest value will not match and the alteration will be detected. Public-key cryptography is typically used in conjunction with a hashing algorithm, such as Secure Hash Algorithm 1 (SHA-1) [SHA-1] or Message Digest 5 (**http://rfc.net/rfc1321.html**), to provide integrity.

Figure 11.7 shows the digital signature creation process. In order to sign a document or any other item of information, the signer first delimits the portion of the document that needs to be signed. The delimited text to be signed is termed the "message." Subsequently, a hashing algorithm in the signer's side computes a message digest. Subsequently, the message digest is encrypted using the digital signature by referring to the signer's private key. The resulting digital signature is thus unique to both the message and the private key

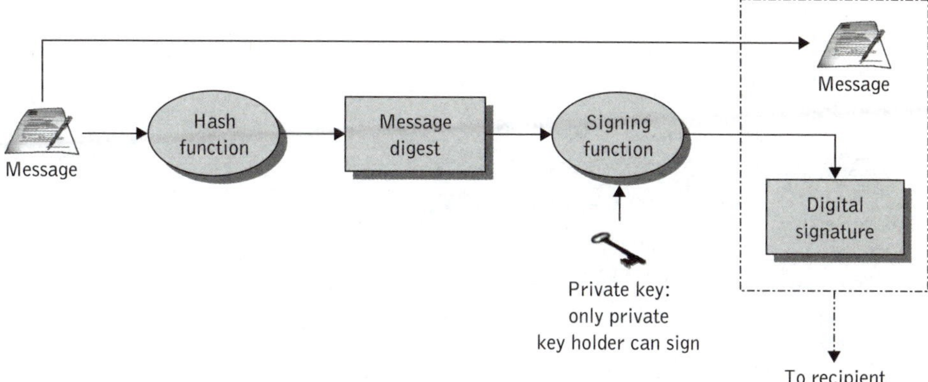

Figure 11.7 Creation of a digital signature

used to create it. Typically, a digital signature is attached to its message and stored or transmitted with its message. However, it may also be sent or stored as a separate data element, so long as it maintains a reliable association with its message. Since a digital signature is unique to its message, it is useless if wholly disassociated from its message.

Figure 11.8 depicts the verification process of a digital signature. This figure shows that the verification process is accomplished by computing a message digest of the original message by means of the same hashing algorithm used in creating the digital signature (which is agreed upon beforehand). The message digest is encrypted by the sender's private key. Subsequently, the message along with the message digest is sent to the recipient. The recipient uses the public key to decrypt the digital signature and check whether the digital signature was created using the corresponding private key. The recipient then uses the same hashing algorithm to calculate its own message digest of the sender's plain text message. Subsequently, the recipient checks whether the newly computed message digest matches the message digest derived from the digital signature. If the signer's private key was used and the message digests are identical, then the digital signature as well as the original message are verified. Verification thus provides two kinds of assurances.

11.3 Application-level security mechanisms

Several applications have intricate security requirements that cannot be met by network-level security measures. The term *application-level security* is used to refer to security safeguards that are built into a particular application and that operate independently of any network-level security measures [Ford 1997].

When considering the application-level security requirements such as authentication, authorization, message integrity, confidentiality, and non-repudiation that we addressed briefly in section 11.1.2, it is important to understand that the fundamental need is for mechanisms and technologies used in any kind of communication between the sender and the recipient to be safe and secure. In the following we describe application-level security

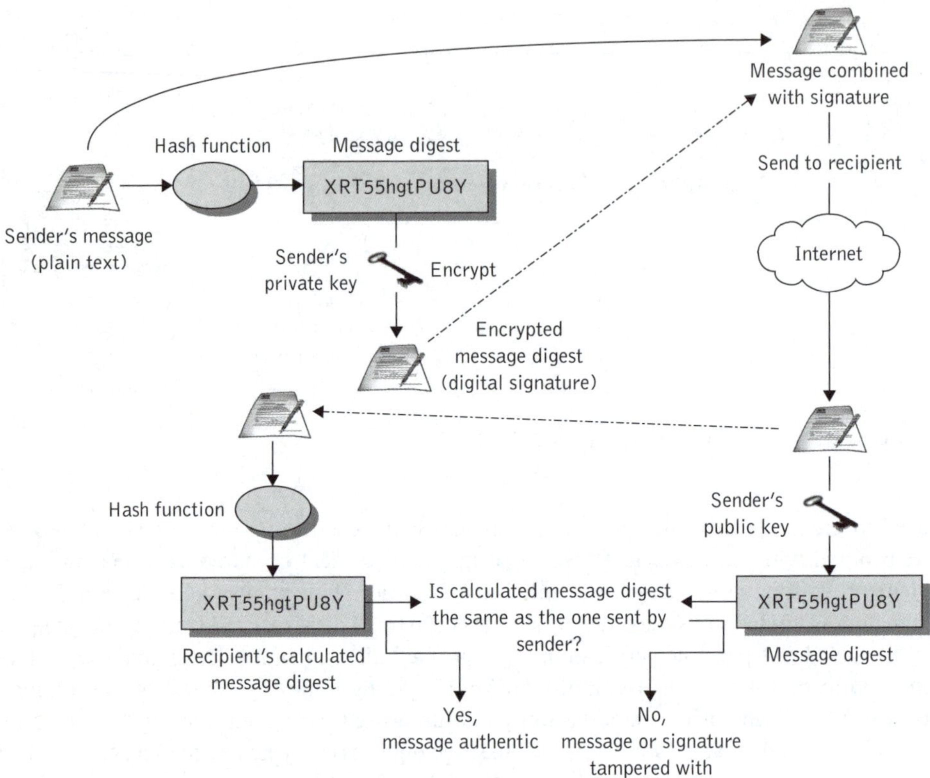

Figure 11.8 Verification of a digital signature

mechanisms that are used in the context of distributed computing environments, such as J2EE, while in sections 11.4 and 11.5 we examine Web-services-related initiatives and solutions.

11.3.1 Authentication

In distributed computing environments, authentication is the mechanism by which clients and service providers prove to one another that they are acting on behalf of specific users or systems [Monzillo 2002], [Singh 2004]. A client usually presents an identifier and the service provider verifies the client's claimed identity. When the proof is bidirectional, it is referred to as mutual authentication. Authentication establishes the call identities and proves that the participants are authentic instances of these identities. For instance, authentication may verify that the identity of entities is provided by the use of public-key certificates and digital signature envelopes. Many authentication methods exist for distributed environments and e-business applications, ranging from simple user names and passwords to stronger methods such as tokens and digital certificates.

Authentication in distributed environments is often achieved in two phases [Monzillo 2002]. First, an *authentication context* is established by performing a service-independent authentication. The authentication context encapsulates the identity and is able to fabricate authenticators (proofs of identity). Subsequently, the authentication context is used to authenticate with other (called or calling) entities. The basis of authentication entails controlling access to the authentication context and thus the ability to authenticate as the associated identity. Most common policies and mechanisms for controlling access to an authentication context include the following:

- Once a client program performs an initial authentication, the processes that the client program starts inherits access to the authentication context.
- When a component is authenticated, access to the authentication context may be available to other related or trusted components, such as those that are part of the same application.

In a distributed environment, when a client program accesses a set of distributed components and resources, e.g., Java Server Pages (JSPs), Enterprise Java Beans (EJBs), databases, etc., the client must present its identity. Subsequently, a container component determines whether the client meets the criteria for access as specified by authorization rules. A container is the run-time environment in which an application runs that provides workload and performance management, resource management, security management, transaction management, deployment, configuration, and administration capabilities (see Chapter 8). A container is synonymous with a J2EE application server. A J2EE application runs inside the container, which has specific responsibilities with respect to the application, e.g., it is interposed on all method calls and provides the standardized environment that supplies specific services to its underlying component. In many cases, processing a client's request to a component might require the component to make a chain of calls to access other components and resources and use an authentication context. Thus, not only does the container enforce authentication and establish an identity when a client calls a component, but it also handles authentication when the component makes an initial chain of calls to these components and resources. The distributed platform allows the client identity established with the authentication of the initial call to be propagated along the chain of calls.

11.3.1.1 Protection domains

Distributed platforms allow entities to be grouped into special domains, called *protection domains*, where they can communicate with each other without requiring authentication [Monzillo 2002], [Singh 2004]. A protection domain is a logical boundary around a set of such entities that are assumed or known to trust each other. When one component interacts with others in the same protection domain, no constraint is placed on the identity that it can associate with its call. In a protection domain authentication is required only for entities that cross the boundary of the protection domain. Interactions that remain within the protection domain do not require authentication.

In a distributed environment such as J2EE, to ensure that unproven or unauthenticated entities do not cross the protection domain boundary, a container provides an authentication boundary between external callers and the components it hosts. In general, it is the job of the container to provide bidirectional authentication functionality to enforce the protection domain boundaries of the deployed applications.

The container ensures that the identity of the call is authenticated before it enters the protection domain. For inbound calls, it is the container's responsibility to make an authentic representation of the caller identity available to the component in the form of a credential. An X.509 certificate and a Kerberos service ticket (see section 11.3.6.3) are examples of credentials used in computing environments. An X.509 certificate is a digital container for the public-key part of a public/private (asymmetric) key pair. A certification authority that assents to the identity related to the public key signs this digital certificate. For outbound calls, the container is responsible for establishing the identity of the calling component.

11.3.1.2 Web resource protection

In distributed environments, such as J2EE, available (exported) application business logic and Web connectivity to clients is provided by a dedicated tier known as the Web tier. The Web tier handles all application communication with Web clients, invoking business logic and transmitting data in response to incoming requests, and provides access to enterprise resources. Web tier resources available to a client may be protected or unprotected. Protected resources are mission-critical resources, e.g., back-end systems, which are distinguished by the presence of authorization rules that restrict access to them to some subset of non-anonymous identities. To access a protected resource, a client must present a credential such that its identity can be evaluated against the resource authorization policy.

With Web tier authentication, the developer specifies an authorization constraint to designate those Web resources, e.g., HTML documents, Web components, image files, archives, and so on, that need to be protected. When a client tries to access a protected Web tier resource, appropriate authentication mechanisms for the component or resource accessed are activated. For example, in the case of J2EE, Web containers support three authentication mechanisms [Singh 2004]: *HTTP basic authentication*, *form-based authentication*, and *HTTPS mutual authentication*.

With HHTP basic authentication the Web server authenticates a principal using the user name and password obtained from the Web client. Form-based authentication lets developers customize the authentication user interface presented by an HTTP browser. Like HTTP basic authentication, form-based authentication is a relatively vulnerable authentication mechanism, since the content of the user dialogue is sent as plain text and the target server is not authenticated [Monzillo 2002]. Finally, with HTTPS mutual authentication both the client and the server use digital certificates to establish their identity, and authentication occurs over a channel protected by SSL.

Distributed environments also provide *single sign-on* among applications within a security policy domain boundary. Single sign-on is a technique that allows a user to use a single password to access all network-based resources that are available to them. In computer networks this is done by the use of so-called tickets. On authentication a user gets a ticket stating their identity and other security-related information. While accessing resources on other servers than the one authenticated on, this ticket is used to state the user's identity. In this way the user does not have to authenticate multiple times at every server they use. In a J2EE application server, single sign-on is provided when a client has authenticated in one application; it is also automatically authenticated for other applications for which that client identity is mapped.

11.3.2 Authorization

Authorization mechanisms for distributed environments allow only authentic caller identities to access resources, such as hosts, files, Web pages, components, and database entries, to name a few. Typical authorization policies permit access to different resources for distinct collections of authenticated clients on the basis of roles, groups, or privileges. Roles represent competencies, authorities, responsibilities, or specific duty assignments, while groups are formed on the basis of organizational affiliation, e.g., division, department, laboratory, etc. Authorization policies may also restrict access based on a global context (e.g., time of day), transactional context (e.g., no more than a certain number or amount of withdrawals per day), or data values. Since distributed platforms focus on permissions that state who can perform what function, authentication and identity need to be established before authorization policies are enforced.

Once the supplied digital certificate or other credentials have authenticated a user's identity, the user's access privileges must be determined. Authorization is meant to limit the actions or operations that authenticated parties are able to perform in a networked environment. The classical solution for restricting access (from either employees or trading partners) to sensitive information is by means of *access control rules* on a resource, such as a Web page or a component, and then evaluating the kind of access requested to determine if the requestor has permission to access the resource. Access control rules can define any security policy expressible in a declarative form without a developer having to hard-code the policy in an application. Essentially, access control refers to the process of ensuring that resources are not used in an unauthorized way. Access control may be applied in a distributed environment for protecting against unauthorized invocations of operations on resources in the context of a particular business process or application. None, read-only, add, edit, or full control access rights can be assigned.

The most common approach to defining access control rules for distributed platforms is on the basis of *permissions*. Permissions focus on who can do what. They can be specified declaratively or programmatically.

With declarative authorization logical privileges called (security) *roles* are defined and are associated with components to specify privileges required for subjects (an entity, either human or computer, that has an identity in some security domain) and to be granted permission to access components, according to identity (established by authentication). Permissions indicate the ability to perform a certain operation according to functional role and/or data sensitivity, e.g., "create an order" or "approve an order," on a component (resource). Security permissions written in this way are static, coarse grained, and not very expressive. Callers are assigned logical privileges based on the values of their security attributes. When a security role is assigned to a security group in the operational environment, any caller whose security attributes indicate membership in the group is assigned the privilege represented by the role.

In addition to declaratively specified security roles, in many cases additional application logic needs to be associated with access control decisions. In such cases *programmatic authorization* is used to associate application logic with the state of a resource, the parameters of a component invocation, or some other relevant information. Programmatic authorization requires access to an application's source code in order to insert the appropriate checks. Programmatic security supports more fine-grained authorization than declarative security, but can restrict the reusability of a component. Assembling an application from several components that use programmatic security will be difficult or impossible if the programmed security model is not consistent between the components. An additional drawback to programmatic security occurs when the security policy changes. Every component must be revisited to verify and possibly update the security authorization.

Mechanisms provided by the distributed platform can be used to control access to Web resources based on identity properties, such as the location and signer of the calling code, and the identity of the user of the calling code. Caller identity is usually established by selecting from the set of authentication contexts available to the calling code. In all cases, a credential is made available to the invoked component (that essentially protects a resource) [Monzillo 2002], [Singh 2004]. As an example, the container-based authorization mechanisms in J2EE require that a container serves as an authorization boundary between the components it hosts and their callers. The authorization boundary exists inside the container's authentication boundary, which identifies the user making the current request. In this way, authorization is considered in the context of successful authentication. For inbound calls, the container compares security attributes from the caller's credential to the access control rules for the target component. If the rules are satisfied, the call is allowed. Otherwise, the call is rejected.

11.3.3 Integrity and confidentiality

In a distributed computing system, a significant amount of information is transmitted through networks in the form of messages. Message content is subject to three main types of attacks. Messages might be intercepted and modified for the purpose of changing the effects they have on their recipients. Messages might be captured and reused one or more times for the benefit of another party. An eavesdropper might monitor messages in an effort to capture information that would not otherwise be available. Using integrity and confidentiality mechanisms can minimize such attacks.

Message (data) integrity comprises two requirements. First, the data received must be the same as the data sent. In other words, data integrity systems must be able to guarantee that a message did not change in transit, either by mistake or on purpose. The second requirement for message integrity is that at any time in the future, it is possible to prove whether different copies of the same document are in fact identical.

Digital signatures can be used to verify if a message has been tampered with. A service requestor can sign a document with the sender's private key and send it along with the payload of the message. The service provider can then verify the signature with the sender's public key to see if any portion of the document has been compromised. Thus Web services applications can ensure data integrity when communicating with each other. For example, the XML Signature standard (see section 11.5.1) provides a means for signing parts of XML documents, providing end-to-end data integrity across multiple systems.

Message integrity ensures that information that is being transmitted has not been altered. Secure transactions are the typical mechanism that guarantees that a message has not been modified while in transit. This is commonly known as *communication integrity* and is often accomplished through hashing algorithms and digitally signed digest codes.

Secure transactions should also guarantee confidentiality. Confidentiality refers to the ability to ensure that messages and data are available only to those who are authorized to view them. Confidentiality can be achieved by making sure the connection between the parties cannot be intercepted, e.g., by using encryption when the data is being sent across untrusted networks. Standard SSL encryption using HTTPS allows point-to-point data privacy between service requestors and service providers. However, in many cases, the service provider may not be the ultimate destination for the message. A service provider may act as a service requestor, sending pieces of information to multiple services. In such situations, the XML encryption standard can be used in conjunction with Web services to permit encryption of portions of the message allowing header and other information to be clear text while encrypting the sensitive payload. Sensitive information can then be left encrypted to the ultimate destination, allowing true end-to-end data privacy.

11.3.4 Non-repudiation

Non-repudiation is of critical importance for carrying out transactions over the Internet. Non-repudiation is a property achieved through cryptographic methods to prevent an individual or entity from denying having performed a particular action related to data. When transactions are performed, it is often a requirement to be able to prove that a particular action took place and that the transaction has been committed with valid credentials. This prevents trading partners from claiming that the transaction never occurred. Digital signatures using digital certificates, e.g., PKI X.509 or Kerberos tickets, are a key element to providing non-repudiation. Digital signatures generated based on asymmetric cryptography have a non-repudiation property, in the sense that the person or organization who created the signature cannot deny that they have done so. Non-repudiation usually combines the use of modification detection with digital signatures. When third-party non-repudiation is required, digital receipts provide independent verification that specific transactions have occurred. Non-repudiation consists of cryptographic receipts that are created so that the author of a message cannot falsely deny sending a message. These tasks fall well within the premises of contract formation and enforcement. Tracking digitally signed messages using a tracking data repository provides an audit trail for guaranteeing non-repudiation. The receiver saves the digital signature together with the message in the repository for later reference in case a dispute arises.

11.3.5 Auditing

Auditing is the practice of recording events, such as failed login attempts and denied requests to use a resource that may indicate attempts to violate enterprise security. The value of auditing is not solely to determine whether security mechanisms are limiting access to a system. When security is breached, security-relevant events are analyzed to determine who has been allowed access to critical data. Knowing who has interacted with a system allows the determination of accountability for a breach of security.

In general, it should be possible for the deployer or system administrator to review the security constraints established for the platform and to associate an audit behavior with each security constraint so that these can be analyzed and audited. It is also prudent to audit all changes (resulting from deployment or subsequent administration) to the audit configuration or the constraints being enforced by the platform. Audit records must be protected so that attackers cannot escape accountability for their actions by expunging incriminating records or changing their content.

11.3.6 Application-level security protocols

Secure communications use a number of authentication and encryption protocols that employ encryption and authentication techniques to ensure secure sessions over the Internet. Traditionally, the Secure Sockets Layer (SSL) along with the *de facto* Transport Layer Security (TLS) and the Internet Protocol Security (IPSec) are some of the common ways of securing distributed application content over the Internet. In this section we shall briefly examine some of the more commonly used protocols that address authentication, integrity, and confidentiality concerns within open networks.

11.3.6.1 Secure Sockets Layer (SSL)

Application-level integrated security requires that individual corporate business applications include functionality for achieving secure communications between a client and application server. SSL, used primarily with Web browsers, is the security protocol most commonly used in this approach. SSL is an open standard Web protocol that provides server authentication, data encryption, and message integrity over TCP/IP connections. SSL is widely used in Internet commerce, being implemented in almost all popular browsers and Web servers.

The purpose of SSL is to serve as an easily deployable, dedicated security protocol that offers full security for multiple applications ensuring that communications between a client and application server remain private and allowing the client to identify the server and vice versa. This form of transport security results in creating a secure pipe between the two interacting servers, see Figure 11.9. Authentication occurs at the time the secure pipe is created, while confidentiality and integrity mechanisms are applied only while the message is in the secure pipe as illustrated in Figure 11.9.

SSL offers a range of security services for client–server sessions including server and client authentication, data integrity, and data confidentiality. SSL-enabled clients and SSL-enabled servers confirm each other's identities using digital certificates. SSL server authentication enables a client to confirm the identity of the server involved in any questioned transaction. This is accomplished in SSL using public-key cryptography techniques that verify that the server's certification is valid and issued by a trusted certification authority. Client authentication allows a server to confirm the identity of a client in the same manner as server authentication. SSL-enabled server software can check that the client's certificate and public key are valid and have been issued by a certification authority listed in the server's list of trusted certification authorities. SSL coordinates the process of encrypting and decrypting all information transmitted between a client and a server. Information transmitted via an encrypted SSL connection remains confidential and tamper-free, ensuring that data received is unchanged and was not seen by others.

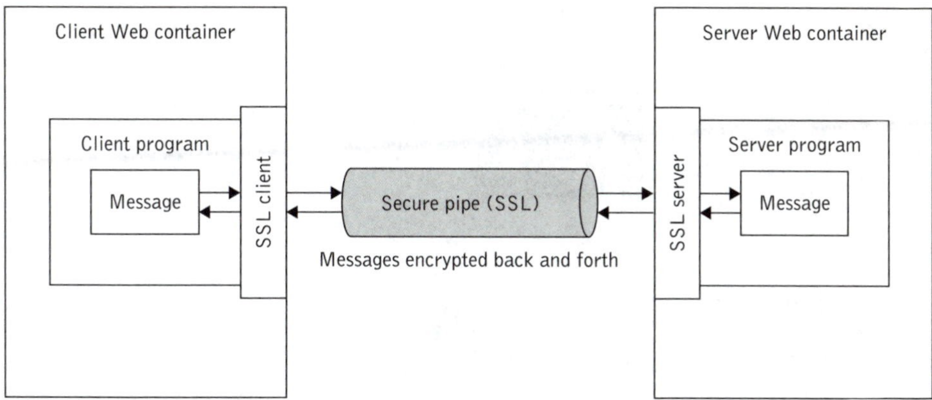

Figure 11.9 Transport security and SSL

As SSL does not support certificate validation, certificate extensions are currently provided to facilitate certificate validation. Additionally, SSL extensions are also providing such features as monitoring, logging, and access control authorization, which are traditionally not supported by conventional SSL technology.

11.3.6.2 Internet Protocol Security (IPSec)

IPSec is another network layer standard for transport security that may become important for distributed and e-business applications. Like SSL/TLS, IPSec also provides secure sessions with host authentication, data integrity, and data confidentiality. However, these are point-to-point technologies. They create a secure tunnel through which data can pass [Mysore 2003]. For instance, SSL is a good solution for server-to-server security but it cannot adequately address the scenario where a message is routed via more than one server. In this case the recipient has to request credentials of the sender and the scalability of the system is compromised.

11.3.6.3 Kerberos

Kerberos was developed to provide a range of authentication and security facilities for computing networks including single sign-on and use of public-key cryptography. The goal of Kerberos is to provide authentication in an insecure distributed environment. Kerberos is a third trusted party authentication protocol that deals with two kinds of security objects: a ticket and a session key. An authentication token (pieces of information used for authentication or authorization that can be added to a SOAP header) called a *ticket* is issued by the Kerberos ticket-granting service for presentation to a particular server, verifying that the client has recently been authenticated by Kerberos. Tickets include an expiry time and a newly generated session key for use by the client and the server. A *session key* is a secret key randomly generated by Kerberos and issued to a client for use when communicating with a particular server. Client processes must posses a ticket and a session key for each server that they use.

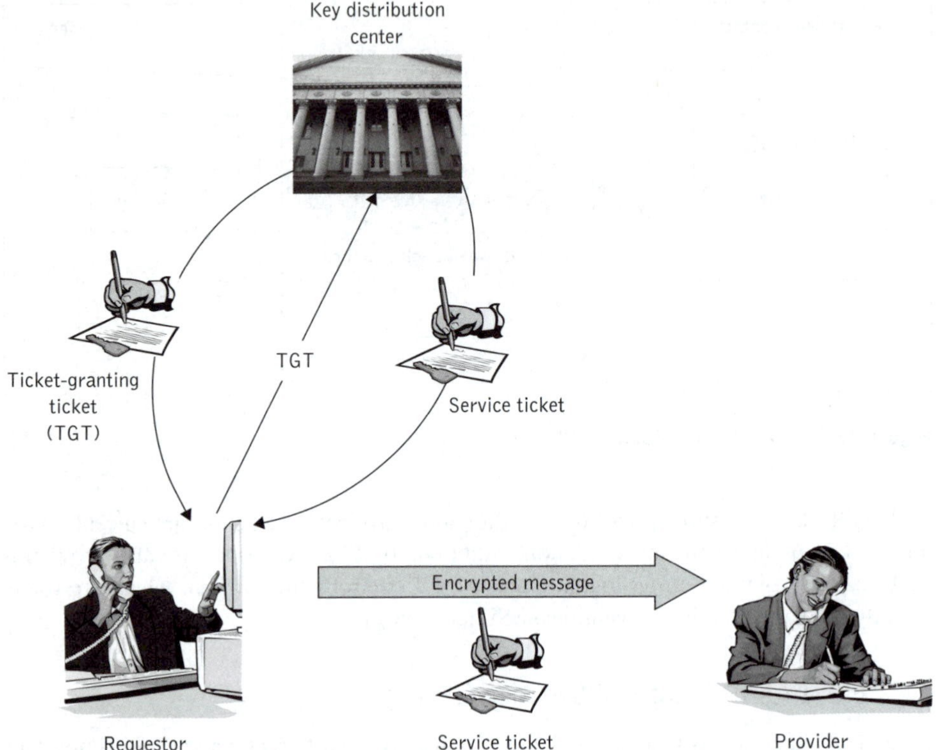

Figure 11.10 Kerberos ticket distribution

In a Web services security application, Kerberos provides a method for a Kerberos (third-party) server to independently verify trust with two parties (via an authentication service) and then to grant shared secret keys that these two parties can use as the basis for a secure interaction [Hall-Gailey 2004]. The Kerberos model performs centralized key management.

Figure 11.10 illustrates the ticket-granting mechanism of Kerberos for a client accessing a Web service. In this scenario a key distribution center (KDC) maintains the principal's credentials. The KDC has a dual function: it first offers an authentication service that accepts the requestor's credentials (typically login and password) from a client process, and subsequently sends back a credential called a ticket-granting ticket (TGT) to the requestor. The TGT contains a temporary secret session key that can be persisted during the session to prevent having to use the permanent credentials. The TGT is encrypted so that only the legitimate principal who possesses the correct password is able to decrypt it and use it at a future time. When the client wishes to access a server application (in this case a particular Web service provided by a specific provider) using Kerberos, the client presents its TGT to the ticket-granting service (TGS) part of the KDC. The TGS then returns a service (or session) ticket, which contains a secret session key, a client identifier, and the TGT expiration time. The client uses the session ticket to establish secure TCP/IP communication with the Web services application in question. The session ticket is protected by encrypting the requestor's information with the provider's private key and is not exposed over the network. As a result only the provider can authenticate the requestor by decrypting the requestor's identification. As long as the TGT is valid the requestor can get various service tickets for different providers without identifying itself again. In this way, single sign-on is achieved.

11.3.7 Security infrastructures

To protect information assets, enterprises are expected to provide gatekeeping functions such as data protection and network isolation, as well as facilitative functions such as exposing enterprise data to outside applications, connecting users for extended collaboration, and enabling on-line transactions and communications. Security infrastructures are distributed infrastructures used as a sound foundation on which applications can communicate and exchange data securely.

11.3.7.1 Public-key infrastructure

The foundation for providing application and network security in distributed multi-faceted environments is public-key infrastructure (PKI) [VeriSign 2003a]. A PKI is a foundation upon which other applications and network security components are built. PKI protects applications that demand the highest level of security, enabling on-line banking and trading, Web-services-based business process automation, digital form signing, enterprise instant messaging, and electronic commerce. In addition, it protects firewalls, VPNs, directories, and enterprise applications. PKI becomes crucial when there is a risk of fraud, a risk of legal ramifications if a transaction is altered or disclosed, or when the confirmed identity of an individual or business entity is essential.

PKI refers to the technology, infrastructure, and practices that support the implementation and operation of digital certificates and certification authorities that verify and authenticate the validity of parties involved in Internet transactions. In a broad sense PKI is an infrastructure of policies, servers, and technologies that provide support for cryptographic solutions to critical security issues related to enterprise computing. PKI capabilities help create and manage asymmetric cryptographic keys or public/private keys required by automated business processes and e-business applications. PKI uses a private key and a public key to encrypt and decrypt confidential information and to generate and verify digital signatures. The main function of PKI is to distribute public keys accurately and reliably to users and applications that need them.

The specific security functions for which a PKI can provide a foundation are confidentiality, integrity, non-repudiation, and authentication, while it also ensures military-grade physical security. PKI also integrates easily with all functions within an enterprise, e.g., marketing, sales, inventory, finance, etc., and with all sorts of internal and external enterprise applications including legacy systems. In this way PKI allows enterprises to easily create communities of trust with partners, customers, and suppliers.

In practice, PKI refers to a system of digital certificates, certification authorities, and other registration authorities that verify and authenticate the validity of each party involved in an electronic transaction. A *public-key certificate* is a digitally signed statement that binds the value of a public key to the identity of the subject (person, device, or service) that holds the corresponding private key. The issuer and signer of the certificate is known as a *certification authority*. The entity being issued the certificate is the *subject* of the certificate. By signing the certificate, the certification authority attests that the private key associated with the public key in the certificate is in the possession of the subject named in the certificate. The certification authority creates and signs digital certificates, maintains certificate revocation lists, makes certificates and revocation lists available, and provides an interface so that administrators can manage certificates. Certificates can be issued for a variety of functions, including Web user authentication, Web server authentication, secure e-mail using Secure/Multipurpose Internet Mail Extensions (S/MIME), IPSec, SSL/TLS, and code signing.

Issuance of a certificate requires verification of the user's identity, usually accomplished by a *registration authority*. Certification and registration authorities are two major PKI components that provide the necessary capabilities to establish, maintain, and protect trusted relationships [Schlosser 1999]. The registration authority evaluates the credentials and relevant evidence that an organization requesting a certificate is indeed the organization which it claims to be. A digitally signed message from the registration authority to the certification authority is required to authenticate the subscriber. One certification authority may operate several registration authorities.

Figure 11.11 illustrates one of the possible ways that a PKI can operate. A requestor first generates a public/private key pair. The public key is then placed into a certificate request signed with the requestor's private key. The self-signed certificate is sent to a registration authority, which verifies the identity of the subscriber. Once the identity of the

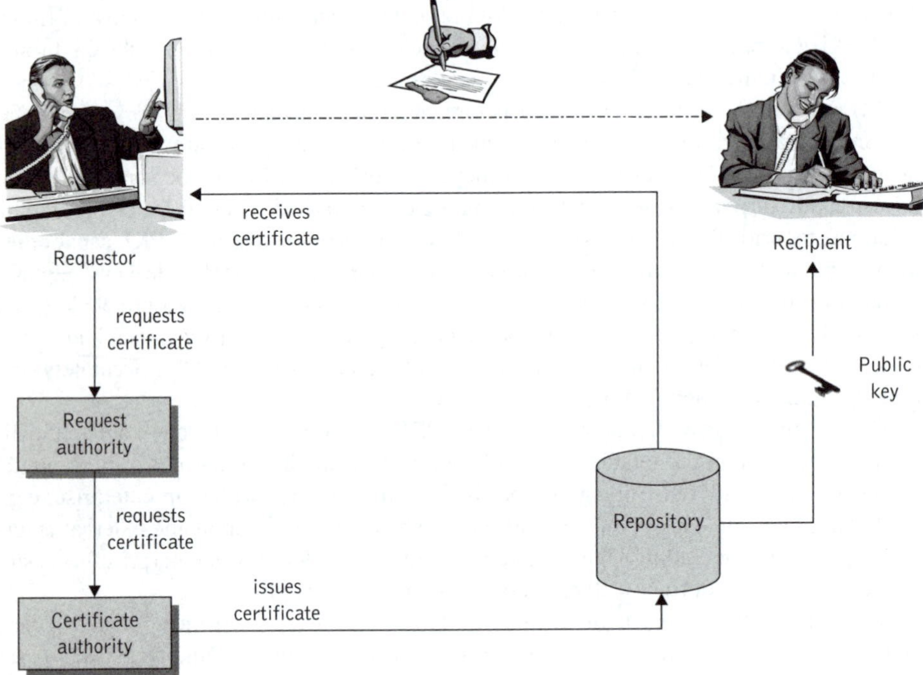

Figure 11.11 PKI

requestor is verified, the certificate is countersigned by the registration authority and sent to the certification authority. The certification authority verifies the registration authority's signature on the certificate request. It additionally verifies that this registration authority is entitled to make this request. Subsequently, the certification authority uses the public key in the certificate request to create a public-key certificate with it, and signs the certificate. The certification authority may also take the certificate and place it in a directory so that any party wishing to communicate with the requestor or wishing to verify the requestor's signature can retrieve the requestor's public key. Finally, the certificate is returned to the requestor which can forward it to a recipient. The recipient receives the digitally signed information from the requestor and needs to use the PKI – in particular, the public-key certificate – to verify the requestor's signature.

One of the most commonly cited PKIs is the PKI X.509 (PKIX) standard that defines the contents of public-key certificates on the basis of the X.509 certificate format with IETF protocols such as SSL, S/MIME, and IPSec. PKI X.509 provides interoperability between digital certificates produced by different vendors.

11.3.7.2 Directory services

PKI applications certificates are published in a public directory, which allows everyone who wishes to send someone an encrypted message to use the receiver's public key that is given in the certificate. Third trusted parties who serve as certification authorities often manage directories.

Directory services for application-level security provide the ability to implement a security policy. As such they may be used to store authorization information such as group membership and access rights, support single sign-on, and in general provide location information and other detailed information about network-available resources and computing infrastructure. Where a PKI is deployed, a directory can be used to distribute certificates, for applications in which an end-user certificate must be obtained before an encrypted message is sent as well as certificate status information, such as certificate revocation lists. The directory can also store private keys, when portability is required in environments where users do not use the same machine each day.

The most popular protocol for accessing the data in network directories is the Lightweight Directory Access Protocol (LDAP). LDAP uses the X.500 data model, which is a comprehensive directory architecture, designed under the auspices of ISO and other international standards organizations. In the X.500 model, the basic unit of data is a directory entry, which consists of one or more attribute–value pairs. LDAP operates over TCP/IP and, consequently, is considerably simpler to implement and deploy. The LDAP distributed architecture supports scalable directory services with server replication capabilities ensuring that directory data is available when needed.

For security, LDAP supports both basic client authentication using a distinguished name and password and SSL services, which provide for mutual authentication between the client and the server and ensure confidentiality and integrity of queries and responses. To enable SSL, a server certificate is required. Certificate-based client authentication using, for example, client certificates issued through PKI is also supported with appropriately configured LDAP directory servers. This restricts access to the directory to only authenticated individuals.

11.4 Security topologies

Security architects in distributed environments are frequently faced with design options and strategies for deploying applications, for instance based on J2EE, in a production demilitarized zone environment. A *demilitarized zone* (DMZ) here signifies a logical partition between two sets of firewalls. The assumption is that the infrastructure residing in the DMZ needs to be accessed directly and therefore is more likely to be compromised [Steel 2006]. The second firewall layer in a DMZ is used to protect against attackers who have compromised servers from gaining access to application servers and back-end applications.

Security topologies define the security requirements of distributed application development in a DMZ environment in a way that addresses architectural capabilities such as availability, scalability, reliability, manageability, and performance. Two such topologies can be identified [Steel 2006]: horizontally and vertically scaled security architectures.

Figure 11.12 illustrates an horizontally scaled security architecture for a J2EE application that is partitioned as a Web tier (employing JSP/Servlets), application-tier (employing EJB components), and back-end resources. The horizontal scalability is achieved by using multiple instances of Web and application servers. The Web tier and the applications tier are separated by a firewall. This enhances security because the traffic between the Web and application servers is required to pass through the firewall. This architecture is not suitable for applications that have a relatively high degree of traffic between the Web tier and the back-end resource tier.

To decouple the Web from back-end resource applications a Web server could be configured with a reverse proxy, which receives HTTP requests from a client on the incoming network side and opens a socket connection on the application server side to perform business application processing [Steel 2006]. This configuration targets environments with less stringent security requirements.

Figure 11.13 shows a vertically scaled security architecture for a J2EE application that is partitioned as a Web tier (employing JSP/Servlets), application tier (employing EJB components), and back-end resources. Adding computing capacity, e.g., processors, memory, etc., achieves vertical scalability. This configuration can lead to an overall system failure if the server infrastructure fails. To avoid this a high-availability cluster can be introduced to provide resilience for both Web and application server infrastructure in the case of failure.

To decouple the Web from back-end resource applications in a vertically scaled security architecture, a Web server could be configured with a reverse proxy that acts in a similar manner as in the case of an horizontally scaled security architecture.

11.5 XML security standards

XML- and Web services-based SOAs facilitate business integration within and across organizational boundaries. However, this benefit comes at a price: security systems themselves must also integrate. Without this security integration, security solutions remain at a per project level, with no central means of configuring, monitoring, analyzing, and controlling integration data flows. The implementation, management, and monitoring of

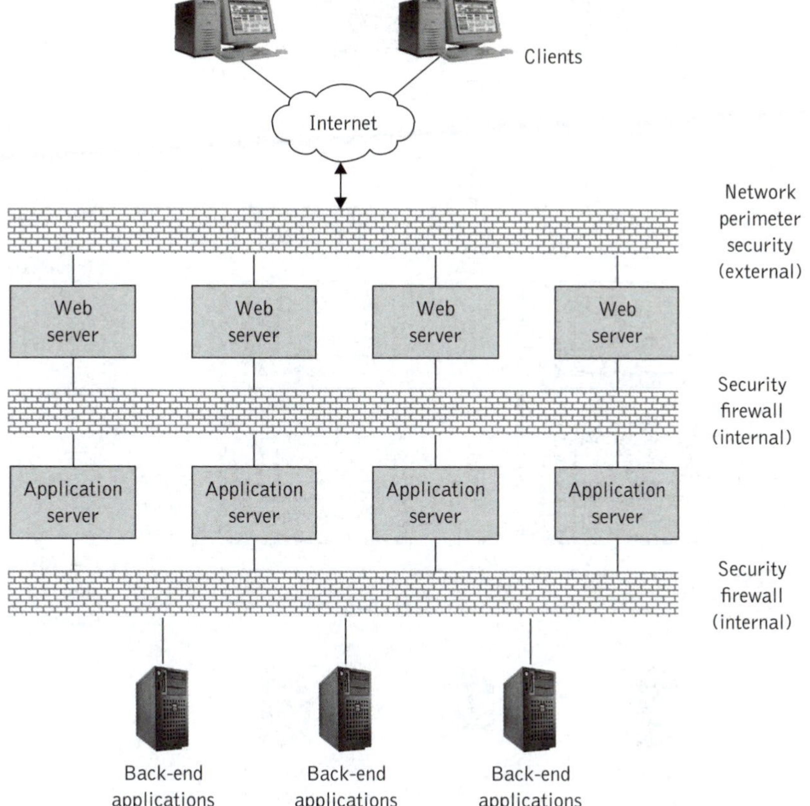

Figure 11.12 Horizontally scaled security architecture
Source: C. Steel, R. Nagappan and R. Lai, *Core Security Patterns: Best Practices and Strategies for J2EE™, Web Services, and Identity Management*, Prentice Hall, 2006. Reproduced with permission.

security policies across enterprise boundaries becomes increasingly vital to the success of integrated enterprises.

As Web services technologies use XML-based messages on Internet-based protocols to interact with other applications in an integrated solution, we shall first concentrate on XML security solutions for integrated enterprises.

XML Trust Services is a suite of open XML specifications for application developers developed in partnership with industry to make it easier to integrate a broad range of XML security services into integrated business applications over the Web. The main technologies for XML Trust Services encompass [VeriSign 2003b]: XML Signature for cryptographically authenticating data, XML Encryption for encrypting data, XML Key Management Specification (XKMS) for managing key registration and key authentication, Security Assertions Markup Language (SAML) for specifying entitlement and identity, and XML Access Control Markup Language (XACML) for specifying fine-grained data access rights.

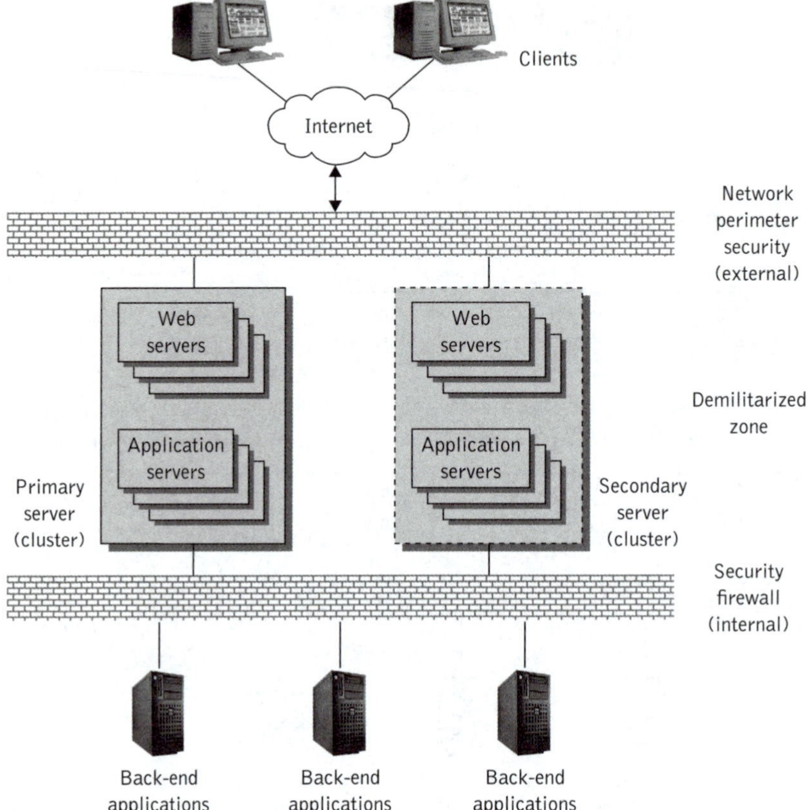

Figure 11.13 Vertically scaled security architecture
Source: C. Steel, R. Nagappan and R. Lai, *Core Security Patterns: Best Practices and Strategies for J2EE™, Web Services, and Identity Management*, Prentice Hall, 2006. Reproduced with permission.

11.5.1 XML Signature

When a single XML document is authored by many parties, then each of them needs to sign the part they authored. This is not possible when using network-level security. It is important to ensure the integrity of certain portions of the document, while leaving open the possibility of further changes and additions to the same document. The XML Signature specification forms the basis for securely exchanging an XML document and conducting business transactions. The objective of XML Signature is to ensure data integrity, message authentication, and non-repudiation of services.

The standard defines a schema for capturing the result of a digital signature operation applied to arbitrary (but often XML) data. XML Signature is applied to arbitrary digital content (data objects) via an indirection [Eastlake 2002a]. Data objects are digested, the resulting value is placed in an element (with other information), which is then digested and cryptographically signed. XML Signature itself will generally indicate the location of the original signed object. XML Signature can sign more than one type of resource, e.g., character-encoded data (HTML), binary-encoded data (a JPG), XML-encoded data, a specific section of an XML document, or external data referenced by an XPointer.

Generally, three types of signatures exist: *enveloping signatures* where the signature envelops the entire document to be signed, *enveloped signatures* where the XML signature is instead embedded within the document, and *detached signatures* where the XML document and signature reside independently and the document is usually referenced by an external URI. A detached signature means that the signed data is not in the signature element – it is elsewhere in the XML document or in some remote location.

Signature validation requires the data object that was signed to be accessible. XML Signature itself will generally indicate the location of the original signed object by referring to enveloping, enveloped, and detached signed objects.

Listing 11.1 illustrates an XML signature example which was developed on the basis of [Simon 2001] and [Eastlake 2002a]. This simplified example shows that the data object signed is a news item identified by the URI attribute of the first `<Reference>` element in Listing 11.1. XML digital signatures are represented by the `<Signature>` element. Information about the original data object that is signed is represented in the element via URIs. In the case of an enveloping signature, the `<Signature>` element becomes the parent of the original data object. In the case of an enveloped signature, the `<Signature>` element becomes the child of the original data object. In the case of a detached signature, the `<Signature>` element could be a sibling of the original data object; alternatively the `<Signature>` element could carry a reference to an external data object. The code fragment in Listing 11.1 represents a detached signature because it is not part of the document being signed.

The `<Signature>` element enables applications to carry additional information along with the digest value and can also carry the key need to validate the signature [Galbraith 2002]. This element contains among other things a `<SignedInfo>` element that provides information about the process that leads to an XML signature and the data objects that are actually signed. It also contains a `<SignatureValue>` element containing the actual value of the digital signature that is the encrypted digest of the `<SignedInfo>` element.

The process of converting an XML document to canonical form is known as *canonicalization*. XML canonicalization is the use of an algorithm to generate the canonical form of an XML document to ensure security in cases where XML is subject to surface representation changes or to processing that discards some information that is not essential to the data represented in the XML, e.g., entities or namespaces with prefixes.

The first sub-element of the `<SignedInfo>` element, `<CanonicalizationMethod>`, is used to specify the canonicalization algorithm that is applied to its associated `<SignedInfo>` element before it is digested and produces the signature. The second sub-element, `<SignatureMethod>`, is the cryptographic algorithm that is used to convert the canonicalized `<SignedInfo>` into the `<SignatureValue>`.

In XML Signature, each referenced resource is specified through a `<Reference>` element, which identifies the data object via its URI attribute and carries the digest value of the data object. Each `<Reference>` element includes a `<DigestMethod>` element. This element specifies the digest algorithm applied to the data object to yield the digest value contained in a `<DigestValue>` element.

```
<?xml version="1.0" encoding="UTF-8"?>
<Signature xmlns="http://www.w3.org/2000/09/xmldsig#">
<SignedInfo Id="2ndDecemberNewsItem">
  <CanonicalizationMethod
    Algorithm="http://www.w3.org/TR/2001/REC-xml-c14n-20010315"/>
  <SignatureMethod
    Algorithm="http://www.w3.org/2000/09/xmldsig#dsa-sha1"/>
  <Reference
    URI="http://www.news_company.com/news/2004/12_02_04.htm">
      <DigestMethod
        Algorithm="http://www.w3.org/2000/09/xmldsig#sha1"/>
      <DigestValue>j6lwx3rvEPO0vKtMup4NbeVu8nk=</DigestValue>
  </Reference>
  <Reference URI="#AMadeUpTimeStamp"
           Type="http://www.w3.org/2000/09/
           xmldsig#SignatureProperties">
     <DigestMethod
       Algorithm="http://www.w3.org/2000/09/xmldsig#sha1"/>
     <DigestValue>k3453rvEPO0vKtMup4NbeVu8nk=</DigestValue>
  </Reference>
   ... ...
</SignedInfo>
<SignatureValue>MC0E~LE=… </SignatureValue>
<KeyInfo>
  <X509Data>
    <X509SubjectName>
      CN=News Items Inc., O=Today's News Items, C=USA
    </X509SubjectName>
    <X509Certificate>
      MIID5jCCA0+gA...lVN
    </X509Certificate>
  </X509Data>
</KeyInfo>
<Object>
  <SignatureProperties>
    <SignatureProperty Id="AMadeUpTimeStamp"
      Target="#2ndDecemberNewsItem">
      <timestamp xmlns="http://www.ietf.org/rfcXXXX.txt">
        <date>2004122</date>
        <time>18:30</time>
      </timestamp>
    </SignatureProperty>
  </SignatureProperties>
</Object>
</Signature>
```

Listing 11.1 XML signature example

The optional <KeyInfo> element provides the ability to verify the signature using the packaged verification key [Eastlake 2002a]. The <KeyInfo> element may contain keys, names, certificates, and other public-key management information, such as in-band key distribution or key agreement data. In Listing 11.1 the keying information contains the X.509 certificate for the sender, which would include the public key needed for signature verification.

The <Object> element in Listing 11.1 is an optional element used mostly in enveloping signatures where the data object is part of the signature element. The <SignatureProperties> element type in <Object> can contain additional information about the signature, e.g., date, time stamp, serial number of cryptographic hardware, and other application-specific attributes.

Signature validation requires the data object that was signed to be accessible. To validate the signature, the recipient decodes the message digest contained in the XML Signature element <SignatureValue> using the signatory's public key. The recipient then compares it to the message digest obtained by following the instructions in <SignedInfo>.

XML Signature provides its own integrity for data. XML Signature is also important for authentication and non-repudiation; however, it does not provide these functions on its own. The WS-Security standard fulfills this role by describing how XML Signature can be used to bind a security token (a representation of security-related information, see section 11.6.3) to a SOAP message, and, by extension, bind the identity of the signer to a SOAP message [O'Neill 2003].

More information about XML Signature as well as examples of enveloping, enveloped, and detached signatures specified in XML Signature can be found in [Galbraith 2002] and [Siddiqui 2003a].

11.5.2 XML Encryption

The XML Signature initiative does not define any standard mechanism for encrypting XML entities, which is another important security characteristic to promote the trusted use of Web applications. This functionality is provided by the XML Encryption specification, a W3C effort, which supports encryption of all or part of an XML document.

The steps for XML Encryption include [Eastlake 2002b]:

1. Selecting the XML document to be encrypted (in whole or in part).
2. Converting the XML document to be encrypted to a canonical form, if necessary.
3. Encrypting the resulting canonical form using public-key encryption.
4. Sending the encrypted XML document to the intended recipient.

Because XML Encryption is not locked into any specific encryption scheme, it requires that additional information be provided on encrypted content and key information. This is accomplished by the <EncryptedData> and <EncryptedKey> elements. The core element in XML Encryption syntax is the <EncryptedData> element which, in conjunction with the <EncryptedKey> element, is used to transport encryption keys from the originator to a known recipient. Data to be encrypted can be arbitrary data, an

XML document, an XML element, an XML element content, or a reference to a resource outside an XML document. The result of encrypting data is an XML encryption element that contains or references the cipher data. When an element or element content is encrypted, the <EncryptedData> element replaces the element or content in the encrypted version of the XML document. The <EncryptedKey> element provides information about the keys involved in the encryption.

```
<?xml version="1.0"?>
 <PaymentInfo xmlns="http://example.org/paymentv2">
  <Name>John Smith</Name>
  <CreditCard Limit="5,000" Currency="USD">
    <Number>4019 2445 0277 5567</Number>
    <Issuer>Example Bank</Issuer>
    <Expiration>04/06</Expiration>
  </CreditCard>
 </PaymentInfo>

----------------------------------------------------------------

<?xml version="1.0"?>
<env:Envelope>
 <env:Body>
   <PaymentInfo xmlns="http://example.org/paymentv2">
     <Name> John Smith </Name>
     <CreditCard Limit="5,000" Currency="USD">
       <EncryptedData xmlns="http://www.w3.org/2001/04/xmlenc#"
         Type="http://www.w3.org/2001/04/xmlenc#Content">
         <CipherData>
           <CipherValue> A23B45C56 </CipherValue>
         </CipherData>
       </EncryptedData>
     </CreditCard>
   </PaymentInfo>
 </env:Body>
</env:Envelope>
```

Listing 11.2 XML encryption example

Listing 11.2 depicts an XML encryption example taken from [Eastlake 2002b]. The first part in Listing 11.2 shows an XML markup representing fictitious payment information, which includes identification information as well as information appropriate to a payment method, e.g., credit card, money transfer, or electronic check. In particular, the example in Listing 11.2 shows that John Smith is using his credit card with a limit of $5,000. The second part in this listing shows that it may be useful for intermediate agents to know that John Smith uses a credit card with a particular limit, but not the card's number, issuer, and expiration date. In this case, the content (character data or children elements) of the credit card element is encrypted. The <CipherData> element is the element that contains the encrypted content. XML Encryption permits the encrypted content to be carried in two ways. If the encrypted content is carried in place, it is carried as content of the `<CipherValue>` element, which exists as a child of the `<CipherData>` element. This is shown in Listing 11.2. Alternatively, XML Encryption permits the encrypted content to be stored at an external location to be referenced by the `<CipherReference>` element, which is a child of the `<CipherData>` element.

An XML (Web services) firewall will receive the contents of Listing 11.2 (SOAP messages with encrypted elements) and translate the contents to a decrypted form before forwarding the decrypted SOAP message request to the SOAP server.

More information about XML Encryption including a variety of examples can be found in [Galbraith 2002].

11.5.3 XML Key Management Specification (XKMS)

XKMS (**http://www.w3.org/TR/xkms/**) is an initiative used to simplify the integration of PKI and management of digital certificates with XML applications. The key objective behind XKMS is to enable the development of XML-based trust (Web) services for the processing and the management of PKI-based cryptographic keys [Galbraith 2002]. XKMS strives to remove the complexity of working with PKI, making it easier for XML-based applications to incorporate security mechanisms into their context.

XKMS facilitates integration of authentication, digital signature, and encryption services, such as certificate processing and revocation status checking, into applications without the constraints and complications associated with proprietary PKI software toolkits. Figure 11.14 shows how XML Signature and Encryption are related to XKMS. With XKMS, trust functions reside in servers accessible via easily programmed XML transactions.

XKMS supports three major services: register service, locate service, and validate service. The register service is used for registering key pairs for escrow services. Once the keys are registered the XKMS service manages the revocation, reissue, and recovery of

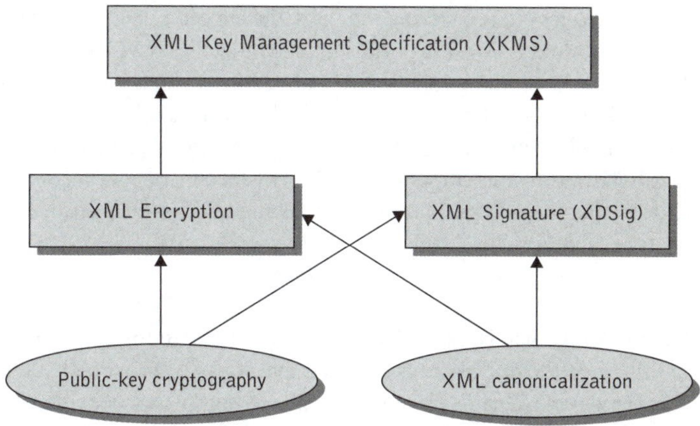

Figure 11.14 Basic building blocks of the XML Trust framework

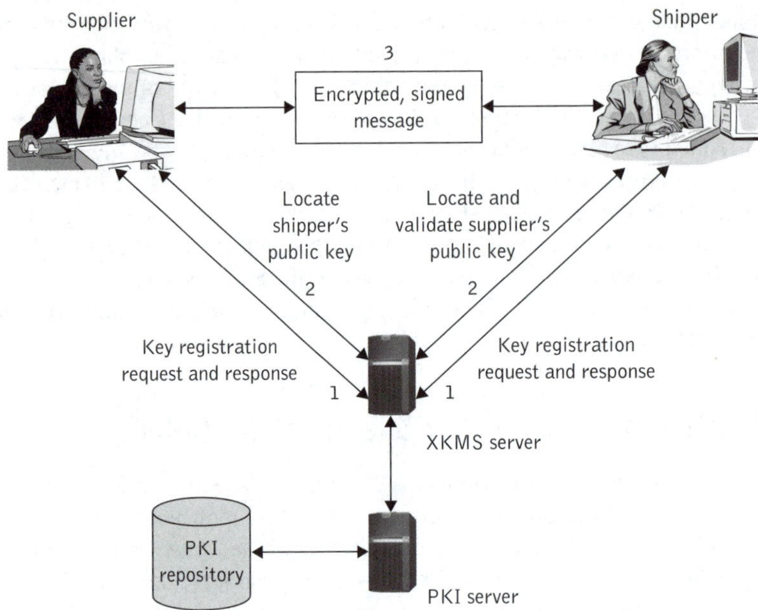

Figure 11.15 Example using XKMS services

registered keys. The locate service is used to retrieve a public key registered with the XKMS service. The validation service provides all the functionality offered by the locate service and in addition supports key validation.

Figure 11.15 depicts an example showing the interactions that take place when a supplier sends a hypothetical encrypted and signed shipment message to a supplier company. The supplier is shown to no longer manage key information and instead consult the XKMS service for key processing activities. The process commences by both the supplier and shipper registering their key pairs with the XKMS trust service using the register service (step 1). Subsequent to registering the keys, the supplier needs to encrypt the message to be sent to the supplier. For this purpose the supplier sends a locate request (step 2) to the XKMS server seeking the public key of the shipper. The server responds with the key given that the shipper has already registered its key with the XKMS service. The supplier then uses this public key to encrypt the message, employs its private key to sign the message, and forwards it to the shipper (step 3). On receipt of the message the shipper passes the XML Signature `<KeyInfo>` element contained in the signed message to the XKMS service for validation.

There are two verification stages for the signature:

1. Local verification that is carried directly by the receiving application (shipper). During this stage the document is checked that it has been correctly signed and not been tampered with during transit. This phase comprises decoding the signature with the signatory's (supplier's) public key and then comparing it to the footprint obtained locally.

2. Contacting the XKMS service and requesting information on the public key transmitted. During this second stage the identity of the signatory (supplier) is made known and it is checked whether the key has been revoked (in case it was stolen) and valid (period of validity has not expired).

XKMS is made up of two major subparts: the XML Key Information Service Specification (X-KISS) and the XML Key Registration Service Specification (X-KRSS). The X-KISS protocol deals with public processing and validation, while the X-KRSS protocol deals with key pair registration.

11.5.3.1 XML Key Information Service Specification (X-KISS)

X-KISS defines protocols to support the processing, by a relying party, of key information associated with an XML digital signature, XML encrypted data, or other public-key usage in an XML-aware application. Functions supported include locating required public keys given identifier information, and binding of such keys to identifier information. Applications that work in conjunction with X-KISS receive messages signed in compliance with XML Signature specifications.

X-KISS provides support for checks by means of two types of service: the locate service, which is used to find out the attached information from the data contained in the XML Signature specification key information element, and the validate service that makes sure that a key is valid.

11.5.3.2 XML Key Registration Service Specification (X-KRSS)

The goal of X-KRSS is to respond to the need for a complete, XML client-focused key lifecycle management protocol. To achieve this X-KRSS defines an XML-based protocol registration of public-key information. It allows an XML-aware application to register its public-key pair and its associated binding information to an XKMS trust service provider.

X-KRSS supports the entire certificate lifecycle by means of the following services:

Key registration: An XML application key pair holder registers its public key with trusted infrastructure by means of a registration server. The public key is sent to the registration server using a digitally signed request in KRSS that may optionally include name and attribute information, authentication information, and proof of possession of a private key.

Key revocation: The revoke service handles the request to revoke a previous registered key binding and any cryptographic credentials associated with it. A key binding may be revoked for different reasons which all end up in the situation where the current key binding may not be considered trustworthy. The revoke service authenticates users who have lost control of their private key by allowing them to specify a special revocation identifier when the key binding is registered. The revocation request is authenticated using the corresponding revocation code.

Key recovery: Because of the design of the encryption used in XML client encryption applications it is statistically impossible to recover encrypted data when a private key needed to decrypt the data is lost. This mandates some form of key recovery provision. In X-KRSS, this function is not supported by standardized protocols but is rather built in. A recovery service in X-KRSS can only recover private keys if they have been previously escrowed. Use of the recovery service is accomplished by sending an authenticated request to the recovery service, which in return sends back an encrypted private key if the requestor is authenticated correctly.

Key reissuing: Because of the need for periodically updating a key binding, X-KRSS provides a reissue service. The use of this service is very similar to the use of the register service with the exception of the request for the renewal of an existing key binding instead of generating a new one. After successful identification a renewed key pair is sent to the requestor.

11.5.4 Security Assertions Markup Language

One of the biggest challenges for XML-based applications (including Web services) is that of user authentication and single sign-on in a distributed environment across a number of disparate applications. Single sign-on in the case of Web services provides the ability to use multiple Web services, or a single Web service made up of multiple services, based on a single authentication.

The Security Assertion Markup Language (SAML) is an OASIS standard, designed around the concept of a Web single sign-on, enabling an identity to be submitted a single time and transported from one enterprise to the next. In version 1.1, the Liberty Alliance standard (**http://www.projectliberty.org/**) developed enhancements that included an identity federation framework cross-domain authentication, and session management. In SAML 2.0, the two versions are merged into a broad framework for identity federation and transport.

SAML is a vendor-neutral, XML-based standard framework for describing and exchanging security-related information, called *assertions* (declarations on facts about subjects), designed to facilitate the exchange of security information between different application components and trust domains [Hughes 2004]. It does so by inserting security information into assertions in XML form. These assertions convey information about an end user's authentication act, their authorization to access a certain resource, or their attributes. SAML assertions may be bound to SOAP messages, to be sent to SAML-aware Web services.

SAML enables disparate security systems to interoperate while allowing individual organizations to retain their own authentication systems. Instead of having an enterprise authenticate all incoming foreign individuals or rely on central authentication registry for every partnership, SAML implementations provide an interoperable XML-based security solution, whereby user information and corresponding authorization information in the form of assertions can be exchanged by collaborating applications or services. To facilitate this undertaking, the SAML specification establishes assertion and protocol schemas for the structure of the documents that transport security. By defining how identity and access information is exchanged, SAML becomes the common language through which organizations can communicate without modifying their own internal security architectures.

The main components of SAML include the following [Cantor 2004]:

1. *Assertions:* SAML defines three kinds of assertions, which are declarations of one or more facts about a subject, e.g., a service requestor. *Authentication assertions* require that the user prove their identity. *Attribute assertions* contain specific details about the user, such as their credit line or citizenship. *Authorization assertions* state whether a client is allowed or denied a request and the scope of the client's privileges. Authorization assertions permit or deny access to specific resources, such as files, devices, Web pages, databases, and so on. For instance, authorization assertions are typically a response to a request such as a "is Plastics Inc. allowed access to confidential Web page information about product design specs and blueprints?" All types of assertions include a common set of elements: the subject, which denotes who the assertion is identifying; the conditions, which denote conditions under which the assertion is valid; and an authentication statement, which denotes advice on how the assertion was made. Each assertion also includes information about the type of request made.

2. *Request/response protocol:* SAML defines a request/response protocol for obtaining assertions. An SAML request can either ask for a specific known assertion or make authentication, attribute, and authorization decision queries, with the SAML response providing back the requested assertions. The XML format for protocol messages and their allowable extensions is defined in an XML schema.

3. *Bindings:* This element details exactly how SAML request/response message exchanges should map into standard messaging or communication protocols. For instance, the SAML SOAP Binding defines how SAML protocol messages can be communicated within SOAP messages while the SAML URI Binding defines how SAML protocol messages can be communicated through URI resolution.

4. *Profiles:* These dictate how SAML assertions can be embedded or transported between communicating systems. Generally, a profile of SAML defines constraints and/or extensions in support of the usage of SAML for a particular application – the goal to enhance interoperability. For instance, the Web browser single sign-on profile specifies how SAML authentication assertions are communicated between an identity provider and service provider to enable single sign-on for a browser user. The Web user authenticates to the identity provider, which then produces an authentication assertion that, on being delivered to the service provider, allows it to establish a security context for the Web user.

Figure 11.16 illustrates the relationship between the SAML components. It also shows an SAML assertion being carried within an SAML response, which itself is embedded within a SOAP Body. Note that an SAML response could contain multiple assertions, although it is more typical to have a single assertion within a response.

Using a protocol defined in SAML, clients can request assertions from SAML authorities and get a response from them in the form of SAML assertions related to these activities. Figure 11.17 illustrates the SAML model. In this model, the subject (client) may authenticate itself with up to three different SAML (authentication, attribute, and authorization) authorities by sending its credentials to them for validation. The subject then

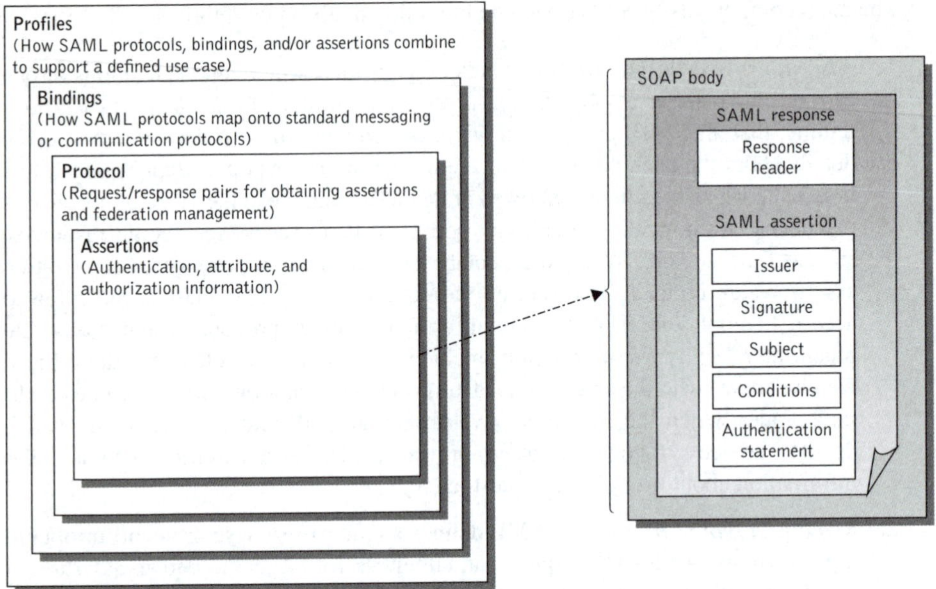

Figure 11.16 SAML components and assertion structure

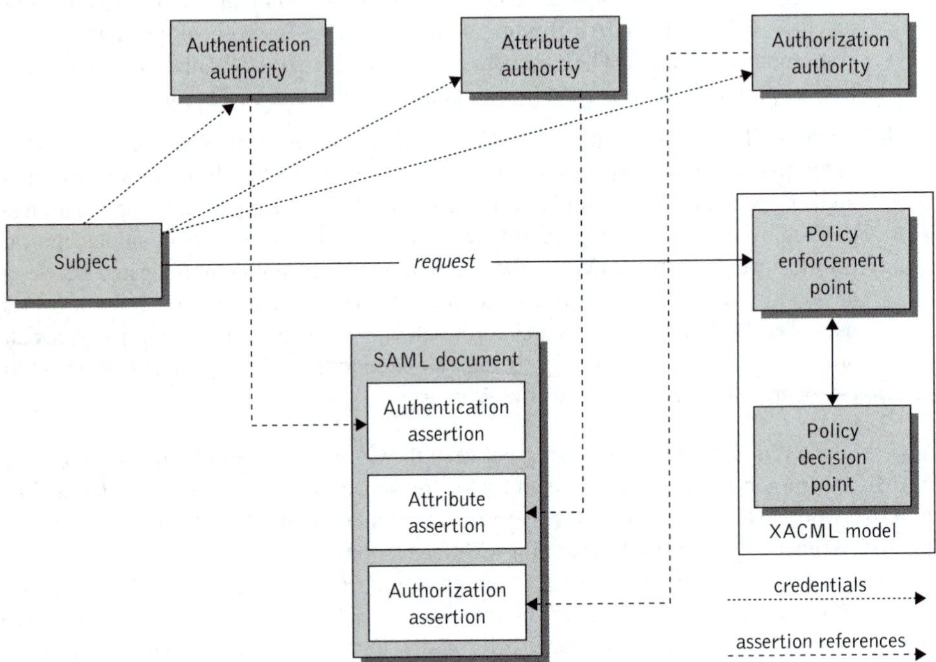

Figure 11.17 SAML and XACML model

obtains assertion references, which it includes in a request for accessing a resource, such as Web service. The subject forwards this information to a policy enforcement point (PEP) module that protects this specific resource. The PEP uses the references to request the actual assertions (authentication decision) from the issuing authority or from a policy decision point (PDP) module. The PEP and PDP modules are part of the XACML access control language that we shall examine in the following section. SAML and XACML are complementary standards that share basic concepts and definitions.

When a client attempts to access some target site, it will forward the SAML assertion from the SAML authentication authority. The target can then verify whether the assertion is from an authority that it trusts, and, if this is so, it can then use the SAML authentication assertion as an assurance that the principal has been authenticated. Subsequently, the target could then go to an SAML attribute authority to request an attribute assertion for the authenticated principal, passing along the authentication assertion. The returned attribute assertion will contain the attributes for the principal, which will be guaranteed to be correct by the SAML attribute authority. Finally, the target may go to an authorization service, and, upon passing the attribute assertion, enquire whether the principal is permitted to perform an activity on a certain resource. The authorization service could be a local service of the target company or an external SAML authorization service. For instance, attribute assertion information may be used at a protected Web service in order to make an access control decision, e.g. "Only users who have authenticated to one of our trusted partners can access this Web service," or "Only users with the attribute 'manager' can access this Web service," etc. SAML authorities can use various sources of information, such as external policy stores and assertions that were received as input in requests, in creating their response.

Listing 11.3 wraps an authentication statement in the format of an SAML assertion. An authentication statement specifies the outcome of an act of authentication which took place in the past. We assume that an SAML authority authenticates a user and issues the security assertion.

Listing 11.3 considers an order processing scenario involving an order message that needs to be forwarded from an order processing service to a shipment processing service and finally to a billing service. Listing 11.3 shows an example assertion with a single authentication statement in the context of the order processing scenario. More specifically, the assertion in the listing states that the entity called name `"OrderProcService"` is the owner of a public key named `"OrderProcServiceKey"`. The asserting authority (`some-trusted-party`) has authenticated the `OrderProcService` using XML digital signatures. The basic information specifies a unique identifier used for the assertion identifier, date and time of issuance, and the time interval for which the assertion is valid.

The root `<Assertion>` element wraps three important sub-elements: a `<Conditions>` element, an `<AuthenticationStatement>` element, and a `<ds:Signature>` element. The `<Conditions>` element specifies the time interval for which the assertion is valid. The `<AuthenticationStatement>` states the outcome (the final result) of an authentication process. The `<ds:Signature>` element contains as usual XML digital signature tags.

The subject that the authentication pertains to is `"OrderProcService"`. The format of the subject could be chosen from a number of predefined formats provided in the SAML specification, including e-mail addresses and X.509 subject names, or alternatively

```
<saml:Assertion
  xmlns:saml="urn:oasis:names:tc:SAML:1.0:assertion"
  MajorVersion="1" MinorVersion="0"
  AssertionID="XraafaacDz6iXrUa"
  Issuer="www.some-trusted-party.com"
  IssueInstant="2004-07-19T17:02:00Z">
       <saml:Conditions
          NotBefore="2004-07-19T17:02:00Z "
          NotOnOrAfter="2004-07-19T17:10:00Z"/>
       <saml:AuthenticationStatement
          AuthenticationMethod="urn:ietf:rfc:3075"
          AuthenticationInstant="2004-07-19T17:02:00Z">
             <saml:Subject>
                <saml:NameIdentifier
                   NameQualifier=http://www.some-trusted-party.com
                   Format="...">
                   uid="OrderProcService"
                </saml:NameIdentifier>
                <saml:SubjectConfirmation>
                   <saml:ConfirmationMethod>
                        urn:oasis:names:tc:SAML:1.0:cm:
                        holder-of-key
                   </saml:ConfirmationMethod>
                      <ds:KeyInfo>
                         <ds:KeyName>OrderProcServiceKey
                            </ds:KeyName>
                         <ds:KeyValue> ... </ds:KeyValue>
                      </ds:KeyInfo>
                </saml:SubjectConfirmation>
             </saml:Subject>
       </saml:AuthenticationStatement>
</saml:Assertion>
```

Listing 11.3 Example of an SAML authentication assertion

could be custom defined. In Listing 11.3 the entity `OrderProcService` was originally authenticated using XML digital signatures (signified by `urn:ietf:rfc:3075`) at `"2004-07-19T17:02:0Z"`. Finally, the `<SubjectConfirmation>` element of an `<AuthenticationStatement>` specifies the relationship between the subject of an assertion and the author of the message that contains the assertion. In the case of Listing 11.3, which contains only a single assertion, the order processing service is the subject of this assertion and the order processing service itself will eventually author the SOAP message to request shipment of the order by the shipment processing service.

Simply providing assertions from an asserting authority to a relying party may not be adequate for a secure system. SAML defines a number of security mechanisms that prevent or detect security attacks. The primary mechanism is for the relying party and asserting party to have a pre-existing trust relationship, typically involving PKI. While use of a PKI is not mandated, it is recommended, and use of particular mechanisms is described for each profile [Hughes 2004].

Although SAML defines mechanisms for user identification, authentication, and authorization, it does not address privacy policies. Rather, partner sites are responsible for developing mutual requirements for user authentication and data protection. SAML, however, defines the structure of the documents that transport security information among services. SAML enables single sign-on and end-to-end security for e-business applications and Web services. Because the SAML standard is designed for the exchange of secure sign-on information between a user, or "relying party," and multiple issuing parties, it allows issuing parties to use their own chosen methods of authentication, e.g., PKI, hash, or password.

While SAML makes assertions about credentials, it does not actually authenticate or authorize users. This is achieved by an authentication server in conjunction with the LDAP directory (see section 11.3.7.2). SAML links back to the actual authentication and makes its assertion based on the results of that event.

Several examples of the use of SAML, including how an application can request an SAML authority for the issuance of an SAML assertion as well as using SAML assertions in WS-Security applications, can be found in [Siddiqui 2003b].

11.5.5 XML Access Control Markup Language (XACML)

SAML can only define how identity and access information is exchanged. How to use that information is the responsibility of XACML, an extension of SAML that allows access control policies to be specified. This language, which uses the same definitions of subjects and actions as SAML, offers a vocabulary for expressing the rules needed to define an organization's security policies and make authorization decisions. In a nutshell, XACML is a general-purpose access control policy language that provides a syntax (defined in XML) for managing authorization decisions.

XACML has two basic components [Proctor 2003]:

1. An access control policy language that lets developers specify the rules about who can do what and when. The access control policy language is used to describe general access control requirements, and has standard extension points for defining new functions, data types, combining logic, and so on.

2. A request/response language that presents requests for access and describes the answers to those queries. The request/response language lets users form a query to ask whether or not a given action should be allowed, and interpret the result. The response always includes an answer about whether the request should be allowed using one of four values: permit, deny, indeterminate (an error occurred or some required value was missing, so a decision cannot be made), or not applicable (the request cannot be answered by this service).

In addition to providing request/response and policy languages, XACML also provides the other pieces of this relationship, i.e., finding a policy that applies to a given request and evaluating the request against that policy to come up with an affirmative or negative answer.

XACML provides for fine-grained control of activities (such as read, write, copy, delete) based on several criteria, including the following:

- Attributes of the user requesting access. Attributes are named values of known types that may include an issuer identifier or an issue date and time, e.g., "Only division managers and above can view this document." A user's name, their security clearance, the file they want to access, and the time of day are all attribute values.
- The protocol over which the request is made, e.g., "This data can be viewed only if it is accessed over secure HTTP."
- The authentication mechanism used.

In a typical XACML usage scenario, a subject, e.g. human user or Web service, may want to take some action on a particular resource. The subject submits its query to the PEP entity that protects the resource, e.g., file system or Web server. The PEP forms a request (using the XACML request language) based on the attributes of the subject, action, resource, and other relevant information. The PEP then forwards this request to a PDP module, which examines the request, retrieves policies (written in the XACML policy language) that are applicable to this request, and determines whether access should be granted according to the XACML rules for evaluating policies. That answer (expressed in the XACML response language) is returned to the PEP, which can then allow or deny access to the requestor. The PEP and PDP might both be contained within a single application, or might be distributed across several servers.

The policy language model of XACML is shown in Figure 11.18. XACML defines a top-level policy element called a `<PolicySet>` which represents a single access control policy. The `<Policy>` element contains a set of `<Rule>` elements linked together using a rule-combining algorithm and an optional set of one or more `<Obligation>`s. Rules are expressions describing conditions under which resource access requests are allowed or denied. A policy can have any number of `<Rule>`s which contain the core logic of an XACML policy. `<Rule>`s comprise a `<Condition>`, which is a Boolean function, and have `<Effect>`s, which indicate the rule writer's intended consequence for a rule that is satisfied. An `<Obligation>` is an operation specified in a policy or policy set that should be performed in conjunction with enforcing an authorization decision. The top-level `<PolicySet>` element `<Policy>` is a container that can hold a set of `<Policy>` or other `<PolicySet>` elements as well as references to policies found in remote locations. Each XACML policy document contains exactly one `<Policy>` or `<PolicySet>` root XML tag.

Given the fact that a `<Policy>` or `<PolicySet>` may contain multiple policies or rules, each of which may evaluate to different access control decisions, XACML needs some way of reconciling the decisions each makes. This is achieved through a collection of combining algorithms. Each algorithm represents a different way of combining multiple decisions into a single decision. There are `<PolicyCombiningAlgorithms>` (used by `<PolicySet>`) and `<RuleCombiningAlgorithms>` (used by `<Policy>`).

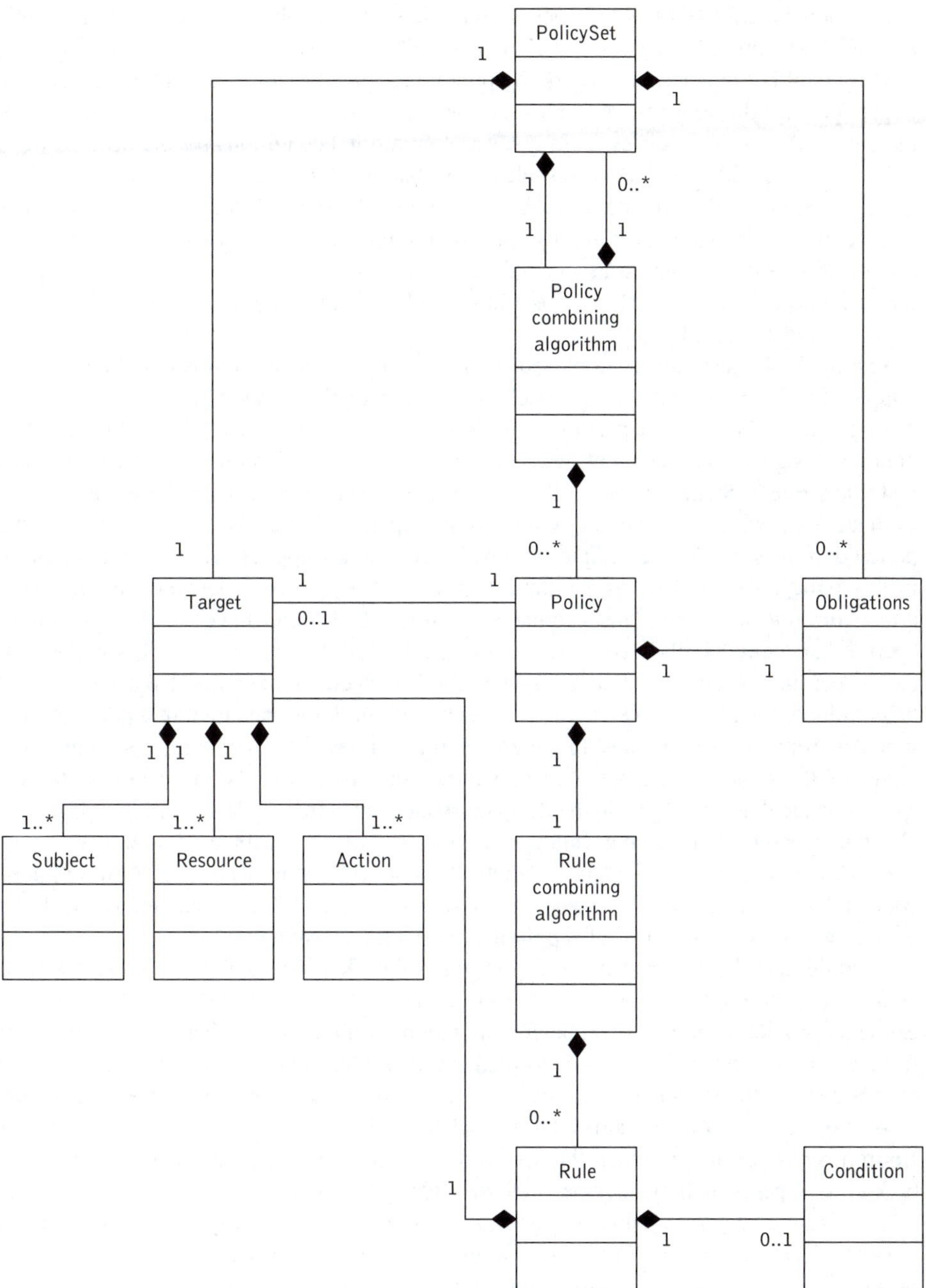

Figure 11.18 XACML policy language model

Part of what an XACML PDP does is find policies that apply to a given request. To this end, XACML provides a `<Target>` element. The `<Target>` of a policy statement is used by the PDP to determine *where* the policy is applicable for a particular request. The target specifies the subjects, resources, and actions (such as read, write, copy, delete) of the policy. A `<Target>` is essentially a set of simplified conditions for the `<Subject>`, `<Resource>`, and `<Action>` sub-elements that must be met for a `<PolicySet>`, `<Policy>`, or `<Rule>` to apply to a given request. These use Boolean functions to compare values found in a request to those included in the `<Target>`. If all the conditions of a `<Target>` are met, then its associated `<PolicySet>`, `<Policy>`, or `<Rule>` applies to the request. Once a `<Policy>` is found, and verified as applicable to a request, its `<Rule>`s are evaluated.

Listing 11.4 illustrates a simple policy from a hypothetical company called Plastics Supply Inc. stating that any subject with an e-mail address in the `plastics_supply.com` domain can perform any action on any resource of this company. The policy is assigned a unique identifier. The deny overrides rule-combining algorithm states that if any rule evaluates to "deny" then the policy must return "deny," whereas if all rules evaluate to "permit" then the policy must return "permit." The `<Target>` section of the policy describes the decision requests to which this policy applies. There is only one rule in this policy, which also has a unique identifier. The `<Rule>` element specifies what effect this rule has if the rule evaluates to "true." Rules can have an effect of either "permit" or "deny." In the case shown in Listing 11.4, if the rule is satisfied, it will evaluate to "permit," meaning that, as far as this rule is concerned, the requested access should be permitted. Finally, the rule `<Target>` section is similar to the target of a policy in that it describes the decision request to which this rule applies. The rule target is similar to the target of the policy itself, but with one important difference. The rule target states a specific value that the subject in the decision request must match. The `<SubjectMatch>` element specifies a matching function in the `MatchId` attribute, a literal value of `"plastics_supply.com"` and a pointer to a specific subject attribute in the request context by means of the `<SubjectAttributeDesignator>` element. Only if the match returns "true" will this rule apply to a particular decision request.

In addition to defining a standard format for policy, XACML defines a standard way of expressing `<Request>`s and `<Response>`s. The `<Request>` and the `<Response>` elements provide a standard format for interacting with a PDP. When a request is sent from a PEP to a PDP, that request is formed almost exclusively of attributes, which will be compared to attribute values in a policy in order to make the appropriate access decisions.

A `<Request>` contains attributes that characterize the subject, resource, action, or environment elements in which the access request is made. Attributes are named values of known types that may include an issuer identifier or an issue date and time. The `<Subject>` element contains one or more attributes of the entity making the access request. There can be multiple subjects, and each subject can have multiple attributes. In addition to attributes, the resource section allows the inclusion of the content of the requested resource, which can be considered in policy evaluation through XPath expressions. The only mandatory `<Attribute>` in a `<Request>` is the resource identifier.

A `<Response>` consists of one or more results, each of which represents the result of an evaluation. Typically, there will only be one result in a `<Response>`. Each `<Result>` contains a decision (permit, deny, not applicable, or indeterminate), some

```
<Policy PolicyId="identifier:example:SimplePolicy1"
         RuleCombiningAlgId="identifier:rule-combining-
           algorithm:deny-overrides">
   <Description>
     Plastics Supply Inc. access control policy
   </Description>
   <Target>
      <Subjects><AnySubject/></Subjects>
      <Resources><AnyResource/></Resources>
      <Actions><AnyAction/></Actions>
   </Target>
   <Rule
     RuleId="identifier:example:SimpleRule1"
     Effect="Permit">
     <Target>
        <Subjects><Subject>
          <SubjectMatch
              MatchId="urn:oasis:names:tc:xacml:1.0:function:
                                                  rfc822Name-match">
             <AttributeValue
              DataType="http://www.w3.org/2001/XMLSchema#string">
              plastics_supply.com
             </AttributeValue>
             <SubjectAttributeDesignator
                AttributeId="urn:oasis:names:tc:xacml:1.0:
                                                 subject:subject-id"
                DataType="urn:oasis:names:tc:xacml:1.0:
                                            data-type:rfc822Name"/>
          </SubjectMatch>
        </Subject></Subjects>
        <Resources><AnyResource/></Resources>
        <Actions><AnyAction/></Actions>
     </Target>
   </Rule>
</Policy>
```

Listing 11.4 Sample XACML policy

status information, e.g., why the evaluation failed, and optionally one or more `<Obligation>`s. An `<Obligation>` element is defined as an action that the PEP is obligated to perform before granting or denying access once the authorization decision is complete. An example of an obligation would be the creation of a digitally signed record every time that a customer's financial records are accessed.

Listing 11.5 shows a hypothetical decision request that might be submitted to a PDP that executes the policy described in Listing 11.4. The access request that generates the decision request may be stated as follows: John Smith, with e-mail name `"jsmith@plastics_supply.com"`, wants to read his tax record at Plastics Supply Inc. In the case of Listing 11.5, there is only one subject involved in the request and the subject has only one attribute: the subject's identity, expressed as an e-mail name.

```
<Request>
 <Subject>
     <Attribute
              AttributeId="urn:oasis:names:tc:xacml:1.0:subject:
              subject-id"
       DataType="identifier:rfc822name">
         <AttributeValue>
            jsmith@plastics_supply.com
         </AttributeValue>
     </Attribute>
  </Subject>
  <Resource>
     <Attribute AttributeId="identifier:resource:resource-uri"
                DataType="xs:anyURI">
        <AttributeValue>
          http://plastics_supply.com/tax-record/employee/JohnSmith
        </AttributeValue>
     </Attribute>
  </Resource>
  <Action>
     <Attribute AttributeId="identifier:example:action"
                DataType="xs:string">
        <AttributeValue>read</AttributeValue>
     </Attribute>
  </Action>
</Request>
```

Listing 11.5 Sample XACML request

The PDP processing this request context locates the policy in its policy repository. It compares the subject, resource, action, and environment in the request context to the subjects, resources, actions, and environments in the policy target. The response context for the request in Listing 11.5 is given in Listing 11.6.

```
<Response>
    <Result>
        <Decision> Permit </Decision>
    </Result>
</Response>
```

Listing 11.6 XACML response

11.6 Securing Web services

So far in this chapter we have concentrated on technologies that are primarily used for XML security, e.g., XML Signature and XML Encryption, or applicable to the application of XML to information security functionality such as key management, authentication, or access control rules, e.g., XKMS, SAML, and XACML. In this section we shall examine how these technologies are used in the context of Web services security. Prior to introducing this subject we shall explain the technology implications and challenges of Web services security.

11.6.1 Web services application-level security challenges

Web services rely on *message security*, which works by applying security technology to the message itself. Message security focuses on two critical security concerns: first, protecting message content from being disclosed to unauthorized individuals (confidentiality), and, second, preventing illegal modification of message content (integrity). Message security also guarantees selectivity by securing portions of the message to different parties (authenticity) and flexibility as different security policies can be applied to request and responses independently [Rosenberg 2004]. An additional requirement is, of course, content access control. As today SSL along with TLS are used to provide transport-level security for Web services applications, we shall first examine the shortcomings of SSL and then reflect on important application (message) level security challenges.

One serious weakness in Web services lies in its use of HTTP. HTTP transport (the basic transport mechanism of the Internet) can tunnel through existing network firewalls and, using SOAP, establish communications with applications within an enterprise infrastructure, thus creating a major break in enterprise virus and hacking defenses. Traditionally, SSL, TLS, VPNs, and IPSec are some of the common ways of securing content. For instance, SSL/TLS (see section 11.3.6.1) offers several security features including authentication, data integrity, and data confidentiality of messages in transit. SSL/TLS enables point-to-point secure sessions and can be used to secure communication from a transport-level perspective. It provides rudimentary, point-to-point data privacy but not full security. SSL/TLS is certainly sufficient to meet the straightforward requirement to secure interactions between Web browsers and Web servers that utilized the stateless HTTP connection protocol, but it cannot adequately address the scenario where a SOAP request is routed via more than one server. For situations where secure messages must pass from one intermediary to another, SSL/TLS is found lacking. Figure 11.19 highlights point-to-point and end-to-end security configurations.

The problem of intermediaries is especially important in the context of Web services, because SOAP is designed to support one or more intermediaries that can forward or reroute SOAP messages based upon information either in the SOAP header or the HTTP header. To maximize the reach of Web services requires *end-to-end* and not just point-to-point security. In the end-to-end security topology, the creator of the message may have written the payload, but intermediaries may inspect or rewrite the message afterwards. Therefore, there must be a way for the intermediary to read the part of the message that instructs it what to do, without compromising the confidential payload of the message. This process becomes even more compound when one considers long-running choreographed

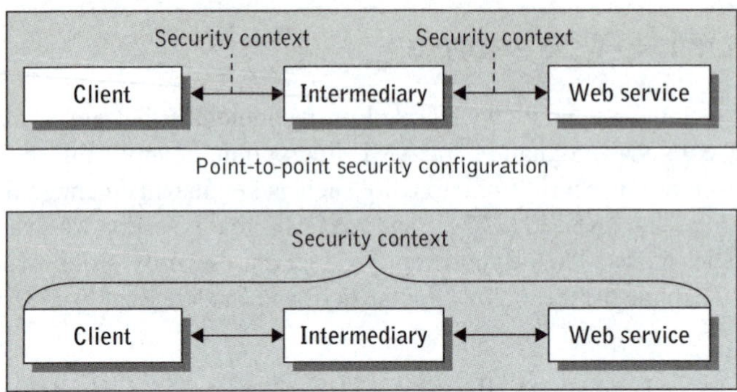

Figure 11.19 Point-to-point versus end-to-end security configuration

Web services conversations involving multiple requests, responses, and forks, and their ensuing security requirements. All of these scenarios rely on the ability of message processing intermediaries to forward messages. When data is received and forwarded by an intermediary beyond the transport layer, both the integrity of data and any security information that flows with it may be lost. This forces any upstream message servers to rely on the security evaluations made by previous intermediaries and to completely trust their handling of the content of messages.

Web services require a high degree of granularity, i.e., different security requirements, for incoming and outgoing messages as well as waypoint visibility, i.e., partial visibility into the message. Web services need to maintain secure context and control it according to their security policies. The infrastructure securing Web services needs XML's granularity for encrypting or digitally signing select document portions and acting on rewritten individual headers. However, the problem is that SSL/TLS can be used for data privacy/encryption, signing/integrity, and for authentication/trust, but only provides transport-level granularity for point-to-point communication and not *granularity on encryption*, such as encrypting sensitive information while exposing routing information in clear text. With SSL/TLS the security of each message is an all-or-nothing proposition: either the entire message is secure, or not. Thus, whenever the security of particular parts of a message is important, for instance in cases where a Web service request might ask for several pieces of information that have different levels of confidentiality, SSL is inadequate.

In addition to the transport-level problems introduced due to the limitations of SSL, Web services face a variety of other application-level security challenges when trying to enable two or more services, running under different security domains, to intercommunicate. For example, one Web service may use Kerberos tickets to authenticate clients, while another might only support client-side SSL certificates. A question that arises is how can these services authenticate to each other? Similarly, as developers start writing enterprise-grade line-of-business applications one problem that surfaces is that when two or more Web services are running under different security domains, it is highly likely that each domain will maintain its own distinct "silo" of user profiles. Such issues require a security mechanism for providing a single point of sign-on and authentication, and a standardized way to obtain suitable security credentials to prove the authenticated identity.

The powerful and flexible security infrastructure that Web services require can be developed by leveraging the transport mechanisms provided by SSL/TLS and extending them with advanced application layer security mechanisms to provide a comprehensive suite of Web services security capabilities that address problems at the message level.

To address this challenge several standards bodies including the W3C, OASIS, the Liberty Alliance, and others have proposed a number of security standards to solve problems related to authentication, role-based access control (RBAC), messaging, and data security. Their aim was to help strengthen Web services security. As a result a number of standards including XML Encryption, XML Signature, and SAML were created and are used in the context of a foundational security standard for Web services called WS-Security, ensuring the integrity, confidentiality, and security of Web services. The remainder of this chapter explores the Web services security model.

11.6.2 Web services security roadmap

To address end-to-end security concerns, IBM and Microsoft have collaborated on a Web services security plan and roadmap for developing a set of Web service security standard specifications and technologies. These are meant to describe a unifying approach for dealing with protection for messages exchanged in a Web services environment [WS-Roadmap 2002]. The proposed security framework and roadmap are sufficient to construct higher-level key exchange, authentication, authorization, auditing, and trust mechanisms, while providing an integrating abstraction allowing systems and applications to build a bridge between diverse security systems and technologies. This security framework is shown in Figure 11.20 to comprise a foundational standard called WS-Security (which in turn is built on XML Signature, XML Encryption, SAML, and various other security standards) followed by other standards that rely on it. Most of the specifications summarized below are still under development, possibly with the exception of WS-Security, which is fairly well defined.

WS-Security: This set of SOAP extensions is focused on implementing message content integrity and confidentiality. The specified mechanisms can be used to accommodate a variety of security models and encryption technologies.

WS-(Security)Policy: WS-SecurityPolicy is an addendum to WS-Security and indicates the policy assertions for WS-Policy that apply to WS-Security. Security policy assertions in WS-SecurityPolicy specify the security requirements of their

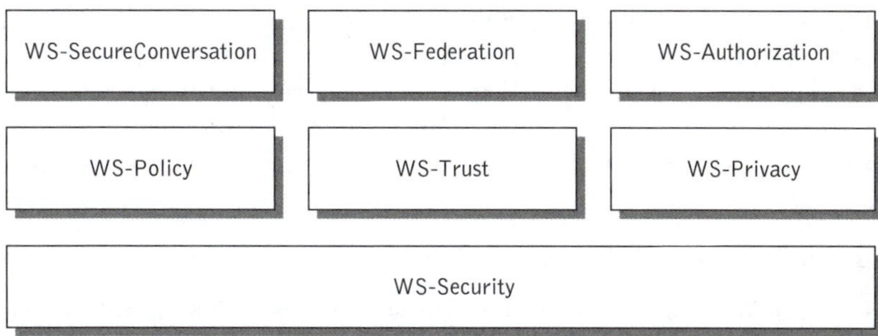

Figure 11.20 Web services security roadmap

Web services. These security requirements include the supported algorithms for encryption and digital signatures, privacy attributes, and how this information may be bound to a Web service.

WS-Trust: This specification defines a series of XML-based primitives for requesting and issuing security tokens, as well as for managing trust relationships.

WS-Privacy: This specification uses a combination of WS-Policy, WS-Security, and WS-Trust to communicate privacy polices. These privacy policies are stated by organizations that deploy Web services and require that incoming SOAP requests contain claims that the sender conforms to these privacy policies.

WS-SecureConversation: WS-SecureConversation defines extensions that build on WS-Security to provide secure communication.

WS-Federation: WS-Federation defines mechanisms that are used to enable identity, attribute, authentication, and authorization federation across different trust realms.

WS-Authorization: This specification has a number of overlaps with XACML, and describes how access policies for a Web service are specified and managed.

In the security roadmap depicted in Figure 11.20, WS-Security serves as the foundation block for a set of composable security building blocks that lean on it. This means that the various building-block standards such as WS-Federation may be constructed using other security building blocks including WS-Security, WS-Policy, WS-Trust, and WS-SecureConversation.

The standards in the security roadmap address distributed message-based security in terms of three broad interrelated security concerns: interoperability, trust, and integration. Interoperability in the context of security means that independent heterogeneous systems that previously did not communicate are able to work together and understand one another. This capability is especially important when communications between disparate systems are secure. The family of security standards that relate to secure interoperability include: WS-Security, WS-SecurePolicy, and WS-SecureConversation. Trust for Web services security is also an important element that needs to be represented in relationships. It can be explicitly established or it may be presumed. The family of security standards that help promote trust include: WS-Trust and WS-Privacy. Integration in the world of Web services security stretches interoperability to address cross-organizational integration by extending and unifying (heterogeneous) system architectures across organizational boarders so that existing services can be reused for new purposes. This means that identities and the trust model under which services operate need to be integrated. The family of security standards that relate to integration include: WS-Federation and WS-Authorization.

We shall first introduce a general Web services security model and then address the security roadmap specifications in turn starting from the interoperability security standards, then moving on to trust standards, and ending with security integration standards.

11.6.3 Web services security model

In the context of Web services, applications need to be able to interoperate despite using their own security infrastructure and mechanisms, such as PKI or Kerberos. To facilitate this, the Web services roadmap specification has defined an abstract security model and

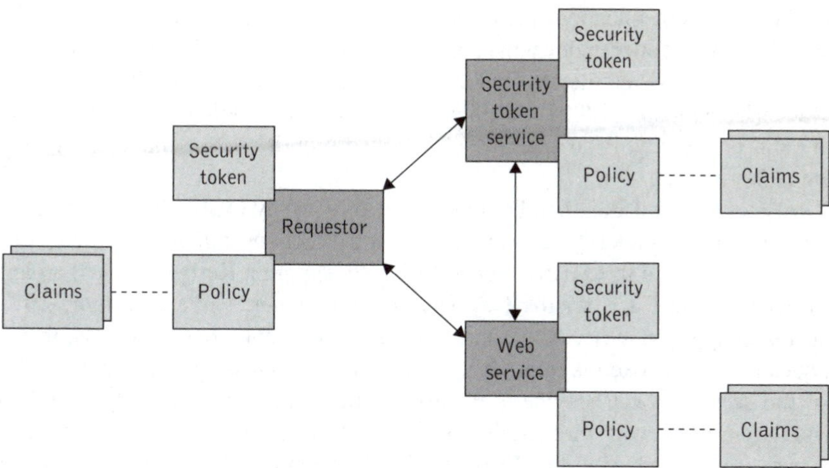

Figure 11.21 The general Web services security and trust model

architecture for this purpose [WS-Roadmap 2002]. This model is generic in the sense that is designed to fit many applications and is shown in Figure 11.21.

The Web services security model should be defined in terms of generic protocols for exchanging generic (token) claims offered by service consumers and generic policy rules regarding such claims enforced by service providers. The advantage of this approach is that only such generic policy and token metadata need be generically exchanged across diverse administrative domains, leaving such domains free to use different concrete policy and token mechanisms, such as PKI, Active Directory, and Kerberos.

Figure 11.21 illustrates that there are three parties involved in the security model for Web services. These are: the requestor, the Web service, and the security token service (the darker shaded modules). The different security technologies in the Web services security model are abstracted into interoperable formats that define a generic policy model, modularized into the following conceptual building blocks: policies, policy assertions, claims, and security tokens. A (security) *policy* determines the security mechanisms that must be present in inbound SOAP messages and the security enhancements that need to be added to outgoing SOAP messages. As usual, *security policy assertions* specify the security requirements of their respective Web services and include the supported algorithms for encryption and digital signatures, privacy attributes, and how this information may be applied to a Web service. A *claim* is a statement about a subject (person, application, or business entity) either by the subject or by a relying party that associates the subject with a property, such as identity of entitlements. Claims can be statements that the security token conveys. For instance, a claim might be used to assert the sender's identity or authorized role.

A security token can be thought of as data (added to a SOAP header), which expresses a claim about an end user or message originator, e.g. their identity, their entitlements and their authorization to access a particular resource for a certain length of time. Examples include user name and password combinations, SSL client certificates, XRML licenses, and Kerberos tickets. Security tokens in Figure 11.21 are used to provide an end-to-end security solution and must be shared, either directly or indirectly between the parties involved in message exchanges. Security tokens assert claims and can be used to assert the binding between authentication secrets or keys and security identities [Nadalin 2004]. An authority can vouch for or endorse the claims in a security token by using its key to sign or encrypt the security token thereby enabling the authentication of the claims in the token. An X.509 [Hallam-Baker 2004] certificate, claiming the binding between a principal's identity and public key, is an example of a signed security token endorsed by the certification authority.

Security token acquisition can be done either directly by explicitly requesting a token from an appropriate authority (as shown in Figure 11.21) or indirectly by delegating the acquisition to a trusted third party. For instance, to acquire a Kerberos ticket, an application needs to contact a Kerberos Key Distribution Center, while to acquire an X.509 certificate, an application needs to contact a certification authority (CA). The third party that issues a security token is referred to as a *security token service* in Figure 11.21. The role of the security token service is to link existing fragmented security islands into a federated security network through the exchange of diverse types of security tokens. The X.509 certification authority, the Kerberos Key Distribution Center, and the certification authority in PKI are good examples of security token services. The security token service does not simply issue and validate tokens, it also exchanges them. The key ability of a security token service as a brokering entity is its ability to exchange one type of token, e.g., X.509 certificate, for another, e.g., Kerberos ticket.

The security model for Web services in Figure 11.21 encompasses a trust model (illustrated by the solid lines interconnecting the heavy shaded modules). The *Web services trust model* defines trust as the characteristic that one entity is willing to rely upon a second entity to execute a set of actions and/or to make a number of assertions about a set of subjects and/or scopes. Trust relationships can be either direct or brokered. Direct trust is when a relying party accepts as true all (or some subset of) the claims in the token sent by the requestor. In the case of brokered trust, a "trust proxy" (second party) is used to read the WS-Policy information and request the appropriate security tokens from an issuer of security tokens, thus vouching for a third party. Trust relationships are based on the exchange and brokering of security tokens and on the support of trust policies that have been established by the corresponding security authorities [Cabrera 2005d]. WS-Security will be used to transfer the required security tokens making use of XML Signature and XML Encryption, which ensures message integrity and confidentiality.

When a requestor wishes to invoke a Web service, it must produce claims such as its identity and privileges. On the other hand, each Web service has a security policy applied to it, which may, for instance, require the encryption and digital signing of messages and identification of the requestor. Such Web services policies specify the security requirements to access the Web service. A Web service receives a message from a requestor that possibly includes security tokens, and may have some protection applied to it using WS-Security mechanisms.

When an application is sending security claims, it will have to consider how to represent them in messages conveyed over SOAP and WS-Security. The Web services security model specifies all claims included in the security token that is attached to a request message [WS-Roadmap 2002]. For example, identity via a password or X.509v3 certificates are security claims. Therefore, they need to be represented as security tokens.

The general security messaging model – claims, policies, and security tokens – subsumes and supports several more specific models, including identity-based security, access control lists, and capabilities-based security [Rosenberg 2004]. It allows use of existing technologies such as passwords, X.509v3 certificates, Kerberos tickets, and so on. This security model in combination with WS-Security and WS-Policy primitives provides sufficient support to construct higher-level key exchanges, authentication, policy-based access decisions, auditing, and complex trust relationships.

11.6.4 WS-Security

WS-Security is an OASIS security standard specification, which proposes a standard set of SOAP extensions that can be used when building secure Web services to provide the ability to send security tokens as part of a message and implement message content integrity and confidentiality [Nadalin 2004]. This specification serves as a building block that can be used in conjunction with other Web services extensions and higher-level application-specific protocols to accommodate a wide variety of security models (including PKI, Kerberos, and SSL) and security technologies.

WS-Security primarily describes how to secure SOAP messages with the use of XML signature and XML encryption. It defines how security tokens are contained in SOAP messages, and how XML security specifications are used to encrypt and sign these tokens as well as how to sign and encrypt other parts of a SOAP message [Nadalin 2004]. The WS-Security model also caters to SOAP endpoints and intermediaries by supporting end-to-end security. It defines scenarios where the integrity and confidentiality of SOAP messages is ensured while the messages traverse intermediaries, even when these intermediaries use security functionality themselves.

Before introducing the elements of WS-Security we shall introduce a simple and intuitive scenario illustrating how the XML-based security mechanisms described in section 11.5 and WS-Security could be applied to protect a simplified order processing transaction involving a relatively simple business dialogue between a client, a seller, a credit rating company, a trusted third party, and a shipment service. Following this we shall describe how Web services standards based around WS-Security help tackle the security challenges faced by enterprises seeking to implement an SOA- or Web-services-based integration deployment. These two topics will help readers to grasp easier and better the material that is related to WS-Security.

11.6.4.1 A use case for WS-Security

The interoperable protocols of the Web services security model that we described in the previous section need to define a generic process model that is abstracted into the following subprocesses:

1. Generating and distributing service security policies via Web services definitions, e.g., WSDL descriptions, and service directories, e.g., UDDI.
2. Generating and distributing security tokens.
3. Presenting tokens in messages and service requests.
4. Verifying whether presented tokens meet required policies. Verification activities verify that the claims in a security token are sufficient to comply with the security

policy and that the message conforms to the security policy; they establish the identity of the claimant and verify that the issuers of the security tokens are trusted to issue the claims they have made [Anderson 2004b]. Only if these verification activities are performed successfully and the requestor is authorized to perform the service operation requested can the Web service process the requested operation.

To understand the above points we make use of the simplified order processing transaction scenario depicted in Figure 11.22. The scenario in Figure 11.22 assumes that a client creates a purchase order and sends the request to fulfill the order to a seller (step 1). The Web services application at the seller's side begins the process of checking the requestor's credit rating and verifying that the ordered parts are available in the product inventory, selecting a shipper and scheduling the shipment for the order, and billing the customer.

Before the order management service (at the seller's side) can interact with other Web services, it must be able to authenticate itself to those services. This will be accomplished by presenting a digital certificate that has been issued by a trusted third party. By providing an interface to a public-key management system, the XKMS server retrieves the order management company's digital certificate (step 2 in Figure 11.22).

The seller submits a request to a credit rating company service to check the creditworthiness of the customer. The order management service (at the seller's side) knows that the credit rating service expects that requests will be digitally signed. This is stated by means of a WS-Policy assertion associated with the WSDL/UDDI description of the credit rating service. When the order management service submits its signed request, the credit rating service accesses the XKMS server to validate the requestor's PKI credentials. Assume that the XKMS server responds that the credentials are valid. The credit rating service then answers the order management application's request with an attribute assertion stating that the applicant has the appropriate credit rating (step 3).

Having verified the client's creditworthiness, the order management service now needs to validate the details of the order in question by checking an inventory/shipment database maintained by a shipping agency. Before granting access, however, the shipping agency checks to verify that the seller has contracted to access this shipping service – and then returns an SAML authorization assertion (step 4). The order management application service submits an order shipment request to the shipping service, with a WS-Security header containing the authorization assertion issued in step 4. A response is returned, indicating that the ordered parts (shipment details in Figure 11.22) fit the description provided by the client and can be shipped (step 5).

Having obtained the necessary assurances about the client and the shipment, the order management application issues a signed bill, billing for the order. XML-Signature and XML-Encryption ensure the integrity and confidentiality of this document.

The following section shows how an end-to-end interoperable Web services scenario such as the one depicted in Figure 11.23 can be realized using a secure SOA implementation.

11.6.4.2 Integrating WS-Security in SOAs

The benefits that can be realized from an integrated end-to-end, interoperable, Web services security framework are compelling enough that enterprises are using a mix of standardized protocols and leading-edge specifications including SSL for communication,

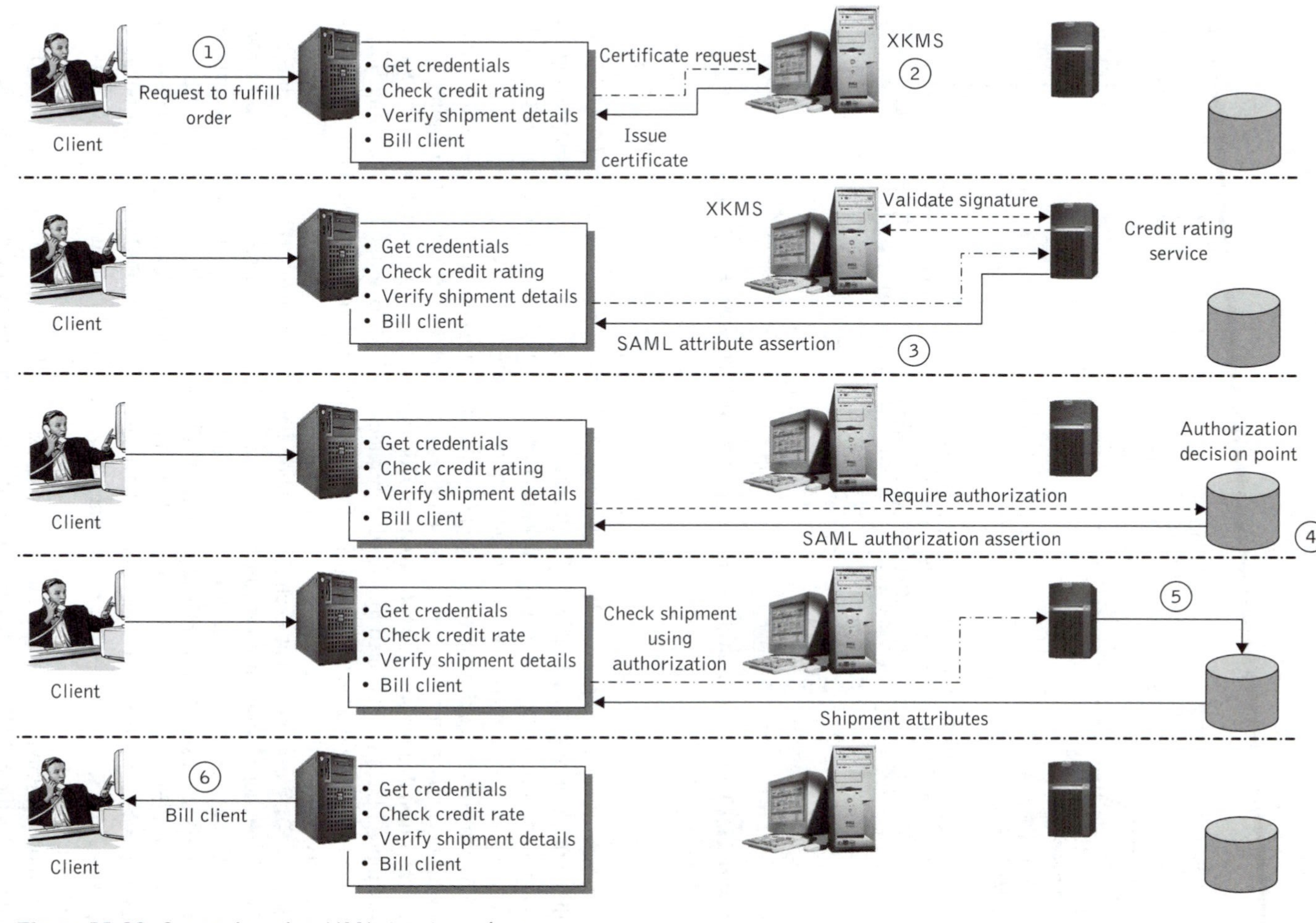

Figure 11.22 Scenario using XML trust services

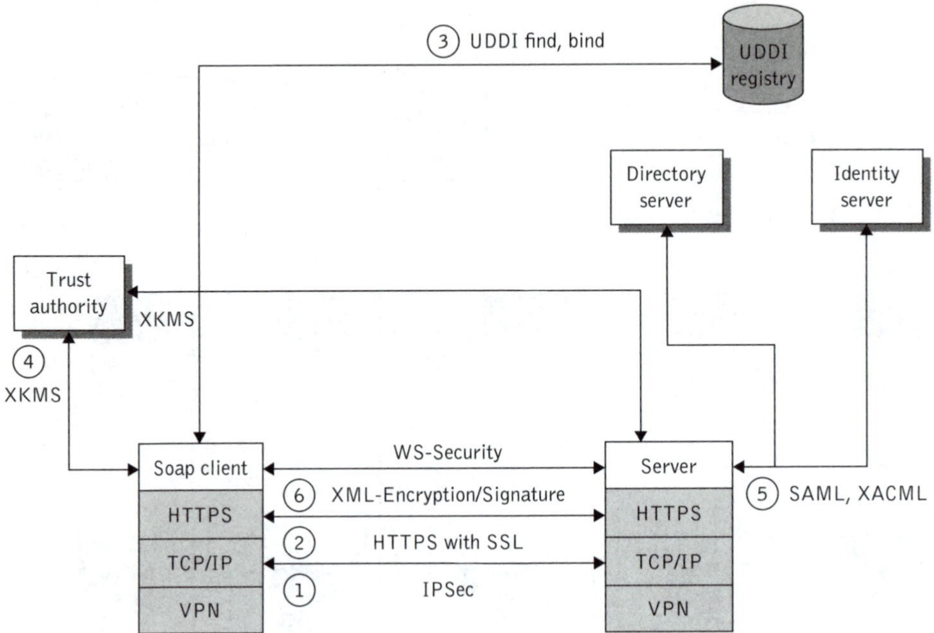

Figure 11.23 Conceptual architecture employing a Web services Security solution
Source: [Lai 2004]

WS-Security (including XML-Encryption and XML-Signature), SAML, and XACML in the context of an SOA. Figure 11.23 illustrates a conceptual architecture employing an integrated Web services security infrastructure that can be used to implement a Web services security scenario such as the one depicted in Figure 11.22.

A Web services call requires different layers of security to achieve end-to-end security connections in an SOA. In the conceptual security architecture depicted in Figure 11.23 it is assumed that the service requestor (a SOAP client initiating the purchase order request in Figure 11.22) is connected to a service provider via VPN over the Internet using IPSec to achieve secure connectivity (step 1). This guarantees network layer security. Transport security within the scope of this architecture is provided by means of HTTP (over SSL/TLS). We assume that each SOAP node has an associated HTTPS node and that SOAP messages between nodes are carried over HTTPS messages. The client also uses HTTPS to secure the connection between the client browser and the server at the provider's site using SSL certificates (step 2). The use of HTTPS with SSL should safeguard the client session. Using a secure HTTPS connection, the client can browse various Web services (business processes) in a UDDI service registry, find the relevant business process, and retrieve the service endpoint URL (step 3). This sequence refers to *service discovery security*.

Upon invoking the relevant business process, e.g., the purchase order process in Figure 11.22, the SOAP client needs to provide its credentials in order to authenticate itself for using the remote Web services in question. Here, we assume that the identity provider is part of a trusted authority that is managed by an external Liberty-Alliance-compliant identity provider. The identity provider then provides an authentication service using XKMS. The client's key is located from the trust authority via XKMS (step 4). The service provider then provides a user identification and password to authenticate itself. Upon successful authentication, the identity provider enables single sign-on for the service client using SAML and XACML protocols (step 5). This means that the service requestor does not need to log in again to use other Web services. This sequence refers to the *service negotiation security*.

When the service requestor invokes a Web service, the client side makes use of the public- and private-key infrastructure using XKMS to encrypt the data content in the SOAP message using XML Encryption. The client then may generate a digital signature using XML Signature to attach to the SOAP envelope. As WS-Security leans on XML Encryption and XML Signature it is used in this security architecture as the message-level security to protect SOAP messages. In this way the service request and data content of the SOAP messages are secured by using the WS-Security standard (step 6).

Due to reasons of simplicity, the conceptual architecture in Figure 11.23 involves only two interacting nodes. In reality, a Web services orchestration would entail a large number of interacting nodes (including many intermediaries). The scenario depicted in Figure 11.22, which involved credit rating, inventory, and shipping services, illustrated this point. In this scenario SOAP messages have to be routed over multiple "hops." Each hop can only authenticate to the next, such that complete end-to-end authentication is unattainable. To establish a single security context between the message originator (client) and target Web services, message-level security needs to be used. To pass security context with XML messages, existing directories with user or policy information in their XML gateways and security servers are used. By inserting end-user credentials inside the message, it is possible for those credentials to be propagated along a chain of Web services or other intermediaries, so that eventually they can be conveyed to the target Web service. Any one of those intermediaries can verify the authenticity of the user's credentials, and can choose not to forward the message onwards for security reasons. For example, the message originator can insert an XML Signature into a SOAP message to ensure that any changes to the message contents will not go unnoticed by any intermediary that chooses to verify the signature.

11.6.4.3 WS-Security key features

As explained at the outset of this section, WS-Security describes enhancements to SOAP messaging to provide quality of protection through message integrity, message confidentiality, and single message authentication. The purpose of WS-Security is not to invent new types of security, but instead to provide a common format to accommodate security in a SOAP message. WS-Security mechanisms can be used to accommodate a wide variety of security models and encryption technologies. It also provides a general-purpose mechanism for associating security tokens with SOAP messages. No specific type of security token is required by WS-Security. It is designed to be extensible, i.e., support multiple security token formats. For example, a client might provide proof of identity and proof that it has a particular business certification.

When securing SOAP messages, a variety of types of threats need to be considered, such as the message being modified or read by an adversary or an adversary sending messages to a service that, while well formed, lacks appropriate security claims to warrant processing. To cater for such threats WS-Security provides a means to protect a message by encrypting and/or digitally signing a body, a header, or any combination of them (parts of them). WS-Security utilizes three core elements, which make up a SOAP security header: security tokens, XML Encryption, and XML Signature. Message integrity is provided by XML Signature [Eastlake 2002a] in conjunction with security tokens to ensure that modifications to messages are detected. The integrity mechanisms are designed to support multiple signatures, potentially by multiple SOAP actors/roles, and to be extensible to support additional signature formats. Message confidentiality leverages XML Encryption [Eastlake 2002a] in conjunction with security tokens to keep portions of a SOAP message confidential. The encryption mechanisms are designed to support additional encryption processes and operations by multiple SOAP actors/roles.

Figure 11.24 shows the WS-Security message structure and its core elements in relation to security tokens, XML Encryption, and XML Signature. The figure shows that the

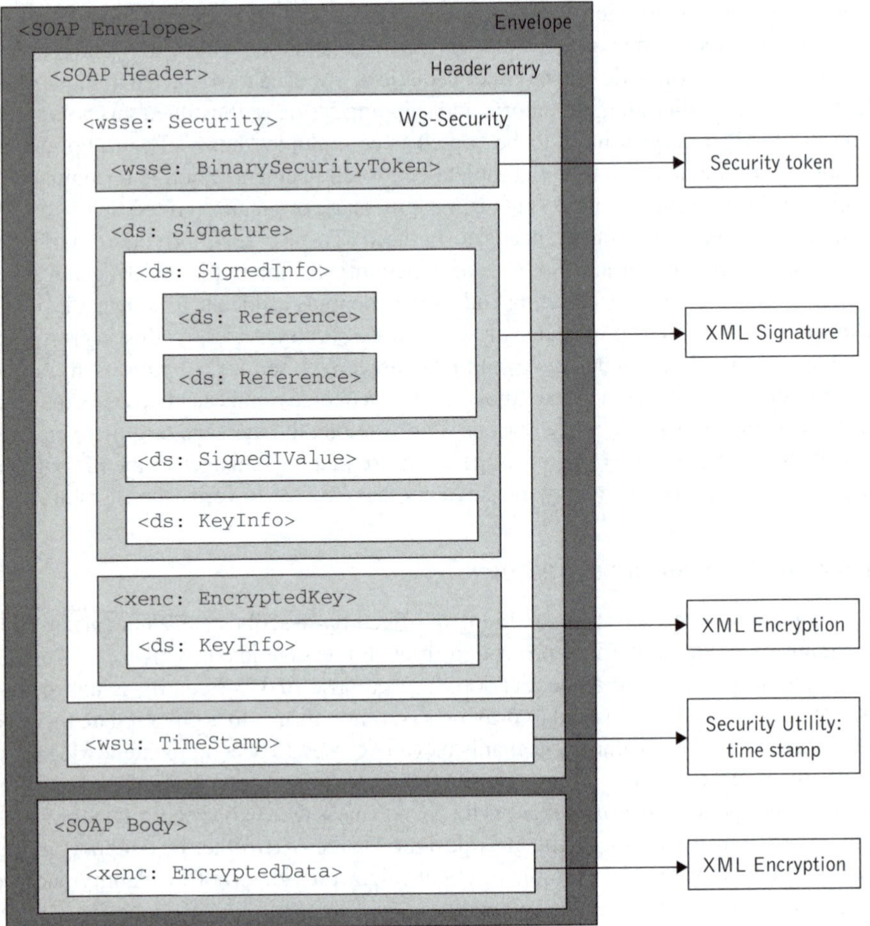

Figure 11.24 WS-Security elements and structure

WS-Security specification encloses security tokens inside SOAP messages and describes how XML Signature and XML Encryption can be used for confidentiality and integrity of these tokens within the SOAP header.

Listing 11.7 shows the basic WS-Security structure within a SOAP envelope. The most fundamental element that WS-Security defines is a `<Security>` element that resides inside the SOAP header. As the simple skeleton listing shows, WS-Security defines its

```
<?xml version="1.0" encoding="utf-8"?>
<env:Envelope
   xmlns:env="http://www.w3.org/2003/05/soap-envelope"
   xmlns:wsse=
   "http://docs.oasis-open.org/wss/2004/01/
                        oasis-200401-wsswssecurity-secext-1.0.xsd"
   xmlns:wsu=
   "http://docs.oasis-open.org/wss/2004/01/
                       oasis-200401-wsswssecurity-utility-1.0.xsd"
   xmlns:ds="http://www.w3.org/2000/09/xmldsig#"
   xmlns:xenc="http://www.w3.org/2001/04/xmlenc#">
 <env:Header>
  <wsse:Security>
    <!-- Security Token -->
    <wsse:UsernameToken wsu:Id="...">
       <wsse:Username>...</wsse:Username>
    </wsse:UsernameToken>
    <!-- XML Signature -->
    <ds:Signature>
       …
       <ds:Reference URI="#MsgBody">
       …
    </ds:Signature>
    <!-- XML Encryption Reference List -->
    <xenc:ReferenceList>
    <xenc:DataReference URI="#bodyID">
    </xenc:ReferenceList>
  </wsse:Security>
 </env:Header>
 <env:Body>
  <!-- XML Encrypted Body -->
  <xenc: EncryptedData Id="bodyID" Type="content">
    <xenc:CipherData>
       <xenc:CipherValue>...</xenc:CipherValue>
    </xenc:CipherData>
  </xenc:EncryptedData>
 </env:Body>
</env:Envelope>
```

Listing 11.7 Structure of basic WS-Security header

own namespace. Still, the creators of WS-Security defer to existing standards and technologies focusing instead on specifying how to use them with SOAP.

Listing 11.7 shows a security header that contains three children: a security token (`UserToken` is just an example of a security token); `<Signature>`, which represents an XML Signature; and an XML Encryption `<ReferenceList>`. As well as enclosing security tokens, the security header block presents information about the use of XML Signature and XML Encryption in the SOAP message. Usually, if an XML signature is included, at a minimum it signs the whole or part of a SOAP body. A security header may also contain `<ReferenceList>` or `<EncryptedKey>` elements. The `<EncryptedData>` element in conjunction with the `<EncryptedKey>` element is used to transport encryption keys from the originator to a known recipient (see section 11.5.2). A `<ReferenceList>` element contains a list to reference all the different `<EncryptedData>` elements. In this way, a WS-Security processor can read the security header and then decrypt all the data to which the `<EncryptedData>` element refers. Listing 11.7 also illustrates that often the SOAP body is also encrypted itself. Finally, the prefix `wsu` denotes the security utility specification that defines several elements (including elements that express time stamp information such as creation and expiration), attributes, and attribute groups which can be reused by other specifications. The `wsu:Id` attribute in this listing is referenced by specifications that require the use of a global identifier.

Security tokens in WS-Security. Authentication in the Web services environment usually involves credentials embedded in either the headers or body of the SOAP message. Standard Web technologies using passwords, X.509 certificates to identify browser-based client identification, Kerberos tickets to authenticate clients, and so on can also be used to authenticate service requestors. Both service requestors and providers should be authenticated for sensitive communication.

WS-Security handles credential management in two ways. It defines a special element, `<UsernameToken>`, to pass the user name and password if the Web service is using custom authentication. WS-Security uses another special element, `<BinarySecurityToken>`, to provide binary authentication tokens. The two classes designated in WS-Security are Kerberos tickets and X.509v3 certificates.

Figure 11.25 illustrates a typical message flow involving security tokens [Seely 2002]. Once a SOAP client requests a security token to add to a SOAP message, a security token returns the appropriate token. The tokens might be Kerberos, PKI, or a user name/password validation service. Returned tokens may not be Web service based. For instance, a Kerberos service ticket granting service might be accessed through the Kerberos protocols using operating system security functions. Once the client gets the tokens it wants to use in the message, the client will embed those tokens within the message (step 2). Subsequently, the client should sign the message with a private key that only the client knows (step 3). SOAP messages must be signed or encrypted if authentication is important. It is not enough that a valid identity token is added to a message as these tokens can be lifted from a valid message and added to messages used by attackers. The receiver (Web service) is able to verify that the client sent the message if the signatures it generates for the message match the signatures contained in the message (step 4). The receiver verifies the signature in a number of ways. For instance, if the client is using a `<UsernameToken>` for

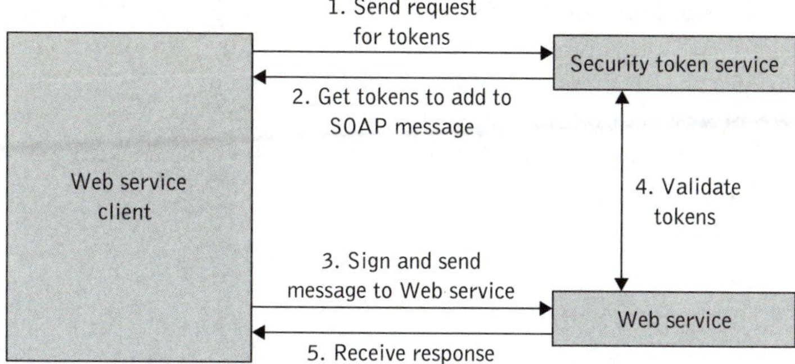

Figure 11.25 Typical message flow involving security tokens

authentication, the receiver expects that the client sends a hashed password and signs the message using that password. Finally the client is able to receive a response from the Web service.

```
<wsse:Security
 xmlns:wsse="http://schemas.xmlsoap.org/ws/2002/12/secext">
 <wsse:BinarySecurityToken
  ValueType="wsse:X509v3"
  EncodingType="wsse:Base64Binary">
   SSphfawHraPle ...
 </wsse:BinarySecurityToken>
</wsse:Security>
```

Listing 11.8 An X.509 certificate embedded in a `<BinarySecurityToken>`

The code snippet in Listing 11.8 shows that an X.509v3 certificate is sent using the more general `<BinarySecurityToken>` element. The `ValueType` attribute of the `<BinarySecurityToken>` indicates that what is being sent is an X.509v3 certificate. The certificate is represented using Base64 encoding, and the certificate itself makes up the content of the `<BinarySecurityToken>` element, which is used to authenticate a client to a particular service.

WS-Security takes a flexible approach to conveying and authenticating identities. However, although two systems can both conform to WS-Security, they might still be incapable of authenticating one another. One system might support only Kerberos, for instance, while the other allows only digital-signature-based authentication using X.509 certificates. Simply agreeing to use WS-Security is not enough; some agreement must also be in place about exactly what kinds of security tokens will be used.

Providing confidentiality in WS-Security. The next major feature of WS-Security to cover is using XML Encryption to ensure confidentiality by providing a means to encrypt some or all of a SOAP message before it gets transmitted. Using the XML Encryption standard, WS-Security allows encrypting all or part of a SOAP message's header information, its body, and any attachments. WS-Security uses only three of the XML elements defined by this standard: `<EncryptedData>`, `<EncryptedKey>`, and `<ReferenceList>` (see section 11.5.2).

```
<env:Envelope>
 <env:Header>
  <wsse:Security>
    <wsse:EncryptedKey>
      <EncryptionMethod
        Algorithm="http://www.w3.org/2001/04/xmlenc#rsa-1_5"/>
        <ds:KeyInfo>
          <wsse:SecurityTokenReference>
            <ds:X509IssuerSerial>
              <ds:X509IssuerName>
                DC=ABC-Corp, DC=com
              </ds:X509IssuerName>
              <ds:X509SerialNumber>12345678</ds:X509SerialNumber>
            </ds:X509IssuerSerial>
          </wsse:SecurityTokenReference>
        </ds:KeyInfo>

      <!-- XML Encryption Reference List -->
      <xenc:ReferenceList>
      <xenc:DataReference URI="#EncryptedBody">
      </xenc:ReferenceList>
    </wsse:EncryptedKey>
  </wsse:Security>
 </env:Header>
 <env:Body>
  <!-- XML Encrypted Body -->
  <xenc: EncryptedData Id=" EncryptedBody" Type="content">
    <xenc:CipherData>
       <xenc:CipherValue>...</xenc:CipherValue>
    </xenc:CipherData>
  </xenc:EncryptedData>
 </env:Body>
</env:Envelope>
```

Listing 11.9 SOAP message with encrypted body

Listing 11.9 shows an example of how a simple SOAP message might look if its sender chose to encrypt elements or element contents within a SOAP envelope with a symmetric key, which is in turn to be encrypted by the recipient's key and embedded in the message. In this example we have removed namespaces to ease reading.

In Listing 11.9 the <EncryptedKey> element uses a public key to encrypt a shared key, which is in turn used to encrypt the SOAP body. This technique is known as *key wrapping* or *digital enveloping* because the shared key is wrapped by the recipient's public key [Rosenberg 2004]. The public key used to do the encryption is found within the <SecurityTokenReference> element in the <KeyInfo> block. The <SecurityTokenReference> element provides the means for referencing security tokens because not all tokens support a common reference pattern.

Providing message integrity in WS-Security. The next major feature of WS-Security to cover is using XML Signature to ensure message integrity. As explained in section 11.5.1, XML Signature provides a detailed mechanism for digitally signing XML documents. XML Signature is used within WS-Security for two main reasons [Rosenberg 2004]. The first is to verify a security token credential such as an X509 certificate or SAML assertion. Another is *message integrity* which verifies that the message has not been modified while in transit.

Listing 11.10 shows the use of XML Signature within WS-Security. In this example we have removed namespaces to ease reading. As usual a <Signature> element includes both the digital signature itself and information about how this signature was produced. A typical instance of <Signature> as used with SOAP will contain the <SignedInfo> and <KeyInfo> elements. The example in Listing 11.10 assumes that an order processing and a shipment service share a secret (symmetric) key, such as a password. Furthermore, it assumes that the order processing service can apply a digest algorithm to its password and arrive at a digest value. The order processing service can then use that digest as a symmetric key to encrypt or sign a message and send the message to the shipment service. The shipment service will use its knowledge of the shared key to repeat the digest calculation and use the digest value (as a key) for decryption and signature verification.

In WS-Security a SOAP header may contain more than one XML signature, and these signatures can potentially overlap. For instance, in an order processing scenario an order message may need to pass through a number of intermediaries. First, the message is directed to an order processing system that inserts a header containing an order identifier and digitally signs it by putting an XML signature into the security header. Following this, the message is forwarded to a shipment processing system where a shipment identifier header is inserted and both the order and shipment identifier headers are digitally signed. Finally, when this message eventually arrives at a billing system, these XML signatures are validated prior to billing the customer.

Several examples of SOAP WS-Service requests involving two actors using different types of security tokens as well as message exchanges involving two actors and a third trusted party can be found in [Siddiqui 2003c].

11.6.5 Managing security policies

Whenever security mechanisms are being used between interacting Web services, security policies must also exist. These policies clarify the specific security requirements for a particular situation. With a Web service using WS-Security a service must describe its

```
<?xml version="1.0" encoding="utf-8"?>
<env:Envelope>
 <env:Header>
  <wsse:Security>
   <wsse:UsernameToken wsu:Id="OrderProcServiceUsernameToken">
      <wsse:Username>ATrustedOrderProcService</wsse:Username>
      <wsse:Nonce>WS3Lhf6RpK...</wsse:Nonce>
      <wsu:Created>2004-09-17T09:00:00Z</wsu:Created>
   </wsse: UsernameToken>
   <ds:Signature xmlns:ds="http://www.w3.org/2000/09/xmldsig#">
    <ds:SignedInfo>
     <ds:CanonicalizationMethod
      Algorithm="http://www.w3.org/2001/10/xml-exc-c14N"/>
     <ds:SignatureMethod
      Algorithm="http://www.w3.org/2000/09/xmldsig#rsa-sha1"/>
     <ds:Reference URI="#Request4Shipment">
      <ds:DigestMethod
        Algorithm="http://www.w3.org/2000/09/xmldsig#sha1"/>
      <ds:DigestValue>
        aOb4Luuk...
      </ds:DigestValue>
     </ds:Reference>
    </ds:SignedInfo>
    <ds:SignatureValue>
      A9qqIrtE3xZ...
    </ds:SignatureValue>
    <ds:KeyInfo>
     <wsse:SecurityTokenReference>
      <wsse:Reference URI="#OrderProcServiceUsernameToken"/>
     </wsse:SecurityTokenReference>
    </ds:KeyInfo>
   </ds:Signature>
  </wsse:Security>
 </env:Header>
 <env:Body>
  <s:ShipOrder
   xmlns:s="http://www.plastics_supply.com/shipping_service/"
   wsu:Id="Request4Shipment">
   <!-- Parameters passed with call -->
   <OrderNumber>PSC0622-X</OrderNumber>
     … … …
  </s:ShipOrder>
 </env:Body>
</env:Envelope>
```

Listing 11.10 SOAP message with digital signature

desired security policy. For instance, it may state that a signature is required on a particular XML element and that particular element must also be encrypted and also state the DSAs that it expects and the encryption algorithms it supports for providing message integrity and confidentiality. The service may also state that it accepts Kerberos tickets for authentication, or X.509 certificates and digital signatures, and so on. Addressing these kinds of issues means defining security policies for Web services.

Policies are useful in areas other than security; for this reason the WS-Policy specification was developed. This standard defines a general approach to specifying policies of all kinds and to associating them with particular services (see Chapter 12). To describe security-conscious policies the WS-SecurityPolicy specification [Della-Libera 2002] is used. This specification is a domain-specific language to represent policies for WS-Security. WS-SecurityPolicy extends the WS-Policy standard to allow organizations initiating a SOAP exchange to discover what type of security tokens are understood at the target, in the same way that WSDL describes a target Web service.

WS-SecurityPolicy defines XML elements that can be used to specify security-related policies. These elements are referred to as assertions because they allow a Web service to specify its policies in an unambiguous way. Assertions allow a developer to specify the types of security tokens, signature formats, and encryption algorithms supported, required, or rejected by a given subject. The assertions defined by WS-SecurityPolicy are summarized in Table 11.1.

The WS-SecurityPolicy specification allows a single `<Policy>` element to contain policies about security tokens, integrity, and confidentiality. A `<Policy>` element has also several other options regarding policies, including ways to specify relative preferences. For example, a Web service can define a `<SecurityToken>` that allows clients to authenticate using either Kerberos (see code snippet in Listing 11.11) or X.509 certificates, then indicate that it prefers Kerberos. By providing an unambiguous way for a Web service to state its security requirements, WS-SecurityPolicy facilitates Web services to make clear what clients must do to access that service.

Table 11.1 Security policy assertions defined by WS-SecurityPolicy

Policy assertion	*Description*
`wsse:SecurityToken`	Specifies a type of security token (defined by WS-Security)
`wsse:Integrity`	Specifies a signature format (defined by WS-Security)
`wsse:Confidentiality`	Specifies an encryption format (defined by WS-Security)
`wsse:Visibility`	Specifies portions of a message that must be able to be processed by an intermediary or endpoint
`wsse:SecurityHeader`	Specifies how to use the `<Security>` header defined in WS-Security
`wsse:MessageAge`	Specifies the acceptable time period before messages are declared "stale" and discarded

```
<wsp:Policy
 xmlns:wsp="http://schemas.xmlsoap.org/ws/2002/12/policy"
 xmlns:wsse="http://schemas.xmlsoap.org/ws/2002/12/secext">
 <wsse:SecurityToken wsp:Usage="wsp:Required">
  <TokenType> wsse:Kerberosv5ST</TokenType>
 </wsse:SecurityToken>
</wsp:Policy>
```

Listing 11.11 Sample security policy

More examples involving WS-SecurityPolicy can be found in section 12.4 where we describe the WS-Policy language.

11.6.6 Managing secure sessions

In cases where an application needs to exchange multiple SOAP messages with some other application, it is useful to create some kind of shared security context between the communicating applications. One common use of this shared context is to define a lifetime for an encryption key that will be used for the context's duration. For example, two communicating parties might want to create a symmetric key and then use it to encrypt the information they exchange over the lifetime of a particular security context.

The WS-SecureConversation standard defines WS-Security extensions to allow security context establishment and sharing, and session-key derivation [Anderson 2004a]. A security context is shared between two or more communicating parties for the lifetime of a session. Session keys are derived from a shared secret, which is used for signing and/or encrypting messages. Session keys are used to decrypt the individual messages sent in the conversation. The security context is represented on the wire as a new type of security token called the *security context token* [Cabrera 2005d]. Like SSL, WS-SecureConversation uses public (asymmetric) encryption to establish a shared secret key and from then on uses shared-key (symmetric) encryption for efficiency.

A security context can be established in three different ways and Web services select the approach that is most appropriate to their needs. First, a security token service may create a security context token and the initiating party has to obtain it to propagate it. Second, one of the communicating parties may create a security context token, which it may propagate to the other party. Third, the security context token may be created via a process of negotiation and exchanges. WS-SecureConversation defines a special binding for security context token requests WS-Trust operations.

The scenario in Listing 11.12 describes the situation where two parties need to negotiate about the contents of the security context token, such as a shared secret. In Listing 11.12 the `<SecurityContextToken>` specifies a security token that is associated with the message and points to the security context (via the unique Id for this context). The next statement in Listing 11.12 specifies the digital signature. In this example, the signature is based on the security context (specifically the secret key associated with the context). The typical contents of the XML digital signature are not shown in this listing.

```
<?xml version="1.0" encoding="utf-8"?>
<Env:Envelope>
 <Env:Header>
     ...
   <wsse:Security>
      <wsc:SecurityContextToken wsu:Id="MyID">
         <wsc:Identifier> uuid:...</wsc:Identifier>
      </wsc:SecurityContextToken>
      <ds:Signature>
          ...
         <ds:KeyInfo>
            <wsse:SecurityTokenReference>
               <wsse:Reference URI="#MyID"/>
            </wsse:SecurityTokenReference>
         </ds:KeyInfo>
      </ds:Signature>
   </wsse:Security>
 </Env:Header>
 <Env:Body wsu:Id="MsgBody">
    <Shipment xmlns:tru="http://shipco.com/services/
     orderShipping">
         <Product Name="Injection Quantity="1" Weight= …/>
         <Product Name="Adjustable Worktable" Quantity="1"
          Weight= …/>
    </Shipment>
 </Env:Body>
</Env:Envelope>
```

Listing 11.12 Shared secret security context as part of WS-SecureConversation

11.6.7 Managing trust

While WS-Security and WS-SecurityPolicy enable a service consumer and provider to directly interoperate in a secure and trusted manner, both assume that identical service token mechanisms are used at both endpoints. Furthermore, they assume that both endpoints are encompassed by a single *trust domain* (sphere of trust). For instance, both sites trust the same certificate authority. This means that these specifications alone are insufficient to define how to send a message from one trust domain using one kind of key security technology, e.g., Kerberos, to a different trust domain using a different key technology, e.g., X.509 certificates.

The WS-Trust specification addresses the above problems. This standard defines extensions to WS-Security with protocols for requesting, issuing, and exchanging security tokens, as well as ways to establish and access the presence of trust relationships [Anderson 2004b]. In particular, operations are defined to acquire, issue, renew, and validate security tokens. Another feature of WS-Trust is mechanisms to broker trust relationships. Using these extensions, applications can engage in secure communication designed to work with the general Web services framework, including WSDL service descriptions, UDDI `<businessServices>` and `<bindingTemplates>`, as well as SOAP messages. WS-Trust also employs conventional network and transport protection mechanisms such as IPSec or TLS/SSL to cater for different security requirements.

The WS-Trust specification defines how security tokens are requested and obtained from security token services and how these services may broker trust and trust policies (refer to the Web services trust model described in section 11.6.3 and Figure 11.21). With WS-Trust a Web services requestor can send messages that demonstrate its ability to prove a required set of claims by associating security tokens with the messages and including signatures of the message that demonstrate proof of possession of (the contents of) the tokens. If the Web services requestor does not have the necessary token(s) to prove the claim, it contacts an appropriate security token service to acquire the tokens. A service can indicate its required claims and related information in its policy as described by WSPolicy and WS-SecurityPolicy specifications.

11.6.8 Managing privacy

Privacy protection is defined as the right of an individual to control the collection and use of personal information by others [Galbraith 2002]. In the context of Web services, WS-Privacy is a forward-looking specification, which is not yet published and which uses a combination of WS-Policy, WS-Security, and WS-Trust to communicate privacy polices that state an organization's privacy practices. These privacy policies are stated by organizations that deploy Web services and require that incoming SOAP requests contain claims that the sender conforms to these privacy policies. The WS-Security specification is used to encapsulate these claims into security tokens which can be verified. WS-Privacy explains how privacy requirements can be included inside WS-Policy descriptions. WS-Trust is used to evaluate the privacy claims encapsulated within SOAP messages against user preferences and organizational policy.

11.6.9 Managing federated identities

A company's value network spans many organizations, systems, applications, and business processes. Several different constituents make up this value network including an enterprise's customers, trading partners, suppliers, and distributors. Organizations which are part of value networks extend their internal systems to external enterprises providing connectivity to customers, partners, and suppliers. Such arrangements result in federated systems that need to interoperate across organizational boundaries and interlink processes utilizing different technologies, security approaches, and programming environments. Federations focus on the notion of identity whereby the requestor or the requestor's delegate (proxy) asserts an identity and the identity provider verifies this assertion.

In a federation, each individual member continues to manage its own identities, but is capable of securely sharing and accepting identities and credentials from other members' sources. A *federated identity* is a collection of agreements for the creation, maintenance, and use of identities and their attributes, as well as credentials and entitlements, plus a supporting infrastructure and standards that make user identity and entitlements portable across autonomous security domains within a federation. Federated identity infrastructure enables cross-boundary single sign-on, dynamic user provisioning, and identity attribute sharing. Federated single sign-on allows users to sign on only once with a member in a federation and subsequently use various services in the federation without signing on again.

The identity federation standard for the Web services security model is based on WS-Federation [Bajaj 2003], which specifies how federated trust scenarios may be constructed using WS-Security, WS-Policy, WS-Trust, and WS-SecureConversation. The WS-Federation specification defines a model and set of messages for brokering trust and the federation of identity and authentication information between participating Web services across different trust realms. The federation model extends the WS-Trust model to describe how identity providers act as security token services and how attributes and pseudonyms can be integrated into the token issuance mechanism to provide federated identity mapping mechanisms. In WS-Federation an attribute service is a Web service that maintains information (attributes) about principals, any system entity or person, within a trust realm or federation. The WS-Federation pseudonym service – a Web service that maintains alternate identity information about principals within a trust realm or federation – provides a mapping mechanism which can be used to facilitate the mapping of trusted identities across federations to protect privacy and identity. WS-Policy and WS-Security are used to determine which tokens are consumed and how to apply for tokens from a security token issuance service, while WS-Federation acts as a layer, above WS-Policy and WS-Trust, indicating how trust relationships are managed.

Figure 11.26 illustrates one possible way that the WS-Trust model may be applied to a simple federation scenario allowing a requestor in one trust domain to interact with a resource (Web service) in a different trust domain using different security models [Kaler 2003]. Here a requestor obtains an identity security token from its identity provider (step 1) and presents/proves this to the security token services for the desired resource (step 2). If successful and if trust exists and authorization is approved, the security token returns an access token to the requestor (step 3). The requestor then uses the access token on request to the Web service (step 4). That is, a token from one security token service is

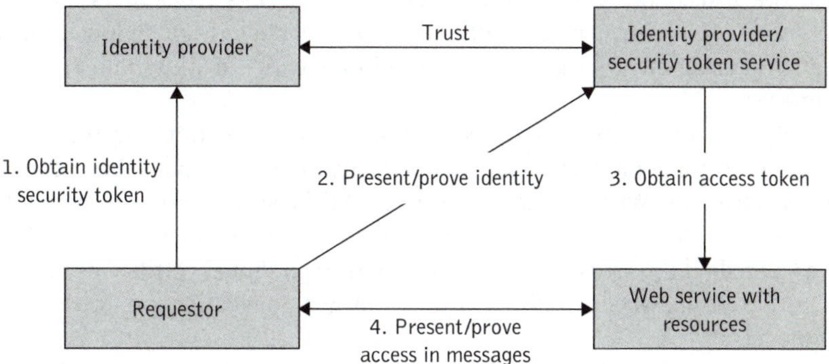

Figure 11.26 Simple federation scenario
Source: [Cabrera 2005d]

exchanged for another at a second security token service or possibly stamped or cross-certified by a second security token service).

Participation in a federation requires knowledge of metadata such as policies and potentially even WSDL descriptions and XML schemas for the services within the federation. Additionally, in many cases mechanisms are needed to identify the identity provider or security token services, and attribute/pseudonym services for the target, i.e., a Web service, of a given policy. To obtain and supply this kind of information, WS-Federation builds on the foundations outlined in WS-MetadataExchange (see Chapter 13), which defines SOAP request/response message types that retrieve different types of metadata associated with a Web service endpoint. More specifically, the request/response pairs retrieve WS-Policy, WSDL, and XML Schema information associated with an endpoint receiving a Web service message, or a given target name space.

11.6.10 Managing authorization

WS-Privacy describes how to state individual and group privacy preferences, and WS-Authorization describes how to manage the data and authorization policies. WS-Authorization deals with authorization decisions in the context of Web services and more specifically it describes how authorization data (access policies) are specified and managed, and how claims in security tokens are interpreted at endpoints.

As of this writing, no specification has been published for WS-Authorization. All that is known is that its objectives are very similar to XACML (see section 11.5.5) and that it will support both access control-based and role-based authorization.

11.7 Summary

The promise of Web services is significant productivity gains as enterprises will be able to participate with their suppliers, partners, and customers in open, collaborative trading communities in which associations can be formed spontaneously and then optimized over time to meet emerging business requirements. However, like most new technology adoption, there are also serious questions about new security risks. To address these concerns the Web services security model introduces a collection of individual, interrelated specifications that describe an approach for layering security facilities into a Web services environment.

The Web services security model is designed to allow mixing and matching of the specifications, enabling implementers to deploy only the specific parts they need. The first of these specifications, Web services security (or WS-Security), provides the fundamental elements necessary to add message integrity and confidentiality facilities to Web services, as well as a method of associating security tokens (e.g., digital certificates and Kerberos tickets) to SOAP messages. WS-Security forms the foundation of the Web services security model.

WS-Security leverages the natural extensibility that is at the core of the Web services model and is built upon foundational technologies such as SOAP, WSDL, XML digital signatures, XML Encryption, and SSL/TLS. This allows Web service providers and requestors to develop solutions that meet the individual security requirements of their applications.

Other security-related specifications address security policies, trust, privacy and authorization, among other things.

Review questions

- What are the most common security threats for Web services?
- What are the most common countermeasures for Web services security threats?
- What is network-level security and what is application-level security?
- Briefly describe the most common firewall architectures.
- What are the most common techniques to protect the security of Internet communications?
- How do symmetric and asymmetric key cryptography differ?
- What are the most widely used application-level security protocols?
- Briefly describe the XML security services and standards XML Encryption, XML Signature, SAML, and XACML.
- Explain how these XML standards are used in the context of Web services.
- What is the purpose of the Web service security and trust model?
- Briefly describe the components of WS-Security.
- How is message integrity and confidentiality achieved in the context of WS-Security?

Exercises

11.1 Develop a simple financial statement of a business customer in XML containing customer name, address, business account balance, and a credit card account where the outstanding balance should be charged. Use this financial statement to illustrate how an enveloped signature can be created in XML Signature.

11.2 Develop an enveloping and detached signature solution for the previous exercise.

11.3 Use a purchase order schema similar to the one defined in Listing 3.6 to show how a customer can encrypt sensitive details of a purchase order, e.g., products and quantities ordered or credit card information.

11.4 Use XACML to define a simple service read request on behalf of a subject that has premium membership to access a security aware URL.

11.5 Define a WS-based SOAP message that contains an X.509 certificate as a binary security token that is digitally signed and encrypted. The SOAP message body should contain an `<EncryptedData>` element to transport encryption keys from the originator to the recipient.

11.6 Define a SOAP message that appropriately combines the three principal WS-Security elements: integrity, confidentiality, and credentials.

CHAPTER 12

Service policies and agreements

Learning objectives

Applications that compose Web services must not only fully understand the service's WSDL contract but also understand additional functional and non-functional service characteristics that relate to requirements (constraints), capabilities, and preferences that allow the configuration of a service to be described. Such features are collectively known as service policies and include authentication, authorization, quality of service, quality of protection, reliable messaging, privacy, and application-specific service options. Interoperability, usability, and reliability of Web services can benefit from use of a common policy language for expressing these types of policies.

In this chapter we describe a comprehensive policy framework and language for Web services that uses other Web services specifications such as WSDL, WS-Security, WS-ReliableMessaging, WS-Addressing, and so forth. After completing this chapter readers will understand the following key concepts:

- The nature of policies and their use in SOA-based applications.
- Different types of policies including versioning, QoS, and security policies.
- The WS-Policy framework.
- Merging and intersecting policies.
- Attaching policies to WSDL.
- Associating standalone policies with policy subjects.
- The role of agreements in SOA-based applications and the WS-Agreement standard.

12.1 What are policies and why are they needed?

While WSDL is designed to describe components of a Web service, such as exposed Web operations, data types, ports, and SOAP message elements, it has proven less useful when it comes to describing choices, preferences, and other requirements not tied directly to the messaging interface itself. It is important to be able to express the fact that if a Web service must reject incoming SOAP requests that do not contain a certain type of security token or that do not have the required signatures, it is equally important to communicate these requirements to clients that want to access the service. Information such as how the Web service implements its interface and what it expects or provides to its requestors is very important to prospective clients that wish to invoke this particular service. Additional information, such as what is expected or provided in a Web services hosting environment, whether the service exhibits transactional behavior, whether its callers must sign and encrypt messages, what kind of security tokens the service is capable of processing, and so on, is extremely important in order to understand the true requirements and capabilities of a service when trying to interact with it. To achieve the promise of an SOA, it becomes important to express, exchange, and process the conditions and requirements governing the interactions between Web services endpoints.

12.1.1 Characteristics of policies

To successfully integrate with a non-trivial Web service, one must not only fully understand the service's XML contract but also understand additional service characteristics which relate to requirements (constraints), capabilities, and preferences that allow the configuration of a service to be described. Such features are collectively known as *service policies*. Typical examples that service policies target include: security issues (including authentication and authorization), reliable messaging, transactional behavior, QoS, quality of protection, reliable messaging, privacy, and application-specific service options, or capabilities and constraints specific to a particular service domain. Web services policies are consumable declarative expressions of service policies required for interaction with a particular Web service. Policies describe in the form of assertions one or more characteristics that a service provider may instruct a client to follow. Policies can range from simple expressions informing a client about the security tokens that a Web service is capable of processing (such as Kerberos tickets or X.509 certificates) to a set of rules evaluated in priority order that determine whether or not a client can interact with a service provider.

The desired objective is for the Web services endpoints (requestor and provider) to communicate any requirements, agreements, or expectations that affect either endpoint when providing a Web service. This includes policies that a Web service implementation declares to express regarding requirements on a hosting environment. This means that among other things policies can express SLAs, which are important for SOA-based applications.

Service policies may affect different domains. *Domains* are contexts that apply to interacting services and are characterized by such factors as security, privacy, management, performance and traffic control, application priorities, and so on. A set of requirements for Web service, i.e., a policy, needs to extend across many domains such as, for instance, security, transaction, and performance. Service policies allow single- and cross-domain applications to implement Web services solutions without having to continuously modify those applications to comply with changing corporate XML policies.

The scope of a policy is the subject to which a specific policy is bound and can range from concrete, low-level artifacts, e.g., the security settings required for messages conforming to a specific input message definition that a Web service offers, to more abstract artifacts, e.g., the frequency with which messages need to be exchanged with a Web service so that a partner agreement can be fulfilled. For example, knowing that a service supports a Web services security standard such as WS-Security is not enough information to enable interaction with this specific service. The client needs to know if the service actually requires WS-Security, what kind of security tokens it is capable of processing (such as `UsernameToken`, Kerberos tickets, or X.509 certificates), and which one it prefers. The client must also determine whether the service requires signed messages and what token type must be used for the digital signatures. And finally, the client must determine when to encrypt the messages, which algorithm to use, and how to exchange a shared key with the service. Trying to orchestrate with a service without understanding these details will inevitably lead to erroneous results.

Policies either can be used in a standalone fashion or are aggregated to perform more elaborate functions. *Standalone policies* are those that can be expressed in a simple statement. These normally include policy rules that represent Web services constraints and capabilities that have a simple character in that they are either required/offered or not, e.g., the WS-Security protocol is offered by a certain Web service. *Aggregate policies* combine policy rules, to model either intricate interactions between service features or the combination of policies originating from diverse services that have complex interdependencies. For instance, they can parameterize and can combine interdependent service features, e.g., a certain canonicalization algorithm needs to be used in combination with a certain security token type when digitally signing a message. While it is possible to use XML and WSDL extensibility to achieve some of these goals, it is preferable to provide a common framework to support Web services constraints and conditions that allows a clear articulation of the available options.

A *standard policy framework* is a common framework for the expression, exchange, and processing of the policies governing the interactions between Web services endpoints. A policy framework provides an additional description layer for services and offers developers a declarative language for expressing and programming policies. To develop a common Web services policy framework, the Web services infrastructure is enhanced with policy-specific extensions in order to understand policies and enforce them at run-time [Skonnard 2003]. For example, a provider could write a policy stating that a given Web service requires Kerberos tokens, digital signatures, and encryption. The infrastructure can then enforce these policy requirements without requiring a developer to develop any additional code. Clients use such policy information to reason about whether they can use the particular service under consideration.

12.1.2 The need for a policy language

It is important for a Web service to rely on a declarative model to indicate in a consistent and declarative way what it is capable of supporting, including the types of protocols that it offers, as well as what requirements it places on its potential requestors. The service implementation should also be able to document requirements on a hosting environment since much of the implementation of the Web service protocols and functions occurs in middleware and operating system functions supporting the service's implementation. Consequently, there must be a consistent way to describe the constraints/conditions derived from the environment hosting a particular Web service. This requirement points in the direction of a Web services policy language in order to express service-related policies.

A Web services policy language should provide expressive power, genericity, extensibility, flexibility, and reusability features to describe a multitude of Web services policy aspects. These features of a policy language for Web services are briefly examined below.

A Web services policy language should be expressive enough to represent Web services constraints and capabilities at different levels of detail addressing both policies that have a simple character as well as complex aggregated policies

A Web services policy language should also attain generic properties by striving to facilitate the definition of a set of common policies and aspects that are common across the various domains. In addition, the policy language should not change whenever new domain-specific policy aspects need to be described. The policy language should support extensibility by allowing for a graceful migration towards supporting the expression of complex domain-specific policies.

The policy language needs to describe both combinations of policies from different domains, e.g., support of a certain reliable messaging protocol in combination with WS-Security, and alternatives between policies from one domain, e.g., use of either X.509 or user name security tokens. The language also needs to provide mechanisms for referencing and including externally defined policies in order to allow reuse of well-known policy patterns.

To cover the requirements described in the previous section, WS-Policy [Bajaj 2006a] and WS-PolicyAttachment [Baja 2006b] have been developed. WS-Policy is a general-purpose, extensible framework and model for expressing all types of domain-specific policy models: transport-level security, resource usage policy, even end-to-end business-process level. WS-Policy expresses requirements, preferences, and capabilities in a Web-services-based environment as policies. Policy expressions allow for both simple declarative assertions as well as more sophisticated conditional assertions. WS-PolicyAttachment offers a flexible way of associating policy expressions with existing and future Web services artifacts. For instance, WS-PolicyAttachment addresses the requirements for associating Web services policy with Web services artifacts such as WSDL artifacts and UDDI entities.

Before we concentrate on describing the characteristics of WS-Policy and WS-PolicyAttachment we shall first examine different types of policies and then explain the relation between policies and other Web services standards.

12.2 Types of policies

We may group Web services policies in three broad categories: versioning policies, QoS policies and security policies. Although security is traditionally considered as part of QoS, it is convenient to think of security policies as a separate category given the fact that the

Web services security model suggests the use of WS-SecurityPolicy assertions (see section 11.6.5) to deal with the requirements of the Web services security domain.

Once services are operational they usually undergo changes throughout their lifecycle. Service changes can impact some or even all of the clients of the given service. Service changes require that the service be designed (versioned) in such a way as to offer differentiated functionality, policies, and QoS, which accommodate the different client requirements. With this approach, service operations can be added, removed, or revised to reflect the different client requirements. *Service versioning* implies that the same service (or operation) can exist in the overall system in multiple guises while keeping exactly the same name. This usually leads to the necessity for SOA to support multiple service versions simultaneously. As an example, consider an Internet shopping Web service which may have a special discount offers for frequent as opposed to new customers. This means that although both frequent and new customers use the same purchase services, their status is detected and different pricing policies apply by invoking different operations for the same service. A *versioning policy* expresses the exact version of the service (operation) that is required for a particular invocation.

A *QoS policy* describes the functional and non-functional service properties that collectively define a service. A QoS policy includes performance requirements, information regarding service reliability, scalability, and availability, transactional requirements, change management and notification, and so on. It also includes factors relating to the Web services hosting environment. A QoS policy also describes technical service characteristics including response times, tolerated system interruption thresholds, levels of message traffic, bandwidth requirements, dynamic rerouting for fail-over or load balancing, and so forth.

Security policies indicate the security requirements and policies of a specific Web service. The Web services security policies describe security tokens, digital signatures, and encryption. An example of a security policy is the requirement that a Web service may expect a requestor to attach a security token when it sends a request to the Web service. For example, an SAML authorization token issued by a trusted authorization authority needs to be presented to access sensitive data. Another example is that a binary security token containing an X.509 certificate needs to be presented for signing purpose. Security policy is also used to indicate a required encryption format for interacting services.

12.3 Policies and Web services standards

The developers of WS-Policy have gone to great lengths to make this standard a stand-alone concept that can be associated with Web services in a variety of ways. For instance, specific parts of WSDL, such as operations or messages, may point to a policy. Another possibility is to have WS-Policy point to the set of the Web services that it covers. As policies are exchanged between trading parties involved in Web service interactions, one can discern three possible policy exchange mechanisms:

1. Sending policies via SOAP messages as a SOAP header.
2. Retrieving policies from a Web service registry such as a UDDI.

3. Retrieving policies from the Web service itself by means of emerging protocols such as WS-MetadataExchange (see section 13.5).

Sending policies via SOAP messages as a SOAP header is the simplest policy exchange mechanism that allows two interacting parties to understand each other's requirements. However, to support more accurate service discovery, WS-Policy proposes a framework that extends the description features already provided through WSDL. More refined service descriptions, qualified by specific Web services policies, support more accurate discovery of compatible services. WS-Policy can be registered itself in UDDI (as tModels). It can also be associated with a UDDI business service (as key in a category bag). Such policies can be accessed via interaction with the UDDI. In a service registry (such as the UDDI registry), querying services described in WS-Policy facilitates the retrieval of services supporting desired/appropriate policies in conjunction with retrieving the correct service interface. For example, a query may request all services that support a `PurchaseOrder` WSDL interface (port type), use Kerberos for authentication purposes, and have an explicitly stated privacy policy. This allows a service requestor to select a service provider on the basis of QoS offerings.

WS-Policy, as well as additional metadata relevant to the service interaction (such as XML Schema and WSDL descriptions), can be dynamically exchanged between interacting endpoints using the Web Services Metadata Exchange protocol. WS-MetadataExchange allows a service requestor to directly ask a service provider for all or part of its metadata, without the mediation of a third-party registry. Using the WS-MetadataExchange protocol service endpoints can exchange policies at run-time to bootstrap their interaction with information about the settings and protocols that apply. This procedure is useful when not all policy information resides in a repository, or when a requestor receives a reference to a service through some mechanism other than a registry query.

The exchanges of policies support the customization of each specific interaction based on a multitude of facts ranging from the identity of the interacting endpoint to any other aspect that characterizes the context under which the interaction takes place. With this kind of flexibility, Web services can then be designed (versioned) to offer differentiated QoSs, e.g., service precision, granularity, timeliness, and scope, depending on the end customers that are targeted. Services can also be differentiated based on technical quality and QoS details such as response time, performance bandwidth used, and reliability.

12.4 WS-Policy framework

The WS-Policy specification defines a common framework and language for services to annotate their interface definitions in order to describe their service assurance qualities and requirements. These can be described in the form of a machine-readable expression containing combinations of individual assertions. The WS-Policy framework fits into the core Web service architecture since it is built on top of XML, XML Schema, WSDL, and UDDI. The WS-Policy framework also allows for algorithms that determine which concrete policies to apply when the requestor, provider, and container support multiple service options.

The WS-Policy framework is a set of three interrelated specifications that together enable the seamless description and communication of Web services policies:

- The Web Services Policy Framework (WS-Policy) specification provides a general-purpose model and corresponding syntax to describe and communicate the policies of a Web service. WS-Policy defines a base set of constructs that can be used and extended by other Web services specifications to describe a broad range of service requirements, preferences, and capabilities.
- WS-PolicyAssertions indicate a set of common message policy assertions that can be specified within a policy.
- The Web Services Policy Attachment (WS-PolicyAttachment) specification indicates three specific attachment mechanisms for using policy expressions with existing Web services technologies. More specifically, it defines how to associate policy expressions with WSDL type definitions and UDDI entities. It also defines how to associate implementation-specific policy with all or part of a WSDL `<portType>` when exposed from a specific implementation.

Figure 12.1 shows how the WS-Policy specifications relate to other Web services standards such WSDL and UDDI. Domain expressions in this figure identify policy subjects that are included in the policy scope, typically using URIs. *Domain expressions* are XML elements that describe the set of policy subjects. The three WS-Policy specifications also set the stage for WS-SecurityPolicy, which provides a set of WS-Security-specific policies that is used to publish information about all aspects of WS-Security. WS-SecurityPolicy is described in section 11.6.5 in this book.

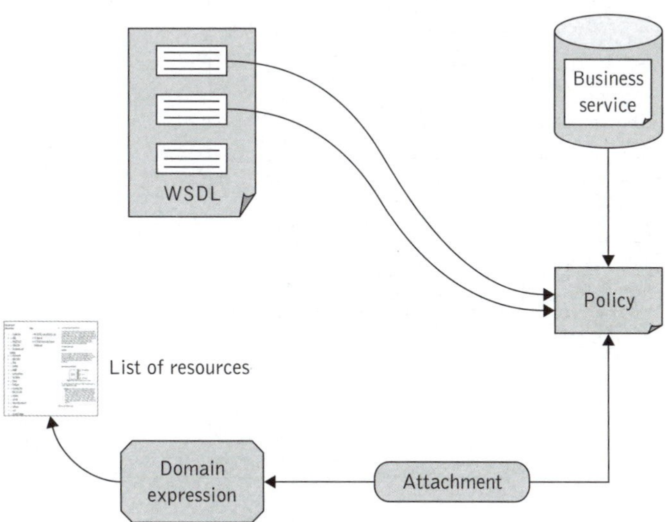

Figure 12.1 Connecting policies with other Web services standards

12.4.1 WS-Policy overview

WS-Policy provides a flexible and extensible XML-based language for expressing the capabilities, requirements, and general functional or non-functional properties of Web services in a declarative manner. WS-Policy defines a framework and a model for the expression of these properties as policies. It enables a service to specify what it expects of callers and how it implements its interface. WS-Policy is critical to achieving interoperability at a higher-level functional operation of the service. Security, transactions, reliable messaging, and other specifications require concrete WS-Policy schemas. These allow services to describe the functional assurance that they expect from and provide to callers.

The WS-Policy abstract model defines a *policy* to be an XML expression that logically combines policy alternatives, where each policy alternative is a collection of policy assertions, see Figure 12.2. Assertions are constructs that specify concrete or abstract service characteristics such as reliable messaging requirements, a required security authentication scheme, or a desired QoS, which characterize an interaction between two Web services' endpoints. In a Web services environment assertions are used to convey such information to the service requestor so that it can successfully invoke the provider's service. Satisfying assertions in the policy usually results in behavior that reflects these conditions. In a Web services interaction scenario, typically the provider of a Web service exposes a policy to convey conditions under which it provides the service. A requestor may then use this policy to decide whether or not to use the service.

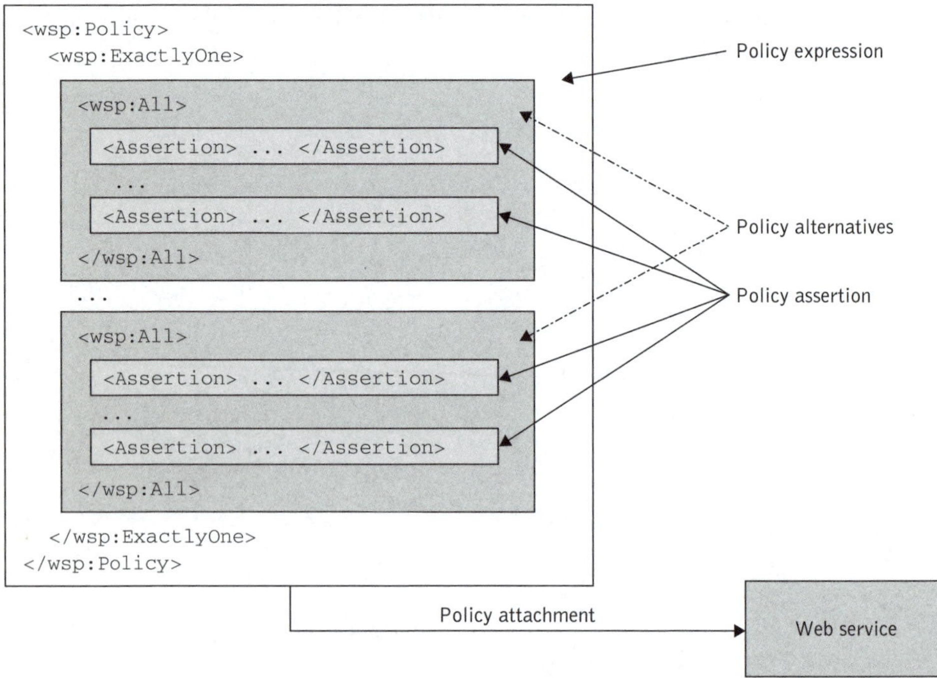

Figure 12.2 Pictorial representation of a WS-Policy statement in normal form

WSPolicy defines three components: policy assertions, policy expressions, and policy operations.

Policy assertions are the building blocks of policies. A *policy assertion* identifies a behavior that is a requirement (or capability) of a *policy subject* [Bajaj 2006a], see Figure 12.2. Each assertion describes an atomic aspect of the requirements of Web service. In particular, an assertion indicates domain-specific (e.g., security, transactions) semantics that are expected to be defined in a separate policy specification and targets an entity to which the policy expression is bound, or, in other words, the resource the policy describes, e.g., a Web service endpoint. Some policy assertions specify traditional requirements and capabilities that will ultimately manifest on the wire, e.g., authentication scheme or transport protocol selection. Other policy assertions have no wire manifestation yet are critical to proper service selection and usage, e.g., privacy policy, QoS characteristics. WS-Policy provides a single policy grammar to allow both kinds of assertions to be reasoned about in a consistent manner.

WS-Policy is about communicating policy, or the requirements for two parties (like a client and a Web service) to work together. There are no assumptions on how the descriptions are associated with the target resource. This language is used for communicating such information as security and authorization requirements, privacy requirements, supported features, preferred ways of invoking the service, and so on, among Web services. This language is declarative and provides descriptions from which a variety of useful information can be extracted. Thus, the policy assertions can come in many different forms and are inherently extensible. There are two additional specifications that define standard sets of policy assertions that can be used within a policy expression. The Web Services Policy Assertions Language (WS-PolicyAssertions) specification defines a set of general message assertions and the Web Services Security Policy Language (WS-SecurityPolicy) specification defines a set of common security-related assertions.

The WS-Policy syntax is used to describe acceptable combinations of assertions to form a complete set of instructions to the policy processing infrastructure, for a given Web service invocation. Each collection of policy assertions is termed a *policy alternative* [Bajaj 2006a], see Figure 12.2. An alternative with one or more assertions indicates behavior characterized only by those assertions. Assertions within an alternative are not ordered, and thus aspects such as the order in which behaviors (indicated by assertions) are applied to a subject are beyond the scope of this specification [Bajaj 2006a]. Another limitation is that although policy alternatives are meant to be mutually exclusive, it cannot be decided in general whether or not more than one alternative can be supported at the same time.

The XML representation of a Web services policy is referred to as a *policy expression*. The mechanism for associating a policy expression with one or more policy subjects is referred to as a *policy attachment*.

Table 12.1 provides a quick reference to the policy terminology that we referred to in this section. The remainder of this section describes the concepts summarized in Table 12.1 in some detail.

WS-Policy defines a set of *policy operators* that enable us to construct different logical combinations of policy assertions to better describe complex policy requirements [Bajaj 2006a]. Policy operators group policy assertions into policy alternatives. The two most frequently used policy operators are `<All>` and `<ExactlyOne>`. The policy operator

Table 12.1 WS-Policy constructs and terminology

Term	*Definition*
Policy	An informal abstraction that is used to refer to the set of information that is being expressed as policy assertions
Policy assertion	Represents an individual preference, requirement, capability, or other property
Policy expression	An XML Infoset representation of one or more policy assertions
Policy operator	Enables construction of different logical combinations of policy assertions
Policy subject	An entity, e.g., an endpoint, object, or resource, to which a policy expression can be bound
Policy attachment	The mechanism for associating policy expressions with one or more subjects.

`<All>` signifies that a message must conform to all of the assertion and operator elements that are direct children of the `<All>` element in a policy statement. The policy operator `<ExactlyOne>` signifies that a message must conform to exactly one of the assertion or operator elements that are direct children of this element. To compactly express complex policies, policy operators may be recursively nested.

```
xmlns:wsp="http://schemas.xmlsoap.org/ws/2004/09/policy"
...
<wsp:Policy>
  <wsp:ExactlyOne>
    <wsse:SecurityToken>
      <wsse:TokenType>
         wsse:Kerberosv5TGT
       </wsse:TokenType>
    </wsse:SecurityToken>
    <wsse:SecurityToken>
       <wsse:TokenType>
         wsse:X509v3
       </wsse:TokenType>
    </wsse:SecurityToken>
  </wsp:ExactlyOne>
</wsp:Policy>
```

Listing 12.1 A sample using WS-Policy

Listing 12.1 illustrates a security policy using assertions defined in WS-SecurityPolicy, see section 11.6.5. In particular, this listing represents a policy for authentication. The listing illustrates the use of the <ExactlyOne> policy operator. This listing represents two specific security policy assertions that indicate that two types of authentication are supported (Kerberos tokens or X.509 certificates). A valid interpretation of the policy in Listing 12.1 would be that an invocation of a Web service under this policy would need to contain one of the security token assertions specified.

Finally a note of caution. Both WS-Policy and XACML use the term "policy" which can be very misleading. This overloaded use of the term "policy" sometimes may confuse readers who are new to these concepts. These two languages are designed for quite different purposes. XACML is a general-purpose access control policy language that provides the syntax for managing authorization decisions and is thus focused on the evaluation of access control policies by a Policy Decision Point module (see section 11.5.5). In contrast to this, WS-Policy is defined for metadata descriptions of properties and capabilities of Web services and Web services endpoints.

12.4.1.1 Policy expressions

A policy expression is the XML representation of a policy. A policy expression is bound to a policy subject. A policy expression comprises three constructs: policy operators, an attribute to qualify an assertion, and a policy reference/inclusion mechanism. WS-Policy provides a normative XML Schema definition that expresses the structure of a policy expression. The WS-Policy schema defines all of the constructs that may be used in a policy expression and it also includes definitions for WS-PolicyAssertions and WS-PolicyAttachment.

Normal form policies. To facilitate interoperability, the WS-Policy specification defines a *normal form* for policy expressions that is a straightforward representation of a policy enumerating each of its alternatives that in turn enumerate each of their assertions. The normal form of policy was defined to simplify the manipulation and to clarify the understanding of policies.

```
<wsp:Policy ... >
  <wsp:ExactlyOne>
    [<wsp:All> [ <assertion ...>... </assertion>]* </wsp:All> ]*
  </wsp:ExactlyOne>
</wsp:Policy>
```

Listing 12.2 Syntax for normal policy form

The schema outline for the normal form of a policy expression is shown in Listing 12.2. In a normal form policy, each valid policy is contained within an <All> element, and all of the alternatives are contained under a single <ExactlyOne> operator. In effect each element within the <ExactlyOne> policy operator is a policy alternative where each policy alternative is encapsulated within an <All> operator. The WS-Policy specification states that the normal form of a policy expression should be used where practical to simplify processing and improve interoperability. For instance, policies must be first described in a standardized normal form before policy aggregation operations can be applied.

```
<wsp:Policy>
  <wsp:ExactlyOne>
     <wsp:All>
       <wsse:SecurityToken>
         <wsse:TokenType>
           wsse:Kerberosv5TGT
         </wsse:TokenType>
       </wsse:SecurityToken>
       <wsse:Algorithm Type ="wsse:AlgSignature"
          URI="http://www.w3.org/2000/09/xmlenc#aes"/>
     </wsp:All>
     <wsp:All>
       <wsse:SecurityToken>
         <wsse:TokenType>
           wsse:X509v3
         </wsse:TokenType>
       </wsse:SecurityToken>
       <wsse:Algorithm Type ="wsse:AlgEncryption"
          URI="http://www.w3.org/2001/04/xmlenc#3des-cbc"/>
     </wsp:All>
  </wsp:ExactlyOne>
</wsp:Policy>
```

Listing 12.3 Normal form of policy in Listing 12.1

Listing 12.3 illustrates the normal form of the policy expression example introduced earlier in Listing 12.1. This listing expresses two alternatives in the policy. This is indicated by the `<ExactlyOne>` policy operator, which specifies that only one of its direct elements must be applicable. Each of these alternatives is shown to be wrapped in an `<All>` operator. The `<All>` operator means that all the assertions enclosed within this operator must be applicable. This means that if the first alternative is chosen, a Kerberos token type and the AES encryption algorithm must be employed. If conversely the second alternative is chosen, an X.509 certificate and the 3DES encryption algorithm must be employed.

Policy identification. A policy expression can also itself be a Web resource, hence identifiable by a URI. The example in Listing 12.4 illustrates how to associate a policy expression with a URI. In this example the URI for the specified policy would be: `"http://www.plastics_supply.com/policies#SecurityTokens"`.

```
<wsp:Policy
       xml:base="http://www.plastics_supply.com/policies"
       wsu:Id="SecurityTokens" >
  <wsse:SecurityToken>
    <wsse:TokenType> wsse:Kerberosv5TGT </wsse:TokenType>
  </wsse:SecurityToken>
  <wsse:Integrity>
    <wsse:Algorithm Type="wsse:AlgSignature"
                    URI="http://www.w3.org/2000/09/
                    xmldsig#rsa-shal" />
    </wsse:Integrity>
</wsp:Policy>
```

Listing 12.4 Associating a policy expression with a URI

Representing optional policies. To indicate the fact that a policy assertion is optional the WS-Policy specification employs the <Optional> attribute. This attribute is a syntactic shortcut for expressing policy alternatives. If the <Optional> attribute defined in a policy is true, the expression of the assertion is semantically equivalent to the following construct:

```
<wsp:ExactlyOne>
  <wsp:All> <Assertion ...> ... </Assertion> </wsp:All>
  <wsp:All />
</wsp:ExactlyOne>
```

The above code snippet indicates that two entries are created for each occurrence of the <Optional> attribute. One entry contains the assertion and the other specifies an empty policy. To represent these two entries, the <ExactlyOne> policy operator is used.

If the <Optional> attribute defined in the schema outline above is false, the expression of the assertion is semantically equivalent to the following construct:

```
<wsp:ExactlyOne>
  <wsp:All> <Assertion ...> ... </Assertion> </wsp:All>
</wsp:ExactlyOne>
```

To exemplify the use of the <Optional> attribute consider the example in Listing 12.5.

```
<wsp:Policy>
   <wsse:SecurityToken wsp:Optional="true" >
      <wsse:TokenType>
         wsse:X509v3
      </wsse:TokenType>
   </wsse:SecurityToken>
</wsp:Policy>
```

Listing 12.5 Compact policy expression using the <optional> attribute

Referencing policies. WS-Policy provides a mechanism for sharing policy assertions across different policy expressions through the <wsp:PolicyReference> element. This element references another policy expression and can be used wherever a policy assertion element is allowed inside a policy expression. The contents of the referenced policy expression conceptually replace the <wsp:PolicyReference> element and are wrapped in a <wsp:All> operator. A policy expression can be referenced by a URI, a digest of the referenced policy expression, or by specifying the digest algorithm being used [Bajaj 2006a].

The example in Listing 12.6 illustrates how to share a policy (with an ID of tokens) across two other policies. The first policy expression is given an identifier ("tokens") and specifies three different types of security tokens. The second and third policy expressions in Listing 12.6 are thus extended by including security token specifications. In particular, the second policy expression specifies a signature format defined by WS-Security (see section 11.6.4) and references the first policy element by URI indicating where the referenced element is placed within the document. Similarly, the third policy expression specifies an encryption format defined by WS-Security and references the first policy element also by URI indicating where the referenced element is placed within the document.

The <wsp:Usage> attribute in Listing 12.6 distinguishes between different types of assertions and assertion processing modes. A value of "wsp:Required" for this attribute indicates that the assertion must be applied to the subject. If the subject does not meet the criteria expressed in the assertion, a fault or error will occur. Usage qualifiers are explained in the following section.

12.4.1.2 Policy assertion usage types

Each assertion is associated with a usage type. The usage type, represented by means of the <wsp:Usage> attribute, stipulates how the assertion should be interpreted in relation to the overall policy. For example, some assertions specify requirements and capabilities that will ultimately manifest on the wire, such as a requirement for digital signatures or encryption. These assertions require cooperation between the Web services of two interacting parties. Other assertions have no wire manifestation but provide additional

```
<wsp:Policy wsu:Id="tokens" xmlns:wsp="..." xmlns:wsse="...">
  <wsp:ExactlyOne wsp:Usage="Required">
     <wsse:SecurityToken>
       <wsse:TokenType> wsse:UsernameToken </wsse:TokenType>
     </wsse:SecurityToken>
     <wsse:SecurityToken>
       <wsse:TokenType>wsse:x509v3</wsse:TokenType>
     </wsse:SecurityToken>
     <wsse:SecurityToken>
       <wsse:TokenType>wsse:Kerberosv5ST</wsse:TokenType>
     </wsse:SecurityToken>
  </wsp:ExactlyOne>
</wsp:Policy>

<wsp:Policy wsu:Id="tokensWithSignature"
   xmlns:wsp="..." xmlns:wsse="...">
  <wsp:PolicyReference URI="#tokens" />
  <wsse:Integrity wsp:Usage="wsp:Required">
    ...
  </wsse:Integrity>
</wsp:Policy>

<wsp:Policy wsu:Id="tokensWithEncryption"
   xmlns:wsp="..." xmlns:wsse="...">
  <wsp:PolicyReference URI="#tokens" />
  <wsse:Confidentiality wsp:Usage="Required">
    ...
  </wsse:Confidentiality>
</wsp:Policy>
```

Listing 12.6 Referencing policies

information to assist in service selection (e.g., support policies, QoS policies, privacy policies, etc.). These assertions have no impact on the message – they simply act as a declaration of agreement between parties. To capture the nature of these differences, WS-Policy defines five possible values for usage qualifiers. These are:

- *Required:* The assertion must be applied to the subject. If the subject does not meet the criteria expressed in the assertion, a fault or error will occur.
- *Rejected:* The assertion is explicitly not supported and, if present, will cause failure.
- *Optional:* The assertion may be made of the subject, but is not required to be applied.
- *Observed:* The assertion will be applied to all subjects, and requestors of the service are informed that the policy will be applied.

- *Ignored:* The assertion is processed but ignored. That is, it can be specified, but no action will be taken as a result of its being specified. Subjects and requestors are informed that the policy will be ignored.

The <Required>, <Rejected>, and <Optional> qualifiers indicate that the assertion is required, not supported, and optional, respectively. The <Observed> qualifier specifies that the assertion has been accepted by both parties and is observed even if there is no wire-level manifestation. The <Ignored> qualifier states that the policy assertion is completely ignored.

```
<wsp:Policy xmlns:wsp="..." xmlns:wsse="...">
  <wsse:SecurityToken wsp:Usage="wsp:Required">
    <wsse:TokenType>wsse:Kerberosv5ST</wsse:TokenType>
  </wsse:SecurityToken>
  <wsse:Integrity wsp:Usage="wsp:Required">
    <wsse:Algorithm Type="wsse:AlgSignature"
        URI="http://www.w3.org/2000/09/xmlenc#aes" />
  </wsse:Integrity>
</wsp:Policy>
```

Listing 12.7 An example using the <Required> usage qualifier

As an example of assertions employing different usage qualifiers, consider the policy expressions in Listings 12.7, 12.8, and 12.9. Details about these policy expressions can be found in [Skonnard 2003].

The policy expression in Listing 12.7 uses the <Required> qualifier and contains two policy assertions defined by the WS-SecurityPolicy specification. This policy expression declares that the subject requires a Kerberos V5 service ticket token and an XML digital signature.

```
<wsp:Policy xmlns:wsp="..." xmlns:wsse="...">
  <wsse:SecurityToken wsp:Usage="wsp:Rejected">
    <wsse:TokenType>wsse:Kerberosv5ST</wsse:TokenType>
  </wsse:SecurityToken>
  <wsse:SecurityToken wsp:Usage="wsp:Rejected">
    <wsse:TokenType>wsse:Kerberosv5TGT</wsse:TokenType>
  </wsse:SecurityToken>
</wsp:Policy>
```

Listing 12.8 An example using the <Rejected> usage qualifier

The policy expression in Listing 12.8 uses the <Rejected> qualifier and contains two policy assertions also defined by the WS-SecurityPolicy specification. The policy expression in Listing 12.8 declares that the subject does not support any type of Kerberos security token, indicating that Kerberos should not be used for authentication purposes.

```
<wsp:Policy xmlns:wsp="..." xmlns:wsse="...">
  <wsse:SecurityToken wsp:Usage="wsp:Optional">
    <wsse:TokenType>wsse:UsernameToken</wsse:TokenType>
  </wsse:SecurityToken>
  <wsse:SecurityToken wsp:Usage="wsp:Optional">
    <wsse:TokenType>wsse:x509v3</wsse:TokenType>
  </wsse:SecurityToken>
</wsp:Policy>
```

Listing 12.9 An example using the <Optional> usage qualifier

Finally, the policy expression in Listing 12.9 declares that the subject supports X.509 certificates as well as UsernameToken, but that both are optional.

12.4.2 Combining and comparing policies

Standalone policies can be aggregated into a more coarse-grained policy to model situations in which services have intricate interdependencies. In many cases, policy combination is the necessary solution to combat the fragmented nature that policies have when they are first developed [Nolan 2004]. To understand this, consider the WS-PolicyAttachment specification which describes how policies can be attached to the elements of a WSDL specification. Very often each element in the WSDL specification may have its own list of policies associated with it (see section 12.4.4). Combining all these policies together to form a single merged policy is a necessary step in policy processing. In addition, combination policies may also need to be compared to each other to determine whether two Web services have common alternatives.

The first requirement for policies that need to be combined or compared is that they must be normalized. Following this, policy compatibility must be determined prior to combining or comparing policies, otherwise policy combination will lead to erroneous results. Determining whether policy alternatives are compatible generally involves domain-specific processing. This is due to the fact that the set of behaviors indicated by an aggregated policy alternative depends on the domain-specific semantics of the assertion instances that comprise this aggregate policy. In particular, in the case of policy comparison, for two policy alternatives to be compatible they must have at least the same vocabulary. The *vocabulary of a policy* is the set of all assertions that appear in a policy statement. Every assertion that is declared within a policy is considered part of the policy's overall vocabulary. Domain-independent algorithms can be employed to determine policy compatibility.

12.4.2.1 Merging policies

Policy merging is the process of combining subpolicies together to form a single policy. Merging is a commutative associative function. The merge operation occurs only when policies have first been converted to normal form. The alternatives from each subpolicy are combined to form the new merged alternative. The combination process follows a cross-product pattern. One alternative is taken from each policy in turn until all permutations have been exhausted [Nolan 2004].

```
<wsp:Policy wsu:id="P1"...>
  <wsp:ExactlyOne>
    <wsp:All>
      <SecurityAssertion/>
    </wsp:All>
    <wsp:All>
      <ReliableMessagingAssertion/>
    </wsp:All>
  </wsp:ExactlyOne>
</wsp:Policy>
```

Listing 12.10 Source policy P_1

Listings 12.10 and 12.11 illustrate two normalized standalone policies P_1, P_2 that can be merged to form an aggregate policy P_3 [Nolan 2004].

```
<wsp:Policy wsu:id="P2"...>
  <wsp:ExactlyOne>
    <wsp:All>
      <TransactionAssertion/>
    </wsp:All>
    <wsp:All>
      <AuditAssertion/>
    </wsp:All>
  </wsp:ExactlyOne>
</wsp:Policy>
```

Listing 12.11 Source policy P_2

Listing 12.12 shows the aggregate policy P_3 that is derived by merging policy P_1 with policy P_2. To derive the merged policy, each alternative from policy P_1 is combined with each alternative from policy P_2. The combination process is simply a matter of taking the cross-product of alternatives (from normalized policies) and forming new alternatives as shown in Listing 12.12. It is the responsibility of the policy framework and run-time system to analyze and determine the meaning of any alternatives that yield duplicate assertions. It is also worth noting that there is the potential for rapid growth in the size of the merged policies if there are multiple choices in each source policy.

```
<wsp:Policy wsu:Id="P3"...>
  <wsp:ExactlyOne>
    <wsp:All>
      <SecurityAssertion/>
      <TransactionAssertion/>
    </wsp:All>
    <wsp:All>
      <SecurityAssertion/>
      <AuditAssertion/>
    </wsp:All>
    <wsp:All>
      <ReliableMessagingAssertion/>
      <TransactionAssertion/>
    </wsp:All>
    <wsp:All>
      <ReliableMessagingAssertion/>
      <AuditAssertion/>
    </wsp:All>
  </wsp:ExactlyOne>
</wsp:Policy>
```

Listing 12.12 Merged policy P_3

12.4.2.2 Policy intersection

Intersection is the process of comparing two Web services policies for common alternatives [Nolan 2004]. Intersection is a commutative, associative function that takes two policies and returns a policy. Policy intersection is an operation that takes place when two or more parties need to express a joint policy and want to limit its alternatives to those that are mutually compatible. For example, when a requestor and a provider express requirements on a message exchange, intersection identifies compatible policy alternatives (if any) included in both requestor and provider policies. The intersection of two policies gives zero or more alternatives on which both parties agree.

Domain-specific knowledge (e.g., transactions, security, etc.) is required in order to be able to complete the process of intersection [Bajaj 2006a], [Nolan 2004]. The process commences with both policies being expanded to normal form. The first phase of the intersection process requires that the normalized policies are now examined an alternative at a time. The intention of the first phase is to eliminate those policy alternatives that are clearly different. This is done by examining the vocabularies of the two alternatives. The vocabulary of an alternative is the `QNames` of the assertions in that alternative. If the vocabularies do not match, then the two alternatives are clearly different and can be discounted from the policy intersection. When two alternatives have a matching vocabulary they are combined to produce a single new alternative in the intersected policy. The process of combining alternatives from two policies is carried out in a cross-product fashion. Each alternative from each policy is compared to every alternative from the other.

It is beyond the scope of the WS-Policy framework specification to define how combined alternatives in a policy intersection are to be interpreted. Domain knowledge is required to rationalize the newly combined alternatives into something meaningful to the underlying policy framework. For example, the WS-SecurityPolicy domain will be the only source of information as to whether two security assertions (one from a requestor and one from a provider) contradict each other or are complementary refinements of each other.

```
<wsp:Policy wsu:Id="Provider_Policy"...>
  <wsp:ExactlyOne>
    <wsp:All>
      <SecurityAssertion level="high"/>
      <ReliableMessagingAssertion/>
    </wsp:All>
    <wsp:All>
      <nsSecurityAssertion level="medium"/>
      <nsTransactionAssertion/>
    </wsp:All>
  </wsp:ExactlyOne>
</wsp:Policy>
```

Listing 12.13 Service provider policy

Listing 12.13 illustrates a normalized service provider policy that is to be compared (intersected) to a normalized service requestor policy. The service requestor policy is shown in Listing 12.14.

```
<wsp:Policy wsu:Id="Requestor_Policy"...>
  <wsp:ExactlyOne>
    <wsp:All>
      <SecurityAssertion/>
      <ReliableMessagingAssertion timeout="100" retries="3"/>
    </wsp:All>
  </wsp:ExactlyOne>
</wsp:Policy>
```

Listing 12.14 Service requestor policy

To intersect these two policies each set of policy assertions in a policy alternative (bound by the `<wsp:All>` operators) must be considered. Only the `QNames` of these assertions are compared. This means that the requestor-side alternative matches only the first alternative from the provider policy. These two alternatives are then combined to produce the intersected alternative shown in Listing 12.15. It is the responsibility of the policy framework and run-time support system to interpret this policy alternative and merge the assertions with identical QNames into assertions that have meaning to the processing modules.

```
<wsp:All>
  <SecurityAssertion level="high"/>
  <SecurityAssertion/>
  <ReliableMessagingAssertion timeout="100" retries="3"/>
  <ReliableMessagingAssertion/>
</wsp:All>
```

Listing 12.15 Intersected policy

12.4.3 Policy attachments

The WS-PolicyAttachment specification [Bajaj 2006b] deals with the important issue of how to associate a particular policy with a specific Web service (subject). This specification defines how to reference policy expressions from XML elements, WSDL definitions, and UDDI entities.

Policies will often be associated with a particular policy subject, see Figure 12.2, using multiple policy attachments. For example, there may be attachments at different points in a WSDL description that apply to a subject, and other attachments may be made by UDDI and other mechanisms. When multiple attachments are made, they must be combined to ascertain the effective policy for a particular policy subject. The term *effective policy* signifies the policy associated with a WSDL element. This is achieved by identifying which policy scopes a particular subject is under and combining the individual policies associated with these scopes using the merge operation (see section 12.4.3.1) to form a merged policy.

A policy can be associated with a policy subject using one of two strategies. One strategy is to define the policy as part of the subject's definition (e.g., within a WSDL document or pointed to from the WSDL document). The second strategy is to have a standalone policy external to the subject's definition that points back to the Web service or services that it is associated with.

12.4.3.1 WSDL policy attachment

It is often desirable to associate policies with the XML elements describing a subject; this allows description formats such as WSDL to be easily used with the WS-Policy framework.

WS-PolicyAttachment defines a global attribute, called wsp:PolicyURIs, that allows policy expressions to be attached to an arbitrary XML element. Alternatively it uses the wsp:Policy and the wsp:PolicyReference elements to point to policies that apply. The wsp:PolicyURIs attribute contains a list of one or more URIs, while wsp:PolicyReferences makes use of QNames, which allow a collection of policies to be associated to any policy subject. When the wsp:PolicyURIs attribute is used, each of the values identifies a policy expression as defined by WS-Policy.

Before we explain the use of WS-PolicyAttachment within a WSDL document, it is useful to understand how to interpret policy attachments when they appear within a WSDL description.

Policies can be associated with several types of WSDL definitions, which serve as policy subjects. These are identified as the *service policy subject*, the *endpoint policy subject*, the *operation policy subject*, and the *message policy subject*, see Figure 12.3. This figure represents how the effective policies, with regard to WSDL, are calculated for each of these policy subjects. Subjects are nested due to the hierarchical nature of WSDL. When attaching a policy to a WSDL element, a policy scope is implied for that attachment. The policy scope only contains the policy subject associated with that element and not those associated with the children of that element. For example, assertions that describe behavior regarding the manipulation of messages should only be contained within policies attached to WSDL message elements. In Figure 12.3, the dashed lines represent policy scopes implied by WSDL elements.

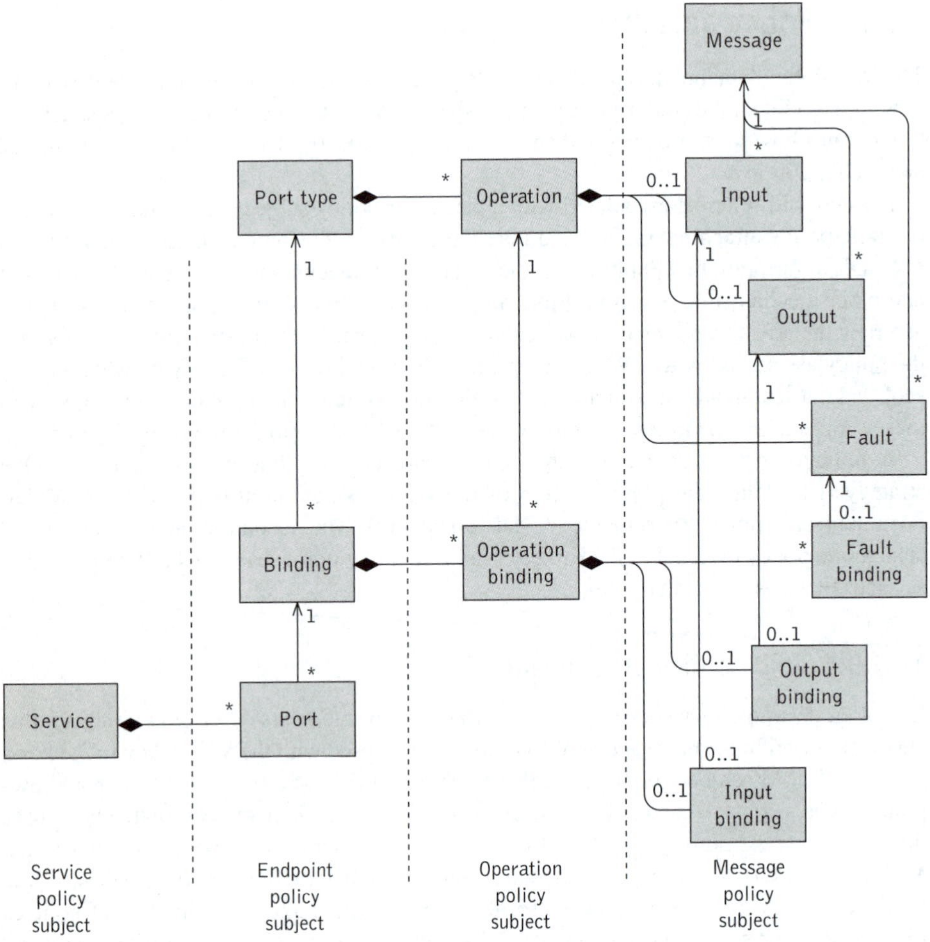

Figure 12.3 Effective policy and policy scopes in WSDL

For a particular policy subject, the effective policy must merge the element policy of each element with a policy scope that contains the policy subject. For example, in Figure 12.3, for a particular input message to a deployed endpoint, there are four policy subjects involved, each with their own effective policy. There is an effective policy for the message, as well as an effective policy for the parent operation of that message, an effective policy for the deployed endpoint, and an effective policy for the service as a whole. All four effective policies are applicable in relation to that specific input message. This indicates that policies which are attached at a higher level in the WSDL hierarchy are inherited. Therefore, for example, a policy attached to a `<portType>` would be inherited by its `<operation>` and subsequently by its `<input>`, `<output>`, and `<fault>` message descendant elements.

Listing 12.16 shows how to associate policies with WSDL elements describing a subject. In particular, this listing shows how the WS-PolicyAttachment `<wsp: PolicyRefs>` attribute is used with `<message>` and `<part>` elements, which are parts of a WSDL definition for a shipment order. For reasons of simplicity we have chosen to attach policies to an `<operation>` and not a `<PortType>` element. The WSDL inheritance properties discussed earlier would also apply to these elements.

Listing 12.16 illustrates two policies attached to a WSDL document, a reliable message and a secure message policy. The `RMPolicy` assertion indicates that the WS-ReliableMessaging must be used to ensure reliable message delivery [Batres 2005]. Specifically, the WS-ReliableMessaging protocol determines invariants maintained by the reliable messaging endpoints and the directives used to track and manage the delivery of a sequence of messages. For endpoints bound to `ShipmentQuoteSoapBinding` the effective policy of the endpoint is found in Listing 12.16, while for the operation `GetShipmentPrice`, an additional message-level effective policy is in effect for the input message. This policy can be found in Listing 12.17.

12.4.3.2 External policy attachment

This mechanism allows standalone policies to be associated with a policy subject independent of that subject's definition and/or representation through the use of a `<wsp:PolicyAttachment>` element. This element has three components: the policy scope of the attachment, the policy expressions being bound, and optional security information. The *policy scope* of the attachment is defined using one or more extensible domain expressions (see Figure 12.1) that identify policy subjects, typically using URIs.

To describe resources that a policy applies to the sub-element `<wsp:AppliesTo>` of `<wsp:PolicyAttachment>` is used. The `<wsp:PolicyAttachment>` sub-element specifies and/or refines the domain expression(s) that define the policy scope. When more than one domain expression is present, the policy scope contains the union of the policy subjects identified by each expression. Listing 12.18 illustrates the use of the external policy attachment mechanism with an `EndpointReference` domain expression for a deployed endpoint as defined in WS-Addressing. In this example, the policy expression (policy assertions) found at `http://plastics_supply.com/acct-policies.xml` applies to all interactions with the `plastics:InventoryService` at the endpoint `http://plastics_supply.com/acct`.

```
<?xml version="1.0"?>
<wsdl:definitions name="Shipment"
  targetNamespace="http://shipco.com/shipment/shipment/binding"
  xmlns:tns="http://shipco.com/shipment/shipment/binding"
  xmlns:ship="http://shipco.com/shipment"
  xmlns:wsdl=http://schemas.xmlsoap.org/wsdl/
  xmlns:rmp="http://schemas.xmlsoap.org/ws/2005/02/rm/policy"
  xmlns:sp="http://schemas.xmlsoap.org/ws/2005/07/securitypolicy"
  xmlns:wsdl="http://schemas.xmlsoap.org/wsdl/"
  xmlns:wsoap12="http://schemas.xmlsoap.org/wsdl/soap12/"
  xmlns:wsp="http://schemas.xmlsoap.org/ws/2004/09/policy"
  xmlns:wsu="http://docs.oasis-open.org/wss/2004/01/oasis-200401-
                                 wsswssecurity-utility-1.0.xsd">

<wsp:Policy wsu:Id="RmPolicy">
  <rmp:RMAssertion>
    <rmp:InactivityTimeout Milliseconds="600000"/>
    <rmp:BaseRetransmissionInterval Milliseconds="3000"/>
    <rmp:ExponentialBackoff />
    <rmp:AcknowledgementInterval Milliseconds="200"/>
  </rmp:RMAssertion>
</wsp:Policy>

<wsp:Policy wsu:Id="SecureMessagePolicy">
  <sp:SignedParts>
  <sp:Body />
  </sp:SignedParts>
  <sp:EncryptedParts>
  <sp:Body />
  </sp:EncryptedParts>

<wsdl:import namespace="http://shipco.com/shipment/shipment"
   location="http://shipco.com/shipment/shipment.wsdl"/>
<wsdl:binding name="ShipmentQuoteSoapBinding" type="ship:Quote">
   <wsoap12:binding style="document"
     transport="http://schemas.xmlsoap.org/soap/http" />
 <wsp:PolicyReference URI="#RmPolicy" wsdl:required="true"/>

 <wsdl:operation name="GetShipmentPrice">
    <wsoap12:operation
       soapAction="="http://shipco.com/shipment/Quote/
       GetShipmentPriceRequest"/>
     <wsdl:input>
       <wsoap12:body use="literal" />
       <wsp:PolicyReference URI="#SecureMessagePolicy"
        wsdl:required="true"/>
     </wsdl:input>
     <wsdl:output>
       <wsoap12:body use="literal" />
       <wsp:PolicyReference URI="#SecureMessagePolicy"
        wsdl:required="true"/>
     </wsdl:output>
  </wsdl:operation>
 </wsdl:binding>
</wsdl:definitions>
```

Listing 12.16 WSDL definition referencing policies

```
<wsp:Policy
   xmlns:sp="http://schemas.xmlsoap.org/ws/2005/07/
                                                  securitypolicy"
   xmlns:wsp="http://schemas.xmlsoap.org/ws/2004/09/policy"
   xmlns:wsu="http://docs.oasis-open.org/wss/2004/01/
                          oasis-200401-wsswssecurity-utility-1.0.xsd"
   wsu:Id="SecureMessagePolicy">
   <sp:SignedParts>
      <sp:Body />
   </sp:SignedParts>
   <sp:EncryptedParts>
      <sp:Body />
   </sp:EncryptedParts>
</wsp:Policy>
```

Listing 12.17 Effective policy for part of the WSDL definition in Listing 12.16

```
<wsp:PolicyAttachment
   xmlns:wsp=" http://schemas.xmlsoap.org/ws/2004/09/policy"
   xmlns:wsa="http://schemas.xmlsoap.org/ws/2004/08/addressing">
  <wsp:AppliesTo>
    <wsa:EndpointReference xmlns:plastics="...">
       <wsa:Address> http://plastics_supply.com/acct
                                                   </wsa:Address>
       <wsa:PortType> plastics:InventoryPortType </wsa:PortType>
       <wsa:ServiceName> plastics:InventoryService
                                                 </wsa:ServiceName>
    </wsa:EndpointReference>
  </wsp:AppliesTo>
  <wsp:PolicyReference URI="http://plastics_supply.com/
                                                acct-policies.xml/>
</wsp:PolicyAttachment>
```

Listing 12.18 Sample external policy attachment

12.5 Service agreements

In addition to policies, in SOAs service clients require guarantees related to services they wish to use. Such guarantees are often related to QoS. Providing service at a specific QoS level depends on the extent at which a specific service is used by its (possibly multiple) clients and the rate at which it consumes resources, e.g., when a requested service operation starts or how long it takes to complete. In many situations different service clients are simultaneously attempting to share, and therefore manage, the same services and consequently their underlying resources, which are maintained by service providers. Therefore, whether service providers can offer and meet QoS guarantees usually depends on their resource situation at the time that the service is requested. To meet these demands common practice is to negotiate an SLA, by which a service provider "contracts" with a client (customer) to provide some measurable capability, see section 1.8. Agreements explicitly state the terms between a service client and service provider allowing service clients to understand what to expect from resources. Based on this agreement, a service provider can allocate the necessary resources to live up to the QoS guarantees. Such an agreement is much more than a simple statement of terms of performance. It should be viewed as a statement of common policy terms to be honored by both parties involved in the agreement [Czajkowski 2005].

An agreement provides a powerful abstraction mechanism by representing an underlying resource strictly in terms of policy terms that it is willing to assert [Czajkowski 2005]. An agreement between a service client and a service provider specifies one or more service-level objectives as both expressions of requirements of the service client and assurances by the service provider on the availability of resources and/or on service qualities. An agreement suppresses complex internal policy details, such as pricing models, detailed configuration information, and so forth. It is thus defined (externally) only by the agreements it is willing to negotiate.

Standard protocols for negotiating and managing agreements are essential for a Web services infrastructure. To achieve this, the Grid Resource Allocation and Agreement Protocol Working Group in the Global Grid Forum is defining WS-Agreement [Andrieux 2005], a standard set of protocols for negotiating, establishing, and managing agreements in a domain- and implementation-independent manner. In the following we shall examine the structure of WS-Agreement, its conceptual model, and its corresponding agreement language.

12.5.1 WS-Agreement structure

WS-Agreement specifies an XML-based language for creating contracts, agreements, and guarantees from offers between a service provider and a client. An agreement may involve multiple services and includes information on the agreement parties, references to prior agreements, service definitions, and guarantee terms. In an agreement the service definition is part of the terms of the agreement and must be established prior to the creation of the agreement. The motivations for the design of WS-Agreement stem out of QoS concerns, especially in the context of load balancing heavy loads on a network of Web services [Andrieux 2005].

Each agreement represents a well-understood policy, capturing a mutual understanding of (future) behavior between the party that initiates an agreement and the party that services this specific agreement. The service and levels of a service are described by agreement terms, which define the content of an agreement. It is expected that most terms will be domain specific, defining qualities such as service description, termination clauses, transferability options, and others. All agreement terms are used to specialize WS-Policy assertions [Andrieux 2005], see section 12.4.1.

The WS-Agreement specification consists of three parts to be used in a composable manner: a schema for specifying an agreement (offer), a schema for specifying an agreement template, and a set of port types and operations for managing agreement lifecycle, including creation, termination, and monitoring of agreement states. The structure of an `<Agreement>` is built upon the following elements:

- *Name:* This attribute identifies the agreement and is used for reference in other agreements.
- *AgreementContext:* This element in the agreement provides information about the agreement that is not specified in the agreement terms, such as who the involved parties are, what the service is that is being agreed to, the length of the agreement, and references to any related agreements.
- *Service description terms:* These provide information needed to instantiate or identify a service to which this agreement pertains.
- *Guarantee terms:* These define the assurance on service quality (or availability) associated with the service described by the service definition terms. For example, an agreement may provide assurances on the bounds on service response time and service availability offered by a service provider to the service consumer. Alternatively, it may provide assurances on the availability of minimum resources such as memory, CPU MIPS, storage, and so forth. Guarantee terms refer to the service description that is the subject of the agreement and define service-level objectives (describing for example the QoS on execution that needs to be met), qualifying conditions (defining for example when those objectives have to be met), and business value expressing the importance of the service level objectives.

The WS-Agreement protocol provides the possibility to create an `<Agreement>`, which is initiated by either the service consumer or by the service provider side. To create an `<Agreement>`, a client makes an offer to an agreement factory, which creates the `<Agreement>`. The agreement factory advertises the types of offers it is willing to accept by means of agreement templates. The `<Agreement>` creation process typically starts with a predefined agreement template specifying customizable aspects of the documents, and rules (creation constraints) that must be followed in creating an agreement. An agreement template is an XML document by the means of which the agreement factory advertises the types of offers it is willing to accept. Like an agreement document, the template is composed of a template name, a context element, and agreement terms, but additionally also includes information on agreement creation constraints. The schema for an agreement template, just like an agreement offer, is schematized in WS-Agreement. A service provider offers an agreement template describing the service and its guarantees. Negotiation then involves a service consumer retrieving the template of an `<Agreement>` for a particular service from the provider and filling in the appropriate fields. The filled template is then sent as an offer to the provider. The provider decides whether to accept or reject the offer, depending on its resources and the QoS it can offer. Although offers and agreements have mostly the same fields, an offer contains choices for an agreement from the service customer for the service provision. In an agreement, the choices in an offer are modified by the service provider to finalize the agreement.

To better understand the implications of WS-Agreement let us consider a simple variant of our order processing example involving a logistics and transport provider. The logistics company in our example provides different service levels associated with the movement of goods (via a Web service interface called goods transportation service) using different modes of transportation. Modes of transportation may include air, ocean, rail or road freight, expedite shipments (premium freight services that meet the time-sensitive shipment needs of customers), direct shipment (freight consolidation, air, ocean, and ground transportation, customs clearance and direct delivery to multiple addresses within the destination country, all through a single source), and specialized shipment services, which meet a customer's specialized transportation and freight needs. Each type of transportation service provides certain QoS characteristics, described via an agreement template, specifying the service and its guarantees, including the QoS options available to the customer. This template offers many options to service consumers. When new customers use the logistics company to transport their goods, they select a transportation service level by customizing the options specified in the corresponding template. Customers can then add availability and response time guarantees to individual logistics operations of the Web service interface. Also, customers can set the time when the service will be available, for instance, during business hours. The performance parameters may refer to the total elapsed time that the transportation process takes from its submission to processing by a freight forwarder. The availability could be measured as a timeout of 30 seconds of a Web service request. The different clients of the logistics provider have different requirements regarding the service's QoS parameters. Since better QoS guarantees require more resources to implement a Web service, QoS guarantees are limited to a certain number of requests per time span, e.g., up to 20 requests per trading day. If more requests are submitted, either another – lower – set of QoS guarantees applies or no performance guarantees are given.

12.5.2 Agreement language

The WS-Agreement language defines the representation of offers that an agreement initiator submits to an agreement responder and of agreement templates. As discussed above, the agreement model is extensible and, hence, the WS-Agreement language does not provide a complete syntax to describe every type of content in an agreement. It provides, however, the main concepts of an agreement and language elements to describe the main elements at a top level. The details of agreement offers can then be filled with other languages as seen fit. For example, WS-Agreement may contain a WSDL definition to define an interface or use a domain-specific expression language to define a response time guarantee.

Listing 12.19 illustrates the XML structure of the content of an `Agreement` offer. This `Agreement` offer has the agreement identifier `<DistributionCapacity123>`, which must be unique between the interacting parties. The `Name` element can illustrate further what is meant. The agreement `<Context>` in Listing 12.19 contains the `<AgreementInitiator>` and `<AgreementResponder>`, and indicates that the `<AgreementResponder>` is the service provider. The expiration time is given in the XML date–time format. An `<Agreement>` offer can contain any number of terms.

```
<wsag:AgreementOffer
                    AgreementId="GoodsTransportationCapacity123">
<wsag:Name>SupplementalAgreementFollowsInDecember</wsag:Name>
<wsag:Context>
  <wsag:AgreementInitiator>
      http://www.logistics-customer.com/
  </wsag:AgreementInitiator>
  <wsag:AgreementResponder>
      http://www.e-logistics_provider.com/
  </wsag:AgreementResponder>
  <wsag:ServiceProvider>AgreementResponder</wsag:ServiceProvider>
  <wsag:ExpirationTime>2005-11-30T14:00:00.000-05:00
  </wsag:ExpirationTime>
    …
</wsag:Context>
<wsag:Terms>
    <wsag:All>
      <wsag:ServiceDescriptionTerm
                  name="GoodsTransportationServiceInterface" … >
        …
      </wsag:ServiceDescriptionTerm>
      <wsag:ServiceDescriptionTerm name=" … " …>
        …
      </wsag:ServiceDescriptionTerm>
       <wsag:ExactlyOne>
              <wsag:GuaranteeTerm
                     name="GoodsTransportationResponseTime" … >
                  …
                  <wsag:QualifyingCondition>
                    <exp:And>
                       <Transportation:BusinessHours/>
                     <exp:Less>
                       <exp:Variable>RequestRate</exp:Variable>
                       <exp:Value>20</exp:Variable>
                     </exp:Less>
                    </exp:And>
                  </wsag:QualifyingCondition>
                     …
              </wsag:GuaranteeTerm>
              <wsag:GuaranteeTerm name=" … " …>
                  …
              </wsag:GuaranteeTerm>
       </wsag:ExactlyOne>
        …
    </wsag:All>
</wsag:Terms>
</wsag:AgreementOffer>
```

Listing 12.19 Structure of a WS-Agreement offer

The term compositors structuring them are equivalent to the WS-Policy compositors `<All>`, `<ExactlyOne>`, and `<OneOrMore>`.

In this example, all `<ServiceDescriptionTerms>` and one of the `<GuaranteeTerms>` must be observed. `<ServiceDescriptionTerms>` describe the services, e.g., goods transportation, that the service provider will render to the service client. This means that as defined in the `<Context>`, the service provider is liable to deliver what is promised in all the `<ServiceDescriptionTerms>`. Both service providers and service customers can give guarantees. The obliged party is defined in each `<GuaranteeTerm>`. This enables a service provider to give guarantees even if the guarantee fulfillment depends on the performance of the service customer. The example may define a response time guarantee for a particular type of good transportation service. The `<QualifyingCondition>` binds the guarantee to business hours and a request rate less than 20.

The WS-Agreement offer language provides significant flexibility to define a rich set of offers. This is particularly the case because domain-specific languages are used to represent expressions and to describe services [Ludwig 2007].

12.6 Summary

Web services applications must rely on a standard policy framework to describe and process polices and available policy options. A standard policy framework is a common framework for the expression, exchange, and processing of the policies governing the interactions between Web services endpoints. This framework provides an additional description layer for services and offers developers a declarative language for expressing and programming policies. To cover these requirements, WS-Policy and WS-PolicyAttachment have been developed.

WS-Policy is a general-purpose, extensible framework and model for expressing all types of domain-specific policy models: transport-level security, resource usage policy, even end-to-end business process level. WS-Policy expresses requirements, preferences, and capabilities in a Web-services-based environment as policies. Policy expressions allow for both simple declarative assertions as well as more sophisticated conditional assertions. WS-PolicyAttachment offers a flexible way of associating policy expressions with existing and future Web services artifacts. For instance, WS-PolicyAttachment addresses the requirements for associating Web services policy with Web services artifacts such as WSDL artifacts and UDDI entities.

In addition to policies in service-oriented environments, service clients require guarantees related to the services they wish to use. Agreements explicitly state the terms between a service client and service provider allowing service clients to understand what to expect from resources. WS-Agreement specifies an XML-based language for creating contracts, agreements, and guarantees from offers between a service provider and a client. An agreement may involve multiple services and includes information on the agreement parties, references to prior agreements, service definitions, and guarantee terms. The WS-Agreement model uses agreement negotiation to capture the notion of dynamically adjusting policies that affect the service environment without necessarily exposing the details necessary to enact or enforce the policies. Policies and agreements are clearly related as all agreement terms in WS-Agreement are listed as WS-Policy assertions.

Review questions

- What are policies and why are they important for Web services applications?
- What are the most common types of policies for Web services?
- How can policies be exchanged?
- What are the main components of the WS-Policy framework?
- What are policy assertions and what are policy alternatives? How are they related?
- Briefly describe the characteristics and role of normalized policies.
- How can policies be referenced?
- Briefly describe policy merging and policy intersection. What are the requirements for merging/intersection of policies?
- Explain how policies can be associated with subjects (Web services).
- Briefly explain what is the purpose of effective policies and policy scopes in WSDL.
- What is the purpose of a Web services agreement? How does an agreement differ from a policy?
- Briefly describe how agreements and templates are created in WS-Agreement.

Exercises

12.1 Use the WS-Policy specification to develop a simple policy ensuring that any request message must contain an X.509-based security token as well as a `UsernameToken`, but both are optional.

12.2 Develop a policy that states that any requesting application must provide one of three kinds of security tokens: `UsernameToken`, Kerberos tickets, or X.509 certificates. The policy should also state its preference to let the requesting application know which types of tokens are preferred. The preference values should indicate that the preferred token type is X.509, followed by Kerberos, followed by `UsernameToken`.

12.3 Modify the policy expression in the previous exercise to indicate that the subject requires `UsernameToken`, X.509, or Kerberos security tokens and that the messages must also have all of the following characteristics: UTF-8 encoding, comply to SOAP 1.1, and must be digitally signed.

12.4 Develop an example of a policy expression that employs two policies which make use of `wsp:PolicyReferences` (that allows a collection of policies to be associated to any policy subject) and which can share a common policy.

12.5 Convert the compact policy expression in Listing 12.5 which uses an `<Optional>` attribute to an equivalent normalized policy expression.

12.6 Modify the example in Listings 12.16 and 12.17 to show how WS-PolicyAttachment can use `<message>` and `<part>` elements rather than an `<operation>` element.

PART VII

Service semantics and business protocols

CHAPTER 13

Semantics and Web services

Learning objectives

To develop complex application-based Web services integration scenarios, individual Web services must appropriately understand the information that is being shared based on their intended meaning. To achieve this purpose Web services must carry a variety of metadata, such as descriptions of the interfaces of a service – the kinds of data entities expected and the names of the operations supported – format of request and response messages, order of interactions, and so on.

This chapter examines the use of metadata associated with Web services and focuses on a declarative metadata description language and mechanisms that discover and retrieve Web-services-related metadata from specified Internet addresses. After completing this chapter readers will understand the following key concepts:

- The semantic interoperability problem.
- The nature of metadata and its use in SOA-based applications.
- XML-based mechanisms for describing Web services metadata beyond WSDL and WS-Policy.
- The Resource Description Framework.
- Mechanisms for querying and retrieving Web services metadata.
- The WS-MetadataExchange Framework.

13.1 The semantic interoperability problem

Web-services-enabled systems can communicate with each other via a platform-independent messaging protocol. However, the underlying data (e.g., customer records) to which the service refers usually remain in a structure and nomenclature unique to the application (e.g., a customer relationship management (CRM) application). This incompatibility can make extraordinarily difficult the assembly of composite applications that source data and business functionality from multiple enterprise systems. For instance, a CRM system using a certain dialect of XML will not necessarily understand the dialect of an order management system.

The challenges of enabling disparate systems to appropriately understand the information that is being shared relates to the logical aspect of using and sharing data and business processes based on their intended meaning. For Web services to interact properly with each other as part of composite applications, which perform more complex functions by orchestrating numerous services and pieces of information, the requestor and provider entities must agree on both the service description (WSDL definition) and semantics that will govern the interaction between them. This is part of a broader problem known as the *semantic interoperability problem*. Semantic interoperability enables Web services to interact with each other despite their semantic nuances.

When an enterprise begins using an SOA (see Chapter 8) to integrate processes across diverse functional areas, a clear requirement is that client services must convert their local definitions to the local definitions of the target services to be able to interoperate with each other. Addressing these semantic concerns involves discovering how information is used differently by each of the members in a trading partnership (or community), and how that information maps to the normative community view. Thus, a data-level integration technique must focus on a complete picture that delivers more than data or messages. It needs to focus on conveying meaning to create fluency. Meaning, in a practical sense, is about metadata, business rules, and user-supplied application context to facilitate robust information transformation between disparate systems and applications.

To understand the semantic interoperability problem at the data level, consider the interpretation of the seemingly simple concept of "order status" as proposed in [Jaenicke 2004]. This concept is vital to the correct execution of many business processes within an enterprise or between collaborating enterprises. However, what are the true semantics of this term? Does it signify the status of issuing a request for a quote, or placing a purchase order? Perhaps "order status" refers to the manufacturing, shipping, delivery, return, or payment status. Moreover, how does "order status" relate to the status of a credit check on the customer? What limitations should be placed on the order if the credit check reveals anomalies? In practice, "order status" is probably all of these things as well as the interdependencies between them. Applications in different functional areas of an enterprise (let alone diverse enterprises) will most likely have different interpretations of "order status" and different data repositories will store different "order status" values. Each database and application within a given area of responsibility, such as order management, manufacturing, or shipping, uses a locally consistent definition of "order status." However, the problem gets particularly acute when different target services, such as order management, manufacturing, and shipping services, each with a different definition of "order status," may need to exchange messages with each other.

The former example illustrates the semantic interoperability problem at the data level. However, the semantic interoperability problem can also be encountered at the business process level.

A complete semantic solution requires that the semantic interoperability problem be addressed not only at the terminology level but also at the level that Web services are used and applied in the context of business scenarios, i.e. at the business process level. This implies that there must be agreement between a service requestor and provider as to the implied processing of messages exchanged between interacting services that are part of a business process. For example, a purchase order Web service is expected – by the requestor which places the order – to process the document containing the purchase order and respond with a quotation as opposed to simply recording it for auditing purposes. This relates to semantic interoperability concerns at the business process level. As semantic interoperability at the business process level raises a multitude of interesting issues that require elaborate treatment, this important topic deserves special treatment. Therefore it is not discussed further in this chapter, but rather examined in depth in a dedicated companion chapter (Chapter 14) in this book. In the remainder of this chapter we shall concentrate exclusively on semantic interoperability issues that arise at the data level.

13.2 The role of metadata

Currently, most semantic interoperability issues are handled by using a common vocabulary of terms that each party must adhere to when communicating to a group of trading partners and/or developing custom-coded, point-to-point bridges that translate one particular vocabulary to the group's vocabulary or to that of a trading partner. Typical semantic interoperability solutions at the data level exhibit the following three key characteristics:

1. *Semantic intermediation:* Semantic interoperability solutions use a common ontology as a mediation layer in order to abstract data terms, vocabularies, and information into a shareable distributed model. This is analogous to creating a model-driven enterprise which uses core information models as a means to reflect enterprise data in whatever form is required.
2. *Semantic mapping:* Mapping to an ontology preserves the native semantics of the data and eliminates the need for custom-developed code. In semantic interoperability solutions, mapping accounts for much more than simple many-to-many data formatting rules or data syntax arbitrations. It is about how the semantics are captured, aligned, and structured in relation to the data itself, thereby creating useful information out of semantically poor data descriptions.
3. *Context sensitivity:* The meaning of any data item is bound to a specific context. Consequently, any semantic interoperability solution must accommodate the fact that the same data item may mean different things from different semantic viewpoints. Typically, the business rules, context definitions, and environmental metadata are captured and stored in metadata repositories so that they can be used during the semantic mapping process.

The core element that is needed to support any semantic-based interoperability solution is metadata. *Metadata* is data describing a data resource, such as schema data, business domain data, company-related data, and so on. Typical metadata includes schema-based data type descriptions, descriptions of data relationships, relations, attributes, primary/foreign key constraints, and other database-centric metadata. The descriptive information metadata supplies allows users and systems to locate, evaluate, access, and manage on-line resources. To fully enable efficient communication and interoperation between systems, extending conventional metadata with human-defined context and business rules is also desirable.

Metadata is organized into fields, where each field represents a characteristic of the data resource, for instance, a resource's title or summary abstract. Each field has a value and some fields may have multiple values. For example, the abstract field may have only a single value, a brief summary of the material, or the field may have multiple values, if the same abstract is provided in several languages. Following a metadata schema creates the actual metadata describing a resource. A *metadata schema* describes a particular set of metadata and the kinds of values that will be used to express the information. Each schema is designed to label a different kind of resource. The organization of the metadata information reflects the manner in which metadata schemas are managed.

The primary drive behind the creation of metadata has traditionally been the need for more effective search methods for locating resources over the Internet and understanding their intended purpose and meaning. Therefore, common metadata fields were used to describe the type of resource so that potential users and applications can discover it.

We can identify four typical kinds of metadata [Ahmed 2001]:

1. *Annotation-based metadata:* This refer to side notes added to a document for a specific purpose. It could be mainly used to add side notes in a variety of literary and linguistic texts for on-line research, teaching, and preservation.

2. *Resource-based metadata:* This kind of metadata is used to associate specific properties and their values with whatever the metadata is about: for example, a metadata record for a manufactured product, giving its name, serial number, weight, production date, and so on. In XML applications, this type of metadata typically holds information about the properties of information resources, leading to the more appropriate name for this type of metadata.

3. *Subject-based metadata:* This refers to data that represents subjects and their interrelationships. It also usually designates specific information resources as belonging to these subjects: for example, a subject index to a record of manufactured products in the form of an "index" Web page that gives collections of links to other documents, with the links organized using a list of subject areas.

4. *Structural mappings:* These resemble annotations and are used to cross-reference documents in ways not foreseen by their original authors. Cross-references may have specific meanings such as "see also," "superseded by," and so on. Structural mappings are also found in engineering product data where, for instance, an interface can be provided for a field engineer that interlinks a maintenance manual for a complex piece of equipment to supplementary data from its design documentation and to a parts manual used for ordering spare parts.

In the following we shall focus only on resource-based metadata. Readers who are interested in other aspects of metadata usage are referred to [Ahmed 2001].

It should be noted that the use of metadata alone is not a complete solution. Metadata has to be connected to an ontology. An *ontology* is a set of vocabulary definitions that express a community's consensus knowledge about a specific domain. This body of knowledge is meant to be stable over time and can be used to solve multiple problems [Gruber 1993]. Formal ontology definitions include a name of a particular concept, a set of relations to other concepts, and a natural language description that serves strictly as documentation. In business-to-business integration, an ontology can serve as the reference model of entities and interactions in some particular domain of application and knowledge, e.g., petrochemicals, financial transactions, transportation, retail, etc. The ontology provides meaning to data because it puts raw structured or unstructured data in the form of a structured conceptual specification.

Ontology-driven tools are emerging to help companies to automate the translation and processing of information. Using these products, companies can leverage standard vocabularies, and add their own domain-specific information classifications, to associate meaning with information expressed in XML. This means that more transformation and processing logic can be driven by business rules, and less of it has to be handled by opaque and hard-to-maintain program code.

The extensive use of metadata is an important part of the SOA approach. It fosters interoperability by requiring increased precision in the documentation of Web services and it permits tools to give a higher degree of automation to the development of Web services. In the Web services world an ontology can serve as the basis to establish a common linguistic understanding of business terminology across individual organizations or even across an entire vertical industry. In this way, the meaning of Web services can be formally expressed through relation to an agreed-upon set of business concepts and terms.

13.3 Resource Description Framework

Agreements about both message syntax and semantics are necessary for organizations or vertical communities to share metadata. Vertical communities may, for instance, agree about the meaning of terms, title, creator, or identifier of a document but until they establish a shared convention for identifying and encoding values, they cannot easily exchange their metadata. Rather than creating bilateral transformations between every pair of messages exchanged, organizations are relying on standard data formats and messages. These intervene between source and target systems and are used to map proprietary source data and messages to target data and messages, and vice versa. Standard data formats and messages are usually enriched with metadata that defines the transformation, aggregation, and validation, and business operations associated with each attribute, element, or the entire schema.

Let us consider the basics of Web services description and discovery. Once a vendor implements a service and wishes to make it available for remote use, the first order of business is to describe the service. In addition to the WSDL definition of a service, other useful elements describing the service may be included. Metadata describing a service typically contains descriptions of the interfaces of a service – the kinds of data entities expected and the names of the operations supported – such as vendor identifier, narrative description of the service, Internet address for messages, format of request and response messages, and may also contain choreographic descriptions of the order of interactions. Such descriptions may range from simple identifiers implying a mutually understood protocol to a complete description of the vocabularies, expected behaviors, and so on. However, a valid use of a service is not equivalent to a permitted use of the service. For example, one may present a syntactically correct request to a service for ordering products from a preferred supplier. If that request is not accompanied by a suitable authentication, then the request is typically denied. Many security considerations and QoS considerations lie in this realm of agreement. Thus metadata for a service should also include QoS as well as policy descriptions (see Chapter 12). Service policy metadata describes the assertions that govern the intent on the part of a participant when a service is invoked. Policies apply to many aspects of services: to security, to privacy, manageability, QoS, and so forth. A service should thus contain a set of metadata declaring all aspects of a service necessary for a service requestor to understand all the externally inspectable aspects of a service.

In general, service metadata should be able to describe service contracts that cover a wide range of aspects of services: QoS agreements, interface and choreography agreements, SLAs, and commercial agreements. The concept of a service contract applies primarily to the requirements for the successful use and provision of services. A service contract is implied when a service requestor makes an invocation request to a service in alignment with the service policy. Figure 13.1 illustrates the various service aspects that require metadata support. These service aspects can be described in a simple declarative metadata description language such as the one offered by the Resource Description Framework [Klyne 2004].

The Resource Description Framework (RDF) promises an architecture for Web-based resource (including Web services) metadata and has been advanced as the primary enabling infrastructure of the Semantic Web activity in the W3C. The Semantic Web activity is a W3C project whose goal is to enable a "cooperative" Web where machines and humans can exchange electronic content that has clear-cut, unambiguous meaning. This vision is based on the automated sharing of metadata terms across Web applications.

The W3C Resource Description Framework [Klyne 2004] has provided the basis for a common approach to declaring schemas in use. At present the RDF Schema (RDFS) specification [Brickley 2004] offers the basis for a simple declaration of schemas. It

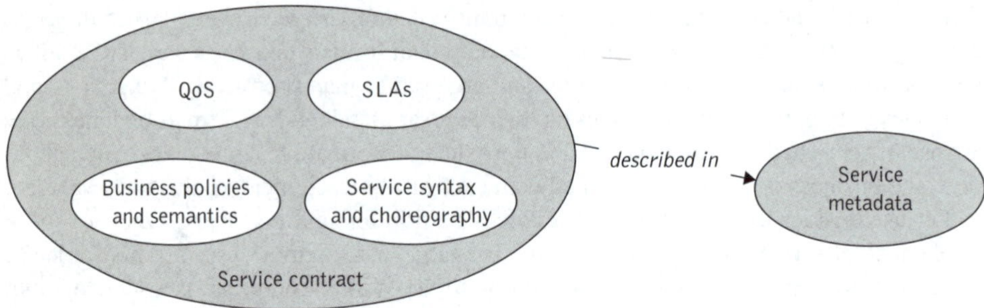

Figure 13.1 Service metadata

provides a common data model and simple declarative language. RDF is an additional layer on top of XML that is intended to simplify the reuse of vocabulary terms across namespaces and is designed to support the reuse and exchange of vocabularies. Most RDF deployment to date has been experimental, though there are significant applications emerging in the world of commerce.

RDF is an infrastructure that enables the encoding, exchange, and reuse of structured metadata. This infrastructure enables metadata interoperability through the design of mechanisms that support common conventions of semantics, syntax, and structure. RDF does not stipulate semantics for each resource description community, but rather provides the ability for these communities to define metadata elements as needed. RDF uses XML as a common syntax for the exchange and processing of metadata.

RDF supports the use of conventions that will facilitate modular interoperability among separate metadata element sets. These conventions include standard mechanisms for representing semantics that are grounded in a simple, yet powerful, data model discussed below. RDF additionally provides a means for publishing both human-readable and machine-processable vocabularies. Vocabularies are the set of properties, or metadata elements, defined by resource description communities. The ability to standardize the declaration of vocabularies is anticipated to encourage the reuse and extension of semantics among disparate information communities.

This introduction to RDF begins by discussing the functionality of RDF and provides an overview of the model, schema, and syntactic considerations.

13.3.1 The RDF data model

The main purpose of RDF is to provide a model for describing resources on the Web. The basic RDF data model consists of three fundamental concepts: resource, properties, and statements.

Resources are the central concept of RDF and are used to describe individual objects of any kind, e.g., an entire Web page, a part of a Web page, or a whole collection of Web pages such as an entire Web site. A resource may also be an object that is not directly accessible via the Web, e.g., a printed book or a travel brochure. RDF defines a resource as any object that is uniquely identifiable by a URI [Klyne 2004], [Manola 2004], which can be a Web address or some other kind of unique identifier. Resources map conceptually to entities or parts of entities.

A *property* is used to express a specific aspect, characteristic, attribute, or relation that is used to describe a resource. The properties associated with resources are identified by property types, which have corresponding values. Property types express the relationships of values associated with resources. In RDF, values may be atomic in nature (text strings, numbers, etc.) or other resources, which in turn may have their own properties. A collection of these properties that refers to the same resource is called a *description*. At the core of RDF is a syntax-independent model for representing resources and their corresponding descriptions. Figure 13.2 illustrates a generic RDF description.

Finally, *statements* are composed of a specific resource, together with a named property and the value of that property for that resource. These three individual parts of a statement are called, respectively, the *subject*, the *predicate*, and the *object*. These three parts (subject,

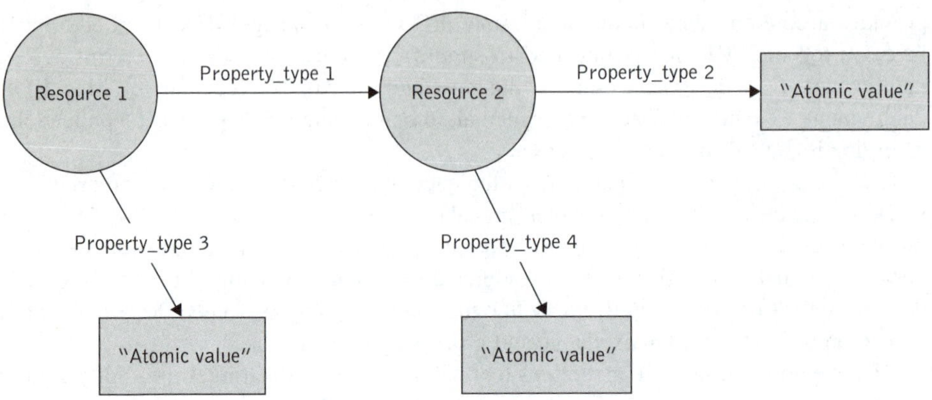

Figure 13.2 Generic RDF description

predicate, object) are often referred to as a *triple*. A triple of the form (x, P, y) corresponds to the logical formula $P(x, y)$, where the binary predicate P relates the subject x to the object y; this representation is used for translating RDF statements into a logical language ready to be processed automatically in conjunction with rules. The object of a statement (the property value) can be another resource or can be a *literal* – a resource (specified by a URI) or a simple string or other primitive data type defined by XML. In RDF terms, a literal may have content that is XML markup but is evaluated no further by the RDF processor.

To distinguish characteristics of the data model, the RDF Model and Syntax specification represents the relationships among resources, property types, and values in a directed labeled graph. The arcs are directed from the resource (the subject of the statement) to the value (the object of the statement); see Figure 13.3. The simple graph in Figure 13.3 shows the data model corresponding to the statement "Document 1 has as author John Smith." This statement has a single resource, Document 1, a property type of author, and a corresponding value of John Smith. In this figure, resources are identified as nodes (ovals), property types are defined as directed label arcs, and string literal values are written in rectangles. In Figure 13.3, Document 1 is the subject, John Smith is the object, and "has as author" is the predicate.

If additional descriptive information regarding the author were desired, e.g., the author's e-mail address and affiliation, an elaboration on the previous example would be required. In this case, descriptive information about John Smith is desired. As was discussed in the first example, before descriptive properties can be expressed about the

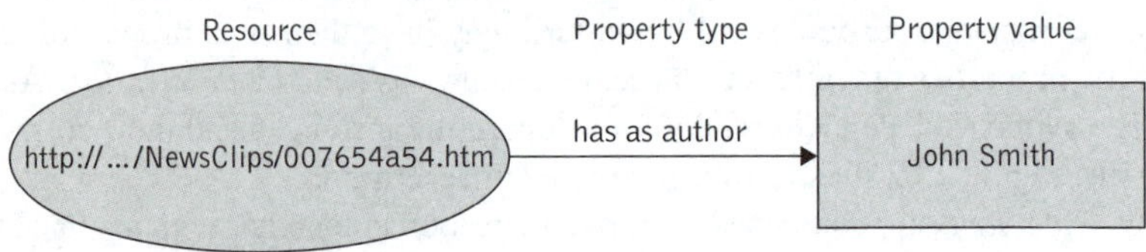

Figure 13.3 Graph-based representation of RDF statement

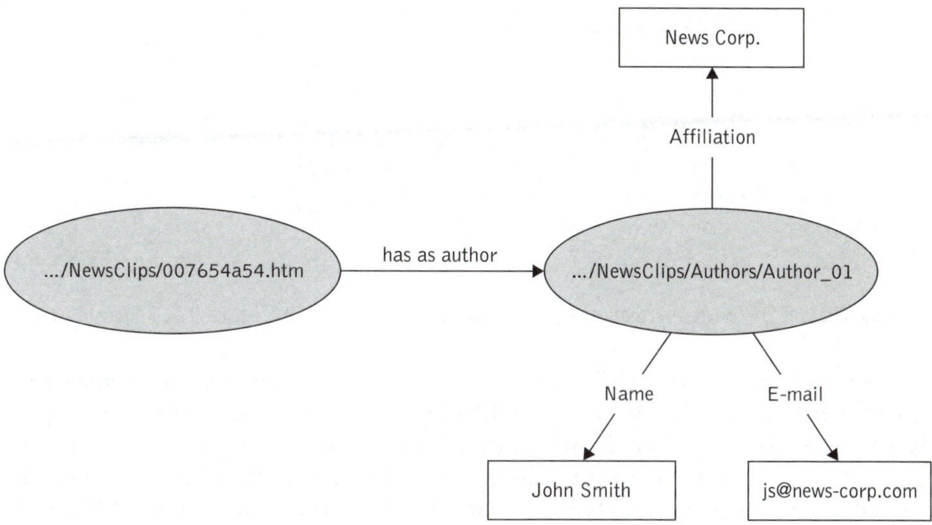

Figure 13.4 Graph-based representation of RDF statement including more details

person John Smith, there needs to be a unique identifiable resource representing him. Given the directed label graph notation in the previous example, the data model corresponding to this description is graphically represented as illustrated in Figure 13.4.

In Figure 13.4, the string "John Smith" is replaced by a uniquely identified resource denoted by Author_01 with the associated property types of name, e-mail, and affiliation. The use of unique identifiers for resources allows for the unambiguous association of properties. This is an important point, as the person John Smith may be the value of several different property types. John Smith may be the author of Document 1, but also may be the value of the CEO of a particular company describing the set of current employees. The unambiguous identification of resources provides for the reuse of explicit, descriptive information.

The RDF model allows for the creation of resources at multiple levels. Concerning the representation of personal names, for example, the creation of a resource representing the author's name could have additionally been described using "first-name," "middle-name," and "surname" property types. Clearly, this iterative descriptive process could continue down many levels.

13.3.2 RDF syntax

In the previous section we explained how RDF models metadata by using graphs. In this section we shall examine how this information is actually represented in XML.

RDF defines a simple, yet powerful model for describing resources. A syntax representing this model is required to store instances of this model into machine-readable files and to communicate these instances among applications. XML is this syntax. RDF imposes formal structure on XML to support the consistent representation of semantics.

```
<rdf:RDF xmlns:rdf="http://www.w3.org/1999/02/22-rdf-syntax-ns#"
         xmlns:ex="http://example.org/staff/">
  <rdf:Description
      rdf:about="http://www.eNews.com/NewsItems/007654a54.htm">
     <ex:has_author> John Smith </ex:has_author>
  </rdf:Description>
</rdf:RDF>
```

Listing 13.1 RDF/XML syntax corresponding to the graph in Figure 13.3

The basic ideas behind the RDF/XML syntax can be illustrated using the examples presented already. Listing 13.1 illustrates the RDF/XML syntax corresponding to the graph in Figure 13.3. The first line in this code snippet is an `<rdf:RDF>` element. The `<rdf:Description>` start tag in Listing 13.1 indicates the start of *a description* of a resource, and goes on to identify the resource the statement is *about* (the subject of the statement) using the `<rdf:about>` attribute to specify the URI reference of the subject resource. Listing 13.1 declares a property element, with the `<QName>` `ex:has_author` as its tag, to represent the predicate and object of the statement. The content of this property element is the object of the statement, the plain literal `John Smith` (the value of the author property of the subject resource).

```
<rdf:RDF xmlns:rdf="http://www.w3.org/1999/02/22-rdf-syntax-ns#"
         xmlns:ex="http://example.org/staff/">
  <rdf:Description
      rdf:about="http://www.eNews.com/NewsItems/007654a54.htm">
     <ex:has_author
         rdf:resource="http://www.eNews.com/NewsItems/
         Authors/Author_01">
  </rdf:Description>

  <rdf:Description
         <rdf:about="http://www.eNews.com/NewsItems/
         Authors/Author_01">
     <ex:name> John Smith </ex:name>
     <ex:e-mail> js@news-corp.com </ex:e-mail>
     <ex:affiliation> News Corp. </ex:affiliation>
  </rdf:Description>
</rdf:RDF>
```

Listing 13.2 RDF/XML syntax corresponding to the graph in Figure 13.4

Listing 13.2 illustrates the RDF/XML syntax corresponding to the graph in Figure 13.4. In Listing 13.2 the `ex:has_author` element represents a property whose value is another resource, rather than a literal. In order to indicate the difference, the `ex:has_author` element is written using what XML calls an empty-element tag (it has no separate end tag), and the property value is written using an `<rdf:resource>`

attribute within that empty element. The <rdf:resource> attribute indicates that the property element's value is another resource, identified by its URIref.

```
<rdf:RDF xmlns:rdf="http://www.w3.org/1999/02/22-rdf-syntax-ns#"
         xmlns:ex="http://example.org/staff/">
  <rdf:Description
   rdf:about="http://www.eNews.com/NewsItems/007654a54.htm">
     <ex:has_author>
        <rdf:Description
            rdf:about="http://www.eNews.com/NewsItems/
              Authors/Author_01">
            <ex:name> John Smith </ex:name>
            <ex:e-mail> js@news-corp.com </ex:e-mail>
            <ex:affiliation> News Corp. </ex:affiliation>
        </rdf:Description>
     </ex:has_author>
  </rdf:Description>
</rdf:RDF>
```

Listing 13.3 Code in Listing 13.2 using a nested <rdf:Description> element

RDF syntax also allows nesting of <rdf:Description> elements. Using this approach, the code in Listing 13.2 is transformed to the equivalent code in Listing 13.3.

Now consider Listing 13.4, which represents an RDF document (say Authors.rdf) listing the various authors who contribute to the News Corp. Website, along with some of

```
<rdf:RDF>
  <rdf:Description rdf:ID="JohnSmith">
     <ex:name> John Smith </ex:name>
     <ex:e-mail> js@news-corp.com </ex:e-mail>
     <ex:affiliation> News Corp. </ex:affiliation>
  </rdf:Description>

  <rdf:Description rdf:ID="FrankJames">
     <ex:name> Frank James </ex:name>
     <ex:e-mail> fj@news-corp.com </ex:e-mail>
     <ex:affiliation> News Corp. </ex:affiliation>
  </rdf:Description>

  <rdf:Description rdf:ID="JimFletcher">
     <ex:name> Jim Fletcher </ex:name>
     <ex:e-mail> jf@news-corp.com </ex:e-mail>
     <ex:affiliation> News Corp. </ex:affiliation>
  </rdf:Description>
</rdf:RDF>
```

Listing 13.4 RDF document listing various authors

their properties. Assume that this RDF document is located at **http://www.eNews.com/NewsItems/Authors.rdf**.

Note that in Listing 13.4 the `<rdf:Description>` element has an `<rdf:ID>` attribute instead of an `<rdf:about>` attribute. Using `<rdf:ID>` specifies a *fragment identifier*, given by the value of the `<rdf:ID>` attribute (`JohnSmith` or `JimFletcher` in this case) as an abbreviation of the complete URI reference of the resource being described.

```
<rdf:RDF xmlns:rdf="http://www.w3.org/1999/02/22-rdf-syntax-ns#"
         xmlns:ex="http://example.org/staff/">
  <rdf:Description rdf:about="http://www.eNews.com/NewsItems
   /007654a54.htm">
     <ex:has_author
         rdf:resource="http://www.eNews.com/NewsItems/
         Authors.rdf#JohnSmith">
  </rdf:Description>

  <rdf:Description rdf:about="http://www.eNews.com/NewsItems/
   007654a42.htm">
     <ex:has_author
        rdf:resource="http://www.eNews.com/NewsItems/
        Authors.rdf#FrankJames">
  </rdf:Description>

  <rdf:Description rdf:about="http://www.eNews.com/NewsItems/
   007654a58.htm">
     <ex:has_author
       rdf:resource="http://www.eNews.com/NewsItems/
       Authors.rdf#JimFletcher">
  </rdf:Description>
</rdf:RDF>
```

Listing 13.5 Referring to the authors' document

In RDF the attribute `<rdf:ID>` is somewhat similar to the `ID` attribute in XML and HTML, in that it defines a name which must be unique relative to the current base URI. Listing 13.5 shows how we can refer to the authors specified in Listing 13.4 within the **eNews.com** Website. This listing shows that a fragment identifier such as `JohnSmith` or `JimFletcher` will be interpreted relative to a base URI.

RDF can classify resources into different kinds or categories in a manner similar to the one used in object-oriented programming language where objects can have different types or classes. RDF supports this concept by providing a predefined property, `<rdf:type>`. The `<rdf:type>` attribute allows us to indicate that a resource is of a particular class. This allows parsers that are able to process this information to glean more about the meta-data [Ahmed 2001].

```
<rdf:RDF xmlns:rdf="http://www.w3.org/1999/02/22-rdf-syntax-ns#"
         xmlns:ex="http://example.org/staff/">
  <rdf:Description
       rdf:about="http://www.eNews.com/NewsItems/007654a54.htm">
       rdf:type="http://www.iptc.org/schema/NITF#NewsArticle">
     <ex:has_author
         rdf:resource="http://www.eNews.com/NewsItems/
         Authors.rdf#JohnSmith">
     <ex:publisher
         rdf:resource="http://www.eNews.com/company_id/3423X0P">
  </rdf:Description>
</rdf:RDF>
```

Listing 13.6 Use of typed attributes in RDF

Listing 13.6 specifies that the resource being referred to is a typed news article resource that adheres to a News Industry Text Format (NITF). NITF (**www.nitf.org**) was developed by the International Press Telecommunications Council (**www.iptc.org**), which is an independent international association of the world's leading news agencies and news industry vendors. NITF uses XML to define the content and structure of news articles and apply metadata throughout the news content making them easily searchable.

RDF uses the concept of *typed element* which is an XML element where a resource that could otherwise be referred to by an `<rdf:type>` property is turned into a namespace-qualified element. Listing 13.7 illustrates the use of an RDF typed element to represent the `<rdf:type>` statement in Listing 13.6. Notice that the `<rdf:Description>` element in Listing 13.6 is replaced by an NITF `NewsArticle` element.

```
<rdf:RDF xmlns:rdf="http://www.w3.org/1999/02/22-rdf-syntax-ns#"
         xmlns:ex="http://example.org/staff/"
         xmlns:ntif="http://www.iptc.org/schema/NITF#">
  <ntif:NewsArticle rdf:about="http://www.eNews.com/NewsItems/
   007654a54.htm">
    <ex:has_author
         rdf:resource="http://www.eNews.com/NewsItems/
         Authors.rdf#JohnSmith">
    <ex:publisher
         rdf:resource="http://www.eNews.com/company_id/3423X0P">
  </ntif:NewsArticle >
</rdf:RDF>
```

Listing 13.7 Using typed elements in RDF

In addition to the <rdf:Description> element that we have examined so far, the RDF syntax introduces three additional elements: property elements, containers, and statements about statements [Ahmed 2001], [Beckett 2004].

In the previous discussion we dealt with and described the properties that the <rdf:Description> element may contain. We have consequently explained that RDF property elements can be expressed in three ways: string literals, resources, and nested RDF statements.

When specifying metadata, there is often a need to describe groups of resources. This is helpful when, for instance, we need to say that a specific book (or article) was written by several authors, or to list the articles that make up a Website, or the software modules in a package. RDF describes such groups of resources by means of containers. A *container* is a list, or collection, of resources. Resources in a container are called *members*. The members of a container may be resources (including blank nodes) or literals. RDF provides a container vocabulary consisting of three predefined types. These are: <rdf:Bag>, <rdf:Seq>, and <rdf:Alt>.

An RDF *bag* (a resource having type <rdf:Bag>) represents a group of resources or literals, possibly including duplicate members, where there is no significance in the order of the members. For example, a bag might be used to describe a group of part numbers in which the order of entry or processing of the part numbers does not matter.

An RDF *sequence* (a resource having type <rdf:Seq>) represents a group of resources or literals, possibly including duplicate members, where the order of the members is significant. For example, a sequence might be used to describe a group that must be maintained in alphabetical order.

An RDF *alternative* (a resource having type <rdf:Alt>) represents a group of resources or literals that are alternatives (typically for a single value of a property). For example, an alternative might be used to describe alternative language translations for the title of a book, or to describe a list of alternative Internet sites at which a resource might be found. An application using a property whose value is an <rdf:Alt> container should be aware that it can choose any one of the members of the group as appropriate.

Listing 13.8 shows the RDF syntax for a bag that enables more than one author to be specified for a specific news item on the eNews Website. The syntax for an RDF bag is simply the enclosing element <rdf:Bag> followed by the list of resources in the bag. This listing also shows that RDF/XML provides the <rdf:li> element (chosen to be mnemonic with the term "list item" from HTML) as a convenience element to identify members of the container, thus avoiding explicitly numbering each membership property.

To describe RDF statements using RDF itself, for instance, to record information about when statements were made, who made them, or other similar information, RDF relies on the concept of reification. RDF provides a built-in vocabulary intended for describing RDF statements. A description of a statement using this vocabulary is called a *reification* of the statement. Reification enables statements to be quoted and have evaluations expressed about them, such as to agree or disagree with them, i.e., to assert whether they are true or false. The RDF reification vocabulary consists of the type <rdf:Statement>, and the properties <rdf:subject>, <rdf:predicate>, and <rdf:object>. Detailed examples of the use of the concept of reification in RDF can be found in [Ahmed 2001], [Manola 2004].

```
<rdf:RDF xmlns:rdf="http://www.w3.org/1999/02/22-rdf-syntax-ns#"
         xmlns:ex="http://example.org/staff/">

   <rdf:Description about="http://www.eNews.com/NewsItems/
    007654a54.htm">
      <ex:has_author>
         <rdf:Bag>
           <rdf:li
            rdf:resource="http://www.eNews.com/NewsItems/
            Authors/JohnSmith">
           <rdf:li
            rdf:resource="http://www.eNews.com/NewsItems/
            Authors/FrankJames">
           <rdf:li
            rdf:resource="http://www.eNews.com/NewsItems/
            Authors/JimFletcher">
         </rdf:Bag>
      </ex:has_author>
   </rdf:Description>
</rdf:RDF>
```

Listing 13.8 RDF/XML example for a bag of authors

This section has served as a brief overview of the RDF syntax and functionality. More details on the RDF syntax as well as examples of its use can be found in [Ahmed 2001], [Beckett 2004], [Manola 2004].

13.3.3 RDF Schema

RDF Schema [Beckett 2004] is used to declare vocabularies, the sets of semantic property types defined by a particular community. RDF Schema defines the valid properties in a given RDF description, as well as any characteristics or restrictions of the property type values themselves. The XML namespace mechanism serves to identify RDF schemas. To understand a particular RDF schema is to understand the semantics of each of the properties in that description. RDF schemas are structured based on the RDF data model.

RDF Schema refers to the metadata entities it describes as classes. A *class* in RDF Schema corresponds to the generic concept of a type or category, somewhat like the notion of a class in object-oriented programming languages such as Java [Manola 2004]. RDF classes can be used to represent almost any category of a modeled entity, such as Web pages, people, document types, databases, or abstract concepts. Classes are defined using the RDF Schema resources `<rdfs:Class>` and `<rdfs:Resource>`, and the properties `<rdf:type>` (see preceding section) and `<rdfs:subClassOf>`.

For example, suppose the organization **example.org** wanted to use RDF to provide information about different kinds of publications. Using RDF Schema, example.org would

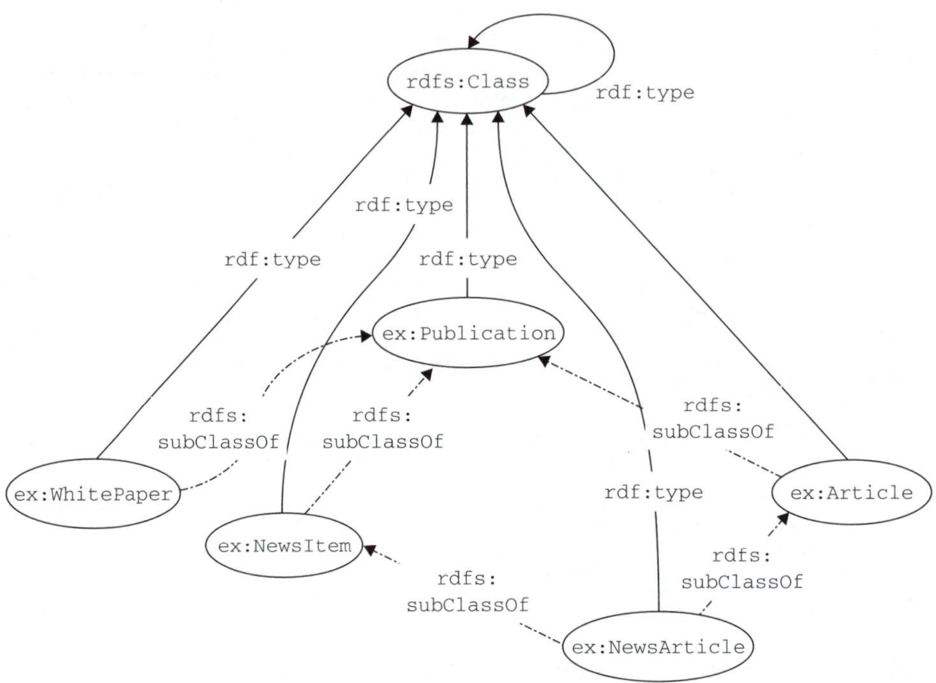

Figure 13.5 The Publication class hierarchy

first need a class to represent the category of entities that are publications. Figure 13.5 depicts such a class hierarchy for publications. In RDF Schema, a class is any resource having an `<rdf:type>` property whose value is the resource `<rdfs:Class>`. Therefore the publication class would be described by assigning the class a URI reference, say `ex:Publication` and describing that resource with an `<rdf:type>` property whose value is the resource `<rdfs:Class>` as shown by the solid line connecting `ex:Publication` to `<rdfs:Class>` in Figure 13.5. This figure also illustrates that there are several other classes such as `ex:Article`, `ex:WhitePaper`, `ex:NewsItem` that are all specializations of class `ex:Publication`. Specialized classes can be described in the same way as class `ex:Publication`, by assigning a URI reference for each new class, and writing RDF statements describing these resources as classes. To indicate that these classes are also specialized classes of the class `ex:Publication`, the predefined `<dfs:subClassOf>` property is used to associate the specialized classes with `ex:Publication`. This is denoted by dot-dashed lines in Figure 13.5. Note that the resource `<rdfs:Class>` itself has an `<rdf:type>` of `<rdfs:Class>`. Moreover, RDF makes use of multiple inheritance to allow a resource to be an instance of more than one class, e.g., the class `NewsArticle` in Figure 13.5. Listing 13.9 illustrates how the schema described in Figure 13.5 can be coded in RDF/XML.

The resources that belong to a class are called its *instances*. In this case, example.org intends for the instances of this class to be resources that are publications. The meaning of the `<rdfs:subClassOf>` relationship dictates that any instance of a class of the

```
<rdf:RDF
      xmlns:rdf="http://www.w3.org/1999/02/22-rdf-syntax-ns#"
      xmlns:rdfs="http://www.w3.org/2000/01/rdf-schema#"
      xml:base="http://www.example.org/schemas/publications">

       <rdf:Description ID="Publication">
             <rdf:type resource="http://www.w3.org/2000/01/
              rdf-schema#Class"/>
       </rdf:Description>
       <rdf:Description ID="WhitePaper">
             <rdf:type resource="http://www.w3.org/2000/01/
              rdf-schema#Class"/>
                     <rdfs:subClassOf rdf:resource="#Publication"/>
       </rdf:Description>
       <rdf:Description ID="NewsItem">
             <rdf:type resource="http://www.w3.org/2000/01/
             rdf-schema#Class"/>
                     <rdfs:subClassOf rdf:resource="#Publication"/>
       </rdf:Description>
       <rdf:Description ID="Article">
             <rdf:type resource="http://www.w3.org/2000/01/
              rdf-schema#Class"/>
                     <rdfs:subClassOf rdf:resource="#Publication"/>
       </rdf:Description>
       <rdf:Description ID="NewsArticle">
             <rdf:type resource="http://www.w3.org/2000/01/
              rdf-schema#Class"/>
                     <rdfs:subClassOf rdf:resource="#Artcle"/>
                     <rdfs:subClassOf rdf:resource="#NewsItem"/>
       </rdf:Description>
</rdf:RDF>
```

Listing 13.9 The publication class hierarchy in RDF/XML

more specialized type, e.g., ex:Article, is also an instance of the class of the more general type with which it is associated, e.g., ex:Publication. Before explaining how instances for the classes defined in Listing 13.9 can be created, we shall first explain how we can define class properties.

In addition to describing specific classes, user communities also need to be able to describe specific properties that characterize those classes (such as the author and title of a publication). In RDF Schema, properties are described using the RDF class <rdf:Property>, and the RDF Schema properties <rdfs:domain>, <rdfs:range>, and <rdfs:subPropertyOf>.

All properties in RDF are described as instances of class <rdf:Property> where a URI identifies the resource which represents the property, and the <rdf:type> of the resource is <rdf:Property>. RDF Schema also provides a vocabulary for describing how properties and classes are intended to be used together in RDF data. The most important information of this kind is supplied by using the RDF Schema properties

`<rdfs:domain>` and `<rdfs:range>` to further describe application-specific properties [Manola 2004]. The `<rdfs:domain>` property is used to indicate that a particular property applies to a designated class. The `<rdfs:domain>` property constraints the classes of subjects (resources) for which this specific property is a valid predicate. For example, we may wish to indicate that the property `ex:Author` applies to instances of class `ex:Publication`. The `<rdfs:range>` property is used to indicate that the values of a

```
<rdf:RDF
      xmlns:rdf="http://www.w3.org/1999/02/22-rdf-syntax-ns#"
     xmlns:rdfs="http://www.w3.org/2000/01/rdf-schema#"
     xml:base="http://www.example.org/schemas/publications">

       <rdf:Class ID="Publication">

       <rdf:Class ID="WhitePaper">
          <rdfs:subClassOf rdf:resource="#Publication"/>
       </rdf:Class>

      <rdf:Class ID="NewsItem">
         <rdfs:subClassOf rdf:resource="#Publication"/>
      </rdf:Class>

      <rdf:Class ID="Article">
         <rdfs:subClassOf rdf:resource="#Publication"/>
      </rdf:Class>

      <rdf:Class ID="NewsArticle">
         <rdfs:subClassOf rdf:resource="#Artcle"/>
         <rdfs:subClassOf rdf:resource="#NewsItem"/>
      </rdf:Class>

     <rdfs:Class rdf:ID="Author"/>
     <rdfs:Class rdf:ID="Publisher"/>
     <rdfs:Datatype rdf:about="&xsd;integer"/>

     <rdf:Property rdf:ID="hasAuthor">
        <rdfs:domain rdf:resource="#Publication"/>
        <rdfs:range rdf:resource="#Author"/>
     </rdf:Property>

     <rdf:Property rdf:ID="hasPublisher">
        <rdfs:domain rdf:resource="#Publication"/>
        <rdfs:range rdf:resource="#Author"/>
     </rdf:Property>

     <rdf:Property rdf:ID="nr_of_pages">
         <rdfs:domain rdf:resource="#Publication"/>
         <rdfs:range rdf:resource="&xsd;integer"/>
     </rdf:Property>

</rdf:RDF>
```

Listing 13.10 Publication schema including properties

particular property are instances of a designated class. The <rdfs:range> property constrains the classes of objects (resources) for which this particular property is a valid predicate. For example, we may indicate that a property such as ex:author may have values that are instances of class ex:Person. The <rdfs:range> property can also be used to indicate that the value of a property is given by a typed literal. For example, we may wish to indicate that the property ex:nr_of_pages has values that are drawn from the XML Schema datatype <xsd:integer>.

Listing 13.10 illustrates a more detailed specification of the publication schema in Listing 13.9. For brevity this listing includes only simple properties for the publication class. Properties for other classes in this listing can be defined in an analogous manner. Note that the schema in Listing 13.10 uses the RDF/XML typed node abbreviation for the definition of classes. This listing also introduces the classes ex:Author and ex:Publisher and explicitly describes the datatype <xsd:integer> as a data type. The ex:hasAuthor property applies to any ex:Publication and its corresponding value is of type ex:Author. The ex:hasPublisher property is defined in a similar manner. Finally, the ex:nr_of_pages property also applies to instances of the class ex:Publication and its value is an <xsd:integer> giving the number of pages in a publication.

We conclude this section by illustrating how we can create instances from a class defined in Listing 13.10. Listing 13.11 describes an instance of the ex:Publication class defined in Listing 13.10, together with some hypothetical values for its properties.

As a final note it is interesting to point out that conceptually RDF is very similar to WSDL, which is simply a collection of metadata about XML-based services. It is therefore quite easy to build a bridge between these two specifications. An example of what a Web service description might look like as an RDF specification can be found in [Ogbuji 2000]. This article also discusses how to take advantage of the simplicity and semantic power of RDF to augment the descriptive ability of WSDL and presents a possible RDF Schema for WSDL.

```
<rdf:RDF
      xmlns:rdf="http://www.w3.org/1999/02/22-rdf-syntax-ns#"
      xmlns:rdfs="http://www.w3.org/2000/01/rdf-schema#"
      xml:ex="http://www.example.org/schemas/publications#"
      xml:base="http://example.org/entities">

      <ex:Publication rdf:ID="JohnSimthsPublication">
          <ex:hasAuthor
               rdf:resource="http://www.example.org/staffid/5583"/>
          <ex:nr_of_pages
               rdf:datatype="&xsd;integer">3</ex:nr_of_pages>
          <ex:hasPublisher
               rdf:resource="http://www.example.org/
               publisherid/3423X0P"/>
     </ex:Publication>
</rdf:RDF>
```

Listing 13.11 Instantiating the publication class

In a similar manner to the preceding section, this section has served only as a brief overview of the RDF Schema declarations. More information on RDF Schema as well as examples of its use, including defining schema constraints, how RDF Schema differs from type systems of object-oriented programming languages such as Java, and details of how statements can be validated using the RDF Schema, can be found in [Ahmed 2001], [Klyne 2004], [Manola 2004].

13.4 Richer schema languages

The expressivity of RDF and RDF Schema that we described in the previous sections is deliberately restricted. RDF is (roughly) limited to binary ground predicates, and RDF Schema is (again roughly) limited to a subclass hierarchy and a property hierarchy, with domain and range definitions of these properties. In particular, RDF Schema provides basic capabilities for describing RDF vocabularies, but additional capabilities are also possible, and can be useful. These capabilities may be provided through further development of RDF Schema, or in other languages based on RDF.

The Web Ontology Working Group (**http://www.w3.org/2001/sw/WebOnt**) identified a number of characteristic use cases for the Semantic Web, which would require much more expressiveness than RDF and RDF Schema.

Some of the richer schema capabilities that have been identified as useful (but that are not provided by RDF Schema) include [Manola 2004]:

- Cardinality constraints on properties, e.g., that a person has exactly one biological father and mother.
- Specifying that a given property (such as `ex:hasAncestor`) is transitive, e.g., that if `A ex:hasAncestor B`, and `B ex:hasAncestor C`, then `A ex:hasAncestor C`.
- Specifying that a given property is a unique identifier (or key) for instances of a particular class.
- Specifying that two different classes (having different URI references) actually represent the same class.
- Specifying that two different instances (having different URI references) actually represent the same individual.
- Specifying cardinality restrictions of a property that depend on the class of resource to which a property is applied, e.g., being able to say that for a soccer team the `ex:hasPlayers` property has 11 values, while for a basketball team the same property should have only 5 values.
- The ability to describe new classes in terms of combinations (e.g., unions and intersections) of other classes, or to say that two classes are disjoint (i.e., that no resource is an instance of both classes).

The capabilities mentioned above, in addition to other semantic constructs, are the targets of ontology languages such as the Ontology Working Language (OWL) [Antoniou 2004],

[McGuiness 2004]. This ontology language is based on RDF and RDF Schema and provides all the additional capabilities mentioned above. The intent of languages such as OWL is to provide additional machine-processable semantics for resources, to provide semantic foundations for situations involving dynamic discovery of businesses and services by relying on knowledge representation and reasoning techniques to represent business concepts, relationships between them, and a set of rules; that is, to make representations of resources more closely mirror the semantics of their intended real-world counterparts. While such capabilities are not necessarily needed to build useful applications using RDF, the development of such languages is a very active subject of work as part of the development of the Semantic Web [Manola 2004].

Currently, there are several attempts to reinvent concepts found in the Semantic Web to provide semantics to Web services in the form WSDL extensions, thereby facilitating dynamic SOA-based applications. Some of the attempts in this direction are OWL and Darpa Agent Markup Language (DAML) [DAML].

13.5 WS-MetadataExchange

Web services use metadata to describe what other endpoints need to know to interact with them. To enable Web services to be self-describing, the Web services architecture defines SOAP-based access protocols for metadata described in the WS-MetadataExchange specification [Ballinger 2006]. Using WS-Addressing, WS-MetadataExchange defines a bootstrap mechanism for metadata-driven message exchange, supporting especially XML Schema, WSDL, and WS-Policy. This enables the creation of an interaction protocol for discovering and retrieving Web services metadata from a specific address. WS-MetadataExchange is not simply a system of additional SOAP headers, but rather a definition of a complete messaging protocol to be carried out independently of and prior to any requestor–provider interaction [Newcomer 2005].

To bootstrap communication with Web services and to retrieve metadata, the WS-MetadataExchange specification defines two request/response interactions. Metadata retrieval is implemented by the metadata request operations "Get Metadata" and "Get." The operation "Get Metadata" is used by for general-purpose metadata queries and is the only required operation for WS-MetadataExchange-compliant endpoints. To retrieve the metadata of a service, a requestor may send a "Get Metadata" request message to the service endpoint. When the type of metadata sought (known as dialect) is known, e.g., WSDL or WS-Policy, a requestor may indicate that only that type should be returned. If additional types of metadata are being used, or are expected, or when a requestor needs to retrieve all of the metadata relevant to subsequent interactions with an endpoint, a requestor may indicate that all available metadata, regardless of its types, is expected. In this case the service endpoint returns to the requestor all metadata that includes any dialects relevant to the interaction with the requestor. The contents of a response message can consist of the actual metadata definitions, address references to metadata definitions, or a combination of both. To retrieve a referenced metadata section (that is probably returned by a "Get Metadata" request message), a requestor may send a "Get" request message to the metadata reference. Metadata reference endpoints are required to support a single operation with the sole purpose of returning a specific set of metadata definitions.

Together these two request/response message pairs allow efficient, incremental retrieval of a Web service's metadata.

The interactions defined in WS-MetadataExchange are intended for the retrieval of metadata (i.e., service description information) only. They are not intended to provide a general-purpose query or retrieval mechanism for other types of data associated with a service, such as state data, properties and attribute values, etc.

```
<env:Envelope
   xmlns:wsa="http://schemas.xmlsoap.org/ws/2004/08/addressing"
   xmlns:wsx="http://schemas.xmlsoap.org/ws/2004/09/mex" >
  <env:Header>
    <wsa:Action>
      http://schemas.xmlsoap.org/ws/2004/09/mex/GetMetadata/Request
    </wsa:Action>
    <wsa:MessageID>
      uuid:73d7edfc-5c3c-49b9-ba46-2480caee43e9
    </wsa:MessageID>
    <wsa:ReplyTo>
      <wsa:Address>http://client.example.com/
       MyEndpoint</wsa:Address>
    </wsa:ReplyTo>
    <wsa:To>http://server.example.org/YourEndpoint</wsa:To>
    <ex:MyRefProp xmlns:ex="http://server.example.org/refs" >
        78f2dc229597b529b81c4bef76453c96
    </ex:MyRefProp>
  </env:Header>
  <env:Body>
    <wsx:GetMetadata>
      <wsx:Dialect>
         http://schemas.xmlsoap.org/ws/2004/09/policy
      </wsx:Dialect>
    </wsx:GetMetadata>
  </env:Body>
</env:Envelope>
```

Listing 13.12 Sample `GetMetadata` request message

Listing 13.12 illustrates a sample `GetMetadata` request for a specific WS-Policy. The `<wsa:Action>` element, which is part of the WS-Addressing specification, identifies that the action denoted by the message in Listing 13.12 is a `GetMetadata` request. As indicated in this listing, addressing may be included in the request and response messages, according to the usage and semantics defined in the WS-Addressing specification (see section 7.2.1). The listing illustrates a pattern where the endpoint is identified by a `<wsa:To>` header block as well as an application-specific header block (identified by `<ex:MyRefProp>`). As the message in the SOAP body indicates, this request is for the policy of the receiver; alternatively, it could include an identifier to request a policy within a given target namespace. If no dialect, e.g., WS-Policy, or identifier is specified in the SOAP body then the request is for all metadata available at the receiver's site.

```
<env:Envelope
    xmlns:s12="http://www.w3.org/2003/05/soap-envelope"
    xmlns:wsa="http://schemas.xmlsoap.org/ws/2004/08/addressing"
    xmlns:wsp="http://schemas.xmlsoap.org/ws/2004/09/policy"
    xmlns:wsx="http://schemas.xmlsoap.org/ws/2004/09/mex" >
   <env:Header>
     <wsa:Action>
       http://schemas.xmlsoap.org/ws/2004/09/mex/GetMetadata/
       Response
     </wsa:Action>
     <wsa:RelatesTo>
       uuid:73d7edfc-5c3c-49b9-ba46-2480caee43e9
     </wsa:RelatesTo>
     <wsa:To>http://client.example.com/MyEndpoint</wsa:To>
   </env:Header>
   <env:Body>
    <wsx:Metadata>
     <wsx:MetadataSection
         Dialect="http://schemas.xmlsoap.org/ws/2004/09/policy" >
      <wsp:Policy
        xmlns:wsse="http://schemas.xmlsoap.org/ws/2002/12/
        secext" >
        <wsp:ExactlyOne>
          <wsse:SecurityToken>
             <wsse:TokenType>wsse:Kerberosv5TGT</wsse:TokenType>
          </wsse:SecurityToken>
          <wsse:SecurityToken>
             <wsse:TokenType>wsse:X509v3</wsse:TokenType>
          </wsse:SecurityToken>
        </wsp:ExactlyOne>
      </wsp:Policy>
     </wsx:MetadataSection>
    </wsx:Metadata>
   </env:Body>
</env:Envelope>
```

Listing 13.13 Sample `GetMetadata` response message

Listing 13.13 illustrates a sample `GetMetadata` response to the `GetMetadata` request in Listing 13.12. The information that is returned in a `GetMetadata` response is included with a `<wsx: Metadata>` element. The children of this element are a variable number of `<wsx: MetadaSection>`s, each of which contains information about either one metadata definition or a set of related definitions of the same dialect and describes a particular aspect of the endpoint behavior [Weerawarana 2005]. Each metadata section includes a `<dialect>` attribute to indicate the type of metadata it carries. The

`<wsa:Action>` element now identifies that the action denoted by the message is a `GetMetadata` response to the message in Listing 13.12. This is identified by the `<wsa:RelatesTo>` element. Note that the code in Listing 13.13 contains a single metadata section. In particular the required dialect attribute specifies that the metadata in this section is of type, or dialect, WS-Policy. Finally, the `<wsp:Policy>` element contains the policy corresponding to the receiver of the `GetMetadata` request in Listing 13.12.

Now let us assume that a requestor specifies a `GetMetadata` request for all metadata for a particular service by omitting to specify a dialect or identifier as part of the `<wsx:GetMetadata>` in Listing 13.11. A sample response to this request may be found in Listing 13.14. This listing indicates that this message is a response to a `GetMetadata` request, and in particular that it is a response to the request identified by the message identifier in our hypothetical request. It is interesting to note that the `<wsx:Metadata>` element in this listing contains two metadata sections. The first section contains a WSDL document that contains an element that describes the target service. Here, we assume that the target service is the purchase order processing service that we described in section 5.2. Listing 13.14 also contains a second metadata section for an XML schema that is sent by reference using the `<wsa:MetadataReference>` element. The metadata requestor may thus fetch the metadata by issuing a `Get` operation against the specified endpoint.

To retrieve a referenced metadata section, a requestor may send a `Get` request message to a metadata reference. `Get` fetches a one-time snapshot of the metadata, according to the metadata type (`Dialect`) and identifier specified in the metadata section.

Listing 13.15 illustrates a sample `Get` request message expressed against the endpoint specified in Listing 13.14. Listing 13.15 indicates that this is a `Get` request message and also that this is associated with the metadata included by reference in the second metadata section in Listing 13.14. A sample response to the request in Listing 13.15 is left as an exercise to the reader (see Exercise 13.4).

13.6 Summary

A Web service may have a variety of metadata associated with it, such as descriptions of the interfaces of a service – the kinds of data entities expected and the names of the operations supported – Internet address for messages, format of request and response messages, and so forth. Such descriptions may range from simple identifiers implying a mutually understood protocol to a complete description of the vocabularies, expected behaviors, and so on. Metadata for a service should also include QoS as well as policy descriptions. Service policy metadata describes the assertions that govern the intent on the part of a participant when a service is invoked. Policies apply to many aspects of services: to security, privacy, manageability, QoS, and so forth.

The various service aspects that require metadata support can be described in a simple declarative metadata description language such as the one offered by the Resource Description Framework. This is an infrastructure that enables the encoding, exchange, and reuse of structured metadata. This infrastructure enables metadata interoperability through the design of mechanisms that support common conventions of semantics, syntax, and structure.

```
<env:Envelope
    xmlns:s12="http://www.w3.org/2003/05/soap-envelope"
    xmlns:wsa="http://schemas.xmlsoap.org/ws/2004/08/addressing"
    xmlns:wsx="http://schemas.xmlsoap.org/ws/2004/09/mex" >
   <env:Header>
     <wsa:Action>
       http://schemas.xmlsoap.org/ws/2004/09/mex/GetMetadata/
       Response
     </wsa:Action>
     <wsa:RelatesTo>
       uuid:a6e37bfb-f324-4e71-b33a-4f6d5c6027f4
     </wsa:RelatesTo>
     <wsa:To>http://client.example.com/MyEndpoint</wsa:To>
   </env:Header>
   <env:Body>
    <wsx:Metadata>
      <wsx:MetadataSection
      Dialect="http://schemas.xmlsoap.org/wsdl">
       <definitions name="PurchaseOrderService"
        targetNamespace="http://supply.com/PurchaseService/wsdl"
        xmlns:tns="http://supply.com/PurchaseService/wsdl"
        xmlns:xsd="http://www.w3.org/2001/XMLSchema"
        xmlns:wsdl="http://schemas.xmlsoap.org/wsdl/"
        xmlns:soapbind="http://schemas.xmlsoap.org/wsdl/soap/">
          .. ..
        <wsdl:portType name="PurchaseOrderPortType">
            <wsdl:operation name="SendPurchase">
                 <wsdl:input message="tns:POMessage"/>
                 <wsdl:output message="tns:InvMessage"/>
             </wsdl:operation>
        </wsdl:portType>
        <wsdl:service name="PurchaseOrderService">
           <wsdl:port
                name="PurchaseOrderPort"
                binding="tns: PurchaseOrderSOAPBinding">
               <soapbind:address
                 location="http://supply.com:8080/
                 PurchaseOrderService"/>
           </wsdl:port>
        </wsdl:service>
       </definitions>
     </wsx:MetadataSection>
     <wsx:MetadataSection
        Dialect="http://www.w3.org/2001/XMLSchema"
        Identifier="urn:plastics_supply:schemas:sq">
       <wsx:MetadataReference>
        <wsa:Address>
           http://www.plastics_supply.com/schemas/sq
        </wsa:Address>
       </wsx:MetadataReference>
      </wsx:MetadataSection>
    </wsx:Metadata>
   </env:Body>
</env:Envelope>
```

Listing 13.14 Sample `GetMetadata` response message to a `GetMetadata` request for all metadata

```
<env:Envelope
    xmlns:s12="http://www.w3.org/2003/05/soap-envelope"
    xmlns:wsa="http://schemas.xmlsoap.org/ws/2004/08/addressing"
    xmlns:wsx="http://schemas.xmlsoap.org/ws/2004/09/mex" >
  <env:Header>
    <wsa:Action>
      http://schemas.xmlsoap.org/ws/2004/09/mex/GetMetadata
      /Request
    </wsa:Action>
    <wsa:MessageID>
      uuid:3e3aac89-ba01-4568-80bf-273c2bc14d1c
    </wsa:MessageID>
    <wsa:ReplyTo>
      <wsa:Address>http://client.example.com/
       MyEndpoint</wsa:Address>
    </wsa:ReplyTo>
    <wsa:To>http://www.plastics_supply.com/schemas/sq</wsa:To>
  </env:Header>
  <env:Body/>
</env:Envelope>
```

Listing 13.15 Sample `Get` request message

WS-MetadataExchange is a specification that discovers and retrieves Web services metadata from a specific Internet address. For a given URI, WS-MetadataExchange defines how to query the network endpoint for WSDL definitions and associated policy information. WS-MetadataExchange is a complete messaging protocol to be carried out independently of and prior to any requestor–provider interaction.

Review questions

- What is the problem of semantic interoperability and why is it important for Web services?
- What is the difference between data-level and process-level semantic interoperability?
- What are the main characteristics of data-level semantic interoperability?
- What are the most typical types of metadata?
- What is the Resource Description Framework?
- Briefly describe the main elements of the RDF data model.
- What are containers and container vocabularies in RDF?
- What is the purpose of richer schema languages?

- What is the purpose of WS-MetadaExchange?
- What are the two request/response mechanisms for retrieving Web services metadata? How do they differ?
- What does a response to a metadata request typically consist of?
- How are endpoint references used in WS-MetadataExchange?

Exercises

13.1 Use RDF to develop a simple schema that describes different types of motor vehicles such as passenger vehicles, trucks, buses, vans, and minivans. All types are subclasses of the class motor vehicle, while minivans are also a subclass of vans.

13.2 Encode the employment scenario in Figure 13.6 in RDF/XML.

13.3 Extend the solution to the previous exercise to describe members of staff in an academic institution. Members of staff are divided into academics, administrative

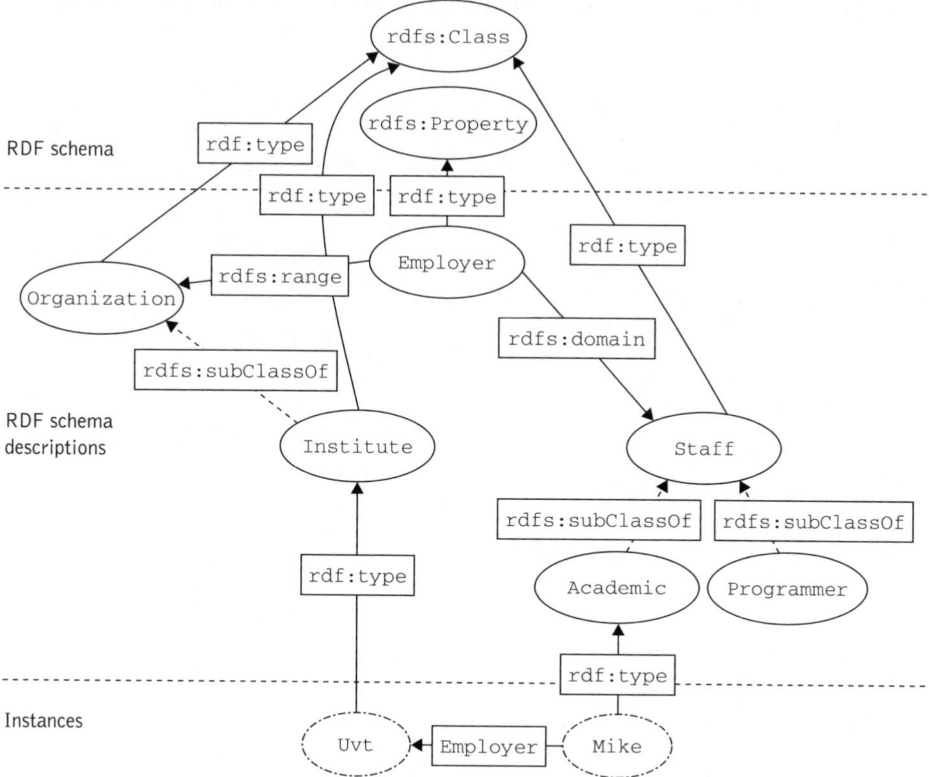

Figure 13.6 The employment hierarachy

staff, and programmers. Common properties are first and last name, room number, telephone number, and e-mail address. Academics have ranks, supervise projects, and author papers, while programmers participate in projects and, finally, administrators manage projects.

13.4 Show a sample response to the WS-MetadataExchange request in Listing 13.15.

13.5 Assume that the procurement system of a manufacturer who needs to order plastics supplies from a supplier, before interacting with an order processing endpoint, needs to retrieve the endpoint's policy description using the operation "GetMeta/Request" in its `<wsa:action>` element. In this way it can verify that all requirements will be met when exchanging messages. Encode a WS-MetadataExchange request sent to endpoint enquiring about security policies. Show a response to this request indicating that the subject requires one of X.509 or Kerberos security tokens.

13.6 The sample request message of Listing 13.16 is a WS-Transfer "Get" request for the retrieval of a resource's representation [Alexander 2004]. In this case, the requested representation is the WS-MetadataExchange element about a Web service endpoint. Develop a sample response message to the request of Listing 13.16. In the response the content of the SOAP body should be a `<mex:Metadata>` element with metadata about the Web service endpoint containing three Metadata sections. The first metadata section should contain the WSDL of the Web service

```
<env:Envelope
    xmlns:wsa="http://schemas.xmlsoap.org/ws/2004/08/addressing"
    xmlns:wsx="http://schemas.xmlsoap.org/ws/2004/09/mex" >
   <env:Header>
     <wsa:Action>
       http://schemas.xmlsoap.org/ws/2004/09/transfer/Get
     </wsa:Action>
     <wsa:MessageID>
       uuid:73d7edfc-5c3c-49b9-ba46-2480caee43e9
     </wsa:MessageID>
     <wsa:ReplyTo>
       <wsa:Address>http://client.example.com</wsa:Address>
     </wsa:ReplyTo>
     <wsa:To>http://supply.com/PurchaseService/metadata</wsa:To>
   </env:Header>
   <env:Body>
     <wsx:GetMetadata>
       <wsx:Dialect>
          http://schemas.xmlsoap.org/ws/2004/09/policy
       </wsx:Dialect>
     </wsx:GetMetadata>
    </env:Body>
</env:Envelope>
```

Listing 13.16 Sample "Get" request message

endpoint. The second metadata section should contain the location of the XML schemas used by the WSDL document. Finally, the third metadata section should contain the WS-Addressing endpoint reference of a resource the representation of which is a WS-Policy. To solve this exercise you will need to refer to the WSDL Listings 4.1 and 4.2.

CHAPTER 14

Business protocols

Learning objectives

Business standardization is about interoperability of business content and message exchange between business processes of different enterprises. Recognizing the need for standardizing these resources, the aim is to provide additional capabilities to baseline XML and service-based solutions in terms of naming and defining data. Moreover, these endeavors must be harnessed with the drive of the emerging communities to build a common understanding of business processes and data that needs to be transferred across existing and future platforms.

This chapter introduces the concept of business standards and protocols. It examines their value, looks at some of their salient features, and briefly introduces two such standards for e-business integration and discusses their convergence with Web services technologies. After completing this chapter readers will understand the following key concepts:

- The semantic interoperability problem for business processes.
- The nature of metadata and their use in SOA-based applications.
- XML-based mechanisms for describing Web services metadata beyond WSDL and WS-Policy.
- The Resource Description Framework.
- Mechanisms for querying and retrieving Web services metadata.
- The WS-MetadataExchange framework.

14.1 The supply-chain business ecosystem

E-business can be defined as the *conduct of transactions by means of electronic communications networks* (e.g., via the Internet and/or possibly private networks) *end to end* [Papazoglou 2006]. E-business does not confine itself to supporting electronic buying and selling but encompasses the exchange of many kinds of information, including online commercial transactions. The basic definition of e-business today is the marriage of traditional supply-chain management techniques with Internet and Web technologies. E-business covers business processes along the whole value chain: electronic purchasing ("e-procurement") and supply-chain management, processing orders electronically, customer service, and cooperation with business partners. E-business applications make extensive use of Internet technologies throughout all the nodes in a supply-chain operation.

E-business requires ensuring a seamless, consistent customer experience achieved by automating inter-organizational business processes that span across trading partners; hence the need for dynamic business-to-business integration that can automate business processes that encompass a diverse range of packaged and legacy applications and systems within the corporation and among supply-chain member organizations. Before we explain how XML and Web services facilitate the conduct of electronic business transactions, we first need to identify the business ecosystems that we are addressing in this chapter.

In e-business, business activity traditionally concentrates within a well-defined business ecosystem known as a supply chain. A *supply chain* is a network of facilities and distribution options that performs the functions of procurement of materials; transformation of these materials into intermediate and finished products; and distribution of these finished products to customers. A supply chain essentially has three main parts: the supply, manufacturing, and distribution. The supply side concentrates on how, from where and when raw materials are procured and supplied to manufacturing. Manufacturing converts these raw materials to finished products and distribution ensures that these finished products reach the final customers through a network of distributors, warehouses, and retailers. The chain can be said to start with the suppliers of an enterprise and end with the customers of its customers. Figure 14.1 illustrates a typical supply chain for physical products. As can be seen from this figure, while the physical transport and handling of goods constitute a flow made up of a straightforward series of activities, the corresponding information flow shows a more varied and complex pattern.

Supply-chain management deals with the planning and execution issues involved in managing a supply chain. *Supply-chain management* is a set of approaches used to efficiently integrate suppliers, manufacturers, warehouses, and customers so that merchandise is produced and distributed at the right quantities, to the right locations, and at the right time in order to minimize system-wide costs while satisfying service-level requirements. Successful supply-chain management allows for an enterprise to anticipate demand and deliver the right product to the right place at the right time, at the lowest price to satisfy its customers.

At the highest level, supply-chain management covers three key processes: planning, execution, and performance measurement. Planning focuses on having the right product at the right place at the right time; execution focuses on the physical movement of goods and services through the supply chain; while performance measurement keeps track of the

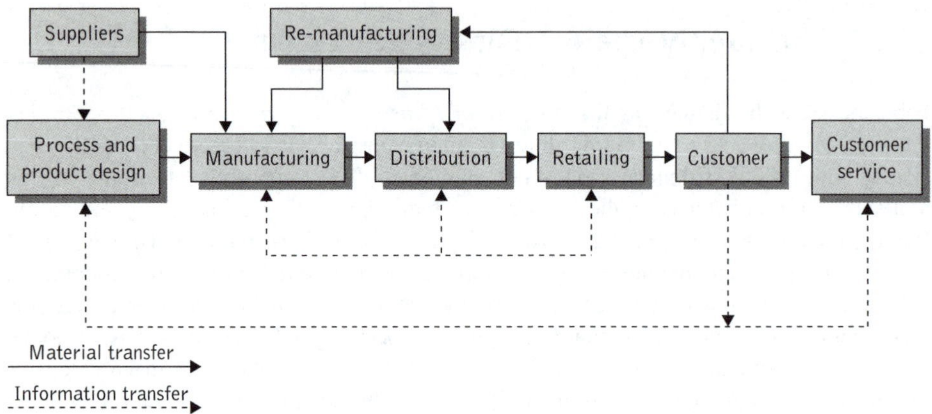

Figure 14.1 Physical product supply chain

health of the supply chain in order to make more informed decisions and respond to changing market conditions. The common theme in all three is the need to optimize processes that extend beyond narrow functional areas, taking into account the needs of the customer. Some key issues in supply chain management include:

- *Network planning:* Focuses on having the right product at the right place at the right time and thus identifies the capacity of each warehouse to determine production requirements and inventory levels at the vendor's facility for each product and develops transportation flows between these facilities to the warehouses. Network capacity is planned in such a way as to minimize total production, inventory, and transportation costs and satisfy service level requirements.
- *Inventory control:* Determines where inventory is held (supplier, warehouse, retailer) and inventory quantities. It also determines the reasons why the inventory is held in such outlets. For instance, it considers whether the inventory held is due to uncertainty in production, distribution, or customer demand. If it is established that the inventory is held due to uncertainty in production, distribution, or customer demand, it then considers possibilities to reduce the uncertainty thereby reducing inventory.
- *Distribution strategies:* Identifies relationships between suppliers and warehouse operators that specify delivery lead times, appointment processes, and hours for receiving, and uses these relationships to optimize supply-chain efficiency.
- *Supply-chain integration and strategic partnering:* Information sharing and operational planning are keys to a successfully integrated supply chain. Supply-chain integration and strategic partnering determines what type of information will be shared between partners, how it will be used, what level of integration is needed between partners, e.g., loose or tight coupling, and what type of partnerships can be implemented.
- *Product design:* Encompasses effective product design and outlines techniques to simplify production and reduce inventory holdings at the vendor's facility. It places

focus on the role that supply-chain management plays in the implementation of product design to simplify production requirements and reduce lead time for inventory replenishment.

- *Customer value:* The measure of a company's performance to its customers based upon the entire range of products, services, and intangibles that constitute the company's offerings. Its objective is to optimize supply-chain management to fulfill the ultimate consumer needs and provide customer value.

The vision of e-business concentrates on enterprises that will have access to a much broader range of trading partners to interact and collaborate and will build supply networks that are far more responsive than the current suboptimal and sequential supply chains. Processes traditionally managed by single enterprises are beginning to spread out across multiple enterprises. Using novel technologies such as Web services and business process management, traditional supply chains are transformed to adaptive supply-chain networks that have the highest visibility, greatest velocity, and best ability to manage product demand and variability.

Special technical standards for e-business that make extensive use of XML have recently emerged to facilitate the exchange of messages and combinations of processes between trading companies in a supply chain. The net effect is to change the linear and rather cumbersome structure of traditional supply chains into a flexible, Internet-based Web of trading partners, encompassing also small- to medium-scale enterprises. Several of these initiatives will be discussed in this chapter including RosettaNet, Electronic Business XML (ebXML), and the application of XML in vertical industries. However, before we examine the XML-based standards for e-business we shall first concentrate on the semantic problems that arise when integrating end-to-end business processes across companies and key partners in a supply chain.

14.2 Semantic problems at the business process level

In addition to the semantic interoperability problems on the data level (see Chapter 13), there exist semantic problems when attempting to integrate business processes that span organizations. Recall that at the process level enterprises need a solution that can cohesively weave together business processes wherever they reside in or across the extended enterprise. The lack of agreement about how business processes are defined and managed can lead to serious problems including serious process re-engineering, corresponding implementation efforts, and organizational changes. These efforts are more about redesigning business processes than about making them easy to change and combine with those of customers, suppliers, and business partners. Although interoperability within a supply chain is an important goal, interoperability *between* supply chains is equally important. An enterprise rarely interacts only within a single supply chain, but rather must connect with several supply chains as product offerings and business dictate.

The lack of effective solutions regarding custom coding, vocabulary, and business process standards has led to limited success among serious e-business projects. We may encounter three types of semantic problems with business process level e-business:

1. Business terminology fluctuations (which are identical to the semantic problems that we examined for data-level integration in Chapter 13).
2. Lack of commonly acceptable and understood processes.
3. Lack of commonly accepted business protocols.

We shall briefly discuss the latter two in the following as we have already discussed business terminology fluctuations in the preceding chapter.

The objective for process-level integration is to provide a method for defining, automating, and managing cross-application and cross-enterprise business processes. Before engaging in such a course of action, it is imperative that collaborating enterprises understand each other's business processes.

In many cases in vertical industries we can identify a *standard* shared set of business processes that have common accepted meaning. We can additionally identify *industry-neutral business processes* that are generic in nature. The generic nature of these business processes enables one to reuse them within a specific context. The context essentially guides how the base set of business information must be adapted for use. On some occasions these shared business processes might require slight modifications to fulfill the requirements that are unique to the business process in a particular context. Consider for example an e-procurement business process used in the European Union versus an e-procurement business process used in the USA or some other part of the world. In such situations it is important that trading partners identify not only such standard and common processes but also various components of a common business process specification that can be reused to create new business processes, e.g., the components for procurement, payment, and shipping for a particular industry. Such core components are defined using identity items that are common across all businesses. Reuse of core components will typically occur at the business process, business collaboration, business transaction, and business document model level. This enables users to define data that is meaningful to their businesses while also maintaining interoperability with other business applications.

Business processes should be able to capture the information and exchange requirements, identifying the timing and order of interactions as well as the purpose of each business collaboration and information exchange. This is the aim of a *business protocol*, which is associated with business processes and governs the exchange of business information and messages between trading partners across differing enterprise information systems, middleware platforms, and organizations. A business protocol specifies the structure and semantics of business messages, how to process the messages, and how to route them to appropriate recipients. It may also specify the characteristics of messages related to persistence and reliability.

14.3 Business standards and protocols

Business standards typically manage the structure for defining form, fit, and function of any product or service, regardless of the industry. They use specialized business and technical dictionaries to provide commonly used domain-specific terminology and accepted values. In addition, they specify the structure and format and semantics of the business content of a message as well as the message exchange requirements between trading partners. A common e-business standard should provide the following functionality [Irani 2002]:

- Definition of common business processes that characterize business transactions, e.g., sending a purchase order.
- Definition of common data interchange formats, i.e., messages that are exchanged in the context of the above processes/transactions.
- Definition of a common terminology at the level of data items and messages seeking a way to bridge varying industry terminologies.
- Definition of a mechanism to describe an enterprise's profile, i.e., the enterprise's capabilities and the business transactions that an enterprise can perform, in such a way that it can be stored in a common repository accessible to all other organizations for querying.
- Definition of a mechanism that allows enterprises to negotiate on the business conditions before they commence transactions.
- Definition of a common transport mechanism for exchanging messages between enterprises.
- Definition of a security and reliability framework.

This functionality not only allows trading partners to integrate more easily with other partners to conduct business electronically, but also results in increased flexibility since an enterprise will have a larger number of potential trading partners to choose from.

Business protocols intend to make it much easier for enterprises to interact in e-business transactions and processes exchanges comprising aggregated Web services and to further develop the global marketplace. This can happen as business protocols define the business intent of business transactions and processes so that they can be easily understood and exchanged between transacting parties. A business protocol is bound to a business conversation definition and a delivery channel for a trading partner. It should also be able to specify collaboration or contractual agreements that exist between two trading partners and contain configuration information required for the partners to interoperate. A business protocol is indirectly bound to such a collaboration agreement through its associated conversation definition and associated trading partner delivery channel. A business protocol must minimally exhibit the following characteristics:

1. It invariably includes data-dependent behavior. For example, an order management protocol depends on data such as the number of line items in an order, the total value of an order, or a delivery by deadline. Defining business intent in these cases requires the use of conditional and timeout constructs.
2. It is able to specify exceptional conditions and their consequences, including recovery sequences.

3. It relies on the support of long-running process interactions that include multiple, often nested units of work (see section 10.4.3.2), each with its own data requirements. Business protocols frequently require cross-partner coordination of the outcome (success or failure) of these units of work at various levels of granularity.

The lack of agreement on the terminology, grammar, and dialogue that constitute e-business processes demonstrates the need for standards. In response to these requirements, organizations have for quite some time started exploring the use of open XML-based standards that help remove the formidable barriers associated with developing a common business process language and process methodology for Internet-based collaboration, communication, and commerce. Without any form of standardization the flexibility of XML will become the biggest single obstacle to implementation within the e-business domain. Flexibility must be managed in a manner which will enable reusability and facilitate harmonization. Without this each non-standard XML dialect will not openly and cost-effectively communicate beyond the boundaries of its own implementation domain.

To develop meaningful business standards and protocols, vendors have begun to work together, facilitated by standards bodies, and in unison with business experts to define global (horizontal) and vertical business standards based on XML. *Horizontal business standards*, like Electronic Business XML (**ebXML.org**), are developed in depth for use within any vertical industry. Horizontal business standards do not apply to any particular industry specifically. On the other hand, *vertical business standards*, like RosettaNet (**www.rosettanet.org**) and business protocols such as the RosettaNet Partner Interface Processes (PIPs), enable the development of process-centric e-business applications within a specific vertical sector.

As Web services constitute the infrastructure for developing complex e-business applications they can be used as an implementation vehicle for implementing business standards such as, for instance, ebXML and RosettaNet. In particular, asynchronous and stateful communication between Web services is critical to the development of e-business applications and the facilitation of next-generation business models. To this extent BPEL provides Web services with the necessary means to enable e-business dialogues between peers and create asynchronous stateful interactions. Figure 14.2 illustrates the technology

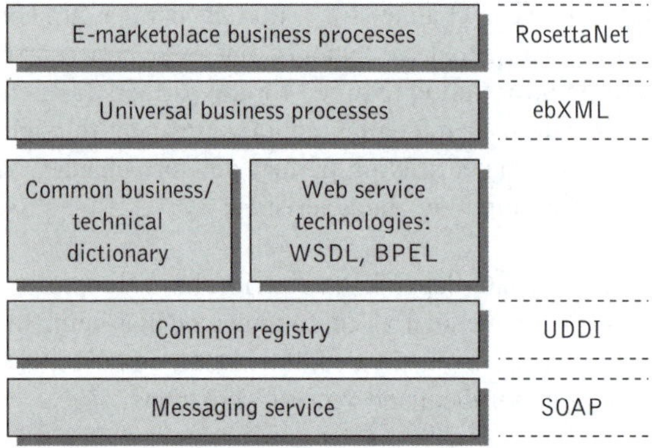

Figure 14.2 Business standards and Web services technologies

stack for supply-chain networks in terms of business standards and protocols and Web services technologies.

In parallel to the preceding standards initiatives, a flurry of distinct industry groups is working to develop their own domain-specific vertical XML standards. These efforts include the Automotive Industry Action Group, the Open Travel Alliance, the Association for Retail Technology Standards, Health Care and Medical Equipment, and the ACORD standards group for the insurance industry, to name but a few. Due to the relatively low barriers to entry, significant cost savings that come from reduced transaction costs and reduced processing costs, the automation of supply chains, and increased productivity, such electronic marketplaces attract smaller companies that establish partnerships with them.

The industry initiatives that we shall briefly examine in the remainder of this chapter provide common business process definitions (promoting industry-based standards through XML formats and defined APIs) and a standard terminology to combat semantic interoperability problems. For reasons of completeness we shall start with Electronic Data Interchange as many industry initiatives are based on modern extensions of this communications protocol.

14.3.1 Electronic Data Interchange

The need for message exchange and interaction among companies and their trading partners did not originate with the Internet. In fact, it has its roots in technologies such as Electronic Data Interchange (EDI), which was first developed in the early 1980s. EDI is a broadly defined communications protocol for exchanging data and documents in a standard format. The development of EDI was motivated by the realization that simple cross-organization business processes such as purchasing, shipment tracking, and inventory queries were tremendously inefficient. EDI is commonly defined as the application-to-application transfer of structured trading data or documents by agreed message standards between computing systems. With EDI, the standards define both the syntax for exchanging data and the business semantics. In operation EDI is the interchange of these agreed messages between trading partners to ensure speed and certainty and better business practice in the supply chain. EDI is a fast and safe method of sending purchase orders, invoices, shipping notices, and other frequently used business data and documents between transacting partners.

EDI has evolved significantly since the 1980s. Initially, it focused on document automation and served as a point-to-point digital communications medium for document transmission. Typical documents included orders, invoices, and payments. The second stage of EDI development began in the early 1990s, driven largely by the automation of internal industrial processes and movement towards just-in-time and continuous production. EDI thus evolved to a many-to-one digital communication medium for inventory replenishment. To support the new automated production processes, EDI was used to eliminate purchase orders and other documents entirely, replacing them with production schedules and inventory balances. Suppliers were sent monthly statements of production requirements and precise scheduled delivery times, and the orders would be fulfilled continuously, with inventory and payments being adjusted at the end of each month. The third stage of EDI development, which began in the mid 1990s, introduced the era of continuous replenishment. Suppliers were given on-line access to parts of the purchasing enterprise's

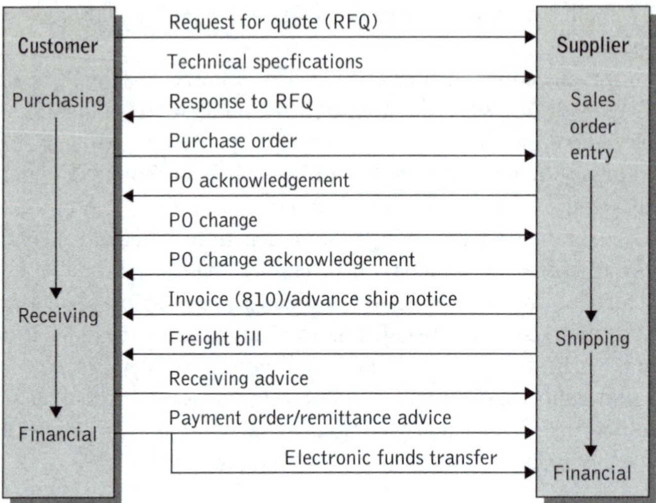

Figure 14.3 Typical EDI message exchange between interacting parties

production and delivery schedules and were required to meet those schedules using automated means. Large manufacturing firms that were implementing ERP systems that required standardization of business processes and resulted in the automation of production, logistics, and many financial processes spurred this development. Such production processes required much closer relationships with suppliers.

Today EDI is viewed as a general enabling technology that provides for the exchange of critical business information between computer applications supporting a wide variety of business processes. A typical example is given in Figure 14.3 where a buyer and a supplier interact by exchanging standard EDI messages. This example illustrates that the two partner organizations need to agree on the exact formats of the documents exchanged between them.

The EDI standards provide definitions of common business documents. Standards are of the utmost importance to EDI. Without predefined, agreed standards EDI is of little value. By using standard messages, organizations can exchange information between many different trading partners and be sure of common understanding throughout the supply chain. EDI formats the structured trading information into a commonly recognized standard published and maintained by a standards body such as ANSI X12 and UN/EDIFACT. The UN/EDIFACT standard (United Nations Electronic Data Interchange for Administration, Commerce, and Transport), which was extended beyond international trade, is the most important format.

Figure 14.4 illustrates a sample EDIFACT order. This order specifies specific purchase order number and orders 500 items of a particular product at a price of $2,500 per item. The order stipulates all 500 items should be delivered by a certain date. Descriptions of the segments that are used with EDIFACT orders can be found at the URL www.unece.org/trade/untdid/do4b/trmd/orders-c.htm.

EDI has always been regarded as a specialized solution, optimized for "heavy" data volume performance between larger enterprises that have the resources to implement it. While traditional EDI had proved that feasibility and efficiencies are possible when using

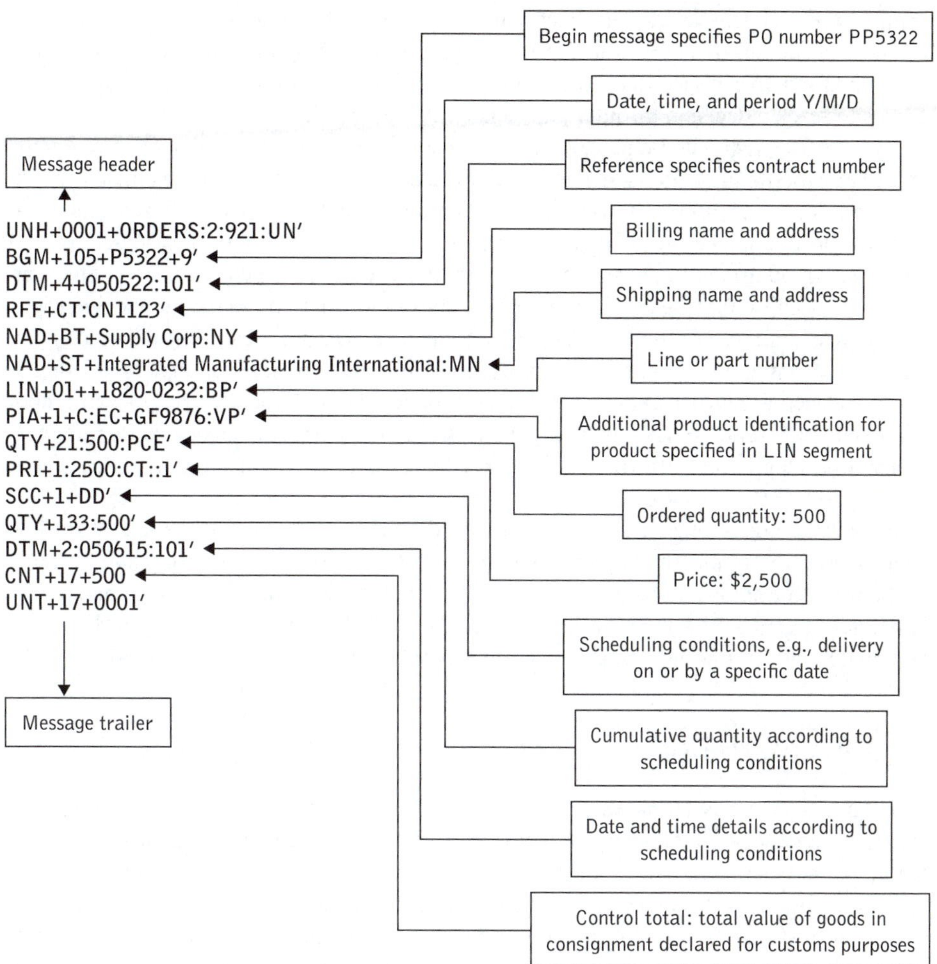

Figure 14.4 EDIFACT sample order

electronic business transactions, the limitations were found to be the cost of integration, deployment, and maintenance to the smaller business partners. EDI supports direct bilateral communications between a small number of companies and does not permit the multilateral dynamic relationships of a true marketplace. It also does not scale easily to include new participants. It involves complex and costly mapping and re-engineering procedures each time a new partner enters the chain. It also involves tremendous operational costs and requires dedicated services, which apart from installation costs consume considerable repeat expenditure by way of maintenance. These facts have meant that EDI has become the preserve for large organizations and has only a meager adoption rate of SMEs (Small to Medium-sized Enterprises). As a result, EDI often cannot provide the agility enterprises need to respond to new business opportunities or integrate with their business partners. Finally, another drawback of EDI is that it is not a means for "interactive" communication [Handfield 2002]. Each time a transaction is sent, it implies that a "decision" has been made: an order for a fixed amount placed, a forecast of future demand fixed, a lead time for delivery specified, and so on. There is no means for the buying and supplying parties to reach a decision through joint, bilateral communication or negotiation.

By contrast, XML can be perceived as a dynamic trading language that enables diverse applications to flexibly and cost-effectively exchange information. The technical implications for e-business information exchange technology are that it must be flexible, in a way that will accommodate the dynamic information requirements between disparate trading partners. An additional requirement is the ability to embrace open standards, which are essential to allow rapid establishment of business information exchange and interoperability. XML is ideally suited to these requirements as it can be used to encode complex business information. For example, XML is well suited to transactional processing in a heterogeneous, asynchronous, open, and distributed architecture that is built upon open standard technologies, such as parsers and interfaces. Not only does this apply to e-business integration with trading partners, but also in terms of enterprise application integration (EAI).

For all the above reasons, XML holds the promise of realizing the original goals of EDI, making it simpler to implement with a relative lower cost of entry and easier to exchange electronic documents over the Internet. It is thus not surprising that several XML developers have already turned to standard EDI messages that map to XML to provide better descriptions and definitions of business operations.

14.3.2 RosettaNet

RosettaNet (**www.rosettanet.org**) is an independent, non-profit consortium of major IT, electronic component and, semiconductor manufacturing companies dedicated to the collaborative development and rapid deployment of industry-wide, open e-business process standards. RosettaNet's supply-chain standards are meant to improve operational efficiencies by forming a common vertical e-business language and aligning processes between supply-chain partners on global high-technology trading networks. Its standards serve the IT, electronic component, and semiconductor manufacturing sectors. RosettaNet's approach is based upon resolving real business issues in a consortium-driven model.

14.3.2.1 The RosettaNet business architecture

The RosettaNet business architecture is based on identifying discrete segments of public business processes and then standardizing the public business interaction processes involved within each of those segments. The segments themselves are broken into subprocesses until an event- or document-based interchange process is defined: a partner interface process. PIPs define business processes between trading partners. PIPs are designed to fit into seven clusters of core business processes that represent the backbone of the trading network. PIPs apply to the following core industry processes: partner, product, and service review; product information; order management; inventory management; marketing information management; service and support; and manufacturing. Each cluster is broken down into segments – cross-enterprise processes involving more than one type of trading partner.

PIPs are specialized system-to-system XML-based dialogues. Each PIP specification includes a business document with the vocabulary, and a business process with the choreography of the message dialogue. As an example of a PIP consider the PIP "Manage Purchase Order" (PIP3A4), a specification of which is given in Figure 14.5. PIP3A4 is a key component for a large number of RosettaNet e-business process standards and serves as a "building block" for a variety of other PIPs. This PIP supports a process for trading partners to issue and acknowledge purchase orders, and cancel and change them based on acknowledgement responses. This PIP encompasses four complementary process segments supporting the entire chain of activities from purchase order creation to tracking and tracing, each of which is further decomposed into multiple individual processes. The provider's acknowledgement may also include related information about delivery expectations. When a provider acknowledges that the status of a purchase order product line item is "pending," the provider may later use PIP3A7, "Notify of Purchase Order Acknowledgment," to notify the buyer when the product line item is either accepted or rejected. The process of issuing a purchase order typically occurs after checking for price and availability and requesting quotes. The process of issuing a purchase order may be followed by changing the purchase order, cancelling the purchase order, querying for purchase order status, and distributing purchase order status.

Figure 14.6 depicts an example of a general business model that consists of demand forecast, forecast reply, and order placement processes in RosettaNet. Demand information is provided using PIP4A3 or 4A4. Moreover, there is also a case where PIP4A1 is used as strategic demand information over a long period of time. The combination of PIP3A4, 3A8, 3A7, and/or 3A9 is used for ordering processes, and PIP3C7 is used for account payable information. The RosettaNet site (**www.rosettanet.org**) provides more details about the usage of demand forecast (PIP4A3, 4A4) and ordering processes (PIP3A4, 3A8, 3A7, 3A9).

To support PIPs the RosettaNet architecture provides specifications for the RosettaNet Implementation Framework (RNIF) and business and technical dictionaries. The RNIF acts as the grammar and provides common exchange protocols while PIPs form the dialogue. The RNIF together with the dictionary, which provides a common set of properties for business transactions and products, form the basis for the implementation of RosettaNet PIPs.

In addition to the RNIF, RosettaNet also provides business and technical dictionaries that contain properties for products and services, a common vocabulary for conducting e-business as well as basic business roles, and elements that are required in fields of business documents or schemas that are necessary to support PIP exchanges. The RosettaNet Business Dictionary designates the properties for defining business transactions between trading partners. These are implemented as business data entities and fundamental business data entities in PIP message guidelines. The RosettaNet Technical Dictionary provides properties for defining products, services, partners, and business transactions. The RNTD eliminates the need for partners to utilize separate dictionaries when implementing multiple PIPs and is not supply chain specific, allowing it to be used in a variety of supply-chain applications.

14.3.2.2 RosettaNet and Web services

Web services can leverage RosettaNet in multiple ways to offer an even higher level of functionality for cross-enterprise supply-chain communications. To cope with semantic

```
<ProcessSpecification xmlns=http://www.ebxml.org/BusinessProcess name="PIP3A4RequestPurchaseOrder">
  <BusinessDocument name="Purchase Order Request"      <-- Definition of business document (POR)
    nameID="Pip3A4PurchaseOrderRequest" specificationLocation="PurchaseOrderRequest.xsd">
  </BusinessDocument>
  <BusinessDocument name="Purchase Order Confirmation" <-- Definition of business document (POC)
    nameID="Pip3A4PurchaseOrderConfirmation" specificationLocation="PurchaseOrderConfirmation.xsd">
  </BusinessDocument>
  <BusinessTransaction name="Request Purchase Order" nameID="RequestPurchaseOrder_BT">
    <RequestingBusinessActivity name="Purchase Order Request Action" nameID="PurchaseOrderRequestAction"
      isAuthorizationRequired="true" isNonRepudiationRequired="true"
      timeToAcknowledgeReceipt="P0Y0M0DT2H0M0S">
      <DocumentEnvelope businessDocument="PurchaseOrderRequest"
          businessDocumentIDRef="Pip3A4PurchaseOrderRequest"/>
    </RequestingBusinessActivity>
    <RespondingBusinessActivity name="Purchase Order Confirmation Action"
      nameID="PurchaseOrderConfirmationAction" isAuthorizationRequired="true" isNonRepudiationRequired="true"
      timeToAcknowledgeReceipt="P0Y0M0DT2H0M0S">
      <DocumentEnvelope businessDocument="Purchase Order Confirmation"
           businessDocumentIDRef="Pip3A4PurchaseOrderConfirmation"/>
    </RespondingBusinessActivity>
  </BusinessTransaction>
  <BinaryCollaboration name="Request Purchase Order" nameID="RequestPurchaseOrder_BC">
    <InitiatingRole name="Buyer" nameID="BuyerId"/>
    <RespondingRole name="Seller" nameID="SellerId"/>
    <StarttoBusinessState="RequestPurchaseOrder"/>
    <BusinessTransactionActivity name="RequestPurchaseOrder" nameID="RequestPurchaseOrder_BTA"
       businessTransaction="RequestPurchaseOrder"businessTransactionIDRef="RequestPurchaseOrder_BT"
       fromAuthorizedRole="Buyer" fromAuthorizedRoleIDRef="BuyerId"
       toAuthorizedRole="Seller" toAuthorizedRoleIDRef="SellerId" timeToPerform="P0Y0M0DT24H0M0S"/>
  </BinaryCollaboration>
</ProcessSpecification>
```

Figure 14.5 Example of a RosettaNet business process "Manage Purchase Order" (PIP3A4)

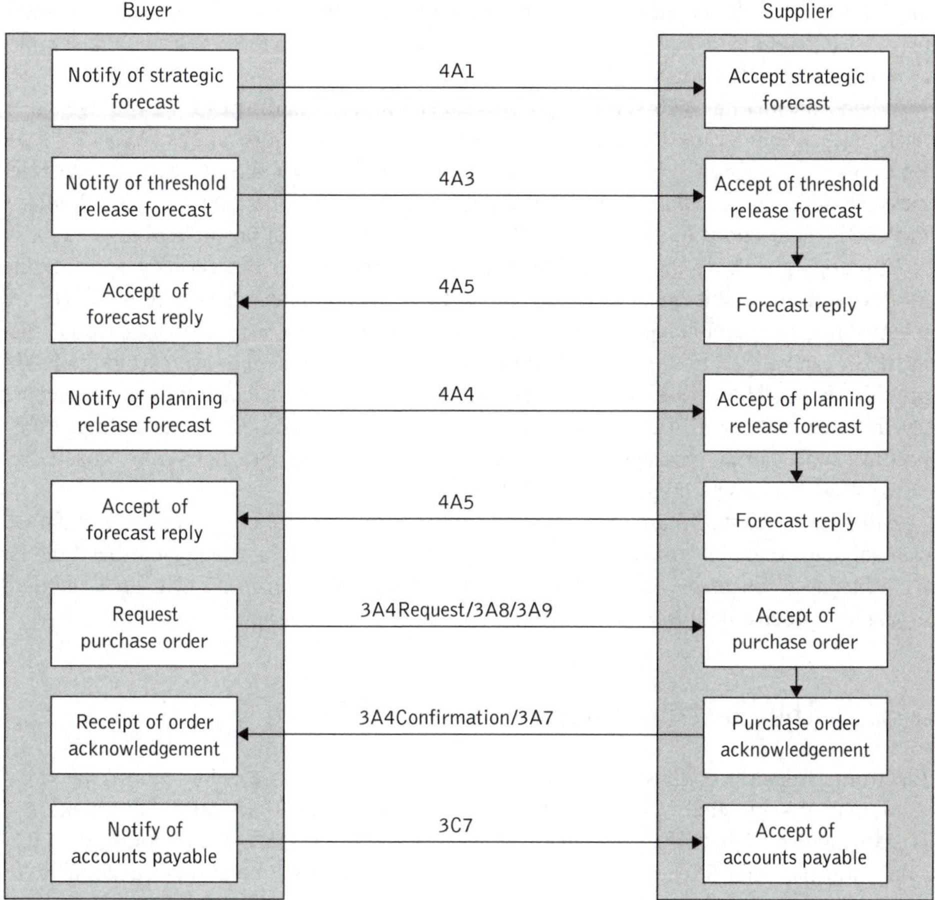

Figure 14.6 Combining demand forecast and order management processes
Source: [RosettaNet 2004]

problems, e-business interactions require standardization at an even higher level (standardized processes, messages, vocabulary, and choreography) than what is currently offered by current Web services technology. It is anticipated that Web services will initially take advantage of the standardization provided by RosettaNet, e.g., business document formats developed by RosettaNet. In this way Web services can permit e-business interactions among multiple partners directly through their applications during the same standardized process, enabling commonly understood concepts such as production balancing between partners and suppliers within or across a supply chain. They will also permit activities such as simultaneously sharing the same purchase order between the supplier, a financial organization, and a carrier to validate all facets of completing an order at once, enabling each participant to work with its relevant portions of the interaction.

RosettaNet can also leverage Web services technology in several ways. Specifically, Web services, itself a standards-based technology, could be incorporated as the underlying infrastructure to enable the deployment of RosettaNet-compliant documents directly onto the Internet, in full accordance with the RosettaNet architecture. RosettaNet e-business processes could then be advertised, discovered, and accessed in the similar public settings as other services [RosettaNet 2003].

When considering Web services as an implementation platform for RosettaNet, it is fairly easy to model the PIP receipt and messages as WSDL operations [Masud 2003]. RosettaNet messages can be mapped to the types definitions of WSDL, while RosettaNet message definitions, including message names, can be mapped to the message definitions in WSDL. The actions in a RosettaNet PIP are mapped to operations in WSDL.

Choreography from the RosettaNet PIP is implemented in the choreography of the abstract and executable business process in BPEL. Exception messages from the RNIF are mapped to the exception handling mechanisms of BPEL. The `<partnerLink>` construct in BPEL can be used to implement PIP partner roles. The messaging layer from the RNIF provides methods for packing and unpacking messages and transporting them in a secure and reliable manner. BPEL and WSDL provide their own methods for encoding, transporting, and securing messages. The workaround is to use best practices from RosettaNet in the Web services paradigm [Masud 2003].

BPEL and RosettaNet are ideally suited for use as a powerful combination, with BPEL as a language to define e-business processes, and RosettaNet to create standardized industry e-business processes. It is conceivable that RosettaNet can use BPEL as a standard e-business process definition language to describe its e-business processes.

14.3.3 The Electronic Business XML initiative

Electronic Business eXtensible Markup Language (ebXML) is a collection of specifications that was initiated by a consortium of businesses, vendors, and governments and is sponsored by UN/CEFACT (United Nations Center for Trade Facilitation and Electronic Business and Structured Information Standards). ebXML consists of a set of XML document type definitions that are common for business-to-business (ANSI X12 EDI) transactions across most industries. Its purpose is to preserve and extend the EDI infrastructure, by leveraging semantics and structure of EDI standards such as X12 and EDIFACT.

The vision of ebXML is to create a single global electronic marketplace where enterprises of any size and in any geographical location can meet and conduct business with each other through the exchange of XML-based messages. To facilitate this, ebXML provides an infrastructure for data communication interoperability, a semantic framework for commercial interoperability, and a mechanism that allows enterprises to find, establish a relationship, and conduct business with each other.

ebXML expresses in a common way several business concepts and constructs, e.g., descriptions of businesses, products, and individuals, measurements, date, time, location, currencies, business classification codes, and so on, which apply to all business domains and are across vendors. A complete business integration solution along the lines of ebXML requires: standardized tags (metadata), for each industry sector; a means for mapping between different metadata descriptions; and means for processing XML documents and invoking business applications and services provided by business processes and workflows.

14.3.3.1 The ebXML reference architecture

The ebXML initiative strives to create a single global electronic marketplace where enterprises of any size and in any geographical location can meet and conduct business with each other through the exchange of XML-based messages. ebXML tackles this problem at two levels:

- At a high level, ebXML identified common cross-industry business processes that characterized business transactions, and defined a structure of those processes that enabled development of a business process specification schema (BPSS). Business processes identify the parties conducting business, their specific roles, the interactions among the parties, the flow of messages in those interactions, and major pieces of data carried in those messages.
- At a more detailed level, ebXML defined core components with perhaps the most potential impact on e-business applications. Core components address semantic interoperability at the level of individual data items, seeking a way to bridge the individual industry terminologies, much as ebXML business processes work at a high level.

It is convenient to think of ebXML in terms of its reference architecture that contains its architectural elements (components) and the systems analysis and development methodology. The latter is referred to as the *process architecture* and has the purpose to provide an analysis and development methodology for the reference architecture.

The ebXML reference architecture is composed of the following five major architectural components [Clark 2001]: messaging service, registry and repository, trading partner information, business process specification schema, and core components. The lower-level layers in this stack support lower-level functionality, e.g., computer processing and message transport details or registry functions, required for the implementation of the higher-level components.

Messaging service. This provides a standard way to exchange business messages between organizations. It provides for means to exchange a payload, which may or may not be an XML business document or traditional and encrypted payloads, over multiple communications services, e.g., SMTP or HTTP, reliably and securely. It also provides means to route a payload to the appropriate internal application once an organization has received it.

The ebXML messaging service evolved into a sophisticated integration component that not only exchanges messages but also checks trading partner profiles to ensure that the exchanges conform to the business agreements and are being routed accordingly. In the latest version it can also perform business rule checking services and interact with Web-services-based components that conform to the ebXML exchange requirements [Webber 2004].

Registry and repository. An ebXML-compliant registry is a component that maintains an interface to metadata for a registered item. It provides a set of services that enable the sharing of information between trading partners. An ebXML-compliant registry is capable of representing a large range of data objects including XML schemas, business process descriptions, ebXML core components, UML models, generic trading partner information, and software components.

The ebXML registry is a document-based e-business registry that also captures descriptive information about each document in the form of metadata. The registry not only holds the ebXML base reference specifications, but also the business process and information meta-models developed by industry groups, SMEs, and other organizations. These meta-models are XML structures that may utilize a classification system and are compatible with the registry and repository architecture requirements. In order to store the models they are converted from UML to XML.

Examples of items in the registry might be XML schemas of business documents, definitions of library components for business process modeling, and trading partner agreements. Both the documents and their associated metadata are stored in the repository. Clients can access the content of the ebXML registry through the registry service interface (APIs exposed by registry services).

Trading partner information. This is known also as the Collaboration Protocol Profile (CPP) and Collaboration Protocol Agreement (CPA). The CPP/CPA defines the capabilities of a trading partner to perform a data interchange and how this data interchange agreement can be formed between two trading partners.

The CPP provides the definition (XML schema) of an XML document that specifies the details of how an organization is able to conduct business electronically. The CPP is published to the ebXML registry and outlines supported technology binding details. The main purpose of the CPP is to ensure interoperability between trading partners relying on the ebXML framework from possibly disparate vendors.

Some of the message exchange details defined by the CPP include specifics such as transport protocol mechanisms, message reliability mechanisms, transport security mechanisms, trust artifacts such as X.509 certificates, and message-level security policy information. In addition to implementation details, the CPP also refers to the set of supported business collaborations that define the supported business transactions.

The CPA is a machine-interpretable version of a trading partner agreement specifying both the technical and business-related agreements. The CPA specifies the details of how two organizations have agreed to conduct business electronically and is formed by combining the CPPs of the two organizations.

Business process specification schema (BPSS). The BPSS of ebXML [Clark 2001] is a relatively simple schema that provides a standard framework for public business process specification. It aims to support the specification of business transactions and their choreography into business collaborations. As such, it works with the ebXML CPP and CPA specifications to bridge the gap between business process modeling and the configuration of ebXML-compliant software, e.g. an ebXML business service interface.

The BPSS provides the definition (in the form of an XML document) that describes how documents can be exchanged between trading organizations. While the CPP/CPA deals with the technical aspects of how to conduct business electronically, the BPSS deals with the actual business process. It identifies such objects as the overall business process, the roles, transactions, identification of the business documents used (the DTDs or schemas), document flow, legal aspects, security aspects, business-level acknowledgements, and status. A BPSS can be used by a software application to configure the business details of conducting business electronically with another organization.

ebXML business processes define the ways in which trading partners engage each other, from the point of configuring their respective systems to actually do business. This is accomplished in such a way that business practices and interactions are represented both accurately and independently of any specific ways of implementing these transactions. Business process specifications are expressed as XML schemas (or DTDs) or in UML.

The business transaction is a key concept in ebXML BPSS. The BPSS supports a long-running business transaction model based on proven e-business transaction patterns used by standards such as RosettaNet. Business transactions within the BPSS are applied to the semantic business level with a simplistic protocol defined for the interaction between two parties (requesting and responding) and determination of success or failure of the transaction. An ebXML business transaction represents business document flows between requesting and responding partners. In any ebXML business transaction there always is a requesting business document, and, optionally, a responding business document. Each business transaction request or response may require that a receipt acknowledgement be returned to the sender. For contract-forming transactions such as purchase order requests, an acceptance acknowledgement may need to be returned to the requester. Time constraints can be applied to the return of responses and acknowledgements.

```
<BusinessTransaction name="Create Order">
    <RequestingBusinessActivity name="SendOrder"
      isNonRepudiationRequired="true"
      timeToAcknowledgeReceipt="P2D"
      timeToAcknowledgeAcceptance="P3D">
    <DocumentEnvelope businessDocument="Purchase Order"/>
    </RequestingBusinessActivity>
    <RespondingBusinessActivity name="SendPOAcknowledgement"
       isNonRepudiationRequired="true"
       timeToAcknowledgeReceipt="P5D">
       <DocumentEnvelope isPositiveResponse="true"
          businessDocument="PO Acknowledgement"/>
     </RespondingBusinessActivity>
</BusinessTransaction>
```

Listing 14.1 Sample ebXML transaction

An ebXML business transaction can be viewed as a type declaration, while business transaction activities (which reference to a unique business transaction type) are the usage of this transaction within a particular choreography. Listing 14.1 defines a business transaction called *create order*. This transaction stipulates that if a supplier accepts a purchase order from a customer, this acceptance is a binding legal agreement for the supplier to deliver the requested products or services to the customer at an agreed price and time, and for the customer to pay the supplier following delivery. The various messages and interactions sent between these external businesses constitute a binding contract between both parties. The BPSS therefore includes the concepts of time periods for business response, plus non-repudiation: neither party can deny its legal obligations to the other party once the purchase order has been issued and accepted. In Listing 14.1 the request message is specified as part of the <RequestingBusinessActivity> element, and the possible response messages are specified as part of the <RespondingBusinessActivity> element. A responding document envelope has a property <isPositiveResponse> that indicates the intent of the response from the respondent's perspective. This property is related to the business failure of a transaction. Ultimately, it is the responsibility of the requestor to identify whether a transaction has been successful by looking at all its aspects (timeouts, signals, and so on). To define the commercial and legal nature of this transaction, the <RequestingBusinessActivity> element requires non-repudiation with the properties *timeToAcknowledgeReceipt="P2D"* and *timeToAcknowledge-Acceptance="P3D"* (where "P2D" is a W3C Schema syntax standard that means Period=2 Days and P3D means Period=3 Days). These periods are all measured from the original sending of the request.

A BPSS business collaboration is essentially the specification of business transaction activities between the two partners, their associated document flow, and the choreography of these business transaction activities. BPSS describes public processes as collaborations between roles, with each role abstractly representing a trading partner. The business collaboration specifies all the business messages that are exchanged between two trading partners, their content, and their precise sequence and timing. All collaborations are composed of combinations of atomic transactions, each between two parties. There are two types of collaborations: binary collaborations and multi-party collaborations. Multi-party collaborations are decomposed to binary collaborations. The sequencing rules contained in a collaboration definition are not between messages but between business transaction activities.

```
<BinaryCollaboration name="Product Fulfillment"
                            timeToPerform="P5D">
  <Documentation>
     timeToPerform = Period: 5 days from start of transaction
  </Documentation>
  <InitiatingRole name="buyer"/>
  <RespondingRole name="seller"/>
  <!-- Transaction: buyer to create an order with seller -->
  <BusinessTransactionActivity name="Create Order"
     businessTransaction="Create Order"
     fromAuthorizedRole="buyer"
     toAuthorizedRole="seller"
     isLegallyBinding="true" />
  <!-- Transaction: buyer to notify seller in case of advance
    shipment -->
  <BusinessTransactionActivity name="Notify Shipment"
     businessTransaction="Notify of advance shipment"
     fromAuthorizedRole="buyer" toAuthorizedRole="seller"/>
</BinaryCollaboration>
```

Listing 14.2 Sample ebXML business collaboration

Listing 14.2 defines a binary collaboration called fulfillment. This collaboration involves a buyer in the initiating role and a seller in the responding role. The collaboration involves two transactions, one creating an order (defined in Listing 14.1) and one defining notification of shipment. In this listing, the transactions are described by the `<BusinessTransactionActivity>` elements and their attributes. These two elements define the names of the two transactions as well as the authorized roles from the sender (from) and recipient (to). If necessary, additional transactions can be added to this binary collaboration to complete the entire data interchange between the buyer and the seller.

- *Core components:* ebXML gives particular attention to business objects that appear in multiple domains, and calls the multiple reusable data items that cut across many industries *core components*. A core component captures information about a business concept, and relationships between that concept and other business concepts. A core component is a piece of basic business information that is designed to take into account commonality across industry business processes and can thus be used to facilitate many different processes across different industry sectors. In the most basic sense a core component is syntax/domain neutral, as it has no business semantics associated with it. Some examples of core components are "date of purchase order," "sales tax," and "total amount." A number of core components can be aggregated to form a building block used to support ebXML business transactions and business processes.

Figure 14.7 illustrates how the elements of the ebXML infrastructure may interact with each other. The CPA and CPP provide means to identify a business process specification governing how the parties do business and parameters for using the ebXML messaging service, but these are both optional and are not required. The BPSS may specify how services offered by the messaging service (such as signaling acknowledgements or requesting digital signatures) are used in the conduct of a business process. The BPSS document is incorporated with or referenced by the ebXML trading partner CPP and CPA. Each CPP declares its support for one or more roles within the BPSS, documented by UML use case diagrams. Within these CPP profiles and CPA agreements are added further technical parameters that result in a full specification of the run-time by ebXML Business Service Interface software at each trading partner. The CPP, CPA, and BPSS may be stored in an ebXML-compliant registry.

The ebXML Message Service Specification provides the infrastructure for message/signal identification, typing, and integrity, as well as placing any one message in sequence with respect to other messages in the choreography. In addition, all communications with the registry must use the ebXML messaging service. The messaging services may be used completely independently, although a message header may contain a reference to a CPA.

14.3.3.2 ebXML functional phases

Three functional phases are defined by the ebXML technical architecture [Clark 2001]: the implementation phase, discovery and retrieval phase, and run-time phase. Each of these phases carries with it its own requirements and processes. The first two phases

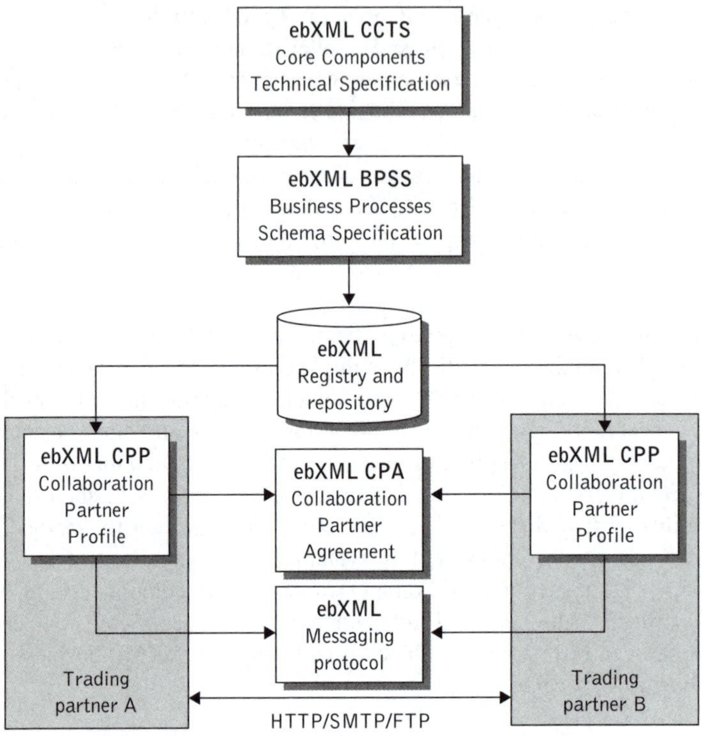

Figure 14.7 Interaction ebXML infrastructure elements

of implementation and retrieval represent a handshake mechanism, while the final phase represents the actual units of business.

Implementation phase. The implementation phase of ebXML is considered the time when a trading partner is making an active decision to do business using the ebXML framework. As shown in Figure 14.8, this phase consists of three steps: request information, implement the ebXML system, and publish the business profile.

The first step in the implementation phase is to request the ebXML specifications (business processes, business scenarios) and understand them. In this phase the trading partner will analyze its business processes in terms of the generalizations provided by the ebXML specification. Subsequently, the trading partner must decide which of its business processes it would implement in accordance with the ebXML specification. During this phase, an actual ebXML implementation must be produced, either built in-house from the core ebXML specifications or obtained from a third-party vendor. The result of the implementation phase is a working ebXML framework including a set of published business processes and interfaces. Once the system is built, the organization is ready to conduct business with other organizations. To achieve this, it needs to publish its profile as a CPP to the ebXML repository for other organizations to discover. As already stated, the CPP describes specific business processes and technology details, including security, transport, and reliability information. Once the CPP is published to the ebXML repository, other

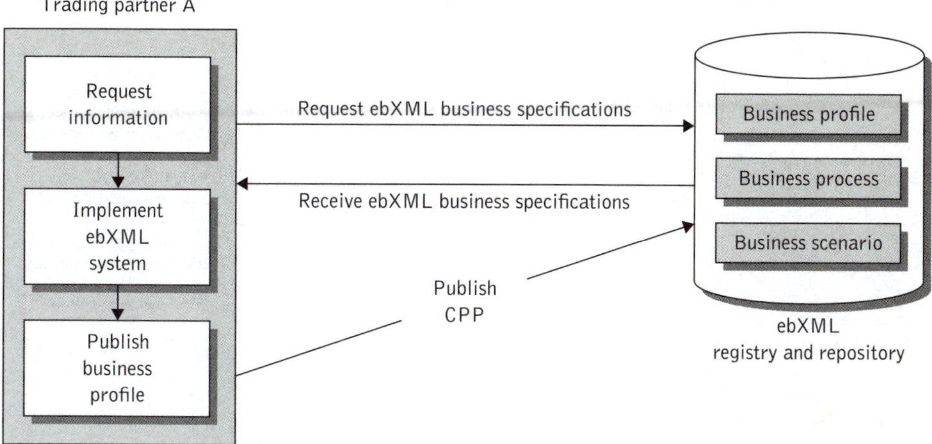

Figure 14.8 Implementation phase

organizations can access it and learn about the capabilities of the organization that published it.

Discovery and retrieval phase. The discovery and retrieval phase of ebXML involves trading partners using the registry to discover business processes and interfaces published by other trading partners. Typically, the CPP for a specific partner or set of partners is exchanged at this time. The specific details denoted in the CPP are used as a basis for messages exchanged during the run-time phase. Figure 14.9 shows two trading partners discovering each other's CPP documents. As shown in Figure 14.9, each trading partner derives the CPA by performing an intersection between each of the partner's CPP instances. The CPA is a special business agreement tied to a specific transactional conversation and makes explicit requirements derived from the intersection of the various CPP instances published by each of the trading partners.

Run-time phase. The last ebXML functional phase is the run-time phase, which concerns itself with the conduct of actual business transactions and choreography of messages exchanged between partners. From the previous phase, the CPP instances published by each participating trading partner are narrowed to form a CPA. As shown in Figure 14.9, the CPA thus contains the negotiated terms and implementation contracts agreed by both trading partners. Before actual ebXML messages are exchanged and before the transaction executes, the CPA instances should match on both ends of the transaction.

Figure 14.10 illustrates that the run-time phase includes three simple steps. In step 1 each trading partner is responsible for obtaining the necessary CPP document for the business partner it would like to engage. In most cases the CPP will be retrieved from an ebXML registry. In step 2, each partner derives the CPA, which makes explicit the range of choices offered in the CPP. Finally, in step 3, the partners can begin business transactions under the governance of the CPA. In this sense there is a policy relation between the ebXML messaging service messages and the derived CPA.

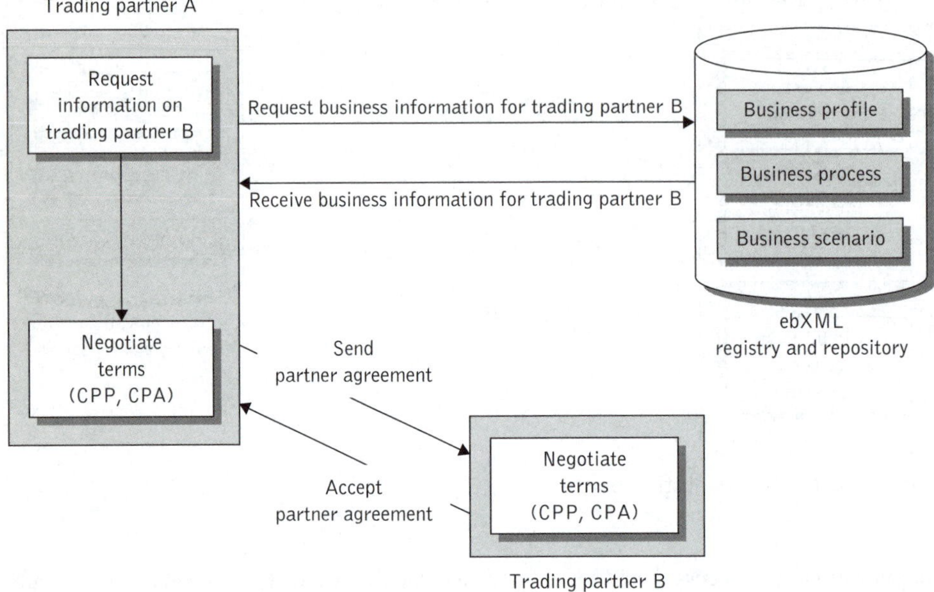

Figure 14.9 Discovery and retrieval phase

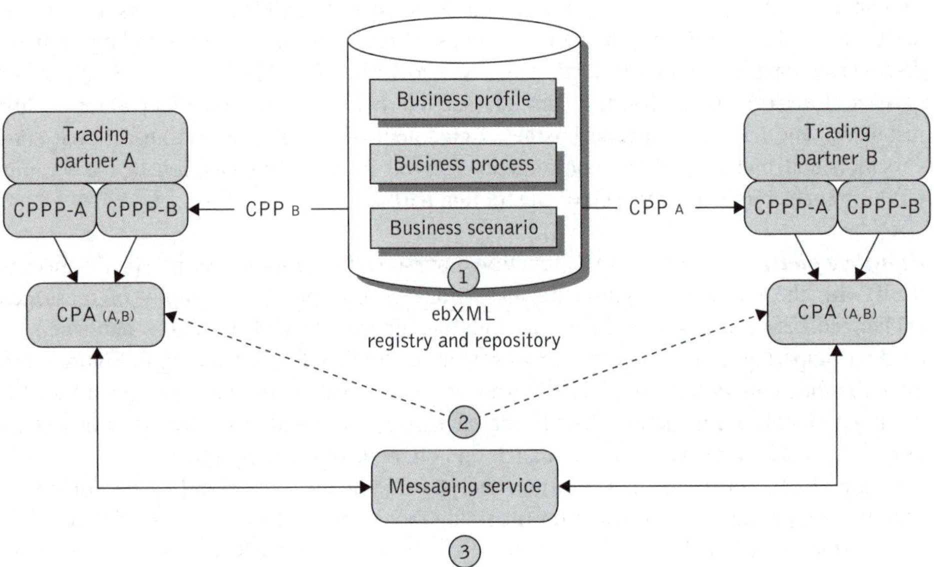

Figure 14.10 Run-time phase

14.3.3.3 ebXML and Web services

As both ebXML and Web services have the same foundational technologies (XML), they have many things in common. Their difference lies in the fact that ebXML provides a complete solution in the e-business integration domain, while Web services are considered as an e-business enabling infrastructure and are broader in scope and include application and e-business integration as well as traditional Web interactions. ebXML addresses several of the layers in the Web services technology stack. At the core layers, the ebXML messaging specification provides secure, reliable communication on any transport, uses SOAP for packaging, and defines a rich set of metadata for carrying out e-business transactions between trading partners [Patil 2003]. At the higher-level layers and in particular the description level, the ebXML collaboration protocol describes the trading partner's business services, the concrete binding where the service can be addressed, and so on. BPSS also defines the collaboration aspects between processes and, thereby, how services are orchestrated. The collaboration protocol covers the business and service-level agreements. Finally, at the publication and discovery level, the ebXML registry allows publication, sharing, and discovery of different business artifacts such as trading partner information, business process definitions, and business document types. When considering Web services as an implementation platform for ebXML, it is fairly easy to use WSDL to describe CPP. BPEL can also be used to implement the BPSS. It can be used to describe the overall business processes and then BPEL can be used to define components in the BPSS. Predefined BPEL components can be included into BPSS diagrams as nodes.

Recently, OASIS (Organization for the Advancement of Structured Information Systems) announced plans to develop an advanced e-business architecture that builds on ebXML and other Web services technology. The new OASIS Electronic Business Service-Oriented Architecture (ebSOA) Technical Committee (http://www.oasis-open.org/committees/) uses ebXML Technical Architecture v1.04 as a starting point for describing an SOA and practical implementation techniques that take into account work done in several standards development organizations including OASIS, the W3C, ISO, UN/CEFACT, and others. The goal of the ebSOA specification is to describe a high-level architecture blueprint and a set of accompanying patterns, which in turn describes an infrastructure facilitating electronic business on a global scale in a secure, reliable, and consistent manner. This will be done in a manner that is not dependent on either ebXML or Web services standards, yet may allow for each to be used in conjunction with another for implementation.

14.4 XML in vertical organizations

Today, trading exchanges are forming at a rapid pace and as a result several industry-specific partnerships have been announced for just about every major manufacturing sector of the economy. The number of vertical industry organizations developing XML data formats that their members can use to interchange information is potentially quite large. Many vertical industry standards groups are working on domain-specific XML standards, including the Automotive Industry Action Group, the Open Travel Alliance, the Association for Retail Technology Standards, Health Care and Medical Equipment, and the ACORD standards group for the insurance industry, and so forth. Due to the relatively low barriers to entry, significant cost savings that come from reduced transaction costs and reduced processing costs, the automation of supply chains, and increased productivity, such on-line marketplaces attract smaller companies that establish partnerships with them.

Most e-marketplaces provide common business process definitions (promoting industry-based standards through XML formats and defined APIs) and a standard terminology to combat semantic interoperability problems. This results in a universal foundation for conducting global electronic business, ensuring the integrity of fast, clean business transactions, guaranteeing common semantics and data integrity across the Internet, backed with the industry representation. Such vertical e-marketplaces are gradually transforming into collaborative trading communities by moving in two directions. First, they handle the full trading lifecycle – from procurement, to supply-chain management, to customer relationship management – spanning raw materials suppliers to consumers. Second, they will move into other product and materials channels, including direct replenishment.

The five recent interesting developments in industry-wide collaboration and industry-based standards that we shall describe in this section come from the aviation industry, automotive industry, retail grocery industry, travel industry and the insurance industry and represent established organizations with considerable membership and traction. These are indicative of the efforts that are currently occurring also in other industry domains.

Aviation industry. Aeroxchange (**www.aeroxchange.com**) is an e-business solutions provider and e-marketplace for the global aviation industry. Aeroxchange includes over 30 airlines, among them Air Canada, Air New Zealand, Cathay Pacific Airways, FedEx, Japan Airlines, KLM, Lufthansa, Northwest Airlines, Scandinavian Airlines, Singapore Airlines, and others, and hundreds of suppliers, all dedicated to maximizing efficiency across the complex aviation supply chain. Aeroxchange was founded to develop and implement next-generation technology that creates value for all trading partners in the aviation supply chain. Its products and services streamline operations and generate efficiencies for all its members.

Aeroxchange provides an open, neutral marketplace for commerce in the aviation supply chain. Aeroxchange is committed to reducing the inefficiencies in the current environment that are created by the different channels of communication between airlines and their suppliers by consolidating EDI, XML, and Web-based communications into a single hub, thus reducing the need for manual communication in the transaction lifecycle.

Aeroxchange provides e-negotiation services, e-procurement, and support services. E-negotiation services include a Web-based negotiation tool, which supports Request for Quotation, Auction and Offer/Counter Offer, and services that extend customers' reach in repair, technical parts, commercial items, catering, and airport services. Aeroxchange also provides an advanced repair service rich with features that create efficiencies for buyers and sellers throughout the service order lifecycle.

Automotive industry. In the automotive distribution value chain the Standards for Technology in Automotive Retail or STAR (**www.starstandard.org**), a non-profit, automotive-industry-wide group, is creating standards for the data elements and transmission format for communication among manufacturers, dealers, and retail system providers. This organization addresses the data interchange and electronic business requirements for distribution of automotive equipment. The aim of the STAR alliance is to define the standard XML message for dealer to original equipment manufacturer business transactions such as parts order, sales lead, and credit application, define a standard IT infrastructure based on ebXML to support these messages between dealers and original equipment manufacturers, and standardize the IT infrastructure at dealerships.

A major focus of STAR is to simplify business transaction processing as this means a more efficient retail automotive industry and eventually more satisfied buyers. To achieve this, STAR has developed a large number of automated tools for highly specific retail processes such as parts locating, labor cost lookups, vehicle model codes, and scheduling service appointments. These business processes are developed in a standard way and are made available to manufacturers, retailers, and retail system providers.

Retail grocery industry. The goal of the Uniform Code Council's (UCC's) retail grocery industry, known as UCCnet (**www.uccnet.org**), is to create a trading community designed to interconnect trading partners with electronic markets and provide enhanced services for its subscribers. UCCnet provides access to industry standards through the adoption of XML technologies and business process models defined by the current trading community. UCCnet shares XML, schemas, process models, and functional and technical specifications with all compliant exchanges and solution providers, standardizing the functionality across a wide range of solutions. It also facilitates data-driven collaboration among trading partners by providing common data definitions, standard formats for data communication, and a data synchronization that ensures that supply-chain information and business processes are correct and updated with the enterprise information systems of trading partners.

Travel industry. To harness the Internet along with established distribution channels, the travel industry also has common technical specifications for the electronic communication of information. The OpenTravel Alliance or OTA (**www.opentravel.org**) brings together all sectors of the travel industry to accomplish this. OTA has specified a set of standard business processes and standard terminology for searching for availability and booking a reservation in the airline, hotel, and car rental industry, as well as the purchase of travel insurance in conjunction with these services. OTA specifications use XML for structured data messages to be exchanged over the Internet or other means of transport. This specification relies upon the work of other standards developing organizations; specifically, the ebXML initiative, and the work of the W3C. OTA specifications also reference standards developed by the ISO, and the International Air Transport Association (IATA), that are used by the travel industry to provide standardized message structures and data for the travel industry. The OpenTravel specifications serve as a common language for travel-related terminology and a mechanism for promoting the seamless exchange of information across all travel industry segments. OTA members are organizations that represent all segments of the travel industry, along with key technology and services suppliers.

Insurance industry. The Association for Cooperative Operations Research and Development or ACORD (**www.acord.org**) is an insurance association that facilitates the development and use of standards for the insurance, reinsurance, and related financial services industries. Affiliated with ACORD are hundreds of insurance and reinsurance companies, and thousands of agents and brokers, related financial services organizations, software providers, and industry organizations. ACORD accomplishes its mission by remaining an objective, independent advocate for sharing information among diverse platforms and by pursuing standards-based, straight-through processing. Through these relationships, ACORD standards are being mapped and harmonized to other industry and cross-industry standards implemented in various countries and regions throughout the world. ACORD's goal is to focus progressively on each link in the insurance value chain to respond to the industry's most pressing business needs. ACORD's participation in global cross-industry groups ensures standards interoperability between industries, and its joint initiatives and working groups seek to achieve interoperability within the insurance and financial services while also preventing duplication of standard-setting efforts.

14.5 Summary

The vision of e-business concentrates on enterprises that will have access to a much broader range of trading partners to interact and collaborate and will build supply-responsive trading networks. Using novel technologies such as Web services and business process management, traditional supply chains are transformed to adaptive supply-chain networks that have the highest visibility, greatest velocity, and best ability to manage product demand and variability.

Within trading networks business processes should be able to capture the information and exchange requirements, identifying the timing, sequence, and purpose of each business collaboration and information exchange. This is the aim of a business protocol, which is associated with business processes and governs the exchange of business information and messages between trading partners across differing enterprise information systems, middleware platforms, and organizations. A business protocol captures the exchange of business information and message exchange requirements, identifying the timing, sequence, and purpose of each business collaboration and information exchange.

Two important standards in the world of e-business are RosettaNet and ebXML that enjoy wide adoption and industry backing. RosettaNet is a widely adopted standard that provides message content, choreography and transport specifications, and standards development processes that target the high-technology manufacturing industry. ebXML is a set of standards developed to enable enterprises to conduct business over the Internet. Its stated objective is similar to RosettaNet, although the specific standards developed are different. It produces specifications for messaging, registries, and business processes. Unlike RosettaNet, ebXML is a horizontal standard, i.e., it is not targeted at any particular industry. Currently, there is complementarity between RosettaNet and ebXML and convergence between these two initiatives is technically feasible, advantageous, and likely at some stage in the future.

RosettaNet, ebXML, and Web services have many things in common. RosettaNet and ebXML both consider Web services as an enabling infrastructure; although they are broader in scope, their focus is on application and e-business integration as well as traditional Web interactions.

Review questions

- What is the purpose of a business ecosystem? What are its main building blocks?
- What are the most common semantic problems at the business process level?
- What kind of functionality should a common business standard/protocol provide to address these semantic problems?
- Briefly describe the functions and major characteristics of an EDI system.
- What are the major drawbacks of EDI with respect to e-business?
- What is the purpose of RosettaNet and what are its major architectural elements?
- What is the purpose of partner interface processes in RosettaNet?
- How does the RosettaNet standard relate to Web services?
- What is the purpose of ebXML?
- What are the major architectural elements of the ebXML reference architecture?
- Describe the major characteristics of ebXML processes and transactions.
- What are the major differences between RosettaNet and ebXML?

Exercises

14.1 Use Figure 14.6 as a basis to develop a simple business model involving a number of RosettaNet PIPs in which a supplier develops replenishment plans for consignment inventory at the buyer's side. As in the case of Figure 14.6, demand information is provided using PIP4A3 or 4A4. Product receipt and inventory information is notified using PIP4B2 and PIP4C1, respectively, between consignment warehouses and suppliers. The other PIPs used in this solution are similar to those used in Figure 14.6. Visit the RosettaNet site (**www.rosettanet.org**) to find more about the definition and usage of these PIPs.

14.2 Modify the scenario in the previous exercise to develop a business model in which a purchase order recipient (supplier) supplies the required stock to a third-party-owned warehouse on the basis of demand information included in purchase orders. The buyer then retrieves the required stock from the warehouse and issues a receipt notification using PIP4B2 to report the status of a received shipment to the warehouse and the supplier.

14.3 Use RosettaNet PIPs to develop a general business model that describes an integrated logistics scenario involving a customer, suppliers, and a logistics service provider. This simplified model consists of forecast notification, forecast acceptance, inventory reporting, shipment receipt, request and fulfill demand, consumption and invoice notification processes. To develop this scenario you need to use the

PIPs described in the following. PIP4A2 "Notify of Embedded Release Forecast" supports a process in which a forecast owner sends forecast data to a forecast recipient. PIP4A5 "Notify of Forecast Reply" provides visibility of available forecasted product quantity between two trading partners. PIP4C1 "Distribute Inventory Report" supports a process in which an inventory information provider reports the status of the inventory to an inventory information user. PIP4B2 "Notify of Shipment Receipt" supports a process used by a consignee to report the status of a received shipment to another interested party, such as a shipper. PIP3B2 "Notify of Advance Shipment" allows a shipper to notify a receiver that a shipment has been assigned. This notification is often a part of the shipment process. PIP3C3 "Notify of Invoice" enables a provider to invoice another party, such as a buyer or financing processor, for goods or services performed.

14.4 The following exercises involve the encoding of ebXML business transactions:

(a) Encode a simple purchase order business transaction in ebXML with a requesting and responding business activity and an attached purchase order document.

(b) Encode a simple delivery notification business transaction in ebXML with a receipt and an acknowledgement for a purchase order. Another requirement is that this transaction should be performed within 3 days.

14.5 Encode a binary collaboration in ebXML regarding the fulfillment of a purchase order. The buyer should be the initiator of this binary collaboration and the seller should act as a responder. The binary collaboration could contain two simple transactions: a create PO transaction and a notify shipment transaction.

14.6 Encode a binary collaboration in ebXML involving the insurance of a given shipment. A client may request the insurance of a shipment; following this the insurer then creates a shipment contact, which is either accepted or rejected by the client.

PART VIII

Service design and development

CHAPTER 15

Web services development lifecycle

Learning objectives

SOA is not simply about deploying software; it also requires that organizations evaluate their business models, come up with service-oriented analysis and design techniques, deployment and support plans, and carefully evaluate partner/customer/supplier relationships. Since SOA is based on open standards and is frequently realized using Web services, developing meaningful services and business process specifications is an important requirement for SOA applications that leverage Web services. A sound development methodology is required for this purpose.

This chapter provides an overview of the methods and techniques that can be used in service-oriented development. The aim of this chapter is to examine a services development methodology and review the range of elements in this methodology. After completing this chapter readers will understand the following key concepts:

- The nature of software development methodologies.
- Differences between conventional and service-oriented development methodologies.
- Milestones of service-oriented design and development.
- Qualities of service-oriented design and development.
- Phases in a service-oriented design and development methodology.
- Services analysis and design techniques.
- Services governance and provisioning.

15.1 Why is a Web services development methodology needed?

The purpose of an SOA-based implementation is to provide an architectural shape in which business processes, information, and enterprise assets can be effectively (re)organized and (re)deployed to support and enable strategic plans and productivity levels that are required by modern business environments. The technology building blocks in an SOA are normally provided by Web services that have a published interface so that they can be discovered and communicate with each other. Service integration is vastly simplified by the use of standards that allow a common way for Web services to communicate so that an enterprise is able to free itself from the constrictions of having to manage business processes as defined by conventional software applications.

Many enterprises in their early use of SOA think that they can port existing components to act as Web services just by creating wrappers and leaving the underlying component untouched. Since component methodologies focus on the interface, many developers assume that these methodologies apply equally well to SOAs. Thus, introducing a thin SOAP/WSDL/UDDI veneer atop existing applications or components that implement Web services is by now widely practiced by the software industry. Yet, this is in no way sufficient to construct commercial-strength enterprise applications. Unless the nature of the component makes it suitable for use as a Web service, and most are not, it takes serious thought and redesign effort to properly deliver component functionality through a Web service. While relatively simple Web services may be effectively built that way, a methodology is of critical importance to specify, construct, refine, and customize highly volatile business processes from internally and externally available Web services. A common concern, though, is that enterprises are spending a significant amount of their time assembling applications that provide Web service functionality rather than worrying about the design principles that guide the development of Web services, the granularity of Web services, or the development of the components that implement them.

The challenge of SOA – and the key to achieving business value – is to elevate service enablement beyond just technology functions. The reality is that an SOA has limited value unless it encompasses disparate applications and platforms, and, most importantly, it moves beyond technology and is orchestrated and controlled in the context of business processes. Developers need to be offered a variety of different services and functions that they can combine at will to create the right set of automated one-of-a-kind processes that can distinctly differentiate themselves from those of competitors. New processes and alliances need to be routinely mapped to services that can be used, modified, built, or syndicated. This requires that business processes be easily designed, assembled, and modified. To achieve such requirements, the internal architecture of an SOA needs to evolve into a multi-tier, service-based system, often with a diversified technical implementation. This diversity is the result of a very broad spectrum of business and performance requirements as well as different execution and reuse contexts and calls for a sound services design and development methodology.

There is a clear need for SOA design methods that allow an organization to avoid the pitfalls of deploying an uncontrolled maze of services and provide a solid foundation for service enablement in an orderly fashion so that Web services can be efficiently used in

SOA-based business applications. However, from the outset, organizations face the challenge of where to start, what services are going to add immediate value, and how are they going to be used by the most important business functions. Identifying the services that are consumed by the most critical business processes in an organization, deciding how they can be assembled into useful business processes, how they can be managed, reused, priced, and metered, can be a daunting proposition. The challenge in selecting and following a services design and development methodology is to provide sufficient principles and regulations to deliver the software quality required for business success, while avoiding steps that waste time, squander productivity, and frustrate developers.

15.2 Web services development and related methodologies

The extent to which an organization has aligned its business and technology strategies is a key determinant of SOA readiness. Service-oriented development requires a well-thought-out strategy that considers the impact of SOA and Web services on technology and tools, organizational alignment, business methodology and process. Successful service-oriented development results in harmonizing the business processes that make internal operations run smoothly in an enterprise, and making these processes interact and collaborate effectively with customer and partner processes. This process harmony is best achieved through well-orchestrated collaboration among the various participants in any given business process.

Existing modeling disciplines such as object-oriented analysis and design (OOAD), component-based development (CBD), and business process modeling, although useful within their own scope, cannot be directly applied to service-oriented development. However, these software development paradigms can assist with the service-oriented development process as they provide sound practices that can support the identification and definition of appropriate abstractions within an SOA. In the following we briefly examine these software development paradigms and explain how they can be used in the context of service-oriented development.

OOAD allows designers to focus attention on units such as classes and objects, which match enterprise or business concepts, and provides modeling facilities to directly represent them. For small, self-contained applications OOAD can provide suitable solutions; however, it concentrates on green-field development and falls short of addressing the needs of large-scale development. The application of OOAD results in the practice of designing rich and complex interfaces on each object, which merely serves to tie the application into a finite set of possible operating modes that are impossible to unravel. The main issue with current object-oriented design practices in relation to service-oriented development is that its level of granularity is focused at the class level, which resides at too low a level of abstraction for business service modeling [Zimmermann 2004]. Strong associations such as inheritance create a rather tight coupling (and, consequently, a dependency) between the involved parties. In contrast, the service-oriented computing paradigm attempts to promote flexibility and agility through loose coupling.

Object-oriented development is an enabler of CBD, which offers a new approach to the design, construction, implementation, and evolution of software applications and provides an opportunity for greater reuse than what is possible with object-oriented development. CBD was devised to address the shortcomings of OOAD such as failure to address large-scale development and application integration problems. CBD introduces a software development approach where all aspects and phases of the development lifecycle, including analysis, design, construction, testing, and deployment, as well as the supporting technical infrastructure, are based on the concept of components [Herzum 2000]. In particular, CBD is a set of technologies, processes, guidelines, and techniques about how business systems should be conceived, analyzed, architected, designed, developed, and evolved. Obviously this approach focuses on its core concept, the business component concept.

Although both CBD and service-oriented computing offer a "separation of internal and external perspectives" and the motivation for both components and services is often expressed in terms of reusability, composability and flexibility, they are quite diverse in nature. In section 1.10 we explained that components and Web services present differences along the dimensions of type of communication, type of coupling, type of interface, type of invocation, and type of request brokering. However, in so far as development is concerned, they also differ fundamentally in the way that they approach flexibility and reusability. Web services are subject to continuous maintenance and improvement in scope and performance so that they can be offered to an ever-increasing number of clients. Providers achieve this by monitoring the use and quality of services and improving it. On the other hand, consumers of Web services have the ability to switch between alternative service implementations offered by diverse providers. The selection of a service is usually done dynamically on the basis of a set of policies. Use of installed components does not allow for the same kind of reuse and dynamic behavior. Moreover, the view that components are merely distributable objects, deployed on some middleware server, carries with it all the difficulties of object modeling and yet multiplies the complexity by increasing the scale of the model, let alone if models are extended across enterprise boundaries.

Business process modeling is a structured methodology for assessing opportunities to improve the business objectives of enterprises such as improving customer satisfaction, carrying out initiatives across an organization, and increasing competitiveness and productivity. It achieves this by systematically examining business processes, identifying ways to improve these processes, and addressing barriers that may be impeding their ability to achieve their business goals in the most efficient manner. The result is a practical action plan that provides a blueprint for achieving an organization's goals and implementing change, while respecting the enterprise's strategic mission.

Most of the first-generation business process methodologies, such as business process re-engineering, the IDEF0 – a standard for functional modeling (**http://www.idef.com/idef0.html**) – the DMAIC (Define–Measure–Analyze–Improve–Control) methodology (**http://www.isixsigma.com/me/dmaic/**), and the various methodologies of consulting companies, such as Catalysis, and those of the various vendors, such as ARIS, approach business process redesign in the same general way [Harmon 2003b]. They all rely on analyzing each new business process as if it were unique. One begins by defining the scope of the process to be analyzed, and then proceeds to decompose the process, identifying its major subprocesses, and then the subprocesses of those, identifying their major activities, and so on down to whatever level of granularity the designer chooses. Once the process is laid out in detail, the analysis team usually considers how to change it.

More interesting from a service-oriented design point of view are second-generation approaches to business modeling which began to emerge a few years ago. These emphasize methodologies that are based on best-in-class business practices and that target the analysis of supply-chain processes. The most notable methodology is the Supply-Chain Operations Reference (SCOR) Framework proposed by the Supply-Chain Council [Supply-Chain Council 2005]. SCOR is a modeling approach that provides standard guidelines for companies. These standard guidelines help to examine the configuration of their supply chains, and identify, and measure metrics in the supply chain. The SCOR model defines common supply-chain management processes, helps match them against "best practices" where deemed appropriate, and assists in improving supply-chain operations. It allows manufacturers, suppliers, distributors, and retailers with a framework to evaluate the effectiveness of their supply-chain operations and to target and measure specific process operations [Supply-Chain Council 2005]. Essentially the SCOR model is a process reference model in that it integrates the well-known concepts of business process re-engineering, benchmarking, and process measurement into a cross-functional framework.

Conventional development methodologies such as the ones that we reviewed so far do not address the three key elements of an SOA: services, service assemblies (composition), and components realizing services. These methodologies can only address part of the requirements of service-oriented computing applications. These practices fail when they attempt to develop service-oriented solutions while being applied independently of each other. Service-oriented design and development requires an interdisciplinary approach fusing elements of object-oriented and component design with elements of business modeling. OOAD and CBD can contribute general software architecture principles such as information hiding, modularization, and separation of concerns. On the other hand, business modeling can contribute conventions that help analyze the structuring of value chains and improve processes, help define amongst other things standardized business processes and operating procedures, and create a shared understanding of how a business functions so that workflow implementations are tested before design and implementation.

15.3 System development lifecycle

System development lifecycle (SDLC) is the overall process of designing and developing software systems through a multi-step process from investigation of initial requirements through analysis, design, implementation, and maintenance. All software development projects can be managed better when segmented into a hierarchy of chunks such as phases, stages, activities, and steps. Although there are many different models and methodologies, each generally consists of a series of defined phases or stages. There are also many variants, on the different models, with some people breaking down the phases while others are merging them. However, they all share a common objective: to form an overall picture of how software systems are developed and brought into production.

The simplest rendition of system development projects is the "waterfall" methodology. This methodology usually has five identifiable phases: analysis, design, implementation, testing, and maintenance. Further, it assumes that all requirements can be specified a priori and once a phase is completed, it cannot be re-entered again. Unfortunately, requirements grow and change throughout the software development process and beyond, calling for considerable feedback and iterative consultation. Thus, while the waterfall methodology offers an orderly structure for software development, it is inappropriate for large-scale and dynamic environments.

The next evolutionary step from the waterfall model is where the various steps are staged for multiple deliveries or handoffs. The ultimate evolution from the waterfall model is the spiral model, taking advantage of the fact that development projects work best when they are both incremental and iterative and where the development team is able to start small and benefit from enlightened trial and error along the way. The *spiral model* emphasizes the need to go back and reiterate earlier stages a number of times as the project progresses. It is actually a series of short waterfall cycles, each producing an early prototype representing a part of the entire project. This approach helps demonstrate a proof of concept early in the cycle, and it more accurately reflects the disorderly evolution of technology. The spiral methodology goes through successive risk analysis and planning, requirements analysis, engineering, and evaluation phases. The engineering phase of the spiral methodology involves design, implementation, and testing. The incremental and iterative nature of this methodology divides the software product into successive design and build activities, where sections of the software under development are created and tested separately. This approach will likely find errors in user requirements quickly, since user feedback is solicited for each stage and because code is tested soon after it is written. The spiral methodology promotes rapid prototyping, increased parallelism, and concurrency in design and build activities. It should nevertheless be planned methodically, with tasks and deliverables identified for each phase in the spiral.

A more recent software development process is the rational unified process (RUP) whose aim is to support the analysis and design of iterative software development. RUP encourages the use of components to assemble a system [Kruchten 2004]. RUP delivers proven best practices and a configurable architecture that enables software developers to select and deploy only the process components needed for each stage of a large-scale software development project. A large part of RUP is about developing and maintaining models of the system under development. The Unified Modeling Language (UML) is used as a graphical aid for this purpose. RUP includes a library of best practices for software engineering, covering everything from project management to detailed test guidance. Proven best practices for the RUP are based on the Capability Maturity Model (CMM) [Paulk 1993], which is a framework that describes the elements of an effective software process.

A key concept in RUP is its phases, which provide project milestones that ensure that iterations make progress and converge on a solution, rather than iterate indefinitely. Figure 15.1 describes the overall architecture of RUP and illustrates that RUP encompasses four broad phases: inception, elaboration, construction, and transition.

The goal of the inception phase is to achieve concurrence among all stakeholders on the lifecycle objectives for the project. The inception phase establishes that the project is worth doing and that one or more feasible candidate solutions exist. During the inception phase, a business case for the system is established and the software development project scope is delimited. The business case includes success criteria, risk assessment, and estimate of the resources needed, and a phase plan showing dates of major milestones [Royce 1998].

The purpose of the elaboration phase is to analyze the problem domain, establish a sound architectural foundation, develop the project plan, and to mitigate risks so that a

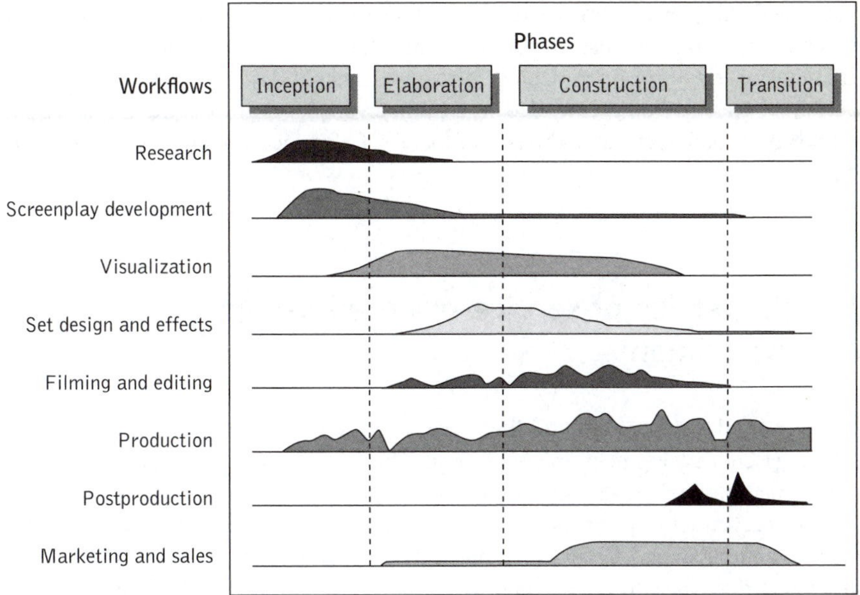

Figure 15.1 Architecture of RUP

single, high-fidelity solution can be identified with a predictable cost and schedule. Architectural decisions have to be made with an understanding of the entire system: its scope, major functionality, and non-functional requirements.

The goal of the construction phase is to achieve a production-quality release ready for its user community. All components and application features are developed and integrated into the software product, and all features are thoroughly tested. The construction phase emphasizes managing resources and controlling operations to optimize costs, schedules, and quality.

The purpose of the transition phase is to field the software product to the user community and provide adequate support. The transition phase is entered when a baseline (description of all the versions of artifacts that make up a product at any time) is mature enough to be deployed in the end-user domain. This typically requires that some usable subset of the system has been completed to an acceptable level of quality and that user documentation is available so that the transition to the user will provide positive results for all parties.

RUP has the principles of OOAD and CBD as its foundation, and therefore does not lend itself readily to be aligned to SOA design [Zimmermann 2004]. RUP views the architecture of a system in terms of the structure of its major components which interact via well-defined interfaces. Furthermore, these components are composed of increasingly smaller components down to a class level of granularity. In contrast, the architecture of an SOA generally comprises fully encapsulated and self-describing services that interact with each other and satisfy a generic business objective that can be easily mapped to a business process modeling solution. Nevertheless since RUP provides support for both the bottom-up and top-down development approaches by acknowledgement of existing design elements and through activities such as architectural analysis to identify architectural elements such as components, several of its milestones can be appropriately adjusted and fitted in the context of service-oriented solutions [Ganci 2006].

Currently, RUP is being extended in a number of places to provide guidance on the development of architectural and design models of a service-oriented solution [Johnston 2005].

15.4 Properties of service-oriented design and development

When software developers are building a service-oriented application, they must rely on a service-based development methodology. This methodology focuses on analyzing, designing, and producing an SOA in such a way that it aligns with business process interactions between trading partners in order to accomplish a common business goal, e.g., requisition and payment of a product, and stated functional and non-functional business requirements, e.g., performance, security, scalability, and so forth. Without a service-based development methodology, projects aiming at building SOA processes are doomed to be over time, violate quality criteria, incorporate designs that infringe basic principles (such as loose coupling), to be hard or virtually impossible to manage, and to be likely to result in systems that are notably intricate, time consuming, and costly to maintain.

Service-oriented solutions should be viewed as a choreographed set of service interactions. Adopting a service-oriented approach to solutions development necessitates a broader review of its impact on how solutions are designed; what it means to assemble them from disparate services; and how deployed services-oriented applications can evolve and be managed. This requires addressing common concerns such as the identification, specification, and realization of services, their flows and composition into processes, as well as the enterprise-scale components needed to realize them and ensure the required QoS.

SOA-based development is facilitated when we view the way that SOA operates as comprising a number of layers of abstract functionality, each with its own category of artifacts that is characterized by its own set of properties and relationships. Each layer helps organize SOA functionality at the most appropriate level of detail. This is illustrated in Figure 15.2, which is an elaboration and refinement of Figure 1.6, where the basic SOA model is divided into six major layers of abstraction: domains, business processes, business services, infrastructure services, service realizations, and operational systems. Starting from the top, each layer relies on its successor layer to accomplish its functional objectives. For instance, the business domain is described by a business model, which describes the business that an enterprise is engaged in. The business process layer provides the artifacts (namely, business processes) that collectively fulfill the functions of this business model. Similarly, design decisions or changes that affect a higher-level layer, such as the definition or modification of processes in the process layer, will most probably lead to cascade of changes in the lower-level layers.

The logical flow employed in the layered SOA development model usually focuses on a top-down, a bottom-up, or a meet-in-the-middle development approach. The top-down

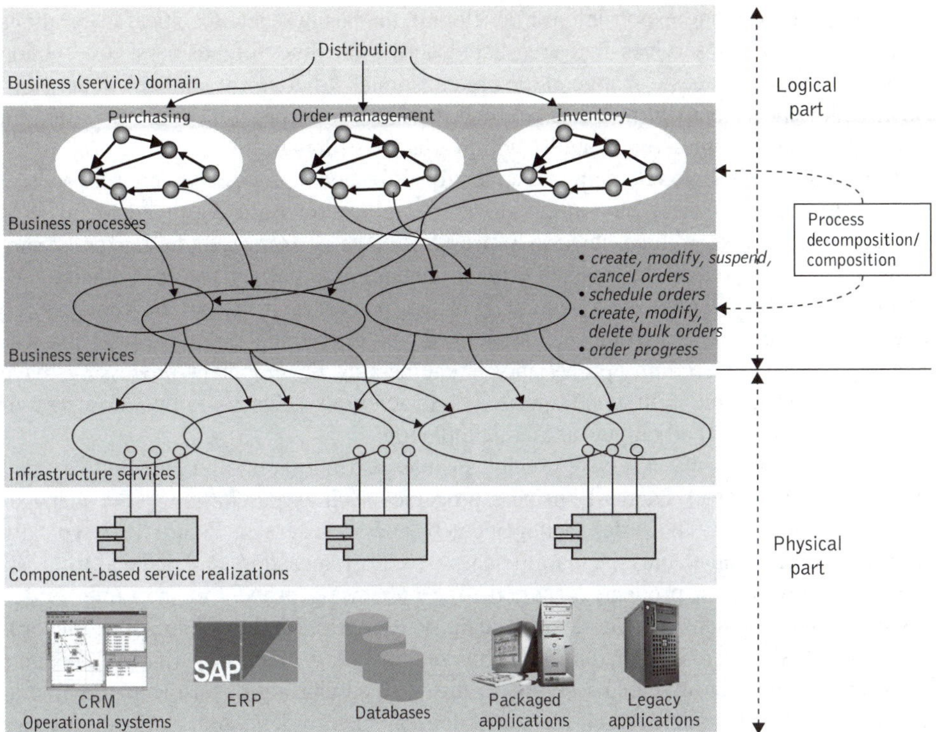

Figure 15.2 SOA layers of abstract functionality

development approach requires an holistic view of business processes and their interactions in an enterprise and emphasizes how business domains are decomposed into a collection of business processes, how business processes are decomposed into constellations of business services, and how these services are implemented in terms of pre-existing enterprise assets. The bottom-up approach emphasizes how existing enterprise assets (e.g., databases, enterprise information systems, legacy systems and applications) are transformed into business services and how business services are in turn composed into business processes. The bottom-up approach can originate on the departmental and group level, starting by exposing existing applications as services and building around those services. The most common approach is, however, to combine top-down and bottom-up approaches, starting at each end and meeting in the middle (see sections 15.9.5 and 15.11.1). In the following we shall concentrate on the layers in the SOA development model without making references to any particular development approach.

Enterprises usually start SOA development by concentrating on the concept of a business domain. An enterprise may comprise one or more business domains. Classifying business processes into logical business domains simplifies an SOA by reducing the number of business processes and services that need to be addressed. Such domains can be leveraged from multiple architectural reasons such as load balancing, access control, and vertical or horizontal partitioning of business logic. Each service domain is overseen by several people who are responsible for developing the business and technical integrations to produce business services that are shared across the lines of business (see section 15.13.1). This introduces a change in the organizational structure for application development (roles and responsibilities), as roles shift from developing functionality within an application to developing functionality within a business domain.

SOA models a business domain as a collection of business processes, which are accessible across the enterprise. Monolithic stovepipe applications are dissolved in favor of self-contained coarse-grained business processes, which perform specific business functions. These processes can be invoked using a standard protocol, thus ensuring their availability across the enterprise and beyond. Business processes are important for a service development methodology as they are associated with operational objectives and business goals, e.g., insurance claims processing or engineering development processing; have defined triggering (initiation) conditions for each new process instance, e.g., the arrival of a claim; and have defined outputs at their completion.

Figure 15.2 shows that a service domain such as distribution is subdivided into a small number of higher-level standard business processes such as purchasing, order management, and inventory. The order management business process in Figure 15.2 typically performs order volume analysis, margin analysis, sales forecasting, and demand forecasting across any region, product, or period. The purchasing process in the same service domain provides purchase order details (quantity, unit price, and extended price) according to purchase order, vendor, buyer, authorizer, inventory item, any chart of accounts combination, and non-invoiced receipts. In this way purchasing departments are able to research purchases made through blanket orders, planned orders, and standard purchase orders and can also analyze vendor performance, lead time based on the promised-by date, and the need-by date. The process can also help analyze goods received and invoice received, and shipped-item costs for distribution to charged accounts. Finally, the distribution inventory process in the service domain helps track the amount of inventory on hand and expected arrival of items, and monitors the movement of physical inventory. It also helps analyze inventory transactions through various accounts, warehouses, and sub-inventories as well as tracking inventory on hand, by warehouse, across the organization at any point in time.

Business processes orchestrate the execution of several finer-grained business services to fulfill the required business functionality and are thus the units of decomposition (top-down approach) or composition (bottom-up approach). Business services represent an activity with significance to the business, e.g., creating a customer record, creating an invoice, or closing an open customer service ticket. For example, the order management process in Figure 15.2 provides business services for creating, modifying, suspending, canceling, querying orders, for creating and tracking orders for a product, a service, or a resource, and capturing customer-selected service details. Business services are the appropriate units of business process and transaction analysis as they identify business processes and transactions and associated business costs, and achieve reuse of resources across enterprises and business units [Marks 2006].

We may collectively think of the service domain, business processes, and business services sections as comprising the *logical part* of Web services development lifecycle, see Figure 15.2. In an SOA the business services layer provides a kind of conceptual bridge between the higher-level business-oriented layers and the lower-level technical implementation layers. Business analysts use the business services layer to identify critical functions that are needed to run the enterprise, while systems developers use this layer to identify and expose technical functions and realizations that match business analysts' requirements [Bieberstein 2006].

Business services are in turn supported by infrastructure, management, and monitoring services such as those providing technical utility, for instance, logging, security, or authentication, and those that manage resources. These services provide the infrastructure enabling the integration of services through the introduction of a reliable set of capabilities, such as intelligent routing, protocol mediation, and other transformation and integration mechanisms, often considered as part of the Enterprise Service Bus (see Chapter 8). The services infrastructure layer also provides technical utility services required for enabling the development, choreography, delivery, maintenance, and provisioning of business services as well as capabilities that monitor, manage, and maintain QoS such as security, performance, and availability. It also provides services that monitor the health of SOA applications, giving insights into the health of systems and networks, and into the status and behavior patterns of applications making them thus more suitable for mission-critical computing environments (see Chapter 16).

At the end of the day, service domains, business processes, and services are layered on a backdrop of a collection of operational functions and data available from resources such as ERP, database, and CRM systems as well as other enterprise resources. The component realization layer in an SOA identifies and characterizes a large number of components that provide service implementations in terms of existing resources. Here, bottom-up analysis of existing applications and systems is required. This reveals component-based service implementations that are candidates of reuse. Components that are revealed in this layer represent the building blocks for business services and processes in an SOA. However, component implementation is an issue that can seriously impact the quality of available services. Both services and their implementation components need to be designed with the appropriate level of granularity. The granularity of components should be the prime concern of the developer responsible for providing component implementations. An implementation component can be of various granularity levels. Fine-grained component (and service) implementations provide a small amount of business process usefulness, such as basic data access. Larger granularities are compositions of smaller-grained components and possibly other artifacts, where the composition taken as a whole conforms to the enterprise component definition. As we shall see later in this chapter, the coarseness of the service operations to be exposed depends on business usage scenarios and requirements and should be at a relatively high level reflecting the requirements of business processes.

In a similar manner to the logical part of Web services development lifecycle, we may think of the infrastructure services, the component-based realizations, and the operational systems sections as comprising the *physical part* of Web services development lifecycle. This physical part of it is intended to accelerate service implementation.

In the remainder of this chapter we shall concentrate on a methodology that focuses on the levels of the web services development lifecycle hierarchy depicted in Figure 15.2. In what follows we shall use the terms *services* and *processes* freely and interchangeably to signify the same concept. We shall make no distinction between these two terms and use the generic term "service" to refer to both, unless we need to refer explicitly to singular business services or business processes.

15.5 Service-oriented design and development milestones

Several important design and development factors drive service-oriented solutions and their underlying SOA implementations. Important design and development milestones that stand out include: reducing costs by reusing existing functionality, minimizing disruption, employing an incremental mode of integration, providing increased flexibility, scalability, and adherence to standards. These are examined briefly below.

Reusing existing functionality: One of the major advantages of SOA is that it promotes the reuse of services or portions of system implementation in order to support a growing and changing set of business requirements. A significant question then arises about which services to build from scratch and which to repurpose to meet changing needs. This depends on the particular circumstances of the business and the scope of the existing services. Service-oriented solutions target reuse of existing functionality and assets such as prepackaged application suites, special-purpose built components, commercial off-the-shelf (COTS) applications or legacy applications, within new applications and policy-based computing. The reusability characteristic of SOA is achieved only by designing services for reuse and by externalizing their operational policies. Services that are useful to more than one application can be reused (repurposed or refactored) once they are identified, implemented, and published. Reusable services can be identified by finding commonly used services and must be implemented with special consideration for reuse. In essence, reusability in the services world is a form of refactoring, which implies that the implementation code is streamlined until it is general enough to address multiple situations. Service reusability is assisted by the fact that application-specific policies such as security (authentication and authorization), SLAs, QoS, and audit information are not included in the service definition but are rather configured and applied outside it using standards such as WS-Policy.

Minimizing costs of disruption: Service-oriented solutions and SOA implementations make use of existing, working technology already in place within the organization. Elements that are part of an enterprise integration solution, such as application servers, integration brokers, databases, messaging products, and so on, can be service enabled and used in the context of an Enterprise Service Bus (see section 8.5.3) as part of an orchestrated service-oriented solution. The adoption of specific "integration logic" functionality that enables orchestration of existing, working technology in the form of services results in minimizing the costs associated with disruption of existing technologies in order to enable the creation of an integration solution.

Employing an incremental mode of integration: One of the key benefits of the service-oriented approach is that integration can be delivered on a gradual, requirements-driven basis, but yet still amount to a cohesive whole in the long term. In this way, tactical decisions can be targeted in the knowledge that the solutions provided could be combined later into an enterprise-wide system. It should also be understood that the architecture itself could be adopted in an incremental fashion.

Providing increased flexibility: Service-oriented solutions provide the ability to quickly and easily evolve and adapt applications in order to meet changing business requirements and new technologies. Service-oriented solutions allow designers to isolate their business processes and services from their applications, which gives them the flexibility to add, upgrade, or replace applications without redefining all of their business process or Web services interfaces.

Providing scalability: Web services solutions may be able to leverage the processing power of multiple application servers – making it potentially possible to process large applications more quickly by spreading the load of processing across many servers. Web services messages may arrive at high burst rates, but since they are using a queuing mechanism they can be consumed by the Web service's application server at whatever rate it can process them. The only requirements are that over some period of time (many hours or even days), the Web service can handle the average traffic load, and that the queue has the capacity to store a sufficient number of transaction messages.

Complying with standards: Business development is being driven by the formation and rapid acceptance of key industry open standards. Standardization leads to commoditization, which is quite attractive to Web services clients as it enables agility through the ability to choose from multiple service providers which all conform to the same standards. Business processes are the top level in a deep and complex technology stack, and rely on the ability of underlying composite Web services to pull together the necessary Web services in a way that is cost effective and of suitable performance. Trying to execute a business process without relying on Web services standards and SOA-based application integration techniques would be out of the question.

Compliance with standards may include business semantics and definitions, standard business processes and protocols, such as the sequencing of messages. This is a topic that we discussed in Chapter 13.

15.6 Quality of service-oriented design and development

A service-oriented design and development methodology focuses on business processes, which it considers as reusable elements that are independent of applications and the computing platforms on which they run. This promotes the idea of viewing enterprise solutions as federations of services connected via well-specified contracts that define service interfaces.

In order to design useful and reliable business processes that are developed on the basis of existing or newly coded services we need to apply sound design principles that guarantee that services are self-contained and come equipped with clearly defined boundaries and service endpoints to allow for service composability. Two key principles serve as the foundation for service design: service coupling and cohesion. The purpose of these two principles is to create services that encompass the right amount of functionality to be useful and to encourage code reuse. Service coupling and cohesion are inextricably associated with service granularity.

15.6.1 Service coupling

It is important that grouping of activities in business processes is as independent as possible from other such groupings in other processes. One way of measuring service design quality is *coupling*, or the degree of interdependence between two business processes. The objective is to minimize coupling: that is, to make (self-contained) business processes as independent as possible by not having any knowledge of or relying on any other business processes. Low coupling between business processes indicates a well-partitioned system that avoids the problems of service redundancy and duplication.

Coupling can be achieved by reducing the number of connections between services in a business process, eliminating unnecessary relationships between them, and by reducing the number of necessary relationships – if possible. As coupling is a very broad concept for service design, it can be partitioned along the following dimensions:

1. *Representational coupling:* Business processes should not depend on specific representational or implementation details and assumptions of one another, e.g., business processes do not need to know the scripting language that was used to compose their underlying services. These concerns lead to the exploitation of interoperability and reusability for service design. Representational coupling is useful for supporting:
   (a) Interchangeable/replaceable services: Existing services may be swapped with new service implementations – or ones supplied by a different provider offering better performance or pricing – without disrupting the overall business process functionality.
   (b) Multiple service versions: Different versions of a service may work best in parts of a business processes depending on the application's needs. For example, a purchase order service may provide different levels of detail, e.g., internal or external requisition details such as internal or external accounts, depending on the ordering options.
2. *Identity coupling:* Connection channels between services should be unaware of who is providing the service. It is not desirable to keep track of the targets (recipients) of service messages, especially when they are likely to change or when discovering the best service provider is not a trivial matter.
3. *Communication protocol coupling:* A sender of a message should rely only on those effects necessary to achieve effective communication. The number of messages exchanged between a sender and addressee in order to accomplish a certain goal should be minimal, given the applied communication model, e.g., one-way, request/response, and solicit/response. For example, a one-way style of communication where a service endpoint receives a message without having to send an acknowledgement places the lowest possible demands on the service performing the operation. The service that performs the operation does not assume anything

about when the effects of the operation hold, or even about the fact that a notification might be needed back to indicate completion.

Low coupling increases the degree of isolation of one business process from changes that happen to another; simplifies design understanding; and increases the reuse potential.

15.6.2 Service cohesion

Cohesion is the degree of the strength of functional relatedness of operations within a service. Service developers should create strong, highly cohesive business processes, business processes whose services and service operations are strongly and genuinely related to one another. A business process with highly related services and related responsibilities, which also has a rather narrow scope, has high design cohesion. The guidelines by which to increase service cohesion are as follows:

1. *Functional service cohesion:* A functionally cohesive business process should perform one and only one problem-related task and contain only services necessary for that purpose. At the same time the operations in the services of the business process must also be highly related to one another, i.e., highly cohesive. Consider services such as "get product price," "check product availability," and "check creditworthiness" in an order management business process.
2. *Communicational service cohesion:* A communicationally cohesive business process is one whose activities and services use the same input and output messages. Communicationally cohesive business processes are cleanly decoupled from other processes as their activities are hardly related to activities in other processes.
3. *Logical service cohesion:* A logically cohesive business process is one whose services all contribute to tasks of the same general category by performing a set of independent but logically similar functions (alternatives) that are tied together by means of control flows. A typical example of this is mode of payment.

Like low coupling, high cohesion is a service-oriented design and development principle to keep in mind during all stages in the methodology. It is an underlying goal to continually consider during all service design aspects. High cohesion increases the clarity and ease of comprehension of the design; simplifies maintenance and future enhancements; achieves service granularity at a fairly reasonable level; and often supports low coupling. Highly related functionality supports increased reuse potential as a highly cohesive service module can be used for very specific purposes.

15.6.3 Service granularity

Decisions about the scope and granularity of services to be implemented and the technical approach taken to realize them must be applied to all service development projects. *Service granularity* refers to the scope of functionality exposed by a service. Services may exhibit different levels of granularity. A coarse-grained interface might be the complete processing for a given service, such as "SubmitPurchaseOrder," where the message contains all of the business information needed to define a purchase order. A fine-grained interface might have separate operations for "CreateNewPurchaseOrder," "SetShippingAddress," "AddItem," and so forth. This example illustrates that fine-grained services might be services that provide basic data access or rudimentary operations. These services are of little value to business applications. Services of the most value are coarse-grained services that are appropriately structured to meet specific business needs. Coarse-grained Web services are composed of finer-grained implementation-based services (that are a straightforward translation of the existing interfaces into Web services). These coarse-grained services can be created from one or more existing systems by defining and exposing interfaces that meet business process requirements.

When Web services are deployed across the Internet the frequency of message exchange becomes an important factor. Sending and receiving more information in a single request is more efficient in a network environment than sending many fine-grained messages. Fine-grained messages result in increased network traffic and make handling errors more difficult. As such, using a small number of coarse-grained messages would reduce the number of transmissions and increase the likelihood of a message arriving and a transaction being completed whilst the connection was still available. Although the quality of connection is improving all the time, this remains good advice when delivering Web services for external use across the Internet. However, there is now much wider internal use of Web services where the network is faster and more stable. A higher number of fine-grained services and messages might therefore be acceptable for EAI applications.

It can sometimes prove difficult to pick the correct granularity of a service component. If the service is too fine grained, it may need to rely constantly on other services – which can lead, in effect, to tight coupling of the interdependent services. By contrast, if a service's functionality is too broad, a company can lose some of the benefits of service reuse and interchangeability. From the perspective of service-oriented design and development it is preferable to create higher-level, coarse-grained interfaces that implement a complete business process. This technique provides the client with access to a specific business service, rather than getting and setting specific data values and sending a large number of messages. Enterprises can use a singular service to accomplish a specific business task, such as billing or inventory control, or they may compose several services together to create a distributed e-business application such as customized ordering, customer support, procurement, and logistical support.

15.7 Overview of Web services development lifecycle

Web services development lifecycle (SDLC), or service-oriented design and development, is a highly iterative and continuous approach to developing, implementing, deploying, and maintaining Web services in which feedback is continuously cycled to and from phases in iterative steps of refinement. To that effect the methodology facilitates designing solutions as assemblies of services in which the assembly description is a managed, first-class aspect of the solution, and, hence, amenable to analysis, change, and evolution. Developers can then view an SOA solution as a choreographed set of service interactions. A service-oriented design and development methodology incorporates many of the advantages of earlier successful development methodologies such as RUP, CBD, and BPM. It builds on valuable lessons learned from applying earlier methodologies and introduces new concepts, patterns, and practices. SDLC concentrates on the SOA layers of functional abstraction depicted in Figure 15.2.

A service-oriented design and development methodology provides models, best practices, standards, reference architectures, and run-time environments that are needed to provide guidance and support through all SOA development, deployment, and production phases. Service-based development incorporates a broad range of capabilities, technologies, tools, and skill sets that include [Arsanjani 2004], [Brown 2005]:

- Managing the entire services lifecycle – including analyzing, identifying, designing, developing, deploying, finding, applying, evolving, and maintaining services.
- Establishing a platform and programming model, which includes connecting, deploying, and managing services within a specific run-time platform.
- Adopting best practices and tools for architecting services-oriented solutions in repeatable, predictable ways that deal with changing business needs. This includes mining existing applications to discover potential services, repurposing existing assets and functionality to extend their utility and make those capabilities accessible as services, creating new services, and "wiring" together services by connecting behavior exposed through their interfaces.
- Delivering high-quality workable service-oriented solutions that respect QoS requirements. These solutions may be implemented as best practices, such as tried and tested methods for implementing security, ensuring performance, compliance with standards for interoperability, and designing for change.

Fundamental to the above capabilities is that business goals and requirements should always drive downstream design, development, and testing to transform business processes into composite applications that automate and integrate enterprises. In this way business requirements can be traced across the entire lifecycle from business goals, through software designs and code assets, to composite applications.

The phases in the SDLC methodology encompass planning, analysis, design, construction, testing, provisioning, deployment, execution, and monitoring (see Figure 15.3). It is a premise of the lifecycle that these phases are traversed iteratively and that feedback is cycled to and from phases in iterative steps of refinement and that the methodology may actually be built using a blend of forward- and reverse-engineering techniques or other means to facilitate the needs of the business. This approach is one of continuous invention, discovery, and implementation with each iteration forcing the development team to drive the software development project's artifacts closer to completion in a predictable and repeatable manner. Usually the partial application is incrementally developed, because it grows gradually with new features, iteration by iteration. This approach considers multiple realization scenarios for business processes and Web services that take into account both technical and business concerns.

In the following, we shall describe a blend of principles and "how-to" guidelines for readers to understand how developers can transition an IT infrastructure into a working SOA solution. We shall present phases that are particular to service-oriented design and development at a level of detail that is appropriate to achieve reader understanding and appreciation. Conventional software development methodology activities such as

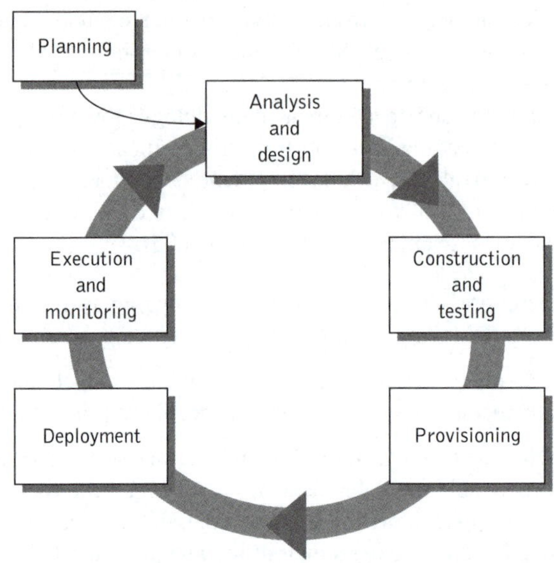

Figure 15.3 Phases of the service-oriented design and development methodology

planning, testing, and execution will be described only briefly as they can be supported by traditional software development techniques such as RUP. The workings of this methodology will be exemplified by means of the order management process that we introduced earlier.

15.8 The planning phase

The planning phase constitutes a preparatory phase that serves to streamline and organize consequent phases in the methodology. During this phase, the project feasibility, goals, rules, and procedures are set and requirements are gathered. More specifically, the planning phase determines the feasibility, nature, and scope of service solutions in the context of an enterprise. A strategic task for any organization is to achieve a service technology "fit" with its current environment. The key requirement in this phase is thus to understand the business environment and to make sure that all necessary controls are incorporated into the design of a service-oriented solution. Activities in this phase include analyzing the business needs in measurable goals, reviewing the current technology landscape, conceptualizing the requirements of the new environment, and mapping those to new or available implementations. Planning also includes a financial analysis of the costs and benefits including a budget and a software development plan of tasks, deliverables, and schedule.

The planning phase is very similar to that found in software development methodologies and has many elements in common with the RUP inception phase, thus we shall not discuss it any further. Several RUP aspects including service identification, existing asset analysis to identify opportunities for asset reuse, software development best practices, and others can be used in the subsequent phases of service analysis described in the remainder of this chapter.

15.9 The analysis phase

The analysis phase is based on a thorough business case analysis whose main purpose is to identify the requirements of an SOA-based implementation. This includes reviewing the business goals and objectives of an enterprise that drive the development of business processes. The analysis phase helps focus SOA initiatives by creating a high-level *process map* that identifies business domains and processes of particular interest to an enterprise. Business processes are ranked by criteria related to business value and impact, reuse and high consumption, feasibility and technical viability [Marks 2006]. From the process map, business analysts can identify candidate business services that relate to these business processes. Candidate business services are services that have potential value for an organization [Marks 2006]. They can be evaluated based on reuse, business impact, and organizational value, and are subsequently analyzed to find what kind of business logic should be encapsulated in each of them and finally designed. Service analysis helps prioritize business processes and services where SOA can contribute to improvements and offer business value potential, and also helps center efforts on business domains within an enterprise that can be mapped to core business processes.

Service analysis aims at identifying, conceptualizing, and rationalizing business processes as a set of interacting Web services. In particular, the analysis phase places emphasis on identifying and describing the processes and services in a business problem domain and on discovering potential overlaps and discrepancies between processes under construction and available system resources that are needed to realize singular Web services and business processes. It therefore examines the existing services portfolio at the service provider's side to understand which patterns are in place and which need to be introduced and implemented.

The ultimate objective of service analysis is to provide an in-depth understanding of the functionality, scope, reuse, and granularity of candidate business processes and services. Three important factors drive the service analysis phase:

1. Viewing the IT capabilities of an organization as a set of services that are assembled to meet specific business requirements. This provides better insight into how business processes can be realized.
2. Assembling singular services into processes and processes into composite applications in turn, as business conditions demand.
3. Focusing on organizational asset reuse and management to obtain greater business efficiency.

To achieve its objective, the analysis phase encourages a more radical view of process (re)design and supports the re-engineering of business processes. Its main objective is the reuse (or repurposing) of business process functionality in new composite applications. To

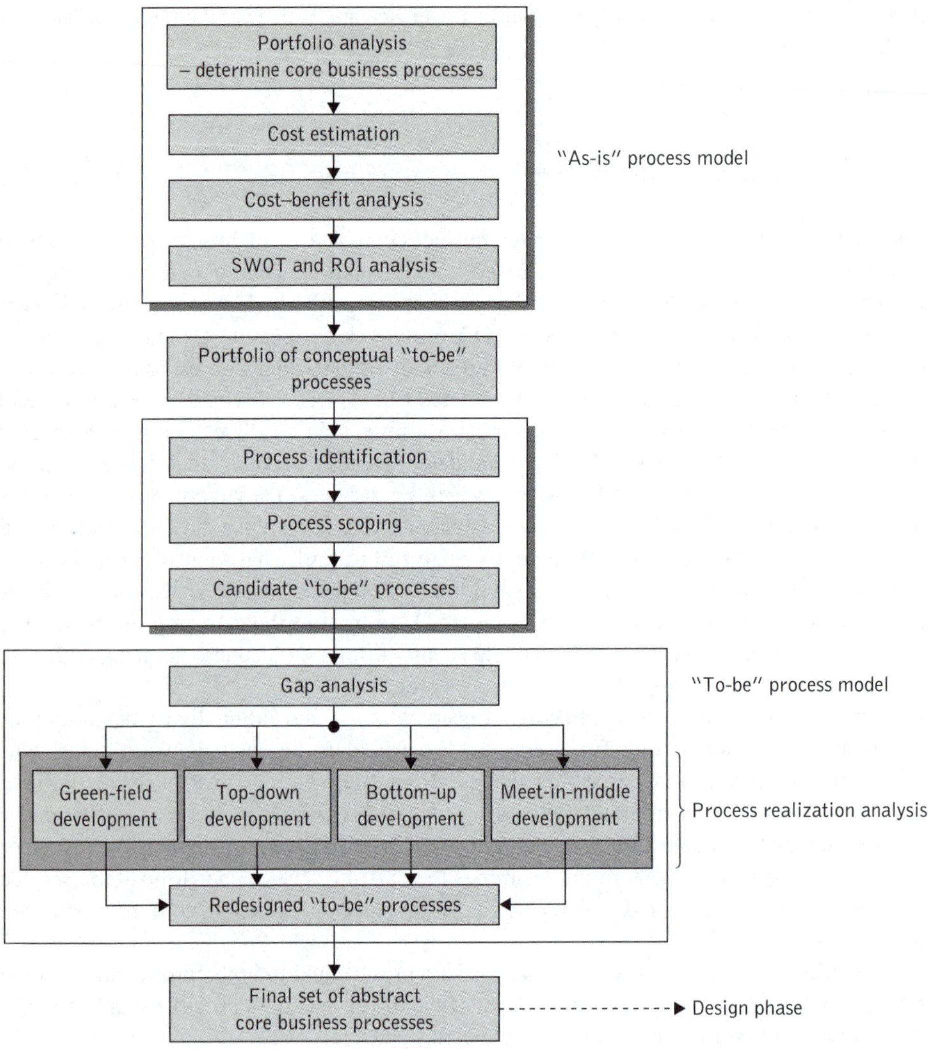

Figure 15.4 Service analysis steps

achieve this objective the analysis phase commences with an "as-is" process model analysis that it follows with four main activities: process identification, process scoping, business gap analysis, and process realization. The steps of the analysis phase are depicted in Figure 15.4.

15.9.1 "As-is" process model analysis

In the service analysis phase the predominant role is that of a business analyst who harvests the functional requirements of business users and provides domain knowledge [Bieberstein 2006]. Business analysts complete an "as-is" process model to allow the various stakeholders to understand the portfolio of available applications and business processes. The "as-is" process model can be used as a basis for conducting a thorough re-engineering analysis of the current portfolio of available software resources. This may involve the following steps:

1. *Portfolio analysis:* Portfolio analysis requires that the applications and business processes that are candidates for re-engineering be prioritized according to their technical quality and business value. Business objectives are derived from business strategies and processes, while technical assets are mapped and weighted against these business objectives and evaluated using a comprehensive set of metrics [Slee 1997]. If an application has low business and technical quality it can be retired. If it has low business value and but high technical quality it should be carefully reassessed. If the application has business value and low technical quality it must be redeveloped. Finally, if an application has high business and technical quality it must be modernized.
2. *Cost estimation:* Cost estimation is a function that involves identifying and weighing all processes to be re-engineered to estimate the cost of the re-engineering project.
3. *Cost–benefit analysis:* In this step, the cost of re-engineering is compared to the expected maintenance cost savings and value increases.

The above steps result in performing a business process strength, weaknesses, opportunities and threats (SWOT) analysis, which may reveal some processes as being significant strengths and other as significant weaknesses. This may have serious consequences for the business model of an organization because it could allow the processes which are major strengths to become the core processes of the organization and lead to further process in-sourcing activities, while processes with significant weaknesses could become the targets of outsourcing [Jeston 2006].

Before an organization commits to any changes to business processes, it needs to design, simulate, and analyze potential changes to the current application portfolio for potential return on investment (ROI). Three activities in an enterprise may help determine IT value: the IT conversion process, the SOA consumption process, and the competitive process [Soh 1995], [Marks 2006]. The IT conversion process represents the conversion of funding and labor into creation of IT assets, such as services and processes. The SOA consumption process involves determining how these services and customers, suppliers, and internal users consume business processes; how they are reused in multiple ways; and how they impact the organization by creating organizational value. The competitive process determines how the organizational value created by the SOA impact on the overall organization results in competitive advantage and better organizational performance.

This part of the analysis phase results in the development of the "to-be" process model that an SOA solution is intended to implement. This is illustrated in Figure 15.4.

15.9.2 Business service identification

Understanding how a business process works and how component functionality differs or can get adjusted between applications is an important milestone when trying to identify suitable business process candidates. When analyzing an application, business analysts must first analyze application functionality and develop a logical model of what an enterprise (or business domain) does in terms of business processes and the services the business requires from them, e.g., what is the shipping and billing address, what is the required delivery time, what is the delivery schedule, etc. The developer may eventually implement these concepts as a blend of singular services. Thus the objective of this step is to identify not only business processes of interest to an enterprise, but also potential singular services that could be aggregated into a highly cohesive business process.

Candidate service identification is a top-down effort required to inspect enterprise core business entities, ascertain business ideas and concepts, and lead to the formation of conceptual business processes and business services [Marks 2006]. During this part of service analysis important issues such as consolidation, decomposition, reuse, simplification, and refactoring of legacy assets should be taken into account. These activities allow transitioning to a set of shared reusable business processes and business services in a way that promotes loose coupling.

The key factor in service analysis is being able to recognize functionality that is essentially self-sufficient for the purposes of a business process. A business process should be specified with an application or the user of the service in mind. It is important to identify the functionality that should be included in it and the functionality that is best incorporated into other business processes. Overlapping services functionality and capabilities, e.g., different services that share identical business logic and rules, should be identified and common functionality should be factored out. Likewise, related services with conflicting functionality should be analyzed and dealt with. Several factors such as encapsulated functionality, business logic and rules, business activities, and organizational influences can serve to determine the granularity of business services and processes. During this procedure, we can also apply the design principles of coupling and cohesion to achieve this effect. For instance, an order management process has low communication protocol coupling with a material requirements process.

It is possible to map business functionality against industry templates to identify a "heat map" of business processes that are candidates for SOA transformation [Bieberstein 2006]. Good candidates for business processes are those that represent commonly required functionality for EAI or e-business, such as sales order management, credit checking, and inventory management. Business processes of this type are designed to provide comprehensive support to very specific business services sharply focused on narrower information and process domains, and can be integrated with existing back-office and custom storefront applications. Process identification could, for instance, start with comparing the abstract business process portfolio (see Figure 15.4) to standard process definitions, such as RosettaNet's "Manage Purchase Order" (PIP3A4). This PIP encompasses four complementary process segments supporting the entire chain of activities from purchase order creation to tracking and tracing, each of which is further decomposed into multiple individual processes. A quick scan of this PIP reveals that Segment 3A "Quote and Order Entry" and Segment 3C "Returns and Finance" may be combined into the process Order Management.

Service identification results in a set of identified candidate business processes and singular business services that exhibit relatively coarse and fine granularity, respectively. The identified candidate services need to be further refined to meet business analysis and design criteria.

15.9.3 Business service scoping

A business process should allow a developer to integrate a precise solution as opposed to one that provides features over and above a basic requirement. Defining the scope of business processes helps ensure that a process does not become monolithic and mimic an entire application. Unbundling functionality into separate business processes will prevent business processes from becoming overly complex and difficult to maintain. For example, designing a business process that handles on-line purchasing would require the removal of packaging and shipping information and costs to different business processes. In this example the three functions are mutually exclusive and should be implemented separately. The functionality included in these business processes is not only discrete and identifiable, but also loosely coupled to other parts of the application.

The scope of a business process is defined as an aggregation of aspects that include where the process starts and ends, the typical customers (users) of the process, the inputs and outputs that the customers of the process expect to see, the external entities that the process is expected to interface with, and the different types of events that start an instance of the process. Process scoping is conceptual in nature and comprises a top-down exercise beginning with the coarse-grained generalized business processes and services that were identified in service analysis. Common contextual relationships of business services are identified and these are grouped accordingly. The scope of the process identifies not only the issues directly related to the flow of the process itself, but also key external entities related to the process, such as users of the process, e.g., suppliers or logistics providers. As usual, services that are internal to a process should be tightly linked activities that belong naturally together.

Figure 15.4 illustrates how business identification and scoping interact. This step results in a set of re-engineered and repurposed business processes that can be reused and are candidates for service design.

15.9.4 Business service gap analysis

Service gap analysis is a technique that purposes a business process and services realization strategy (see the following section) by incrementally adding more implementation details to an abstract service/process. Gap analysis commences with comparing candidate "to-be" service functionality to potentially available software service implementations that may be assembled within the enclosures of a newly conceived business process.

A gap analysis strategy may be developed in stages and results in a recommendation to do development work, reuse, or purchase Web services. There might exist software components internal to an organization that provide a good match to implement candidate service functionality. These may include service implementations previously developed by the enterprise, externally supplied service realizations available on a subscription or pay per use basis, and so forth. In this way, portfolios of services possibly accessible on a global scale will complement and sometimes even entirely replace monolithic applications as the new fabric of business processes.

Service gap analysis is assisted by a *reusability strategy* that is based on asset reuse characteristics of individual environments and leads to specific reuse disciplines appropriate for a given organization [Marks 2006]. More specifically, gap analysis tries to match descriptions of available software assets, such as legacy systems, COTS, and ERP packages (and possible component implementations of these) against descriptions of candidate Web services that can be used to construct a new business process. During gap analysis it is ascertained which existing resources and applications can become service enabled to provide service content. Following this, organizational fitness needs to be assessed. This is required for accommodating a graceful transition from the existing to the planned business processes. Several factors internal and external to an organization need to be considered at this stage. Internal factors may include understanding best practices, maturity of business processes and type of organization, training issues, staffing and organizational culture, while external factors may include continuity and trustworthiness of service providers.

15.9.5 Business service realization analysis

Service gap analysis results in a realization architecture that describes at a high level how a Web service usage interface could be connected to a portfolio of existing services and service-enabled applications which are assembled to form service orchestration specification interfaces. This correspondence is illustrated in Figure 15.5. Service content in Figure 15.5 can be provided in several ways: as a separate software component (simple Web service), as an existing resource that can be service enabled, or as an assembly of existing singular services into a higher-order business process. Service-enabled content may include software components such as legacy systems, COTS components, ERP packages, and the like.

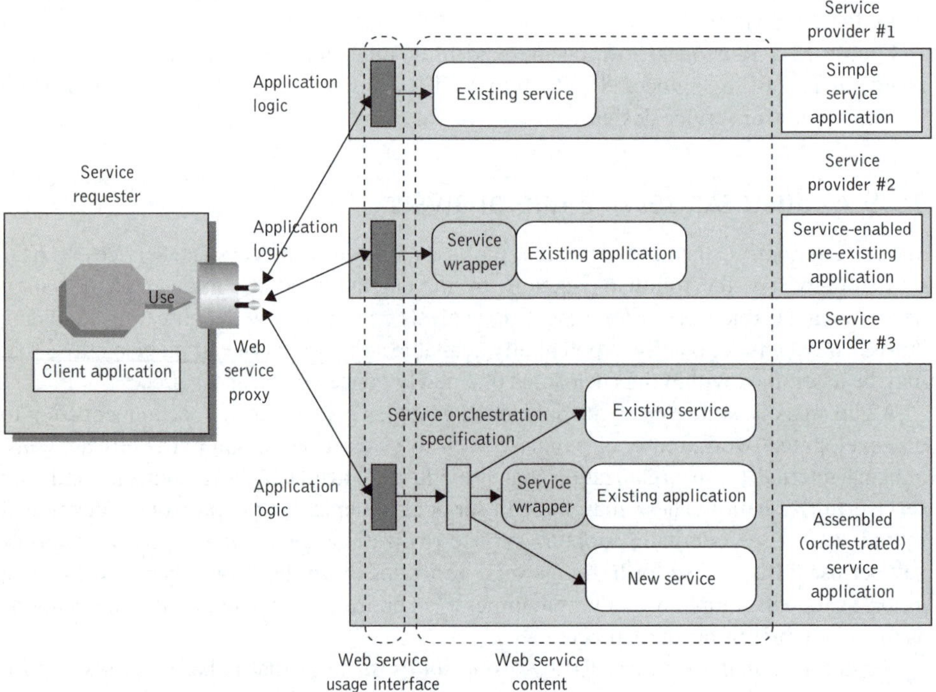

Figure 15.5 Web services realization architecture and Web services portfolio in gap analysis

Process realization analysis is an approach that considers diverse business process realization scenarios evaluated in terms of costs, risks, benefits, and ROI in accordance with business requirements and priorities. During process realization, analysis decisions are made whether to reuse a particular enterprise asset, e.g., a COTS or legacy application. To determine the quality of a specific asset, quality metrics are used that evaluate its flexibility, extensibility, maintainability, and level of cohesion and coupling. The process realization analysis estimates existing and expected operational costs, integration costs, service and process customization costs, service and process provisioning costs, and architecture costs for each realization scenario. Business analysts and developers could use automated tools to gain insight into the business benefits, costs, and risks of the SOA services implementation portfolio.

Service providers consider the following four realization options (which may be mixed in various combinations) to develop new business processes [Brittenham 2001]:

1. *Green-field development:* This step involves describing how a new interface for a singular Web service will be created on the basis of the Web service implementation. Green-field development assumes that first a service is implemented and subsequently the service interface is derived from the new Web service implementation. During this step the programming languages and models that are appropriate for implementing the new Web service are also determined.

2. *Top-down development:* Using this realization option a new singular service can be developed that conforms to an existing service interface. This type of service interface is usually part of an industry standard that can be developed by any number of service providers. Processes are usually deployed in a top-down fashion from a business-level process blueprint. The main benefit of the top-down service development is the consistency of the applications and integration mechanisms. It is also rather easy to evolve the service-oriented solution across the enterprise as the industry evolves. Main problems with this realization option are the costs involved in development as well as the costs of achieving consensus on a high-level SOA architecture throughout the enterprise [Graham 2005].

3. *Bottom-up development:* SOA implementation strategy rarely starts on a green field and almost always integrates existing systems at the physical part of the SOA layers of abstraction in Figure 15.2. Using this option a new singular service interface is developed for an existing application. The existing application can be coded as a Java, C++ program, Enterprise Java Beans (EJB), etc., or could be a back-end legacy application. This option usually involves creating a Web service interface from the API of the application that implements the Web service. Bottom-up development is well suited for an environment that includes several heterogeneous technologies and platforms or uses rapidly evolving technologies.

4. *Meet-in-the-middle development:* This option is used when an already existing Web service interface – for which an implementation already exists – is partially mapped onto a new service or process definition. This option involves service realizations that mix services and service-enabled implementations. This approach may thus involve creating a wrapper for the existing applications that need to be service enabled and that are to be combined with the already existing Web service

interface. Meet-in-the-middle development realization strategies offer a middle ground that attempts to take advantage of some of the benefits of the other approaches while extenuating some of the most notable problems and risks.

Use of the above service realization options results in removing service redundancy and creates opportunities for business services. However, one of the issues with the top-down, bottom-up, and meet-in-the-middle development options is that they are rather ambiguous regarding which business processes an enterprise should start from and how these can be combined to form business scenarios. To address this problem, service development solutions need to target specific focal points and common practices within the enterprise, such as those that are specified by its corresponding sector reference models. Reference models, a typical example of which is RosettaNet, address a common large proportion of the basic "plumbing" for a specific sector, from a process, operational function, integration, and data point of view. Such a *verticalized development model* presents the ideal architecture for supporting service development. This ensures that the software development team is aware of known best practices and standard processes so that it does not reinvent the wheel. For example, developers could use RosettaNet's standard processes PIP4B2 ("Notify of Shipment Receipt") and PIP4C1 ("Distribute Inventory Report") for applications in which suppliers develop replenishment plans for consignment inventory. Product receipt and inventory information is notified using PIP4B2 and PIP4C1, respectively between consignment warehouses and suppliers.

Semantic issues come into play at the level of end-to-end business processes that span multiple organizations, see Chapter 13. To address terminology and semantic mismatch problems, consistent definitions of typical business objects such as a purchase order or an invoice can be used for business processes to achieve cognitive consistency among relevant business communities. This is essential to the business relationships that enable the extended enterprise. A standard business language such as the Universal Business Language (UBL), which is intended to provide a library of standard electronic XML business documents (e.g., purchase orders and invoices) to be exchanged using standard messages, is an important initiative in achieving semantic confluence. UBL is used for capturing business information for use in integrating business processes and sharing data with trading partners.

The various options for process realization analysis emphasize the separation of specification from implementation that allows Web services to be realized in different ways, e.g., top-down or meet-in-the-middle development. It then becomes important to plan effectively when deciding how to realize or provision services. The service realization strategy involves choosing from an increasing diversity of realization alternatives and requires making the right choice. The different options for service realization may be mixed in various combinations. Service realization alternatives include:

1. Reusing or repurposing already existing Web services, business processes, or business process logic.
2. Developing new Web services or business processes logic from scratch.
3. Purchasing/leasing/paying per use for services. This option is covered in section 15.13.3, which concentrates on service metering and billing.

4. Outsourcing service design and implementation regarding Web services or (parts of) business processes. Once a service is specified, the design of its interfaces or sets of interfaces and the coding of its actual implementation may be outsourced.

5. Using wrappers and/or adapters to revamp existing enterprise (COTS) components or existing (ERP/legacy) systems. Revamping software components including database functionality or legacy software results in introducing service-enabling implementations for these systems in the form of adapters or wrappers.

Process realization results in a business process architecture represented by business processes and the set of normalized business functions extracted from the analysis of these processes, see Figure 15.4. The process architecture includes an end-to-end process model that provides an overview of the core processes for an organization. It also includes such information as ownership of the process, scope of the process, core processes, support processes (processes that support the core processes), outsourced processes, types of processes that need to be provided from external organizations, and process reference models.

15.10 The service design phase

This phase is logically succeeded by service design, during which conceptual processes and services are transformed from abstract entities into a set of concrete service interfaces. Designing a service-oriented application requires developers to define related well-documented interfaces for all conceptual services identified by the analysis phase prior to constructing them.

The design phase encompasses the steps of singular service specification, business process specification, and policy specification for both singular services as well as business processes. Service design is based on a twin-track design approach that provides two production lines, one along the logical part and one along the physical part of the SOA abstraction layers in Figure 15.2. The purpose of logical service design is to define singular services and assemble (compose) services out of reusable singular service constellations. This calls for a business process model that forces developers to determine how services combine and interact jointly to produce higher-level services. The physical design trajectory focuses on how to design component implementations that implement services at an acceptable level of granularity. Physical design is based on techniques for leveraging legacy applications (see section 8.5.6) and CBD techniques. CBD falls outside the scope of this book. Readers interested in this topic can find an overview of CBD methodologies and a wealth of ideas in the following sources: [Allen 2001], [Atkinson 2002], [Cheesman 2001], [Veryard 2001], [Whitehead 2002]. In the following we shall concentrate on logical service design only. We shall first start by describing a broad set of service design guidelines.

15.10.1 Service design concerns

A number of important concerns exist, which are driven by the factors outlined in section 15.6 and which influence design decisions and result in an efficient design of service interfaces, if taken seriously. These concerns bring into operation the design principles for service-enabled processes. Prime concerns include managing service granularity, designing for service reuse, and designing for service composability.

15.10.1.1 Managing service and component granularity

The granularity of business services and service implementation components should be the prime concern of the developer responsible for providing service and component implementations realizing the service content. Just like a service, a component implementation can be of various granularity levels.

Services analysis provides an initial granularity assessment based on the top-down logical analysis of services functionality and scope, which can be used as a starting point for designing concrete service interfaces. There are several heuristics that can be used to identify the right level of granularity for business services (as well as implementation components). These include clearly identifiable business concepts, highly usable and reusable concepts, concepts that have a high degree of cohesion and low degree of coupling, and concepts that relate to service integration and interoperability. Many vertical sectors, e.g., automotive, travel industry, and so on, have already started standardizing business entities and processes by choosing their own levels of granularity, see section 15.6.3. It is important that the developer who implements the service still thinks about granularity so they can change parts of the implementation with the minimum of disruption to other components, applications, and services.

15.10.1.2 Designing for service reusability

When designing services it is important to be able to design them for reuse so that they can perform a given function wherever this function is required within an enterprise. To design for service reuse one must make services more generic, abstracting away from differences in requirements between one situation and another, and attempting to use the generic service in multiple contexts where it is applicable. Designing a solution that is reusable requires keeping it as simple as possible. There are intuitive techniques that facilitate reuse and that are related to design issues such as identification and granularity of services. These include looking for common behavior that exists in more than one place in the system and trying to generalize behavior so that it is reusable.

When designing a service-based application, it is possible to extract common behavior and provide it by means of a generic service so that multiple clients can use it directly. It is important, however, when designing enterprise services that business logic is kept common and consistent across the enterprise. Nevertheless there are cases where fine tuning, specialization, or variation of business logic functionality is required. Consider, for instance, discounting practices that differ depending on the type of customer being handled. In those cases it is customary to produce a generalized solution with customization points to allow for service variations.

15.10.1.3 Designing for service composability

In order to design useful and reliable services we need to apply sound service design principles that guarantee that services are self-contained, modular, and support service composability. The design principles that underlie component reusability revolve around the two well-known software design guidelines of service coupling and cohesion that we examined in section 15.6.

15.10.2 Specifying services

An important design requirement for SOA-based applications is providing a formal interface contract in some service description language (e.g., WSDL) defining the service signature as well the necessary pre- and postconditions, and invariants. Singular service design results in the definition and the interface signature of the service; the schema of the messages the service exchanges, including its service data; the dependencies the service has on other services; and integrity constraints that are appropriate to service implementation assumptions. Semantics must also be addressed if strongly cohesive services are to be specified. RDF can therefore be used to model semantics when inserted as annotations for the WSDL syntactic types.

A service specification is a set of three specification elements, all equally important. These are [Johnston 2005]:

1. *A structural specification:* This focuses on defining the service types, messages, port types, and operations.

2. *A behavioral specification:* This entails understanding the effects and side effects of service operations and the semantics of input and output messages. If, for example, we consider an order management service we might expect to see a service that lists "place order," "cancel order," and "update order," as available operations. The behavioral specification for this ordering service might then describe how a user cannot update or cancel an order they did not place, or that after an order has been cancelled it *cannot be updated.*

3. *A policy specification:* In addition to service syntax and semantics, QoS considerations must also be addressed. To this end a policy specification mechanism is necessary. Policy specification describes policy assertions and constraints on the service. Policy assertions may cover security, manageability, etc. A policy specification may require that certain elements of the order need be encrypted, denoting the encryption techniques to be used, certificates to use, and so forth. Such nonfunctional requirements can be specified using appropriate constructs from the WS-Policy specification framework.

Like services analysis, service design is greatly facilitated when reference models, such as SCOR or RosettaNet (see Chapter 14), are available. Service interfaces can then be derived on their basis.

In the remainder of this section we shall describe the elements of service design in terms of a sample purchase order business process based on RosettaNet's order management PIP cluster. By applying the dominant cohesion criterion, namely functional cohesion, this process may be decomposed into several subprocesses such as "Quote and Order Entry," "Transportation and Distribution," and "Returns and Finance," which conform to RosettaNet's segments 3A, 3B, and 3C respectively. The "Quote and Order Entry" subprocess allows partners to exchange price and availability information, quotes, purchase orders, and order status, and enables partners to send requested orders to other partners. The "Transportation and Distribution" subprocess enables communication of shipping- and delivery-related information with the ability to make changes and handle exceptions and claims. Finally, the "Returns and Finance" subprocess provides for issuance of billing, payment and reconciliation of debits, credits and invoices between partners, as well as supporting product return and its financial impact. By applying functional cohesion again, the "Quote and Order Entry" subprocess may be decomposed into several services such "Request Quote," "Request Price and Availability," "Request Purchase Order," and "Query Order Status." The "Request Quote" service provides a buyer with quotes and referrals used to select suppliers and prepare purchase orders. The "Request Price and Availability" service provides a quick, automated process for trading partners to request and provide product price and availability. The "Request Purchase Order" service supports a process for trading partners to issue and acknowledge new purchase orders. Finally, the "Query Order Status" service allows trading partners to cancel and change purchase orders, and acknowledge changes, as well as allows product sellers to report order status on all open orders. These three services conform to RosettaNet's PIPs 3A1, 3A2, 3A4, and 3A5, respectively.

In the following we shall briefly examine the course of specifying an interface for a singular Web service in the WSDL standard. The effects of service message exchanges will be also examined. Following this the service programming style will be determined. Service policy specifications will be introduced after we examine business process specification.

15.10.2.1 Structural and behavioral service specification

Singular Web service interface specification comprises four steps: describing the service interface, specifying operation parameters, designating the messaging and transport protocol, and finally fusing port types, bindings, and actual location (a URI) of the Web services. These steps themselves are rather trivial and already described in depth in the literature, e.g., in [Siddiqui 2001], where a detailed approach for specifying services is outlined. While performing these steps, the developer should apply the design guidelines and principles that we outlined in the previous section. In particular, the following guidelines guarantee that a service encapsulates the required amount of business logic and that loose coupling is introduced between interacting services:

- From a structural point of view the service interface should only contain port types (operations) that are logically related or functionally cohesive. For example, the service "Request Purchase Order" captures the operations "Purchase Order Request" and "ReceiptAcknowledgement" as they are functionally cohesive.
- From a behavioral point of view, messages within a particular port type should be tightly coupled by using representational coupling and communication protocol coupling. For example, the operation "Purchase Order Request" may have one input message (`PurchaseOrderID`) and one output message (`PurchaseOrder`) sharing the same communication protocol (e.g., SOAP) and representation (atomic XML Schema data types).

- From a behavioral point of view, coupling between services should be minimized. For example, the services "Request Purchase Order" and "Query Order Status" are autonomous, having no interdependencies.

These singular service design guidelines are examined in turn below.

Specifying the service interface. A WSDL specification outlines operations, messages, types, and protocol information. Listing 15.1 shows an abridged specification for a service interface and operation parameters for the "Request Purchase Order" service. The WSDL example in Listing 15.1 illustrates that the Web service defines two `<portType>`s named `"CanReceive3A42_PortType"` and `"CanSend3A42_PortType"`. The `<portType>` `"CanReceive3A42_PortType"` supports two `<operation>`s, which are called `"PurchaseOrderRequest"` and `"ReceiptAcknowledgement"`.

```
… … … …
<portType name="CanReceive3A42_PortType">
     <!-- name of operation is same as name of message -->
     <operation name="PurchaseOrderRequest">
            <output message="tns:PurchaseOrderRequest"/>
     </operation>
     <operation name="ReceiptAcknowledgement">
            <output message="tns:ReceiptAcknowledgment"/>
     </operation>
</portType>

<portType name="CanSend3A42_PortType">
     <!-- name of operation is same as name of message -->
     <operation name="PurchaseOrderConfirmation">
            <input message="tns:PurchaseOrderConfirmation"/>
     </operation>
     <operation name="ReceiptAcknowledgment">
            <input message="tns:ReceiptAcknowledgment"/>
     </operation>
     <operation name="Exception">
            <input message="tns:Exception"/>
     </operation>
</portType>
  … … … …
```

Listing 15.1 WSDL excerpt for "Request Purchase Order"

Specifying operation parameters. After having defined the operations, designers need to specify the parameters they contain. A typical operation defines a sequence containing an input message followed by an output message. When defining operation parameters (messages) it is important to decide whether simple or complex types will be used. The `<operation>` `"PurchaseOrderRequest"` in Listing 15.1 is shown to contain an output message `"PurchaseOrderRequest"` which includes a single part named

"PO-body". This part is shown in Listing 15.2 to be associated with the complex type "PIP3A4PurchaseOrderRequest" that is further specified to the level of atomic (XSD) types in the compartment that is embraced with the <wsdl:types> tag. As Listing 15.2 indicates, well-factored Web services often result in a straightforward <portType> element where the business complexity is moved into the business data declaration.

Several graphical Web services development environments and toolkits exist today. These enable developers to rapidly create, view, and edit services using WSDL and manage issues such as correct syntax and validation, inspecting and testing Web services, and accelerating many common XML development tasks encountered when developing Web-service-enabled applications.

15.10.2.2 Service programming style

In addition to structural and behavioral service specifications, the service programming style must also be specified during the service design phase. Determining the service programming style is largely a design issue as different applications impose different programming-style requirements for Web services. Consider for example an application that deals with purchase order requests, purchase order confirmations, and delivery information. This application requires that request messages should contain purchase orders in the form of XML documents, while response messages should contain purchase order receipts or delivery information, again in the form of XML documents. Moreover, there is no real urgency for a response message to follow a request immediately, if at all. This type of application uses document-oriented or asynchronous Web services. In contrast to this, consider an application that provides businesses with up-to-the-instant credit standings. Before completing a business transaction, a business may require to check a potential customer's credit standing. In this scenario, a request would be sent to the credit check Web service provider, e.g., a bank, and a response indicating the potential customer's credit rating would be returned. This type of Web service relies on an RPC or synchronous programming style. In this type of application the client invoking the Web service needs an immediate response or may even require that the Web services interact in a back-and-forth conversational way.

Using document-based messaging results in loose coupling, since the message constructs the document, but does not indicate the steps to process that document. With document-based messaging, it is only the receiver that knows the steps to handle an incoming document. Thus, the receiver can add additional steps, delete steps, and so on, without impacting the client. In general, there is no reason for the Web service client to know the name of the remote methods.

15.10.3 Specifying business processes

Following the specification of concrete singular services, business processes must be designed. Business process design means explicitly modeling, designing, simulating, and redesigning processes in an enterprise. A service-oriented design and development methodology provides the ability to restructure, compose, and decompose processes as systems and business interfaces are re-engineered internally or with partners and must support reuse, generalization, and specialization of process elements. In particular, designers

```
<wsdl:types>
      <xsd:complexType name = "PIP3A4PurchaseOrderRequest">
            <xsd:sequence>
                  <xsd:element ref = "PurchaseOrder"/>
                  <xsd:element ref = "fromRole"/>
                  <xsd:element ref = "toRole"/>
                  <xsd:element ref =
                               "thisDocumentGenerationDateTime"/>
                  <xsd:element ref = "thisDocumentIdentifier"/>
                  <xsd:element ref = "GlobalDocumentFunctionCode"/>
            </xsd:sequence>
      </xsd:complexType>

      <xsd:complexType name = "PurchaseOrder">
            <xsd:sequence>
                  <xsd:element ref = "deliverTo" minOccurs = "0"/>
                  <xsd:element ref = "comment" minOccurs = "0"/>
                  <xsd:element ref = "packListRequirements"
                                     minOccurs = "0"/>
                  <xsd:element ref = "ProductLineItem"
                                     maxOccurs = "unbounded"/>
                  <xsd:element ref = "GlobalShipmentTermsCode"/>
                  <xsd:element ref = "RevisionNumber"/>
                  <xsd:element ref = "prePaymentCheckNumber"
                                     minOccurs = "0"/>
                  <xsd:element ref = "QuoteIdentifier"
                                     minOccurs = "0"/>
                  <xsd:element ref = "WireTransferIdentifier"
                                     minOccurs = "0"/>
                  <xsd:element ref = "AccountDescription"
                                     minOccurs = "0"/>
                  <xsd:element ref =
                            "generalServicesAdministrationNumber"
                                    minOccurs = "0"/>
                  <xsd:element ref =
                           "secondaryBuyerPurchaseOrderIdentifier"
                                    minOccurs = "0"/>
                  <xsd:element ref = "GlobalFinanceTermsCode"/>
                  <xsd:element ref = "PartnerDescription"
                                     maxOccurs = "unbounded"/>
                  <xsd:element ref = "secondaryBuyer"
                                     minOccurs = "0"/>
                  <xsd:element ref = "GlobalPurchaseOrderTypeCode"/>
            </xsd:sequence>
      </xsd:complexType>
</wsdl:types>
   … … … …
<message name="PurchaseOrderRequest">
      <part name="PO-body" type="tns:PIP3A4PurchaseOrderRequest"/>
</message>
```

Listing 15.2 Specifying operation parameters for operations in Listing 15.1

should be able to compose (or decompose) and relate to each other's process models that are developed in different parts of the enterprise, or by partners. They also should be in a position to incrementally refine processes and export process improvements achieved in one part of the business to other parts of the business with adaptation as required. Industry best practices and patterns must also be taken into account when designing processes and abstract process models can act as blueprints for subsequent concrete models.

Once business processes are extracted and their boundaries are clearly demarcated, they need to be described in the abstract in terms of constellations of interacting singular services that were specified according to the guidelines described in the previous section. Prior to describing business processes in the abstract, designers must determine the type of service composition. The choice is between orchestration and choreography (see section 9.6). If a choice for orchestration is made three tasks follow to orchestrate a process. These are defined using BPEL (see section 9.7). In the following we shall emphasize orchestration given that today there are several implementations for BPEL while WS-CDL is still being specified.

The step of describing processes in the abstract comprises three separate tasks: one deriving the process structure and behavior (including the process workflow logic); one linking it to business roles, which reflect responsibilities of the trading partners, e.g., a buyer, a seller, and a shipper in the order management process; and one specifying policies and non-functional characteristics of business processes (see section 15.10.4).

Finally, an SOA integration model is required to describe processes that span organizational boundaries comprehensibly. This integration model describes interaction relationships, transportation, and delivery patterns between service consumers and providers and achieves service integration in the context of an inter-organizational SOA. The SOA integration model is described in some detail in section 15.10.5. In the following we shall describe how to define process logic in terms of processes scripted in BPEL without putting any particular emphasis on integration considerations.

15.10.3.1 Describing the business process structure

The next step in the service design methodology is to describe the business structure and the functions (behavior) of the business process. The business process structure refers to the logical flow or progression of a business process. A business process reveals how an individual process activity (`<portType>`) is linked with another such activity in order to achieve a business objective. To assemble a higher-level service (process) by composing existing singular Web services, the service aggregator needs to select potential services that need to be composed depending on how these services and their operations fit within the enclosures of a business process and how they relate to one another. Subsequently, the service provider needs to connect the process interface to the interfaces of imported services and plug them together. Business processes can be scripted using BPEL.

The abstract description of a process encompasses the following tasks:

1. *Identify, group, and describe the activities and services that together implement a business process:* The objective of this action is to identify the services that need to be assembled and composed in order to generate a business process and then describe the usage interface of the overall business process. The functions of a business process are expressed in terms of the activities or the services that need to

be performed by a specific business process. For instance, the registration of a new customer is an activity in a sales order process. The structure of a business process describes how an individual process activity (`<portType>`) is linked with another in order to assemble a higher-level service in terms of singular Web services. During this procedure the service designer needs to:

(a) Select the services to compose by looking at how these services and their operations fit within the context of a business process and how they relate to one another.

(b) Connect the usage interface of the business process to the interfaces of imported services and plug them together.

2. *Describe activity dependencies, conditions, or synchronization:* A process definition can organize activities into varying structures such as hierarchical, conditional, and activity dependency definitions. In a hierarchical definition, process activities have a hierarchical structure. For instance, the activity of sending an insurance policy for a shipped order can be divided into three sub-activities: "compute the insurance premium," "notify insurance," and "mail insurance premium to customer." In process definitions that have a conditional activity structure activities are performed only if certain conditions are met. For instance, it may be company policy to send a second billing notice to a trading partner when an invoice is more than 2 months overdue. Activity dependency definitions signify synchronization dependencies between activities and sub-activities in a process. In any process definition, sub-activities can execute only after their parent activity has commenced. This means that sub-activities are implicitly dependent on their parent activity. In other cases there might be an explicit synchronization dependency between activities: an activity may only be able to start when another specific activity has completed. For instance, a shipment cannot be sent to a customer if the customer has not been sent an invoice.

3. *Describe the implementation of the business process:* Provide a BPEL definition, which maps the operations and interfaces of imported services to those of another in order to create the usage interface of the business process.

Listing 15.3 illustrates a snippet of the BPEL specification for the order management process. This is an abbreviated version of Listing 9.4. The first step in the process flow is the initial buyer request. The listing shows that three activities are planned in parallel. An inventory service is contacted in order to check the inventory, and a credit service is contacted in order to receive a credit check for the customer. Finally, a billing service is contacted to bill the customer. Upon receiving the responses back from the credit, inventory, and billing services, the supplier would construct a message back to the buyer.

15.10.3.2 Describing business roles

The second step during business process design is to identify responsibilities associated with business process activities and the roles that are responsible for performing them. Each service provider is expected to properly fulfill the business responsibility of implementing a business activity as one or more port types of a Web service, which perform a specific role. The result of this phase actually constitutes the foundation for implementing business policies, notably role-based access control and security policies (see following section).

```
<sequence>
    <receive  partner="Manufacturer"
                   portType="lns:PurchaseOrderPortType"
                   operation="Purchase"  variable="PO"
                   createInstance="yes" >
    </receive>
  <flow>
        <links>
              <link name="inventory-check"/>
              <link name="credit-check"/>
        </links>
      <!- Check inventory -->
      <invoke partner="inventoryChecker"
                  portType="lns:InventoryPortType"
                  operation="checkInventory"
                  … … …
              <source linkName="inventory-check"/>
          …
      <invoke/>
      <!- Check credit -->
      <invoke partner="creditChecker"
                  portType="lns:CreditCheckPortType"
                  operation="checkCredit"
                  … … …
              <source linkName="credit-check"/>
          ….
      <invoke/>
      <!- Issue bill once inventory and credit checks are successful -->
      <invoke partner="BillingService"
                  portType="lns:BillingPortType"
                                         operation="billClient"
                  inputVariable="billRequest"
                                     outputVariable="Invoice" >
                  joinCondition="getLinkStatus("inventory-
                  check") AND getLinkStatus("credit-check")" />
              <target linkName="inventory-check"/>
              <target linkName="credit-check"/>
          ….
      <invoke/>
  </flow>
    ...
  <reply partnerLink="Purchasing" portType="lns:purchaseOrderPT"
                      operation="Purchase" variable="Invoice"/>
</sequence>
```

Listing 15.3 BPEL process flow for the "Purchase Order" process

Listing 15.4 illustrates the different parties that interact within the business process in the course of processing a client's purchase order. This listing describes how the "PurchaseOrder" service is interfaced with the port types of associated service specifications including a credit check and price calculation (billing) service (not shown in

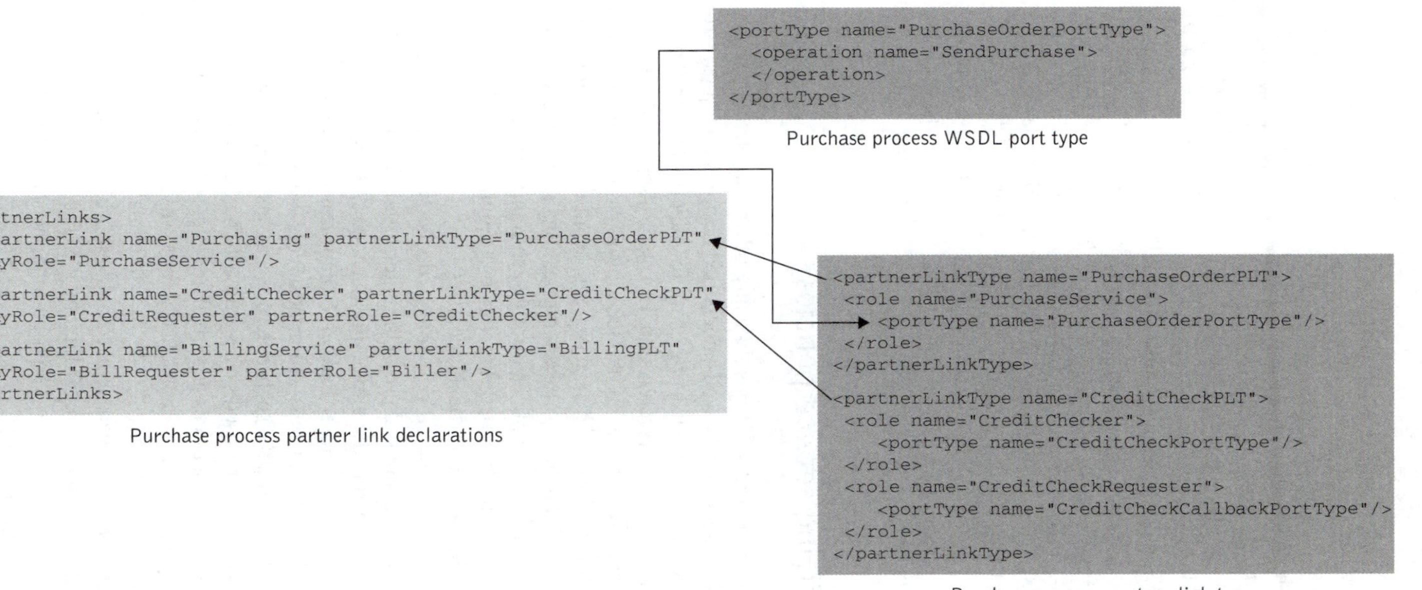

Listing 15.4 Defining roles in BPEL

this figure) to create an order management process. Each <partnerLink> definition in this listing is characterized by a <partnerLinkType>.

Developers can use automated tools to assist them with designing and developing business processes. Toolsets enable analysts to model, simulate, and analyze complex business processes quickly and effectively. Such toolsets can be used to model "as-is" and "to-be" business processes, allocate resources, and perform "what-if" simulations to optimize and estimate business benefits [Brown 2005]. These models can then be transformed into UML and BPEL models to jumpstart integration activities.

Developers may also rely on specialized graphical notations, such as the Business Process Modeling Notation (BPMN), which can be used for modeling business processes and directly produce fully executable BPEL scripts. BPMN is an attempt at a standards-based business process modeling language that can unambiguously define business logic and information requirements to the extent that the resultant models are executable [White 2004], [Owen 2004]. BPMN is intended for allowing users to express the complex semantics of business processes. The net result is that business logic and information requirements are maintained in a model that is consistent with and reflects the requirements of business.

15.10.4 Specifying service policies

The design of service-oriented solutions, like any other complex structure, requires early architectural decisions supported by well-understood design techniques, structural patterns, and styles that that go far beyond ensuring "simple" functional correctness, and deal with non-functional service concerns (see section 1.8). Non-functional design concerns focus around four areas that include business and technology constraints, run-time and non-run-time qualities [Bieberstein 2006]. These have significant impact on the overall design and deployment of an SOA and have enormous implications regarding how consumers accept business services. This section examines briefly each non-functional design aspect.

Business constraints include operating ranges, regulatory and legal constraints, or standards established in specific vertical industries.

Technology constraints are based on choices, decisions, and commitments to specific technologies in current and continued use in the enterprise infrastructure [Bieberstein 2006]. This may include choice of specific application packages, legacy applications, decision to use original equipment manufacturer hardware platforms, and commitments to industry-specific standards. All these decisions can impose constraints on the design and development of SOAs. To service-enable such enterprise assets adaptation, re-engineering and repurposing mechanisms may be used (see sections 8.5.5 and 8.5.6).

Run-time qualities explore services aspects that are directly related to system dynamics such as performance, scalability, transactional integrity, security, and fault tolerance, which are examined in turn below. In SOAs run-time qualities are captured by SLAs.

Service performance is perceived as a combination of response time and throughput and can be impacted by decisions regarding such factors as service granularity, service binding choices, message passing and data volume, network bandwidth, scalability, and security choices [Bieberstein 2006].

The granularity of exposed services needs to be carefully designed. As already explained, fine-grained services lead to a lot of interactions and introduce performance overheads; on the other hand, services that are unnecessarily coarse grained lead to very large information exchanges also impacting performance.

Using WSDL as a service description medium allows services to be invoked using different binding options. To improve performance, binding optimization policies could be introduced supporting, for instance, multiple service bindings with faster protocols.

The network and processing nodes between service consumer and provider endpoints may severely impact the level of service. This requires that network capability with guaranteed bandwidth and propagation delays must be utilized whenever appropriate.

Scalability is an important issue for SOA applications and was addressed in the context of the ESB (see section 8.5.7). Scalable services can be designed effectively only when capacity planning, service provisioning, and policy-based routing is carefully controlled [Bieberstein 2006]. Capacity planning is determined from existing transaction measurements and is largely relevant to internal use of services within an enterprise. Capacity planning for SOA must gracefully introduce additional processing power. Service providers that expose their services to clients or partners usually need to define a provisioning mechanism that enables them to evaluate the number and type of additional resources required to deliver services complying with SLA stipulations. Finally, policy-based routing allows different SLAs that include agreements ranging from best-effort delivery to guaranteed response time to be applied per service customer group. In this way, better scalability control can be exercised.

Since Web services should allow access to sanctioned clients, security is a first-order business consideration. Normally, an integrated approach to security is required whereby all technical system aspects as well as business policies and processes are taken into consideration. There are several unique security-related characteristics that need to be addressed by a service design methodology. For example, a service provider could specify a policy stating that a given Web service requires Kerberos tokens, digital signatures, and encryption. Potential clients use such policy information to determine whether they can use this particular service. In many cases an SLA is used to bundle security policies to protect multi-party collaborations. Knowing that a new business process adopts a Web services security standard such as WS-Security is not enough information to enable successful composition. The client needs to be aware of the transport security policies that state the type of protection offered in the actual delivery protocols, e.g., use of SSL; message-level security policies that specify end-to-end message protection by using encryption and digital signatures; and security token policies that specify the type of security token used during interactions. Trying to orchestrate services without understanding these technical details will inevitably lead to erroneous results. For example, the purchase order service in the order management process may indicate that it only accepts user name tokens that are signed using an X.509 certificate that is cryptographically endorsed by a specific third party.

In addition to security concerns, SLAs are also concerned with authorization. Increasingly authorization capabilities are emerging as a major security requirement for business collaborations. An enterprise not only needs to know who the requestors accessing its services are; it also needs to control what Web services that requestor has access to, what factors affect availability of the Web services to that customer, and what auditing is required to ensure the non-repudiation of transactions with that requestor. Client authentication may rely on different authentication policies. For instance, an authentication policy may require that a client authenticates itself by presenting its encoded credentials or may require that XML signatures be generated for Web service requests.

A good source for designing robust security models that secure business applications (including SOA-enabled ones) end to end at all levels is [Steel 2006]. This reference covers the rationale for adopting a security methodology, the process steps of a security methodology, and how to create and use security patterns within that methodology.

Non-functional service design requirements such as the ones described in the previous section can be described using WS-Policy assertions, which were described in section 12.4.

15.10.5 Services integration model

An SOA services integration model facilitates the design of a service integration strategy that applies Web services to solving integration and interoperability problems mainly between interacting enterprises. This strategy includes such subjects as service design models, policies, SOA governance options (see section 15.13.1), and organizational and industry best practices and conventions. All these need to be taken into account when designing integrated end-to-end business processes that span organizational boundaries. The SOA integration model is based on four broad service integration principles. These are service relationship, transportation, delivery, and process flow principles and are described in great length in [Marks 2006]. In the following we shall briefly introduce these principles and explain how they relate to the SOA services integration model design phases.

The *service relationship principle* examines the services relationships that are founded in business processes in terms of service producers and consumers during service design. Relationships can be characterized as message exchange relationships, where services that exchange messages are related according to their responsibilities in the message exchange in a similar manner to business roles in BPEL, and link dependencies, which are characterized by business or technological links between service consumers and producers. Link dependencies are characterized as one-to-one (binary), one-to-many, and many-to-many depending on how many service providers and consumers interacts with each other.

The *service transportation principle* examines the message interceptors or brokers interposed between service consumers and providers. Three main SOA message transportation patterns can be utilized when designing service-oriented integration [Marks 2006]: direct access pattern, brokered interception pattern, and service bus pattern. These largely coincide with the business integration patterns examined in Exercises 8.4 and 8.5. In the direct access pattern, service providers and consumers communicate directly. In the broker interception pattern, one or more intermediaries are interposed between consumers and providers. Finally, the service bus pattern supports federated ESB configurations enabling loose coupling and providing increased scalability and high-volume transportation.

The *service delivery principle* describes the mechanisms which service intermediaries, consumers, and producers use to deliver messages to various endpoints. The service delivery principle is characterized by three delivery patterns. In-order delivery patterns are delivery patterns in which messages are delivered sequentially between participant parties in a business process. Same-time delivery patterns are delivery patterns in which parallel broadcasting of messages to multiple subscribers is used. Finally, synchronous and asynchronous delivery patterns coincide with the services programming style in section 15.10.2.

The final principle is the *process flow principle*, which describes how service conversations and behavioral activities in which service providers and consumers are engaged are influenced by business, technical, and environmental requirements. The process flow principle exhibits four interaction patterns. The direct conversation pattern describes a conversation path and process flow between service consumers and providers. The indirect conversation pattern describes message and business process redirection to a number of service consumers and providers to accomplish a single business transaction. The final two conversation patterns are the one-way message transmission pattern, which is identical to one-way SOAP messaging (see Figure 4.3), and, the two-way message transmission pattern, which is identical to one-way SOAP messaging (see Figure 4.4).

The service integration principles described above help define four corresponding service integration design phases, which are traversed iteratively. The first phase, the *service integration relationship*, identifies service associations in an SOA environment. This phase includes steps that identify transaction ownership and partnership and establish integration relationships between service consumers and providers involved in a single business transaction. The *service integration transportation definition* phase identifies message transmitters and conversation enablers. It includes steps that determine service responsibilities, assign duties to intermediaries, such as performing and facilitating message interception, message transformation, load balancing, routing, and so on, and produce a transportation integration map by utilizing the service integration strategy principle patterns. The *service integration delivery definition* phase applies connectivity and message distribution patterns. It includes steps that determine message distribution needs, delivery-responsible parties, and provides a service delivery map. The final phase of service integration, *process flow definition*, is concerned with message and process orchestration utilizing appropriate transportation mechanisms. This phase includes steps that establish network routes; verify network and environment support, e.g., validate network topology and environmental capacity as well as routing capabilities; and employ integration flow patterns to facilitate the flow of messages and transactions.

The design of the SOA services integration model ends when the process architecture is completely expressed and validated against technological specifications provided mainly by infrastructure, management/monitoring services, and technical utility services (see section 15.4).

15.11 The service construction phase

Service construction is a phase at the physical SOA level that involves implementing Web services and business processes using the specifications that were developed during the design phase. The construction phase of the services lifecycle requires the creation of the hosting environment for SOA-based applications and the actual deployment of those applications. This includes resolving the application's resource dependencies, operational conditions, capacity requirements, integrity and access constraints. The specialized nature of SOA run-time platform elements is the primary differentiating factor in the creation phase. Applications built within SOA initiatives require a specialized run-time platform. This platform may include application servers, which provide advanced facilities for publishing service interfaces and hosting their implementations; ESB implementations which can transparently apply QoS policies and transformations to service requests and replies; service orchestration engines; and so on.

The construction phase of the lifecycle methodology includes development of the Web service implementation, the definition of the service interface description, and the definition of the service implementation description [Brittenham 2001]. This phase may involve green-field code development; however, in most cases it will consist of modifying existing (J2EE or .NET) services or constructing wrappers on top of existing legacy applications and is supported by infrastructure, management/monitoring services, and technical utility services.

Service construction is a two-pronged activity. It involves constructing services at both the service provider and the service client sides. On the provider side the implementation of a Web service can be provided by creating a new Web service, or by transforming existing applications into Web services, or by composing new Web services from other (reusable) Web services and applications. Unlike the previous phases that focus only on the provider, the service construction phase also considers service requestors. On the service client side, although the service requestor progresses through similar lifecycle stages as the service provider, different tasks are performed during each construction step. In the following we shall concentrate on the development concepts for a singular Web service for reasons of brevity and simplicity. Business process can be created in a similar manner.

15.11.1 Constructing a service: the provider perspective

When new Web services are created they may be either allocated directly to component-based containers for realization of their functionality, or realized by adapting existing legacy functionality. Likewise, when transforming existing applications into Web services (service-enabling applications) the service functionality may be realized by appropriately adapting existing legacy functionality. In summary, when creating a Web service there are two possible implementation paths [Wahli 2004]:

1. There is an already existing implementation (service content) for the Web service, e.g., in Java code. By using this implementation the developer can build the service definition (WSDL document). Once the WSDL definition has generated the WSDL document, the developer can assemble the Web service application.

2. A service definition already exists in the form of a WSDL document. By using this WSDL document the designer can build or adapt the implementation (Java) code to realize that service. Once the code is implemented, the developer can assemble the Web service application.

In the following we shall briefly examine how the four service realization options that were identified during service analysis in section 15.9.5 are constructed, starting with green-field development. There are two ownership possibilities as regards the service realization options. The service provider could own both the WSDL interface and the service implementation. Alternatively, the service provider could own a WSDL interface whose implementation was constructed and owned by an application service provider.

The green-field development method considers how a new service is created and comprises two steps [Brittenham 2001]:

1. *Develop the new Web service content:* This step includes the design and coding of the service content required to implement the service, and the testing to verify that all the interfaces of the service implementation components work correctly. For example, a Web service provider may construct an artifact, e.g., a Java program, which contains the business logic and code to access the required back-end systems in an enterprise to develop the implementation component of a new Web service.
2. *Define a new Web service interface:* Once the new Web service has been designed and developed, its interface definition in WSDL can be generated from the implementation of the service. The WSDL interface for the Web service cannot be created unless the artifact that represents the implementation and business logic underlying the Web service is complete. This is due to the fact that the WSDL interface matches the exact implementation of the service.

Figure 15.6 illustrates the green-field development approach and distinguishes between the logical and the physical part of the services lifecycle methodology. The WSDL specification in Figure 15.6 corresponds to a business service in Figure 15.2 and the service implementation corresponds to the physical layers in the same figure.

The top-down approach is commonly used when we have a standard Web service definition for which there exists no service implementation. The developer then needs to build a service implementation conforming to the service interface. The top-down realization option is divided into two distinct steps:

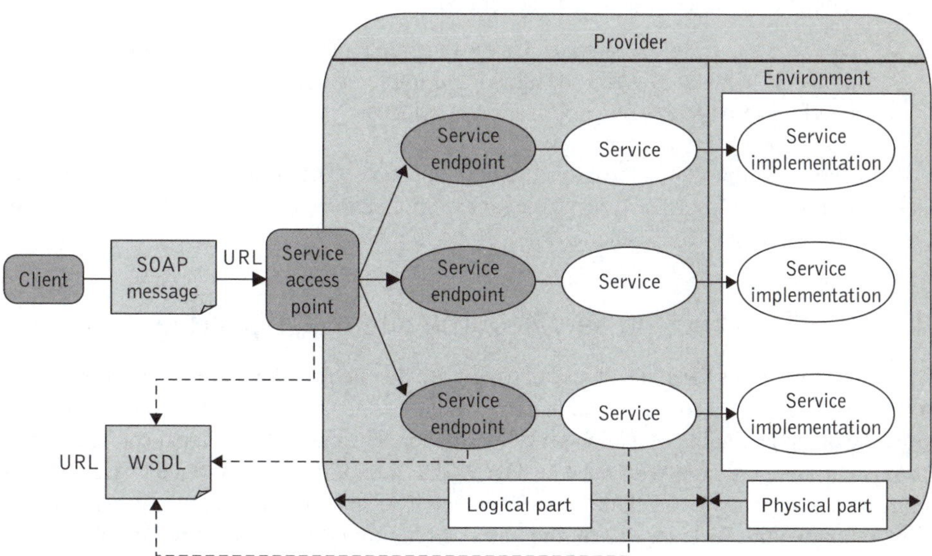

Figure 15.6 The provider perspective on service construction

1. *Generate the Web service implementation skeleton:* An implementation skeleton for the Web service is generated using the Web service interface definition. This skeleton contains all the methods and parameters that must be used so that a compliant implementation of the Web service interface can be realized.
2. *Develop the new Web service:* Using the implementation template created in the previous step, design and develop the application and business logic that implements the Web service. This step includes the design and coding required to implement the service, and the testing verifying that all the interfaces of the service implementation components work correctly.

The bottom-up approach is the most common way to build a Web service. Designers start with the Web service content which comes in the form of a business application that is already developed, tested, and running in an enterprise. The bottom-up realization option comprises only one step: developing the Web service interface. The Web service interface is derived from the API of the non-service application that represents the Web service content by creating a wrapper. Therefore, developers start with the Web service content and generate a WSDL definition document for it, providing all the desired functionality that needs to be externally exposed as a Web service. Depending of the implementation model (J2EE, for instance), designers may also have to generate the deployment descriptors.

The meet-in-the-middle realization option is used when a Web service interface and service content already exist. The prime concern of the meet-in-the-middle development is to map existing application interfaces to those specified in the Web service WSDL interface definition. We can distinguish two steps for this realization option:

1. *Generate the service implementation skeleton:* Using the service interface definition that is going to be used to implement the Web service, an implementation template of the Web service is generated.
2. *Develop the service wrapper:* Using the implementation skeleton created in the previous step, a wrapper is designed and implemented which will map the service interface into the existing application interface.

All processes follow the same construction trajectory. The designer composes process parts from new Web services, service-enabled applications, or existing Web services, or from a combination of those elements.

15.11.2 Constructing services: the client perspective

The build-time tasks for the service requestor are dictated by the method for binding to a Web service. On the provider side, the construction-time tasks are dictated on the basis of how the client is binding to a Web service provider. The client uses a local service stub or proxy to access a remote Web service. The WSDL definition of the service is used to generate a stub or proxy at the client's environment. The stub or proxy knows at request time how to invoke the Web service on the basis of binding information. Binding to a service could happen either statically or dynamically. This results in distinguishing between two types of Web service clients: static clients versus dynamic clients.

A *static client* is created at construction time by locating the service implementation definition for the single Web service that will be used by the service requestor. The service implementation definition contains a reference to the service interface, service binding, and service endpoint that will be used to generate the service proxy code. The service proxy contains a complete implementation of the client application that can be used by the service requestor to invoke Web service operations.

There are three steps involved in this realization option. First, the service requestor must acquire the service definition either directly from the provider or by consulting the UDDI. Following this step, the designer generates a proxy or stub using the information contained in the WSDL document. This stub is a local representation of the remote Web service. There are currently several tools available that automatically generate stubs from WSDL definitions. Finally, the service is tested and subsequently deployed in the client run-time environment.

A *dynamic client* is used when a service requestor wants to use a specific type of Web service with a known service definition whose implementation is not known until run-time or can change at run-time. This means that service operations, the parameters associated with the operations, and the way to bind to the service are already known; however, the endpoint where this service is provided is not known at design time. A typical example of this is when a vertical industry defines a service interface that is implemented by several providers. In that case, a service requestor may wish to choose at run-time out of a pool of providers a particular provider on the basis of specific quality criteria such as performance, cost, and so forth. The use of a public, private, or shared UDDI registry is involved in the process to dynamically provide to the client a range of entry points available at a given time.

There are three steps involved in this realization option. First, the service requestor must acquire the service definition document obtaining information about the types, the messages, the port type with the operations, and the binding of the WSDL document using the same mechanisms as in the case of a static client. Following this step, the designer generates a proxy using the information contained in the WSDL document. This proxy is a local representation of the remote Web service and can be used to access any implementation of the service interface. The only difference between the service proxy of a dynamic client and the one generated for a static client is that the static client uses a service proxy that has knowledge of only a single specific service implementation, while the dynamic client uses a generic service proxy that contains the code to locate a service implementation by searching a service registry. Finally, the service is tested and subsequently deployed in the client run-time environment.

Figure 15.7 shows the construction approach from the perspective of a requestor. Notice that, just like the case of the provider in Figure 15.6, the client also must be concerned both with the logical and the physical aspects of proxy services.

15.12 The service test phase

Testing is arguably one of the most important phases in any software development project. The goal of testing is to analyze or operate the implementation in a test environment in order to expose any failures that are latent in the code as it is integrated, configured, and

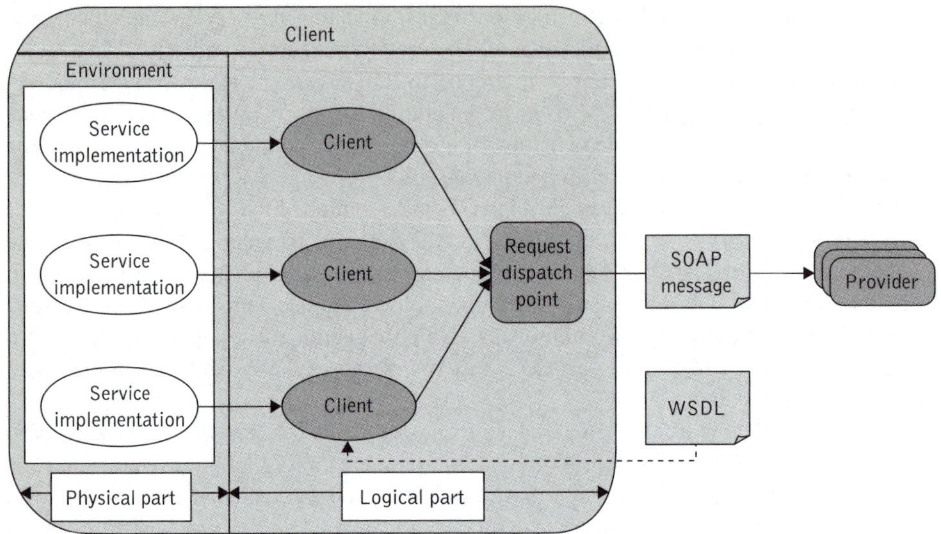

Figure 15.7 The client perspective on service construction

run on diverse platforms. *Service testing* is generally characterized as a validation exercise at the physical level, ascertaining that requirements have been met and that the deliverables are at an acceptable level and in accordance with existing standards during the analysis, design, and construction phases of the services lifecycle. The result of testing is a "healthy" service-oriented application that performs well enough to satisfy the needs of its customers.

Enterprises normally start out with pilots and proof-of-concept implementations to test the performance and availability of their Web services. Pilot projects offer an excellent opportunity for enterprises to set informal QoS goals for their applications and track against them. For instance, an enterprise can determine whether or not it can provide 99% 24/7 availability for a claims processing service that is used by its worldwide partners. This enterprise can then evaluate the test results from its pilot project and if it is satisfied with the QoS levels attained, it may decide to roll out the claims processing service to its brokers in multiple phases, with each phase including a larger number of external users. Using the service testing approach, this enterprise can gradually fine tune its applications, set realistic expectations with its community of brokers, and reduce any potential business risks.

Service testing spans various forms of testing including dynamic testing, functional testing, performance testing, interface testing, and assembly testing. These are examined in turn below.

The most interesting type of testing for service implementations is *dynamic testing*, which consists of running the implementation and comparing its actual to its expected behavior before it is deployed. If the actual behavior differs from the expected behavior, a defect has been found. In the context of services, dynamic testing is used to perform a variety of types of tests such as functional tests, performance and stress tests, assembly tests, and interface tests.

Functional testing covers how well the service executes the functions it is expected to execute – including user commands, data manipulation, searches, and integration activities. The objective of functional testing in service-oriented environments is to ensure that the business process design has been correctly implemented. Functional testing covers the obvious service interface and operations, as well as the ensuing operations on back-end systems, including security functions, database transactions, and how upgrades affect the service-oriented system [Culbertson 2001].

The focus of *performance testing* in service-oriented environments is monitoring service on-line response times and transaction rates under peak workload conditions. It also involves load testing, which measures the service's ability to handle varied workloads. Performance testing is related to stress testing, which looks for errors produced by low resources or competition for resources. It is also related to volume testing, which subjects the service to larger and larger amounts of data to determine its point of failure. During performance testing it is important to document all of the testing performed, issues that were encountered, and fixes that were made.

The objective of *interface testing* is to ensure that any service is developed to properly interface with other service functions outside of its surrounding process. Interface testing should be performed while testing the function that is affected, e.g., an order management process calling an inventory service.

Finally, *assembly testing* ensures that all services function properly when assembled into business processes. It also verifies that services that interact and interoperate function properly when assembled as parts of business processes.

In addition to functional tests, performance and stress tests, assembly tests, and interface tests, there are a variety of other tests that may need to be performed during the service test phase. These include network congestion tests, security tests, installation tests, compatibility tests, usability tests, and upgrade tests. For instance, security tests have to be conducted to ensure service security requirements such as privacy, message integrity, authentication, authorization, and non-repudiation.

15.13 The service provisioning phase

The provisioning requirements for Web services impose serious implications for SDLC. Service provisioning is a complex mixture of technical and business aspects for supporting service client and provider activities and involves choices for service governance, service certification, service enrollment, service auditing, metering, billing, and managing operations that control the behavior of a service during its use. We provide an overview of the most salient features of service provisioning in what follows.

15.13.1 Service governance

Enterprises that progress towards SOA development wish to ensure continuity of their business operations, manage their security exposure, align technology implementation with business requirements, manage liabilities and dependencies, and, in general, reduce the cost of operations. Many successful enterprises have created value by selecting the right investments and successfully managing them from concept through implementation to realizing the expected value. Such decisions are generally made on the basis of what is known as IT governance.

IT governance is a formalization of the structured relationships, procedures, and policies that ensure the IT functions in an organization support and are aligned to business functions. IT governance aligns IT activities with the goals of the organization as a whole and includes the decision-making rights associated with IT investment, as well as the policies, practices, and processes used to measure and control the way IT decisions are prioritized and executed [Holley 2006].

The IT Governance Institute (**http://www.itgi.org/**) has established a value IT framework that consists of a set of guiding principles, and a number of processes conforming to those principles, which are further defined as a suite of key management practices. To obtain ROI, the ITGI recommends that the stakeholders of the IT-enabled investments apply these guiding principles in terms of three core processes: value governance, portfolio management, and investment management. The goal of *value governance* is to optimize the value of an organization's IT-enabled investments by establishing the governance, monitoring, and control framework, providing strategic direction for the investments and defining the investment portfolio characteristics. The goal of *portfolio management* is to ensure that an organization's overall portfolio of IT-enabled investments is aligned with and contributes optimal value to the organization's strategic objectives by establishing and managing resource profiles; defining investment thresholds; evaluating, prioritizing, and selecting, managing the overall portfolio; and monitoring, and reporting on portfolio performance. Finally, the goal of *investment management* is to ensure that an organization's individual IT-enabled investment programs deliver optimal value at an affordable cost with a known and acceptable level of risk by identifying business requirements, analyzing the alternatives, assigning clear accountability and ownership, managing the program through its full economic lifecycle, and so forth.

A significant challenge to widespread SOA adoption is for SOAs to deliver value. To achieve this, there must be control in areas ranging from how a service is built and the process of service deployment, to granular items such as XSD schemas and WSDL creation. Moreover, the cross-organizational nature of end-to-end business processes that are composed out of variety of service fragments (which may need to be maintained separately by different organizations) makes the management of QoS a factor of paramount importance. QoS must not only be enforced but also be proven and demonstrated to service consumers to gain their trust and create an effective shared-service environment. To implement an efficient services strategy at the enterprise level, more than just technical know-how is needed. It requires efficient SOA governance. Therefore, not surprisingly, SOA has been a key driver in the increasing emphasis on, and interest in, governance in recent years. Consequently, identifying, specifying, creating, and deploying enterprise services, and overseeing their proper maintenance and growth needs SOA governance to oversee the entire lifecycle of an enterprise's service portfolio [Mitra 2005]. Only when SOA-enabled business investments are managed well within an effective governance framework can enterprises harvest significant opportunities to create value.

SOA governance is an extension of IT governance and guiding principles, such as the ones described above, which focus on the lifecycle of services and is designed to enable enterprises to maximize business benefits of SOA such as increased process flexibility, improved responsiveness, and reduced IT maintenance costs. SOA governance refers to the organization, process, policies, and metrics that are required to manage an SOA successfully [Marks 2006]. SOA governance is a lifecycle approach that integrates an organization's people, processes, information, and assets. It mitigates many of the business risks inherent in SOA adoption by establishing decision rights, guiding the definition of appropriate services, managing assets, and measuring effectiveness.

The goal of SOA governance is to align the business strategy and imperatives of an enterprise with its IT initiatives. When applied to service-oriented applications, SOA governance may involve internal development project-specific reviews as well external reviews from the perspective of the service providers. Typical issues for internal reviews include whether the right types of services have been selected, whether all requirements for new services have been identified, and so forth. To this end SOA governance may use as input the findings of the business gap analysis subphase that we covered earlier in this chapter. Other internal review issues also include whether the use of a particular service within an application would conform to enterprise-specific or government-mandated privacy rules, whether service implementation does not compromise QoS requirements as stipulated in SLAs or enterprise-specific intellectual property, and so on. To achieve its stated objectives and support an enterprise's business objectives on strategic, functional, and operational levels, SOA governance provides a well-defined structure. It defines the rules, processes, metrics, and organizational constructs needed for effective planning, decision making, steering, and control of the SOA engagement to meet the business requirements of an enterprise and its customers [Balzer 2004].

The SOA lifecycle methodology is layered on a backdrop of a set of governance processes that ensure that compliance and operational polices are enforced, and that change occurs in a controlled fashion and with appropriate authority as envisioned by the business design. An enterprise can address the service governance challenge most effectively by establishing an internal governance body comprising business analysts, line of business decision makers, security specialists, network operations experts, users, and others. Such teams can play a crucial role in engineering an SOA environment which functions for the greater benefit of the enterprise.

The essential responsibilities of the governance body include strategic alignment, value delivery, risk, resource, and performance management [Mitra 2005]. *Strategic alignment* concentrates on aligning the business vision, goals, and requirements with IT efforts. *Value delivery* concentrates on how results including profitability, expense reduction, error reduction, improved company image, branding, and so on prove the value of IT. *Risk management* concentrates on business continuity and measures to be taken to protect the IT assets of an enterprise. *Resource management* focuses on optimizing infrastructure services that are a part of the environment supporting the application services. Finally, *performance management* concentrates on monitoring the services that run in an enterprise environment. An enterprise's SOA governance body ensures that the enterprise's IT sustains and extends its strategies and objectives by laying down service-related policies and decides about which people in the enterprise are empowered to make those decisions and can thus monitor, define, and authorize the changes to the existing suite of services supported within the enterprise.

Services that flow between enterprises must also have defined owners with established ownership and governance responsibilities. These owners are responsible for gathering requirements, development, deployment, and operations management for any mission-critical or revenue-generating service [Bieberstein 2005]. The service must meet the functional and QoS objectives both within the context of the business unit and the enterprises within which it operates. To this end, SOA governance introduces the notion of *business domain ownership*, where domains are managed sets of services sharing some business context. Typical examples of such business scopes are customer relationship management, customer information and entitlements, order management, financing, taxes, and so forth.

Two different governance models are possible. These are central governance versus federated governance and are discussed below:

> *Central governance:* With central governance, the governing body within an enterprise has representation from each business domain as well as from independent parties that do not have direct responsibility for any of the service domains. There is also representation from the different business units in the organization and subject matter experts who can talk to the developers who implement key technological components of the services solution. The central governance council reviews any additions or deletions to the list of services, along with changes to existing services, before authorizing the implementation of such changes. Central governance suits an entire enterprise.
>
> *Federated governance:* With federated governance each business unit has autonomous control over how it provides the services within its own enterprise. This requires a functional service domain approach. A central governance committee can provide guidelines and standards to different teams. This committee has an advisory role in that it makes only recommendations and it does not have to authorize changes to the existing service infrastructure within any business unit. Federated governance suits enterprise chains better.

Figure 15.8 was inspired by [Wilkes 2005] and illustrates the role that the ESB plays with respect to SOA governance. As illustrated in this figure, the ESB can play an important role in SOA governance by monitoring business activities and handling exceptions, by providing run-time monitoring capabilities to check policy compliance and provide audit trails, facilitating service management, resource, and business process optimization.

Finally, excellent overviews of SOA governance processes and principles can be found in [Bieberstein 2006], [Marks 2006].

15.13.2 Service certification

In the early development phases we have stressed the fact that enough information should be provided in order to determine whether a service is useful within the context for which it is being evaluated. An item of importance is whether one can trust the QoS. *Service certification* deals with this service aspect and may involve establishing that a service possesses particular properties, most often in conformance with some specification against which the service or business process is certified [Bachmann 2000]. This ensures that application developers work with "known quantities." To establish that a service possesses some desired property we need to use knowledge to predict the overall properties that an assembled application may attain.

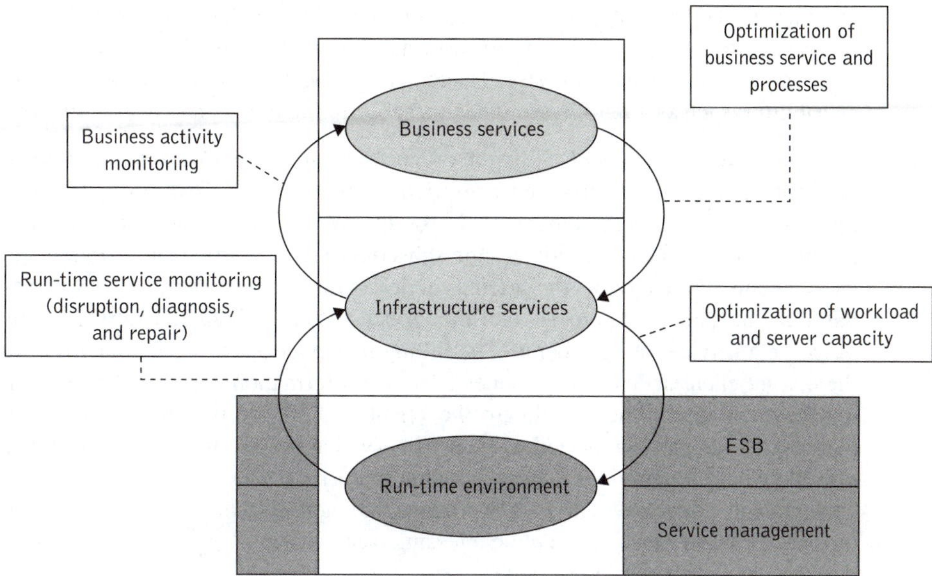

Figure 15.8 The role of the ESB in SOA governance

Certification identifies which properties of services are material for predicting or achieving some end-system properties, such as performance, safety, scalability, and so on, and how to predict the "values" of end-system properties from service properties. Measurement techniques must be in place to determine, to a desired level of confidence, the degree to which a service exhibits these properties.

It is foreseeable that an independent trusted group within an organization or even a third party might certify that services and processes are fit for their stated purpose and attest to the truth of this conformance. This has consequences for the development of consumer trust.

15.13.3 Service metering and rating

A service-oriented design methodology should take into account several important aspects relating to the accounting process for service provisioning. This process requires that service providers come up with viable business models that address factors such as service metering, rating, and billing, as explained in the following:

> *Service metering model:* Use of a service by a client must be metered if the service provider requires usage-based billing. In this case the service provider needs to audit the service as it is used and bill for it. This could typically be done on a periodic basis and requires that a metering and accounting model for the use of the service be established. The model could allow the establishment of a service contract for each new subscriber as well as tracking and billing for using the subscribed hosted services. To achieve this, the service metering model could operate on the assumption that Web services with a high degree of value are contracted via, for example, SLAs. This implies that both the service provider and requestor agree to a contract

and they are bound to it. The service contract lays the foundation for metering the services to be used, by covering all aspects of how they will be offered by the provider and used by the requestor. The metering model can cover diverse payment possibilities such as a fee-for-use model, a subscription model, and a lease model.

Service rating/billing model: Software organizations that are used to the traditional up-front license/ongoing maintenance pricing structure for software should come up with annuity-based pricing models for the Web services they provide. The pricing (rating) model could determine subscriber rates based on subscription and usage events. For example, the pricing model could calculate charges for services based on the quality and precision of the service and on individual metering events based on a service rating scheme. The billing model associates rating details with the correct client account. It provides adequate information to allow the retrieval and payment of billing details by the client and the correct disbursement of payments to the service provider's suppliers (which are in turn service providers offering wholesale services to the original provider).

Service charging alternatives may include: payment on a per use basis, payment on a subscription basis, payment on a leasing basis, lifetime services, free services, and free services with hidden value.

15.14 The service deployment phase

Once the provisioning model has been established, the Web services may be deployed and advertised. Deployment means rolling out new processes to all the participants, including other enterprises, applications, and other processes. SDLC promotes a separation between service creation and deployment activities, which are grouped into separate phases that can occur at different times, and that different individuals with different skills can perform. This yields a true separation of concerns, enabling developers to repurpose software components, services, and business processes.

The tasks associated with the deployment phase of the Web service development lifecycle include the publication of the service interface and service implementation definition. Services are deployed at the service provider side according to the four service realization options that were examined in section 15.11.1.

For services that were developed in a green-field fashion we can distinguish the following four deployment steps [Brittenham 2001]:

1. *Publish the service interface:* Service providers publish their Web service definition in a service registry, such as UDDI, so that service requestors can use it to determine how to bind to the service.

2. *Deploy the Web service:* The run-time code for the service and any deployment metadata that is required to run it are deployed during this step. Some Web services will require a deployment environment that provides support for functions such as service billing, service auditing, service security, and logging. After a Web service has been deployed, service requestors can use it.

3. *Create the service implementation definition:* Service providers provide a service content implementation definition based on how and where the service was deployed. The service implementation definition can contain references to more than one version of the deployed Web service. This allows the service provider to implement different levels of service to suit the requirements of multiple service requestors.
4. *Publish the service implementation definition:* The service implementation definition contains the definition of the network-accessible endpoint or endpoints where the Web service can be invoked. After the service implementation definition has been published, service requestors can discover the service definition and use it to bind to the Web service.

For services that were developed in a top-down fashion we can distinguish the following three deployment steps [Brittenham 2001]:

1. *Deploy the Web service:* The run-time code for the service and any deployment metadata that is required to run it are deployed during this step.
2. *Create the service implementation definition:* The service implementation definition is created based on how and where the service was deployed.
3. *Publish the service implementation definition:* The service implementation definition contains the definition of the network-accessible endpoint or endpoints where the Web service can be invoked.

For services that were developed in a bottom-up fashion we can distinguish the following four deployment steps [Brittenham 2001]:

1. *Deploy the Web service:* This step is the same as step 2 in green-field service development.
2. *Create the service implementation definition:* This step is the same as step 3 in green-field service development.
3. *Publish the service interface definition:* The service interface definition must be published first and then publication of the service implementation can follow.
4. *Publish the service implementation definition:* This step is the same as step 4 in green-field service development.

The deployment steps for the meet-in-the-middle method are similar to those for the bottom-up option. The only difference is that the service interface is already published.

15.15 The service execution phase

The service execution phase in the SDLC methodology deals with the execution of Web services. This phase includes the actual binding and run-time invocation of the deployed services as well as managing and monitoring their lifecycle. Execution means ensuring that the new process is carried out by all participants – people, other organizations, systems, and other processes. During the execution phase, Web services are fully deployed and operational. During this stage of the lifecycle, a service requestor can find the service definition and invoke all defined service operations. The run-time functions include static and dynamic binding, service interactions as a function of SOAP serialization/deserialization and messaging, and interactions with back-end legacy systems (if necessary).

15.16 The service monitoring phase

Once services and business processes become operational, their progress needs to be managed and monitored to gain a clear view of how services perform within their operational environment, make management decisions, and perform control actions to modify and adjust the behavior of Web-services-enabled applications. Service-level monitoring is a disciplined methodology for establishing acceptable levels of service that address business objectives, processes, and costs.

The service monitoring phase concerns itself with service-level measurement; monitoring is the continuous and closed loop procedure of measuring, monitoring, reporting, and improving the QoS of systems and applications delivered by service-oriented solutions. Service monitoring involves several distinct activities including logging and analysis of service execution details, obtaining business metrics by analyzing service execution data, detecting business situations that require management attention, determining appropriate control actions to take in response to business situations, whether in mitigating a risk or taking an opportunity, and using historical service performance data for continuous service improvement.

The service monitoring phase targets continuous evaluation of service-level objectives, monitoring the services layer for availability and performance, managing security policies, tracking interconnectivity of loosely coupled components, analyzing the root cause, and correcting problems. To achieve this objective, service monitoring requires that a set of QoS metrics be gathered on the basis of SLAs, given that an SLA is an understanding of expectation of service. In addition, workloads need to be monitored and service weights for request queues might need to be readjusted. This allows a service provider to ensure that the promised performance level is being delivered, and to take appropriate actions to rectify non-compliance with an SLA, such as reprioritizing and reallocating resources.

To determine whether an objective has been met, SLA-available QoS metrics are evaluated based on measurable data about a service (e.g., response time, throughput, availability, and so on), performance during specified times, and periodic evaluations, see Chapter 16. SLAs include other observable objectives, which are useful for service monitoring. These include compliance with differentiated service-level offerings, i.e., providing differentiated QoS for various types of customers, individualized service-level offerings, and requests policing which ensures that the number requests per customer stays within a predefined limit. All these also need to be monitored and assessed. A key aspect of defining measurable objectives is to set warning thresholds and alerts for compliance failures. This results in pre-emptively addressing issues before compliance failures occur. For instance, if the response time of a particular service is degrading then the client could be automatically routed to a backup service.

15.17 Summary

Service orientation reinforces general software engineering principles such as modularization and separation of the interfaces from their implementations, in addition to introducing concepts such as service choreography and message-oriented and event-driven interactions. To build a system that conforms to SOA principles, a Web services development lifecycle methodology needs to be followed. This methodology allows the design and development of solutions as assemblies of services which are amenable to analysis, change, and evolution.

A service-oriented design and development methodology is based on an iterative and incremental process that comprises one preparatory and eight distinct main phases that concentrate on business processes and may be traversed iteratively. These are planning, analysis, design, construction, testing, provisioning, deployment, execution, and monitoring.

The planning phase determines the feasibility, nature, and scope of service solutions in the context of an enterprise. A strategic task for any organization is to achieve a service technology "fit" within its current environment. The phase of service-oriented analysis identifies the requirements of new applications. It includes reviewing the business goals and objectives that drive the development of business processes. The service design phase requires modeling and defining well-documented interfaces for all major service components prior to constructing the services themselves. It considers both functional and non-functional service characteristics and provides two production lines: one to produce services (possibly out of pre-existing components), and another to assemble (compose) services out of reusable service constellations.

The construction phase includes development of the Web service implementation, the definition of the service interface description, and the definition of the service implementation description. Testing analyzes the service implementation in a test environment in order to expose any failures that are latent in the code as services are integrated, configured, and run on diverse platforms. Service provisioning involves choices for service governance, service certification, service enrollment, service auditing, metering, billing, and managing operations that control the behavior of a service during its use. The service deployment phase includes the service implementation definition and the publication of the service interface. Finally, during the execution phase Web services are fully deployed and operational, while during the monitoring phase services are monitored to gain a clear view of how they behave within their operational environment and address any deviations in their behavior.

Review questions

- How does a Web services development methodology compare to traditional methodologies such as object-oriented analysis and design and component-based development?
- What are business services and how do they relate to infrastructure services and implementation components?

- Briefly describe the milestones of service-oriented design development.
- What is service coupling, service cohesion, and service granularity?
- Briefly describe the phases of the Web services development lifecycle.
- What is the purpose of "as-is" process analysis?
- What is service gap analysis?
- What are the major service design concerns?
- What are the steps for specifying Web services and business processes?
- What is the purpose of the services integration model?
- What is the purpose of the service test phase?
- What are the objective and the major elements of SOA governance?

Exercises

15.1 Consider an enterprise that is operating a coordination system for aircraft landing activities. This system comprises interconnected older-generation systems for ticket booking, crew management, flight coordination, and flight operation, which are implemented on mainframe computers that typically run COBOL/CICS transactions. These four systems are responsible for retrieving passenger details from the ticket booking system, crew information from the crew management system, flight schedule and arrival information from the flight coordination system, and cockpit information from the flight operation system. The application also checks safety of the airport parking spot and the status of the unloaded cargo. In the current implementation, events are tightly coupled and business logic for collaboration between the four systems is hard-coded so that the integration functionality cannot adapt to new business requirements. This enterprise wishes to migrate to SOA-based integration for its applications and develop modern business processes on an ESB platform. In particular, the enterprise requires that data from the crew management, ticket booking, and flight operation be merged and the landing management process be notified of flight arrivals before checking the parking spot. Flight arrival is a typical event that requires detection by the flight operation system. Conduct an "as-is" and "to-be" analysis for this SOA-based application and produce a high-level view of the service components and their interconnections in the ESB platform.

15.2 Consider a simple retail inventory process that offers integration with warehouses, suppliers, or third-party fulfillment centers. First the client selects a product from a catalogue by specifying its product number. Then the availability of this product is checked in a local store inventory against the appropriate quantities. If the product is not available, then the order recipient forwards the request to a warehouse by specifying demand information. If the warehouse cannot meet the requirements of the quote, it may then identify another supplier for the customer. In this case, a referral is sent to the customer. Decompose this process into a number of discrete services and design their interfaces according to the service design steps in section 15.10.2. Finally, design the process and specify it abstractly in BPEL according to the process design steps in section 15.10.3.

15.3 EU-Rent is a fictitious car rental company that has over 1000 branches worldwide (**http://www.businessrulesgroup.org/egsbrg.shtml**). At each branch vehicles, classified by vehicle group, are available for rental. The company offers a wide variety of current-model vehicles on a short-term rental basis including daily, weekly, and monthly at a variety of locations such as airports, residential areas, and resorts. Most rentals are by advance reservation; the rental period and the car group are specified at the time of reservation. Assume that EU-Rent implements its vehicle rental processes using older-generation technologies and now wishes to implement an SOA solution for added flexibility. Further, assume that EU-Rent has conducted an "as-is", ROI, and SWOT analysis and has come up with a "to-be" process model that contains the following core vehicle rental business processes: vehicle rental reservation, vehicle handover, vehicle return from rental, and payment processing. Conduct business service identification, business scoping, gap analysis, and realization analysis (including functional and non-functional, e.g., security, requirements) for the four core EU-Rent vehicle rental processes.

15.4 Consider a loan processing application. This application comprises a loan management service that receives requests from clients and is responsible for managing a request for a new loan application or an extension of a current loan; a new account service which is responsible for opening new loan applications; a loan application service which is responsible for processing new and existing loan applications; and a credit verifier service for verifying customer credibility. Develop a service integration transportation model employing two transportation patterns, service broker interceptor and service bus for the loan processing application. Subsequently, define a service integration process flow for the service integration transportation model.

15.5 Consider the brokered enterprise topology in Exercise 8.5. This topology, just like any other, impacts SOA governance. Describe the responsibilities of business analysts and service developers in implementing an appropriate SOA governance solution for this ESB topology.

15.6 Describe an SOA governance model that applies to large enterprises. Explain the role and responsibilities of teams that are involved in implementing this SOA governance model. Common activities within this model include among other things determining SOA architecture oversight, establishing SOA policies, implementing SOA governance processes, governing services definition, creation and publishing, and establishing policies and processes for QoS enforcement. Finally, explain how the governance model can be launched in this enterprise. Some useful ideas regarding governance principles and launching the governance model can be found in [Balzer 2004].

PART IX

Service management

CHAPTER 16

Web services management

Learning objectives

In SOA solutions, service usage patterns, SLA criteria and metrics, and failure data should be continuously collected and analyzed. Without such information, it is often quite challenging to understand the root cause of an SOA-based application's performance or stability problems. In particular, enterprises need to manage and monitor business operations, identifying opportunities and diagnosing problems as they occur so as to ensure that the Web services supporting a given business task are performing in accordance with service-level objectives. To tackle these challenges there is a critical need for a Web services measurement and management infrastructure and associated toolset.

This chapter explores traditional distributed management approaches and their underlying architectural concepts and relates them to Web services management techniques and upcoming standards. After completing this chapter readers will understand the following key concepts:

- The necessity for managing distributed computing infrastructures.
- The nature and architectural types of Enterprise Management Systems.
- Conceptual management architectures and standard management frameworks.
- The features of Web services management.
- Architectural approaches for the management of Web services.
- The Web Services Distributed Management standard.

16.1 Managing distributed systems

Distributed (or composite) applications are increasingly being used in mission-critical roles and the need to monitor, track, and measure them has never been greater. Distributed applications spread functionality and components over a variety of resources including Web servers, application servers, messaging backbones, legacy resources, applications, and so on. These elements must work together seamlessly to support the implementation and delivery of business processes necessary for business operations. This requires new management approaches and capabilities.

Although most organizations have traditional monitoring tools to manage individual resources at a high level, many lack an integrated solution to automatically monitor, analyze, and resolve problems (failures) at the service, transaction, application, and resource levels. Distributed applications are more difficult to monitor and measure than applications running on a centralized computing system within a single system image. Any procedure for linking processing activities on multiple systems to a single business transaction must operate across an especially complex environment. As a result, when users experience application problems, e.g., service brownouts and slowdowns, it is difficult and time consuming to trace and identify the cause of the failure to an individual server, network link, or software element and fix the problems.

Problems arise because there is no generalized method for tracing the flow of transactions from one system image to another. It would be useful for an administrator to know unambiguously when transactions begin and end, both those that are visible to the user as well as the component transactions that invoke local transactions on remote servers. Distributed systems management addresses such issues by monitoring and controlling the activities of a distributed system, making management decisions and performing control actions to modify the behavior of the system.

16.1.1 Purpose of distributed systems management

Traditional distributed systems and network management has evolved from the need to manage successive layers of new technologies and devices as they have been deployed into distributed computing environments. A *managed (or manageable) resource* in a distributed environment could be any type of a hardware or software component that can be managed and that can maintain embedded management-related metadata. A managed resource could be a server, storage unit, database, application server, service, application, or any other entity that needs to be managed.

A bewildering array of standalone utilities has gradually been merged into comprehensive management suites that are integrated through the ability to share events and common data and are controlled through a consistent interface. A distributed application management system controls and monitors an application throughout its lifecycle, from installing and configuring to collecting metrics and tuning the application to ensure responsive execution [Papazoglou 2005b]. The system's functionality must cover all operational activities – including starting and stopping processes, and rerouting operations – as well as problem-detection functions, such as application tracing and message editing.

Distributed application manageability in this context signifies the ability to exercise administrative and supervisory actions and receive information that is relevant to such actions on a variety of distributed resources. Manageability can be distinguished by three functional parts [Murray 2002]:

1. *Monitoring:* The ability to capture run-time and historical events from a particular component, for reporting and notification.
2. *Tracking:* The ability to observe aspects of a single unit of work or thread of execution across multiple resources.
3. *Control:* The ability to alter the run-time behavior of a managed resource.

Manageability provides a mechanism to ensure that an application is both active and functioning properly, as well as that of checking an application's performance over time. Any management solution must address four necessary management questions [Mehta 2003]:

1. What resources need to be managed?
2. What are their properties?
3. How is the management information exchanged (operations, notifications, and kinds of protocols needed)?
4. What are the relationships among the managed resources?

In distributed systems management, management tool suites and utilities monitor distributed system activities to facilitate management decisions and system behavior modifications. Such toolsets provide tools, programs, and utilities that give systems administrators and network managers insights into system and network health, as well as into application status and behavior patterns.

Figure 16.1 shows management toolsets that have been developed to support both systems administration functions, e.g., client–server management, configuration management, and the like, and network management functions, e.g., LAN/WAN management, and remote access management. Distributed systems management tools can, for instance, provide an analysis of processing activities on multiple systems that link to a single business transaction that is providing meaningful service to an end user.

Although toolsets and utilities have existed in traditional distributed computing environments for many years, we have yet to develop equivalent technologies for the complex world of loosely coupled, Web-services-based applications.

16.1.2 Distributed management for Web services

Businesses orchestrate distributed services nowadays into many different configurations to support multiple business processes. An orchestrated service implementation forms a logical network of services layered over the infrastructure (including software environments, servers, legacy applications, and back-end systems) and the physical connectivity

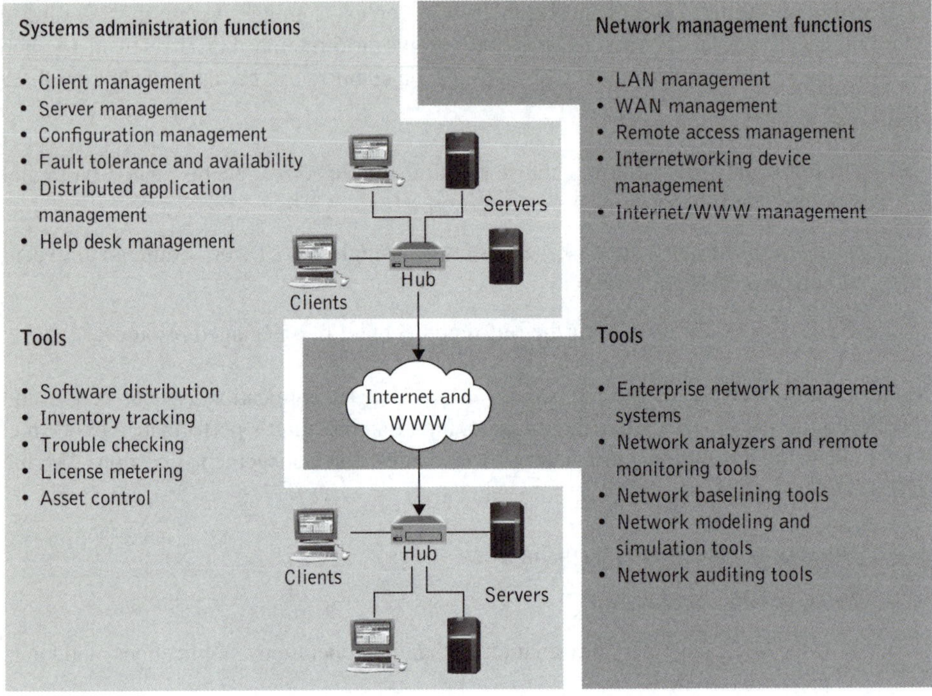

Figure 16.1 Distributed computing infrastructure administration and management

network. As such a Web services network grows, its existence and performance become as relevant to the business's core activities as other critical computing resources. This has changed the enterprise traffic patterns and increased the dependency on mission-critical enterprise services and infrastructures. Consequently, any such environment should be managed in order to provide the security, usability, and reliability needed in today's business environment.

Traditionally, distributed systems and network management focused on managing successive layers of new technologies and devices as they were deployed into distributed computing environments. However, such techniques concentrate on providing solutions at the systems and network management levels and fail to meet enterprise requirements in a service-centric world because they lack the business-awareness functions required by services management products. Also, many existing system management infrastructures do not support SLA reporting or collect specific service information from Web services applications for troubleshooting purposes.

Distributed management solutions for Web services should offer a clear view of how services perform within their operational environment to enable management decisions and to perform control actions to modify and adjust the behavior of Web-services-enabled applications. Some of the essential components needed for proper management of a service-centric architectures are briefly outlined below and depicted in Figure 16.2:

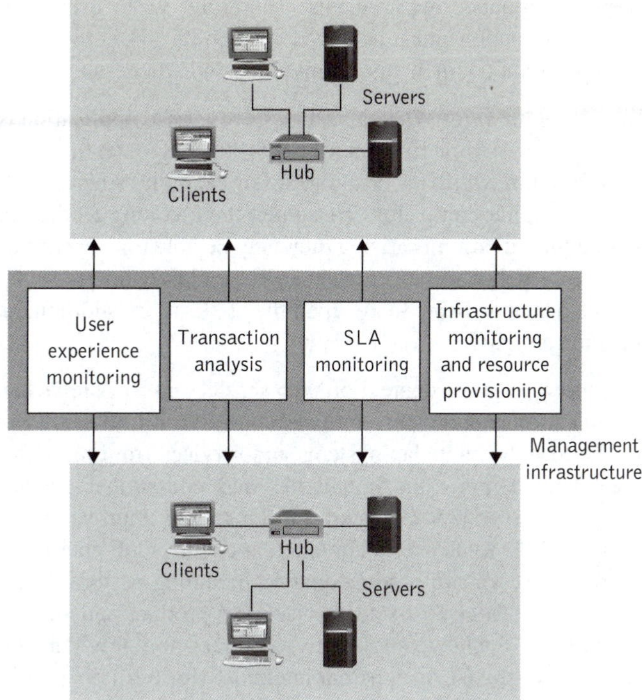

Figure 16.2 Essential components of a service-centric management architecture

User experience monitoring: Services must be monitored for availability and performance from the application user's perspective so that the management infrastructure and administrators understand when the user experience is failing to meet objectives. Front-end processing, e.g., on-line purchasing, can be understood by monitoring actual user transactions, while back-end processing, e.g., account billing, can be captured by monitoring the back-end fulfillment processes for timeliness and completion.

Infrastructure monitoring: Distributed resources must be monitored for availability, performance, and utilization so that developing problems can be quickly detected. This includes not only servers and networks, but also critical software infrastructure. The management infrastructure must know how many instances of a service are running, whether a service is performing adequately and when it has stopped functioning, and how to readily connect and disconnect services and their clients without breaking applications or infrastructure. For systems administrators to tackle these challenges, they require management capabilities specific to the Web services environment.

Transaction monitoring: The growing complexity of global Web services brings together large numbers of services, suppliers, and technologies, all with potentially different performance requirements. Therefore, when user experience degrades, individual transactions must be traced through the system to see which servers and which application components are involved and where the problem lies.

Resource provisioning: When a Web-services-based application is running, careful monitoring of system activity can help to identify potential problems before they are manifested in overloads or failures. For example, when a particular resource is in danger of being completely consumed then as long as the operations staff are aware that this situation is arising they may be able to take corrective action before a failure occurs. For instance, when a server cluster no longer has the capacity to handle the demands being made upon the application, additional servers are provisioned and configured.

SLA monitoring: In the context of Web services an SLA reflects the most rigorous requirements for the key performance indicators for all services supported by the SLA. The SLA ties together systems and services from multiple groups and multiple vendors, defining the boundaries and operational characteristics of these groups. The enterprise SLA's goal is ultimately to improve the service's quality of experience (QoE) to its internal or external clients. QoE entails a shared foundation for measuring service or product quality, including performance, overall customer satisfaction, pre- and post-sale service, and product and service delivery [Open Group 2004]. To achieve an effective contract, the provider often must establish and monitor several SLAs, whether internally (for business or end users) or externally (for service providers, partners, outsourcers, suppliers, and so on). For every tier or peer SLA, one party can be considered a supplier or provider and the other a customer. An SLA can add value in providing the business application to an end customer only when the individual service applications are instrumented adequately so that metrics can be determined. Such metrics ensure conformance, attempt to prevent or warn of non-conformance, and measure non-conformance. Thus, the goal of establishing and managing an end-to-end enterprise SLA is only possible by mapping the requirements and objectives of the amalgamated SLA to measurable parameters at the SLA tiers.

Ensuring quality, service-focused management requires measurable key performance indicators (KPIs) for applications and services. Generic KPIs for business applications include service availability, response time, transaction rate, service throughput, service idle time, and security. The service provider must know whether the services it has contracted to deliver are meeting its KPI objectives and issue warnings and alarms, if they fail to do so. Service providers must therefore set the service KPIs and their objectives, and be able to measure, analyze, and report on the KPI values achieved against these objectives.

To tackle the above challenges there is a critical need for a Web services measurement and management infrastructure and associated toolset, which exists external to the application Web services to address the needs listed above. However, before we introduce the concept of Web services management, to better understand the concepts behind it we shall first introduce the topic of enterprise management systems and describe standard management frameworks that are currently in wide use for the development of distributed applications.

Subsequently, we shall describe a conceptual architecture for the management of distributed resources.

16.2 Enterprise management frameworks

Enterprise Management Systems are network management systems capable of managing devices, independent of vendors and protocols, in IP-based enterprise networks [Kakadia 2002]. Enterprise Management Systems are software solutions that allow systems administrators to manage a vast set of heterogeneous devices in their data centers. This section provides a brief summary of typical architectures of Enterprise Management Systems and functionality to help the reader better understand Web services management solutions.

Most Enterprise Management Systems (EMSs) use common functions such as fault management, configuration management, accounting management, performance management, and security management [Kakadia 2002]. Fault management applications include processing all events and determining if a fault is detected. Fault detection requires other functions, including filter events, logging to maintain historical records that detect long-term trends, monitoring, notification, and reporting by generating alarms. Configuration management allows the operator to verify and modify the configuration of managed devices. Accounting management maintains usage-based statistics for billing purposes. Performance management provides utilities to the operator to define and periodically measure performance-related variables. Security management allows network services to be accessed in a secure manner in a distributed network and includes authentication, authorization, data integrity – to verify the integrity of the cryptographic data checksum that confirms the integrity of unaltered data – and auditing (historical tracking of logs used in post-mortem investigations as a result of security incidents or proactive precautionary measures).

To describe how an EMS is deployed, a network architecture is employed. EMSs can be organized in a variety of architectures depending on how network managers are organized. Models can be a single central manager, hierarchical managers, distributed peer managers, and so on. A network architecture also includes the management protocols that are used to communicate information about the management resource between network managers and agents. The choice of architecture has a direct impact on scalability, availability, performance, and security.

Figure 16.3 provides an overview of the main types of Enterprise Management System architectures. In this figure, network management systems (NMSs) manage a particular device, often implemented by the device manufacturer. Figure 16.3(a) illustrates a centralized architecture, where a single NMS manages all the devices on an enterprise network. The single NMS has limited performance and scalability, in terms of network and computing capabilities. All management applications that carry out one or more fault, configuration, accounting, performance, and security functions are preformed on the central server. The single network connection is a single point of failure that quickly becomes congested as the number of managed devices increases and the management server also reaches its limits in terms of polling for events and processing traps. The NMS console in Figure 16.3 is the management console for the display and manipulation of all distributed network-related management information. Management consoles are capable

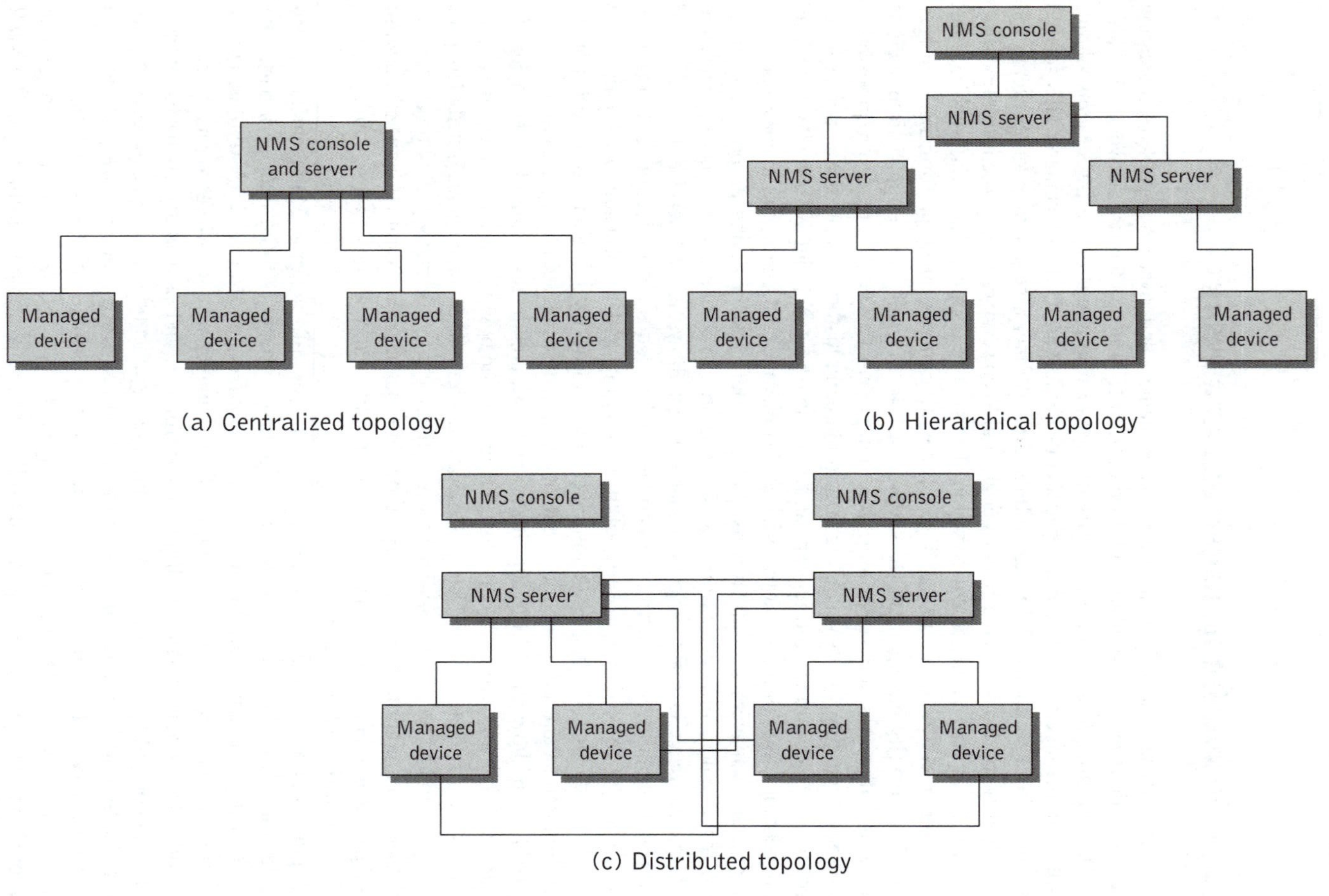

Figure 16.3 Overview of the main types of Enterprise Management System topologies

of displaying management information in a human-comprehensible manner. The console will typically provide a number of topological views into the distributed network platform and the associated management environment, suitable for different types and levels of operations and administrative staff. Figure 16.3(b) illustrates a hierarchical architecture, where there are many local management servers managing small local networks and propagating important events to a higher central management system. This model offers better network and server processing performance capabilities. The bulk of the network traffic is localized, because only filtered and correlated events and information are forwarded to the central server. This architecture provides increased availability and avoids the problems of the centralized server architecture. Finally, Figure 16.3(c) depicts a highly distributed system, where any management server can communicate with any managed device. This architecture offers a highly availability and scalability, and also permits specialization of services.

16.3 Conceptual management architecture

Distributed systems management technologies monitor and respond to managed-resource-related situations in the environment, basically functioning as a control loop. They collect details regarding a managed resource and act accordingly. Figure 16.4 shows that we can view the management infrastructure in terms of a conceptual management architecture that fuses together various components, including managed resources, resource managers, and a management console.

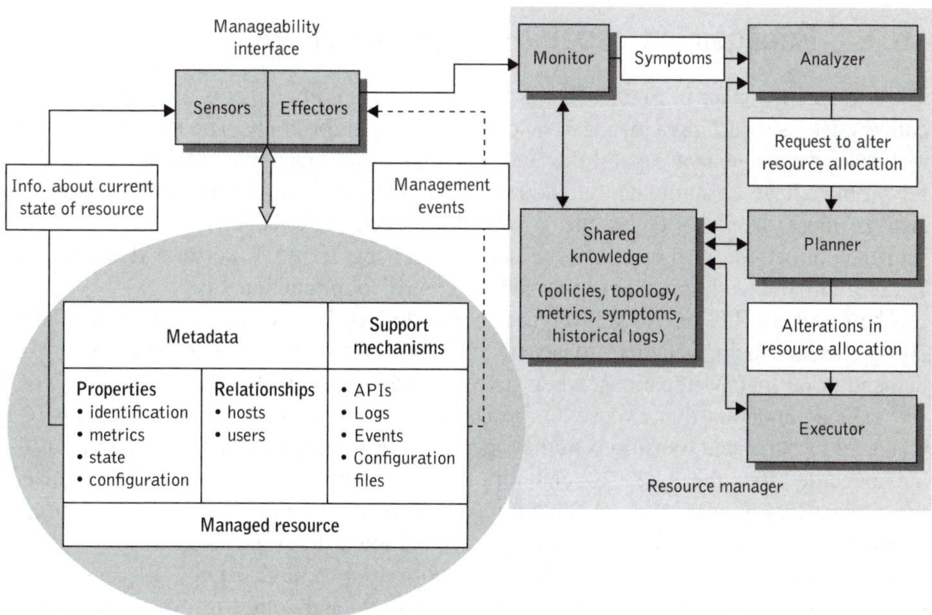

Figure 16.4 Conceptual management architecture

The management console displays management information through its management interface, which lets administrators control and supervise managed resources and change their behaviors. Manageable resources are all kinds of hardware and software resources, both physical and logical, such as software applications, business processes, services, hardware devices, networks, servers, etc., whose management capabilities could be exposed as Web services that implement various management interfaces, such as those defined in Web Services Distributed Management (see section 16.6). A management interface of a resource could be described by a corresponding WSDL definition, resource properties schema, metadata information, and potentially a set of management-related policies [Kreger 2005a]. A services provider then exposes this management interface. As the oval in Figure 16.4 shows, the interface also uses metadata about the resource's properties, including:

- *identification*, which denotes an instance of the managed resource;
- *metrics*, which provide information and operations for resource measurements, such as throughput, utilization, and so on; and
- *configuration*, which provides information and operations for the configurable attributes of a managed resource.

Management interfaces also require information about a resource's relationships with its immediate environment, including its users and hosts. Finally, the interface retrieves information about the current state of a managed resource and the management events (notifications) that might occur when the resource undergoes significant state changes.

16.3.1 Management capabilities and functions

The resource manager in Figure 16.4 is a component that implements a control loop that collects details regarding a managed resource and acts accordingly. The resource manager realizes the management capabilities and functions of management solutions. To achieve this, it must have an automated method to collect the details it needs from the system; to analyze those details to determine if something needs to change; to create a plan, or sequence of actions, that specifies the necessary changes; and to perform those actions. These four parts work together to provide the control loop functionality.

The manageability interface in Figure 16.4 is divided into sensors and effectors [IBM 2004]. Sensors help managers to access the state of the managed resource, either on demand or through notifications, when state changes occur [IBM 2004]. An example of a sensor is an endpoint that exposes information about the current operational status of a managed resource and transitions in that operational state. Effectors provide the means for a manager to affect the state and behavior of the managed resource by means of management operations or configuration capabilities. For instance, it may provide an operation to stop the managed resource; that is, change its operational status to "stopped."

The sensor and effector interfaces support four unique styles of interaction: request/response, send notification, perform operation, and solicit/response. A resource manager uses the request/response interaction mode when it needs to retrieve details about a managed resource through its interface. In a similar fashion a managed resource uses the notification interaction mode when it needs to inform its corresponding resource manager of impending events that may affect the status of the resource.

The monitor module in Figure 16.4 collects, aggregates, filters, and reports managed resource details, e.g., metrics, collected from a managed resource [IBM 2004]. The collected managed resource metadata can include such information as metrics, topology information, configuration property settings, offered capacity, throughput, and so on. The monitor aggregates, correlates, and filters the metadata and organizes it into symptoms that require analysis. For example, the monitor function could collect details about initiating and completing transactions. It then calculates the response time for the transaction measurements. If the response time exceeds a prespecified threshold, the monitor module could produce a "missed response time" symptom. Such transaction measurements are passed to the resource manager through the retrieve-state and receive-notification interaction modes of the management interface. A resource manager could subsequently use the monitored data, e.g., during the analysis process, to generate a change request or the execute function to perform system self-optimization. Selected monitored data also could be presented to a systems administrator on a management console.

The analyzer module provides the mechanisms that observe, correlate, and analyze complex situations (e.g., employing prediction techniques such as time series forecasting and queuing models) [IBM 2004]. These mechanisms allow the resource manager to learn about the computing environment and help predict future situations where changes may eventually need to be made. For example, the analyzer module may determine that some policy is not being met or is violated. In many cases, the analyzer module models complex behavior so that it can employ prediction techniques such as time series forecasting and queuing models to allow a resource manager to learn about the environment surrounding a managed resource and help predict future behavior. Policies are coded by system analysts and specify the criteria that a resource manager uses to realize a definite goal or to accomplish a course of action. For instance, a resource manager involved in workload management uses the specified workload policies to guide its analysis and decisions. These workload policies might include QoS goals for accomplishing the workload. Using the symptom data delivered by the monitor module, the analyzer module can understand how the involved systems commit their resources to execute the workload and how changes in allocation affect performance over time. It then uses the transaction measurements from the monitor component and performance goals from prespecified workload policies to generate a change request to alter resource allocations. For example, the analyzer module could add or delete a resource to optimize performance across these multiple systems.

The plan module provides the mechanisms that construct the actions needed to achieve goals and objectives [IBM 2004]. It achieves this by creating or selecting a procedure to enact a desired alteration in the managed resource on the basis of policy information. The plan module passes the appropriate change plan, which represents a desired set of changes for the managed resource, to the executor module. A plan can take on many forms, ranging from a single command to a complex workflow. For instance, the plan module could use a change request created by the analyzer to generate or select a change plan for improving workload management. It might produce a workflow that will add or delete specific resources or redistribute portions of the workload to different resources.

The executor module provides the mechanisms to schedule and perform the necessary changes to the system [IBM 2004]. These mechanisms control the execution of a plan with considerations for dynamic updates. For instance, an executor module involved in workload management may use the change plan delivered by the plan function to make the necessary modifications to the managed resource.

The four parts of a resource manager that provide the control loop functionality rely on shared knowledge represented in a uniform (standard) way to perform their tasks. Shared management knowledge includes data such as topology information, historical logs, metrics, symptoms and policies, and so on. Shared system knowledge can be divided into three general types: solution topology knowledge, policy knowledge, and problem determination [IBM 2004]. Solution topology knowledge captures knowledge about the components and their construction and configuration for a solution or business system. The planner module can use this knowledge for installation and configuration planning. Policy knowledge is knowledge that needs to be consulted to determine whether or not changes need to be made in the system. Finally, problem determination knowledge includes monitored data, symptoms, and decision trees. The problem determination process also may create knowledge. As the management system responds to actions taken to correct problems, learned knowledge can be accumulated and stored in an appropriate format for use by the resource manager modules.

The conceptual management architecture that we examined in the previous section accomplishes three main functions: repair, adaptation, and optimization. The conceptual management architecture can discover, diagnose, and react to managed resource disruptions. It can detect system malfunctions and initiate policy-based corrective action without disrupting the existing computing environment. Corrective action could involve a product altering its own state or effecting changes in other components in the environment. The conceptual management architecture can also adapt to changes in the environment, using policy-based configuration actions. Such changes could include the deployment of new components or the removal of existing ones or changes in the system characteristics and configuration. The conceptual management architecture can monitor and tune resources to meet end-user or business needs. Finally, the tuning actions could mean reallocating resources – such as in response to dynamically changing workloads – to improve overall resource utilization, or ensure that particular business transactions can be completed in a timely fashion. For instance, optimization actions could divert excess server capacity to lower-priority work when an application does not fully use its assigned computing resources. Optimization helps provide a high standard of service for both system and application end users.

16.4 Standard distributed management frameworks

Diverse technologies that are currently in wide use and relevant to Web services management are suitable for building application manageability. The two most prominent include the Simple Network Management Protocol (SNMP), the Common Information Model, and the Web-Based Enterprise Management (CIM/WBEM). Of these two distributed management frameworks, we shall give a brief overview of SNMP and concentrate on CIM/WBEM as it comes closer to Web services management.

16.4.1 Simple Network Management Protocol

The IETF's SNMP is an application layer protocol that was developed for TCP/IP-based networks and facilitates the exchange of management information between network devices [Case 1999]. SNMP's network elements are devices – such as hosts, gateways, and terminal servers – with management agents that perform the functions requested by network management stations. The SNMP framework lets network administrators manage network performance, find and solve network problems, and plan for network growth. SNMP is today's *de facto* industry standard for network management.

SNMP defines a client–server relationship. The client program (called the network manager) makes virtual connections to a server program (called the SNMP agent) that executes on a remote network entity (often a device, but this could be an application platform also). Agents provide information to the network manager regarding the remote entity's status. An SNMP agent is therefore required on each machine on which an application is running, to monitor that application or component. An SNMP agent is a network management software module that resides in a managed device, which is a network node. Managed devices collect and store management information and make this information available to network managers using SNMP. Managed devices can be routers and access servers, switches and bridges, hubs, computer hosts, or printers. An agent has local knowledge of management information and translates that information into a form compatible with SNMP. A network manager executes applications that monitor and control managed devices and provides services to management applications. Network managers provide the bulk of the processing and memory resources required for network management. One or more network managers must exist on any managed network. SNMP is used for exchanging messages between network managers and agents by encoding management information in basic encoding rules. The database of management information that is used and controlled by the SNMP agent is referred to as the SNMP Management Information Base (MIB), and is a standard set of statistical and control values. Finally, SNMP uses a management information model defining all managed resources in a pseudo object-oriented manner – a manner where all objects are stored virtually in a management information base.

SNMP is essentially a protocol. The management information structure of SNMP has its network transport protocol very closely tied to the representation of management information. This prevents SNMP from significantly moving forward because of the backward-compatibility co-existence requirements it has to meet [Cole 2002].

16.4.2 The Common Information Model/Web-Based Enterprise Management

CIM, developed by the Distributed Management Task Force (DMTF), describes managed elements across the enterprise, including systems, networks, and applications. CIM includes schemas for systems, networks, operating systems, applications, and devices. It provides mapping techniques for interchange of CIM data with MIB data from SNMP agents. CIM is implementation independent, allowing different management applications to collect the required data from a variety of sources. One of the main functions CIM offers is the ability to define the associations between components. CIM's object-oriented approach makes it easier to track the relationships and interdependencies between managed objects.

The CIM specification details a language and methodology for describing management data. The CIM schema enables applications from developers on different platforms to describe management data in a standard format that can be shared between varieties of management applications. It supplies a set of classes with properties and associations that provide a well-understood conceptual framework within which it is possible to organize the available information about the managed environment.

The CIM schema itself is structured into three distinct layers: the core schema, common schemas, and extension schemas.

The core schema is an information model that captures notions that are applicable to all areas of management. Common schemas are information models that capture notions that are common to particular management areas, but independent of a particular technology or implementation. The common areas are systems, devices, networks, applications, metrics, databases, the physical environment, event definition and handling, users and security, policy, and so forth. Extension schemas represent organizational or vendor-specific extensions of the common schema. These schemas can be specific to environments, such as operating systems (e.g., UNIX or Microsoft Windows).

The formal definition of the CIM schema is expressed in a managed object file (MOF), which is the standard textual syntax for specifying the description of managed resources. The function of MOF is analogous to MIB for SNMP.

Having a common model such as the one advocated by CIM does not achieve interoperability. A common protocol and a standard encoding scheme are also required. To address these requirements DMTF members developed the WBEM (Web-Based Enterprise Management) to deliver an integrated set of standards-based management tools leveraging emerging Web technologies. WBEM is a standard that uses XML, HTTP, and SSL to manage systems and networks throughout the enterprise. XML provides the information encoding, HTTP provides transport – thereby creating a platform-independent, distributed management infrastructure – and SSL provides for security requirements.

WBEM provides a rich model of manageable entities featuring inheritance and associations, an extensible set of operations that can be performed on these objects, and a protocol to encode the objects and operations for communication over a network. To use a WBEM approach, the developer is required to first model the required managed objects in an object-oriented style. Then the developer maps their managed application objects into the CIM, or a derived extension of it.

Existing management standards (such as SNMP and CIM) primarily focus on data collection and not on supporting rich management applications for the adaptive infrastructure required by Web services. Moreover, they are too low level to allow flexible, coordinated interaction patterns involving business processes.

16.4.3 Java Management Extensions

Java Management Extensions (JMX) technology (**http://java.sun.com/products/JavaManagement/**) provides the tools for building distributed, Web-based, modular, and dynamic solutions for managing and monitoring devices, applications, and service-driven networks. Typical uses of the JMX technology include inspecting and modifying application configuration, accumulating statistics about application behavior, and notifying state changes and erroneous conditions. This standard is suitable for adapting legacy systems, implementing new management and monitoring solutions, and plugging into future solutions.

The JMX environment is composed of three layers: the instrumentation, the agent, and the distributed services layers.

The instrumentation layer provides the means to expose managed resources to the agent layer. It allows agents to query the state of resources and invoke operations exposed by those resources. Also, it allows resources to send events to other parts of the management architecture. At the instrumentation layer, one or more Java objects known as Managed Beans, or MBeans, can instrument a given resource. These MBeans are registered in a core-managed object server, known as an MBean server, which acts as a management agent and can run on most devices enabled for the Java programming language.

JMX agents are used to manage resources instrumented in compliance with the specification. A JMX agent consists of an MBean server, in which MBeans are registered, and a set of services for handling MBeans. In this way, JMX agents directly control resources and make them available to remote management applications at the distributed services layer. Management protocols link together the two layers.

The distributed services layer includes application connectors and protocol adapters as well as all-important application-level management support. This layer allows developers to write management applications that take action in response to changing conditions and instruct management agents to perform tasks such as replicate a service or change a resource allocation policy. JMX technology defines standard connectors (JMX connectors) that allow accessing JMX agents from remote management applications. JMX connectors using different protocols provide the same management interface. Hence, a management application can manage resources transparently, regardless of the communication protocol used.

16.5 Web services management

As traditional, centralized management applications transition to highly distributed and dynamic SOAs, they can more flexibly deploy essential management functions. With SOAs, a standard Web services management framework can provide support for discovering, introspecting, securing, and invoking managed resources, management functions, and management infrastructure services and toolsets [Papazoglou 2005b]. This section describes the architectural characteristics, structure, and responsibilities of the Web services management and support infrastructure.

16.5.1 Features of Web services management

In the previous sections we have talked about enterprise management frameworks, distributed management concepts, and architectures as well as standard distributed management initiatives that are currently in use and relevant to Web services management. In what follows we shall explain how the initiatives and approaches to distributed systems management have influenced Web services management.

Currently, management vendors offer only instrumentation at SOAP endpoints and intermediaries or at UDDI servers. Although this provides information about Web services while such applications use them, the view is clearly incomplete and lacks critical information regarding the state and characteristics of Web services. For example, many existing system management infrastructures, e.g., SNMP, CIM, and JMX, do not support SLA reporting or the collection of specific service information from (Web services) applications for troubleshooting purposes. To derive such information, Web services must become measurable and much more manageable. This can only be achieved by a standard approach to managing Web services, which can provide, among other things, end-to-end visibility and control over all parts of a long-lived, multi-step transaction spanning multiple applications, human actors, and enterprises. Only by watching over business operations can analysts and administrators identify opportunities and diagnose problems as they occur, and can ensure that the Web services supporting a given business task are performing in accordance with service-level objectives. Web services management is therefore expected to become a critical component of production-quality Web services applications in the near future.

Web services need to be managed in at least two dimensions. There is the operational management dimension, in which a systems administrator starts and stops Web services and keeps track of how many instances of a Web service are running, in which containers, and on which remote systems. There is also a tactical (or business management) dimension that provides a number of business activity monitoring and analytical capabilities that enable some human agent to watch over business operations, identifying opportunities and diagnosing problems as they occur so as to ensure that the Web services supporting a given business task are performing in accordance with service-level objectives. *Tactical Web services management* provides end-to-end visibility and control over all parts of a long-lived, multi-step information request or transaction/process that spans multiple applications and human actors in one or more enterprises. Tactical management is directly related to the concept of business process management and monitoring that we covered in sections 8.5.2 and 8.5.3 in the context of the Enterprise Service Bus. Therefore, in the remainder of this section we shall concentrate only on the activities and features of operational service management.

Operational Web services management (henceforth referred to simply as Web services management) is defined as the functionality required for discovering the existence, availability, performance, health, patterns of usage, extensibility, as well as the control and configuration, lifecycle support, and maintenance of a Web service or business process within the context of SOAs. This definition implies that Web services can be managed using Web services technologies. In particular, it suggests a manageability model that applies to both Web services and business processes in terms of manageability topics (identification, configuration, state, metrics, and relationships) and the aspects (properties, operations, and events) used to define them [Potts 2003]. In fact, these abstract concepts apply to understanding and describing the manageability information and behavior of any managed resource, including business processes and Web services.

16.5.2 Functional characteristics of Web services management

A Web services management framework is a set of components and objects that enable SLA management, auditing, monitoring, troubleshooting, dynamic service provisioning, and service management for Web services infrastructure and applications. A Web services management framework performs four activities as part of end-to-end Web services management:

1. Measuring end-to-end levels of service for user-based units of work, e.g., individual Web services, business processes, application transactions, and so on.
2. Breaking such units of work down into identifiable, measurable components, e.g. requests for application transactions.
3. Attributing end-to-end service levels and resource consumption to such units and their components. This involves tracing and monitoring them through multi-domain, geographical, technological, application, and supplier infrastructures.
4. Identifying and predicting current problems and future requirements in user terms.

To perform the above activities a Web services management framework must take into consideration a number of interrelated Web services management aspects. The most prominent functions of service management include the following:

Metrics/performance indicators: Key operational metrics of a Web service at the operational level include the number of request messages that the Web service endpoint has received, the number of successful requests handled by a Web service endpoint, the total elapsed time (in seconds) that the Web service endpoint has taken to process all requests (successfully or not), the maximum time duration (in seconds) between all requests received and their completion or failure, and the last recorded time duration (in seconds) between the last request received and its completion or failure. This set of basic metrics for a Web service revolves mainly around the concept of response time and is currently provided by Web services management initiatives such as the WSDM (see section 16.6). In addition to the above basic Web service metrics, additional useful Web service metrics include connect time, response time, round-trip delay, transaction rate, and throughput. Connect time denotes how long a service takes to start. Round-trip delay denotes the time taken between making a request and seeing the response. Transaction rate is the rate that the system can service requests. It is important to understand how the system or service reacts when presented with transaction rates higher than the value required. Burst rates and sustained rates and their periods should be defined. Finally, throughput is the total amount of information that is offered to the system.

Auditing, monitoring, and troubleshooting: This item may include providing service performance and utilization statistics, measurement of transaction arrival rates and response time loads (number of bytes per incoming and outgoing transaction), load balancing across servers, measuring the health of services, and troubleshooting. Web services should be audited and these measurements can be used to compare against SLAs. Resources should be monitored for bottlenecks and for user-defined thresholds that exceed the prescribed limits. These measurements can be recorded and the historical performance data collected and used for capacity planning. Today, several toolsets found in platforms for developing, deploying, and managing service applications provide process monitoring capabilities.

SLA management: This may include QoS (e.g., sustainable network bandwidth with priority messaging service), service reporting (e.g., acceptable system response time), and service metering.

Service redeployment/dynamic rerouting and graceful degradation: The Web services management framework should allow the service to be redeployed (moved) around the network for performance, redundancy for availability, or any other reasons. The management framework should support dynamic rerouting for fail-over or load balancing. In case a service fails or is overloaded, it should fail in a controlled and gradual manner, servicing the highest-priority tasks for as long as possible.

Service lifecycle and state management: The Web services management framework should expose the current state of a service and permit lifecycle management including the ability to start and stop a service, the ability to configure a deployed Web service, and to support versioning of Web services. The management framework must be able to affect the lifecycle state and configuration parameters of a Web service or a group of related Web services. In addition, it should have some control over the versions of deployed Web services. Multiple versions of the same Web service can be active simultaneously in the framework controlled by the services management system. Further, the management system must be able to route a client request to an appropriate version of the Web service.

Service change management and notification: The Web services management framework should support the description of versions of Web services and notification of a change or impending change to the service interface or implementation.

Scalability/extensibility/availability: The Web services management framework should be extensible and must permit discovery of supported management functionality in a given instantiation.

Dynamic services (and resources) provisioning: Provisioning occurs at all phases of running a solution, ranging from bringing solutions into production, managing production execution, and removing them from production [Kreger 2005b]. Provisioning moves solutions into production by automatically triggering deployment, installation, configuration, and activation of the solution and all of its elements. The Web services management framework should support the provisioning of services and resources to authorized personnel, dynamic allocation/deallocation of hardware, installation/deinstallation of software, changing of workloads of "on-demand" basis, while ensuring SLAs, management policies for messaging routing and security, and reliable SOAP messaging delivery.

Security management: Like Web services, manageable services architecture implementations need to be secure, including support for authorization, confidentiality, integrity, non-repudiation, and so on. These were discussed in some detail in Chapter 11 that deals with security aspects of Web services.

Service maintenance: The Web services management framework should allow for the management and correlation of new versions of the service.

A Web services management framework that is based on the above services management functionality can provide end-to-end, cross-architecture, business-level and process-level monitoring and management facilities. These can be used to determine whether an organization is realizing desired benefits from a particular service or composite application.

16.5.3 Service management architectural approaches

A standard Web services management framework provides an abstraction layer that allows discovery of and interaction with managed resources, as well as a standard, model-agnostic way of describing resource capabilities. The preferred model is an abstraction layer on top of physical resources that presents the "capabilities" of the system, encapsulating the details of the physical resources. The abstraction layer pushes down onto the aggregation of the lower-level physical resource sensors and actuators and enables standardization of how developers view resource consumption and how they measure baseline metrics. In this way, there is no need for every new type of resource to have individual software written in order to communicate with each management application, and developers and system administrators need not understand many different control protocols in order to provide efficient systems management. As such, the same Web services technologies that are used to define and execute business processes can now interact directly with resource managers, management infrastructure services, and managed resources.

In a Web services environment, all essential communication between service providers and consumers is carried out using standardized SOAP messages. SOAP messages can facilitate Web services management in several ways. First, developers can use SOAP messages to mark the beginning and endpoints of service transactions. Also, because a SOAP message's source and destination are readily identifiable, it is easy to obtain detailed performance measures for applications that span platforms and enterprises by sniffing and altering SOAP messages – which can be intercepted at many points in the network of applications connected via Web services. Service containers facilitate the request/response message flow environment (see section 8.3). As already explained in Chapter 8, the Web service containers entail the physical manifestation of an abstract service endpoint and provide the service interface implementation.

Administrators can inject service management capabilities into the SOAP pipeline using a container-based and/or intermediary approach. These two approaches are composable in that we can have management functions incorporated in both containers and intermediaries.

Container-based service management reflects a purely container-based style of Web services management. Here, the platform's native Web service container hosts the management capabilities. From an architectural perspective, the container can leverage the infrastructure configuration of the Web services node (the application server), which administrators can cluster and secure for required service levels. The container-based management scenario is shown in Figure 16.5.

In the *intermediary-based management* approach, an intermediary or broker acts as the client endpoint and passes the request to the actual service endpoint (see Figure 16.6). This comes in contrast to the container-based scenario, which directly links the Web services management servers to containers. In Figure 16.6 capabilities are deployed on the intermediary, which acts as a client endpoint. Following monitoring and control, the intermediary passes the request to the service endpoint. Administrators deploy management capabilities

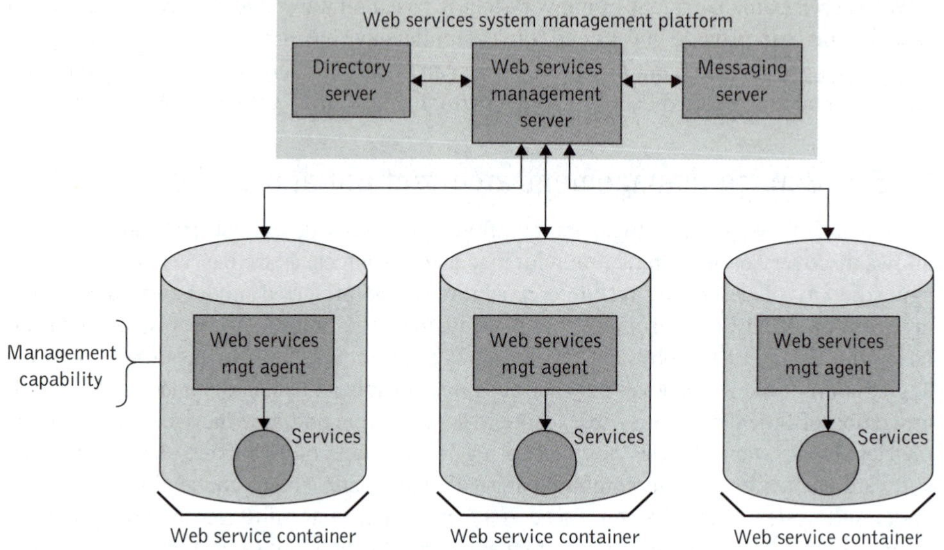

Figure 16.5 Container-based management scenario

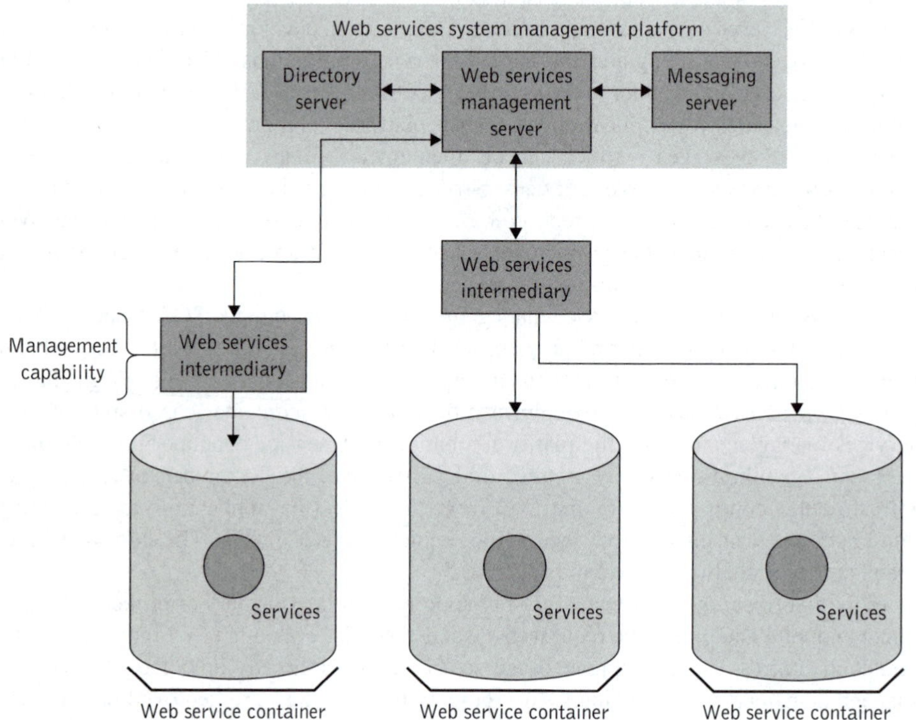

Figure 16.6 Intermediary-based management scenario

on the intermediary, allowing for monitoring and control. The intermediary model is completely decoupled from the Web services nodes, and can be used in any environment. Services from multiple platforms can be routed through the intermediary, which also facilitates central management and configuration.

The intermediary model is particularly useful in simplifying administration and technical support without requiring a container for each individual Web services node. However, intermediaries do require network address reconfiguration. Also, if there is no infrastructure to cluster the Web services intermediaries, they can constitute single points of failure and thus create problems in environments that require high reliability.

In conclusion, there is no distinctive functional difference between the container-based and intermediary-based scenarios to Web services management apart from the standalone (intermediary) versus server plug-in (container) configuration.

16.5.4 Management infrastructure services

To manage services, the Web services management framework uses the *manageability capabilities* of various architecture resources. These capabilities define standard schemas, metadata, and WSDL interfaces that describe resource-specific behavior that resources use to advertise – and provide access to – manageability information [Kreger 2005b]. Typically, resources implement only applicable selections rather than all of their standard manageability capabilities. Basic computing resource manageability capabilities include operational status, metrics, and relationships. Manageability capabilities are realized through a *manageability information model* that represents resource manageability and related information, such as state, configuration, and relationships [Potts 2003]. The service management framework uses this model's information to retrieve information and exert control. Manageability information might, for example, indicate that a SOAP message header contained a digital certificate of the client's identity. The Web services management framework would then extract that information and translate it into the client's identification for later use (such as when counting a particular client's SOAP messages to a particular Web service).

A Web service is manageable if its manageability capabilities are exposed via standard management interfaces, which are similar to a Web service's functional interfaces [Potts 2003]. The management interfaces differ only in that they convey management-related semantics and that a Web services management system, rather than a client, uses them.

The Web services management framework uses management infrastructure services to define standard interfaces for commonly available functions in the infrastructure's information [Kreger 2005b]. Management infrastructure services include metering, metric and event mediation, monitoring, system scanning, policy enforcement and management, and model bridges. The standard management interfaces enable higher-value utility functions, management of end-to-end processes, or management applications such as availability and performance management, optimization, capacity planning, billing, configuration management, asset protection, problem determination, and business analytics. These mechanisms also offer interfaces and content for management consoles.

Figure 16.7 shows the management interfaces (management channel) exposed by a manageable Web service and accessible by the Web services management framework. This management framework is positioned between Web services clients and providers

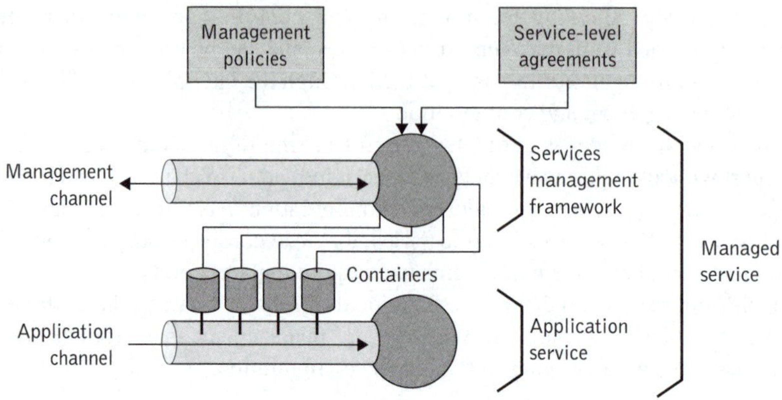

Figure 16.7 Integrating application and management-based services

(application channel) and offers a centralized management and policy framework. In this figure application channels are developed in accordance with SOA principles and are continuously connected and directed into the management channel. A WSDL document describes the management interfaces and the endpoints to which the Web services management framework can send messages with management-related payloads. A management service could be a Web service based on the Web Service Distributed Management model described in section 16.6.

To manage event-driven processes, the management service might support an event mechanism for notification push. Because they are in the same memory space, the containers and management service interact via direct message calls. In the memory space, information from the management channel controls the containers. Any information that the containers collect is passed to the management service, which then makes it available on the management channel.

As Figure 16.7 shows, along with distributed monitoring and policy enforcement, the Web services management framework offers a centralized management and policy framework. This framework works in concert with service directories and identity management solutions both in receiving information (such as service performance statistics, alerts, and service interdependency information) and in sending information. Policy, in the form of rule sets, is sent to the service management components. These rules define service management component behavior – that is, when to raise alerts, how to process transiting message traffic, where to route messages, how to enforce security policies and SLAs, and so on.

16.5.5 Connecting service management and application channels

In addition to traditional application service development facilities, a Web-services-based SOA requires two key features to effectively manage systems and applications [Papazoglou 2005b]:

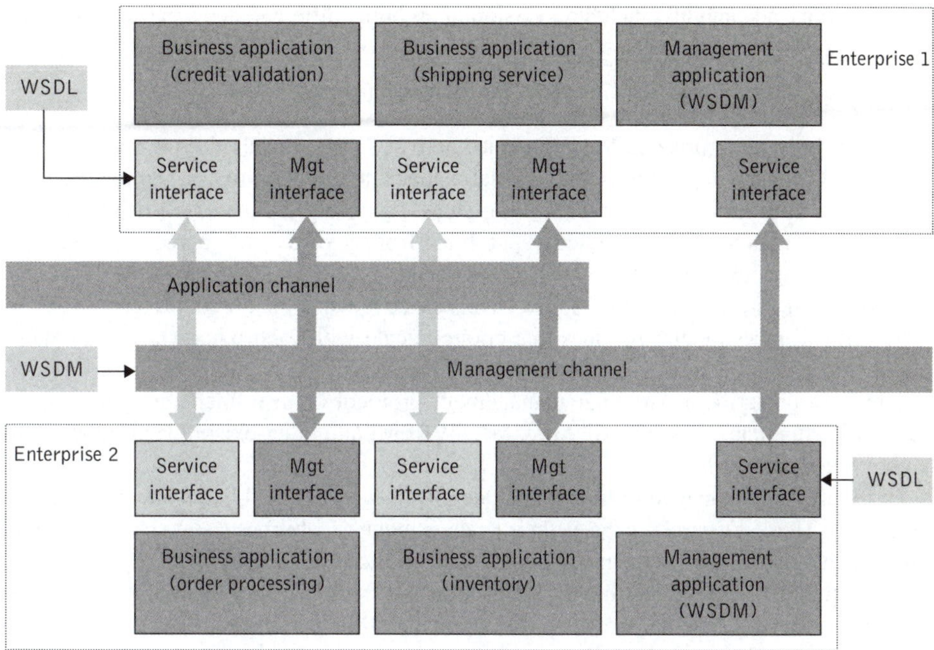

Figure 16.8 Developing and managing Web-services-based applications

- A management framework that is consistent across an increasingly heterogeneous set of participating component systems.
- Support for complex, cross-component management scenarios, such as SLA enforcement and dynamic resource provisioning.

Figure 16.8 shows the conceptual architecture components that combine service management and application channels developed in accordance with SOA principles. This architecture continuously connects to the Web services application channel and directs it into the management channel. The architecture depicted in Figure 16.8 provides the connection points between different functional units. The use of Web services as an implementation platform of an integrated SOA-based management and application development solution among other things encourages implementers to leverage existing approaches and support multiple binding and marshaling techniques. This means that the management channel enables the use of common management services. Typical management services that are common across both the applications and management channels include:

1. SLA and QoS management, including the measurement of performance and availability, as well as alerting services.
2. Visibility and control capabilities, including interactive monitoring, administration, and reporting.

3. Service adaptability, including versioning, routing, differentiated services, and message transformation.
4. Web-services- and XML-based security mechanisms.

Accordingly, an enterprise building a service delivery structure based on this architecture can extend business applications with special management capabilities or add management capabilities as required. This ensures the greatest flexibility for the enterprise because it can mix and match standards-based capabilities from a variety of sources to create the service delivery environment that best suits its needs.

In the architecture depicted in Figure 16.8, service management involves a collection of management infrastructure services that communicate with each other – passing data or coordinating some activity – to facilitate the delivery of one or more business services. Rather than prescribe a particular management protocol or instrumentation technology, the architecture can work with SNMP, JMX, WBEM, and other existing and future technologies and standards.

In Figure 16.8, managed resources include physical and logical hardware and software resources. These resources expose their management capabilities as Web services that implement various management interfaces, such as those defined in WSDM (see the following section). A resource's management interface is described by a WSDL document, resource properties schema, metadata documents, and (potentially) a set of management-related policies. Resource managers interact with managed resources and management infrastructure services using the Web services interfaces. In addition, service managers leverage Web services technologies, such as WS-BPEL, to describe and execute management processes that perform a "scripted" management function [Kreger 2005a]. The use of management processes based on Web services enables reuse of the business process infrastructure as well as invocation of resource services, management infrastructure services, and business components.

Resource managers can directly access managed resources as part of a business or management process. As Figure 16.8 shows, a business process integrates basic services such as credit validation, shipping, order processing, and inventory services originating from two collaborating enterprises. The architecture's management applications, such as performance management, capacity planning, asset protection, and job control, manage resources through their management interfaces or management infrastructure services [Kreger 2005a].

In large-scale enterprises where manageability capabilities and interfaces are standardized, multiple managers may be used to manage individual services. The two most common multiple resource manager scenarios are [Potts 2003]:

1. Separation of responsibilities between managers. This means that, for instance, one manager performs performance monitoring while another one takes care of deployment changes.
2. Installations that include management software from various vendors.

In those circumstances, the management interface and the manageability model must enable operational consistency. In addition, the management architecture must ensure consistency of simultaneously executed operations, and that managers do not execute operations that conflict with each other.

To avoid conflicting operations that are associated with the manageability of a Web service, managers must coordinate and negotiate usage of these operations among themselves. Coordination strategies could be introduced among peers. This includes federated coordination based on negotiation or delegated coordination by means of a trusted third party coordinating usage. Finally, a hierarchal structure of managers may be introduced. In all such cases standards must be used to coordinate and negotiate usage of service manageability. For example, federated coordination may be supported by WS-Agreement and delegated coordination by WS-Coordination.

16.6 The Web Services Distributed Management Initiative

While standards such as SNMP or CIM are effective in managing specific resources within the enterprise, they do not address the management of business processes and the underlying application services they rely on. There is no distributed management standard available for expressing the relationships that exist between resources, business processes, and related services. And there is a significant gap for management standards to provide a means to correlate business and systems development activities. In many cases a management solution is driven by systems-based goals and metrics, which may not be optimally aligned with the overall business goals. In addition, management solutions based on the preceding standards provide a single point of control for resources within the scope of a specific set of management tasks or processes. While this approach may work well, particularly within the confines of a single management system, it can be difficult to integrate different enterprise management systems to provide an overall view of cross-application (end-to-end) business processes.

Consistent end-to-end Web services management is impossible without industry-wide standards development. To address this, OASIS is actively developing the Web Services Distributed Management (WSDM) standard (**http://www.oasis-open.org/committees/tc_home.php?wg_abbrev=wsdm**) to provide end-to-end Web services management. WSDM is leveraging many of the capabilities provided by the WS-Resource Framework and WS-Notification standard families (see sections 7.2 and 7.3), such as the ability to expose properties, expose several resources in a collection, and standardize faults and notifications. WSDM defines a protocol for the interoperability of management information and capabilities via Web services. To resolve distributed system management problems, WSDM focuses on two distinct tasks: Management Using Web Services (MUWS) and Management of Web Services (MOWS). MUWS addresses the use of Web services technologies as the foundation of a modern distributed systems management framework. With MOWS, the WSDM addresses the specific requirements for managing Web services themselves. The MOWS specification is based on the MUWS specification's concepts and definitions. As with MUWS, MOWS aims to build on existing model frameworks to define a Web service's management model, rather than reinvent a general managed resource object model scheme.

The WSDM specifications depend on the WS-I Basic Profile as well as other Web services foundation specifications being standardized in OASIS [Kreger 2005a]. These include WS-Addressing (WSA) for service references (see section 7.2.1), WS-Resource

Framework (WS-RF) Resource Properties (WSRP) for properties (see section 7.2.3), and WS-Notification (WSN) Base Notifications (WSBN) (see section 7.3.1) for management event transport. WSDM also utilizes WS-RF Service Groups (WSSG) (see section 7.2.5) and WS-Notification WS-Topics (WST) (see section 7.3.2) in optional functions. It is expected that WSDM will evolve as it depends on other evolving Web services standards.

WSDM can be used to monitor the end-to-end response time of a BPEL process as well as the time taken by each step. Business analysts can use this information to monitor timely delivery of (telecommunications or financial) services to their customers. In addition, WSDM-based notifications can be forwarded to the business analysts when exceptional circumstances occur. In this way, WSDM can be used to monitor a business process and correlate that process with systems-level associated events.

The following two sections provide readers with a brief overview of the MUWS and MOWS and their major characteristics.

16.6.1 Management Using Web Services (MUWS)

MUWS facilitates the management of distributed computing resources using Web services. The purpose of MUWS is to achieve universal management interoperability across the many different varieties of distributed computing resources. In particular, MUWS defines how to describe the manageability capabilities of managed resources using WSDL documents. Expressing capabilities enables more efficient discovery of and introspection of resources since managers typically focus on a particular management task or domain, and therefore need to be able to easily and efficiently determine the relevant capabilities of a managed resource.

MUWS is not creating a new model for representing managed resources. Rather, the requirement is that MUWS must be able to work with multiple, existing, domain-specific models. CIM from DTMF is the most prominent, but not the exclusive, model for this work. SNMP information models will also be considered. The objective is to bind a unifying layer on top of these various models to facilitate consistent management in a heterogeneous distributed environment.

MUWS defines a set of foundation manageability capabilities generally expected in distributed computing management systems [Kreger 2005a]. Examples of manageability functions that can be performed via MUWS include: monitoring QoSs, enforcing SLAs, controlling tasks, and managing resource lifecycles. New or domain-specific capabilities can extend existing foundational capabilities as appropriate.

Access to the manageability for a resource is provided by a Web service endpoint. A simple example of a managed resource could be a server that indicates when its storage capacity is low, or a Web server that reports congestion due to an excessively high number of hits. The Web service endpoint providing access to some managed resource is called a *manageability endpoint*. A manageability endpoint realizes a number of management interfaces. Each management interface represents all or part of a manageability capability. Similarly, a single manageability capability may be represented in one or more interfaces.

A manageability consumer discovers the Web service endpoint and exchanges messages with the endpoint in order to request information, subscribe to events, or control the managed resource associated with the endpoint. An example of a manageability consumer is a management system, or a business automation process, or simply any Web service application. In order to discover the Web service endpoint providing access to a particular managed resource, a manageability consumer first obtains an endpoint reference as defined by the WS-Addressing specification (see section 7.2.1), and then obtains any other required descriptions, including, but not limited to, a WSDL document, an XML schema, or a policy document. MUWS uses the same mechanisms, for obtaining references and their associated descriptions, as used by regular Web service implementations, and their applications.

To exchange messages with a manageability endpoint, a manageability consumer needs to understand all of the required descriptions for the endpoint. The manageability consumer sends messages targeted to the managed resource by using information contained in the endpoint reference, e.g., an address and other reference properties in accordance with WS-Addressing conventions.

In MUWS manageability is composed of a number of capabilities. Each capability has its own distinct semantics. In MUWS each manageability capability is identified by a standard URI and has a WS-Notification topic used to identify and categorize capability-specific notifications. In addition, each capability has metadata defined for its properties and operations.

WSDM MUWS 1.0 defines several standard capabilities. These include an identity that is used only to determine whether two resources being managed are the same resource; a description capability that describes a managed resource; a manageability characteristics capability that describes the properties of the management interface of a resource; a correlatable properties capability that defines a set of properties that together determine whether two managed resources with different identities are the same resource; and a metrics, a configuration, and a state capability. An operational status capability defines three very simple status levels (available, unavailable, and unknown) as well as events for status changes for interoperability. And finally, an advertisement capability defines a standard event to be sent when a new managed resource is created.

MUWS uses composability of capabilities to allow for additional manageability capabilities to be gradually introduced, based upon the availability of management functions and processing power within an implementation of a managed resource. Manageability consumers can discover and make use of composed capabilities as these capabilities become available. This is illustrated in Figure 16.9, which shows how composability is used to combine service implementation aspects provided by the Web services platform with manageability capabilities and resource-specific manageability capabilities. Common manageability capabilities contain identity, relationships, availability, and so on.

A relationship in MUWS is an *n*-ary association between resources. MUWS supports two kinds of relationships: relationships that are simple data representations of some actual relationship that exists between resources, and relationships between resources that have their own properties and behavioral characteristics. One of these properties is a type that conveys the semantics of the relationship. The resources involved in the relationship are called participants. Each participant has a role in the relationship. The participants may or may not be managed resources in the MUWS sense.

Listing 16.1 is an example of a relationship information instance taken from [Vambenepe 2005a]. The relationship is a WSDM-manageable network host called `myhost.myorg.org` containing an attached SCSI disk. The SCSI disk is not manageable by itself, but is exposed as a functional or operational endpoint of a Web service, e.g., to read/write from the disk.

In Listing 16.1 `muws-p2-xs:Name` is a human-readable name for a relationship, while `muws-p2-xs:Type` is the relationship type to which this relationship belongs. Examples of such types include linkage, containment, or dependency. MUWS does not

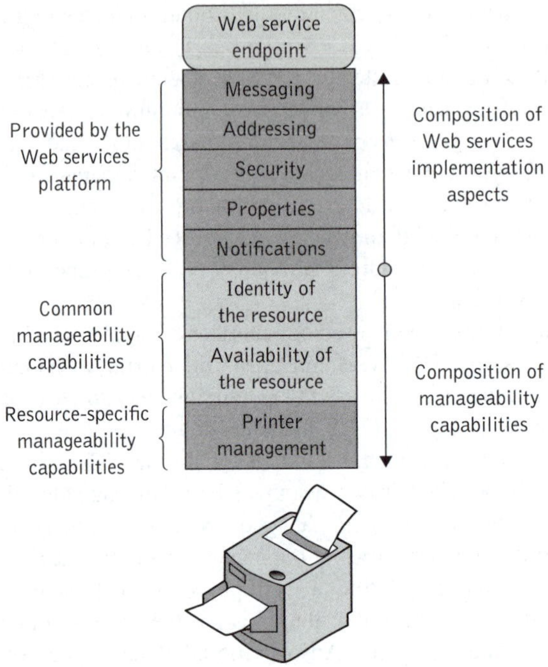

Web service endpoint
Messaging
Addressing
Security
Properties
Notifications
Identity of the resource
Availability of the resource
Printer management
Provided by the Web services platform
Common manageability capabilities
Resource-specific manageability capabilities
Composition of Web services implementation aspects
Composition of manageability capabilities

Figure 16.9 MUWS composability
Source: W. Vambenepe (ed) 'Web services distributed management: management using web services (MUWS 1.0) Part 1', *OASIS Standard*, March 2005.

define any specific relationship type. This is left to domain-specific models. The construct `muws-p2-xs:Participant` contains information about a participant in the relationship. There must be at least two participants, but there may be more than two participants. The construct `muws-p1-xs:ManageabilityEndpointReference` is a reference to a WSDM manageability endpoint, while `muws-p1-xs:ResourceID` is a WSDM-managed resource identifier. The construct `muws-p2-xs:Role` is a URI which identifies the role that a participant plays in a relationship. A participant role must be unique within a given instance of the relationship. A relationship type defines the set of valid roles.

WSDM defines interfaces to query a managed resource about its resource properties and the relationships it participates in directly, such as a containment relationship. In addition, WSDM also defines an interface for a service that offers relationship information for many managed resources enabling a relationship registry.

WSDM also provides an extensible XML event format that carries management event information [Vambenepe 2005a]. The format defines a set of basic, consistent data elements that allow different types of management event information to be carried in a consistent manner. The WSDM Event Format provides a basis for programmatic processing, correlation, and interpretation of events from different products, platforms, and management technologies. To be effective, the WSDM Event Format must provide the identification of the resource experiencing an event, called the source, and the identification of the reporter of an event. In most cases the source reports its own event; thus the identity of the reporter and the source are the same.

```
<muws-p2-xs:Relationship>
     <muws-p2-xs:Name>SCSI disk attached to the host
      computer</muws-p2-xs:Name>
     <muws-p2-xs:Type>
           <scsi:Attached>
                 <bus:Connected>
                      <generally:Linked/>
                 </bus:Connected>
           </scsi:Attached>
     </muws-p2-xs:Type>
     <muws-p2-xs:Participant>
          <muws-pl-xs:ManageabilityEndpointReference>
              ... EPR1 ...
          </muws-pl-xs:ManageabilityEndpointReference>
          <muws-pl-xs:ResourceID>urn:uuid:123
          </muws-pl-xs:ResourceID>
          <muws-p2-xs:Role>urn:role:bus:host</muws-p2-xs:Role>
          <netop-xs:HostName>myhost.myorg.org</netop
           xs:NostName>
     </muws-p2-xs:Participant>
     <muws-p2-xs:Participant>
           <muws-p2-xs:Role>urn:role:bus:device</muws-p2-xs:Role>
           <scsi-xs:Port>2</scsi-xs:Port>
           <scsi-xs:CH>0</scsi-xs:CH>
           <scsi-xs:BusID>5</scsi-xs:BusID>
           <scsi-xs:LUN>0</scsi-xs:LUN>
           <mows-xs:EndpointReference>
              ... EPR2 ...
           </mows-xs:EndpointReference>
     </muws-p2-xs:Participant>
</muws-p2-xs:Relationship>
```

Listing 16.1 Sample relationship in WSDM MUWS

Both management applications and resources will need a unified means of advertising and discovering each other in heterogeneous environments. The advertisement capability in WSDM facilitates discovery via events. The advertisement capability is exposed by a Web service that is able to provide a notification on the creation or the destruction of a managed resource [Vambenepe 2005b]. Since a consumer cannot register for a notification on a resource before the resource is created, a creation event is reported for some other resource by the implementer of a "lifetime notification" capability.

The goal of discovery is to obtain the endpoint reference (as defined by WS-Addressing) of an advertised manageability endpoint. Discovery methods commonly used for Web services will be used as discovery methods for manageability services. There are two ways by means of which discovery of manageability services is conducted [Vambenepe 2005b]: discovery using relationships and discovery using registries.

There are at least two scenarios in which a relationship can be used to discover an advertised managed resource. The first scenario is when a managed resource points to some other managed resource through a relationship. A managed resource that supports the relationship capability enables discovery of an endpoint reference for some other resource that participates in a relationship with the managed resource. This is done by using the relationship capability or invoking the operations that query manageability relationships. The relationship capability of WSDM facilitates resource discovery, root cause analysis, and finding the set of resources participating to offer a higher-level service. The second scenario is when a consumer has access to a WS-Resource representing a relationship and the relationship has a managed resource as a member. A consumer can then use the properties of the relationship resource capability to retrieve any endpoint references of a managed resource participating in the relationship. Finally, a resource can be advertised to a registry by invoking an insertion interface of a registry. A consumer can then discover a managed resource by invoking a query interface of the registry. A registry of this type can make use of the WS-RF WS-SG specification (see section 7.2.5), which can be used to define the registry itself along with the message exchanges used to interact with it.

More information and examples regarding the WSDL MUWS can be found in [Vambenepe 2005b], [Kreger 2005a].

16.6.2 Management of Web Services (MOWS)

To manage the Web services network, an administrator needs to manage the components that form the network – the Web services endpoints. The MOWS part of the WSDM specification addresses management of the Web services endpoints using Web services protocols. The MOWS specification is based on the concepts and definitions expressed in the MUWS specification. Like MUWS activities, MOWS aims to build on existing model frameworks (such as, for instance, DMTF CIM) in its definition of the management model of a Web service, rather than reinventing a general managed resource object model scheme.

The model requirements are being primarily driven by a set of management tasks that should be supported. These management tasks are numerous and include such varied activities as service metering, auditing, billing, performance profiling, SLA management, problem detection, root cause failure diagnosis, service deployment, and lifecycle management. Explicit in MOWS is the requirement that it be described and accessible in a way consistent with MUWS. Application of MOWS to MUWS gives an interesting combination of the "manageable" management. Using both specifications, it is possible to build reliable and accountable management systems.

WSDM MOWS defines the following MUWS capabilities applicable to Web services endpoints [Sedukhin 2005]:

- *Identity:* The MUWS identity capability defines a unique identity for the Web service.
- *Identification:* The identification capability is used to help establish the Web service endpoint being managed. The identity capability may be used to determine whether two manageability endpoints provide manageability of the same resource or not.
- *Metrics:* The MOWS metrics capability defines a set of basic metrics for a Web service; these include `NumberOfRequests`, `NumberOfFailedRequests`, `NumberOfSuccessfulRequests`, `ServiceTime`, `MaxResponseTime`, and `LastResponseTime`.

- *OperationalState:* The MOWS operational state capability provides the current operational state of the service. A valid state is Up which indicates that a service endpoint is capable of receiving new requests. The Up state has the substates of Busy, which means that the Web service endpoint is capable of accepting new requests during processing of other requests, and Idle, which means that that the Web service endpoint is capable of accepting new requests and is not processing any other requests. Another valid state is Down, which indicates that a service endpoint is not capable of accepting new requests. Down has as substates Stopped, which indicates that the Web service endpoint is not capable of accepting new requests and was intentionally stopped by an administrator; Crashed, which indicates that the Web service endpoint is not capable of accepting new requests as a result of some internal failure; and Saturated, which indicates that the Web service endpoint is not capable of accepting new requests due to lack of resources.
- *OperationalStatus:* The MUWS operational status capability provides the high-level status of the services: all Up states return Available and all Down states return as status of Unavailable, except for Saturated which returns PartiallyAvailable.
- *RequestProcessingState:* The MOWS request processing state capability defines a request state diagram and provides a mechanism to define events to be sent when request processing states change.

Figure 16.10 shows how a manageable Web printer service could be composed, according to the MOWS specification. A resource may support both manageability and functional capabilities. For example, a printer can obviously print, but the same printer may also be able to indicate if it is on-line and may be able to notify when the toner is running out. A managed resource may allow access to its manageability capabilities and functional capabilities via Web services. The functional interface for the printer is a simple Print operation defined and accessed as a WSDL operation. The resource management interface, which manages the printer device itself, offers two properties – PrintedPageCount and AvailableTonerCapacity – and an Enable operation. The properties are advertised in the resource properties document and are accessible through the WS-RF GetResourceProperty operation (see section 7.2.3). Finally the manageability capability for managing the printer Web service offers the MOWS metrics, NumberOfRequests, and the additional operational status control operations: Start and Stop.

Composition of manageability and functional capabilities makes it easy to distinguish between a management-oriented and a business-oriented resource capability perspective [Sedukhin 2005]. Management-oriented clients may thus gain visibility into functional aspects of a resource while business-oriented clients gain visibility into management aspects of a resource. For example, a Web-services-based business process may involve a selection of an on-line printer with a good amount of toner in order to print an urgent report. Composability makes it easy for implementers of resource services to offer an appropriate set of functional capabilities along with an appropriate set of manageability capabilities guided by the appropriate model for authorization of these requests. Composability also makes it easy to produce a resource properties document that defines

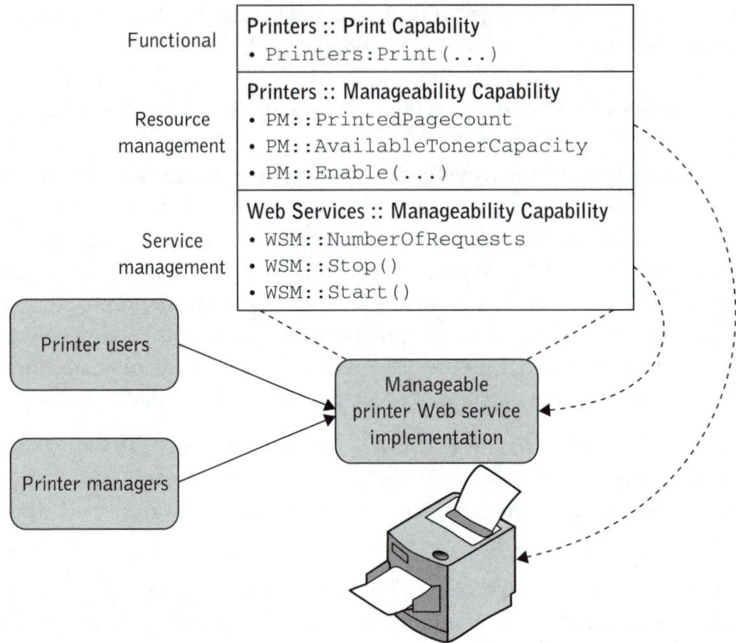

Figure 16.10 Printer exposed as Web service according to MOWS
Source: I. Sedukhin, 'Web services distributed management: management of web services (WSDM-MOWS) 1.0', *OASIS Standard*, March 2005. Copyright © OASIS Open 2003–2006. All rights reserved. Reproduced with permission.

both the resource manageability capability and Web services manageability properties as global element declarations in the schema. These are specified in Listing 16.2 for the printer example in Figure 16.10.

```
<xs:element name="ResourceId" type="xs:anyURI"/>
<xs:element name="PrintedPageCount" type="xsd:positiveInteger" />
<xs:element name="AvailableTonerCapacity"
 type="xsd:positiveInteger" />
<xs:element name="NumberOfRequests" type="mows-xs:
 IntegerCounter" />
<xs:element name="NumberOfSuccessfulRequests" type="mows-
 xs:IntegerCounter" />
<xs:element name="NumberOfFailedRequests" type="mows-
 xs:IntegerCounter" />
<xs:element name="ServiceTime" type="mows-xs:DurationMetric" />
<xs:element name="MaxResponseTime" type="mows-xs:DurationMetric" />
<xs:element name="LastResponseTime" type="mows-xs:DurationMetric" />
```

Listing 16.2 Printer manageability properties

Listing 16.3 shows the WSDL interface for the manageable printer defined in Listing 16.2. The WSDL interface is shown to contain four operations and the WS-RF `GetResourceProperty` operations.

```
<portType name="ManageablePrinter"
wsrf-rp:ResourceProperties="Printers:PrinterProperties">
  <wsdl:operation name="Print" >
     <wsdl:input … />
     <wsdl:output … />
  </wsdl:operation>
  <wsdl:operation name="Enable" >
      <wsdl:input … />
      <wsdl:output … />
  </wsdl:operation>
  <wsdl:operation name="Start" >
      <wsdl:input … />
      <wsdl:output … />
  </wsdl:operation>
  <wsdl:operation name="Stop" >
      <wsdl:input … />
      <wsdl:output … /></wsdl:operation>
      <wsdl:operation name="GetResourceProperty">
      <wsdl:input name="GetResourcePropertyRequest"
            message="wsrp:GetResourcePropertyRequest" />
      <wsdl:output name="GetResourcePropertyResponse"
            message="wsrp:GetResourcePropertyResponse" />
      <wsdl:fault name="UnknownResource"
            message="wsrp:ErrorMessage" />
      <wsdl:fault name="InvalidResourcePropertyQName"
            message="wsrp:ErrorMessage" />
  </wsdl:operation>
     … … …
</portType>
```

Listing 16.3 Sample operations for the manageable printer defined in Listing 16.2

More details and examples regarding the MOWS can be found in [Sedukhin 2005], [Kreger 2005a].

16.7 Summary

In the world of Web services, distributed management becomes a clear requirement because the growing complexity of global Web services brings together large numbers of services, suppliers, and technologies, all with potentially different performance requirements. However, many existing system management infrastructures do not support service-level agreement reporting or collect specific service information from Web services applications for troubleshooting purposes. Existing management standards (such as SNMP, CIM, OMI) primarily focus on data collection and not on supporting rich management applications for the adaptive infrastructure required by Web services.

Web services management provides the necessary infrastructure to help enterprises monitor, optimize, and control the Web services infrastructure. A Web services management system provides visibility into the Web services run-time environment to enable: monitoring of availability, accessibility, performance of Web services, SLA-compliance tracking, and error detection, resolution, and auditing.

OASIS Web Services Distributed Management is a key standard for Web services management. It allows the exposure of management functionality in a reusable way through two specifications: one for Management Using Web Services and the other for Management of Web Services. The MUWS specification provides a framework that defines how to represent and access the manageability interfaces of resources as Web services. MOWS builds on MUWS to define how to manage a Web service as a resource. It defines WSDL interfaces, which allows management events and metrics to be exposed, queried, and controlled by a broad range of management tools.

Review questions

- What is distributed computing systems management?
- How does Web services management differ from conventional distributed computing systems management?
- Briefly describe the three main topologies of Enterprise Management Systems.
- What are the main ingredients of a conceptual management architecture?
- Briefly describe the main characteristics of standard distributed management frameworks.
- What is operational and what is tactical services management?
- What are the most prominent functions of service management?
- Briefly describe the container-based and the intermediary-based architectural approach.
- How are the application and management channels interlinked in a Web services management architecture?
- What is the purpose and main characteristics of the Management Using Web Services specification?
- What is the purpose and main characteristics of the Management of Web Services specification?
- How are the Management Using Web Services and Management of Web Services specifications related?

Exercises

16.1 Consider the example of a company that would like to streamline its manufacturing and fulfillment processes across multiple factories and warehouses, as well as suppliers' facilities. The company has decided to outsource the manufacturing of low-margin parts that are not in inventory when orders are placed. Depending on the available-to-promise inventory levels, the company will either fulfill the order from one of its warehouses or place the order directly with one of its established suppliers for outsourced manufacturing. This end-to-end order fulfillment process covers multiple inter- and intra-company independently controlled Web services that rely on other services and processes to complete a task. How can this manufacturer apply service management solutions to effectively manage end-to-end quality objectives in a manner that aligns desired business objectives and guarantees acceptable level of service? Your solution should leverage the content and context of the messages that are exchanged between Web services and combined with system-level information in a way that ensures that business tasks are performing in accordance with service-level objectives.

16.2 Use the Management EJB (MEJB) component (Chapter JSR77.7, "J2EE Management EJB Component") technology to develop an application that accesses the attributes of a managed object of the J2EEApplication type through the MEJB.

16.3 Implement an application that illustrates how a J2EE component creates an MEJB session object, how managed objects of a certain type are found, and how the attributes of a managed object can be retrieved and their values determined.

16.4 Implement an application that illustrates how a method with a specific signature can be invoked.

16.5 Define and implement a manageable resource and create a management interface for it. The resource should be an abstract construct that represents purchase orders and stores such information as purchase order ID, shipping and billing addresses, and dates.

16.6 Consider an implementation which creates a large number of many management services at run-time. This application would clearly suffer from bad performance as management services consume sizeable chunks of the CPU time because of their operation execution times. Eventually the excessive use of management services will dominate consumption of resources over the business functions of the application – a clear case of overusing management services technology. Explain what decisions you need to make to overcome this problem.

PART X

Emerging trends

CHAPTER 17

Recent trends and developments

Learning objectives

As upcoming Web services standards, such as security, composition, policy, and so on, begin to crystallize and mature and robust industrial strength applications begin to appear, Web services technologies are expected to influence several other technological fields. In many cases this phenomenon is already happening. Among the many recent developments, most notable are grid services and mobile services.

In this chapter we shall overview these two important developments, describe their merits, architectural features, and related upcoming standards, and examine the consanguinity between Web services grid and mobile technologies. After completing this chapter readers will understand the following key concepts:

- Grid computing.
- Grid computing architectures.
- Grid services.
- Mobile computing.
- Mobile services.
- Mobile services protocols and framework.

17.1 Grid computing

Computing infrastructure in most organizations must accommodate multiple concurrent projects with differing schedules and milestones. Computing problems often occur in such organizations due to processing large volumes of data and/or performing repetitive computations and require massive amounts of computing power to the extent that the workload requirements exceed existing server platform capabilities. Product development teams often share the same finite set of computational resources. In response, grids containing thousands of inexpensive processors have been installed at academic, national laboratory, and commercial technical computing centers. The concept behind grid computing is simple and intuitive: a grid is a network of tens, hundreds, or even thousands of interconnected computers that work on common tasks. Grid computing has the design goal of solving problems that are far too big and complex for any single supercomputer, while retaining the flexibility to work on multiple smaller problems. In many cases, the results have been spectacular. For several applications, computer runs that used to take days or weeks to complete on large supercomputing systems now take minutes or hours.

17.1.1 A brief overview of grid computing

Grid computing is way of organizing large numbers of networked computers belonging to diverse organizations so that they can be flexibly and dynamically allocated and accessed and used as an ensemble to solve massive computational problems that require many collaborating resources [Banks 2003]. Grid computing involves sharing heterogeneous resources (based on different platforms, hardware/software architectures, and computer languages), located in different places belonging to different administrative domains over a network using open standards. Shareable resources include hardware and software resources and applications, such as central processors, storage, network bandwidth, databases, applications, sensors, scientific instruments, firmware implementations, and networking services, all available within an enterprise or service provider environment. Rather than keeping these resources isolated within an individual organization, they are available to authenticated users on a "demand" basis for resolving specific problems.

Conceptually, a grid is composed of a collection of computing resources connected through a network along with grid middleware that aggregates these resources and provides transparent, remote, and secure access to computing power wherever and whenever it is needed. Grid computing aggregates resources and delivers computing power to every user in the network. Gateway servers running grid engine software accomplish coordination between grid resources. These management servers receive requests for service from outside the grid, parcel out the jobs, and assemble the results. They also constantly monitor the systems in the grid to make sure all servers are on-line and ready for work. Grid engines monitor member systems for utilization status and steer new workloads towards servers that are underutilized.

Specific problems that require grid computing support may be a software capability problem, e.g., modeling, simulation, or hardware availability and/or computing capacity shortage problems, e.g., processor computing resources, data storage/access needs, and so on [Joseph 2004]. On another level, problems may be related to a networking bandwidth availability problem, the need for immediate circuit provisioning of a network, a security event, or other event correlation issue. Most of these problems might take an excessively long time to solve on a single installation's resources. A grid computing solution can reduce the turnaround time to a few minutes with the right kind of parallelization and distribution of the tasks involved. This reduction in turnaround time has opened up areas and styles for computing applications that have previously been impractical.

There are a variety of business areas and applications that can benefit from the use of grid infrastructure. These include life sciences, financial services, higher-education services, collaborative engineering, government services, industrial manufacturing, data exploration, high-throughput computing, and of course distributed supercomputing.

Grid computing can be used in a variety of ways to address various kinds of application requirements. Often, grids are categorized according to the type of solutions that they best address. Functionally, one can distinguish between two primary types of grids: computational grids (including CPU scavenging grids) and data grids.

The term *computational grid* comes from an analogy with the electric power utility grid. A computational grid is focused on setting aside resources specifically for computing power and uses networks of computers as a single, unified computing resource. It is possible to cluster or couple a wide variety of resources including supercomputers, storage systems, data sources, and special classes of devices distributed geographically and use them as a single unified resource. Such pooling requires significant hardware infrastructure to achieve the necessary interconnections and software infrastructure to monitor and control the resulting ensemble. The majority of the computational grids are centered on major scientific experiments and collaborative environments. Computational grid applications exhibit several functional computational requirements. These include the ability to: manage a variety of computing resources; select computing resources capable of running a user's job; predict loads on grid resources; decide about resource availability, dynamic resource configuration, and provisioning [Joseph 2004]. Other useful mechanisms for the management of resources include failure detection, fail-over, and security mechanisms.

The requirement for managing large data sets is a core underpinning of any grid computing environment. These data sources can be databases, file systems, and storage devices. A *data grid* is responsible for housing and providing access to data across multiple organizations and makes them available for sharing and collaboration purposes. Data grids can also be used to create a single, virtual view of a collection of data sources for large-scale collaboration. This process is called "data federation." In data grids, the focus is on the management of data which is being held in a variety of data storage facilities in geographically dispersed locations. For example, medical data grids are designed to make large data sets, such as patient records containing clinical information and associated digital X-rays, medication history, doctor reports, symptoms history, genetic information, and so on, available to many processing sites. By coupling the availability of these massive data sets with the large processing capability of grid computing, scientists can create applications to analyze the aggregated information. Searching the information for patterns or signatures enables scientists to potentially reach new insights regarding the environmental or genetic causes of diseases. Data grid systems must be capable of providing data virtualization services to provide the ability to discover data, transparency for data access, integration, and processing as well as the ability to support flexible data access and data filtering mechanisms. In addition, the provision of security and privacy mechanisms for all respective data in a grid system is an essential requirement for data grids.

It is important to note that there are no hard boundaries between these two grid types and often grids may be a combination of computational and data grids. Rather than regarding them as being separate problems to solve, we should regard them as being particular cases along a continuum – data grids have more activity around data, and compute grids have more activity around computation.

In general, grid computing environments must be constructed upon the following three foundations [Foster 2002a]:

1. *Coordinated resources:* Grid systems should come equipped with the appropriate infrastructure for coordination among computing resources on the basis of respective policies and SLAs instead of relying on a centralized control.
2. *Open standard protocols and frameworks:* Grid systems should be built around open standards that promote interoperability and integration facilities; for instance, protocols and interfaces that address such fundamental issues as authentication, authorization, resource discovery, and resource coordination.
3. *Non-trivial QoSs:* Another basic requirement of a grid computing system is the ability to provide the QoS requirements necessary for the end-user community. A grid system should allow its constituent resources to be used in a coordinated fashion to deliver various QoSs, relating for example to response-time measures, aggregated performance, security fulfillment, resource scalability, availability, autonomic features such as event correlation and configuration management, and partial fail-over mechanisms in such a way that the utility of the combined system is significantly greater than that of the sum of its parts. QoS validations must be done in congruence with the available resource metrics.

17.1.2 Features and requirements of grid systems

Essentially, grid computing involves virtualizing computing resources. A grid federates a large number of resources contributed by individual machines into a greater total virtual resource. The objective is to share information and processing capacity so that it can be more efficiently exploited.

The various kinds of shareable resources on the grid are usually accessed via an executing application or job. Usually we reserve the term *application* to signify the highest level of a piece of work on the grid. A *grid application* is a collection of work items to solve a certain problem or to achieve desired results using a grid infrastructure. For example, a grid application can be the simulation of business scenarios, like stock market development, which requires a large amount of data as well as a high demand for computing resources in order to calculate and handle the large number of variables and their effects. For each set of parameters a complex calculation needs to be performed. A grid application that is organized as a collection of jobs is usually designed to have these jobs execute in parallel on different machines in the grid. For instance, the simulation of a large-scale scenario, such as stock market development, can be divided into a number of calculation steps (or jobs) that together fulfill the entire task. A job is considered as a single unit of work within a grid application. It is typically submitted for execution on the grid, and has defined input and output data and execution requirements in order to complete its task. A single job can launch one or many processes on a specified grid node. It can perform complex calculations on large amounts of data or might be relatively simple in nature. However, in many cases jobs may have specific dependencies that may prevent them from executing in parallel.

There are a number of requirements needed for grid computing architectures utilized by virtual organizations. These include [Joseph 2004]:

- The need for dynamic discovery of computing resources based on their capabilities and functions.
- The allocation and provisioning of these resources based on their availability and user requirements.
- The management of computing resources to meet the required SLAs.
- The provisioning of multiple autonomic features for the resources, such as self-diagnosis, self-healing, self-configuring, and self-management.
- The provisioning of secure access methods to the resources and bindings with the local security mechanisms.

Such requirements are addressed by specialized grid middleware that not only provides transparent, remote, and secure access to computing resources, but also aggregates, monitors, and manages them.

Figure 17.1 shows a simplified view of a grid computing architecture executing a number of jobs on behalf of an application (client). A scheduler is used in this architecture

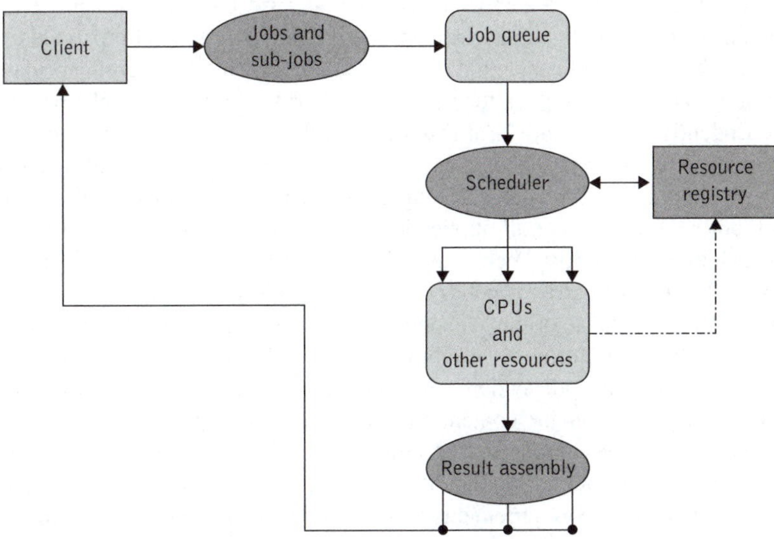

Figure 17.1 Simplified view of a grid computing architecture

for the management of jobs, fulfilling functions such as allocating resources needed for any specific job, partitioning of jobs to schedule parallel execution of tasks, data management, event correlation, and service-level management capabilities. Resource registries are used to discover those resources needed for the execution of a job. Multiple sources may need to be consulted to locate all the resources needed for a computation. Once these have been located, the grid management system contacts the owning resource manager to request allocations for CPUs, secondary storage, and/or other required resources. Assuming the discovery and allocation steps were successful, the management system (node) then sends the client input data and executables, receiving a reference to the execution in return. As resources are allocated, the resource manager may need to update the information in the registry to enable reasonable bids for resource allocation from other clients. Lastly, the grid management system monitors execution of the task using the reference it previously received. It can retrieve the results, or be sent status of the task as it progresses.

In a "scavenging" grid system, any machine that becomes idle would typically report its idle status to the grid management node [Ferreira 2002]. This management node would assign to this idle machine the next job that is satisfied by the machine's resources. Grid resources can also be "reserved" in advance for a designated set of jobs. Such reservations are done to meet deadlines and guarantee QoS. When policies permit, resources reserved in advance could also be scavenged to run lower-priority jobs when they are not busy during a reservation period, yielding to jobs for which they are reserved. Thus, various combinations of scheduling, reservation, and scavenging can be used to more completely utilize the grid.

17.1.3 Grid application considerations

Grid applications require partitioning that involves breaking a complex problem into discrete pieces. There are many factors to consider in grid enabling an application. New computation-intensive applications written today are being designed for parallel execution and these can be easily grid enabled, if they do not already follow emerging grid protocols and standards. These grid applications are usually written so that they can be partitioned into independently running parts. For instance, a CPU-intensive grid application can consist of a number of small sub-jobs, each of which executes on a different machine in the grid. The grid application is scalable as long as these sub-jobs do not need to communicate with each other. However, not all applications can be transformed to run in parallel on a grid and achieve scalability. There are several barriers that hinder perfect scalability [Ferreira 2002]. The first barrier depends on the algorithms used for splitting the application among many CPUs. If the algorithm can only be split into a limited number of independently running parts, then that forms a scalability barrier. The second barrier appears if the parts are not completely independent; this can cause contention, which can again limit scalability. Sources of inter-job contention in a parallel grid application include message communications latencies among the jobs, network communication capacities, synchronization protocols, input/output bandwidth to devices and storage devices, and latencies interfering with real-time requirements. Although there are some practical tools that skilled application designers can use to write a parallel grid application, automatic transformation of applications is still a long way away.

Several considerations need to be made when evaluating, designing, or converting applications for use in a grid computing environment. These fall into two main categories: CPU considerations and data considerations [Ferreira 2002]. CPU considerations focus on applications that consume large amounts of CPU time. Data considerations focus on the amounts of data that are needed to be sent to the node performing a calculation and the time required to send the data when splitting applications for use on a grid.

17.1.4 Grid services

The vision of grid computing is that the diverse resources that make up a modern computing environment can be discovered, accessed, allocated, monitored, accounted for, billed for, etc., and in general managed as a single virtual system [Foster 2005]. This should be irrespective of whether services are confined to a single enterprise or extending to encompass external resource sharing and service provider relationships. Key to the realization of the grid vision is the need for open standards that define this kind of grid interaction and encourage interoperability between components supplied from different sources. This need for standardization was the motivation for the Open Grid Services Architecture (OGSA), specified by the Open Grid Services Infrastructure Working Group of the Global Grid Forum (GGF). The main objectives of OGSA are to [Unger 2003]:

- Manage resources across distributed heterogeneous platforms.
- Deliver seamless end-to-end QoSs when running on top of different native platforms.
- Provide a common base for autonomic management solutions to manage grids that contain many resources with numerous combinations of configurations, interactions, and changing state and failure modes.
- Define open standard interfaces and protocols (e.g., OGSA) to guarantee interoperability of diverse resources.
- Exploit industry-standard integration technologies. The foundation of OGSA is Web services.

Work on OGSA seeks to address these challenges by defining an integrated set of Web-service-based definitions designed both to simplify the creation of secure, robust grid systems, and to enable the creation of interoperable, portable, and reusable components and systems via the standardization of key interfaces and behaviors [Foster 2005]. The OGSA architectural concept is a result of the alignment of existing grid standards with emerging Web services standards. OGSA provides a uniform way to describe grid services and define a common pattern of behavior for these services. It defines grid service behavior, service description mechanisms, and protocol binding information by using Web services as the technology enabler.

As Figure 17.2 illustrates, four main layers comprise the OGSA architecture. These are [Unger 2003]: resources, Web services (and in addition the OGSI extensions that define grid services), OGSA architected services, and grid applications.

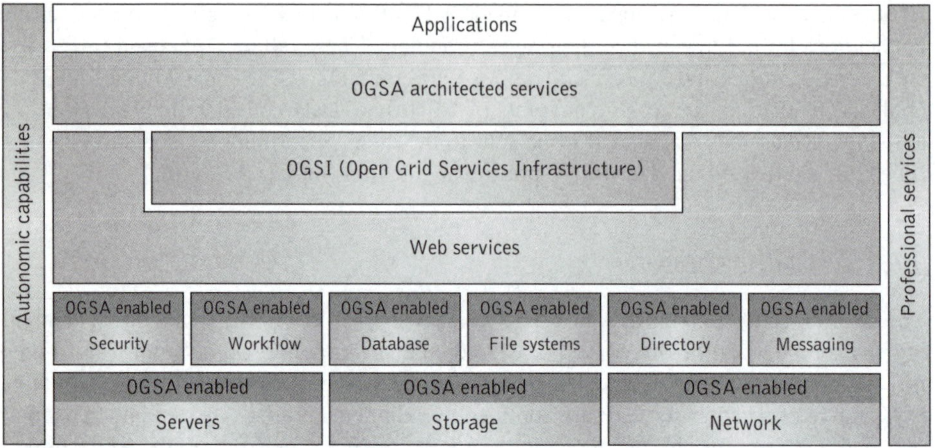

Figure 17.2 Overview of OGSA
Source: [Unger 2003]

Resources comprise the capabilities of the grid, and are of physical and logical types. Physical resources include servers, storage, and network. Logical resources reside above the physical resources in the architecture, see Figure 17.2. They provide a virtualization layer and additional functions for virtualizing and aggregating the resources in the physical layer. General-purpose middleware facilities such as file systems, database managers, directories, and workflow managers provide these abstract services on top of the physical grid.

The second layer in the OGSA architecture uses Web services to model all grid resources – both logical and physical. These grid resources are modeled as services defined by the Open Grid Services Infrastructure (OGSI) [Tuecke 2003]. The OGSI specification is a companion standard that defines the interfaces and protocols that will be used between the various services in a grid environment. The OGSI is the standard that will provide the interoperability between grids designed using OGSA. For this purpose, OGSI extends WSDL to provide capabilities for dynamic, stateful, and manageable Web services that are required to model the resources of the grid. OGSI version 1.0 defines a set of conventions and extensions on the use of WSDL and XML Schema to enable stateful Web services.

At the core of OGSI is a *grid service* [Foster 2002b], a Web service that conforms to a set of conventions in a grid system for such purposes as creating, naming, and managing the lifetime of instances of services; for declaring and inspecting service state data; for asynchronous notification of service state change; for representing and managing collections of service instances; and for common handling of service invocation faults. OGSI also introduces standard factory and registration interfaces for creating and discovering grid services.

Grid services resemble Web services especially from a programmatic view. A grid service is (in practice) a Web service that conforms to a particular set of coding practices, namely a set of XML coding conventions in the form of standards. For example, grid services can be defined in terms of standard XML-based WSDL, with perhaps some minor XML language extensions. These grid services can now take advantage of standard Web services binding technologies (for messaging, reliability, providing standardized access to and management of resources that are exposed via Web services, addressing, notification, transactions, and security), such as SOAP, WS-ReliableMessaging, WS-Resource Framework, WS-Addressing, WS-Notification, WS-Transaction, and WS-Security.

The Web services layer along with its OGSI extensions provides a base infrastructure for the next layer, the architected grid services. The Global Grid Forum is currently working to define many of these architected grid services in areas like program execution, data services, and core services.

Grid applications comprise the topmost layer of the architecture. They make use of the architected grid services.

OGSA concerns itself with the provision of an infrastructure fulfilling the goal of supporting virtual organizations. Concretely, this goal requires that, among other tasks, the access to and management of grid resources can be virtualized. To achieve this objective OGSA defines the following functionalities [Ferreira 2004]:

Interoperability: Seamless integration of services architected on OGSA is addressed by separating the interfaces definition and the protocol bindings through WSDL and the usage of SOA for the OGSA framework. A layer of abstraction that hides the platform-specific implementation supports uniform service interface definition. This adds up to the concept of virtualization of services and adds to the fluidity of virtual organization. The QoS is handled as the properties of bindings.

Registration, discovery, and access of resources: The three parts are a standard representation of service data, containing information about grid service instances; a standard operation to retrieve service data from individual grid service instances; and a standard interface registry for registering and querying information about the grid service instances.

Services state: OGSA manages service states by defining service data elements that store the service states and maintain them until the end of the service lifetime. The stored service state is accessible via the grid service interfaces defined in OGSA. In the grid architecture, the service definition is separate from the actual service instances. One single interface can have more than one instance active at the same time, serving multiple client services.

Dynamic service creation: One of the most important characteristics of the OGSA is its acknowledgement of the need to create and manage new grid service instances dynamically. To this end OGSA defines an interface called "Factory" for creating new grid service instances.

Lifetime management: In a dynamic environment, services are created and need to be destroyed when no longer needed. The grid services architecture addresses this lifecycle issue through a soft state approach where grid services are created with a specified initial lifetime (that can be extended) and the host itself can discard a grid service instance if the stream of "keep-alive" messages that reaffirm the need for it to be retained dries up.

Notification: Common abstractions and service interfaces for subscription to, and delivery of, event notifications are supported through the OGSA notification sink and source port types, so that grid services can asynchronously notify each other of relevant changes to their state.

As already stated, OGSA realizes virtualization functions in terms of services, the interfaces these services expose, the individual and collective state of resources belonging to these services, and the interaction between these services within an SOA. To realize virtualization functionality OGSA provides a series of services that include execution management services, data services, resource management services, security services, self-management, and information services.

17.2 Mobile computing

Mobile technology has made notable progress over the past few years, due to the development of new handheld devices, improved wide area celullar data coverage and bandwidth, and the seamless integration of wireless data access into personal digital assistants (PDAs) that offer improved connectivity to the Internet. Enterprises can now attempt large-scale deployments of field service, route management, and field sales projects, thus automating and tightly integrating a field-based workforce into a company's stationary IT infrastructure. The recent advances in wireless technologies coupled with more powerful handhelds and cell phones have given birth to the mobile computing paradigm. Mobile computing represents a fundamentally new paradigm in enterprise computing. *Mobile computing* enables operating a job- and role-specific application loaded on a handheld or tablet device that passes only relevant data between a field worker and the relevant back-end enterprise systems regardless of connectivity availability. This comes in contrast to conventional distributed enterprise applications that can be accessed via a machine in a fixed network connection from a remote location.

Mobile computing contributes to the vision of pervasive computing. The essence of *pervasive computing* is the creation of environments saturated with computing and wireless communication, yet gracefully integrated with human users [Satyanarayanan 2001]. The pervasive computing space can be envisioned as a combination of mobile and stationary devices that draw on powerful services embedded in the network [Dertouzos 1999]. In this environment mobile and stationary devices will dynamically connect and coordinate to help users accomplish their tasks. The overall goal is to provide users with universal and immediate access to information, no matter whether it is available on a fixed or wireless network, and to transparently support them in their tasks. Pervasive computing devices are not personal computers as we tend to think of them, but very tiny – even invisible – devices, either mobile or embedded in almost any type of object imaginable, including cars, tools, appliances, and various consumer goods – all communicating through increasingly interconnected networks.

17.2.1 Elements of mobile infrastructure

The mobile Web differs from the fixed Web in some significant ways. Mobile terminals suffer from several notable limitations: mobile handset processing power is restricted in terms of CPU capabilities, addressable memory, and permanent memory. At the same time the user interface is limited in terms of both screen and input device and the network is constrained in both data throughput and latency. However, recently there have been

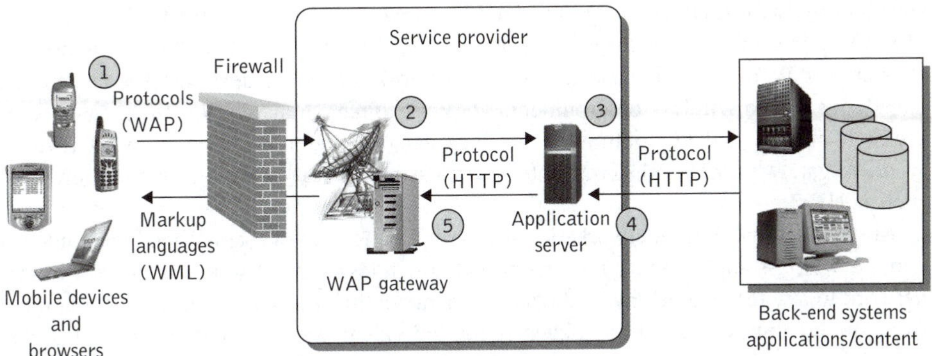

Figure 17.3 Typical elements in mobile infrastructure

several dramatic improvements in mobile technology. Mobile operating systems and user interfaces are becoming increasingly powerful and sophisticated. These advanced terminal platforms have opened up their local resources to host third-party applications. Current and widely deploying wireless packet switching protocols, such as General Packet Radio Service (GPRS), offer greater capacity, higher bit rates, and always-connected functionality.

Wireless systems can be configured in a variety of topologies to meet the needs of specific applications and installations. Configurations can range from peer-to-peer networks suitable for a small number of users to full-fledged networks of large numbers of users that enable roaming over vast areas.

Figure 17.3 illustrates the typical elements in a networked wireless infrastructure. The architecture is shown to encompass a network-aware application residing on a wireless device (the client), the wireless network and the Internet, corresponding communication protocols, a secure private network that includes one or more firewalls, a proxy gateway or Web server, and back-end applications and servers.

Mobile devices and microbrowsers in Figure 17.3 are used to access the wireless network. A wireless device in this context is a device that has connectivity to the Internet without being physically plugged into a network with a wire. Each wireless device uses a browser to display information. Mobile browser applications provide an interface to key enterprise systems from a variety of mobile devices. A mobile salesperson can, for instance, use a mobile browser application to obtain customer and latest product availability and pricing information, while on the move, without the need for a laptop. Mobile browser access provides highly optimized wireless access to collaboration information from any mobile device with browser capabilities. Users have a choice of selecting any native client browser (e.g., XHTML, HTML, Wireless Markup Language (WML), Handheld Device Markup Language (HDML), Compact HTML (cHTML), tinyHTML) on any phone, PDA, or laptop with a wireless Internet connection. All mobile applications are optimized to take full advantage of the device form factor, browser capabilities, data entry options, and available network bandwidth.

Microbrowsers use one of several markup languages designed specifically for mobile devices. The three general-use markup languages currently used in data-enabled mobile devices are: WML specified by the Wireless Application Protocol (WAP), cHTML specified by the i-mode protocol, and HDML. Newer devices tend to use WML instead of HDML. Special wireless data protocols such as WAP, i-mode, and others were created to transport Web-based data on a wireless network and were designed for the unique constraints of the wireless environment. They use binary transmission for greater compression of data and are optimized for long latency and low to medium bandwidth. Wireless gateways are used to translate a wireless protocol request to a standard protocol such as HTTP.

At the other end of the networked wireless application are the server and back-end systems. A wireless application server connects the wireless content source over the wireless network to a wireless gateway or device. To achieve this, the server retrieves the content from the content source, personalizes it for individual users, and transforms it to the specific markup language understood by the wireless device being used.

When a wireless device requests a mobile application the device's browser first forwards the request to a wireless network base station (step 1 in Figure 17.3). The request can be sent over a protocol such as WAP, depending on the type of device being used. As soon as the wireless network base station receives the mobile device's request, it proceeds to authenticate it. Once a session with this specific device is established, the WAP gateway passes the information regarding the specific request to the wireless application server (step 2 in Figure 17.3). Subsequently, a connection is established with the mobile device and the request is transferred over the wireless network using a standard wireless transfer protocol, e.g., the Wireless Transport Protocol (WTP). This request is translated by the WAP gateway before it is passed to the server and back-end systems.

The WAP gateway not only performs translations from one protocol to another but also knows how to relay a message from the wireless network to a traditional stationary network. The converted message is sent as a standard Internet request to the wireless application server (step 3 in Figure 17.3). It receives the message header – which encodes information such as the user's identity, the device that the user is using to access the wireless network, and the geographical location of the user – and the message body. The application server then interprets the user's identity, the location, and other identification information that is passed to it, retrieves the content of the application being accessed, and customizes it for the user (step 4 in Figure 17.3). Customization of services occurs on the basis of information provided by the user. This may include choosing which services the user wishes to invoke, setting up notification services, and personalizing the services based on the device the user is employing and the user's geographical location (location-based services). Finally, the application server transforms the content of the output result to a format understood by the user's wireless device (step 5 in Figure 17.3). The transformed response is subsequently transported to the user.

There is a list of factors that developers need to consider when writing applications for wireless clients. Content should be personalized based on the location of the device and/or the type of the device. Microbrowsers in mobile devices are usually not HTML based; some are WML based, some are cHTML based or HDML based, and some use Web Clipping. Mobile devices have small display and limited user input facilities, narrowband network connection, and limited memory and computational resources. Some devices have additional advanced features such as Bluetooth, power keys, and SMS messaging that can be used to enhance an application. A few of the devices are limited in the amount of data that can be transmitted to them for a page. Wireless networks are constrained by low bandwidth, high latency, and unpredictable availability and stability given that connectivity is often lost when the device is mobile. Finally, mobile devices usually have no PKI security capability.

17.2.2 Wireless protocols

Currently, there are two popular protocols for the presentation and delivery of wireless information and telephony services on mobile phones. These are WAP and i-mode and are briefly examined below.

WAP [WAP Forum 2002] is an open standard for the presentation and delivery of wireless information and telephony services on mobile phones and other wireless terminals that works across differing wireless network technology types. WAP addresses wireless network characteristics by adapting several data handling approaches already in use by Web protocols, and introducing new ones, where appropriate, to the special requirements of handheld wireless devices. The reuse of existing Web technologies eases the development of WAP applications, and makes it similar to developing HTML-based Web applications since WAP is browser based.

The WAP specification addresses the limitations of wireless networks (low bandwidth, low memory, high latency, and unpredictable availability and stability) and wireless devices (limited CPU, memory, and battery life, and a simple user interface). WAP specifies two essential elements of wireless communication: an over-the-air wireless protocol and an application environment. In essence, it is a standardized technology for cross-platform, distributed computing.

Two of the main components of the WAP application environment are Wireless Markup Language (WML) (**http://www.wapforum.org/what/technical.htm**) and WMLScript. WML for WAP applications is analogous to HTML for TCP/IP applications. WML is a markup language based on XML, and is intended for use in specifying content and user interface for microbrowsers that exist in WAP-enabled devices, e.g., cellular phones and pagers. WML was thus designed with the constraints of small narrowband devices in mind to provide the appropriate presentational services for wireless devices. A WML document is a collection – referred to as a deck – of one or more cards. Each card in a deck of cards is considered a well-defined unit of interaction. A card is the WAP equivalent of an HTML page and carries enough information to fit onto one screen of a wireless device.

The WAP solution can leverage investments in Web servers, Web development tools, Web programmers, and Web applications while solving the unique problems associated with the wireless domain.

I-mode is a wireless Internet service that was inspired by WAP and was developed by NTT DoCoMo and designed to be closely aligned with Internet standards so as not to require content developers to learn new languages and tools for the wireless Internet (**www.nttdocomo.com**).

I-mode uses NTT DoCoMo's 3G network called FOMA. This high-speed cellular network allows speeds of up to 384 kbit/s download (typically 200 kbit/s) and 64 kbit/s upload in best conditions and therefore allows video telephony. I-mode uses a packet switched system where users are charged for the information downloaded and not for the connection time.

I-mode is based on fixed Internet protocols such as cHTML, which is derived from HTML, as well as DoCoMo proprietary protocols ALP (HTTP) and TLP (TCP, UDP). I-mode also uses HTTP for content transmission. It is committed to support the WAP 2.0 standard and also uses a wireless-profiled version of TCP. Secure communication is achieved with SSL connection between mobile terminals and content servers, while data packets are tunneled through a mobile network gateway.

17.2.3 Mobile Web services

With the proliferation of advanced reliable wireless networks and devices, mobile operators and enterprises can now provide a variety of types of services to their users. Recently, wireless and voice platforms have started to emerge, offering comprehensive support for mobile browser applications (PDAs, smartphones, and so on), mobile messaging applications (one-way/two-way SMS, MMS, and so on), location-based services (mobile positioning, tracking, mapping, routing, and so on), interactive voice applications, and sensor-based services (RFID). Such wireless platforms allow developers to leverage middleware technology to develop, deploy, and manage new mobile applications and integrate with existing fixed enterprise systems and applications where appropriate. When combined with sophisticated software running on wireless devices, these services provide near-real-time access to a broad range of information, from simple text messages and e-mail to corporate data.

At the same time, with Web services being widely deployed as the SOA of choice for internal processes in organizations, there is also an emerging demand for using Web services enabling mobile working and e-business. By integrating Web services and mobile computing technologies, consistent business models can be enabled on a broad array of endpoints: not just on mobile devices operating over mobile networks, but also on servers and computing infrastructure operating over the Internet. To make this integration happen at a technical level, mechanisms are required to expose and leverage existing mobile network services. Also, practices for how to integrate the various business needs of the mobile network world and their associated enablers such as security must be developed. The result is a framework, such as the Open Mobile Alliance (see section 17.2.4.1), that demonstrates how the Web service specifications can be used and combined with mobile computing technology and protocols to realize practical and interoperable solutions.

The aim of the mobile Web services effort is two-fold. First, to create a new environment that enables the IT industry and the mobile industry to create products and services that meet customer needs in a way not currently possible within the existing Web services practices. Second, to help create Web services standards that will enable new business opportunities by delivering integrated services across stationary (fixed) and wireless networks. Mobile Web services use existing industry-standard (XML)-based Web services architecture to expose mobile network services to the broadest audience of developers. Developers will be able to access and integrate mobile network services such as messaging, location-based content delivery, syndication, personalization, identification, authentication, and billing services into their applications. This will ultimately enable solutions that work seamlessly across stationary networks and mobile environments. Customers will be able to use mobile Web services from multiple devices on both wired and wireless networks.

17.2.3.1 Mobility considerations

Successful mobile solutions that help architect customers' service infrastructures need to address security availability and scalability concerns both at the functional level and at the end-to-end solution level, rather than just offering fixed-point products. What is required is a standard specification and an architecture (as will be explained in section 17.2.4) that tie together service discovery, invocation, authentication, and other necessary components – thereby adding context and value to Web services. In this way operators and enterprises will be able to leverage the unique capabilities of each component of the end-to-end network and shift the emphasis of service delivery from devices to the human user. Using a combination of wireless, broadband, and wireline devices, users can then access any service on demand, with a single identity and single set of service profiles, personalizing service delivery as dictated by the situation. There are three important requirements to accomplish user (mobile-subscriber)-focused delivery of mobile services: federated identity, policy, and federated context [Sun Microsystems 2003]. We shall explain these requirements in brief in what follows.

In a mobile environment users are not seen as individuals (e.g., mobile subscribers) to software applications and processes who are tied to a particular domain, but rather as entities that are free to traverse multiple service networks. This requirement demands a complete *federated network identity model* to tie the various "personas" of an individual without compromising privacy or loss of ownership of the associated data. The federated network identity model allows the implementation of seamless single sign-on for users interacting with applications [Nokia 2004]. It also ensures that user identity, including transactional information and other personal information, is not tied to a particular device or service, but rather is free to move with the user between service providers. Furthermore, it guarantees that only appropriately authorized parties are able to access protected information.

User policy, including roles and access rights, is an important requirement for allowing users not only to have service access within their home network, but also to move outside it and still receive the same access to services. Knowing who the user is and what role they fulfill at the moment they are using a particular service is essential to providing the right service at the right instance. The combination of federated identity and policy enables service providers and users to strike a balance between access rights and user privacy [Sun Microsystems 2003].

Understanding what the user is doing, what they ask, why it is being requested, where they are, and what device they are using is an essential requirement. The notion of *federated context* means accessing and acting upon a user's current location, availability, presence, and role, e.g., at home, at work, on holiday, etc., and other situational attributes. This requires the intelligent synthesis of information available from all parts of the end-to-end network and allows service providers and enterprises to deliver relevant and timely applications and services to end users in a personalized manner. For example, information about the location and availability of a user's device may reside on the wireless network, the user's calendar may be on the enterprise intranet, and preferences may be stored in a portal.

Integrating identity, policy, and context into the overall mobile services architecture enables service providers to differentiate the user from the device, and deliver the right service to the right user on virtually any device [Sun Microsystems 2003].

17.2.3.2 Field Web services

Wireless services are evolving towards the goal of delivering the right service to whoever needs it, e.g., employees, suppliers, partners, and customers, at the right place, at the right time, and on any device of their choice. The combination of wireless handheld devices and service delivery technologies poses the opportunity for an entirely new paradigm of information access that in the enterprise context can substantially reduce delays in the transaction and fulfillment process and lead to improved cash flow and profitability. Companies that can outfit their employees with devices like PDAs, laptops, multi-function smart phones, or pagers will begin to bridge the costly chasm between the field and the back office. For example, transportation costs for remote employees can be significantly reduced and productivity can be significantly improved by eliminating needless journeys back to the office to file reports, collect parts, or simply deliver purchase orders.

A field Web services solution automates, standardizes, and streamlines manual processes in an enterprise and helps centralize disparate systems associated with customer service lifecycle management including customer contact, scheduling and dispatching, mobile workforce communications, resource optimization, work order management, time, labor, material tracking, billing, payroll, and so on. A field Web services solution links seamlessly all elements of an enterprise's field service operation – customers, service engineers, suppliers, and the office – to the enterprise's stationary infrastructure, wireless communications, and mobile devices. Field Web services provide real-time visibility and control of all calls and commitments, resources, and operations. They effectively manage business activities such as call taking and escalation, scheduling and dispatching, customer entitlements and SLAs, work orders, service contracts, time sheets, labor and equipment tracking, pre-invoicing, resource utilization, reporting and analytics.

Field service optimization solutions try to automatically match the most cost-effective resource with each service order, based on prioritized weightings assigned to every possible schedule constraint. To accommodate evolving business priorities, most optimization solutions allow operators to reorder these weightings and to execute ad hoc "what-if" scenario analyses to test the financial and performance impacts of scheduling alternatives. In this way, they help enhance supply-chain management by enabling real-time response to changing business conditions.

Of particular interest to field services are location-based services, notification services, and service disambiguation as these mechanisms enable developers to build more sophisticated field service applications by providing accessible interfaces to advanced features and "intelligent" mobile features.

Location-based services provide information specific to a location using the latest positioning technologies and are a key part of the mobile Web services suite [Bennett 2002]. Dispatchers can use GPS or network-based positioning information to determine the location of field workers and optimally assign tasks (push model) based on geographic proximity. Location-based services and applications enable enterprises to improve operational efficiencies by locating, tracking, and communicating with their field workforce in real time. For example, location-based services can be used to keep track of vehicles and employees, whether they are conducting service calls or delivering products. Trucks could be pulling in or out of a terminal, visiting a customer site, or picking up supplies from a manufacturing or distribution facility. With location-based services applications can get such things such as real-time status alerts, e.g., estimated time of approach, arrival, departure, duration of stop, current information on traffic, weather, and road conditions for both home-office and en route employees.

Notification services allow critical business to proceed uninterrupted when employees are away from their desks, by delivering notifications to their preferred mobile device. Employees can thus receive real-time notification when critical events occur, such as when incident reports are completed. The combination of location-based and notification services provides added value by enabling such services as proximity-based notification and proximity-based actuation. Proximity-based notification is a push or pull interaction model that includes targeted advertising, automatic airport check-in, sightseeing information, and so on. Proximity-based actuation is a push–pull interaction model, whose most typical example is payment based upon proximity, e.g., toll watch.

Finally, service instance disambiguation helps distinguish between many similar candidate service instances, which may be available inside close perimeters. For instance, there may be many on-device payment services in proximity of a single point of sale. Convenient and natural ways for identifying appropriate service instances are then required, e.g., relying on closeness or pointing rather than identification by cumbersome unique names.

The topic of user location, which is a key element for field Web services, is treated at some length in [Pashtan 2005]. This book provides a detailed description of handset-based and network-based approaches to determine mobile user locations.

17.2.4 Mobile Web services standard initiatives

Delivering appealing, low-cost mobile data services, including ones that are based on mobile Internet browsing and mobile commerce, is proving increasingly difficult to achieve. The existing infrastructure and tools as well as the interfaces between Internet/Web applications and mobile network services remain largely fragmented, characterized by tightly coupled, costly, and close alliances between value-added service providers and a complex mixture of disparate and sometimes overlapping standards (WAP, MMS, Presence, Identity, etc.) and proprietary models (e.g., propriety interfaces). This hinders interoperability solutions for the mobile sector and at the same time drives up the cost of application development and ultimately the cost of services offered to mobile users. Such problems have given rise to initiatives for standardizing mobile Web services. The most important of these initiatives are the Open Mobile Alliance and the mobile Web services frameworks that are examined below.

17.2.4.1 The Open Mobile Alliance Initiative

Recently, much effort has been expended to standardize over-the-air interfaces between wireless devices and elements in the mobile network. This has led to the creation of the Open Mobile Alliance (**www.openmobilealliance.org**). OMA is a group of wireless vendors, IT companies, mobile operators, and application and content providers, who have come together to drive the growth of the mobile industry. The objective of OMA is to deliver open technical specifications, based upon market requirements, for the mobile industry, that enable interoperable solutions across different devices, geographies, service providers, operators, and networks. OMA includes all key elements of the wireless value chain, and contributes to the timely availability of mobile service enablers. For enterprises already using a multi-tiered network architecture based on open technologies, such as Web services, that implement wireless services, OMA is a straightforward extension of existing wireline processes and infrastructures. In this way wireless services become simply another delivery channel for communication, transactions, and other value-added services.

The technical working groups within OMA address the need to support standardized interactions. To achieve this OMA is currently addressing how mobile operators can leverage Web services and defines a set of common protocols, schemas, and processing rules using Web services technologies that are the elements that can be used to create or interact with a number of different services.

In order to mitigate the challenge developers face in achieving robust, distributed, decentralized, and interoperable implementations with rapid time to market, the OMA Web Services Enabler (OWSER) specification [OMA 2004] defines capabilities that are expected to be common across Web services within OMA. The OWSER specification capitalizes on all the benefits of Web services technologies to simplify the task of integrators, developers, and implementers of service enablers by providing them with common mechanisms and protocols for interoperability of service enablers. Examples of functionality common across service enablers range from transport and message encoding definitions, to security concerns, service discovery, charging, definition, and management of SLAs, as well as management, monitoring, and provisioning of the service enablers that exist within a service provider's network.

The OMA Web service interfaces are intended to enhance a service provider's data for a particular mobile subscriber. A common scenario starts with a data request from some application (perhaps a mobile browser) to a service provider. The service provider then uses Web services to interact with a subscriber's mobile operator to retrieve some relevant data about the subscriber such as location or presence. This data can be used to enhance the service provider's response to the initial request. Mobile Web services are envisioned to support server-to-server, server-to-mobile terminal, mobile terminal-to-server, and mobile terminal-to-mobile terminal (or peer-to-peer) interactions.

Currently, the OMA is defining core services such as location, digital rights, and presence services; use cases involving mobile subscribers, mobile operators, and service providers; an architecture for the access and deployment of core services; and a Web services framework for using secure SOAP.

17.2.4.2 Mobile Web services framework

In parallel with the OMA activities, Microsoft and Vodafone Group Services have proposed a framework for mobile Web services to meet the requirements for bridging stationary enterprise infrastructure and the mobile world [Jeal 2003]. The objective of the mobile Web services framework is to enable the application of Web services specifications, SOA implementations, and tools to the problem of exposing mobile network services in a commercially viable way to the mass market of developers. The focus of the work concentrates on mechanisms to orchestrate the calls to mobile Web services.

The mobile Web services framework concentrates specification work around a set of core mechanisms that will be used by dependent services within their own specifications.

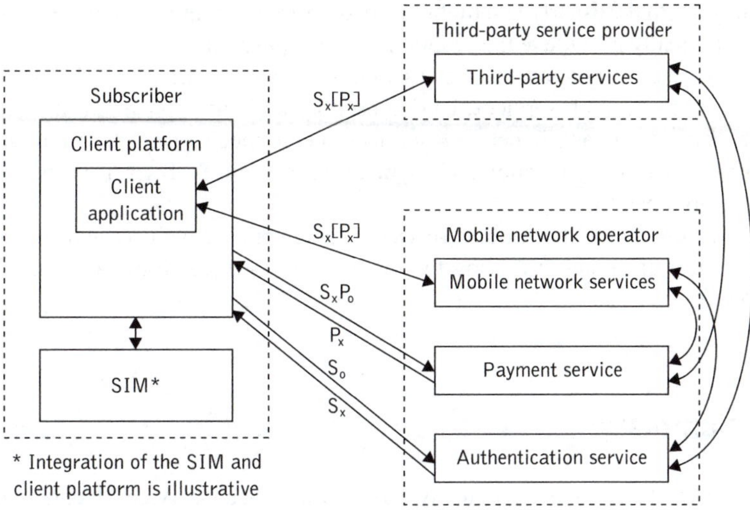

Figure 17.4 Overview of the mobile Web services architecture

The mobile Web services framework places particular emphasis on core mechanisms such as security, authentication, and payment. Core security mechanisms are offered which apply WS-Security to mobile network security services, such as the use of a GSM-style SIM security device within a Web services endpoint to provide a means for authentication. In addition, a set of core payment mechanisms within the Web services architecture has been proposed that understands how to interact with the participating Web services endpoints. It is expected that a number of services dependent on the mobile Web services framework and that rely on its core mechanisms will be developed.

Presently, SMS services, MMS services, and location-based services have been identified as common services that are candidates for specification activity. Specification work will include profiling and optimization of the core Web services protocols so that they can easily be realized over any bearer, on any device, or both. This addresses the inefficiencies that current Web services specifications exhibit when used over a narrowband and possibly intermittent bearer, or when being processed by a low-performance mobile device.

The mobile Web services architecture depicted in Figure 17.4 is shown to link subscribers to third-party service providers and mobile network operators. The architecture also supports variations of these roles. A subscriber is an end user or entity which has a business relationship with a mobile network operator. The architecture distinguishes between services of a third-party service provider and those of a mobile network operator that provides authentication and payment services as well as its own services. Third-party services are general-purpose Web services that provide access to a wide variety of functionality, some of which may be well defined within a particular industry and some of which may be proprietary in nature. Mobile network services are Web services that provide access to functionality within a mobile network that may either be well defined within the mobile industry, such as SMS, MMS, location-based functionality, or offer proprietary functionality. Both third-party and mobile network services require a subscriber to authenticate and optionally provide authorization to make a payment.

Security and authentication services as well as chargeable transaction services, developed on the basis of Web services, can be used by a client application interacting with third-party services or mobile network services. These mechanisms are supported by the client platform. The authentication and payment services are Web services operated by the mobile network operator.

Further details about the mobile services framework as well as authentication and payment request examples involving the mobile Web services framework can be found in [Jeal 2003].

17.3 Summary

In recent years there have been many cases where Web services technologies were successfully amalgamated with other technologies and applied to diverse application fields, e.g., agent technologies, ontologies, and medical information systems, to name a few. Among these recent developments, the most notable are grid services and mobile services.

Grid computing focuses on providing dynamic coordinated sharing in a multi-user environment. This results in innovative applications making use of high-throughput computing for dynamic problem solving. Grid services are special kinds of Web services that conform to a set of conventions in a grid system for such purposes as creating, naming, and managing the lifetime of instances of services; for declaring and inspecting service state data; for asynchronous notification of service state change; for representing and managing collections of service instances; and for common handling of service invocation faults.

Mobile computing represents a fundamentally new paradigm in enterprise computing which enables operating a job- and role-specific application loaded on a handheld or tablet device that passes relevant data between a field worker and relevant back-end enterprise systems regardless of connectivity availability. Mobile Web services help create Web services standards that will enable new business opportunities by delivering integrated services across stationary (fixed) and wireless networks. To achieve this goal they use existing industry-standard (XML)-based Web services architecture to expose mobile network services to the broadest audience of developers.

Review questions

- What is grid computing?
- What is the concept of the computational and the data grid?
- Briefly describe the main characteristics of a typical grid computing architecture.
- What are grid services and what are their most typical characteristics?

- What is mobile computing?
- Briefly describe the main elements in a typical mobile infrastructure.
- Which are the two main wireless protocols and how are they related?
- What is the purpose of mobile services?
- What are location-based services?
- What are notification services? How do they interact with location-based services?
- What is the purpose of the Open Mobile Alliance Initiative?
- What are the main components of the mobile Web services framework?

References

[Ahmed 2001] K. Ahmed *et al.*, "XML Metadata", Wrox Press, 2001.

[Aldrich 2002] S. E. Aldrich, "Anatomy of Web Services", Patricia Seybold Group, Inc. 2002, available at:
www.psgroup.com.

[Alexander 2004] J. Alexander *et al.*, "Web Services Transfer (WS-Transfer)", September 2004, available at:
http://www.w3.org/Submission/2006/SUBM-WS-Transfer-20060315/.

[Allen 2001] P. Allen, *Realizing e-Business with Components*, Addison-Wesley, 2001.

[Alonso 2004] G. Alonso *et al.*, *Web Services: Concepts, Architectures and Applications*, Springer, 2004.

[Anagol-Subbaro 2005] A. Anagol-Subbaro, *J2EE Web Services on BEA WebLogic*, Prentice Hall, 2005.

[Anderson 2004a] S. Anderson *et al.*, "Web Services Secure Conversation Language (WS-SecureConversation)", Version 1.1, May 2004, available at:
ftp://www6.software.ibm.com/software/developer/library/ws-secureconversation.pdf.

[Anderson 2004b] S. Anderson *et al.* "Web Services Trust Language (WS-Trust)", Version 1.1, May 2004, available at:
ftp://www6.software.ibm.com/software/developer/library/ws-trust.pdf.

[Andrews 2003] T. Andrews *et al.* (eds.), "Business Process Execution Language for Web Services", May 2003, available at:
http://www.ibm.com/developerworks/library/ws-bpel.

[Andrieux 2005] A. Andrieux *et al.*, "Web Services Agreement Specification (WS-Agreement)", Technical Report, Grid Resource Allocation Agreement Protocol (GRAAP) WG, September 2005, available at:
http://www.gridforum.org/Public_Comment_Docs/Documents/Oct-2005/WS-AgreementSpecificationDraft050920.pdf.

[Antoniou 2004] G. Antoniou, F. van Harmelen, *A Semantic Web Primer*, MIT Press, 2004.

[Arkin 2001] A. Arkin, "Business Process Modelling Language", March 2001, bpmi.org.

[Arkin 2002] A. Arkin, "Business Process Modelling Language (BPML) specification", BPMI, June 2002, available at:
http://www.bpmi.org/index.esp.

[Arsanjani 2004] A. Arsanjani, "Service-oriented Modeling and Architecture", IBM developerWorks, Novemeber 2004, available at:
http://www-106.ibm.com/developerworks/library/ws-soa-design1/.

[Atkinson 2002] C. Atkinson *et al.*, *Component-based Product Line Engineering with UML*, Addison-Wesley, 2002.

[Austin 2004] D. Austin *et al.* (eds.), "Web Services Choreography Requirements", W3C Working Draft, March 2004, available at:
http://www.w3.org/TR/ws-chor-reqs/.

[Bachmann 2000] F. Bachmann *et al.*, "Technical Concepts of Component-Based Software Engineering", Technical Report, Carnegie-Mellon University, CMU/SEI-2000-TR-008 ESC-TR-2000-007, 2nd edition, May 2000.

[Bajaj 2003] S. Bajaj *et al.* (eds.), "Web Services Federation Language (WS-Federation) Version 1.0", July 2003, available at:
http://www-128.ibm.com/developerworks/library/specification/ws-fed/.

[Bajaj 2006a] S. Bajaj *et al.*, "Web Services Policy Framework (WS-Policy) Version 1.2", March 2006, available at:
http://xml.coverpages.org/ws-policy200603.pdf.

[Bajaj 2006b] S. Bajaj *et al.*, "Web Services Policy Attachment (WS-PolicyAttachment)", March 2006, available at:
http://specs.xmlsoap.org/ws/2004/09/policy/ws-policyattachment.pdf.

[Ballinger 2006] K. Ballinger *et al.*, "Web Services Metadata Exchange (WS-MetadataExchange), Version 1.1", August 2006, available at:
http://msdn.microsoft.com/library/en-us/dnglobspec/html/ws-metadataexchange.pdf.

[Balzer 2004] Y. Balzer, "Improve your SOA project plans", IBM developerWorks, July 2004, available at:
http://www-106.ibm.com/developerworks/library/ws-improvesoa/.

[Banks 2003] T. Banks (ed.), "Open Grid Service Infrastructure Primer", GWD-I (draft-ggf-ogsi-gridserviceprimer-1), Open Grid Services Infrastructure (OGSI), June 2003, available at:
https://forge.gridforum.org/projects/ogsi-wg.

[Bass 2001] L. Bass, M. Klein, G. Moreno, "Applicability of General Scenarios to the Architecture Tradeoff Analysis Method", Technical Report CMU/SEI-2001-TR-014, Software Engineering Institute, Carnegie-Mellon University, 2001.

[Bass 2003] L. Bass, P. Clements, R. Kazman, *Software Architecture in Practice*, 2nd edition, Addison-Wesley, 2003.

[Batres 2005] S. Batres *et al.*, "Web Services Reliable Messaging Policy Assertion (WS-RM Policy) Version 1.0", February 2005, available at:
http://www.oasis-open.org/committees/download.php/16889/.

[Bean 2003] J. Bean, *XML for Data Architects: Designing for Re-use and Integration*, Morgan Kaufmann, 2003.

[Beckett 2004] D. Beckett (ed.), "RDF/XML Syntax Specification (Revised)", W3C Recommendation, February 2004, available at:
http://www.w3.org/TR/rdf-syntax-grammar/.

[Bellwood 2003] T. Bellwood *et al.*, "Universal Description, Discovery and Integration specification (UDDI) 3.0", December 2003, available at:
http://uddi.org/pubs/uddi-v3.00.

[Bennett 2002] V. Bennett, A. Capella, "Location-based Services", IBM developerWorks, March 2002, available at:
http://www-106.ibm.com/developerworks/library/i-lbs/.

[Berners-Lee 1998] T. Berners-Lee, R. Fielding, L. Masinter, "RFC 2396: Uniform Resource Identifiers (URI): Generic Syntax", August 1998, available at:
http://www.ietf.org/rfc/rfc2396.txt.

[Bieberstein 2005] N. Bieberstein *et al.*, "Impact of Service-Oriented Architecture on Enterprise Systems, Organizational Structures, and Individuals", IBM Systems Journal, vol. 44, no. 4, pp. 691–708, 2005.

[Bieberstein 2006] N. Bieberstein *et al.*, *Service-Oriented Architecture (SOA) Compass*, IBM Press, 2006.

[Bilorusets 2005] R. Bilorusets *et al.*, "Web Services Reliable Messaging Protocol (WS-ReliableMessaging)", February 2005, available at:
http://msdn.microsoft.com/library/default.asp?url=/library/en-us/dnglobspec/html/wsrmspecindex.asp.

[Bloch 2003] B. Bloch *et al.* (eds.), "Web Services Business Process Execution Language", OASIS Open Inc. Working Draft 01, October 2003, available at:
http://www.oasis-open.org/apps/org/workgroup/wsbpel/.

[Bloomberg 2004] J. Bloomberg, "Events vs. Services", ZapThink White Paper, October 2004, available at:
www.zapthink.com.

[Bosworth 2004] A. Bosworth *et al.*, "Web Services Addressing (WS-Addressing)", August 2004, available at:
http://msdn.microsoft.com/ws/2004/08/ws-addressing/.

[Box 2003] D. Box *et al.*, "Reliable Message Delivery in a Web Services World: A Proposed Architecture and Roadmap", Joint IBM Corporation and Microsoft Corporation White Paper, March 2003, available at:
http://msdn.microsoft.com/library/default.asp?url=/library/en-us/dnglobspec/html/ws-rm-exec-summary.asp.

[BRCommunity 2005] "A Brief History of the Business Rule Approach", Business Rule Community 2005, available at:
http://www.BRCommunity.com.

[Brickley 2004] D. Brickley, R. V. Guha (eds.), "RDF Vocabulary Description Language 1.0: RDF Schema", W3C Recommendation, February 2004, available at:
http://www.w3.org/TR/rdf-schema/.

[Brittenham 2001] P. Brittenham, F. Curbera, D. Ehnebuske, and S. Graham, "Understanding WSDL in a UDDI Registry", IBM developerWorks, September 2001, available at:
http://www-106.ibm.com/developersworks/library/.

[Brown 2005] A. Brown *et al.*, "SOA Development Using the IBM Rational Software Development Platform: A Practical Guide", Rational Software, September 2005.

[Bunting 2003a] D. Bunting *et al.*, "Web Services Composite Application Framework (WS-CAF)", July 2003, available at:
http://developers.sun.com/techtopics/webservices/wscaf/index.html.

[Bunting 2003b] D. Bunting *et al.*, "Web Service Context (WS-CTX)", July 2003, available at:
http://developers.sun.com/techtopics/webservices/wscaf/wsctx.pdf.

[Bunting 2003c] D. Bunting *et al.*, "Web Service Coordination Framework (WS-CF)", July 2003, available at:
http://developers.sun.com/techtopics/webservices/wscaf/wscf.pdf.

[Bunting 2003d] D. Bunting *et al.*, "Web Services Transaction Management (WS-TXM)", July 2003, available at:
http://developers.sun.com/techtopics/webservices/wscaf/wstmx.pdf.

[Cabrera 2005a] L. F. Cabrera *et al.*, "Web Service Coordination: (WS-Coordination)", August 2005, available at:
http://schemas.xmlsoap.org/ws/2004/10/coord.

[Cabrera 2005b] L. F. Cabrera *et al.*, "Web Services Atomic Transaction: (WS-AtomicTransaction)", August 2005, available at:
http://schemas.xmlsoap.org/ws/2004/10/at.

[Cabrera 2005c] L. F. Cabrera *et al.*, "Web Services Business Activity Framework (WS-BusinessActivity)", August 2005, available at:
http://schemas.xmlsoap.org/ws/2004/10/ba.

[Cabrera 2005d] F. Cabrera, C. Kurt, *Web Services Architecture and its Specifications*, Microsoft Press, 2005.

[Candadai 2004] A. Candadai, "A Dynamic Implementation Framework for SOA-based Applications", *Web Logic Developers Journal: WLDJ*, September/October 2004.

[Cantor 2004] S. Cantor *et al.* (eds.), "Assertions and Protocols for the OASIS Security Assertion Markup Language (SAML) V2.0", OASIS, Committee Draft 03, December 2004, available at: **http://www.oasis-open.org/committees/documents.php?wg_abbrev=security**.

[Carzaniga 2000] A. Carzaniga, D. S. Rosenblum, A. L. Wolf, "Content-based Addressing and Routing: A General Model and its Application", Technical Report CU-CS-902-00, Department of Computer Science, University of Colorado, January 2000.

[Carzaniga 2001] A. Carzaniga, D. S. Rosenblum, A. L. Wolf, "Design and Evaluation of a Wide-Area Event Notification Service", ACM Transactions on Computer Systems, vol. 19, no. 3, pp. 332–83, August 2001.

[Case 1999] J. D. Case *et al.*, "Introduction to Version 3 of the Internet-standard Network Management Framework", Internet Engineering Task Force (IETF), RFC 2570, April 1999, available at:
www.rfc-editor.org/rfc/rfc2570.txt.

[Cauldwell 2001] P. Cauldwell *et al.*, *XML Web Services*, Wrox Press, 2001.

[Channabasavaiah 2003] K. Channabasavaiah, K. Holley, E. M. Tuggle, Jr., "Migrating to a Service-Oriented Architecture", IBM developerWorks, December 2003, available at: **http://www-106.ibm.com/developerworks/library/ws-migratesoa/**.

[Chappell 2004] D. A. Chappell, *Enterprise Service Bus*, O'Reilley, 2004.

[Chappell 2005a] D. Chappell, "ESB Myth Busters: Clarity of definition for a growing phenomenon", *Web Services Journal*, pp. 22–6, February 2005.

[Chappell 2005b] D. Chappell, Private communication, April 2005.

[Chatterjee 2004] S. Chatterjee, J. Webber, *Developing Enterprise Web Services*, Prentice Hall, 2004.

[Cheesman 2001] J. Cheesman, J. Daniels, *UML Components: A Simple Process for Specifying Component-based Software*, Addison-Wesley, 2001.

[Clark 2001] J. Clark *et al.* (eds.), "ebXML Business Process Specification Schema: Version 1.01", OASIS, May 2001, available at:
www.ebxml.org/specs/ebBPSS.pdf.

[Colan 2004] M. Colan, "Service-Oriented Architecture expands the vision of Web services, Part 2", IBM developerWorks, April 2004, available at:
http://www-106.ibm.com/developerworks/library/ws-soaintro2/.

[Cole 2002] G. Cole, "SNMP vs. WBEM – The Future of Systems Management", available at: **http://www.wbem.co.uk**.

[Colgrave 2003a] J. Colgrave, "A new approach to UDDI and WSDL: Introduction to the new OASIS UDDI WSDL", IBM developerWorks, August 2003, available at: **http://www-106.ibm.com/developersworks/library/**.

[Colgrave 2003b] J. Colgrave, "A new approach to UDDI and WSDL, Part 2: Queries supported by the new OASIS UDDI WSDL Technical Note", IBM developerWorks, September 2003, available at: **http://www-106.ibm.com/developersworks/library/**.

[Colgrave 2004] J. Colgrave, K. Januszewski, "Using WSDL in a UDDI Registry, Version 2.0.2 – Technical Note Using WSDL in a UDDI Registry, Version 2.0.2", OASIS, June 2004, avaialble at: **http://www.oasis-open.org/committees/uddi-spec/doc/tn/uddi-spec-tc-tn-wsdl-v202-20040631.htm**.

[Comella-Dorda 2000] S. Comella-Dorda *et al.*, "A Survey of Legacy System Modernization Approaches", Technical Note CMU/SEI-2000-TN-003, Software Engineering Institute, Carnegie-Mellon University, April 2000, available at:
http://www.sei.cmu.edu/publications/pubWeb.html.

[Coulouris 2001] G. Coulouris, J. Dollimore, T. Kindberg, *Distributed Systems: Concepts and Design*, 3rd edition, Addison-Wesley, 2001.

[Culbertson 2001] R. Culbertson, C. Brown, G. Cobb, *Rapid Testing*, Prentice Hall, 2001.

[Curbera 2003] P. Curbera *et al.*, "Web services, the next step: A framework for robust service composition", Communications of the ACM, Special Section on Service-Oriented Computing, M. P. Papazoglou and D. Georgakopoulos (eds.), October 2003.

[Czajkowski 2004] K. Czajkowski *et al.*, "The WS-Resource Framework, Version 1.0", March 2004, available at:
www-106.ibm.com/developerworks/library/ws-resource/ws-wsrf.pdf.

[Czajkowski 2005] K. Czajkowski, I. Foster, C. Kesselman, "Agreement-Based Resource Management", *Proceedings of the IEEE*, vol. 93, no. 3, March 2005.

[DAML] Darpa Agent Markup Language, available at:
http://www.daml.org.

[Davis 2004] M. Davis *et al.*, "WS-I Security Scenarios Document Status", Web Services Interoperability Organisation Working Group Draft Version 0.15, February 2004, available at:
http://www.ws-i.org.

[Della-Libera 2002] G. Della-Libera *et al.*, "Web Services Security Policy (WS-SecurityPolicy)", IBM, Microsoft, RSA Security, VeriSign, Draft, December 2002, available at:
http://www.ibm.com/developerworks/library/ws-secpol/.

[Dertouzos 1999] M. L. Dertouzos, "The future of computing", Scientific American, August 1999.

[Duftler 2002] M. Duftler, R. Khalaf, "Business Process with BPEL4WS: Learning BPEL4WS, Part 3", IBM developmentworks, October 2002, available at:
http://www-106.ibm.com/developerworks/Webservices/library/.

[Eastlake 2002a] D. Eastlake, J. Reagle, D. Solo (eds.), "XML-Signature Syntax and Processing", W3C Recommendation, February 2002, available at:
http://www.w3.org/TR/2002/REC-xmldsig-core-20020212/.

[Eastlake 2002b] D. Eastlake, J. Reagle (eds.), "XML Encryption Syntax and Processing", W3C Recommendation, December 2002, available at:
http://www.w3.org/TR/2002/REC-xmlenc-core-20021210/.

[Elmagarmid 1992] A. Elmagarmid (ed.), *Database Transaction Models for Advanced Applications*, Morgan Kaufmann, 1992.

[Endrei 2004] M. Endrei *et al.*, "Patterns: Service-Oriented Architecture and Web Services", IBM Redbooks SG24-6303-00, April 2004, available at:
http://publib-b.boulder.ibm.com/Redbooks.nsf/redbooks/.

[Eswaran 1976] K. Eswaran *et al.*, "The Notion of Consistency and Predicate Locks in Database Systems", *Communications of the ACM*, vol. 19, no. 11, pp. 624–33, November 1976.

[Ferreira 2002] L. Ferreira, V. Berestis, "Fundamentals of Grid Computing", IBM Redbooks paper REDP-3613-00, November 2002, available at:
http://www.redbooks.ibm.com/redpapers/pdf/redp3613.pdf.

[Ferreira 2004] L. Ferreira *et al.*, "Grid Services Programming and Application Enablement", IBM Redbooks, May 2004, available at:
ibm.com/redbooks.

[Ford 1997] W. Ford, M. S. Baum, *Secure Electronic Commerce: Building the infrastructure for digital signatures and encryption*, Prentice Hall, 1997.

[Foster 2002a] I. Foster, "What is the Grid? A Three Point Checklist", *GRIDToday*, July 2002, available at:
http://www.globus.org/alliance/publications/papers.php#Overview%20Papers.

[Foster 2002b] I. Foster *et al.*, "The Physiology of the Grid: An Open Grid Services Architecture for Distributed Systems Integration", Globus Project, 2002, available at:
www.globus.org/research/papers/ogsa.pdf.

[Foster 2004] I. Foster *et al.* (eds.), "Modeling Stateful Resources with Web Services Version 1.1", March 2004, available at:
http://www.ibm.com/developerworks/library/ws-resource/ws-modelingresources.pdf.

[Foster 2005] I. Foster, H. Kishimoto, A. Savva (eds.), "The Open Grid Services Architecture, Version 1.0", GFD-I.030, available at:
http://forge.gridforum.org/projects/ogsa-wg, January 2005.

[Galbraith 2002] B. Galbraith *et al.*, *Professional Web Services Security*, Wrox Press, 2002.

[Ganci 2006] J. Ganci *et al.*, *Patterns: SOA Foundation Service Creation Scenario*, IBM Redbooks, September 2006.

[Garcia-Molina 2002] H. Garcia-Molina, J. D. Ullman, J. Widom, *Database Systems*, Prentice Hall, 2002.

[Garcia-Molina 1987] H. Garcia-Molina, K. Salem, Proceedings of the ACM SIG on Management of Data, 1987 Annual Conference, San Francisco, May 1987, ACM Press, pp. 249–59.

[Gardner 2002] J. Gardner, Z. Rendon, *XSLT and XPath*, Prentice Hall, 2002.

[Goldfarb 2001] C. Goldfarb, P. Prescod, *The XML Handbook*, 3rd edition, Prentice Hall 2001.

[Graham 2004a] S. Graham *et al.*, *Building Web Services with Java*, SAMS Publishing, 2004.

[Graham 2004b] S. Graham, P. Niblett (eds.), "Publish-Subscribe Notification for Web Services", March 2004, available at:
http://docs.oasis-open.org/committees/dowload.php/6661/WSNpubsub-1-0.pdf.

[Graham 2004c] S. Graham, J. Treadwell (eds.), "Web Services Resource Properties 1.2 (WS-ResourceProperties)", OASIS Working Draft 04, June 2004, available at:
http://docs.oasis-open.org/wsrf/2004/11/wsrf-WS-ResourceProperties-1.2-draft-05.pdf.

[Graham 2004d] S. Graham, P. Murray (eds.), "Web Services Base Notification (WS-BaseNotification 1.2)", OASIS Working Draft 03, June 2004, available at:
http://docs.oasis-open.org/wsn/2004/06/wsn-WS-BaseNotification-1.2-draft-03.pdf.

[Graham 2005] S. Graham *et al.*, *Building Web Services with Java*, 2nd edition, SAMS Publishing, 2005.

[Gray 1993] J. Gray, A. Reuter, *Transaction Processing: Concepts and Techniques*, Morgan Kaufmann, 1993.

[Gruber 1993] T. R.Gruber, "Toward Principles for the Design of Ontologies used for Knowledge Sharing", KSL-93-04. Knowledge Systems Laboratory, Stanford University, 1993.

[Gudgin 2003] M. Gudgin *et al.* (eds.), "SOAP 1.2 Part 1: Messaging Framework", Martin Gudgin, W3C Recommendation, June 2003, available at:
http://www.w3.org/TR/2003/REC-soap12-part1-20030624/.

[Hall-Gailey 2004] J. Hall-Gailey, *Understanding Web Services Specifications and the WSE*, Microsoft Press, 2004.

[Hallam-Baker 2004] P. Hallam-Baker *et al.* (eds.), "Web Services Security X.509 Certificate Token Profile", OASIS Standard 200401, March 2004, available at:
http://docs.oasis-open.org/wss/2004/01/oasis-200401-wss-x509-token-profile-1.0.

[Handfield 2002] R. B. Handfield, E. L. Nichols, *Supply Chain Redesign*, Prentice Hall, 2002.

[Harmon 2003a] P. Harmon, "Analyzing Activities", *Business Process Trends*, vol. 1, no. 4, pp. 1–12, April 2003.

[Harmon 2003b] P. Harmon, "Second Generation Business Process Methodologies", *Business Process Trends*, vol. 1, no. 5, pp. 1–13, May 2003.

[Herzum 2000] P. Herzum, O. Sims, *Business Component Factory*, John Wiley & Sons, 2000.

[Holley 2006] K. Holley, J. Palistrant, S. Graham, "Effective SOA Governance", IBM OnDemand Business, March 2006, available at:
http://www-306.ibm.com/software/solutions/soa/gov/lifecycle/.

[Hughes 2004] J. Hughes *et al.*, "SAML Technical Overview", OASIS-SSTC, July 2004, available at:
http://www.oasis-open.org/committees/security/.

[IBM 2004] IBM Corporation, "An architectural blueprint for autonomic computing", IBM Autonomic Computing White Paper, October 2004, available at:
http://www-03.ibm.com/autonomic/pdfs/ACBP2_2004-10-04.pdf.

[Irani 2002] R. Irani, "An Introduction to ebxml", in *Web Services Business Strategies and Architectures*, P. Fletcher, M. Waterhouse (eds.), ExpertPress, 2002.

[Iwasa 2004] K. Iwasa *et al.* (eds.), "Web Services Reliable Messaging TC WS-Reliability 1.1", OASIS Standard, OASIS, November 2004, available at: **http://docs.oasis-open.org/wsrm/ws-reliability/v1.1/wsrm-ws_reliability-1.1-spec-os.pdf**.

[Jaenicke 2004] C. Jaenicke, "Canonical Message Formats: Avoiding the Pitfalls", WebLogic Journal, September/October 2004.

[Jeal 2003] D. Jeal *et al.*, "Mobile Web Services Roadmap", Microsoft Corporation and Vodafone Group Services, 2003.

[Jeston 2006] J. Jeston, J. Nelis, "Business Process Management: Practical Guidelines to Successful Implementations", Butterworth–Heinemann, 2006.

[Jin 2002] L. J. Jin, V. Machiraju, A. Sahai, "Analysis on Service Level Agreement of Web Services", Technical Report HPL-2002-180, Software Technology Laboratory, HP Laboratories Palo Alto, June 2002, available at: **www.hpl.hp.com/techreports/2002/HPL-2002-180.pdf**.

[Johnston 2005] S. Johnston, "Modelling Service-oriented Solutions", IBM developerWorks, July 2005, available at: **http://www-128.ibm.com/developerworks/rational/library/johnston/**.

[Joseph 2004] J. Joseph, M. Ernset, C. Fellenstein, "Evolution of grid computing architecture and grid adoption models", *IBM Systems Journal*, vol. 43, no. 4, pp. 624–45, 2004.

[Juric 2006] M. Juric, B. Matthew, P. Sarang, *Business Process Execution Language for Web Services*, 2nd edition, PACKT Publishing, 2006.

[Kakadia 2002] D. Kakadia *et al.*, "Enterprise Management Systems: Architectures and Standards", Sun Microsystems, April 2002, available at: **http://www.sun.com/blueprints/0402/ems1.pdf**.

[Kaler 2003] C. Kaler, A. Nadalin (eds.), "Web Services Federation Language (WS-Federation) Version 1.0", July 2003, available at: **http://www-106.ibm.com/developerworks/Webservices/library/ws-fed/**.

[Kaufman 1995] C. Kaufman, R. Perlman, M. Speciner, "Network Security, Private Communication in a Public World", Prentice Hall, 1995.

[Kavantzas 2004] N. Kavantzas *et al.*, "Web Services Choreography Description Language 1.0", Editor's Draft, April 2004, available at: **http://lists.w3.org/Archives/Public/www-archive/2004Apr/att-0004/cdl_v1-editors-apr03-2004-pdf.pdf**.

[Keen 2004] M. Keen *et al.*, "Patterns: Implementing an SOA Using an Enterprise Service Bus", IBM Redbooks SG24-6346-00, July 2004, available at: **http://publib-b.boulder.ibm.com/Redbooks.nsf/redbooks/**.

[Kifer 2005] M. Kifer, A. Bernstein, P. M. Lewis, *Database Systems: An Application-Oriented Approach*, 2nd edition, Addison-Wesley, 2005.

[Klyne 2004] F. Klyne, J. J. Carroll, "Resource Description Framework (RDF): Concepts and Abstract Syntax", W3C Recommendation, February 2004, available at: **http://www.w3.org/TR/rdf-concepts/**.

[Kreger 2005a] H. Kreger, "A Little Wisdom about WSDM", IBM developerWorks, available at: **http://www-128.ibm.com/developerworks/library/ws-wisdom**.

[Kreger 2005b] H. Kreger *et al.*, "Management Using Web Services: A Proposed Architecture and Roadmap", IBM, HP, and Computer Associates, June 2005, available at: **www-128.ibm.com/developerworks/library/specification/ws-mroadmap**.

[Kruchten 2004] P. Kruchten, *Rational Unified Process – An Introduction*, 3rd edition, Addison-Wesley, 2004.

[Kurose 2003] J. F. Kurose, K. W. Ross, *Computer Networking: A Top-Down Approach Featuring the Internet*, 2nd edition, Addison-Wesley, 2003.

[Lai 2004] R. Lai, *J2EE Platform Web Services*, Prentice Hall, 2004.

[Leymann 2000] F. Leymann, D. Roller, *Production Workflow*, Prentice Hall, 2000.

[Leymann 2001] F. Leymann, "Web Services Flow Language", May 25, 2001, available at: **http://xml.coverpages.org/wsft.html**.

[Leymann 2002] F. Leymann, D. Roller, "A Quick Overview of BPEL4WS", IBM developerWorks, August 2002, available at: **http://www-106.ibm.com/developerworks/**.

[Linthicum 2003] D. Linthicum, *Next Generation Application Integration: From Simple Information to Web Services*, Addison-Wesley, 2003.

[Little 2003a] M. Little, J. Webber, "Introducing WS-CAF – More than just transactions", *Web Services Journal*, vol. 3, no. 12, December 2003.

[Little 2003b] M. Little, J. Webber, "Introducing WS-Transaction", *Web Services Journal*, vol. 3, no. 6, pp. 28–33, June 2003.

[Little 2004] M. Little, J. Maron, G. Pavlik, *Java Transaction Processing*, Prentice Hall, 2004.

[Lubinsky 2001] B. Lubinsky, M. Farrel, "Enterprise Architecture and J2EE", *eAI Journal*, November 2001.

[Ludwig 2007] H. Ludwig, "WS-Agreement Concepts and Use-Agreement-Based Service-Oriented Architectures", in *Readings in Service Oriented Computing*, D. Georgakopoulos, M.P. Papazoglou (eds.), MIT Press, 2007.

[Maguire 2005] T. Maguire, D. Snelling (eds.), "Web Services Service Group 1.2 (WS-ServiceGroup)", OASIS Working Draft 04, February 2005, available at: **http://docs.oasis-open.org/wsrf/2005/03/wsrf-WS-ServiceGroup-1.2-draft-04.pdf**.

[Malan 2002] R. Malan, D. Bredemeyer, "Software Architecture: Central Concerns, Key Decisions", 2002, available at: **http://www.ruthmalan.com/**.

[Manes 2004] A. T. Manes, *The Role of Web Services Registries in Service Oriented Architectures*, Burton Group, November 2004.

[Mani 2002] A. Mani, A. Nagarajan, "Understanding quality of service for Web services", IBM developerWorks, January 2002, available at: **http://www-106.ibm.com/developerworks/library/ws-quality.html**.

[Manola 2004] F. Manola, E. Miller (eds.), "RDF Primer", W3C Recommendation, February 2004, available at: **http://www.w3.org/TR/rdf-primer/**.

[Marks 2006] E. A. Marks, M. Bell, *Service-oriented Architecture: A Planning and Implementation Guide for Business and Technology*, John Wiley & Sons, 2006.

[Masud 2003] S. Masud, "RosettaNet Based Web Services", IBM developerWorks, July 2003, available at: **http://www-128.ibm.com/developerworks/webservices/library/ws-rose1/**.

[McGoveran 2004] D. McGoveran, "An Introduction to BPM and BPMS", *Business Integration Journal*, April 2004.

[McGuiness 2004] D. McGuiness, F. van Harmelen, "OWL Web Ontology Language Overview", W3C Recommendation, February 2004, available at: **http://www.w3.org/TR/owl-features**.

[McKee 2001] B. McKee, D. Ehnebuske, "Providing a Taxonomy for Use in UDDI Version 2.0", UDDI.org, June 2001.

[Mehta 2003] T. Mehta, "Adaptive Web Services Management Solutions", *Enterprise Networks and Servers*, vol. 17, no. 5, May 2003, available at: **http://www.enterprisenetworksandservers.com/monthly/toc.php?4**.

[Mitra 2003] N. Mitra (ed.), "SOAP Version 1.2 Part 0: Primer 1.1", W3C Recommendation, June 2003 available at: **http://www.w3.org/TR/soap12-part0/**.

[Mitra 2005] T. Mitra, "A Case for SOA Governance", IBM developerWorks, August 2005, available at:
http://www-106.ibm.com/developerworks/webservices/library/ws-soa-govern/index.html.

[Monson-Haefel 2001] R. Monson-Haefel, D. A. Chappell, *Java Message Service*, O'Reilley, 2001.

[Monson-Haefel 2004] R. Monson-Haefel, *J2EE Web Services*, Addison-Wesley, 2004.

[Monzillo 2002] R. Monzillo, "Security", in *Designing Enterprise Applications with the J2EE Platform*, 2nd edition, I. Singh, B. Stearns, M. Johnson (eds.), Addison-Wesley 2002.

[Moss 1985] E. Moss, *Nested Transactions: An Approach to Reliable Distributed Computing*, MIT Press, 1985.

[Moss 1997] J. Moss, "Understanding TCP/IP", PC Network Advisor, no. 87, September 1997.

[Murray 2002] J. Murray, "Designing Manageable Applications", Web Developer's Journal, October 2002, available at:
http://www.webdevelopersjournal.com/articles/design_man_app/.

[Mysore 2003] S. Mysore, "Securing Web Services – Concepts, Standards, and Requirements", Sun Microsystems, October 2003, available at:
sun.com/software.

[Nadalin 2004] A. Nadalin *et al.* (eds.), "Web Services Security: SOAP Message Security 1.0 (WS-Security)", OASIS Standard 200401, OASIS Open, March 2004, available at:
http://docs.oasis-open.org/wss/2004/01/oasis-200401-wss-soap-message-security-1.0.

[Newcomer 2005] E. Newcomer, G. Lomow, *Understanding SOA with Web Services*, Addison-Wesley, 2005.

[Niblett 2005] P. Niblett, S. Graham, "Events and Service-Oriented Architecture: The OASIS Web Services Notification Specifications", *IBM Systems Journal*, vol. 44, no. 4, pp. 869–86, 2005.

[Nokia 2004] Nokia Corporation and Sun Microsystems, "Identity Federation and Web Services – technical use cases for mobile operators", Nokia and Sun Microsystems White Paper, 2004, available at:
www.nokia.com.

[Nolan 2004] P. Nolan, "Understand WS-Policy Processing: Explore Intersection, Merge, and Normalization in WSPolicy", IBM developerWorks, December 2004, available at:
http://www-106.ibm.com/developerworks/library/ws-policy.html.

[OASIS 2004] OASIS: Organization for the Advancement of Structured Integration Standards, "Introduction to UDDI: Important Features and Functional Concepts", October 2004, available at:
http://xml.coverpages.org/UDDI-TechnicalWhitePaperOct28.pdf.

[Ogbuji 2000] S. Ogbuji, "Supercharging WSDL with RDF: Managing structured Web service metadata", IBM developerWorks, November 2000, available at:
http://www-4.ibm.com/software/developer/library/ws-rdf/index.html.

[OMA 2004] Open Mobile Alliance, "OMA Web Services Enabler (OWSER): Core Specifications Version 1.0", OMA-OWSER-Core-Specification-V1_0-20040715-A, July 2004.

[O'Neill 2003] M. O'Neill *et al.*, *Web Services Security*, McGraw-Hill Osborne, 2003.

[Open Group 2004] "SLA Management Handbook: Enterprise Perspective", version 2, volume 4, issue 0.8, November 2004, available at:
www.opengroup.org/pubs/catalog/go45.htm.

[Owen 2004] M. Owen, J. Raj, "BPMN and Business Process Management: An Introduction to the New Business Process Modelling Standard", Business Process Trends, March 2004, available at:
www.bptrends.com.

[Pallickara 2004] S. Pallickara, G. Fox, "An Analysis of Notification Related Specifications for Web/Grid applications", Community Grids Laboratory, Indiana University, 2004, available at:
http://grids.ucs.indiana.edu/ptliupages/publications/WSNotifyEventComparison.pdf.

[Papazoglou 2003] M. P. Papazoglou, G. Georgakapoulos, "Introduction to the Special Issue about Service-Oriented Computing", *Communications of the ACM*, vol. 46, no. 10, pp. 24–8, October 2003.

[Papazoglou 2005a] M. P. Papazoglou, "Extending the Service Oriented Architecture", *Business Integration Journal*, February 2005.

[Papazoglou 2005b] M. P. Papazoglou, W. J. van den Heuvel, "Web Services Management: A Survey", *IEEE Internet Computing*, November/December 2005.

[Papazoglou 2006] M. P. Papazoglou, P. M. A. Ribbers, *e-Business: Organizational and Technical Foundations*, John Wiley & Sons, 2006.

[Pashtan 2005] A. Pashtan, *Mobile Web Services*, Cambridge University Press, 2005.

[Patil 2003] S. Patil, E. Newcomer, "ebXML and Web Services", *IEEE Internet Computing*, May 2003.

[Paulk 1993] M. Paulk *et al.*, "Capability Maturity Model for Software", version 1.1, Software Engineering Institute, Pittsburgh, Technical Report SE-93 TR-024, 1993.

[Pelz 2003] C. Pelz, "Web Services Orchestration and Choreography", *Web Services Journal*, July 2003.

[Pilz 2003] G. Pilz, "A New World of Web Services Security", *Web Services Journal*, March 2003.

[Potts 2003] M. Potts, I. Sedukhin, H. Kreger, "Web Services Manageability – Concepts (WS-Manageability)", IBM, Computer Associates International, Inc., Talking Blocks, Inc, September 2003, available at:
www3.ca.com/Files/SupportingPieces/web_service_manageability_concepts.pdf.

[Proctor 2003] S. Proctor, "A Brief Introduction to XACML", March 2003, available at:
http://www.oasis-open.org/committees/download.php/2713/Brief_Introduction_to_XACML.html.

[Rana 2004] R. Rana, S. Kumar, "Service on Demand Portals: A Primer on Federated Portals", *Web Logic Developers Journal: WLDJ*, September/October 2004.

[Robinson 2004] R. Robinson, "Understand Enterprise Service Bus Scenarios and Solutions in Service-Oriented Architecture", IBM developerWorks, June 2004, available at:
http://www-106.ibm.com/developerworks/library/ws-esbscen/.

[Roch 2002] E. Roch, "Application Integration: Business and Technology Trends", *eAI Journal*, August 2002.

[Rodriguez 2001] A. Rodriguez, "TCP/IP Tutorial and Technical Overview", IBM Redbooks, August 2001, available at:
ibm.com/redbooks/.

[Rosenberg 2004] J. Rosenberg, D. Remy, "Securing Web Services with WS-Security", SAMS Publishing, 2004.

[Rosenblum 1997] D. S. Rosenblum, A. L. Wolf, "A design framework for Internet-scale event observation and notification", Proceedings of the Sixth European Software Engineering Conference, Lecture Notes in Computer Science 1301, Springer, 1997.

[RosettaNet 2003] "RosettaNet and Web Services", 2003, available at:
http://www.rosettanet.org/RosettaNet/Doc/0/IP0QL046K55KFBSJ60M9TQCPB3/RosettaNet+Web+ServicesFINAL+.pdf.

[RosettaNet 2004] RosettaNet Implementation Guide, "Cluster 3: Order Management Segment A: Quote and Order Entry PIPs 3A4, 3A7, 3A8, 3A9", April 2004, available at:
www.rosettanet.org/usersguides/.

[Royce 1998] W. Royce, "Software Project Management: A Unified Framework", Addison-Wesley, 1998.

[Shapiro 2002] R. Sahapiro, "A Comparison of XPDL, BPML and BPEL4WS", March 2002, available at:
xml.coverpages.org/Shapiro-XPDL.pdf.

[Satyanarayanan 2001] M. Satyanarayanan, "Pervasive Computing: Vision and Challenges", *IEEE Personal Communications*, August 2001.

[Schlosser 1999] M. Schlosser, "IBM Application Framework for e-Business: Security", November 1999, available at:
http://www-4.ibm.com/software/developer/library/security/index.html.

[Schmelzer 2002] R. Schmelzer *et al.*, *XML and Web Services*, SAMS Publishing, 2002.

[Scribner 2000] K. Scribner, M. C. Stiver, *Understanding SOAP*, SAMS Publishing, 2000.

[Scribner 2002] K. Scribner, M. C. Stiver, *Applied SOAP*, SAMS Publishing, 2002.

[Seacord 2001] R. C. Seacord *et al.*, "Legacy System Modernization Strategies", Technical Report, CMU/SEI-2001-TR-025, ESC-TR-2001-025, Software Engineering Institute, Carnegie-Mellon University, July 2001, available at:
http://www.sei.cmu.edu/publications/pubWeb.html.

[Sedukhin 2005] I. Sedukhin, "Web Services Distributed Management: Management of Web Services (WSDM-MOWS) 1.0", OASIS-Standard, March 2005, available at:
http://docs.oasis-open.org/wsdm/2004/12/wsdm-mows-1.0.pdf.

[Seely 2002] S. Seely, "Understanding WS-Security", Microsoft Corporation, October 2002, available at:
http://msdn.microsoft.com/library/default.asp?url=/library/en-us/dnwssecur/html/understw.asp.

[SHA-1] "FIPS PUB 180-1 Secure Hash Standard", US Department of Commerce National Institute of Standards and Technology, available at:
http://csrc.nist.gov/publications/fips/fips180-1/fip180-1.txt.

[Shaikh 2004] H. Saikh, "Managing the Life Cycle of WS-Resources", IBM developerWorks, May 2004, available at:
http://www-106.ibm.com/developerworks/library/ws-statefulws2/.

[Sharma 2001] P. Sharma, B. Stearns, T. Ng, *J2EE Connector Architecture and Enterprise Application Integration*, Addison-Wesley, 2001.

[Shaw 1996] M. Shaw, D. Garlan, *Software Architecture: Perspectives on an Emerging Discipline*, Prentice Hall, 1996.

[Siddiqui 2001] B. Siddiqui, "Deploying Web services with WSDL", available at:
http://www-106.ibm.com/developerworks/library/ws-intwsdl/.

[Siddiqui 2003a] B. Siddiqui, "Web Services Security, Part 2", O'Reilly XML.com, April 2003, available at:
http://Webservices.xml.com/lpt/a/ws/2003/04/01/security.html.

[Siddiqui 2003b] B. Siddiqui, "Web Services Security, Part 3", O'Reilly XML.com, May 2003, available at:
http://Webservices.xml.com/lpt/a/ws/2003/05/13/security.html.

[Siddiqui 2003c] B. Siddiqui, "Web Services Security, Part 4", O'Reilly XML.com, July 2003, available at:
http://Webservices.xml.com/lpt/a/ws/2003/07/22/security.html.

[Silver 2003] B. Silver, "BPM 2.0: Process Without Programming", Bruce Silver Associates, September 2003, available at:
www.brsilver.com.

[Simon 2001] E. Simon, P. Madsen, C. Adams, "An Introduction to XML Digital Signatures", XML.com August 2001, available at:
http://www.xml.com/pub/a/2001/08/08/xmldsig.html.

[Singh 2004] J. Singh *et al.*, *Designing Web Services with the J2EE 1.4 Platform*, Addison-Wesley, 2004.

[Skonnard 2002] A. Skonnard, M. Gudgin, *Essential XML Quick Reference*, Addison-Wesley, 2002.

[Skonnard 2003] A. Skonnard, "Understanding WS-Policy", Web Services Policy Framework (WS-Policy), Version 1.01, June 2003, available at:
http://www.ibm.com/developerworks/library/ws-polfram/.

[Slee 1997] C. Slee, M. Slovin, "Legacy Asset Management", Information Systems Management. Winter 1997.

[Soh 1995] C. Soh, M. L. Markus, "How IT Creates Business Value: A Theory Synthesis", Proceedings of 16th International Conference on Information Systems, Amsterdam, December 1995.

[Soni 1995] D. Soni, R. Nord, C. Hofmeister, "Software Architectures in Industrial Applications", in Proceedings of the 17th International Conference on Software Engineering, IEEE CS Press, pp. 196–207, September 1995.

[Srinivasan 2004] L. Srinivasan, T. Banks (eds.), "Web Services Resource Lifetime (WS-ResourceLifetime)", OASIS Working Draft 04, November 2004, available at:
http://docs.oasis-open.org/wsrf/2004/11/wsrf-WS-ResourceLifetime-1.2-draft-04.pdf.

[Steel 2006] C. Steel, R. Nagappan, R. Lai, *Core Security Patterns: Best Practices and Strategies for J2EE™, Web Services, and Identity Management*, Prentice Hall, 2006.

[Sun Microsystems 2003] Sun Microsystems, "The Sun Common Mobility Architecture: Delivering Mobile Services – A Technical Overview", 2003, available at:
www.sun.com/wireless.

[Supply-Chain Council 2005] Supply-Chain Council, "Supply-Chain Operations Reference-model: SCOR Version 7.0 Overview", 2005, available at:
www.supply-chain.org.

[Tennison 2001] J. Tennison, *XSLT and XPath*, M & T Books, 2001.

[Tuecke 2003] S. Tuecke *et al.*, "Open Grid Service Infrastructure (OGSI)", Global Grid Forum OGSI-WG, GFD-R-P.15, June 2003.

[Ullman 1988] J. Ullman, *Principles of Database and Knowledge Based Systems*, Computer Science Press, 1998.

[Ulrich 2002] W. Ulrich, *Legacy Systems – Transformation Strategies*, Prentice Hall, 2002.

[Unger 2003] J. Unger, M. Haynos, "A visual tour of Open Grid Services Architecture", IBM developerWorks, August 2003, available at:
http://www-106.ibm.com/developerworks/grid/library/gr-visual/.

[Valentine 2002] C. Valentine, L. Dykes, E. Tittel, *XML Schemas*, Sybex, 2002.

[Vambenepe 2004] W. Vambenepe (ed.), "Web Services Topics (WS-Topics) v. 1.2", OASIS Working Draft 01, July 2004, available at:
http://docs.oasis-open.org/wsn/2004/06/wsn-WS-Topics-1.2-draft-01.pdf.

[Vambenepe 2005a] W. Vambenepe (ed.), "Web Services Distributed Management: Management Using Web Services (MUWS 1.0) Part 1", *OASIS Standard*, March 2005, available at:
http://docs.oasis-open.org/wsdm/2004/12/wsdm-muws-part1-1.0.pdf.

[Vambenepe 2005b] W. Vambenepe (ed.), "Web Services Distributed Management: Management Using Web Services (MUWS 1.0) Part 2", *OASIS Standard*, March 2005, available at:
http://docs.oasis-open.org/wsdm/2004/12/wsdm-muws-part2-1.0.pdf.

[VeriSign 2003a] VeriSign Inc., "VeriSign Digital Trust Services", April 2003, available at:
www.verisign.com.

[VeriSign 2003b] VeriSign Inc., "Managed PKI: Securing Your Business Applications", White Paper, May 2003, available at:
www.verisign.com.

[Veryard 2001] R. Veryard, *The Component-Based Business: Plug and Play*, Springer, 2001.

[Vinovski 2004] S. Vinoski, "More Web Services Notifications", *IEEE Internet*, May/June 2004.

[vonHalle 2002] B. von Halle, *Business Rules Applied*, John Wiley & Sons, 2002.

[Wahli 2004] U. Wahli *et al.*, "WebSphere Version 5.1 Application Developer 5.1.1 Web Services Handbook", IBM Redbooks, February 2004, available at:
ibm.com/redbooks.

[Walmsley 2002] P. Walmsley, *Definitive XML Schema*, Prentice Hall, 2002.

[WAP Forum 2002] WAP Forum, "Wireless Application Protocol WAP 2.0", Technical White Paper, January 2002, available at:
www.wapforum.org.

[Webber 2001] J. Webber *et al.*, "Making Web Services Work", *Application Development Advisor*, pp. 68–71, November/December 2001.

[Webber 2003a] J. Webber, M. Little, "Introducing WS-Coordination", *Web Services Journal*, vol. 3, no. 5, pp. 12–16, May 2003.

[Webber 2003b] J. Webber, M. Little, "Introducing WS-CAF: More than just Transactions", *Web Services Journal*, vol. 3, no. 12, pp. 52–5, December 2003.

[Webber 2004] D. R. Webber *et al.*, "The Benefits of ebXML for e-Business", International Conference of XML (XML'04), August 2004.

[Weerawarana 2005] S. Weerawarana *et al.*, *Web Services Platform Architecture*, Prentice Hall, 2005.

[WfMC 1999] Workflow Management Coalition, "Terminology & Glossary", Document Number WFMC-TC-1011, February 1999.

[White 2004] S. A. White, "Introduction to BPMN", *Business Process Trends*, July, 2004, available at:
www.bptrends.com.

[Whitehead 2002] K. Whitehead, *Component-based Development*, Addison-Wesley, 2002.

[Wilkes 2005] M. Wilkes, "Modernizing Application Integration with Service Oriented Architecture", CBDI Report, CBDI Forum 2005, available at:
www.cbdiforum.com.

[WS-Roadmap 2002] "Security in a Web Services World: A Proposed Architecture and Roadmap", IBM developerWorks, April 2002, available at:
http://www-128.ibm.com/developerworks/library/specification/ws-secmap.

[Zimmermann 2003] O. Zimmermann *et al.*, *Perspectives on Web Services*, Springer, 2003.

[Zimmermann 2004] O. Zimmermann, P. Krogdahl, C. Gee, "Elements of Service-oriented Analysis and Design", IBM developerWorks, June 2004, available at:
http://www-106.ibm.com/developerworks/library/ws-soad1/.

Index